Second Canadian Edition

Earth

An Introduction to Physical Geology

Edward J. Tarbuck
Illinois Central College, Emeritus

Frederick K. Lutgens
Illinois Central College, Emeritus

Cameron J. Tsujita
University of Western Ontario

Stephen R. Hicock
University of Western Ontario

PEARSON
Prentice Hall
Toronto

Library and Archives Canada Cataloguing in Publication

Earth: an introduction to physical geology/Edward J. Tarbuck ... [et al.].—2nd Canadian ed.

Includes index.
ISBN 978-0-13-613865-5

1. Physical geology—Textbooks. I. Tarbuck, Edward J.

QE28.2.T37 2009 550 C2007-906617-8

ISBN-13: 978-0-13-613865-5
ISBN-10: 0-13-613865-9

Vice-President, Editorial Director: Gary Bennett
Marketing Manager: Marlene Olsavsky
Acquisitions Editor: Michelle Sartor
Developmental Editor: Paul Donnelly
Production Editor: Marisa D'Andrea
Copy Editor: Dawn Hunter
Proofreader: Claudia Forgas
Production Coordinator: Patricia Ciardullo
Indexer: Belle Wong
Photo and Permissions Researcher: Lisa Brant
Compositor: Hermia Chung
Art Director: Julia Hall
Interior and Cover Design: Anthony Leung
Cover Image: Daryl Benson/Mastefile

For permission to reproduce copyrighted material, the publisher gratefully acknowledges the copyright holders listed underneath figures and tables, which are considered an extension of this copyright page.

2 3 4 5 12 11 10 09

Printed and bound in the United States.

PEARSON
Prentice Hall

To our wives, Joanne and Nancy,
for their support and patience.

—E.J.T. and F.K.L.

This edition of Earth: An Introduction to Physical Geology *is dedicated to all Canadian geoscientists—past and present—who have contributed to the education of the Canadian public.*

—C.J.T. and S.R.H.

Brief Contents

GEODe: Earth CD-ROM Contents

This icon for the GEODe: Earth CD-ROM appears whenever a text discussion has a corresponding GEODe: Earth activity.

Contents

This icon for the GEODe: Earth CD-ROM appears whenever a text discussion has a corresponding GEODe: Earth activity.

Preface

Earth is a very small part of a vast universe and a fairly small planet within our solar system, but it is our home. Like Goldilocks, on Earth we enjoy just the right combination of conditions and ingredients necessary to maintain life and support our activities. The science of geology is important in our quest for understanding how planet Earth works.

Media reports keep us aware of the geologic forces at work on our planet. News stories graphically portray the violent force of volcanic eruptions, the devastation generated by strong earthquakes, and the large numbers of people left homeless by landslides and flooding. In the three years that have elapsed between the writing of the first and second Canadian editions of this textbook, the world witnessed the horrible aftermath of the earthquake-generated tsunami that swept across the Indian Ocean on Boxing Day of 2004, and millions watched helplessly as 80 percent of New Orleans became flooded when Hurricane Katrina hit the U.S. Gulf Coast in 2005. Both events clearly caught human populations off guard. Such tragedies are grim reminders that in order to be better prepared for such events, we must gain an awareness of their nature, not only in context of their damaging effects on human populations, but also in terms of their underlying causes and their frequency of occurrence over long periods of time. Aspects of geology can aid in the understanding of where, why, and how such events occur and how to lessen their impact on human populations through long-range planning.

Geology can also yield clues to help us understand, prevent, and repair environmental problems. Just as an auto mechanic must have a good working knowledge of the interactions among the parts in a car in order to fix it, the knowledge of our planet is critical to our well-being and is, indeed, vital to our survival.

The second Canadian edition of *Earth: An Introduction to Physical Geology* is a university-level text that is intended to be a meaningful, non-technical primer for students taking their first course in geology. In addition to being informative and up to date, a major goal of *Earth* is to meet the needs of students for a readable and user-friendly text, a book that is an effective resource for learning the basic principles and concepts of geology.

Distinguishing Features

Readability

The language of the book is straightforward and written to be understood by the layperson. Featuring clear, readable discussions with a minimum of technical language is the rule. Frequent headings and subheadings throughout the book help students follow discussions and identify the important ideas presented in each chapter. Significant portions of the text were rewritten and condensed from the first Canadian edition in an effort to make the material less repetitive, more understandable, and more relevant to a Canadian audience. The result is a much more streamlined text that will serve as an even better tool for learning than its predecessor.

Illustrations and Photographs

Geology is a highly visual and spatially oriented science. Therefore, photographs and artwork are a very important part of an introductory book in this discipline. Following the tradition of previous versions of this textbook, *Earth* contains hundreds of photographs, many of which are new to the second Canadian edition. These have been carefully selected to aid understanding and add realism while contributing a Canadian perspective to geologic concepts.

The illustrations in *Earth* have been renowned for their quality. The original art program for the U.S. editions, from which the Canadian editions of the text are adapted, was carried out by Dennis Tasa, a gifted artist and respected geologic illustrator. In addition to Tasa's excellent illustrations, this edition features many pieces of new or substantially redesigned line art. The new art illustrates ideas and concepts more clearly and realistically than ever before; many of these were custom designed by the co-authors together with the outstanding graphics teams at Pearson Education Canada and ArtPlus Limited.

Focus on Learning

When a chapter has been completed, three useful devices help students review. First, the Chapter Summary recaps all the major points. Next are Review Questions that help students examine their knowledge of significant facts and ideas. These are followed by a checklist of Key Terms with page references. Learning the language of geology helps students learn the material. Each chapter closes with a reminder to visit the Companion Website for *Earth* (**www.pearson.ca/tarbuck**), which contains many excellent opportunities for review and exploration.

Earth as a System

An important occurrence in modern science, particularly in geology, has been the realization that Earth is a giant multidimensional system. Our planet consists of many distinct but interacting parts. The Earth system responds to changes in any of its constituent parts, often in ways that are neither obvious nor immediately apparent. Although it is not possible to study the entire system at once, it is possible to develop an awareness and appreciation for the concept and for many of the system's important interrelationships. Therefore, the theme of "Earth as a system" recurs at appropriate places throughout the book. It is a thread that weaves through the chapters and helps tie them together.

New and revised special-interest boxes relate to "Earth as a system." To remind the reader of this important theme, the small icon you see at the beginning of this section is used to mark these boxes.

People and the Environment

Because knowledge about our planet and how it works is necessary to our survival and well-being, the treatment of environmental issues plays an important part in *Earth*. Such discussions serve to illustrate the relevance and application of geologic knowledge. This theme is given considerable prominence in the second Canadian edition. The text integrates a great deal of information about the relationship between people and the natural environment and explores applications of geology to understanding and solving problems that arise from these interactions. In addition to many basic text discussions, several of the text's special-interest boxes involve the "people and the environment" theme and are quickly recognized by the distinctive icon you see at the beginning of this section.

Canadian Profile

Many of the people, places, issues, and ideas that play pivotal roles in understanding physical geology also happen to originate in Canada. Of course, this theme pervades the second Canadian edition, but we have also highlighted certain topics for discussion in special-interest boxes in almost every chapter. You can identify these in the text by the small icon you see at the beginning of this section.

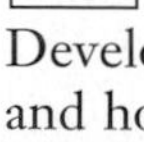

Understanding Earth

Developing an understanding of how science is done and how scientists work is another important theme that appears throughout this book. The Understanding Earth boxes encourage students to explore not only the reasoning behind current interpretations of geologic phenomena, but also some of the difficulties encountered by scientists as they have attempted to answer various questions about our planet. These boxes also provide opportunities to examine some of the topics in greater detail than would otherwise be possible in the main part of the chapters.

Basic Structure of the Textbook

The organization of chapters in this textbook is intended to be a compromise between the traditional approach of covering plate tectonics as a culmination of the understanding of geologic principles, and the more "systems-based" approach in which plate tectonics is generally covered at the beginning of the text. This particular organization was selected largely to accommodate the study of minerals and rocks in the laboratory (which usually comes early in an introductory-level geology course), while exploring how each component fits into the basic idea of plate tectonics. By revisiting plate tectonics after covering the fundamental components of geology (minerals, rocks, time, etc.), the user of this text will hopefully have a better appreciation of why plate tectonics is the central paradigm of modern geology.

The book begins with a rudimentary view of geology and a brief glimpse of plate tectonics as a general concept. We then turn to a discussion of Earth materials, from minerals to rocks and rocks to lithosphere. Next to be covered is the element of time—how time is classified, how Earth materials can be dated, and the sheer immensity of geologic time as revealed in the geologic record. From here, we examine the manner in which rocks are deformed and the dynamic nature of Earth's surface as observed in earthquakes. Related to the study of earthquakes is the use of seismic waves in deducing the internal structure of our planet. To improve the flow of the text, we have decided to incorporate this topic into the chapter on earthquakes. We then proceed to an examination of the ocean floor and the significant role played by oceanic exploration to the understanding of the mechanisms responsible for the movement of tectonic plates. Finally, all of the components of Earth discussed to this point, from minerals to features of the ocean floor, are brought together within the context of plate tectonics. By revisiting plate tectonics in greater detail, the reader can now truly appreciate how the "little pictures" fit into the "big picture."

The second section of the book deals with surficial processes and features, including mass wasting, streamflow, groundwater flow, glaciation, wind, and waves and currents. Because these processes are dependent on the force of gravity, and thus also the differences in topography that are commonly produced by plate tectonic activity, we have chosen to cover these topics after plate tectonics. Finally, we discuss mineral and energy resources, from the viewpoint of both resource use and value, and in the context of the environment. As many of the predicted effects of climate change centre on issues related to processes near *Earth's* surface, and also because resource exploration is often viewed as the "bottom line" of geology, we feel its placement at the end of the book is most appropriate.

More about the Second Canadian Edition

The second Canadian edition of *Earth* represents a robust revision of both its U.S. counterparts and the first Canadian edition. Every part of the book was examined carefully with the goals of keeping topics current, addressing Canadian perspectives and issues, and improving the clarity of text discussions.

Here are some examples of what is new in the second Canadian edition of *Earth:*

- More than 30 new photos, maps, and illustrations have been added, with a stronger focus on Canadian examples.
- Although more Canadian examples have been included in the text, we have been careful to retain the best of the examples from the rest of the world. A few additional international examples have also been added, from places as far away as Antarctica.
- The best of the Canadian Profile boxes, focussing on notable Canadian geologists, important geologic sites, and other aspects of Canadian geology, have been retained and improved with new images. A number of new boxes have also been added. Among these is a biographic article on Canadian geologist Norman L. Bowen (Chapter 3); a special feature on cosmogenic dating, a field that has been significantly advanced by Canadian geologists (Chapter 8); and in anticipation of the 2010 Winter Olympics at Whister, B.C., a look at geologic hazards along the Sea-to-Sky Highway in British Columbia.
- Chapter 3, Igneous Rocks, has been reorganized to provide a more logical progression from magma evolution to rock classification.
- Chapter 4, Volcanoes and Other Igneous Bodies, features new photos that stress the relevance of the chapter content to Canadian geology.
- Chapter 5, Weathering and Soil, has been modified for greater clarity in the explanations of concepts and also contains new Canadian photos.
- Chapter 6, Sedimentary Rocks, has been reorganized so that a discussion of sedimentary environments appears before the section on rock classification.
- Chapter 7, Metamorphism and Metamorphic Rocks, contains new photos and improved artwork.
- Chapter 8, Geologic Time, features the most recent version of the geologic time scale approved and published by the International Commission on Stratigraphy. One of the more controversial decisions made by the Commission has been to adopt the Paleogene and Neogene as periods of the Cenozoic Era, in place of the Tertiary and Quaternary. Existing first-year-level geology texts (at the time of writing) continue to cling to the older, traditional scheme. We thus regard the adoption of the new time scale as a bold, but progressive, move. Although it may take some time for the "older generation" to get used to the new scheme, we feel it's important to provide the most up-to-date information for the benefit of the next generation of Canadian geologists.
- Chapter 9, Crustal Deformation, features improved artwork to better convey concepts relating to geologic structures.
- Chapter 10, Earthquakes and Earth's Interior, has undergone the most extensive modification of all the chapters in this second Canadian edition of *Earth*. Formerly two separate chapters (Chapters 15 and 16 in the first Canadian edition), this chapter has been considerably condensed and streamlined to reduce repetition and provide a stronger connection between the dual importance of seismic information in the study of earthquakes and as a basis for interpreting the properties and structure of Earth's interior. We also begin the chapter with an account of one of the most disastrous geologic events witnessed in the past century—the 2004 Sumatran earthquake and resulting Indian Ocean tsunami. This event, relatively fresh in the public's memory, sets the stage for understanding the relationships between plate tectonics, earthquakes, and human society. It effectively reinforces an important message about our awareness of violent geologic events. Rather than wondering *if* such events will happen, we should be asking ourselves *what* these events represent, *when* and *where* they will

happen, *whom* they will affect, and *how* they are likely to affect human populations. We have also placed greater emphasis on earthquakes in Canada, with new Canadian examples.

- Chapter 11, The Ocean Floor, features new Canadian photos and has been condensed for improved readability. This chapter also sets the stage for the development of more advanced concepts in plate tectonics to be covered in Chapter 12.
- Chapter 12, Plate Tectonics: The Framework for Modern Geology, revisits the paradigm from the viewpoint of how concepts covered in Chapters 2 (Minerals: The Building Blocks of Rocks) through 11 (The Ocean Floor) fit into the big picture. We have removed much of the repetition that existed in the equivalent chapter of the first Canadian edition, making for a more succinct discussion of plate tectonics as a synthesis of many smaller conceptual components.
- Chapter 13, Mountain Building and Continental Frameworks, has undergone relatively little modification, but improvements in the art quality will be immediately apparent to the reader. We believe the placement of this chapter after plate tectonics provides an improved flow of concepts, connecting product (mountains) to process (plate tectonics).
- Chapter 14, Mass Wasting: The Work of Gravity, has been streamlined, clarified, and further Canadianized to emphasize the relevance of mass wasting processes to the Canadian reader. At the request of previous users of the book, we have also included a new section on periglacial phenomena.
- Chapter 15, Running Water, has been reorganized and some sections have been rewritten for a more logical flow of concepts. Following a basic discussion of the hydrologic cycle, the chapter progresses from the flow characteristics of streams to the significance of streams as agents of erosion, sediment transport, and deposition. From here, the graded stream concept forms the basis of examining streams on a larger scale, focussing on valleys, channel systems and floodplains, and the alluvial fans and deltas where streams end. Streams are then discussed in terms of their drainage patterns. Finally, the significance of streams to human populations is examined, especially with regard to floods.
- Chapter 16, Groundwater, has been condensed, and additional graphics have been added to better convey concepts relating to groundwater processes.
- Chapter 17, Glaciers and Glaciation, has been improved with the addition of spectacular new photos focussing on Canadian examples. In places, the text has been clarified and simplified to provide a clearer explanation of glacial processes and products.
- Chapter 18, Deserts and Winds, has been further condensed to focus on essential concepts and to remove some of the repetition that remained in the first Canadian edition.
- Chapter 19, Shorelines, contains more photos of Canadian examples, as well as improved art.
- Chapter 20, Mineral and Energy Resources, has been updated in terms of statistics and recent developments in mining activity (e.g., new diamond mines in the Northwest Territories and Ontario).

The Teaching and Learning Package

We have prepared an excellent supplements package to accompany the text. This package includes the traditional supplements that students and professors have come to expect from authors and publishers, as well as some new kinds of supplements that involve electronic media.

For the Student

Geode: Earth CD-ROM. Each copy of *Earth*, Second Canadian Edition, comes with GEODe: Earth, by Edward Tarbuck, Fredrick Lutgens, and Dennis Tasa of Tasa Graphic Arts, Inc. GEODe: Earth is a dynamic program that reinforces key concepts by using animations, tutorials, and interactive exercises. A special GEODe: Earth icon appears throughout the text wherever a discussion has a corresponding GEODe: Earth activity. This special offering gives students two valuable products (GEODe: Earth and the textbook) for the price of one.

Companion Website. This site, created specifically for the text, contains numerous review exercises (from which students get immediate feedback), exercises to expand one's understanding of geology, and resources for further exploration. It provides an excellent platform from which to start using the internet for the study of geology. Please visit the site at **www.pearsoned.ca/tarbuck.**

For the Professor

Instructor's Resource CD-ROM. This aid provides quick and easy access to a wealth of valuable teaching tools, including the following:

- Instructor's Manual.
- Test Generator. Contains more than 3,000 questions in multiple-choice, true/false, short-answer, word-analysis, critical-thinking, and visualization formats, a selection of which you can link to actual figures from the text.
- Customizable PowerPoint® lecture presentations with Digital Image Libary.
- The Prentice Hall Geoscience Animations. A library of more than 30 Flash animations for physical geography, meteorology, physical geology, and Earth sciences. Created through a unique collaboration among four of Prentice Hall's leading geoscience authors, these animations make some key physical processes visual and accessible.

Acknowledgments

Writing or revising a textbook requires the talents and cooperation of many individuals. When approached by Pearson Education Canada to produce a second Canadian edition of *Earth* for Canadian use, we both enthusiastically accepted the challenge. Pearson Education and its Canadian branch, Pearson Education Canada, are world-renowned for their exceptional educational publications, and we are honoured to work with them on this project. The excellent graphics and user-friendly explanations of geologic processes from both the U.S and first Canadian editions provided an excellent framework for this textbook and we thank all those who were instrumental in their production.

We are indebted to the many friends and colleagues who enthusiastically contributed material to both the first and second Canadian editions of *Earth*; such enthusiasm for this project is a testament to the dedication of the geologic community in Canada toward the promotion of geologic literacy in this country. We are also deeply thankful to the many professors who influenced our academic philosophies during our academic careers and to our students, whose insightful questions and comments ultimately improve the way we communicate concepts to those who follow them.

Many other colleagues generously contributed material for the new Canadian Profile boxes found throughout the textbook. Many thanks are extended to these individuals:

Rick Cheel
Claudia Cochrane
Matt Devereux
David Eaton
John Gosse
Brian Hart
Richard Léveillé
Mike Powell
Rob Schincariol
Gordon Southam
Keith Tinkler
Vic Tyrer
Gordon Winder
Grant Young

Several colleagues and other individuals were also very generous in providing photographs for both the first and second Canadian editions of *Earth*, and in many cases, allowed us to use multiple images from their personal collections. We would particularly like to thank Christopher Collom, Catherine Hickson, Bob Hodder, Alfred Lenz, Mike Schering, Kristin Singh, Guy Plint, Denis Tetreault, Grant Young, John Clague, and John Gosse for their cooperation in this regard. Although too numerous to mention here, several other people contributed individual images that enhance the tangibility of the concepts covered in the textbook, and we are grateful for their permission to showcase their photographic work.

Special thanks go to those colleagues who prepared in-depth reviews for the second Canadian edition. Their critical comments and thoughtful input helped guide our work and strengthen the text. We wish to thank the following reviewers:

Dileep J. A. Athaide, University of British Columbia
Rick Cheel, Brock University
Fred Clark, University of Alberta
Jaroslav Dostal, Saint Mary's University
Simone Dumas, University of Ottawa
Robbie Dunlop, Simon Fraser University
Jennifer S. Getsinger, Capilano College
Sandra L. McBride, Queen's University
Ken Munyikwa, Athabasca University
Mungandi Nasitwitwi, Kwantlen University College
J. Victor Owen, Saint Mary's University
Nicholas Vlachopoulos, Royal Military College of Canada
Lucy Wilson, University of New Brunswick at Saint John

We would also like to acknowledge the publishing team at Pearson Education Canada. Many thanks are due to Michelle Sartor, Acquisitions Editor, who brought us on board, and once again to Paul Donnelly, Senior Developmental Editor, who skilfully and meticulously coordinated this project and helped us stay on track (and who didn't nag too much when the deadlines made that "whooshing sound" as they flew by). We also express our gratitude to the production team, led by Marisa D'Andrea and Patricia Ciardullo, and to our copyeditor, Dawn Hunter, and our technical reviewer, Fred Clark, for their outstanding work. The professionalism and eye for detail that all of you contributed to the production of this textbook is greatly appreciated by us and will also surely be appreciated by our readers. Many thanks as well to Editorial Director Gary Bennett and Marketing Manager Marlene Olsavsky for having faith in the value of this product (and for selling enough of the first edition to allow us to write this one!).

Cam extends his heartfelt thanks to his father (James Tsujita), mother (Lilly Tsujita), and sister (Kimberly Kaszas), who have provided unwavering support throughout his academic career. Special thanks to Cam's wife, Erica Tsujita, and his three sons Jeremy, Casey, and Warner, who persevered through his long work hours and frequent absences from home during the preparation of this textbook.

Steve gives heartfelt thanks to his wife Fran and two daughters, Brenda and Robyn, for their patience and understanding when work on the textbook meant spending evenings and weekends away from home.

Cam Tsujita and Steve Hicock

The Pearson Education Canada **COMPANION WEBSITE**

A Great Way to Learn and Instruct Online

The Pearson Education Canada Companion Website is easy to navigate and is organized to correspond to the chapters in this textbook. Whether you are a student in the classroom or a distance learner you will discover helpful resources for in-depth study and research that empower you in your quest for greater knowledge and maximize your potential for success in the course.

Companion Website

[www.pearsoned.ca/tarbuck]

Enter

Jump to... http://www.pearsoned.ca/tarbuck

Home Search Help Profile

Home >

Companion Website

Earth: An Introduction to Physical Geology, Second Canadian Edition, by Tarbuck, Lutgens, Tsujita, and Hicock

Student Resources

The modules in this section provide students with tools for learning course material. These modules include:

- Chapter review summaries
- Self-assessment quizzes
- Virtual field trips
- Links to Research Navigator

In the quiz modules students can send answers to the grader and receive instant feedback on their progress through the Results Reporter. Coaching comments and references to the textbook may be available to ensure that students take advantage of all available resources to enhance their learning experience.

Instructor Resources

The modules in this section provide instructors with additional teaching tools. Downloadable PowerPoint Presentations, Test Generator, and an Instructor's Manual are just some of the materials that may be available in this section. Where appropriate, this section will be password protected. To get a password, simply contact your Pearson Education Canada Representative or call Faculty Sales and Services at 1-800-850-5813.

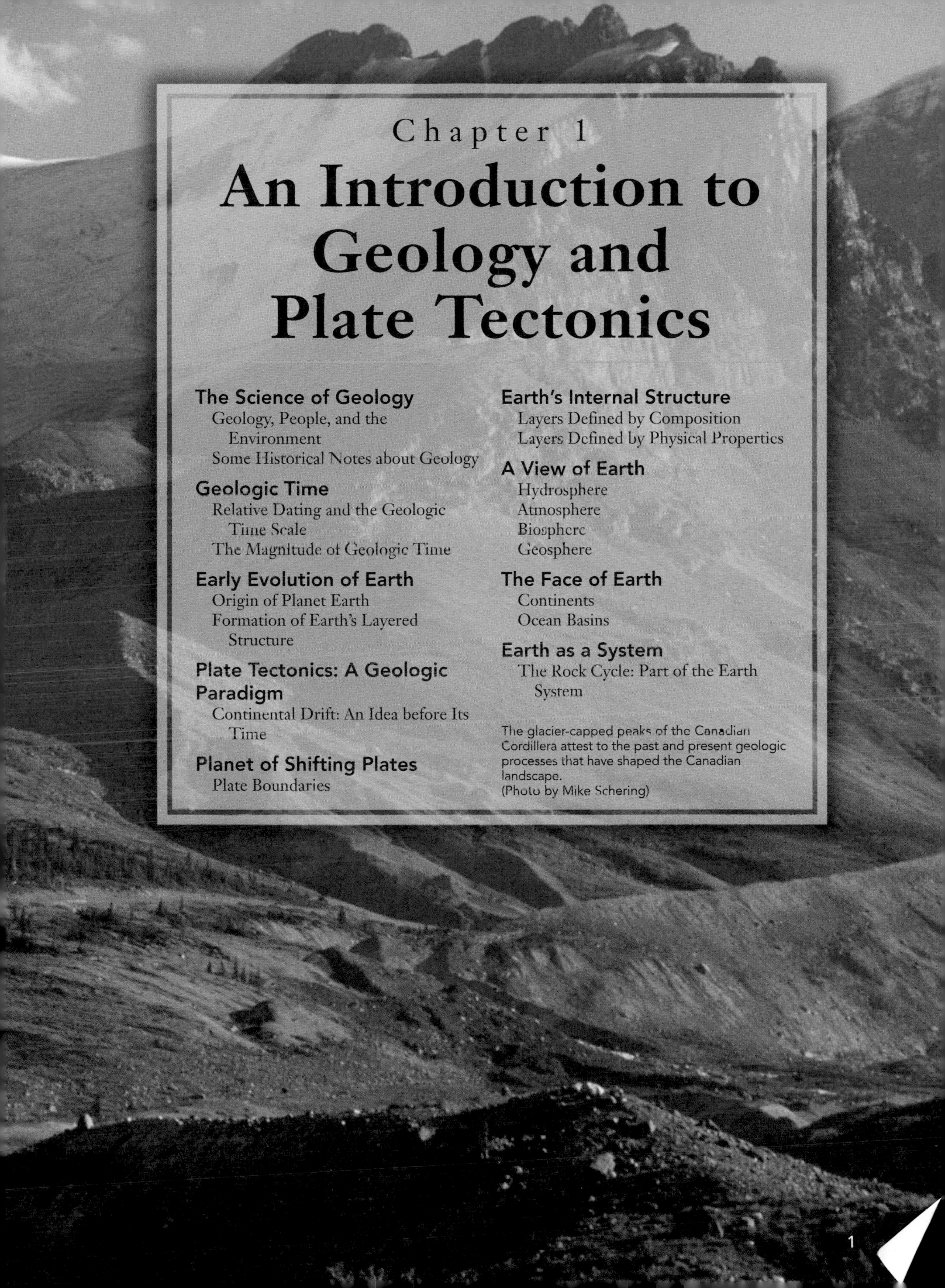

Chapter 1

An Introduction to Geology and Plate Tectonics

The glacier-capped peaks of the Canadian Cordillera attest to the past and present geologic processes that have shaped the Canadian landscape.
(Photo by Mike Schering)

The spectacular eruption of a volcano, the terror caused by an earthquake, the magnificent scenery of a mountain valley, and the destruction created by a landslide* are all subjects for the **geologist** (Figure 1.1). The study of geology deals with many fascinating and practical questions about our physical environment. What forces produce mountains? Will there soon be a great earthquake on the Canadian west coast? What was the Ice Age like? Will there be another? How are ore deposits formed? Should we look for water here? Is strip mining practical in this area? Where is the best place to drill the next oil well?

◆ **Figure 1.1** These sharp peaks in the French Alps are being sculpted by alpine glaciers. Geologists study the processes that create and modify these mountains. (Photo by St. Clair Renard, Felix/Getty Images, Inc./Image Bank)

THE SCIENCE OF GEOLOGY

The subject of this text is **geology**, from the Greek *geo*, "Earth," and *logos*, "discourse." It is the science that pursues an understanding of planet Earth. Geology is traditionally divided into two broad areas—physical and historical. **Physical geology**, the primary focus of this book, examines the materials composing Earth to gain an understanding of the many processes that operate both on and beneath its surface. The aim of **historical geology**, conversely, is to understand the origin of Earth and its development through time. Thus, it strives to establish an orderly, chronologic arrangement of the multitude of physical and biologic changes that have occurred in the geologic past. The study of physical geology logically precedes the study of Earth history because we must first understand how Earth works before we attempt to unravel its past.

To understand Earth is challenging because our planet is a dynamic body with many interacting parts and a complex history. Throughout its long existence, Earth has been changing. In fact, it is changing as you read this page and will continue to do so in the future. Sometimes the changes are rapid and violent, as when landslides or volcanic eruptions occur. Conversely, change can take place so slowly that it goes unnoticed during a lifetime. Scales of size and space also vary greatly among the phenomena that geologists study. Sometimes they must focus on phenomena that are submicroscopic, and at other times they must deal with features that are continental or global in scale.

Geology is perceived as a science that is done outdoors, and rightly so. A great deal of geology is based on observations and experiments conducted in the field. Typically, this information comes from **outcrops** (e.g., Figure 1.1), where bedrock is exposed at the surface. But geology is also done in the laboratory where, for example, the study of various Earth materials provides insights into many basic processes. Frequently, geology requires an understanding of and the application of knowledge and principles from physics, chemistry, and biology. Geology is a science that seeks to expand our knowledge of the natural world and our place in it. This basic philosophy has endured since the time of the pioneers of geology, including the knighted Canadian geologist, Sir William Logan (Box 1.1).

---

*Throughout this book, the term *landslide* is used informally, in a general sense, to describe various gravity-driven slope processes that are classified in Chapter 14.

BOX 1.1

Canadian Profile
Sir William Logan: Canada's Premier Geologist

C. Gordon Winder*

In a 1998 list of the 100 most important Canadians in history, a **geologist** was cited as the number-one scientist. William Edmond Logan (1798–1875) was born in Montreal, the third child and second son of Scottish immigrants (see Figure 1.A). His education started in Montreal and finished in Edinburgh. In 1816, he registered for medicine at the University of Edinburgh and completed the first year. He had the highest mark in his geometry class of 200 students and was awarded a brass octant, engraved with his name.

In 1817, Logan started working in London for his uncle, a commodity broker. He travelled to Northern Ireland, Paris, Spain (to view copper deposits), and Rome, where his diary records types of building stone. He was reading the available geology books and continued with lessons in geometry, languages, painting, and the flute.

In 1830, Logan's uncle purchased a copper smelter at Swansea, Wales, and Logan was appointed business manager. Coal was mined around Swansea, but the supply was sporadic. Logan started mapping the area's geology. He used precise surveying instruments and his map proved to be so superior that the British Geological Survey adopted it as its official map. On the basis of upright petrified tree trunks and stumps in the strata, he proposed a theory for the origin of coal, a theory that is still valid today.

In the early 1840s, the Government of Canada decided to establish a geologic survey. Logan applied for the directorship, was appointed on April 20, 1842, and was headquartered in Montreal. In 1843, he measured the rocks with coal at Joggins, Nova Scotia. In 1844, he examined the Gaspé Peninsula, looking for coal. His collections of rock chips and fossils were wrapped in paper; he counted paces and used a Rochon micrometer to measure distance, a compass for direction, and mercury barometers for elevation; and he recorded his observations in leather-bound notebooks during the evenings beside a campfire.

His accommodation was a blanket thrown over saplings, and he was assisted by Aboriginal people who moved the camp and constructed birchbark canoes. He ate salt pork, sea biscuits, berries, fish, birds, and wild game, and drank tea with sugar. On one occasion, local people, puzzled by this aimlessly wandering mumbler, attempted to deliver him to an insane asylum.

In subsequent years, Logan traversed the Ottawa River to Lake Temiskaming; surveyed the areas around Lake Superior and Lake Huron for copper and iron deposits; and studied the complex geology of the Quebec Eastern Townships, where copper deposits were being explored. No coal deposit was ever discovered.

Logan trained his assistants himself. Alexander Murray was a retired naval officer who mapped southern Ontario (including the Petrolia oil fields) and later the area north of Lake Huron. Sterry Hunt was a university-trained chemist who analyzed rocks, minerals, and water. Elkanah Billings, a lawyer and amateur paleontologist, identified fossils. Logan had two map-makers and a handyman, who was once mistaken for the survey director in his elegant clothes. The director, commonly dressed in field clothes, looked more like a handyman.

Logan drew attention to Canada's potential mineral wealth at international exhibitions in London (1851) and Paris (1855). The Canadian rock and mineral specimens were the largest and most spectacular at the exhibitions. In January 1856, he was knighted by Queen Victoria and was the first individual born in Canada to be so honoured. He received numerous other awards in his lifetime.

As the Geological Survey director, Logan did administrative work, including writing field reports, doing cost accounting, answering letters (including some from swindlers), and sending requests to the government for funds. Occasionally, the government reduced the funding and Logan, convinced the Geological Survey was essential, paid the additional costs

◆ **Figure 1.A** Sir William Logan. (Photo reproduced with the permission of the Minister of Public Works and Government Services Canada, 2004, and courtesy of Natural Resources Canada, Geological Survey of Canada)

with his own money. Logan wrote the four copies of all reports, scientific and administrative, by hand. He worked day and night in the Survey office and had a folding chair that, with blankets, served as a bed—though some people wondered if he ever slept. His worn-out field boots lined the walls.

In 1863, a 983-page text, *Geology of Canada*, was published and included a small atlas with a coloured geologic map of Canada, including parts of Newfoundland, the Maritime provinces, the adjacent areas of the United States, and areas west of Lake Superior. In 1869, a large, scale map was published; all copies were hand-coloured, probably by Logan, which contributed to eyestrain.

On November 30, 1869, Logan retired as the Geological Survey director and went to Llechryd, Wales, to live with his sister Eliza. Each summer he returned to the Eastern Townships to examine the complex geology. He died in Wales on June 22, 1875, and is buried in the Anglican churchyard at Cilgerran, Wales. His name was given to Canada's highest mountain, Mount Logan (5959 metres), located in the southwest corner of Yukon.

---

*C. Gordon Winder is a professor emeritus in the Department of Earth Sciences, the University of Western Ontario.

Geology, People, and the Environment

The primary focus of this book is to help you develop an understanding of basic geologic principles, but along the way, we will explore numerous important relationships between people and the natural environment. Many of the problems and issues addressed by geology are of practical value.

Natural hazards are a part of living on Earth. Every day they adversely affect millions of people worldwide and are responsible for staggering damage (e.g., Figure 1.2). Among the hazardous Earth processes studied by geologists are volcanoes, floods, earthquakes, and landslides. Of course, geologic hazards are simply *natural* processes; they become hazards only when people try to live where these processes occur (Figure 1.3).

Resources represent another important focus of geology that is of great practical value. Resources include water and soil, a great variety of metallic and nonmetallic minerals, and energy. Together, they form the very foundation of modern civilization. Geology deals not only with the formation and occurrence of these vital resources but also with maintaining their supplies and with the environmental impact of their extraction and use.

Complicating all environmental issues is rapid world population growth and everyone's aspiration to a better standard of living. Earth is now gaining about 100 million people each year. This means a skyrocketing demand for resources and a growing pressure for people to dwell in environments that have significant geologic hazards.

Geologic processes have an impact on people, but we humans can dramatically influence geologic processes as well. For example, river flooding is natural, but the magnitude and frequency of flooding can be changed significantly by human activities, such as clearing forests, building cities, and constructing dams. Unfortunately, natural systems do not always adjust to artificial changes in ways that we can anticipate. Thus, an alteration to the environment that is intended to benefit society often has the opposite effect.

Throughout this book, you will examine different aspects of our relationship with the physical environment. Almost all chapters address some aspect of natural hazards, environmental issues, or resources. Significant parts of some chapters provide the basic geologic knowledge and principles needed to understand environmental problems. Moreover, a number

◆ **Figure 1.2** Two geologic hazards are represented in this image. On January 13, 2001, an earthquake (magnitude 7.6) caused considerable damage in El Salvador. A landslide was triggered by the earthquake and caused the damage pictured here. As many as 1000 people were buried under 8 metres of landslide debris.
(Photo by Reuters/STR/Archive Photos)

◆ **Figure 1.3** This is an image of Italy's Mt. Vesuvius in September 2000. This major volcano is surrounded by the city of Naples and Bay of Naples. In A.D. 79, Vesuvius explosively erupted, burying the towns of Pompeii and Herculanaeum in volcanic ash. Will it happen again?
(Image courtesy of NASA)

of the book's special-interest boxes focus on geology, people, and the environment by providing case studies or highlighting topical issues, particularly those of interest to Canadians.

Some Historical Notes about Geology

The nature of Earth—its materials and processes—has been a focus of study for centuries. Writings about such topics as fossils, gems, earthquakes, and volcanoes date back more than 2300 years to the early Greeks, whose primitive ideas survived through the Middle Ages.

Catastrophism In the mid-seventeenth century, James Ussher, Anglican Archbishop of Armagh, Primate of all Ireland, published a major work that had an immediate and a profound influence. A respected scholar of the Bible, Ussher constructed a chronology of human and Earth history in which he determined that Earth was only a few thousand years old, having been created in 4004 B.C. Ussher's treatise earned widespread acceptance among Europe's scientific and religious leaders, and his chronology was soon printed in the margins of the Bible itself.

During the seventeenth and eighteenth centuries the doctrine of **catastrophism** strongly influenced people's thinking about Earth. Briefly stated, catastrophists believed that Earth's landscapes had been shaped primarily by great catastrophes. Features, such as mountains and canyons, which today we know take long periods to form, were explained as having been produced by sudden and often worldwide disasters produced by unknown causes that no longer operate. This philosophy was an attempt to force-fit the rates of Earth processes to the then-current ideas on the age of Earth.

The relationship between catastrophism and the age of Earth has been summarized as follows:

> That the earth had been through tremendous adventures and had seen mighty changes during its obscure past was plainly evident to every inquiring eye; but to concentrate these changes into a few brief millenniums required a tailor-made philosophy, a philosophy whose basis was sudden and violent change.*

---

*H. E. Brown, V. E. Monnett, and J. W. Stovall, *Introduction to Geology* (New York: Blaisdell, 1958).

Uniformitarianism Modern geology began in the late eighteenth century when James Hutton, a Scottish physician and gentleman farmer, published his *Theory of the Earth*. In this work, Hutton put forth a fundamental principle that is a pillar of geology today: **uniformitarianism**. It states that the *physical, chemical, and biologic laws that operate today have also operated in the geologic past.* This means that the forces and processes that we observe presently shaping our planet have been at work for a very long time. This idea is summarized in the statement "the present is the key to the past."

Before Hutton's *Theory of the Earth*, no one had effectively demonstrated that geologic processes occur over extremely long intervals. However, Hutton persuasively argued that forces that appear small could, over long spans, produce effects that were just as great as those resulting from sudden catastrophic events. Unlike his predecessors, Hutton carefully cited verifiable observations to support his ideas.

For example, when he argued that mountains are sculpted and ultimately destroyed by weathering and the work of running water, and that their wastes are carried to the oceans by processes that can be observed, Hutton said, "We have a chain of facts which clearly demonstrates ... that the materials of the wasted mountains have travelled through the rivers ... There is not one step in all this progress ... that is not to be actually perceived." He then went on to summarize this thought by asking a question and immediately providing the answer: "What more can we require? Nothing but time."

Today the basic tenets of uniformitarianism are just as viable as in Hutton's day. Indeed, we realize more strongly than ever that the present gives us insight into the past and that the physical, chemical, and biologic laws that govern geologic processes remain unchanging through time. However, we also understand that the doctrine should not be taken too literally. To say that geologic processes in the past were the same as those occurring today is not to suggest that they always had the same relative importance or that they operated at precisely the same rate. Moreover, some important geologic processes are not currently observable, but evidence that they occur is well established. For example, we know that Earth has experienced impacts from large meteorites even though we have no human witnesses. Such events altered Earth's crust, modified its climate, and strongly influenced life on the planet.

The acceptance of uniformitarianism meant understanding that Earth is very old. Although Earth processes vary in intensity, they still take a long time to create or destroy major landscape features (Figure 1.4).

◆ **Figure 1.4** Geologist Dr. Gerd Westermann contemplates how weathering and erosion have sculpted the spectacular hoodoos of the Drumheller area in southern Alberta. Some geologic processes act so slowly that changes may not be visible during an entire human lifetime.
(Photo by C. Tsujita)

For example, geologists have established that mountains once existed in portions of the present-day Maritimes and Canadian Shield. Today these regions consist of low hills and plains. Erosion (processes that wear land away) gradually destroyed these peaks. Estimates indicate that the North American continent is being lowered at a rate of about 3 centimetres per 1000 years. At this rate it will take 100 million years for water, wind, and ice to lower mountains that are 3000 metres high.

But even 100 million years is a relatively short span on the time scale of Earth history, for the rock record contains evidence that shows Earth has experienced many cycles of mountain building and erosion. Concerning the ever-changing nature of Earth through great expanses of geologic time, Hutton made a statement that was to become his most famous. In concluding his classic 1788 paper published in the *Transactions of the Royal Society* of Edinburgh, he stated, "The results, therefore, of our present enquiry is, that we find no vestige of a beginning—no prospect of an end." A quote from William L. Stokes sums up the significance of Hutton's basic concept:

> In the sense that uniformitarianism implies the operation of timeless, changeless laws or principles, we can say that nothing in our incomplete but extensive knowledge disagrees with it.*

In the chapters that follow, we will be examining the materials that compose our planet and the processes that modify it. It is important to remember that although many features of our physical landscape may seem to be unchanging over the decades we observe them, they are nevertheless changing, but on time scales of hundreds, thousands, or even many millions of years.

GEOLOGIC TIME

Although Hutton and others recognized that geologic time is exceedingly long, they had no methods to accurately determine the age of Earth. However, in 1896 radioactivity was discovered. The use of radioactivity for dating was first attempted in 1905 and has been undergoing refinement ever since. Geologists are now able to assign fairly accurate dates to events in Earth history.**

For example, we know the dinosaurs became extinct about 65 million years ago. Today the age of Earth is estimated at 4.6 billion years.

Relative Dating and the Geologic Time Scale

During the nineteenth century, long before the advent of radiometric dating, a geologic time scale was developed by using principles of relative dating. **Relative dating** means that events are placed in their proper sequence or order without knowing their age in years. This is done by applying such principles as the **law of superposition** (*super* = over, *positum* = to place), which states that in layers of sedimentary rocks or lava flows, the youngest layer is on top and the oldest is on the bottom (assuming that nothing has turned the layers upside down, which sometimes happens). Arizona's Grand Canyon provides a fine example in which the oldest rocks are located in the inner gorge and the youngest rocks are found on the rim (Figure 1.5). The law of superposition establishes the *sequence* of rock layers—not their numeric ages. Today such a proposal appears to be elementary, but 300 years ago it was a major breakthrough in scientific reasoning to establish a rational basis for relative time measurements.

Fossils, the remains or traces of prehistoric life (Figure 1.6), were also essential to the development of the geologic time scale. Fossils are the basis for the **principle of fossil succession**, which states that *fossil organisms succeed one another in a definite and determinable order, and therefore any time span can be recognized by its fossil content*. This principle was laboriously worked out over decades by collecting fossils from countless rock layers around the world. Once established, it allowed geologists to identify rocks of the same age in widely separated places and to build the geologic time scale shown in Figure 1.7.

Notice that units with the same designations do not necessarily extend for the same number of years. For example, the Cambrian Period lasted about 50 million years, whereas the Silurian Period spanned only about 26 million years. As we will emphasize again in Chapter 8, this situation exists because the basis for establishing the time scale was not the regular rhythm of a clock, but the changing character of life forms through time. Numeric ages were added long after the time scale was established. A glance at Figure 1.7 also reveals that the Phanerozoic Eon is divided into many more units than earlier eons even though it encompasses only about 12 percent of Earth history. The meagre fossil record for the earlier eons is the primary reason for

---

*W. L. Stokes, *Essentials of Earth History* (Englewood Cliffs, New Jersey: Prentice Hall, 1966), p. 34.

**Chapter 8 is devoted to a much more complete discussion of geologic time.

◆ **Figure 1.5** These rock layers were exposed by the downcutting of the Colorado River as it created the Grand Canyon. The relative ages of these layers can be determined by applying the law of superposition. The youngest rocks are on top, and the oldest are at the bottom.
(Photo by Marc Muench/David Muench Photography, Inc.)

the lack of detail on this portion of the time scale. Without abundant fossils, geologists lose their primary tool for subdividing geologic time.

The Magnitude of Geologic Time

The concept of geologic time is new to many nongeologists. People are accustomed to dealing with increments of time that are measured in hours, days, weeks, and years. History books commonly examine events over spans of centuries, but even a century is difficult to appreciate fully. For most of us, someone or something that is 90 years old is *very old*, and a 1000-year-old artifact is *ancient*.

By contrast, those who study geology must routinely deal with vast time spans—millions or bil-

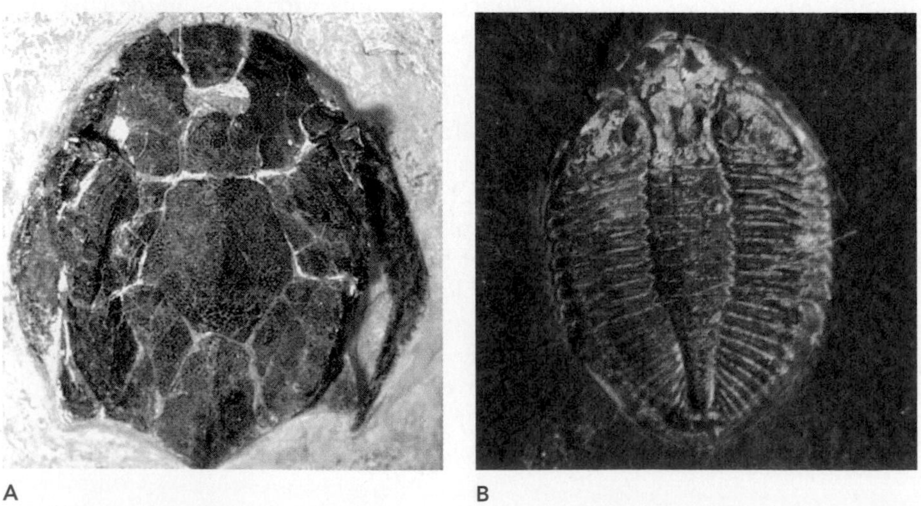

◆ **Figure 1.6** **A.** Armoured head region of a primitive Devonian fossil fish from Quebec. **B.** An Ordovician trilobite from the Georgian Bay area of Ontario.
(Photo **A** courtesy of Terry Ciotka, Canada Fossils Inc.; photo **B** by Denis Tetreault)

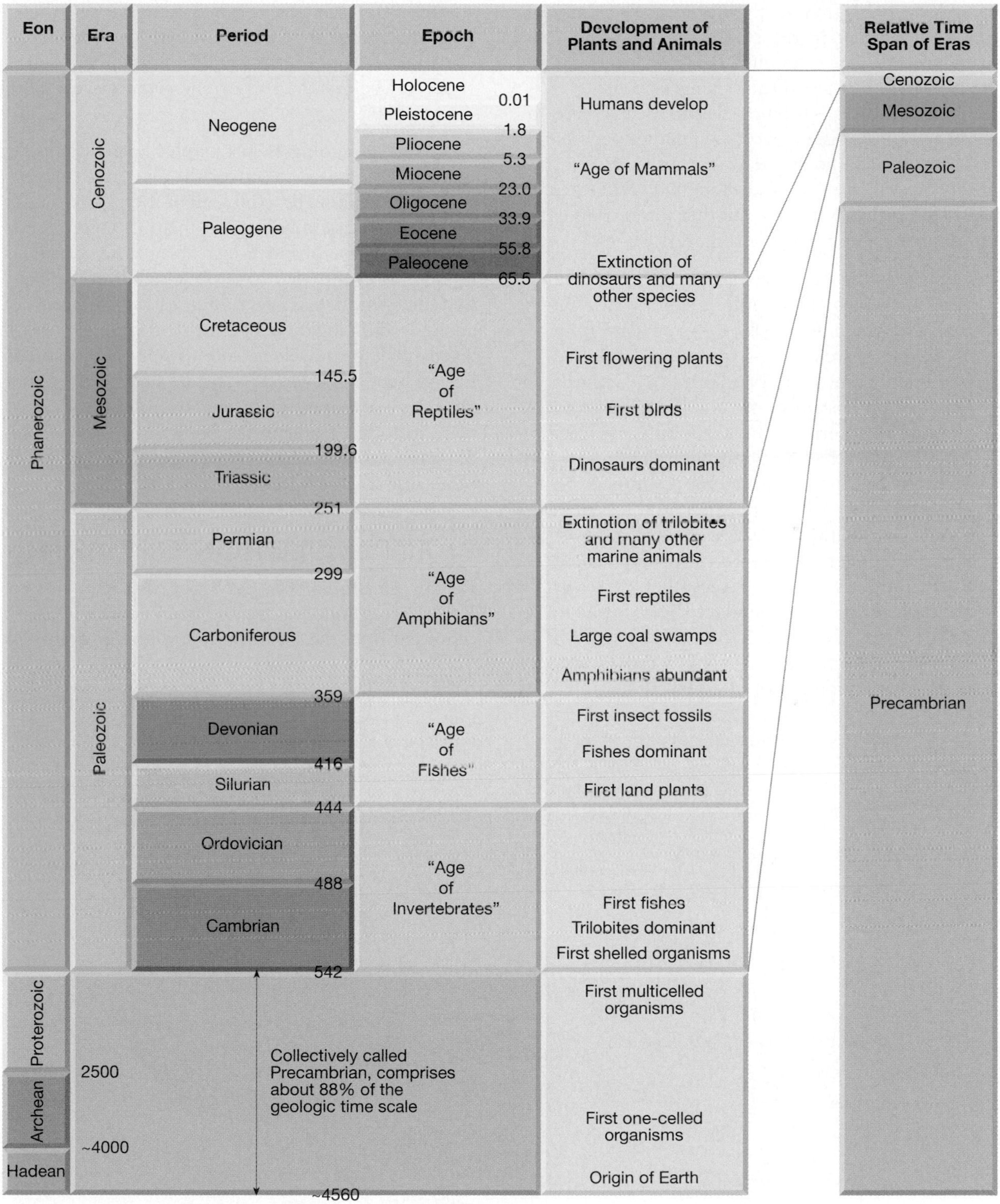

◆ **Figure 1.7** The geologic time scale. Numbers on the time scale represent time in millions of years before the present. These ages were added long after the time scale had been established by using relative dating techniques. The Precambrian accounts for more than 88 percent of geologic time.
(Modified after the International Commission on Stratigraphy)

lions (thousands of millions) of years. When viewed in the context of Earth's 4.6-billion-year history, a geologic event that occurred 100 million years ago may be characterized as "recent" by a geologist and a rock sample that has been dated at 10 million years may be called "young."

An appreciation for the magnitude of geologic time is important in the study of geology because many processes are so gradual that vast spans of time are needed before significant changes occur.

How long is 4.6 billion years? If you were to begin counting at the rate of one number per second and continued 24 hours a day, seven days a week and never stopped, it would take about two lifetimes (150 years) to reach 4.6 billion! Another interesting basis for comparison is as follows (Figure 1.8):

> Compress, for example, the entire 4.6 billion years of geologic time into a single year. On that scale the oldest rocks we know date from about mid-March. Living things first appeared in the sea in late April. Land plants and animals emerged on December 1st and the widespread swamps that formed the Carboniferous coal deposits flourished for about four days in early December. Dinosaurs became dominant in mid-December but disappeared on the 27th at about the time the Rocky Mountains were first uplifted. Human-like creatures appeared about 8 P.M. on the evening of December 31st, and the most recent continental ice sheets began to recede from the Great Lakes area and from northern Europe about 1 minute and 25 seconds before midnight on the 31st. Rome ruled the Western world for 5 seconds from 11:59:45 to 11:59:50. Columbus discovered North America 3 seconds before midnight, and the science of geology was born with the writings of James Hutton just slightly more than one second before the end of our eventful year of years.*

The foregoing is just one of many analogies that have attempted to convey the magnitude of geologic time. Although helpful, all of them—no matter how clever—can only begin to help us comprehend the vast expanse of Earth history and the enormous number of events that have occurred. Nevertheless, now that you have some notion of the evolution of geologic thinking, and of Earth's antiquity, we will briefly review how scientists think our planet came to be and how it is layered before we peek at the major geologic development of the twentieth century—plate tectonics. Later in the book we present details of plate tectonics, which frames the context in which other topics are discussed.

EARLY EVOLUTION OF EARTH

Recent earthquakes caused by displacements of Earth's crust and lava erupted from active volcanoes represent only the latest in a long line of events by

*Modified from D. L. Eicher, *Geologic Time*, 2nd ed. (Englewood Cliffs, New Jersey: Prentice Hall, 1978), pp. 18–19. Reprinted by permission.

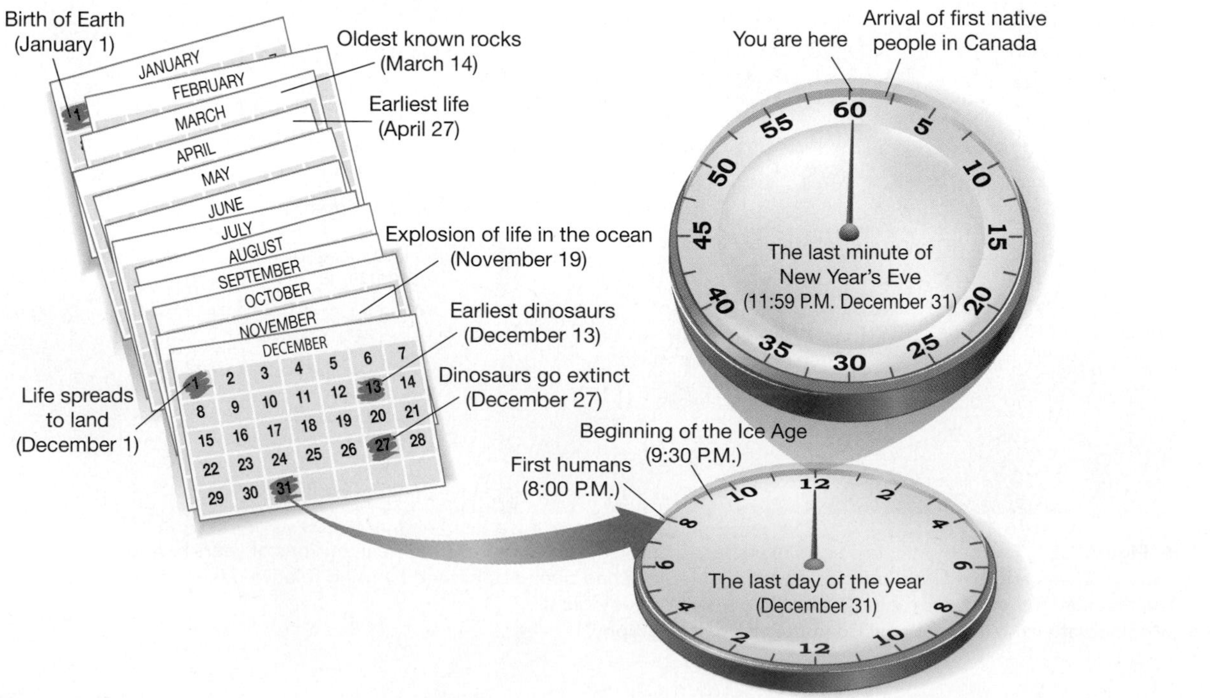

◆ **Figure 1.8** The 4.6 billion years of Earth history squeezed into just one year. (Adapted from Clague, J., and R. Turner. 2003. *Vancouver, City on the edge: Living with a dynamic geological landscape.* Vancouver, BC: Tricouni Press. Permission from Tricouni Press Ltd.)

which our planet has attained its present form and structure. The geologic processes operating in Earth's interior can be best understood when viewed in the context of much earlier events in Earth history.

Origin of Planet Earth

Earth's story began about 12 billion to 15 billion years ago with the *Big Bang*, an incomprehensibly large explosion that sent all matter of the universe flying outward at incredible speeds. In time, the debris from this explosion, which was almost entirely hydrogen and helium, began to cool and condense into the first stars and galaxies. It was in one of these galaxies, the Milky Way, that our solar system and planet Earth took form.

Earth, along with other planets, several dozen moons, and numerous smaller bodies, revolve around the Sun. The orderly nature of our solar system leads most researchers to conclude that Earth and the other planets formed at essentially the same time and from the same primordial material as the Sun. The **nebular hypothesis** suggests that the bodies of our solar system evolved from an enormous rotating cloud called the *solar nebula*, composed mostly of hydrogen and helium, with a small percentage of the heavier elements (Figure 1.9).

About 5 billion years ago this huge cloud of gases and minute particles began to gravitationally contract (what triggered the collapse is not known). As this slowly spiralling nebula contracted, it rotated faster and faster for the same reason ice skaters do when they draw their arms toward their bodies. Eventually the inward pull of gravity came into balance with the outward force caused by the rotational motion of the nebula (Figure 1.9). By this time the once vast cloud had assumed a flat disk shape with a large concentration of material at its centre called the *protosun* (pre-Sun).

During the collapse, gravitational energy was converted to thermal energy (heat), causing the temperature of the inner portion of the nebula to dramatically rise. However, the formation of the Sun marked the end of the period of contraction and thus the end of gravitational heating. Temperatures in the region where the inner planets now reside began to decline. The decrease in temperature caused those substances with high melting points to coalesce (join together). Such materials as iron and nickel and the elements of which the rock-forming minerals are composed—silicon, calcium, sodium, and so forth—formed metallic and rocky clumps that orbited the Sun. Repeated collisions caused these fragments to coalesce into larger asteroid-sized bodies, which in a few tens of millions of years accreted into the four

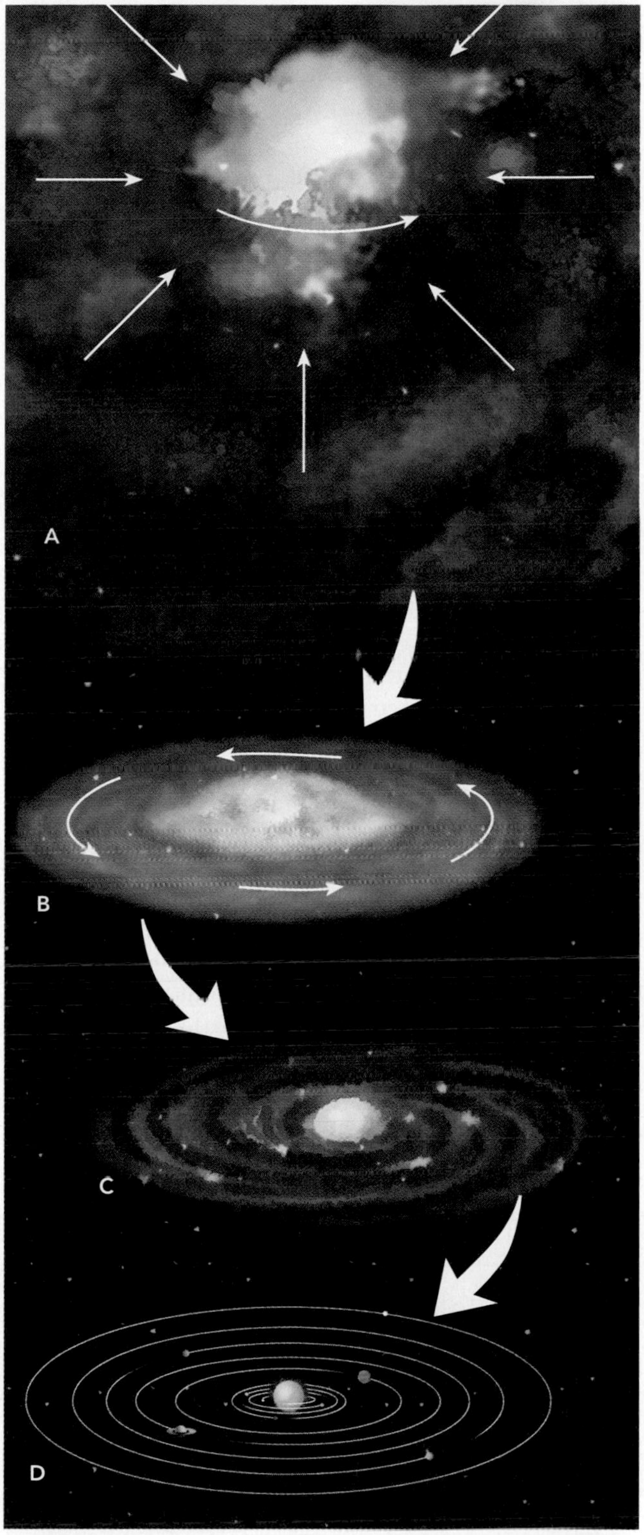

◆ **Figure 1.9** Nebular hypothesis. **A.** A huge rotating cloud of dust and gases (nebula) begins to contract. **B.** Most of the material is gravitationally swept toward the centre, producing the Sun. However, owing to rotational motion, some dust and gases remain orbiting the central body as a flattened disk. **C.** The planets begin to accrete from the material that is orbiting within the flattened disk. **D.** In time most of the remaining debris collected into the planets and their moons.

inner planets, including Earth. Not all of these clumps of matter were incorporated into the *protoplanets* (pre-planets). Those that remained in orbit are called *meteorites* when they survive an impact with Earth.

Formation of Earth's Layered Structure

As material accumulated to form Earth (and for a short period afterward), the high-velocity impact of nebular debris and the decay of radioactive elements caused the temperature of our planet to steadily increase. During this time of intense heating, Earth became hot enough to melt iron and nickel. Melting produced liquid blobs of heavy metal that sank toward the centre of the planet. This process occurred rapidly on the scale of geologic time and produced Earth's dense iron-rich **core**.

The early episode of heating resulted in another process of chemical differentiation, whereby melting formed buoyant masses of molten rock that rose toward the surface, where they solidified to produce a primitive **crust**. These rocky materials were enriched in oxygen and oxygen-seeking elements, particularly silicon and aluminum, along with lesser amounts of calcium, sodium, potassium, iron, and magnesium. In addition, some heavy metals, such as gold, lead, and uranium, which have low melting points or were highly soluble in the ascending molten masses, were scavenged from Earth's interior and concentrated in the developing crust. This early period of chemical segregation established the three basic divisions of Earth's interior: the iron-rich *core*, the thin *primitive crust*, and Earth's largest layer, called the **mantle**, which is located between the core and crust and is also dominated by iron, magnesium, and oxygen-seeking elements.

An important consequence of this early interval of chemical differentiation is that large volumes of gases were allowed to escape from Earth's interior, as happens today during volcanic eruptions. By this process a primitive atmosphere gradually evolved. It was on this planet, with this atmosphere, that life as we know it came into existence. We will elaborate on Earth's interior after we introduce the most important development in geologic thinking in recent times—plate tectonics.

PLATE TECTONICS: A GEOLOGIC PARADIGM

Earth is a dynamic planet! If we could go back in time a few hundred million years, we would find the face of our planet dramatically different from what we see today. There would be no Great Lakes, Rocky Mountains, or prairies. Moreover, we would find continents having different sizes and shapes and located in different positions than today's landmasses. In contrast, over the past few billion years, the Moon's surface has remained essentially unchanged—only a few craters have been added.

Within the past several decades a great deal has been learned about the workings of our dynamic planet. This episode has witnessed an unequalled revolution in our understanding of Earth. The revolution began in the early part of the twentieth century with the radical proposal by Alfred Wegener (Figure 1.10) of **continental drift**—the idea that the continents moved about the face of the planet. This proposal contradicted the established view that the continents and ocean basins are permanent and stationary features on the face of Earth. For that

◆ **Figure 1.10** Alfred Wegener shown waiting out the 1912–1913 Arctic winter during an expedition to Greenland, where he made a 1200-kilometre traverse across the widest part of the island's ice sheet. (Photo courtesy of Bildarchiv Preussischer Kulturbesitz, Berlin)

reason, the notion of drifting continents was received with great skepticism and even ridicule. More than 50 years passed before enough data were gathered to transform this controversial hypothesis into a **paradigm** (comprehensive theory held with a very high degree of confidence and respect) that wove together the basic processes known to operate on Earth. The paradigm that finally emerged, called **plate tectonics** (*tekton* = to build), provided geologists with the first comprehensive model of Earth's internal workings.*

Thus, the paradigm of plate tectonics did not appear overnight; it evolved gradually over several decades from its first incarnation as continental drift. We'll briefly review Wegener's evidence, then introduce the main components of the plate tectonics paradigm.

Continental Drift: An Idea Before Its Time

The idea that continents, particularly South America and Africa, fit together like pieces of a jigsaw puzzle originated with the development of reasonably accurate world maps. However, little significance was given to this idea until 1915, when Alfred Wegener, a German meteorologist and geophysicist, published *The Origin of Continents and Oceans*. In this book, Wegener set forth the basic outline of his radical hypothesis of continental drift.

Wegener suggested that a single *supercontinent* called **Pangaea** (*pan* = all, *gaea* = Earth) once existed (Figure 1.11). He further hypothesized that about 200 million years ago this supercontinent began breaking into smaller continents, which then "drifted" to their present positions, based on the following evidence.

Fit of the Continents Like a few others before him, Wegener first suspected that the continents might once have been joined when he noticed the remarkable similarity between the coastlines on opposite sides of the South Atlantic. However, his use of present-day shorelines to make a fit of the continents was challenged immediately by other Earth scientists. These opponents correctly argued that shorelines are continually modified by erosional, depositional, and tectonic processes.

Many years later, a much better approximation of the true outer boundary of the continents was used—the **continental shelf**, a gently sloping platform of continental material extending seaward from the shore. Today the seaward edge of the continental shelf lies submerged, a few hundred metres below sea level. In the early 1960s, Sir Edward Bullard and two associates produced a map that attempted to fit the edges of the continental shelves of South America and Africa at a depth of 900 metres. The remarkable fit that was obtained is shown in Figure 1.12. Although the continents overlap in a few places, these are regions where streams have deposited large

*Plate tectonics can be defined as the composite of various ideas explaining the observed motion of Earth's lithosphere through the mechanisms of subduction and seafloor spreading, which in turn generate Earth's major features, including continents and ocean basins (terms will be explained shortly).

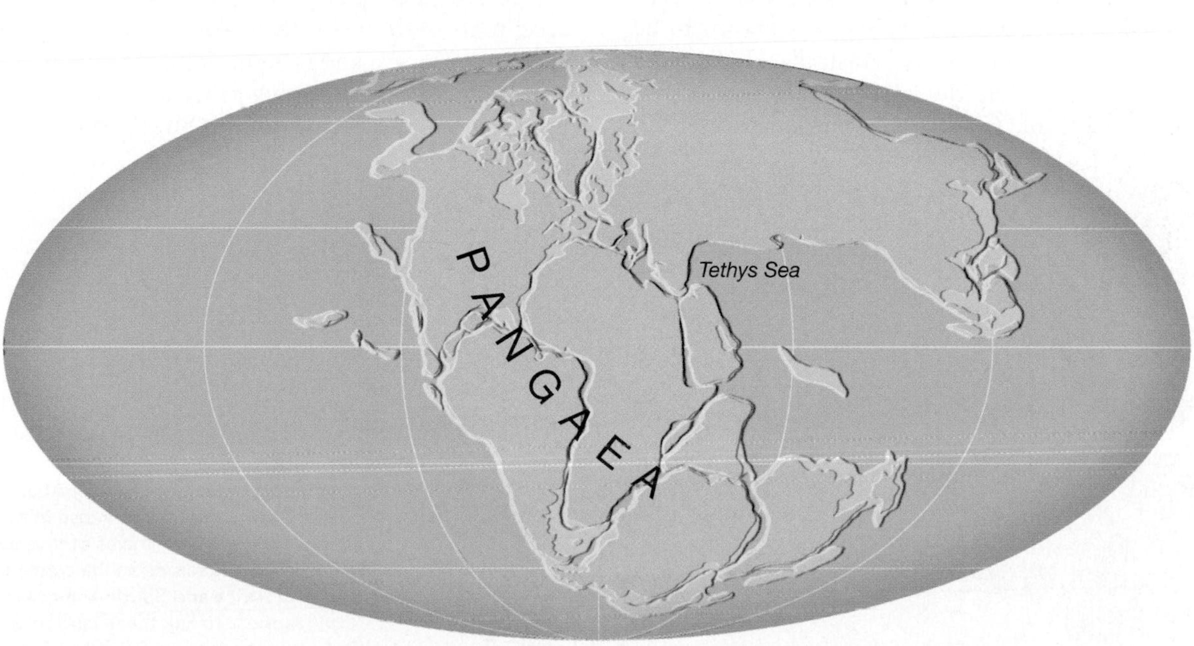

◆ **Figure 1.11** Reconstruction of Pangaea as it is thought to have appeared 200 million years ago.

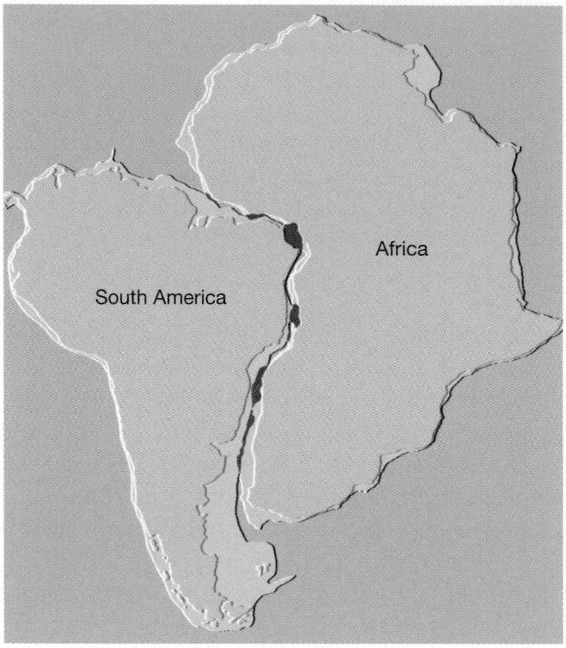

◆ **Figure 1.12** This figure shows the best fit of South America and Africa along the continental slope at a depth of about 900 metres. The areas where continental blocks overlap appear in brown.
(After A. G. Smith, "Continental Drift." In *Understanding the Earth*, edited by I. G. Gass)

quantities of sediment, thus enlarging the continental shelves.

Fossil Evidence To add credibility to his argument for the existence of the supercontinent Pangaea, Wegener cited the distribution of the fossil fern *Glossopteris*. This plant, identified by its large seeds that could not be blown very far, was known to be widely dispersed in Africa, Australia, India, and South America during the late Paleozoic Era. Later, fossil remains of *Glossopteris* were discovered in Antarctica as well. Wegener also learned that these seed ferns and associated flora grew only in a subpolar climate. Therefore, he concluded that the landmasses must have been joined, because they are presently located in climatic zones that are far too diverse to support these cold-loving plants. For Wegener, fossils were convincing evidence that a supercontinent had existed.

Wegener also came across an article citing fossil evidence for the existence of a land bridge connecting South America and Africa. Through a search of the literature, Wegener learned that most paleobotanists (scientists who study the fossilized remains of plants) agreed that some type of land connection was needed to explain the existence of identical fossils on widely separated landmasses. This requirement was particularly true for late Paleozoic and early Mesozoic life forms.

Wegener cited documented cases of several fossil organisms that had been found on different landmasses but that could not have crossed the vast oceans presently separating the continents. The classic example is *Mesosaurus*, a presumably aquatic, snaggle-toothed reptile whose fossil remains are limited to eastern South America and southern Africa (Figure 1.13). If *Mesosaurus* had been able to swim well enough to cross the vast South Atlantic Ocean, its remains should be more widely distributed. As this was not the case, Wegener argued that South America and Africa must have been joined somehow.

How did scientists during Wegener's era explain the discovery of identical fossil organisms in places separated by thousands of kilometres of open ocean? The idea of land bridges was the most widely accepted solution to the problem of migration (Figure 1.14). We know, for example, that during the recent Ice Age, the lowering of sea level allowed animals to cross the narrow Bering Strait between Asia

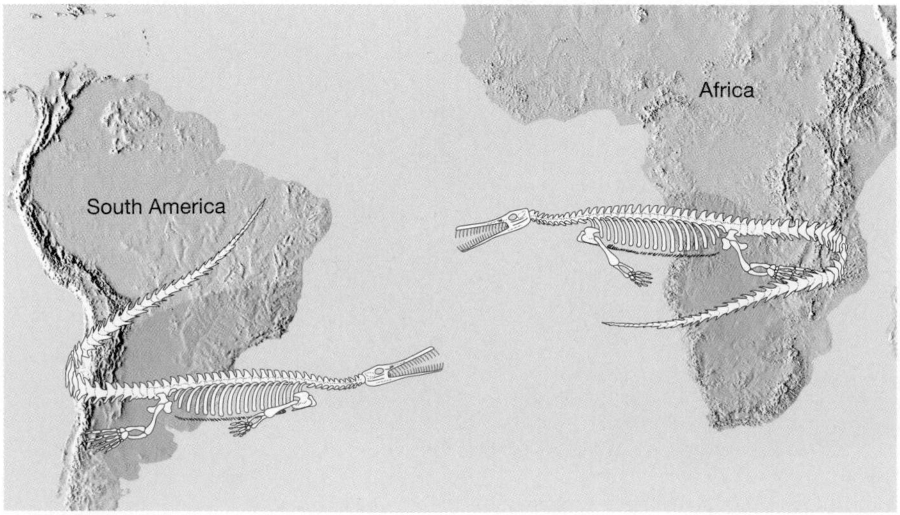

◆ **Figure 1.13** Fossils of *Mesosaurus* have been found on both sides of the South Atlantic Ocean and nowhere else in the world. Fossil remains of this and other organisms on the continents of Africa and South America appear to link these landmasses during the late Paleozoic Era and early Mesozoic Era.

◆ **Figure 1.14** These sketches by John Holden illustrate various explanations for the occurrence of similar species on landmasses that are presently separated by vast oceans. (Reprinted with permission of John Holden)

and North America. Was it possible that land bridges once connected Africa and South America? We are now quite certain that land bridges of this magnitude did not exist. If they had, their remnants should still lie below sea level, but they are nowhere to be found.

Rock Type and Structural Similarities Anyone who has worked a jigsaw puzzle knows that in addition to the pieces fitting together, the picture must be continuous as well. The picture that must match in the continental drift puzzle is one of rock types and mountain belts found on the continents. If the continents were once together, as the supercontinent of Pangaea, the rocks found in a particular region on one continent should closely match in age and type with those found in adjacent positions on the adjoining continent.

Such evidence exists in the form of mountain belts that terminate at one coastline, only to reappear on a landmass across the ocean. For instance, the mountain belt that includes the Appalachians trends northeastward through eastern North America and disappears off the coast of Newfoundland and Labrador (Figure 1.15A). Mountains of comparable

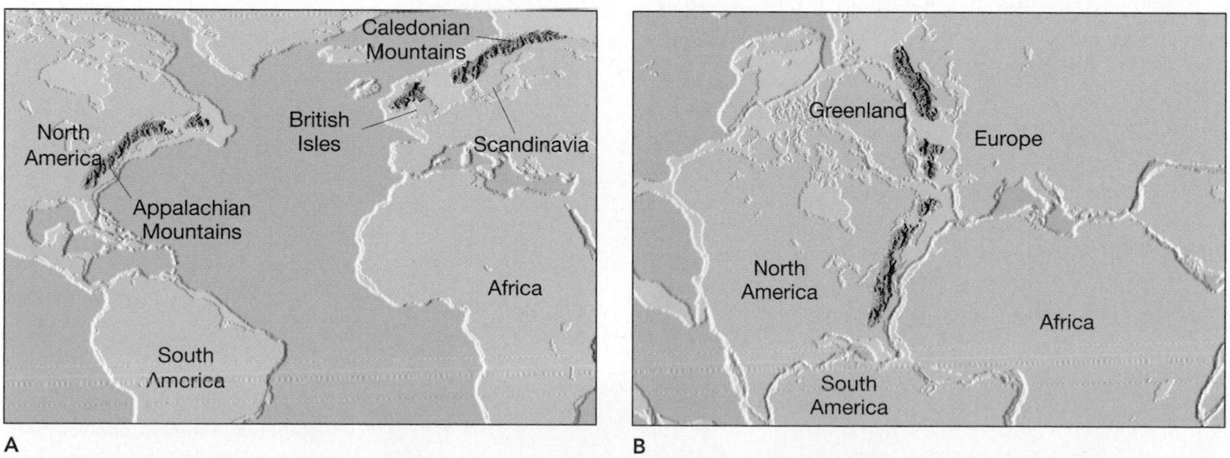

◆ **Figure 1.15** Matching mountain ranges across the North Atlantic. **A.** The Appalachian Mountains trend along the eastern flank of North America and disappear off the coast of Newfoundland and Labrador. Mountains of comparable age and structure are found in the British Isles and Scandinavia. **B.** When these landmasses are placed in their pre-drift locations, these ancient mountain chains form a nearly continuous belt. These folded mountain belts formed roughly 300 million years ago as the landmasses collided during the formation of the supercontinent of Pangaea.

age and structure are found in the British Isles and Scandinavia. When these landmasses are reassembled, as in Figure 1.15B, the mountain chains form a nearly continuous belt.

Wegener was very satisfied that the similarities in rock structure on both sides of the Atlantic linked these landmasses. In his own words, "It is just as if we were to refit the torn pieces of a newspaper by matching their edges and then check whether the lines of print run smoothly across. If they do, there is nothing left but to conclude that the pieces were in fact joined in this way."*

Paleoclimatic Evidence Because Alfred Wegener was a meteorologist by profession, he was keenly interested in obtaining paleoclimatic (*palaios* = ancient, *climatic* = climate) data in support of continental drift. His efforts were rewarded when he found evidence for apparently dramatic global climatic changes. In particular, he learned of ancient glacial deposits that indicated that near the end of the Paleozoic Era (between 300 million and 220 million years ago), ice sheets covered extensive areas of the Southern Hemisphere. Layers of ancient glacial rock called *tillite*, of the same age, were found in southern Africa and South America, as well as in India and Australia. Below these beds of glacial rock lay striated and grooved rock. In some locations the striations and grooves indicated that the ice had moved from what is now the sea onto land. Much of the land area containing evidence of this late Paleozoic glaciation presently lies within 30 degrees of the equator in a subtropical or tropical climate.

Could Earth have gone through an episode of sufficient cooling to have generated extensive continental ice sheets in what is presently a tropical region? Wegener rejected this explanation because during the late Paleozoic Era, large tropical swamps existed in the Northern Hemisphere. These swamps, with their lush vegetation, eventually became the major coalfields of eastern North America, Europe, and Siberia.

Wegener believed that a more plausible explanation for the late Paleozoic glaciation was provided if the landmasses were fitted together as a supercontinent, with South Africa centred over the

*A. Wegener, *The Origin of Continents and Oceans*. Translated from the 4th revised German edition of 1929 by J. Birman (London: Methuen, 1966).

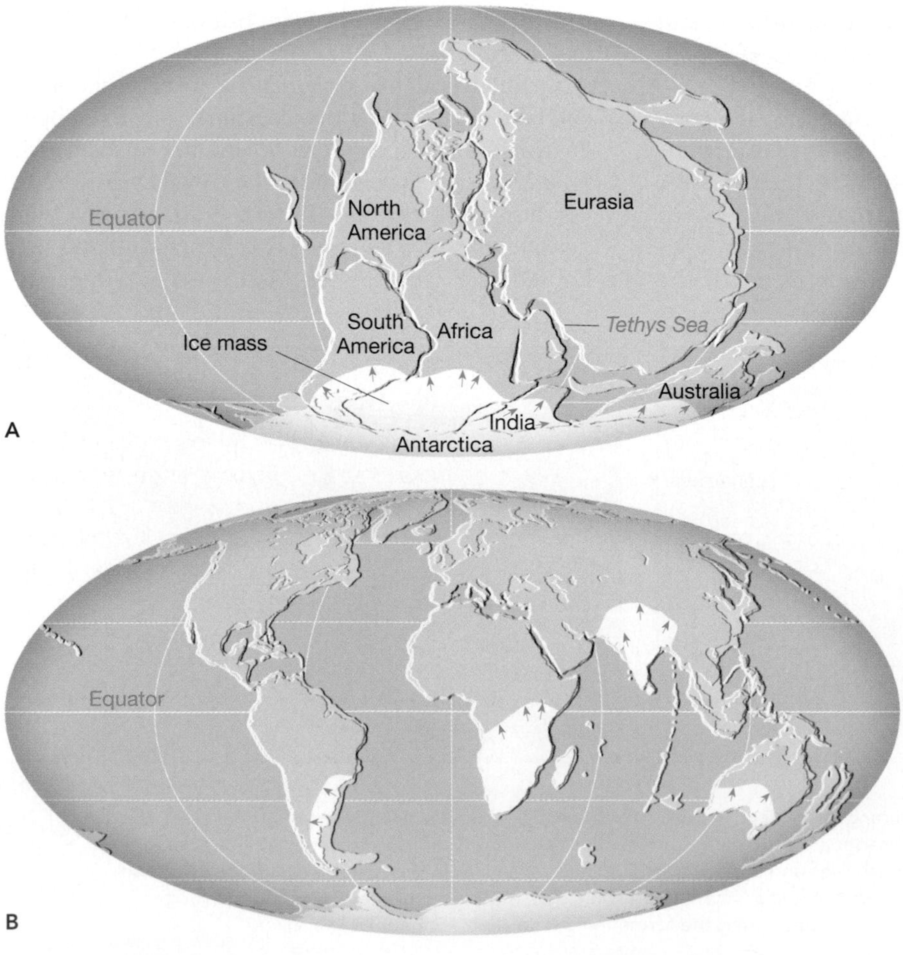

◆ **Figure 1.16** **A.** The supercontinent Pangaea, showing the area covered by glacial ice 300 million years ago. **B.** The continents as they are today. White areas contain evidence of the old ice sheet.

South Pole (Figure 1.16). This would account for the conditions necessary to generate extensive expanses of glacial ice over much of the Southern Hemisphere. At the same time, this geography would place today's northern landmasses nearer the equator and account for their vast coal deposits. Wegener was so convinced that his explanation was correct that he wrote, "This evidence is so compelling that by comparison all other criteria must take a back seat."

How does a glacier develop in hot, arid Australia? How do land animals migrate across wide expanses of open water? As compelling as this evidence may have been, 50 years passed before most of the scientific community would accept it and the logical conclusions to which it led. Unfortunately Alfred Wegener perished on the Greenland Ice Sheet in 1930 and did not live to see his idea vindicated.

PLANET OF SHIFTING PLATES

GEODe EARTH Plate Tectonics
↳ Introduction

According to the plate tectonics model, Earth's rigid outer shell, called the **lithosphere** (sphere of rock) by geologists, is broken into numerous slabs called **plates**, which are in motion and are continually changing shape and size. As shown in Figure 1.17, seven major lithospheric plates are recognized. They are the North American, South American, Pacific, African, Eurasian, Australian-Indian, and Antarctic plates. Intermediate-size plates include the Caribbean, Nazca, Philippine, Arabian, Cocos, Juan de Fuca, and Scotia plates. In addition, over a dozen smaller plates have been identified but are not shown in Figure 1.17. Note that several large plates include an entire continent plus a large area of seafloor (for example, the South American plate). However, none of the plates are defined entirely by the margins of a single continent.

The lithospheric plates move relative to one another at a very slow but continuous rate that averages about 5 centimetres a year. This movement is ultimately driven by the unequal distribution of heat within Earth, resulting in mantle **convection** (*con* = with, *vect* = carried). Hot material found deep in the mantle moves slowly upward and serves as one part of our planet's internal convective system. Concurrently, cooler, denser slabs of lithosphere descend back into the mantle, setting Earth's rigid outer shell in motion. Ultimately, the titanic movements of Earth's lithospheric plates generate earthquakes, create volcanoes, and deform large masses of rock into mountains.

Plate Boundaries

Lithospheric plates move as coherent units relative to all other plates. Although the interiors of plates may experience some deformation, all major interactions among individual plates (and therefore most deformation) occurs along their *boundaries*. In fact, the first attempts to outline plate boundaries were made by using the locations of earthquakes. Later work showed that plates are bounded by three distinct types of boundaries, which are distinguished by the type of relative movement they exhibit. These boundaries are depicted at the bottom of Figure 1.17 and briefly described here:

1. In **divergent boundaries**, plates move apart, resulting in upwelling of material from the mantle to create new seafloor (Figure 1.17A). Plate spreading (divergence) occurs mainly at a **mid-ocean ridge** (e.g., Mid-Atlantic Ridge, East Pacific Rise) but can also occur under rift valleys on continents. This mechanism has created the floor of the Atlantic Ocean during the past 160 million years and is appropriately called **seafloor spreading**. Along mid-ocean ridges molten rock emerges and the oceanic lithosphere is elevated and buoyant because it is hot and occupies more volume than do cooler rocks. Worldwide, this interconnected ridge system extends for more than 70,000 kilometres through all major ocean basins. As new lithosphere is formed along the oceanic ridge, it is slowly yet continually displaced away from the zone of upwelling along the ridge axis. In addition, cooling causes the hot material just below the seafloor to strengthen (become more rigid), thereby adding to the thickness of the plate (oceanic lithosphere in this case). Therefore, as that part of the plate moves farther away from the mid-ocean ridge with seafloor spreading, it becomes older, cooler, and thicker.
2. In **convergent boundaries**, plates move together, resulting in the descent (consumption) of oceanic lithosphere into the mantle (Figures 1.17B and 1.18), or two continental margins collide to create a major mountain system (Figure 1.18). Although new lithosphere is continually being added at the oceanic ridges, the planet is not growing in size—its total surface area remains essentially constant. To accommodate the newly created lithosphere, older oceanic plates return to Earth's interior along *convergent boundaries*. As two plates slowly converge, the leading edge of an oceanic slab is bent downward, allowing it to slide beneath the other slab by a process called **subduction**. Plate margins at which oceanic crust is being consumed are called **subduction zones**.

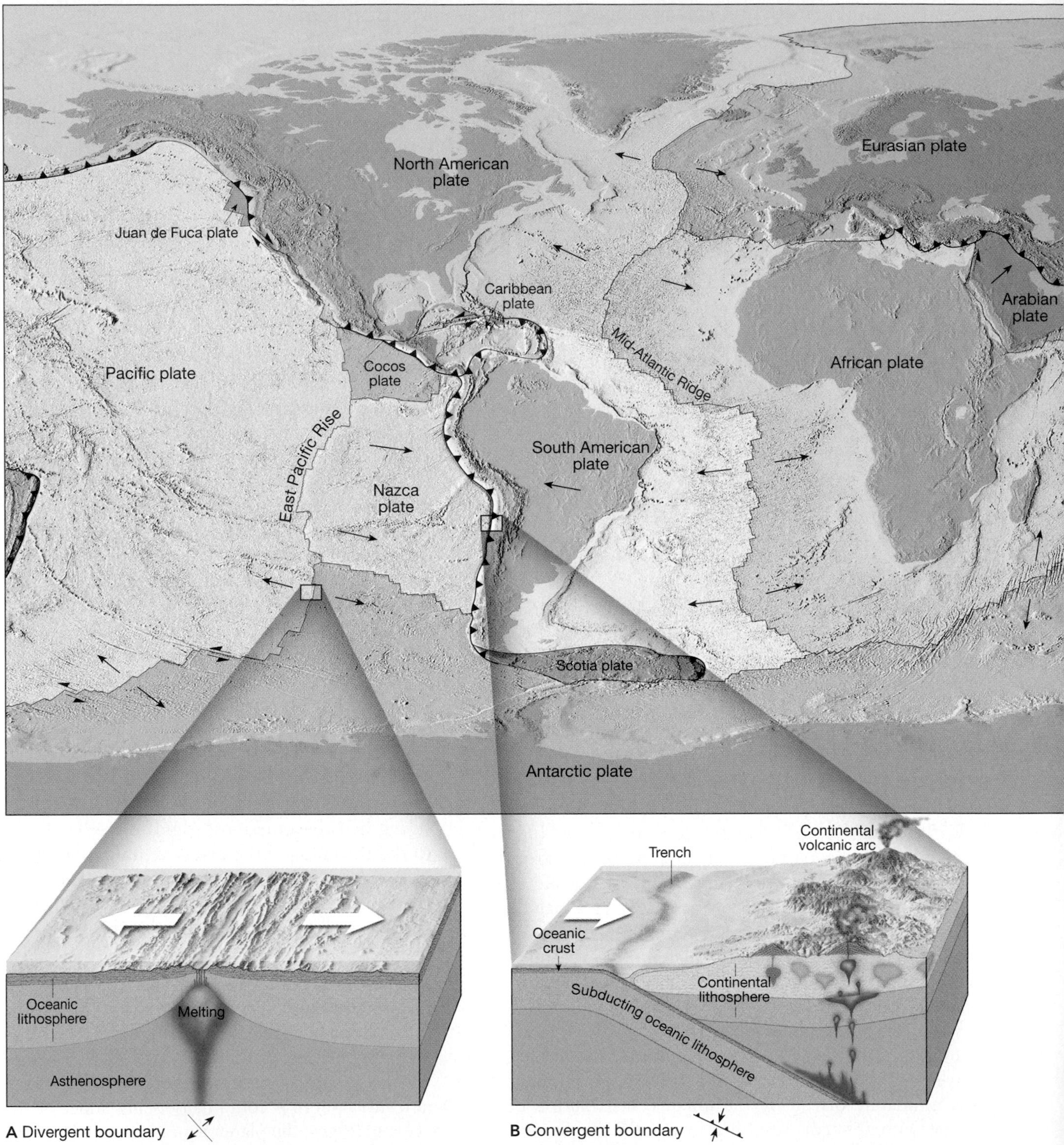

◆ **Figure 1.17** Mosaic of rigid lithospheric plates that constitute Earth's outer shell. (After W. B. Hamilton, U.S. Geological Survey)

3. In **transform fault boundaries**, plates slide past each other without the production or destruction of lithosphere (Figure 1.17C). These faults form in the direction of plate movement and were first discovered in association with offsets in oceanic ridges by Canadian John Tuzo Wilson. Although most transform faults are located along oceanic ridges, some slice through the continents (e.g., San Andreas Fault, Alpine Fault of New Zealand) and can cause devastating earthquakes.

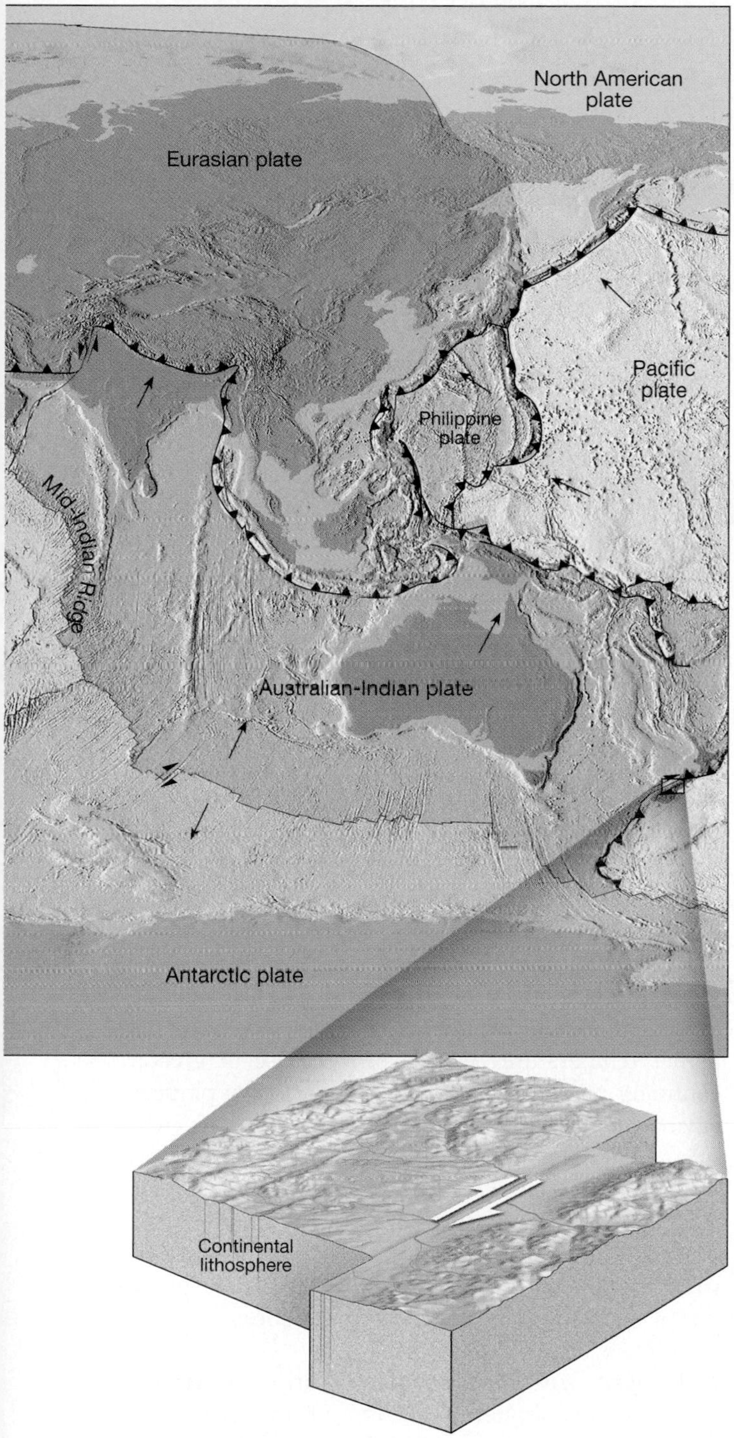

C Transform fault boundary

If you examine Figure 1.17, you can see that each large plate is bounded by a combination of these boundaries. Movement along one boundary requires that adjustments be made at the others.

Now that you have the basic idea of continental drift and plate tectonics, we will leave this topic to examine the internal structure, major spheres, and dominant surface features of our planet. In subsequent chapters we relate topics to plate tectonics, and in Chapter 12 we revisit the paradigm in detail (including paleomagnetic evidence), after gaining more background knowledge of minerals, rocks, dating methods, and internal Earth processes.

EARTH'S INTERNAL STRUCTURE

GEODe EARTH An Introduction to Geology
↳ Earth's Layered Structure

The segregation of material that began early in Earth's history resulted in the formation of three layers defined by their chemical composition: the crust, mantle, and core. In addition to these compositionally distinct layers, Earth can be divided into layers based on physical properties. The physical properties used to define such zones include whether the layer is solid or liquid and how weak or strong it is, based on criteria discussed later in Chapter 10. Knowledge of both types of layered structures is essential to our understanding of basic geologic processes, such as plate tectonics, volcanism, earthquakes, and mountain building (Figure 1.19).

Layers Defined by Composition

Crust The crust, Earth's comparatively thin, rocky outer skin, is generally divided into oceanic and continental crust. The oceanic crust is roughly 7 kilometres thick and composed of dark rocks called *basalt* (see Chapter 3). By contrast, the continental crust averages 35–40 kilometres thick but may exceed 70 kilometres in some mountainous regions. Unlike the oceanic crust, which has a relatively homogeneous chemical composition, the continental crust consists of many rock types. The upper crust has an average composition similar to a rock called *granite* (see Chapter 3), whereas the composition of the lowermost continental crust is more similar to basalt. Continental rocks have an average density of about 2.7 g/cm^3, and some have been discovered in the Northwest Territories that are 4 billion years old. The rocks of the oceanic crust are generally younger (180 million years or less) and denser (about 3.0 g/cm^3) than continental rocks.*

*Liquid water at sea level has a density of 1 g/cm^3; therefore, the density of basalt is three times that of water.

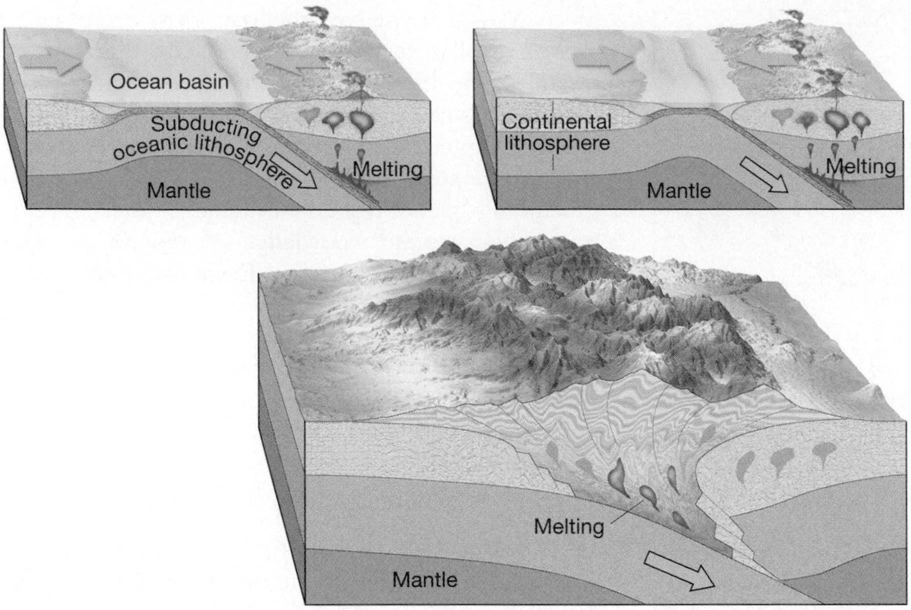

◆ **Figure 1.18** When two plates containing continental lithosphere collide, complex mountains are formed. The formation of the Himalayas represents a relatively recent example.

Mantle More than 82 percent of Earth's volume is contained in the mantle, a solid rocky shell that extends to a depth of 2900 kilometres. The boundary between the crust and mantle represents a marked change in chemical composition. The dominant rock type in the uppermost mantle is *peridotite* (see Chapter 3), which has a density of 3.3 g/cm^3. At greater depth peridotite changes by assuming a more compact crystalline structure and hence a greater density.

Core The composition of the core is thought to be an iron-nickel alloy with minor amounts of oxygen, silicon, and sulphur—elements that readily form compounds with iron. At the extreme pressure found in the core, this iron-rich material has an average density of nearly 11 g/cm^3 and approaches 14 times the density of water at Earth's centre.

Layers Defined by Physical Properties

Earth's interior is characterized by a gradual increase in temperature, pressure, and density with depth. Estimates put the temperature at a depth of 100 kilometres at between 1200°C and 1400°C, whereas the temperature at Earth's centre may exceed 6700°C. Clearly, Earth's interior has retained much of the energy acquired during its formative years, despite the fact that heat is continuously transferred to the surface, where it is lost to space. The increase in pressure with depth causes a corresponding increase in rock density.

The gradual increase in temperature and pressure with depth affects the physical properties and hence the mechanical behaviour of Earth materials. When a substance is heated, its chemical bonds weaken and its mechanical strength (resistance to deformation) is reduced. If the temperature exceeds the melting point of an Earth material, the material's chemical bonds break and melting ensues. If temperature were the only factor that determined whether a substance melted, our planet would be a molten ball covered with a thin, solid outer shell. However, pressure also increases with depth and tends to increase rock strength. Furthermore, because melting is accompanied by an increase in volume, it occurs at higher temperatures with depth because of greater confining pressure. Thus, depending on the physical environment (temperature and pressure), a particular Earth material may behave like a brittle solid, deform in a puttylike manner, or even melt and become liquid.

Earth can be divided into five main layers based on physical properties and hence mechanical strength: the lithosphere, asthenosphere, mesosphere (lower mantle), outer core, and inner core.

Lithosphere and Asthenosphere Earth's outermost layer (the lithosphere) consists of the crust and uppermost mantle and forms a relatively cool, rigid, and brittle shell. Although this layer is composed of materials with markedly different chemical compositions, it tends to act as a unit that exhibits rigid behaviour, mainly because it is cool and thus strong. The lithosphere averages about 100 kilometres in thickness but may be more than 250 kilometres thick below the older portions of the continents (Figure 1.19). Within the ocean basins, the lithosphere is only a few kilometres thick along the

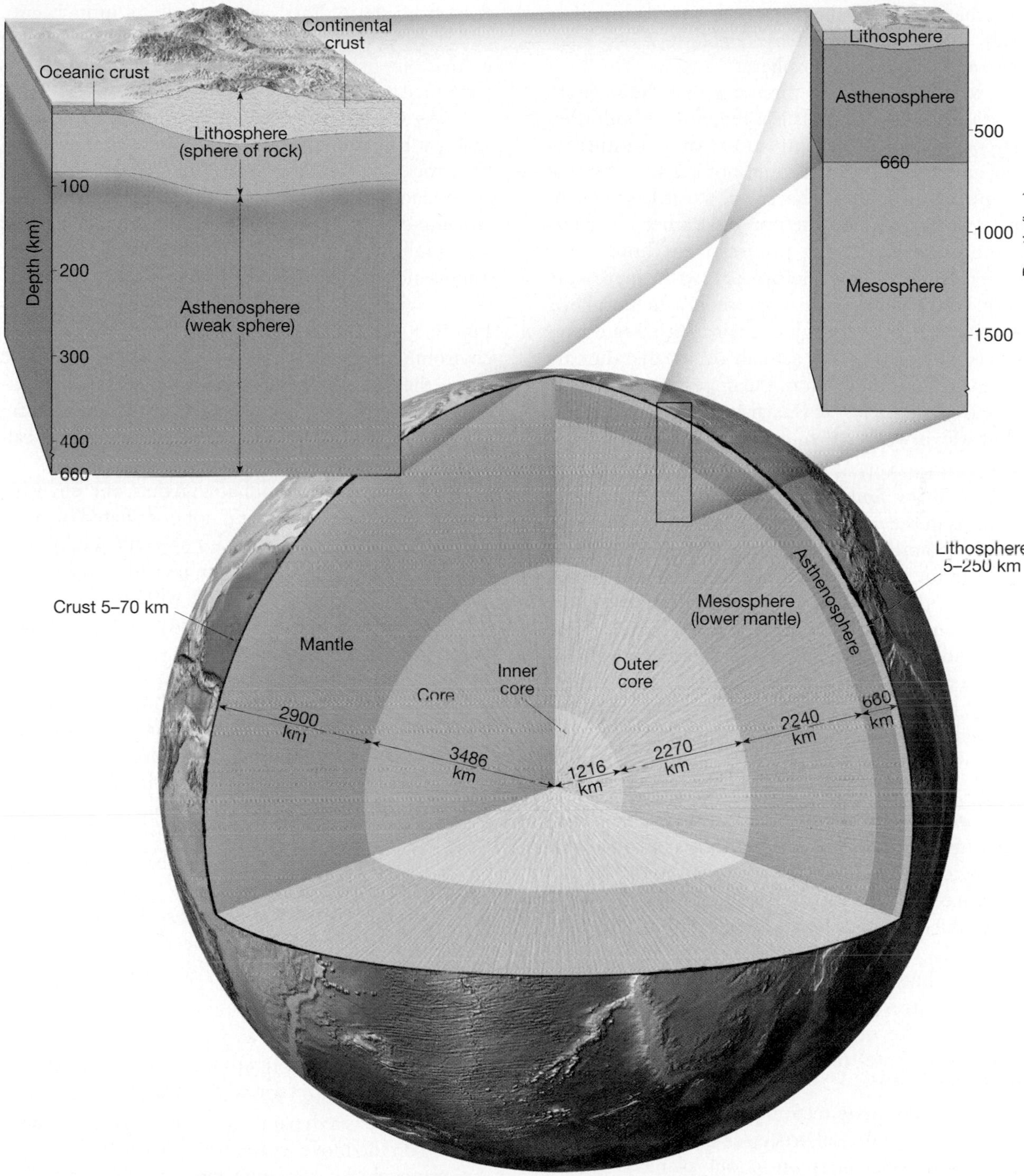

◆ **Figure 1.19** Views of Earth's layered structure. The left side of the large cross-section shows that Earth's interior is divided into three different layers based on compositional differences: the crust, mantle, and core. The right side of the large cross section depicts the five main layers of Earth's interior, based on physical properties and hence mechanical strength: the lithosphere, asthenosphere, mesosphere, outer core, and inner core. The block diagrams above the large cross-section show an enlarged view of the upper portion of Earth's interior.

oceanic ridges but increases to perhaps 100 kilometres in regions of older and cooler oceanic crust.

Beneath the lithosphere, in the upper mantle (to a depth of about 660 kilometres) lies the soft, comparatively weak **asthenosphere** ("weak sphere"). The top portion of the asthenosphere has a temperature/pressure regime that results in a small amount of melting. Within this very weak zone the lithosphere is mechanically detached from the layer below. The result is that the lithosphere is able to move independently of the asthenosphere.

It is important to emphasize that the strength of various Earth materials is a function of both their composition and the temperature and pressure of their environment. You should not get the idea that the entire lithosphere behaves like a brittle solid similar to rocks found on the surface. Rather, the rocks of the lithosphere get progressively hotter and weaker (more easily deformed) with increasing depth. At the depth of the uppermost asthenosphere, the rocks are close enough to their melting temperatures (some melting may actually occur) that they are very easily deformed. Thus, the uppermost asthenosphere is weak because it is near its melting point, just as hot wax is weaker than cold wax.

Mesosphere or Lower Mantle Below the zone of weakness in the uppermost asthenosphere, increased pressure counteracts the effects of higher temperature, and the rocks gradually strengthen with depth. Between the depths of 660 kilometres and 2900 kilometres a more rigid layer is found, called the **mesosphere** (*middle sphere*) or **lower mantle**. Despite their strength, the rocks of the mesosphere are still very hot and capable of very gradual flow, an essential component of the heat transfer mechanism that drives plate tectonics.

Inner and Outer Core The core, which is composed mostly of an iron-nickel alloy, is divided into two regions that exhibit very different mechanical strengths. The **outer core** is a *liquid layer* 2270 kilometres thick. It is the convective flow of metallic iron within this zone that generates Earth's magnetic field (Box 1.2). The **inner core** is a sphere with a radius of 1216 kilometres. Despite its higher temperature, the material in the inner core is stronger (because of immense pressure) than the outer core and behaves like a *solid*.

From the plate tectonics introduction, we can see that Earth's internal processes are intimately connected with what goes on at our planet's surface, which we will look at next.

A VIEW OF EARTH

GEODe EARTH An Introduction to Geology ↳ A View of Earth

A view of Earth, such as the one in Figure 1.20A, provided the *Apollo 8* astronauts and the rest of humanity with a unique perspective of our home. Seen from space, Earth is breathtaking in its beauty and startling in its solitude. Such an image reminds us that our home is, after all, a planet—small, self-contained, and fragile.

As we look more closely at our planet from space, it becomes apparent that Earth is much more than rock and soil (Figure 1.20B). In fact, the most conspicuous features are not the continents but the swirling clouds suspended above the surface and the vast global ocean. These features emphasize the importance of air and water to our planet.

The closer view of Earth from space, shown in Figure 1.20B, helps us appreciate why the physical environment is traditionally divided into three major parts: the water portion of our planet, the hydrosphere; Earth's gaseous envelope, the atmosphere; and, of course, the solid Earth, which geologists call the geosphere.

It needs to be emphasized that our environment is highly integrated and not dominated by rock, water, or air alone. Rather, it is characterized by continuous interactions as air comes in contact with rock, rock with water, and water with air. Moreover, the biosphere, which is the totality of all plant and animal life on our planet, interacts with each of the three physical realms and is an equally integral part of the planet. Thus, Earth can be thought of as consisting of four major spheres: the hydrosphere, atmosphere, biosphere, and geosphere.

The interactions among Earth's four spheres are uncountable. The photo on the cover of this book and Figure 1.21 provide us with examples. The shoreline is an obvious meeting place for rock, water, and air. Ocean waves created by the drag of air moving across open water break against the rocky shore. The force of the water can be powerful and the erosional work that is accomplished can be great.

Hydrosphere

Earth is sometimes called the *blue* planet. Water, more than anything else, makes Earth unique. The **hydrosphere** is a dynamic mass of water that is continually on the move, evaporating from the oceans to the atmosphere, precipitating on the land, and returning to the ocean again. The global ocean is certainly the most prominent feature of the hydrosphere (Figure 1.20B), blanketing nearly 71 percent of Earth's surface to an average depth of about 3800 metres. It accounts for about 97 percent of Earth's water. However, the hydrosphere also includes the fresh water found underground and in streams, lakes, and glaciers that are responsible for sculpting and creating many of our planet's varied landforms.

BOX 1.2

Understanding Earth
Why Does Earth Have a Magnetic Field?

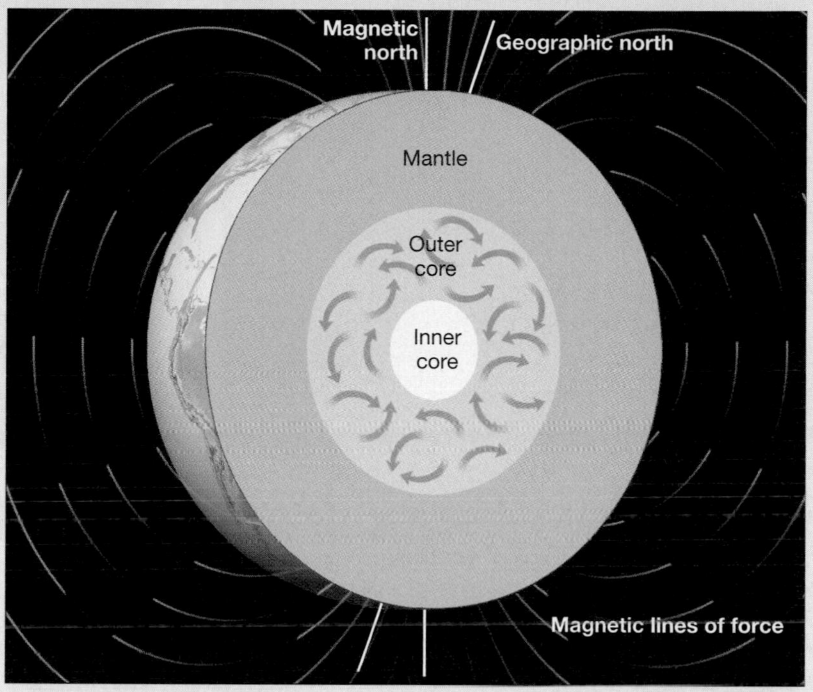

◆ **Figure 1.B** Earth's magnetic field is thought to be generated by convection of molten iron alloy in the liquid outer core.

Anyone who has used a compass to find direction knows that Earth's magnetic field has a north pole and a south pole. In many respects our planet's magnetic field resembles that produced by a simple bar magnet. Invisible lines of force pass through Earth and out into space while extending from one pole to the other (Figure 1.B). A compass needle, which is a small magnet free to move about, becomes aligned with these lines of force and points toward the magnetic poles. Note that Earth's magnetic poles do not coincide exactly with the geographic poles. The north magnetic pole is located in northeast Canada, near Hudson Bay, while the south magnetic pole is located near Antarctica in the Indian Ocean south of Australia.

In the early 1960s, geophysicists learned that Earth's magnetic field periodically (every million years or so) reverses polarity; that is, the north magnetic pole becomes the south magnetic pole, and vice versa. The cause of these reversals is apparently linked to the fact that Earth's magnetic field experiences long-term fluctuations in intensity. Recent calculations indicate that the magnetic field has weakened by about 5 percent over the past century. If this trend continues for another 1500 years, Earth's magnetic field will become very weak or even nonexistent.

It has been suggested that the decline in magnetic intensity is related to changes in the convective flow in the core. In a similar manner, magnetic reversals may be triggered when something disturbs the main convection pattern of the fluid core. After a reversal takes place, the flow is re-established and builds a magnetic field with opposite polarity.

Magnetic reversals are not unique to Earth. The Sun's magnetic field regularly reverses polarity, having an average period of about 22 years. These solar reversals are closely tied to the well-known 11-year sunspot cycle.

When Earth's magnetic field was first described in 1600, it was thought to originate from permanently magnetized materials located deep within Earth. We have since learned that except for the upper crust, the planet is much too hot for magnetic materials to retain their magnetism. Furthermore, permanently magnetized materials are not known to vary their intensity in a manner that would account for the observed long-term waxing and waning of Earth's magnetic field.

The details of how Earth's magnetic field is produced are still poorly understood. Nevertheless, most investigators agree that the gradual flow of molten iron in the outer core is important to the process. The most widely accepted view proposes that the core behaves like a self-sustaining *dynamo*, a device that converts mechanical energy into magnetic energy. The driving forces of this system are Earth's rotation and the unequal distribution of heat in the interior, which propels the highly conductive molten iron in the outer core. As the iron churns in the outer core, it interacts with Earth's magnetic field. This interaction generates an electric current, just as moving a wire past a magnet creates a current in the wire. Once established, the electric current produces a magnetic field that reinforces Earth's magnetic field. As long as the flow within the molten iron outer core continues, electric currents will be produced and Earth's magnetic field will be sustained.

Atmosphere

Earth is surrounded by a life-giving gaseous envelope called the **atmosphere**. Compared with the geosphere, the atmosphere is thin and tenuous (Figure 1.20B). Fifty percent lies below an altitude of 5.6 kilometres, and 90 percent occurs within just

A

B

◆ **Figure 1.20** **A.** View that greeted the *Apollo 8* astronauts as their spacecraft emerged from behind the Moon. **B.** Africa and Arabia are prominent in this image of Earth taken from *Apollo 17*. The tan cloud-free zones over the land coincide with major desert regions. The band of clouds across central Africa is associated with a much wetter climate that in places sustains tropical rain forests. The dark blue of the oceans and the swirling cloud patterns remind us of the importance of the oceans and the atmosphere. Antarctica, a continent covered by glacial ice, is visible over the South Pole. (Photo **A** by NASA Headquarters; photo **B** by NASA/Science Source/Photo Researchers, Inc.)

16 kilometres of Earth's surface. By comparison, Earth's lithosphere averages 100 kilometres in thickness! Despite its modest dimensions, this thin blanket of air is a crucial part of the planet. It not only provides the air that we breathe but also protects us from the Sun's intense heat and dangerous ultraviolet radiation. The energy exchanges that continually occur between the atmosphere and Earth's surface and between the atmosphere and space produce the effects we call weather and climate. Without weather and climate there would be no weathering and little erosion of Earth's surface.

Biosphere

The **biosphere** includes all life on Earth. It is concentrated near the surface in a zone that extends from the ocean floor upward for several kilometres into the atmosphere. Plants and animals depend on the physical environment for the basics of life. However, organisms do more than just respond to

◆ **Figure 1.21** The shoreline is one obvious meeting place for rock, water, and air. The rocks that dominate this scene were smoothed by ocean waves created by the force of moving air. The calm conditions apparent in this photograph of Peggy's Cove, Nova Scotia, are deceptive, for the force of the water can be powerful during storms, and the erosional work that is accomplished can be great.
(Photo by Mike Schering)

their physical environment. Through countless interactions, life forms help maintain and alter their physical environment. Without life, the makeup and nature of the geosphere, hydrosphere, and atmosphere would be very different.

Geosphere

Lying beneath the atmosphere and oceans is the geosphere. Much of our study of the geosphere focuses on more accessible surface features that we will briefly examine next before concluding the chapter by considering Earth as a system with a rock cycle.

THE FACE OF EARTH

GEODe EARTH An Introduction to Geology
↳ Features of the Continents and Floor of the Ocean

The two principal divisions of Earth's surface are the continents and the ocean basins (Figure 1.22). A significant difference between these two areas is their relative levels. The average elevation of the continents above sea level is about 840 metres, whereas the average depth of the oceans is about 3800 metres. Thus, the continents stand, on average, 4640 metres above the level of the ocean floor.

◆ **Figure 1.22** Major physical features of some continents and ocean basins. The diversity of features on the ocean floor is as great as on the continents.

Although land and sea meet at the shoreline, this is not the boundary between the continents and the ocean basins; the real boundary is marked by the outer edge of the continental shelf, a gently sloping platform of continental material that extends seaward from the shore. A glance at Figure 1.22 shows that the width of the continental shelf is variable. For example, it is broad along the East and Arctic coasts of North America but relatively narrow along the Pacific margin of the continent.

The boundary between the continents and the deep-ocean basins lies along the **continental slope**, which is a steep drop-off that extends from the outer edge of the continental shelf to the floor of the deep ocean (Figure 1.22). Using this as the dividing line, we find that about 60 percent of Earth's surface is represented by ocean basins and the remaining 40 percent by continents.

Continents

The most prominent topographic features of the continents are linear mountain belts. Although the distribution of mountains may appear to be random, this is not the case. When the youngest mountains are considered, we find that they are located principally in two zones. The circum-Pacific belt (the region surrounding the Pacific Ocean) includes the mountains of the western Americas and continues into the western Pacific in the form of volcanic island arcs. Island arcs are active mountainous regions composed largely of deformed volcanic rocks and include the Aleutian Islands, Japan, the Philippines, and New Guinea.

The other major mountain belt extends eastward from the Alps through Iran and the Himalayas, and then dips southward into Indonesia. Careful examination of mountainous terrains reveals that most are places where thick sequences of rocks have been squeezed and highly deformed as if placed in a gigantic vise.

Older mountain ranges are also found on the continents. Examples include the Appalachians in eastern North America and the Urals in Russia. Their formerly lofty peaks are now worn low, the result of millions of years of erosion. Still older are the stable continental interiors. Within these stable interiors are areas known as **shields**, extensive and relatively flat expanses composed largely of crystalline material. Radiometric ages of minerals contained in some shield rocks exceed 4 billion years. Even these oldest-known rocks exhibit evidence of enormous forces that have folded and deformed them.

Ocean Basins

The ocean-basin floor has a wide diversity of features, including linear chains of volcanoes, deep canyons, and large plateaus. The topography is nearly as varied as that on the continents.

The ocean basins contain one of the most prominent topographic features on Earth: the oceanic ridge system. In Figure 1.22 the Mid-Atlantic Ridge and the East Pacific Rise are parts of this system. This broad elevated feature forms a continuous belt that winds for more than 70,000 kilometres around the globe in a manner similar to the seam of a baseball. Rather than consisting of highly deformed rock, such as most of the mountains found on the continents, the oceanic ridge system consists of layer upon layer of volcanic rock that has been fractured and uplifted.

The ocean floor also contains extremely deep depressions that can exceed 11,000 metres below sea level. Although these deep-ocean **trenches** are relatively narrow and represent only a small fraction of the ocean floor, they are very significant features. Some trenches are located adjacent to young mountains that flank the continents. For example, in Figure 1.22 the Peru–Chile Trench off the west coast of South America parallels the Andes Mountains. Other trenches parallel linear island chains called volcanic island arcs.

EARTH AS A SYSTEM

GEODe EARTH An Introduction to Geology
↳ A View of Earth and Rock Cycle

As we study Earth, it becomes clear that our planet can be viewed as a dynamic body with many separate but interacting parts or *spheres*. The hydrosphere, atmosphere, biosphere, and geosphere and all of their components can be studied separately. However, the parts are not isolated. Each is related in some way to the others to produce a complex and continuously interacting whole that we call the *Earth system*.

A **system** is a group of interacting, or interdependent, parts that form a complex whole. Most of us hear and use the term frequently. We may service our car's cooling *system*, make use of the city's transportation *system*, and be a participant in the political *system*. A news report might inform us of an approaching weather *system*. Further, we know that Earth is just a small part of a large system known as the *solar system*.

The parts of the Earth system are linked: a change in one part can produce changes in any or all of the other parts. For example, when a volcano erupts, lava from Earth's interior may flow out at the surface and block a nearby valley. This new obstruction influences the region's drainage system by creating a lake or causing streams to change course. The large quantities of volcanic ash and gases that can be emitted during an eruption might be blown high into the atmosphere and influence the amount of solar energy that can reach Earth's surface. The result could be a drop in air temperatures over the entire hemisphere. Where the surface is covered by lava flows (or a thick layer of volcanic ash), existing soils are buried. This causes the soil-forming processes to begin anew to transform the new surface material into soil (Figure 1.23). The Earth system is characterized by processes that vary on spatial scales from fractions of millimetres to thousands of kilometres. Time scales for Earth's processes range from milliseconds to billions of years.

The Earth system is powered by energy from two sources. The Sun drives external processes that occur in the atmosphere, in the hydrosphere, and at Earth's surface. Weather and climate, ocean circulation, and erosional processes are driven by energy from the Sun. Earth's interior is the second source of energy. Heat remaining from when our planet formed, and heat that is continuously generated by radioactive decay, powers the internal processes that produce volcanoes, earthquakes, and mountains.

Humans are *part of* the Earth system—a system in which the living and nonliving components are entwined and interconnected. Therefore, our actions produce changes in all of the other parts. When we burn gasoline and coal, build seawalls along the shoreline, dispose of our wastes, and clear the land, we cause other parts of the system to respond, often in unforeseen ways. Throughout this book you will learn about many of Earth's subsystems: the hydrologic system, the tectonic (mountain-building) system, and the rock cycle, to name a few. Remember that these components *and we humans* are all part of the Earth system.

The Rock Cycle: Part of the Earth System

The Earth system has a nearly endless array of cycles (e.g., water, chemical, biologic) in which matter is recycled over and over again. Viewed over long time spans, the rocks of the geosphere are constantly forming, changing, and reforming. The cycle that involves the processes by which one type of rock changes to another is called the **rock cycle.** This cycle allows us to view many of the interrelationships among different parts of the Earth system. It helps us understand the origin of igneous, sedimentary, and metamorphic rocks (see Chapters 3, 6, and 7) and to see that each type is linked to the others by the processes that act on and within the planet.

The Basic Cycle We will begin our look at the rock cycle at the bottom of Figure 1.24. *Magma* is molten

◆ **Figure 1.23** When Mount St. Helens erupted in May 1980, the area shown here was buried by a volcanic mudflow. Now plants are re-established and new soil is forming.
(Photo by Jack W. Dykinga Associates)

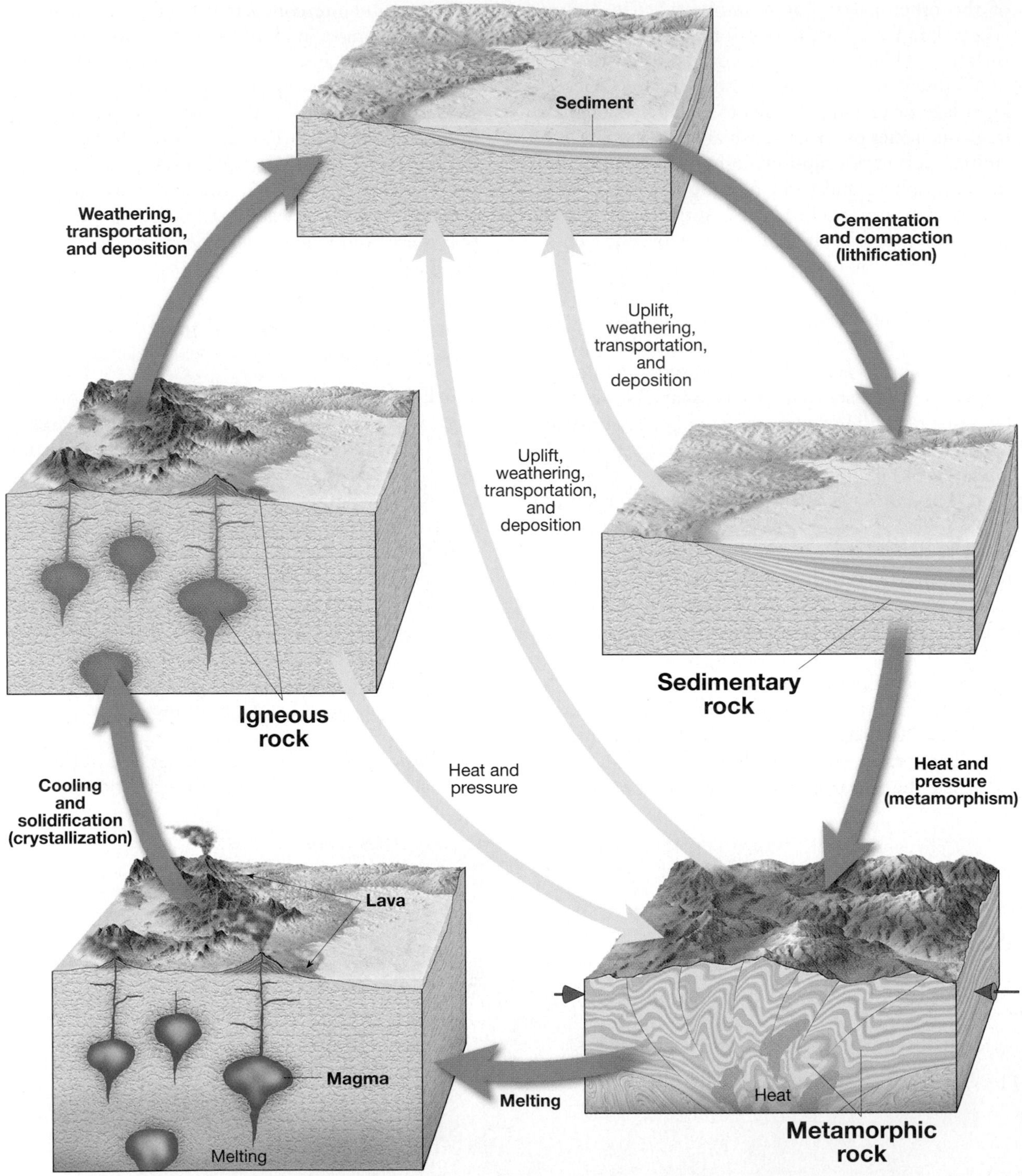

◆ **Figure 1.24** Viewed over long spans, rocks are constantly forming, changing, and reforming. The rock cycle helps us understand the origin of the three basic rock groups. Arrows represent processes that link each group to the others.

material that forms in certain environments of Earth's interior where temperatures and pressures are such that rock melts. Once formed, magma migrates upward into Earth's outer layer or crust. Eventually, magma cools and solidifies. This process, called *crystallization*, can occur either beneath the surface or, following a volcanic eruption, at the surface. In either situation the resulting rocks are called **igneous rocks** (*ignis* = fire, *ous* = full of).

If igneous rocks are exposed at the surface, they will undergo *weathering*, in which the day-to-day influences of the atmosphere slowly disintegrate and decompose rocks. The materials that result are often moved downslope by gravity (see Chapter 14) before being picked up and transported by any of a number of erosional agents: running water, glaciers, wind, or waves (see Chapters 15–19). Eventually, these particles and dissolved substances are deposited as **sediment**. Although most sediment ultimately comes to rest in the ocean, other sites of deposition include river floodplains, swamps, desert basins, and dunes.

Next, the sediments undergo *lithification*, a term meaning "conversion into rock." Sediment is usually lithified into **sedimentary rock** when compacted by the weight of overlying layers or when cemented as percolating water fills the pores (open spaces between particles) with mineral matter.

If the resulting sedimentary rock is buried deep within Earth and involved in the dynamics of mountain building, or intruded by a mass of magma, it will be subjected to great pressures and intense heat. The sedimentary rock will react to the changing environment and turn into the third rock type, **metamorphic rock** (*meta* = change, *morph* = form). When metamorphic rock is subjected to additional pressure changes or to still higher temperatures, it will melt, creating magma, which will eventually crystallize into igneous rock.

Processes driven by heat from Earth's interior are responsible for creating igneous and metamorphic rocks. Weathering and erosion—external processes powered by a combination of energy from the Sun and gravity—produce the sediment from which sedimentary rocks form.

Alternative Paths The paths shown in the basic cycle (purple arrows) are not the only ones that are possible. Indeed, other paths are just as likely to be followed as those described in the preceding section. These alternatives are indicated by the blue arrows in Figure 1.24.

Igneous rocks, rather than being exposed to weathering and erosion at Earth's surface, may remain deeply buried. Eventually, these masses may be subjected to the strong compressional forces and high temperatures associated with mountain building. When this occurs, they are transformed directly into metamorphic rocks.

Metamorphic and sedimentary rocks, as well as sediment, do not always remain buried. Rather, overlying layers may be stripped away, exposing the once-buried rock. When this happens, the material is attacked by weathering processes and turned into new raw materials for sedimentary rocks.

Although rocks might seem to be unchanging masses, the rock cycle clearly shows that they are not. The changes, however, take time—great amounts of geologic time (see Chapter 8).

In the remaining chapters we will examine in more detail the workings of our dynamic planet in the context of plate tectonics and the rock cycle. In Chapter 2 we will start this process with the basic building blocks of rocks—the minerals.

Chapter Summary

- *Geology* means "the study of Earth." The two broad areas of the science of geology are (1) *physical geology*, which examines the materials composing Earth and the processes that operate beneath and on its surface; and (2) *historical geology*, which seeks to understand the origin of Earth and its development through time.
- The relationship between people and the natural environment is an important focus of geology. This includes natural hazards, resources, and human influences on geologic processes.
- During the seventeenth and eighteenth centuries, *catastrophism* influenced the formulation of explanations about Earth. Catastrophism states that Earth's landscapes have been developed primarily by great catastrophes. By contrast, *uniformitarianism*, one of the fundamental principles of modern geology advanced by James Hutton in the late eighteenth century, states that the physical, chemical, and biologic laws that operate today have also operated in the geologic past. The idea is commonly summarized as "the present is the key to the past." Hutton argued that processes that appear to be slow acting could, over long spans of time, produce effects that were just as great as those resulting from sudden catastrophic events.
- Using the principles of *relative dating*—the placing of events in their proper sequence or order without knowing their age in years—scientists developed a geologic time scale during the nineteenth century. Relative dates can be established by applying such principles as the *law of superposition* and the *principle of fossil succession*.
- The *nebular hypothesis* describes the formation of the solar system. The planets and Sun began forming about 5 billion years ago from a large cloud of dust and gases. As the cloud contracted,

it began to rotate and assume a disk shape. Material that was gravitationally pulled toward the centre became the protosun. Within the rotating disk, small centres, called protoplanets, swept up more and more of the cloud's debris.

- In the early twentieth century Alfred Wegener set forth the *continental drift* hypothesis. One of its major tenets was that a supercontinent called *Pangaea* began breaking apart into smaller continents about 200 million years ago. The smaller continental fragments then "drifted" to their present positions. To support the claim that the now-separate continents were once joined, Wegener and others used the fit of South America and Africa, fossil evidence, rock types and structures, and ancient climates.
- The theory of *plate tectonics* provides a comprehensive model of Earth's internal workings. It holds that Earth's rigid outer *lithosphere* consists of several segments called *plates* that are slowly and continually in motion relative to one another. Most earthquakes, volcanic activity, and mountain building are associated with the movements of these plates.
- The three distinct types of plate boundaries are (1) *divergent boundaries*, at which plates move apart; (2) *convergent boundaries*, at which plates move together, causing one to go beneath the other or at which plates of continental crust collide; and (3) *transform fault boundaries*, at which plates slide past each other.
- Earth's internal structure is divided into layers based on differences in chemical composition and on the basis of changes in physical properties. Compositionally, Earth is divided into a thin outer *crust*, a solid rocky *mantle*, and a dense *core*. Based on physical properties, the layers of Earth are (1) the lithosphere, the cool, rigid outermost layer that averages about 100 kilometres thick; (2) the *asthenosphere*, a relatively weak layer located in the mantle beneath the lithosphere; (3) the more rigid *mesosphere*, where rocks are very hot and capable of very gradual flow; (4) the liquid *outer core*, where Earth's magnetic field is generated; and (5) the solid *inner core*.
- Earth's physical environment is traditionally divided into three major parts: the solid Earth or *geosphere*; the water portion of our planet, the *hydrosphere*; and Earth's gaseous envelope, the *atmosphere*. In addition, the *biosphere*, the totality of life on Earth, interacts with each of the three physical realms and is an equally integral part of Earth.
- Two principal divisions of Earth's surface are the continents and ocean basins. The *continental shelf* and *continental slope* mark the continent–ocean basin transition. Major continental features include mountains and *shields*. Important zones on the ocean floor are trenches and the extensive oceanic ridge system.
- Although Earth's four spheres can be studied separately, they are all related in a complex and continuously interacting whole that we call the Earth system. Changing one part of the Earth system can produce changes in any or all of the other parts.
- The two sources of energy that power the Earth system are (1) the Sun, which drives the external processes that occur in the atmosphere, in the hydrosphere, and at Earth's surface; and (2) heat from Earth's interior, which powers the internal processes that produce volcanoes, earthquakes, and mountains.
- The *rock cycle* is one of many cycles of the Earth system in which matter is recycled. The rock cycle is a means of viewing many of the interrelationships of geology. It illustrates the origin of the three basic rock types (*sedimentary*, *igneous*, and *metamorphic*) and the role of various geologic processes in transforming one rock type into another.

Review Questions

1. Geology is traditionally divided into two broad areas. Name and describe these two subdivisions.
2. How did the proponents of catastrophism perceive the age of Earth?
3. Describe the doctrine of uniformitarianism. How did the advocates of this idea view the age of Earth?
4. About how old is Earth?
5. The geologic time scale was established without the aid of radiometric dating. What principles were used to develop the time scale?
6. Briefly describe the events that led to the formation of the solar system.
7. Contrast the asthenosphere and the lithosphere.
8. What first led scientists, such as Alfred Wegener, to suspect that the continents were once joined?

9. What was Pangaea?
10. List the evidence that Wegener and his followers gathered to support the continental drift hypothesis.
11. Early in the twentieth century, what was the prevailing view of how land animals migrated across vast expanses of ocean?
12. How does evidence for a late Paleozoic glaciation in the Southern Hemisphere support the continental drift hypothesis?
13. Briefly explain why the recent acceptance of plate tectonics has been described as a scientific "revolution."
14. With which type of plate boundary is each of the following associated: subduction zone, San Andreas Fault, seafloor spreading, and Mount St. Helens?
15. List and briefly describe Earth's compositional divisions.
16. List and briefly describe the four "spheres" that constitute our environment.
17. What are the two sources of energy for the Earth system?
18. Using the rock cycle, explain the statement "One rock is the raw material for another."

Key Terms

asthenosphere (p. 21)
atmosphere (p. 23)
biosphere (p. 24)
catastrophism (p. 5)
continental drift (p. 12)
continental shelf (p. 13)
continental slope (p. 26)
convection (p. 17)
convergent boundary (p. 17)
core (p. 12)
crust (p. 12)
divergent boundary (p. 17)
fossil succession, principle of (p. 7)
geologist (p. 2)
geology (p. 2)
historical geology (p. 2)
hydrosphere (p. 22)
igneous rock (p. 28)
inner core (p. 22)
lithosphere (p. 17)
lower mantle (p. 22)
mantle (p. 12)
mesosphere (p. 22)
metamorphic rock (p. 29)
mid-ocean ridge (p. 17)
nebular hypothesis (p. 11)
outcrops (p. 2)
outer core (p. 22)
Pangaea (p. 13)
paradigm (p. 13)
physical geology (p. 2)
plate (p. 17)
plate tectonics (p. 13)
relative dating (p. 7)
rock cycle (p. 27)
seafloor spreading (p.17)
sediment (p. 29)
sedimentary rock (p. 29)
shield (p. 26)
subduction (p. 17)
subduction zone (p. 17)
superposition, law of (p. 7)
system (p. 26)
transform fault boundary (p. 18)
trench (p. 26)
uniformitarianism (p. 6)

Web Resources

The *Earth* website uses the resources and flexibility of the internet to aid in your study of the topics in this chapter. Written and developed by geology instructors, this site will help improve your understanding of geology. Visit **www.pearsoned.ca/tarbuck** and click on the cover of the text to find

- online review quizzes
- Web-based critical thinking and writing exercises
- links to chapter-specific Web resources
- internet-wide key-term searches

www.pearsoned.ca/tarbuck

Chapter 2

Minerals: The Building Blocks of Rocks

Minerals

The Composition of Minerals
- Atomic Structure
- Bonding
- Isotopes and Radioactive Decay

The Structure of Minerals

Physical Properties of Minerals
- Crystal Form
- Lustre
- Colour
- Streak
- Hardness
- Cleavage
- Fracture
- Specific Gravity
- Other Properties of Minerals

Mineral Groups
- The Silicates
- Common Silicate Minerals
- Important Nonsilicate Minerals

A cluster of colourful quartz crystals (variety: amethyst) from Las Vigas, Mexico. (Photo by Jeff Scovil)

Earth's crust and oceans are the source of a wide variety of useful and essential minerals (Figure 2.1). In fact, practically every manufactured product contains materials obtained from minerals. Most people are familiar with the common uses of many basic metals, including aluminum in beverage cans, copper in electrical wiring, and gold and silver in jewellery. But some people are not aware that pencil lead contains the greasy-feeling mineral graphite and that baby powder comes from the mineral talc. Moreover, many do not know that drill bits covered with diamonds are employed by dentists to drill through tooth enamel, or that the common mineral quartz is the source of silicon for computer chips. As the mineral requirements of modern society grow, the need to locate additional supplies of useful minerals also grows and becomes more challenging.

In addition to the economic uses of rocks and minerals, all of the processes studied by geologists are in some way dependent on the properties of these basic Earth materials. Such events as volcanic eruptions, plate tectonics and mountain building, weathering and erosion, and even earthquakes involve rocks and minerals. Consequently, a basic knowledge of Earth materials is essential to the understanding of all geologic phenomena.

MINERALS

GEODe EARTH Minerals: Building Blocks of Rocks
↳ Introduction

We begin our discussion of Earth materials with an overview of **mineralogy** because minerals are the building blocks of rocks. Geologists define **minerals**

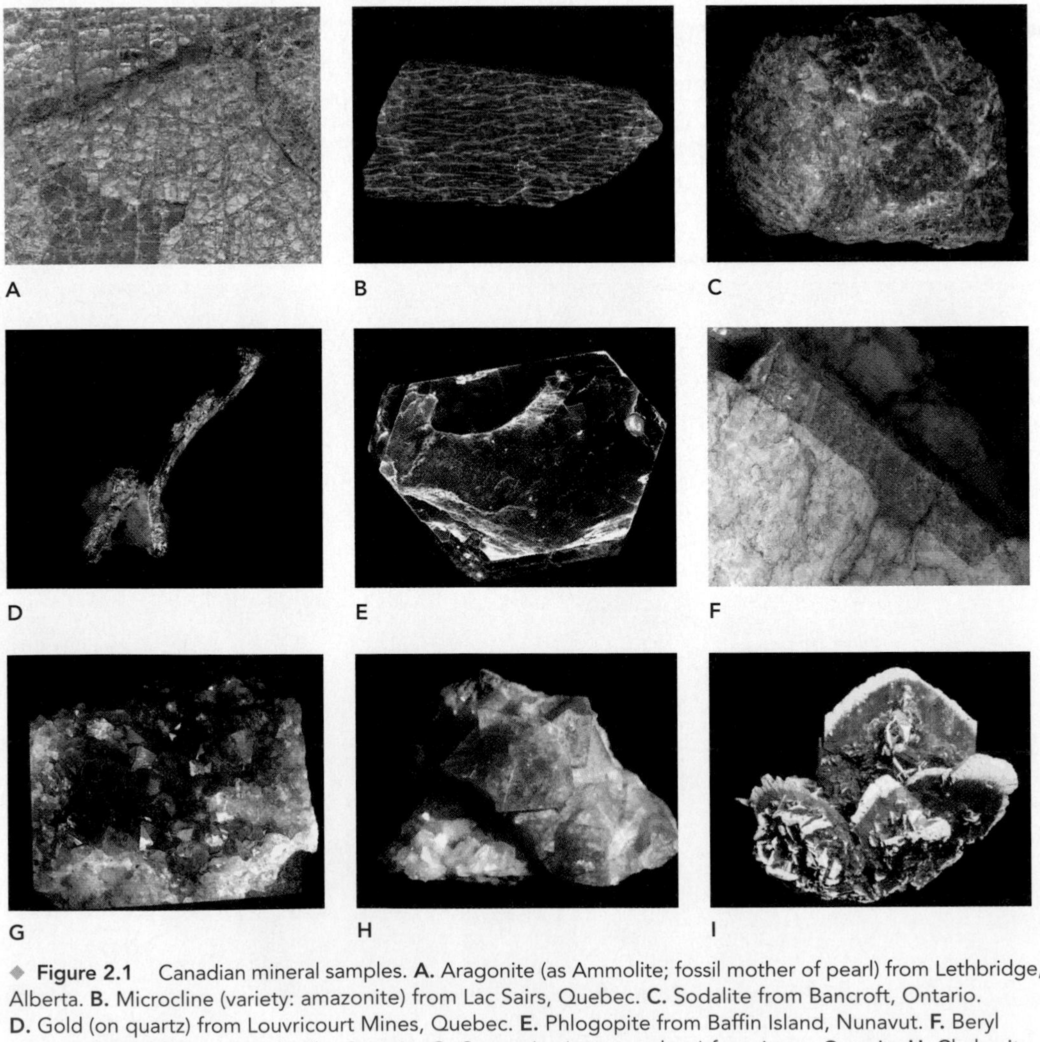

◆ **Figure 2.1** Canadian mineral samples. **A.** Aragonite (as Ammolite; fossil mother of pearl) from Lethbridge, Alberta. **B.** Microcline (variety: amazonite) from Lac Sairs, Quebec. **C.** Sodalite from Bancroft, Ontario. **D.** Gold (on quartz) from Louvricourt Mines, Quebec. **E.** Phlogopite from Baffin Island, Nunavut. **F.** Beryl (variety: emerald) from Quadeville, Ontario. **G.** Quartz (variety: amethyst) from Loon, Ontario. **H.** Chabazite from Wasson's Bluff, Nova Scotia. **I.** Gypsum (variety: selenite) from Swift Current Creek, Saskatchewan. (Photos **A–G** by C. Tsujita; photos **H** and **I** by Arnim Walter; specimens **B–I** courtesy of the Department of Earth Sciences, the University of Western Ontario)

as any naturally occurring inorganic solids that possess an orderly internal structure and a definite chemical composition. Thus, for any Earth material to be considered a mineral it must exhibit the following characteristics:

1. It must occur naturally.
2. It must be inorganic.
3. It must be a solid.
4. It must possess an orderly internal structure; that is, its atoms must be arranged in a definite pattern.
5. It must have a definite chemical composition that can vary within specified limits.

When geologists use the term *mineral*, only substances that meet these five criteria are considered minerals. Consequently, synthetic diamonds and other useful materials produced by chemists are not considered minerals. Further, the gemstone *opal* is classified as a *mineraloid*, rather than a mineral, because it lacks an orderly internal structure.

Rocks, however, are more loosely defined. Simply, a **rock** is any solid mass of mineral or mineral-like matter that occurs naturally as part of our planet. A few rocks are composed almost entirely of one mineral. A common example is the sedimentary rock *limestone*, which is composed of impure masses of the mineral calcite. However, most rocks, like the common rock granite (shown in Figure 2.2), occur as aggregates of several kinds of minerals. Here, the term *aggregate* implies that the minerals are joined in such a way that the properties of each mineral are retained. Note that you can easily distinguish the mineral constituents of the sample of granite shown in Figure 2.2.

A few rocks are composed of nonmineral matter. These include the volcanic rocks *obsidian* and *pumice*, which are noncrystalline, glassy substances; and *coal*, which consists of solid organic debris.

Although this chapter deals primarily with the nature of minerals, keep in mind that most rocks are simply aggregates of minerals. Because the properties of rocks are determined largely by the chemical composition and internal structure of the minerals they contain, we will first consider these Earth materials. Subsequent chapters describe the major rock types.

◆ **Figure 2.2** Most rocks are aggregates of several kinds of minerals.

THE COMPOSITION OF MINERALS

Each of Earth's approximately 4000 minerals is uniquely defined by its chemical composition and internal structure. In other words, every sample of the same mineral contains the same elements joined together in a consistent, repeating pattern. We will first review the basic building blocks of minerals, the *elements*, and then examine how elements bond to form mineral structures.

At present, 112 elements are known. Of these, 92 are naturally occurring (Figure 2.3). Some minerals, such as gold and sulphur, consist entirely of one element. But most minerals are a combination of two or more elements joined to form a chemically stable compound. To understand better how elements combine to form molecules and compounds, we must first consider the **atom** (*a* = not, *tomos* = cut), the smallest part of matter that still retains the characteristics of an element. It is this extremely small particle that does the combining.

Atomic Structure

Two simplified models illustrating basic atomic structure are shown in Figure 2.4. Note that atoms have a central region, called the **nucleus** (*nucleos* = a little nut), which contains very dense **protons** (particles with positive electrical charges) and equally dense **neutrons** (particles with no electrical charges). Surrounding the nucleus are very light particles called **electrons,** which travel at high speeds and are negatively charged. For simplicity, we often depict atoms with the electrons in orbits around the nucleus (Figure 2.4A), like the orbits of the planets around the Sun. However, electrons *do not* travel in the same plane, the way planets do. Further, because of their rapid motion, electrons create spherically shaped negatively charged zones around the nucleus called **energy levels**, or **shells**. Hence, a more realistic picture of the atom can be obtained by envisioning cloudlike shells of fast-moving electrons surrounding a central nucleus (Figure 2.4B). As you will see, an important fact about these shells is that each can accommodate a specific number of electrons.

The number of protons found in an atom's nucleus determines the **atomic number** and name of the element. For example, all atoms with six protons are carbon atoms, those with eight protons are oxygen atoms, and so forth. Because atoms have the same number of electrons as protons, the atomic number also equals the number of electrons surrounding the nucleus (Table 2.1). Moreover, because neutrons have no charge, the positive charge of the protons is exactly balanced by the negative charge of the electrons. Consequently, atoms are electrically neutral. Thus, an **element** is a large collection of electrically neutral atoms, all having the same atomic number.

The simplest element, hydrogen, is composed of atoms that have only one proton in the nucleus and one electron surrounding the nucleus. Each successively heavier atom has one more proton and one more electron, in addition to a certain number of neutrons. Studies of electron configurations have shown that each electron is added systematically to a particular energy level or shell. In general, electrons enter higher energy levels after lower energy levels have been filled to capacity.*

The first principal shell holds a maximum of two electrons, while each of the higher shells holds eight or more electrons. As you will see, it is generally the outermost electrons, also referred to as **valence electrons**, that are involved in chemical bonding.

Bonding

Elements combine with each other to form a wide variety of more complex substances. The strong attractive force linking atoms together is called a *chemical bond*. When chemical bonding joins two or more elements together in definite proportions, the substance is called a **compound**. Most minerals are chemical compounds.

Why do elements join together to form compounds? Experimentation has revealed that the forces holding the atoms together are electrical and that chemical bonding results in a change in the electron configuration of the bonded atoms. As we noted earlier, the valence electrons (outer-shell electrons) are generally involved in chemical bonding. Other than the first shell, which contains two electrons, *a stable configuration occurs when the valence shell contains eight electrons*. Only the so-called noble gases, such as neon and argon, have a complete outermost electron shell. Hence, the noble gases are the least chemically reactive and thus their designation as "inert." However, all other atoms seek a valence shell containing eight electrons like the noble gases.

The **octet rule**, literally "a set of eight," refers to the concept of a complete outermost energy level. Simply, the octet rule states that atoms combine to form compounds and molecules in order to obtain the stable electron configuration of the noble gases. To satisfy the octet rule, an atom can gain, lose, or share electrons with one or more atoms (see Figure 2.5). The result of this process is the formation

*This principle holds for the first 18 elements.

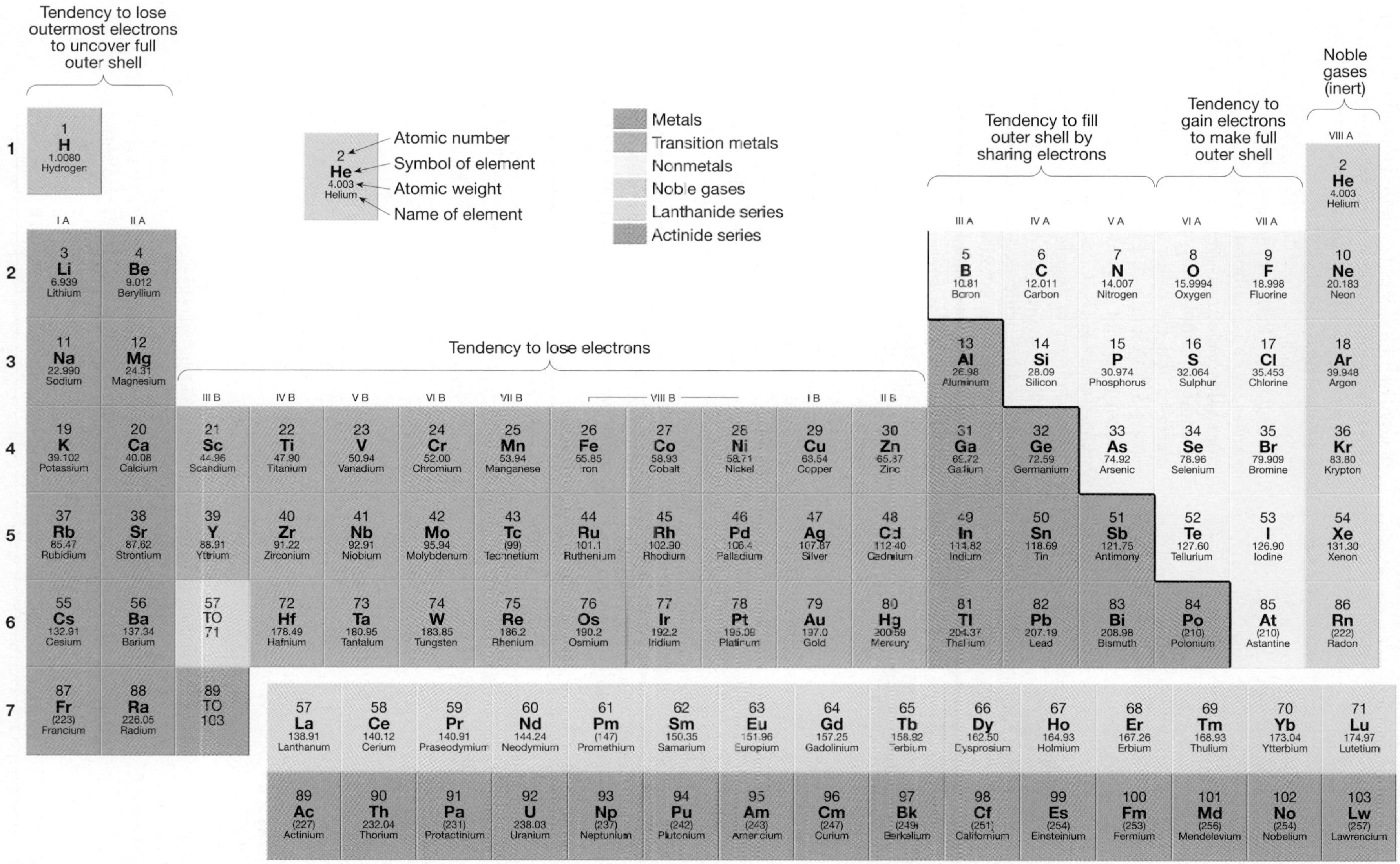

◆ **Figure 2.3** Periodic table of the elements.

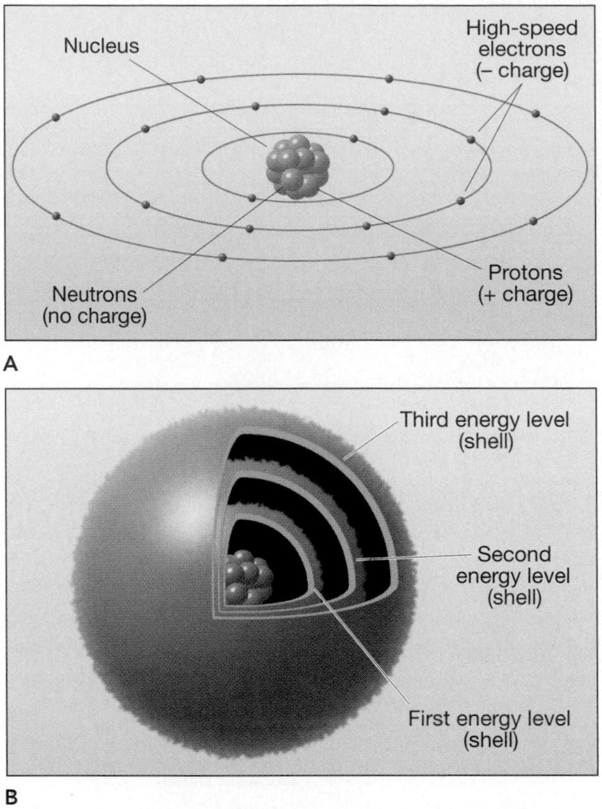

◆ **Figure 2.4** Two models of the atom. **A.** A very simplified view of the atom, which consists of a central nucleus comprising protons and neutrons encircled by high-speed electrons. **B.** Another model of the atom showing spherically shaped electron clouds (energy level shells). Note that these models are not drawn to scale. Electrons are minuscule in size compared with protons and neutrons, and the relative space between the nucleus and electron shells is much greater than illustrated.

of electrical "glue" that bonds the atoms. In summary, *most atoms are chemically reactive and bond to achieve the stable noble-gas configuration while retaining overall electrical neutrality.*

Ionic Bonds Perhaps the easiest type of bond to visualize is an **ionic bond.** In ionic bonding, one or more valence electrons are transferred from one atom to another. Simply, one atom gives up its valence electrons and the other uses them to complete its outer shell. A common example of ionic bonding is sodium (Na) and chlorine (Cl) joining to produce sodium chloride (NaCl or common table salt). This bond is shown in Figure 2.5. Notice that sodium gives up its single outer electron to chlorine. As a result, sodium achieves a stable configuration with eight electrons in its outermost shell. By acquiring the electron that sodium loses, chlorine—which has seven valence electrons—completes its outermost shell. Thus, through the transfer of a single electron, both the sodium and chlorine atoms have acquired the stable noble-gas configuration.

Once electron transfer occurs, atoms are no longer electrically neutral. By giving up one electron, a neutral sodium atom (11 protons/11 electrons) becomes *positively charged* (11 protons/10 electrons). Similarly, by acquiring one electron, the neutral chlorine atom (17 protons/17 electrons) becomes *negatively charged* (17 protons/18 electrons). Such atoms, which have an electrical charge because of the unequal numbers of electrons and protons, are called **ions**. An atom that picks up an extra electron and

TABLE 2.1 **Atomic Number and Distribution of Electrons**

			Number of Electrons in Each Shell			
Element	**Symbol**	**Atomic Number**	**1st**	**2nd**	**3rd**	**4th**
Hydrogen	H	1	1			
Helium	He	2	2			
Lithium	Li	3	2	1		
Beryllium	Be	4	2	2		
Boron	B	5	2	3		
Carbon	C	6	2	4		
Nitrogen	N	7	2	5		
Oxygen	O	8	2	6		
Fluorine	F	9	2	7		
Neon	Ne	10	2	8		
Sodium	Na	11	2	8	1	
Magnesium	Mg	12	2	8	2	
Aluminum	Al	13	2	8	3	
Silicon	Si	14	2	8	4	
Phosphorus	P	15	2	8	5	
Sulphur	S	16	2	8	6	
Chlorine	Cl	17	2	8	7	
Argon	Ar	18	2	8	8	
Potassium	K	19	2	8	8	1
Calcium	Ca	20	2	8	8	2

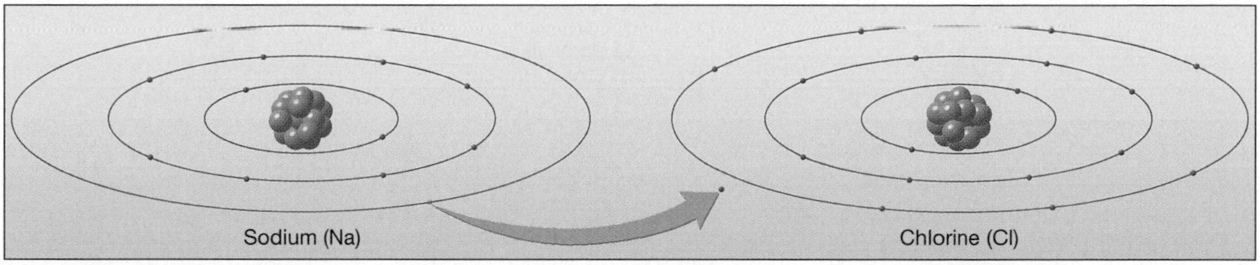

◆ **Figure 2.5** Chemical bonding of sodium and chlorine through the transfer of the lone outer electron from a sodium atom to a chlorine atom. The result is a positive sodium ion (Na^+) and a negative chloride ion (Cl^-). Bonding to produce sodium chloride (NaCl) is due to electrostatic attraction between the positive and negative ions. In this process note that both the sodium and the chlorine atoms have achieved the stable noble-gas configuration (eight electrons in their outer shell).

becomes negatively charged is called an *anion*. An atom that loses an electron and becomes positively charged is called a *cation*.

We know that particles (ions) with like charges repel and those with unlike charges attract. Thus, an *ionic bond* is the attraction of oppositely charged ions to one another, producing an electrically neutral compound. Figure 2.6 illustrates the arrangement of sodium and chloride ions in ordinary table salt. Notice that salt consists of alternating sodium and chloride ions, positioned in such a manner that each positive ion is attracted to and surrounded on all sides by negative ions, and vice versa. This arrangement maximizes the attraction between ions with unlike charges while minimizing the repulsion between ions with like charges. Thus, *ionic compounds consist of an orderly arrangement of oppositely charged ions assembled in a definite ratio that provides overall electrical neutrality*.

The properties of a chemical compound are *dramatically different* from the properties of the elements composing it. For example, chlorine is a green, poisonous gas that is so toxic it was used during World War I as a chemical weapon. Sodium is a soft, silvery metal that reacts vigorously with water and, if held in your hand, can burn severely. Together, however, these atoms produce the compound sodium chloride (table salt), a clear crystalline solid that is essential for human life. This example also illustrates an important difference between a rock and a mineral. Most *minerals* are *chemical compounds* with unique properties that are very different from the elements that compose them. A *rock*, however, is a *mixture* of minerals, with each mineral retaining its own identity.

Covalent Bonds Not all atoms combine by transferring electrons to form ions. Other atoms *share* electrons. For example, the gaseous elements oxygen (O_2), hydrogen (H_2), and chlorine (Cl_2) exist as stable molecules consisting of two bonded atoms, without a complete transfer of electrons.

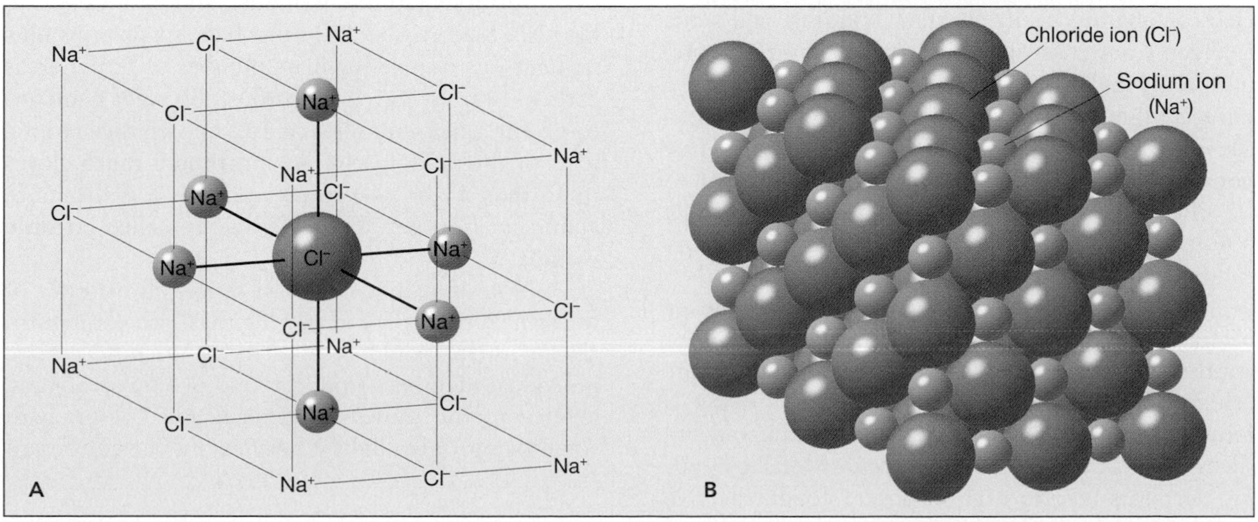

◆ **Figure 2.6** Schematic diagrams illustrating the arrangement of sodium and chloride ions in table salt. **A.** Structure has been opened up to show arrangement of ions. **B.** Actual ions are closely packed.

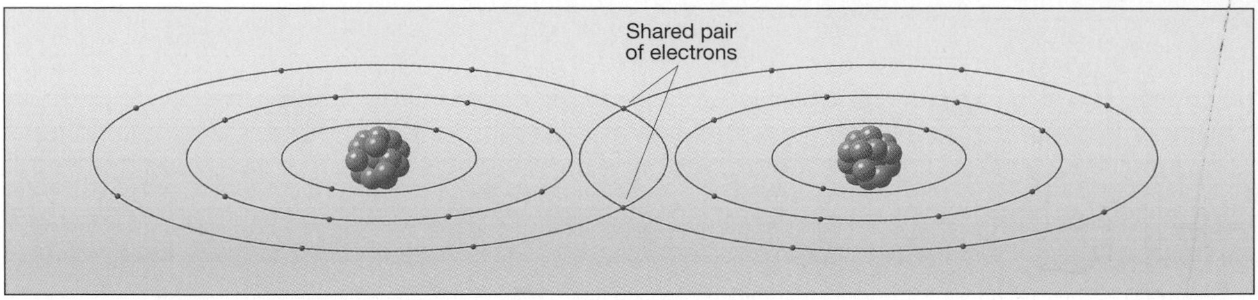

◆ **Figure 2.7** Illustration of the sharing of a pair of electrons between two chlorine atoms to form a chlorine molecule. Notice that by sharing a pair of electrons, both chlorine atoms have eight electrons in their valence shell.

Figure 2.7 illustrates the sharing of a pair of electrons between two chlorine atoms to form a molecule of chlorine gas (Cl_2). By overlapping their outer shells, these chlorine atoms share a pair of electrons. Thus, each chlorine atom has acquired, through cooperative action, the needed eight electrons to complete its outer shell. The bond produced by the sharing of electrons is called a **covalent bond**.

A common analogy can help you visualize a covalent bond. Imagine two people at opposite ends of a dimly lit room, each reading under a separate lamp. By moving the lamps to the centre of the room, they are able to combine their light sources so each can see more clearly. Just as the overlapping light beams meld, the shared electrons that provide the "electrical glue" in covalent bonds are indistinguishable from each other. The most common mineral group, the silicates, contains the element silicon, which readily forms covalent bonds with oxygen.

Other Bonds As you might suspect, many chemical bonds are actually hybrids. They consist of some electron sharing, as in covalent bonding, and some electron transfer, as in ionic bonding. Furthermore, both ionic and covalent bonds may occur within the same compound. This occurs in many silicate minerals, in which silicon and oxygen atoms are covalently bonded to form the basic building block common to all silicates. These structures in turn are ionically bonded to metallic ions, producing various electrically neutral chemical compounds.

Another chemical bond exists in which valence electrons are free to migrate from one ion to another. The mobile valence electrons serve as the "electrical glue." This type of electron sharing is found in metals, such as copper, gold, aluminum, and silver, and is called a **metallic bond**. Metallic bonding accounts for the high electrical conductivity of metals, the ease with which metals are shaped, and numerous other special properties of metals.

Isotopes and Radioactive Decay

Subatomic particles are so incredibly small that a special unit was devised to express their mass. A proton or a neutron has a mass just slightly more than one *atomic mass unit*, whereas an electron is only about 1/2000 of an atomic mass unit. Thus, although electrons play an active role in chemical reactions, they do not contribute significantly to the mass of an atom.

The **mass number** of an atom is simply the total of its neutrons and protons in the nucleus. Atoms of the same element always have the same number of protons but commonly have varying numbers of neutrons. This means that an element can have more than one mass number. These variants of the same element are called **isotopes** of that element.

For example, carbon has three well-known isotopes. One has a mass number of 12 (carbon-12), another has a mass number of 13 (carbon-13), and the third, carbon-14, has a mass number of 14. All atoms of the same element must have the same number of protons (atomic number), and carbon always has six. Hence carbon-12 must have six protons plus *six* neutrons to give it a mass number of 12, whereas carbon-14 must have six protons plus *eight* neutrons to give it a mass number of 14. The *average* atomic mass of any random sample of carbon is much closer to 12 than 13 or 14 because carbon-12 is the more abundant isotope. This average is called **atomic weight**.*

Note that in a chemical sense, all isotopes of the same element are nearly identical. To distinguish among them would be like trying to differentiate individual members from a group of similar objects, all having the same shape, size, and colour, with some being only slightly heavier. Further, different

*The term *weight* as used here is a misnomer that has been sanctioned by long use. The correct term is atomic *mass*.

isotopes of an element are generally found together in the same mineral.

Although the nuclei of most atoms are stable, some elements do have isotopes in which the nuclei are unstable. Unstable isotopes, such as carbon-14, disintegrate through a process called **radioactive decay**. During radioactive decay, unstable nuclei spontaneously break apart, giving off subatomic particles or electromagnetic energy similar to X-rays. The rate at which the unstable nuclei decay is steady and measurable, thus making such isotopes useful clocks for dating the events of Earth history. A discussion of radioactive decay and its applications in dating past geologic events occurs in Chapter 8.

THE STRUCTURE OF MINERALS

A mineral is composed of an ordered array of atoms chemically bonded to form a particular crystalline structure. This orderly packing of atoms is reflected in the regularly shaped objects we call crystals (see chapter-opening photo).

What determines the particular crystalline structure of a mineral? For those compounds formed by ions, the internal atomic arrangement is determined partly by the charges on the ions, but even more so by the size of the ions involved. To form stable ionic compounds, each positively charged ion is surrounded by the largest number of negative ions that will fit, while maintaining overall electrical neutrality, and vice versa. Figure 2.8 shows ideal packing arrangements for ions of various sizes.

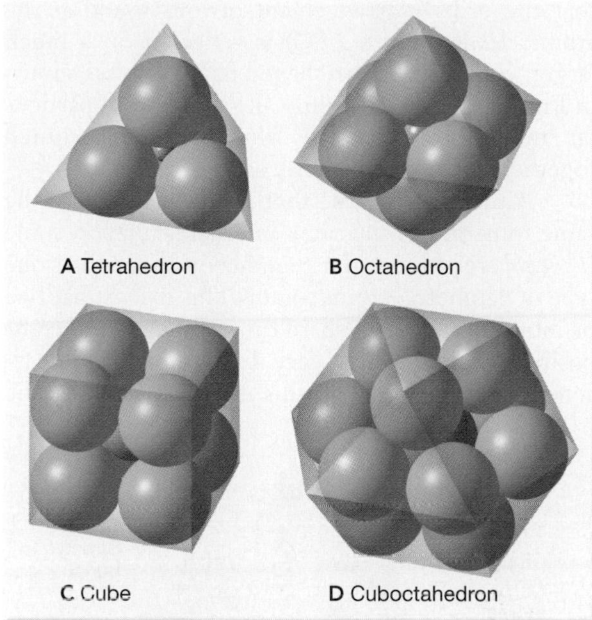

◆ **Figure 2.8** Ideal geometric packing for positive (purple) and negative (green) ions of various size ratios.

Let's examine the geometric arrangement of sodium and chloride ions in the mineral halite (Figure 2.9). We see in Figure 2.9A that the sodium and chloride ions pack together to form a cube-shaped internal structure (Figure 2.9B). Also note

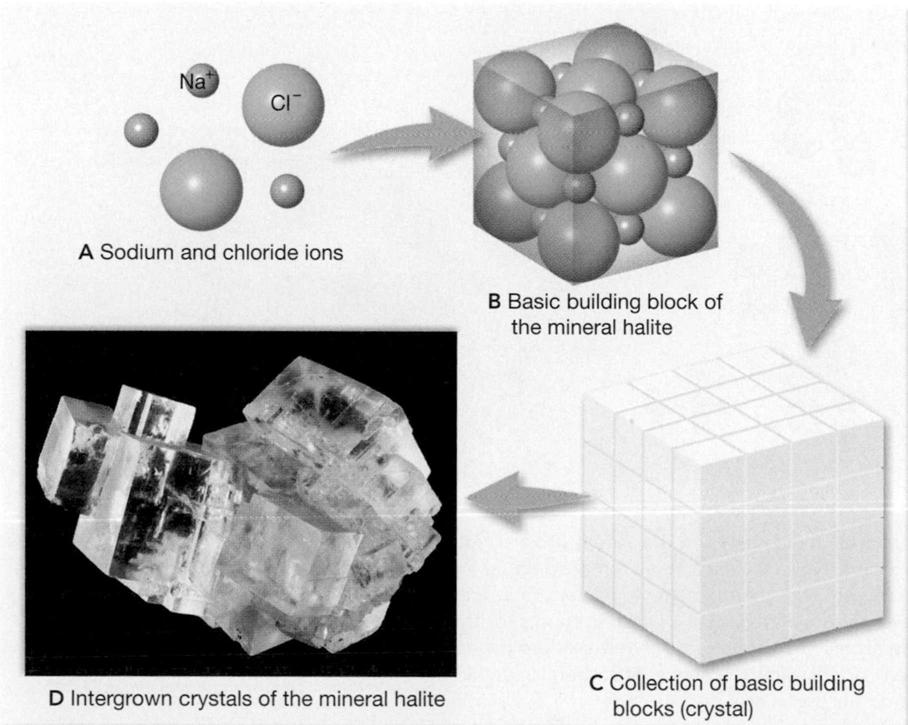

◆ **Figure 2.9** The structure of sodium chloride. **A, B**. The orderly arrangement of sodium and chloride ions in the mineral halite. **C, D**. The orderly arrangement at the atomic level produces the regularly shaped salt crystals shown in this photograph. (Photo by M. Claye/Jacana Scientific Control/Photo Researchers, Inc.)

that the orderly arrangement of ions found at the atomic level (Figure 2.9C) is reflected on a much larger scale in the cube-shaped halite crystals shown in Figure 2.9D. Like halite, all samples of a particular mineral contain the same elements, joined together in the same orderly arrangement.

Although it is true that every specimen of the same mineral has the same internal structure, some *elements* are able to join together in more than one type of geometric arrangement. This means that two or more minerals can share the same chemical composition and yet exhibit very different physical characteristics. Minerals of this type are said to be **polymorphs** (*poly* = many, *morph* = form). Graphite and diamond are particularly good examples of polymorphism because they both consist exclusively of carbon yet have drastically different properties (Figure 2.10). Graphite is the soft, grey material of which pencil lead is made, whereas diamond is the hardest known mineral. The differences between these minerals can be attributed to the conditions under which they were formed. Diamonds form at depths approaching 200 kilometres, where the compact structure shown in Figure 2.10A is produced by extreme pressures. Graphite, conversely, forms under low pressure and temperature and consists of

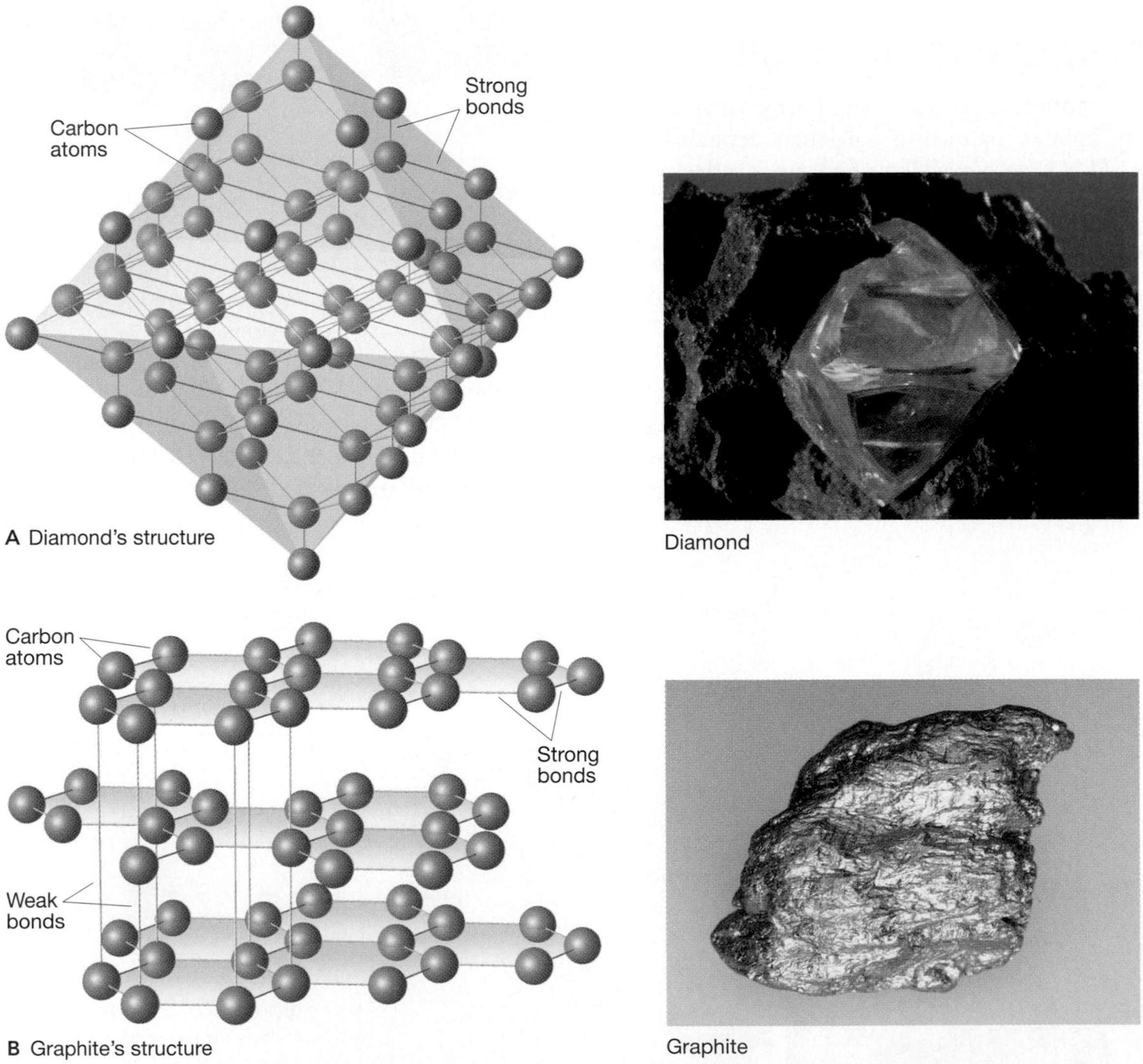

◆ **Figure 2.10** Comparing the structures of diamond and graphite. Both are natural substances with the same chemical composition: carbon atoms. Nevertheless, their internal structure and physical properties reflect the fact that each forms in a very different environment. **A.** All carbon atoms in diamond are covalently bonded into a compact, three-dimensional framework, which accounts for the extreme hardness of the mineral. **B.** In graphite the carbon atoms are bonded into sheets that are joined in a layered fashion by very weak electrical forces. These weak bonds allow the sheets of carbon to readily slide past each other, making graphite soft and slippery, and thus useful as a dry lubricant.
(Photo **A** by photographer Dane Pendland, courtesy of Smithsonian Institution; photo **B** by E. J. Tarbuck)

sheets of carbon atoms that are widely spaced and weakly held together (Figure 2.10B). Because these carbon sheets will easily slide past one another, graphite makes an excellent lubricant.

Scientists have learned that by heating graphite under high pressure, they can produce diamonds. Although synthetic diamonds are generally not gem quality, they have many industrial uses. The transformation of one polymorph to another is called a *phase change*. In nature, certain minerals go through phase changes as they move from one environment to another. For example, when rocks are carried to greater depths by a subducting plate, the mineral *olivine* changes to a more compact form called *spinel*.

PHYSICAL PROPERTIES OF MINERALS

GEODe EARTH Matter and Minerals
↳ Physical Properties of Minerals

Minerals are solids formed by inorganic processes. Each mineral has an orderly arrangement of atoms (crystalline structure) and a definite chemical composition, which give it a unique set of physical properties. Because the internal structure and chemical composition of a mineral are difficult to determine without the aid of sophisticated tests and apparatuses, the more easily recognized physical properties are frequently used in identification. A discussion of some useful physical properties follows.

Crystal Form

Most people think of a crystal as a rare commodity, when, in fact, most inorganic solid objects are composed of crystals. The reason for this misconception is that most crystals do not exhibit good crystal form. The **crystal form** is the external expression of a mineral that reflects the orderly internal arrangement of atoms. Figure 2.11A illustrates the characteristic form of the iron-bearing mineral pyrite.

Generally, whenever a mineral is permitted to form without space restrictions, it will develop individual crystals with well-formed crystal faces. Some crystals, such as those of the mineral quartz, have a very distinctive crystal form that can be helpful in identification (Figure 2.11B). However, most of the time, crystal growth is interrupted because of competition for space, resulting in an intergrown mass of crystals, none of which exhibits its crystal form.

Lustre

Lustre is the appearance or quality of light reflected from the surface of a mineral. Some minerals, such as pyrite (Figure 2.11A), that have the appearance of polished metal, regardless of colour, are said to have a *metallic lustre*. Others, such as quartz (Figure 2.11B), have a *nonmetallic lustre* and can be further described by various adjectives, including vitreous (glassy), pearly, silky, resinous, and earthy (dull). Still other minerals appear partially metallic in lustre and can be said to be submetallic.

A B

◆ **Figure 2.11** Crystal form is the external expression of a mineral's orderly internal structure. **A.** Pyrite, commonly known as "fool's gold," often forms cubic crystals. They may exhibit parallel lines (striations) on the faces. **B.** Quartz sample that exhibits well-developed hexagonal crystals with pyramid-shaped ends. (Photo **A** courtesy of E. J. Tarbuck; photo **B** by Breck P. Kent)

Colour

Although **colour** is an obvious feature of a mineral, it is often unreliable as a diagnostic property. For example, in its purest form the common mineral quartz is clear and colourless (see Figure 2.11B), but slight impurities can give it a variety of colours (Figure 2.12) including purple (amethyst, as shown in the chapter-opening photo and Figure 2.1), pink (rose quartz), yellowish orange (citrine), and even dark brown.

Streak

Streak is the colour of a mineral in its powdered form and is obtained by rubbing the mineral across a piece of unglazed porcelain known as a *streak plate* (Figure 2.13). Although the colour of a mineral can vary from sample to sample, the streak usually does not and is therefore the more reliable property.

Hardness

One of the most useful properties is **hardness**, a measure of a mineral's resistance to abrasion or scratching. This property is determined by rubbing a mineral of unknown hardness against one of known hardness, or vice versa. A numeric value can be obtained by using the **Mohs scale** of hardness, which consists of 10 minerals arranged in order from 1 (softest) to 10 (hardest), as shown in Table 2.2.

Any mineral of unknown hardness can be compared with these or with other objects of known hardness. For example, a fingernail has a hardness of 2.5, a copper penny 3, and a piece of glass 5.5. The mineral gypsum, which has a hardness of 2, can be easily scratched with your fingernail. The mineral calcite, which has a hardness of 3, will scratch your fingernail but will not scratch glass. Quartz, the hardest of the common minerals, will scratch glass.

◆ **Figure 2.12** Because of the presence of slight impurities, minerals, such as quartz, can occur in a wide range of colours.

◆ **Figure 2.13** Although the colour of a mineral may not be helpful in identification, the streak, which is the colour of the powdered mineral, can be very useful.

Cleavage

Within the crystal structure of a mineral, some bonds are weaker than others. When a mineral is stressed, it will break at these bonds. **Cleavage** (*kleiben* = carve) is the tendency of a mineral to break along planes of weak bonding. Not all minerals have definite planes of weak bonding, but those that possess cleavage can be identified by the distinctive smooth surfaces that are produced when the minerals are broken.

The simplest type of cleavage is exhibited in the micas (Figure 2.14). Because the micas have weak bonds in one direction, they cleave to form thin, flat sheets. Some minerals have several cleavage planes, which produce smooth surfaces when broken, while others exhibit poor cleavage and still others, such as quartz, have no cleavage at all. When minerals break evenly in more than one direction, cleavage is described as the *number of planes* exhibited and the *angles at which they meet* (Figure 2.15). Common cleavages found in minerals are presented in Figure 2.15.

TABLE 2.2 **Mohs Scale of Hardness**

Relative Scale	Mineral	Hardness of Some Common Objects
10 (Hardest)	Diamond	
9	Corundum	
8	Topaz	
7	Quartz	6.5 streak plate
6	Potassium feldspar	5.5 glass
5	Apatite	5 knife blade
4	Fluorite	4.5 wire nail
3	Calcite	3 copper penny
2	Gypsum	2.5 fingernail
1 (Softest)	Talc	

◆ **Figure 2.14** The thin sheets shown here were produced by splitting a mica (muscovite) crystal parallel to its perfect cleavage. (Photo by Chip Clark)

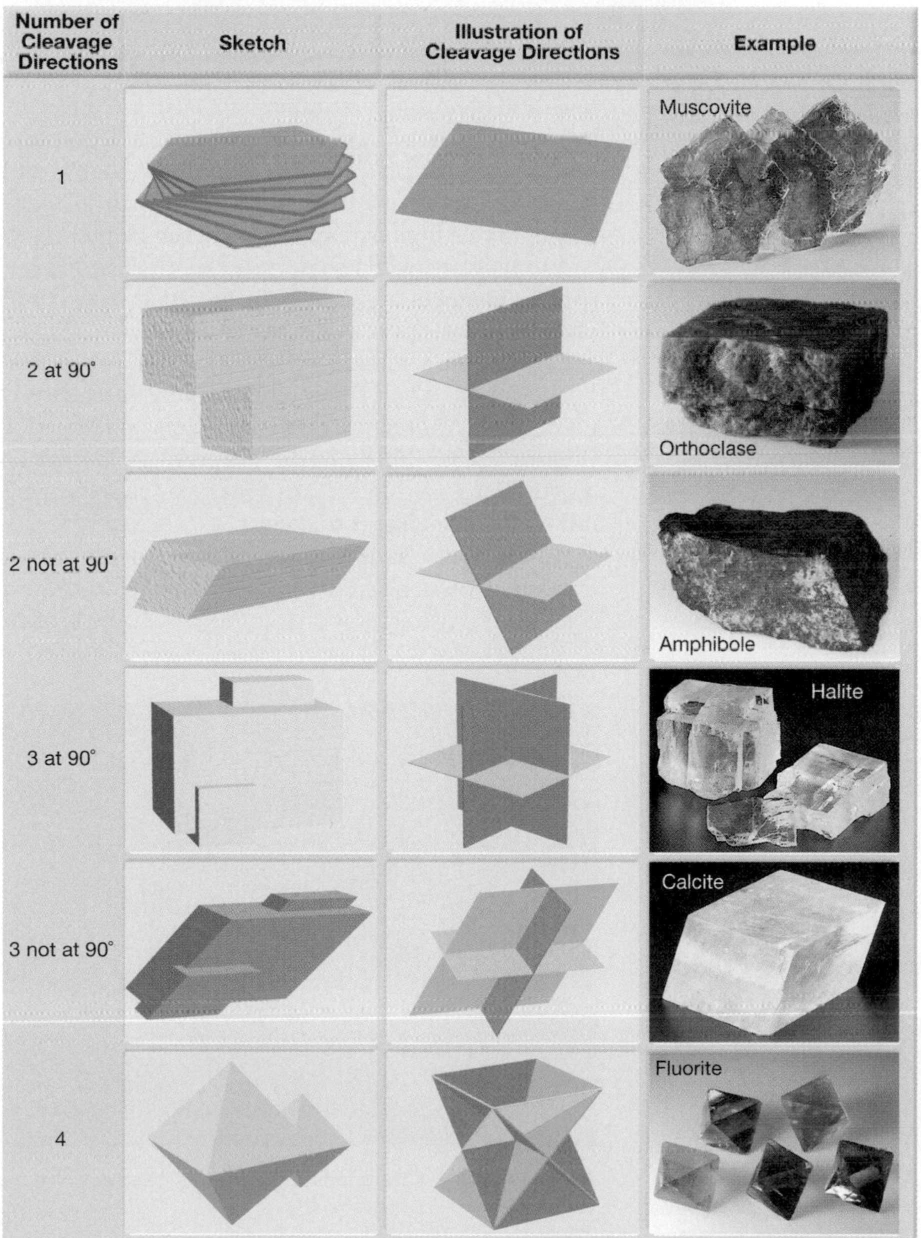

◆ **Figure 2.15** Common cleavage directions exhibited by minerals. (Photos courtesy of E. J. Tarbuck)

Do not confuse cleavage with crystal form. When a mineral exhibits cleavage, it will break into pieces, *each of which has the same geometry*. By contrast the quartz crystals shown in Figure 2.11B do not have cleavage. If broken, they fracture into shapes that do not resemble each other or the original crystals.

Fracture

Minerals that do not exhibit cleavage when broken, such as quartz, are said to **fracture**. Those that break into smooth curved surfaces resembling broken glass have a *conchoidal fracture* (Figure 2.16). Others break into splinters or fibres, but most minerals fracture irregularly (uneven fracture).

◆ **Figure 2.17** Galena is lead sulphide and, like other metallic ores, has a relatively high specific gravity. (Photo courtesy of E. J. Tarbuck)

Specific Gravity

Specific gravity is a number representing the ratio of the mass of a mineral to the weight of an equal volume of water. For example, if a mineral weighs three times as much as an equal volume of water, its specific gravity is 3. With a little practice you can estimate the specific gravity of minerals by hefting them in your hand. For example, if a mineral feels as heavy as the common rocks you have handled, its specific gravity will probably be somewhere between 2.5 and 3. Some metallic minerals have a specific gravity two or three times that of common rock-forming minerals. Galena, which is an ore of lead (Figure 2.17), has a specific gravity of roughly 7.5, whereas the specific gravity of 24-karat gold is approximately 20.

Other Properties of Minerals

In addition to the properties already discussed, some minerals can be recognized by other distinctive properties. For example, halite is ordinary salt so it is quickly identified with your tongue. Thin sheets of mica will bend and elastically snap back. Gold is malleable and can be easily shaped. Talc and graphite both have distinctive feels; talc feels soapy and graphite feels greasy. A few minerals, such as magnetite, have a high iron content and can be picked up with a magnet, while some varieties (lodestone) are natural magnets and will pick up small iron-based objects, such as pins and paper clips.

Some minerals exhibit special optical properties. For example, when a transparent piece of calcite is placed over printed material, the letters appear twice (Figure 2.18). This optical property is known as *double refraction*. The streak of many sulphur-bearing minerals smells like rotten eggs.

One very simple chemical test to identify a mineral involves placing a drop of dilute hydrochloric acid from a dropper bottle onto a freshly broken

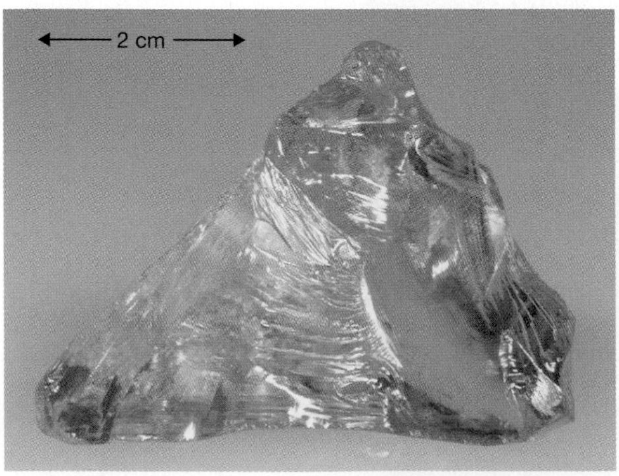

◆ **Figure 2.16** Conchoidal fracture. The smooth curved surfaces result when minerals break in a glasslike manner. (Photo by E. J. Tarbuck)

◆ **Figure 2.18** A transparent specimen of calcite showing the property of double refraction. (Photo by S. R. Hicock)

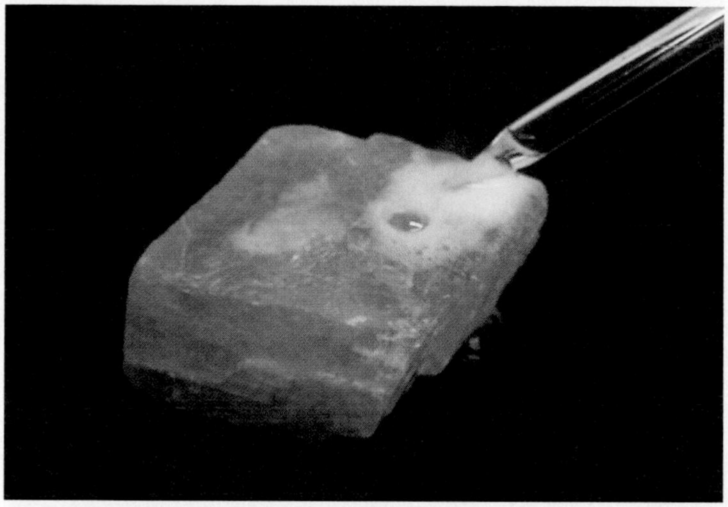

◆ **Figure 2.19** Calcite vigorously effervesces when brought into direct contact with acid.
(Photo by C. Tsujita)

mineral surface. Carbonate minerals will effervesce (fizz) with hydrochloric acid (Figure 2.19). This test is useful in identifying calcite, which is a common carbonate mineral.

In summary, a number of special physical and chemical properties are useful in identifying certain minerals. These include taste, smell, elasticity, malleability, feel, magnetism, double refraction, and chemical reaction to hydrochloric acid. Remember that each of these properties depends on the composition (elements) of a mineral and its structure (how the atoms are arranged).

MINERAL GROUPS

GEODe EARTH Minerals: Building Blocks of Rocks
↳ Mineral Groups

Approximately 4000 minerals have been named and several new ones are identified each year. Fortunately, for students who are beginning to study minerals, no more than a few dozen are abundant! Collectively, these few make up most of the rocks of Earth's crust and, as such, are classified as the *rock-forming minerals*. Only *eight elements* make up the bulk of these minerals, and they represent more than 98 percent (by weight) of the continental crust (Figure 2.20). These elements in order of abundance are oxygen (O), silicon (Si), aluminum (Al), iron (Fe), calcium (Ca), sodium (Na), potassium (K), and magnesium (Mg).

Silicon and oxygen combine to form the framework of the most common mineral group, the **silicates**. The next most common mineral group is the carbonates, of which calcite is the most prominent member. Other common rock-forming minerals include gypsum and halite.

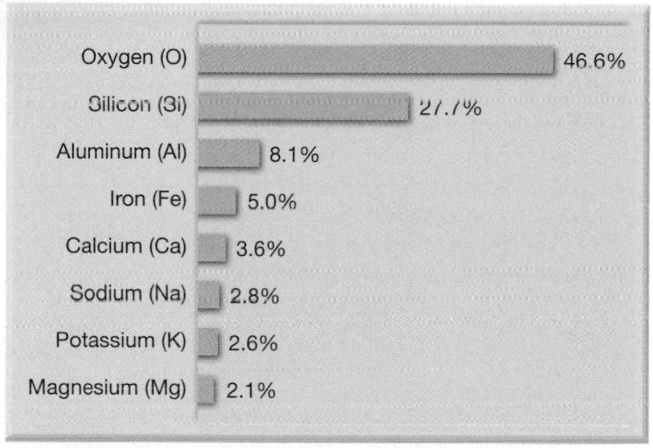

◆ **Figure 2.20** Relative abundance of the eight most abundant elements in the continental crust.

We will first discuss the most common mineral group, the silicates, and then consider some of the other prominent mineral groups.

The Silicates

Every silicate mineral contains the elements oxygen and silicon. Except for a few minerals, such as quartz, a silicate mineral includes one or more additional elements that are needed to produce electrical neutrality. These additional elements give rise to the great variety of silicate minerals and their varied properties (Box 2.1).

The Silicon–Oxygen Tetrahedron All silicates have the same fundamental building block, the **silicon–oxygen tetrahedron** (*tetra* = four, *hedra* = a base). This structure consists of four oxygen ions surrounding a much smaller silicon ion (Figure 2.21). The silicon–oxygen tetrahedron is a complex ion (SiO_4^{4-}) with a charge of –4.

BOX 2.1

People and the Environment
Asbestos: What Are the Risks?

Asbestos is a commercial term applied to a variety of silicate minerals that readily separate into thin, strong fibres that are highly flexible, heat resistant, and relatively inert. These properties make asbestos a desirable material for the manufacture of a wide variety of products including insulation, fireproof fabrics, cement, floor tiles, and car brake linings.

The mineral chrysotile, marketed as "white asbestos," belongs to the serpentine mineral group and accounts for the vast majority of asbestos sold commercially (Figure 2.A). Canada's only currently mined source of chrysotile is in eastern Quebec in the vicinity of Thetford Mines. Still, Canada is the world's top exporter and second-largest producer of chrysotile. All other forms of asbestos are amphiboles (defined shortly) and constitute only a minor proportion of asbestos used commercially. The two most common amphibole asbestos minerals are amosite and crocidolite, informally called brown asbestos and blue asbestos, respectively.

Health concerns about asbestos, raised in the 1980s, stem largely from claims of high death rates attributed to asbestosis (lung scarring from asbestos fibre inhalation), mesothelioma (cancer of the chest and abdominal cavity), and lung cancer among asbestos mine workers. The degree of concern generated by these claims has been well demonstrated by the growth of an entire industry built around asbestos removal from buildings.

◆ **Figure 2.A** Chrysotile asbestos. This sample is a fibrous form of the mineral serpentine. **Inset:** Thetford Mines, Quebec, the source of all Canadian chrysotile asbestos. (Photo by E. J. Tarbuck)

The stiff, straight fibres of brown and blue (amphibole) asbestos are known to readily pierce, and remain lodged in, the linings of human lungs. The fibres are physically and chemically stable and are not broken down in the human body. These forms of asbestos are therefore a genuine cause for concern. White asbestos, however, being a different mineral, has different properties. The curly fibres of white asbestos are readily expelled from the lungs and, if they are not expelled, can dissolve within a year. Studies conducted on people living in the Thetford Mines area exposed to high levels of white asbestos dust suggest little, if any, difference in mortality rates from mesothelioma and lung cancer relative to the general public. Despite the fact that more than 90 percent of all asbestos used commercially is white asbestos, a number of countries have banned the use of asbestos in many applications, as the different mineral forms of asbestos are not distinguished. Still, the health hazards of chrysotile at low doses remain controversial.

One of the simplest ways in which these tetrahedra join together to become neutral compounds is through the addition of cations (Figure 2.22). In this way, a chemically stable structure is produced, consisting of individual tetrahedra linked by cations.

More Complex Silicate Structures In addition to cations providing the opposite electrical charge needed to bind the tetrahedra, the tetrahedra can link with other tetrahedra in a variety of configurations. For example, the tetrahedra can be joined to form *single chains*, *double chains*, or *sheet structures*, as shown in Figure 2.23. The joining of tetrahedra in each of these configurations results from the sharing of a different number of oxygen atoms between silicon atoms in adjacent tetrahedra.

To understand better how this sharing takes place, select one of the silicon ions (small blue spheres) near the middle of the single-chain structure shown in Figure 2.23A. Notice that this silicon ion is completely surrounded by four larger oxygen ions (you are looking *through* one of the four to see

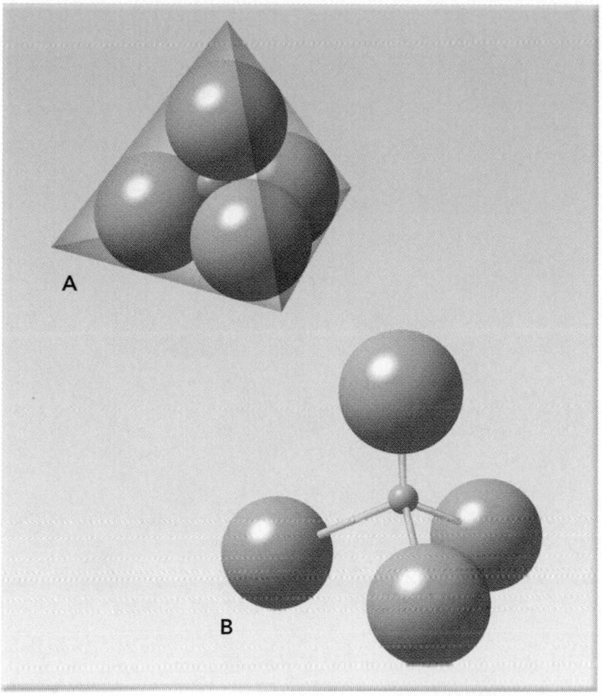

◆ **Figure 2.21** Two representations of the silicon–oxygen tetrahedron. **A.** The four large spheres represent oxygen ions, and the blue sphere represents a silicon ion. The spheres are drawn in proportion to the radii of the ions. **B.** An expanded view of the tetrahedron using rods to depict the bonds that connect the ions.

the blue silicon ion). Also notice that of the four oxygen ions, two are joined to other silicon ions, whereas the other two are not shared in this manner. *It is the linkage across the shared oxygen ions that joins the tetrahedra as a chain structure.* Now examine a silicon ion near the middle of the sheet structure and count the number of shared and unshared oxygen ions surrounding it (Figure 2.23C). The increase in the degree of sharing accounts for the sheet structure. Other silicate structures exist, and the most common has all of the oxygen ions shared to produce a complex three-dimensional framework.

The ratio of oxygen ions to silicon ions differs in each of the silicate structures. The isolated tetrahedron has four oxygen ions for every silicon ion. In the single chain the oxygen-to-silicon ratio is 3:1, and in the three-dimensional framework, this ratio is 2:1. Consequently, as more of the oxygen ions are shared, the percentage of silicon in the structure increases. Silicate minerals are therefore described as having a high or low silicon content based on their ratio of oxygen to silicon. This difference in silicon content is important, as you will see in Chapter 3, when we consider the formation of igneous rocks.

Most silicate structures, including single chains, double chains, and sheets, are not neutral chemical compounds. Thus, like the individual tetrahedra, they are all neutralized by the inclusion of metallic cations that bond them together into a variety of complex crystalline configurations. The cations that most often link silicate structures are those of the elements iron (Fe), magnesium (Mg), potassium (K), sodium (Na), aluminum (Al), and calcium (Ca).

Notice that in Figure 2.22 each of these cations has a particular atomic size and a particular charge. Generally, ions of approximately the same size are able to substitute freely for one another. For instance, ions of iron (Fe^{2+}) and magnesium (Mg^{2+}) are nearly the same size and substitute for each other without altering the mineral structure. This also holds true for calcium and sodium ions, which can occupy the same site in a crystalline structure. In addition, aluminum (Al^{3+}) often substitutes for silicon in the silicon–oxygen tetrahedron.

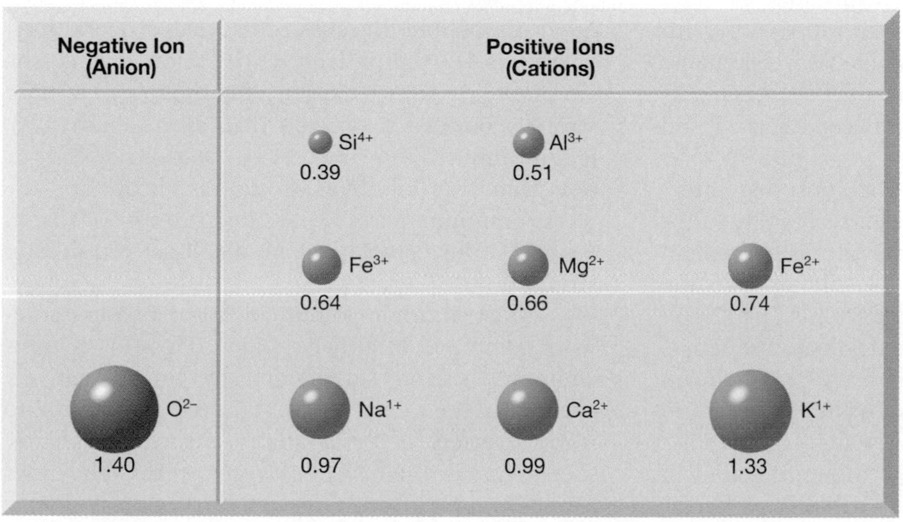

◆ **Figure 2.22** Relative sizes and electrical charges of ions of the eight most common elements in Earth's crust. These are the most common ions in rock-forming minerals. Ionic radii are expressed in angstroms (1 angstrom equals 10^{-8} cm).

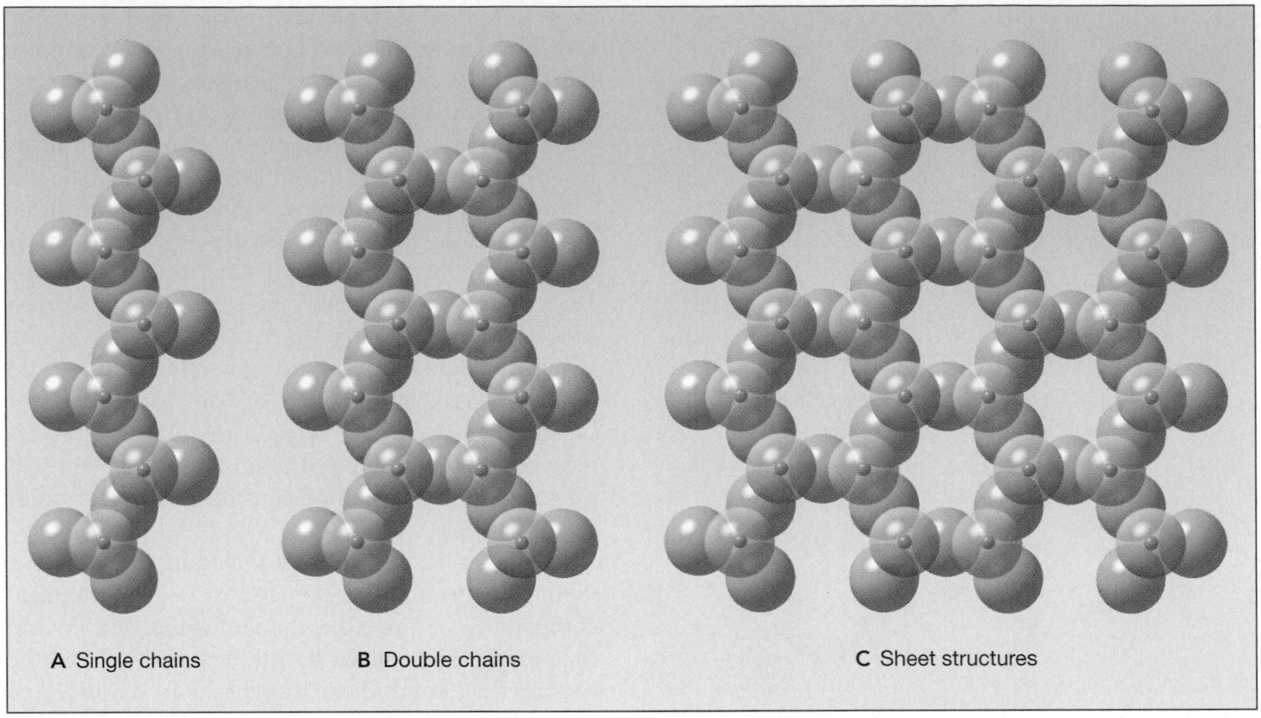

◆ **Figure 2.23** Three types of silicate structures.

Because of the ability of silicate structures to readily accommodate different cations at a given bonding site, individual specimens of a particular mineral can contain varying amounts of certain elements. A mineral of this type is often expressed by a chemical formula that uses parentheses to show the variable component. A good example is the mineral olivine, $(Mg,Fe)_2SiO_4$, which is magnesium–iron silicate. As you can see from the formula, the iron (Fe^{2+}) and magnesium (Mg^{2+}) cations in olivine freely substitute for each other. At one extreme, olivine may contain iron without any magnesium (Fe_2SiO_4, or iron silicate), and at the other, iron is totally lacking (Mg_2SiO_4, or magnesium silicate). Between these end members, any ratio of iron to magnesium is possible. Thus, olivine, as well as many other silicate minerals, is actually a *family* of minerals with a range of composition between the two end members.

In certain substitutions, the ions that interchange do not have the same electrical charge. For instance, when calcium (Ca^{2+}) substitutes for sodium (Na^{+}), the structure gains a positive charge. One way in which this substitution is accomplished, while still maintaining overall electrical neutrality, is the simultaneous substitution of aluminum (Al^{3+}) for silicon (Si^{4+}). This particular double substitution occurs in the mineral plagioclase feldspar, which is a member of the most abundant family of minerals found in Earth's crust. The end members of this particular feldspar series are a calcium–aluminum silicate (anorthite, $CaAl_2Si_2O_8$), and a sodium–aluminum silicate (albite, $NaAlSi_3O_8$).

You are now prepared to review silicate structures in light of what you know about chemical bonding. An examination of Figure 2.22 shows that among the major constituents of the silicate minerals, only oxygen is an anion (negatively charged). Because oppositely charged ions attract (and similarly charged ions repel), the chemical bonds that hold silicate structures together form between oxygen and oppositely charged cations. Thus, cations arrange themselves so that they can be as close as possible to oxygen while remaining as far apart from each other as possible. Because of its small size and high charge (+4), the silicon (Si) cation forms the strongest bonds with oxygen. Aluminum (Al) is more strongly bonded to oxygen than are calcium (Ca), magnesium (Mg), iron (Fe), sodium (Na), or potassium (K), but not as strongly as silicon. In many ways, aluminum plays a role similar to that of silicon by being the central ion in the basic tetrahedral structure.

Most silicate minerals consist of a basic framework composed of either a single silicon or a single aluminum cation surrounded by four negatively charged oxygen ions. These tetrahedra often link to form a variety of other silicate structures (chains, sheets, etc.) through shared oxygen atoms. The other cations bond with the oxygen atoms of these silicate structures to create the more complex crystalline structures that characterize the silicate minerals.

Common Silicate Minerals

To reiterate, the silicates are the most abundant mineral group and have the silicate ion (SiO_4^{4-}) as their basic building block. The major silicate groups and common examples are given in Figure 2.24. The feldspars (*feld* = field, *spar* = mineral) are by far the most abundant silicate minerals, composing more than 50 percent of Earth's crust. Quartz, the second most abundant mineral in the continental crust, is the only common mineral made completely of silicon and oxygen.

Notice in Figure 2.24 that each mineral *group* has a particular silicate *structure* and that a relationship exists between the internal structure of a mineral and the *cleavage* it exhibits. Because the silicon–oxygen bonds are strong, silicate minerals

Mineral		Idealized Formula	Cleavage	Silicate Structure
Olivine		$(Mg, Fe)_2SiO_4$	None	Single tetrahedron 
Pyroxene group (Augite)		$(Mg,Fe)SiO_3$	Two planes at 90°	Single chains 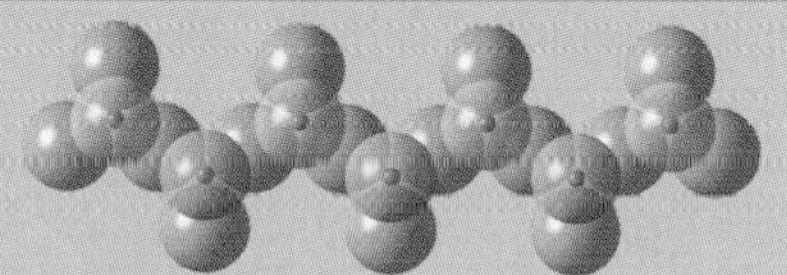
Amphibole group (Hornblende)		$Ca_2(Fe,Mg)_5Si_8O_{22}(OH)_2$	Two planes at 60° and 120°	Double chains 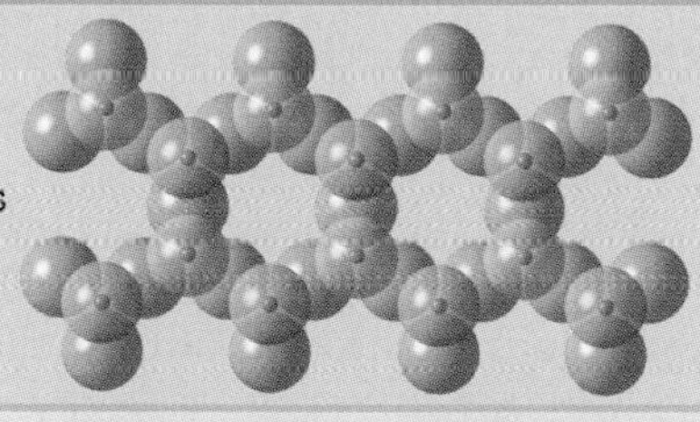
Micas	Biotite	$K(Mg,Fe)_3AlSi_3O_{10}(OH)_2$	One plane	Sheets 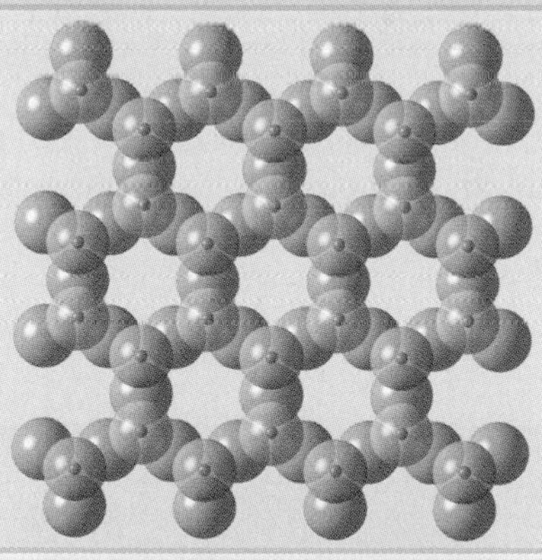
	Muscovite	$KAl_2(AlSi_3O_{10})(OH)_2$		
Feld-spars	Orthoclase	$KAlSi_3O_8$	Two planes at 90°	Three-dimensional networks 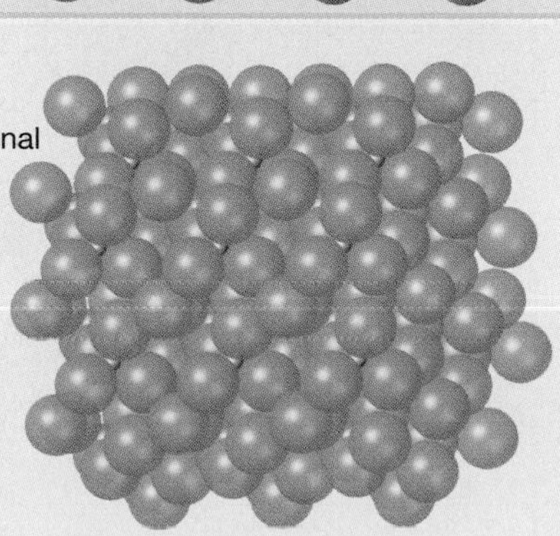
	Plagioclase	$(Ca,Na)AlSi_3O_8$		
Quartz		SiO_2	None	

◆ **Figure 2.24** Common silicate minerals. Note that the complexity of the silicate structure increases down the chart.

tend to cleave between the silicon–oxygen structures rather than across them. For example, the micas have a sheet structure and thus tend to cleave into flat plates (see Figure 2.14). Quartz, which has equally strong silicon–oxygen bonds in all directions, has no cleavage and fractures instead.

Most silicate minerals form (crystallize) as molten rock is cooling. This cooling can occur at or near Earth's surface (low temperature and pressure) or at great depths (high temperature and pressure). The environment during crystallization and the chemical composition of the molten rock determine, to a large degree, which minerals are produced. For example, the silicate mineral olivine crystallizes at high temperatures, whereas quartz crystallizes at much lower temperatures.

In addition, some silicate minerals form at Earth's surface from the weathered products of existing silicate minerals. Still other silicate minerals are formed under the extreme pressures associated with mountain building. Each silicate mineral, therefore, has a structure and a chemical composition that *indicate the conditions under which it formed*. Thus, by carefully examining the mineral constituents of rocks, geologists can often determine the circumstances under which the rocks formed.

We will now examine some of the most common silicate minerals, which we divide into two major groups on the basis of their chemical makeup.

Ferromagnesian (Dark) Silicates The **dark silicates,** or **ferromagnesian silicates,** are those minerals containing ions of iron (iron = *ferro*) or magnesium or both in their structure. Because of their iron content, ferromagnesian silicates are dark in colour and have a greater specific gravity, between 3.2 and 3.6, than nonferromagnesian silicates. The most common dark silicate minerals are olivine, the pyroxenes, the amphiboles, the dark mica (biotite), and garnet.

The *olivine* family of high-temperature silicate minerals are black to olive green and have a glassy lustre and a conchoidal fracture. Rather than developing large crystals, olivine commonly forms small, rounded crystals that give rocks consisting largely of olivine a granular appearance. Olivine is composed of individual tetrahedra that are bonded by a combination of iron and magnesium ions positioned so as to link the oxygen atoms with the magnesium and iron atoms. Because the three-dimensional network generated in this fashion does not have its weak bonds aligned, olivine does not possess cleavage.

The *pyroxenes* are a group of complex minerals thought to be important components of Earth's mantle. The most common member, *augite*, is a dark opaque mineral with two directions of cleavage that meet at a nearly 90-degree angle. Its crystalline structure consists of single chains of tetrahedra bonded by ions of iron and magnesium. Because the silicon–oxygen bonds are stronger than the bonds joining the adjacent silicate chain, augite cleaves parallel to (between) the silicate chains. Augite is one of the dominant minerals in basalt, a common igneous rock of the oceanic crust and volcanic areas on the continents.

Amphibole is a chemically complex group of minerals whose most common member is *hornblende* (Figure 2.25). Like the pyroxene mineral augite, hornblende is usually dark green to black and has two directions of cleavage. In contrast to augite, whose two cleavage directions intersect at 90 degrees, hornblende always cleaves at angles of approximately 60 and 120 degrees (Figure 2.26). As in pyroxene minerals, the cleavage angles in amphibole minerals

◆ **Figure 2.25** Hornblende variety of amphibole. Hornblende is a common dark silicate mineral having two cleavage directions that intersect at roughly 60° and 120°. (Photo courtesy of E. J. Tarbuck)

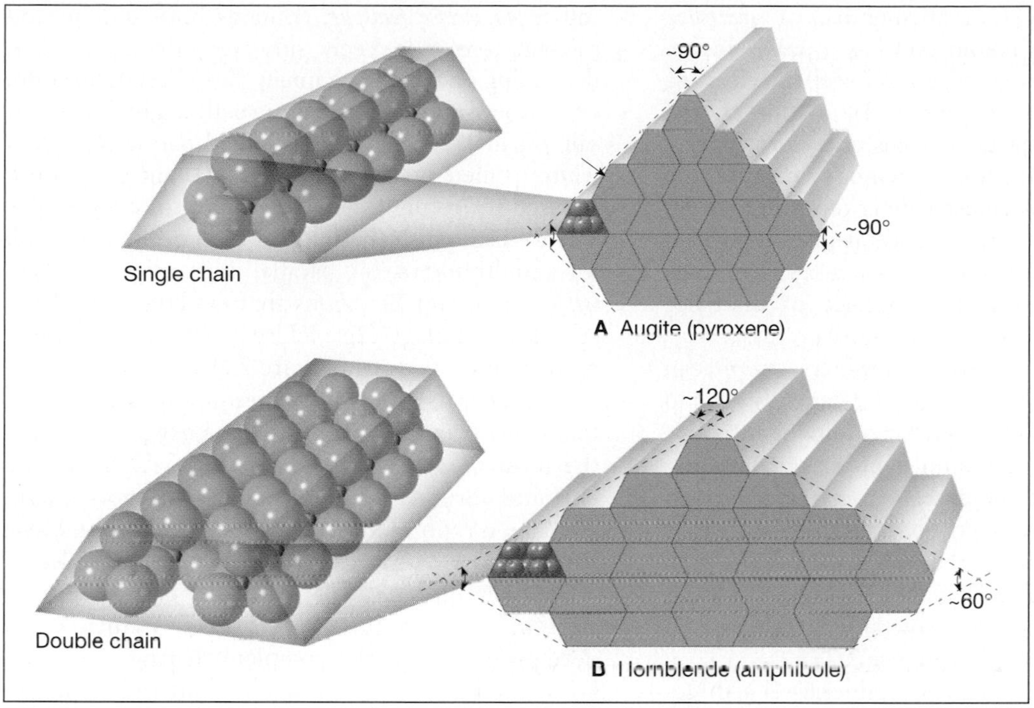

◆ **Figure 2.26** Cleavage angles for augite and hornblende.

reflect the weaker nature of the ionic bonds holding the silicate chains together, relative to the strong covalent bonds existing within the silica chain structures themselves. Because of differences in the cross-sectional dimensions of double chained versus single-chained units of tetrahedra, the planes of weakness in an amphibole mineral, such as hornblende, intersect at different angles than in a pyroxene mineral, such as augite. The cleavage angles corresponding to the relative orientations of these planes of weakness differ accordingly. Note that hornblende often forms elongate crystals, whereas augite tends to form rather stubby, blocky crystals. Hornblende is found predominantly in continental rocks, where it commonly makes up the dark portion of an otherwise light-coloured rock.

Biotite is the dark iron-rich member of the mica family. Like other micas, biotite possesses a sheet structure that gives it excellent cleavage in one direction. Biotite also has a shiny black appearance that helps distinguish it from the other dark ferromagnesian minerals. Like amphibole, biotite is a common constituent of continental rocks, including the igneous rock granite.

Garnet is similar to olivine in that its structure is composed of individual tetrahedra linked by metallic ions. Also like olivine, garnet has a glassy lustre, lacks cleavage, and possesses conchoidal fracture. Although the colours of garnet are varied, this mineral is most commonly brown to deep red. Garnet readily forms equidimensional crystals that are most commonly found in metamorphic rocks (Figure 2.27). When garnets are transparent, they can be used as gemstones.

Nonferromagnesian (Light) Silicates As the name implies, the **light silicates**, or **nonferromagnesian silicates**, are generally light in colour and have a specific gravity of about 2.7, which is considerably less than the ferromagnesian silicates. As indicated earlier, these differences are mainly attributable to the presence or absence of iron and magnesium. The light silicates contain varying amounts of aluminum, potassium, calcium, and sodium rather than iron and magnesium.

◆ **Figure 2.27** A deep-red garnet crystal embedded in a light-coloured, mica-rich metamorphic rock.
(Photo by E. J. Tarbuck)

Muscovite is a common member of the mica family. It is light in colour and has a pearly lustre. Like other micas, muscovite has excellent cleavage in one direction (see Figure 2.14). In thin sheets, muscovite is transparent to translucent, a property that accounts for its use in windows during the Middle Ages. Because muscovite is very shiny, it can often be identified by the sparkle it gives a rock. If you have ever looked closely at beach sand, you may have seen the glimmering brilliance of the mica flakes scattered among the other sand grains.

Feldspar, the most common mineral group, can form under a very wide range of temperatures and pressures, a fact that partially accounts for its abundance. All feldspars have similar physical properties: they have two planes of cleavage meeting at or near 90-degree angles, are relatively hard (6 on the Mohs scale), and have a lustre that ranges from glassy to pearly. As one component in a rock, feldspar crystals can be identified by their rectangular shape and rather smooth, shiny faces (Figure 2.28).

The structure of feldspar minerals is a three-dimensional framework formed when oxygen atoms are shared by adjacent silicon atoms. In addition, one quarter to one half of the silicon atoms in the feldspar structure are replaced by aluminum atoms. The difference in charge between aluminum (+3) and silicon (+4) is made up by the inclusion of one or more of the following ions into the crystal lattice: potassium (+1), sodium (+1), or calcium (+2). Because of the large size of the potassium ion as compared with the size of the sodium and calcium ions, two different feldspar structures exist. *Orthoclase feldspar* is a common member of a group of feldspar minerals that contains potassium ions in its structure and is therefore often referred to as *potassium feldspar*. The other group, called *plagioclase feldspar*, contains both sodium and calcium ions that freely substitute for each other, depending on the environment during crystallization.

Potassium feldspar is usually light cream to salmon pink. The plagioclase feldspars range from white to medium grey. However, colour should not be used to distinguish these groups. The only sure way to distinguish the feldspars physically is to look for a multitude of fine parallel lines, called *striations* (*striat* = a streak). Striations are found on some cleavage planes of plagioclase feldspar but are not present on orthoclase feldspar (Figure 2.29).

Quartz is the only common silicate mineral that consists entirely of silicon and oxygen. As such, the term *silica* is applied to quartz, which has the chemical formula SiO_2. As the structure of quartz contains a ratio of two oxygen ions (O^{2-}) for every silicon ion (Si^{4+}), no other positive ions are needed to attain neutrality.

In quartz a three-dimensional framework is developed through the complete sharing of oxygen by adjacent silicon atoms. Thus, all the bonds in quartz are of the strong silicon–oxygen (covalent) type. Consequently, quartz is hard, resistant to weathering, and does not have cleavage. When broken, quartz generally exhibits conchoidal fracture. In a pure form quartz is clear and, if allowed to solidify without interference, will form hexagonal crystals that develop pyramid-shaped ends (see the chapter-opening photo and Figure 2.11B). However, like most other clear minerals, quartz is commonly coloured by the inclusion of various ions (impurities) and forms without developing good crystal faces. The most common varieties of quartz are milky (white), smoky (grey), rose (pink), amethyst (purple), and rock crystal (clear) (Figure 2.12).

◆ **Figure 2.28** Sample of the mineral orthoclase feldspar. (Photo courtesy of E. J. Tarbuck)

◆ **Figure 2.29** These parallel lines, called striations, are a distinguishing characteristic of the plagioclase feldspars. (Photo by E. J. Tarbuck)

Clay is a term used to describe a variety of complex minerals that, like the micas, have a sheet structure. The clay minerals are generally very fine grained and can be studied only microscopically. Most clay minerals originate as products of the chemical weathering of other silicate minerals. Thus, clay minerals make up a large percentage of the surface material we call soil. Because of the importance of soil in agriculture, and because of its role as a supporting material for buildings, clay minerals are extremely important to humans.

One of the most common clay minerals is *kaolinite*, which is used in the manufacture of fine chinaware and in the production of high-gloss paper, such as that used in this textbook. Further, some clay minerals absorb large amounts of water, which allows them to swell to several times their normal size. These swelling clays have been used commercially in a variety of ingenious ways, including as an additive to thicken milkshakes in fast-food restaurants and as a clumping agent in cat litter.

Important Nonsilicate Minerals

Other mineral groups are scarce when compared with the silicates, although many are extremely important geologically and economically. Table 2.3 lists examples of several nonsilicate mineral groups of economic value. A discussion of a few of the more common nonsilicate rock-forming minerals follows.

The *carbonate* minerals are much simpler structurally than are the silicates. This mineral group is composed of the carbonate ion (CO_3^{2-}) and one or more kinds of cations. The two most common carbonate minerals are *calcite*, $CaCO_3$ (calcium carbonate), and *dolomite*, $CaMg(CO_3)_2$ (calcium–magnesium carbonate). Because these minerals are similar both physically and chemically, they are difficult to distinguish from each other. Both have a vitreous lustre, a hardness of 3 to 4, and nearly perfect rhombic cleavage (in three directions, not at 90 degrees; see Figure 2.15). They can, however, be distinguished by

TABLE 2.3 **Common Nonsilicate Mineral Groups**

Group	Member	Formula	Economic Use
Oxides	Hematite	Fe_2O_3	Ore of iron, pigment
	Magnetite	Fe_3O_4	Ore of iron
	Corundum	Al_2O_3	Gemstone, abrasive
	Ice	H_2O	Solid form of water
	Chromite	$FeCr_2O_4$	Ore of chromium
	Ilmenite	$FeTiO_3$	Ore of titanium
Sulphides	Galena	PbS	Ore of lead
	Sphalerite	ZnS	Ore of zinc
	Pyrite	FeS_2	Sulphuric acid production
	Chalcopyrite	$CuFeS_2$	Ore of copper
	Bornite	Cu_5FeS_4	Ore of copper
	Cinnabar	HgS	Ore of mercury
Sulphates	Gypsum	$CaSO_4 \cdot 2H_2O$	Plaster
	Anhydrite	$CaSO_4$	Plaster
	Barite	$BaSO_4$	Drilling mud
Native elements	Gold	Au	Trade, jewellery
	Copper	Cu	Electrical conductor
	Diamond	C	Gemstone, abrasive
	Sulphur	S	Sulpha drugs, chemicals
	Graphite	C	Pencil lead, dry lubricant
	Silver	Ag	Jewellery, photography
	Platinum	Pt	Catalyst
Halides	Halite	$NaCl$	Common salt
	Fluorite	CaF_2	Component of steelmaking
	Sylvite	KCl	Fertilizer
Carbonates	Calcite	$CaCO_3$	Portland cement, lime
	Dolomite	$CaMg(CO_3)_2$	Portland cement, lime
	Malachite	$Cu_2CO_3(OH)_2$	Gemstone
	Azurite	$Cu_3(CO_3)_2(OH)_2$	Gemstone
Hydroxides	Limonite	$FeO(OH) \cdot nH_2O$	Ore of iron, pigments
	Bauxite	$Al(OH)_3 \cdot nH_2O$	Ore of aluminum
Phosphates	Apatite	$Ca_5(PO_4)_3(F,Cl,OH)$	Fertilizer
	Turquoise	$CuAl_6(PO_4)_4(OH)_8$	Gemstone

◆ **Figure 2.30** Thick beds of potash (potassium-rich salt deposit) in an underground mine in Saskatchewan. (Photo by Jisuo Jin)

using dilute hydrochloric acid. As noted earlier, calcite reacts vigorously with this acid; dolomite reacts much more slowly. Calcite and dolomite are usually found together as the primary constituents in the sedimentary rocks limestone (in which calcite dominates) and dolostone (in which dolomite dominates). Limestone has numerous economic uses as road aggregate, building stone, and the main ingredient in portland cement.

Three other nonsilicate minerals found in sedimentary rocks are *halite*, *sylvite*, and *gypsum*. These minerals are commonly found in thick layers, which are the last vestiges of ancient seas that have long since evaporated (Figure 2.30). Like limestone, both are important nonmetallic resources. Halite is the mineral name for common table salt ($NaCl$), whereas sylvite (KCl) is the principal mineral of potash. Gypsum ($CaSO_4 \cdot 2H_2O$), calcium sulphate with water bound into the structure, is the mineral from which plaster and other similar building materials are made.

A number of other minerals are prized for their economic value (see Table 2.3 and Box 2.2). Included in this group are the ores of metals, such as hematite (iron), sphalerite (zinc), and galena (lead); the native (free-occurring, not in compounds) elements, including gold, silver, and carbon (diamonds); and a host of others, such as fluorite, corundum, and uraninite (a uranium source).*

In the chapters that follow we will see that minerals combine under different pressure and temperature conditions in the rock cycle (see Chapter 1) to form various rocks. Some minerals are found together because they are formed under similar conditions.

*For more on the economic significance of these and other minerals, see Chapter 20.

BOX 2.2

Understanding Earth
Gemstones

Precious stones have been prized since antiquity. But misinformation abounds regarding gems and their mineral makeup. This stems partly from the ancient practice of grouping precious stones by colour rather than by mineral makeup. For example, *rubies* and red *spinels* are very similar in colour, but they are completely different minerals. Classifying by colour led to the more common spinels being passed off as rubies to royalty. Even today, with modern identification techniques, common *yellow quartz* is sometimes sold as the more valuable gemstone *topaz*.

Naming Gemstones

Most precious stones have common names that are different from their parent mineral. For example, *sapphire* is one of two names given to the mineral *corundum*. Minute amounts of foreign elements can produce vivid sapphires of nearly every colour (Figure 2.B). Traces of titanium and iron in corundum produce the most-prized: blue sapphires. When corundum contains a sufficient quantity of chromium, it exhibits a brilliant red colour, and the gem is called *ruby*. If a specimen is not suitable as a gem, it simply goes by the mineral name *corundum*. Because of its hardness, corundum that is not of gem quality is often crushed and sold as an abrasive.

To summarize, when corundum exhibits a red hue, it is called *ruby*, but if it exhibits any other colour, the gem is called *sapphire*. Whereas corundum is the base mineral for two gems, quartz is the parent of more than a dozen gems. Table 2.A lists some well-known gemstones and their parent minerals.

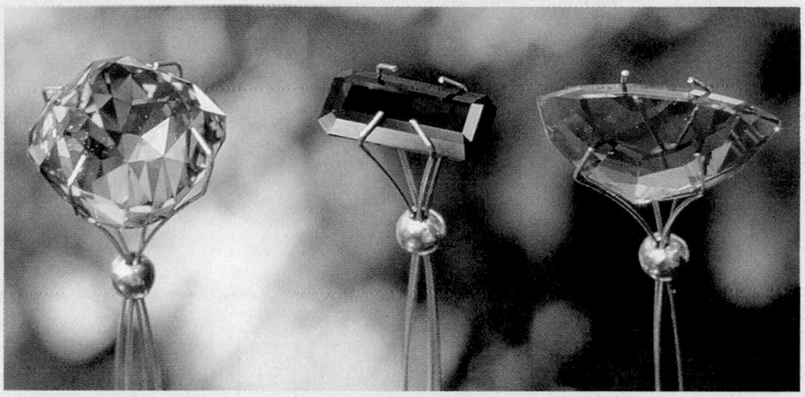

◆ **Figure 2.B** Australian sapphires showing variation in cuts and colours. (Photo by Fred Ward, Black Star)

TABLE 2.A **Important Gemstones**

Gem	Mineral Name	Prized Hues
Precious		
Diamond	Diamond	Colourless, yellows
Emerald	Beryl	Greens
Opal	Opal	Brilliant hues
Ruby	Corundum	Reds
Sapphire	Corundum	Blues
Semiprecious		
Alexandrite	Chrysoberyl	Variable
Amethyst	Quartz	Purples
Cat's-eye	Chrysoberyl	Yellows
Chalcedony	Quartz (agate)	Banded
Citrine	Quartz	Yellows
Garnet	Garnet	Reds, greens
Jade	Jadeite or nephrite	Greens
Moonstone	Feldspar	Transparent blues
Peridot	Olivine	Olive greens
Smoky quartz	Quartz	Browns
Spinel	Spinel	Reds
Topaz	Topaz	Purples, reds
Tourmaline	Tourmaline	Reds, blue-greens
Turquoise	Turquoise	Blues
Zircon	Zircon	Reds

What Constitutes a Gemstone?

When found in their natural state, most gemstones are dull and would be passed over by most people as just another rock. Gems must be cut and polished by experienced professionals before their true beauty is displayed (Figure 2.B). Only those mineral specimens that are of such quality that they can command a price in excess of the cost of processing are considered gemstones.

Gemstones can be divided into two categories: precious and semiprecious. A *precious* gem has beauty, durability, size, and rarity, whereas a *semiprecious* gem generally has only one or two of these qualities. The gems traditionally held in highest esteem are diamonds, rubies, sapphires, emeralds, and some varieties of opal (Table 2.A). All other gemstones are classified as semiprecious. However, large high-quality specimens of semiprecious stones often command a very high price.

Today translucent stones with evenly tinted colours are preferred. The most favoured hues are red, blue, green, purple, rose, and yellow. The most-prized stones are pigeon-blood rubies, blue sapphires, grass-green emeralds, and canary-yellow diamonds. Colourless gems are generally less than desirable, except for diamonds that display flashes of colour known as *brilliance*.

The durability of a gem depends on its hardness, that is, its resistance to abrasion by objects normally encountered in everyday living. For good durability, gems should be as hard as or harder than quartz as defined by the Mohs scale of hardness. One notable exception is opal, which is comparatively soft (hardness of 5 to 6.5) and brittle. Opal's esteem comes from its "fire," which is a display of a variety of brilliant colours, including greens, blues, and reds.

It seems to be human nature to treasure what is rare. In the case of gemstones, large high-quality specimens are much rarer than smaller stones. Thus, large rubies, diamonds, and emeralds, which are rare in addition to being beautiful and durable, command the very highest prices.

Chapter Summary

- A *mineral* is a naturally occurring inorganic solid that possesses a definite chemical structure that gives it a unique set of physical properties. Most *rocks* are aggregates composed of two or more minerals.
- The building blocks of minerals are *elements*. An *atom* is the smallest particle of matter that still retains the characteristics of an element. Each atom has a *nucleus*, which contains *protons* (particles with positive electrical charges) and *neutrons* (particles with no electrical charges). Orbiting the nucleus of an atom in regions called *energy levels*, or *shells*, are *electrons* which have negative electrical charges. The number of protons in an atom's nucleus determines its *atomic number* and the name of the element. An element is a large collection of electrically neutral atoms, all having the same atomic number.
- Atoms combine with each other to form more complex substances called *compounds*. Atoms bond by gaining, losing, or sharing electrons with other atoms. In *ionic bonding*, one or more electrons are transferred from one atom to another, giving the atoms a net positive or negative charge. The resulting electrically charged atoms are called *ions*. Ionic compounds consist of oppositely charged ions assembled in a regular, crystalline structure that allows for the maximum attraction of ions, given their sizes. Another type of bond, the *covalent bond*, is produced when atoms share electrons.
- *Isotopes* are variants of the same element but with different *mass numbers* (the total number of neutrons plus protons found in an atom's nucleus). Some isotopes are unstable and disintegrate naturally through a process called *radioactive dating*.
- The properties of minerals include *crystal form*, *lustre*, *colour*, *streak*, *hardness*, *cleavage*, *fracture*, and *specific gravity*. In addition, a number of special physical and chemical properties (taste, smell, elasticity, malleability, feel, magnetism, double refraction, and chemical reaction to hydrochloric acid) are useful in identifying certain minerals. Each mineral has a unique set of properties that can be used for identification.
- Of the approximately 4000 minerals, no more than a few dozen make up most of the rocks of Earth's crust and, as such, are classified as rock-forming minerals. Eight elements (oxygen, silicon, aluminum, iron, calcium, sodium, potassium, and magnesium) make up the bulk of these minerals and represent more than 98 percent (by weight) of Earth's continental crust.
- The most common mineral group is the *silicates*. All silicate minerals have the negatively charged *silicon–oxygen tetrahedron* as their fundamental building block. In some silicate minerals the tetrahedra are joined in chains (the pyroxene and amphibole groups); in others the tetrahedra are arranged into sheets (the micas: biotite and muscovite) or three-dimensional networks (the feldspars and quartz). The tetrahedra and various silicate structures are commonly bonded by the positive ions of iron, magnesium, potassium, sodium, aluminum, and calcium. Each silicate mineral has a structure and a chemical composition that indicates the conditions under which it formed.
- The *nonsilicate* mineral groups, which contain several economically important minerals, include the *oxides* (e.g., hematite, mined for iron), *sulphides* (e.g., sphalerite, mined for zinc; and galena, mined for lead), *sulphates* (e.g., gypsum), *halides* (e.g., halite, sylvite), and *native elements* (e.g., gold and silver). The more common nonsilicate rock-forming minerals include the *carbonate minerals*: calcite and dolomite.

Review Questions

1. Define the term *rock*.
2. List the three main particles of an atom and explain how they differ from one another.
3. If the number of electrons in a neutral atom is 35 and its mass number is 80, calculate the following:
   (a) the number of protons
   (b) the atomic number
   (c) the number of neutrons
4. What is the significance of valence electrons?
5. Briefly distinguish between ionic and covalent bonding.
6. What occurs in an atom to produce an ion?
7. What is an isotope?
8. Although all minerals have an orderly internal arrangement of atoms (crystalline structure),

most mineral samples do not exhibit their crystal form. Why?

9. Why might it be difficult to identify a mineral by its colour?
10. If you find a glassy-appearing mineral while rock hunting, and hope it is a diamond, what simple test might help you identify it?
11. Explain the use of corundum, as given in Table 2.3, in terms of the Mohs hardness scale.
12. Gold has a specific gravity of almost 20. If a 25-litre pail of water weighs 25 kilograms, how much would a 25-litre pail of gold weigh?
13. Explain the difference between the terms *silicon* and *silicate*.
14. What do ferromagnesian minerals have in common? List examples of ferromagnesian minerals.
15. What do muscovite and biotite have in common? How do they differ?
16. Should colour be used to distinguish between orthoclase feldspar and plagioclase feldspar? What is the best means of distinguishing between these two types of feldspar?
17. Each of the following statements describes a silicate mineral or mineral group. In each case, provide the appropriate name:
    (a) the most common member of the amphibole group
    (b) the most common nonferromagnesian member of the mica family
    (c) the only silicate mineral made entirely of silicon and oxygen
    (d) a high-temperature silicate with a name that is based on its colour
    (e) one silicate mineral or group that is characterized by striations
    (f) one silicate mineral or group that originates as a product of chemical weathering
18. What simple test can be used to distinguish calcite from dolomite?

Key Terms

atom (p. 36)
atomic number (p. 36)
atomic weight (p. 40)
cleavage (p. 44)
colour (p. 44)
compound (p. 36)
covalent bond (p. 40)
crystal form (p. 43)
dark silicates (p. 52)
electron (p. 36)
element (p. 36)
energy levels (p. 36)
ferromagnesian silicates (p. 52)
fracture (p. 46)
hardness (p. 44)
ion (p. 38)
ionic bond (p. 38)
isotope (p. 40)
light silicates (p. 53)
lustre (p. 43)
mass number (p. 40)
metallic bond (p. 40)
mineral (p. 35)
mineralogy (p. 34)
Mohs scale (p. 44)
neutron (p. 36)
nonferromagnesian silicates (p. 53)
nucleus (p. 36)
octet rule (p. 36)
polymorph (p. 42)
proton (p. 36)
radioactive decay (p. 41)
rock (p. 35)
shell (p. 36)
silicates (p. 47)
silicon–oxygen tetrahedron (p. 48)
specific gravity (p. 46)
streak (p. 44)
valence electron (p. 36)

Web Resources

The *Earth* website uses the resources and flexibility of the internet to aid in your study of the topics in this chapter. Written and developed by geology instructors, this site will help improve your understanding of geology. Visit **www.pearsoned.ca/tarbuck** and click on the cover of the text to find

- online review quizzes
- Web-based critical thinking and writing exercises
- links to chapter-specific Web resources
- internet-wide key-term searches

www.pearsoned.ca/tarbuck

Smokey the Bear
Hat

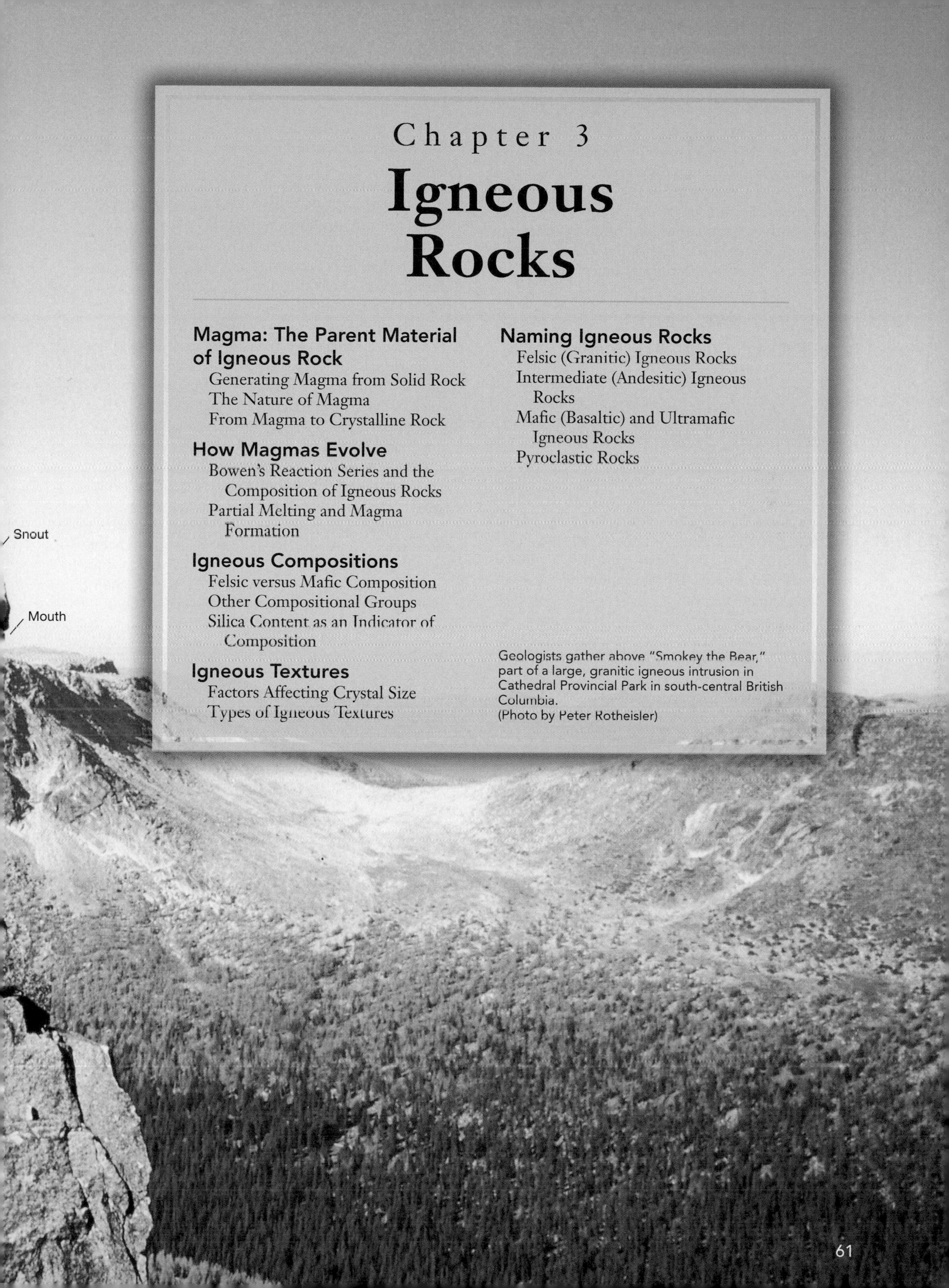

Chapter 3
Igneous Rocks

Geologists gather above "Smokey the Bear," part of a large, granitic igneous intrusion in Cathedral Provincial Park in south-central British Columbia.
(Photo by Peter Rotheisler)

Igneous rocks make up the bulk of Earth's crust. In fact, with the exception of Earth's core, the remaining solid portion of our planet is basically a huge mass of igneous rock that is partially covered by a thin veneer of sedimentary and metamorphic rocks. Consequently, a basic knowledge of igneous rocks is essential to our understanding of the structure, composition, and internal workings of our planet.

MAGMA: THE PARENT MATERIAL OF IGNEOUS ROCK

GEODe EARTH Igneous Rocks
↳ Introduction

In our discussion of the rock cycle (Chapter 1), it was pointed out that **igneous rocks** (*ignis* = fire) form as molten rock cools and solidifies. Abundant evidence indicates that the parent material for igneous rocks—called *magma*—is formed by a process called **partial melting**. Partial melting occurs at various levels within Earth's crust and upper mantle to depths of perhaps 250 kilometres. We will explore the origin of magma in the next section.

Once it is formed, a magma body buoyantly rises toward the surface because it is less dense than the surrounding rocks. Occasionally molten rock breaks through, producing a volcanic eruption. Magma that reaches Earth's surface is called **lava**. The lava fountain shown in Figure 3.1 was produced when escaping gases propelled molten rock from a magma chamber. Sometimes magma is explosively ejected from a vent, producing a catastrophic eruption. However, not all eruptions are violent; many volcanoes emit quiet outpourings of very fluid lava.

Igneous rocks that form when magma solidifies *at the surface* are classified as **extrusive** (*ex* = out, *trudere* = thrust), or **volcanic** (after the fire god Vulcan). Extrusive igneous rocks are abundant in western portions of the Americas, including the volcanic cones of the Cascade Range and the extensive lava flows of the Columbia Plateau. In addition, many oceanic islands, such as the Hawaiian chain, are composed almost entirely of volcanic igneous rocks.

Magma that loses its mobility before reaching the surface eventually crystallizes at depth. Igneous rocks that *form at depth* are termed **intrusive** (*in* = into, *trudere* = thrust), or **plutonic** (after Pluto, the god of the lower world in classical mythology). A body of

◆ **Figure 3.1** Recent eruption of Hawaii's Kilauea Volcano. (Photo by Soames Summerhays/Science Source/Photo Researchers, Inc.)

plutonic rock is called a *pluton*. Intrusive igneous rocks would rarely be exposed at the surface if portions of the crust were not uplifted and the overlying rocks stripped away by erosion. Exposures of intrusive igneous rocks occur in many places, including much of western and central British Columbia, the St. Lawrence region of Quebec (e.g., Mount Royal in Montreal), the highlands of the Maritimes, and in the Sweetgrass Hills area of Montana just south of Alberta. Very ancient igneous intrusions are also exposed throughout the Canadian Shield, which includes much of Nunavut; the Northwest Territories; much of Manitoba, Ontario, and Quebec; and parts of Alberta and Saskatchewan.

Generating Magma from Solid Rock

Although some magmas show evidence of at least some components that were derived from melting of crustal rocks, geologists are now confident that most magma originates from melting in Earth's mantle. It is also clear that plate tectonics play a major role in the generation of most magma. The greatest amount of igneous activity occurs at divergent plate boundaries in association with seafloor spreading. Substantial amounts of magma are also produced at subduction zones where oceanic lithosphere descends into the mantle. The magma generated here contains components of the mantle as well as subducted crust and subducted sediments. In addition, some magma appears to be generated deep in the mantle where it is not influenced directly by plate motions.

Based on available scientific evidence, *Earth's crust and mantle are composed primarily of solid, not molten, rock*. Although the outer core is a fluid, its iron-rich material is very dense and remains deep within Earth. So, what is the source of magma that produces igneous activity?

Geologists conclude that magma originates when essentially solid rock, located in the crust and upper mantle, melts. The most obvious way to generate magma from solid rock is to raise the temperature above the rock's melting point.

Role of Heat What source of heat is sufficient to melt rock? Workers in underground mines know that temperatures get higher as they go deeper. Although the rate of temperature change varies from place to place, it *averages* between 20°C and 30°C per kilometre in the *upper* crust. This change in temperature with depth is known as the **geothermal gradient** (Figure 3.2). Estimates indicate that the temperature at a depth of 100 kilometres ranges between 1200°C and 1400°C. At these high temperatures, rocks in the lower crust and upper mantle are near their melting points; they are very hot but still essentially solid.

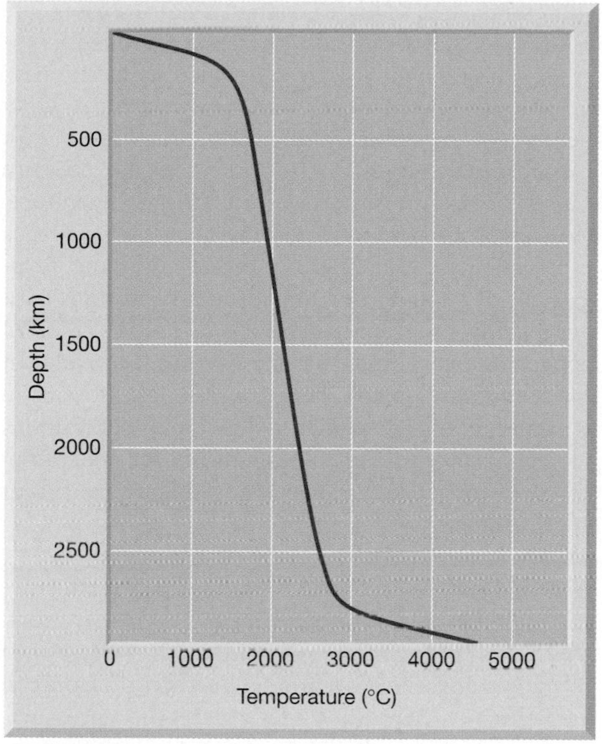

◆ **Figure 3.2** This graph illustrates the estimated temperature distribution for the crust and mantle. Notice that temperature increases significantly from the surface to the base of the lithosphere (100-kilometre depth) and that the temperature gradient (rate of change) is much less in the mantle. Because the temperature difference between the top and bottom of the mantle is relatively small, geologists conclude that slow convective flow (hot material rising and cool material sinking) must occur in the mantle.

Enough additional heat can be generated within the crust or upper mantle to produce some magma in several ways. First, at subduction zones, friction generates heat as huge slabs of crust slide past one another. Second, crustal rocks are heated as they descend into the mantle during subduction. Third, hot mantle rocks can rise and intrude crustal rocks. Although all of these processes generate some magma, the quantities produced are relatively small and the distribution is very limited.

As you will see, the vast bulk of magma forms without the aid of an additional heat source. Rock that is near its melting point can begin to melt if the confining pressure drops or if **volatiles** (fluids, gases) are introduced. We will now consider the roles that pressure and volatiles play in generating magma.

Role of Pressure If temperature were the only factor that determined whether or not rock melts, our planet would be a molten ball covered with a thin, solid outer shell. This, of course, is not the case. The reason is that pressure also increases with depth.

Melting, which is accompanied by an increase in volume, *occurs at higher temperatures at depth* because of greater confining pressure (Figure 3.3). Consequently, an increase in confining pressure causes a rise in the rock's melting temperature. Conversely, reducing confining pressure lowers a rock's melting temperature. When confining pressure drops enough, **decompression melting** is triggered. This can occur when rock *ascends* as a result of convective upwelling, thereby moving into zones of lower pressure. (Recall that even though the mantle is a solid, it does flow at very slow rates over millions of years.) This process is responsible for generating magma along ocean ridges where plates are rifting apart (Figure 3.4).

Role of Volatiles Another important factor affecting the melting temperature of rock is its water content. Water and other volatiles (mainly gases) cause rock to melt at lower temperatures. Further, the effect of volatiles is magnified by increased pressure. Consequently, "wet" rock buried at depth has a much lower melting temperature than does "dry" rock of the same composition and under the same confining pressure (see Figure 3.3). Therefore, in addition to a rock's composition, its temperature, depth (confining pressure), and water content determine whether it exists as a solid or liquid.

Volatiles play an important role in generating magma in regions where cool slabs of oceanic lithosphere descend into the mantle (Figure 3.5). As an oceanic plate sinks, both heat and pressure drive water from the subducting crustal rocks. These volatiles, which are very mobile, migrate into the wedge of hot mantle that lies above. This process is believed to lower the melting temperature of mantle rock sufficiently to generate some melt. Laboratory studies have shown that the melting point of basalt can be lowered by as much as 100°C by the addition of only 0.1 percent water.

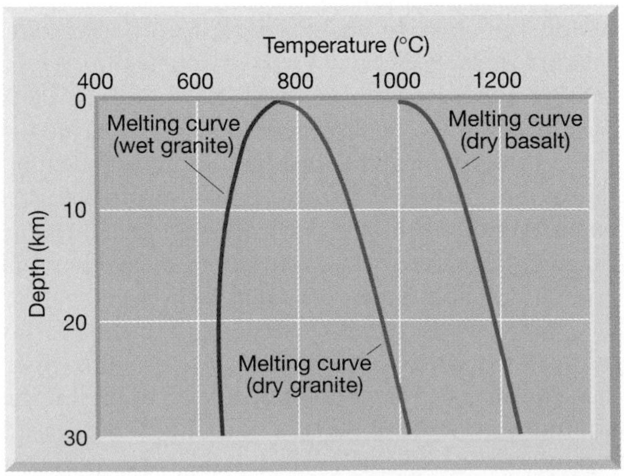

◆ **Figure 3.3** Idealized melting temperature curves. These curves portray the minimum temperatures required to melt rock within Earth's crust. Notice that dry granite and dry basalt melt at higher temperatures with increasing depth. By contrast, the melting temperature of wet granite actually decreases as the confining pressure increases.

When enough mantle-derived **mafic** (from *ma*gnesium and *f*errum, the Latin name for iron) magma forms, it will buoyantly rise toward the surface. In a continental setting, mafic magma may pond beneath crustal rocks, which have a lower density and are already near their melting temperature. This pooling can result in some melting of the crust and the formation of a secondary, silica-rich or **felsic** (from *fel*dspar and *si*lica) magma.

In summary, magma can be generated under three sets of conditions: (1) *heat* can be added, for example, by a magma body from a deeper source intruding and melting crustal rock; (2) *a decrease in pressure* (without the addition of heat) can result in *decompression melting*; and (3) the *introduction of volatiles* (mainly water) can lower the melting temperature of mantle rock sufficiently to generate magma.

The Nature of Magma

Magma is completely or partly molten material that, on cooling, solidifies to form an igneous rock. Most magmas consist of three distinct parts: a liquid component, a solid component, and a gaseous phase.

The liquid portion, called **melt**, is composed of mobile ions of those elements commonly found in Earth's crust. Melt is made up mostly of ions of silicon and oxygen, as well as lesser amounts of aluminum, potassium, calcium, sodium, iron, and magnesium.

The solid components (if any) in magma are silicate minerals that have already crystallized from the melt. As a magma body cools, the size and number of crystals increases. During the last stage of cooling, a magma body is mostly a crystalline solid with only minor amounts of melt.

Water vapour (H_2O), carbon dioxide (CO_2), and sulphur dioxide (SO_2) are the most common volatile components of magma and are confined by the immense pressure exerted by the overlying rocks. These volatiles are dissolved within the melt and will readily vaporize (form a gas) at surface pressures. Volatiles remain part of the magma until it either moves near the surface (low-pressure environment), or until the magma body is essentially crystallized, at which time any remaining volatiles freely migrate away. These hot fluids play an important role in metamorphism and will be considered further in Chapter 7.

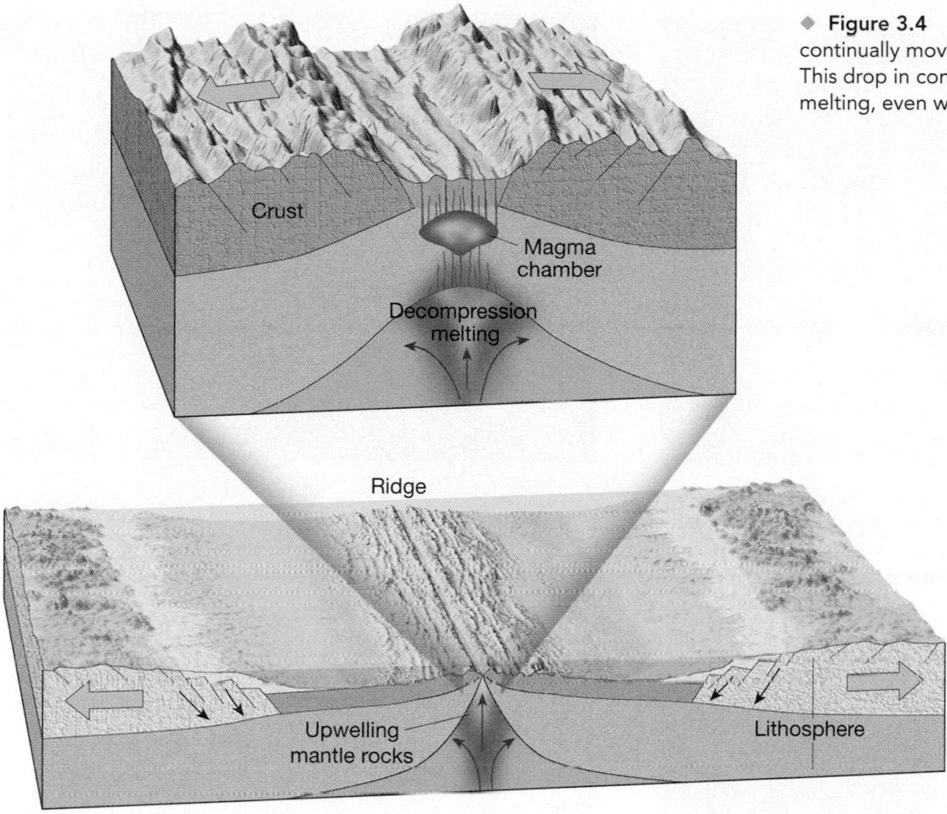

◆ **Figure 3.4** As hot mantle rock ascends, it continually moves into zones of lower pressure. This drop in confining pressure can trigger melting, even without additional heat.

From Magma to Crystalline Rock

As magma cools, the ions in the melt begin to lose their mobility and arrange themselves into orderly crystalline structures. This process, called **crystallization**, generates various silicate minerals that reside within the remaining melt.

When magma cools, it is generally the silicon and oxygen atoms that link together first to form silicon–oxygen tetrahedra, the basic building blocks of the silicate minerals (Chapter 2). As magma continues to lose heat to its surroundings, the tetrahedra join with each other and with other ions to form embryonic crystal nuclei. Slowly, each nucleus grows as ions lose their mobility and join the crystalline network.

The earliest formed minerals have space to grow and tend to have better developed crystal faces than do the later ones that fill the remaining space. Eventually, all of the melt is transformed into a solid mass of interlocking silicate minerals that we call an igneous rock (Figure 3.6).

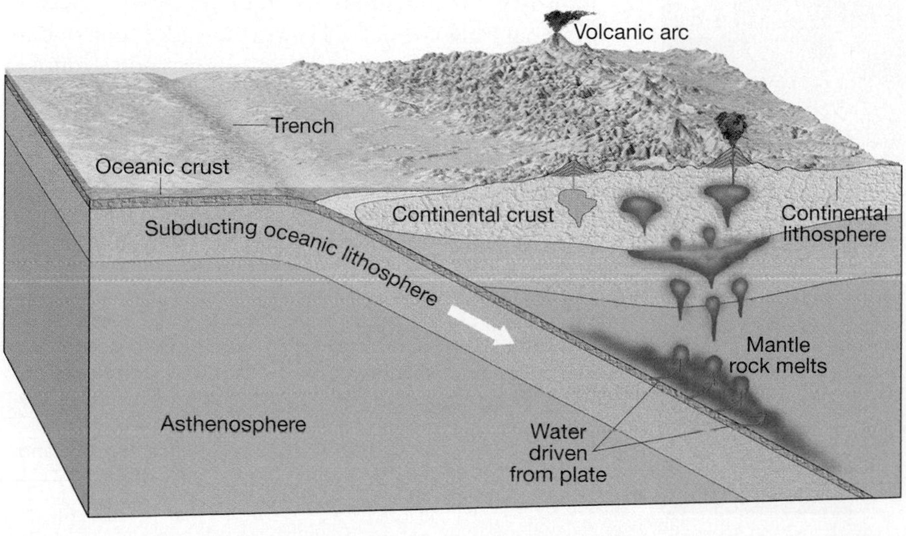

◆ **Figure 3.5** As a plate of oceanic lithosphere descends into the mantle, water and other volatiles are driven from the subducting crustal rocks. These volatiles lower the melting temperature of mantle rock sufficiently to generate melt.

A

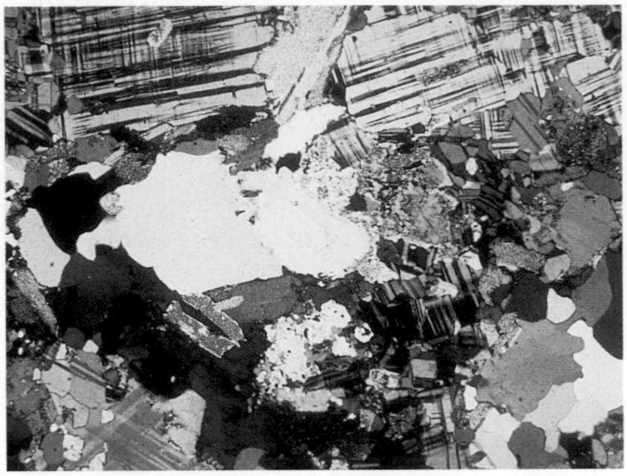

B

◆ **Figure 3.6** **A.** Close-up of interlocking crystals in a coarse-grained igneous rock. The largest crystals are about 1 centimetre in length. **B.** Photomicrograph (photo taken through a microscope) of interlocking crystals in a coarse-grained igneous rock.
(Photos by E. J. Tarbuck)

As you will see later, the crystallization of magma is much more complex than just described. Whereas a single compound, such as water, crystallizes at a specific temperature, solidification of magma, with its diverse chemistry, spans a temperature range of at least 200°C. During crystallization, the composition of the melt continually changes as ions are selectively removed and incorporated into the earliest formed minerals. If the melt should separate from the earliest formed minerals, its composition will be different from that of the original magma. Thus, a single magma can generate rocks with widely differing compositions. Consequently, a great variety of igneous rocks exist.

HOW MAGMAS EVOLVE

Because of the large variety of igneous rocks, it is logical to assume that an equally large variety of magmas also exist. However, geologists have observed that a single volcano can extrude a number of lavas that exhibit quite different compositions (Figure 3.7). Data of this type led geologists to exam-

◆ **Figure 3.7** Ash and pumice ejected during a large eruption of Mt. Mazama (Crater Lake). Notice the gradation from light-coloured, silica-rich ash near the base to dark-coloured rocks at the top. It is likely that before this eruption the magma began to segregate as the less dense silica-rich (felsic) magma migrated toward the top of the magma chamber. The zonation seen in the rocks resulted because a sustained eruption tapped deeper and deeper levels of the magma chamber. Thus, this rock sequence is an inverted representation of the compositional zonation in the magma body; that is, the magma from the top of the chamber erupted first and is found at the base of these ash deposits and vice versa.
(Photo by E. J. Tarbuck)

ine the possibility that magma might change (evolve) and thus become the parent to a variety of igneous rocks. To explore this idea, a pioneering investigation into the crystallization of magma was carried out by Canadian scientist N. L. Bowen (Box 3.1) in the first quarter of the twentieth century.

Bowen's Reaction Series and the Composition of Igneous Rocks

Recall that ice freezes at a single temperature whereas magma crystallizes through at least 200°C of cooling. In a laboratory setting Bowen and his co-workers

BOX 3.1

Canadian Profile

Norman Bowen and His Reaction Series

Based on his high-temperature, high-pressure experiments and microscopic studies of igneous rocks (Figure 3.A), Norman Bowen's reaction series provides a visual representation of the order in which minerals crystallize from a magma of average composition (see Figure 3.8). This model assumes that the magma cools slowly at depth in an otherwise unchanging environment. Notice that Bowen's reaction series is divided into two branches: a discontinuous series and a continuous series. Discontinuous refers to the changing crystal structures of minerals within the series, whereas all the minerals in the continuous series have the same crystal structure.

Discontinuous Reaction Series

The upper left branch of Bowen's reaction series, called the *discontinuous reaction series*, indicates that as a magma cools, olivine is the first mineral to crystallize. Once formed, olivine chemically reacts with the remaining melt to form pyroxene (see Figure 3.8). In this reaction, olivine, which is composed of individual silicon–oxygen tetrahedra, incorporates more silica into its structure, thereby linking its tetrahedra into single-chain structures of pyroxene. (Note: Pyroxene has a lower crystallization temperature than olivine and is more stable at lower temperatures.) As the magma body cools further, pyroxene crystals react with the melt to generate the double-chain structure of amphibole, which in turn reacts with the melt to form the sheet-silicate biotite. These reactions do not usually run to completion, so various amounts of each mineral in the series may exist at any given time. In fact, some minerals, such as biotite, may never form.

Continuous Reaction Series

The right branch of the reaction series, called the *continuous reaction series*, illustrates that calcium-rich plagioclase feldspar crystals react with the sodium ions in the melt to become progressively more sodium rich (see Figure 3.8). Here, the sodium ions diffuse into the feldspar crystals and displace the calcium ions in the crystal lattice.

During the last stage of crystallization, after much of the magma has solidified, potassium feldspar forms. Finally, if the remaining melt has excess silica, the mineral quartz forms.

Testing Bowen's Reaction Series

During an eruption of Hawaii's Kilauea volcano in 1965, mafic lava poured into a pit crater, forming a lava lake that became a natural laboratory for testing Bowen's reaction series. When the surface of the lava lake cooled enough to form a crust, geologists drilled through it into the magma and periodically removed samples that were quenched to preserve the melt and minerals that were growing within it. By sampling the lava at successive stages of cooling, a history of crystallization was recorded.

As Bowen's reaction series predicts, olivine crystallized early but later ceased to form and was partly reabsorbed into the cooling melt. (In a larger magma body that cooled more slowly, we would expect most, if not all, of the olivine to react with the melt and change to pyroxene.) Most importantly, the melt changed composition throughout the course of crystallization. In contrast to the original mafic lava, which contained about 50 percent silica (SiO_2), the final melt contained more than 75 percent silica and had a composition similar to granite.

◆ **Figure 3.A** Norman Levi Bowen (1887–1956) studying his reaction series with a polarizing microscope. Bowen was born in Kingston, Ontario, graduated from Queen's University, completed his Ph.D. at MIT, then spent most of his professional life at the Geophysical Laboratory, Carnegie Institution, Washington, DC. He was considered the leading expert on igneous rocks. (Photo courtesy of the Geophysical Laboratory, Carnegie Institution of Washington)

Although the lava in this setting cooled rapidly compared with rates experienced in deep magma chambers, it was slow enough to verify that minerals do crystallize in a systematic fashion that roughly parallels Bowen's reaction series. Further, had the melt been separated at any stage in the cooling process, it would have formed a rock with a composition much different from that of the original lava.

demonstrated that as a mafic magma cools, minerals tend to crystallize in a systematic fashion based on their melting points. As shown in Figure 3.8, the first mineral to crystallize from a mafic magma is the ferromagnesian mineral olivine. Further cooling generates calcium-rich plagioclase feldspar as well as pyroxene, and so forth down the diagram.

During the crystallization process, the composition of the liquid portion of the magma continually changes. For example, at the stage when about a third of the magma has solidified, the melt will be nearly depleted of iron, magnesium, and calcium because these elements are constituents of the earliest-formed minerals. The removal of these elements from the melt will cause it to become enriched in sodium and potassium. Further, because the original mafic magma contained about 50 percent silica (SiO_2), the crystallization of the earliest-formed mineral, olivine, which is only about 40 percent silica, leaves the remaining melt richer in SiO_2. Thus, the silica component of the melt becomes enriched as the magma evolves.

Magmatic Differentiation Bowen demonstrated that minerals crystallize from magma in a systematic fashion. But how do Bowen's findings account for the great diversity of igneous rocks? It has been shown that, at one or more stages during crystallization, a separation of the solid and liquid components of a magma can occur. One example is called **crystal settling**. This process occurs when the earlier-formed minerals are denser (heavier) than the liquid portion and sink toward the bottom of the magma chamber, as shown in Figure 3.9. When the remaining melt solidifies—either in place or in another location if it migrates into fractures in the surrounding rocks—it will form a rock with a chemical composition much different from the parent magma (Figure 3.9). The formation of one or more secondary magmas from a single parent magma is called **magmatic differentiation.**

At any stage in the evolution of a magma, the solid and liquid components can separate into two chemically distinct units. Further, magmatic differentiation within the secondary melt can generate additional chemically distinct fractions. Consequently, magmatic differentiation and separation of the solid and liquid components at various stages of crystallization can produce several chemically diverse magmas and ultimately a variety of igneous rocks (see Figure 3.9). Bowen also demonstrated that if the solid components of a magma remain in contact with the remaining melt, they will chemically react and evolve into the next mineral in the sequence shown in Figure 3.8. For this reason, this arrangement of minerals became known as **Bowen's reaction series** (see Box 3.1). As explained above, in some natural settings the earliest-formed minerals can be separated from the melt, thus halting any further chemical reaction.

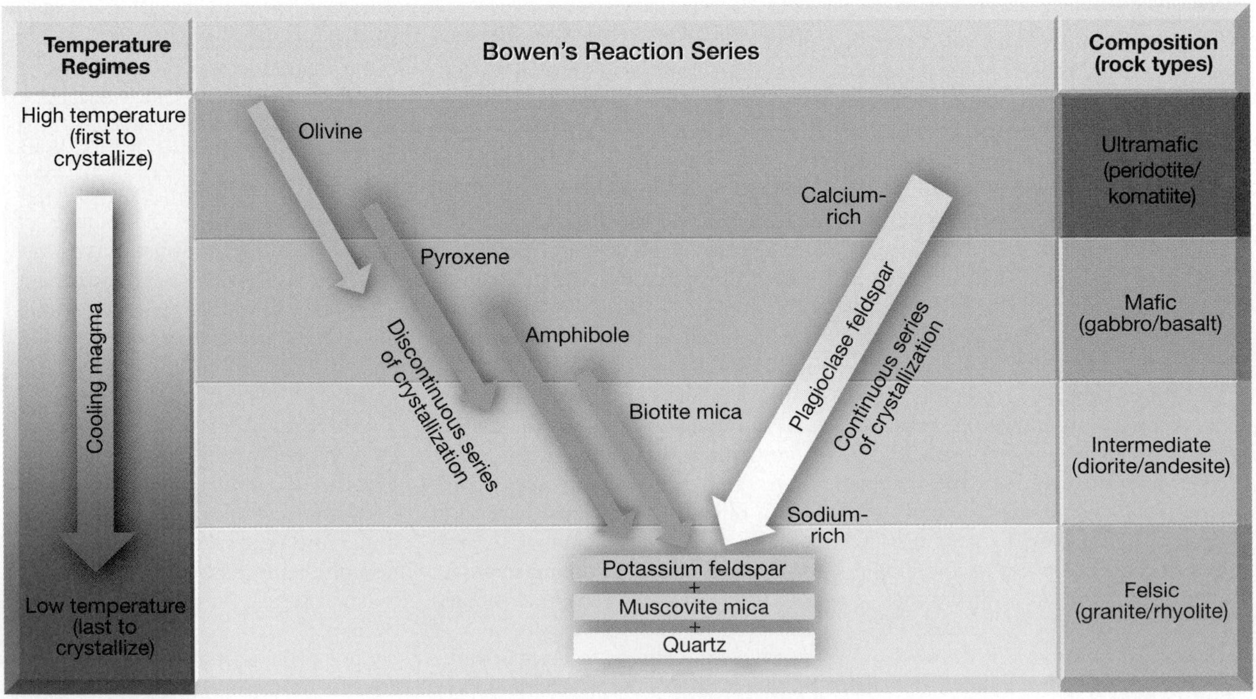

◆ **Figure 3.8** Bowen's reaction series shows the sequence in which minerals crystallize from magma. Note that each rock group consists of minerals that crystallize in the same temperature range.

The diagram of Bowen's reaction series in Figure 3.8 depicts the sequence that minerals crystallize from a magma of average composition under laboratory conditions. Evidence that this highly idealized crystallization model approximates what can happen in nature comes from the analysis of igneous rocks. In particular, we find that minerals that form in the same general temperature regime on Bowen's reaction series are found together in the same igneous rocks. For example, notice in Figure 3.8 that the minerals quartz, potassium feldspar, and muscovite, which are located in the same region of Bowen's diagram, are typically found together as major constituents of the plutonic igneous rock granite.

Bowen successfully demonstrated that through magmatic differentiation, a parent magma can generate several mineralogically different igneous rocks. However, more recent work indicates that magmatic differentiation by crystal settling cannot by itself account for the entire compositional spectrum of igneous rocks; other mechanisms must be involved.

Assimilation Once a magma body forms, its composition can change through the incorporation of foreign material. For example, as magma migrates upward, it may incorporate some of the surrounding host rock, a process called **assimilation** (Figure 3.10). This process can operate in a near-surface environment, where rocks are brittle. As the magma pushes upward, stress causes numerous cracks in the overlying rock. The force of the injected magma is often sufficient to dislodge blocks of "foreign" rock and incorporate them into the magma body. In deeper environments, the magma may be hot enough to simply melt and assimilate some of the surrounding host rock, which is near its melting temperature.

Magma Mixing Another means by which the composition of a magma body can be altered is called **magma mixing**. This process occurs whenever one magma body intrudes another (Figure 3.10). Once combined, convective flow can stir the two magmas and generate a fluid with an intermediate composition. Magma mixing can occur during the ascent of two chemically distinct magma bodies, when the more buoyant mass overtakes the slower moving mass.

In summary, Bowen successfully demonstrated that through crystal settling and magmatic differentiation, a single parent magma can generate several mineralogically different igneous rocks. Thus, this process, in concert with magma mixing and contamination by crustal rocks, accounts in part for the great diversity of magmas and igneous rocks. We will next look at another important process, partial melting, which also generates magmas that have varying compositions.

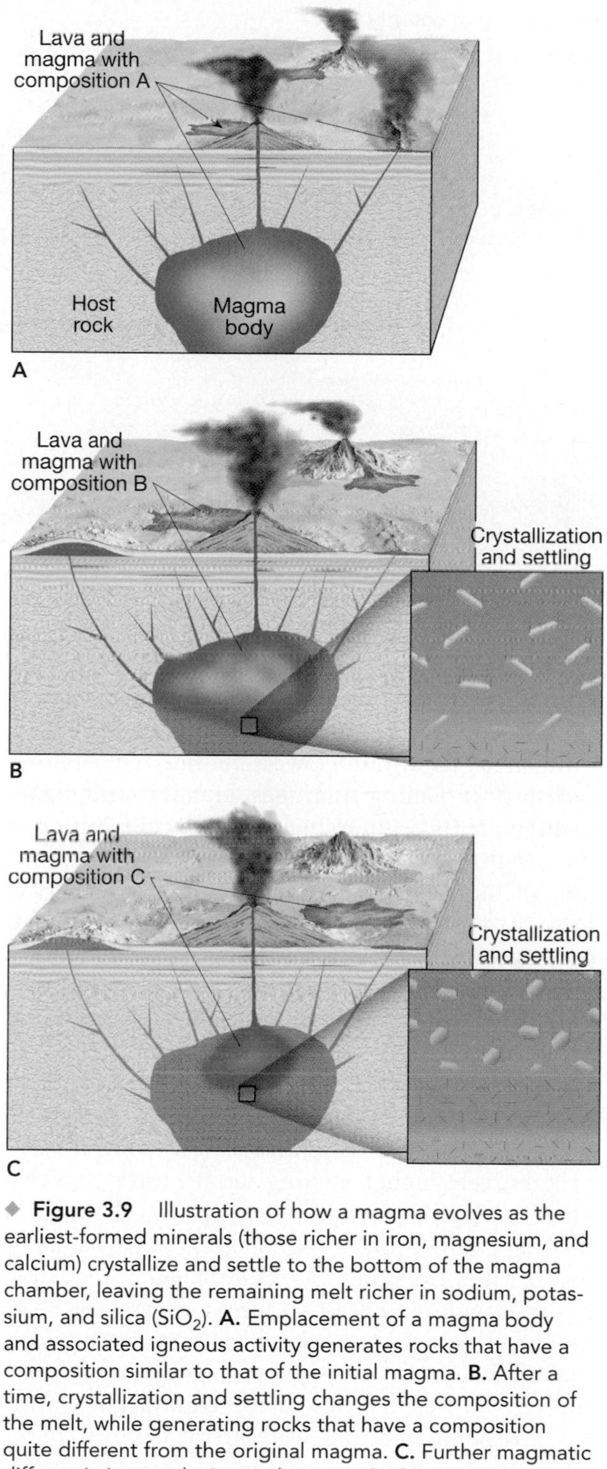

◆ **Figure 3.9** Illustration of how a magma evolves as the earliest-formed minerals (those richer in iron, magnesium, and calcium) crystallize and settle to the bottom of the magma chamber, leaving the remaining melt richer in sodium, potassium, and silica (SiO_2). **A.** Emplacement of a magma body and associated igneous activity generates rocks that have a composition similar to that of the initial magma. **B.** After a time, crystallization and settling changes the composition of the melt, while generating rocks that have a composition quite different from the original magma. **C.** Further magmatic differentiation results in another more highly evolved melt with its associated rock types.

Partial Melting and Magma Formation

Recall that the crystallization of a magma occurs over a temperature range of at least 200°C. As you

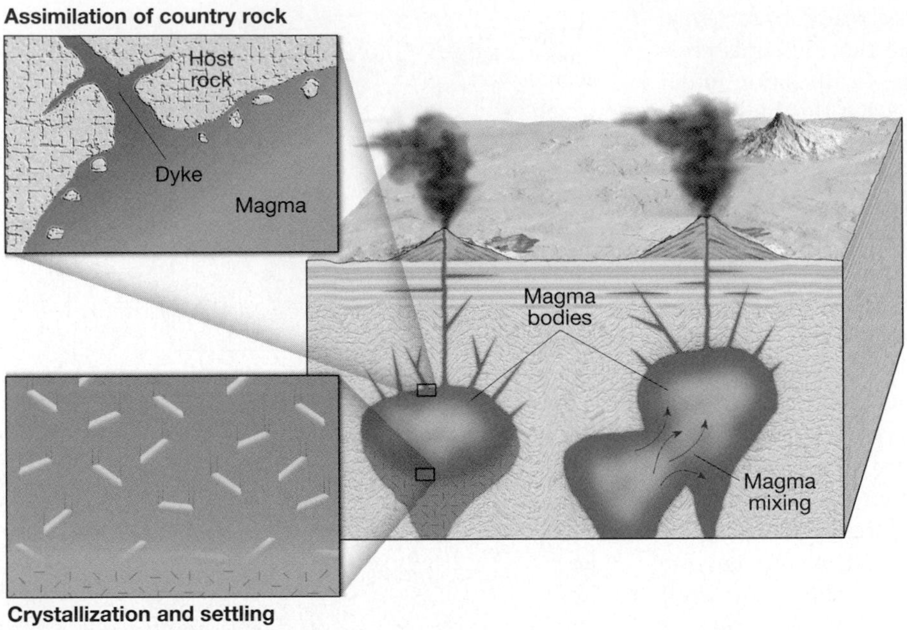

◆ **Figure 3.10** This illustration shows three ways that the composition of a magma body can be altered: magma mixing, assimilation of host (country) rock, and crystallization and settling (magmatic differentiation).

might expect, melting, the reverse process, spans a similar temperature range. As rock begins to melt, those minerals with the lowest melting temperatures melt first. If melting continues, minerals with higher melting points begin to melt and the composition of the magma steadily approaches the overall composition of the rock from which it was derived. Most often, however, melting is not complete. The incomplete melting of rocks is known as partial melting, a process that produces most, if not all, magma.

Notice in Figure 3.8 that rocks with a felsic composition are composed of minerals with the lowest melting (crystallization) temperatures—namely, quartz and potassium feldspar. Also note that as we move up Bowen's reaction series, the minerals have progressively higher melting temperatures and that olivine, which is found at the top, has the highest melting point. When a rock undergoes partial melting, it will form a melt that is enriched in ions from minerals with the lowest melting temperatures. The unmelted crystals are those of minerals with higher melting temperatures. Separation of these two fractions would yield a melt with a chemical composition that is richer in silica and nearer to the felsic end of the spectrum than the rock from which it was derived.

Formation of a Mafic Magma Most mafic magmas probably originate from partial melting of *peridotite*, a dark-coloured igneous rock that is thought to be the main constituent of the upper mantle. Mafic magmas that originate from direct melting of mantle rocks are called *primary* magmas because they have not yet evolved. Melting to produce these mantle-derived magmas can be triggered by a reduction in confining pressure (decompression melting). This can occur, for example, where mantle rock ascends as part of slow-moving convective flow at mid-ocean ridges (see Figure 3.4). Recall that mafic magmas can also be generated at subduction zones, where water driven from the descending slab of oceanic crust promotes partial melting of mantle rocks (see Figure 3.5).

Because most mafic magma forms between about 50 and 250 kilometres below the surface, we might expect that this material would cool and crystallize at depth. However, as mafic magma migrates upward, the confining pressure steadily diminishes and reduces its melting temperature. As you will see in the next chapter, environments exist in which mafic magmas ascend rapidly enough that the heat loss to the surrounding environment is offset by the drop in the melting temperature. Consequently, large outpourings of mafic lavas are common at Earth's surface. In some situations, however, mafic magmas that are comparatively dense will collect beneath crustal rocks and crystallize at depth.

Formation of Andesitic and Felsic Magmas If partial melting of mantle rocks generates mafic magmas, what is the source of the magma that generates intermediate and felsic rocks? Intermediate and felsic magmas are not erupted from volcanoes in the deep-ocean basins; rather, they are found only within, or adjacent to, the continental margins (Figures 3.5 and 3.11). Strong evidence suggests that interactions between mantle-derived mafic magmas and more silica-rich components of Earth's crust generate these magmas. For example, as a mafic magma migrates upward, it may melt and assimilate some of

◆ **Figure 3.11** Eruption in 1996 of Mount Ruapehu, Tongariro National Park, New Zealand. Volcanoes that border the Pacific Ocean are fed largely by magmas that have intermediate or felsic compositions. These silica-rich magmas often erupt explosively, generating large plumes of volcanic dust and ash. (Photo by Tui De Roy/Minden Pictures)

the crustal rocks through which it ascends. The result is the formation of a more silica-rich magma of **intermediate composition** or **andesitic composition** (between mafic and felsic).

Magma of intermediate composition can also evolve from a mafic magma by the process of magmatic differentiation. Recall from our discussion of Bowen's reaction series that as mafic magma solidifies, it is the silica-poor ferromagnesian minerals that crystallize first. If these iron-rich components are separated from the liquid by crystal settling, the remaining melt, now enriched in silica, will have a composition more akin to andesite. These evolved (changed) magmas are termed *secondary magmas*.

Felsic rocks are found in much too large a quantity to be generated solely from the magmatic differentiation of primary mafic magmas. Most likely they are the end product of the crystallization of an intermediate magma, or the product of partial melting of silica-rich continental rocks. The heat to melt crustal rocks often comes from hot mantle-derived mafic magmas that formed above a subducting plate within the crust.

Felsic melts are higher in silica and thus more viscous (thicker) than other magmas. Felsic magmas are also formed at lower temperatures than other magmas. Therefore, in contrast to mafic magmas that frequently produce vast outpourings of lava, felsic magmas usually lose their mobility before reaching the surface and tend to produce large plutonic bodies. On those occasions when silica-rich magmas do reach the surface, explosive eruptions, such as those from Mount St. Helens, are the result.

IGNEOUS COMPOSITIONS

GEODe EARTH Igneous Rocks
↳ Igneous Compositions

Igneous rocks are mainly composed of silicate minerals. Furthermore, the mineral makeup of a particular igneous rock is ultimately determined by the chemical composition of the magma from which it crystallizes. Recall that magma is composed largely of the eight elements that are the major constituents of the silicate minerals. Chemical analysis shows that silicon and oxygen (usually expressed as the silica [SiO_2] content of a magma) are by far the most abundant constituents of igneous rocks. These two elements, plus ions of aluminum (Al), calcium (Ca), sodium (Na), potassium (K), magnesium (Mg), and iron (Fe), make up roughly 98 percent by weight of most magmas. In addition, magma contains small amounts of many other elements, including titanium and manganese, and trace amounts of much rarer elements, such as gold, silver, and uranium.

As magma cools and solidifies, these elements combine to form two major groups of silicate minerals. The dark (or ferromagnesian) silicates are rich in iron or magnesium or both and comparatively low in silica. Olivine, pyroxene, amphibole, and biotite mica (Figure 3.8) are the common dark silicate minerals of Earth's crust. By contrast the light (or nonferromagnesian) silicates contain greater amounts of potassium, sodium, and calcium rather than iron and magnesium. As a group these minerals are richer in silica than are the dark silicates. The light silicates include quartz, muscovite mica, and the most abundant mineral group, the feldspars. The feldspars make up at least 40 percent of most igneous rocks. Thus, in addition to feldspar, igneous rocks contain some combination of the other light and dark silicates listed above.

Felsic versus Mafic Compositions

Despite their great compositional diversity, igneous rocks (and the magmas from which they form) can be divided into broad groups according to their proportions of light and dark minerals (Figure 3.12). At one end of the continuum are rocks composed almost entirely of light-coloured silicates: quartz and feldspar. Igneous rocks in which these are the dominant minerals are said to be felsic. In addition to quartz and feldspar, most felsic rocks contain about 10 percent dark silicate minerals, usually biotite mica and amphibole. Felsic rocks are rich in silica (about 70 percent) and are major constituents of the continental crust. Because granite is the most common type of felsic rock, some geologists refer to felsic rocks as having a **granitic** composition.

Rocks that contain substantial dark silicate minerals and calcium-rich plagioclase feldspar (but no quartz) are said to be mafic (Figure 3.12). This is because they contain a high percentage of ferromagnesian minerals. Because of their iron content, mafic rocks are typically darker and denser than felsic rocks. Mafic rocks are also referred to as having a

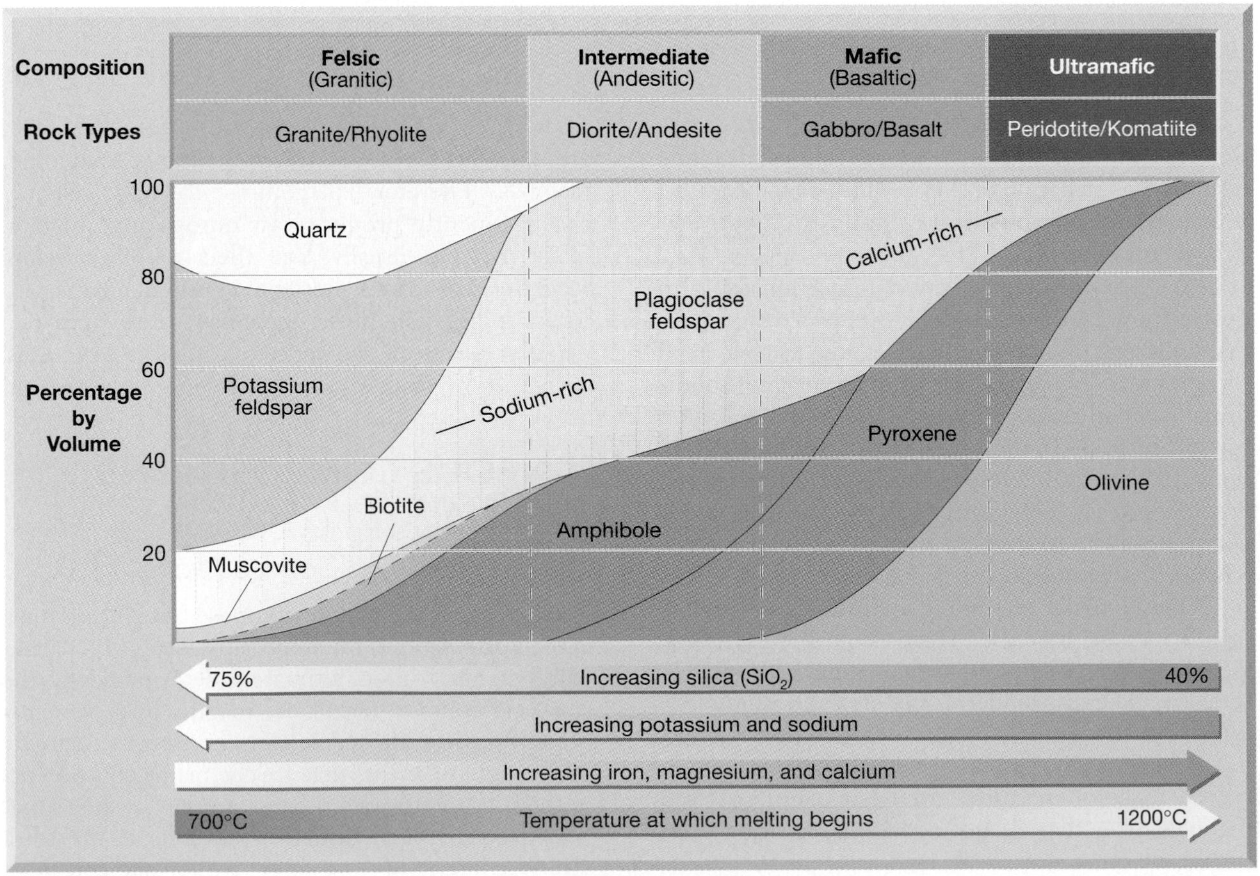

◆ **Figure 3.12** Mineralogy of common igneous rocks and the magmas from which they form. (After Dietrich, Daily, and Larsen)

basaltic composition because the most common rock type of this composition is basalt. Mafic rocks make up the ocean floor as well as many of the volcanic islands located within the ocean basins, and they are also found on the continents.

Other Compositional Groups

As you can see in Figure 3.12, rocks with a composition between felsic and mafic are said to have an intermediate or andesitic composition after the common volcanic rock *andesite*. Intermediate rocks contain at least 25 percent dark silicate minerals, mainly amphibole, pyroxene, and biotite mica, with the other dominant mineral being plagioclase feldspar. This important category of igneous rocks is associated with volcanic activity that is typically confined to the margins of the continents (see Figure 3.5).

Another important igneous rock, peridotite, contains mostly olivine and pyroxene and thus falls on the opposite side of the compositional spectrum from felsic rocks (see Figure 3.12). Because peridotite is composed almost entirely of ferromagnesian minerals, its chemical composition is referred to as **ultramafic**. Although ultramafic rocks are rare at Earth's surface, peridotite is believed to be the main constituent of the upper mantle. The volcanic equivalent of peridotite is komatiite.

Silica Content as an Indicator of Composition

An important aspect of the chemical composition of igneous rocks is their silica (SiO_2) content. Recall that silicon and oxygen are the two most abundant elements in igneous rocks. Typically the silica content of crustal rocks ranges from a low of about 45 percent in ultramafic rocks to a high of more than 70 percent in felsic rocks (Figure 3.12). The percentage of silica in igneous rocks actually varies in a systematic manner that parallels the abundance of other elements. For example, rocks comparatively low in silica contain large amounts of iron, magnesium, and calcium. By contrast, rocks high in silica contain very small amounts of those elements but are enriched instead in sodium and potassium. Consequently, the chemical makeup of an igneous rock can be inferred directly from its silica content.

Further, the amount of silica present in magma strongly influences its behaviour. Felsic magma, which has a high silica content, is quite viscous and exists as a liquid at temperatures as low as 700°C. Conversely, mafic magmas are low in silica and are generally more fluid. Also, mafic magmas crystallize at higher temperatures than felsic magmas and are completely solid when cooled to 1000°C.

In summary, igneous rocks can be divided into broad groups according to the proportions of light and dark minerals they contain. Felsic rocks, which are almost entirely composed of the light-coloured minerals quartz and feldspar, are at one end of the compositional spectrum (Figure 3.12). Mafic rocks, which contain abundant dark silicate minerals in addition to plagioclase feldspar, make up the other major igneous rock group of Earth's crust. Between these groups are rocks with an intermediate (andesitic) composition, while ultramafic rocks, which lack light-coloured minerals, lie at the other end of the compositional spectrum from felsic rocks.

Although the crystallization of magma is complex, it is nevertheless possible to classify igneous rocks based on their mineral composition and the conditions under which they formed. Their environment during crystallization can be roughly inferred from the size and arrangement of the mineral grains, a property called *texture*. Consequently, *igneous rocks are most often classified by their mineral composition and texture*. We will consider these two rock characteristics in the following sections.

IGNEOUS TEXTURES

GEODe EARTH Igneous Rocks
↳ Igneous Textures

The term **texture**, when applied to an igneous rock, is used to describe the overall appearance of the rock based on the size, shape, and arrangement of its interlocking crystals (Figure 3.13). Texture is an important characteristic because it reveals a great deal about the environment in which the rock formed. This permits geologists to make inferences about a rock's origin while working in the field (Figure 3.13A), where sophisticated equipment is not available.

Factors Affecting Crystal Size

Three factors contribute to the textures of igneous rocks: (1) *the rate at which magma cools* (e.g., glassy texture), (2) *the amount of silica present*, and (3) *the amount of volatiles in the magma* (e.g., pegmatitic texture). Of these, the rate of cooling is the dominant factor, but like all generalizations, this one has numerous exceptions.

As a magma body loses heat to its surroundings, cooling can occur rapidly (for example, in a thin lava flow) and the ions quickly combine to form crystals. The result is a solid mass of many small, intergrown crystals. Conversely, a very large magma body located at great depth will cool over perhaps

◆ **Figure 3.13** Igneous rock textures. **A.** Outcrop of dark basalt (solidified lava flow) intruded by pink bodies of granite on Baffin Island (note backpack for scale). **B.** Aphanitic (fine-grained) hand specimen of basalt. **C.** Phaneritic (coarse-grained) hand specimen of granite. **D.** Porphyritic (large crystals embedded in a finer-grained groundmass). **E.** Glassy (cooled too rapidly to form crystals). Photomicrographs (the coloured circular photos taken through a microscope; see Box 3.2) are magnified about 27 times.
(Photo **A** by S. R. Hicock; photos **B–E** by E. J. Tarbuck)

BOX 3.2

Understanding Earth
Thin Sections and Rock Identification

Igneous rocks are classified on the basis of their mineral composition and texture. When analyzing specimens, geologists examine them closely to identify the minerals present and to determine the size and arrangement of the interlocking crystals. When out in the field, geologists use megascopic techniques to study rocks. The *megascopic* characteristics of rocks are those features that can be determined with the unaided eye or by using a low-magnification (×10) hand lens. When practical to do so, geologists collect hand samples that can be taken back to the laboratory where *microscopic*, or high-magnification, methods can be employed. Microscopic examination is important to identify trace minerals, as well as those textural features that are too small to be visible with the unaided eye.

Because most rocks are not transparent, microscopic work requires the preparation of a very thin slice of rock known as a *thin section* (Figure 3.B). First, a saw containing diamonds embedded in its blade is used to cut a narrow slab from the sample. Next, one side of the slab is polished by using grinding powder and then cemented to a microscope slide. Once the mounted sample is firmly in place, the other side of it is ground to a thickness of about 0.03 millimetre. When a slice of rock is that thin, it is usually transparent. Nevertheless, some metallic minerals, such as pyrite and magnetite, remain opaque.

Once produced, thin sections are examined under a *polarizing microscope*. Such an instrument has a polarized light source beneath the stage so that light can be transmitted upward through the thin section in one (plane-polarized) or two (cross-polarized) directions. Because minerals have crystalline structures that influence polarized light, this procedure allows for even the smallest components of a rock to be identified. Part C of Figure 3.B is a photomicrograph (photo taken through a microscope) of a thin section of granite shown under cross-polarized light. The mineral constituents are identified by their unique optical properties. In addition to assisting in the study of igneous rocks, microscopic techniques are also used in analyzing sedimentary and metamorphic rocks.

◆ **Figure 3.B** Thin sections are very useful in identifying the mineral constituents in rocks. **A.** A slice of rock is cut from a hand sample by using a diamond saw. **B.** This slice is cemented to a microscope slide and ground until it is transparent to light (about 0.03 millimetre thick). **C.** A thin section of granite viewed under cross-polarized light.
(Photos by E. J. Tarbuck)

tens or hundreds of thousands of years. Slow cooling permits ions to join one of the existing crystalline structures. Consequently, slow cooling promotes the growth of fewer but larger crystals.

At the opposite extreme, when molten material is quenched quickly, there may not be sufficient time for the ions to arrange into a crystalline network. Rocks that consist of unordered ions are referred to as **glass**.

Types of Igneous Textures

The effect of cooling on rock textures is fairly straightforward: rapid cooling tends to generate small crystals, whereas slow cooling promotes the growth of large crystals. We will consider the other two factors affecting crystal growth as we examine the major textural types.

Aphanitic (Fine-Grained) Texture Igneous rocks that form at the surface or as small masses within the upper crust where cooling is relatively rapid possess a very fine-grained texture termed **aphanitic** (*a* = not, *phaner* = visible). By definition, the crystals that make up aphanitic rocks are so small that individual minerals can only be distinguished with the aid of a microscope (Figure 3.13B). Because mineral identification is not possible, we commonly characterize fine-grained rocks as being light, intermediate, or dark in colour. Using this system of grouping, light-coloured aphanitic rocks are those containing primarily light-coloured nonferromagnesian silicate materials and so forth (see the section titled "Common Silicate Minerals" in Chapter 2).

◆ **Figure 3.14** Vesicular texture displayed in an outcrop of solidified lava. Vesicles are small holes left by escaping gas bubbles.
(Photo courtesy of E. J. Tarbuck)

Commonly seen in many aphanitic rocks are the voids left by gas bubbles that attempt to escape as lava solidifies. These spherical or elongate openings are called *vesicles*, and the rocks that contain them are said to have a **vesicular** texture. Rocks that exhibit a vesicular texture usually form in the upper zone of a lava flow, where cooling occurs rapidly enough to "freeze" the lava, thereby preserving the cavities produced by the expanding gas bubbles (Figure 3.14).

Phaneritic (Coarse-Grained) Texture When large masses of magma slowly solidify far below the surface, they form igneous rocks that exhibit a coarse-grained texture described as **phaneritic** (*phaner* = visible). These coarse-grained rocks consist of a mass of intergrown crystals, which are roughly equal in size and large enough so that the individual minerals can be identified without the aid of a microscope (Figure 3.13C). Geologists often use a small magnifying lens to aid in identifying coarse-grained minerals. Because phaneritic rocks form deep within Earth's crust, their exposure at Earth's surface results only after erosion removes the overlying rocks that once surrounded the magma chamber.

Porphyritic Texture A large mass of magma located at depth may require tens to hundreds of thousands of years to solidify. Because different minerals crystallize at different temperatures (as well as at differing rates), it is possible for some crystals to become quite large before others even begin to form. If magma containing some large crystals should change environments—for example, by erupting at the surface—the remaining liquid portion of the lava would cool relatively quickly. The resulting rock, which has large crystals embedded in a matrix of smaller crystals, is said to have a **porphyritic** texture (Figure 3.22A). The large crystals in such a rock are referred to as **phenocrysts** (*pheno* = show, *cryst* = crystal) whereas the matrix of smaller crystals is called **groundmass**. A rock with such a texture is termed a **porphyry**.

Glassy Texture During some volcanic eruptions, molten rock is extruded into water or ejected into the atmosphere, where it is quenched quickly. Rapid cooling of this type may generate rocks having a **glassy** texture. As we indicated earlier, glass results when unordered ions are "frozen" before they are able to form crystals. *Obsidian*, a common type of natural glass, is similar in appearance to a dark chunk of manufactured glass (Figure 3.13E).

Lava flows composed of obsidian several tens of metres thick occur in some places (Figure 3.15). Thus, rapid cooling is not the only mechanism by which a glassy texture can form. As a general rule,

◆ **Figure 3.15** This obsidian flow was extruded from a vent along the south wall of Newberry Caldera, Oregon. Note the road for scale.
(Photo by E. J. Tarbuck)

magmas with high silica content tend to form long, chainlike structures before crystallization is complete. These structures in turn impede ionic transport and increase the magma's viscosity. *Viscosity* is a measure of a fluid's resistance to flow.

A magma that is rich in silica may be extruded as an extremely viscous mass that eventually solidifies to form obsidian. By contrast, a magma that is low in silica forms very fluid lavas that on cooling usually generate fine-grained crystalline rocks. However, the surface of silica-poor lava may be quenched rapidly enough to form a thin, glassy skin. Moreover, Hawaiian volcanoes sometimes generate lava fountains, which spray mafic lava tens of metres into the air. Such activity can produce strands of volcanic glass called *Pele's hair*, after the Hawaiian goddess of volcanoes.

◆ **Figure 3.16** Pyroclastic (fragmental) texture. This volcanic rock consists of angular rock fragments embedded in a light-coloured matrix of ash.
(Photo by E. J. Tarbuck)

Pyroclastic (Fragmental) Texture Some igneous rocks are formed from the consolidation of individual rock fragments that are ejected during a violent volcanic eruption. The ejected particles might be very fine ash, molten blobs, or large angular blocks torn from the walls of the vent during the eruption. Igneous rocks composed of these rock fragments are said to have a **pyroclastic or fragmental** texture (Figure 3.16).

A common type of pyroclastic rock called *welded tuff* is composed of fine fragments of glass that remained hot enough during their flight to fuse together on impact. Other pyroclastic rocks are composed of fragments that solidified before impact and became cemented together at some later time. Because pyroclastic rocks are made of individual particles or fragments rather than interlocking crystals, their textures often appear to be more similar to sedimentary rocks than to other igneous rocks.

Pegmatitic Texture Under special conditions, exceptionally coarse-grained igneous rocks, called **pegmatites**, may form. These rocks, which are composed of interlocking crystals all larger than a centimetre in diameter, are said to have a **pegmatitic** texture. Most pegmatites are found as small masses around the margins of large plutons or thin dykes and veins that extend into the adjacent host rock.

Pegmatites form in the late stages of crystallization, when water and other volatiles, such as chlorine, fluorine, and sulphur, make up an unusually high percentage of the melt. Because ion migration is enhanced in these fluid-rich environments, the crystals that form are abnormally large. Thus, the large crystals in pegmatites are not the result of inordinately long cooling histories: rather, they are the consequence of the fluid-rich environment in which crystallization takes place.

The composition of most pegmatites is similar to that of granite. Thus, pegmatites contain large crystals of quartz, feldspar, and muscovite. However, some contain significant quantities of comparatively rare and hence valuable minerals (see Box 3.3).

NAMING IGNEOUS ROCKS

GEODe EARTH Igneous Rocks
↳ Naming Igneous Rocks

As was stated previously, igneous rocks are most often classified, or grouped, on the basis of their mineral composition and texture (Figure 3.17). The various igneous textures result mainly from different cooling histories, whereas the mineral composition of an igneous rock is the consequence of the chemical makeup of its parent magma. Because igneous rocks are classified on the basis of their mineral composition and texture, two rocks may have similar mineral constituents but have different textures and hence different names. For example, granite, a coarse-grained plutonic rock, has a fine-grained volcanic equivalent called *rhyolite*. Although these rocks are mineralogically the same, they have different cooling histories and do not look at all alike (Figure 3.18).

Felsic (Granitic) Igneous Rocks

Granite Granite is perhaps the best known of all igneous rocks (Figure 3.18A). This is partly because of its natural beauty, which is enhanced when it is polished, and partly because of its abundance in the

BOX 3.3

Understanding Earth
Pegmatites

Pegmatite is a name given to an igneous rock composed of abnormally large crystals (Figure 3.C). How large is *large*? Crystals in most pegmatite samples are more than 1 centimetre in diameter. In some specimens, crystals that are 1 metre or more across are common. Gigantic hexagonal crystals of muscovite measuring a few metres across have been found in Ontario. In the Black Hills of South Dakota, crystals as large as telephone poles of the lithium-bearing mineral spodumene have been mined. The largest of these was more than 12 metres long. Further, feldspar masses the size of houses have been quarried from a pegmatite located in North Carolina.

Most pegmatites have the composition of granite and contain unusually large crystals of quartz, feldspar, and muscovite. In addition to being an important source of excellent mineral specimens, large granitic pegmatites have been mined for their mineral constituents. Feldspar, for example, is used in the production of ceramics, and muscovite is used for electrical insulation and glitter. Although granitic pegmatites are most common, pegmatites with chemical makeup similar to those of other igneous rocks are also known. Further, pegmatites can contain significant amounts of some of the least abundant elements. Thus, in addition to the common silicates, pegmatites with minerals containing the elements lithium, cesium, and uranium are known. Also, semiprecious gems, such as beryl, topaz, and tourmaline, are occasionally found.

◆ **Figure 3.C** This pegmatite in the Black Hills of South Dakota was mined for its large crystals of spodumene, an important source of lithium. Arrows are pointing to impressions left by crystals. Note person in upper centre of photo for scale. (Photo by James G. Kirchner)

Chemical Composition	Felsic (Granitic)	Intermediate (Andesitic)	Mafic (Basaltic)	Ultramafic
Dominant Minerals	Quartz Potassium feldspar Sodium-rich plagioclase feldspar	Amphibole Sodium- and calcium-rich plagioclase feldspar	Pyroxene Calcium-rich plagioclase feldspar	Olivine Pyroxene
Accessory Minerals	Amphibole Muscovite Biotite	Pyroxene Biotite	Amphibole Olivine	Calcium-rich plagioclase feldspar
Rock Colour (based on % of dark minerals)	0% to 25%	25% to 45%	45% to 85%	85% to 100%
TEXTURE: Phaneritic (coarse-grained)	**Granite**	**Diorite**	**Gabbro**	**Peridotite**
TEXTURE: Aphanitic (fine-grained)	**Rhyolite**	**Andesite**	**Basalt**	**Komatiite** (rare)
TEXTURE: Porphyritic	"Porphyritic" precedes any of the above names whenever there are appreciable phenocrysts			Uncommon
TEXTURE: Glassy	**Obsidian** (compact glass) **Pumice** (frothy glass)			
TEXTURE: Pyroclastic (fragmental)	**Tuff** (fragments smaller than 2 mm) **Volcanic Breccia** (fragments larger than 2 mm)			

◆ **Figure 3.17** Classification of the major groups of igneous rocks based on their mineral composition and texture. Phaneritic (coarse-grained) rocks are plutonic, solidifying deep underground. Aphanitic (fine-grained) rocks are volcanic, or solidify as shallow, thin plutons (plutonic outcrops).

A Granite

Close up

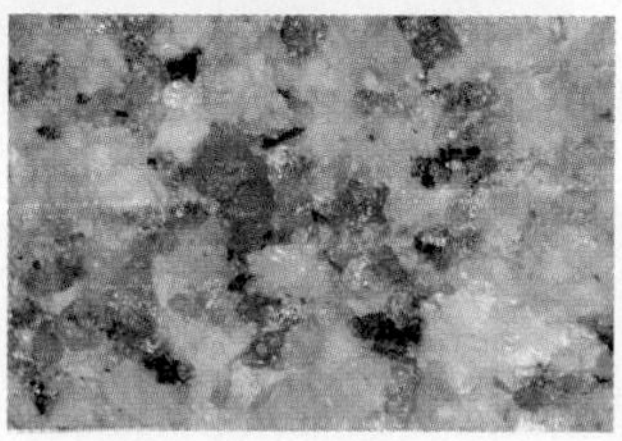

B Rhyolite

Close up

◆ **Figure 3.18** **A.** Granite, one of the most common phaneritic igneous rocks. **B.** Rhyolite, the aphanitic equivalent of granite, is less abundant.
(Photos by E. J. Tarbuck)

continental crust. Slabs of polished granite are commonly used for tombstones, monuments, and construction. Kenora, Ontario, is one well-known area in Canada where granite is quarried.

Granite is a phaneritic rock composed of about 25 percent quartz and roughly 65 percent feldspar, mostly potassium- and sodium-rich varieties. Quartz crystals, which are irregular in shape, are commonly glassy and clear to light grey in colour. By contrast, feldspar crystals are not as glassy, are generally white to grey or salmon pink, and exhibit a rectangular rather than irregular shape. When potassium feldspar is dominant and dark pink in colour, granite appears almost reddish. This variety is popular as a building stone. However, the feldspar grains are commonly white to grey so that when mixed with lesser amounts of dark silicates, granite appears light grey in colour.

Other minor constituents of granite are muscovite and some dark silicates, particularly biotite and amphibole. Although the dark components make up less than 10 percent of most granites, dark minerals appear to be more prominent than their percentage would indicate.

Granite can also have a porphyritic texture (Figure 3.13D). These specimens contain feldspar crystals of a centimetre or more in length that are scattered among the finer-grained groundmass of quartz, feldspar, and amphibole.

Granite and other related crystalline rocks are often the by-products of mountain building (as in the Coast Mountains of British Columbia). Because granite is very resistant to weathering, it frequently forms the core of eroded mountains (chapter-opening photo and Figure 3.19).

Granite is a very abundant rock. However, it has become common practice among geologists to apply the term *granite* to any coarse-grained intrusive rock composed predominantly of light silicate materials that contain quartz. We will follow this practice for the sake of simplicity. You should keep in mind that this use of the term *granite* covers rocks that have a wide range of mineral compositions.

Rhyolite Rhyolite is the extrusive equivalent of granite and, like granite, is composed essentially of the light-coloured silicates (Figure 3.18B). This fact accounts for its colour, which is usually buff to pink or occasionally very light grey. Rhyolite is aphanitic and frequently contains glass fragments and voids, indicating rapid cooling in a surface environment. When rhyolite contains phenocrysts, they are small and composed of either quartz or potassium feldspar. In contrast to granite, which is widely distributed as large plutonic masses, rhyolite deposits are less common and generally less voluminous. Yellowstone Park is one well-known exception. Here rhyolite lava flows and thick ash deposits of similar composition are extensive.

Obsidian Obsidian is a dark-coloured glassy rock that usually forms when silica-rich lava is quenched quickly

◆ **Figure 3.19** Stawamus Chief, a large igneous monolith located near Squamish, British Columbia. Granite bedrock is exposed over much of the area whose steep rock faces attract climbers from around the world. (Photo courtesy of Gunter Marx/Alamy)

A Obsidian flow

B Hand sample of obsidian

◆ **Figure 3.20** Obsidian is a dark-coloured, glassy rock formed from silica-rich lava. The scene in photo **A** shows the base of a lava dome south of Mono Lake, California.
(Photos courtesy of E. J. Tarbuck)

(Figure 3.20). In contrast to the orderly arrangement of ions characteristic of minerals, *the ions in glass are unordered*. Consequently, glassy rocks such as obsidian are not composed of minerals in the strict sense.

Although usually black or reddish-brown in colour (Figure 3.20), obsidian has a high silica content. By itself, silica is clear like window glass; the dark colour results from the presence of metallic ions. If you examine a thin edge of a piece of obsidian, it will be nearly transparent. Because of its excellent conchoidal fracture and ability to hold a sharp, hard edge, obsidian was a prized material from which Aboriginal peoples chipped arrowheads and cutting tools.

Pumice *Pumice* is a volcanic rock with a frothy texture. Usually found with obsidian, pumice forms when large amounts of gas escape through lava to generate a grey, frothy mass (Figure 3.21). Because of the large percentage of voids, many samples of pumice will float when placed in water. Flow lines are commonly visible in pumice, indicating that some movement occurred before solidification was complete. Moreover, pumice and obsidian can often be found interlayered.

Intermediate (Andesitic) Igneous Rocks

Andesite Andesite is a medium-grey fine-grained rock of volcanic origin. Its name comes from South

◆ **Figure 3.21** Pumice, a glassy rock containing numerous vesicles.
(Photo courtesy of E. J. Tarbuck)

America's Andes Mountains, where numerous volcanoes are composed of this rock type. In addition to those of the Andes, many of the other volcanic structures encircling the Pacific Ocean are of andesitic composition. Andesite commonly exhibits a porphyritic texture (Figure 3.22). When this is the case, the phenocrysts are commonly light, rectangular crystals of plagioclase feldspar or black, elongate amphibole crystals. Andesite often resembles rhyolite, so identification usually requires microscopic examination to verify the abundance, or lack, of quartz crystals. Andesite contains minor amounts of quartz, whereas rhyolite is composed of about 25 percent quartz.

Diorite *Diorite* is the plutonic equivalent of andesite. It is a coarse-grained intrusive rock that looks somewhat similar to grey granite. However, it can be distinguished from granite by the absence of visible quartz crystals and a higher percentage of dark silicate minerals. The mineral makeup of diorite is primarily sodium-calcium plagioclase feldspar and amphibole, with lesser amounts of biotite. Because the light-coloured feldspar grains and dark amphibole crystals appear to be roughly equal in abundance, diorite has a salt-and-pepper appearance (Figure 3.23).

Mafic (Basaltic) and Ultramafic Igneous Rocks

Basalt *Basalt* is a very dark green to black fine-grained volcanic rock composed primarily of pyroxene and calcium-rich plagioclase feldspar, with lesser amounts of olivine and amphibole (Figure 3.24A). Porphyritic basalt commonly contains small light-coloured feldspar phenocrysts or glassy-appearing olivine phenocrysts embedded in a dark groundmass.

Basalt is the most common extrusive igneous rock (Figure 3.24A). Many volcanic islands, such as the Hawaiian Islands and Iceland, are composed mainly of basalt (Figure 3.25). Further, the upper layers of the oceanic crust consist of basalt. In Canada, areas of south-central British Columbia were the sites of significant basaltic outpourings. Farther south, in Oregon and Washington, basalt flows have accumulated to thicknesses approaching 3 kilometres (see Figure 4.24).

A Andesite porphyry

B Close up

◆ **Figure 3.22** Andesite porphyry. **A.** Hand sample of andesite porphyry, a common volcanic rock. **B.** Photomicrograph of a thin section of andesite porphyry to illustrate texture. Notice that the few large crystals (phenocrysts) are surrounded by much smaller crystals (groundmass).
(Photo courtesy of E. J. Tarbuck)

Diorite

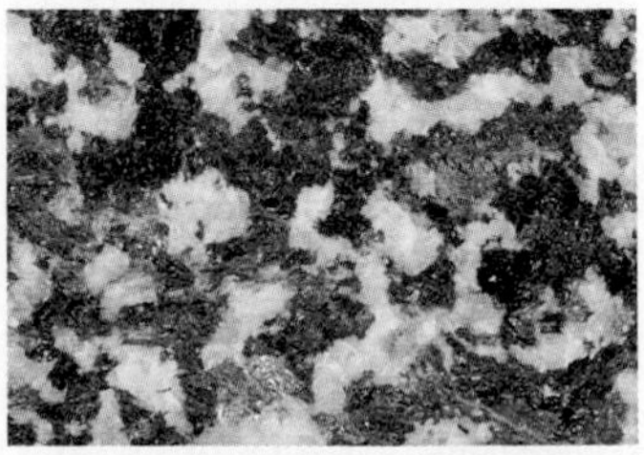

Close up

◆ **Figure 3.23** Diorite is a phaneritic igneous rock of intermediate composition. The white crystals are plagioclase feldspar and the black crystals are amphibole and biotite.
(Photo courtesy of E. J. Tarbuck)

A Basalt

Close up

B Gabbro

Close up

C Peridotite

◆ **Figure 3.24** These dark-coloured mafic and ultramafic rocks are composed primarily of pyroxene and calcium-rich plagioclase. **A.** Basalt is aphanitic and a very common extrusive rock. **B.** Gabbro, the phaneritic equivalent of basalt, is less abundant. **C.** Peridotite is an ultramafic phaneritic rock. (Photos **A** and **B** by E. J. Tarbuck; photo **C** by S. R. Hicock)

Gabbro *Gabbro* is the intrusive equivalent of basalt (Figure 3.24B). Like basalt, it is very dark green to black in colour and composed primarily of pyroxene and calcium-rich plagioclase feldspar. Although gabbro is not a common constituent of the continental crust, it undoubtedly makes up a significant percentage of the oceanic crust. Here large portions of the magma found in subsurface magma chambers that once fed basalt flows eventually solidified at depth to form gabbro.

Peridotite The upper mantle is dominated by a phaneritic rock called peridotite (Figure 3.24C), which has an ultramafic composition; it is primarily composed of olivine, pyroxene, and calcium-rich plagioclase feldspar. Occurrences of peridotite are limited to rare slivers of mantle rock that are pushed up to Earth's surface in some forms of mountain building and to small chunks of material that are transported to the surface by basaltic (mafic) magma.

Pyroclastic Rocks

Pyroclastic rocks are composed of fragments ejected during a volcanic eruption. One of the most common pyroclastic rocks, called *tuff*, is composed mainly of tiny ash-size fragments (smaller than two millimetres) that are later cemented together (Figure 3.26). In situations where the ash particles remained hot enough to fuse, the rock is called *welded tuff*.

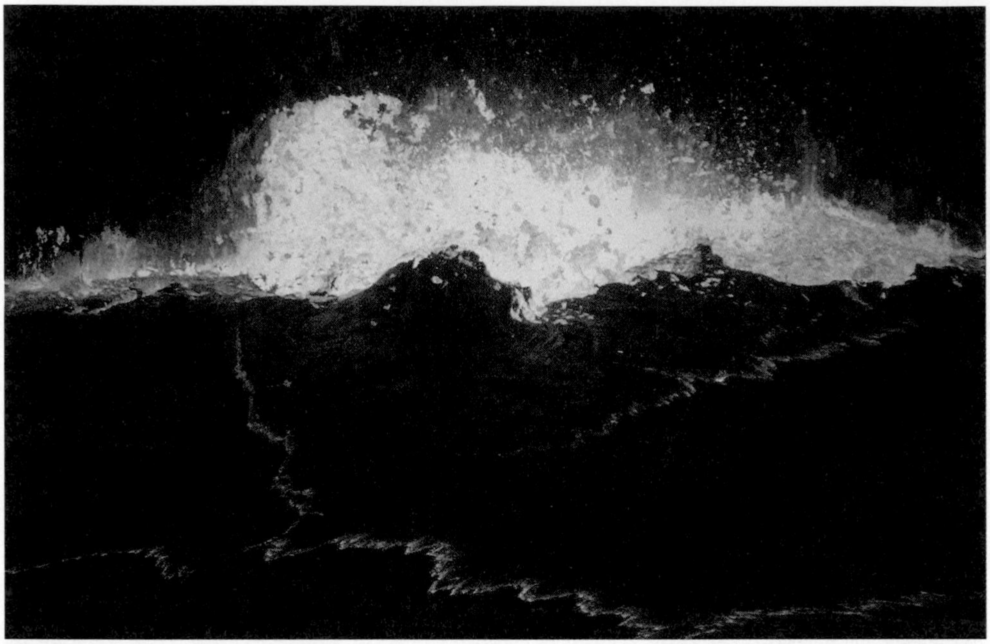

◆ **Figure 3.25** Fluid mafic lava moving down the slopes of Hawaii's Kilauea Volcano. (Photo by Tim Davis/ Photo Researchers, Inc.)

Although welded tuff consists mostly of tiny glass shards, it may contain walnut-size pieces of pumice and other rock fragments.

Welded tuffs blanket vast portions of once volcanically active areas of western North America. Some of these tuff deposits are hundreds of metres thick and extend for tens of kilometres from their source. Most formed millions of years ago as volcanic ash spewed from large volcanic structures (calderas) in an avalanche style, spreading laterally at speeds

◆ **Figure 3.26** River bank exposure of tuff with walnut-sized balls of pumice resting on granitic bedrock in Lillooet Valley, British Columbia. Note the brown stump of a tree that was killed and buried by the pyroclastic material. Tuff is composed mainly of ash-sized particles and may contain larger fragments of pumice or other volcanic rocks.
(Photo by S. R. Hicock)

approaching 100 kilometres per hour. Early investigators of these deposits incorrectly classified them as rhyolite lava flows. Today we know that this silica-rich lava is too viscous to flow more than a few kilometres from a vent.

Pyroclastic rocks composed mainly of particles larger than ash are called *volcanic breccia*. The particles in volcanic breccia can consist of streamlined fragments that solidified in air, blocks broken from the walls of the vent, crystals, and glass fragments.

Unlike most igneous rock names, such as granite and basalt, the terms *tuff* and *volcanic breccia* do not imply mineral composition. Thus, they are frequently used with a composition modifier, as, for example, rhyolite tuff.

Chapter Summary

- *Igneous rocks* form when *magma* cools and solidifies. *Extrusive*, or *volcanic*, igneous rocks result when *lava* cools at the surface. Magma that solidifies at depth produces *intrusive*, or *plutonic*, igneous rocks.
- Magma originates from essentially solid rock of the crust and mantle. In addition to a rock's composition, its temperature, depth (confining pressure), and water content determine whether it exists as a solid or liquid. Thus, magma can be generated by raising a rock's temperature, as occurs when a hot mantle plume collects beneath crustal rocks. A decrease in pressure can cause *decompression melting*. Further, the introduction of *volatiles* (mainly water) can lower a rock's melting point sufficiently to generate magma. Because melting is generally not complete, a process called *partial melting* produces a *melt* made of the minerals that melt at the lowest temperatures, which are higher in silica than the original rock. Thus, magmas generated by partial melting are nearer to the *felsic* end of the compositional spectrum than are the rocks from which they formed.
- As magma cools, the ions that compose it arrange themselves into orderly patterns during a process called *crystallization*. Slow cooling results in the formation of rather large crystals. Conversely, when cooling occurs rapidly, the outcome is a solid mass consisting of tiny intergrown crystals. When molten material is quenched instantly, a mass of unordered atoms, referred to as *glass*, forms.
- The mineral makeup of an igneous rock is ultimately determined by the chemical composition of the magma from which it crystallizes. N. L. Bowen discovered that as magma cools in the laboratory, those minerals with higher melting points crystallize before minerals with lower melting points. *Bowen's reaction series* illustrates the sequence of mineral formation within magma.
- During the crystallization of magma, if the earlier-formed minerals are denser than the liquid portion, they will settle to the bottom of the magma chamber during a process called *crystal settling*. Owing to the fact that crystal settling removes the earlier-formed minerals, the remaining melt will form a rock with a chemical composition much different from that of the parent magma. The process of developing more than one magma type from a common magma is called *magmatic differentiation*.
- Once a magma body forms, its composition can change through the incorporation of foreign material, a process termed *assimilation*, or by *magma mixing*.
- The mineral composition of an igneous rock is the consequence of the chemical makeup of the parent magma and the environment of crystallization. Igneous rocks are divided into broad compositional groups based on the percentage of dark and light silicate minerals they contain. Felsic rocks (e.g., granite and rhyolite) are composed mostly of the light-coloured silicate minerals potassium feldspar, sodium plagioclase feldspar, and quartz. Rocks of *intermediate composition* (e.g., andesite and diorite) contain mostly plagioclase feldspar and amphibole. *Mafic* rocks (e.g., basalt and gabbro) contain abundant olivine, pyroxene, and calcium plagioclase feldspar. They are high in iron, magnesium, and calcium, low in silicon, and dark grey to black in colour.
- Igneous rocks are most often classified by their mineral composition and *texture*.
- The texture of an igneous rock refers to the overall appearance of the rock based on the size and arrangement of its interlocking crystals. The most important factor affecting texture is the rate at which magma cools. Common igneous rock textures include *aphanitic*, with grains too small to be distinguished without the aid of a microscope; *phaneritic*, with intergrown crystals that are roughly equal in size and large enough to be identified with the unaided eye; *porphyritic*, which has large crystals (*phenocrysts*) interbedded in a matrix of smaller crystals (*groundmass*); and *glassy*.

Review Questions

1. What is magma?
2. How does lava differ from magma?
3. What is the geothermal gradient?
4. Describe the three conditions that are thought to cause rock to melt.
5. How does the rate of cooling influence the crystallization process?
6. In addition to the rate of cooling, what two other factors influence the crystallization process?
7. What is magmatic differentiation? How might this process lead to the formation of several different igneous rocks from a single magma?
8. Relate the classification of igneous rocks to Bowen's reaction series.
9. What is partial melting?
10. How does the composition of a melt produced by partial melting compare with the composition of the parent rock?
11. How are most mafic magmas generated?
12. Mafic magma forms at great depth. Why doesn't most of it crystallize as it rises through the relatively cool crust?
13. Why are rocks of intermediate (andesitic) and felsic (granitic) composition generally *not* found in the ocean basins?
14. How are granite and rhyolite different? In what way are they similar?
15. The classification of igneous rocks is based largely on two criteria. Name these criteria.
16. The statements that follow relate to terms describing igneous rock textures. For each statement, identify the appropriate term.
    - **(a)** Openings are produced by escaping gases.
    - **(b)** Obsidian exhibits this texture.
    - **(c)** A matrix of fine crystals surrounding phenocrysts.
    - **(d)** Crystals are too small to be seen without a microscope.
    - **(e)** A texture characterized by two distinctly different crystal sizes.
    - **(f)** The rock is coarse-grained, with crystals of roughly equal size.
    - **(g)** The rock has exceptionally large crystals exceeding 1 centimetre in diameter.
17. Why are the crystals in pegmatites so large?
18. What does a porphyritic texture indicate about an igneous rock?
19. Compare and contrast the rocks in each of the following pairs:
    - **(a)** granite and diorite
    - **(b)** basalt and gabbro
    - **(c)** andesite and rhyolite
20. How do tuff and volcanic breccia differ from other igneous rocks such as granite and basalt?

Key Terms

andesitic composition (p. 71)
aphanitic (p. 76)
assimilation (p. 69)
basaltic (p. 73)
Bowen's reaction series (p. 68)
crystallization (p. 65)
crystal settling (p. 68)
decompression melting (p. 64)
extrusive (p. 62)
felsic (p. 64)
fragmental (p. 77)
geothermal gradient (p. 63)
glass (p. 76)
glassy (p. 76)
granitic (p. 72)
groundmass (p. 76)
igneous rocks (p. 62)
intermediate composition (p. 71)
intrusive (p. 62)
lava (p. 62)
mafic (p. 64)
magma (p. 63)
magma mixing (p. 69)
magmatic differentiation (p. 68)
melt (p. 64)
partial melting (p. 62)
pegmatite (p. 77)
pegmatitic (p. 77)
phaneritic (p. 76)
phenocrysts (p. 76)
plutonic (p. 62)
porphyritic (p. 76)
porphyry (p. 76)
pyroclastic (p. 77)
texture (p. 73)
ultramafic (p. 73)
vesicular (p. 76)
volatiles (p. 63)
volcanic (p. 62)

Web Resources

The *Earth* website uses the resources and flexibility of the internet to aid in your study of the topics in this chapter. Written and developed by geology instructors, this site will help improve your understanding of geology. Visit **www.pearsoned.ca/tarbuck** and click on the cover of the text to find

- online review quizzes
- Web-based critical thinking and writing exercises
- links to chapter-specific Web resources
- internet-wide key-term searches

www.pearsoned.ca/tarbuck

Chapter 4

Volcanoes and Other Igneous Bodies

Nature's fireworks: twin fountains spew lava and volcanic bombs.
(Photo by George Shelley/The Stock Market)

On Sunday, May 18, 1980, the largest volcanic eruption to occur in North America in recorded history transformed a picturesque volcano into a decapitated remnant (Figure 4.1). On that date in southwest Washington State, Mount St. Helens erupted with tremendous force. The blast blew out the entire north flank of the volcano, leaving a gaping hole. In an instant, a prominent volcano whose summit had been more than 2900 metres above sea level was lowered by more than 400 metres.

The event devastated a wide swath of timber-rich land on the north side of the mountain. Trees within a 400-square-kilometre area lay intertwined and flattened, stripped of their branches and appearing from the air like toothpicks strewn about. The accompanying mudflows carried ash, trees, and water-saturated rock debris 29 kilometres down the Toutle River. The eruption claimed 59 lives, some dying from the intense heat and the suffocating cloud of ash and gases, others from being hurled by the blast, and still others from entrapment in the mudflows.

The eruption ejected nearly a cubic kilometre of ash and rock debris. Following the devastating explosion, Mount St. Helens continued to emit great quantities of hot gases and ash. The force of the blast was so strong that some ash was propelled more than 18,000 metres into the atmosphere. During the next few days, this very fine-grained material was carried around Earth by strong upper-air winds. Measurable deposits were reported well into southern Alberta,

◆ **Figure 4.1** Before (this page) and after (next page) photographs show the transformation of Mount St. Helens caused by the May 18, 1980, eruption. The dark area in the "after" photo is debris-filled Spirit Lake, partially visible in the "before" photo.
(Photos courtesy of U.S. Geological Survey)

with crop damage into central Montana. Meanwhile, ash fallout in the immediate vicinity exceeded 2 metres in depth. The air over Yakima, Washington (130 kilometres to the east), was so filled with ash that residents experienced midnight-like darkness at noon.

Not all volcanic eruptions are as violent as the 1980 Mount St. Helens event. Some volcanoes, such as Hawaii's Kilauea volcano, generate relatively quiet outpourings of fluid lavas. However, these "gentle" eruptions are not without some fiery displays; occasionally fountains of incandescent lava spray hundreds of metres into the air (Figure 4.2). Such events, however, typically pose minimal threat to human life and property, and the lava generally falls back into a lava pool.

Testimony to the quiet nature of Kilauea's eruptions is the fact that the Hawaiian Volcanoes Observatory has operated on its summit since 1912. Further, the longest and largest of Kilauea's eruptions began in 1983 and remains active, although it has received only modest media attention.

Why do volcanoes like Mount Garibaldi (Canada, Figure 4.3) and Mount St. Helens (United States) erupt explosively, whereas others, like Kilauea, are relatively quiet? Why do volcanoes occur in chains, like the Aleutian Islands or the Cascade Range? Why do some volcanoes form on the ocean floor, while others occur on the continents? This chapter will deal with these and other questions as we explore the nature and movement of magma and lava.

◆ **Figure 4.2** Fluid mafic lava erupting from Kilauea Volcano, Hawaii.
(Photo by Douglas Peebles)

◆ **Figure 4.3** Mount Garibaldi, located in southwest British Columbia. Mount Garibaldi has been dormant since the last Ice Age and has suffered some erosion since then.
(Photo by S. Irwin. Reproduced with the permission of the Minister of Public Works and Government Services Canada, 2008, and courtesy of Natural Resources Canada)

THE NATURE OF VOLCANIC ERUPTIONS

GEODe EARTH Volcanoes and Other Igneous Activity
↳ The Nature of Volcanic Eruptions

Volcanic activity is commonly perceived as a process that produces a picturesque, cone-shaped structure that periodically erupts in a violent manner, like Mount St. Helens (Box 4.1). Although some eruptions are very explosive, many are not. What determines whether a volcano extrudes magma violently or gently? The primary factors include the magma's *composition*, its *temperature*, and the amount of *dissolved gases* it contains. To varying degrees, these factors affect the magma's mobility, or **viscosity** (*viscos* = sticky). The more viscous the material, the greater is its resistance to flow. (For example, maple syrup is more viscous than water.) Magma associated with an explosive eruption may be five times more viscous than magma extruded in a quiescent manner.

Factors Affecting Viscosity

The effect of temperature on viscosity is easily seen. Just as heating maple syrup makes it more fluid (less viscous), the mobility of lava is strongly influenced by temperature. As lava cools and begins to congeal, the flow decreases in mobility and eventually halts.

A more significant factor influencing volcanic behaviour is the chemical composition of the magma. Recall from Chapter 3 that a major difference among various igneous rocks is their silica (SiO_2) content (Table 4.1). Magmas that produce mafic rocks, such as basalt, contain about 50 percent silica, whereas magmas that produce felsic rocks (granite and its extrusive equivalent, rhyolite) contain more than 70 percent silica. The intermediate

BOX 4.1

Understanding Earth
Anatomy of an Eruption

The events leading to the May 18, 1980, eruption of Mount St. Helens began about two months earlier as a series of minor Earth tremors centred beneath the mountain (Figure 4.A, part A). The tremors resulted from the upward movement of magma within the mountain. The first volcanic activity took place a week later, when a small amount of ash and steam rose from the summit. Over the next several weeks, sporadic eruptions of varied intensity occurred. Before the main eruption, the primary concern had been the potential hazard of mudflows. Such moving lobes of saturated soil and rock are created as ice and snow on the mountain is melted by the heat emitted from the magma within the volcano.

The only warning of a potential eruption was a bulge on the volcano's north flank (Figure 4.A, part B). Careful monitoring of this dome-shaped structure indicated a very slow but steady growth rate of a few metres per day. If the growth rate of the bulge changed appreciably, an eruption might quickly follow. Unfortunately, no such variation was detected before the explosion. In fact, the seismic activity decreased during the two days preceding the huge blast.

Dozens of scientists were monitoring the mountain when it exploded. "Vancouver, Vancouver, this is it!" was the only warning—and the last words from one scientist—that preceded the unleashing of tremendous quantities of pent-up gases. The trigger was a medium-sized earthquake. Its vibrations sent the north slope of the cone plummeting into the Toutle River, removing the overburden that had trapped the magma below (Figure 4.A, part C). With the pressure reduced, the water in the magma vaporized and expanded, causing the mountainside to rupture like an overheated steam boiler. Because the eruption originated around the bulge, several hundred metres below the summit, the initial blast was directed laterally rather than vertically. Had the full force of the eruption been upward, far less destruction would have occurred.

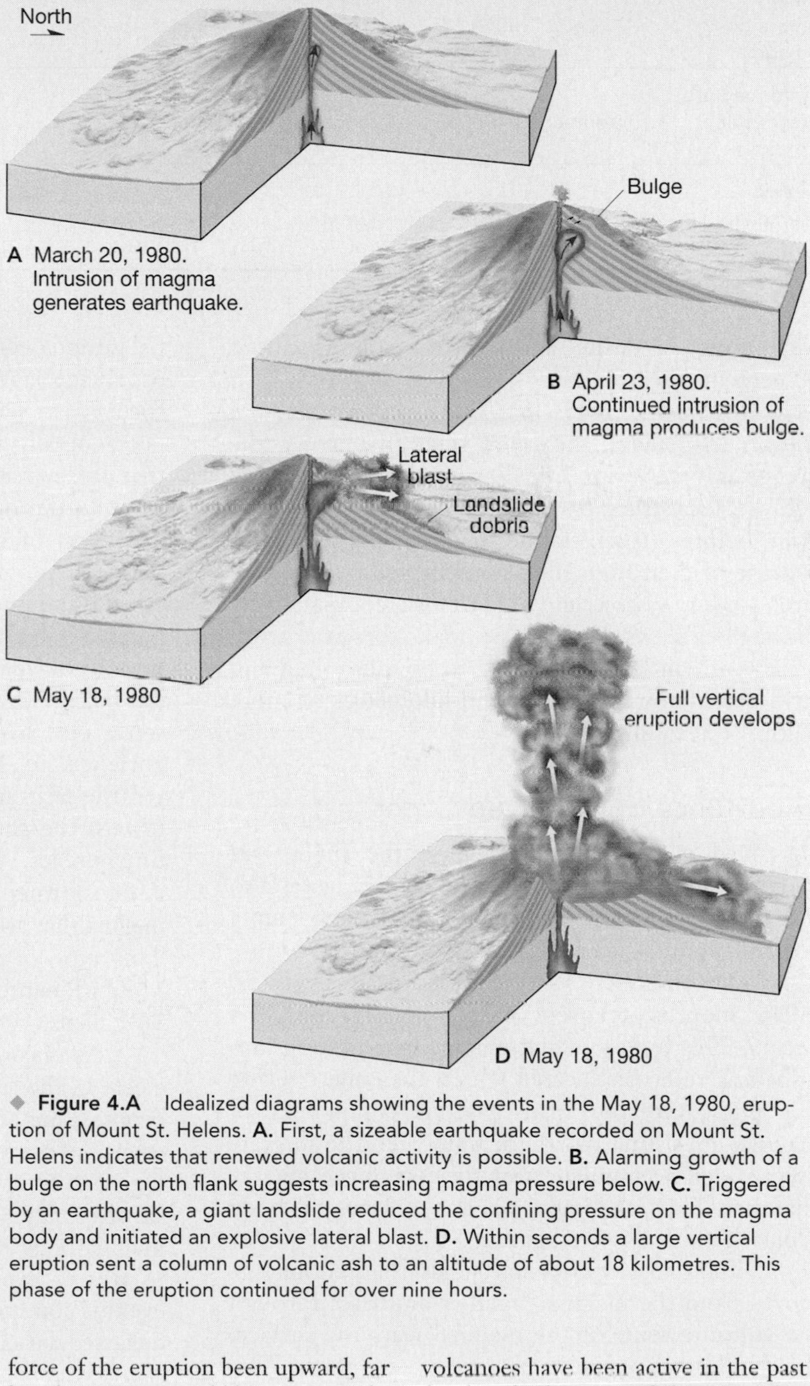

◆ **Figure 4.A** Idealized diagrams showing the events in the May 18, 1980, eruption of Mount St. Helens. **A.** First, a sizeable earthquake recorded on Mount St. Helens indicates that renewed volcanic activity is possible. **B.** Alarming growth of a bulge on the north flank suggests increasing magma pressure below. **C.** Triggered by an earthquake, a giant landslide reduced the confining pressure on the magma body and initiated an explosive lateral blast. **D.** Within seconds a large vertical eruption sent a column of volcanic ash to an altitude of about 18 kilometres. This phase of the eruption continued for over nine hours.

Mount St. Helens is one of 15 large volcanoes and innumerable smaller ones that compose the Cascade Range, which extends from British Columbia to northern California (see Figure 4.18). Eight of the largest volcanoes have been active in the past few hundred years. Of the remaining seven active volcanoes, the most likely to erupt again are Mount Baker (just south of Vancouver, British Columbia) and Mount Rainier in Washington, Mount Hood in Oregon, and Mount Shasta and Lassen Peak in California.

TABLE 4.1 **Magmas Have Different Compositions, Which Cause Their Properties to Vary**

Composition	Silica Content	Viscosity	Gas Content	Tendency to Form Pyroclastics	Volcanic Landform
Mafic (basaltic) magma	Least (~50%)	Least	Least (1%–2%)	Least	Shield volcanoes Basalt plateaus Cinder cones
Intermediate (andesitic) magma	Intermediate (~60%)	Intermediate	Intermediate (3%–4%)	Intermediate	Composite cones
Felsic (granitic) magma	Most (~70%)	Greatest	Most (4%–6%)	Greatest	Volcanic domes Pyroclastic flows

rock types—andesite and diorite—contain about 60 percent silica.

A magma's viscosity is directly related to its silica content. In general, the more silica in magma, the greater is its viscosity. The flow of magma is impeded because silica structures link together into long chains, even before crystallization begins. Consequently, because of their high silica content, felsic (rhyolitic) lavas are very viscous and tend to form comparatively short, thick flows. By contrast, mafic (basaltic) lavas, which contain less silica, tend to be quite fluid and have been known to travel 150 kilometres or more before congealing.

Importance of Dissolved Gases

Dissolved gases tend to increase the fluidity of magma. On their escape from the magma, gases also provide enough force to propel molten rock from a volcanic **vent**, a surface opening, or **conduit**.

The summits of volcanoes often begin to inflate months, or even years, before an eruption occurs. This indicates that magma is migrating into a shallow reservoir located within the cone. During this phase, volatiles (the gaseous component of magma, consisting mostly of water) tend to migrate upward and accumulate near the top of the magma chamber. Thus, the upper portion of a magma body is enriched by dissolved gases.

When an eruption starts, gas-charged magma moves from the magma chamber and rises through the volcanic vent. As the magma nears the surface, the confining pressure is greatly reduced. This reduction in pressure allows the dissolved gases to be released suddenly, just as opening a warm can of pop will allow carbon dioxide gas bubbles to expand and escape.

Very fluid mafic magmas allow the expanding gases to migrate upward and escape from the vent with relative ease. As they escape, the gases can propel incandescent lava hundreds of metres into the air, producing lava fountains (see Figure 4.2). Although spectacular, such fountains are mostly harmless and not generally associated with major eruptive events that cause great loss of life and property.

At the other extreme, highly viscous magmas expel jets of hot ash-laden gases that evolve into buoyant plumes called **eruption columns** that extend thousands of metres into the atmosphere (Figure 4.4). Before such an eruption, an extended period of magmatic differentiation (Chapter 3) occurs, in which iron-rich minerals crystallize and settle out, leaving the upper part of the magma enriched in silica and dissolved gases. As this volatile-rich magma moves up the volcanic vent toward the surface, these gases begin to collect as tiny bubbles. At some point in the vent, this mixture is transformed into a gas jet containing tiny bits of magma that are explosively ejected from the volcano. This type of violent eruption was exemplified by Mount Pinatubo in the Philippines (1991) and Mount St. Helens (1980).

As magma in the upper portion of the vent is ejected, the pressure on the underlying magma drops. Thus, rather than a single "bang," volcanic eruptions are really a series of explosions. The soluble gases in a viscous magma migrate upward quite slowly. Only within the uppermost portion of the magma body does the gas content build sufficiently to trigger explosive eruptions. Thus, an explosive event is commonly followed by the quiet emission of degassed lavas. However, once this eruptive phase ceases, the process of gas buildup begins anew. This time lag may partially explain the sporadic eruptive patterns of volcanoes that eject viscous lavas.

To summarize, the viscosity of magma, plus the quantity of dissolved gases and the ease with which they can escape, determines the nature of a volcanic eruption. We can now begin to explain the gentle volcanic eruptions of hot, fluid lavas in Hawaii

◆ **Figure 4.4** Huge eruption column produced as Mount St. Helens erupted on July 22, 1980, two months after the most destructive event.
(Photo by David Weintraub/Photo Researchers, Inc.)

and the explosive and sometimes catastrophic eruptions of viscous lavas from such volcanoes as Mount St. Helens.

MATERIALS EXTRUDED DURING AN ERUPTION

GEODe EARTH Volcanoes and Other Igneous Activity
↳ Materials Extruded during an Eruption

Volcanoes extrude lava, large volumes of gas, and pyroclastic materials (broken rock, lava "bombs," fine ash, and dust). In this section we will examine each of these materials.

Lava Flows

Because of their low silica content, hot mafic lavas are usually very fluid. They flow in thin, broad sheets or streamlike ribbons. On the island of Hawaii, such lavas have been clocked at speeds of 30 kilometres per hour down steep slopes, but flow rates of 10 to 300 metres per hour are more common. In contrast, the movement of silica-rich (rhyolitic) lava can be too slow to perceive.

When fluid mafic lavas of the Hawaiian type congeal, they commonly form a relatively smooth skin that wrinkles as the still-molten subsurface lava continues to advance (Figure 4.5A). These are known as **pahoehoe** (pronounced *pah-hoy-hoy*) **flows** and resemble the twisting braids in ropes.

Another common type of mafic lava, called an **aa** (pronounced *ah ah*) **flow**, has a surface of rough, jagged blocks with dangerously sharp edges and spiny projections (Figure 4.5B). Active aa flows are relatively cool and thick and advance at rates from 5 to 50 metres per hour. Moreover, gases escaping from the surface produce numerous voids and sharp spines in the congealing lava. As the molten interior advances, the outer crust is broken further, giving the flow the appearance of an advancing mass of lava rubble.

Hardened lava flows commonly contain tunnels that once were channels carrying lava from the volcanic vent to the flow's leading edge. These openings develop in the interior of a flow where temperatures remain high long after the surface congeals. Under these conditions, the still-molten lava within the conduits continues its forward motion, leaving behind the cavelike tunnels called **lava tubes** (Figure 4.6). Lava tubes are important because they allow fluid lavas to advance great distances from their source. Good examples of lava tubes, pahoehoe and aa flows, and a crater are well preserved in Nisga'a Memorial Lava Bed Park in northeast British Columbia. The eruption of basalt that produced these features 250 years ago destroyed two villages and killed more than 2000 members of the Nisga'a band. Local legend states that the eruption occurred because a child showed disrespect to the salmon, which are vital to the tribe's survival.

When lava enters the ocean, or when outpourings of lava actually originate underwater, the flow's outer skin quickly congeals. However, the lava is usually able to move forward by breaking through the hardened surface. This process occurs over and over, generating a lava flow composed of elongate structures resembling large pillows stacked atop one

◆ **Figure 4.5** **A.** Typical pahoehoe (ropy) lava flow, Kilauea, Hawaii. **B.** Typical slow-moving aa flow. **C.** Typical outcrop of solidified pillow lavas on south Vancouver Island.
(Photos **A** and **B** by J. D. Griggs, U.S. Geological Survey; photo **C** by S. R. Hicock)

another (Figure 4.5C). These structures, called **pillow lavas**, are useful in the reconstruction of Earth history (see Figure 11.15) because they indicate deposition in an underwater environment.

Gases

Magmas contain varying amounts of volatiles held in the molten rock by confining pressure, just as carbon dioxide is held in pop or beer. As with carbonated drinks, as soon as the pressure is reduced, the gases begin to escape.

The gaseous portion of most magmas composes 1 percent to 6 percent of the total weight, with most of this in the form of water vapour. Although the percentage may be small, the actual quantity of emitted gas can exceed thousands of tonnes per day.

The composition of volcanic gases is important because they contribute significantly to the gases that make up our planet's atmosphere. Analyses of samples taken during Hawaiian eruptions indicate that the gases are about 70 percent water vapour, 15 percent carbon dioxide, 5 percent nitrogen, 5 percent sulphur dioxide, and lesser amounts of chlorine, hydrogen, and argon. Sulphur compounds are easily recognized by their pungent odour. Volcanoes are a natural source of air pollution, including sulphur dioxide, which readily combines with water to form sulphuric acid. A famous example was the Philippines volcano, Mount Pinatubo, which erupted in June 1991, injecting up to 27 million tonnes of sulphur dioxide into the atmosphere. The haze of aerosols that remained in the atmosphere after the eruption lowered global temperatures by 0.5°C over the following year.

In addition to propelling magma from a volcano, gases play an important role in creating the narrow passageway or conduit that connects the magma

A

B

◆ **Figure 4.6** Lava streams that flow in confined channels often develop a solid crust and become flows within lava tubes. **A.** Thurston Lava Tube, Hawaii Volcanoes National Park. **B.** View of an active lava tube as seen through its collapsed roof.
(Photo **A** by Douglas Peebles; photo **B** by Jeffrey Judd, U.S. Geological Survey)

chamber to the surface. First, high temperatures and the buoyant force from the magma body crack the rock above. Then, hot blasts of high-pressure gases expand the cracks and develop a passageway to the surface. Once the passageway is completed, hot gases armed with rock fragments erode its walls, producing a larger conduit. Because these erosive forces are concentrated on any protrusion along the pathway, the volcanic conduits that are produced are circular. As the conduit enlarges, magma moves upward to the surface. Following an eruptive phase, the conduit often becomes choked with congealed magma and debris that was not thrown clear of the vent. Before the next eruption, a new surge of explosive gases may again clear the conduit.

Occasionally, eruptions emit colossal amounts of volcanic gases that rise high into the atmosphere, where they can reside for several years. Some of these eruptions have an impact on Earth's climate, on a local to regional scale, by spewing volcanic ash and gases into the atmosphere and blocking out sunlight for a short period. However, it has yet to be proven that volcanic eruptions have a long-term impact on global climate.

Pyroclastic Materials

When mafic lava is extruded, dissolved gases escape freely and continually. These gases propel incandescent blobs of lava to great heights (see Figure 4.2). Some of this ejected material lands near the vent and builds a cone-shaped structure, whereas smaller particles tend to be carried great distances by the wind. By contrast, viscous (granitic) magmas are highly charged with gases; on release, they expand a thousand-fold as they blow pulverized rock, lava, and glass fragments from the vent. The particles produced in both situations are called **pyroclastic materials** (*pyro* = fire, *clast* = fragment). These ejected fragments range in size from dust and sand-sized volcanic ash (less than 2 millimetres) to pieces that weigh several tonnes.

Ash and dust particles are produced from gas-laden viscous magma during an explosive eruption (see Figure 4.4). As magma moves up in the vent, the gases rapidly expand, generating a froth of melt. As the hot gases expand explosively, the froth is blown into very fine glassy fragments. When the hot ash falls, the glassy shards often fuse to form a rock called welded tuff (Chapter 3, Figure 3.26). Sheets of this material, as well as ash deposits that later consolidate, cover vast portions of North America.

Also common are pyroclasts that range from the size of small beads to about the size of walnuts, termed *lapilli* ("little stones"; see Figure 3.26) or *cinders* (2 to 64 millimetres). Particles larger than 64 millimetres in diameter are called *blocks* when they are made of hardened lava and *bombs* when they are ejected as incandescent lava. Because bombs are semi-molten on ejection, they often assume a

◆ **Figure 4.7** Volcanic bombs forming during an eruption of Hawaii's Kilauea volcano. Ejected lava fragments take on a streamlined shape as they sail through the air. The bomb in the insert is about 10 centimetres long. (**Main** photo by Arthur Roy/ National Audubon Society; **inset** photo by E. J. Tarbuck)

streamlined shape as they hurtle through the air (Figure 4.7). Because of their size, bombs and blocks usually fall on the slopes of a cone; however, they are occasionally propelled far from the volcano by the force of escaping gases. For instance, bombs 6 metres long and weighing about 200 tonnes were blown 600 metres from the vent during an eruption of the Japanese volcano Asama.

So far we have distinguished various pyroclastic materials based largely on the size of the fragments. Some materials are also identified by their texture and composition. In particular, **scoria** is the name applied to vesicular (containing voids) ejecta derived from mafic magma (Figure 4.8). These black to reddish-brown fragments are generally found in the size range of lapilli. When magma with an intermediate or silica-rich composition generates vesicular ejecta, it is called **pumice** (see Figure 3.21). Pumice is usually lighter in colour and less dense than scoria. Some pumice fragments have so many vesicles that they float in water for prolonged periods.

Nuée Ardente: A Deadly Pyroclastic Flow

The extrusion of **pyroclastic flows** consisting of hot gases infused with incandescent ash and larger rock fragments can be devastating. The most destructive of these fiery flows, called **nuées ardentes** (also referred to as *glowing avalanches*), are capable of racing down steep volcanic slopes at speeds that can approach 200 kilometres per hour (Figure 4.9). An infamous one wiped out the port town of St. Pierre on the Caribbean island of Martinique in 1902 (Figure 4.10). Only one of the 28,000 inhabitants (a

◆ **Figure 4.8** Scoria is a volcanic rock that exhibits a vesicular texture. Vesicles are small holes left by escaping gas bubbles. (Photo by E. J. Tarbuck)

◆ **Figure 4.9** Nuée ardente races down the slope of Mount St. Helens on August 7, 1980, at speeds exceeding 100 kilometres per hour.
(Photo by Peter W. Lipman, U.S. Geological Survey)

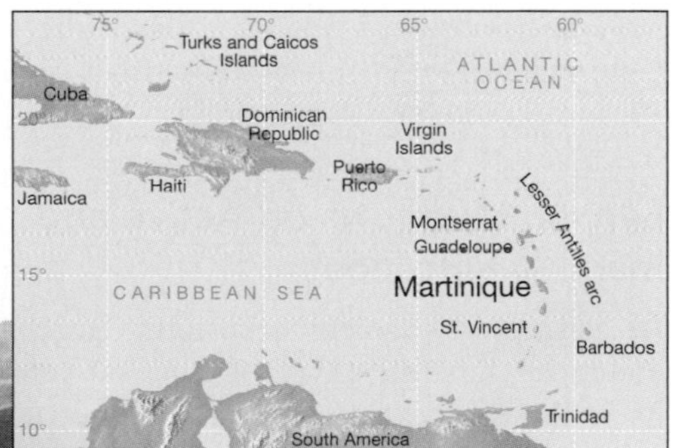

◆ **Figure 4.10** St. Pierre as it appeared shortly after the eruption of Mount Pelée, 1902.
(Reproduced from the collection of the Library of Congress)

prisoner protected in a dungeon) survived that devastating eruption of Mount Pelée.

The ground-hugging portion of a nuée ardente is rich in particulate matter, which is suspended by jets of buoyant gases passing upward through the flow. Some of these gases have escaped from newly erupted volcanic fragments. In addition, air that is overtaken and trapped by an advancing flow can be heated sufficiently to provide buoyancy to the particulate matter of the nuée ardente. Thus, this flow, which can include large rock fragments in addition to ash, travels downslope in a nearly frictionless environment. This helps to explain why some nuée ardente deposits are found more than 100 kilometres from their source.

Gravity causes these flows, which are heavier than air, to sweep downslope, much like a snow avalanche. Some pyroclastic flows result when a powerful eruption blasts pyroclastic material laterally out the side of a volcano (e.g., Mount St. Helens, 1980). More often, nuées ardentes form from the collapse of tall eruption columns that form over a volcano during an explosive event. Once gravity overcomes the initial upward thrust provided by the escaping gases, the ejecta begin to fall. Massive amounts of incandescent blocks, ash, and pumice fragments that fall onto the summit area begin to cascade downslope under the influence of gravity. The largest fragments have been observed bouncing down the flanks of a cone, while the finer materials travel rapidly as an expanding tongue-shaped cloud.

Lahars: Mudflows on Active and Inactive Volcanoes

In addition to violent eruptions, large composite cones can generate a type of mudflow referred to by its Indonesian name **lahar**. These destructive flows occur when volcanic debris becomes saturated with water and rapidly moves down steep volcanic slopes, generally following gullies and stream valleys. Some lahars are triggered when large volumes of ice and snow melt during an eruption. Others are generated when heavy rainfall saturates weathered volcanic deposits. Thus, lahars can occur even when a volcano is *not* erupting.

When Mount St. Helens erupted in 1980, several lahars formed. These flows and accompanying floodwaters raced down the valleys of the north and south forks of the Toutle River at speeds exceeding 30 kilometres per hour. Water levels in the river rose to 4 metres above flood stage, destroying or severely damaging nearly all the homes and bridges along the affected area. Fortunately, the area was not densely populated. This was not the case in 1985, when Nevado del Ruiz, an ice-capped volcano in the Andes, erupted and generated lahars that killed nearly 20,000 people (see the section entitled "Debris Flow" in Chapter 14).

VOLCANIC STRUCTURES AND ERUPTIVE STYLES

GEODe EARTH Volcanoes and Other Igneous Activity
↳ Volcanic Structures and Eruptive Styles

The popular image of a volcano is that of a solitary, graceful, snow-capped cone, such as (pre-1980) Mount St. Helens of Washington State (Figure 4.1). These picturesque, conical mountains are produced by volcanic activity that occurred intermittently over thousands, or even hundreds of thousands, of years. However, many volcanoes do not fit this image. Some volcanoes are only 30 metres high and were formed during a single eruptive phase that may have lasted only a few days. Other volcanic landforms are not volcanoes at all.

Volcanic landforms come in a wide variety of shapes and sizes, and each structure has a unique eruptive history. Nevertheless, volcanologists have been able to classify volcanic landforms and determine their eruptive patterns. In this section we will consider the general anatomy of a volcano and look at three major volcanic types: shield volcanoes, cinder cones, and composite cones. This discussion will be followed by an overview of other significant volcanic landforms.

Anatomy of a Volcano

Volcanic activity frequently begins when a fissure (crack) develops in the crust as magma moves forcefully toward the surface. As the gas-rich magma moves up this linear fissure, its path is usually localized into a circular conduit, or **pipe**, that terminates at a vent (Figure 4.11). Successive eruptions of lava, pyroclastic material, or frequently a combination of both, often separated by long periods of inactivity eventually build the structure we call a **volcano**.

Located at the summit of many volcanoes is a steep-walled depression called a **crater** (*crater* = a bowl). Craters are constructional features that are built upward as ejected fragments collect around the vent to form a doughnut-like structure. Some volcanoes have multiple summit craters, whereas others have very large, more or less circular, depressions called **calderas** (*caldaria* = a cooking pot). Calderas are

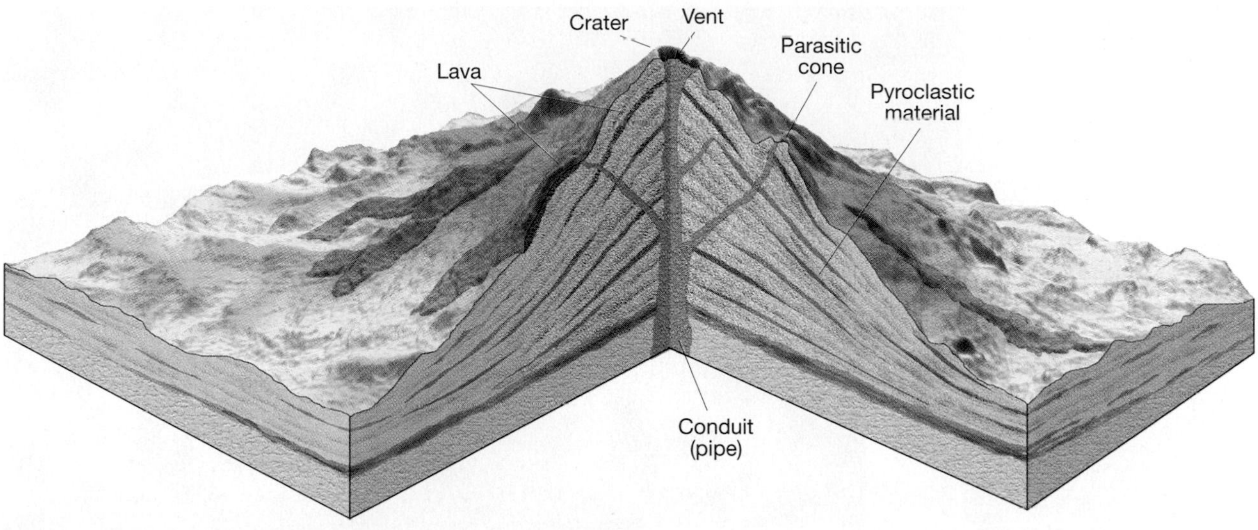

◆ **Figure 4.11** Anatomy of a typical composite cone (see also Figures 4.12 and 4.15 for a comparison with a shield and cinder cone, respectively).

large collapse structures that may or may not form in association with a volcano. (We will consider the formation of various types of calderas later.)

During early stages of growth most volcanic discharges come from a central summit vent. As a volcano matures, material also tends to emerge from fissures that develop along the flanks, or base, of the volcano. Continued activity from a flank eruption may produce a small **parasitic cone** (*parasitus* = one who eats at the table of another). Mount Etna in Italy, for example, has more than 200 secondary vents, some of which have built cones. Many of these vents, however, emit only gases and are appropriately called **fumaroles** (*fumus* = smoke).

The form of a particular volcano is largely determined by the composition of the contributing magma. As you will see, fluid Hawaiian-type lavas tend to produce broad structures with gentle slopes, whereas more viscous silica-rich lavas (and some gas-rich mafic lavas) tend to generate cones with moderate to steep slopes.

Shield Volcanoes

Shield volcanoes are produced by the accumulation of fluid mafic lavas and are broad, slightly domed structures that resemble a warrior's shield, with slopes typically less than 5 degrees (Figure 4.12). Most shield volcanoes have grown up from the deep ocean floor to form islands or seamounts, such as the islands of the Hawaiian chain, Iceland, and the Galapagos. Some shield volcanoes, however, occur

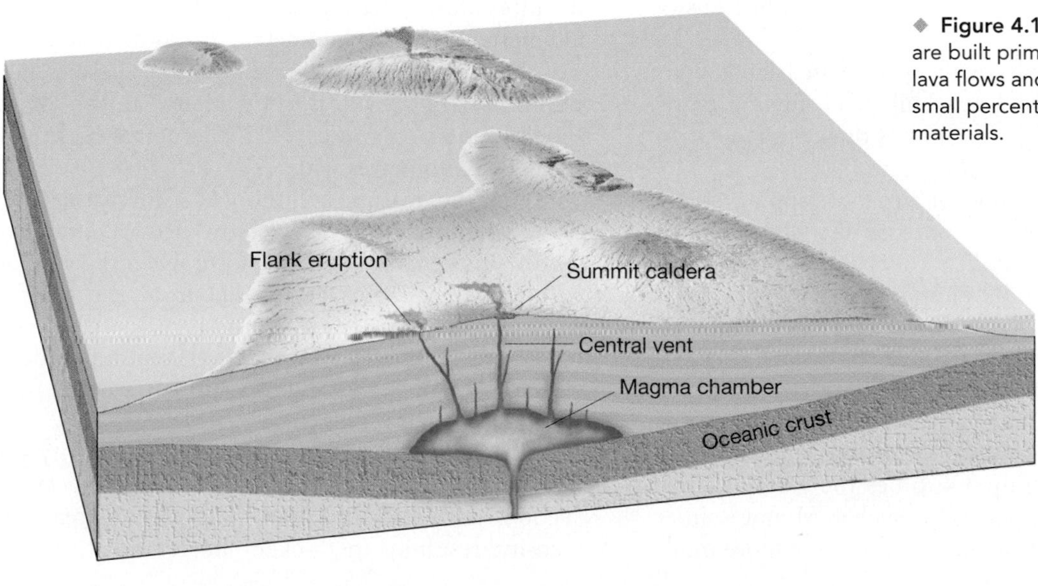

◆ **Figure 4.12** Shield volcanoes are built primarily of fluid mafic lava flows and contain only a small percentage of pyroclastic materials.

A

B

◆ **Figure 4.13** **A.** Mauna Loa is one of five shield volcanoes that together make up the island of Hawaii. **B.** The Ilgachuz Range is a large shield volcano located in western British Columbia. The irregular top of this old volcano is due to erosion. (Photo **A** by Greg Vaughn; photo **B** by Catherine Hickson, Geological Survey of Canada)

on continents. Included in this group are rather massive structures located in East Africa, like Suswa in Kenya.

Extensive study of the Hawaiian Islands confirms that each shield was built from myriad mafic lava flows averaging a few metres thick with less than about 1 percent pyroclastic ejecta.

Mauna Loa is one of five overlapping shield volcanoes that together compose the Big Island of Hawaii (Figure 4.13A). From its base on the floor of the Pacific Ocean to its summit, Mauna Loa is more than 9 kilometres high, exceeding the height of Mount Everest. This massive pile of basaltic rock has a volume of 40,000 cubic kilometres that was extruded over a period of nearly a million years. For comparison, the volume of material composing Mauna Loa is roughly 200 times the amount composing a large composite cone, such as Mount Rainier (Figure 4.14). Most shields, however, are more modest in size. For example, the classic Icelandic shield, Skjaldbreidur, rises to a height of only about 600 metres and is 10 kilometres across its base.

Despite its enormous size, Mauna Loa is not the largest known volcano. Olympus Mons, a huge shield volcano on Mars, is 25 kilometres high and nearly 600 kilometres wide.

Another feature common to a mature, active shield volcano is a large steep-walled caldera that occupies its summit. Calderas form when the roof of the volcano collapses as magma from the central magma reservoir migrates to the flanks, often feeding fissure eruptions. Mauna Loa's summit caldera measures 2.6 by 4.5 kilometres and has a depth that averages about 150 metres.

In their final stage of growth, the activity on mature shields is more sporadic, and pyroclastic ejections are more prevalent. The lavas increase in viscosity, resulting in thicker, shorter flows. These

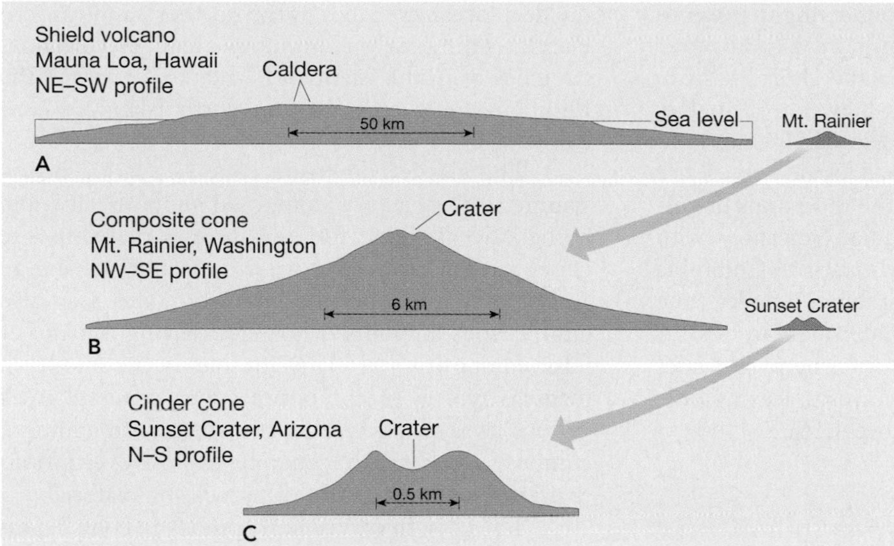

◆ **Figure 4.14** Profiles of volcanic landforms. **A.** Profile of Mauna Loa, Hawaii, the largest shield volcano in the Hawaiian chain. Note size comparison with Mount Rainier, Washington, a large composite cone. **B.** Profile of Mount Rainier, Washington. Note how it dwarfs a typical cinder cone. **C.** Profile of Sunset Crater, Arizona, a typical steep-sided cinder cone.

eruptions tend to steepen the slope of the summit area, which often becomes capped with clusters of cinder cones. This explains why Mauna Kea, a very mature volcano that has not erupted in recorded history, has a steeper summit than Mauna Loa, which erupted as recently as 1984.

Cinder Cones

As the name suggests, **cinder cones** (also called **scoria cones**) are built from ejected lava fragments that harden while in flight. These fragments range in size from fine ash to bombs but consist mostly of pea- to walnut-size lapilli. Usually a product of relatively gas-rich mafic magma, cinder cones consist of scoria. Occasionally, an eruption of silica-rich magma will generate a cinder cone composed of ash and pumice fragments. Although cinder cones are composed mostly of loose pyroclastic material, they sometimes extrude lava at their base.

Cinder cones have a very simple, distinctive shape determined by the slope that loose pyroclastic material maintains as it comes to rest (Figure 4.15). Because cinders have a high angle of repose (the steepest angle at which material remains stable), young cinder cones are steep-sided, having slopes between 30 and 40 degrees. In addition, cinder cones have large, deep craters in relation to the overall size of the structure. Although relatively symmetrical, many cinder cones are elongate, and higher on the side that was downwind during the eruptions.

Cinder cones are usually the product of a single eruptive episode that sometimes lasts only a few weeks and rarely exceeds a few years. Once this event

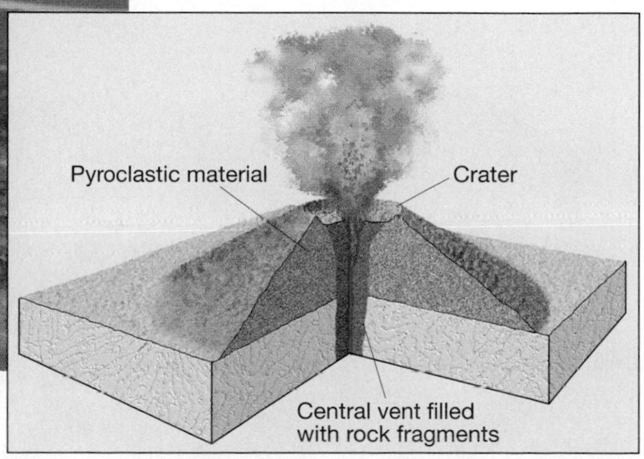

◆ **Figure 4.15** Eve Cone, a cinder cone of the Mt. Edziza Volcanic Complex, British Columbia.
(Photo by Catherine Hickson, Geological Survey of Canada)

ceases, the magma in the pipe connecting the vent to the magma chamber solidifies, and the volcano never erupts again. As a consequence of this short life span, cinder cones are small, usually between 30 metres and 300 metres, and they rarely exceed 700 metres in height (see Figure 4.14C). Small cinder cones are common features occurring in the thousands of volcanoes around the globe. Canadian volcanoes with cinder cones include Mt. Edziza in British Columbia (Figure 4.15). Probably the most famous cinder cone (Parícutin) erupted in a Mexican cornfield in 1943. A nearby village was eventually buried by pyroclastics and lava flows over the next nine years, leaving only the church towers exposed (Figure 4.16).

Composite Cones

Earth's most picturesque yet potentially dangerous volcanoes are **composite cones** or **stratovolcanoes** (Figure 4.17). Most are located in a relatively narrow zone that rims the Pacific Ocean, appropriately called the *Ring of Fire* (see Figure 4.33). This active zone includes a chain of continental volcanoes that are distributed along the west coast of South and North America, including the large cones of the Andes and the Cascade Range of western North America. The latter group includes Mount St. Helens and Mount Rainier in Washington State and Mount Garibaldi in British Columbia. The most active regions in the Ring of Fire are located along curved belts of volcanic islands situated adjacent to the deep ocean trenches of the northern and western Pacific. This nearly continuous chain of volcanoes stretches from the Aleutian Islands to Japan and the Philippines and ends on the North Island of New Zealand.

The classic composite cone is a large, nearly symmetrical structure composed of both lava and pyroclastic deposits. For the most part, composite cones are the product of gas-rich magma having an andesitic composition. (Composite cones may also emit various amounts of material having a mafic or felsic composition.) Relative to shields, the silica-rich magmas typical of composite cones generate thick viscous lavas that travel short distances. In addition, composite cones can generate explosive eruptions that eject huge quantities of pyroclastic material.

The growth of a typical composite cone begins with both pyroclastic material and lava being emitted from a central vent. As the structure matures, lavas tend to flow from fissures that develop on the lower flanks of the cone. This activity may alternate with explosive eruptions that eject pyroclastic material from the summit crater. Sometimes both activities occur simultaneously.

A conical shape, with a steep summit area and more gradually sloping flanks, is typical of many large composite cones. This classic profile is partially a consequence of the way viscous lavas and pyroclastic ejecta contribute to the growth of the cone. Coarse fragments ejected from the summit crater tend to accumulate near their source. Because of

◆ **Figure 4.16** The village of San Juan Parangaricutiro engulfed by lava from Parícutin, shown in the background. Only the church towers remain. (Photo by Tad Nichols)

◆ **Figure 4.17** These two volcanoes, Pomerape and Parinacota, exhibit the classic shape of a composite cone. Lauca National Park, Chile.
(Photo by Michael Giannechini/Photo Researchers, Inc.)

their high angle of repose, coarse materials contribute to the steep slopes of the summit area. Finer ejecta are deposited as a thin layer over a large area, which acts to flatten the flank of the cone. In addition, during the early stages of growth, lavas tend to be more abundant and flow greater distances from the vent than do later lavas. This contributes to the cone's broad base. As the volcano matures, the short flows that come from the central vent armour and strengthen the summit area. Consequently, steep slopes exceeding 40 degrees are sometimes possible. Mount St. Helens in Washington State (Figure 4.1) had the classic form we expect of a composite cone, with its steep summit and gently sloping flanks.

Despite their symmetrical form, most composite cones have a complex history. Huge mounds of volcanic debris surrounding many cones provide evidence that, in the distant past, a large section of the volcano slid downslope as a massive landslide. Others develop horseshoe-shaped depressions at their summits as a result of explosive eruptions or, as occurred during the 1980 eruption of Mount St. Helens, a combination of a landslide and the eruption of magma that left a gaping void on one side of the cone. Often, so much rebuilding has occurred since these eruptions that no trace of the amphitheatre-shaped scar remains. Following are examples of the danger that comes with living near composite cone volcanoes.

Living in the Shadow of a Composite Cone More than 50 volcanoes have erupted in North America in the past 200 years (Figure 4.18). Fortunately, the most explosive of these eruptions, except for Mount St. Helens in 1980, occurred in sparsely inhabited regions of Alaska. On a global scale, numerous destructive eruptions have occurred during the past few thousand years, a few of which may have influenced the course of human civilization.

In the case of the Santorini composite cone in the Aegean Sea, all that remains after its catastrophic eruption about 1600 B.C. is the scar of the caldera (Figure 4.19). It has been suggested that this event gave rise to Plato's legend of the sinking of the island empire of Atlantis that may have occupied Santorini. Another famous composite cone eruption was Italy's Vesuvius, which wiped out the Roman towns of Pompeii and Herculaneum in A.D. 79. The casts of victims that were buried by pyroclastic debris during that eruption can be seen today (Figure 4.20). Geologic evidence indicates a super-eruption occurred in Toba, Indonesia, about 73,500 years ago that reached heights of 30 kilometres and spread volcanic ash more than 1000 kilometres away from the

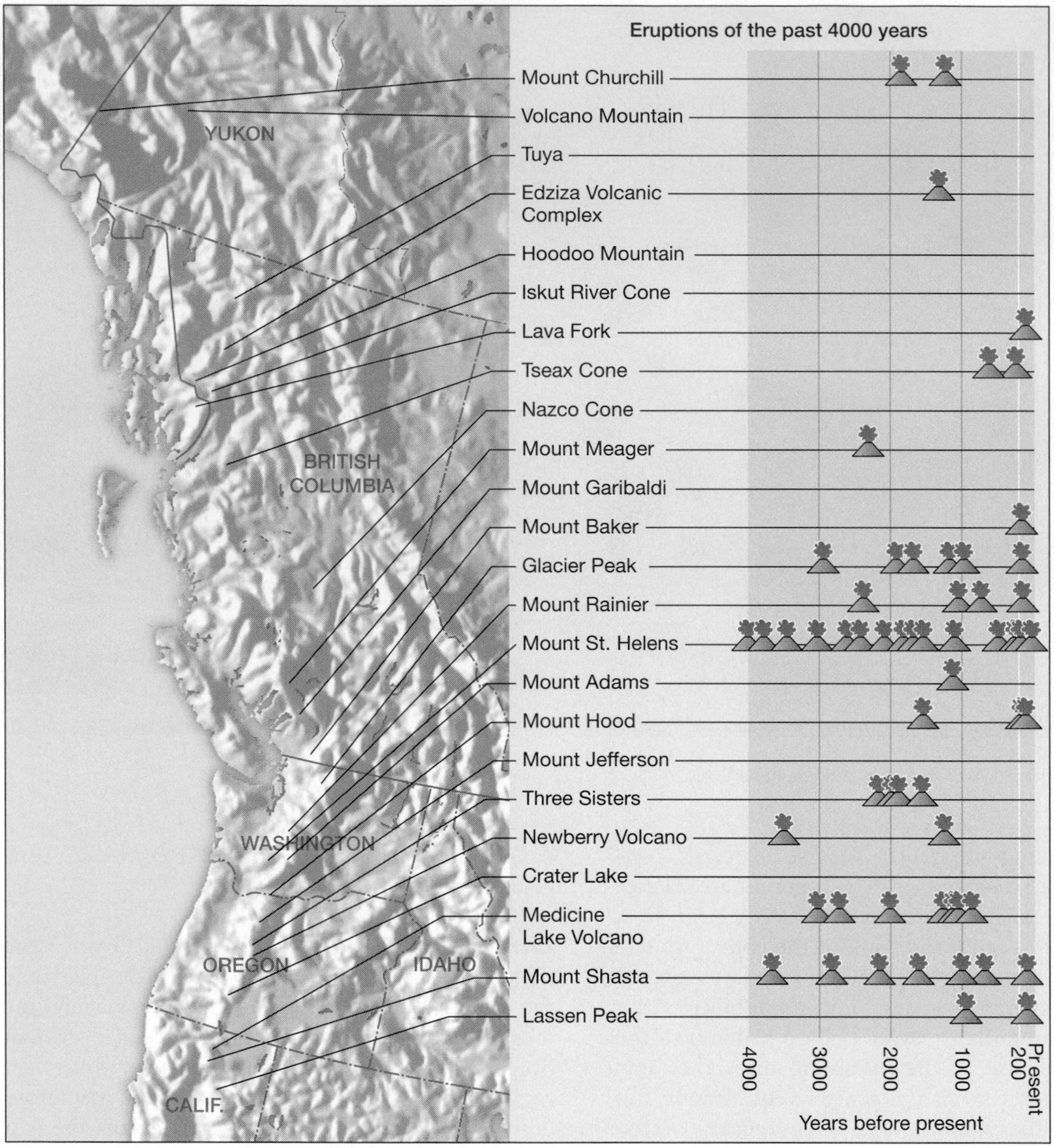

◆ **Figure 4.18** The locations of volcanoes along the west coast of North America. Each eruption symbol in the diagram represents from one to several dozen eruptions closely spaced in time. (After U.S. Geological Survey and Geological Survey of Canada)

volcano. Computer models suggest that, while airborne, the ash drove tropical temperatures to freezing for a period lasting from days to weeks.

The most obvious volcanic structure is a cone. But other distinctive and important landforms are also associated with volcanic activity.

Calderas

Calderas are large collapse depressions having a more or less circular form. Their diameters exceed 1 kilometre, and many are tens of kilometres across. (Those less than 1 kilometre across are called *collapse pits*.) Most calderas are formed by one of the following processes: (1) the collapse of the summit of a large composite volcano following an explosive eruption of silica-rich pumice and ash fragments (Crater Lake type; Figure 4.21); (2) the collapse of the top of a shield volcano caused by subterranean drainage from a central magma chamber (Hawaiian type); and (3) the collapse of a large area, independent of any existing volcanic structures, caused by the discharge of colossal volumes of silica-rich pumice and ash along ring fractures (Yellowstone type).

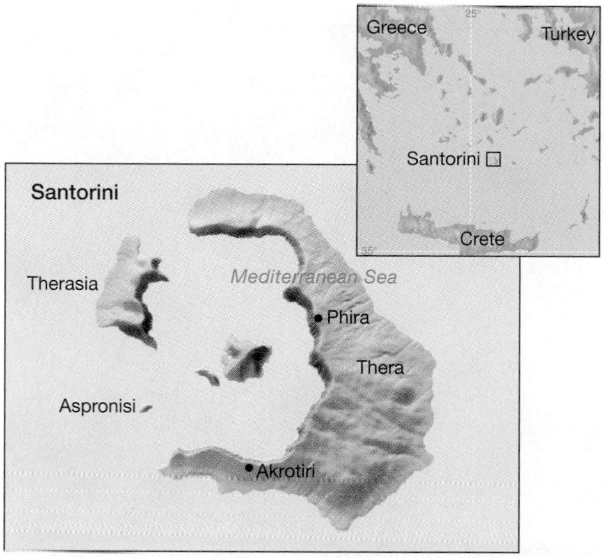

◆ **Figure 4.19** Map showing the remains of the volcanic island of Santorini after the top of the cone collapsed into the emptied magma chamber following an explosive eruption. The location of the recently excavated Minoan town of Akrotiri is shown. Volcanic eruptions over the last 500 years built the central islands. Despite the fact that another destructive eruption is likely, the city of Phira was built on the flanks of the caldera.

Another distinctive feature associated with most large calderas is a slow upheaval, or *resurgence*, of the floor of the caldera following an eruptive phase. Thus, these structures consist of a large, somewhat circular depression containing a central elevated region (such as Wizard Island in Crater Lake, Figure 4.22). Most large calderas exhibit a complex history. Geologic evidence suggests that a magma reservoir still exists beneath Yellowstone; thus, another caldera-forming eruption is likely, but not imminent.

Calderas of the type located on the Yellowstone Plateau of northwest Wyoming are the largest volcanic

◆ **Figure 4.20** Plaster casts of several victims of the A.D. 79 eruption of Mount Vesuvius that destroyed the Roman city of Pompeii.
(Photo by Leonard von Matt/Photo Researchers, Inc.)

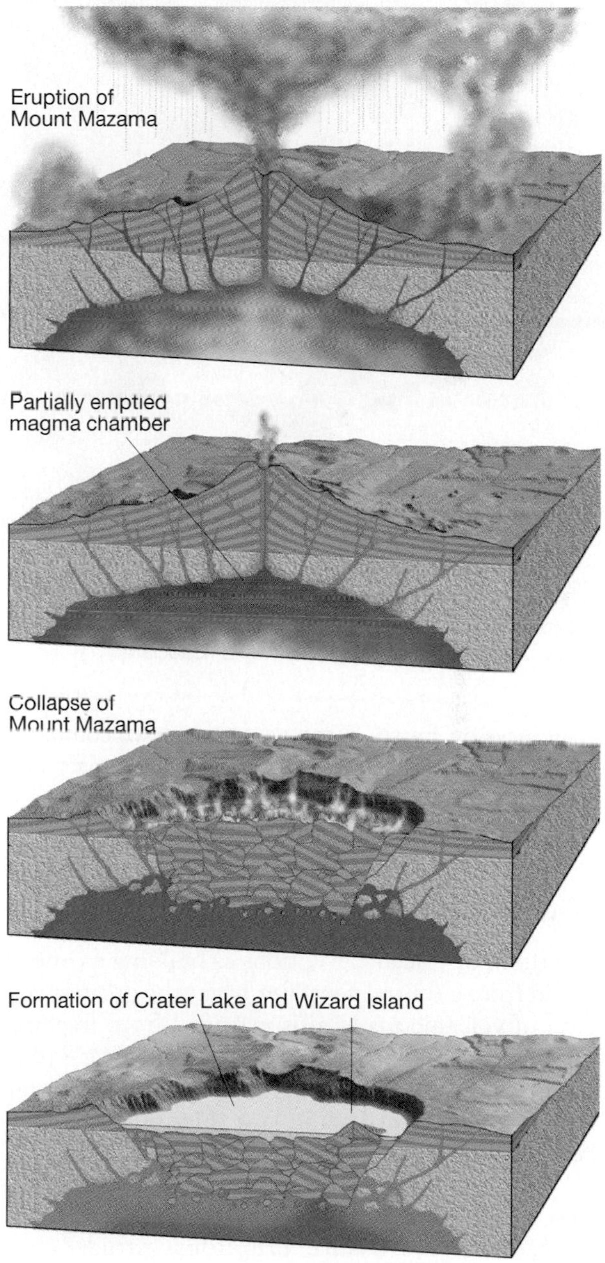

◆ **Figure 4.21** Sequence of events that formed Crater Lake, Oregon. About 7000 years ago, a violent eruption partly emptied the magma chamber, causing the summit of former Mount Mazama to collapse. Rainfall and groundwater contributed to form Crater Lake, the deepest lake in the United States. Subsequent eruptions produced the cinder cone called Wizard Island.
(After H. Williams, *The Ancient Volcanoes of Oregon*, p. 47. Courtesy of the University of Oregon)

◆ **Figure 4.22** Crater Lake occupies a caldera about 10 kilometres in diameter. The small cinder cone in the foreground is Wizard Island.
(Photo by Greg Vaughn/Tom Stack and Associates)

structures on Earth. Some geologists have compared their destructive force with that of the impact of a small asteroid. Fortunately, no eruption of this type has occurred in recorded history.

Fissure Eruptions and Lava Plateaus

We think of volcanic eruptions as building a cone or shield from a central vent. But by far the greatest volume of volcanic material is extruded from fractures in the crust called **fissures** (*fissura* = to split). Rather than building a cone, these long, narrow cracks can emit a low-viscosity mafic lava (Figure 4.23), blanketing a wide area.

The extensive Columbia Plateau in the northwest United States was formed this way (Figure 4.24). Here, numerous **fissure eruptions** extruded very fluid mafic lava between 17 million and 6 million years ago (Figures 4.25A and 4.25B). Successive flows, some 50 metres thick, buried the existing landscape as they built a lava plateau nearly 1.5 kilometres thick. The fluid nature of the lava is evident, because some remained molten long enough to flow 150 kilometres from its source. Although less extensive in terms of area, basaltic lavas of similar age to those of the Columbia Plateau occur in south-central British Columbia (Figure 4.25C). The term **flood basalts** appropriately describes these flows.

One of the largest accumulations of flood basalt in the world is the Deccan Traps, a thick sequence of flat-lying basalt flows covering nearly 500,000 square kilometres of west central India. When the Deccan Traps formed about 66 million years ago, nearly 2 million cubic kilometres of lava was extruded in fewer than 1 million years. This event coincided with the demise of the dinosaurs (at the end of the Cretaceous Period), and some believe the two events are connected. Another huge deposit of flood basalts, called the Ontong Java Plateau, is found on the floor of the Pacific Ocean.

Iceland, which is located astride the Mid-Atlantic Ridge (see Chapter 1), regularly experiences fissure eruptions. The largest Icelandic eruptions in recorded history occurred in 1783 and were named the Laki eruptions. A rift 25 kilometres long generated more than 20 separate vents, which initially extruded sulphurous gases and ash deposits that built several small cinder cones. This activity was followed by huge outpourings of very fluid mafic lava. The total volume of lava extruded by the Laki eruptions

◆ **Figure 4.23** Lava extruded along the East Rift Zone, Kilauea, Hawaii. (Photo by Greg Vaughn)

was in excess of 12 cubic kilometres. Volcanic gases poisoned and stunted grasslands and directly killed 75 percent of Iceland's livestock. The ensuing famine caused 10,000 deaths, representing 25 percent of Iceland's population at the time.

Lava Domes

In contrast to mafic lavas, silica-rich lavas near the felsic (rhyolitic) end of the compositional spectrum are so viscous they hardly flow. As the thick lava is "squeezed" out of the vent, it may produce a steep-sided dome-shaped mass of congealed lava called a **lava dome**.

Lava domes typify the late stages of activity of mature, chiefly andesitic composite cones (see Box 4.2). Here these rhyolitic structures form in the summit crater and as parasitic structures on the flanks of these cones following an explosive eruption of a gas-rich magma. This is exemplified by the volcanic dome that continues to grow from the vent of the 1980 eruption of Mount St. Helens (Figure 4.26).

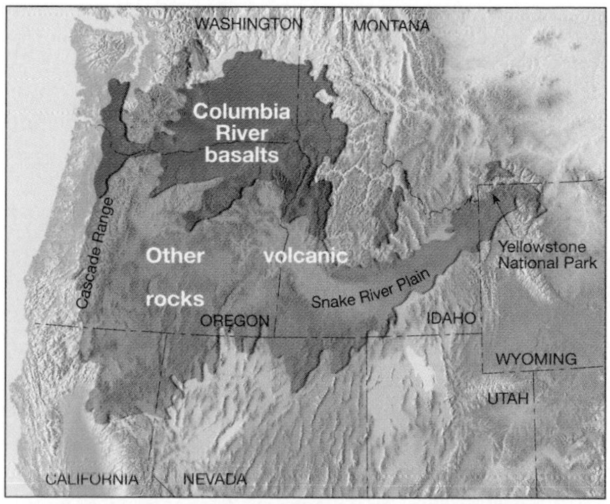

◆ **Figure 4.24** Volcanic areas that compose the Columbia Plateau in the U.S. Pacific Northwest. The Columbia River basalts cover an area of nearly 200,000 square kilometres. Activity here began about 17 million years ago as lava began to pour out of large fissures, eventually producing a basalt plateau with an average thickness of nearly 1.5 kilometre. (After U.S. Geological Survey)

◆ **Figure 4.25** Basaltic fissure eruption. **A.** Lava fountaining from a fissure and formation of fluid lava flows called flood basalts. **B.** Photo of basalt flows near Idaho Falls. **C.** Plateau basalts exposed in canyon walls of Chasm Provincial Park, south-central British Columbia. The canyon was carved by meltwater at the end of the Ice Age.
(Photo **B** by John S. Shelton; photo **C** by S. R. Hicock)

Although most lava domes form in association with existing composite cones or shield volcanoes, some form independently, such as the line of rhyolitic and obsidian domes at Mono Craters, California.

Volcanic Pipes and Necks

Most volcanoes are fed magma through short conduits, called *pipes*, that connect a magma chamber to the surface. In rare circumstances, pipes may extend to depths exceeding 200 kilometres. When this occurs, the ultramafic magmas that migrate up these structures produce rocks that are thought to be samples of the mantle that have undergone very little alteration during their ascent. Geologists consider these unusually deep conduits to be "windows" into Earth, for they allow us to view rock normally found only at great depth.

Well-known volcanic pipes are the diamond-bearing structures of South Africa and Northwest Territories (see Chapter 20). Here, the rocks filling the pipes originated at depths of at least 150 kilometres, where pressure is high enough to generate diamonds and other high-pressure minerals. The task of transporting essentially unaltered magma (along with diamond inclusions) through 150 kilometres of solid rock is exceptional and accounts for the scarcity of natural diamonds.

Volcanoes on land are continually being lowered by weathering and erosion. Cinder cones are easily eroded, because they are composed of unconsolidated materials. However, all volcanoes eventually succumb to relentless erosion over geologic time. As erosion progresses, the rock occupying the volcanic pipe is commonly more resistant and may remain standing above the surrounding terrain long after most of the cone has vanished. Shiprock, New Mexico, is such a feature and is called a **volcanic neck** (Figure 4.27). This structure, higher than many skyscrapers, is but one of many such landforms that protrude conspicuously from the red desert landscapes of the American Southwest.

BOX 4.2

People and the Environment
Volcanic Crisis on Montserrat

The Caribbean's Lesser Antilles are mostly volcanic in origin and extend from near the northeast coast of South America in an arc toward Puerto Rico and the Virgin Islands (Figure 4.B). Near the beginning of the twentieth century, devastating eruptions occurred when volcanoes on Martinique (Mt. Pelée) and St. Vincent (Soufrière) killed more than 30,000 people. As the twentieth century came to a close, the Caribbean was once again a focus for volcanologists. This time their attention was on the island of Montserrat.

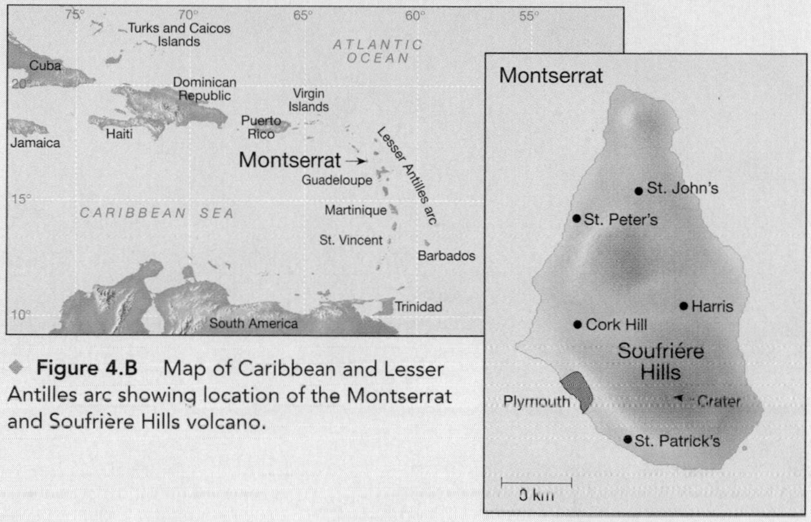

◆ **Figure 4.B** Map of Caribbean and Lesser Antilles arc showing location of the Montserrat and Soufrière Hills volcano.

This small island is dominated by the Soufrière Hills volcano, which began erupting in July 1995 after thousands of years of inactivity. The volcano, like most in the Caribbean, erupts viscous lava that oozes out at the surface, forming a lava dome. Such domes have the potential to produce devastating nuées ardentes. Because there may be little warning, such eruptions are extremely dangerous (Figure 4.C).

The activity at Soufrière Hills volcano included many large nuées ardentes that eventually covered large parts of the island. Moreover, plumes of volcanic ash were sometimes erupted to heights of 6000 metres or more. By January 1998, many of the island's nearly 12,000 residents had been evacuated to neighbouring islands. To say the least, the erupting volcano caused serious hardship and economic distress to the people of Montserrat. On the positive side, loss of life was small.

◆ **Figure 4.C** The August 20, 1997, eruption of Soufrière Hills volcano on the Caribbean island of Montserrat. This is one of several volcanoes in the region that owes its existence to the melting of a subducting plate. (Photo by Kevin West/Gamma Liaison)

Since the onset of eruptive activity, Soufrière Hills has become one of the most closely monitored volcanoes in the world. Almost immediately after the unexpected activity began, the Montserrat Volcano Observatory was established. Staffed by scientists from the University of the West Indies and the British Geological Survey, the mountain was wired with seismometers, tiltmeters, and gas analyzers. The valuable data being gathered may one day contribute to a reliable method of predicting volcanic eruptions.

◆ **Figure 4.26** Following the May 1980 eruption of Mount St. Helens, a lava dome began to develop. (Photo by David Falconer/DRK Photo)

◆ **Figure 4.27** Shiprock, New Mexico, is a volcanic neck. This structure, which stands more than 420 metres high, consists of igneous rock that crystallized in the vent of a volcano; the volcano itself has long since been eroded away. (Photo by Tom Bean)

INTRUSIVE IGNEOUS BODIES

GEODe EARTH Volcanoes and other Igneous Activity
↳ Intrusive Igneous Activity

Although volcanic eruptions can be among the most violent and spectacular events in nature, and therefore worthy of detailed study, most magma is emplaced at depth. Thus, an understanding of intrusive igneous activity is as important to geologists as the study of volcanic events.

Many of the structures that result from the emplacement of igneous material at depth are called **plutons**, named for Pluto, the god of the lower world in classical mythology. Because all plutons form out of view beneath Earth's surface, they can be studied only after uplift and erosion have exposed them. The challenge lies in reconstructing the events that generated these structures millions or even hundreds of millions of years ago.

For the sake of clarity, we have separated our discussions of volcanism and plutonic activity. Keep in mind, however, that these diverse processes occur simultaneously and involve basically the same materials.

Nature of Plutons

Plutons occur in a great variety of sizes and shapes. Some of the most common types are illustrated in Figure 4.28. Notice that some of these structures have a tabular (tabletop) shape, whereas others are quite massive or shapeless. Also, observe that some of these bodies cut across existing structures, such as layers of sedimentary rock; others form when magma is injected between sedimentary layers. Because of these differences, intrusive igneous bodies are generally classified according to their shape as either **tabular** or **massive** and by their orientation with respect to the host rock. Intrusive rocks are said to be **discordant** (*discordare* = to disagree) if they cut across existing structures and **concordant** (*concordare* = to agree) if they form parallel to features, such as sedimentary layers. As you can see in Figure 4.28A, plutons are closely associated with volcanic activity. Many of the largest intrusive bodies are the remnants of magma chambers that once fed ancient volcanoes. Large intrusive bodies of particular significance in Canada include plutons in the Coast Mountains of British Columbia, the Monteregian intrusions in the Montreal region of Quebec, and the Sweetgrass Hills just south of Alberta.

Dykes

Dykes are tabular discordant bodies that are produced when magma is injected into fractures (Figure 4.29). The force exerted by the emplaced magma can be great enough to further separate the walls of the fracture. Once crystallized, these wall-like structures have thicknesses that range from less than 1 centimetre to more than 1 kilometre. The largest have lengths of hundreds of kilometres. Most dykes, however, are a few metres thick (Figure 4.29B) and extend laterally for no more than a few kilometres.

Dykes are commonly found in groups (e.g., Mackenzie Dyke Swarm of the Canadian Shield) that once served as vertically oriented pathways followed by molten rock that fed ancient lava flows. The parent pluton is generally not observable. Some dykes are found radiating, like spokes on a wheel, from an eroded volcanic neck (e.g., Figure 4.27). In these situations the active ascent of magma is thought to have generated fissures in the volcanic cone out of which lava flowed.

Sills

Tabular intrusions formed when magma is injected along sedimentary bedding surfaces are called **sills** (Figure 4.30). Horizontal sills are the most common (e.g., Purcell Sill of Waterton Lakes National Park, Alberta), but sills can occur in other orientations if the sedimentary layers within which they are hosted have been tilted. Because of their relatively uniform thickness and large areal extent, sills are likely the product of very fluid magmas. Magmas having a low silica content are more fluid, so most sills are mafic in composition.

The emplacement of a sill requires that the overlying sedimentary rock be lifted to a height equal to the thickness of the sill. Although this is a formidable task, in shallow environments it often requires less energy than forcing the magma up the remaining distance to the surface. Consequently, sills form only at shallow depths, where the pressure exerted by the weight of overlying rock layers is low. Although sills are intruded between layers, they can be locally discordant.

In many respects, sills closely resemble buried lava flows. Both are tabular and commonly exhibit columnar jointing (Figure 4.31). **Columnar joints** form as igneous rocks cool and develop shrinkage fractures that produce elongate, pillar-like columns.

When attempts are made to reconstruct the geologic history of a region, it becomes important to differentiate between sills and buried lava flows. Fortunately, under close examination these two

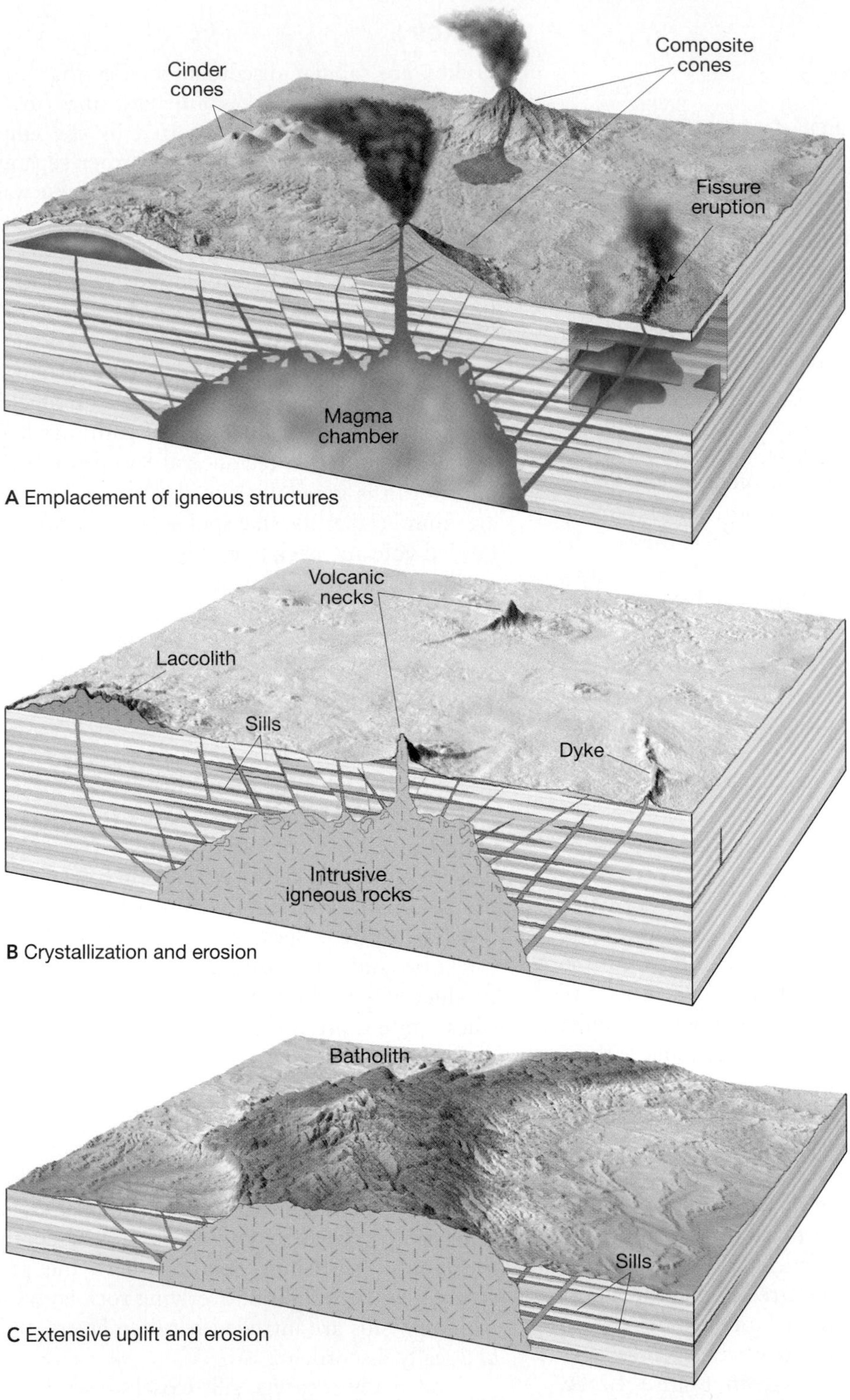

◆ **Figure 4.28** Illustrations showing basic igneous bodies. **A.** This block diagram shows the relationship between volcanism and intrusive igneous activity. **B.** This view illustrates the basic plutons, some of which have been exposed by erosion long after their formation. **C.** After millions of years of uplifting and erosion, a batholith is exposed at the surface.

phenomena can be readily distinguished. The upper portion of a buried lava flow usually contains voids produced by escaping gas bubbles (vesicular texture; see Figure 3.14), and only the rocks beneath a lava flow show evidence of metamorphic alteration. Sills, however, form when magma has been forcefully intruded between sedimentary layers. Thus, fragments of the overlying rock can be found only in sills. Lava

A

B

◆ **Figure 4.29** Light- and dark-coloured dykes. **A.** Dykes of felsic composition cut through dark-coloured mafic volcanic rocks near Lakelse, British Columbia. **B.** Dark coloured dyke of mafic composition cuts through light-coloured granitic rock north of Sudbury, Ontario.
(Photos by S. R. Hicock)

A

B

◆ **Figure 4.30** **A.** The dark-coloured rock layer in this photograph is a sill made of gabbro. It is located in the Upper Brock River Canyon, near Paulatuk, Northwest Territories. **B.** Dark mafic sill in mountains made of lighter coloured sedimentary rock in the Dry Valleys area of Antarctica.
(Photo **A** by R. Rainbird. Reproduced with the permission of the Minister of Public Works and Government Services Canada, 2008, and courtesy of Natural Resources Canada; photo **B** by S. R. Hicock)

◆ **Figure 4.31** Columns north of Vancouver, British Columbia, show the characteristic hexagonal patterns of joints in basalt. These are produced by the contraction and fracturing that result as a lava flow or sill gradually cools. (Photo by Catherine Hickson, Geological Survey of Canada)

flows, conversely, are extruded before the overlying strata are deposited. "Baked" zones in the rock above and below are trademarks of a sill and are only found on the rock below a lava flow, not on the overlying rock.

Laccoliths

Laccoliths (*lakkos* = pond, *lithos* = stone) are similar to sills because they form when magma intrudes between sedimentary layers in a near-surface environment. However, the magma that generates laccoliths is more viscous and collects as a blister-like mass that arches the overlying strata upward (see Figure 4.28B). Consequently, a laccolith can occasionally be detected because of the dome-shaped bulge it creates at the surface. Most large laccoliths are probably not much wider than a few kilometres.

Batholiths

By far the largest intrusive igneous bodies are **batholiths** (*bathos* = depth, *lithos* = stone). Most commonly, batholiths occur in groups that form linear structures several hundreds of kilometres long and up to 100 kilometres wide, as shown in Figure 4.32. Indirect evidence gathered from gravitational studies indicates that batholiths are also very thick, possibly extending dozens of kilometres into the crust.

By definition, a plutonic body must have a surface exposure greater than 100 square kilometres to be considered a batholith. Smaller plutons of this type are termed **stocks**. Many stocks appear to be portions of batholiths that are not yet fully exposed.

Batholiths usually consist of rock types having chemical compositions toward the felsic end of the spectrum, although diorite is commonly found. Smaller batholiths can be rather simple structures composed almost entirely of one rock type. However, studies of large batholiths have shown that they consist of several distinct plutons that were intruded over millions of years. The plutonic activity that created the Sierra Nevada batholith, for example, occurred nearly continuously over 130 million years that ended about 80 million years ago, during the Cretaceous Period.

Batholiths may compose the core of mountain systems. Uplifting and erosion have removed the surrounding rock, thereby exposing the resistant igneous body (see Figure 3.19 and Chapter 3's opening photo). Large expanses of granitic rock also occur in the stable interiors of the continents, such as the Canadian Shield. These relatively flat exposures are the remains of ancient mountains that have long since been levelled by erosion. The exposed rocks that make up the batholiths of youthful mountain ranges, such as the Sierra Nevada, were generated near the top of a magma chamber, whereas in shield

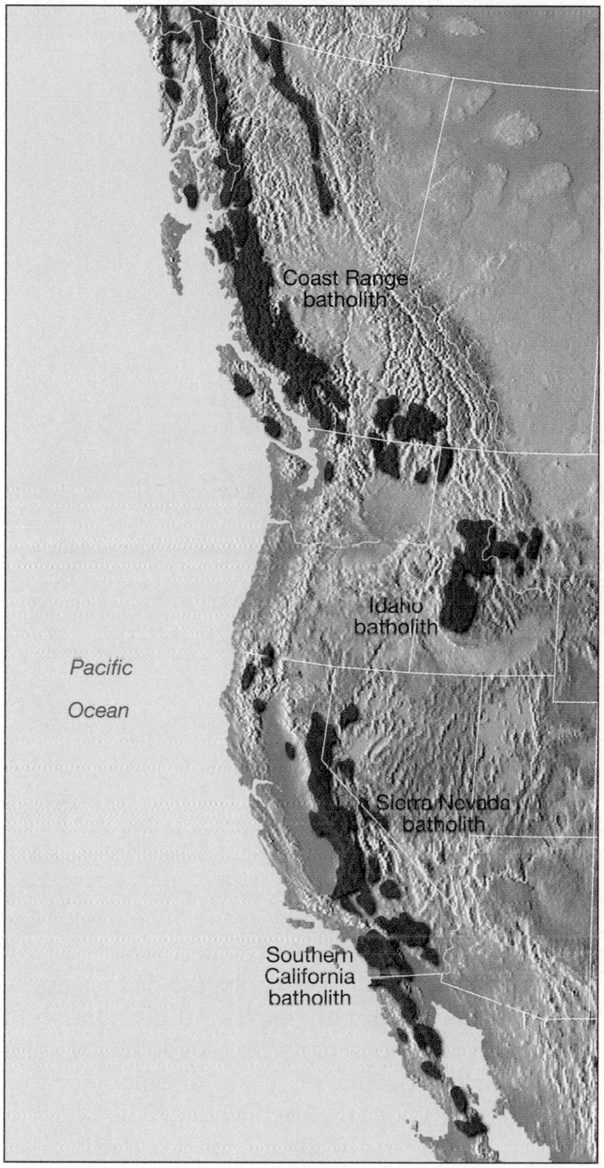

◆ **Figure 4.32** Granitic batholiths that occur along the western margin of North America. These gigantic, elongate bodies consist of numerous plutons that were emplaced during the last 150 million years of Earth history.

areas, the roots of former mountains and, thus, the lower portions of batholiths are exposed. In Chapter 13 we will further consider the role of igneous activity as it relates to mountain building.

Emplacement of Batholiths An interesting problem geologists faced was trying to explain how large granitic batholiths came to reside within only moderately deformed sedimentary and metamorphic rocks. What happened to the rock that was displaced by these igneous masses? How did the magma body make its way through several kilometres of solid rock?

We know that magma rises because it is less dense than the surrounding rock, much like a cork held at the bottom of a container of water will rise when it is released. But Earth's crust is made of solid rock. Nevertheless, at depths of several kilometres, where temperature and pressure are high, even solid rock deforms by flowing. Thus, at great depths, a mass of buoyant, rising magma can forcibly make room for itself by pushing aside the overlying rock. As the magma continues to move upward, some of the host rock that was shouldered aside will fill in the space left by the magma body as it passes.*

As a magma body nears the surface, it encounters relatively cool, brittle rock that resists deformation. Further upward movement is accomplished by *stoping*. In this process, fractures that develop in the overlying host rock allow magma to rise and dislodge blocks of rock. Once incorporated into the magma body, these blocks may melt, thereby altering the composition of the magma body. Eventually, the magma body will cool sufficiently so that upward movement comes to a halt. Evidence supporting the fact that magma can move through solid rock occurs in the form of **xenoliths**. Xenoliths are unmelted pieces of the host rock found in the pluton after it has been exhumed by erosion.

PLATE TECTONICS AND IGNEOUS ACTIVITY

GEODe EARTH Plate Tectonics
↳ Introduction

Geologists have known for decades that the global distribution of volcanism is not random. Of the more than 800 active volcanoes that have been identified, most are located along the margins of the ocean basins—most notably along the circum-Pacific belt known as the *Ring of Fire* (Figure 4.33).** This group of volcanoes is associated with convergent plate boundaries and consists mainly of composite cones that emit volatile-rich magma of intermediate

*An analogous situation occurs when a can of oil-based paint is left in storage. The oily component of the paint is less dense than the pigments used for coloration; thus, oil collects into drops that slowly migrate upward, while the heavier pigments settle to the bottom.

**For our purposes, active volcanoes include those with eruptions that have been dated. At least 700 other cones exhibit geologic evidence that they have erupted within the past 10,000 years and are regarded as potentially active. Further innumerable active submarine volcanoes are hidden from view in the depths of the ocean and are not counted in these numbers.

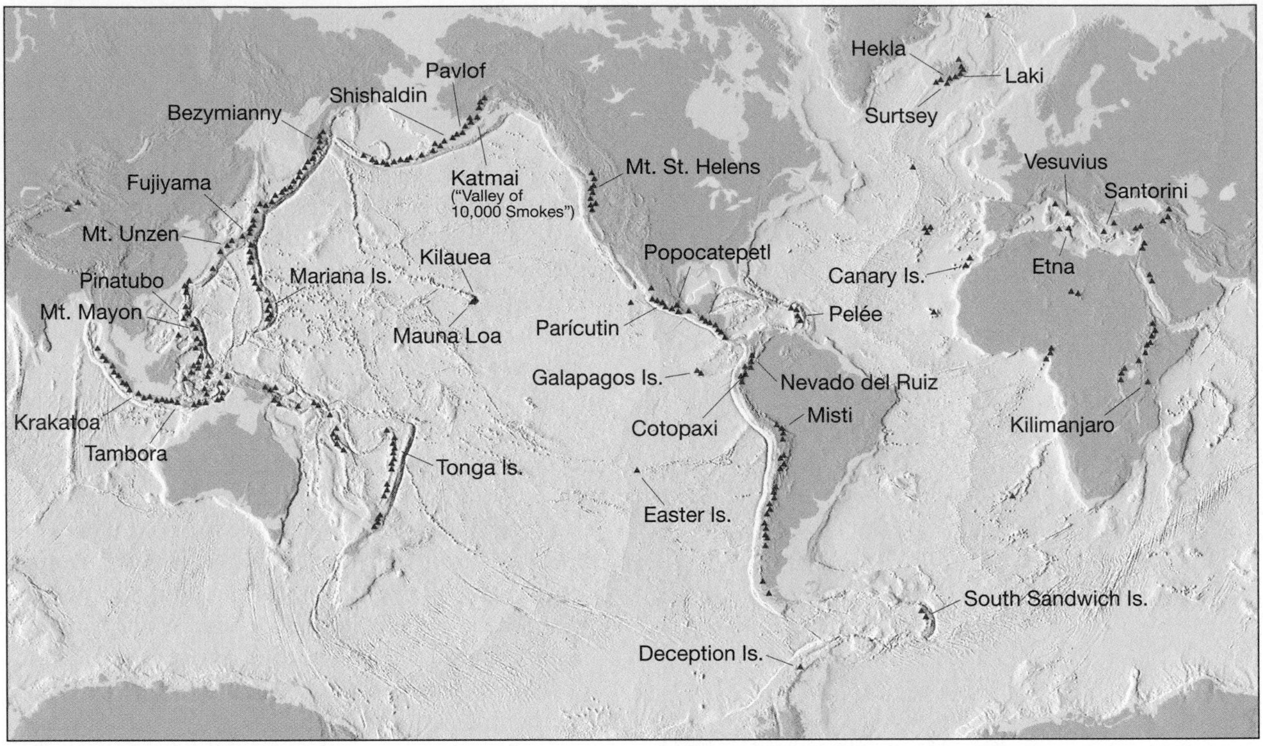

◆ **Figure 4.33** Locations of some of Earth's major volcanoes.

(andesitic) composition and occasionally produce awe-inspiring eruptions.

The volcanoes composing a second group emit very fluid mafic lavas at divergent plate boundaries (mid-ocean ridges; e.g., Iceland) and are confined to the deep ocean basins. This group also contains many active submarine volcanoes that dot the ocean floor; particularly notable are the innumerable small seamounts that form linear patterns. At these depths the pressures are so great that seawater does not boil explosively, even in contact with hot lavas. Thus, firsthand knowledge of these eruptions is limited, coming mainly from deep-diving submersibles.

A third group of volcanoes, produced by **intraplate volcanism** (meaning "within the plate"), are irregularly distributed and lack obvious associations with convergent and divergent plate boundaries. Such volcanoes form as a result of magma generation associated with ascending plumes of hot mantle rock. One of the best-known volcanoes belonging to this group is Hawaii's Kilauea, which is situated in the middle of the vast Pacific plate, thousands of kilometres from the nearest plate boundary. Among other examples are the Canary Islands, Yellowstone, Mount Kilimanjaro, and several volcanic centres in the Sahara Desert of northern Africa. Intraplate volcanoes situated on oceanic lithosphere typically erupt mafic lava, whereas the lava erupted from similar volcanoes on continents can range from mafic to felsic in composition.

Until the late 1960s, geologists had no explanation for the apparently haphazard distribution of continental volcanoes, nor were they able to account for the almost continuous chain of volcanoes that circles the margin of the Pacific basin. The development of the theory of plate tectonics clarified the picture. Recall that all primary (unaltered) magma originates in the upper mantle and that the mantle is essentially solid, *not molten*, rock. The basic connection between plate tectonics and volcanism is that *plate motions provide the mechanisms by which mantle rocks melt to generate magma*; this connection will be further discussed in Chapters 11 through 13 where we will examine the three regions of igneous activity in more detail, and their relationship to plate boundaries.

Before we examine the next major group of rocks (sedimentary), we must first study the breakdown of rock that produces the materials that make up sedimentary rocks. This rock breakdown is called *weathering* and is presented in the next chapter.

Chapter Summary

- The primary factors that determine the nature of volcanic eruptions include the magma's composition, its temperature, and the amount of dissolved gases it contains. As lava cools, it begins to congeal and, as *viscosity* increases, its mobility decreases. The viscosity of magma is directly related to its silica content. Felsic (rhyolitic) lava, with its high silica content (more than 70 percent), is very viscous and forms short, thick flows. Mafic (basaltic) lava, with a lower silica content (about 50 percent), is more fluid and may travel a long distance before congealing. Dissolved gases tend to increase the fluidity of magma and, as they expand, provide the force that propels molten rock from the *vent* of a *volcano*.
- The materials associated with a volcanic eruption include (1) lava flows (*pahoehoe flows*, which resemble twisted braids; and *aa flows*, consisting of rough, jagged blocks; both form from mafic lavas); (2) gases (primarily water vapour); and (3) *pyroclastic material* (pulverized rock and lava fragments blown from the volcano's vent, which include ash, pumice, lapilli, cinders, blocks, and bombs). Composite cones produce some of the most violent volcanic activity. Often associated with a violent eruption is a *nuée ardente*, a fiery cloud of hot gases infused with incandescent ash that races down steep volcanic slopes. Large composite cones may also generate a type of mudflow known as a *lahar*.
- Successive eruptions of lava from a central vent result in a mountainous accumulation of material known as a volcano. Located at the summit of many volcanoes is a steep-walled depression called a *crater*. *Shield volcanoes* are broad, slightly domed volcanoes built primarily of fluid, mafic lava. *Cinder cones* have steep slopes composed of pyroclastic material. *Composite cones*, or *stratovolcanoes*, are large, nearly symmetrical structures built of interbedded lavas and pyroclastic deposits.
- Most volcanoes are fed by *conduits* or *pipes*. As erosion progresses, the rock occupying the pipe is often more resistant and may remain standing above the surrounding terrain as a *volcanic neck*. The summits of some volcanoes have large, nearly circular depressions called *calderas* that result from collapse following an explosive eruption. Calderas also form on shield volcanoes by subterranean drainage from a central magma chamber, and the largest calderas form by the discharge of colossal volumes of silica-rich pumice along ring fractures. Although volcanic eruptions from a central vent are the most familiar, by far the largest amounts of volcanic material are extruded from cracks in the crust called *fissures*. The term *flood basalts* describes fluid, runny, mafic lava flows that cover extensive regions. When silica-rich magma is extruded, *pyroclastic flows* consisting largely of ash and pumice fragments usually result.
- Intrusive igneous bodies are classified according to their shape and by their orientation with respect to the host rock, generally sedimentary rock. The two general shapes are *tabular* (sheet-like) and *massive*. Intrusive igneous bodies that cut across existing sedimentary beds are said to be *discordant*; those that form parallel to existing sedimentary layers are *concordant*.
- *Dykes* are tabular, discordant igneous bodies produced when magma is injected into fractures that cut across rock layers. Tabular, concordant bodies, called *sills*, form when magma is injected along the bedding surfaces of sedimentary rocks. In many respects, sills closely resemble buried lava flows. *Laccoliths* are similar to sills but form from less fluid magma that collects as a lens-shaped mass that arches the overlying strata upward. *Batholiths*, the largest intrusive igneous bodies with surface exposures of more than 100 square kilometres, frequently make up the cores of mountains.
- Most active volcanoes are associated with plate boundaries. Active areas of volcanism are found along mid-ocean ridges, where seafloor spreading is occurring (divergent plate boundaries), in the vicinity of ocean trenches where one plate is being subducted beneath another (convergent plate boundaries), and in the interiors of plates themselves (because of *intraplate volcanism*). Rising plumes of hot mantle rock are the source of most intraplate volcanism.

Review Questions

1. What event triggered the May 18, 1980, eruption of Mount St. Helens? (See Box 4.1.)

2. List three factors that determine the nature of a volcanic eruption. What role does each play?

3. Why is a volcano fed by highly viscous magma likely to be a greater threat than a volcano supplied with very fluid magma?

4. Describe pahoehoe and aa lava.

5. List the main gases released during a volcanic eruption. Why are gases important in eruptions?

6. How do volcanic bombs differ from blocks of pyroclastic debris?

7. What is scoria? How is scoria different from pumice?

8. Compare a volcanic crater with a caldera.

9. Compare and contrast the three main types of volcanoes (size, composition, shape, and eruptive style).

10. Name a prominent volcano for each of the three types.

11. Explain why in Canada volcanoes are only found in British Columbia and Yukon Territory.

12. What are the largest volcanic structures on Earth?

13. What is Shiprock, New Mexico, and how did it form?

14. How do the eruptions that created the Columbia Plateau differ from eruptions that create volcanic peaks?

15. Where are fissure eruptions most common?

16. Extensive pyroclastic flow deposits are most often associated with which volcanic structures?

17. Describe each of the four intrusive features discussed in the text (dyke, sill, laccolith, and batholith).

18. Why might a laccolith be detected at Earth's surface before being exposed by erosion?

19. What is the largest of all intrusive igneous bodies? Is it tabular or massive? concordant or discordant?

20. Describe how batholiths are emplaced.

21. What is the Ring of Fire?

Key Terms

aa flow (p. 95)
batholith (p. 116)
caldera (p. 100)
cinder cone (p. 103)
columnar joints (p. 113)
composite cone (p. 104)
concordant (p. 113)
conduit (p. 94)
crater (p. 100)
discordant (p. 113)
dyke (p. 113)
eruption column (p. 94)
fissure (p. 108)
fissure eruption (p. 108)
flood basalt (p. 108)
fumarole (p. 101)
intraplate volcanism (p. 118)
laccolith (p. 116)
lahar (p. 100)
lava dome (p. 109)
lava tube (p. 95)
massive (p. 113)
nuée ardente (p. 98)
pahoehoe flow (p. 95)
parasitic cone (p. 101)
pillow lava (p. 96)
pipe (p. 100)
plutons (p. 113)
pumice (p. 98)
pyroclastic flow (p. 98)
pyroclastic material (p. 97)
scoria (p. 98)
scoria cone (p. 103)
shield volcano (p. 101)
sill (p. 113)
stock (p. 116)
stratovolcano (p. 104)
tabular (p. 113)
vent (p. 94)
viscosity (p. 92)
volcanic neck (p. 110)
volcano (p. 100)
xenolith (p. 117)

Web Resources

The *Earth* website uses the resources and flexibility of the internet to aid in your study of the topics in this chapter. Written and developed by geology instructors, this site will help improve your understanding of geology. Visit **www.pearsoned.ca/tarbuck** and click on the cover of the text to find

- online review quizzes
- Web-based critical thinking and writing exercises
- links to chapter-specific Web resources
- internet-wide key-term searches

www.pearsoned.ca/tarbuck

Chapter 5

Weathering and Soil

The spectacular badland topography of southern Alberta is a testament to the processes of weathering and erosion. (Photo by Mike Schering)

Earth's surface is constantly changing. Rock is disintegrated and decomposed; moved to lower elevations by gravity; and carried away by water, wind, or ice. In this manner, Earth's physical landscape is sculpted. This chapter focuses on the first step of this ongoing process: weathering. What causes solid rock to crumble, and why does the type and rate of weathering vary from place to place? Soil, an important product of the weathering process and a vital resource, is also examined.

EARTH'S EXTERNAL PROCESSES

GEODe EARTH Weathering and Soil
↳ Earth's External Processes

Weathering, mass wasting, and erosion are called **external processes** because they occur at or near Earth's surface and are powered by energy from the Sun or Earth's gravity. External processes are a basic part of the rock cycle because they are responsible for transforming solid rock into sediment.

To most people, the face of Earth appears to be unchanging. In fact, a mere 200 years ago most people fervently believed that mountains, lakes, and deserts were permanent features of a young Earth no more than a few thousand years old. Today, we know that Earth is at least 4.6 billion years old and that mountains eventually wear down, lakes fill with sediment or are drained by streams, and deserts come and go with changes in climate.

Earth is a dynamic body. Some parts of Earth's surface are gradually elevated through plate tectonics, mountain building, and volcanic activity. These **internal processes** derive their energy from Earth's interior. Meanwhile, opposing external processes are continually breaking rock apart and moving the debris to lower elevations (Figure 5.1) through the following processes:

1. **Weathering:** the physical breakdown (disintegration) and chemical alteration (decomposition) of rock at or near Earth's surface
2. **Mass wasting:** the transfer of rock and soil downslope under the influence of gravity
3. **Erosion:** the physical removal of material by mobile agents, such as water, wind, or ice

In this chapter we will focus on rock weathering and the products generated by this activity. However, weathering cannot be easily separated from mass wasting and erosion because erosion and mass wasting remove the rock debris as weathering breaks rocks apart. This transport of material by erosion

◆ **Figure 5.1** This is an interesting example of the weathering of cross-bedded sandstone in Writing-on-Stone Provincial Park, Davis Coulee, Alberta. When weathering accentuates differences in rocks, spectacular landforms are sometimes created. As the rock gradually disintegrates and decomposes, mass wasting and erosion remove the products of weathering. (Photo by Rudi Meyer)

and mass wasting promotes further disintegration and decomposition of the rock.

WEATHERING

GEODe EARTH Weathering and Soil
↳ Types of Weathering

Weathering goes on all around us, but it seems so slow and subtle that it is easy to underestimate its importance. However, weathering is an essential part of the rock cycle and thus a key process in the Earth system.

All materials are subject to weathering. Consider, for example, the fabricated product concrete. A newly poured concrete sidewalk has a smooth, fresh look. However, a few years later the same sidewalk will appear chipped, cracked, and rough, with pebbles exposed at the surface. Roots of nearby trees may heave and buckle the concrete as well. The same natural processes that break apart a concrete sidewalk also break down rock.

Weathering occurs when rock is mechanically fragmented (disintegrated) or chemically altered (decomposed). **Mechanical weathering** is accomplished by physical forces that break rock into smaller and smaller pieces without changing the rock's mineral composition. **Chemical weathering** involves a chemical transformation of rock into one or more new compounds. These two concepts can be illustrated with a piece of paper. As an analogy, paper can be disintegrated by tearing it into smaller and smaller pieces, whereas decomposition occurs when the paper is burned.

Why does rock weather? Simply, weathering is the response of Earth materials to a changing environment. For instance, after millions of years of uplift and erosion, the rocks overlying a large, intrusive igneous body (pluton) may be removed, exposing it at the surface (see Figures 3.19, 5.4, and 5.5). This mass of crystalline rock—formed deep below ground where temperatures and pressures are high—is now subjected to a very different and comparatively hostile surface environment. In response, this rock mass will gradually change. This transformation of rock is what we call weathering.

In the following sections, we will discuss the various modes of mechanical and chemical weathering. Although we consider these two processes separately, keep in mind that they usually work simultaneously in nature and enhance each other's effectiveness.

MECHANICAL WEATHERING

GEODe EARTH Weathering and Soil
↳ Mechanical Weathering

When a rock undergoes *mechanical weathering*, it is broken into smaller and smaller pieces, each retaining the characteristics of the original material. The end result is many small pieces from a single large one. Figure 5.2 shows that breaking a rock into smaller pieces increases the surface area available for chemical attack. An analogous situation occurs when sugar is added to tea. In this situation, a cube of sugar will dissolve much more slowly than will an equal volume of sugar granules because the cube has much less surface area available for dissolution. Hence, by breaking rocks into smaller pieces, mechanical weathering increases the amount of surface area available for chemical weathering.

In nature, three important physical processes lead to the fragmentation of rock: frost wedging, expansion resulting from unloading, and biologic activity. In addition, although the work of erosional agents, such as wind, glacial ice, and running water, is usually considered separately from mechanical weathering, it is nevertheless important. As these mobile agents move rock debris, they relentlessly disintegrate these materials.

Frost Wedging

Repeated freezing and thawing are important processes of mechanical weathering. Liquid water has the unique property of expanding about 9 percent on freezing, because water molecules in the regular crystalline structure of ice are farther apart than they are in liquid water near the freezing point. As a result, water freezing in a confined space exerts tremendous outward pressure on the walls of its container. To verify this, consider an unopened plastic bottle of pop that is placed in the freezer. As the water in the pop freezes, the bottle may crack.

In nature, water works its way into cracks in rock and, on freezing, expands and enlarges these openings. After many freeze–thaw cycles, the rock is broken into angular fragments. This process is appropriately called **frost wedging** (Figure 5.3). Frost wedging is most pronounced in mountainous regions where a daily freeze–thaw cycle often exists. Here, sections of rock are wedged loose and may

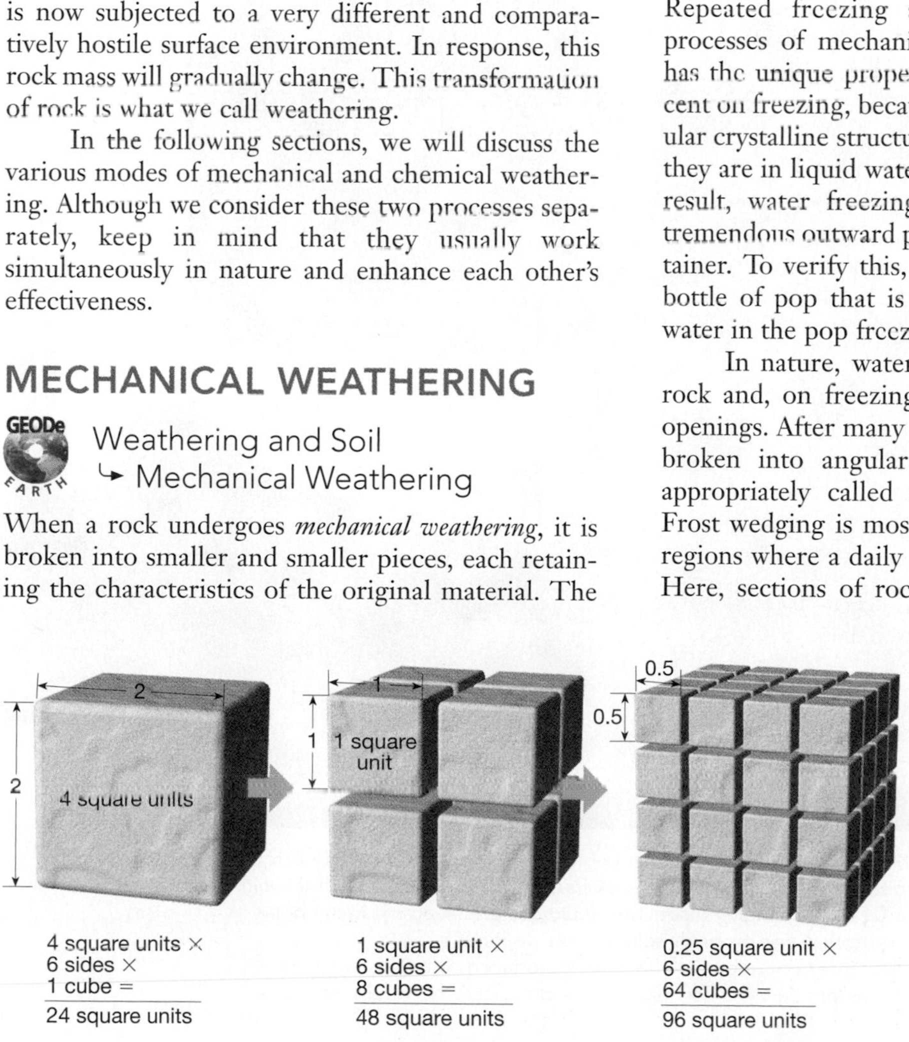

◆ **Figure 5.2** Chemical weathering can occur only to those portions of a rock that are exposed to the elements. Mechanical weathering breaks rock into smaller and smaller pieces, thereby increasing the surface area available for chemical attack.

tumble into large piles called **talus slopes** that commonly form at the base of steep rock outcrops (Figure 5.3).

Frost wedging also causes great destruction to highways in Canada, particularly in the early spring, when the freeze–thaw cycle is well established. Roadways acquire numerous potholes and are occasionally heaved and buckled by this destructive force. Another type of wedging in rock fractures is caused by the crystallization of salt (such as sodium sulphate, calcium chloride, and sodium chloride) through the evaporation of saline solutions that seep into cracks and joints, especially in hot arid climates. As the salt crystals grow, they can force the fractures apart and thus contribute to rock disintegration.

Unloading

When large masses of igneous rock, particularly granite, are exposed by erosion, concentric slabs begin to break loose. The process generating these onion-like layers is called **sheeting**. It is thought that this occurs, at least in part, because of the great reduction in pressure when the overlying rock is eroded away, a process called *unloading*. Accompanying this unloading, the outer layers expand more than the rock below and thus separate from the rock body (Figure 5.4). Continued weathering eventually causes the slabs to separate and spall off (flake away), creating **exfoliation domes** (*ex* = off, *folium* = leaf). Excellent examples of exfoliation domes are Stawamus

◆ **Figure 5.3** Frost wedging. As water freezes, it expands, exerting a force great enough to break rock. When frost wedging occurs in such a setting as this, the broken rock fragments fall to the base of the cliff and create a cone-shaped accumulation known as *talus*. **Inset:** This boulder, a glacial erratic in the polar desert conditions of the Northwest Territories, was probably split by frost wedging.
(**Main** photo by Tom & Susan Bean, Inc.; **inset** photo by C. Jefferson. Reproduced with the permission of the Minister of Public Works and Government Services Canada, 2008, and courtesy of Natural Resources Canada)

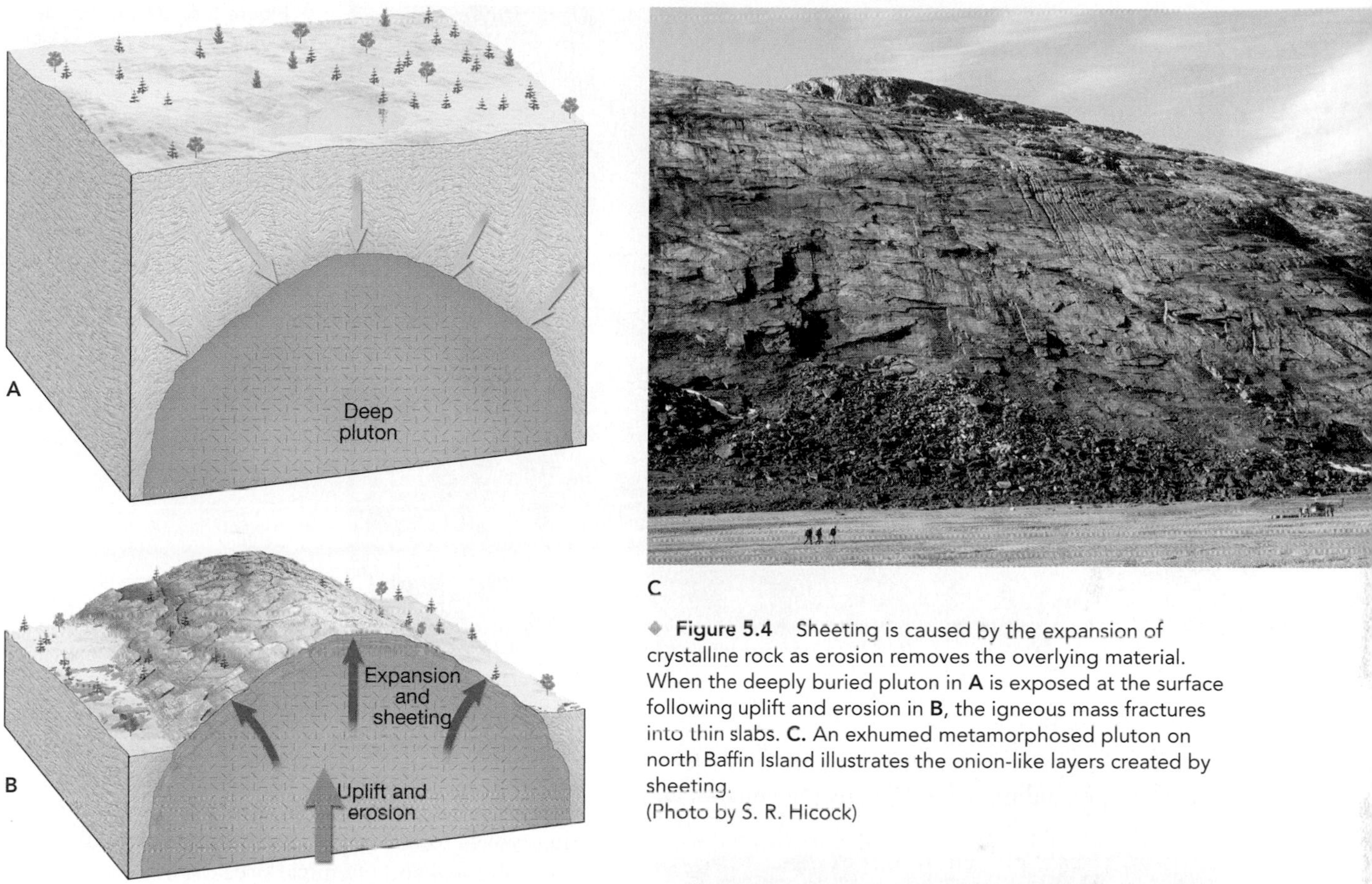

◆ **Figure 5.4** Sheeting is caused by the expansion of crystalline rock as erosion removes the overlying material. When the deeply buried pluton in **A** is exposed at the surface following uplift and erosion in **B**, the igneous mass fractures into thin slabs. **C.** An exhumed metamorphosed pluton on north Baffin Island illustrates the onion-like layers created by sheeting.
(Photo by S. R. Hicock)

Chief in British Columbia (see Figure 3.19); Sugarloaf in Rio de Janeiro; and Half Dome and Liberty Cap in Yosemite National Park in California (Figure 5.5).

Deep underground mining provides us with another example of how rocks behave once the confining pressure is removed. Large rock slabs have been known to explode off the walls of newly cut mine tunnels because of the abruptly reduced pressure. Evidence of this type, plus the fact that fracturing occurs parallel to the floor of a quarry when large blocks of rock are removed, strongly supports the process of unloading as the cause of sheeting.

Although many fractures are created by expansion, others are produced by contraction during the crystallization of magma (see Figure 4.31), and still others by tectonic forces during mountain building. Fractures produced by these activities generally form a definite pattern and are called *joints* (Figure 5.6). Joints allow water to penetrate deeply and start the process of weathering long before the rock is exposed. Finally, fracturing of rocks by frequent drastic temperature changes in deserts has been suggested but not yet proven.

◆ **Figure 5.5** Summit of Half Dome, an exfoliation dome in Yosemite National Park, California.
(Photo by Breck Kent)

◆ **Figure 5.6** Nearly parallel vertical joints in granitic rock on the south side of Grouse Mountain, British Columbia. (Photo by S. R. Hicock)

Biologic Activity

Weathering is also accomplished by the activities of organisms, including plants, burrowing animals, and humans. Plant roots and seedlings in search of nutrients and water grow into and expand fractures (Figure 5.7), providing a pathway for water and chemical infiltration. Lichens and mosses attach themselves to bare rock surfaces, thereby enhancing their physical and chemical breakdown.

Burrowing animals further break down rock by moving fresh material to the surface, where physical and chemical processes can more effectively attack it. Decaying organisms also aid in chemical weathering by producing acids that break down elements, like aluminum, so that rainwater can easily remove them.

◆ **Figure 5.7** Roots of cedar trees work their way into fractures in the dolostone that caps the Niagara Escarpment in the Beaver Valley of Ontario. Root wedging widens fractures in rock and aids the process of mechanical weathering. (Photo by C. Tsujita)

CHEMICAL WEATHERING

GEODe EARTH Weathering and Soil
↳ Chemical Weathering

Chemical weathering involves the complex processes that break down rock components and the internal structures of minerals. Such processes convert the constituents to new minerals or release them to the surrounding environment. During this transformation, the original rock decomposes into substances that are stable in the surface environment. Consequently, the products of chemical weathering remain essentially unchanged as long as they remain in an environment similar to the one in which they formed.

Water is by far the most important agent of chemical weathering. Pure water alone is a good solvent, and small amounts of dissolved materials result in increased chemical activity for weathering solutions. The major processes of chemical weathering are dissolution, oxidation, and hydrolysis. Water plays a leading role in each.

Dissolution

Perhaps the easiest type of decomposition to envision is the process of **dissolution**. Just as sugar dissolves in water, so too do certain minerals. One of the most water-soluble minerals is halite (common salt), which is composed of sodium and chloride ions. Halite readily dissolves in water because although this compound maintains overall electrical neutrality, the individual ions retain their respective charges.

Moreover, the surrounding water molecules are polar—that is, the oxygen end of the molecule has a small residual negative charge; the end with hydrogen has a small positive charge. As the water molecules come in contact with halite, their negative ends approach sodium ions and their positive ends cluster about chloride ions. This disrupts the attractive forces in the halite crystal and releases the ions to the water solution (Figure 5.8).

Although most minerals are, for all practical purposes, insoluble in pure water, the presence of even a small amount of acid dramatically increases the corrosive force of water. (An acidic solution contains the reactive hydrogen ion, H^+.) In nature, acids are produced by a number of processes. For example, carbonic acid is created when carbon dioxide in the atmosphere dissolves in raindrops. As acidic rainwater soaks into the ground, carbon dioxide in the soil may increase the acidity of the weathering solution. Various organic acids are also released into the soil as organisms decay, and sulphuric acid is introduced as acid rain (Box 5.1) and produced by the weathering of pyrite and other sulphide minerals.

Regardless of the source of the acid, this highly reactive substance readily decomposes most rocks and produces certain products that are water soluble. For example, the mineral calcite, $CaCO_3$, which makes up the common building stones marble and limestone, is easily attacked by even a weakly acidic solution:

$$\underset{\text{calcium carbonate}}{CaCO_3} + \underset{\text{hydrogen ions}}{2H^+} \rightarrow \underset{\text{calcium ion (soluble)}}{Ca^{2+}} + \underset{\text{carbon dioxide}}{CO_2\uparrow} + \underset{\text{water}}{H_2O}$$

During this process, the insoluble calcium carbonate is transformed into soluble products. In nature, over thousands of years, large quantities of limestone are dissolved and carried away by underground water. This activity is clearly evidenced by the large number of subsurface caverns found in limestone regions throughout North America. Monuments and buildings made of limestone or marble are also subjected to the corrosive work of acids, particularly in industrial areas that have smoggy, polluted air (see Box 5.1).

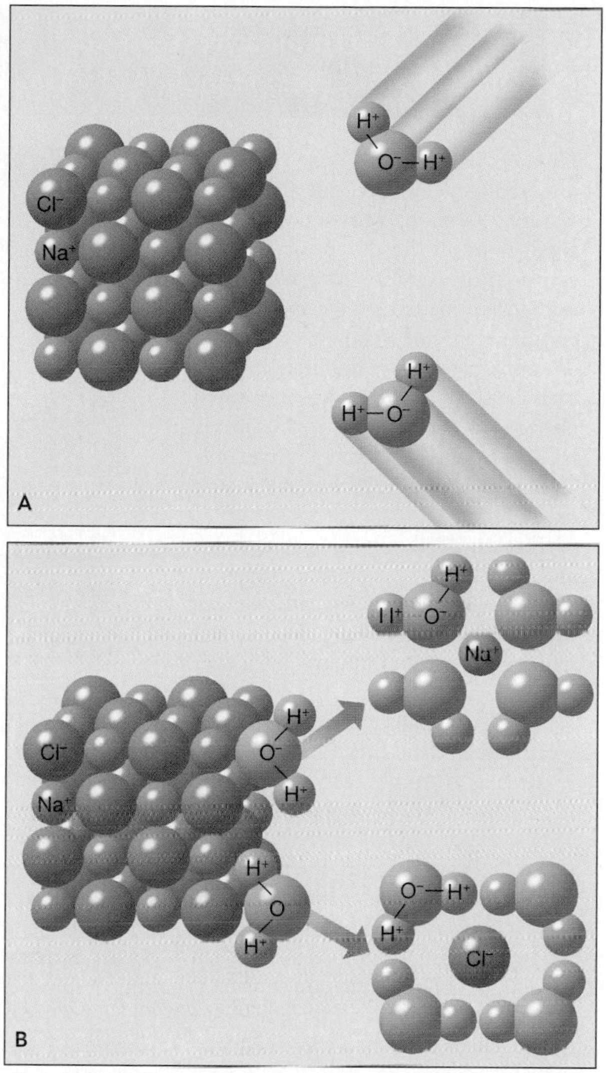

◆ **Figure 5.8** Illustration of halite dissolving in water. **A.** Polar water molecules attack sodium and chloride ions. **B.** Once removed, these ions are surrounded and held by a number of water molecules, as shown.

The soluble ions from reactions of this type are retained in our underground water supply. These dissolved ions are responsible for the so-called hard water found in many locales. Simply, hard water is undesirable because the active ions react with soap to produce an insoluble material that renders soap nearly useless in removing dirt. To solve this problem, a water softener can be used to remove these ions, generally by replacing them with others that do not chemically react with soap.

BOX 5.1

Earth as a System

Acid Precipitation: A Human Impact on the Earth System

Humans are part of the complex interacting whole we call the Earth system. As such, our actions cause changes to all the other parts of the system. For example, by going about our normal activities, we modify the composition of the atmosphere. These atmospheric modifications in turn cause unintended and unwanted changes to occur in the hydrosphere, biosphere, and geosphere. Acid precipitation is one small but significant example.

Decomposed stone monuments and structures are common sights in many cities (Figure 5.A). Although we expect rock to gradually decompose, many of these monuments have succumbed prematurely. An important cause of this accelerated chemical weathering is acid precipitation.

◆ **Figure 5.A** Acid rain accelerates the chemical weathering of stone monuments and structures, including this building facade in Leipzig, Germany. (Photo by Doug Plummer/Photo Researchers, Inc.)

Rain is naturally somewhat acidic (i.e., lower than 7 on the pH scale). When carbon dioxide from the atmosphere dissolves in water, the product is weak carbonic acid. However, the term *acid precipitation* refers to precipitation that is much more acidic than natural, unpolluted rain and snow.

As a consequence of burning large quantities of fossil fuels, like coal and petroleum products, 40 million tonnes of sulphur and nitrogen oxides are released into the atmosphere each year in North America alone. The major sources of these emissions include power-generating plants, industrial processes, such as ore smelting and petroleum refining, and vehicles of all kinds. Through a series of complex chemical reactions, some of these pollutants are converted into acids that then fall to Earth's surface as rain or snow. Another portion is deposited in dry form and subsequently converted into acid after coming in contact with precipitation, dew, or fog.

Northern Europe and eastern North America have experienced widespread acid rain for some time. Studies have also shown that acid rain occurs in many other regions, including western North America, Japan, China, Russia, Europe, and South America. In addition to local pollution sources, a portion of the acidity found in the northeast United States and eastern Canada originates hundreds of kilometres away in industrialized regions to the south and southwest. This situation occurs because many pollutants remain in the atmosphere for as long as five days, during which time they can be transported great distances.

The damaging environmental effects of acid rain are thought to be considerable in some areas and imminent in others. The best-known effect is an increased acidity in thousands of lakes in Scandinavia and eastern North America. Accompanying this have been substantial increases in dissolved aluminum leached from the soil by the acidic water, which is toxic to fish. Consequently, some lakes are virtually devoid of fish, and others are approaching this condition. Ecosystems are characterized by many interactions at many levels of organization, which means that evaluating the effects of acid precipitation on these complex systems is difficult and expensive, and far from complete.

In addition to the many lakes that can no longer support fish, research indicates that acid precipitation may also reduce agricultural crop yields and impair the productivity of forests. Acid rain not only harms the foliage but also damages roots and leaches nutrient minerals from the soil. Finally, acid precipitation promotes the corrosion of metals and contributes to the destruction of stone structures.

Oxidation

Everyone has seen iron and steel objects that rusted when exposed to water (Figure 5.9). The same thing can happen to iron-rich minerals. The process of rusting occurs when oxygen combines with iron to form iron oxide as follows:

$$\underset{\text{iron}}{4Fe} + \underset{\text{oxygen}}{3O_2} \rightarrow \underset{\text{iron oxide (hematite)}}{2Fe_2O_3}$$

◆ **Figure 5.9** Iron reacts with oxygen to form iron oxide, as seen on this rusted tram winch on the Chilkoot Trail, Yukon. (Photo by Mike Schering)

This type of chemical reaction, called **oxidation**,* occurs when electrons are lost from one element during the reaction. In this case, we say that iron was oxidized because it lost electrons to oxygen. Although the oxidation of iron progresses very slowly in a dry environment, the addition of water greatly speeds the reaction.

Oxidation is important in decomposing such ferromagnesian minerals as olivine, pyroxene, and amphibole. Oxygen readily combines with the iron in these minerals to form the reddish-brown iron oxide called *hematite* (Fe_2O_3) or, in other cases, a yellowish-coloured rust called *goethite* [FeO(OH)]. These products are responsible for the rusty colour on the surfaces of dark, iron-rich igneous rocks, such as basalt, as they begin to weather (see Figure 5.11). However, oxidation can occur only after iron is freed from the silicate structure by another process, called hydrolysis (explained below).

Another important oxidation reaction occurs when sulphide minerals, such as pyrite, decompose. Sulphide minerals are major constituents in many metallic ores, and pyrite is frequently associated with coal deposits as well. In a moist environment, chemical weathering of pyrite (FeS_2) yields sulphuric acid (H_2SO_4) and goethite [FeO(OH)]. In many mining locales, this weathering process creates a serious environmental hazard, particularly in humid areas where abundant rainfall infiltrates spoil banks (waste material left after coal or other minerals are removed). This so-called *mine acid* eventually makes its way to streams, killing aquatic organisms and degrading aquatic habitats (see Box 20.2).

Hydrolysis

The most common mineral group, the silicates, is decomposed primarily by the process of **hydrolysis** (*hydro* = water, *lysis* = a loosening), which basically is the reaction of any substance with water. Ideally, the hydrolysis of a mineral would take place in pure water, as some of the water molecules dissociate to form the very reactive hydrogen (H^+) and hydroxyl (OH^-) ions. It is the tiny hydrogen ion that attacks and replaces other larger cations found in the crystal lattice. With the introduction of hydrogen ions into the crystalline structure, the original orderly arrangement of atoms collapses and the mineral decomposes.

In nature, water usually contains other substances that contribute additional hydrogen ions, thereby greatly accelerating hydrolysis. The most common of these substances is carbon dioxide, CO_2, which dissolves in water to form carbonic acid, H_2CO_3. Rain dissolves some carbon dioxide in the atmosphere, and additional amounts, released by decaying organic matter, are acquired as the water percolates through the soil.

In water, carbonic acid ionizes to form hydrogen ions (H^+) and bicarbonate ions (HCO_3^-). To illustrate how a rock undergoes hydrolysis in the presence of carbonic acid, let's examine the chemical weathering of granite, a common continental rock. Recall that granite consists mainly of quartz and potassium feldspar. The weathering of the potassium feldspar component of granite is as follows:

$$\underset{\text{potassium feldspar}}{2KAlSi_3O_8} + \underset{\text{carbonic acid}}{2(H^+ + HCO_3^-)} + \underset{\text{water}}{H_2O} \rightarrow$$

$$\underset{\text{kaolinite (residual clay)}}{Al_2Si_2O_5(OH)_4} + \underbrace{\underset{\text{potassium ion}}{2K^+} + \underset{\text{bicarbonate ion}}{2HCO_3^-}}_{\text{in solution}} + \underset{\text{silica}}{4SiO_2}$$

*Note that *oxidation* is a term referring to any chemical reaction in which a compound or radical loses electrons. The element oxygen is not necessarily present.

In this reaction, the hydrogen ions (H^+) attack and replace potassium ions (K^+) in the feldspar structure, thereby disrupting the crystalline network. Once removed, the potassium is available as a nutrient for plants or becomes the soluble salt potassium bicarbonate ($KHCO_3$), which may be incorporated into other minerals or carried to the ocean.

The most abundant product of the chemical breakdown of potassium feldspar is the clay mineral kaolinite. Clay minerals are the end products of weathering and are very stable under surface conditions. Consequently, clay minerals make up a high percentage of the inorganic material in soils. Moreover, the most abundant sedimentary rock, shale, contains a high proportion of clay minerals. Industrial uses of clay minerals are presented in Chapter 20.

In addition to the formation of clay minerals during the weathering of potassium feldspar, some silica is removed from the feldspar structure and carried away by groundwater. This dissolved silica will eventually precipitate, producing nodules of chert or flint, or it will fill in the pore spaces between grains of sediment, or it will be carried to the ocean, where microscopic animals will remove it from the water to build hard silica shells.

To summarize, the weathering of potassium feldspar generates a residual clay mineral, a soluble salt (potassium bicarbonate), and some silica, which enters into solution.

Quartz, the other main component of granite, is very resistant to chemical weathering; it remains substantially unaltered when attacked by weak acidic solutions. As a result, when granite weathers, the feldspar crystals dull and slowly turn to clay, releasing the once interlocked quartz grains, which still retain their fresh, glassy appearance. Although some of the quartz remains in the soil, much is eventually transported to the sea or to other sites of deposition, where it becomes the main constituent of such features as sandy beaches and sand dunes. In time these quartz grains may be lithified to form the sedimentary rock *sandstone*.

Table 5.1 lists the weathered products of some of the most common silicate minerals. Remember that silicate minerals make up most of Earth's crust and that these minerals are composed mostly of only eight elements. When chemically weathered, the silicate minerals yield sodium, calcium, potassium, and magnesium ions that form soluble products, which can be removed from groundwater. The element iron combines with oxygen, producing relatively insoluble iron oxides, most notably hematite and limonite, which give soil a reddish-brown or yellowish colour. Under most conditions, the three remaining elements—aluminum, silicon, and oxygen—join with water to produce residual clay minerals. However, even the highly insoluble clay minerals are very slowly removed by subsurface water.

TABLE 5.1 **Products of Weathering**

Mineral	Residual Products	Material in Solution
Quartz	Quartz grains	Silica
Feldspars and Micas	Clay minerals	Silica K^+, Na^+, Ca^{2+}
Amphibole (hornblende)	Clay minerals Limonite Hematite	Silica Ca^{2+}, Mg^{2+}
Olivine	Limonite Hematite	Silica Mg^{2+}

Alterations Caused by Chemical Weathering

As noted earlier, the most significant result of chemical weathering is the decomposition of unstable minerals and the generation or retention of those materials that are stable at Earth's surface. This accounts for the predominance of certain minerals in the surface material we call soil.

In addition to altering the internal structure of minerals, chemical weathering causes physical changes as well. For instance, when angular rock fragments are attacked by water flowing through joints, the fragments tend to take on a spherical shape. The gradual rounding of the corners and edges of angular blocks is illustrated in Figure 5.10. The corners are attacked most readily because of the greater surface area for their volume as compared with the edges and faces. This process, called **spheroidal weathering**, gives the weathered rock a more rounded or spherical shape (Figure 5.10).

Sometimes during the formation of spheroidal boulders, successive shells separate from the rock's main body (Figure 5.11). Eventually the outer shells break off, allowing the chemical weathering activity to penetrate deeper into the boulder. This spherical scaling results because as the minerals in the rock weather to clay, they increase in size through the addition of water to their structure. This increased bulk exerts an outward force that causes concentric layers of rock to break loose and fall off.

Hence, chemical weathering does produce forces great enough to cause mechanical weathering. This type of spheroidal weathering in which shells spall off should not be confused with the phenomenon of sheeting discussed earlier. In sheeting, the

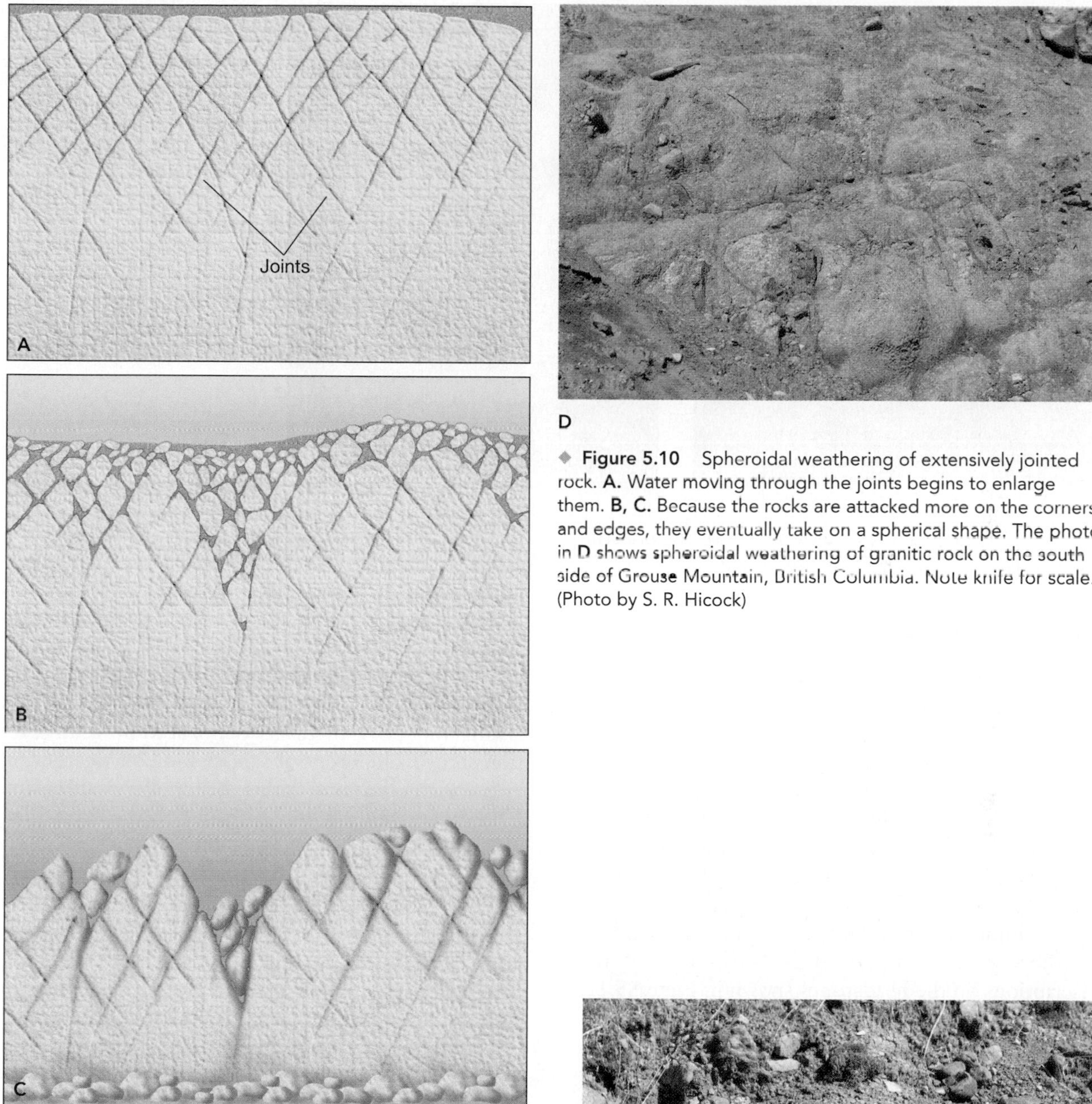

◆ **Figure 5.10** Spheroidal weathering of extensively jointed rock. **A.** Water moving through the joints begins to enlarge them. **B, C.** Because the rocks are attacked more on the corners and edges, they eventually take on a spherical shape. The photo in **D** shows spheroidal weathering of granitic rock on the south side of Grouse Mountain, British Columbia. Note knife for scale. (Photo by S. R. Hicock)

fracturing occurs as a result of unloading, and the rock layers that separate from the main body are largely unaltered at the time of separation.

RATES OF WEATHERING

GEODe EARTH Weathering and Soil
↳ Rates of Weathering

Several factors influence the type and rate of rock weathering. We have already seen how mechanical weathering affects the rate of weathering. By breaking rock into smaller pieces, the amount of surface area exposed to chemical weathering increases.

◆ **Figure 5.11** Successive shells are loosened as the weathering process continues to penetrate ever deeper into this ancient lava flow on south Vancouver Island. Note the orange oxidation on the surface of the basalt sphere (underneath the piece of rock held in hand).
(Photo by S. R. Hicock)

◆ **Figure 5.12** An examination of headstones reveals the rate of chemical weathering of diverse rock types. The granite headstone (left) was erected a few years after the marble headstone (right). The inscription date of 1885 on the marble monument is nearly illegible.
(Photos by E. J. Tarbuck)

Other important factors examined here include the roles of rock characteristics and climate.

Rock Characteristics

Rock characteristics encompass all of the chemical traits of rocks, including mineral composition and solubility. In addition, any physical features, such as joints, can be important because they influence the ability of water to penetrate rock (see Figure 5.6).

The variations in weathering rates because of the mineral constituents can be demonstrated by comparing old headstones made from different rock types. Headstones of granite, which is composed of silicate minerals, are relatively resistant to chemical weathering. We can see this by examining the inscriptions on the headstones shown in Figure 5.12. In contrast, the marble headstone shows signs of extensive chemical alteration over a relatively short period. Marble is composed of calcite (calcium carbonate), which readily dissolves in even a weakly acidic solution.

The most abundant mineral group, the silicates, weathers in the order shown in Figure 5.13. This arrangement of minerals is identical to Bowen's reaction series. The order of silicate mineral weathering is essentially the same as their order of crystallization. The explanation for this is related to the crystalline structure of silicate minerals. Silicon–oxygen bonds are very strong. Because quartz is composed entirely of these strong covalent bonds, it is very resistant to weathering. By contrast, olivine has fewer silicon–oxygen bonds and is not nearly as resistant to chemical weathering. Furthermore, olivine crystallizes at a

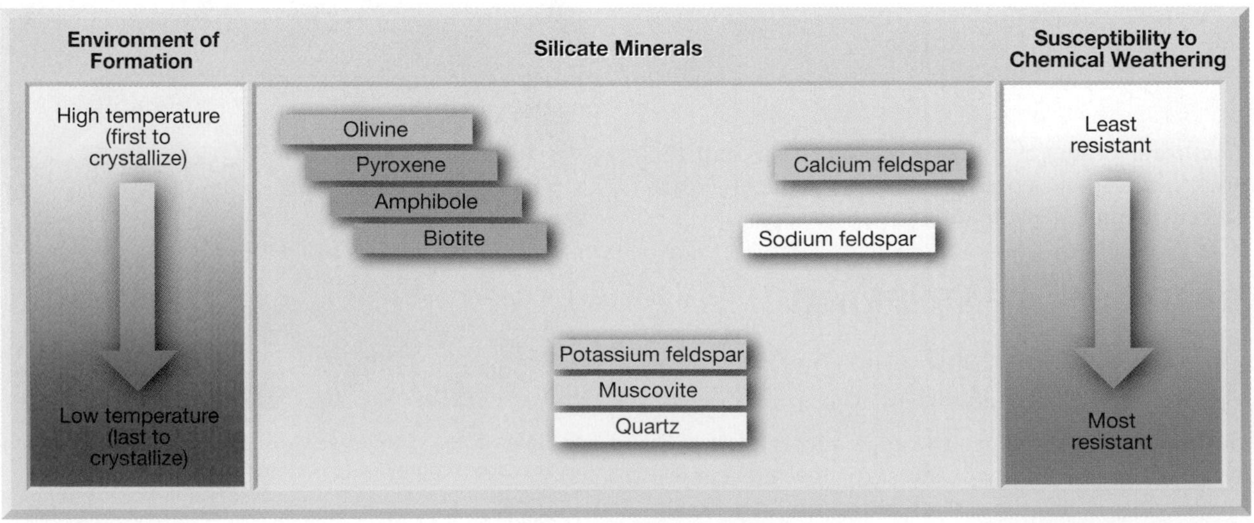

◆ **Figure 5.13** The weathering of common silicate minerals. The order in which the silicate minerals chemically weather is essentially the same as their order of crystallization in Bowen's reaction series (Chapter 3).

much higher temperature than quartz, whose melting point is closer to weathering temperatures. Because they are already the products of weathering, oxides, hydroxides, and clay minerals tend to be most resistant to weathering.

Climate

Climatic factors, particularly temperature and moisture, are crucial to the rate of rock weathering. One important example from mechanical weathering is that the frequency of freeze–thaw cycles greatly affects the amount of frost wedging. Temperature and moisture also exert a strong influence on rates of chemical weathering and on the kind and amount of vegetation present. Regions with lush vegetation generally have a thick mantle of soil rich in decayed organic matter from which chemically active fluids containing carbonic acid and humic acids are derived.

The optimum environment for chemical weathering is a combination of warm temperatures and abundant moisture. In polar regions, chemical weathering is ineffective because frigid temperatures keep the available moisture locked up as ice; in arid regions, there is insufficient moisture to foster rapid chemical weathering.

As discussed in Box 5.1, human activities influence the composition of the atmosphere, which in turn affects the rate of chemical weathering.

Differential Weathering

Masses of rock do not weather uniformly; they do so unevenly. This is called **differential weathering**. Look back at the photo of a volcanic neck in Figure 4.27. The durable igneous mass stands above the surrounding terrain like a stone tower. Figure 5.1 shows an additional example of the phenomenon of differential weathering. The results vary in scale from the rough, uneven surface of the marble headstone in Figure 5.12, to the boldly sculpted exposures of Drumheller, Alberta (Figure 1.4), to the steep cliffs of Mount Robson, Castle Mountain, and Mount Rundle in the Rocky Mountains of Alberta.

Many factors influence the rate of rock weathering. Among the most important are variations in the composition of the rock, including the size of its particles. More resistant rock protrudes as ridges or pinnacles, or as steeper cliffs on an irregular hillside, whereas finer rocks, like shale, tend to erode more easily. The number and spacing of joints can also be a significant factor (see Figures 5.6 and 5.10). Differential weathering and subsequent erosion are responsible for creating many unusual and sometimes spectacular rock formations and landforms.

SOIL

Soil covers most land surfaces. Along with air and water, it is one of our most indispensable resources (Figure 5.14). Like air and water, soil is taken for granted by many of us. The following quote helps put this vital layer in perspective.

> Science, in recent years, has focused more and more on the Earth as a planet, one that for all we know is unique—where a thin blanket of air, a thinner film of water, and the thinnest veneer of soil combine to support a web of life of wondrous diversity in continuous change.*

Soil has accurately been called "the bridge between life and the inanimate world." All life—the entire biosphere—owes its existence to a dozen or so elements that ultimately come from Earth's crust. Once weathering and other processes create soil, plants carry out the intermediary role of assimilating the necessary elements and making them available to animals, including humans.

An Interface in the Earth System

Within the Earth system, soil is an important *interface*—a common boundary at which different parts of

◆ **Figure 5.14** Soil is an essential resource that we often take for granted. Soil is not a living entity, but it contains a great deal of life. Moreover, this complex medium supports nearly all plant life, which, in turn, supports animal life. (Photo by Tom Bean/Corbis/Stock Market)

*J. Eddy, "A Fragile Seam of Dark Blue Light," in *Proceedings of the Global Change Research Forum*. U.S. Geological Survey Circular 1086, 1993, p. 15.

a system interact. Indeed, soil forms where the geosphere, the atmosphere, the hydrosphere, and the biosphere meet. Soil forms through complex environmental interactions among different parts of the Earth system. Over time, soil evolves toward equilibrium with the environment. Soil is sensitive to environmental changes, such as climate, vegetative cover, and animal (including human) activity.

What Is Soil?

With few exceptions, Earth's land surface is covered by **regolith** (*rhegos* = blanket, *lithos* = stone), the layer of rock and mineral fragments produced by weathering. Some would call this material soil. By definition, however, **soil** is a combination of mineral and organic matter, water, and air—that portion of the regolith that supports the growth of plants. Although the proportions of the major components in soil vary, the same four components always are present to some extent (Figure 5.15). About one half of the total volume of a good-quality surface soil is a mixture of disintegrated and decomposed rock (mineral matter) and **humus**, the decayed remains of animal and plant life (organic matter). The remaining half consists of pore spaces among the solid particles where air and water circulate.

Although the mineral portion of the soil is usually much greater than the organic portion, humus is an essential component. In addition to being an important source of plant nutrients, humus enhances the soil's ability to retain water. Because plants require air and water to live and grow, the portion of the soil consisting of pore spaces that allow for the circulation of these fluids is as vital as the solid soil constituents.

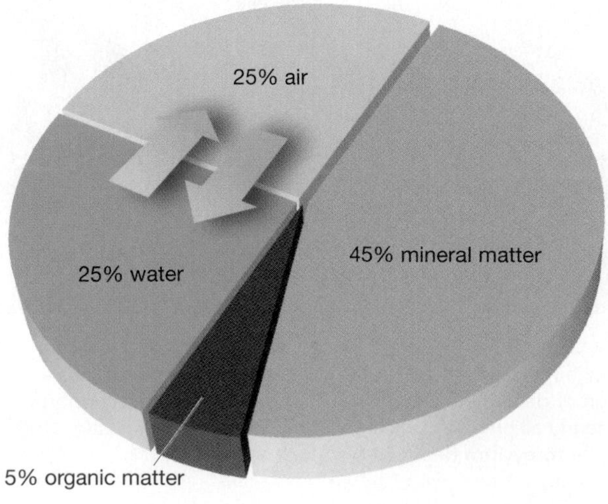

◆ **Figure 5.15** Composition (by volume) of a soil in good condition for plant growth. Although the percentages vary, each soil is composed of mineral and organic matter, water, and air.

Soil water is far from "pure" water; instead, it is a complex solution containing many nutrients. Soil water not only provides the necessary moisture for the chemical reactions that sustain life but also supplies plants with nutrients in a form they can use.

The open spaces not filled with water contain air. This air is the source of necessary oxygen and carbon dioxide for most microorganisms and plants that live in the soil.

CONTROLS OF SOIL FORMATION

Soil is the product of the complex interplay of several factors, including parent material, time, climate, plants and animals, and topography. Although all these factors are interdependent, their roles will be examined separately.

Parent Material

The source of the weathered mineral matter from which soils develop is called the **parent material** and is a major factor influencing a newly forming soil. Gradually, it undergoes physical and chemical changes as the soil develops. Parent material can either be bedrock or a layer of unconsolidated deposits. When the parent material is bedrock, the soils are termed *residual soils*. By contrast, those developed on unconsolidated sediment transported from elsewhere are called *transported soils* (Figure 5.16)—that is, the soil develops in place on transported parent material, such as the glacial deposits that cover much of Canada.

The nature of the parent material influences soils in two ways. First, the type of parent material will affect the rate of weathering and thus the rate of soil formation. Also, because unconsolidated deposits are already partly weathered, soil development on such material progresses more rapidly than on bedrock. Second, the chemical makeup of the parent material affects the soil's fertility. This influences the character of the natural vegetation the soil can support.

At one time the parent material was believed to be the primary factor causing differences among soils. Today, soil scientists realize that other factors, especially climate, are more important. In fact, it has been found that similar soils are often produced from different parent materials and that dissimilar soils can develop from the same parent material. For example, an organic-rich soil formed on granite in a temperate climate, such as Nova Scotia or northern Ontario, will be quite different from a soil formed on granite in a desert. Such discoveries reinforce the importance of other soil-forming factors.

Figure 5.16 The parent material for residual soils is the underlying bedrock, whereas transported soils form on unconsolidated deposits. Also note that as slopes become steeper, soil becomes thinner.

Time

Time is an important component of every geologic process, and soil formation is no exception. The nature of soil is strongly influenced by the length of time that soil-forming processes have been operating. If weathering has been going on for a comparatively short time, the character of the parent material determines to a large extent the characteristics of the soil. As weathering processes continue, the influence of parent material on soil is overshadowed by the other soil-forming factors, especially climate. The amount of time required for various soils to evolve cannot be listed, because the soil-forming processes act at varying rates under different circumstances. However, as a rule, the longer a soil has been forming, the thicker it becomes and the less it resembles the parent material.

Climate

Climate is considered to be the most influential control of soil formation. Temperature and precipitation are the elements that exert the strongest impact on soil formation. Variations in temperature and precipitation determine whether chemical or mechanical weathering will predominate and also greatly influence the rate and depth of weathering. For instance, a hot, wet climate may produce a thick layer of chemically weathered soil in the same amount of time that a cold, dry climate produces a thin mantle of mechanically weathered debris. The amount of precipitation influences the degree to which various materials are leached from the soil, thereby affecting soil fertility. Finally, climatic conditions are an important control on the type of plant and animal life present.

Plants and Animals

Plants and animals play a vital role in soil formation. The types and abundance of organisms present have a strong influence on the physical and chemical properties of a soil. In fact, for well-developed soils in many regions, the significance of natural vegetation in influencing soil type is frequently implied in the description used by soil scientists. Such phrases as *prairie soil*, *forest soil*, and *tundra soil* are common.

Plants and animals supply organic matter to the soil. Certain bog soils are composed almost entirely of organic matter, whereas desert soils might contain less than 1 percent. Although the quantity of organic matter varies substantially among soils, only rarely does soil lack it completely.

The primary source of organic matter in soil is plants, although animals and an incredible number of microorganisms also contribute. When organic matter is decomposed, important nutrients are supplied to plants, animals, and microorganisms living in the soil. Consequently, soil fertility is in part related to the amount of organic matter present. Furthermore, the decay of plant and animal remains causes the formation of various organic acids. These complex acids hasten the weathering process. Organic matter also absorbs water and thus aids water retention in a soil.

Microorganisms, including fungi, bacteria, and single-celled protozoa, play an active role in the decay of plant and animal remains. The end product is humus, an earthy looking material that no longer resembles the plants and animals from which it is formed. In addition, certain microorganisms aid soil fertility because they have the ability to convert atmospheric nitrogen into soil nitrogen.

Earthworms and other burrowing animals mix the mineral and organic portions of a soil. Earthworms, for example, feed on organic matter and thoroughly mix soils in which they live, often moving and enriching tonnes per hectare each year. Burrows and holes also aid the passage of water and air through the soil.

Topography

The slope of the land can vary greatly over short distances. Such variations, in turn, can lead to the development of a variety of localized soil types. Many of the differences exist because slope strongly influences the amount of erosion and the water content of soil.

On steep slopes, soils are often poorly developed. In such situations little water soaks in and, as a result, the moisture content of the soil may be insufficient for vigorous plant growth. Further, because of accelerated erosion on steep slopes, the soils are thin or in some cases nonexistent (Figure 5.16).

In contrast, poorly drained and waterlogged soils found in lowlands have a much different character. Such soils are usually thick and dark. The dark colour results from the large quantity of organic matter that accumulates because saturated conditions retard the decay of vegetation. The optimum terrain for soil development is a flat to undulating upland surface, which produces good drainage, minimum erosion, and sufficient infiltration of water into the soil.

Slope orientation is another factor we should note. In the mid latitudes of the Northern Hemisphere, a south-facing slope will receive a great deal more sunlight than a north-facing slope. In fact, a steep north-facing slope may receive no direct sunlight at all. The difference in the amount of solar radiation received will cause differences in soil temperature and moisture, which in turn influence the nature of the vegetation and the character of the soil.

Although this section deals separately with each of the soil-forming factors, remember that they all interact to form soil. No single factor is responsible for a soil's character; it is the combined influence of parent material, time, climate, plants and animals, and topography.

THE SOIL PROFILE

Because soil-forming processes operate from the surface downward, variations in composition, texture, structure, and colour gradually evolve at varying depths. These vertical differences, which usually become more pronounced as time passes, form distinctive zones or layers known as **horizons**. A vertical section through all of the soil horizons, as would be observed in a trench, constitutes the **soil profile** (Figure 5.17).

Figure 5.18 presents an idealized view of a well-developed soil profile with five distinct horizons. From the surface downward, they are designated as *O*, *A*, *E*, *B*, and *C*. These five horizons are common in soil profiles of temperate regions. The characteristics and extent of development of horizons vary in different environments. Thus, different localities can exhibit soil profiles that contrast greatly with one another.

The *O* soil horizon consists largely of organic material. This is in contrast to the layers beneath it, which consist mainly of mineral matter. The upper portion of the *O* horizon is primarily plant litter, such as loose leaves and other organic debris that are still recognizable. By contrast, the lower portion of the *O* horizon is made up of partly decomposed organic matter (humus) with no identifiable plant structures. In addition to plants, the *O* horizon is teeming with microscopic life, including bacteria, fungi, protozoa, and insects, that contribute oxygen, carbon dioxide, and organic acids to the developing soil.

Underlying the organic-rich *O* horizon is the *A* horizon. This zone is largely mineral matter, yet biologic activity is high, and humus is generally present—up to 30 percent in some instances. Together, the *O* and *A* horizons make up what is commonly called the *topsoil*. Below the *A* horizon, the *E* horizon is a light-coloured layer that contains little organic material. As water percolates downward through this zone, finer particles are carried away, a process called **eluviation** (*elu* = get away from, *via* =

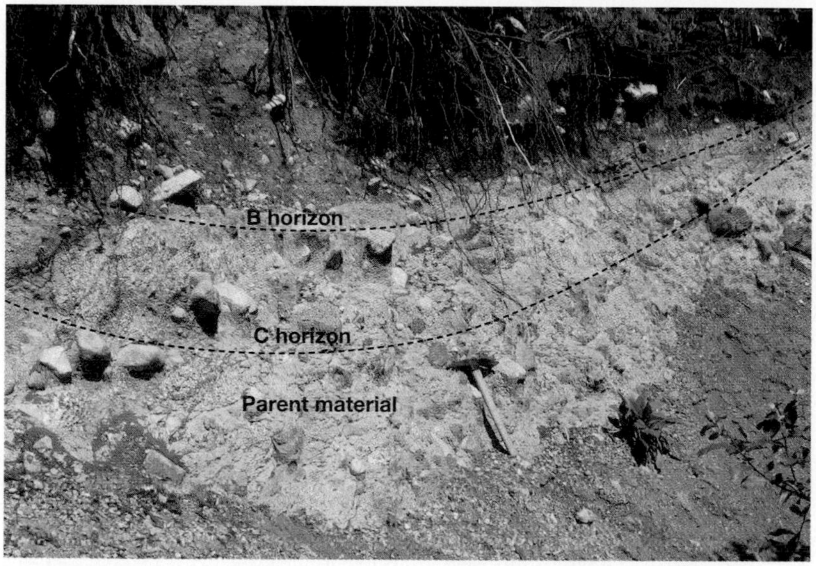

◆ **Figure 5.17** A soil profile is a vertical cross-section from the surface down to the parent material (grey sediment in this case). Well-developed soils show distinct layers called horizons. In this photo an upper rusty horizon (B horizon) rests on a lower pale horizon (C horizon) underlain by grey parent material (in this case, glacial till). (Photo by S. R. Hicock)

a way). Downward percolation of water also dissolves soluble inorganic soil components and carries them to deeper zones. This process is called **leaching**.

Immediately below the *E* horizon is the *B* horizon, or *subsoil*. Much of the material removed from the *E* horizon by eluviation is deposited in the *B* horizon, or *zone of accumulation*. The accumulation of the fine clay particles enhances water retention in the subsoil. The *O*, *A*, *E*, and *B* horizons together constitute the **solum**, or "true soil." It is in the solum that the soil-forming processes are active and that living roots and other plant and animal life are largely confined. In Figure 5.17 the upper rusty *B* horizon is visible above the pale *C* horizon; the *O*, *A*, and *E* horizons occur above the *B*, just out of view.

Below the solum and above the unaltered parent material is the *C* horizon, a layer characterized by partially altered parent material. Whereas the *O*, *A*, *E*, and *B* horizons bear little resemblance to the parent material, it is easily identifiable in the *C* horizon (Figure 5.17). Although this material is undergoing changes that will eventually transform it into soil, it has not yet crossed the threshold that separates regolith from soil.

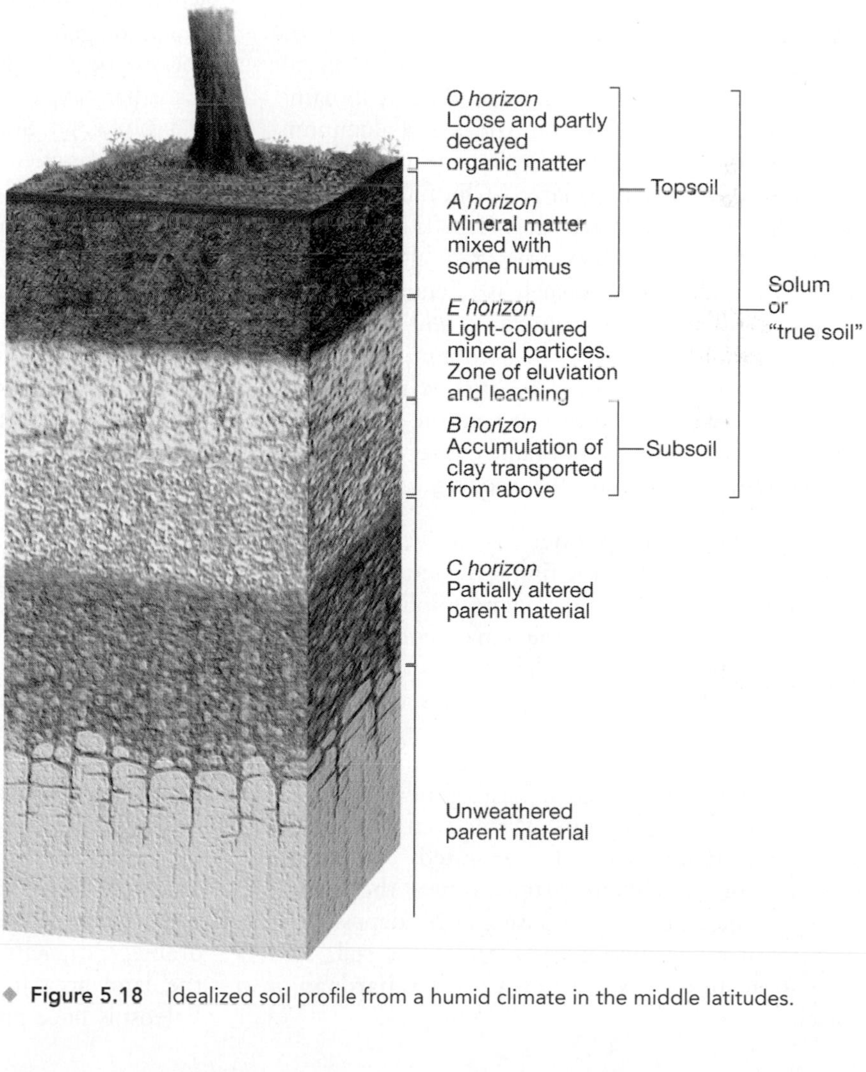

◆ **Figure 5.18** Idealized soil profile from a humid climate in the middle latitudes.

The characteristics and extent of development can vary greatly among soils in different environments. The boundaries between soil horizons can be sharp or gradual. Consequently, a well-developed soil profile indicates that environmental conditions have been relatively stable over an extended time span and that the soil is *mature*.

By contrast, some soils lack horizons altogether. Such soils are called *immature* because soil building has been going on for only a short time. Immature soils are also common on steep slopes, where erosion continually strips away the soil, preventing full development.

SOIL TYPES

We have many ways to classify soils, and literally hundreds of names are applied to soils in different areas of the world. Excluding the poorly developed soils of cold and dry regions, most soils can be classified in the context of three soil types, according to prevailing climatic conditions: pedalfer, pedocal, and laterite.

Pedalfer The term **pedalfer** is derived from the Greek *pedon* (soil) plus the chemical symbols for aluminum (Al) and iron (Fe). As implied by its name, a pedalfer is enriched in iron oxides and aluminum-rich clays in the *B* horizon of the soil profile. This soil type develops in relatively humid temperate climates of Pacific and southeast Canada and the eastern United States. In these areas, rainfall is sufficient to leach soluble minerals, such as calcium carbonate, from the soil and carry iron oxides and clays downward to produce a rusty brown-coloured *B* horizon (Figure 5.17). These soils are organic-rich and are best developed under forest vegetation, where large amounts of decomposing organic matter produce the acid conditions necessary for leaching.

Pedocal The term **pedocal** is derived from the Greek *pedon* (soil), plus the first three letters of calcite (calcium carbonate). As the name implies, pedocals are characterized by a high calcium carbonate content. This soil type is found in the prairies of southwest Canada and the western United States, where vegetation is dominated by temperate grassland and brush vegetation. Because chemical weathering is less intense in drier areas, pedocals generally contain less clay than do pedalfers. Water contained in the soil is drawn upward and evaporated, causing the precipitation of calcium carbonate near the surface. In high concentrations, calcite can be deposited as nodules or a continuous layer within the soil. This type of calcite-cemented soil is known as **hardpan** or **caliche**.

Laterite In the hot, wet climates of the tropics, soils called **laterites** (after the Latin *latericius*, meaning "brick") may develop. Because chemical weathering is intense under such conditions, these soils are much deeper and denser (like brick) than soils developing over a similar period in temperate regions. Not only does leaching remove soluble materials, such as calcite, but the great quantities of percolating water also remove much of the silica, resulting in the concentration of the upper soil profile with iron and aluminum. The iron gives the soil a distinctive red colour. As bacterial activity is very high in the tropics, laterites contain practically no humus. This fact, coupled with the highly leached and bricklike nature of these soils, makes laterites poor for growing crops. The infertility of this soil has been demonstrated repeatedly in tropical countries where cultivation has expanded into such areas.

The Canadian Soil Classification System

Although the classification of soils by climate is useful when discussing soils in a global context, it becomes much too general when considering the types of soils specific to a single country, such as Canada. In the Canadian soil classification system, coordinated by the Canadian Soil Classification Working Group, soils are classified in a hierarchical system, similar to that used to study organisms in biology. The levels of hierarchy are, from highest to lowest: orders, great groups, groups, subgroups, families, and series. Attributes of the 10 major categories, or orders, of Canadian soils are summarized in Table 5.2 and their geographic distribution in Canada is shown in Figure 5.19. Other countries use similar classification schemes that are tailored to the climatic conditions and zones of vegetation of those nations.

Ancient Soils: Paleosols

In the past couple of decades, geologists have come to appreciate the significance of *paleosols* ("ancient soils") that record soil-forming conditions of Earth's past. Paleosols serve as valuable indicators of past land areas and many have been found to contain features that are similar to those observed in various modern soils. Such features include traces and remains of plant roots, cracks produced by repeated wetting and drying, horizons showing the reduction or oxidation of iron, and beds of caliche. Specific combinations of such features preserved in any given paleosol can provide information on water content, drainage capacity, fertility, and other attributes of the land area in which the original soil formed. Paleosols have proven particularly useful in studies

TABLE 5.2 **Generalized Descriptions of Canadian Soils According to the Canadian Soil Classification System**

Soil Order	Distinguishing Features of Soil Profile	Environments of Soil Formation
Regosolic	Very poor development of *A* and *B* horizons	Areas where mass wasting or repeated influx of parent material prevents significant maturation of soil profile
Chernozemic	Dark, brown to black-coloured (organic-rich) *A* horizon grading downward into *B* horizon	Cool subarid to subhumid grasslands and forest-grassland transition zones
Brunisolic	Brown-coloured *B* horizon	Young forested areas affected by relatively dry climatic conditions and long winters
Gleysolic	*B* horizon, commonly grey or mottled with grey and red	Areas affected by frequent flooding or poor drainage where iron reduction is prevalent
Luvisolic	Strongly leached *A* horizon and a clay-rich *B* horizon	Areas hosting deciduous or mixed forest with moderate to cool climate and calcareous parent material
Podzolic	Poorly decomposed organic layer, strongly leached *A* horizon, clay- and aluminum/iron-rich *B* horizon	Cool, moist, temperate areas dominated by coniferous forest and strongly affected by leaching
Solonetzic	High salt content at or near soil surface, iron-stained *B* horizons, salt-rich *C* horizon	Semi-arid climates where evaporation is extreme; vegetation is dominated by grass or mixed grass-forest cover
Organic	Very high organic content and low mineral content	Cool, wet areas where organic matter accumulation is high
Cryosolic	Layer of permafrost within 1 metre of the soil surface; disruption of soil horizons by repeated freezing and thawing	Tundra landscape dominated by moss and lichens
Vertisolic	Clay rich, with deep cracks and other disruptive features because of repeated shrinking and swelling	Semi-arid regions of Canadian Prairies underlain by parent material rich in swelling clays; distribution highly localized

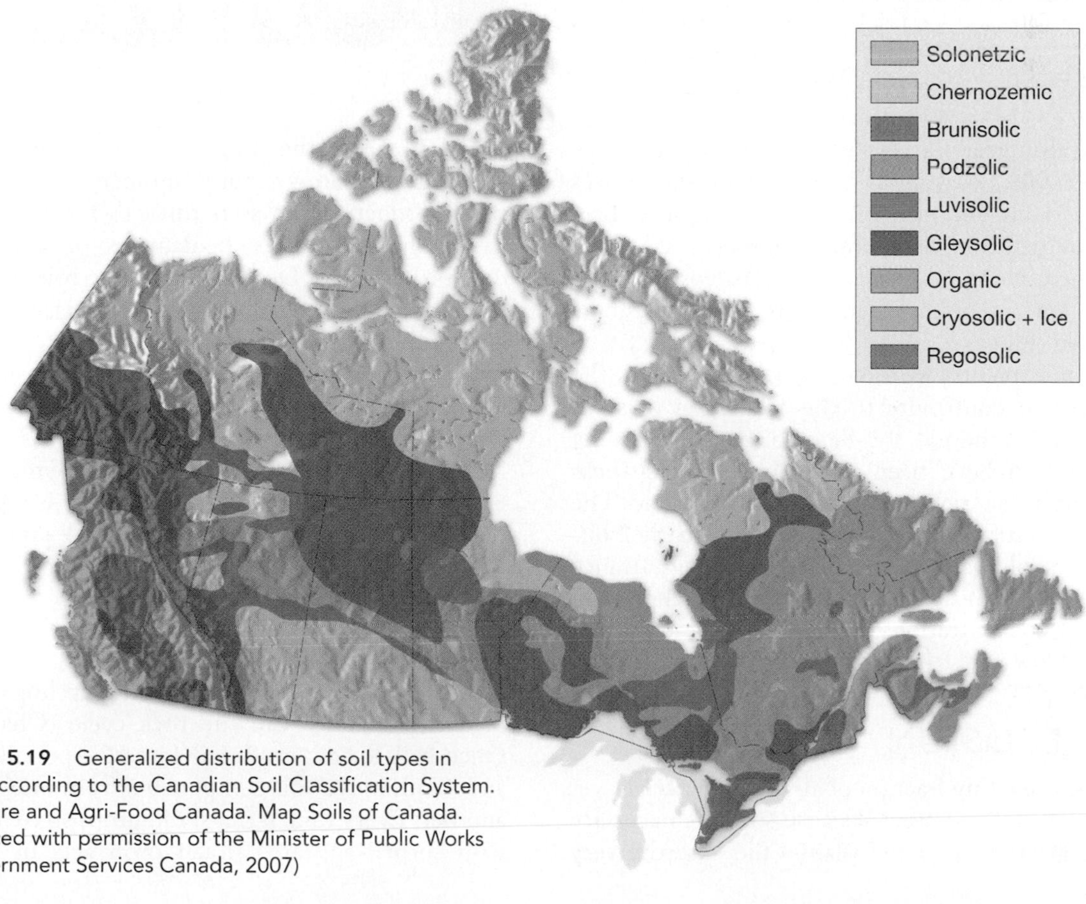

◆ **Figure 5.19** Generalized distribution of soil types in Canada according to the Canadian Soil Classification System. (Agriculture and Agri-Food Canada. Map Soils of Canada. Reproduced with permission of the Minister of Public Works and Government Services Canada, 2007)

A

B

◆ **Figure 5.20** **A.** Exhumed rusty paleosol developed on ancient pillow lavas during a warm interglacial episode on south Vancouver Island, early in the last Ice Age. **B.** A paleosol preserved in a Cretaceous coastal plain deposit of British Columbia. In this case, soil development occurred in mudstone with alternating organic-rich (dark-coloured) and organic-poor (light-coloured) layers. The drab colour of the paleosol indicates that iron in the soil was not oxidized, probably because of poor soil drainage on a coastal plain. The thin, dark-coloured lines are fossil plant roots that penetrate through the sedimentary layers of the parent material of the soil. The small increments of the scale bar represent centimetres.
(Photo **A** by S. R. Hicock; photo **B** by Guy Plint)

of glacial-interglacial cycles of the last Ice Age (Figure 5.20A), serving as indicators of fluctuations in temperature and rates of precipitation. To be preserved in the geologic record, a soil must reside in an area where it can be buried. Thus, paleosols developed in lowland or coastal areas are most likely to be preserved (Figure 5.20B).

Land plants were not present before the Paleozoic to contribute to the formation of soils. However, weathered, soil-like horizons containing oxidized iron have been noted in very old rocks extending as far back in time as the Proterozoic. The oldest of such horizons, estimated to be nearly 2 billion years old, are of great geologic significance because they indicate that oxygen levels had reached sufficient concentrations in the atmosphere by that time to allow iron to rust on land.

SOIL EROSION

Soils are just a tiny fraction of all Earth materials, yet they are a vital resource. Because soils are necessary for the growth of rooted plants, they are the very foundation of the human life-support system. Although human ingenuity can increase the agricultural productivity of soils through fertilization and irrigation, soils can also be damaged or destroyed by careless activities. Despite their basic role in providing food, fibre, and other basic materials, soils are among our most abused resources.

Perhaps this neglect and indifference has occurred because a substantial amount of soil seems to remain even where soil erosion is serious. Nevertheless, although the loss of fertile topsoil may not be obvious to the untrained eye, it is a growing problem as human activities expand and disturb more and more of Earth's surface.

How Soil Is Eroded

Soil erosion is part of the constant recycling of Earth materials that we call the rock cycle (Chapter 1). Once soil forms, erosional forces, especially water and wind, move soil components from one place to another. Every time it rains, raindrops strike the land with surprising force. Each drop acts like a tiny

◆ **Figure 5.21** When it is raining, millions of water drops are falling at velocities approaching 10 metres per second (35 kilometres per hour). When water drops strike an exposed surface, soil particles may splash as high as 1 metre into the air and land more than a metre away from the point of raindrop impact. Soil dislodged by splash erosion is more easily moved by sheet erosion.
(Photo courtesy of Soil Conservation Service/ U.S. Department of Agriculture)

bomb, blasting moveable soil particles out of their positions in the soil mass (Figure 5.21).

Then, water flowing across the surface carries away the dislodged soil particles. Because the soil is moved by thin sheets of water, this process is termed *sheet erosion*.

After flowing as a thin, unconfined sheet for a relatively short distance, threads of current typically develop, and tiny channels called *rills* begin to form. When normal farm cultivation cannot eliminate the channels, we know the rills have grown large enough to be called *gullies* (Figure 5.22). Although most dislodged soil particles move only a short distance during each rainfall, substantial quantities eventually leave the fields and make their way downslope to a stream. Once in the stream channel, these soil particles, which can now be called *sediment*, are transported downstream and eventually deposited.

Rates of Erosion

We know that soil erosion is the ultimate fate of practically all soils. In the past, erosion occurred at slower rates than it does today because more of the land surface was covered and protected by trees, shrubs, grasses, and other plants. However, human activities, such as farming, logging, and construction, which remove or disrupt the natural vegetation, have greatly accelerated the rate of soil erosion. Without the stabilizing effect of plants, the soil is more easily swept away by the wind or carried downslope by sheet wash.

◆ **Figure 5.22** Gully erosion in poorly protected laterite soil, southern Colombia.
(Photo by Carl Purcell/Photo Researchers, Inc.)

Natural rates of soil erosion vary greatly from one place to another and depend on soil characteristics, as well as on such factors as climate, topography, and type of vegetation. Over a broad area, erosion caused by surface runoff can be estimated by determining the sediment loads of streams that drain the region. When studies of this kind were made on a global scale, they indicated that before the appearance of humans, sediment transport by rivers to the ocean amounted to more than 9 billion tonnes per year. By contrast, the amount of material currently transported to the sea by rivers is about 24 billion tonnes per year—more than two and a half times the earlier rate.

It is more difficult to measure the loss of soil through wind erosion. Soil removal by wind is generally much less significant than by water erosion, except during periods of prolonged drought. When dry conditions prevail, strong winds can remove large quantities of soil from unprotected fields. Such was the case in the 1930s in the prairie lands that came to be called the Dust Bowl (see Box 5.2).

In many regions the rate of soil erosion is significantly greater than the rate of soil formation.

BOX 5.2

People and the Environment

Return to the Dust Bowl?

During a span of dry years in the 1930s, large dust storms plagued the Canadian Prairies and Great Plains of the United States. Because of the size and severity of these storms, the region came to be called the Dust Bowl, and the decade, the Dirty Thirties. The heart of the Dust Bowl was nearly 40 million hectares in the panhandles of Texas and Oklahoma and adjacent parts of Colorado, New Mexico, and Kansas.

Meanwhile, in Canada, low rainfall rates in the early thirties caused severe shortages of surface water and groundwater. Farmers desperately planted seed in the dry fields only to see it blown away along with the topsoil. Many Canadian farmers fell deeply into debt and moved to cities to look for new jobs. Between the late 1920s and early 1930s, the average income of Prairie families dropped more than 90 percent.

◆ **Figure 5.B** Dust storm near Edmonton, Alberta, in the summer of 2000. (Photo by L. Peleshok)

What caused the Dust Bowl? Clearly, the fact that portions of the Prairies and Great Plains experience some of North America's strongest winds is important. However, it was the expansion of agriculture that set the stage for the disastrous period of soil erosion. Thanks to mechanization, cultivation expanded nearly tenfold between the 1870s and 1930. When precipitation was adequate, the soil remained in place. However, the prolonged drought conditions of the 1930s rendered the unprotected fields prone to wind erosion. Only in the late 1930s, when precipitation rates increased, was soil erosion again reduced.

Soil conservation practices have greatly improved since the Dust Bowl era. In particular, farmers minimize tilling and leave a layer of stubble on the ground to reduce soil erosion. Still, the severity of summer droughts in the past couple of decades serves as an eerie reminder of the Dust Bowl years (Figure 5.B), and 2001 and 2002 were reportedly the driest years in more than a century for parts of Alberta and Saskatchewan, significantly reducing hay and grain productivity. The hay shortage forced many cattle ranchers to sell much of their herd. Forest fires, grasshopper epidemics, and dust storms were commonplace. Despite an abnormally wet summer in 2005, the Prairies again experienced severe drought in 2007, when a heat wave spread over much of western North America during the summer months. Many fear that global warming is contributing to the severe conditions recently witnessed in the Prairies, signalling a possible return to Dust Bowl conditions in the future.

This means that a renewable resource has become non-renewable in these places. At present, it is estimated that topsoil is eroding faster than it forms on more than one third of the world's croplands. The result is lower productivity, poorer crop quality, reduced agricultural income, and an uncertain future.

Sedimentation and Chemical Pollution

Another problem related to excessive soil erosion involves the deposition of sediment. Each year in North America hundreds of millions of tonnes of eroded soil are deposited in lakes, reservoirs, and streams. The detrimental impact of this process can be significant. For example, as more and more sediment is deposited in a reservoir, the capacity of the reservoir is diminished, limiting its usefulness for flood control, water supply, and hydroelectric power generation. In addition, sedimentation in streams and other waterways can restrict navigation and lead to costly dredging operations.

In some cases soil particles are contaminated with pesticides used in farming. When these chemicals are introduced into a lake or reservoir, the quality of the water supply is threatened and aquatic organisms may be endangered. In addition to pesticides, nutrients found naturally in soils, as well as those added by agricultural fertilizers, make their way into streams and lakes, where they stimulate the growth of plants. Over time, excess nutrients accelerate the process by which plant growth and subsequent decay lead to the depletion of oxygen and death of the lake.

The availability of good soils is critical if the world's rapidly growing population is to be fed. On every continent unnecessary soil loss occurs as a result of a lack of conservation measures. Although it is a recognized fact that soil erosion can never be completely eliminated, soil conservation programs can substantially reduce its severity. Windbreaks (rows of trees), terracing, and plowing along the contours of hills are effective measures, as are special tillage practices and crop rotation. Innovative experiments on the use of waste material in soil remediation also hold great promise for the sustainability of soils (see Box 5.3).

BOX 5.3

People and the Environment

"Waste" Materials as Possible Resources for Land Regeneration

Brian Hart*

Land degradation is a concept that reflects the needs of humans and is typically a result of misuse through human-based activities (e.g., agricultural practices, overgrazing by livestock, and deforestation). In fact, there is really no such thing as "degraded" land. Even for land classified as "severely degraded" (beyond the point of regeneration—approximately 10 percent of the total degraded land worldwide), the only real constraints on regeneration are the amount and kind of financial inputs and sources that can be availed.

As population increases and soil conditions worsen, the perception of the amount of money that should be used to rejuvenate degraded soil will probably increase. This scenario is one of the major challenges facing the world today, and new technologies are drastically needed to meet the challenge. In a country like India, the health of soils and their ability to produce vegetative matter is a key issue for quality of life, especially when 75 percent of the population is rural and the vast majority of daily living requirements come from the land.

Inputs for increasing soil productivity have historically been confined to chemical fertilizers and water management. However, recent work has shown that the use of fertilizers can have negative effects on soil pH, microorganisms, groundwater, and surface water. Alternative measures to enhance the biotic function of soil by using various types of organic and inorganic additives are becoming increasingly more appealing and, because many of these materials are considered waste, they are also becoming more available.

Common by-products of human activities, such as composted sewage sludge (SS) and coal combustion ash (fly ash: FA) can be used as additives. Combined, they contain large amounts of organic matter, along with nitrogen, phosphorus, potassium, calcium, magnesium, and numerous beneficial trace elements. They can also act as conditioners to improve soil properties, such as aeration, bulk density, microbial activity, and water retention. This makes them favourable for use as amendments in poor quality soils.

The use of these materials does, however, have the potential to create environmental problems. Both materials can contain high concentrations of potentially toxic trace metals. These can accumulate in the soil, be mobilized into groundwater, taken up by plants, or transported to drinking water supplies, eventually entering the food chain. Therefore, with the potential for environmental damage, the importance of rigorous and

---

*Brian Hart is a research scientist at Surface Science Western and adjunct Professor in Earth Sciences, at the University of Western Ontario.

detailed analyses of the raw materials (SS and FA) and continual monitoring of the amended sites cannot be overemphasized.

What follows is a brief summary of an ongoing project conducted by scientists at the University of Western Ontario that seeks to demonstrate the technology of mixing FA with SS as a soil amendment to regenerate degraded lands in India. Amended sites were used to establish tree plantations and carry out edible crop trials. Growth rates, biomass production, and soil and vegetation analyses were conducted regularly over four years to assess the impact of the amendment.

◆ **Figure 5.C** Kandai plantation site, Chhattisgarh, India: a view of the area before the plantation was established. The soil is a highly weathered laterite, rich in Fe and Al (hence the red colour), very low in organic material, low in pH, low in nutrient availability, and poor in productivity. Soil temperatures in the summer months reach 60°C.
(Photo by Brian Hart)

Tree Plantations

Approximately 400 hectares of wasteland were brought under mixed plantation with more than 100 different tree species in various agricultural zones of India (Figure 5.C).

For the majority of the species planted at different sites, plant growth has proven successful (Figure 5.D). The four-year-old standing tree volume of *Gmelina arborea* (gamhar) shows 1.6 times more wood yield than that of the traditional methods and is estimated to rise to around two times in six years. The average survival rate of plants at all the sites on amended lateritic soil is around 85 percent.

Soil and vegetation analyses reveal no buildup of any heavy metal in the soil at any of the sites after four years of amendment application. The concentrations of most of the potentially toxic elements were within the normal ranges. No accumulation of any trace metal (beyond their respective threshold values) was found in vegetative tissues of plants on amended soils.

Edible Crop Trials

In addition to the 400 hectares of plantation, 3 hectares of agricultural trials were established to test the suitability of the technology on edible crops, like peanuts. Applications improved soil quality, resulting in crop growth responses better than, or similar to, traditional fertilizer inputs. Metal loading in soils was not observed after amendment application and metal content in crops and crop residues did not exceed recommended guidelines. Based on the trials, crop responses vary according to amendment composition, soil types, climatic conditions, and individual crops. For example, alkaline soils responded much better to high proportions of sludge in the mix; sludges tend to have a high content of organic acids and hence a low pH. However, for neutral or slightly acidic soils, high proportions of sludge in the mix reduce peanut production. Presumably, lower pH reduces the ability of soil microorganisms to promote the formation of root nodules and so nut production falls off.

For the most part, the results from the project were positive; the production of biomass in vegetation grown in mixtures of sludge and ash was equal to or greater than vegetation grown in traditionally fertilized soils. Furthermore, potential toxicity arising from metal accumulation after amendment was not observed. However, reduced nut production shows that the technology is not without its drawbacks. It is important to recognize that soils (degraded or not) are extremely variable and therefore amendments should be tailored for the soil to which they are applied.

◆ **Figure 5.D** The Kandai plantation 2.5 years after establishment. These trees (in treatments of soil amended with sludge and ash) are on average 1.5 times greater in girth than the trees planted with traditional amendments. Toxicity was not detected in the trees, nor was metal accumulation detected in the soil after amendment.
(Photo by Brian Hart)

Chapter Summary

- External processes include (1) *weathering*—the disintegration and decomposition of rock at or near Earth's surface, (2) *mass wasting*—the transfer of rock material downslope under the influence of gravity, and (3) *erosion*—the removal of material by a mobile agent, usually water, wind, or ice. They are called *external processes* because they occur at or near Earth's surface and are powered by energy from the Sun or Earth's gravity. By contrast, *internal processes*, such as volcanism and mountain building, derive their energy from Earth's interior.
- *Mechanical weathering* is the physical breaking up of rock into smaller pieces. Rocks can be broken into smaller fragments by *frost wedging* (where water works its way into cracks or voids in rock and, on freezing, expands and enlarges the openings), *unloading* (expansion and breaking because of a great reduction in pressure when the overlying rock is eroded away), and *biologic activity* (by humans, burrowing animals, plant roots, etc.).
- *Chemical weathering* alters a rock's chemistry, changing it into different substances. Water is by far the most important agent of chemical weathering. *Dissolution* occurs when water-soluble minerals, such as halite, become dissolved in water. Oxygen dissolved in water will oxidize iron-rich minerals. When carbon dioxide (CO_2) is dissolved in water, it forms carbonic acid, which accelerates the decomposition of silicate minerals by *hydrolysis*. The chemical weathering of silicate minerals frequently produces (1) soluble products containing sodium, calcium, potassium, and magnesium ions, and silica in solution; (2) insoluble iron oxides; and (3) clay minerals.
- The rate at which rock weathers depends on such factors as (1) particle size—small pieces generally weather faster than large pieces; (2) mineral makeup—calcite readily dissolves in mildly acidic solutions, and silicate minerals that form first from magma are least resistant to chemical weathering; and (3) climatic factors, particularly temperature and moisture. Frequently, rocks exposed at Earth's surface do not weather at the same rate. This *differential weathering* of rocks is influenced by such factors as mineral makeup and degree of jointing.
- *Soil* is a combination of mineral and organic matter, water, and air, and is the portion of the *regolith* (the layer of rock and mineral fragments produced by weathering) that supports the growth of plants. About half of the total volume of a good-quality soil is a mixture of disintegrated and decomposed rock (mineral matter) and *humus* (the decayed remains of animal and plant life); the remaining half consists of pore spaces, where air and water circulate. The most important factors that control soil formation are *parent material, time, climate, plants and animals*, and *topography*.
- Soil-forming processes operate from the surface downward and produce zones or layers in the soil that are called *horizons*. From the surface downward, the soil horizons are, respectively, designated as *O* (largely organic matter), *A* (largely mineral matter), *E* (where the fine soil components and soluble materials have been removed by *eluviation* and *leaching*), *B* (or subsoil, often referred to as the zone of accumulation), and *C* (partially altered parent material). Together the *O* and *A* horizons make up what is commonly called the topsoil.
- Although hundreds of soil types and subtypes exist worldwide, the three generic types are (1) *pedalfer*—characterized by an accumulation of iron oxides and aluminum-rich clays in the *B* horizon; (2) *pedocal*—characterized by an accumulation of calcium carbonate; and (3) *laterite*—deep soils that develop in the hot, wet tropics and are poor for growing crops because they are highly leached.
- Soil erosion is a natural process; it is part of the constant recycling of Earth materials that we call the rock cycle. Once in a stream channel, soil particles are transported downstream and eventually deposited. Rates of soil erosion vary from one place to another and depend on the soil's characteristics, as well as on such factors as climate, topography, and type of vegetation.

Review Questions

1. Describe the role of external processes in the rock cycle.
2. If two identical rocks were weathered, one mechanically and the other chemically, how would the products of weathering differ?
3. In what type of environment is frost wedging most effective?
4. Describe the processes of sheeting and spheroidal weathering. How are they different and how are they similar?
5. How does mechanical weathering add to the effectiveness of chemical weathering?
6. Suppose that granite and basalt are exposed at the surface in a hot, wet region.
   (a) Which type of weathering will predominate?
   (b) Which of these rocks will weather most rapidly? Why?
7. Heat speeds up a chemical reaction. Why then does chemical weathering proceed slowly in a hot desert?
8. How is carbonic acid (H_2CO_3) formed in nature? What results when this acid reacts with potassium feldspar?
9. List some possible environmental effects of acid precipitation (see Box 5.1).
10. What is the difference between soil and regolith?
11. What factors might cause different soils to develop from the same parent material, or similar soils to form from different parent materials?
12. Which of the controls of soil formation is most important? Explain.
13. How can slope affect the development of soil? What is meant by the term *slope orientation*?
14. List the characteristics associated with each horizon in a well-developed soil profile. Which of the horizons constitute the solum? Under what circumstances do soils lack horizons?
15. Distinguish between pedalfers and pedocals.
16. What soil type is associated with tropical rainforests? This soil is associated with luxuriant natural vegetation, but is it also excellent for growing crops? Briefly explain.
17. List three detrimental effects of soil erosion other than the loss of topsoil from croplands.
18. Briefly describe the conditions that led to the Dust Bowl of the 1930s (see Box 5.2).

Key Terms

caliche (p. 140)
chemical weathering (p. 125)
differential weathering (p. 135)
dissolution (p. 129)
eluviation (p. 138)
erosion (p. 124)
exfoliation dome (p. 126)
external process (p. 124)
frost wedging (p. 125)
hardpan (p. 140)
horizon (p. 138)
humus (p. 136)
hydrolysis (p. 131)
internal process (p. 124)
laterite (p. 140)
leaching (p. 138)
mass wasting (p. 124)
mechanical weathering (p. 125)
oxidation (p. 131)
parent material (p. 136)
pedalfer (p. 140)
pedocal (p. 140)
regolith (p. 136)
sheeting (p. 126)
soil (p. 136)
soil profile (p. 138)
solum (p. 139)
spheroidal weathering (p. 132)
talus slope (p. 126)
weathering (p. 124)

Web Resources

The *Earth* website uses the resources and flexibility of the internet to aid in your study of the topics in this chapter. Written and developed by geology instructors, this site will help improve your understanding of geology. Visit **www.pearsoned.ca/tarbuck** and click on the cover of the text to find

- online review quizzes
- Web-based critical thinking and writing exercises
- links to chapter-specific Web resources
- internet-wide key-term searches

www.pearsoned.ca/tarbuck

Chapter 6

Sedimentary Rocks

Cambrian sedimentary rocks exposed below Popes Peak near Lake Louise, Alberta. (Photo by Christopher Collom)

Chapter 5 gave you the background needed to understand the origin of sedimentary rocks. Recall that weathering of existing rocks begins the process. Next, erosional agents, such as running water, wind, waves, and ice, remove the products of weathering and carry them to a new location, where they are deposited. Usually the particles are broken down further during the transport phase. Following deposition, this material, which is now called **sediment**, becomes lithified. In most cases, the sediment is lithified into solid sedimentary rock by the processes of compaction and cementation.

WHAT IS A SEDIMENTARY ROCK?

GEODe EARTH Sedimentary Rocks
↳ Introduction

The products of mechanical and chemical weathering constitute the raw materials for sedimentary rocks. The word *sedimentary* indicates the nature of these rocks, for it is derived from the Latin *sedimentum*, which means "to settle," a reference to solid material settling out of a fluid (water or air). Most sediment is deposited in this fashion. Weathered debris is continuously being swept from bedrock, carried away, and eventually deposited in lakes, river valleys, seas, and countless other places. The particles in a desert sand dune, the mud on the floor of a swamp, the gravel in a streambed, and even household dust are examples of this never-ending process. Because the weathering of bedrock and the transport and deposition of the weathering products are continuous, sediment is found almost everywhere. As piles of sediment accumulate, the materials near the bottom are compacted. Over long periods, these sediments become cemented together by mineral matter deposited in the spaces between particles, forming solid rock.

Geologists estimate that sedimentary rocks account for only about 5 percent (by volume) of Earth's outer 16 kilometres. However, the importance of this group of rocks is far greater than this percentage would imply. If we were to sample the rocks exposed at the surface, we would find that the great majority are sedimentary. Indeed, about 75 percent of all rock outcrops on the continents are sedimentary (Figure 6.1). Therefore, we can think of sedimentary rocks as being a relatively thin and somewhat discontinuous layer in the uppermost portion of the crust. This fact is readily understood when we consider that sediment accumulates at the surface.

Because sediments are deposited at Earth's surface, the rock layers that they eventually form contain evidence of past events that occurred at the

◆ **Figure 6.1** These eroded sedimentary rocks near Cheltenham, Ontario, are very colourful. Sedimentary rocks are exposed at the surface more than igneous and metamorphic rocks. Because they contain fossils and other clues about our geologic past, sedimentary rocks are important in the study of Earth history.
(Photo by C. Tsujita)

surface. By their very nature, sedimentary rocks contain within them indications of past environments in which their particles were deposited and, in some cases, clues to the mechanisms involved in their transport. Furthermore, it is sedimentary rocks that contain fossils, which are vital to the relative dating and correlation of rock units. Thus, it is largely from this group of rocks that geologists must reconstruct the details of Earth history.

Finally, it should be mentioned that many sedimentary rocks are very important economically. Coal, which is burned to provide a significant portion of energy in North America, is classified as a sedimentary rock. Our other major energy sources, petroleum and natural gas, are associated with sedimentary rocks, as are major sources of iron, aluminum, manganese, and fertilizer, and numerous materials essential to the construction industry (more details are given in Chapter 20).

TURNING SEDIMENT INTO SEDIMENTARY ROCK: DIAGENESIS AND LITHIFICATION

A great deal of change can occur to sediment from the time it is deposited until it becomes a sedimentary rock and is subsequently subjected to the temperatures and pressures that convert it to metamorphic rock. The term **diagenesis** (*dia* = change, *genesis* = origin) is a collective term for all of the chemical, physical, and biologic changes that take place after sediments are deposited and during and after lithification but before metamorphism.

Burial promotes diagenesis because as sediments are buried, they are subjected to increasingly higher temperatures and pressures. Diagenesis occurs within the upper few kilometres of Earth's crust at temperatures that are generally between 150°C and 200°C. Beyond this somewhat arbitrary threshold, metamorphism is said to occur.

One example of diagenetic change is *re-crystallization*, the development of more stable minerals from less stable ones. It is illustrated by the mineral aragonite, the less stable form of calcium carbonate ($CaCO_3$). Aragonite is secreted by many marine organisms, which use it to form shells and other hard parts, such as the skeletal structures produced by modern corals. In some environments, large quantities of these solid materials accumulate as sediment. As burial takes place, aragonite recrystallizes to the more stable form of calcium carbonate, calcite (the main constituent in the sedimentary rock limestone).

Diagenesis includes **lithification**, the processes by which unconsolidated sediments are transformed into solid sedimentary rocks (*lithos* = stone, *fic* = making). Basic lithification processes include compaction and cementation.

As sediment accumulates, the weight of overlying material compresses the deeper sediments. This process is called **compaction**. The deeper sediment is buried, the more it is compacted, and the firmer it becomes. As the grains are pressed closer and closer together, there is considerable reduction in **pore space** (the open space between rock particles or in rock fractures). For example, when clays are buried beneath several thousand metres of material, the volume of clay can be reduced by as much as 40 percent. As pore space decreases, much of the water that was trapped in the sediments is driven out. Because sands and other coarse sediments are less compressible, compaction is most significant as a lithification process in fine-grained sedimentary rocks.

Cementation is the most important process by which sediments are converted to sedimentary rock. It is a chemical diagenetic change that involves the precipitation of minerals among the individual sediment grains. The cementing materials are carried in solution by water percolating through the pore spaces between particles. Through time, the cement precipitates onto the sediment grains, fills the pore spaces, and joins the particles. Just as the amount of pore space is reduced during compaction, the addition of cement into a sedimentary deposit reduces its porosity as well.

Calcite, silica, and iron oxide are the most common cements. It is often a relatively simple matter to identify the cementing material. Calcite cement will effervesce with dilute hydrochloric acid. Silica is the hardest cement and thus produces the hardest sedimentary rocks. An orange or dark red colour in a sedimentary rock means that iron oxide is present (Figure 6.1).

Most sedimentary rocks are lithified by means of compaction and cementation. However, some initially form as solid masses of intergrown crystals rather than beginning as accumulations of separate particles that later become solid. Other crystalline sedimentary rocks do not begin that way but are transformed into masses of interlocking crystals sometime after the sediment is deposited.

For example, with time and burial, loose sediment consisting of delicate calcareous skeletal debris may be re-crystallized into a relatively dense crystalline limestone. Because crystals grow until they fill all the available space, pore spaces are frequently lacking in crystalline sedimentary rocks.

Unless the rocks later develop joints and fractures, they will be relatively impermeable to fluids, like water and oil.

Now that you know basically how sediment turns into rock, we will briefly look at where sediment is deposited or precipitated, before detailing how sedimentary rocks are named and classified.

SEDIMENTARY ENVIRONMENTS

GEODe EARTH Sedimentary Rocks
↳ Sedimentary Environments

Sedimentary rocks are important in the interpretation of Earth history. By understanding the conditions under which sedimentary rocks form, geologists can often deduce the history of a rock, including information about the origin of its component particles, the method and length of sediment transport, and the nature of the place where the grains eventually came to rest; that is, the environment of deposition.

An **environment of deposition** or **sedimentary environment** is simply a geographic setting where sediment is accumulating. Each site is characterized by a particular combination of geologic processes and environmental conditions. Some kinds of sediment, such as the salt that precipitates from seawater as it evaporates, are solely the product of their sedimentary environment. That is, their component minerals originate and are deposited in the same place. Other sediments accumulate in places far from where they originated, their constituents having been transported great distances by some combination of gravity, water, wind, and ice.

At any given time, the geographic setting and environmental conditions of a sedimentary environment determine the nature of the sediments that accumulate. Therefore, geologists carefully study the sediments in present-day depositional environments because the features they find can also be observed in ancient sedimentary rocks. In fact, this is an application of the principle of *uniformitarianism* (Chapter 1).

By applying a thorough knowledge of present-day conditions, geologists attempt to reconstruct the ancient environments and geographic relations of an area at the time a particular set of sedimentary layers were deposited. Such analyses often lead to the creation of maps, which depict the geographic distribution of land and sea, mountains and river valleys, deserts and glaciers, and other environments of deposition.

Types of Sedimentary Environments

Sedimentary environments are commonly placed into one of three categories: continental, transitional (shoreline), or marine. Each category includes many specific subenvironments. Figure 6.2 is an idealized diagram illustrating a number of important sedimentary environments associated with each category. Realize that this is just a sampling of the great diversity of depositional environments. The remainder of this section provides a brief overview of each category. Later, Chapters 14, 15, 17, 18, and 19, as well as portions of Chapter 11, will examine many of these environments in greater detail. Each is an area in which sediment accumulates and in which organisms live and die. Each produces a characteristic sedimentary rock or assemblage that reflects prevailing conditions.

Continental Environments Continental environments are dominated by the erosion and deposition associated with streams. In some cold regions, moving masses of glacial ice replace running water as the dominant process. In arid regions (as well as some coastal settings) wind takes on greater importance. Clearly, the nature of the sediments deposited in continental environments is strongly influenced by climate.

In frigid high-latitude or high-altitude settings, glaciers pick up and transport huge volumes of sediment. Materials deposited directly from ice are typically poorly sorted mixtures of particles that range in size from clay to boulders. Water from melting glaciers transports and re-deposits some of the glacial sediment, creating stratified, sorted accumulations.

Streams are the dominant agent of landscape alteration, eroding more land and transporting and depositing more sediment than any other process. The agitation of sediment by running water within channels of a river system tends to separate sedimentary particles according to density and grain size. As a consequence, sediment deposited in the turbulent headwaters of such a system is commonly dominated by gravel, whereas mud tends to predominate in more distant, and typically less turbulent, parts of a stream's course. Where streams emerge from a mountainous area onto a flatter surface, coarse-grained sediment sourced from the nearby highlands can accumulate at the toe of the slope to form a distinctive cone-shaped feature called an *alluvial fan*. In lowlands distant from such sediment source areas, significant volumes of mud and sand settle out from floodwaters that inundate flat areas of land called *floodplains*.

The work of wind and its resulting deposits are referred to as *aeolian*, after Aeolus, the Greek god of wind. Unlike glacial deposits, aeolian sediments are well sorted. Wind can lift fine dust high into the atmosphere and transport it great distances. Where winds are strong and the surface is not anchored by vegetation, sand is transported closer to the ground, where it accumulates in *dunes*. Deserts and coasts are common sites for this type of deposition.

In addition to being areas where dunes sometimes develop, desert basins are the sites at which shallow *playa lakes* occasionally form following heavy rains or periods of snowmelt in adjacent mountains. They rapidly dry up, sometimes leaving behind evaporites and other characteristic deposits. In humid regions lakes are more enduring features, and their quiet waters are excellent sediment traps. Small deltas, beaches, and bars form along the lakeshore, with finer sediments coming to rest on the lake floor.

Transitional Environments In transition zones characterized by low gradients or quiet water conditions, fine-grained sediment may be alternately deposited under shallow sheets of water and exposed to air, producing mud-dominated *tidal flats*. At the other extreme, where the shoreline is characterized by energetic wave and current action, sediments delivered to the sea by streams can be sorted and deposited to produce a sand or gravel *beach*. Further reworking and redistribution of sand by waves and currents along a shoreline can produce linear sand bodies, such as *spits*, *bars*, and *barrier islands*. Finally, a sheltered, calm-water area called a *lagoon* may develop behind an offshore bar or reef, within which fine-grained sediments may be deposited.

Deltas are among the most significant deposits associated with transitional environments. The complex accumulations of sediment build outward into the sea when rivers experience an abrupt loss of velocity and drop their load of detritus.

Marine Environments Marine depositional environments are divided according to depth. The *shallow marine* environment reaches to depths of about 200 metres and extends from the shore to the outer edge of the continental shelf. The *deep marine* environment lies seaward of the continental shelf in waters deeper than 200 metres.

The shallow marine environment borders all of the world's continents. Its width varies greatly, from practically nonexistent in some places to broad expanses extending as far as 1500 kilometres in other locations. On the average this zone is about 80 kilometres wide. The kind of sediment deposited here depends on several factors, including distance from shore, the elevation of the adjacent land area, water depth, water temperature, and climate.

Because of the ongoing erosion of the adjacent continent, the shallow marine environment receives huge quantities of land-derived sediment. Where the influx of such sediment is small and the seas are relatively warm, carbonate-rich muds may be the predominant sediment. Most of this material consists of the skeletal debris of carbonate-secreting organisms mixed with inorganic precipitates. Coral *reefs* are also associated with warm, shallow marine environments. In hot regions where the sea occupies a basin with restricted circulation, evaporation triggers the precipitation of soluble materials and the formation of marine evaporite deposits.

Deep marine environments include all the floors of the deep ocean. Far from landmasses, tiny particles from many sources remain adrift for long spans. Gradually these small grains "rain" down on the ocean floor, where they accumulate very slowly as *pelagic ooze*. An accumulation composed only of the tiny skeletons of planktonic marine organisms is called *biogenic ooze*. Significant exceptions are thick deposits of relatively coarse sediment that occur at the base of the continental slope. These materials are moved down from the continental shelf by *turbidity currents*—dense gravity-driven masses of sediment and water—and are deposited as turbidites in *deep-sea fans*.

Sedimentary Facies

By studying a series of sedimentary layers, we can see the changes in environmental conditions that occurred at a particular place with the passage of time. Changes in past environments can also be seen when a single unit of sedimentary rock is traced laterally. This is true because at any one time many different depositional environments can exist over a broad area. For example, when sand is accumulating in a beach environment, finer muds are often being deposited in quieter offshore waters. Still farther out, perhaps in a zone where biologic activity is high and land-derived sediments are scarce, the deposits consist largely of the calcareous remains of small organisms. In this example, different sediments are accumulating adjacent to one another at the same time. Each unit possesses a distinctive set of characteristics reflecting the conditions in a particular environment. To describe such sets of sediments, the term **sedimentary facies** is used. When a sedimentary unit is examined in cross-section from one end to the other, each facies can grade laterally into another that formed at the same time but that exhibits different characteristics (Figure 6.3).

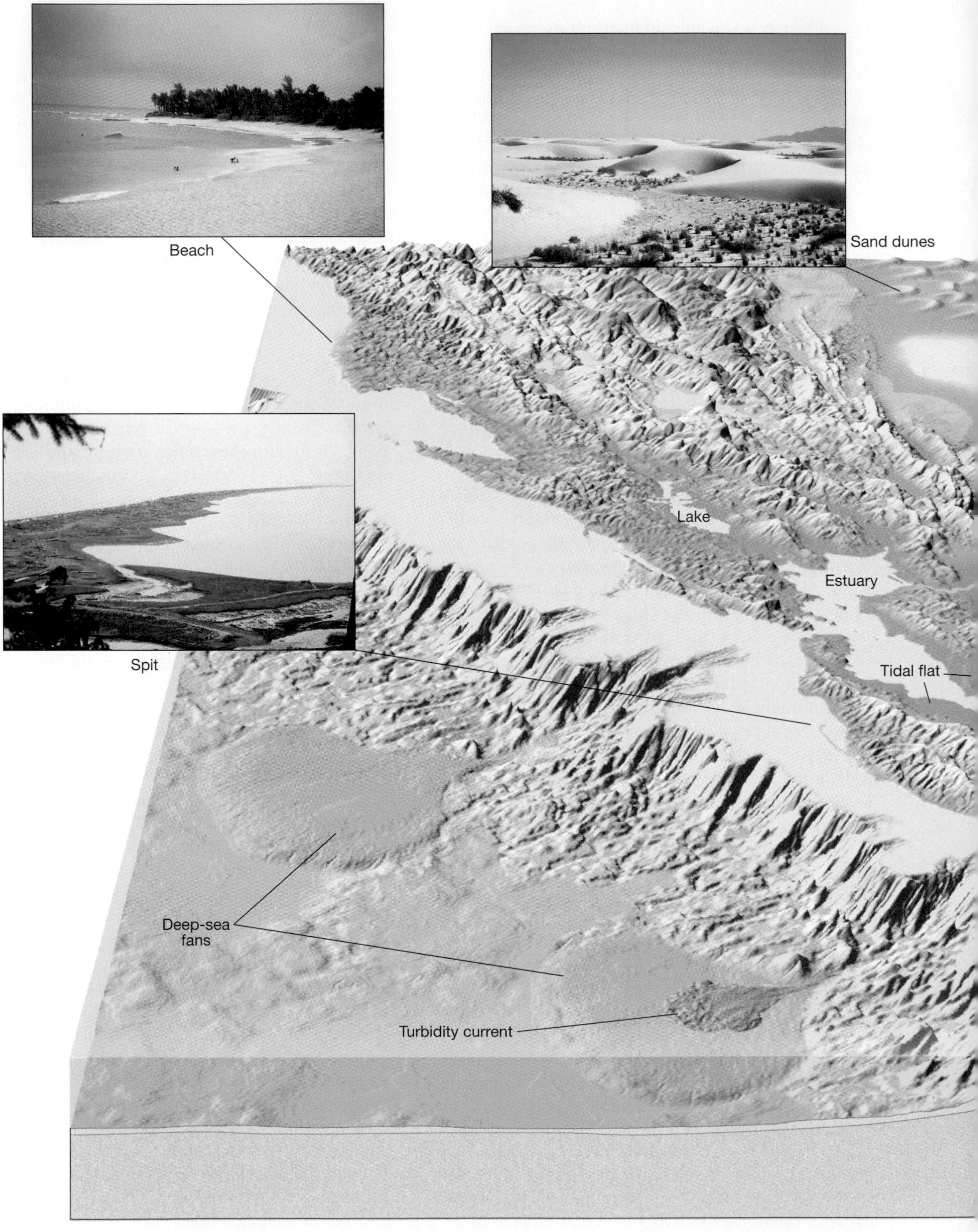

◆ **Figure 6.2** Sedimentary environments are those places where sediment accumulates. Each is characterized by certain physical, chemical, and biologic conditions. Because each type of sediment contains clues about the environment in which it was deposited, sedimentary rocks are important in the interpretation of Earth history. A number of important continental, transitional, and marine sedimentary environments are represented in this idealized diagram.
(Alluvial fans photo by Marli Miller; all other photos by E. J. Tarbuck)

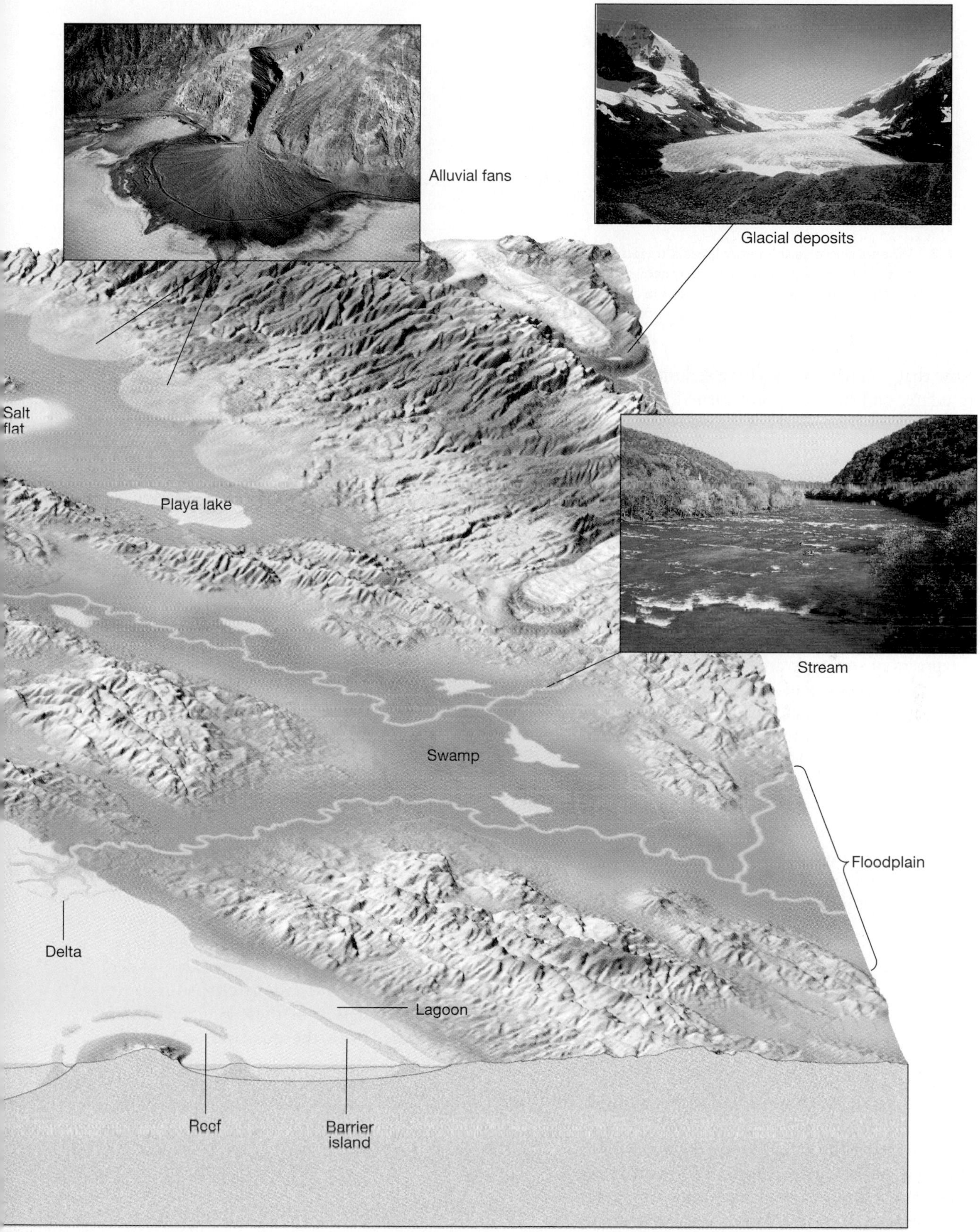
Alluvial fans
Glacial deposits
Salt flat
Playa lake
Stream
Swamp
Floodplain
Delta
Lagoon
Reef
Barrier island

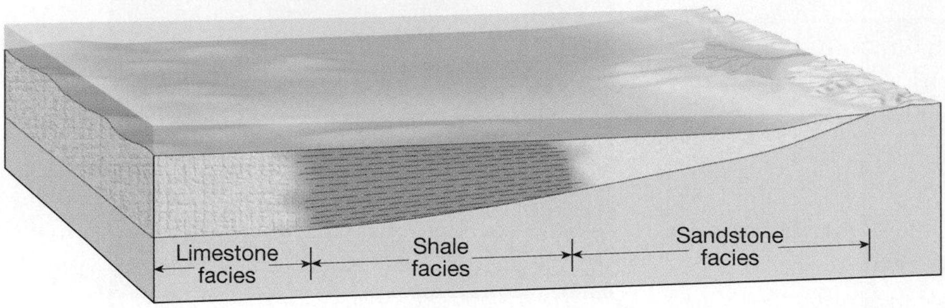

◆ **Figure 6.3** When a single sedimentary layer is traced laterally, we may find that it is made up of several different rock types. This can occur because many sedimentary environments can exist at the same time over a broad area. The term *facies* is used to describe such sets of sedimentary rocks. Each facies grades laterally into another that formed at the same time but in a different environment.

Now that you have seen where sediments tend to accumulate, and how they are turned into sedimentary rock, you are now ready to study the rocks themselves.

TYPES OF SEDIMENTARY ROCKS

Sediment has two principal sources. First, sediment can be an accumulation of material that originates and is transported as solid particles derived from both mechanical and chemical weathering of existing rocks. Deposits of this type are termed *detrital*, and the sedimentary rocks that they form are called **detrital sedimentary rocks**. The second major source of sediment is soluble material produced largely by chemical weathering. When these dissolved substances are precipitated by either inorganic or organic processes, the material is known as chemical sediment and the rocks formed from it are called **chemical sedimentary rocks**.

We will now look at each type of sedimentary rock and some examples of each.

DETRITAL SEDIMENTARY ROCKS

GEODe EARTH Sedimentary Rocks
↳ Types of Sedimentary Rocks

Though a wide variety of minerals and rock fragments can be found in detrital rocks, the silicate minerals clay and quartz are the chief constituents of most sedimentary rocks in this category; for this reason, these rocks can also be referred to as *siliciclastic* sedimentary rocks. Recall from Chapter 5 that clay minerals are the most abundant product of the chemical weathering of silicate minerals, especially the feldspars. Clays are fine-grained minerals with sheet-like crystalline structures similar to the micas. The other common mineral, quartz, is abundant because it is extremely durable and is very resistant to chemical weathering. Thus, when igneous rocks, such as granite, are attacked by weathering processes, individual quartz grains are freed.

Other common minerals in detrital rocks are feldspars and micas. Because chemical weathering rapidly transforms these minerals into new substances, their presence in sedimentary rocks indicates that erosion and deposition were fast enough to preserve some of the primary minerals from the source rock before they could be decomposed.

Particle size is the primary basis for distinguishing among various detrital sedimentary rocks. Table 6.1 presents the size categories for particles making up detrital rocks. Particle size is more than just a convenient criterion for dividing detrital rocks; the sizes of the component grains also provide useful information about environments of deposition (Figure 6.2). Currents of water or air sort the particles by size: the stronger the current, the larger the particle size carried. Gravels, for example, are moved by swiftly flowing rivers as well as by landslides and glaciers. Less energy is required to transport sand; thus, it is common to such features as windblown dunes and some river deposits and beaches. Very little energy is needed to transport clay, so it settles very slowly. Accumulation of these tiny particles is generally associated with the quiet water of a lake, lagoon, swamp, or certain marine environments.

Common detrital sedimentary rocks, in order of increasing particle size, are mudrocks, sandstone, and conglomerate or breccia. We will now look at each type and how it forms.

Shale and Other Mudrocks

Mudrocks, the group of sedimentary rocks that include shale, mudstone, and siltstone, consist of clay- to silt-sized particles (Figure 6.4). These fine-grained detrital rocks account for more than half of

TABLE 6.1 Particle Size Classification for Detrital Rocks

Size Range (mm)	Particle Name	Common Sediment Name	Detrital Rock
>256	Boulder		
64–256	Cobble	Gravel	Conglomerate or breccia
4–64	Pebble		
2–4	Granule		
1/16–2	Sand	Sand	Sandstone
1/256–1/16	Silt	Mud	Mudrocks (Shale, mudstone, or siltstone)
< 1/256	Clay		

10 20 30 40 50 60

Scale in millimetres

all sedimentary rocks. The particles in these rocks are so small that they cannot be readily identified without strong magnification. For this reason mudrocks are more difficult to study and analyze than most other sedimentary rocks.

Much of what can be learned is based on particle size. The tiny grains in mudrocks indicate that deposition occurs as the result of gradual settling from relatively quiet, non-turbulent currents. Such environments include lakes, river floodplains, lagoons, and portions of the deep-ocean basins (Figure 6.2). Even these "quiet" environments usually experience enough turbulence to keep clay size particles suspended almost indefinitely. Consequently, much of the clay is deposited only after the individual particles coalesce to form larger aggregates.

◆ **Figure 6.4** Shale is a type of mudrock. Mudrocks are by far the most abundant of all sedimentary rocks. Dark shales containing plant remains are relatively common. (Photo courtesy of E. J. Tarbuck)

Sometimes the chemical composition of the rock provides additional information. One example is black shale, which is black because it contains abundant organic matter (carbon). When such a rock is found, it strongly implies that deposition occurred in an oxygen-poor environment, such as a swamp, where organic materials do not readily oxidize and decay.

As silt and clay accumulate, they tend to form thin layers, which are commonly referred to as *laminae* (*lamin* = a thin sheet). Initially the particles in the laminae are oriented randomly. This disordered arrangement leaves a high percentage of pore space that is filled with water. However, this situation usually changes with time as additional layers of sediment pile up and compact the sediment below.

During compaction the clay and silt particles take on a more nearly parallel alignment and become tightly packed. This rearrangement of grains reduces the size of the pore spaces and forces out much of the water. Once the grains are pressed closely together, the tiny spaces between particles do not readily permit solutions containing cementing material to circulate. Therefore, shales are often described as being weak because they are poorly cemented and therefore not well lithified.

The inability of water to penetrate its microscopic pore spaces explains why shale commonly forms barriers to the subsurface movement of water and petroleum. Indeed, rock layers that contain groundwater are commonly underlain by shale beds, which block further downward movement. The opposite is true for underground reservoirs of petroleum. They are commonly capped by shale beds that effectively prevent oil and gas from escaping to the surface.*

It is common to apply the term *shale* to all fine-grained sedimentary rocks, especially in a nontechnical context. It should be emphasized that shale is a type of mudrock that must exhibit the ability to split into thin layers along well-developed closely spaced planes (e.g., the top of the slab in Figure 6.4). This property is termed **fissility** (*fissilis* = something that can be cleft or split). If the rock breaks into chunks or blocks, the name mudstone is applied. Another fine-grained sedimentary rock that, like mudstone, is often grouped with shale but lacks fissility is *siltstone*. As its name implies, siltstone is composed largely of

*The relationship between impermeable beds and the occurrence and movement of groundwater is examined in Chapter 16. Shale beds as cap rocks in oil traps are discussed in Chapter 20.

silt-size particles and contains less clay-size material than shale and mudstone.

Although mudrocks are far more common than other sedimentary rocks, they do not usually attract as much notice as other less abundant members of this group. The reason is that mudrocks do not form prominent outcrops as sandstone and limestone commonly do. Rather, mudrocks crumble easily and usually form a cover of soil that hides the unweathered rock below (see differential weathering in Chapter 5). This is illustrated nicely in the Niagara Gorge, where the gentler slopes of weathered shale are quite inconspicuous and overgrown with vegetation, in sharp contrast with the bold cliffs produced by more durable rocks, such as dolostone and sandstone (Figure 6.5).

Although shale beds do not form striking cliffs and prominent outcrops, some deposits have economic value. Certain mudrocks, such as the red shales of the Queenston Formation that underlie more resistant dolostones of the Niagara Escarpment in Ontario, have been a valuable clay source in the brick-making industry for several decades. Clay extracted from mudrocks also represents the raw material for pottery and tile in many parts of the world. More details are given in Chapter 20.

Sandstone

Sandstone is the name given to rocks in which sand-size grains dominate (Figure 6.6). After shale, sandstone is the most abundant sedimentary rock, accounting for approximately 20 percent of the entire group. Sandstones form in a variety of environments (Figure 6.2) and commonly contain significant clues about their origin, including sorting, particle shape, and composition.

Sorting is the degree of similarity in particle size in a sedimentary rock. For example, if all the grains in a sample of sandstone are about the same size, the sand is considered *well sorted* (Figure 6.6). Conversely, if the rock is a mixture of large and small particles, the sand is considered *poorly sorted*. By studying the degree of sorting, we can learn much about the depositing flow rates. Deposits of wind-blown sand (Figure 6.7) are usually better sorted

◆ **Figure 6.5** Sedimentary rock layers exposed in the walls of the Niagara River valley. Beds of resistant sandstone and dolostone produce bold cliffs. By contrast, weaker, poorly cemented shale crumbles and produces a gentler slope of weathered debris in which some vegetation is growing. This is also a good example of differential weathering, as discussed in Chapter 5.
(Photo by Denis Tetreault)

◆ **Figure 6.6** Quartz sandstone. After mudrock, sandstone is the most abundant sedimentary rock. This thick layer of sandstone, called the Navajo Sandstone, is exposed in and near Utah's Zion National Park. The hand sample comes from this layer.
(**Main** photo by Tom & Susan Bean, Inc.; **hand sample** photos by E. J. Tarbuck)

◆ **Figure 6.7** Sorting is the degree of similarity in particle size. The wind-transported sand grains in this sand dune are well sorted because they are all practically the same size. Athabasca Sand Dunes, Saskatchewan.
(Photo courtesy of Parkland Publishing)

than deposits sorted by wave activity. Particles washed by waves are commonly better sorted than materials deposited by streams.

Sediment accumulations that exhibit poor sorting usually result when particles are transported for only a relatively short time and then rapidly deposited. For example, when a turbulent stream reaches the gentler slopes at the base of a steep mountain, its velocity is quickly reduced, and poorly sorted sands and gravels are deposited.

The shapes of sand grains can also help decipher the history of a sandstone. When streams, winds, or waves move sand and other sedimentary particles, the grains lose their sharp edges and corners and become more rounded as they collide with other particles during transport. Usually, the degree of rounding indicates the distance or time involved in the transportation of sediment by currents of air or water. Highly rounded grains indicate that a great deal of abrasion and hence a great deal of transport has occurred.

Very angular grains, conversely, imply two things: that the materials were transported only a short distance before they were deposited, and that some other medium may have transported them. For example, when glaciers move sediment, the particles can be made more irregular by the crushing of colliding particles near the glacier bed.

In addition to affecting the degree of rounding and the amount of sorting that particles undergo, the length of transport by turbulent air and water currents also influences the mineral composition of a sedimentary deposit. Substantial weathering and long transport lead to the gradual destruction of weaker and less stable minerals, including the feldspars and ferromagnesians. Because quartz is very durable, it is usually the mineral that survives the long trip in a turbulent environment.

The origin and history of sandstone can often be deduced by examining the sorting, roundness, and mineral composition of its constituent grains. Knowing this information allows us to infer that a well-sorted quartz-rich sandstone consisting of highly rounded grains must be the result of a great deal of transport. Such a rock, in fact, may represent several cycles of weathering, transport, and deposition. We can also conclude that a sandstone containing significant amounts of feldspar and angular grains of ferromagnesian minerals underwent little chemical weathering and transport and was probably deposited close to the source area of the particles.

Owing to its durability, quartz is the predominant mineral in most sandstones. When this is the case, the rock may simply be called *quartz sandstone*. When a sandstone contains appreciable quantities of feldspar, the rock is called *arkose*. In addition to feldspar, arkose usually contains quartz and sparkling bits of mica. The mineral composition of arkose indicates that the grains were derived from granitic source rocks. The particles are generally poorly sorted and angular, which suggests short-distance transport, minimal chemical weathering in a relatively dry climate, and rapid deposition and burial.

A third variety of sandstone is known as *wacke*. Along with quartz and feldspar, this dark-coloured rock contains abundant rock fragments and matrix. *Matrix* refers to the silt- and clay-size particles found in spaces between larger sand grains. More than 15 percent of a wacke's volume is matrix. The poor sorting and angular grains characteristic of wacke suggest that the particles were transported only a relatively short distance from their source area and then rapidly deposited. Before the sediment could be reworked and sorted further, it was buried under additional layers of sediment. Wacke is frequently associated with submarine deposits made by dense sediment-choked torrents called turbidity currents.*

Conglomerate and Breccia

Conglomerate consists largely of rounded pebbles and cobbles (Figure 6.8). As Table 6.1 indicates, these particles can range in size from large boulders to particles as small as garden peas. The particles are commonly large enough to be identified as distinctive rock types; thus, they can be valuable in identifying the source areas of sediments. Many conglomerates are poorly sorted because the spaces between the large gravel particles contain trapped sand or mud.

Gravels accumulate in a variety of environments and usually indicate the existence of steep slopes or very turbulent currents. The coarse particles in a conglomerate may reflect the action of energetic mountain streams or the strong wave activity along a rapidly eroding rocky coast (Figure 6.2). Some glacial and landslide deposits also contain plentiful gravel.

If the large particles are angular rather than rounded, the rock is called *breccia* (Figure 6.9). Because large particles abrade and become rounded very rapidly during transport, the pebbles and cobbles in a breccia indicate that they did not travel far from their source area before they were deposited.

Thus, like other sedimentary rocks, conglomerates and breccias contain clues to their history. Their particle sizes reveal the strength of the currents

*More on these currents and the *graded beds* they create is found in the section "Submarine Canyons and Turbidity Currents" in Chapter 11.

A

B

Close up

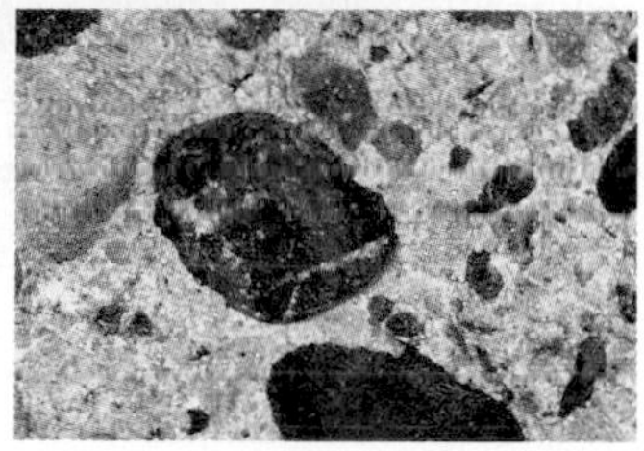

◆ **Figure 6.8** **A.** As shown in this example near Ville-Marie, Quebec, conglomerate is composed primarily of rounded, gravel-sized particles. Note compass for scale. **B.** Hand specimen of conglomerate. (Photo **A** by S. R. Hicock; photo **B** by E. J. Tarbuck)

Close up

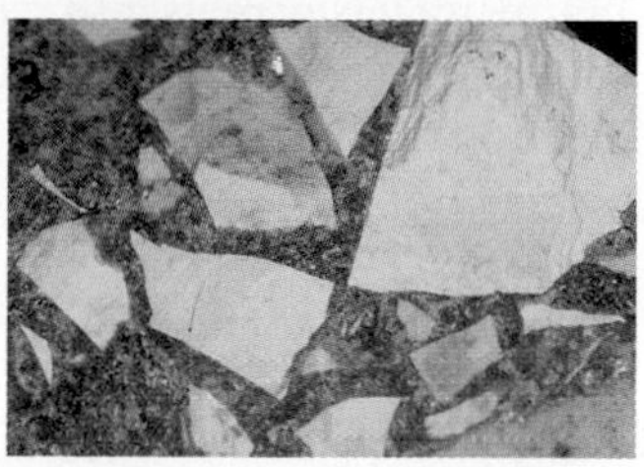

◆ **Figure 6.9** When the gravel-sized particles in a detrital rock are angular, the rock is called breccia. (Photo by E. J. Tarbuck)

that transported them, whereas the degree of rounding indicates how far or how long the particles traveled. The fragments within a sample identify the source rocks that supplied them.

CHEMICAL SEDIMENTARY ROCKS

GEODe EARTH Sedimentary Rocks
↳ Types of Sedimentary Rocks

In contrast to detrital rocks, which form from the solid products of weathering, chemical sediments derive from material that is carried *in solution* to lakes and seas (Figure 6.2). This material does not remain dissolved in the water indefinitely, however. Some of it precipitates to form chemical sediments. These become rocks, such as limestone, chert, rock salt, and potash.

This precipitation of material occurs in two ways. *Inorganic* (*in* = not, *organicus* = life) processes, such as evaporation and chemical activity, can produce chemical sediments. *Organic* (life) processes of aquatic organisms also form chemical sediments, said to be of **biochemical** origin.

One example of a deposit resulting from inorganic chemical processes is the white crust that develops on the bottom of a teakettle. Another is the dripstone that decorates many caves (Figure 6.10), and another still is the salt left behind as a body of

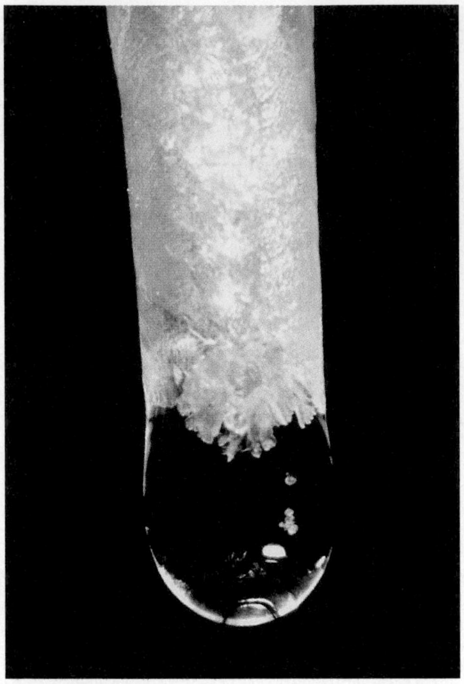

◆ **Figure 6.10** Because many cave deposits are created by the seemingly endless dripping of water over long time spans, they are commonly called *dripstone*. The material being deposited is calcium carbonate ($CaCO_3$) and the rock is a form of limestone called *travertine*. The calcium carbonate is precipitated when some dissolved carbon dioxide escapes from a water drop.
(Photo by Clifford Stroud/Wind Cave National Park)

◆ **Figure 6.11** This rock, called *coquina*, consists of shell fragments; therefore, it has a biochemical origin.
(Photo by E. J. Tarbuck)

seawater evaporates. In contrast, many water-dwelling animals and plants extract dissolved mineral matter to form shells and other hard parts. After the organisms die, their skeletons collect by the millions on the floor of a lake or ocean as biochemical sediment (Figure 6.11). In fact, deposition of carbonate sediment is an integral part of Earth's carbon cycle (see Box 6.1).

Limestone

Representing about 10 percent of the total volume of all sedimentary rocks, *limestone* is the most abundant chemical sedimentary rock. It is composed chiefly of the mineral calcite ($CaCO_3$) and forms either by inorganic means or as the result of biochemical processes. Regardless of its origin, the mineral composition of all limestone is similar, yet many different types exist. This is true because limestones are produced under a variety of conditions. Those forms having a marine biochemical origin are by far the most common.

Reefs Corals are important examples of organisms that are capable of creating large quantities of marine limestone. These relatively simple invertebrate animals secrete a calcareous (calcium carbonate–rich) external skeleton. Although they are small, corals are capable of creating massive structures called *reefs* (Figures 6.12 and 6.2). Modern reefs consist of coral colonies made up of great numbers of individuals that live side by side on a calcareous structure secreted by the animals. In addition, other organisms live with the corals and help cement the entire structure into a solid mass. A wide variety of other organisms also live in and near the reefs.

Certainly the best-known modern reef is Australia's Great Barrier Reef, 2000 kilometres long, but many lesser reefs also exist. They develop in the shallow, warm waters of the tropics and subtropics equator-ward of about 30° latitude. Striking examples exist in the Bahamas and Florida Keys.

Reefs are not restricted to the present day, and corals have not built all reefs. In Canada, reefs made by microbes are common features in the Precambrian and Early Paleozoic rock successions of the Rocky Mountains and Arctic archipelago. Sponge-like organisms called archaeocyathids formed small reefs in the Cambrian sequences of British Columbia and Newfoundland and Labrador. Coral-dominated reefs of Silurian and Devonian age occur in rocks of the Niagara Escarpment of Ontario and parts of Arctic Canada (Figure 6.12B). Significant to Canada's

BOX 6.1

Earth as a System
The Carbon Cycle and Sedimentary Rocks

To illustrate the movement of material and energy in the Earth system, we will look at the *carbon cycle* (Figure 6.A). Pure carbon is rare in nature, occurring mainly as diamond and graphite. Most carbon is bonded chemically to other elements to form compounds, such as carbon dioxide, calcium carbonate, and hydrocarbons in coal and petroleum. Carbon is also the basic building block of life as it readily combines with hydrogen and oxygen to form the organic compounds that compose living things.

In the atmosphere, carbon occurs mainly as carbon dioxide (CO_2). Atmospheric carbon dioxide is significant because it is a greenhouse gas, being an efficient absorber of energy emitted by Earth, and thus influences atmospheric heating.*

Because many processes that operate on Earth involve carbon dioxide, this gas constantly moves into and out of the atmosphere. For example, in photosynthesis, plants absorb carbon dioxide from the atmosphere to produce the organic compounds needed for growth. Animals that consume these plants (or other animals that eat plants) use the compounds as a source of energy and, through the process of respiration, return carbon dioxide to the atmosphere. (Plants also return some CO_2 to the atmosphere via transpiration.) Further, when plants die and decay or are burned, this biomass is oxidized, and carbon dioxide is returned to the atmosphere.

Not all dead plant material is immediately converted back to carbon dioxide. A small percentage is deposited as sediment. Over geologic time, considerable biomass is buried with sediment. Under the right conditions, some of this biomass is converted to fossil fuel—coal, petroleum, or natural gas. Eventually some of the fuels are recovered (mined or pumped from a well) and burned to run factories and fuel our transportation system. One result of fossil-fuel combustion is the release of huge quantities of CO_2 into the atmosphere. Thus, CO_2 is transferred from the atmosphere to the biosphere and back again.

Carbon also moves from the lithosphere and hydrosphere to the atmosphere and back again. For example, volcanic activity early in Earth's history is thought to be the source of most of the carbon dioxide found in the atmosphere. Carbon dioxide makes its way back to the hydrosphere and then to the solid Earth by first combining with water to form carbonic acid (H_2CO_3), which then attacks rocks of the lithosphere. One product of this chemical weathering of solid rock is the soluble bicarbonate ion ($2HCO_3^-$), which is carried by groundwater and streams to the ocean. Here, marine organisms extract this dissolved material to secrete calcium carbonate ($CaCO_3$) shells. Dead organisms contribute skeletal remains to the biochemical sediment of the ocean floor and become sedimentary rock. Eventually these rocks may be exposed at Earth's surface, where chemical weathering causes carbon stored in the rock to be released to the atmosphere as CO_2.

In summary, carbon moves among all four of Earth's major spheres. It is essential to every living thing in the biosphere. In the atmosphere carbon dioxide is an important greenhouse gas. In the hydrosphere, carbon dioxide is dissolved in lakes, rivers, and the ocean. In the lithosphere carbon is contained in rocks and is stored as organic matter in deposits of coal and petroleum.

*For more on this idea, see the section on "Carbon Dioxide and Global Warming" in Chapter 20.

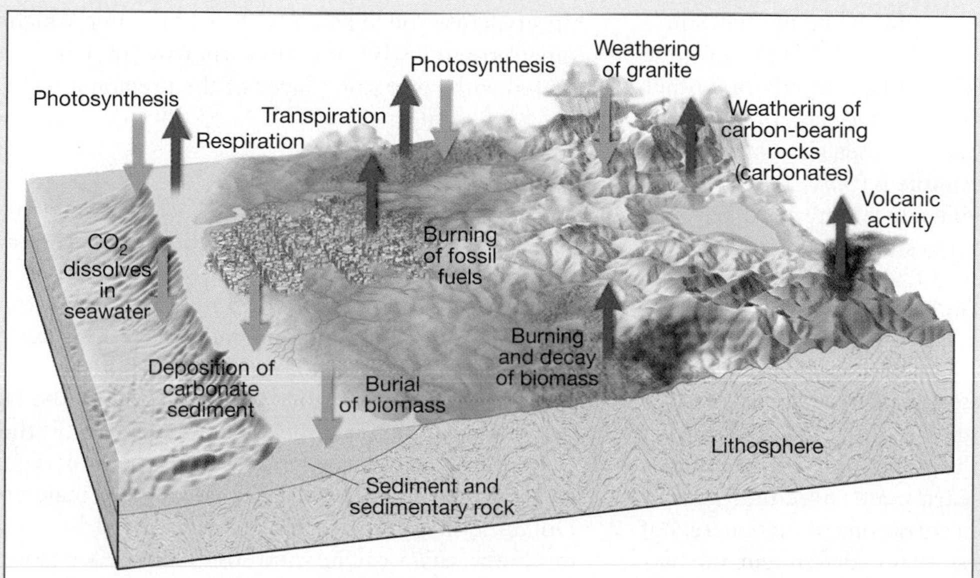

◆ **Figure 6.A** Simplified diagram of the carbon cycle with emphasis on the flow of carbon among the atmosphere, hydrosphere, geosphere, and biosphere. The coloured arrows show whether the flow of carbon is into or out of the atmosphere.

A

B

◆ **Figure 6.12** **A.** This modern coral reef is at Bora Bora in French Polynesia. **B.** Paleozoic fossil reef in Arctic Canada containing tubular to cone-shaped corals.
(Photo **A** by Nancy Sefton/Photo Researchers, Inc.; photo **B** by Jisuo Jin)

economy, much of Alberta's petroleum is hosted by Devonian reefs that were made chiefly by hard sponges called stromatoporoids.

Coquina, Fossiliferous Limestone, and Chalk Although most limestone is the product of biologic processes, this origin is not always evident, because shells and skeletons can undergo considerable change before becoming lithified into rock. However, one easily identified biochemical limestone is *coquina*, a coarse rock composed of poorly cemented shells and shell fragments (see Figure 6.11). Limestone consisting of visible shells, shell fragments, and other skeletal components, as well as calcareous mud, is called *fossiliferous limestone*. Another less obvious, but nevertheless familiar, example is *chalk*, a soft, porous rock made up almost entirely of the hard parts of microscopic marine organisms. Among the most famous chalk deposits are those exposed along the southeast coast of England (Figure 6.13).

Inorganic Limestones Limestones having an inorganic origin form when chemical changes or high water temperatures increase the concentration of calcium carbonate to the point that it precipitates. Microbes can assist carbonate precipitation by increasing dissolved concentrations of carbonate, but the precipitation process is not dependent on biologic activity. Travertine, the type of limestone commonly seen in caves, is an example (see Figure 6.10). When travertine is deposited in caves, groundwater is the source of the calcium carbonate. As water droplets become exposed to the air in a cavern, some of the carbon dioxide dissolved in the water escapes, causing calcium carbonate to precipitate.

Another variety of inorganic limestone is *oolitic limestone*. It is a rock composed of small spherical grains called *ooids*. Ooids form in shallow marine waters as tiny "seed" particles (commonly small shell fragments) are moved back and forth by currents. As the grains are rolled about in the warm water, which is supersaturated with calcium carbonate, they become coated with layer upon layer of the precipitate.

Dolostone

Closely related to limestone is *dolostone*, which is composed of the calcium–magnesium carbonate mineral dolomite. Although dolostone can form by direct precipitation from seawater, most dolostone probably originates when magnesium in seawater or groundwater replaces some of the calcium in limestone. The latter hypothesis is reinforced by the fact that there is practically no young dolostone. Rather, most dolostones are ancient rocks in which there was ample time for magnesium to replace calcium. Dolomite is less prone to being dissolved by acidic rainwater than calcite and therefore often forms prominent cliff faces, such as those at the Niagara Escarpment in southern Ontario.

◆ **Figure 6.13** The White Cliffs of Dover. This prominent chalk deposit underlies large portions of southern England as well as parts of northern France.
(Photo by Laguna Photo/Liaison Agency, Inc.)

Chert

Chert is a name used for a number of very compact and hard rocks made of microcrystalline silica (SiO_2). One well-known form is *flint*, whose dark colour results from the organic matter it contains. *Jasper*, a red variety, gets its bright colour from the iron oxide it contains. The banded form is usually referred to as *agate*.

Chert deposits are commonly found in one of two situations: as irregularly shaped nodules in limestone/dolostone (Figure 6.14A) and as tabular layers of rock (Figure 6.14B). The silica composing many chert nodules may have been deposited directly from water. Such nodules have an inorganic origin. However, it is unlikely that a very large percentage of chert layers were precipitated directly from seawater, because seawater is seldom saturated with silica. Hence, some beds of chert are thought to have originated largely as biochemical sediment.

Most water-dwelling organisms that produce hard parts make them of calcium carbonate. But some, such as diatoms and radiolarians, produce glasslike silica skeletons. These tiny organisms are able to extract silica even though seawater contains only tiny quantities. It is from their remains that most chert beds are believed to originate. Some bedded cherts, however, occur in association with lava flows and layers of volcanic ash. For these occurrences it is probable that the silica was derived from the decomposition of the volcanic ash and not from biochemical sources. Note that when a hand specimen of chert is being examined, there are few reliable criteria by which the mode of origin (inorganic versus biochemical) can be determined. Chert is also found interbedded with iron-rich deposits in a type of chemical sedimentary rock known as *banded iron formation*, indicating there was a greater amount of dissolved silica in the sea during Precambrian times than today (Figure 6.14B).

Like glass, most chert has a conchoidal fracture. Its hardness, ease of chipping, and ability to hold a sharp edge made chert a favourite of First Nations peoples for fashioning points for spears and arrows. Because of chert's durability and extensive use, arrowheads made from it are found in many parts of North America.

Evaporites

Very often, evaporation is the mechanism triggering deposition of chemical precipitates in places like salt flats, playa lakes, and lagoons (Figure 6.2). Minerals commonly precipitated in this fashion include halite (sodium chloride, NaCl), the chief component of rock salt, and gypsum (hydrous calcium sulphate, $CaSO_4 \cdot 2H_2O$), the main ingredient of *rock gypsum*. Both have significant importance. Halite is familiar to everyone as the common salt used in cooking and seasoning foods. In Canada, rock salt is used widely for de-icing roads during the winter months. Of course, it has many other uses and has been considered important enough that people have sought, traded, and fought over it for much of human history. Gypsum is the basic ingredient of plaster of Paris and is used most extensively in the construction industry for drywall and interior plaster (see Chapter 20).

A B

◆ **Figure 6.14** **A.** Chert commonly forms beds and blob-shaped nodules. This chert nodule in dolostone near Hamilton, Ontario, contains a fossil sponge, the silica-rich skeleton of which acted as a "seed" for dissolved silica to precipitate around. **B.** Banded iron formation from northern Ontario, showing alternating bands of magnetite/hematite (purple) and iron-bearing chert (red).
(Photo **A** by Denis Tetreault; photo **B** by Grant Young)

In the geologic past, many areas that are now dry land were basins submerged under shallow arms of a sea that had only narrow connections to the open ocean (Figure 6.2). Under these conditions, seawater continually moved into the bay to replace water lost by evaporation. Eventually the waters of the bay became saturated and salt deposition began. Such deposits are called **evaporites**.

When a body of seawater evaporates, the minerals that precipitate do so in a sequence that is determined by their solubility. Less soluble minerals precipitate first and more soluble minerals precipitate later, as salinity increases. For example, gypsum precipitates when about two thirds to three quarters of the seawater has evaporated, and halite settles out when nine tenths of the water has been removed. During the last stages of this process, potassium and magnesium salts precipitate. One of these last-formed salts, the mineral sylvite, is mined as a significant source of potassium (potash) for fertilizer.

◆ **Figure 6.15** The Bonneville Salt Flats in Utah are a well-known example of evaporite deposits.
(Photo by Tom & Susan Bean, Inc.)

On a smaller scale, evaporite deposits can be seen in such places as the Great Salt Lake of Utah. Here, following rains or periods of snowmelt in the mountains, streams flow from the surrounding mountains into an enclosed basin. As the water evaporates, **salt flats** form when dissolved materials are precipitated as a white crust on the ground (Figure 6.15). Salt flats also develop in saline lakes and sloughs of the Canadian Prairies.

Coal

Coal is quite different from other rocks. Unlike limestone and chert, which are made of calcite and silica, coal is made of organic matter. Close examination of coal under a magnifying glass often reveals plant structures, such as leaves, bark, and wood, that have been chemically altered but are still identifiable. This supports the conclusion that coal is the end product of large amounts of plant material buried for millions of years (Figure 6.16).

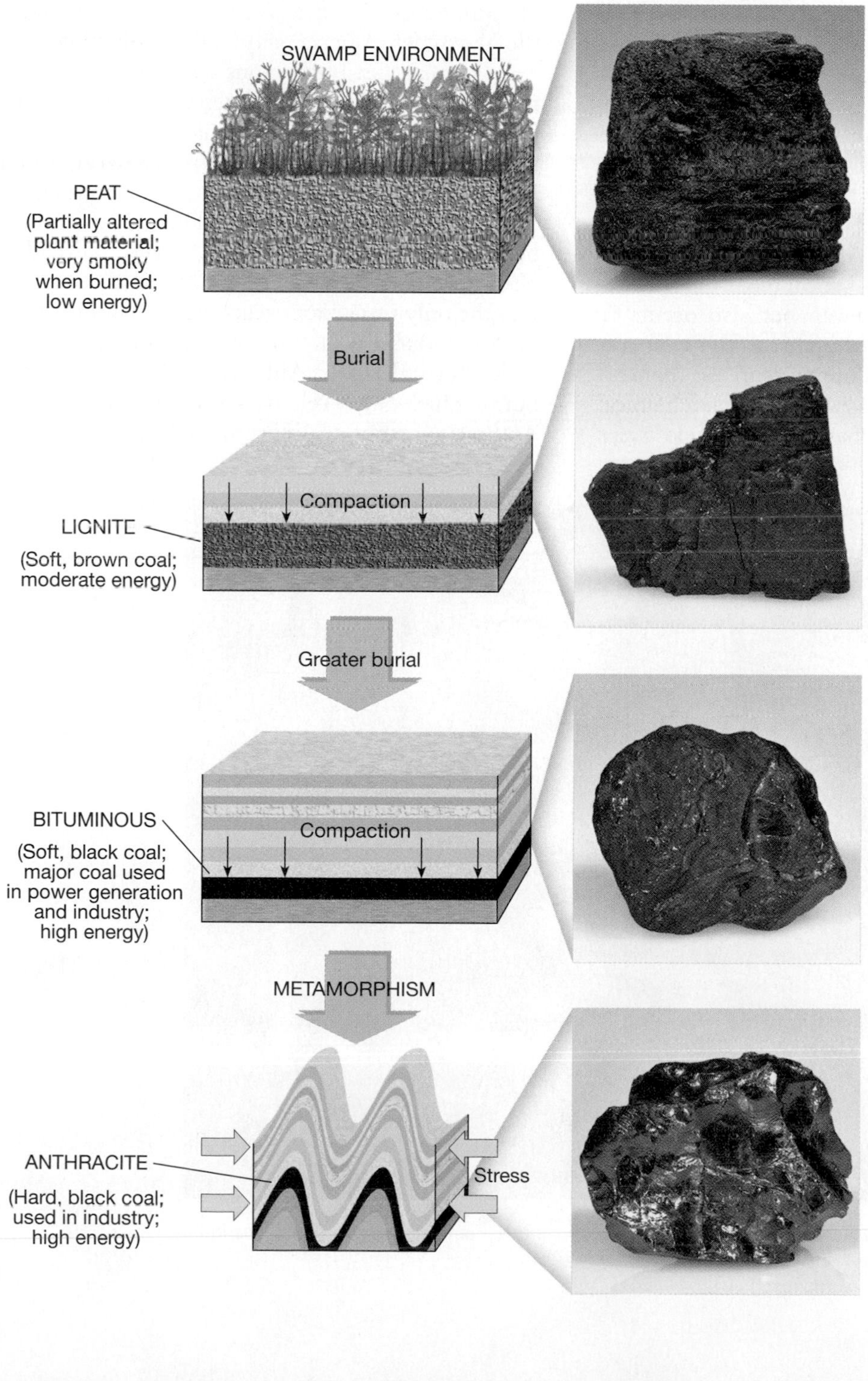

◆ **Figure 6.16** Successive stages in the formation of coal.
(Photos by E. J. Tarbuck)

The initial stage in coal formation is the accumulation of large quantities of plant remains. However, special conditions are required for such accumulations, because dead plants readily decompose when exposed to the atmosphere or other oxygen-rich environments. One important environment that allows for the buildup of plant material is a swamp (Figures 6.17 and 6.2).

Stagnant swamp water is oxygen-deficient, so complete decay (oxidation) of the plant material is not possible. Instead, the plants are attacked by certain bacteria, which partly decompose the organic material and liberate oxygen and hydrogen. As these elements escape, the percentage of carbon gradually increases. The bacteria are not able to finish the job of decomposition because they are destroyed by acids liberated from the plants.

The partial decomposition of plant remains in an oxygen-poor swamp creates a layer of *peat*, a soft, brown material in which plant structures are still easily recognized. With shallow burial, peat slowly changes to *lignite*, a soft brown coal. Lignite is actively mined in Saskatchewan but also occurs in Alberta and Manitoba. Burial increases the temperature of sediments as well as the pressure on them.

The higher temperatures bring about chemical reactions within the plant materials and yield water and organic gases (volatiles). As the load increases from more sediment on top of the developing coal, the water and volatiles are pressed out and the proportion of *fixed carbon* (the remaining solid combustible material) increases. The greater the carbon content, the greater is the coal's energy ranking as a fuel. During burial, the coal also becomes increasingly compact. For example, deeper burial transforms lignite into a harder, more compacted black rock called *bituminous* coal. Compared with the peat from which it formed, a bed of bituminous coal may be only one tenth as thick. Canada is a major producer of bituminous coal, the largest deposits occurring in the Maritimes, Alberta, and British Columbia.

Lignite and bituminous coals are sedimentary rocks. However, when sedimentary layers are subjected to the folding and deformation associated with mountain building, the heat and pressure cause a further loss of volatiles and water, thus increasing the concentration of fixed carbon. This metamorphoses bituminous coal into *anthracite*, a very hard, shiny black metamorphic rock. Accordingly, it is no accident that the only Canadian occurrences of anthracite are in the mountainous regions of northern British Columbia and Yukon. Although anthracite is a clean-burning fuel, only a relatively small amount is mined. Anthracite is not widespread (although it is more

◆ **Figure 6.17** Because stagnant swamp water does not allow plants to completely decay, large quantities of plant material can accumulate in a swamp.

common in the U.S. Appalachians) and is more difficult and expensive to extract than the relatively flat-lying layers of bituminous coal.

Coal is a major energy resource. Its role as a fuel and some of the problems associated with burning coal are discussed in Chapter 20.

CLASSIFICATION OF SEDIMENTARY ROCKS

The classification scheme in Figure 6.18 divides sedimentary rocks into two major groups: detrital and chemical. The main criterion for subdividing the detrital rocks is particle size, whereas the primary basis for distinguishing among different rocks in the chemical group is their mineral composition.

As is the case with many (perhaps most) classifications of natural phenomena, the categories presented in Figure 6.18 are more rigid than the actual state of nature. In reality, many of the sedimentary rocks classified into the chemical group also contain at least small quantities of detrital sediment. Many limestones, for example, contain varying amounts of mud or sand, giving them a "sandy" or "shaley" quality. Conversely, because practically all detrital rocks are cemented with material that was originally dissolved in water, they too are far from being pure.

As was the case with the igneous rocks examined in Chapter 3, texture is a part of sedimentary rock classification. There are two major textures used in the classification of sedimentary rocks: clastic and nonclastic. The term **clastic** is taken from the Greek *klastos*, meaning "broken." Rocks that display a clastic texture consist of discrete fragments and particles that are cemented and compacted together. Although cement is present in the spaces between particles, these openings are rarely filled completely. Figure 6.18 shows that *all* detrital rocks have a clastic texture. The table also shows that some chemical sedimentary rocks exhibit this texture, too. For example, coquina, the limestone composed of shells and shell fragments, is obviously as clastic as a conglomerate or sandstone. When the origin of the clastic particles is definitely of biological origin, the term **bioclastic** is commonly used (e.g., shell fragments).

Some chemical sedimentary rocks have a **nonclastic** texture (also called crystalline texture) in which the minerals form a pattern of interlocking

Detrital Sedimentary Rocks			
Clastic Texture Particle Size		Sediment Name	Rock Name
Coarse (over 2 mm)	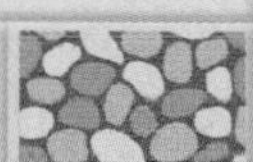	Gravel (Rounded particles)	Conglomerate
		Gravel (Angular particles)	Breccia
Medium (1/16 to 2 mm)	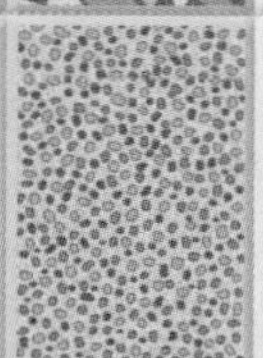	Sand (If abundant feldspar is present the rock is called Arkose)	Sandstone
Fine (1/256 to 1/16 mm)		Silt	Siltstone
Very fine (less than 1/256 mm)		Clay	Shale

Chemical Sedimentary Rocks				
Composition	Texture		Rock Name	
Calcite, $CaCO_3$	Bioclastic	Visible, similar-sized shells (and/or other skeletal components)	Coquina	Biochemical Limestone
		Visible, variously sized shells (and/or other skeletal components) and calcareous mud	Fossiliferous Limestone	
		Microscopic skeletal components	Chalk	
	Nonclastic	Crystalline, may be banded and/or porous	Inorganic Limestone (e.g., Travertine)	
Quartz, SiO_2		Very fine crystalline	Chert	
Gypsum $CaSO_4 \cdot 2H_2O$		Fine to coarse crystalline	Rock Gypsum	
Halite, NaCl		Fine to coarse crystalline	Rock Salt	
Altered plant fragments		Fine-grained organic matter	Coal	

◆ **Figure 6.18** Identification of sedimentary rocks. Sedimentary rocks are divided into two major groups, detrital and chemical, based on their source of sediment. The main criterion for naming detrital sedimentary rocks is particle size, whereas the primary basis for distinguishing among chemical sedimentary rocks is their mineral composition.

A

Close up

B

◆ **Figure 6.19** **A.** Rock salt, the substance that made Goderich, Ontario, famous, is said to have a nonclastic texture because it is composed of intergrown crystals. **B.** A similar crystalline texture is seen in this sample of potash from Saskatchewan. (Photo **A** by E. J. Tarbuck; photo **B** by C. Tsujita)

crystals. The crystals may be microscopically small or large enough to be visible without magnification. Common examples of rocks with nonclastic textures are those deposited when seawater evaporates (Figure 6.19). The materials that make up many other nonclastic rocks may actually have originated as detrital deposits. In these instances, the particles probably consisted of shell fragments and other hard parts rich in calcium carbonate or silica. The clastic nature of the grains was subsequently obliterated or obscured because the particles re-crystallized when they were consolidated into limestone or chert.

Nonclastic rocks consist of intergrown crystals, and some may resemble igneous rocks, which are also crystalline. The two rock types are usually easy to distinguish because the minerals contained in nonclastic sedimentary rocks are quite unlike those found in most igneous rocks. For example, rock salt, gypsum, and some forms of limestone consist of intergrown crystals, but the minerals within these rocks (halite, gypsum, and calcite) are seldom associated with igneous rocks and they scratch easily.

SEDIMENTARY STRUCTURES

In addition to variations in grain size, mineral composition, and texture, sediments exhibit a variety of structures. Some, such as graded beds, are created when sediments are accumulating and are a reflection of the transporting medium. Others, such as *mud cracks*, form after the materials have been deposited and result from processes occurring in the environment. When present, sedimentary structures provide additional information that can be useful in the interpretation of Earth history and in the search for oil and natural gas (see Chapter 20).

Sedimentary rocks form as layer upon layer of sediment accumulates in various depositional environments. These layers, called **strata**, or **beds**, are probably *the single most common and characteristic feature of sedimentary rocks*. Each stratum is unique. It may be coarse sandstone, a fossil-rich limestone, a black shale, and so on. When you look at Figure 6.20 or look back through this chapter at the title page photo, Figure 6.5, and Figure 6.14B, you see many such layers, each different from the others. The variations in texture, composition, and thickness reflect the different conditions under which each layer was deposited.

The thickness of beds ranges from microscopically thin to tens of metres thick. Separating the strata are **bedding planes**, flat surfaces along which rocks tend to separate or break. Changes in the grain size or in the composition of the sediment being deposited can create bedding planes. Pauses in deposition can also lead to layering because chances are slight that newly deposited material will be exactly the same as previously deposited sediment. Generally,

◆ **Figure 6.20** These Cretaceous strata exposed near Drumheller, Alberta, illustrate the characteristic layering of sedimentary rocks. The dark-coloured beds are composed of organic-rich mudstone, whereas the light-coloured beds are composed of sandstone. (Photo by S. R. Hicock)

each bedding plane marks the end of one episode of sedimentation and the beginning of another.

Because sediments usually accumulate as particles that settle from a fluid, most strata are originally deposited as horizontal layers. There are circumstances, however, when sediments do not accumulate in horizontal beds. Sometimes when a bed of sedimentary rock is examined, we see layers within it that are inclined to the horizontal. When this occurs, it is called **cross-bedding** and is most characteristic of sand dunes, river deltas, and certain stream channel deposits (Figure 6.21).

A

B

◆ **Figure 6.21** **A.** The cut-away section of this sand dune shows cross-bedding. **B.** The cross-bedding of this sandstone indicates it was once a sand dune (see Chapter 18). (Photo **A** by John S. Shelton; photo **B** by David Muench Photography, Inc.)

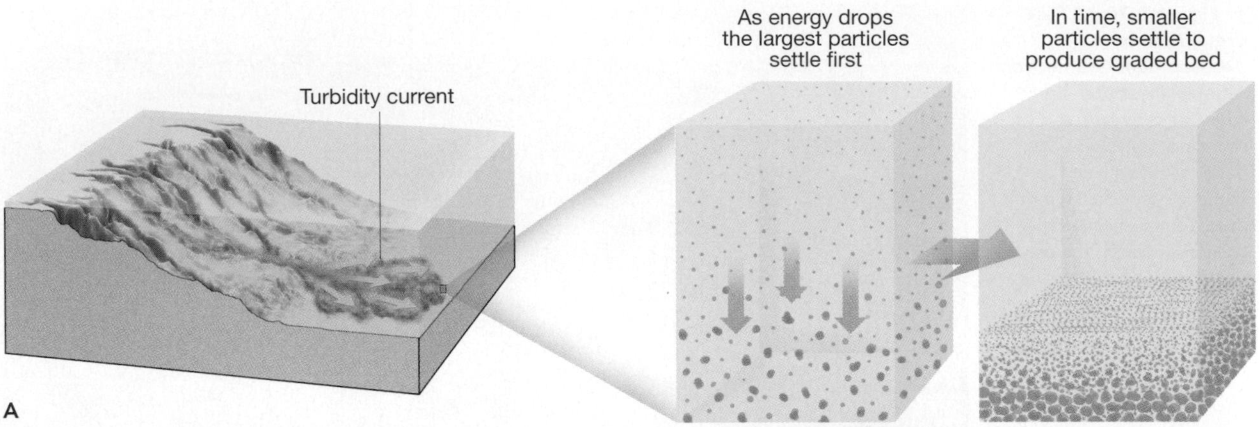

B

◆ **Figure 6.22** **A.** Graded beds. Each layer grades from coarse at its base to fine at the top. **B.** A graded bed in a Proterozoic turbidite deposit of northern Ontario. Note how the grain size decreases upward, from granules at the base of the bed to fine sand at the top. (Photo by Grant Young)

Graded beds represent another special type of bedding. In this case the particles within a single sedimentary layer gradually change from coarse at the bottom to fine at the top (Figure 6.22). Graded beds are most characteristic of rapid deposition from water containing sediment of varying sizes. When a current experiences a rapid energy loss, the largest particles settle first, followed by successively smaller grains. The deposition of a graded bed is most commonly associated with a turbidity current (Figure 6.2), a mass of sediment-choked water that is denser than clear water and that moves downslope along the bottom of a lake or ocean.* Graded beds can also be produced when sediment particles thrown into suspension during a storm settle out after the storm passes.

Geologists can deduce much when they examine sedimentary rocks. A conglomerate, for example, can indicate a high-energy environment, such as a surf zone or rushing stream, where only coarse materials settle out and finer particles are kept suspended (Figures 6.23 and 6.22). If the rock is arkose, it may signify a dry climate in which little chemical alteration of feldspar is possible. Carbonaceous shale is a sign of a low-energy, organic-rich environment, such as a swamp or lagoon (Figure 6.2).

Knowledge of how sedimentary structures form in modern sedimentary deposits provides additional clues to the environments represented by sedimentary rocks (uniformitarianism again). For example, wet mud is observed to shrink on exposure to air, forming **mud cracks** (Figure 6.24). **Ripple marks** are small waves of sand that develop on the surface of a sediment layer by the action of moving water or air (Figure 6.25). The ridges form at right angles to the direction of motion. If the ripple marks were formed by air or water moving in essentially one direction, their form will be asymmetrical. These *current ripple marks* will have steeper sides in the down-current direction and more gradual slopes on the up-current side. Ripple marks produced by a stream flowing across a sandy channel or by wind blowing over a

*More on these currents and graded beds can be found in the section "Submarine Canyons and Turbidity Currents" in Chapter 11.

◆ **Figure 6.23** In a turbulent stream channel, only large particles settle out. Finer sediments remain suspended and continue their downstream journey. This energetic river is in the Rocky Mountains of British Columbia. (Photo by Mike Schering)

sand dune are two common examples of current ripples. When present in solid rock, they can be used to determine the direction of movement of ancient wind or water currents. Other ripple marks have a symmetrical form. These features, called *oscillation ripple marks*, result from the back-and-forth movement of surface waves in a shallow near-shore environment.

The significance of storms in the deposition of sediment in the sea has become apparent in the past couple of decades. Storms are capable of eroding, transporting, and depositing large volumes of sediment in a very short time, only hours to days. This contrasts greatly with the small volumes of sediment that are generally observed during calm water intervals. A common type of sedimentary structure found in sandy storm deposits is **hummocky cross-stratification**, characterized by low-angle laminations that define wavelike undulations up to 1 metre long in cross-section (Figure 6.26A).

A

B

◆ **Figure 6.24** **A.** Mud cracks developed on a modern riverbank. This example is from the Thames River, London, Ontario. **B.** Mud cracks preserved in mudstone. (Photo **A** courtesy of R. W. Hodder; photo **B** by Gary Yeowell/Stone)

A

B

◆ **Figure 6.25** **A.** Ripple marks in sand of a river channel. **B.** Ripple marks preserved in Proterozoic sandstone. (Photo **A** by Galen Rowell/Mountain Light Photography Inc.; photo **B** by Guy Plint)

A

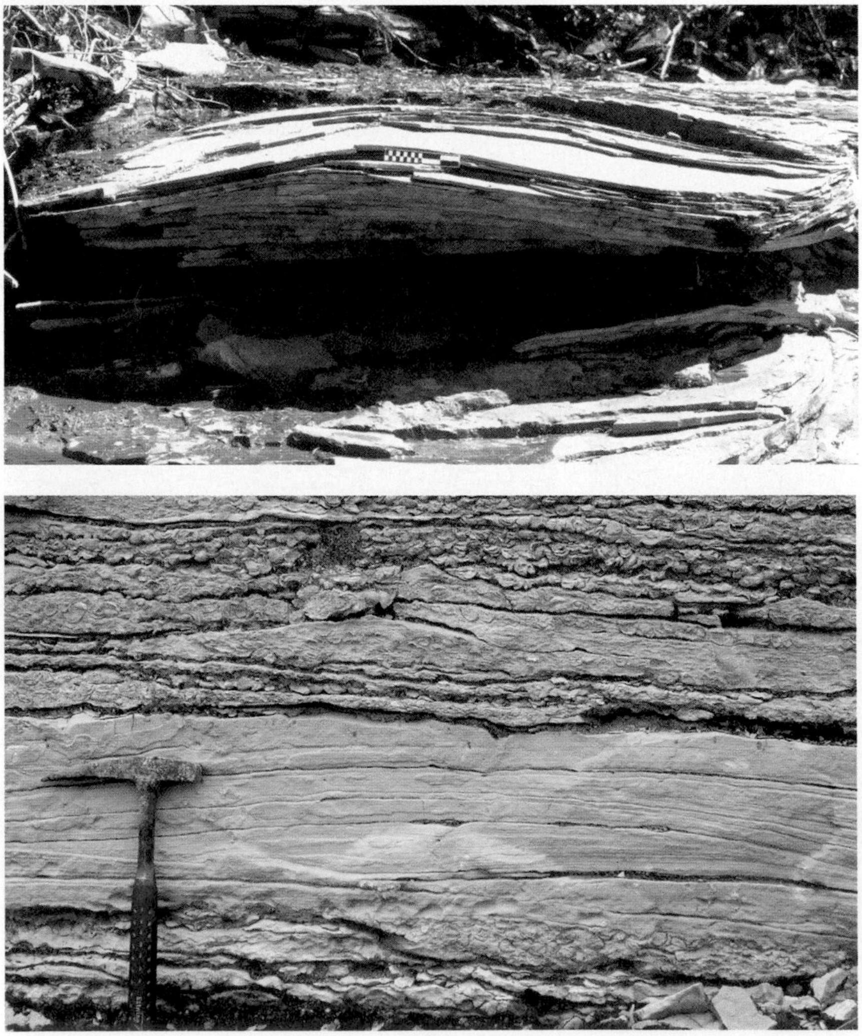

B

◆ **Figure 6.26** **A.** Hummocky cross-stratification, as seen in this Cretaceous sandstone, is a sedimentary structure believed to reflect wave and current action generated by storms. Smallest increments of scale bar are in centimetres. **B.** Storms can also concentrate coarse-grained material, such as shell debris, while washing away much of the mud they were once buried in. Note that the lowermost shell-rich horizon in this photograph marks the base of a limestone bed containing hummocky cross-stratification. (Photo **A** by Guy Plint; photo **B** by Jisuo Jin)

This type of structure is probably formed by large storm waves in the shallow marine environment. Erosion and sorting of sediment on the seafloor by storms can also form concentrations of pebbles, shells, and other coarse-grained debris on areas of the seafloor that are otherwise dominated by fine-grained sediment (Figure 6.26B).

FOSSILS: EVIDENCE OF PAST LIFE

Fossils, the remains or traces of prehistoric life, are important inclusions in sediment and sedimentary rocks (Figure 6.27). Fossils can provide information on sedimentary environments, such as water salinity, temperature, turbidity, depth, and sediment softness/firmness, that may not otherwise be obvious in the physical characteristics of the host rocks. Further, fossils are important time indicators and play a key role in correlating rocks of similar ages among different areas of the world. Fossils can be loosely classified into two categories: *body fossils*, which preserve evidence of the tissues of an organism, and *trace fossils*, which preserve evidence of an organism's activities.

Only a tiny fraction of the organisms that lived during the geologic past have left evidence of their tissues as body fossils. Normally, the remains of an animal or a plant are totally destroyed. Under what circumstances are they preserved?

The preservation of any organic remains requires their isolation from scavengers and microbes that consume and disturb dead tissue and from the physical and chemical agents that assist in the breakdown of mineralized tissues. This means that fossil preservation is more likely to occur when the remains are rapidly entombed, or better yet, when rapid entombment is accompanied by the suppression of scavenging and decomposition. Such conditions were apparently met in the soft-tissue preservation of organisms in amber (fossil resin; Figure 6.27A), tar, and permafrost. However, these cases are exceptional. More commonly, the remains of dead organisms are buried in sediment, where scavengers and microbes degrade the remains to some degree.

Very rarely, the combination of rapid burial of remains and severely low oxygen levels that slow down the decomposition process allow soft tissues to be preserved. These remarkable circumstances were responsible for the soft tissue preservation observed in the famous Cambrian strata of the Burgess Shale in Yoho National Park, British Columbia (see Box 6.2). It is believed that the Burgess Shale organisms were rapidly buried by sediment slumps at the foot of a large, submarine escarpment, a deep-water site with little or no oxygen to support decomposition. The Burgess Shale fossils are preserved as a result of both *carbonization*, the preservation of tissue as a carbon film upon the loss of volatile tissue components, and precipitation of clay or mica minerals on the tissue surfaces. The fossil assemblage of the Burgess Shale is extremely important because it provides a fairly faithful snapshot of the communities (dominated by soft-bodied organisms) that existed shortly after the initial explosive diversification of life at the beginning of the Paleozoic Era.

Soft tissue can also be represented in the fossil record by *imprints* despite not being preserved itself (Figure 6.27B). This type of preservation is typical

A

B

◆ **Figure 6.27** **A.** The soft tissues of this insect are beautifully preserved in amber. **B.** Imprints of spindle- and frond-shaped soft-bodied Ediacaran animals from Mistaken Point, Newfoundland and Labrador. (Photo **A** by Breck P. Kent; photo **B** by Guy Narbonne)

BOX 6.2

Canadian Profile

The Burgess Shale: Yoho National Park, British Columbia

Matt Devereux*

The fossil record can be rich with the remains of durable skeletal materials, such as shell, bone, teeth, and wood. Only in extremely rare circumstances are the softest tissues, like skin, muscle, and gut, ever preserved; consequently, there are very few localities in the world where soft tissue remains are found. The best known of these is the Middle Cambrian (515-million-year-old) Burgess Shale of Yoho National Park in British Columbia (Figure 6.B).

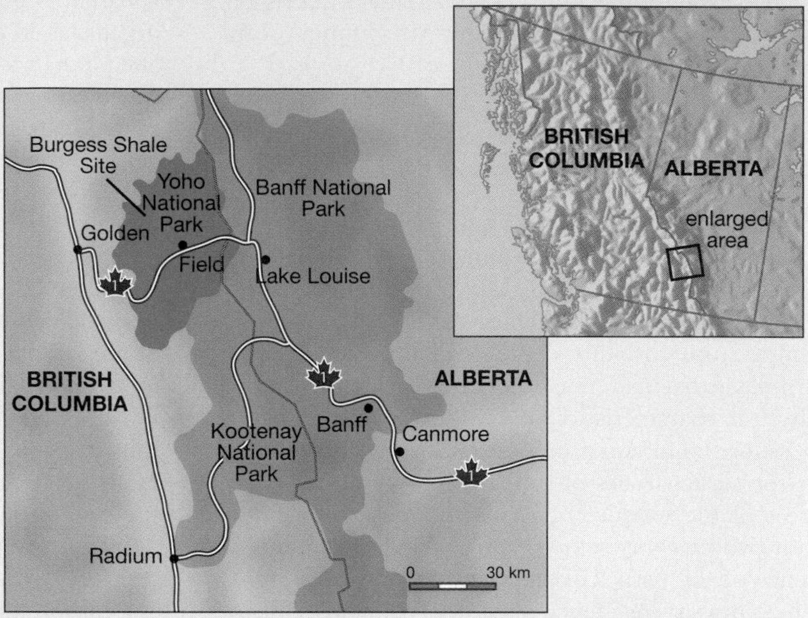

◆ **Figure 6.B** The Burgess Shale is exposed near the town of Field in Yoho National Park in British Columbia.

A prominent American scientist by the name of Charles Doolittle Walcott discovered the Burgess Shale in 1909. In seven summer collecting seasons between 1909 and 1924, he managed to excavate more than 60,000 specimens representing more than 100 different animals. These fossils now reside at the Smithsonian Institution in Washington, DC. More recent excavations, led by Desmond Collins of the Royal Ontario Museum, were just as successful, and many new species have been identified since Walcott's time.

Additional fossils have come from a few hundred cubic metres of shale excavated from a mountain ridge within walking distance of the town of Field, British Columbia (Figure 6.B). The shales were originally deposited as fine mud along the base of an ancient underwater cliff near the continental margin of ancient North America. This cliff has been traced over a distance of some 20 kilometres south of Walcott's quarry, along which other fossil localities have been identified. Though new and important discoveries have been made, none yet rival the original discovery of the Burgess Shale.

◆ **Figure 6.C** A reconstruction of what the seafloor may have looked like in the Middle Cambrian, based on fossil remains preserved in the Burgess Shale. (Photo courtesy of the Royal Tyrrell Museum, Drumheller, Alberta)

The incredibly well-preserved fossils give us a glimpse of life as it was shortly after the "big bang" of animal evolution known as the Cambrian Explosion (Figure 6.C). Some of the animals were probably ancestors of modern sea life, but a significant proportion are so strange that they continue to baffle scientists almost a century after their initial discovery. For example, one animal called *Opabinia* had five eyes on the top of its head and a long snout ending in a claw. Another animal, *Wiwaxia*, looks like a computer mouse armed with blade-like spines. Many animals reveal delicate appendages and others have even been found with their last meal still visible in their gut cavities (Figure 6.D). More remarkable still, components of some of the gut remains are still identifiable (Figure 6.E).

*Matt Devereux studied the Burgess Shale fauna as part of his M.Sc. thesis and is currently the Science Outreach Coordinator at the University of Western Ontario.

A

B

C

◆ **Figure 6.D** The delicate remains of a wide variety of lightly skeletonized organisms are preserved in exquisite detail in the Burgess Shale. Examples shown here are **A.** *Wiwaxia*; **B.** *Marrella*; and **C.** *Canadia*.
(With permission of the Royal Ontario Museum and Parks Canada © ROM. Photo credits: **A** ROM2007_9581_1–J. B. Caron; **B** ROM2006_8107_38–Brian Boyle; **C** ROM2007_9643_2–J. B. Caron)

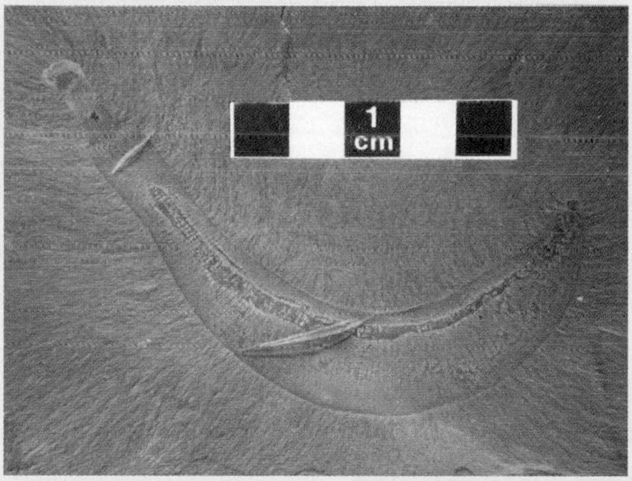

◆ **Figure 6.E** An example of exceptional preservation of soft tissues in the Middle Cambrian Burgess Shale animal *Ottoia*. The animal's gut, containing partly digested food, is represented by the dark-coloured, U-shaped band that follows the length of the animal's body. (Photo by Matt Devereux)

in Precambrian fossils of the oldest complex multicellular animals known (collectively known as Ediacaran fauna), all of which lacked hard skeletons. Were it not for this type of preservation, the existence of complex life before the Paleozoic would be known only from the tracks and trails of a select few organisms.

Hard parts (e.g., shells, bones, and teeth) have a much higher preservation potential than soft tissue because of their physical and chemical durability. Therefore, these parts represent the vast majority of body fossils in the geologic record. If the hard parts are physically and chemically stable in their host sediments, they can be preserved unaltered from their original state. For example, shells composed of calcite or silica are commonly preserved without significant changes in their composition. However, hard parts composed of less stable materials (e.g., calcium carbonate in the form of aragonite) may re-crystallize or be completely dissolved away. Even hard parts have varying degrees of preservational quality.

The preservation of hard parts can follow a number of pathways, depending on the processes they are subjected to both before and after burial. In

◆ **Figure 6.28** Petrified dinosaur bone from southern Alberta. Pores that were once occupied by blood vessels have been infilled with *siderite* (iron carbonate) that precipitated from the porewaters of the surrounding sediment.
(Photo by Denis Tetreault)

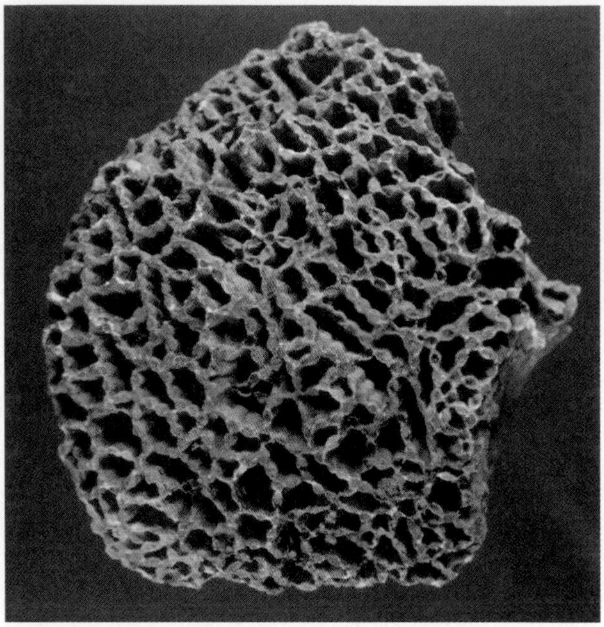

◆ **Figure 6.29** Fossil coral replaced by silica (Manitoulin Island, Ontario). Note that the calcite matrix has dissolved away, leaving only the silicified (silica-replaced) fossil.
(Photo by Denis Tetreault)

some cases, fossilization merely involves the filling of pores in the hard parts by minerals that are precipitated from sediment porewaters. This simple addition of minerals to the original remains is called *petrifaction*, or *permineralization*, and is a common mode of preservation observed in highly porous remains, such as bone and wood (Figure 6.28).

Alternatively, the original minerals in the hard parts may undergo *replacement*, a process that involves the substitution of original material by a different substance. The process of replacement is poorly understood but appears to operate at a molecular level and can faithfully preserve even the most delicate structures. It is not uncommon to find originally calcareous fossil remains replaced by silica (Figure 6.29) or pyrite. Cases in which both hard and soft tissues have been replaced by phosphate are also known.

Body fossils can also be preserved by virtue of the moulding properties of their surrounding sediments (Figure 6.30). For example, a buried bivalved organism with its valves clamped shut will leave an

A B

◆ **Figure 6.30** **A.** Internal moulds of brachiopod shells, surrounded by empty spaces where the shells were dissolved. Internal moulds represent moulds of the interior surface of a fossilized object. Each of these particular shells contained a vertical plate that supported a feeding apparatus. This has been dissolved away to leave a v-shaped slit in each specimen. **B.** An external mould of a bivalve (clam) shell, showing external ribs and growth lines that adorned the outer surface of the shell.
(Photos by Denis Tetreault)

external mould in the sediment surrounding it. If soft sediment is able to fill the empty space between the valves, it will form an *internal mould*, preserving internal features of the shell, such as muscle scars. If the shell completely dissolves away, an internal mould, an external mould, and an empty space where the original shell existed is observed. If the empty space is not filled and is later filled by minerals, a *cast*, or replica of the external form of the original shell will be produced within the external mould (Figure 6.31).

Trace fossils do not represent the actual remains of organisms but rather record their activities. Such traces include footprints (Figure 6.32A), burrows, borings, trails, fossil excrement (Figure 6.32B), and gastroliths ("gizzard stones" of dinosaurs). As in body fossils, the preservation of trace fossils in sediment requires isolation from agents of disturbance that would otherwise obscure the evidence left by the organism. Burrows are commonly preserved because they automatically reside within the sediment and are therefore protected from surface processes. The trace in question is either formed within the sediment or, if produced on the surface, is rapidly buried to avoid being obscured by potential agents of disturbance.

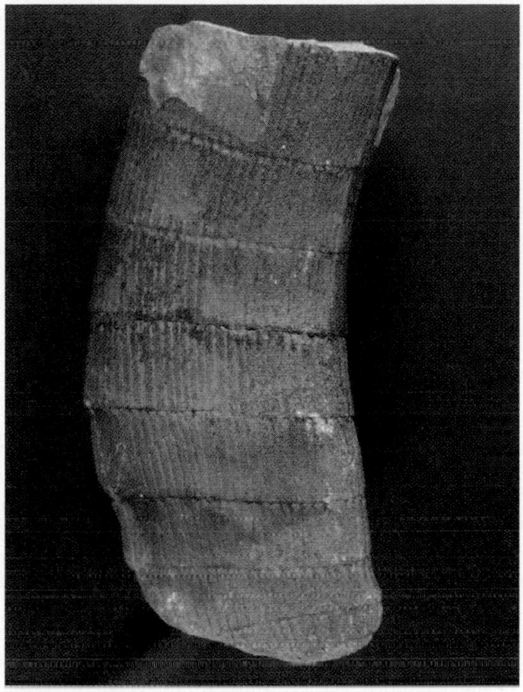

◆ **Figure 6.31** Cast of the stem of a fossil horsetail plant from sandstone of Joggins, Nova Scotia. The space once occupied by wood was filled in with sediment and produced a replica of the original exterior surface of the stem. (Photo by Denis Tetreault)

A

B

◆ **Figure 6.32** **A.** Footprint of an ancient amphibian from Nova Scotia. **B.** Coprolite (fossil excrement), from Cretaceous rocks of Saskatchewan, possibly produced by a small dinosaur. The coprolite is approximately 15 centimetres long.
(Photo by Denis Tetreault)

Chapter Summary

- Sedimentary rock consists of *sediment* that in most cases has been lithified into solid rock by the processes of compaction and cementation. Sediment has two principal sources: (1) as detrital material, which originates and is transported as solid particles from both mechanical and chemical weathering, and, when lithified, forms *detrital sedimentary rocks*; and (2) from soluble material produced largely by chemical weathering, which, when precipitated, forms *chemical sedimentary rocks*.
- *Diagenesis* refers to all of the physical, chemical, and biologic changes that occur after sediments are deposited and during and after the time they are turned into sedimentary rock. Burial promotes diagenesis. Diagenesis includes lithification.
- *Lithification* refers to the processes by which unconsolidated sediments are transformed into solid sedimentary rock. Most sedimentary rocks are lithified by means of *compaction* or *cementation*. Compaction occurs when the weight of overlying materials compresses the deeper sediments. Cementation, the most important process by which sediments are converted to sedimentary rocks, occurs when soluble cementing materials, such as calcite, silica, and iron oxide, are precipitated onto sediment grains, fill open spaces, and join the particles. Although most sedimentary rocks are lithified by compaction or cementation, certain chemical rocks, such as the *evaporites*, initially form as solid masses of intergrown crystals.
- *Sedimentary environments* are those places in which sediment accumulates. They are grouped into continental, transitional (shoreline), and marine environments. Each is characterized by certain physical, chemical, and biologic conditions. Because sediment contains clues about the environment in which it was deposited, sedimentary rocks are important in the interpretation of Earth's history.
- Particle size is the primary basis for distinguishing among various detrital sedimentary rocks. The size of the particles in a detrital rock indicates the energy of the medium that transported them. For example, gravels are moved by swiftly flowing rivers, whereas less energy is required to transport sand. Common detrital sedimentary rocks include mudrocks (silt- and clay-size particles), sandstone, and conglomerate (rounded gravel-size particles) or breccia (angular gravel-size particles).
- Precipitation of chemical sediments occurs in two ways: (1) by inorganic processes, such as evaporation and chemical activity; or (2) by organic processes of water-dwelling organisms that produce sediments of biochemical origin. Limestone, the most abundant chemical sedimentary rock, consists of the mineral calcite ($CaCO_3$) and forms either by inorganic means or as the result of biochemical processes. Inorganic limestones include travertine, which is commonly seen in caves, and oolitic limestone, consisting of small spherical grains of calcium carbonate. Other common chemical sedimentary rocks include dolostone (composed of the calcium-magnesium carbonate mineral dolomite), chert (made of microcrystalline silica), evaporites (such as rock salt and rock gypsum), and coal (lignite and bituminous).
- Sedimentary rocks can be divided into two main groups: detrital and chemical. All detrital rocks have a *clastic* texture, which consists of discrete fragments and particles that are cemented and compacted together. The main criterion for subdividing the detrital rocks is particle size. Common detrital rocks include conglomerate, sandstone, and mudrocks. The primary basis for distinguishing among different rocks in the chemical group is their mineral composition. Some chemical rocks, such as those deposited when seawater evaporates, have a *nonclastic* texture in which the minerals form a pattern of interlocking crystals. However, in reality, many of the sedimentary rocks classified into the chemical group also contain at least small quantities of detrital sediment. Common chemical rocks include limestone, rock gypsum, and coal (e.g., lignite and bituminous).
- Sedimentary rocks are particularly important in interpreting Earth's history because, as layer upon layer of sediment accumulates, each records the nature of the environment at the time the sediment was deposited. These layers, called *strata*, or *beds*, are probably the single most characteristic feature of sedimentary rocks. Other features found in some sedimentary rocks, such as *ripple marks*, *mud cracks*, *cross-bedding*, and *fossils*, also provide clues to past environments.

Review Questions

1. How does the volume of sedimentary rocks in Earth's crust compare with the volume of igneous rocks in the crust? Are sedimentary rocks evenly distributed throughout the crust?
2. What is diagenesis? Give an example.
3. Compaction is most important as a lithification process with which sediment grain size?

4. List three common cements for sedimentary rocks. How can each be identified?
5. List three categories of sedimentary environments. Provide one or more examples for each category.
6. What minerals are most common in detrital sedimentary rocks? Why are these minerals so abundant?
7. What is the primary basis for distinguishing among various detrital sedimentary rocks?
8. Why does shale usually crumble easily?
9. How are the degree of sorting and the amount of rounding related to the transportation of sand grains?
10. Distinguish between conglomerate and breccia.
11. Distinguish between the two categories of chemical sedimentary rocks.
12. What are evaporite deposits? Name a rock that is an evaporite.
13. When a body of seawater evaporates, minerals precipitate in a certain order. What determines this order?
14. Each of the following statements describes one or more characteristics of a particular sedimentary rock. For each statement, name the sedimentary rock that is being described.
    (a) An evaporite used to make plaster
    (b) A fine-grained detrital rock that exhibits *fissility*
    (c) Dark-coloured sandstone containing angular rock particles as well as clay, quartz, and feldspar
    (d) The most abundant chemical sedimentary rock
    (e) A dark-coloured hard rock made of microcrystalline quartz
    (f) A variety of limestone composed of small spherical grains
15. How is coal different from other biochemical sedimentary rocks?
16. What is the primary basis for distinguishing among different chemical sedimentary rocks?
17. Distinguish between clastic and nonclastic textures. What type of texture is common to all detrital sedimentary rocks?
18. Some nonclastic sedimentary rocks closely resemble igneous rocks. How can the two be distinguished easily?
19. What is probably the single most characteristic feature of sedimentary rocks?
20. Distinguish between cross-bedding and graded bedding.
21. How do current ripple marks differ from oscillation ripple marks?
22. List two conditions that favour the preservation of organisms as fossils.
23. What type of fossilization is indicated by each of the following statements for body fossils? Which one is an example of a trace fossil?
    (a) A leaf preserved as a thin carbon film
    (b) Small internal cavities and pores of a log filled with mineral matter
    (c) Fossil dung
    (d) This is created when a mould is filled with mineral matter

Key Terms

bedding plane (p. 172)
beds (p. 172)
biochemical (p. 163)
bioclastic (p. 171)
cementation (p. 153)
chemical sedimentary rock (p. 158)
clastic (p. 171)
compaction (p. 153)
cross-bedding (p. 173)
detrital sedimentary rock (p. 158)
diagenesis (p. 153)
environment of deposition (p. 154)
evaporite deposit (p. 168)
fissility (p. 159)
fossil (p. 177)
graded bed (p. 174)
hummocky cross-stratification (p. 175)
lithification (p. 153)
mud crack (p. 174)
nonclastic (p. 171)
pore space (p. 153)
ripple mark (p. 174)
salt flat (p. 169)
sediment (p. 152)
sedimentary environment (p. 154)
sedimentary facies (p. 155)
sorting (p. 160)
strata (p. 172)

Web Resources

The *Earth* website uses the resources and flexibility of the internet to aid in your study of the topics in this chapter. Written and developed by geology instructors, this site will help improve your understanding of geology. Visit **www.pearsoned.ca/tarbuck** and click on the cover of the text to find

- online review quizzes
- Web-based critical thinking and writing exercises
- links to chapter-specific Web resources
- internet-wide key-term searches

www.pearsoned.ca/tarbuck

Chapter 7

Metamorphism and Metamorphic Rocks

Deformed Precambrian metamorphic rocks north of Barrie, Ontario. (Photo by Mike Schering)

As we have seen in the previous chapters, igneous and sedimentary processes are relatively straightforward. Igneous rocks result from the intrusion or extrusion of magma generated within Earth, whereas sedimentary rocks result from deposition of particles derived from existing rock or by the precipitation of minerals from a solution. Metamorphism, however, involves some very complex physical and chemical processes that can affect existing rocks through heat, changes in pressure, the flow of fluids deep below Earth's surface, or a combination of these factors.

The conditions and time scales involved in metamorphism are difficult to comprehend. To begin to appreciate the dynamics of metamorphism we need only consider the belt of metamorphic rocks that stretches from the northern Georgian Bay area of Ontario, through the northern St. Lawrence Region of Quebec, and into Newfoundland and Labrador. Around 1 billion years ago, these rocks lay several kilometres below the surface and were subjected to temperatures in excess of 800°C. This is because these very rocks occupied the roots of a mountain chain that may have risen as high as the present-day Himalayas. Incredibly, the intense deformation (Figure 7.1) and radical mineral changes in these rocks occurred entirely while the rock was solid.

Metamorphism occurs under extreme conditions, and almost always deep below Earth's surface, so we cannot directly observe active metamorphic processes. Because of this, our understanding of metamorphic processes is largely built on observations of ancient metamorphic rocks and experiments conducted in special high-temperature/high-pressure laboratories.

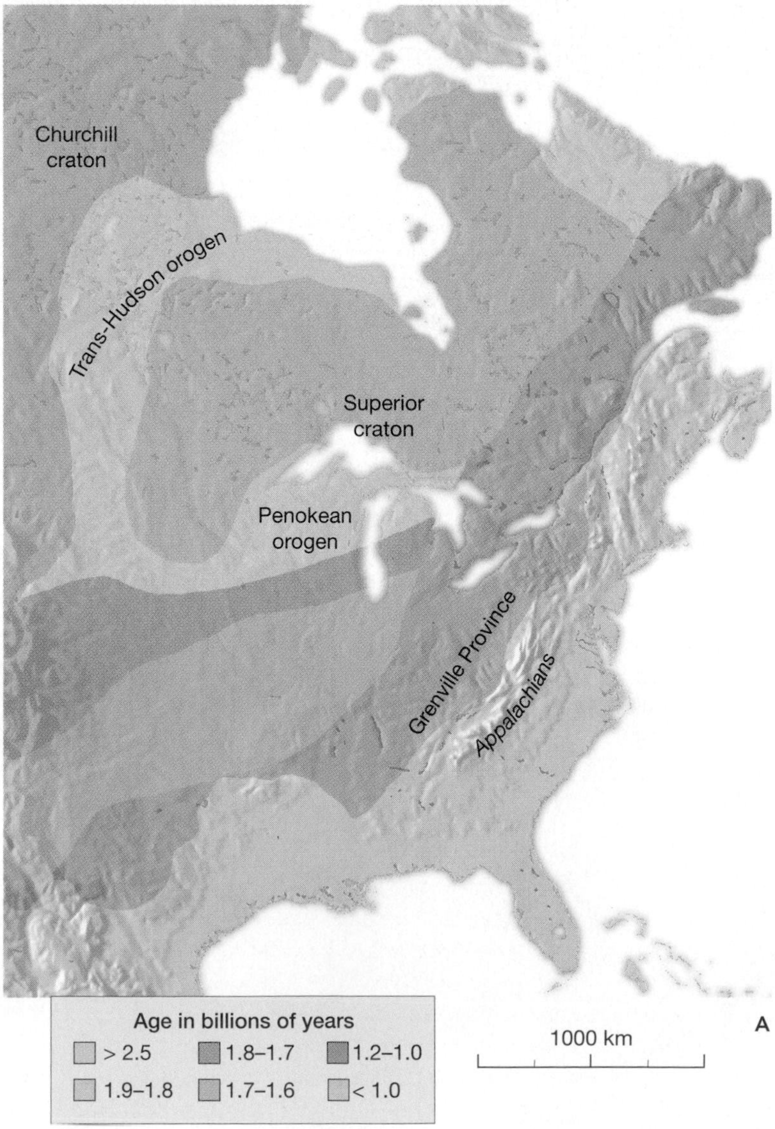

A

B

◆ **Figure 7.1** **A.** Metamorphic rocks of the Grenville Province were formed in the roots of a Precambrian mountain chain that formed 1 billion years ago and may have risen as high as the Himalayas. Most of these metamorphic rocks are now covered with a thick pile of younger sedimentary rocks. **B.** Folded Precambrian metamorphic rocks of the Grenville Province at Parry Sound, Ontario. (Photo by W. R. Church)

METAMORPHISM

GEODe EARTH Metamorphic Rocks
↳ Introduction

The term **metamorphism**, meaning to "change form," collectively refers to the changes that take place *when a rock is subjected to temperatures or pressures markedly different from those in which it originally formed.* These changes happen in a solid state, although hot fluids migrating through the rock may play a key role in the process. Physical and chemical characteristics of the rock change in order to establish equilibrium with the new temperature/pressure conditions it encounters.

The type and degree of change in the transformation of an existing **parent rock** to a metamorphic rock depends on the type and intensity of individual or combined metamorphic processes involved. On one hand, lightly metamorphosed slate can be difficult to distinguish from its shale parent rock. On the other hand, metamorphism can be so severe that all of the distinguishing characteristics of the parent rock, including its original mineral content, become unrecognizable (Figure 7.2).

◆ **Figure 7.2** Deformed metamorphic rocks exposed in southern Greenland.
(Photo by Carl Ozyer)

CONTROLLING FACTORS IN METAMORPHISM

GEODe EARTH Metamorphic Rocks
↳ Agents of Metamorphism

The overall chemical composition of a metamorphic rock largely reflects that of its parent rock, but the **texture** and *specific mineral makeup* of the rock depend on the particular physical processes involved in the metamorphic transformation. The main factors controlling metamorphism are heat, pressure, and chemically active fluids. In this section, we will examine the significance of these fundamental factors.

Composition of the Parent Rock

All metamorphic rocks ultimately originate from existing parent rocks. Accordingly, the composition of a parent rock greatly determines the characteristics of the resultant metamorphic rock. Even though elements can be redistributed between minerals and some elements or volatiles, such as water, may leak in or out during metamorphism, the chemical composition of a metamorphic rock is usually inherited largely from its parent. For example, the metamorphism of a mafic igneous rock will result in the formation of a metamorphic rock that is relatively rich in iron- and magnesium-bearing minerals, whereas the metamorphism of a felsic igneous rock will result in a metamorphic rock that is depleted in such minerals but rich in feldspar and quartz. Likewise, clay minerals contained in shale can re-crystallize to form micas, and the calcite in marble is obviously derived from a limestone parent. It is only in extreme cases of element loss or gain because of fluid migration that a metamorphic rock becomes substantially different in composition from its parent rock.

Heat as a Metamorphic Agent

Heat is one of the most important agents of metamorphism. Not only does heat drive the basic chemical reactions that transform minerals into new forms, but it also influences the mobility and reactivity of chemically active fluids. The heating of parent rocks can occur in two ways. First, heat given off by an intrusive igneous body can locally bake the rocks surrounding it. Second, rocks can be cooked by Earth's internal heat (geothermal gradient) if they are brought to great depths below the surface, as in a subduction zone (Figure 7.3).

Keep in mind that different minerals are stable at different temperatures and therefore do not all change at the same time. For example, at temperatures between 150°C and 200°C, clay minerals become unstable and start changing into micas. Conversely, such minerals as quartz remain stable at these temperatures and can remain so in environments with much higher temperatures.

Pressure (Stress) as a Metamorphic Agent

Whereas the primary role of heat in metamorphism is to change the distribution of chemical components within a rock, pressure is primarily responsible for changing the physical characteristics of the rock. Pressure does, however, also influence the temperature at which certain minerals are stable and therefore plays a role in dictating the distribution of elements within a metamorphic rock. When discussing the deformation of rocks, the term *stress* is sometimes substituted for *pressure*.

Confining Pressure (Uniform Stress) **Confining pressure**, also called **uniform stress**, involves the squeezing of a rock in all directions, "confining" the material into the smallest possible volume with no change in shape. Water pressure is a familiar form of confining pressure that increases with water depth under the weight of the overlying water mass. When you dive into deep water, you can feel the increasing water pressure in your ears, but your body is certainly not pressed flat. This is because the pressure is not only transmitted through the water from above but is also applied from all directions. In the same way, a rock below Earth's surface experiences uniform pressure from all directions under the weight of the overlying rock column (Figure 7.4A). Accordingly, confining pressure increases with increasing depth of burial. At great depths, confining pressure can force mineral grains to crowd together and crystal arrangements to become more compact. Because no internal deformation is involved, these simple changes form metamorphic rocks that are harder and denser and contain new minerals but are otherwise similar in appearance to their parent rocks (Figure 7.5A).

Directed Pressure (Differential Stress) **Directed pressure**, also called **differential stress**, refers to the unequal application of pressure, resulting in the distortion of a body (Figure 7.4B). Within the Earth, directed pressure is largely associated with the hori-

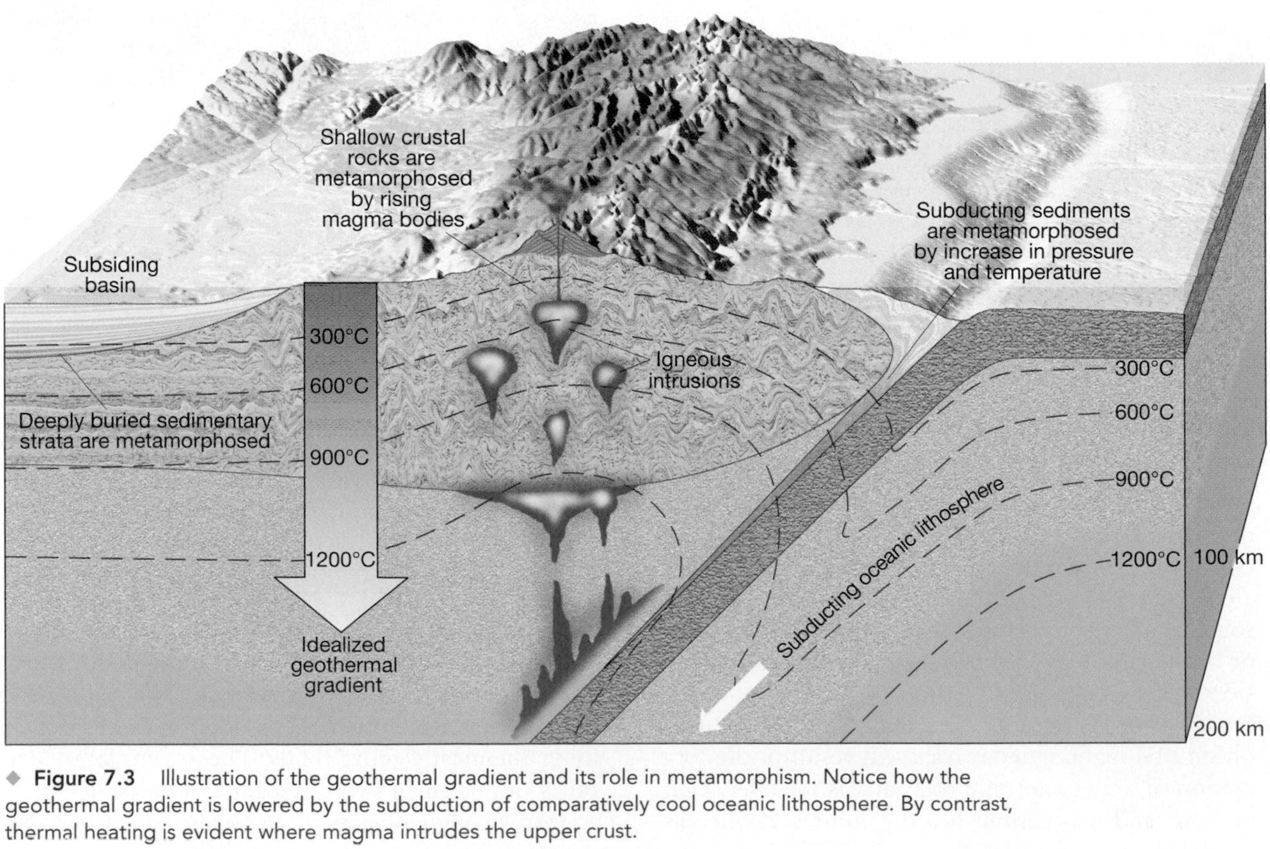

◆ **Figure 7.3** Illustration of the geothermal gradient and its role in metamorphism. Notice how the geothermal gradient is lowered by the subduction of comparatively cool oceanic lithosphere. By contrast, thermal heating is evident where magma intrudes the upper crust.

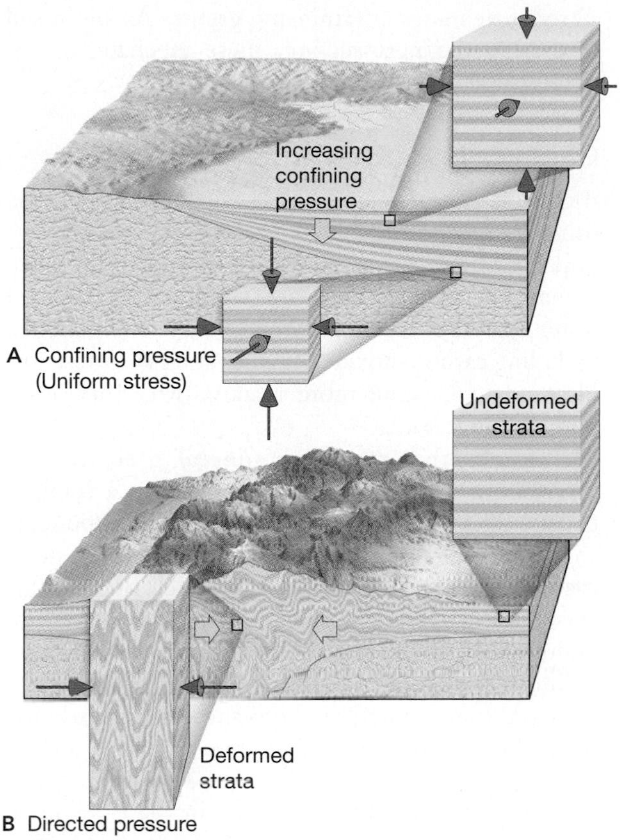

◆ **Figure 7.4** The effects of pressure on the texture of metamorphic rocks. **A.** If solely affected by confining pressure (uniform stress), metamorphic rocks retain features of their parent rock, such as bedding. **B.** Directed pressure (differential stress) causes rocks to crumple in the plane of least stress.

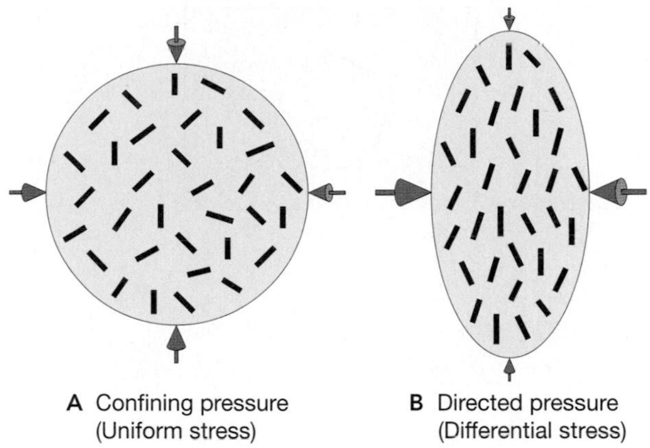

◆ **Figure 7.5** **A.** Confining pressure (uniform stress) acts to push mineral grains from all directions, allowing them to remain in their original orientation. **B.** Directed pressure (differential stress) causes grains to become preferentially aligned toward the plane of least stress.

zontal shortening and stretching of Earth's crust caused by plate tectonic activity.

Three basic types of directed pressure are recognized. Perhaps the most obvious type is compressional stress that is characterized by a "pushing together" motion and results in crustal shortening (Figure 7.4B). Tensional stress involves a "pulling apart" motion that results in crustal stretching. Finally, in shear stress, forces are parallel but are directed in opposite directions, causing layers of material to slide parallel to one another like cards in a deck.

In surface environments where temperatures are comparatively low, rocks are *brittle* and tend to fracture when subjected to directed pressure. Continued deformation under such conditions grinds and pulverizes the mineral grains into small fragments. By contrast, in higher temperature environments, rocks are ductile. When rocks exhibit *ductile* behaviour, their mineral grains tend to flatten and elongate when subjected to directed pressure, and the rock tends to respond to directed pressure by flowing (rather than fracturing). The vast majority of metamorphic rocks affected by directed pressure show evidence of ductile deformation.

The results of directed pressure and ductile deformation are clearly manifested in the spectacular folds and other structures found in many metamorphic rocks (Figure 7.2). However, on a much smaller (microscopic) scale, directed pressure also greatly affects the texture of metamorphic rocks. Under directed pressure, platy (sheet-like to tablet-shaped) and elongate grains of minerals tend to become aligned so that they are oriented parallel to the direction of minimum stress (Figure 7.5B). You can probably imagine what the internal texture of a pile of leaves would look like if you and all your friends sat on the pile. In the same way, the preferred orientation of platy and elongate mineral grains in a metamorphic rock affected by directed pressure forms a layered or banded texture that is, quite fittingly, called **foliation** (*folium* = leaf). Three main factors influence the development of foliation:

1. Rotation of platy and/or elongate mineral grains into a new orientation
2. Changing the shape of equidimensional grains into elongate shapes that are aligned in a preferred orientation
3. Re-crystallization of minerals to form new grains growing in the direction of preferred orientation

The rotation of existing mineral grains is the easiest of these mechanisms to envision. Figure 7.5B illustrates the mechanics by which platy/elongate minerals are rotated. The new alignment is parallel to the direction of least stress and perpendicular to the direction of maximum stress. Although physical

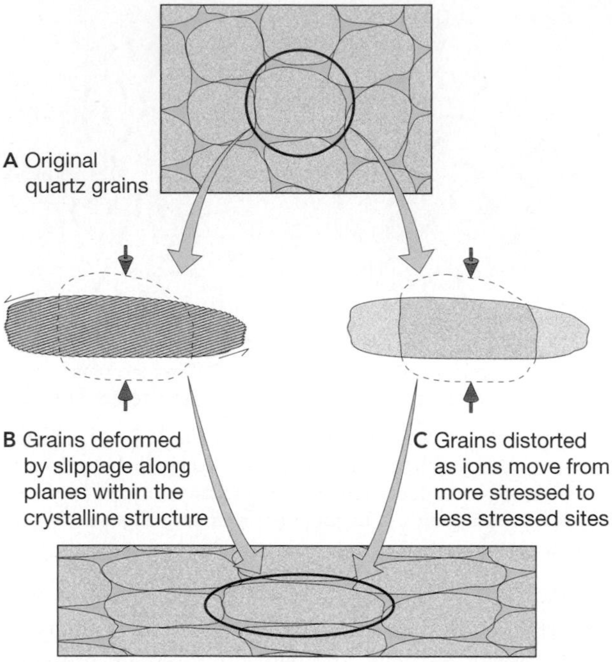

◆ **Figure 7.6** Development of preferred orientations of such minerals as quartz, calcite, and olivine. **A.** Ductile deformation leading to the flattening and elongation of these roughly equidimensional mineral grains can occur in one of two ways. **B.** The first mechanism is a solid-state plastic flow that involves intracrystalline gliding of individual units within each grain. **C.** The second mechanism involves dissolving material from areas of high stress and depositing that material in locations of low stress. **D.** Both mechanisms change the shape of the grains, but the volume and composition of each grain remains essentially unchanged.

rotation of platy minerals contributes to the development of foliation under low to moderate stress conditions, other mechanisms dominate in more extreme environments.

Grain elongation, another factor that can impart a foliated appearance to a rock, results from internal deformation along planes within the crystal structure of mineral grains (Figure 7.6B). This type of elongation is well illustrated by the rock metaconglomerate. In this rock type, the drastic change in the shape of the pebbles is the net result of internal deformation within constituent mineral crystals of the pebbles (Figure 7.7).

Re-crystallization involves the creation of new mineral grains from old ones. In some cases, mineral components can be dissolved, transported to a different site, and re-precipitated on other mineral grains. In others, re-crystallization involves the mass transfer of mineral material from highly stressed to less stressed areas on individual mineral grains (Figure 7.6C). In both cases, crystal growth is focused in the direction of least stress, resulting in the preferred orientation of mineral grains. As discussed further in the next section, these mechanisms are greatly aided by chemically active fluids.

Chemically Active Fluids

Although all true metamorphic change occurs in the solid state, **chemically active fluids** can play an important role in some types of metamorphism. Chemically active fluids are composed mainly of water but also contain other volatile components, including carbon dioxide. As a general rule, these fluids tend to become more reactive with increasing temperature.

Fluids that surround mineral grains act as catalysts to promote textural changes in a rock by enhancing the migration of chemical components without being consumed in the process. A good example of this is the manner in which fluids influence mineral re-crystallization. When two mineral grains are squeezed together, the parts of their crystalline structures that touch are the most highly stressed. Ions located at these sites are readily dissolved by the hot fluids and migrate along the surface of the grain to locations where the two grains are not in direct contact. Thus, fluids aid in the crystallization of mineral grains by dissolving material from regions of high stress and then precipitating it in areas of low stress (Figure 7.6C). As a result, *minerals tend to crystallize and grow longer in a direction perpendicular to compressional stresses.*

Fluid components not only are important as catalysts but can also play significant roles in changing the overall chemical composition of a rock. For example, water that permeates rocks in mid-ocean ridges reacts with anhydrous (water-free) high-temperature

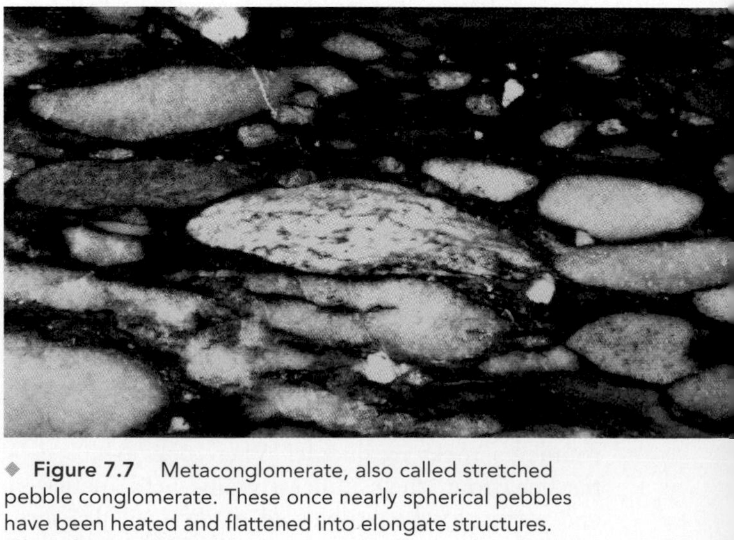

◆ **Figure 7.7** Metaconglomerate, also called stretched pebble conglomerate. These once nearly spherical pebbles have been heated and flattened into elongate structures. (Photo by E. J. Tarbuck)

minerals, such as olivine, to produce hydrated minerals, such as *serpentine*:

$$\underset{\text{olivine}}{2Mg_2SiO_4} + \underset{\text{water}}{2H_2O} \rightarrow \underset{\text{serpentine}}{Mg_3Si_2O_5(OH)_4} + \underset{\text{(in solution)}}{MgO}$$

Fluids are also essential transport media for chemical components that are released by some metamorphic reactions. These dissolved components can react with minerals elsewhere to produce new minerals or can be carried out of the metamorphic environment altogether. It is largely because some elements can be transported by fluids that the chemical composition of a metamorphic rock is sometimes different from its parent rock.

What is the source of these chemically active fluids? Water occurs in the pore spaces of sedimentary rocks and in fractures of igneous rocks and can contribute to the fluid system in a metamorphic environment. Water also occurs within minerals of the parent rocks themselves. Many minerals, such as clays, micas, and amphiboles, are *hydrated* (*hydra* = water), meaning that they naturally contain water in their crystal structures. When a rock is heated during metamorphism, these minerals become dehydrated. For example, heating of muscovite mica produces potassium feldspar, corundum, and water:

$$\underset{\text{muscovite}}{KAl_2(AlSi_3O_{10})(OH)_2} + \text{heat} \rightarrow \underset{\text{potassium feldspar}}{KAlSi_3O_8} + \underset{\text{corundum}}{Al_2O_3} + \underset{\text{water}}{H_2O}$$

The water driven off by mineral dehydration can migrate to areas of lower temperature and pressure, where it can participate in the metamorphic reactions discussed above. Of equal significance, however, is the slowing down of chemical reactions in rocks that have lost water through mineral dehydration. It is because mineral reactions slow down significantly with progressive water loss that anhydrous high-temperature minerals tend not to revert back to their original hydrous forms.

METAMORPHIC GRADE AND INDEX MINERALS

GEODe EARTH Metamorphic Rocks
↳ Textural and Mineralogical Changes

Now that we have considered the various factors that influence the formation of metamorphic rocks, we can take a closer look at environments below Earth's surface where most metamorphism takes place. As you will see, observations of mineral composition and texture are key to understanding how metamorphic rocks form.

Metamorphic rocks are often described in terms of their **metamorphic grade**, or intensity of metamorphism they have experienced. In general, an increase in metamorphic grade is indicated by the sequential appearance of minerals that are stable at progressively higher temperatures and, in some cases, progressively higher pressures. In some metamorphic rocks, texture can also be used as an indicator of grade.

As determined in laboratory studies, some metamorphic minerals form, and remain stable, within relatively narrow, well-defined ranges of temperature and pressure. Some of these minerals are used as **index minerals** to define the grade of a metamorphic rock (Figure 7.8). For example, the mineral *chlorite* begins to form at relatively low temperatures, cooler than 200°C. Thus, rocks that contain chlorite are referred to as *low grade*. At the opposite end of the spectrum, the mineral *sillimanite* forms only in extreme environments where temperatures exceed 600°C; and rocks containing sillimanite are considered *high grade*. *Intermediate grade* metamorphic rocks record conditions between these opposite ends of the spectrum and can contain metamorphic minerals, such as biotite and garnet.

The formation of some metamorphic minerals depends on a combination of temperature and pressure conditions. Among such minerals are *andalusite*, *kyanite*, and *sillimanite* (Figure 7.8). These three minerals have the same chemical composition (Al_2SiO_5), but each is distinguished by a unique set of mineral properties, including crystal form. Because they have well-defined fields of stability with respect to both temperature and pressure, they are particularly useful as index minerals for some metamorphic rocks.

Because metamorphism may or may not involve significant changes in pressure as a rock is heated, and some rocks may not contain pressure-sensitive index minerals, it is important to consider the texture of a metamorphic rock when interpreting its conditions of formation (Figure 7.9). In rocks that have simply been heated without significant increases in directed pressure, increasing metamorphic grade is simply indicated by the appearance of higher temperature index minerals. In such cases, the more or less uniform pressure conditions allow platy and elongate mineral grains to remain randomly oriented regardless of the degree of heating, and the rock will retain a **nonfoliated** appearance. However, the increasing metamorphic grade of a rock subjected to significant increases in both temperature and

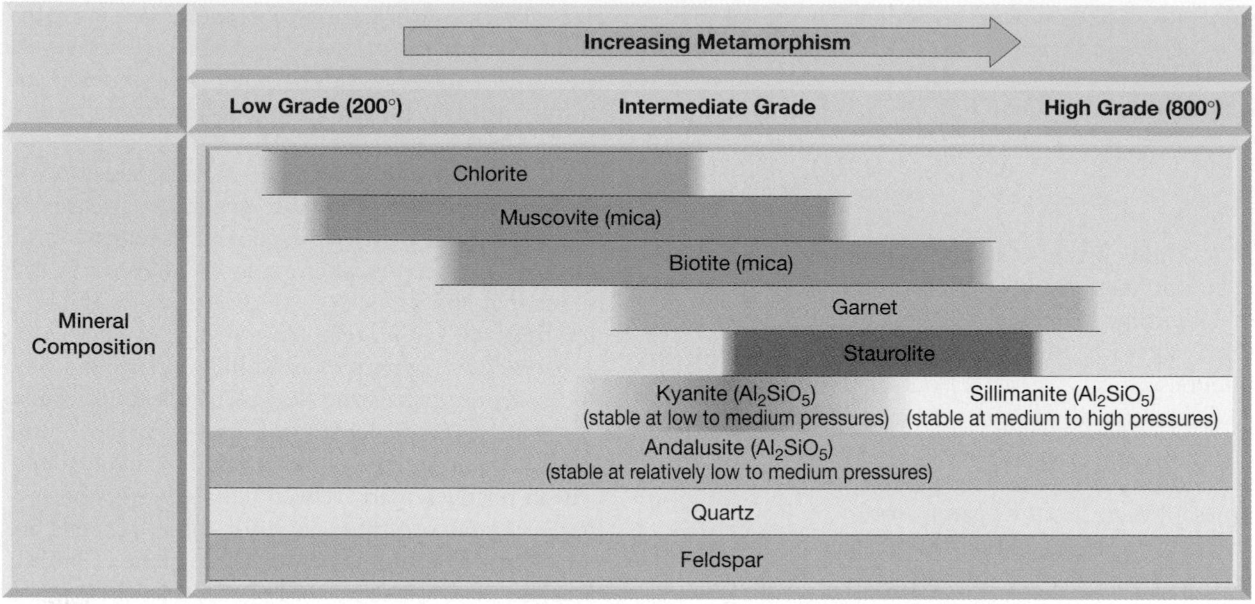

◆ **Figure 7.8** Index minerals provide information on the temperature and pressure conditions experienced by a rock during metamorphism. The parent rock in this case is shale. This diagram shows the temperature ranges in which selected index minerals are stable. Note that the stabilities of andalusite, kyanite, and sillimanite are sensitive to both temperature and pressure, making them useful index minerals for metamorphic rocks affected by both factors.

directed pressure is reflected by the appearance of higher-temperature minerals, as well as increased grain size of the constituent minerals and the progressive development of foliation.

The basic spectrum of metamorphic conditions dictated by temperature and pressure changes are those classified in the categories of burial, contact, regional, and subduction zone metamorphism. The

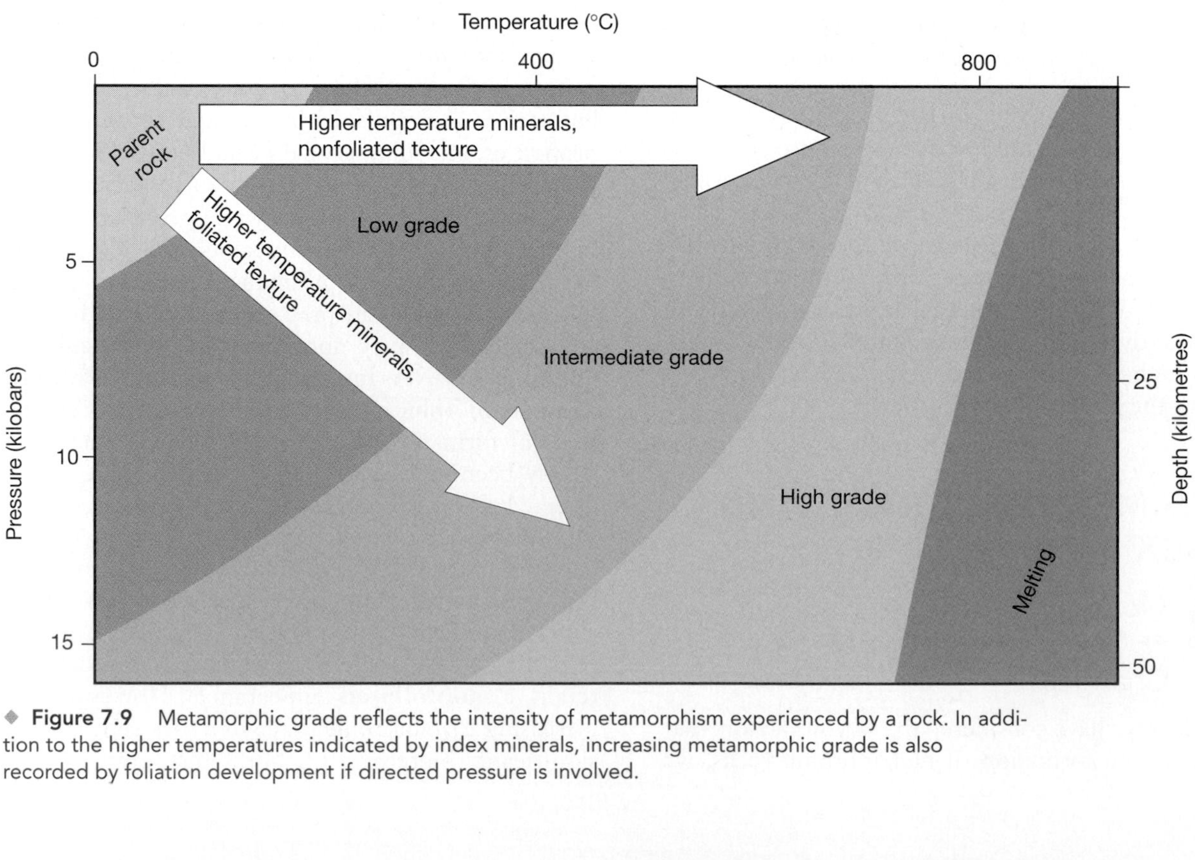

◆ **Figure 7.9** Metamorphic grade reflects the intensity of metamorphism experienced by a rock. In addition to the higher temperatures indicated by index minerals, increasing metamorphic grade is also recorded by foliation development if directed pressure is involved.

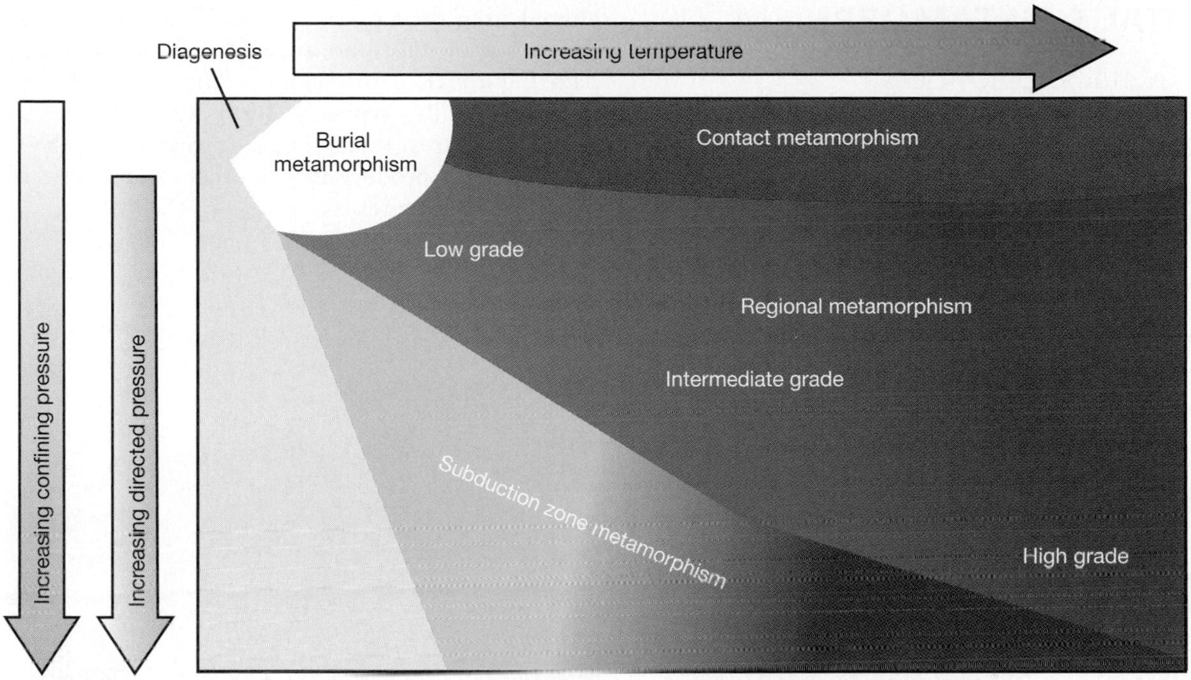

◆ **Figure 7.10** Basic types of metamorphism associated with changes in temperature and pressure. Note that true metamorphism occurs at temperatures higher than those experienced by sedimentary rocks during diagenesis.

relative importance of these factors for each basic type of metamorphism is illustrated in Figure 7.10.

BURIAL METAMORPHISM

Burial metamorphism involves the mild alteration of rock (usually sedimentary, but sometimes volcanic) by an increase in temperature and confining pressure and can essentially be viewed as a step beyond sediment diagenesis (Figure 7.10). Such conditions are met in the deepest areas of sedimentary basins, ocean trenches, and passive margins where geothermal heat is sufficient to re-crystallize minerals in sedimentary parent rocks to form low-grade metamorphic minerals, such as *zeolites* (from hydration of silicates) and chlorite (altered from clay; Figure 7.11). As a result of increased confining pressure and minimal directed pressure, rocks become denser but are not distorted. They therefore resemble rocks affected by low-temperature contact metamorphism. The effects of this type of metamorphism can be so mild that such features as bedding and grain size variations are preserved.

The specific depth required for burial metamorphism varies according to differences in geothermal gradient from place to place. On average, low-grade metamorphism usually begins at depths of about 8 kilometres, where temperatures reach up to 200°C. However, burial metamorphism can occur closer to the surface in areas with steeper geothermal gradients.

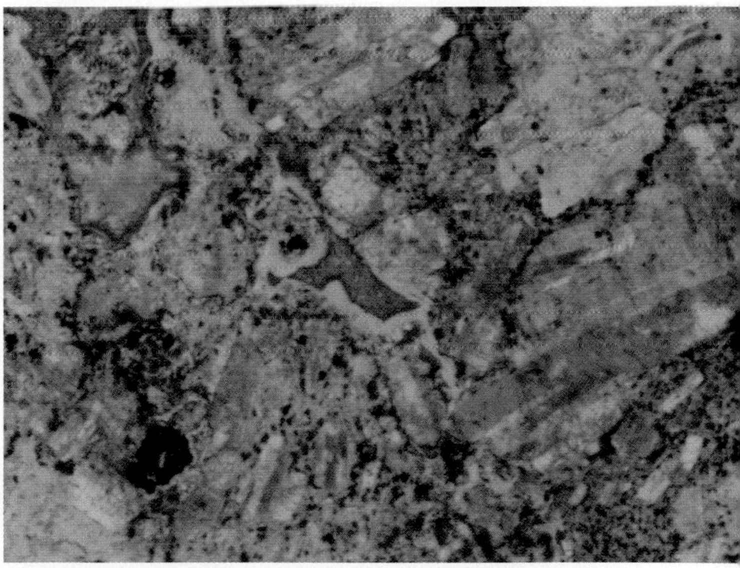

◆ **Figure 7.11** Sample of volcanic tuff from South Island, New Zealand, subjected to burial metamorphism. Because this rock has been affected by confining pressure only, the individual grains of the rock (including shards of volcanic glass and grains of feldspar) have retained their original shape. However, metamorphic minerals, such as zeolites and chlorite (imparting a greenish colour), are present in the groundmass. The width of the image is approximately 5 millimetres. (Photo by David Dillon)

CONTACT METAMORPHISM

GEODe EARTH Metamorphic Rocks
↳ Common Metamorphic Rocks

Contact metamorphism (also known as *thermal metamorphism*) occurs when rocks immediately surrounding an igneous body are cooked and therefore altered from their original state. The altered rocks define a zone called an **aureole** (*aureolus* = golden halo; Figure 7.12). Although small intrusions, such as dykes and sills, typically form aureoles only a few centimetres thick, large intrusions, such as batholiths, can produce aureoles that extend outward for several kilometres.

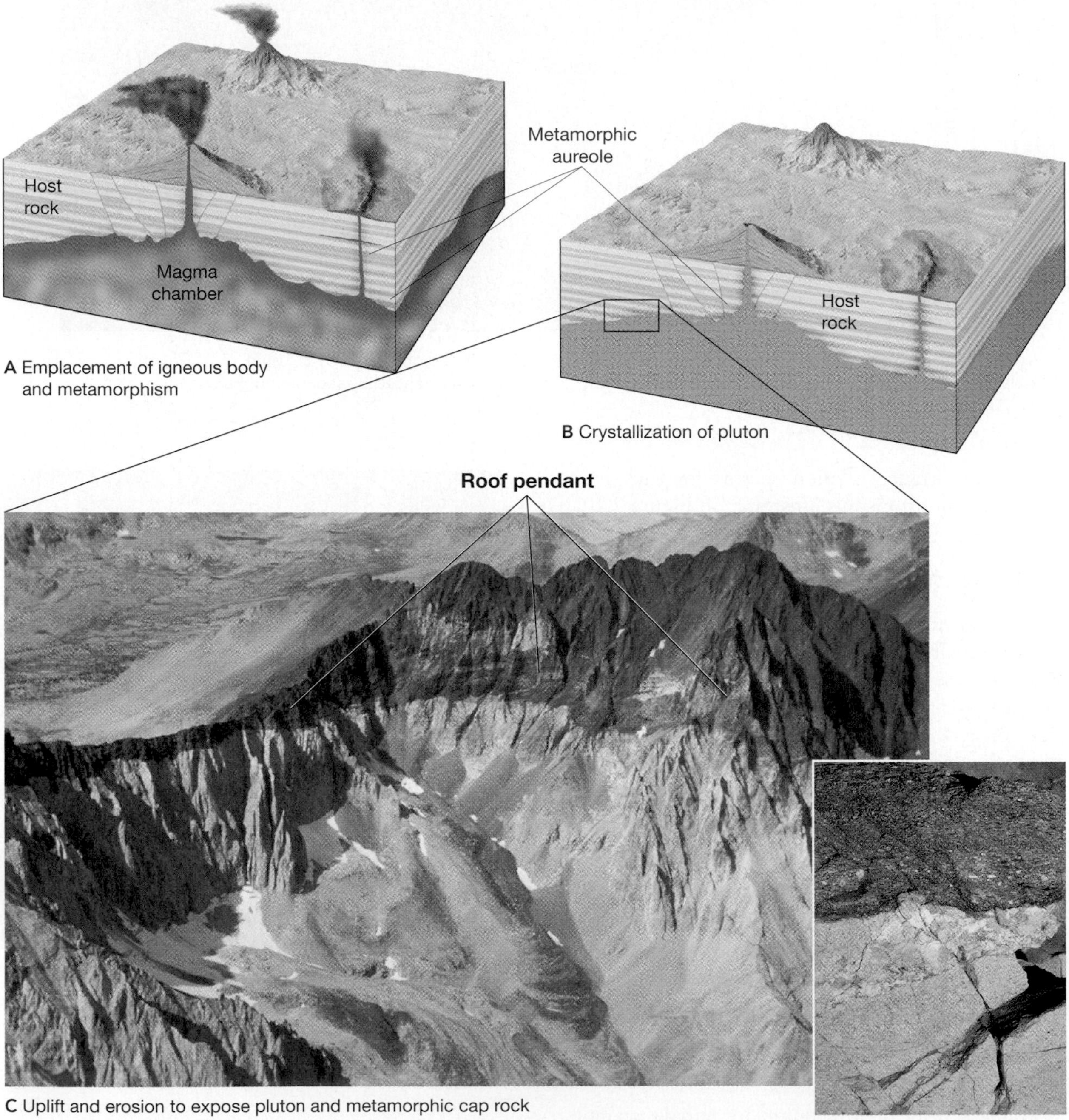

◆ **Figure 7.12** Sierra Nevada, near Bishop, California. Contact metamorphism produces a zone of alteration called an aureole around an intrusive igneous body. In the photo, the dark layer, called a roof pendant, consists of metamorphosed host rock adjacent to the upper part of the light-coloured igneous pluton. The term *roof pendant* implies that the rock was once the roof of a magma chamber. **Inset:** close-up view of the igneous pluton and dark hornfels resulting from the metamorphism of the host rock.
(Photos by John S. Shelton)

Although contact metamorphism is not entirely restricted to shallow crustal depths, it is most easily recognized when it has occurred near the surface. Here, the temperature contrast between the intrusion and the host rock is greatest and confining pressure is low. Because contact metamorphism does not involve directed pressure, all mineral crystals within the metamorphic aureole are more or less randomly oriented, regardless of the minerals present.

Metamorphic rocks produced by contact metamorphism are characteristically nonfoliated. This is because contact metamorphism involves the simple baking of a parent rock in the absence of directed pressure, allowing mineral grains to crystallize in random orientations. Random crystal orientation is most obvious in metamorphic rocks that contain many platy or elongate mineral crystals. Parent rocks that produce such minerals when metamorphosed include sedimentary mudrocks, such as shale, and mafic igneous rocks, such as basalt. Heating can both transform clay minerals of shale into platy micas and encourage ferromagnesian components of basalt to form elongate crystals of amphibole. In both cases, a dark-coloured, nonfoliated, and rather homogeneous-looking rock is produced. This type of metamorphic rock is called *hornfels*. In some cases, large grains of metamorphic minerals, called *porphyroblasts*, impart a spotted appearance or **porphyroblastic texture** to the rock (Figure 7.13). Although various types of metamorphic rocks can have a porphyroblastic texture, a distinguishing feature of this texture in contact metamorphic rocks is that neither the porphyroblasts nor platy/elongate crystals within the surrounding matrix exhibit preferred orientation.

◆ **Figure 7.13** Hornfels is a metamorphic rock produced by contact metamorphism. The hornfels has a spotted appearance because of the presence of large crystals (porphyroblasts) of the mineral *cordierite*. This hornfels was produced when a mud-rich parent rock was baked by heat released from a felsic intrusive body (preserved as a light-coloured igneous rock at the bottom of the photograph). Scale bar: 1 centimetre. (Photo by W. R. Church)

Metamorphic grade, in this case reflecting the intensity of heating without a major influence from pressure variation, decreases away from the igneous intrusion that acted as a heat source. Thus, a zone of high metamorphic grade, containing such index minerals as garnet and sillimanite, would be expected to lie well within a metamorphic aureole near the central intrusion, whereas a zone of low metamorphic grade, containing such minerals as chlorite, would be expected to occur near the outer edge of the aureole (Figure 7.14).

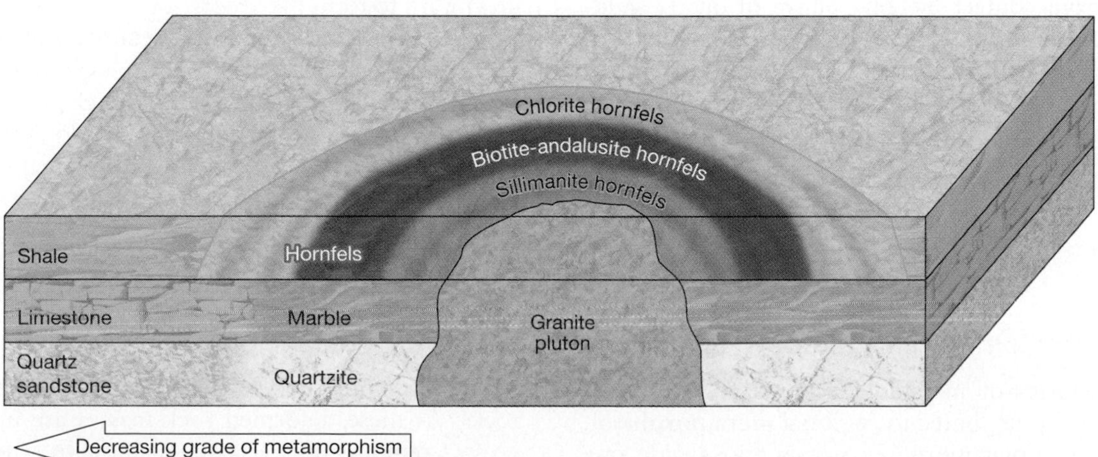

◆ **Figure 7.14** Metamorphic grade within a metamorphic aureole decreases away from the intrusive body, as indicated by the distribution of temperature-sensitive index minerals (see Figure 7.8).

◆ **Figure 7.15** **A.** Quartzite is a nonfoliated metamorphic rock formed from quartz sandstone. The photomicrograph shows the interlocking quartz grains typical of quartzite. **B.** Marble, a crystalline rock formed by the metamorphism of limestone. Photomicrograph shows interlocking calcite crystals using cross-polarized light. (Photos by E. J. Tarbuck)

Not all parent rocks contain the mineral components to produce platy and elongate minerals and therefore a number of other nonfoliated metamorphic rock types can result from contact metamorphism. Two common types of rocks produced together with hornfels during contact metamorphism are *quartzite* (Figure 7.15A) and marble (Figure 7.15B), which result from contact metamorphism of quartz sandstone and limestone, respectively. At the same time, we emphasize that although quartzite and marble are commonly associated with contact metamorphism, they are not diagnostic of this type of metamorphism.

REGIONAL METAMORPHISM

Metamorphic Rocks
↳ Common Metamorphic Rocks

The majority of metamorphic rocks observed on Earth can be attributed to **regional metamorphism**. This type of metamorphism occurs over a wide area and is closely tied to the increased pressures and temperatures associated with convergent plate boundaries. During convergence, large segments of Earth's crust are squeezed in a horizontal direction, imposing substantial directed pressure (Figure 7.16). As the rocks are deformed, the crust is shortened and thickened, like a rumpled carpet. This thickening causes crust above sea level to be pushed up to form mountains and crust below sea level to be forced downward to form the "roots" of the mountains. It is here that the most intense metamorphic activity occurs. Along with the increases in directed pressure, the rocks undergo deep burial, which means that confining pressures also increase. In addition, rocks are subjected to elevated temperatures that accompany both deep burial and the emplacement of magma from the mantle.

The intensity of regional metamorphism becomes greatest when continents collide. The cores of many mountain ranges resulting from continental collision consist of folded and faulted metamorphic rocks, commonly intermixed with intruded igneous rocks. As these deformed rock masses are uplifted, erosion removes the overlying material to expose the igneous and metamorphic rocks that compose the central core of the mountain range.

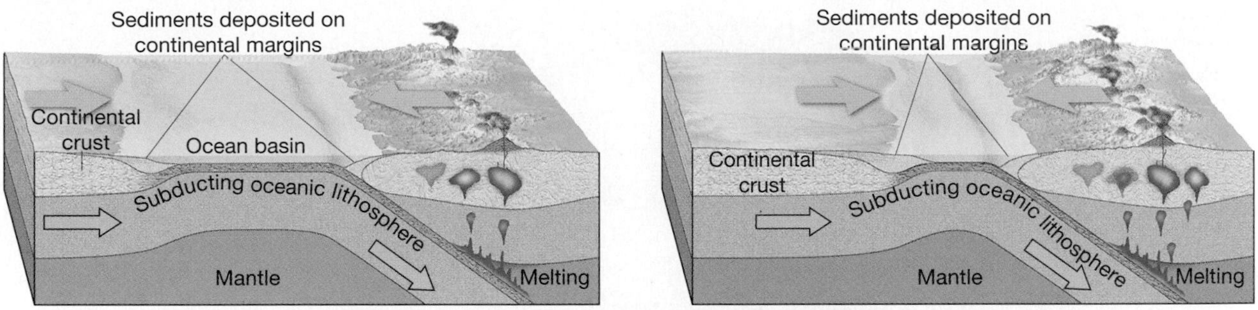

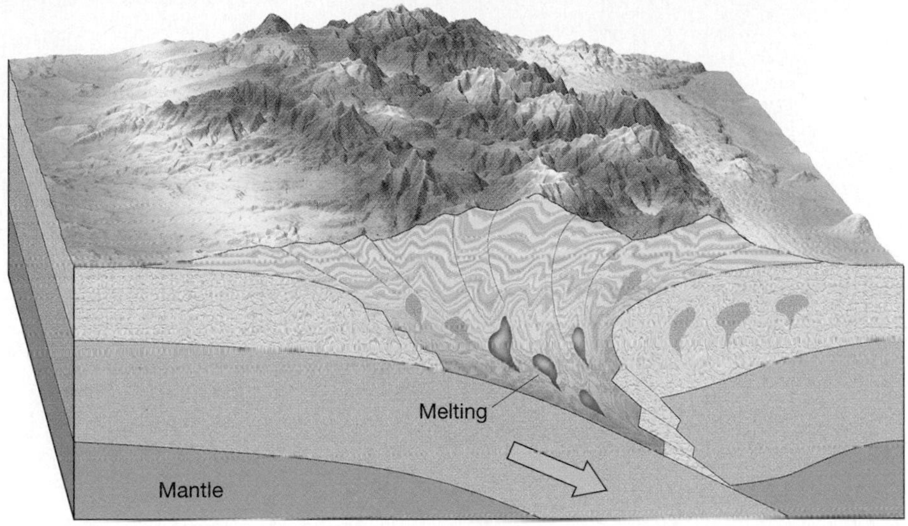

◆ **Figure 7.16** Regional metamorphism occurs where rocks are squeezed between two converging continental lithospheric plates during mountain building.

As with contact metamorphism, the rocks that best display the effects of regional metamorphism are those containing lots of platy or elongate mineral grains, whose orientations provide clues to the nature of pressure applied. Because mudrocks, such as shale, can produce large quantities of such minerals when metamorphosed, they are the best parent rocks to consider when examining the manner in which rocks change during regional metamorphism. As you will see, the increased intensity of directed pressure that accompanies the progressive elevation of temperature and confining pressure causes platy and elongate minerals to attain a preferred orientation. It is because of this preferred orientation that foliated rocks are characteristic of regional metamorphism. The metamorphism of shale is emphasized in this section because it is widespread and contains the necessary chemical ingredients to produce the platy and elongate mineral crystals that best define foliation.

In regional metamorphism, metamorphic index minerals and texture change systematically with increasing temperatures and pressures. So although temperature is the main factor influencing metamorphic grade in contact metamorphism, metamorphic grade in regionally metamorphosed rocks reflects significant changes in both temperature and pressure.

Regional Metamorphism of Shale

In this section, we track the transformation of shale into the metamorphic rock types *slate* (Figure 7.17A), *phyllite* (Figure 7.17B), *schist* (Figure 7.17C), and *gneiss* (Figure 7.17D) with increasing temperature and pressure. The relative depths at which these rock types might be formed within an active mountain belt are illustrated in Figure 7.17.

Slate Slate is a very fine-grained foliated rock primarily composed of mica flakes that are too small to be seen with the unaided eye (Figure 7.17A). It is typically produced by the low-grade metamorphism of clay-rich mudrocks, such as shale, but in rare instances it can also form from volcanic ash.

Slate looks similar to shale but is much harder and commonly has a slight sheen. Slate can be readily distinguished from sedimentary mudrock, such as shale, by its lack of an earthy smell when rubbed and the ringing sound it produces when struck by a fingernail or other hard object. Shale, in contrast, usually has an earthy smell because of its volatile content and produces a dull thud when struck because the platy minerals are not held together as tightly. Because of the preferred orientation of platy minerals in the direction of weakest stress, slate develops **rock cleavage** (also known as *slaty* cleavage; Figure 7.18),

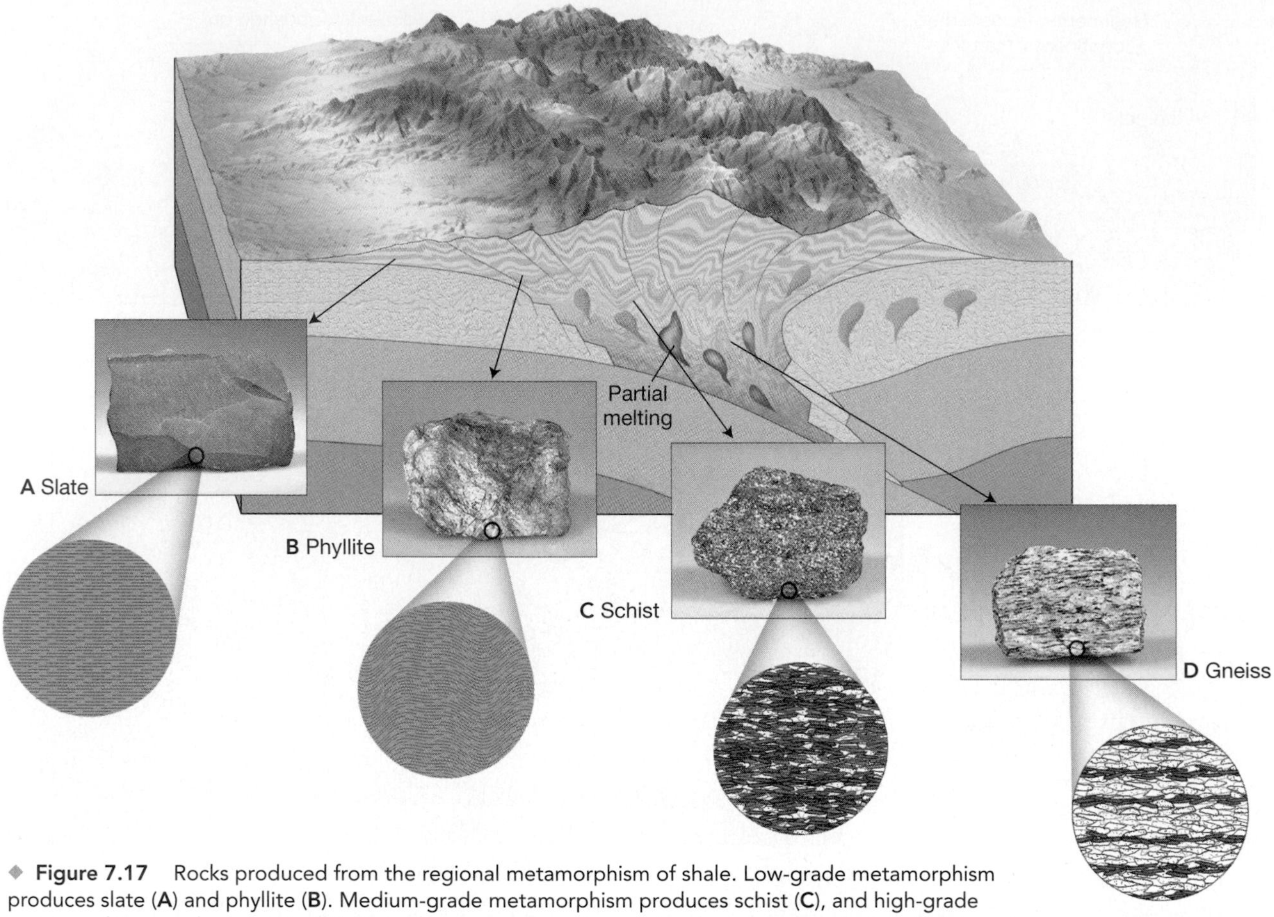

◆ **Figure 7.17** Rocks produced from the regional metamorphism of shale. Low-grade metamorphism produces slate (**A**) and phyllite (**B**). Medium-grade metamorphism produces schist (**C**), and high-grade metamorphism produces gneiss (**D**). Note the progressive alignment and increased grain size of platy and elongate minerals with increasing temperature and directed pressure associated with mountain building. (Photos by E. J. Tarbuck)

which allows it to be broken into very thin, flat slabs (Figure 7.19). Rock cleavage must not be confused with bedding, which you will recall is a sedimentary feature. Bedding, along with most other sedimentary features, is commonly obliterated when platy minerals align themselves in response to directed stress. The resulting planes of rock cleavage almost never coincide with bedding (Figure 7.18). Rock cleavage is also not to be confused with mineral cleavage, which is dictated by the arrangement of atoms *within*, rather than *between*, individual mineral crystals.

The colour of slate is dependent on the specific minerals it contains. Black (carbonaceous) slate contains organic material, red slate contains iron oxide, and green slate usually contains chlorite.

Phyllite Phyllite is a low-grade metamorphic rock produced at slightly higher temperatures and pressures than slate. Its constituent platy minerals are larger than those of slate, giving it a glossy sheen, but are still too small to be seen by the unaided eye. Phyllite also exhibits rock cleavage, but the cleavage surfaces commonly have a slightly wavy appearance, which reflects the higher degree of directed pressure it has experienced relative to slate (Figure 7.17B). Phyllite is commonly either grey, indicating a high muscovite content, or green, indicating the presence of chlorite.

Schist Schist is a medium- to coarse-grained metamorphic rock dominated by platy mica minerals (biotite and muscovite) large enough to be seen by the unaided eye (Figure 7.17C) and represents a medium metamorphic grade, one step higher than phyllite. These platy minerals have an obvious preferred orientation that defines a distinctive schistose foliation or **schistosity** in this rock type. In addition to platy minerals, schists contain smaller amounts of blocky and tabular minerals, such as feldspar, and can also contain elongate grains of minerals, such as amphibole.

The term *schist* refers to the texture of the rock. To indicate the composition, names of constituent minerals are used. For example, schists composed primarily of muscovite and biotite are called mica schists. Depending on the intensity of metamorphism and composition of their parent rocks, mica

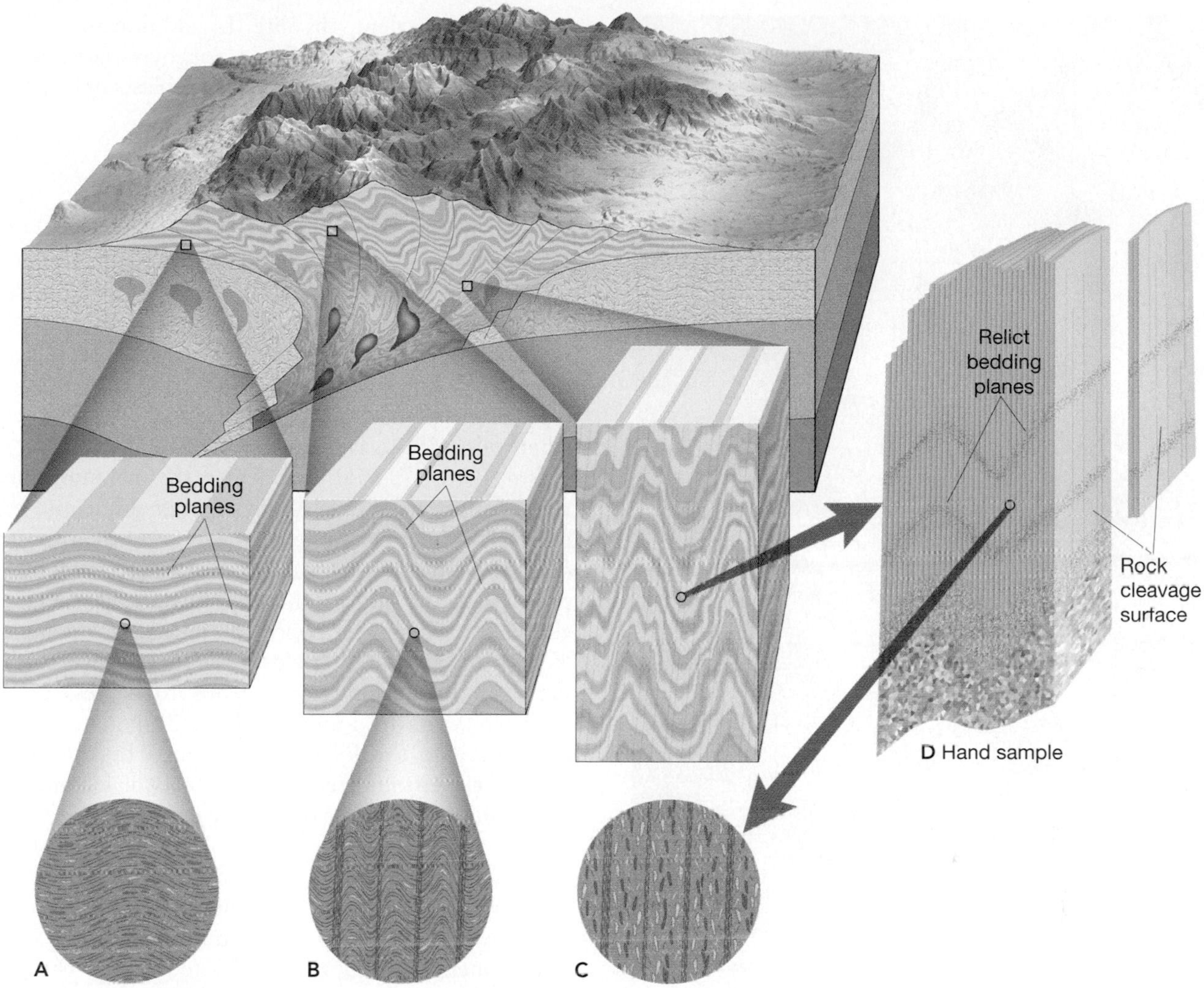

◆ **Figure 7.18** Development of one type of rock cleavage. As shale is strongly folded (**A, B**) and metamorphosed to form slate, the developing mica flakes are bent into microfolds. **C.** Further metamorphism results in the re-crystallization of mica grains along the limbs of these folds to enhance the foliation. **D.** Hand sample of slate illustrates rock cleavage and its orientation to relic bedding surfaces.

schists commonly contain accessory minerals, some of which are unique to metamorphic rocks. Common metamorphic minerals include garnet, *staurolite*, and sillimanite, in which case the rock is called garnet-mica-schist, staurolite-mica schist, and so on. In addition to schistosity, some schists show striking examples of porphyroblastic texture, in which mica grains appear to be wrapped around large crystals of minerals, such as garnet.

Gneiss Gneiss is the term applied to medium- to coarse-grained banded metamorphic rocks in which granular and elongate (as opposed to platy) minerals predominate. It is of high metamorphic grade. The most common minerals in gneiss are quartz, potassium feldspar, and sodium-rich plagioclase feldspar. Most gneisses contain lesser amounts of biotite, amphibole, and muscovite that develop a preferred orientation. Some gneisses will split along layers of platy minerals, but most break into irregular pieces.

During high-grade metamorphism, the light and dark components separate into layers, giving gneiss their characteristic banded or layered appearance, called **gneissic texture** or *gneissosity*. Thus, most gneisses consist of alternating bands of white or pink feldspar-rich zones and layers of dark ferromagnesian minerals (Figures 7.2 and 7.17D). These banded gneisses commonly show evidence of deformation (Figure 7.2).

Gneiss forms from the high-grade metamorphism of shale and represents the highest grade reached by such rocks during regional metamorphism before the onset of melting. Like schists, gneisses can also include large crystals of metamorphic minerals, such as garnet and staurolite. Gneisses can also form by the regional metamorphism of granite or its

◆ **Figure 7.19** Slaty cleavage is exhibited by this metamorphic rock. The parallel mineral alignment in this rock allows it to split easily along the flat plates visible in the photo.
(Photo by E. J. Tarbuck)

aphanitic equivalent, rhyolite. In addition to gneissosity, some gneisses exhibit a porphyroblastic texture, with large eye-shaped porphyroblasts of quartz, feldspar, or garnet.

Regional Metamorphism of Basalt

Unlike shale, which is primarily composed of hydrous clay minerals, basalt is predominantly composed of anhydrous minerals, such as plagioclase feldspar and the ferromagnesian minerals olivine and pyroxene. A basalt parent rock therefore produces different mineral assemblages, and hence different types of metamorphic rocks, than a shaly parent rock when subjected to conditions of regional metamorphism (Figure 7.20). In particular, the metamorphic rocks derived from basalt have a higher abundance of minerals containing iron and magnesium than those derived from mudrocks. It is only at low metamorphic grades that platy mineral grains are sufficiently abundant to produce obvious foliation. At medium to high metamorphic grades, the foliation in basalt-derived metamorphic rocks tends to be less pronounced than in mudrock-derived metamorphic rocks because the foliation is defined by the preferred orientation of elongate crystals of ferromagnesian minerals, rather than platy crystals of mica.

Greenschist At low grades of metamorphism ferromagnesian minerals, such as olivine and pyroxene, contained in the parent basalt are hydrated to form such minerals as chlorite. Chlorite imparts both a phyllite-like foliation and a green colour to the rock. This type of rock, called greenschist (Figure 7.20A), is of equivalent metamorphic grade to slate and phyllite.

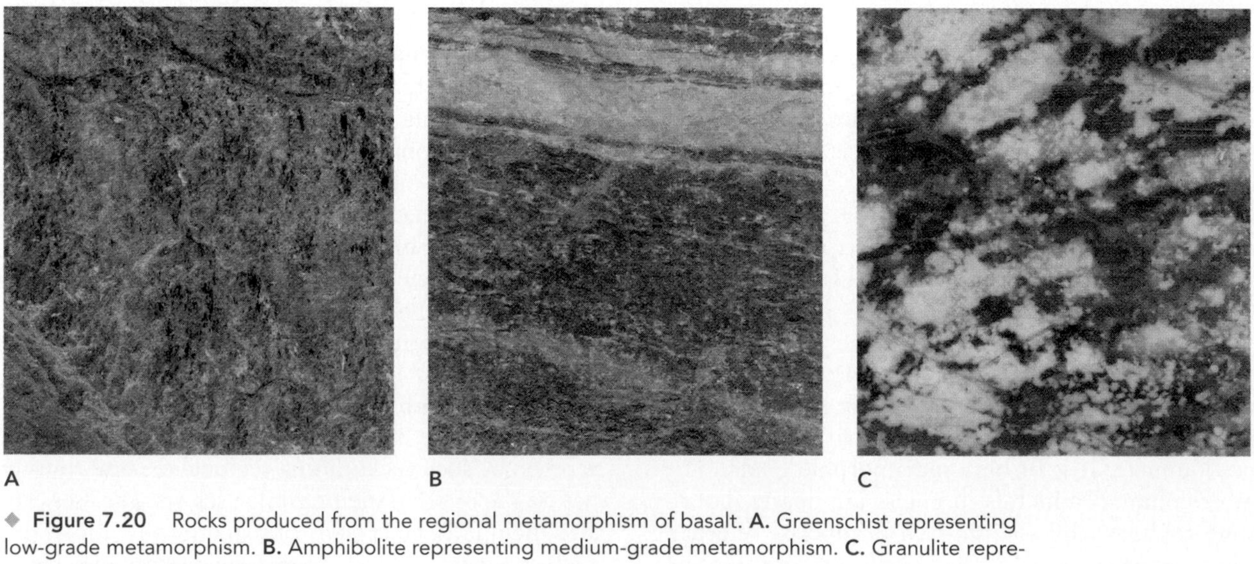

◆ **Figure 7.20** Rocks produced from the regional metamorphism of basalt. **A.** Greenschist representing low-grade metamorphism. **B.** Amphibolite representing medium-grade metamorphism. **C.** Granulite representing high-grade metamorphism.
(Photos by C. Tsujita)

Amphibolite When subjected to higher temperatures and pressures, chlorite and associated hydrated minerals lose water and are converted to amphiboles. The resulting rock, called *amphibolite* (Figure 7.20B), is of equivalent metamorphic grade to the schist produced from a shale parent. The preferred orientation of needle-like amphibole crystals produces a foliation that is less distinct than in greenschist.

Granulite At even higher temperatures and pressures, the amphibole minerals contained in amphibolite are further dehydrated to produce pyroxenes and garnets. The high-grade metamorphic rock thus produced, called *granulite* (Figure 7.20C), is equivalent to gneiss produced from mudrock parents but has a very coarse-grained granular texture. The constituent mineral crystals, including those of pyroxene, are typically blocky in shape. Because of the low degree of elongation in the mineral crystals, little preferred orientation of grains is apparent.

◆ **Figure 7.21** Migmatite near West Vancouver, British Columbia. The lightest-coloured parts are igneous rock composed of quartz, feldspar, and biotite, while the dark angular foliated pieces have a metamorphic origin.
(Photo by S. R. Hicock)

The Upper Limit of Regional Metamorphism

In the extreme environments in regional metamorphism, rocks begin to partially melt and pass into a transition zone between metamorphism and the igneous realm. In such environments, part of the rock remains solid and can be considered as part of the metamorphic process, but part of it is melted to form magma. Rocks called **migmatites** represent this somewhat ambiguous state and include both metamorphic and igneous components. They are generally included in metamorphic rocks because they represent the very last possible step a metamorphic rock can take in its passage through conditions of progressively higher temperature and pressure. Recall from our discussion of igneous rocks that different minerals melt at different temperatures. Light-coloured silicates, such as quartz and potassium feldspar, have the lowest melting temperatures and begin to melt first, whereas the mafic silicates, such as amphibole and biotite, remain solid. When the partially melted rock cools, the light bands have an igneous appearance, whereas the dark bands consist of solid metamorphic components. The igneous bands commonly form tortuous folds and sometimes contain angular fragments of the dark components (Figure 7.21).

Regional Metamorphism and Nonfoliated Rocks

The fact that many rocks produced by regional metamorphism are foliated does not mean that all of them show this texture, because some parent rocks lack the necessary elements to produce the platy or elongate mineral grains that define foliation in metamorphic rocks. Such minerals as quartz and calcite occur in various shapes and therefore do not define a foliation as readily as do such minerals as micas. As in contact metamorphism, regional metamorphism transforms quartz sandstone to quartzite and limestone to marble. As a result of the lack of platy and elongate minerals, pure quartzites (Figure 7.15A) and marbles (Figure 7.15B) produced by regional metamorphism can look identical to ones produced by contact metamorphism, at least to the unaided eye. However, in some cases impurities, such as clay in the host rocks, produce some faint banding in regionally metamorphosed rocks that are otherwise homogeneous in appearance.

SUBDUCTION ZONE METAMORPHISM

Subduction zone metamorphism is technically a form of regional metamorphism but is discussed here in a separate category because of the special conditions involved. Metamorphism in the region of a subducted slab is characterized by very high pressures and relatively low temperatures (Figures 7.3 and 7.10). Rocks lying on both sides of the plate boundary are affected. Because a subducted oceanic slab is cold and is a poor heat conductor, rocks on the top of the subducted slab and on the underside of the overlying plate encounter a large increase in pressure at a rapid rate but remain relatively cool. Under these conditions, a peculiar, sodium-rich, blue-coloured amphibole forms, called *glaucophane*. Because of the preferred orientation of elongate glaucophane grains, the rock exhibits foliation and is called *blueschist* (Figure 7.22A). Continued subduction drags rocks into the mantle, where the blueschist is further transformed into a rock called *eclogite*, characterized by pyroxene and garnet (Figure 7.22B).

Other localized types of metamorphism also occur, such as the reaction of rocks with hot fluids of igneous activity, and the pulverizing of rocks along faults and through the impact of asteroids and comets. Box 7.1 explains the latter.

METAMORPHIC FACIES AND PLATE TECTONICS

A **metamorphic facies** is defined by a distinctive assemblage of minerals that can be used to designate a particular set of metamorphic environmental conditions recorded in the rocks (Figure 7.23). One advantage of this scheme is that rocks produced by different types of metamorphism can be interpreted within a single, unified context.

The names of metamorphic facies refer to metamorphic rocks derived specifically from a basaltic parent rock. This is because Pentti Eskola, the geologist who proposed the metamorphic facies scheme in 1915, concentrated on the metamorphism of basalts, and his basic terminology, although now slightly modified, has stuck ever since. The names of Eskola's facies serve as convenient labels for a particular combination of temperature and pressure values. In other words, even if a non-basaltic parent rock produces indicator minerals other than a basalt would under a given set of metamorphic conditions, the names of Eskola's facies are used for the purpose of denoting the temperature and pressure ranges embodied by the metamorphic rock.

Comparison of Figure 7.23 and Figure 7.10 illustrates the usefulness of the metamorphic facies concept in the interpretation of metamorphic environments. Figure 7.24 shows how facies fit into the context of plate tectonics. The *hornfels facies*, not surprisingly, is associated with the high temperatures and low pressures involved in contact metamorphism. The *zeolite facies* reflects very low grade metamorphism involving low heat and low pressure and is generally associated with burial metamorphism and the very lowest grade of regional metamorphism. The increasing temperatures and pressures associated with regional metamorphism are recorded by the *greenschist-amphibolite-granulite facies* sequence. Subduction zone metamorphism is characterized by the *blueschist facies*, representing relatively low temperatures but high pressures. Finally, rocks of the *eclogite facies* are diagnostic of very high temperatures and pressures encountered by a deeply subducted slab of oceanic lithosphere.

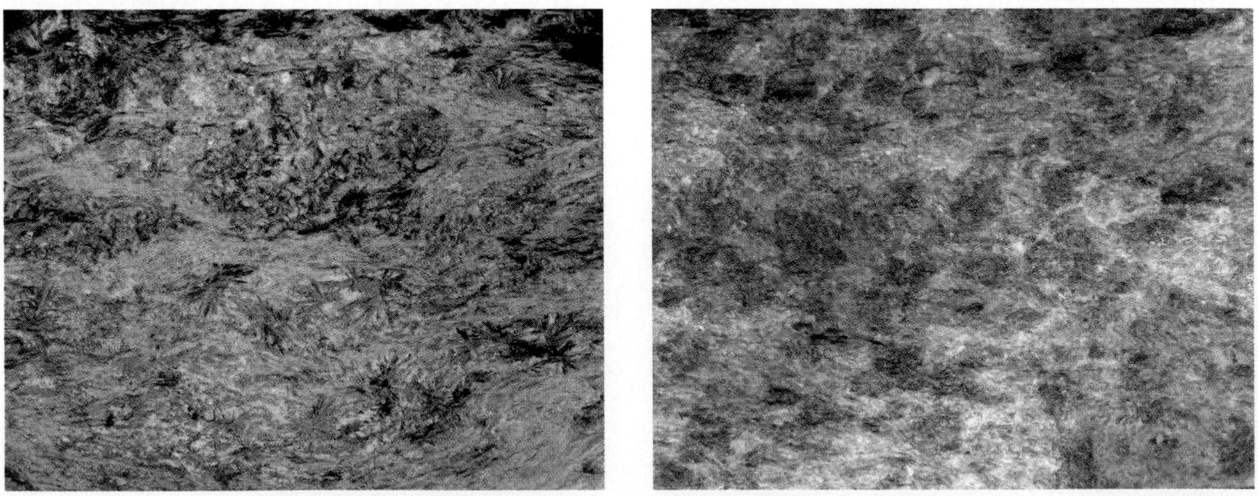

A B

◆ **Figure 7.22** Rocks produced by subduction zone metamorphism. **A.** Blueschist, representing low-temperature, high-pressure conditions (note the blue-coloured amphibole, called glaucophane). **B.** Eclogite, representing high-temperature, high-pressure conditions of the mantle. Note the pink grains of garnet and green grains of pyroxene.
(Photos by C. Tsujita)

BOX 7.1

Understanding Earth
Impact Metamorphism

It is now clear that comets and asteroids have collided with Earth far more frequently than previously thought, based on more than 100 giant impact structures called astroblemes (*astro* = star, *blema* = wound from a projectile) that have been found worldwide. The Barringer Crater in Arizona bears the familiar bowl-like shape that we generally associated with impact craters (Figure 7.A). Many astroblemes also exist in Canada, and include the Manicouagan Crater in Quebec, the Sudbury Basin in Ontario, and the Eagle Butte structure in Alberta.

When high-velocity projectiles (comets, asteroids) hit Earth's surface, pressures reach millions of atmospheres and temperatures exceed 2000°C momentarily. The result is pulverized, shattered, and melted rock. Where impact craters are relatively fresh, shock-melted ejecta and rock fragments ring the impact site. Although most material is deposited close to its source, some ejecta can travel great distances. One example is tektites (*tektos* = molten), beads of silica-rich glass up to a few centimetres in size resulting from rapid quenching of blobs of the molten ejecta. These can fall hundreds of kilometres away from the impact site.

Shock metamorphism produces some distinctive deformation features. At the microscopic end of the scale are shock lamellae, linear features developed because of small-scale partial melting. Shock lamellae are recognized relatively easily in such minerals as quartz that do not have planar cleavage or fracture planes that the shock lamellae could otherwise be confused with. On the large scale of deformation features are *shatter cones*. These are nested cone-like structures that emanate from the point of impact and can be compared with the small-scale patterns produced in glass when a rock damages the windshield of a car. The presence of these structures in rocks surrounding the Sudbury Basin provides evidence suggesting that Sudbury Basin represents the site of a large meteorite impact that occurred during the Precambrian (Figure 7.B). Because the Sudbury Basin has been deformed, the orientations of shatter cones vary from place to place, but it is assumed that before this deformation, the pointed ends of all the shatter cones were consistently oriented toward the site of impact.

◆ **Figure 7.A** Barringer Crater, located west of Winslow, Arizona. (Photo by Michael Collier)

◆ **Figure 7.B** Upward-pointing shatter cones made in Precambrian greywacke, near Sudbury, Ontario. **Inset:** Close-up view of a single shatter cone cross-section. (**Main** photo by Grant Young; **inset** photo by S. R. Hicock)

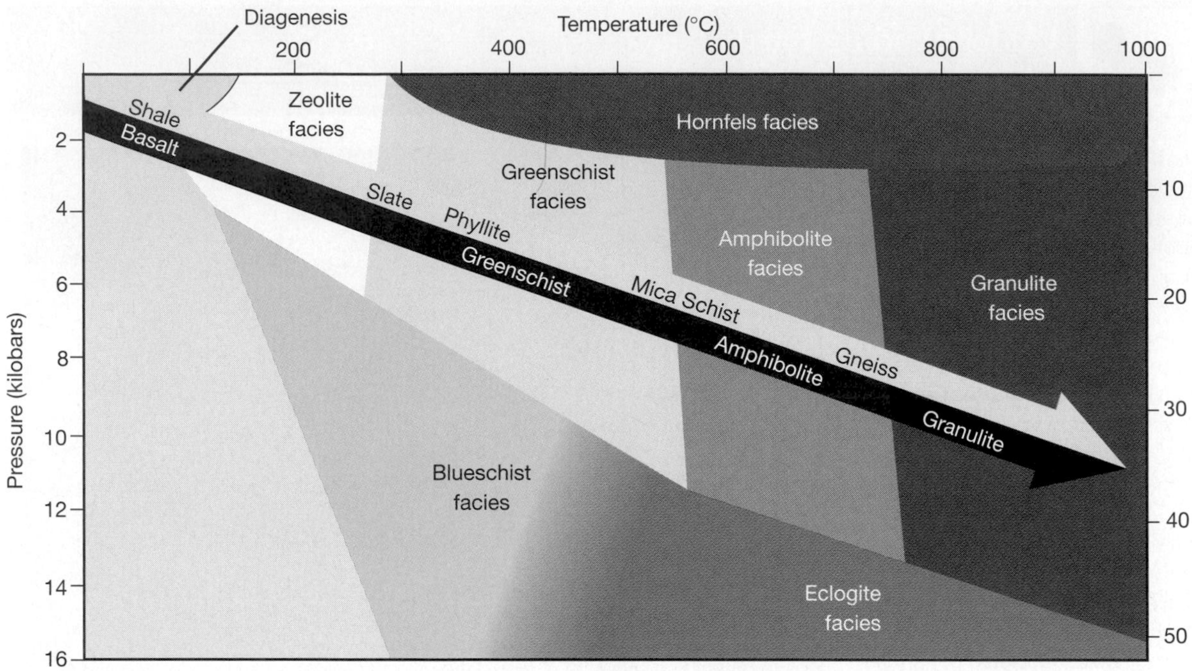

◆ **Figure 7.23** Metamorphic facies and corresponding temperature and pressure conditions. Note the equivalent metamorphic rocks produced from regional metamorphism of shale and basalt parent rocks.

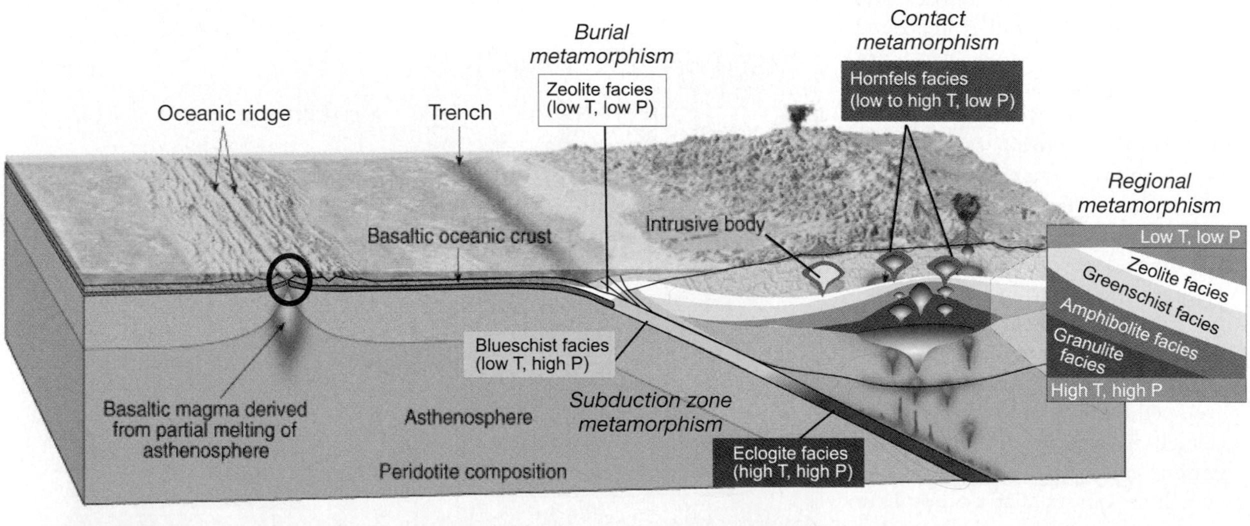

◆ **Figure 7.24** The association of metamorphic facies with plate tectonic environments.

ANCIENT METAMORPHIC ENVIRONMENTS

In addition to the linear belts of metamorphic rocks that are found along the axes of most mountain belts, even larger expanses of metamorphic rocks exist within the stable continental interiors (Figure 7.25). These relatively flat expanses of metamorphic rocks and associated igneous rocks are called **shields**. One such region, the Canadian Shield, has very little topographic expression and forms the bedrock over much of Canada. Radiometric dating of rocks in the Canadian Shield indicates that it is composed of rocks that range in age from 1.8 billion to about 4 billion years. Rocks of the Acasta Gneiss Complex, exposed just east of Great Slave Lake in the Northwest Territories, have yielded radiometric dates of up to 4.03 billion years and currently represent the oldest known rocks in the world (Figure 7.26).

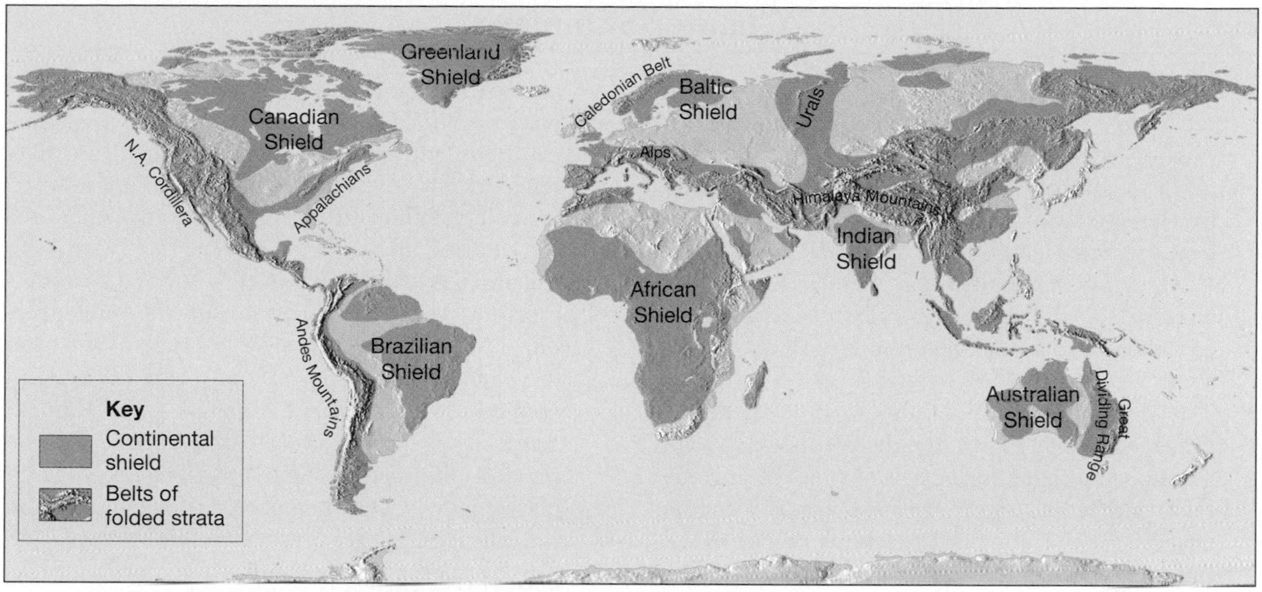

◆ **Figure 7.25** Occurrences of metamorphic rocks. The continental shields of the world are composed largely of metamorphic rocks and associated igneous intrusions. In addition, the deformed portions of many mountain belts are also metamorphic. The remaining area shown in this map is the stable continental interior, which generally consists of undeformed sedimentary beds that overlie metamorphic and igneous basement rocks that are buried extensions of the shields.

Because shields are ancient and their rock structure is similar to that found in the cores of younger, deformed mountainous terrains, they are assumed to be remnants of much earlier periods of mountain building (Figure 7.25). This evidence strongly supports the generally accepted view that Earth has been a dynamic planet throughout most of its history. Studies of these vast areas of metamorphism in the context of the plate tectonic model have given geologists new insights into the problem of discerning just how the continents came to exist. We will consider this topic further in Chapter 13.

◆ **Figure 7.26** Ancient metamorphic and igneous rocks on the shore of Great Slave Lake, Northwest Territories. These rocks, which are part of the Canadian Shield, are among the most ancient on Earth. **Inset:** A sample of the Acasta Gneiss, determined by radiometric dating to be 4.03 billion years old and currently representing the oldest known rock in North America (scale bar: 1 centimetre).
(**Main** photo by Tom and Susan Bean, Inc.; **inset** photo by C. Tsujita)

Chapter Summary

- *Metamorphism* is the transformation of one rock type into another. Metamorphic rocks form from existing rocks (either igneous, sedimentary, or other metamorphic rocks) that have been altered by the agents of metamorphism, which include heat, pressure (stress), and *chemically active fluids*. During metamorphism the material essentially remains solid. The changes that occur in metamorphosed rocks are textural as well as mineralogic.
- The mineral makeup of the *parent rock* determines, to a large extent, the degree to which each metamorphic agent will cause change. Heat is the most important agent because it provides the energy to drive chemical reactions that result in the re-crystallization of minerals. Pressure, like temperature, also increases with depth. When subjected to *confining pressure* (*uniform stress*), minerals may re-crystallize into more compact forms. During mountain building, rocks are subjected to *directed pressure* (*differential stress*), which tends to shorten them in the direction pressure is applied from and lengthens them in the direction perpendicular to that force. At depth, rocks are warm and ductile, which accounts for their ability to deform by flowing when subjected to directed pressures. Chemically active fluids, usually dominated by water, also enhance the metamorphic process by acting as catalysts in chemical reactions, by transporting dissolved substances, and, in some cases, by becoming incorporated into the chemical makeup of certain minerals.
- The grade of metamorphism is reflected in the texture and mineralogy of metamorphic rocks. In terms of mineralogy, *metamorphic grade* is indicated by the presence of certain *index minerals*, which reflect the temperature/pressure conditions experienced by the rock during metamorphism. In terms of texture, rocks affected by temperature alone retain a *nonfoliated* texture regardless of grade, whereas those affected by both temperature and differential stress show a general increase in the degree of preferred orientation among platy and elongate minerals.
- The preferred orientation of platy and elongate minerals defines the *foliation* of rocks affected by regional metamorphism. Foliation develops as platy or elongate minerals are rotated into parallel alignment, are plastically deformed into flattened grains that exhibit a planar alignment, or are re-crystallized to form new grains with a preferred orientation.
- Foliation is particularly well displayed in metamorphic rocks produced from the metamorphism of shale. *Rock cleavage* is a type of foliation in which rocks split cleanly into thin slabs along surfaces where platy minerals are aligned. *Schistosity* is a type of foliation defined by the parallel alignment of medium- to coarse-grained platy minerals. During high-grade metamorphism, ion migrations can cause minerals to segregate into distinct layers or bands. Metamorphic rocks with a banded texture are called *gneiss*. Metamorphism of basalt produces rocks that are similarly foliated but contain different minerals. The regional metamorphism of basalt produces, in order of increasing grade, *greenschist*, *amphibolite*, and *granulite*.
- Metamorphic rocks composed of only one mineral forming equidimensional crystals often appear nonfoliated, regardless of the specific pressure conditions involved in their formation. Both marble (metamorphosed limestone) and quartzite are examples of such rocks. Hornfels is a nonfoliated rock that is diagnostic of contact metamorphism.
- A *metamorphic facies* is defined by a distinctive assemblage of minerals and is used to designate a particular set of metamorphic environmental conditions recorded in the rocks (Figure 7.23). The metamorphic facies concept provides a convenient context within which many different types of metamorphism can be interpreted in terms of temperature and pressure conditions.
- Metamorphism most often occurs in two settings: (1) when rock is in contact with magma, *contact metamorphism* occurs; (2) when continental convergence and mountain building occur, extensive areas of rock undergo *regional metamorphism* and *subduction zone metamorphism*. However, metamorphism can also occur during the simple burial of rocks (*burial metamorphism*).

Review Questions

1. What is metamorphism? What are the agents that change rocks?
2. Why is heat such an important agent of metamorphism?
3. How is confining pressure (uniform stress) different from directed pressure (differential stress)?
4. What role do chemically active fluids play in metamorphism?
5. How does the parent rock affect the metamorphic process?
6. What is foliation? Distinguish between schistosity and gneissic textures.
7. Briefly describe the three mechanisms by which minerals develop a preferred orientation.
8. List some changes that might occur to a rock in response to metamorphic processes.
9. Slate and phyllite resemble each other. How can you distinguish one from the other?
10. Each of the following statements describes one or more characteristics of a particular metamorphic rock. For each statement, name the metamorphic rock that is being described.
    - **(a)** Is calcite-rich and nonfoliated
    - **(b)** Represents a grade of metamorphism between slate and schist
    - **(c)** Is very fine-grained and foliated; excellent rock cleavage
    - **(d)** Is foliated and composed predominantly of platy minerals
    - **(e)** Is composed of alternating bands of light and dark silicate minerals
    - **(f)** Is hard, nonfoliated rock resulting from contact metamorphism
11. Distinguish between contact metamorphism and regional metamorphism. Which creates the greatest quantity of metamorphic rock?
12. Describe burial metamorphism.
13. How do geologists use index minerals?
14. Briefly describe the textural changes that occur in the transformation of slate to phyllite to schist and then to gneiss.
15. How are gneisses and migmatites related?
16. With which type of plate boundary is regional metamorphism associated?
17. Why do the cores of Earth's major mountain chains contain metamorphic rocks?
18. Explain the concept of metamorphic facies. Why are metamorphic facies useful in the interpretation of metamorphic conditions rocks have experienced?
19. What are shields? How are these relatively flat areas related to mountains?

Key Terms

aureole (p. 194)
burial metamorphism (p. 193)
chemically active fluids (p. 190)
confining pressure (p. 188)
contact metamorphism (p. 194)
differential stress (p. 188)
directed pressure (p. 188)
foliation (p. 189)
gneissic texture (p. 199)
index mineral (p. 191)
metamorphic facies (p. 202)
metamorphic grade (p. 191)
metamorphism (p. 187)
migmatite (p. 201)
nonfoliated (p. 191)
parent rock (p. 187)
porphyroblastic texture (p. 195)
regional metamorphism (p. 196)
rock cleavage (p. 197)
schistosity (p. 198)
shield (p. 204)
subduction zone metamorphism (p. 201)
texture (p. 187)
uniform stress (p. 188)

Web Resources

The *Earth* website uses the resources and flexibility of the internet to aid in your study of the topics in this chapter. Written and developed by geology instructors, this site will help improve your understanding of geology. Visit **www.pearsoned.ca/tarbuck** and click on the cover of the text to find

- online review quizzes
- Web-based critical thinking and writing exercises
- links to chapter-specific Web resources
- internet-wide key-term searches

www.pearsoned.ca/tarbuck

Chapter 8

Geologic Time

Geology Needs a Time Scale

Relative Dating: Key Principles
- Law of Superposition
- Principle of Original Horizontality
- Principle of Cross-Cutting Relations
- Inclusions
- Unconformities

Correlation of Rock Layers
- Correlation by Physical Criteria
- Fossils and Correlation

Dating with Radioactivity
- Radioactivity
- Half-Life
- Radiometric Dating
- Dating with Carbon-14
- Importance of Radiometric Dating

The Geologic Time Scale
- Structure of the Time Scale
- Precambrian Time

Difficulties in Dating the Geologic Time Scale

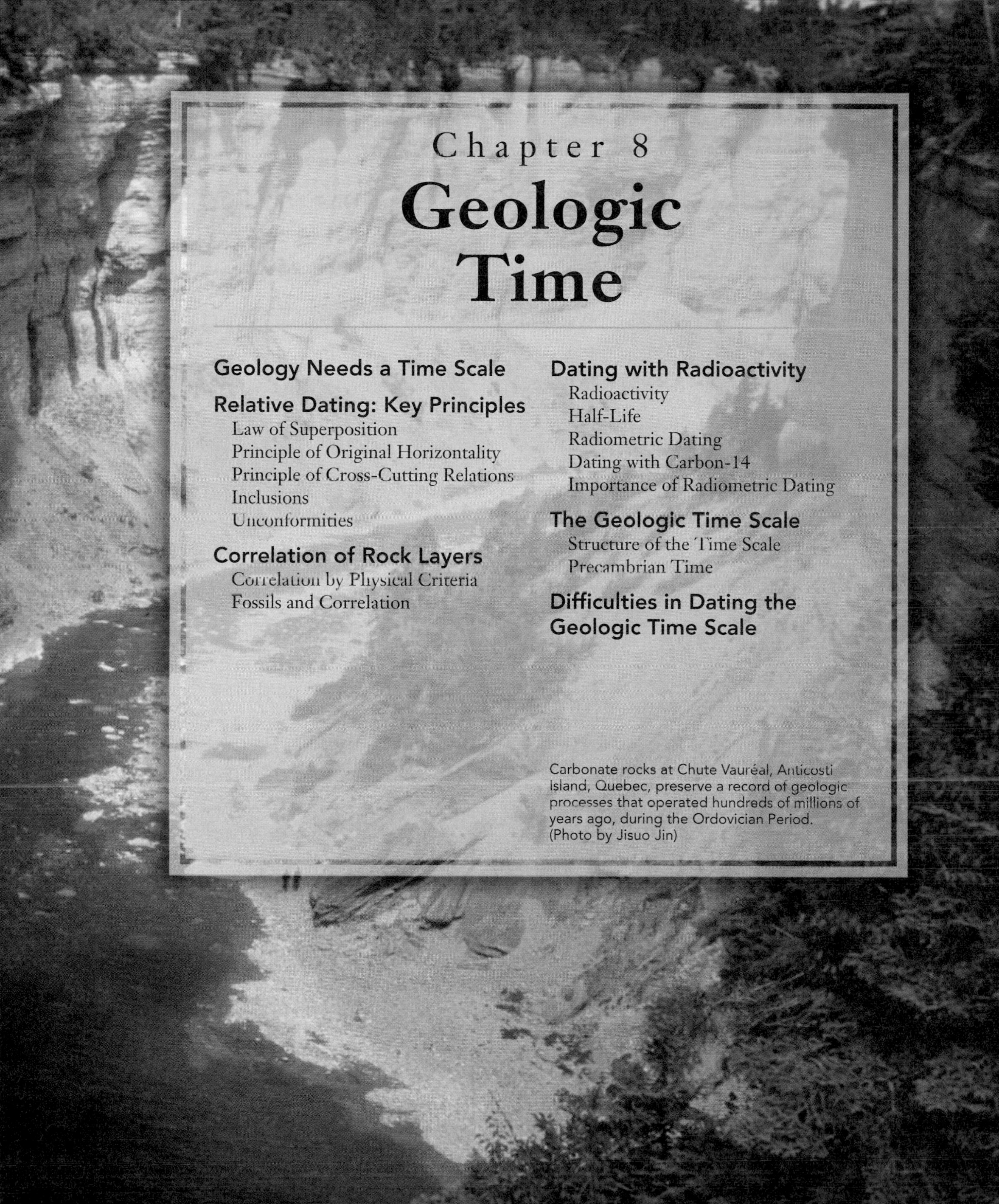

Carbonate rocks at Chute Vauréal, Anticosti Island, Quebec, preserve a record of geologic processes that operated hundreds of millions of years ago, during the Ordovician Period. (Photo by Jisuo Jin)

In the late eighteenth century, James Hutton recognized the immensity of Earth history and the importance of time as a component in all geologic processes. In the nineteenth century, Sir Charles Lyell and others effectively demonstrated that Earth had experienced many episodes of mountain building and erosion, which must have required great spans of geologic time. Although these pioneering scientists understood that Earth was very old, they had no way of knowing its true age. Was it tens of millions, hundreds of millions, or even billions of years old? A geologic time scale was developed that showed the sequence of events based on relative dating principles. What are these principles? What part do fossils play? With the discovery of radioactivity and radiometric dating techniques, geologists now can assign fairly accurate dates to many of the events in Earth history. What is radioactivity? Why is it a good clock for dating the geologic past?

GEOLOGY NEEDS A TIME SCALE

Like the pages in a long and complicated history book, rocks record the geologic events (Figure 8.1) and changing life forms of the past. The book, however, is not complete. Many pages, especially in the early chapters, are missing. Others are tattered, torn, or smudged. Yet enough of the book remains to allow much of the story to be deciphered, much like the rock record.

Interpreting Earth history is a prime goal of the science of geology. Like a sleuth, the geologist must interpret the clues found preserved in the rocks. By studying rocks, especially sedimentary rocks, and the features they contain, geologists can unravel the complexities of the past.

Geologic events by themselves, however, have little meaning until they are put into a time perspective. Studying history, whether it is that of humans or dinosaurs, requires a clock. Among geology's major contributions to science are the *geologic time scale* and the discovery that Earth history is exceedingly long.

◆ **Figure 8.1** The history of this large boulder illustrates the immensity of geologic time. The boulder is composed of metamorphic rock that once lay several kilometres below Earth's surface in the roots of a great Precambrian mountain chain. Uplift and erosion over hundreds of millions of years exposed the rock at the surface. During the last Ice Age, the boulder was dislodged from the bedrock surface and transported to a site near its present location. It now lies on this rocky beach, near Port Severn, Ontario, where it is being slowly broken down by physical and chemical weathering. (Photo by Mike Schering)

RELATIVE DATING: KEY PRINCIPLES

GEODe EARTH Geologic Time
↳ Relative Dating—Key Principles

The geologists who developed the geologic time scale revolutionized the way people think about time and perceive our planet. They learned that Earth is much older than anyone had previously imagined and that its surface and interior have been changed over and over again by the same geologic processes that operate today.

During the late nineteenth century and early twentieth century, attempts were made to determine Earth's age. Although some of the methods appeared promising at the time, none of these early efforts proved to be reliable. What these scientists were seeking was a **numeric date**. Such dates specify the actual number of years that have passed since an event occurred. Today our understanding of radioactivity allows us to accurately determine numeric dates for rocks that represent important events in Earth's distant past. We will study radioactivity later in this chapter. Before the discovery of radioactivity, geologists had no reliable method of numeric dating and had to rely solely on relative dating.

Relative dating means that rocks are placed in their proper *sequence of formation*—which ones formed first, second, third, and so on. Relative dating cannot tell us how long ago something took place, only that it followed one event and preceded another. The relative dating techniques that were developed are valuable and still widely used.

Numeric dating methods did not replace these techniques; they simply supplemented them. To establish a relative time scale, a few basic principles or rules had to be discovered and applied. Although they may seem obvious to us today, they were major breakthroughs in thinking at the time, and their discovery was an important scientific achievement.

Law of Superposition

Nicolaus Steno, a Danish anatomist, geologist, and priest (1638–1686), is credited with being the first to recognize a sequence of historical events in an outcrop of sedimentary rock layers. Working in the mountains of western Italy, Steno applied a very simple rule that has come to be the most basic principle of relative dating—**the law of superposition** (*super* = above, *positum* = to place). The law simply states that in an undeformed sequence of sedimentary rocks, each bed is older than the one above and younger than the one below. Although it may seem obvious that a rock layer could not be deposited with nothing beneath it for support, it was not until 1669 that Steno clearly stated this principle.

This rule also applies to other surface-deposited materials, such as lava flows and beds of ash from volcanic eruptions. Applying the law of superposition to the beds exposed in the upper portion of the Grand Canyon (Figure 8.2), we can easily place the layers in their proper order. Among those that are pictured, the sedimentary rocks in the Supai Group are the oldest, followed in order by the Hermit Shale, Coconino Sandstone, Toroweap Formation, and Kaibab Limestone.

Principle of Original Horizontality

Steno is also credited with recognizing the importance of another basic principle, called the **principle of original horizontality**. Simply stated, it means that layers of sediment are generally deposited in a horizontal position. Thus, if we observe rock layers that are flat, it means they have not been disturbed and still have their *original* horizontality. The layers in the Chute Vauréal illustrate this in the chapter-opening photo, as do those of the Grand Canyon (Figure 8.2). But if the layers are folded or inclined at a steep angle, they must have been moved into that position by crustal disturbances some time after their deposition (Figure 8.3).

Principle of Cross-Cutting Relations

When a fault cuts through other rocks, or when magma intrudes and crystallizes, we can assume that the fault or intrusion is younger than the rocks affected. For example, in Figure 8.4, the faults and dykes clearly must have occurred after the sedimentary layers were deposited.

This is the principle of **cross-cutting relations**. By applying the cross-cutting principle, you can see that fault A occurred *after* the sandstone layer was

◆ **Figure 8.2** Applying the law of superposition to these layers exposed in the upper portion of the Grand Canyon, the Supai Group is the oldest, and the Kaibab Limestone is the youngest.
(Photo by E. J. Tarbuck)

◆ **Figure 8.3** Most layers of sediment are deposited in a nearly horizontal position. Thus, when we see rock layers that are inclined, we can assume that they must have been moved into that position by crustal disturbances after their deposition. Hartland Quay, Devon, England.
(Photo by Tom Bean/DRK Photo)

deposited because it "broke" the layer. Likewise, fault A occurred *before* the conglomerate was laid down, because that layer is unbroken.

We can also state that dyke B and its associated sill are older than dyke A because dyke A cuts the sill. In the same manner, we know that the batholith was emplaced after movement occurred along fault B but before dyke B was formed. This is true because the batholith cuts across fault B, while dyke B cuts across the batholith.

Inclusions

Sometimes inclusions can aid the relative dating process. **Inclusions** (*includere* = to enclose) are fragments of one rock unit that have been enclosed within another. The basic principle is logical and straightforward. The rock mass adjacent to the one containing the inclusions must have been there first to provide the rock fragments. Therefore, the rock mass containing inclusions is the younger of the two. Figure 8.5 provides an example: the inclusions of intrusive igneous rock in the adjacent sedimentary layer indicate that the sedimentary layer was deposited on top of a weathered igneous mass rather than being intruded from below by magma that later crystallized.

Unconformities

When we observe layers of rock that have been deposited essentially without interruption, we call them **conformable**. Particular sites exhibit conformable beds representing certain spans of geologic time. However, no place on Earth has a complete set of conformable strata.

Throughout Earth history, the deposition of sediment has been interrupted over and over again. All such breaks in the rock record are termed unconformities. An **unconformity** is a gap in the record produced by erosion and /or non-deposition. In each case, uplift and erosion are followed by subsidence and renewed sedimentation. Unconformities are important features because they represent significant geologic events in Earth history. Moreover, their recognition helps us identify what intervals of time

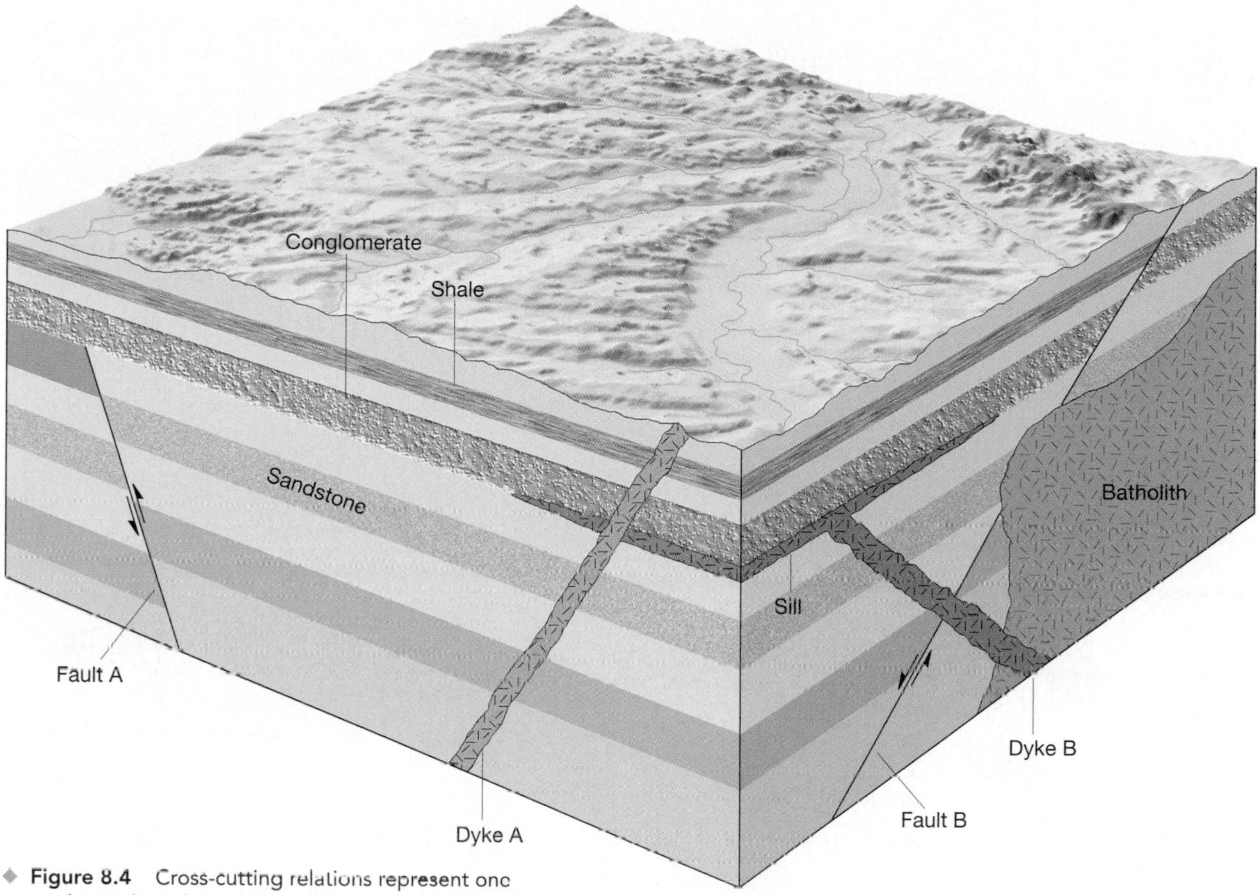

◆ **Figure 8.4** Cross-cutting relations represent one principle used in relative dating. An intrusive rock body is younger than the rocks it intrudes. A fault is younger than the rock layers it cuts.

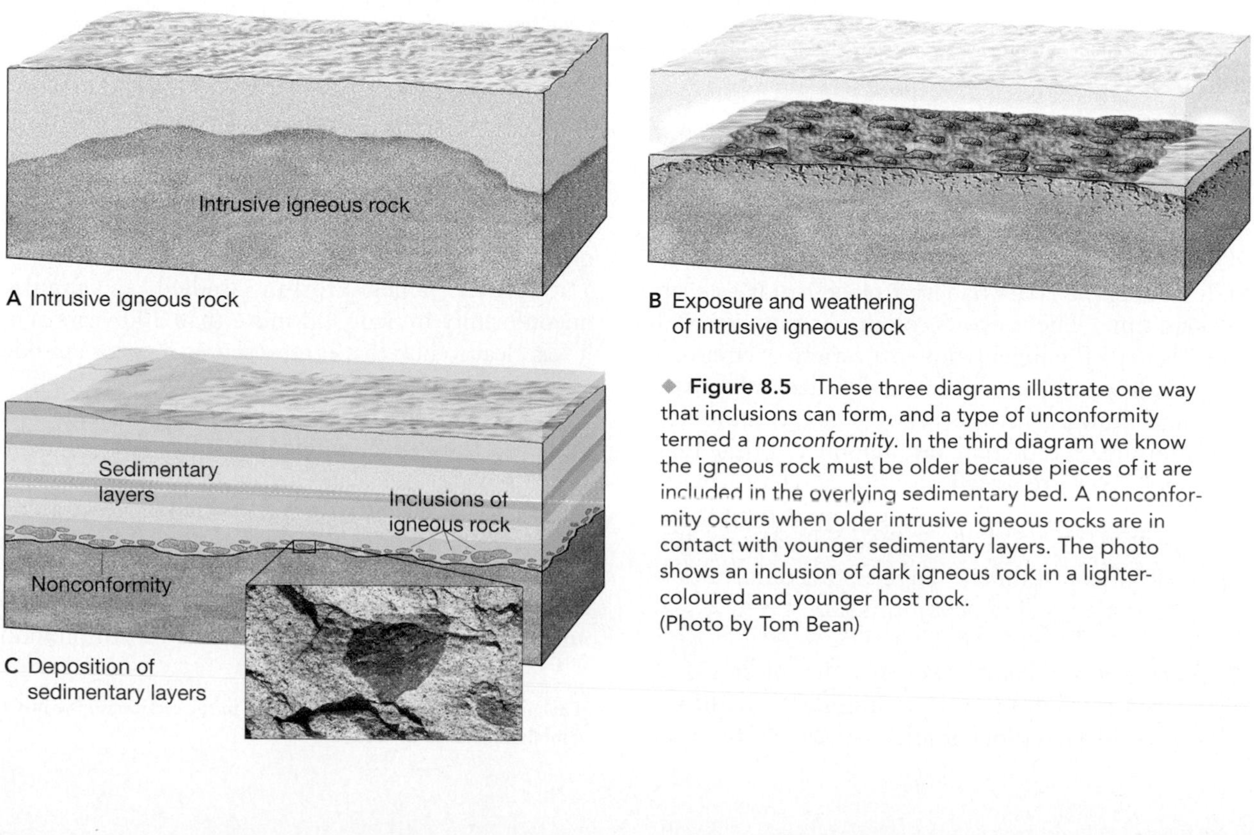

◆ **Figure 8.5** These three diagrams illustrate one way that inclusions can form, and a type of unconformity termed a *nonconformity*. In the third diagram we know the igneous rock must be older because pieces of it are included in the overlying sedimentary bed. A nonconformity occurs when older intrusive igneous rocks are in contact with younger sedimentary layers. The photo shows an inclusion of dark igneous rock in a lighter-coloured and younger host rock.
(Photo by Tom Bean)

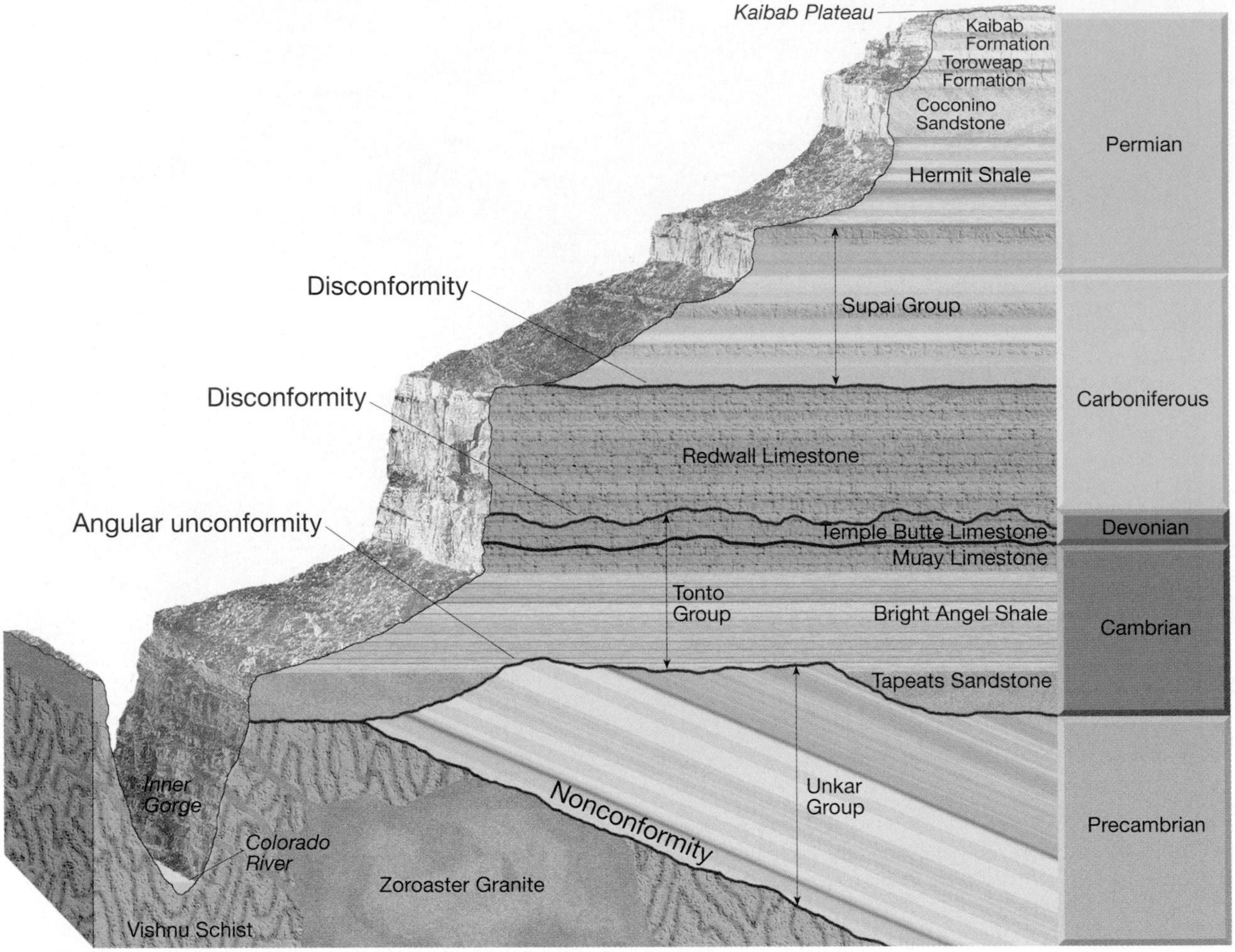

◆ **Figure 8.6** This cross-section through the Grand Canyon illustrates the three basic types of unconformities. An angular unconformity can be seen between the tilted Precambrian Unkar Group and the Cambrian Tapeats Sandstone. Two disconformities are marked, above and below the Redwall Limestone. A nonconformity occurs between the igneous and metamorphic rocks of the Inner Gorge and the sedimentary strata of the Unkar Group.

are not represented by strata and thus are missing from the geologic record.

The rocks exposed in the Grand Canyon of the Colorado River represent a tremendous span of geologic history. It is a wonderful place to take a trip through time. The canyon's colourful strata record a long history of sedimentation in a variety of environments: advancing seas, rivers, and deltas, tidal flats, and sand dunes. But the record is not continuous. Unconformities represent vast amounts of time that have not been recorded in the canyon's layers. Figure 8.6 is a geologic cross-section of the Grand Canyon. Refer to it as you read about the three basic types of unconformities: angular unconformities, disconformities, and nonconformities.

Angular Unconformity Perhaps the most easily recognized unconformity is an **angular unconformity**. It consists of tilted or folded sedimentary rocks that are overlain by younger, more flat-lying strata. An angular unconformity indicates that during the pause in deposition, a period of deformation (folding or tilting) and erosion occurred (Figure 8.7).

When James Hutton studied an angular unconformity in Scotland more than 200 years ago, it was clear to him that it represented a major episode of geologic activity.*

He and his colleagues also appreciated the immense time span implied by such relationships. When a companion later wrote of their visit to this site, he stated that "the mind seemed to grow giddy by looking so far into the abyss of time."

Disconformity When contrasted with angular unconformities, **disconformities** are more common

*This pioneering geologist is discussed in the section on the birth of modern geology in Chapter 1.

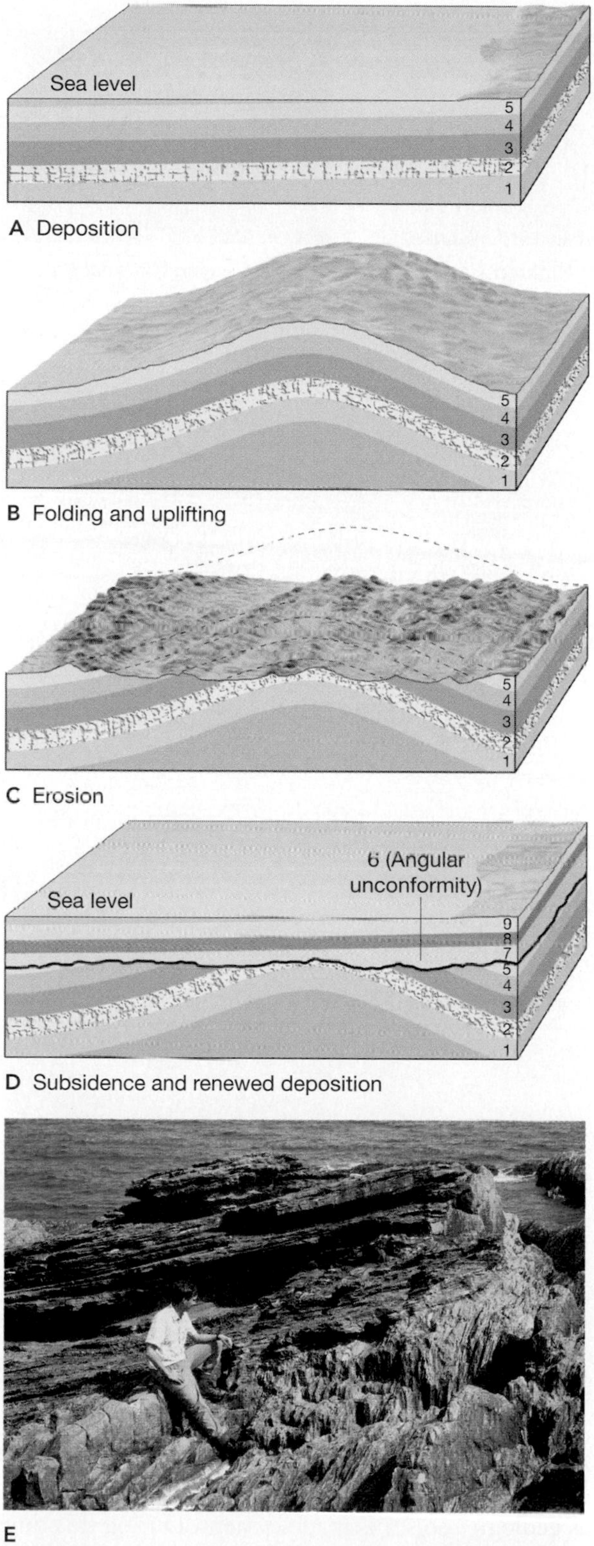

◆ **Figure 8.7** Formation of an angular unconformity. An angular unconformity represents an extended span during which deformation and erosion occurred. Part **E** shows an angular unconformity at Siccar Point, Scotland, that was first described by James Hutton more than 200 years ago. (Photo by A. P. Trujillo/APT Photos)

but usually far less conspicuous because the strata on either side are essentially parallel. Many disconformities are difficult to identify because the rocks above and below are similar and they show little evidence of erosion. Such a break commonly resembles an ordinary bedding plane but can represent a significant time gap. Other disconformities are easier to identify because the ancient erosion surface is cut deeply into the older rocks below.

Nonconformity The third basic type of unconformity is a **nonconformity**. Here the break separates older metamorphic or intrusive igneous rocks from younger sedimentary strata (Figures 8.5 and 8.6). Just as angular unconformities and disconformities imply crustal movements, so too do nonconformities. Intrusive igneous masses and metamorphic rocks originate far below the surface. Thus, for a nonconformity to develop, an episode of uplift and the erosion of overlying rocks must occur. Once exposed at the surface, the igneous or metamorphic rocks are subjected to weathering and erosion before subsidence and the renewal of sedimentation.

CORRELATION OF ROCK LAYERS

To develop a geologic time scale that is applicable to the entire Earth, rocks of similar age in different regions must be matched up. Such a task is referred to as **correlation**.

Correlation by Physical Criteria

Within a limited area, correlating rocks of one locality with those of another can be done simply by walking along the outcropping edges. However, this may not be possible when the rocks are mostly concealed by soil and vegetation. Correlation over short distances is often achieved by noting the position of a bed in a sequence of strata. Or a layer may be identified in another location if it is composed of distinctive or uncommon minerals.

By correlating the rocks from one place to another, a more comprehensive view of the geologic history of a region is possible. Figure 8.8, for example, shows the correlation of strata at three sites on the Colorado Plateau in southern Utah and northern Arizona. No single locale exhibits the entire sequence, but correlation reveals a more complete picture of the sedimentary rock record.

Many geologic studies involve relatively small areas. Although they are important in their own right, their full value is realized only when they are correlated with other regions. Although the methods just described are sufficient to trace a rock formation over relatively short distances, they are not adequate

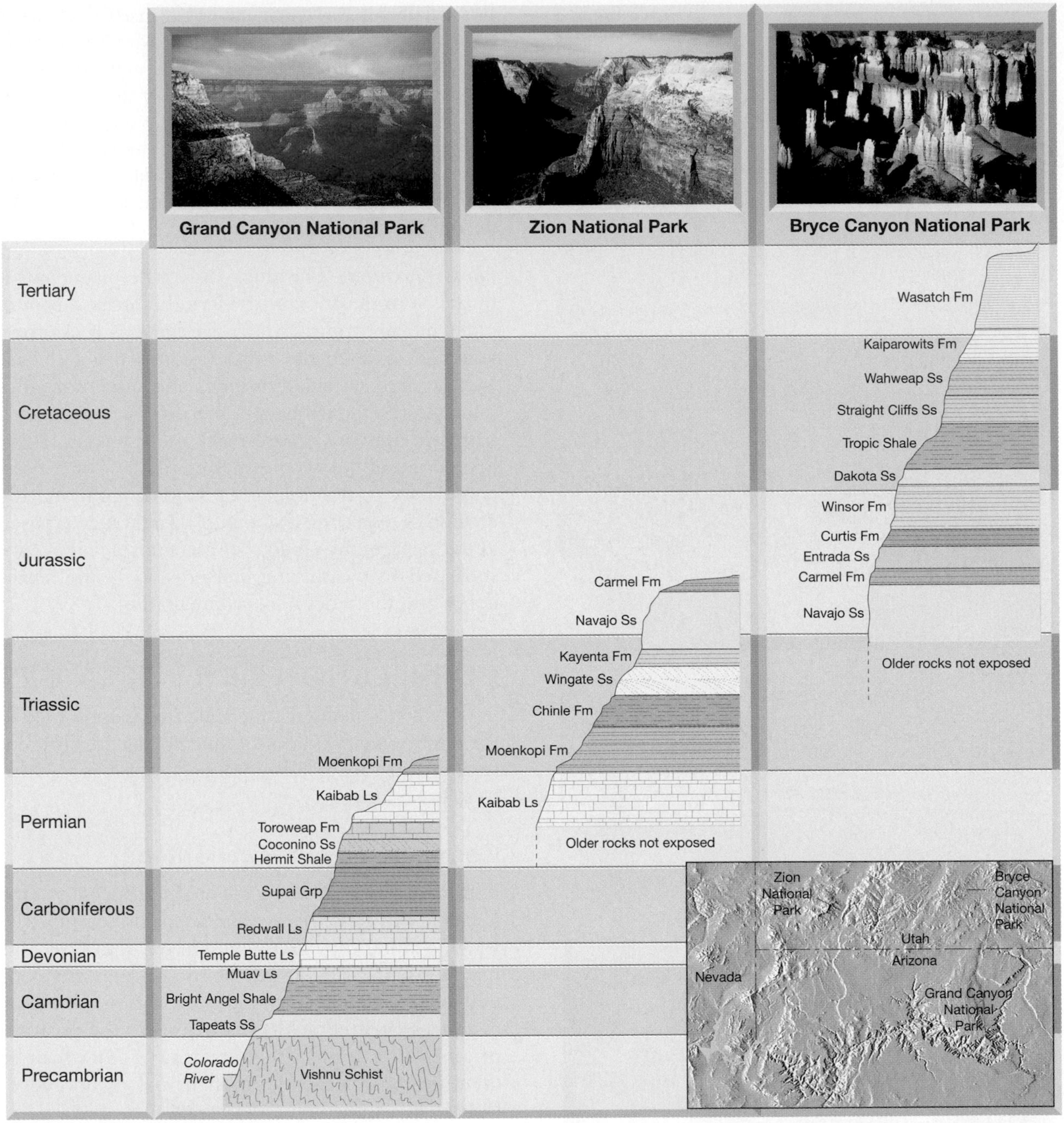

◆ **Figure 8.8** Correlation of strata at three locations on the Colorado Plateau reveals the total extent of sedimentary rocks in the region.
(After U.S. Geological Survey; photos by E. J. Tarbuck)

for matching up rocks that are separated by great distances. When correlation between widely separated areas or between continents is the objective, geologists must rely on fossils.

Fossils and Correlation

The existence of fossils (Chapter 6) had been known for centuries, yet it was not until the late eighteenth and early nineteenth centuries that their significance as geologic tools was made evident. During this time an English engineer and canal builder, William Smith, discovered that each rock formation in the canals he worked on contained fossils unlike those in the beds either above or below. Further, he noted that sedimentary strata in widely separated areas could be identified—and correlated—by their distinctive fossil content.

Based on Smith's classic observations and the findings of many geologists who followed, one of the most important and basic principles in historical geology was formulated: *Fossil organisms succeed one another in a definite and determinable order, and therefore any time interval can be recognized by its fossil content.* This has come to be known as the **principle of fossil succession**. In other words, when fossils are arranged according to their age, they do not present a random or haphazard picture. On the contrary, fossils document the evolution of life through time.

For example, an Age of Trilobites is recognized quite early in the fossil record. Then, in succession, paleontologists recognize an Age of Fishes, an Age of Coal Swamps, an Age of Reptiles, and an Age of Mammals. These ages pertain to groups that were especially plentiful and characteristic during particular episodes. Within each of the ages are many subdivisions that are based, for example, on certain species of trilobites and certain types of fish, reptiles, and so on. This same succession of dominant organisms, never out of order, is found on every continent.

When fossils were found to be time indicators, they became the most useful means of correlating rocks of similar age in different regions. Geologists pay particular attention to certain fossils called **index fossils**. These fossils are widespread geographically and are limited to a short span of geologic time, so their presence provides an important method of matching rocks of the same age (see Box 8.1). Rock formations, however, do not always contain a specific index fossil. In such situations, groups of fossils are

BOX 8.1

Understanding Earth

Index Fossils and Ecology of Organisms

At a very basic level, the degree to which the remains of marine organisms are distributed over the globe depends on the life habits of their owners. For example, whereas an organism that lives in well-sorted sand in shallow water would probably be restricted to a very narrow geographic zone near the coastline, an organism that lives its entire life in the plankton of marine surface waters would be able to drift over wide expanses of the sea. Furthermore, the shell of an organism living in a beach environment pounded by waves would be less likely to be preserved than that of an organism whose remains settle on a quiet, muddy seafloor. An added practical advantage of many of these forms is that they are microscopic in size and therefore many individuals can be extracted from a relatively small sample of rock. Consistent with these factors, most of the index fossils that form the basis of global correlations represent the remains of drifting or swimming organisms that lived in the water column (Figure 8.A). Some particularly important index fossils are described below.

Planktonic Drifters

Foraminifera are amoeba-like animals that construct a calcium carbonate shell. Small (less than 1 millimetre) planktonic forms are important Mesozoic and Cenozoic index fossils. Bottom-dwelling forms of foraminifera range from the Paleozoic to the present and are also important index fossils, particularly in Paleozoic strata, but are less widespread than planktonic forms.

Coccoliths are very tiny (0.002–0.02 millimetres) plates of calcium carbonate that cover single-celled, planktonic algae called coccolithophores. They are important index fossils of the mid to late Mesozoic and the Cenozoic.

Organic-walled cysts of planktonic algae known as *acritarchs* and *dinoflagellates* are commonly used in relative dating. Acritarchs range from the Proterozoic to the present day but are primarily used in pre-Mesozoic strata. Dinoflagellates are extensively used as index fossils for strata of Cretaceous age to the present. The cysts are bodies that represent the resting stage of otherwise planktonic organisms.

Chitinozoans are tiny (0.05–0.4 millimetres) flask-shaped fossils of unknown biologic affinity that are important Paleozoic index fossils (Early Ordovician to Late Devonian).

Swimmers

Conodonts are microscopic (0.2–5 millimetres), phosphatic, tooth-like objects that were elements of the feeding apparatus of small eel-like animals that were active swimmers. The conodont animal is tentatively classified as a primitive, extinct chordate. Conodonts are important index fossils for the Paleozoic and Early Mesozoic (Triassic).

Graptolites are extinct colonial animals that formed long, saw-blade-shaped, organic-walled skeletons and are classified in the group of animals called hemichordates. Forms that were passive floaters are useful in the relative dating of Paleozoic strata, particularly those of Ordovician to Silurian age.

Ammonoids are extinct molluscs related to squids and octopuses and were probably active swimmers. Their calcareous shells are important index fossils for the late Paleozoic and the Mesozoic.

Throughout much of the Phanerozoic Eon, an important factor that restricted the geographic distribution of many bottom-dwelling organisms was the stagnation of bottom waters in deep water areas of sedimentary basins; at times, this prevented much of the seafloor from being colonized by organisms. During times of adverse seafloor conditions, the remains of most bottom-dwelling organisms tend to have a patchy distribution on a global scale and are therefore undesirable for correlation. Even so, a few organisms had an unusually high tolerance of low-oxygen conditions on the seafloor and are used as index fossils for regional correlations. Some of these are described below.

Bottom Dwellers

Trilobites are extinct arthropods, the group of organisms that include present day crabs, shrimps, lobsters, insects, spiders, scorpions, and barnacles. Their calcium carbonate skeletons are used as index fossils primarily in Cambrian to Devonian strata.

Bivalves (known less formally as clams) are molluscs that construct a bivalved shell of calcium carbonate. A group of clams informally known as "flatclams" were extremely abundant and very tolerant of hostile seafloor conditions during the Mesozoic. Various forms of flatclams are important index fossils of the Mesozoic. Scallop-like flatclams called monotids are important in Triassic strata, whereas oyster-like forms called inoceramids serve as index fossils in Cretaceous strata.

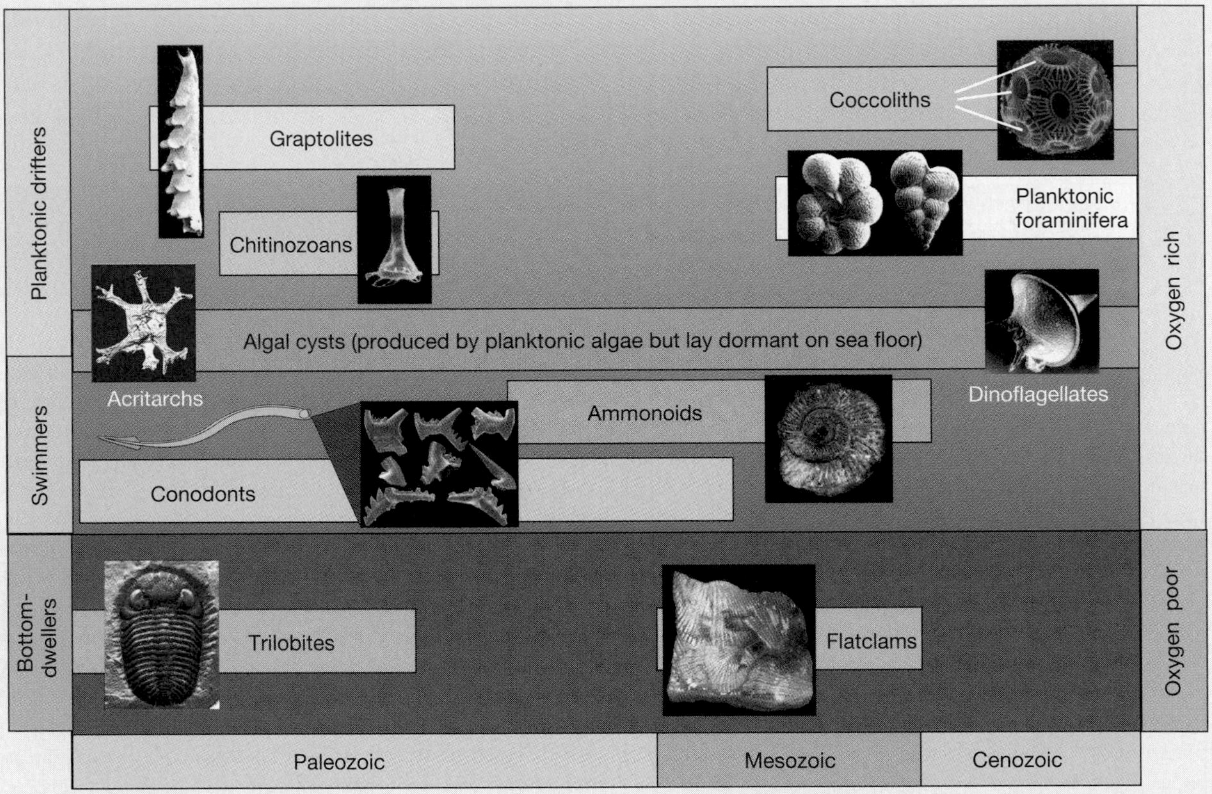

◆ **Figure 8.A** Some important index fossils of the Phanerozoic Eon, life habits of organisms whose remains are represented, and their time ranges. Among planktonic drifters are coccolithophores (containing coccoliths), planktonic foraminifera, graptolites, chitinozoans, acritarchs, and dinoflagellates. Among the remains of swimming organisms are conodonts and ammonoids. Two types of bottom-dwelling organisms that are extensively used as index fossils are trilobites and flatclams.
(Photo of coccolithophore by Jeremy Young; foraminifera reproduced with permission of the Geological Association of Canada (GAC) from *Cretaceous Rocks and Their Foraminifera in the Manitoba Escarpment*, by D. H. McNeil and W. G. E. Caldwell, GAC Special Paper 21(1981); graptolite by Alfred Lenz; chitinozoan courtesy of Esther Asselin, Geological Survey of Canada; acritarch by Andrew MacRae; dinoflagellate by Graham Williams; conodonts by Godfrey Nowlan, Geological Survey of Canada; ammonoid and flatclams by C. Tsujita; trilobite by Denis Tetreault)

used to establish the age of the bed. Figure 8.9 illustrates how an assemblage of fossils can be used to date rocks more precisely than could be accomplished by the use of any one of the fossils.

In addition to being important and often essential tools for correlation, fossils are important environmental indicators (see Box 8.1). Although much can be deduced about past environments by studying the nature and characteristics of sedimentary rocks, a close examination of the fossils present can usually provide a great deal more information.

When the remains of certain clam shells are found in limestone, for example, the geologist quite reasonably assumes that the region was once covered

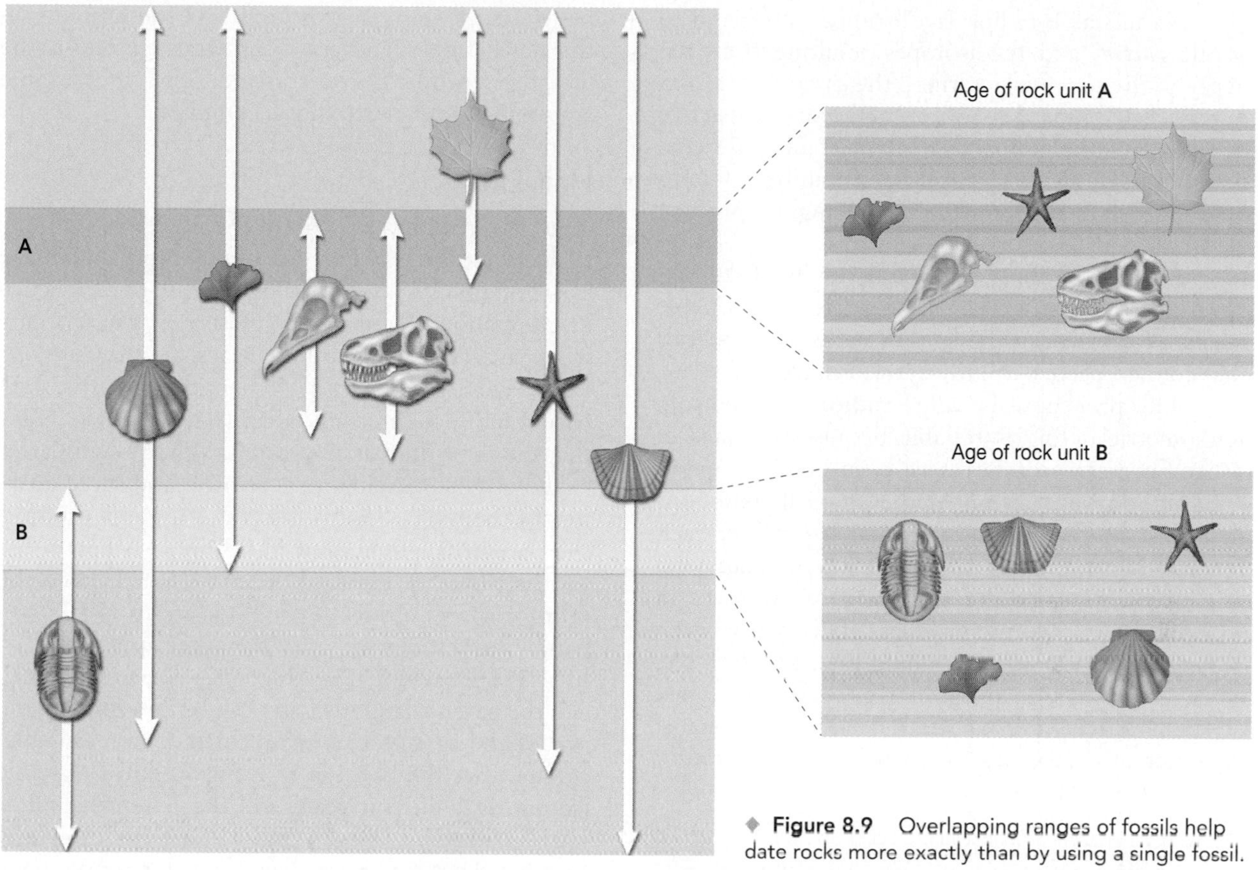

◆ **Figure 8.9** Overlapping ranges of fossils help date rocks more exactly than by using a single fossil.

by a shallow sea. Also, by using what we know of living organisms, we can conclude that fossil animals with thick shells capable of withstanding pounding and surging waves inhabited shorelines. Conversely, animals with thin, delicate shells probably indicate deep, calm offshore waters. Hence, by looking closely at the types of fossils, the approximate position of an ancient shoreline can be identified.

Fossils can also be used to indicate the former temperature of the water. Certain kinds of present-day corals must live in warm and shallow tropical seas, like those around Florida and the Bahamas. When similar types of coral are found in ancient limestones, they indicate the marine environment that must have existed when they were alive. These examples illustrate how fossils can help unravel the complex story of Earth history.

DATING WITH RADIOACTIVITY

GEODe EARTH Geologic Time
↳ Dating with Radioactivity

In addition to establishing relative dates by using the principles described in the preceding sections, it is also possible to obtain reliable numeric dates for events in the geologic past. For example, we know that Earth is about 4.6 billion years old and that the dinosaurs became extinct about 66 million years ago. Dates that are expressed in millions and billions of years truly stretch our imagination, because our personal clocks involve time measured in hours, weeks, and years. Nevertheless, the vast expanse of geologic time is a reality, and it is radiometric dating that allows us to measure it. In this section you will learn about radioactivity and its application in radiometric dating.

Radioactivity

Recall from Chapter 2 that each atom has a nucleus containing protons and neutrons and that the nucleus is orbited by electrons. Electrons have a negative electrical charge, and protons have a positive charge. A neutron is actually a proton and an electron combined, so it has no charge (it is neutral or balanced in charge).

The forces that bind protons and neutrons together in the nucleus are usually strong. However, in some isotopes, the nuclei are unstable because the forces binding protons and neutrons together are not strong enough. As a result, the nuclei spontaneously break apart, or decay, in a process called **radioactivity**.

An unstable radioactive isotope is referred to as the *parent*, and the isotopes resulting from the decay of the parent are termed the *daughter products*. Figure 8.10 provides an example of radioactive decay. When the radioactive parent uranium-238 (its mass number) decays, it follows a number of steps before finally becoming the stable daughter product lead-206.

Among the most important results of the discovery of radioactivity is that it provided a reliable means of calculating the ages of rocks and minerals that contain particular radioactive isotopes.

The procedure is called **radiometric dating**. Radiometric dating is reliable because the rates of decay for many isotopes have been precisely measured and do not vary under the physical conditions that exist in Earth's outer layers. Therefore, each radioactive isotope used for dating has been decaying at a fixed rate since the formation of the rocks in which it occurs, and the products of decay have been accumulating at a corresponding rate. For example, when uranium is incorporated into a mineral that crystallizes from magma, there is no lead (the stable daughter product) from previous decay. The radiometric clock starts at this point. As the uranium in this newly formed mineral disintegrates, atoms of the daughter product are trapped, and measurable amounts of lead eventually accumulate.

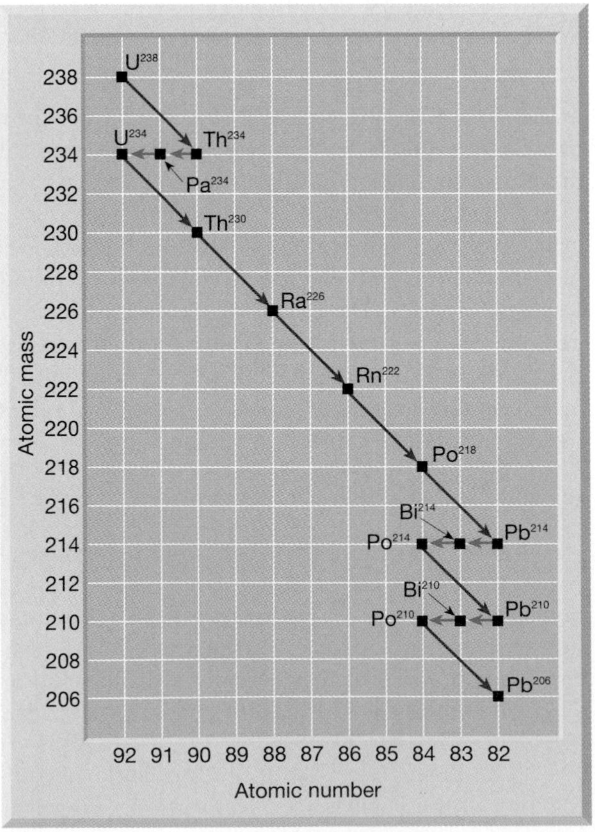

◆ **Figure 8.10** The most common isotope of uranium (U-238) is an example of a radioactive decay series. Before the stable end product (Pb-206) is reached, many different isotopes are produced as intermediate steps.

Half-Life

The time required for half of the nuclei in a sample to decay is called the **half-life** of the isotope. Half-life is a common way of expressing the rate of radioactive disintegration. Figure 8.11 illustrates what occurs when a radioactive parent decays directly into its stable daughter product. When the quantities of parent and daughter are equal (ratio 1:1), we know that one half-life has transpired. When one quarter of the original parent atoms remain, and three quarters of them have decayed to the daughter product, the parent/daughter ratio is 1:3 and we know that two half-lives have passed. After three half-lives, the ratio of parent atoms to daughter atoms is 1:7 (one parent atom for every seven daughter atoms).

If the half-life of a radioactive isotope is known and the parent/daughter ratio can be determined, the age of the sample can be calculated. For example, assume that the half-life of a hypothetical unstable isotope is 1 million years and the parent/daughter ratio in a sample is 1:15. Such a ratio indicates that four half-lives have passed and that the sample must be 4 million years old.

Radiometric Dating

Notice that the *percentage* of radioactive atoms that decay during one half-life is always the same: 50 percent. However, the *actual number* of atoms that decay with the passing of each half-life continually decreases. Thus, as the percentage of radioactive parent atoms declines, the proportion of stable daughter atoms rises, with the increase in daughter atoms just matching the drop in parent atoms. This fact is the key to radiometric dating.

Of the many radioactive isotopes that exist in nature, five have proved particularly useful in providing radiometric ages for ancient rocks (Table 8.1). Rubidium-87, thorium-232, and the two isotopes of uranium are used only for dating rocks that are millions of years old, but potassium-40 is more versatile. Canadians are leading the way in using cosmic ray–generated isotopes to date exposed rock surfaces and to reconstruct landscape evolution (see Box 8.2).

Potassium-Argon Although the half-life of potassium-40 is 1.3 billion years, analytical techniques make possible the detection of tiny amounts of its stable daughter product, argon-40, in some rocks that are younger than 100,000 years. Another impor-

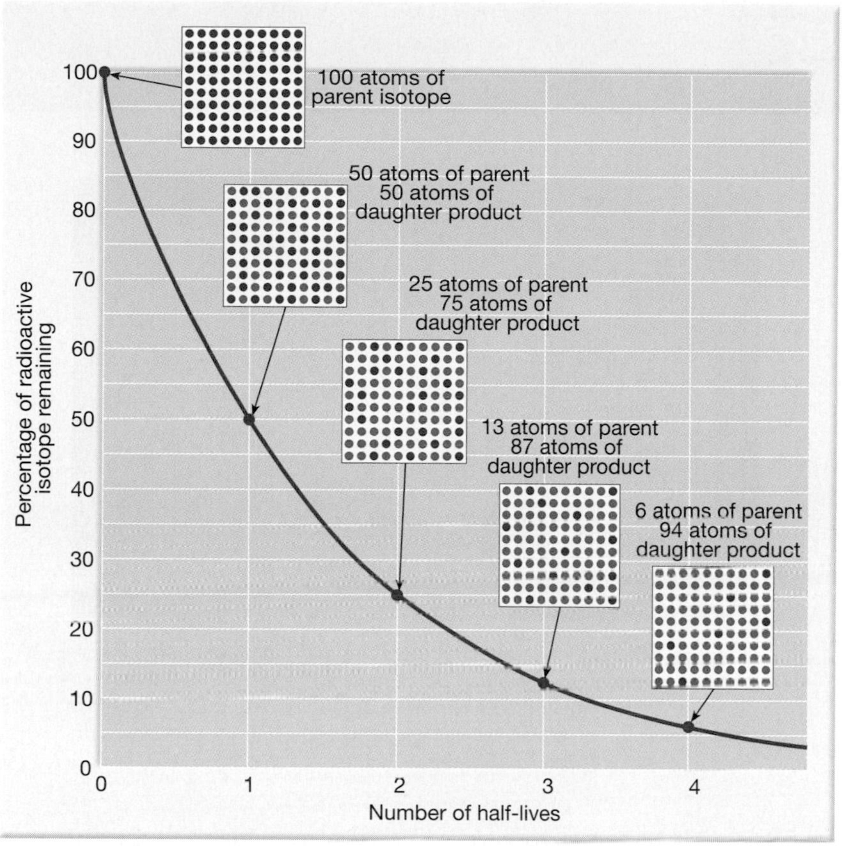

◆ **Figure 8.11** The radioactive-decay curve shows change that is exponential. Half of the radioactive parent remains after one half-life. After a second half-life one quarter of the parent remains, and so forth.

tant reason for its frequent use is that potassium is an abundant constituent of many common minerals, particularly micas and feldspars.

Although potassium (K) has three natural isotopes, K^{39}, K^{40}, and K^{41}, only K^{40} is radioactive. When K^{40} decays, it does so in two ways. About 11 percent changes to argon-40 (Ar^{40}). The remaining 89 percent of K^{40} decays to calcium-40 (Ca^{40}). The decay of K^{40} to Ca^{40}, however, is not useful for radiometric dating, because the Ca^{40} produced by radioactive disintegration cannot be distinguished from calcium that may have been present when the rock formed.

The potassium-argon clock begins when potassium-bearing minerals crystallize from magma or form within a metamorphic rock. At this point the new minerals will contain K^{40} but will be free of Ar^{40}, because this element is an inert gas that does not chemically combine with other elements. As time passes, the K^{40} steadily decays. The Ar^{40} produced by this process remains trapped within the mineral's crystal lattice. Because no Ar^{40} was present when the mineral formed, all of the daughter atoms trapped in the mineral must have come from the decay of K^{40}. To determine a sample's age, the K^{40}/Ar^{40} ratio is measured precisely and the known half-life for K^{40} applied.

Sources of Error It is important to realize that an accurate radiometric date can be obtained only if the mineral remained a closed system during the entire period since it formed. A correct date is not possible unless there was neither the addition nor loss of parent or daughter isotopes. This is not always the case. In fact, an important limitation of the potassium-argon method arises from the fact that argon is a gas and it can leak from minerals, throwing off measurements. Indeed, losses can be significant if the rock is subjected to relatively high temperatures. Of course, a reduction in the amount of Ar^{40} leads to an underestimation of the rock's age. Sometimes temperatures

TABLE 8.1 **Isotopes Frequently Used in Radiometric Dating**

Radioactive Parent	Stable Daughter Product	Currently Accepted Half-Life Values
Uranium-238	Lead-206	4.5 billion years
Uranium-235	Lead-207	713 million years
Thorium-232	Lead-208	14.1 billion years
Rubidium-87	Strontium-87	47.0 billion years
Potassium-40	Argon-40	1.3 billion years

BOX 8.2

Canadian Profile
Dating Earth's Surface with Terrestrial Cosmogenic Nuclides

John Gosse[*]

Earth is continuously bombarded by radiation that originates from outside our solar system. Fortunately, the geomagnetic field deflects much of the radiation, but even at the equator where the field is strongest some of the highest energy particles can still penetrate. When the cosmic particles, or rays, enter the atmosphere, they interact with the nuclei of nitrogen and oxygen and create a secondary flux of radiation. The secondary rays include such particles as neutrinos, electrons, muons, pions, neutrons, protons, and heavier particles called nuclides, which are nuclei of atoms without electrons. The secondary particles may have enough energy to continue to interact with matter deeper into the atmosphere and even in the lithosphere, biosphere, and hydrosphere. For instance, carbon-14, used for radiocarbon dating, is produced cosmogenically in the atmo-sphere. Cosmic-ray-produced (cosmogenic) beryllium-10 is a terrestrial cosmogenic nuclide (TCN) that is produced in quartz when an energetic secondary neutron annihilates the nucleus of a silicon-28 or oxygen-16 nucleus during a type of interaction called spallation. Although many cosmogenic nuclides are so unstable that they decay quickly, many are stable (^{3}He, ^{21}Ne, ^{38}Ar) or have a long enough half-life that they are useful for geologic dating (^{10}Be $t_{\frac{1}{2}}$ = 1.4 Ma, ^{26}Al $t_{\frac{1}{2}}$ = 0.7 Ma, ^{36}Cl $t_{\frac{1}{2}}$ = 0.3 Ma, ^{14}C $t_{\frac{1}{2}}$ = 5.7 ka).

◆ **Figure 8.B** A former lake that filled this basin in north central Baffin Island was rapidly drained about 8000 years ago after glacier ice that dammed the lake melted. The exposure age on emerged shorelines and delta indicate when glacial retreat occurred and when the lake drained. (Photo courtesy of John C. Gosse)

The average energy of secondary cosmic radiation decreases approximately exponentially with depth so in rock and sediments in the upper few metres of Earth's surface, the concentration of TCN also decreases with depth. The rate that these TCN are produced in rocks depends on how thick the atmosphere is above the sample (cosmic ray flux to mountain tops or airplanes is greater than the flux at sea level). For example, at sea level ^{10}Be is produced at the rate of five ^{10}Be atoms per gram of quartz per year. Consider that our tans get darker with longer exposure to solar rays. Similarly, the TCN concentration (atoms per gram) in minerals increases with time with greater exposure to cosmic rays. Because there are so few TCN atoms among the 10^{24} atoms of a gram of a mineral, TCNs are usually measured by using high precision accelerator or atom-grade noble gas mass spectrometry. By measuring the concentrations of these rare nuclides we can calculate the time since a rock surface was exposed at Earth's surface. For a stable TCN,

Time = Concentration/Production rate

The cosmic clock begins as soon as the rock is exposed, so the technique is useful for dating lavas, fault scarps, emerged beaches, and deltas (Figure 8.B), deglaciated landforms

are high enough for a sufficiently long interval that all argon escapes. When this happens, the potassium-argon clock is reset and dating the sample will give only the time of thermal resetting, not the true age of the rock. For other radiometric clock, a loss of daughter atoms can occur if the rock has been subjected to weathering or leaching. To avoid such a problem, one simple safeguard is to use only fresh, unweathered material and not samples that may have been chemically altered.

Dating with Carbon-14

To date geologically recent events, carbon-14 is used. Carbon-14 is the radioactive isotope of carbon. The process is often called **radiocarbon dating**. Because the half-life of carbon-14 is only 5730 years, it can be used for dating events from recorded history as well as those from very recent geologic history (see Box 8.3). In some cases carbon-14 can be used to date events as far back as 70,000 years.

◆ **Figure 8.C** Exposure dates of 15,900 years on large erratic boulders near Peggy's Cove, Nova Scotia, record when the last ice sheet margin retreated from the continental shelf and onto land. Samples were collected with a cutoff saw in order to remove pieces 2 centimetres thick from the centre of the top surface. (Photo courtesy of Fiona H. McDonald)

◆ **Figure 8.D** By exposure dating stream-polished surfaces down the wall of Granite Gorge of the Grand Canyon, researchers can determine how fast the Colorado River incised through the Grand Canyon.
(Photo courtesy of Laura Crossey)

and erratic boulders (Figure 8.C), alluvial fans, stream terraces, stream-eroded canyon walls (Figure 8.D), and landslides. Surfaces as young as decades, and as old as tens of millions of years, have been measured in the Dry Valleys of Antarctica and hyper-arid deserts where erosion has not removed much of the cosmic ray exposure record. The technique is useful for helping determine the recurrence intervals of volcanic eruptions, earthquake faulting, flooding, and landsliding, and the influence of climate change on global glacial ice volumes.

*John Gosse is a professor in the department of Earth Sciences and Canada Research Chair in Earth System Evolution at Dalhousie University.

Carbon-14 is continuously produced in the upper atmosphere as a consequence of cosmic ray bombardment. This isotope of carbon quickly becomes incorporated into carbon dioxide, which circulates in the atmosphere and is absorbed by living matter. As a result, all organisms contain a small amount of carbon-14, including you.

As long as an organism is alive, the decaying radiocarbon is continually replaced and the proportions of carbon-14 and carbon-12 remain constant. Carbon-12 is the stable and most common isotope of carbon. However, when any plant or animal dies, the amount of carbon-14 gradually decreases as it decays to nitrogen-14. By comparing the proportions of carbon-14 and carbon-12 in a sample, radiocarbon dates can be determined.

Although carbon-14 is only useful in dating the last small fraction of geologic time, it has become a very valuable tool for anthropologists, archaeologists, and historians, as well as for geologists who study very recent Earth history. In fact, the development of radiocarbon dating was considered so important that the chemist who discovered this application, Willard F. Libby, received a Nobel Prize in 1960.

Importance of Radiometric Dating

Bear in mind that although the basic principle of radiometric dating is simple, the actual procedure is quite complex. The analysis that determines the quantities of parent and daughter must be painstakingly precise. In addition, some radioactive materials do not decay directly into the stable daughter product, as was the case with our hypothetical example, a fact that may further complicate the analysis. Uranium-238 forms 13 intermediate unstable daughter products formed before the 14th and last daughter product, the stable isotope lead-206, is produced (see Figure 8.10).

Radiometric dating methods have produced literally thousands of dates for events in Earth history. Rocks from several localities have been dated at more than 3 billion years, and geologists realize that still-older rocks exist. For example, granite from

BOX 8.3

Understanding Earth
Using Tree Rings to Date and Study the Recent Past

If you look at the top of a tree stump or at the end of a log, you will see that it is composed of a series of concentric rings. Each of these *tree rings* becomes larger in diameter outward from the centre (Figure 8.E). Every year in temperate regions, trees add a layer of new wood under the bark. Characteristics of each tree ring, such as size and density, reflect the environmental conditions (especially climate) that prevailed during the year when the ring formed. Favourable growth conditions produce a wide ring; unfavourable ones produce a narrow ring. Trees growing at the same time in the same region show similar tree-ring patterns.

Because a single growth ring is usually added each year, the age of the tree when it was cut can be determined by counting the rings. If the year of cutting is known, the age of the tree and the year in which each ring formed can be determined by counting back from the outside ring.*

This procedure can be used to determine the dates of recent geologic events, for example, the minimum number of years since a new land surface was created by a landslide or a flood. The dating and study of annual rings in trees is called *dendrochronology*.

To make the most effective use of tree rings, extended patterns known as ring chronologies are established. If the same pattern can be identified in two samples, one of which has been dated, the second sample can be dated from the first by matching the ring pattern common to both. This technique, called *cross-dating*, is illustrated in Figure 8.F. Tree-ring chronologies extending back for thousands of years have been established for some regions. To date a timber sample of unknown age, its ring pattern is matched against the reference chronology—a unique archive of environmental and climate history.

*Scientists are not limited to working with trees that have been cut down. Small, nondestructive core samples can be taken from living trees.

◆ **Figure 8.E** Each year a growing tree produces a layer of new cells beneath the bark. If the tree is felled and the trunk examined (or if a core is taken, to avoid cutting the tree), each year's growth can be seen as a ring. Because the amount of growth (thickness of a ring) depends on precipitation and temperature, tree rings are useful records of past climates. (Photo by Stephen J. Krasemann/DRK Photo)

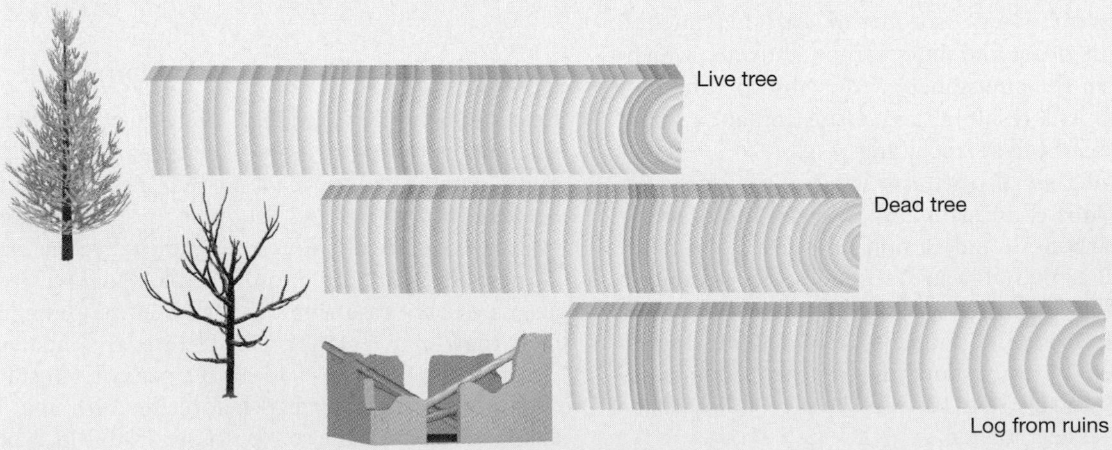

◆ **Figure 8.F** Cross-dating is a basic principle in dendrochronology. Here it was used to date an archaeological site by correlating tree-ring patterns for wood from trees of three different ages. First, a tree-ring chronology for the area is established by using cores extracted from living trees. This chronology is extended further back in time by matching overlapping patterns from older, dead trees. Finally, cores taken from beams inside the ruin are dated by using the chronology established from the other two sites.

South Africa has been dated at 3.2 billion years and contains inclusions of quartzite. (Remember that inclusions are older than the rock containing them.) Quartzite, a metamorphic rock, was originally the sedimentary rock sandstone. Sandstone, in turn, is the product of the lithification of sediments produced by the weathering of existing rocks. Thus, we have a positive indication that even older rocks existed.

Radiometric dating has vindicated the ideas of Hutton, Darwin, and others, who more than 150 years ago inferred that geologic time must be immense. Indeed, radiometric dating has proved that there has been enough time for the processes we observe to have accomplished tremendous tasks.

THE GEOLOGIC TIME SCALE

GEODe EARTH Geologic Time
↳ The Geologic Time Scale

Geologists have divided the whole of geologic history into units of varying magnitude. Together, they compose the **geologic time scale** of Earth history (Figure 8.12). The major units of the time scale were

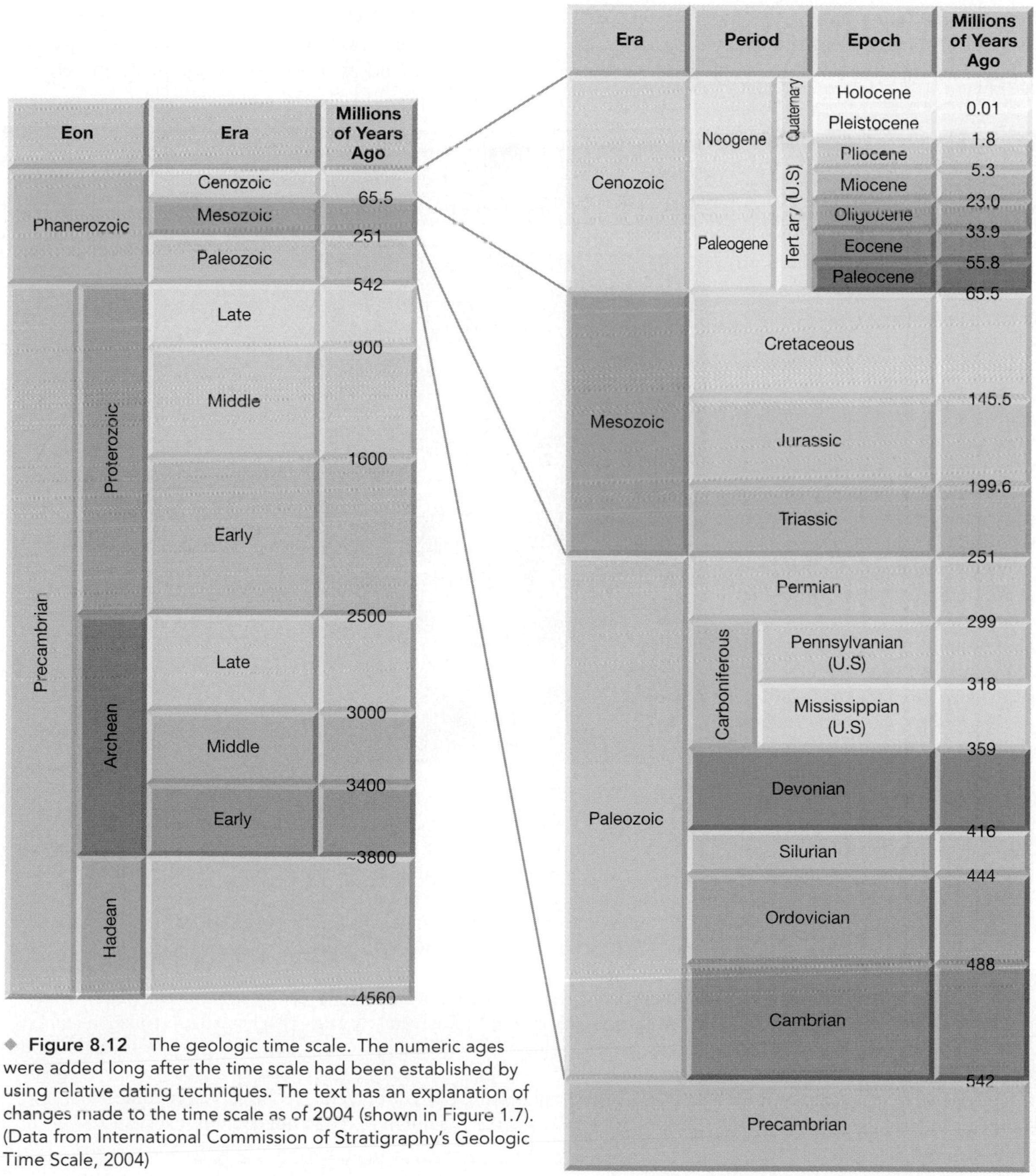

◆ **Figure 8.12** The geologic time scale. The numeric ages were added long after the time scale had been established by using relative dating techniques. The text has an explanation of changes made to the time scale as of 2004 (shown in Figure 1.7). (Data from International Commission of Stratigraphy's Geologic Time Scale, 2004)

delineated during the nineteenth century, principally by workers in Western Europe and Great Britain. Because radiometric dating was unavailable at that time, the entire time scale was created by using methods of relative dating. It was only in the twentieth century that radiometric methods permitted numeric dates to be added.

Structure of the Time Scale

The geologic time scale subdivides the 4.6-billion-year history of Earth into many different units and provides a meaningful time frame within which the events of the geologic past are arranged. As shown in Figure 8.12, **eons** represent the greatest expanses of time. The eon that began about 542 million years ago is the **Phanerozoic**, a term derived from Greek words meaning *visible life*. It is an appropriate description because the rocks and deposits of the Phanerozoic eon contain abundant fossils that document major evolutionary trends.

The Phanerozoic Eon is divided into **eras**. The three eras within the Phanerozoic are the **Paleozoic** (*palaios* = ancient, *zoe* = life), the **Mesozoic** (*meso* = middle, *zoe* = life), and the **Cenozoic** (*ceno* = recent, *zoe* = life). As the names imply, the eras are bounded by profound worldwide changes in life forms (see Box 8.4).

Each era is subdivided into time units known as **periods**. The Paleozoic has six, the Mesozoic three, and the Cenozoic two. Each of these dozen periods is characterized by a somewhat less profound change

BOX 8.4

Earth as a System
Demise of the Dinosaurs

The boundaries between divisions on the geologic time scale represent times of significant geologic and biologic change. Of special interest is the boundary between the Mesozoic Era ("middle life") and Cenozoic Era ("recent life"), about 65.5 million years ago. Around this time, more than half of all plant and animal species died out in a *mass extinction*. This boundary (Figure 8.12) marks the end of the era in which dinosaurs (Figure 8.G) and other reptiles dominated the landscape and the beginning of the era when mammals become very important.

The extinction of the dinosaurs is generally attributed to this group's inability to adapt to some radical change in environmental conditions. What event could have triggered the rapid extinction of the dinosaurs—one of the most successful groups of land animals ever to have lived?

◆ **Figure 8.G** Dinosaurs dominated the North American landscape through much of the Mesozoic Era. *Tyrannosaurus* was one of the last meat-eating dinosaurs to have roamed North America just before the great mass extinction that occurred at the end of the Cretaceous Period. (Photo used with permission from the Royal Tyrrell Museum, Drumheller, Alberta)

The most strongly supported hypothesis proposes that about 65.5 million years ago, a large meteorite approximately 10 kilometres in diameter collided with Earth (Figure 8.H). The speed at impact was about 90,000 kilometres per hour! The force of the impact vaporized the meteorite and trillions of tonnes of Earth's crust. Huge quantities of dust and other metamorphosed debris were blasted high into the atmosphere. For a year or two the encircling dust cloud greatly restricted the sunlight reaching Earth's surface. With insufficient sunlight for photosynthesis, delicate food chains most likely would have collapsed. Large plant-eating dinosaurs would have been affected more adversely than smaller life forms because of the tremendous volume of vegetation they consumed. Next would have come the demise of large carnivores. When the sunlight returned, more than half of the species on Earth, including numerous marine organisms, had become extinct.

This period of mass extinction appears to have affected all land animals larger than dogs. Supporters of the catastrophic-event scenario suggest that small, rat-like mammals were able to survive a breakdown in their food chains lasting perhaps several months. Large dinosaurs, they contend, could not survive this event.

The loss of these large reptiles opened a habitat for the small mammals that remained. This new habitat, along with evolutionary forces, led to the development of the large mammals that occupy our modern world.

What evidence points to such a catastrophic collision 65.5 million years ago? First, a thin layer of sediment nearly 1 centimetre thick marks the boundary between Cretaceous and Paleogene strata worldwide. This sediment contains a high level of the element *iridium*, rare in Earth's crust but found in high proportions in stony meteorites. Could this layer be the scattered remains of the meteorite that was responsible for the environmental changes that led to the demise of many reptile groups?

Despite its growing support, some scientists disagree with the impact hypothesis. They suggest instead that huge volcanic eruptions led to the breakdown in the food chain. To support their hypothesis, they cite enormous outpourings of lavas in the Deccan Plateau of northern India about 65.5 million years ago.

Whatever caused the end-Cretaceous extinction, we now have a greater appreciation of the role of catastrophic events in shaping the history of our planet and the life that occupies it. Could a catastrophic event having similar results occur today? This possibility may explain why an event that occurred 65.5 million years ago has captured the interest of so many.

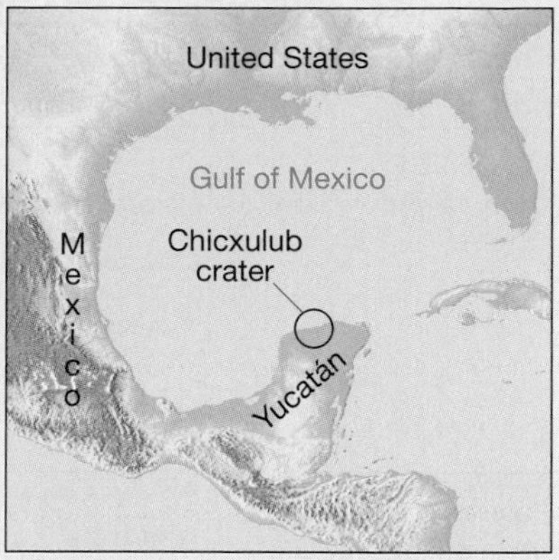

◆ **Figure 8.H** Chicxulub crater is a giant impact crater that formed about 65.5 million years ago and has since been filled with sediments. About 180 kilometres in diameter, Chicxulub crater is regarded by some researchers as the impact site of the meteorite that resulted in the demise of the dinosaurs.

in life forms as compared with the eras. The eras and periods of the Phanerozoic, with brief explanations of each, are presented in Table 8.2.

Finally, each of the 12 periods is divided into still smaller units called **epochs**. As you can see in Figure 8.12, seven epochs have been named for the periods of the Cenozoic. The epochs of other periods usually are simply termed *early*, *middle*, and *late*.

Precambrian Time

Notice that the detail of the geologic time scale does not begin until about 542 million years ago, the date for the beginning of the Cambrian Period. The nearly 4 billion years before the Cambrian are divided into three eons, the **Hadean** (*Hades* = mythological subterranean world of departed spirits), the **Archean** (*archaios* = ancient), and the **Proterozoic** (*proteros* = before, *zoe* = life). It is also common for this vast expanse of time to simply be referred to as the **Precambrian**. Although it represents about 88 percent of Earth history, the Precambrian is not divided into nearly as many smaller time units as the Phanerozoic Eon.

Why is the huge expanse of Precambrian time not divided into numerous eras, periods, and epochs? The reason is that Precambrian history is not known in great enough detail. The quantity of information geologists have deciphered about Earth's past is somewhat analogous to the detail of human history. The farther back we go, the less that is known. Certainly more data and information exist about the past 10 years than for the first decade of the twentieth century; the events of the nineteenth century have been documented much better than the events of the first century A.D.; and so on. So it is with Earth history. The more recent past has the freshest, least disturbed, and more observable record. The further back in time geologists go, the more fragmented the record and clues become. Other reasons help explain our lack of a detailed time scale for this vast segment of Earth history:

1. The first abundant fossil evidence does not appear in the geologic record until the beginning of the Cambrian Period. Before the Cambrian, simple life forms, such as algae, bacteria, fungi, and worms, predominated. All of these organisms lack hard parts, an important condition favouring preservation. For this reason, only a meagre Precambrian fossil record exists. Many exposures of Precambrian rocks have been studied in some detail, but correlation is often difficult when fossils are lacking.
2. Because Precambrian rocks are very old, most have been subjected to a great many changes. Much of the Precambrian rock record is composed of highly distorted metamorphic rocks. This makes the interpretation of past environments difficult, because many of the clues present in the original sedimentary rocks have been destroyed.

Radiometric dating has provided a partial solution to the troublesome task of dating and correlating

TABLE 8.2 **Major Divisions of Geologic Time**

Cenozoic Era (Age of Recent Life)	Neogene Period* Paleogene Period*	From the Greek words *neo* = new and *genes* = born From the Greek words *palaios* = ancient and *genes* = born
Mesozoic Era (Age of Middle Life)	Cretaceous Period	Derived from Greek word for chalk (*kreta*) and first applied to extensive deposits that form white cliffs along the English Channel (see Figure 6.13); extinction of the dinosaurs at the end of this period
	Jurassic Period	Named for the Jura Mountains, located between France and Switzerland, where rocks of this age were first studied; age of dinosaurs
	Triassic Period	Taken from the word *trias* in recognition of the threefold character of these rocks in Europe; dinosaurs first appeared
Paleozoic Era (Age of Ancient Life)	Permian Period	Named after the province of Perm, Russia, where these rocks were first studied
	Carboniferous Period**	The literal meaning of this term is "carbon-bearing" and refers to the extensive coal measures of Western Europe that are of this age
	Devonian Period	Named after Devonshire County, England, where these rocks were first studied
	Silurian Period Ordovician Period	Named after Celtic tribes, the Silures and the Ordovices, that lived in Wales during the Roman Conquest
	Cambrian Period	Taken from Roman name for Wales (Cambria), where rocks containing the earliest evidence of complex forms of life were first studied
Precambrian		The time between the birth of the planet and the appearance of skeletonized forms of life; about 88 percent of Earth's estimated 4.6 billion years fall into this span.

Sources: U.S. Geological Survey and the International Commission of Stratigraphy

*According to the International Commission of Stratigraphy, the terms Quaternary and Tertiary (Figure 8.12), which are still widely used, are no longer considered periods of the Cenozoic; many geologists remain opposed to this controversial ruling.

**In North America, the Carboniferous Period is divided into the Mississippian and Pennsylvanian subperiods (Figure 8.12). The names of these subperiods (formerly considered periods in the United States) refer to the extensive exposures of rocks representing this interval of time in the Mississippi River Valley and the state of Pennsylvania, respectively.

Precambrian rocks. But untangling the complex Precambrian record still remains a daunting task.

DIFFICULTIES IN DATING THE GEOLOGIC TIME SCALE

Although reasonably accurate numeric dates have been worked out for the periods of the geologic time scale (Figure 8.12), the task is not without difficulty. The primary difficulty in assigning numeric dates to units of time is the fact that not all rocks can be dated by radiometric methods. Recall that for a radiometric date to be useful, all the minerals in the rock must have formed at about the same time. For this reason, radioactive isotopes can be used to determine when minerals in an igneous rock crystallized and when pressure and heat created new minerals in a metamorphic rock.

However, samples of sedimentary rock can only rarely be dated directly by radiometric means. Although a detrital sedimentary rock can include particles that contain radioactive isotopes, the rock's age cannot be accurately determined because the grains composing the rock are not the same age as the rock in which they occur. Rather, the sediments have been weathered from rocks of diverse ages.

Radiometric dates obtained from metamorphic rocks can also be difficult to interpret, because the age of a particular mineral in a metamorphic rock does not necessarily represent the time when the rock initially formed. Instead, the date might indicate any one of a number of subsequent metamorphic phases in which the clock may have been reset.

If samples of sedimentary rocks rarely yield reliable radiometric ages, how can numeric dates be assigned to sedimentary layers? Usually, the geologist must relate the strata to datable igneous masses, as in Figure 8.13.

This is one example of literally thousands that illustrate how datable materials are used to bracket the various episodes in Earth history within specific time intervals. It shows the necessity of combining laboratory dating methods with field observations of rocks.

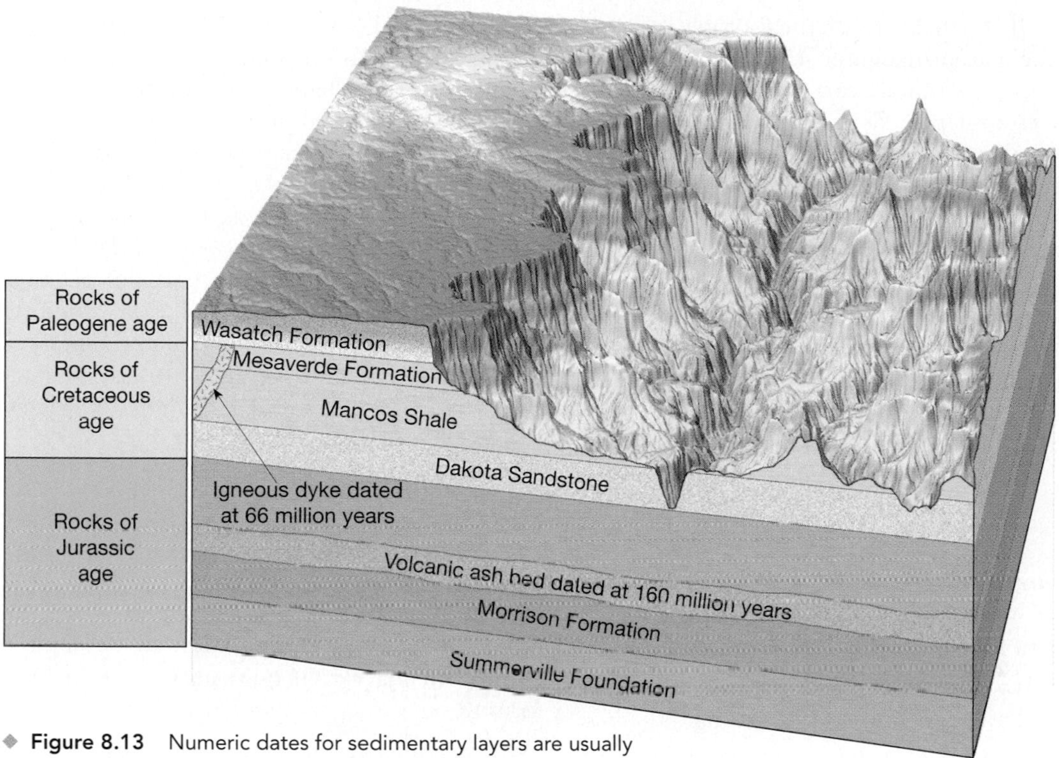

◆ **Figure 8.13** Numeric dates for sedimentary layers are usually determined by examining their relationship to igneous rocks. (After U.S. Geological Survey)

Chapter Summary

- The two types of dates used by geologists to interpret Earth history are (1) *relative dates*, which put events in their proper sequence of formation, and (2) *numeric dates*, which pinpoint the time in years when an event occurred.
- Relative dates can be established by using the *law of superposition* (in an undeformed sequence of sedimentary rocks or surface-deposited igneous rocks, each bed is older than the one above, and younger than the one below), *principle of original horizontality* (most layers are deposited in a horizontal position), *cross-cutting relations* (when a fault or intrusion cuts through another rock, the fault or intrusion is younger than the rocks cut through), and *inclusions* (the rock mass containing the inclusion is younger than the rock that provided the inclusion).
- *Unconformities* are gaps in the rock record. Each represents a long span during which deposition ceased, erosion may have removed previously formed rocks, and then deposition resumed. The three basic types of unconformities are *angular unconformities* (tilted or folded sedimentary rocks that are overlain by younger, flat-lying strata), *disconformities* (the strata on either side of the unconformity are essentially parallel), and *nonconformities* (where a break separates older metamorphic or intrusive igneous rocks from younger sedimentary strata).
- *Correlation*, the matching of two or more geologic phenomena in different areas, is used to develop a *geologic time scale* that applies to the whole Earth.
- Fossils are used to correlate sedimentary rocks that are from different regions by using the rocks' distinctive fossil content and applying the *principle of fossil succession*. It is based on the work of William Smith in the late eighteenth century and states that fossil organisms succeed one another in a definite and determinable order, and, therefore, any time period can be recognized by its fossil content. The use of *index fossils*, those that are widespread geographically and are limited to a short span of geologic time, provides an important method for matching rocks of the same age.
- An unstable radioactive isotope, called the parent, will decay and form stable daughter products. The length of time for half of the nuclei of a radioactive isotope to decay is called the *half-life*

of the isotope. If the half-life of the isotope is known, and the parent/daughter ratio can be measured, the age of a sample can be calculated. An accurate radiometric date can only be obtained if the mineral containing the radioactive isotope has remained a closed system during the entire time since its formation.

- The geologic time scale divides Earth's history into units of varying magnitude. It is commonly presented in chart form, with the oldest time and event at the bottom and the youngest at the top. The principal subdivisions of the geologic time scale, called *eons*, include the *Hadean*, *Archean*, *Proterozoic* (together, these three eons are commonly referred to as the *Precambrian*), and, beginning about 542 million years ago, the *Phanerozoic*. The Phanerozoic (meaning "visible life") Eon is divided into the following *eras: Paleozoic* ("ancient life"), *Mesozoic* ("middle life"), and *Cenozoic* ("recent life").
- A significant problem in assigning numeric dates is that not all rocks can be *radiometrically dated*. A sedimentary rock can contain particles of many ages that have been weathered from different rocks that formed at various times. One way geologists assign numeric dates to sedimentary rocks is to relate them to datable igneous masses, such as volcanic ash beds.

Review Questions

1. Distinguish between numeric and relative dating.
2. What is the law of superposition? How are cross-cutting relations used in relative dating?
3. Refer to Figure 8.4 (p. 213) and answer the following questions:
   (a) Is fault A older or younger than the sandstone layer?
   (b) Is dyke A older or younger than the sandstone layer?
   (c) Was the conglomerate deposited before or after fault A?
   (d) Was the conglomerate deposited before or after fault B?
   (e) Which fault is older, A or B?
   (f) Is dyke A older or younger than the batholith?
4. When you observe an outcrop of steeply inclined sedimentary layers, what principle allows you to assume that the beds were tilted after they were deposited?
5. A mass of granite is in contact with a layer of sandstone. Using a principle described in this chapter, explain how you can determine whether the sandstone was deposited on top of the granite, or whether the granite was intruded from below after the sandstone was deposited?
6. Distinguish among angular unconformity, disconformity, and nonconformity.
7. What is meant by the term *correlation*?
8. Describe William Smith's important contribution to the science of geology.
9. Why are fossils such useful tools in correlation?
10. Figure 8.14 is a block diagram of a hypothetical area in Canada. Place the lettered features in the proper sequence, from oldest to youngest. Identify an angular unconformity and a nonconformity.
11. Why is radiometric dating the most reliable method of dating the geologic past?
12. A hypothetical radioactive isotope has a half-life of 10,000 years. If the ratio of radioactive parent to stable daughter product is 1:3, how old is the rock containing the radioactive material?
13. Briefly describe why tree rings might be helpful in studying the geologic past (see Box 8.3).
14. To provide a reliable radiometric date, a mineral must remain a closed system from the time of its formation until the present. Why is this true?
15. What precautions are taken to ensure reliable radiometric dates?
16. To make calculations easier, let us round the age of Earth to 5 billion years for this question.
    (a) What fraction of geologic time is represented by recorded history (assume 5000 years for the length of recorded history)?
    (b) The first abundant fossil evidence does not appear until the beginning of the Cambrian Period (540 million years ago, rounded down). What percentage of geologic time is represented by abundant fossil evidence?
17. What subdivisions make up the geologic time scale?
18. Explain the lack of a detailed time scale for the vast span known as the Precambrian.
19. Briefly describe the difficulties in assigning numeric dates to layers of sedimentary rock.

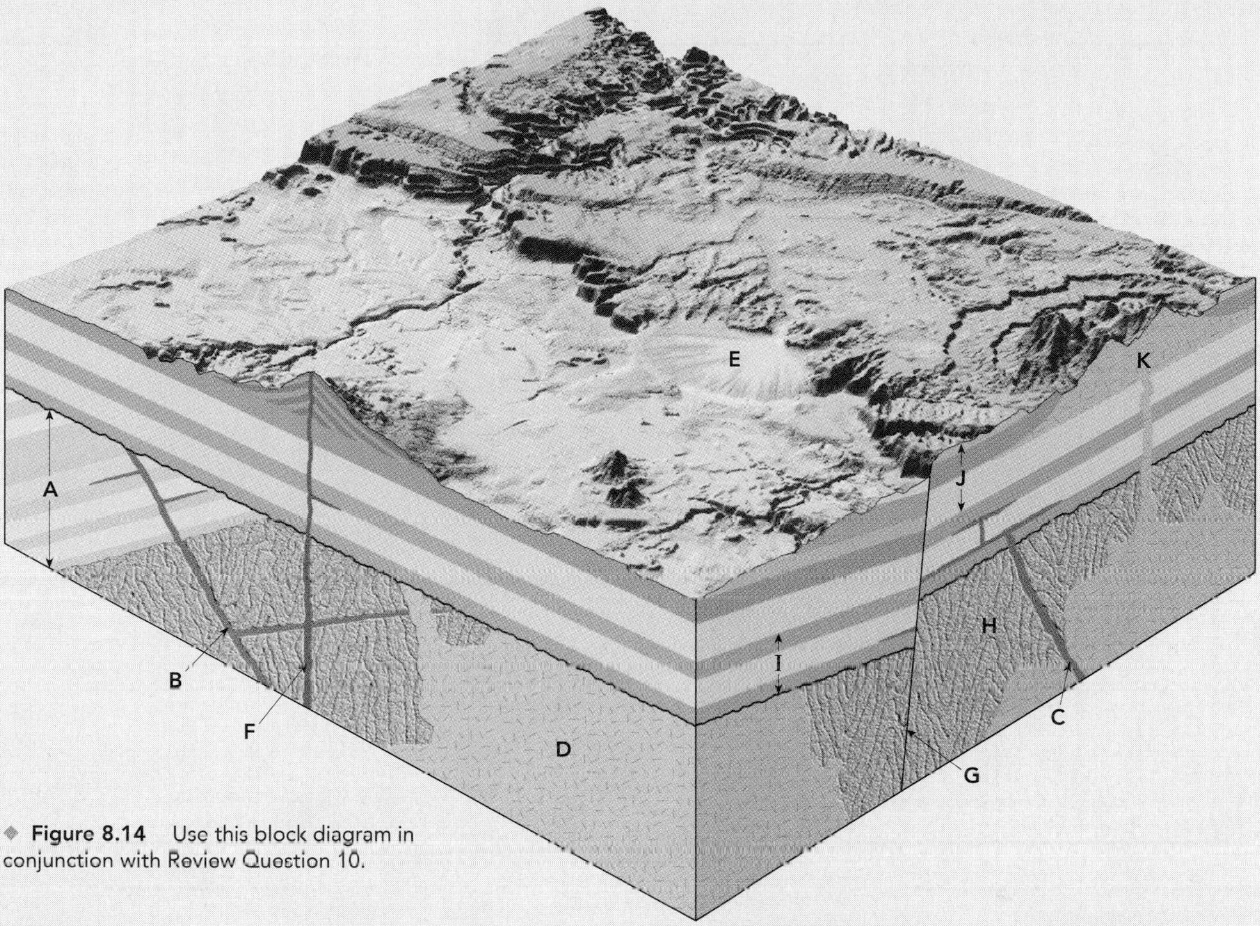

◆ **Figure 8.14** Use this block diagram in conjunction with Review Question 10.

Key Terms

angular unconformity (p. 214)
Archean Eon (p. 227)
Cenozoic Era (p. 226)
conformable (p. 212)
correlation (p. 215)
cross-cutting relations (p. 211)
disconformity (p. 214)
eon (p. 226)
epoch (p. 227)
era (p. 226)
fossil succession, principle of (p. 217)
geologic time scale (p. 225)
Hadean Eon (p. 227)
half-life (p. 220)
inclusions (p. 212)
index fossil (p. 217)
Mesozoic Era (p. 226)
nonconformity (p. 215)
numeric date (p. 210)
original horizontality, principle of (p. 211)
Paleozoic Era (p. 226)
period (p. 227)
Phanerozoic Eon (p. 226)
Precambrian (p. 227)
Proterozoic Eon (p. 227)
radioactivity (p. 219)
radiocarbon dating (p. 222)
radiometric dating (p. 220)
relative dating (p. 210)
superposition, law of (p. 211)
unconformity (p. 212)

Web Resources

The *Earth* website uses the resources and flexibility of the internet to aid in your study of the topics in this chapter. Written and developed by geology instructors, this site will help improve your understanding of geology. Visit **www.pearsoned.ca/tarbuck** and click on the cover of the text to find

- online review quizzes
- Web-based critical thinking and writing exercises
- links to chapter-specific Web resources
- internet-wide key-term searches

www.pearsoned.ca/tarbuck

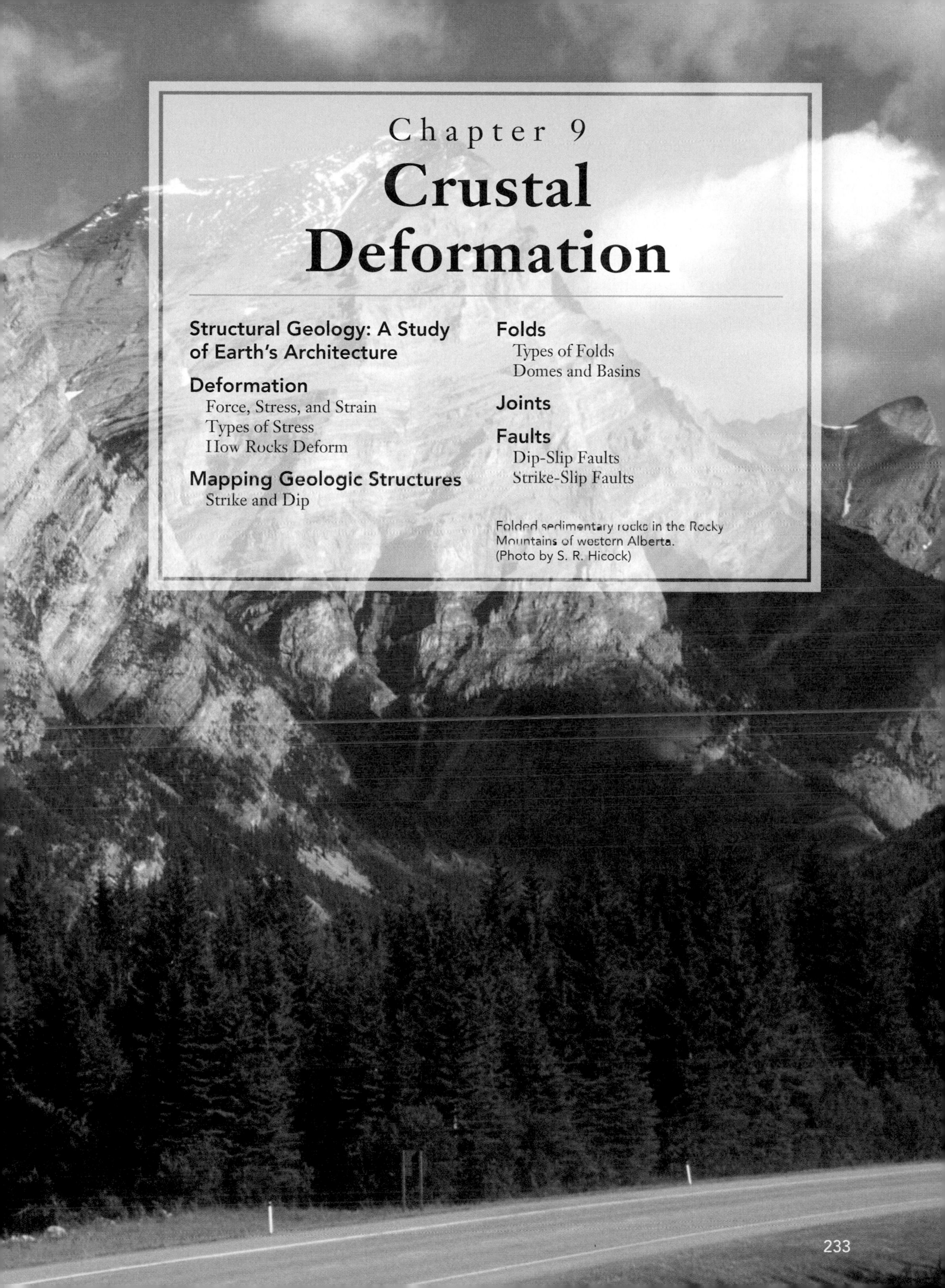

Chapter 9

Crustal Deformation

Structural Geology: A Study of Earth's Architecture

Deformation
- Force, Stress, and Strain
- Types of Stress
- How Rocks Deform

Mapping Geologic Structures
- Strike and Dip

Folds
- Types of Folds
- Domes and Basins

Joints

Faults
- Dip-Slip Faults
- Strike-Slip Faults

Folded sedimentary rocks in the Rocky Mountains of western Alberta. (Photo by S. R. Hicock)

Tectonic forces deform rocks in the crust. Evidence demonstrating the operation of enormous forces within Earth includes thousands of kilometres of rock layers that are bent, contorted, overturned, and sometimes riddled with fractures (Figure 9.1). In the Canadian Rockies, for example, some rock units have been thrust for dozens of kilometres over other layers. On a smaller scale, crustal movements of a few metres occur along faults during major earthquakes. In addition, rifting (spreading) and extension of the crust produce elongate depressions; over long spans of geologic time, they can even create ocean basins.

STRUCTURAL GEOLOGY: A STUDY OF EARTH'S ARCHITECTURE

The results of tectonic activity are strikingly apparent in Earth's major mountain belts (see chapter opening photo). Here, rocks containing fossils of marine organisms can be found thousands of metres above sea level, and massive rock units show evidence of having been intensely fractured and folded, as though they were made of putty. Even in the stable interiors of the continents, rocks reveal a history of deformation that shows they have been uplifted from much deeper levels in the crust.

Structural geologists study the architecture of Earth's crust and the influence of deformation on that architecture. By studying the orientations of faults and folds, as well as small-scale features of deformed rocks, structural geologists can often reconstruct the original geologic setting and the nature of the forces that generated these rock structures. In this way, the complex events of Earth's geologic history are revealed.

An understanding of rock structures is not only important in deciphering Earth's history, but it is also basic to our economic well-being. For example, many occurrences of oil and natural gas are associated with geologic structures that act to trap these fluids in valuable "reservoirs" (see Chapter 20). Furthermore, rock fractures are sites of hydrothermal mineralization, which means they can be sites of metallic ore deposits. Moreover, the orientation of fracture surfaces, which represent zones of weakness

◆ **Figure 9.1** Uplifted and folded sedimentary strata at Stair Hole, near Lulworth, Dorset, England. These layers of Jurassic rock, originally deposited in horizontal beds, have been folded as a result of the collision between the African and European lithospheric plates.
(Photo by Tom & Susan Bean, Inc.)

in rocks, must be considered when selecting sites for major construction projects, such as bridges, hydroelectric dams, and nuclear power plants. In short, a working knowledge of rock structures is essential to our modern way of life.

In this chapter we will examine the forces that deform rock, as well as the structures that result. The basic geologic structures associated with deformation are folds, joints, faults, and foliation (including rock cleavage). Because rock cleavage and foliation were examined in Chapter 7, this chapter will be devoted to the remaining rock structures and the tectonic forces that produce them.

DEFORMATION

GEODe EARTH Crustal Deformation
↳ Deformation

Every body of rock, no matter how strong, has a limit beyond which it will fracture or flow. **Deformation** (*de* = out, *forma* = form) is a general term that refers to all changes in the original form or size of a rock body. Deformation can also produce changes in the location and orientation of rock. Most crustal deformation occurs along or near plate margins. Recall from Chapter 1 that the lithosphere consists of large segments (plates) that move relative to one another. Plate motions and the interactions along plate boundaries generate tectonic forces that cause rock units to deform.

Force, Stress, and Strain

Force is any influence that tends to put stationary objects in motion or change the motions of moving bodies. From everyday experience, you know that if a door is stuck (stationary), you apply force to open it (put it in motion).

To describe the forces that deform rocks, structural geologists use the term **stress**—the amount of force applied to a given area. The magnitude of stress is not simply a function of the amount of force applied; it also relates to the area on which the force acts. For example, if you are walking barefoot on a hard, flat surface, the force (weight) of your body is distributed across your entire foot, so the stress acting on any one point of your foot is low. However, if you step on a small pointed rock (ouch!), the stress concentration at a single point on your foot will be high. Thus, you can think of stress as a measure of how concentrated the force is. As discussed in Chapter 7, stress can be applied uniformly from all directions (uniform stress) or non-uniformly (differential stress from directed pressure).

Types of Stress

When stress is applied unequally from different directions, it is termed **differential stress**. Differential stress that shortens a rock body is known as **compressional** (*com* = together, *premere* = to press) **stress**. Compressional stresses associated with plate collisions tend to shorten and thicken Earth's crust by folding, flowing, and faulting (Figure 9.2B). Recall from our discussion of metamorphic rocks that compressional stress is more concentrated at places where mineral grains are in contact, causing mineral matter to migrate from areas of high stress to areas of low stress (see Figure 7.6). As a result, the mineral grains (and the rock unit) tend to shorten in the direction parallel to maximum stress and elongate perpendicular to the direction of greatest stress.

When stress tends to elongate or pull apart a rock unit, it is known as **tensional** (*tendere* = to stretch) **stress** (Figure 9.2C). Where plates are being rifted apart (divergent plate boundaries), tensional stresses tend to lengthen those rock bodies located in the upper crust by displacement along faults. At depth, however, displacement is accomplished by a type of puttylike flow.

Differential stress can also cause rock to **shear** (Figure 9.2D). Shearing is similar to the slippage that occurs between individual playing cards when the top of the deck is moved relative to the bottom (Figure 9.3). In near-surface environments, shearing often occurs on closely spaced parallel surfaces of weakness, such as bedding planes, foliation, and microfaults. Further, at transform fault boundaries, shearing stresses produce large-scale offsets along major fault zones. By contrast, at great depths where temperatures and confining pressures are high, shearing is accomplished by solid-state flow.

Strain Whereas stress is the force applied to a given area, **strain** is the visible result of that force. Like the circle shown in Figure 9.3, *strained bodies do not retain their original configuration during deformation.* Figure 9.1 illustrates the strain (deformation) exhibited by rock units near Dorset, England. When studying strained rock units like those shown in Figure 9.1, geologists ask, "What do these deformed structures indicate about the original arrangement of these rocks, and how have they been deformed?"

How Rocks Deform

When rocks are subjected to stresses greater than their own strength, they begin to deform, usually by flowing (folding) or fracturing (faulting) (Figure 9.4).

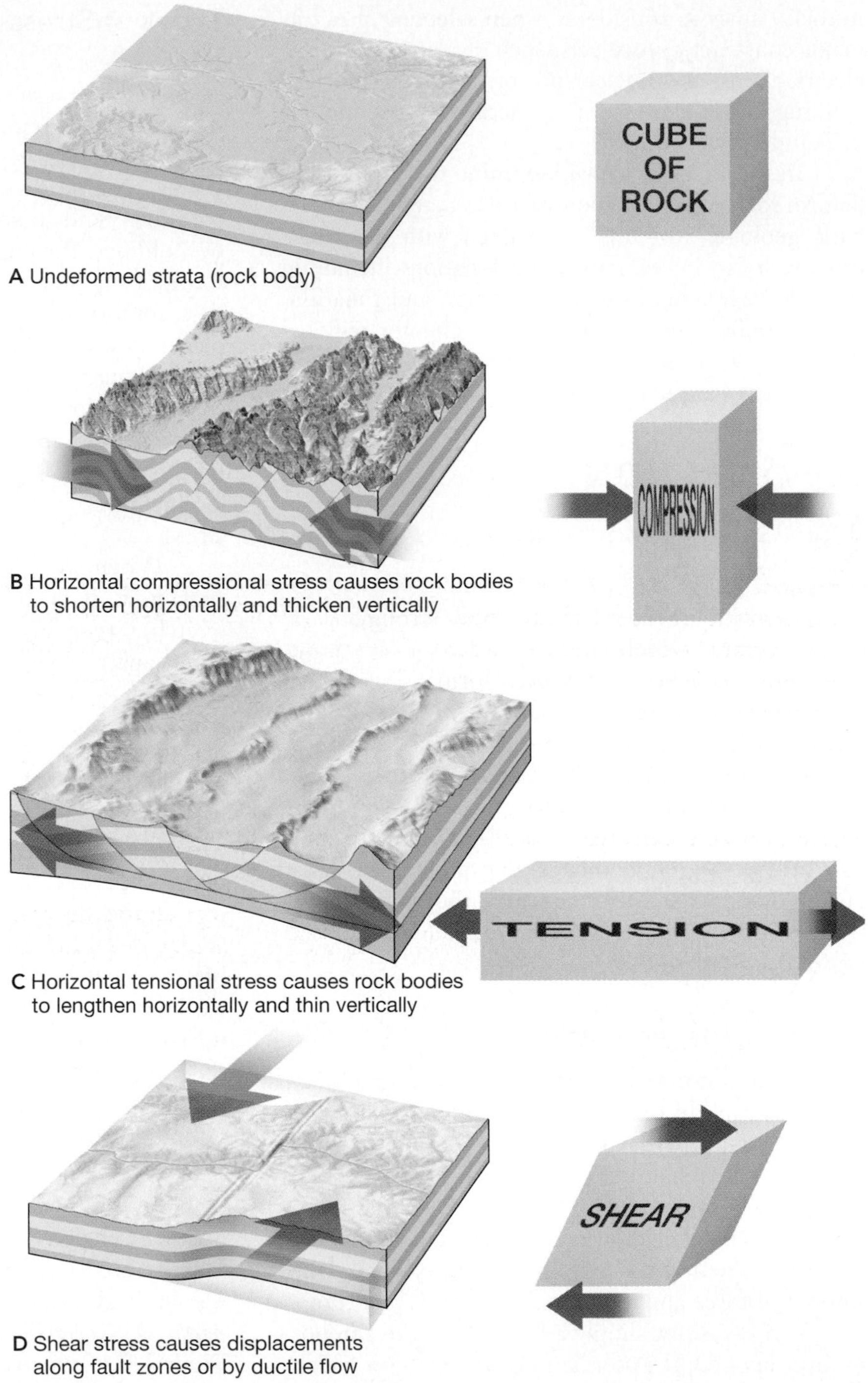

◆ **Figure 9.2** Deformation of Earth's crust caused by tectonic forces and associated stresses resulting from the movement of lithospheric plates. **A.** Strata before deformation. **B.** Compressional stresses associated with plate collisions tend to shorten and thicken Earth's crust by folding, flowing, and faulting. **C.** Tensional stresses at divergent plate boundaries tend to lengthen rock bodies by displacement along faults in the upper crust and ductile flow at depth. **D.** Shear stresses at transform plate boundaries tend to produce offsets along fault zones. The right side of the diagram illustrates the deformation (strain) of a cube of rock in response to the differential stresses illustrated in corresponding diagrams to the left.

It is easy to visualize how rocks break, because we normally think of them as being brittle. But how can rock units be *bent* into intricate folds without being broken during the process? To answer this question, structural geologists performed laboratory experiments in which rocks were subjected to differential stress under conditions that simulated those existing at various depths within the crust (Figure 9.5).

Although each rock type deforms somewhat differently, the general characteristics of rock deformation were determined from these experiments. Geologists discovered that when stress is gradually applied, rocks first respond by deforming elastically. Changes that result from *elastic deformation* are recoverable; that is, like a rubber band, the rock will return to nearly its original size and shape when the stress is removed. (As you will see in the next chapter, the energy for most earthquakes comes from stored elastic energy that is released as rock snaps back to its original shape.)

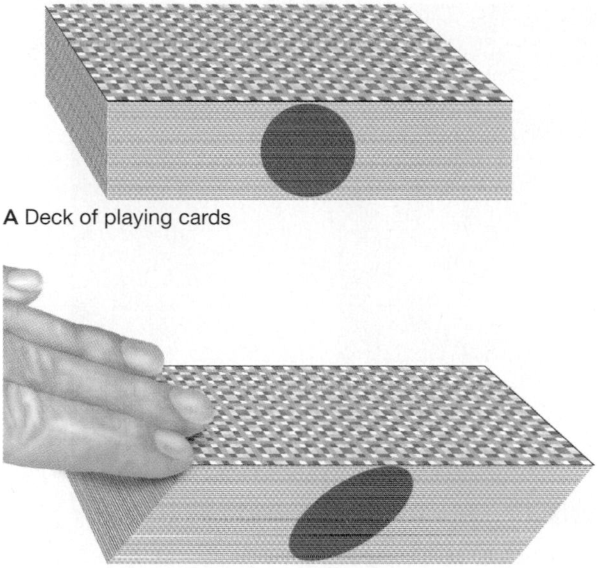

A Deck of playing cards

B Shearing occurs when hand pushes top of deck

◆ **Figure 9.3** Illustration of shearing and the resulting deformation (strain). **A.** An ordinary deck of playing cards with a circle embossed on its side. **B.** By sliding the top of the deck relative to the bottom, we can illustrate the type of shearing that commonly occurs along closely spaced planes of weakness in rocks. Notice that the circle becomes an ellipse, which can be used to measure the amount and type of strain. Additional displacement (shearing) of the cards would result in further strain and would be indicated by a change in the shape of the ellipse.

Temperature and Confining Pressure Rocks near the surface, where temperatures and confining pressures are low, tend to behave like a brittle solid and fracture once their strength is exceeded. This type of deformation is called **brittle** (*bryttian* = to shatter) **failure** or **brittle deformation**. From our everyday experience, we know that glass objects, wooden pencils, china plates, and even our bones exhibit brittle failure once their strength is surpassed. By contrast, at depth, where temperatures and confining pressures are high, rocks exhibit *ductile* behaviour. **Ductile deformation** is a type of solid-state flow that produces a change in the size and shape of an object without fracturing. Ordinary objects that display ductile behaviour include modelling clay, beeswax, caramel candy, and most metals. For example, a copper penny placed on a railroad track will be flattened and deformed (without breaking) by the force applied by a passing train. Ductile deformation of a rock—strongly aided by high temperature and high confining pressure (Figure 9.5)—is somewhat similar to the deformation of a penny flattened by a train. One way this type of solid-state flow is accomplished within a rock is by gradual slippage and recrystallization along planes of weakness within the crystal lattice of mineral grains (see Figure 7.6B). This microscopic form of gradual solid-state flow

◆ **Figure 9.4** Deformed sedimentary strata exposed in a road cut near Palmdale, California. In addition to the obvious folding, light-coloured beds are offset along a fault located on the right side of the photograph. (Photo by E. J. Tarbuck)

◆ **Figure 9.5** A marble cylinder deformed in the laboratory by applying thousands of kilograms of load from above. Each sample was deformed in an environment that duplicated the confining pressure found at various depths. Notice that when the confining pressure was low (left cylinders), the sample deformed by brittle fracture, whereas when the confining pressure was high (right cylinders), the sample deformed in a ductile or plastic manner.
(Photo courtesy of M. S. Patterson, Australian National University)

involves slippage that disrupts the crystal lattice and immediate re-crystallization that repairs the structure. Rocks that display evidence of ductile flow usually were deformed at great depth and can exhibit contorted folds that give the impression that the strength of the rock was akin to soft putty (Figure 9.6).

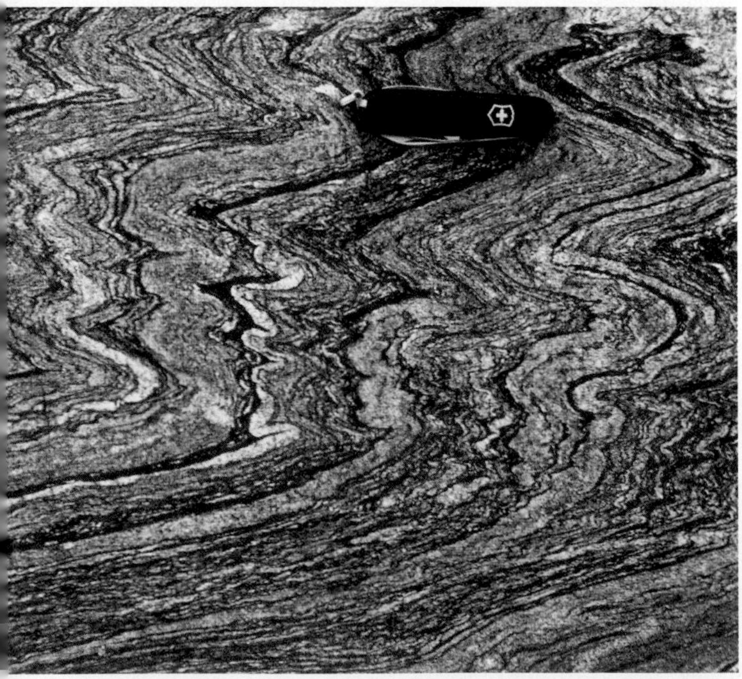

◆ **Figure 9.6** Rocks in Colorado exhibiting the results of ductile behaviour. These rocks were deformed at great depth and were subsequently exposed at the surface.
(Photo by Marli Miller/Visuals Unlimited)

Rock Type In addition to the physical environment, the mineral composition and texture of a rock greatly influence how it will deform. For example, crystalline rocks composed of minerals that have strong internal molecular bonds tend to fail by brittle fracture. By contrast, sedimentary rocks that are weakly cemented, or metamorphic rocks that contain zones of weakness, such as foliation, are more susceptible to ductile flow. Rocks that are weak and thus most likely to behave in a ductile manner when subjected to differential stress include rock salt, gypsum, and shale. Limestone, schist, and marble are of intermediate strength. Rock salt is so weak that it deforms under small amounts of differential stress and rises like stone pillars through beds of sediment that lie in and around the Gulf of Mexico, and off the east coast of Canada (see Chapter 20).

Perhaps the weakest naturally occurring solid to exhibit ductile flow on a large scale is glacial ice. By comparison, quartzite, granite, and basalt are strong and brittle. In a near-surface environment, strong, brittle rocks will fail by fracturing when subjected to stresses that exceed their strength.

Time One key factor that researchers are unable to duplicate in the laboratory is how rocks respond to small amounts of stress applied over long spans of *geologic time*. However, insights into the effects of time on deformation are provided in everyday settings. For example, marble benches have been known to sag under their own weight over a hundred years or so, and wooden bookshelves can bend after being loaded with books for a relatively short time. In nature small stresses applied over long spans surely play an important role in the deformation of rock. Forces that are unable to deform rock when initially applied may cause rock to flow if the stress is maintained over an extended time.

It is important to note that the processes by which rocks deform occur along a continuum that ranges from pure brittle fracture at one end to ductile (viscous to plastic) flow at the other. No sharp boundaries exist between different types of deformation. We also need to remind ourselves that the elegant folds and flow patterns we see in deformed rocks are generally achieved by the combined effect of distortion, sliding, and rotation of the individual grains that make up a rock. Further, this distortion and reorganization of mineral grains takes place in rock that is essentially solid.

MAPPING GEOLOGIC STRUCTURES

GEODe Crustal Deformation
↳ Mapping Geologic Structures

The processes of deformation generate features at many different scales. At one extreme are Earth's major mountain systems. At the other extreme, highly localized stresses create minor fractures in bedrock. All of these phenomena, from the largest folds in the Alps to the smallest fractures in a slab of rock, are referred to as **rock structures**. Before beginning our discussion of rock structures, let us examine the way geologists describe and map them.

When conducting a study of a region, a geologist identifies and describes the dominant structures. A structure is commonly so large that only a small portion is visible from any particular vantage point. In many situations, most of the bedrock is concealed by vegetation or by recent sedimentation. Consequently, the reconstruction must be done by using data gathered from a limited number of *outcrops*, which are sites where bedrock is exposed at the surface. Despite such difficulties, a number of mapping techniques enable geologists to reconstruct the orientation and shape of the existing structures. In recent years this work has been aided by advances in aerial photography, satellite and GIS (geographic information system) imagery, and the development of the global positioning system (GPS). In addition, seismic reflection profiling (see Box 10.4) and drill holes provide data on the composition and structure of rocks that lie at depth.

Geologic mapping is most easily accomplished where sedimentary strata are exposed. This is because sediments are usually deposited in horizontal layers. If the sedimentary rock layers are still horizontal, this tells geologists that the area is probably undisturbed structurally. But if strata are inclined, bent, or broken, this indicates deformation occurred following deposition.

Strike and Dip

Geologists use measurements called strike (bearing) and dip (inclination) to help determine the orientation or attitude of a rock layer, joint, or fault surface (Figure 9.7). By knowing the strike and dip of rocks at the surface, geologists can predict the nature and structure of rock units and faults that are hidden beneath the surface, beyond their view.

Strike is the compass direction of the line produced by the intersection of an inclined rock layer or fault, with a horizontal plane (Figure 9.7). The strike, or compass bearing, is generally expressed in azimuth form, as a three-digit angle clockwise from north. For example, (010°) means the line of strike is 10° clockwise from north. The strike of the rock units illustrated in Figure 9.7 is approximately 075°.

Dip is the angle of inclination of the surface of a rock unit or fault measured from a horizontal plane. In Figure 9.7 the dip angle of the rock layer is 30°. A good way to visualize dip is to imagine that water will always run down the rock surface parallel to the dip direction, which will always be at a 90° angle to the strike.

In the field, geologists measure the strike and dip of sedimentary rocks at as many outcrops as practical. These data are then plotted on a topographic map or an aerial photograph, along with a colour-coded description of the rock. From the orientation of the strata, an inferred orientation and shape of the structure can be established, as shown in Figure 9.8. By using this information, the geologist can reconstruct the pre-erosional structures and begin to interpret the region's geologic history.

FOLDS

GEODe Crustal Deformation
↳ Folds

During mountain building, flat-lying sedimentary and volcanic rocks are often bent into a series of

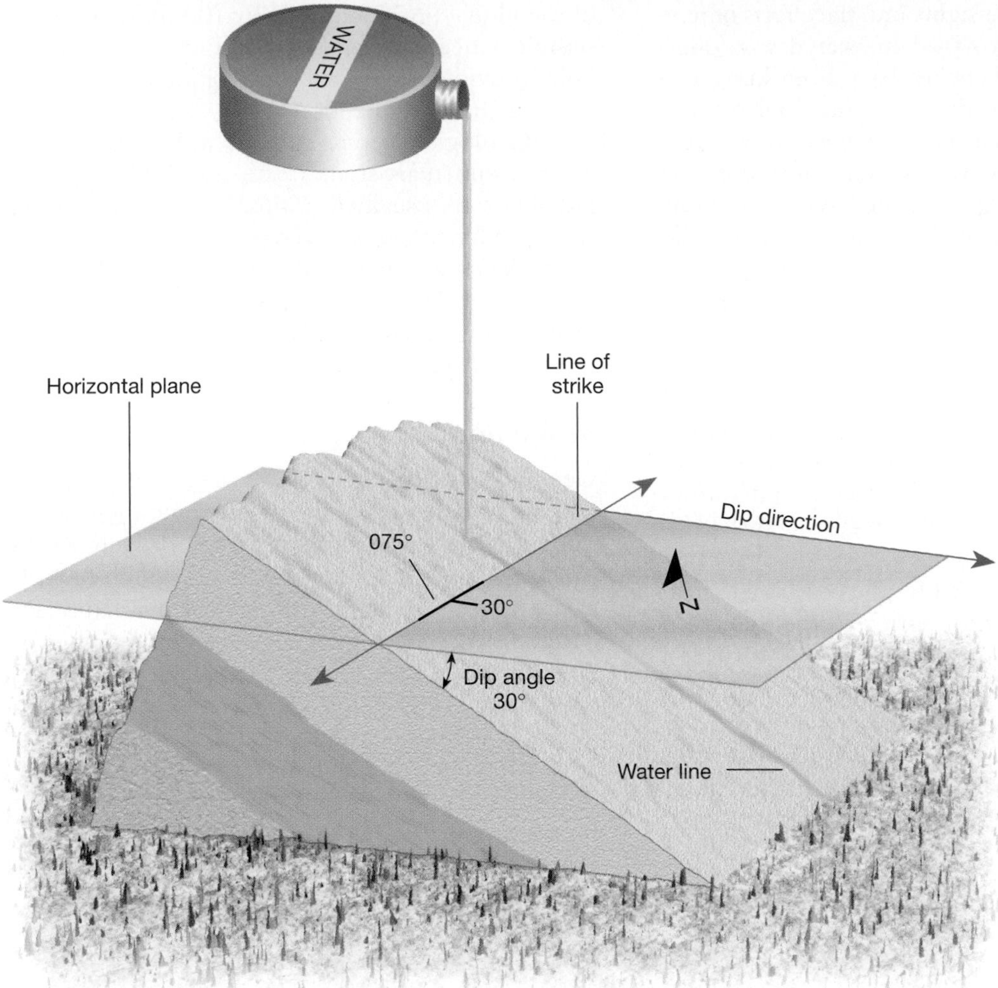

◆ **Figure 9.7** Strike and dip of a rock layer.

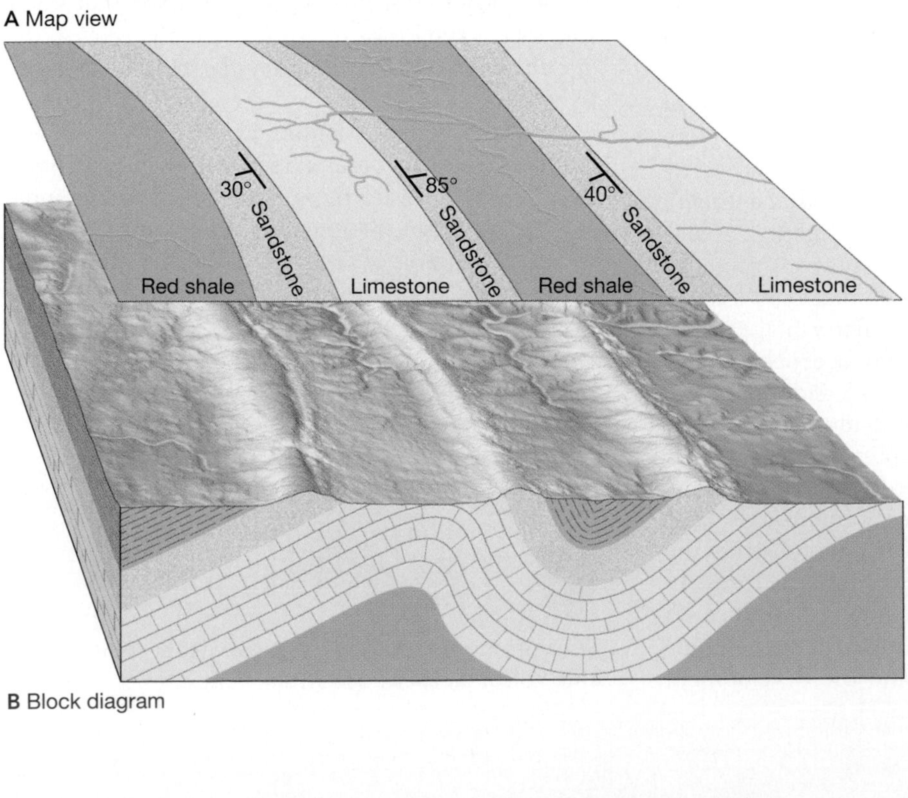

◆ **Figure 9.8** By establishing the strike and dip of outcropping sedimentary beds on a map (**A**) geologists can infer the orientation of the structure below ground (**B**).

wavelike undulations called **folds**. Folds in sedimentary strata are much like those that would form if you were to hold the ends of a sheet of paper and then push them together. In nature, folds come in a wide variety of sizes and configurations. Some folds are broad flexures in which rock units hundreds of metres thick have been slightly warped. Others are very tight microscopic structures found in metamorphic rocks. Size differences notwithstanding, most folds are the result of compressional stresses that result in the shortening and thickening of the crust. Occasionally, folds are found singly, but most often they occur as a series of undulations.

To aid our understanding of folds and folding, we need to become familiar with the terminology used to name the parts of a fold. As shown in Figure 9.9, the two sides of a fold are called *limbs*. A line drawn along the points of maximum curvature of each layer is termed the *axis* of the fold. In some folds, as Figure 9.9A illustrates, the axis is horizontal, or parallel to the surface. However, in more complex folding, the fold axis is often inclined at an angle known as the *plunge* (Figure 9.9B). Further, the *axial plane* is an imaginary surface that divides a fold as symmetrically as possible.

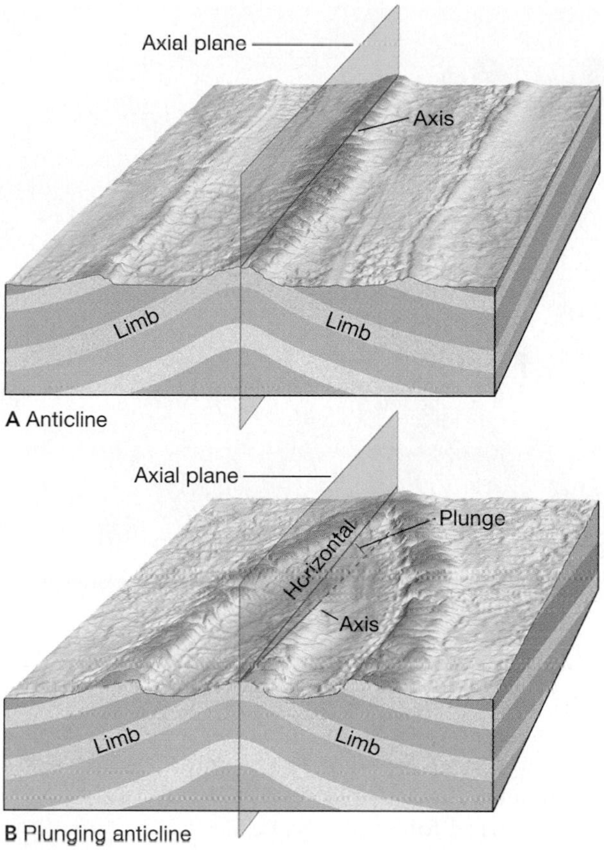

◆ **Figure 9.9** Idealized sketches illustrating the features associated with symmetrical folds. The axis of the fold in **A** is horizontal, whereas the axis of the fold in **B** is plunging.

Types of Folds

The two most common types of folds are called anticlines and synclines (Figure 9.10). An **anticline** is most commonly formed by the upfolding, or arching, of rock layers.* Figure 9.9 is an example of an anticline. Anticlines are sometimes spectacularly displayed where highways have been cut through deformed strata. Commonly found in association with anticlines are downfolds, or troughs, called **synclines**. Notice in Figure 9.11 that the limb of an anticline is also a limb of the adjacent syncline.

*By strict definition, an anticline (antiform) is a structure in which the oldest strata are found in the centre of the structure. This most typically occurs when strata are upfolded. Further, a syncline (synform) is strictly defined as a structure in which the youngest strata are found in the centre. This occurs most commonly when strata are downfolded.

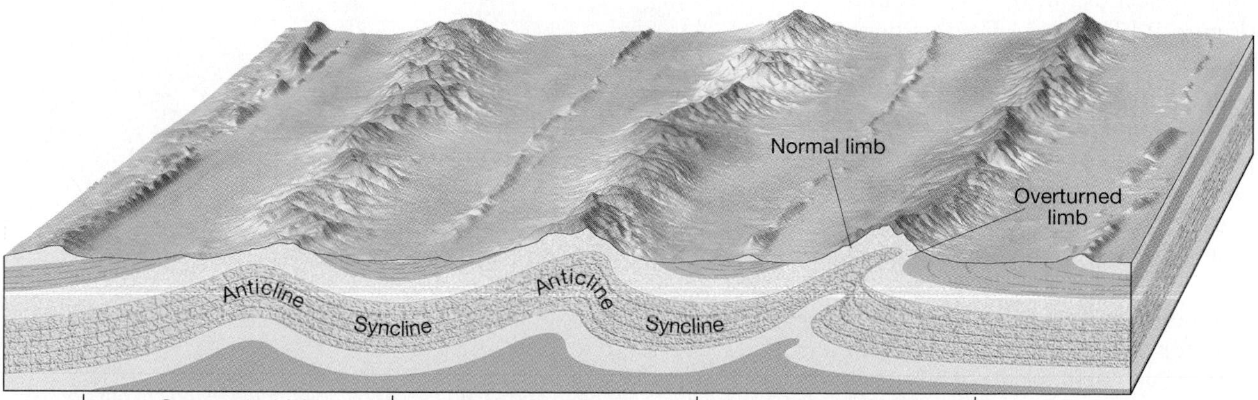

◆ **Figure 9.10** Block diagram of principal types of folded strata. The upfolded, or arched, structures are anticlines. The downfolds, or troughs, are synclines. Notice that the limb of an anticline is also the limb of the adjacent syncline.

◆ **Figure 9.11** Syncline (left) and anticline (right) share a common limb.
(Photo by E. J. Tarbuck)

Depending on their orientation, these basic folds are described as *symmetrical* when the limbs are mirror images of each other and asymmetrical when they are not. An asymmetrical fold is said to be *overturned* if one limb is tilted beyond the vertical (see Figure 9.10). An overturned fold can also lie on its side so that the axial plane of the fold would actually be horizontal. These *recumbent* folds are common in mountainous regions, such as the Alps of Europe.

Folds do not continue forever; rather, their ends die out much like the wrinkles in cloth. Some folds plunge because the axis of the fold descends into the ground (Figure 9.12). As the figure shows, both anticlines and synclines can plunge. Figure 9.13 shows an example of a plunging anticline and the pattern produced when erosion removes the upper layers of the structure and exposes its interior. Note that the outcrop pattern of an anticline points in the direction it is plunging, whereas the opposite is true for a syncline. The kind of topography that results when erosional forces attack folded sedimentary strata are schematically illustrated in Figures 9.10 and 9.12.

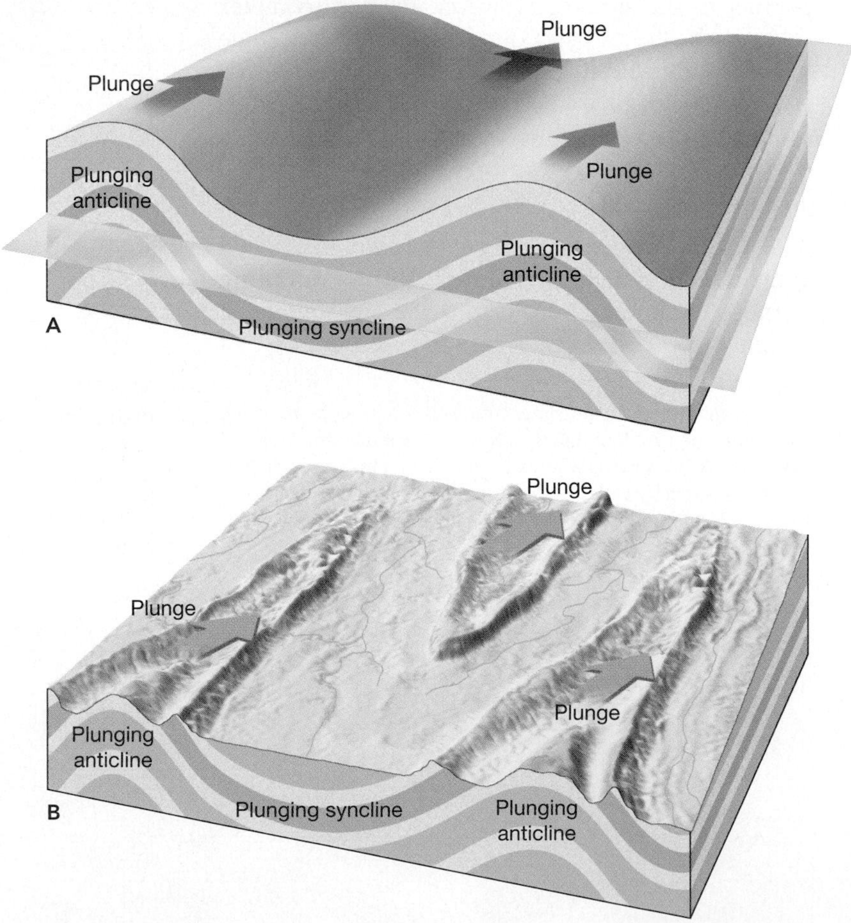

◆ **Figure 9.12** Plunging folds. **A.** Idealized view of plunging folds in which a horizontal surface has been added. **B.** View of plunging folds as they might appear after extensive erosion. Notice that in a plunging anticline the outcrop pattern "points" in the direction of the plunge, while the opposite is true of plunging synclines.

It is important to understand that ridges are not necessarily associated with anticlines, and valleys are not necessarily related to synclines. Rather, ridges and valleys result because of differential weathering and erosion (see Chapter 5). For example, in the Valley and Ridge Province of the southern Appalachians, resistant sandstone beds remain as imposing ridges separated by valleys cut into more easily eroded shale or limestone beds.

Although we have separated our discussion of folds and faults, in the real world, folds are generally intimately coupled with faults. Examples of this close association are broad regional features called monoclines. Particularly prominent features of the Colorado Plateau, **monoclines** (*mono* = one, *kleinen* = incline) are large, steplike folds in otherwise horizontal sedimentary strata (Figure 9.14). These folds appear to be the result of the reactivation of steeply dipping fault zones located in basement rocks beneath the plateau. As large blocks of basement rock were displaced upward along ancient faults, the comparatively ductile sedimentary strata above responded by folding. On the Colorado Plateau, monoclines display a narrow zone of steeply inclined beds that flatten out to form the uppermost layers of large elevated areas, including the Zuni Uplift, Echo Cliffs Uplift, and San Rafael Swell (see Figure 9.14). Displacement along these reactivated faults commonly exceeds 1 kilometre, and the very largest monoclines exhibit displacements that approach 3 kilometres.

◆ **Figure 9.13** Sheep Mountain, a doubly plunging anticline. Note that erosion has cut the flanking sedimentary beds into low ridges that make a V pointing in the direction of plunge. (Photo by John S. Shelton)

◆ **Figure 9.14** Monocline. **A.** The San Rafael monocline, Utah. **B.** Monocline consisting of bent sedimentary beds that were deformed by faulting in the bedrock below.
(Photo **A** by Stephen Trimble)

Domes and Basins

Broad upwarps in basement rock can deform the overlying cover of sedimentary strata and generate large folds. When this upwarping produces a circular or elongate structure, the feature is called a **dome** (Figure 9.15A). Downwarped structures having a similar shape are termed **basins** (Figure 9.15B).

The Black Hills area of western South Dakota is a large structural dome thought to be caused by upwarping. Here erosion has stripped away the highest portions of the upwarped sedimentary beds, exposing older igneous and metamorphic rocks in the centre (Figure 9.16). Remnants of these once continuous sedimentary layers are visible, flanking the crystalline core of this mountain range. The more resistant strata are easy to identify because differential erosion has left them in outcrops as prominent angular ridges called **hogbacks** (see Box 13.1). Because hogbacks can form whenever resistant strata are steeply inclined, they are also associated with other types of folds.

Domes can also be formed by the intrusion of magma (laccoliths), as shown in Figure 4.28B. In addition, the upward migration of salt formations can produce salt domes that are common in the Gulf of Mexico.

Several large basins exist in North America. The Michigan (Figure 9.17) and Williston basins have very gently sloping beds similar to saucers. These basins are thought to be the result of lithospheric thinning or plume activity that caused the crust to subside (see Figure 13.16). A few structural basins may have been the result of giant asteroid impacts (e.g., Sudbury, Ontario, and Manicouagan, Quebec).

Because large basins contain sedimentary beds sloping at such low angles, they are usually identified by the age of the rocks composing them. The youngest rocks are found near the centre, and the

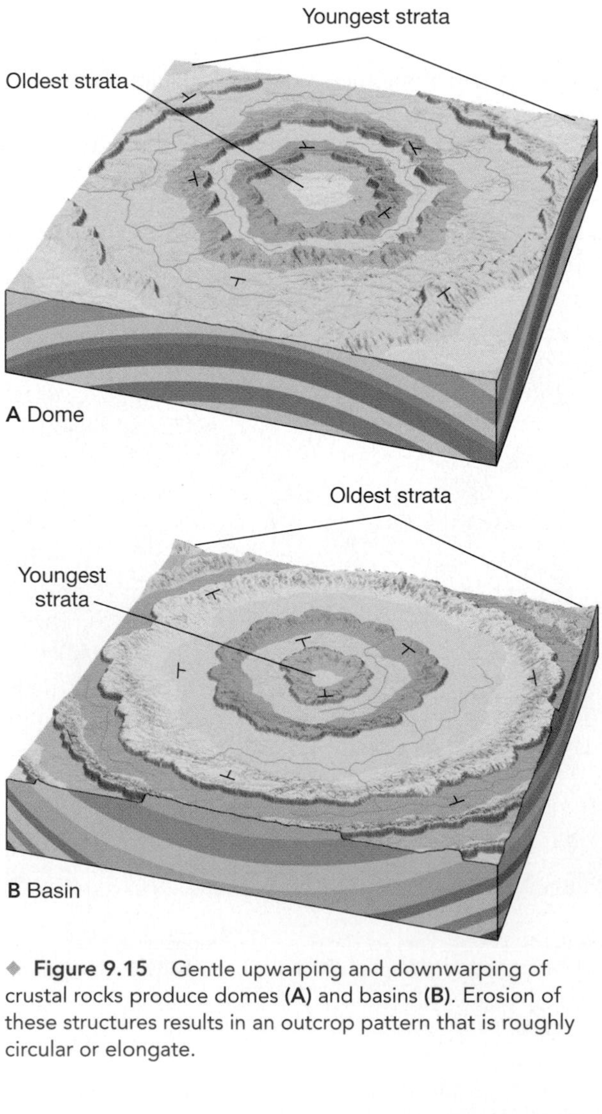

◆ **Figure 9.15** Gentle upwarping and downwarping of crustal rocks produce domes **(A)** and basins **(B)**. Erosion of these structures results in an outcrop pattern that is roughly circular or elongate.

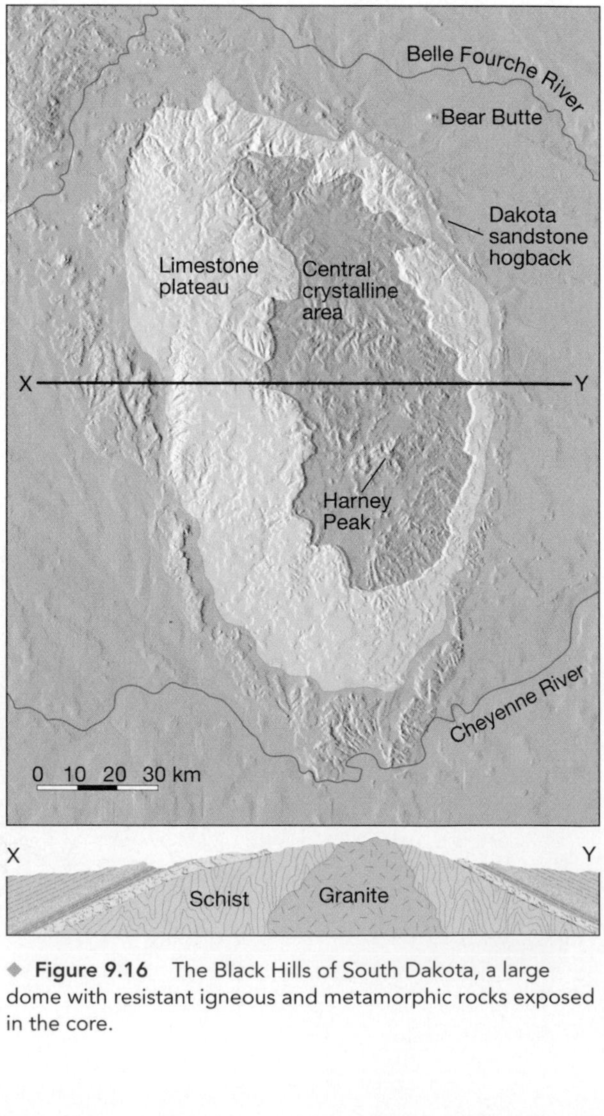

◆ **Figure 9.16** The Black Hills of South Dakota, a large dome with resistant igneous and metamorphic rocks exposed in the core.

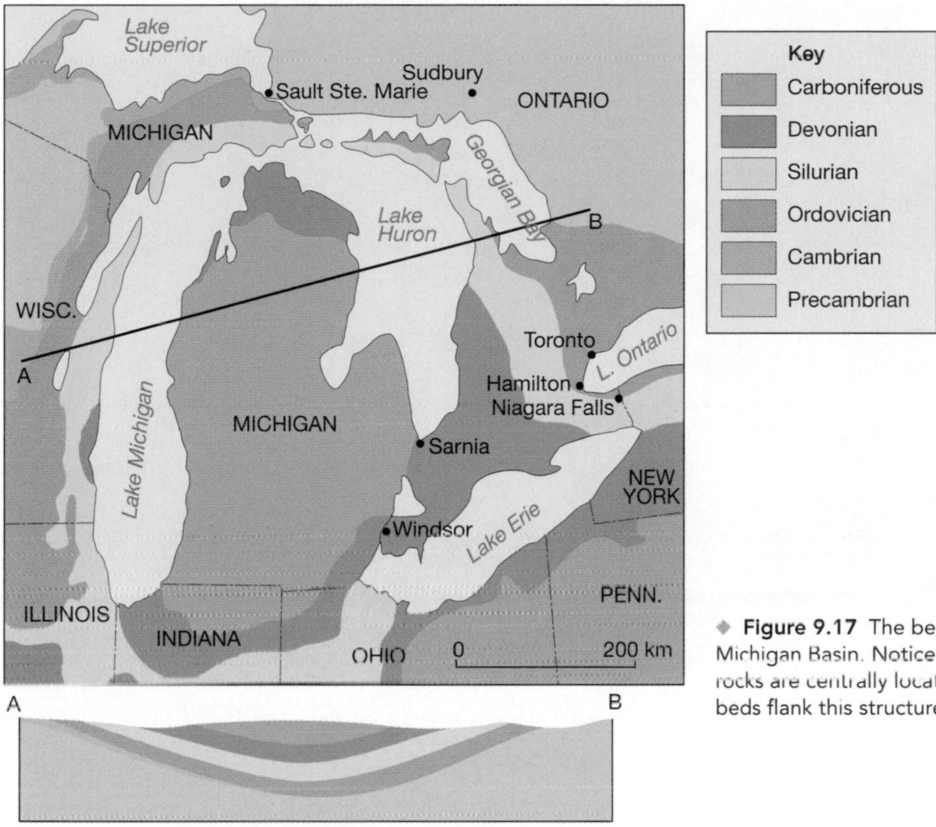

◆ **Figure 9.17** The bedrock geology of the Michigan Basin. Notice that the youngest rocks are centrally located, while the oldest beds flank this structure.

oldest rocks are at the flanks. This is just the opposite order of a dome, such as the Black Hills, where the oldest rocks form the core.

JOINTS

GEODe EARTH Crustal Deformation
↳ Faults and Fractures

Among the most common rock structures resulting from brittle deformation are fractures called **joints**. Unlike faults, joints are fractures along which no appreciable displacement has occurred. Although some joints have a random orientation, most occur in roughly parallel groups (see Figure 5.6).

We have already considered two types of joints. In Chapter 4 you learned that *columnar joints* form when igneous rocks cool and develop shrinkage fractures that produce elongate, pillarlike columns (Figures 4.31 and 9.18). Also recall that sheeting produces a pattern of gently curved joints that develop more or less parallel to the surface of large exposed igneous bodies, such as batholiths (e.g., Figures 5.4 and 5.5). Here the jointing results from the gradual expansion that occurs when erosion removes the overlying load (unloading).

In contrast to the situations just described, most joints are produced when rocks in the outermost crust are deformed. Here tensional and shearing stresses associated with crustal movements cause the rock to fail by brittle fracture. For example, when folding occurs, rocks situated at the axes of the folds are elongate and pulled apart to produce tensional joints. Extensive joint patterns can also develop in response to relatively subtle, and often barely perceptible, regional upwarping and downwarping of the crust. In many cases, the cause for jointing at a particular locale is not readily apparent.

Many rocks are broken by two or even three sets of intersecting joints that slice the rock into numerous regularly shaped blocks. These joint sets commonly exert a strong influence on other geologic processes. For example, chemical weathering tends to be concentrated along joints, and in many areas groundwater movement and the resulting dissolution in soluble rocks is controlled by the joint pattern (Figure 9.19). Moreover, a system of joints can influence the direction that stream courses follow. The rectangular drainage pattern described in Chapter 15 is such a case.

Joints may also be significant from an economic standpoint. Some of the world's largest and most important mineral deposits were emplaced

◆ **Figure 9.18** This felsic igneous intrusion exposed on the Burlington Peninsula of Newfoundland and Labrador exhibits columnar joints.
(Photo courtesy of R. W. Hodder)

◆ **Figure 9.19** These Silurian dolostones exposed in a roadcut south of Meaford, Ontario, have broken along joints to produce sheer vertical surfaces.
(Photo by C. Tsujita)

along joint systems. Hydrothermal solutions, which are basically mineralized fluids, can migrate into fractured host rocks and precipitate economically important amounts of copper, silver, gold, zinc, lead, and uranium (see Chapter 20).

Further, highly jointed rocks present a risk to the construction of engineering projects, including highways and dams. On June 5, 1976, 14 lives were lost and nearly US$1 billion in property damage occurred when the Teton Dam in Idaho failed. This earthen dam was constructed of very erodible clays and silts and was situated on highly fractured volcanic rocks. Although attempts were made to fill the voids in the jointed rock, water gradually penetrated the subsurface fractures and undermined the dam's foundation. Eventually, the moving water cut a tunnel into the clays and silts. Within minutes the dam failed, sending a 20-metre-high wall of water down the Teton and Snake rivers.

FAULTS

GEODe EARTH Crustal Deformation
↳ Faults and Fractures

Faults are fractures in the crust along which appreciable displacement has taken place. Occasionally, small faults can be recognized in road cuts where sedimentary beds have been offset a few metres, as shown in Figure 9.20. Faults of this scale usually occur as single discrete breaks. By contrast, large faults, like the San Andreas Fault in California, have displacements of hundreds of kilometres and consist of many interconnecting fault surfaces (see Box 9.1). These *fault zones* can be several kilometres wide and are often easier to identify from high-altitude photographs than at ground level.

Sudden movements along faults are the cause of most earthquakes. However, many faults are inactive and thus are remnants of past deformation. Along active faults, rock is often broken and pulverized as crustal blocks on opposite sides of a fault slip past one another. The loosely coherent, clayey material that results from this activity is called *fault gouge*. On some fault surfaces the rocks become highly polished and striated, or grooved, as the crustal blocks slide past one another. These polished, streaked, and striated surfaces with tiny straight parallel ridges, called *slickensides* (*slicken* = smooth), provide geologists with evidence for the direction of the most recent displacement along the fault. Geologists classify faults by these relative movements, which can be predominantly horizontal, vertical, or oblique.

◆ **Figure 9.20** Faulting caused the vertical displacement of these beds located near Kanab, Utah. Beds on the left side of the fault have moved downward relative to those on the right side.
(Photo by Tom Bean/DRK Photo)

Dip-Slip Faults

Faults in which the movement is primarily parallel to the dip (or inclination) of the fault surface are called **dip-slip faults**. Up and down displacements along dip-slip faults can produce long, low cliffs called **fault scarps** (*scarpe* = a slope). Fault scarps, such as the one shown in Figure 9.21, are produced by displacements that generate earthquakes.

It has become common practice to call the rock surface that is immediately above the fault the *hanging wall* and to call the rock surface below it the *footwall* (Figure 9.22). This nomenclature arose from prospectors and miners who excavated shafts and tunnels along fault zones because these are commonly sites of ore deposits. In these tunnels, the miners would walk on the rocks below the mineralized fault zone (the footwall) and hang their lanterns on the rocks above (the hanging wall).

Two major types of dip-slip faults are **normal faults** and **reverse faults**. In addition, when a reverse fault has an angle of dip of less than 45°, it is called a **thrust fault**. We will consider these types of dip-slip faults next.

Normal Faults Dip-slip faults are classified as normal faults when the hanging wall block moves down relative to the footwall block (Figure 9.23). Most normal faults have steep dips of about 60°, which tend to flatten out with depth. However, some dip-slip faults have much lower dips, with some approaching

BOX 9.1

People and the Environment
The San Andreas Fault System

The San Andreas, the best-known and largest fault system in North America, first attracted wide attention after the great 1906 San Francisco earthquake and fire. Following this devastating event, geologic studies demonstrated that a displacement of as much as 5 metres along the fault had accompanied the earthquake. It is now known that this dramatic event is just one of many thousands of earthquakes that have resulted from repeated movements along the San Andreas throughout its 29-million-year history.

Where is the San Andreas fault system located? As shown in Figure 9.A, it trends in a northwesterly direction for nearly 1300 kilometres through much of western California. At its southern end, the San Andreas connects with a spreading centre located in the Gulf of California. In the north, the fault enters the Pacific Ocean at Point Arena, where it is thought to continue its northwesterly trend, eventually joining the Mendocino fracture zone. In the central section, the San Andreas is relatively simple and straight. However, at its two extremities, several branches spread from the main trace, so that in some areas the fault zone exceeds 100 kilometres in width.

Over much of its extent, a linear trough reveals the presence of the San Andreas Fault. When the system is viewed from the air, linear scars, offset

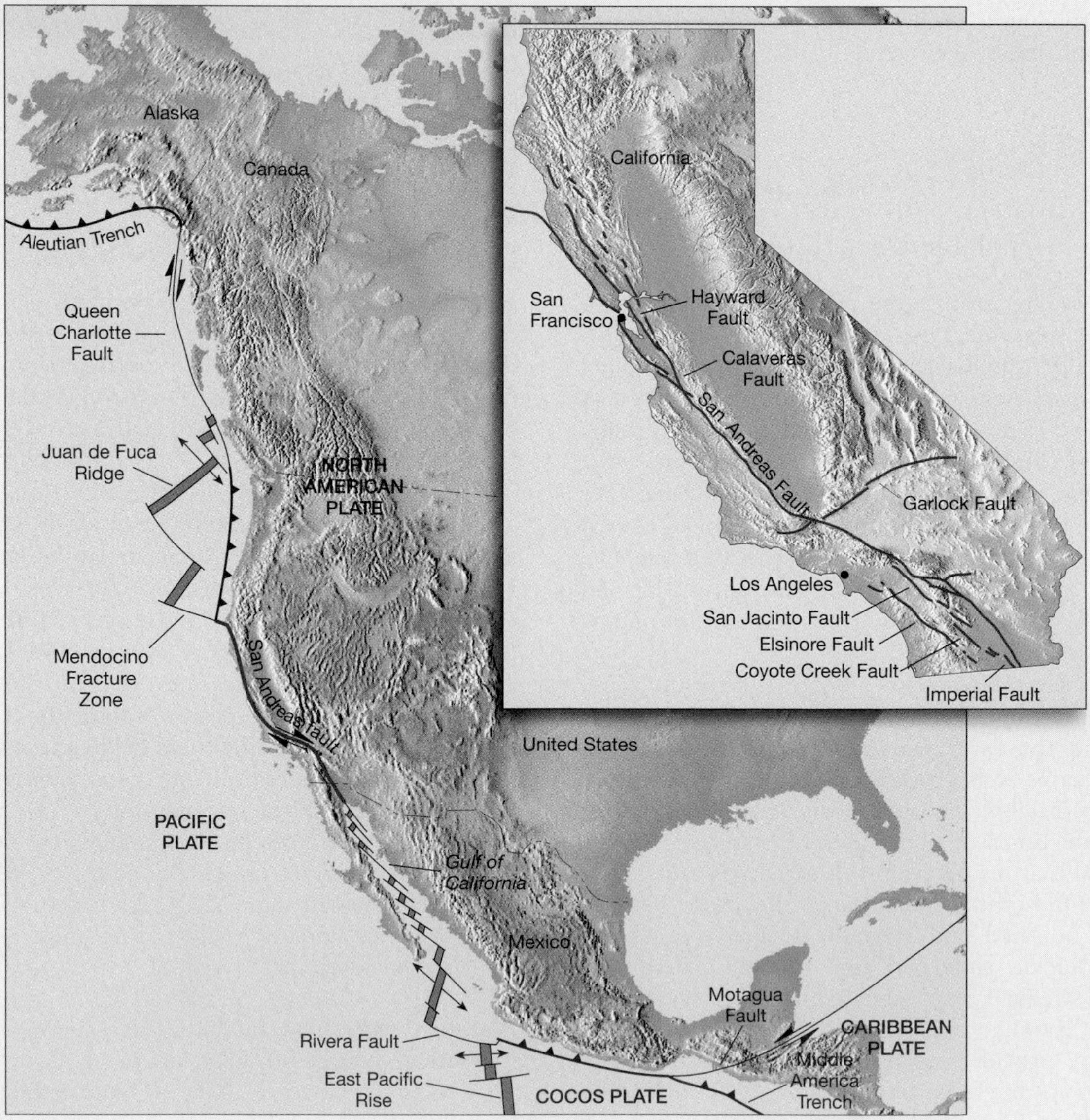

◆ **Figure 9.A** Map showing the extent of the San Andreas fault system. **Inset** shows only a few of the many splinter faults that are part of this great fault system.

TABLE 9.A **Major Earthquakes on the San Andreas Fault System**

Date	Location	Magnitude	Remarks
1812	Wrightwood, CA	7	Church of San Juan Capistrano collapsed, killing 40 worshippers
1812	Santa Barbara channel	7	Churches and other buildings wrecked in and around Santa Barbara
1838	San Francisco peninsula	7	At one time thought to have been comparable with the great earthquake of 1906
1857	Fort Tejon, CA	8.25	One of the greatest U.S. earthquakes; occurred near Los Angeles, then a city of 4000
1868	Hayward, CA	7	Rupture of the Hayward Fault caused extensive damage in San Francisco Bay area
1906	San Francisco, CA	8.25	The great San Francisco earthquake; as much as 80 percent of the damage caused by fire
1940	Imperial Valley	7.1	Displacement on the newly discovered Imperial Fault
1952	Kern County	7.7	Rupture of the White Wolf Fault; largest earthquake in California since 1906 did US$60 million in damage and killed 12 people
1971	San Fernando Valley	6.5	US$500 million in damage and 58 lives lost
1989	Santa Cruz Mountains	7.1	Loma Prieta earthquake; US$6 billion dollars in damage, 62 lives lost, and 3757 people injured
1994	Northridge (Los Angeles area)	6.9	More than US$15 billion in damage, 51 lives lost, and more than 5000 injured

stream channels, and elongate ponds mark the trace in a striking manner. On the ground, however, surface expressions of the faults are much more difficult to detect. Some of the most distinctive landforms include long, straight escarpments, narrow ridges, and sag ponds formed by the settling of blocks within the fault zone. Further, many stream channels characteristically bend sharply to the right where they cross the fault (Figure 9.B).

With the formulation of the theory of plate tectonics, geologists began to realize the significance of this great fault system. The San Andreas Fault is a transform boundary separating two lithospheric plates that move very slowly. The Pacific plate, located to the west, moves northwestward relative to the North American plate, causing earthquakes along the fault (Table 9.A).

The San Andreas is undoubtedly the most studied of any fault system in the world. Although many questions remain unanswered, geologists have learned that each fault segment exhibits somewhat different behaviour. Some portions of the San Andreas exhibit a slow creep with little noticeable seismic activity. Other segments regularly slip, producing small earthquakes, while still other segments seem to store elastic energy for hundreds of years and rupture in great earthquakes. This knowledge is useful when assigning earthquake hazard potential to a given segment of the fault zone.

Because of the great length and complexity of the San Andreas Fault, it is more appropriately referred to as a "fault system." This major fault system consists primarily of the San Andreas Fault and several major branches, including the Hayward and Calaveras faults of central California and the San Jacinto and Elsinore faults of southern California (see Figure 9.A). These major segments, plus a vast number of smaller faults that include the Imperial Fault, San Fernando Fault, and the Santa Monica Fault, collectively accommodate the relative motion between the North American and Pacific plates.

Blocks on opposite sides of the San Andreas Fault move horizontally in opposite directions, such that if a person stood on one side of the fault, the block on the opposite side would appear to move to the right when slippage occurred. This type of displacement is known as **right-lateral strike-slip** by geologists (see Figure 9.B).

Ever since the great San Francisco earthquake of 1906, when as much as 5 metres of displacement occurred, geologists have attempted to establish the cumulative displacement along this fault over its 29-million-year history. By matching rock units across the fault, geologists have determined that the total accumulated displacement from earthquakes and creep exceeds 560 kilometres, for an average rate of just less than 2 centimetres per year.

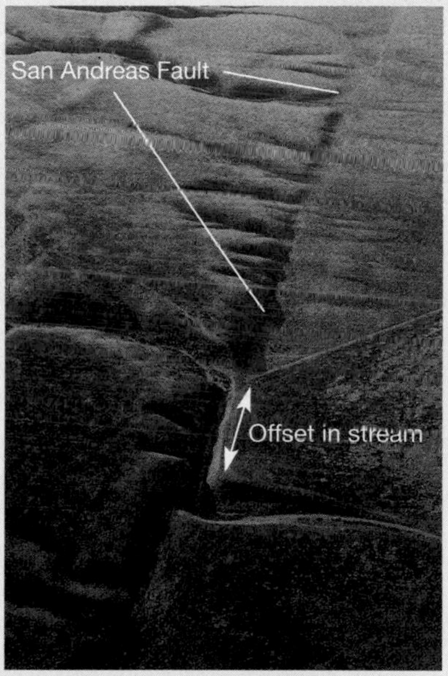

◆ **Figure 9.B** Aerial view showing offset stream channel across the San Andreas Fault on the Carrizo Plain west of Taft, California.
(Photo by Michael Collier/DRK Photo)

◆ **Figure 9.21** A fault scarp located near Ville-Marie, Quebec. (Photo by S. R. Hicock)

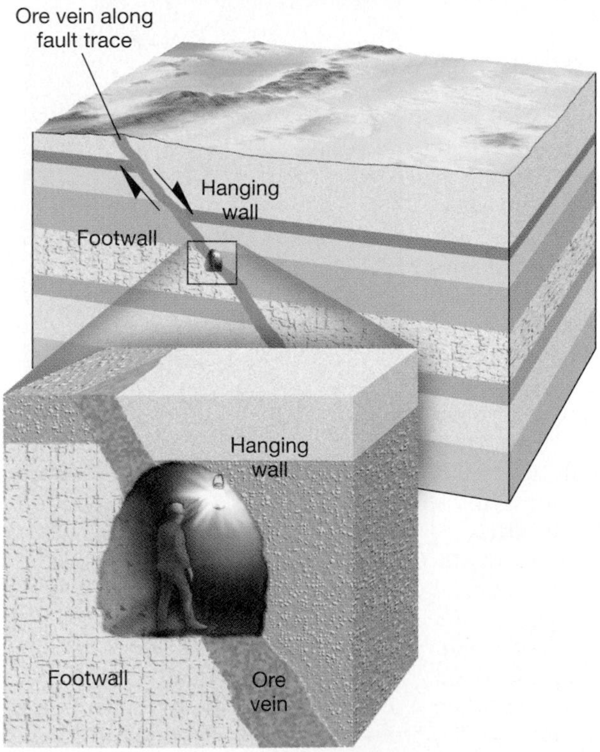

◆ **Figure 9.22** The rock immediately above a fault surface is the *hanging wall*, and that below is called the *footwall*. These names came from miners who excavated ore along fault zones. The miners hung their lanterns on the rocks above the fault trace (hanging wall) and walked on the rocks below the fault trace (footwall).

horizontal. Because of the downward motion of the hanging wall, normal faults accommodate lengthening, or extension, and thinning of the crust.

Normal faulting is prevalent at spreading centres where plate divergence occurs. Here, a central block called a **graben** (*graben* = ditch) is bounded by normal faults and drops as the plates separate (Figure 9.24). These grabens produce an elongate valley bounded by relatively uplifted structures called **horsts**. The Rift Valley of East Africa is made up of several large grabens, above which tilted horsts produce a linear mountainous topography. This valley, nearly 6000 kilometres long, contains the excavation sites of some of the earliest human fossils. Examples of inactive rift valleys include the Rhine Valley in Germany and the Triassic-age grabens of the eastern United States. Even larger inactive normal fault systems are the rifted continental margins, such as along the east coasts of the Americas and the west coasts of Europe and Africa.

Fault motion provides geologists with a method of determining the nature of the forces at work within Earth. Normal faults indicate the existence of tensional stresses that pull the crust apart. This "pulling apart" can be accomplished either by uplifting that causes the surfaces to stretch and break or by diverging horizontal forces.

Reverse and Thrust Faults Reverse faults and thrust faults are dip-slip faults in which the hanging wall

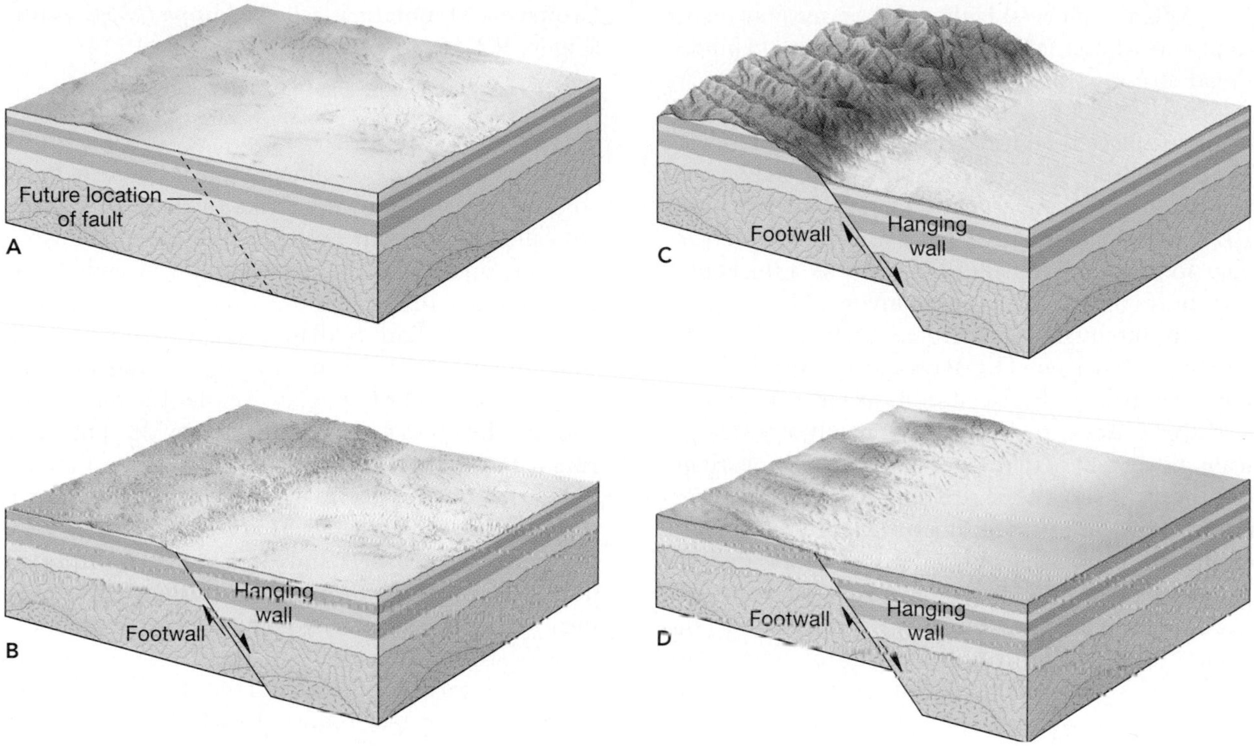

◆ **Figure 9.23** Block diagrams illustrating a normal fault. **A.** Rock strata before faulting. **B.** The relative movement of displaced blocks. Displacement can continue in a fault-block mountain range over millions of years and consist of many widely spaced episodes of faulting. **C.** How erosion might alter the upfaulted block. **D.** Eventually the period of deformation ends and erosion becomes the dominant geologic process.

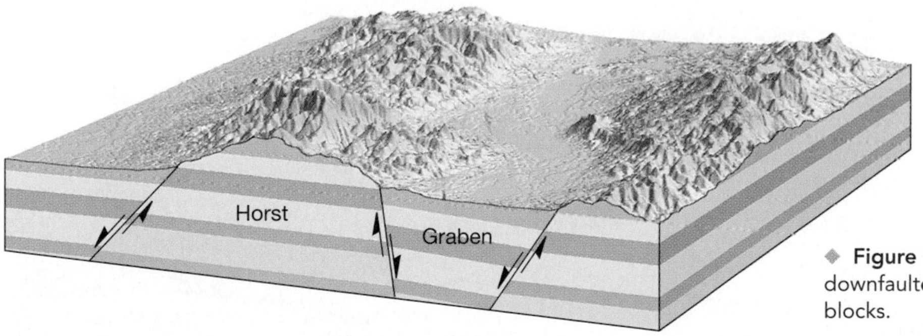

◆ **Figure 9.24** Diagrammatic sketch of downfaulted (graben) and upfaulted (horst) blocks.

block moves up relative to the footwall block (Figure 9.25). Recall that reverse faults have dips greater than 45° and thrust faults have dips less than 45° (typically much less). Because the hanging wall block moves up and over the footwall block, reverse and thrust faults accommodate shortening of the crust.

Most high-angle reverse faults are small and accommodate local displacements in regions dominated by other types of faulting. Thrust faults, conversely, exist at all scales. Small thrust faults exhibit displacement of millimetres to a few metres. Some large thrust faults have displacements of tens of kilometres.

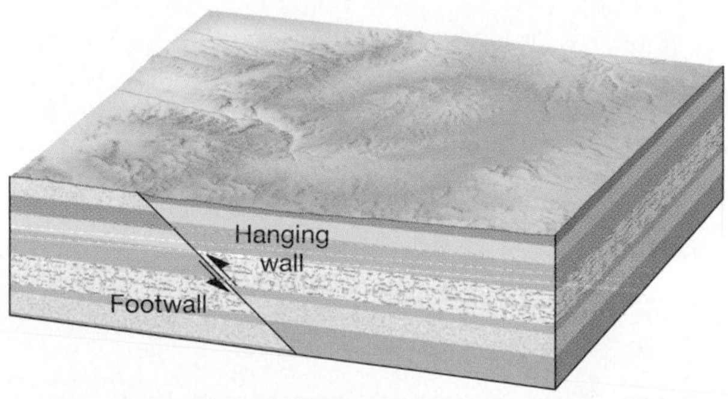

◆ **Figure 9.25** Block diagram showing the relative movement along a reverse fault.

Whereas normal faults occur in tensional environments, thrust faults result from strong compressional stresses. In these settings, crustal blocks are displaced *toward* one another, with the hanging wall being displaced upward relative to the footwall. Thrust faulting is most pronounced in subduction zones and other convergent boundaries where plates are colliding. Compressional forces generally produce folds as well as faults and result in a thickening and shortening of the material involved.

In mountainous regions, such as the Alps, Northern Rockies, Himalayas, and Appalachians, thrust faults have displaced strata as far as 50 kilometres over adjacent rock units. The result of this large-scale movement is that older strata end up overlying younger rocks. A classic site of thrust faulting occurs in the Crowsnest Pass of Alberta (Figure 9.26). Here, mountain peaks that provide the area's majestic scenery have been carved from Paleozoic rocks that were displaced over much younger Cretaceous strata. At the eastern edge of the Crowsnest Pass is an outlying peak called Crowsnest Mountain. This structure is an isolated remnant of the thrust sheet that was severed by the erosional forces of glacial ice and running water. An isolated block, such as Crowsnest Mountain, is called a **klippe** (*klippe* = cliff) (Figure 9.27).

Strike-Slip Faults

Faults in which the dominant displacement is horizontal and parallel to the strike of the fault surface are called **strike-slip faults**. Because of their large size and linear nature, many strike-slip faults produce a trace that is visible over a great distance (Figure 9.28). Rather than a single fracture along which movement takes place, large strike-slip faults consist of a zone of roughly parallel fractures. The zone can be up to several kilometres wide. The most recent movement, however, is often along a strand only a few metres wide, which may offset features, such as stream channels (Figures 9.29 and 9.B). Furthermore, crushed and broken rocks produced during faulting are more easily eroded, often producing linear valleys or troughs that mark the locations of strike-slip faults.

The earliest scientific records of strike-slip faulting were made following surface ruptures that produced large earthquakes. One of the most noteworthy of these was the great San Francisco earth-

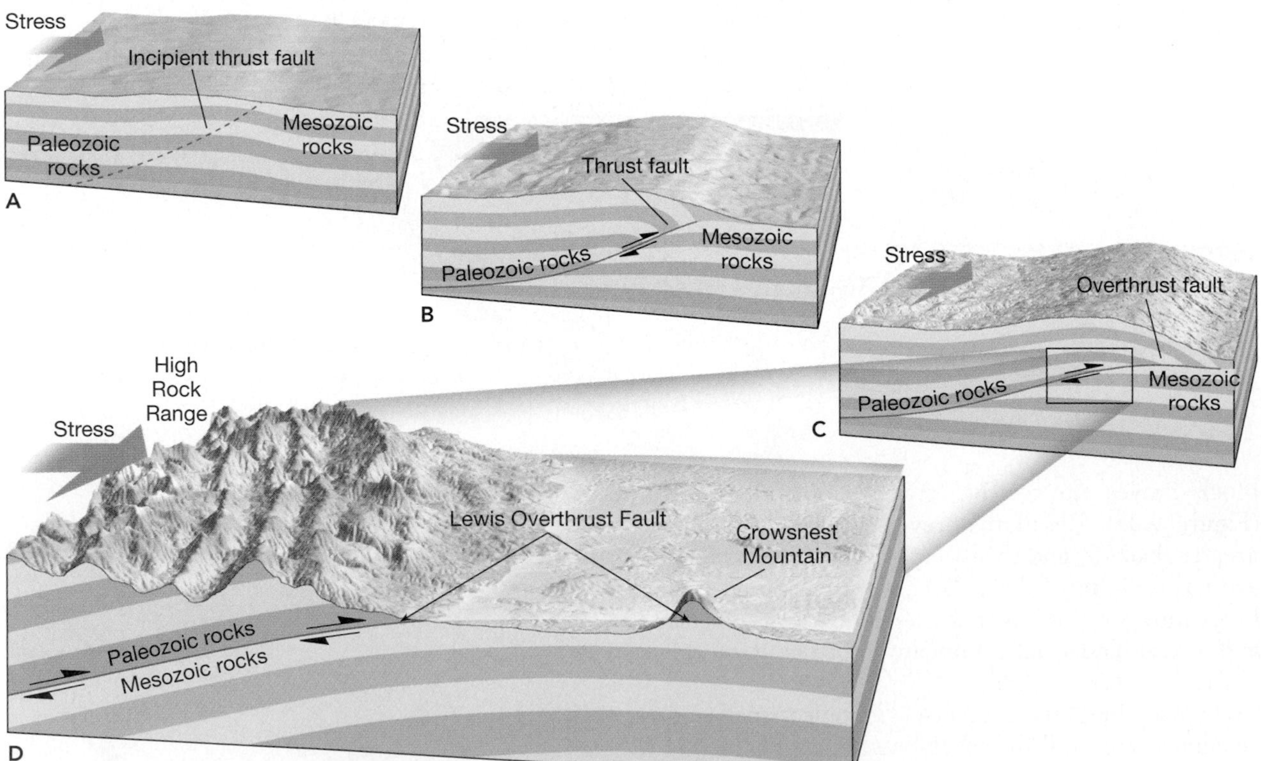

◆ **Figure 9.26** Idealized development of the Lewis Overthrust fault near Crowsnest Pass, Alberta. **A.** Geologic setting before deformation. **B., C.** Large-scale movement along a thrust fault displaced Paleozoic rock over Mesozoic strata in the region of the Crowsnest Pass, Alberta. **D.** Erosion by glacial ice and running water sculpted the thrust sheet into a majestic landscape and isolated remnants of the thrust sheet, such as Crowsnest Mountain.

◆ **Figure 9.27** Crowsnest Mountain in the Crowsnest Pass area of southwest Alberta is a klippe.
(Photo by Thelma Pirot)

◆ **Figure 9.28** Aerial view of strike-slip (right-lateral) fault in Southern Nevada.
(Photo by Marli Miller)

quake of 1906. During this strong earthquake, structures, such as fences, that were built across the San Andreas Fault were displaced by as much as 5 metres. Because the movement along the San Andreas causes the crustal block on the opposite side of the fault to move to the right as you face the fault, it is called a *right-lateral* strike-slip fault. The Great Glen Fault in Scotland is a well-known example of a *left-lateral* strike-slip fault, which exhibits the opposite sense of displacement. The total displacement along the Great Glen Fault is estimated to exceed 100 kilometres. Also associated with this fault trace are numerous lakes, including Loch Ness, the home of the legendary monster.

Many major strike-slip faults cut through the lithosphere and accommodate motion between two large lithospheric plates. In Chapter 1 you learned that this special kind of strike-slip fault is called a **transform** (*trans* = across, *forma* = form) **fault**. Numerous transform faults cut the oceanic lithosphere and link spreading oceanic ridges. Others accommodate displacement between continental plates that move horizontally with respect to each other. One of the best-known transform faults is California's San Andreas Fault (Box 9.1). This plate-bounding fault can be traced for about 950 kilometres from the Gulf of California to a point along the Pacific Coast north of San Francisco, where it

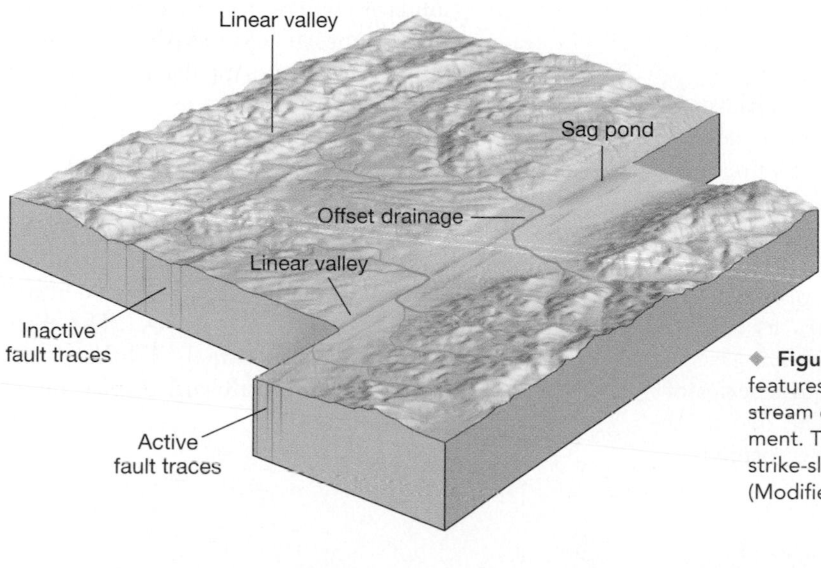

◆ **Figure 9.29** Block diagram illustrating the features associated with strike-slip faults. Note how stream channels have been offset by fault movement. The faults in this diagram are right-lateral strike-slip faults.
(Modified after R. L. Wesson and others)

continues out to sea. Since its formation, about 29 million years ago, displacement along the San Andreas Fault has exceeded 560 kilometres. This movement has accommodated the northward displacement of southwest California and the Baja Peninsula of Mexico in relation to the remainder of North America. The nature of these important structures will be discussed in more detail in Chapter 12.

Chapter Summary

- *Deformation* refers to changes in the shape or volume of a rock body and is most pronounced along plate margins. To describe the forces that deform rocks, geologists use the term *stress*, which is the amount of *force* applied to a given area. Stress that is uniform in all directions is called confining pressure, whereas *differential stresses* are applied unequally in different directions. Differential stresses that shorten a rock body are *compressional stresses*; those that elongate a rock unit are *tensional stresses*. *Strain* is the change in size and shape of a rock unit caused by stress.
- Rocks deform differently depending on the environment (temperature and confining pressure), the composition and texture of the rock, and the length of time stress is maintained. Rocks first respond by deforming elastically and will return to their original shape when the stress is removed. Once their elastic limit (strength) is surpassed, rocks either deform by ductile flow or they fracture. *Ductile deformation* is a solid-state flow that results in a change in size and shape of an object without fracturing. Ductile flow can be accomplished by gradual slippage and re-crystallization along planes of weakness within the crystal lattice of mineral grains. Ductile deformation occurs in a high-temperature, high-pressure environment. In a near-surface environment, most rocks deform by *brittle failure*.
- The orientation of rock units or fault surfaces is established with measurements called strike and dip. *Strike* is the compass direction of a line produced by the intersection of an inclined rock layer or fault with a horizontal plane. *Dip* is the angle of inclination of the surface of a rock unit or fault measured from a horizontal plane.
- The most basic geologic structures associated with rock deformation are *folds* (flat-lying sedimentary and volcanic rocks bent into a series of wavelike undulations) and *faults*. The two most common types of folds are *anticlines*, formed by the upfolding, or arching, of rock layers, and *synclines*, which are downfolds. Most folds are the result of horizontal compressional stresses. Folds can be symmetrical, asymmetrical, or, if one limb has been tilted beyond the vertical, overturned. *Domes* (upwarped structures) and *basins* (downwarped structures) are circular or somewhat elongate folds formed by vertical displacements of strata.
- *Joints* are fractures along which no appreciable displacement has occurred. Joints generally occur in groups with roughly parallel orientations and are the result of brittle failure of rock units located in the outermost crust.
- Faults are fractures in the crust along which appreciable displacement has occurred. Faults in which the movement is primarily up and down are called *dip-slip faults*. Dip-slip faults include both *normal* and *reverse faults*. Low-angle reverse faults are called *thrust faults*. Normal faults indicate tensional stresses that pull the crust apart. Along the spreading centres of plates, divergence can cause a central block called a *graben*, bounded by normal faults, to drop as the plates separate.
- Reverse and thrust faulting indicate that compressional forces are at work. Large thrust faults are found along subduction zones and other convergent boundaries where plates are colliding. In mountainous regions, such as the Alps, Northern Rockies, Himalayas, and Appalachians, thrust faults have displaced strata as far as 50 kilometres over adjacent rock units.
- *Strike-slip faults* exhibit mainly horizontal displacement parallel to the strike of the fault surface. Large strike-slip faults, called *transform faults*, accommodate displacement between plate boundaries. Most transform faults cut the oceanic lithosphere and link spreading centres. The San Andreas Fault cuts the continental lithosphere and accommodates the northward displacement of southwest California.

Review Questions

1. What is rock deformation? How does a rock body change during deformation?
2. List five geologic structures associated with deformation.
3. How is *stress* related to *force*?
4. Contrast compressional and tensional stresses.
5. Describe how shearing can deform a rock in a near-surface environment.
6. Compare *strain* and *stress*.
7. How is brittle deformation different from ductile deformation?
8. List three factors that determine how rocks will behave when exposed to stresses that exceed their strength. Briefly explain the role of each.
9. What is an outcrop?
10. What two measurements are used to establish the orientation of deformed strata? Distinguish between them.
11. Distinguish between anticlines and synclines; domes and basins; anticlines and domes.
12. How is a monocline different from an anticline?
13. How are joints different from faults?
14. Crowsnest Mountain in southwest Alberta is an example of what type of geologic feature?
15. Contrast the movements that occur along normal and reverse faults. What type of stress is indicated by each fault?
16. Is the fault shown in Figure 9.20 a normal or a reverse fault?
17. Describe a horst and a graben. Explain how a graben valley forms and name one.
18. How are reverse faults different from thrust faults? In what way are they the same?
19. The San Andreas Fault is an excellent example of a _______________ fault.
20. At which of the three types of plate boundaries does normal faulting predominate? At which does reverse faulting predominate? At which does strike-slip faulting predominate?

Key Terms

anticline (p. 241)
basin (p. 244)
brittle deformation (p. 237)
brittle failure (p. 237)
compressional stress (p. 235)
deformation (p. 235)
differential stress (p. 235)
dip (p. 239)
dip-slip fault (p. 247)
dome (p. 244)
ductile deformation (p. 237)
fault (p. 247)
fault scarp (p. 247)
fold (p. 241)
force (p. 235)
graben (p. 250)
hogback (p. 244)
horst (p. 250)
joint (p. 245)
klippe (p. 252)
monocline (p. 243)
normal fault (p. 247)
reverse fault (p. 247)
right-lateral strike-slip (p. 249)
rock structure (p. 239)
shear (p. 235)
strain (p. 235)
stress (p. 235)
strike (p. 239)
strike-slip fault (p. 252)
syncline (p. 241)
tensional stress (p. 235)
thrust fault (p. 247)
transform fault (p. 253)

Web Resources

The *Earth* website uses the resources and flexibility of the internet to aid in your study of the topics in this chapter. Written and developed by geology instructors, this site will help improve your understanding of geology. Visit **www.pearsoned.ca/tarbuck** and click on the cover of the text to find

- online review quizzes
- Web-based critical thinking and writing exercises
- links to chapter-specific Web resources
- internet-wide key-term searches

www.pearsoned.ca/tarbuck

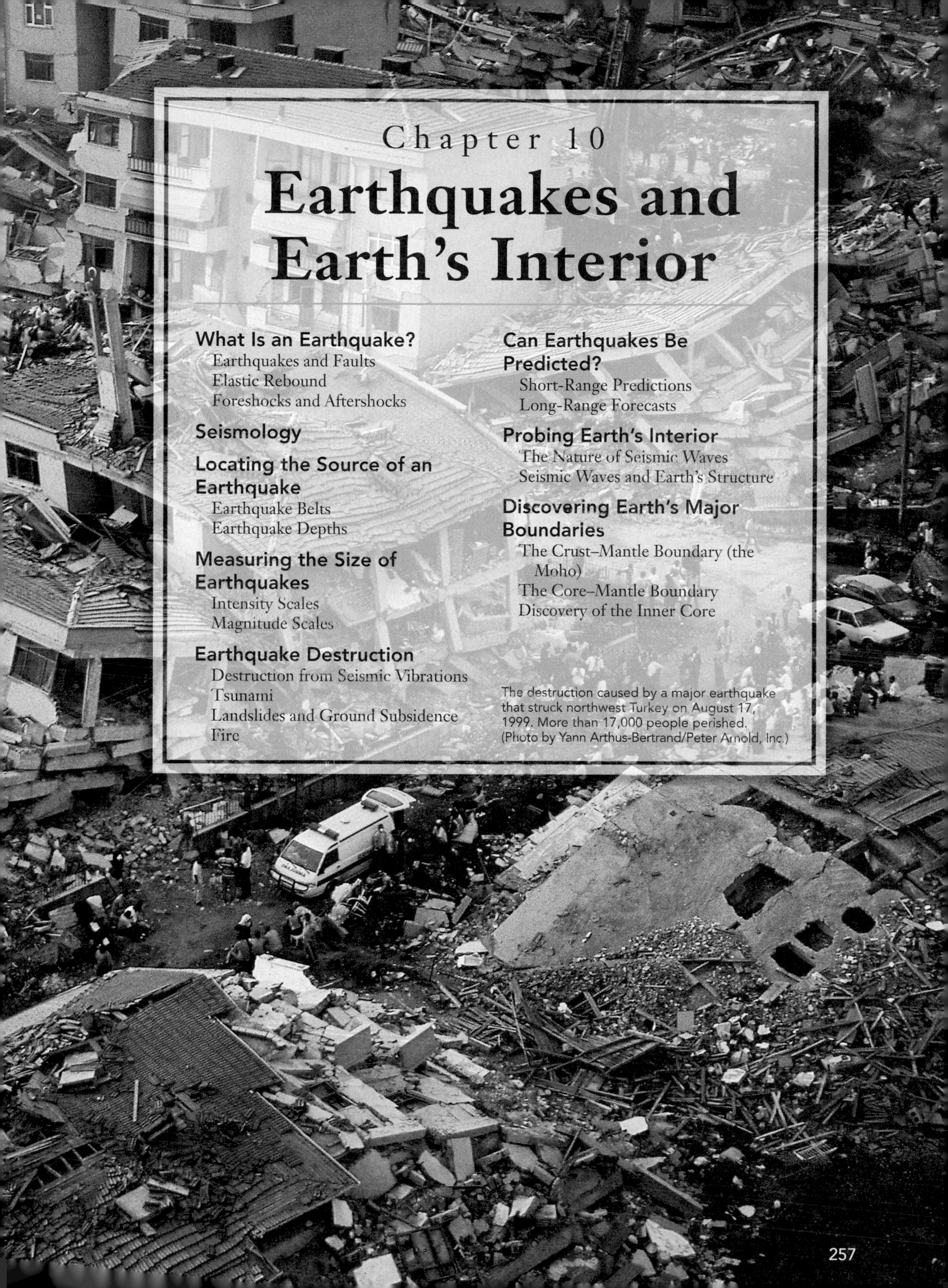

Chapter 10

Earthquakes and Earth's Interior

What Is an Earthquake?
Earthquakes and Faults
Elastic Rebound
Foreshocks and Aftershocks

Seismology

Locating the Source of an Earthquake
Earthquake Belts
Earthquake Depths

Measuring the Size of Earthquakes
Intensity Scales
Magnitude Scales

Earthquake Destruction
Destruction from Seismic Vibrations
Tsunami
Landslides and Ground Subsidence
Fire

Can Earthquakes Be Predicted?
Short-Range Predictions
Long-Range Forecasts

Probing Earth's Interior
The Nature of Seismic Waves
Seismic Waves and Earth's Structure

Discovering Earth's Major Boundaries
The Crust–Mantle Boundary (the Moho)
The Core–Mantle Boundary
Discovery of the Inner Core

The destruction caused by a major earthquake that struck northwest Turkey on August 17, 1999. More than 17,000 people perished. (Photo by Yann Arthus-Bertrand/Peter Arnold, Inc.)

It was peak tourist season at the beachfront hotels on the island of Phuket, Thailand; thousands of foreign travellers had flocked to the island for a relaxing vacation. Late-night revellers who had slept in on that morning of December 26, 2004, awoke to the shaking of their beds at 7:58 A.M. local time. The tremors, which lasted for about three minutes, were mild and few people thought anything more of them once the shaking had stopped. To those people who had already ventured out to the beach for a walk, the morning seemed blissfully uneventful.

About two hours later, a great commotion erupted on the west coast beaches of Phuket; to the many onlookers gathered there, it appeared that the water was being pulled away from the shoreline and into the Andaman Sea. Within a few minutes, it appeared that the water was returning with a vengeance. Observers gazed seaward at a swelling wave that was quickly advancing toward the beach. Curiosity quickly turned to panic as the swell transformed into a wall of water more than 5 metres high. The wave hit the shore with explosive force (Figure 10.1A). Water surged inland, rushing through beachfront hotels and into the streets of the town (Figure 10.1B). Individuals who had escaped the deluge in the upper floors of their hotels watched in horror as debris and people were swept up in the torrent of water. At 30-minute intervals, the resort areas were inundated a second, third, and

◆ **Figure 10.1** **A.** It is obvious in this picture that people were taken by surprise as the first wave of the 2004 Boxing Day tsunami hit Ao Nang Beach on Phuket Island, Thailand. **B.** This photo, taken immediately after the first wave of the tsunami struck the beach at a tourist resort on Phuket Island, shows water surging inland from the ocean. To appreciate the severity of the surge, one need only consider the water level relative to the tops of the palm trees. The image in **C** highlights the crests (red) and troughs (blue) of the tsunami generated by the great Sumatra earthquake of 2004. To the east of the Andaman and Nicobar Islands, the waves travelled across the Andaman Sea to hit Thailand and Malaysia. Simultaneously, the waves that were generated westward into the Indian Ocean hit Sri Lanka (as depicted here), India, and the eastern coast of Africa. (Photo **A** by David Rydevik; photo **B** by CP/FotoGro Storteig/SCANPIX; part **C** modified from an image courtesy of the Geological Survey of Japan, AIST)

fourth time; the second wave was the largest to hit the coast.

Even before the waves hit Thailand, they had already claimed thousands of lives in Indonesia. To the west, the waves travelled across the Indian Ocean, claiming many more victims in Sri Lanka, Bangladesh, India, and the east coast of Africa. Only later would survivors of the disaster on Phuket Island learn that the minor tremors they felt that morning were from seismic waves produced more than 700 kilometres away, near Sumatra, Indonesia, by the second-largest earthquake recorded by modern instruments. This event was responsible for generating the killer waves that arrived in Thailand two hours later.

Earthquakes and their associated phenomena, such as tsunami, are tangible reminders that Earth is a highly dynamic system, both above and below its surface. Each year, more than a thousand earthquakes occur in Canada alone, although the majority of these produce vibrations that are simply too weak to be felt by humans and can be detected only by sensitive instruments.

Occasionally, media reports alert us to particularly strong earthquake events. The most severe earthquake disasters in recent times have included those centred in İzmit, Turkey (August 17, 1999; more than 17,000 deaths), Gujarat, India (January 26, 2001; more than 20,000 deaths), and the Bam region of Iran (December 26, 2003; more than 25,000 deaths). A disaster of this size is difficult for most Canadians to comprehend; indeed, many Canadians have never even *felt* an earthquake in their lifetime. The events that occurred in the Indian Ocean on the morning of December 26, 2004, are particularly significant in that they changed the consciousness of millions of people worldwide. Victims in at least eight countries bordering the Indian Ocean were reported, with a death toll of more than 200,000 people. Among the victims were native citizens of the affected countries and travellers from several other countries, including Canada. In this sense, the disaster was one that was truly felt by the global community. Before the disaster, few people had even heard the term *tsunami*; by the next day, it had become a household word. It was a strong reminder that earthquake hazards can extend far beyond the area in which an earthquake itself is generated. It was also a wake-up call to the many nations that, having not experienced an earthquake for some time, had become complacent about preparing for such a disaster.

Ancient stories of the Aboriginal peoples of Vancouver Island, historical documents from Japan, computer-modelling methods, and a variety of geologic evidence indicate that an earthquake of similar magnitude to the Sumatra-Andaman earthquake occurred in 1700. Canada is not immune from tsunami: a rare Atlantic tsunami associated with the 1929 Grand Banks, Newfoundland and Labrador, earthquake was responsible for at least 10 deaths—historically, the largest number of deaths attributed to a single Canadian earthquake. Thus, the question is not "will another earthquake occur in Canada?" but rather "when will the next big earthquake happen—and where?" Answering this question will require knowledge of past earthquake events and the study of current earthquake activity.

In this chapter, we examine what earthquakes are, how they are produced, the damage they cause, and how they are studied. We also explore the positive side of earthquakes—how the behaviour of seismic waves has been used to deduce the structure of Earth's interior.

WHAT IS AN EARTHQUAKE?

GEODe EARTH Earthquakes
↳ What Is an Earthquake?

An **earthquake** is the vibration of Earth produced by the rapid release of energy. Most often, earthquakes are caused by slippage along a fault in Earth's crust. The energy released radiates in all directions from its source, the **focus** (*focus* = a point), in the form of seismic waves. These waves are analogous to those produced when a stone is dropped into a calm pond (Figure 10.2). Just as the impact of the stone sets water waves in motion, an earthquake generates seismic waves that radiate throughout Earth. Even though the energy dissipates rapidly with increasing distance from the focus, sensitive instruments located around the world record the event.

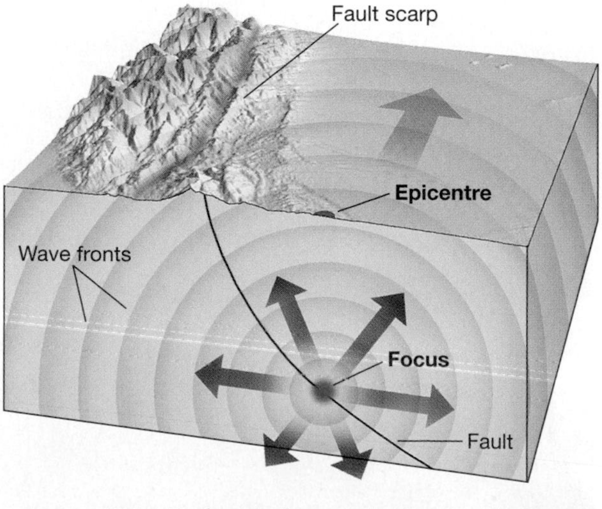

◆ **Figure 10.2** Earthquake focus and epicentre. The focus is the zone within Earth at which the initial displacement occurs. The epicentre is the surface location directly above the focus.

Earthquakes and Faults

The tremendous energy released by atomic explosions or by volcanic eruptions can produce earthquakes, but these events are relatively weak and infrequent. What mechanism produces a destructive earthquake? Ample evidence exists that Earth is not a static planet. We know that Earth's crust has been uplifted at times, because we have found numerous ancient wave-cut benches many metres above the level of the highest tides. Other regions exhibit evidence of extensive subsidence. In addition to these vertical displacements, offsets in fence lines, roads, and other structures indicate that horizontal movement is common (Figure 10.3). These movements are usually associated with faults (Chapter 9).

Most of the motion along faults can be satisfactorily explained by plate tectonic theory, as introduced in Chapter 1. Mobile plates of lithosphere interact with neighbouring plates, straining and deforming the rocks at their margins. In fact, it is along the faults associated with plate boundaries that most earthquakes occur. Furthermore, earthquakes are repetitive: as soon as one is over, the continuous motion of the plates resumes, adding strain to the rocks until they fail again.

Elastic Rebound

The actual mechanism of earthquake generation eluded geologists until H. F. Reid of Johns Hopkins University conducted a study following the great 1906 San Francisco earthquake. The earthquake was accompanied by horizontal surface displacements of several metres along the northern portion of the San Andreas Fault. This 1300-kilometre fracture extends northwest–southeast through southern California. It is a large fault zone that separates two great sections of Earth's crust: the North American plate and the Pacific plate. Field investigations determined that during this single earthquake, the Pacific plate lurched as much as 5 metres northward past the adjacent North American plate.

The mechanism for earthquake formation that Reid deduced from this information is illustrated in Figure 10.4. In part A of the figure, you see an existing fault. In part B, tectonic forces slowly deform the crustal rocks on both sides of the fault, as demonstrated by the bent features. Under these conditions, rocks bend and store elastic energy, much like a wooden stick does if bent. Eventually, the frictional resistance holding the rocks together is overcome. As slippage occurs at the weakest point (the focus), displacement exerts stress farther along the fault, where additional slippage occurs (Figure 10.4C) until most of the built-up strain is released (Figure 10.4D). This slippage allows the deformed rock to "snap back." The vibrations we know as an earthquake occur as the rock elastically returns to its original shape. The springing back of the rock was termed **elastic rebound** by Reid because the rock behaves elastically, much like a stretched rubber band does when it is released. After release, stress builds up again along the fault as the earthquake cycle continues.

In summary, most earthquakes are produced by the rapid release of elastic energy stored in rock that has been subjected to great stress. Once the strength of the rock is exceeded, it suddenly ruptures, causing the vibrations of an earthquake. Earthquakes most commonly occur along existing faults whenever the frictional forces on the fault surfaces are overcome.

◆ **Figure 10.3** This fence was offset 2.5 metres during the 1906 San Francisco earthquake. (Photo by G. K. Gilbert, U.S. Geological Survey)

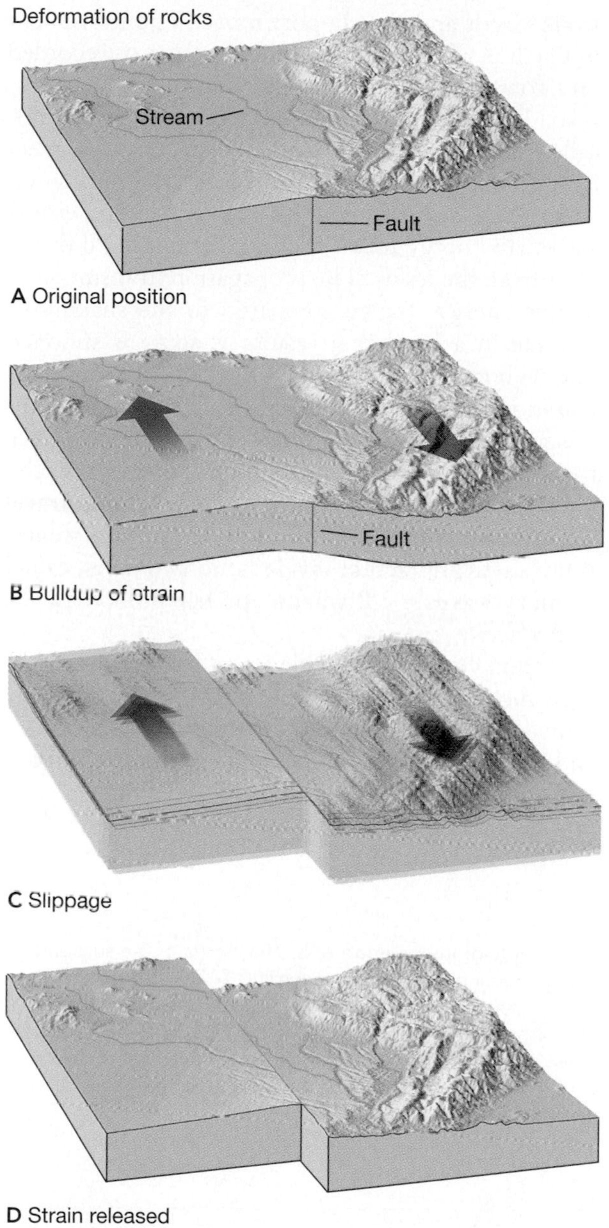

◆ **Figure 10.4** Elastic rebound. As rock is deformed, it bends, storing elastic energy. Once strained beyond its breaking point, the rock fails (breaks), releasing the stored-up energy as earthquake waves.

Foreshocks and Aftershocks

The intense vibrations of the 1906 San Francisco earthquake lasted about 40 seconds. Although most of the displacement along the fault occurred in this rather short span, additional movements along this and other nearby faults lasted for several days following the main quake. The adjustments that follow a major earthquake often generate smaller earthquakes called **aftershocks**. Although these aftershocks are usually much weaker than the main earthquake, they can sometimes destroy already badly weakened structures. This occurred, for example, during a 1988 earthquake in Armenia. A large aftershock collapsed many structures that had been weakened by the main tremor.

In addition, small earthquakes called **foreshocks** often precede a major earthquake by days or, in some cases, by as much as several years. Monitoring of these foreshocks has been used as a means of predicting forthcoming major earthquakes, with mixed success. We will consider the topic of earthquake prediction later in this chapter.

SEISMOLOGY

GEODe EARTH
Earthquakes
↳ Seismology

The study of earthquake waves, **seismology** (*seismos* = shake, *ology* = the study of) dates back to attempts made by the Chinese almost 2000 years ago to determine the direction from which these waves originated. The seismic instrument used by the Chinese was a large hollow jar that contained a suspended mass (similar to a clock pendulum) connected in some fashion to the jaws of several large dragon figurines that encircled the container (Figure 10.5). The jaws of each dragon held a metal ball. When earthquake waves reached the instrument, the relative motion between the suspended mass and the jar would dislodge some of the metal balls into the waiting mouths of frog figurines directly below.

The Chinese were probably aware that the first strong ground motion from an earthquake is directional, and when it is strong enough, all poorly supported items will topple over in the same direction. Apparently the Chinese used this fact, plus the position of the dislodged balls, to detect the direction to an earthquake's source. However, the complex motion of seismic waves makes it unlikely that the actual direction to an earthquake was determined with any regularity.

In principle, modern **seismographs** (*seismos* = shake, *graph* = write), instruments that record seismic waves, are not unlike the device used by the early Chinese. Seismographs have a mass freely suspended from a support that is attached to the ground (Figure 10.6). When the vibration from a distant earthquake reaches the instrument, the **inertia*** (*iners* = idle) of the mass keeps it relatively stationary

*Inertia: Simply stated, objects at rest tend to stay at rest, and objects in motion tend to remain in motion, unless acted on by an outside force. You probably have experienced this phenomenon when an automobile you were in stopped quickly and your body continued to move forward.

◆ **Figure 10.5** Ancient Chinese seismograph. During an Earth tremor, the dragons located in the direction of the main vibrations would each drop a ball into the mouth of the frog below it.

while Earth and the support move. The movement of Earth in relation to the stationary mass is recorded on a rotating drum or magnetic tape.

The records obtained from seismographs, called **seismograms** (*seismos* = shake, *gramma* = what is written), provide a great deal of information concerning the behaviour of seismic waves. Seismic waves are energy forms that radiate out in all directions from the focus. The propagation (transmission) of this energy can be compared to the shaking of gelatine in a bowl that results as some is spooned out. Whereas the gelatine will have one mode of vibration, seismograms reveal that two main groups of seismic waves are generated by the slippage of a rock mass. The wave types that travel through Earth's interior are called **body waves**. The types that travel along the outer part of Earth are called **surface waves**. Body waves are further divided into two types, called **primary waves,** or **P waves,** and **secondary waves,** or **S waves**.

Body waves are divided into P and S waves by their mode of travel through intervening materials. P waves are "push-pull" waves—they push (compress) and pull (expand) rocks in the direction the wave is travelling (Figure 10.7A). Imagine holding someone by the shoulders and shaking that person. This

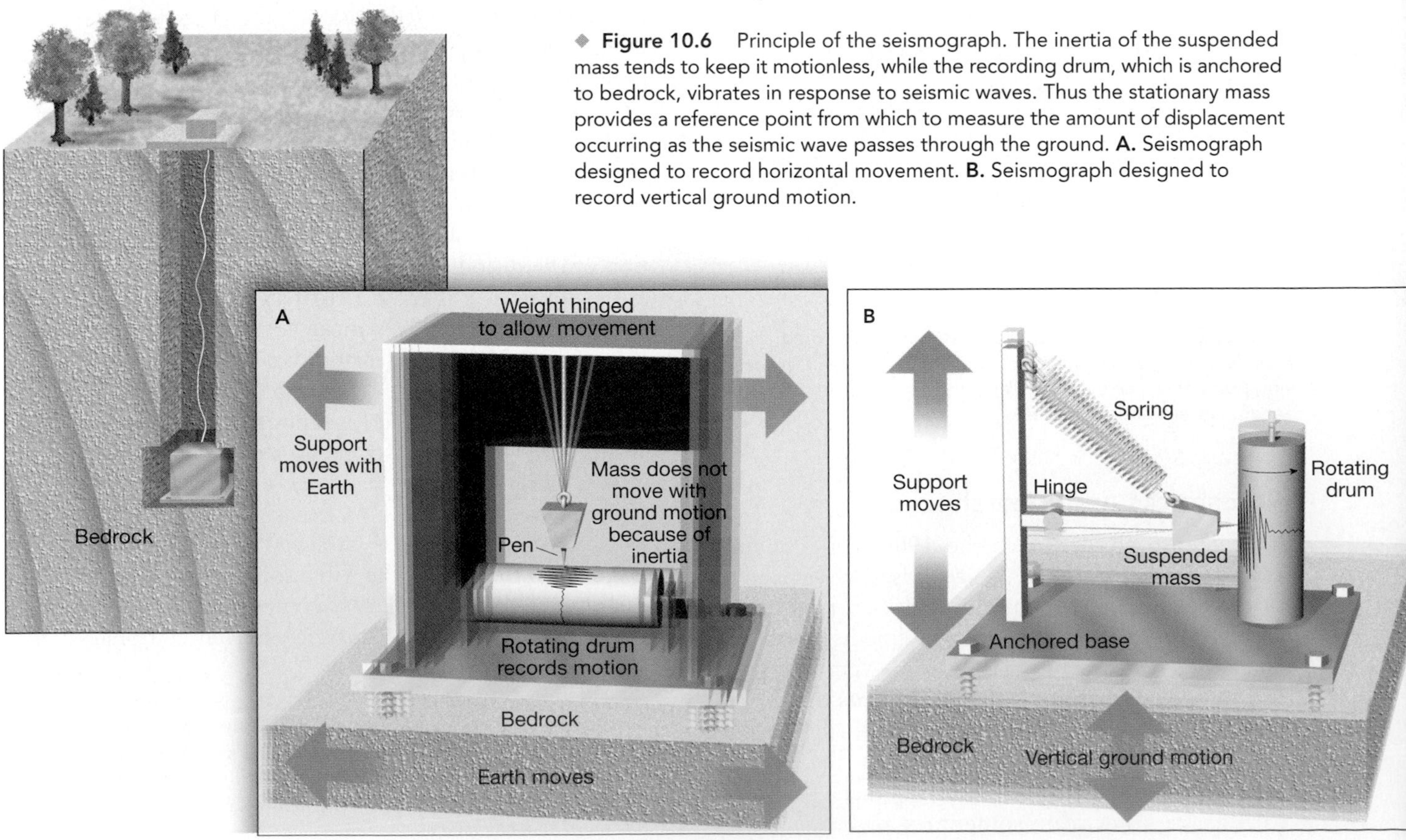

◆ **Figure 10.6** Principle of the seismograph. The inertia of the suspended mass tends to keep it motionless, while the recording drum, which is anchored to bedrock, vibrates in response to seismic waves. Thus the stationary mass provides a reference point from which to measure the amount of displacement occurring as the seismic wave passes through the ground. **A.** Seismograph designed to record horizontal movement. **B.** Seismograph designed to record vertical ground motion.

push-pull movement is how P waves move through Earth. Solids, liquids, and gases resist a change in volume when compressed and will elastically spring back once the force is removed. Therefore, P waves, which are compressional waves, can travel through all these materials.

Conversely, S waves "shake" the particles at right angles to their direction of travel. This can be

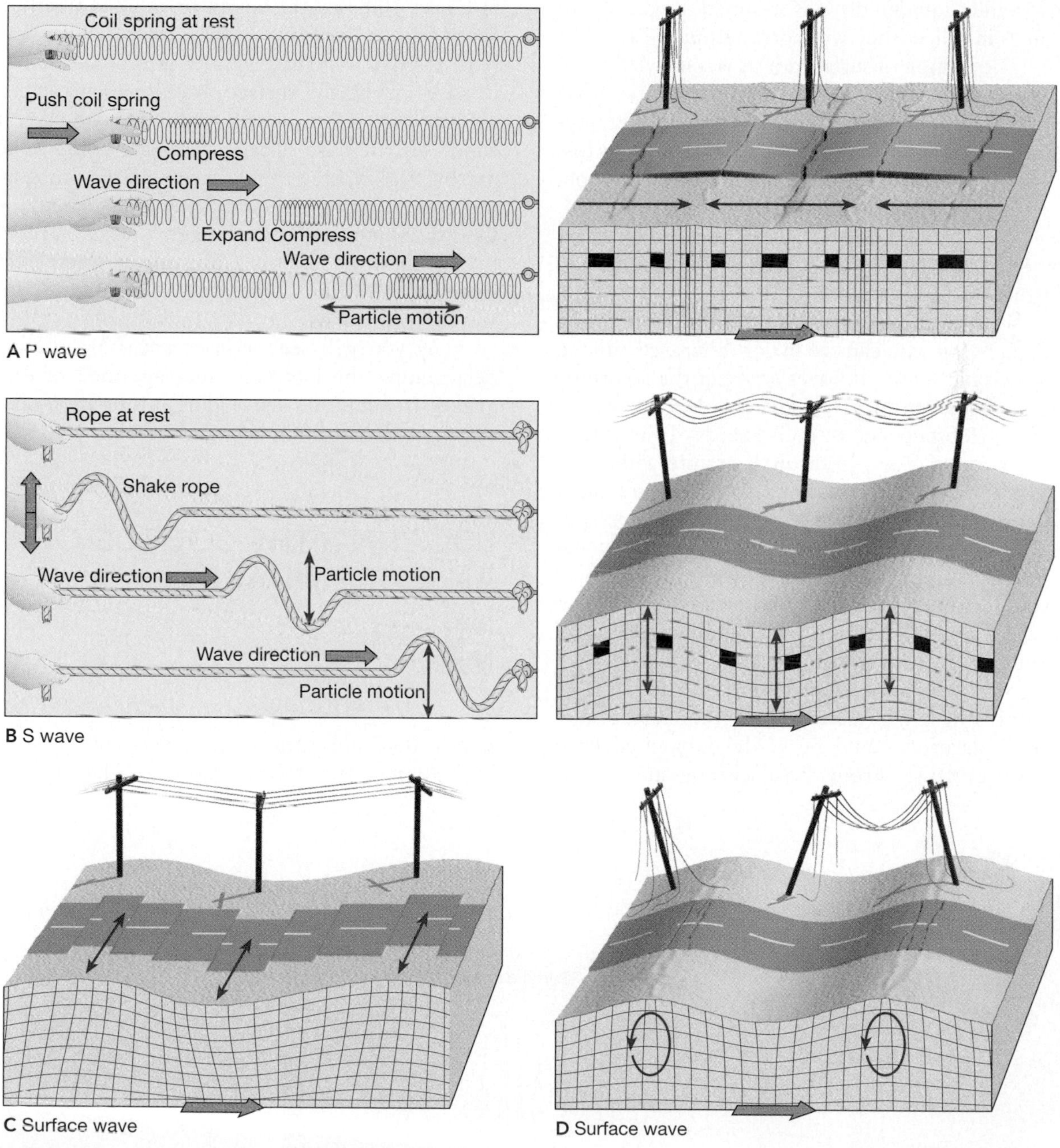

◆ **Figure 10.7** Basic types of seismic waves and their characteristic motion. (Note that during a typical earthquake, ground shaking consists of a combination of various kinds of seismic waves that have complex movements in three dimensions.) **A.** As illustrated by a coil spring, P waves are compressional waves that alternately compress and expand the material through which they pass. The back-and-forth motion produced as compressional waves travel along the surface can cause the ground to buckle and fracture, and they can cause power lines to break. **B.** S waves cause material to oscillate at right angles to the direction of wave motion. Because S waves can travel in any plane, they produce up-and-down and sideways shaking of the ground. **C.** One type of surface wave is essentially the same as that of an S wave that exhibits only horizontal motion. This kind of surface wave moves the ground from side to side and can be particularly damaging to the foundations of buildings. **D.** Another type of surface wave travels along Earth's surface, much like rolling ocean waves. The arrows show the elliptical movement of rock as the wave passes.

illustrated by fastening one end of a rope and shaking the other end, as shown in Figure 10.7B. Unlike P waves, which temporarily change the *volume* of intervening material by alternately compressing and expanding it, S waves temporarily change the *shape* of the material that transmits them. Because fluids (gases and liquids) do not respond elastically to changes in shape, they will not transmit S waves.

The motion of surface waves is somewhat more complex (Figure 10.7C). As surface waves travel along the ground, they cause the ground and anything resting on it to move, much as ocean swells toss a ship. In addition to their up-and-down motion, surface waves have a side-to-side motion similar to an S wave oriented in a horizontal plane. This latter motion is particularly damaging to the foundations of structures.

By observing a "typical" seismic record, as shown in Figure 10.8, you can see major differences among these seismic waves: P waves arrive at the recording station first, then S waves, and then surface waves. This is a consequence of their speeds. To illustrate, the velocity of P waves through granite within the crust is about 6 kilometres per second. S waves under the same conditions travel at 3.6 kilometres per second. Differences in density and elastic properties of the rock greatly influence the velocities of these waves. Generally, in any solid material, P waves travel 1.7 times as fast as S waves, and S waves travel 1.1 times as fast as surface waves.

A system was developed for locating earthquake epicentres by using seismograms from earthquakes whose epicentres could be easily pinpointed from physical evidence. From these seismograms, travel-time graphs were constructed (Figure 10.9). The first travel-time graphs were greatly improved when seismograms became available from nuclear explosions, because the precise location and time of detonation were known.

In addition to velocity differences, also notice in Figure 10.8 that the height or, more correctly, the amplitude of these wave types varies. The S waves tend to have a slightly greater amplitude than the P waves, while the surface waves, which cause the greatest destruction, tend to exhibit an even greater amplitude. Because surface waves are confined to a narrow region near the surface and are not spread throughout Earth as P and S waves are, they retain their maximum amplitude longer. Surface waves also have longer periods (time intervals between crests); therefore, they are commonly referred to as **long waves**, or **L waves**.

As you will see, seismic waves are useful in determining the location and magnitude of earthquakes, in addition to providing information on the nature of Earth's internal characteristics.

LOCATING THE SOURCE OF AN EARTHQUAKE

GEODe EARTH Earthquakes
↳ Locating the Source of an Earthquake

Recall that the *focus* is the place within Earth where earthquake waves originate. The **epicentre**

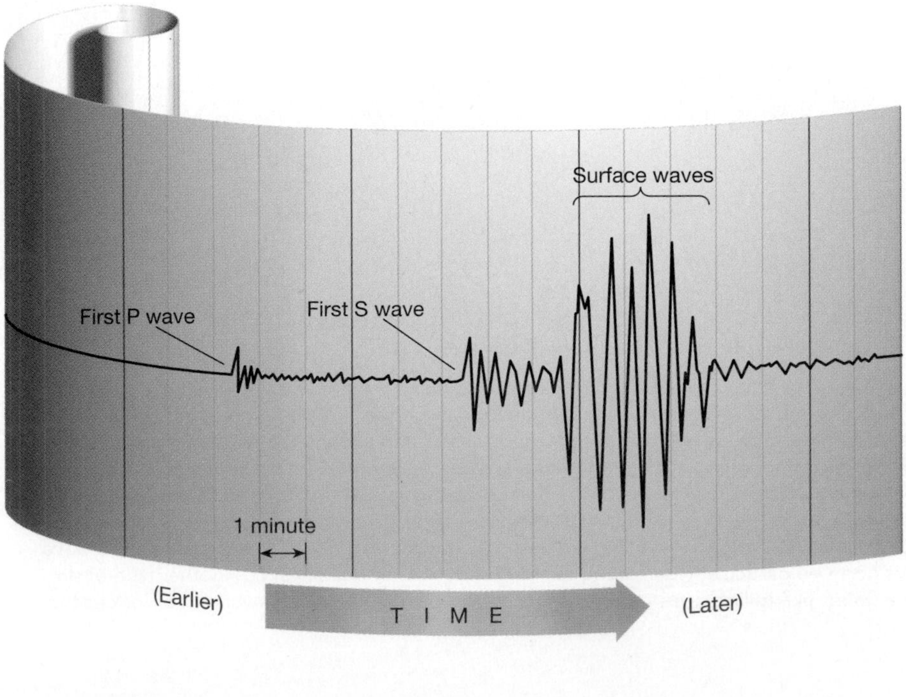

◆ **Figure 10.8** Typical seismogram. Note the time interval (about 5 minutes) between the arrival of the first P wave and the arrival of the first S wave.

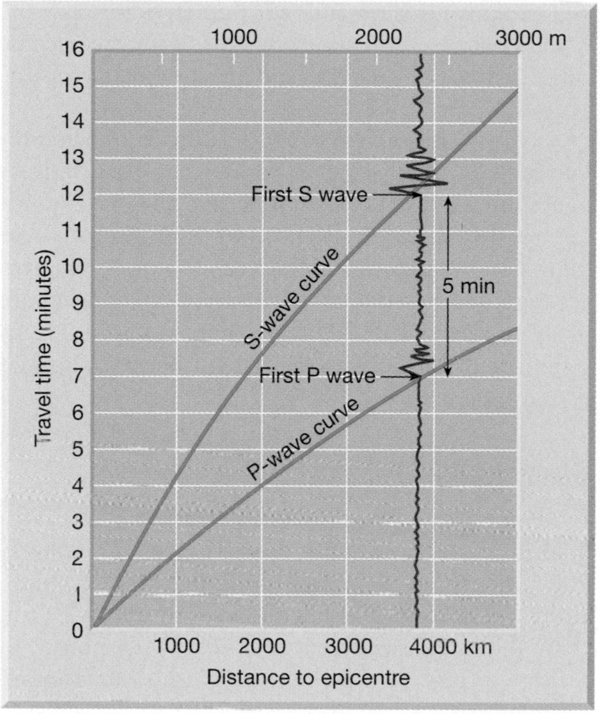

◆ **Figure 10.9** A travel-time graph is used to determine the distance to the epicentre. The difference in arrival times of the first P and S waves in the example is 5 minutes. Thus, the epicentre is roughly 3800 kilometres away.

(*epi* = upon, *centr* = a point) is the location on the surface directly above the focus (see Figure 10.2).

The difference in velocities of P and S waves provides a method for locating the epicentre. The principle used is analogous to a race between two vehicles, one faster than the other. The P wave always wins the race, arriving ahead of the S wave. But the greater the length of the race, the greater will be the difference in the arrival times at the finish line (the seismic station). Therefore, the greater the interval measured on a seismogram between the arrival of the first P wave and the first S wave, the greater the distance to the earthquake source. By using the sample seismogram in Figure 10.8 and the travel-time curves in Figure 10.9, we can determine the distance separating the recording station from the earthquake in two steps: (1) determine the time interval between the arrival of the first P wave and the first S wave, and (2) find on the travel-time graph the equivalent time spread between the P and S wave curves. From this information, we can determine that this earthquake occurred 3800 kilometres from the recording instrument.

Now we know the *distance* but what *direction*? The epicentre could be in any direction from the seismic station. As shown in Figure 10.10, the precise location can be found when the distance is known from three or more different seismic stations. On a globe, we draw a circle around each seismic station. Each circle represents the epicentre distance for each station. The point at which the three circles intersect is the epicentre of the quake. This method is called *triangulation*.

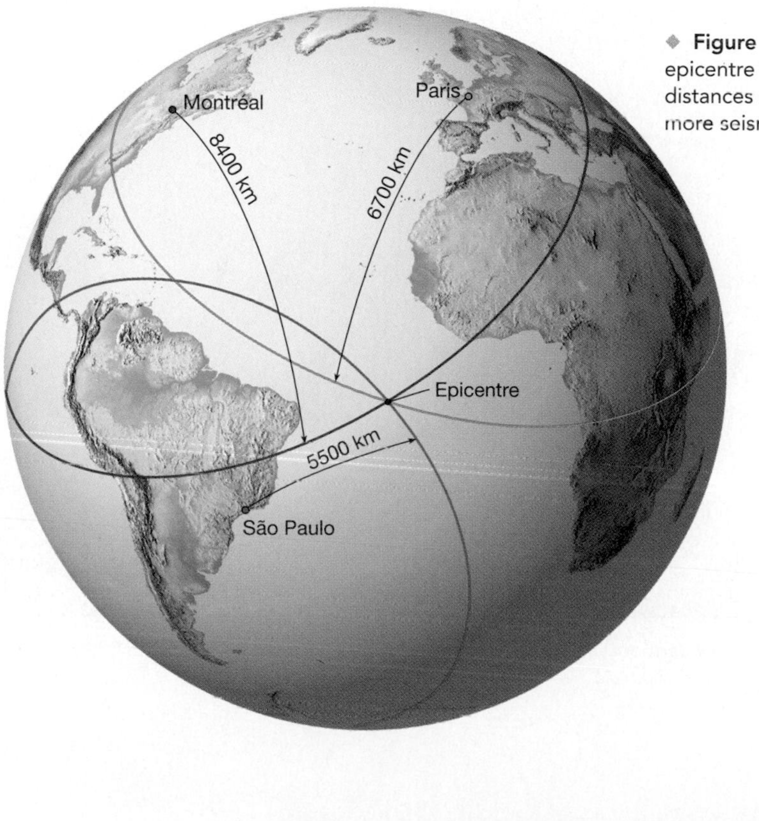

◆ **Figure 10.10** An earthquake epicentre is located by using the distances obtained from three or more seismic stations.

The study of earthquakes was greatly bolstered during the 1960s through efforts to discriminate between underground nuclear explosions and natural earthquakes. A worldwide network of more than 100 seismic stations is coordinated through Golden, Colorado. The largest of these, located in Billings, Montana, consists of an array of 525 instruments grouped in 21 clusters covering a region 200 kilometres in diameter. By using data from this array and high-speed computers, seismologists are able to differentiate between nuclear blasts and natural earthquakes, as well as determine the position of an earthquake's epicentre.

Earthquake Belts

About 95 percent of the energy released by earthquakes originates in a few relatively narrow zones that wind around the globe (Figure 10.11). The greatest energy is released along a path around the outer edge of the Pacific Ocean known as the *circum-Pacific belt*. Included in this zone are regions of great seismic activity, such as Japan, the Philippines, Chile, and numerous volcanic island chains, as exemplified by the Aleutian Islands.

Another major concentration of strong seismic activity extends through the mountainous regions that flank the Mediterranean Sea and continues through Iran and on past the Himalayan complex. Figure 10.11 indicates that yet another continuous belt extends for thousands of kilometres through the world's oceans. This zone coincides with the oceanic ridge system, an area of frequent but weaker seismic activity.

Areas of North America included in the circum-Pacific belt lie adjacent to California's San Andreas Fault and along the western coastal regions extending to the Aleutian Islands. In addition to these high-risk areas, other sections of North America are regarded as regions where strong earthquakes are likely to occur. In Canada earthquakes are concentrated in British Columbia but do occur elsewhere (Box 10.1).

Earthquake Depths

Evidence from seismic records reveals that earthquakes originate at depths ranging from 5 to nearly 700 kilometres. In a somewhat arbitrary fashion, earthquake foci have been classified according to their depth of occurrence. Those with points of origin within 70 kilometres of the surface are referred to as *shallow*, while those generated between 70 and 300 kilometres are considered *intermediate*, and those with a focus deeper than 300 kilometres are classified as *deep*. About 90 percent of all earthquakes occur at depths of less than 100 kilometres, and nearly all very damaging earthquakes appear to originate at shallow depths.

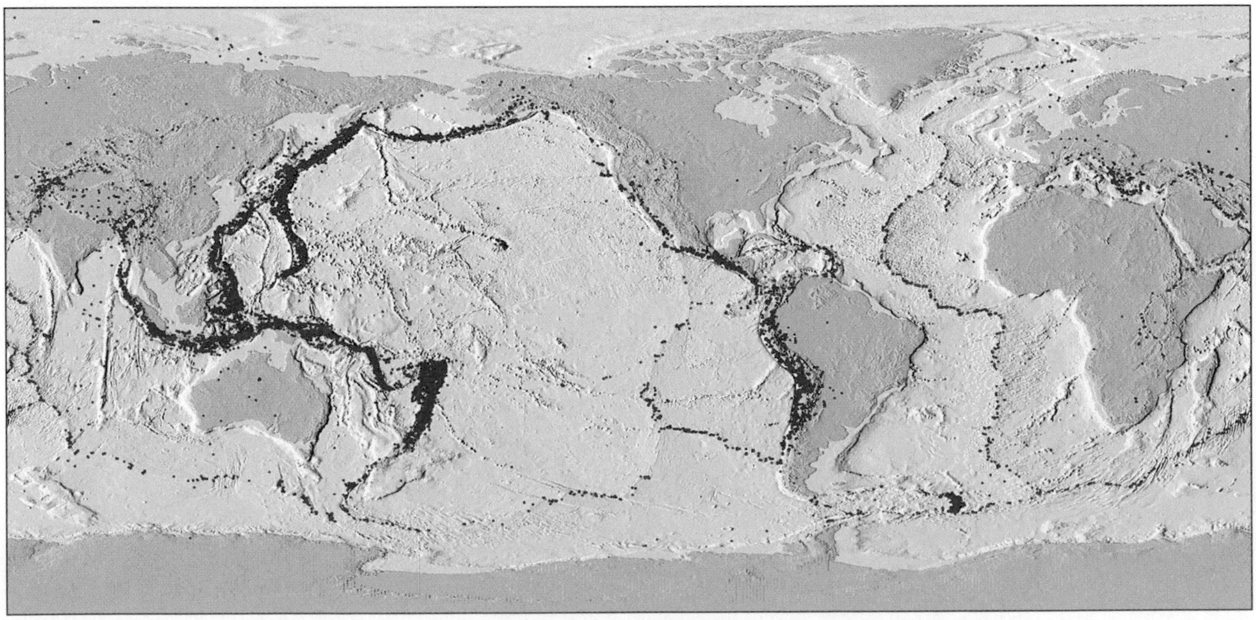

◆ **Figure 10.11** Distribution of the 14,229 earthquakes with magnitudes of at least 5 between 1980 and 1990. (Data from National Geophysical Data Center/NOAA)

BOX 10.1

Canadian Profile
Earthquakes in Canada

David Eaton*

On August 22, 1949, residents of the Queen Charlotte Islands were jolted by Canada's largest measured earthquake. With a magnitude of 8.1, this offshore tremor ranks as one of the great earthquakes of the twentieth century, well recorded around the globe. The earthquake knocked cows off their feet and caused an oil tank at Cumshewa Inlet to collapse. Even 300 kilometres away in Terrace, British Columbia, the ground shaking was so intense that standing on the street was described as "like being on the heaving deck of a ship at sea." Fortunately, the sparse population of the region meant that casualties and property damage were light in comparison with other earthquakes of similar magnitude, such as the 1946 Vancouver Island earthquake (Figure 10.12B).

The 1949 earthquake ruptured a major segment of the Queen Charlotte fault system, an active right-lateral transform fault along Canada's west coast (Figure 10.A). Across the fault, the Pacific plate is creeping slowly northward relative to North America, in a manner analogous to lithospheric movement along the San Andreas Fault system in California. Friction across the fault resists this motion, causing stress to accumulate during aseismic intervals. The sudden release of stored energy during an earthquake (elastic rebound) starts the earthquake cycle once again.

In southwest British Columbia, a different plate-tectonic setting exists, more akin to Japan than California (Figure 10.A). From southern Vancouver Island to northern California, the oceanic Juan de Fuca plate is subducting beneath the North American plate within a system known as the Cascadia subduction zone. Although large earthquakes have taken place, such as the widely felt Nisqually earthquake near Seattle, Washington, on February 28, 2001, the Cascadia subduction zone is unusual because no large historical earthquake has occurred along the dipping plate boundary. (The Nisqually earthquake took place within the oceanic slab as it breaks apart during descent into the mantle). There is now compelling scientific evidence, however, that a so-called megathrust earthquake took place with an estimated magnitude of 9.0 along the plate boundary on January 26, 1700, before settlement of the region by Europeans. The timing of this earthquake is known from the oral traditions of the Cowichan people of Vancouver Island, from the study of tree rings in remnant stumps of drowned forests in estuaries along the Oregon and Washington coast, and from meticulous Japanese written records of a devastating tsunami. By using computer simulations, scientists have demonstrated that the tsunami must have originated near the west coast of North America.

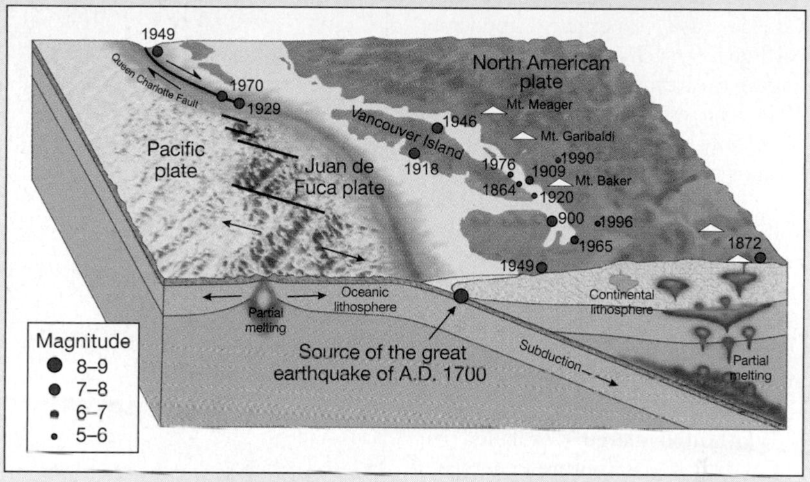

Figure 10.A Configuration of lithospheric plates and locations of significant earthquakes that have been recorded in British Columbia. (Modified from R. J. W. Turner, J. J. Clague, and B. J. Groulx, *Geoscape Vancouver, Living with Our Geological Landscape III*, Geological Survey of Canada, 1998, Open File 3309; reproduced with the permission of the Minister of Public Works and Government Services Canada, 2008, and courtesy of Natural Resources Canada)

The giant Cascadia earthquake of 1700 was not a unique event. Studies of shoreline sediments from Oregon to Vancouver Island reveal a cyclic pattern of sudden downdrop of the coast, followed by a slow rebound in elevation. In the last 6000 years, 13 such great earthquakes have been documented. We are presently in the midst of a long span of episodic stress buildup between megathrust earthquake events, producing coastal uplift and a squeezing of Vancouver Island that is measurable by using modern survey techniques. The next offshore megathrust earthquake will happen, perhaps hundreds of years in the future, and residents of southwest British Columbia and adjacent areas need to be ready for it.

The tectonically active west coast is not the only part of Canada that experiences earthquakes. Figure 10.B shows a map of earthquakes in Canada since 1980, catalogued as part of the National Earthquake Hazards Program of the Geological Survey of Canada. In western Canada, zones of earthquake activity are found in the Rocky Mountains of southwest Alberta and the Mackenzie Mountains of the Northwest Territories, where earthquakes of magnitudes up to 6.6 have been recorded. These bands of seismicity are thought to be the result of transmission of plate boundary stresses from convergent margins (Cascadia and Alaska), far into the North American plate.

Although very far from any active plate boundary, parts of eastern Canada also experience moderate earthquakes, such as the magnitude 5.9 Saguenay earthquake on November 25, 1988. The seismicity of eastern Canada is mainly concentrated along the Ottawa and St. Lawrence River valleys, and in the Appalachians of Quebec and New Brunswick. Like intraplate earthquakes in the United States, including the New Madrid earthquake sequence in 1811–1812, the cause of these earthquakes is not well understood. The zones of seismicity appear to be associated with the locations of ancient rifted margins or failed rift zones, which may rupture (reactivate) in response to the slow movement of North America away from the spreading mid-Atlantic ridge.

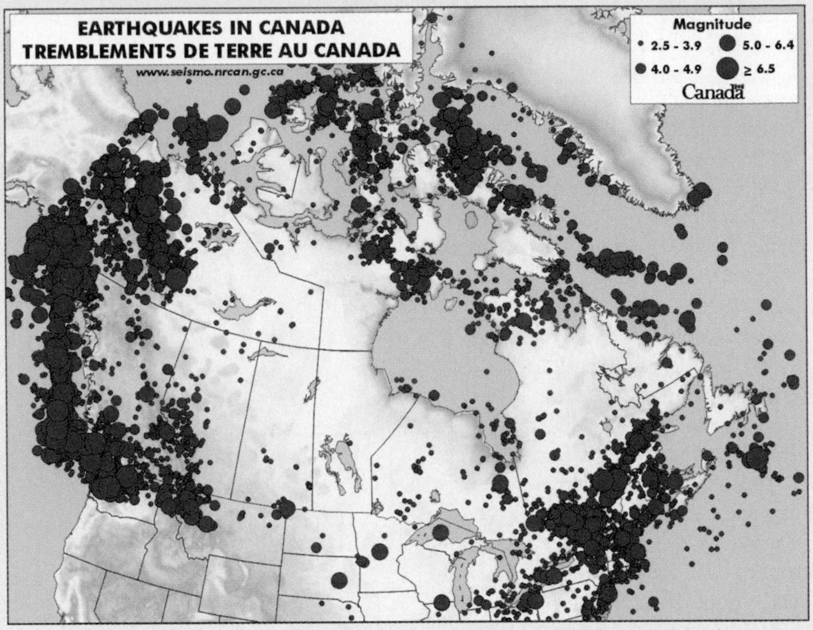

◆ **Figure 10.B** The distribution and magnitudes of earthquakes in Canada since 1980. (Reproduced with the permission of the Minister of Public Works and Government Services Canada, 2008, and courtesy of Natural Resources Canada)

*David Eaton is a professor in the Department of Earth Sciences at the University of Calgary.

MEASURING THE SIZE OF EARTHQUAKES

Historically, seismologists have employed a variety of methods to obtain two fundamentally different measures that describe the size of an earthquake: intensity and magnitude. The first to be used was **intensity**—a measure of the degree of earthquake shaking at a given locale based on the amount of damage. With the development of seismographs, it was possible to obtain a quantitative measure of an earthquake based on seismic records rather than uncertain personal estimates of damage. The measurement that was developed, called **magnitude**, relies on calculations that use data provided by seismic records (and other techniques) to estimate the amount of energy released at the source of the earthquake.

As it turns out, both intensity and magnitude provide useful, although quite different, information about earthquake strength. Consequently, both measures are still used to describe the relative sizes of earthquakes.

Intensity Scales

Until a little more than a century ago, historical records provided the only accounts of the severity of earthquake shaking and destruction. The use of these descriptions—which were compiled without any established standards for reporting—made accurate comparisons of earthquake sizes difficult, at best. To standardize the study of earthquake severity, early earthquake investigators developed various intensity scales that considered damage done to buildings, as well as individual descriptions of the event, and secondary effects—landslides and the extent of ground rupture. By 1902, Giuseppe Mercalli had developed a relatively reliable intensity scale, which in a modified form is still used today. The **Modified Mercalli Intensity Scale** (Table 10.1) was developed by using California buildings as its standard, but it is appropriate for use throughout most of the United States and Canada to estimate the strength of an earthquake (see Figure 10.12). For example, if some well-built wooden structures and most masonry buildings are destroyed by an earthquake, a region would be assigned an intensity of X on the Mercalli scale (Table 10.1).

Despite their usefulness in providing seismologists with a tool to compare earthquake severity, particularly in regions without seismographs, intensity scales have severe drawbacks. In particular, intensity scales are based on effects of earthquakes (largely destruction) that depend not only on the severity of

TABLE 10.1 **Modified Mercalli Intensity Scale**

I	Not felt except by a very few under especially favourable circumstances.
II	Felt by a few persons at rest, especially on upper floors of buildings.
III	Felt quite noticeably indoors, especially on upper floors of buildings.
IV	During the day, felt indoors by many, outdoors by few. Sensation like heavy truck striking building.
V	Felt by most people, many awakened. Disturbances of trees, poles, and other tall objects sometimes noticed.
VI	Felt by all; many frightened and run outdoors. Some heavy furniture moved; few instances of fallen plaster or damaged chimneys. Damage slight.
VII	Everybody runs outdoors. Damage negligible in buildings of good design and construction; slight to moderate in well-built ordinary structures; considerable in poorly built or badly designed structures.
VIII	Damage slight in specially designed structures; considerable in ordinary substantial buildings with partial collapse; great in poorly built structures (fall of chimneys, factory stacks, columns, monuments, walls).
IX	Damage considerable in specially designed structures. Buildings shifted off foundations. Ground cracked conspicuously.
X	Some well-built wooden structures destroyed. Most masonry and frame structures destroyed. Ground badly cracked.
XI	Few, if any (masonry) structures remain standing. Bridges destroyed. Broad fissures in ground.
XII	Waves seen on ground surfaces. Objects thrown upward into air. Damage total.

ground shaking but also on external factors, such as population density, building design, and the nature of surface materials. In British Columbia, for example, the 1946 Vancouver Island earthquake caused more property damage (Figure 10.12B) than the much stronger earthquake that occurred west of the Queen Charlotte Islands in 1949, largely because it affected a more densely populated area.

Magnitude Scales

To compare earthquakes across the globe, a measure was needed that does not rely on parameters that vary considerably from one part of the world to another, such as types of construction. As a consequence, the Richter scale was developed.

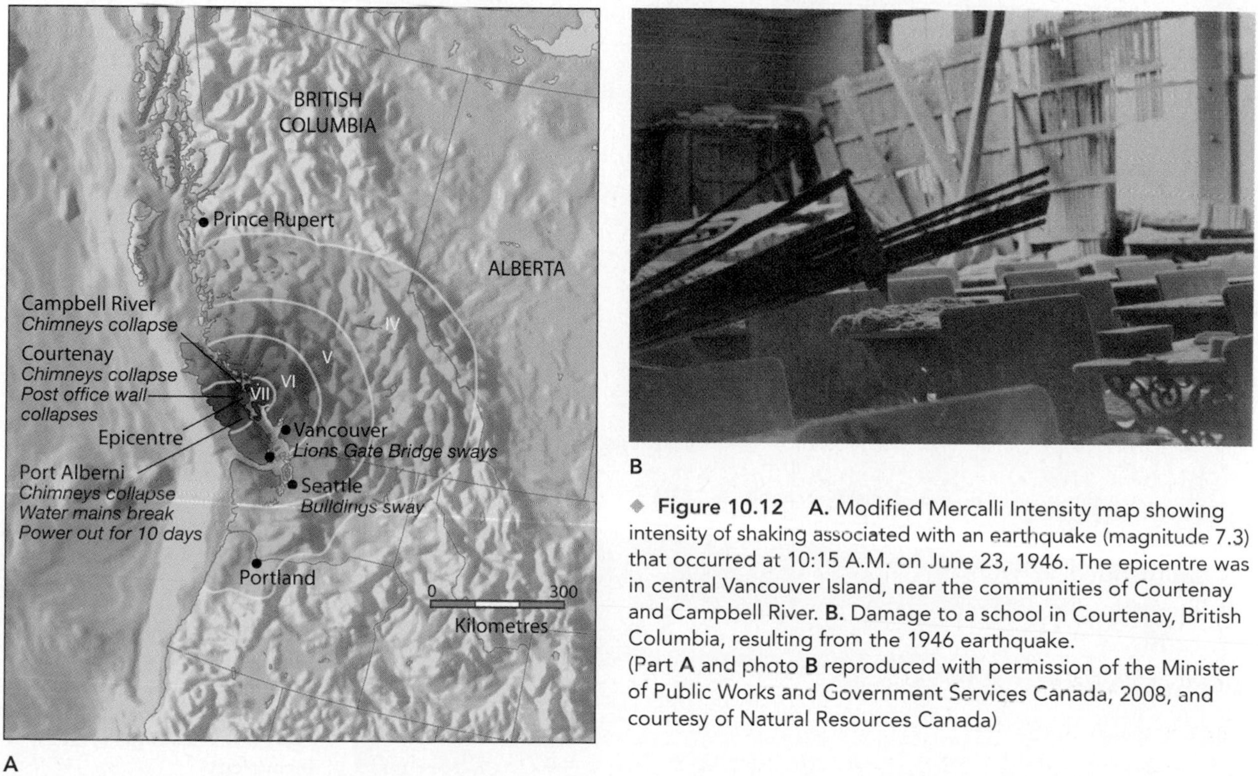

◆ **Figure 10.12** **A.** Modified Mercalli Intensity map showing intensity of shaking associated with an earthquake (magnitude 7.3) that occurred at 10:15 A.M. on June 23, 1946. The epicentre was in central Vancouver Island, near the communities of Courtenay and Campbell River. **B.** Damage to a school in Courtenay, British Columbia, resulting from the 1946 earthquake.
(Part **A** and photo **B** reproduced with permission of the Minister of Public Works and Government Services Canada, 2008, and courtesy of Natural Resources Canada)

Richter Magnitude In 1935 Charles Richter of the California Institute of Technology developed the first magnitude scale by using seismic records to estimate the relative sizes of earthquakes. As shown in Figure 10.13, the **Richter scale** is based on the amplitude of the largest seismic wave (P, S, or surface wave) recorded on a seismogram. Because seismic waves weaken as the distance between the earthquake epicentre and the seismograph increases (in a manner similar to light), Richter developed a method that accounted for the decrease in wave amplitude with increased distance. Theoretically, as long as the same, or equivalent, instruments were used, monitoring stations at various locations would obtain the same Richter magnitude for every recorded earthquake (Richter selected the Wood-Anderson seismograph as the standard recording device). In practice, however, different recording stations often obtained slightly different Richter magnitudes for the same earthquake—a consequence of the variations in rock types through which the waves travelled.

Although the Richter scale has no upper limit, the largest magnitude recorded on a Wood-Anderson seismograph was 8.9. These great shocks released approximately 10^{26} ergs of energy—roughly equivalent to the detonation of 1 billion tonnes of TNT. Conversely, earthquakes with a Richter magnitude of less than 2.0 are not felt by humans. With the development of more sensitive instruments, tremors of a magnitude of –2 were recorded.

Earthquakes vary enormously in strength, and great earthquakes produce wave amplitudes that are thousands of times larger than those generated by weak tremors. To accommodate this wide variation, Richter used a *logarithmic scale* to express magnitude, where a *tenfold* increase in wave amplitude corresponds to an increase of 1 on the magnitude scale. Thus, the amount of ground shaking for a magnitude 5 earthquake is 10 times greater than that produced by a magnitude 4 earthquake.

In addition, each unit of Richter magnitude equates to roughly a *32-fold energy increase*. Thus, an earthquake with a magnitude of 6.5 releases 32 times as much energy as one with a magnitude of 5.5, and roughly 1000 times as much energy as one with a magnitude of 4.5 (Table 10.2). A major earthquake with a magnitude of 8.5 releases millions of times as much energy as the smallest earthquakes felt by humans.

Other Magnitude Scales Richter's original goal was modest in that he only attempted to rank the earth-

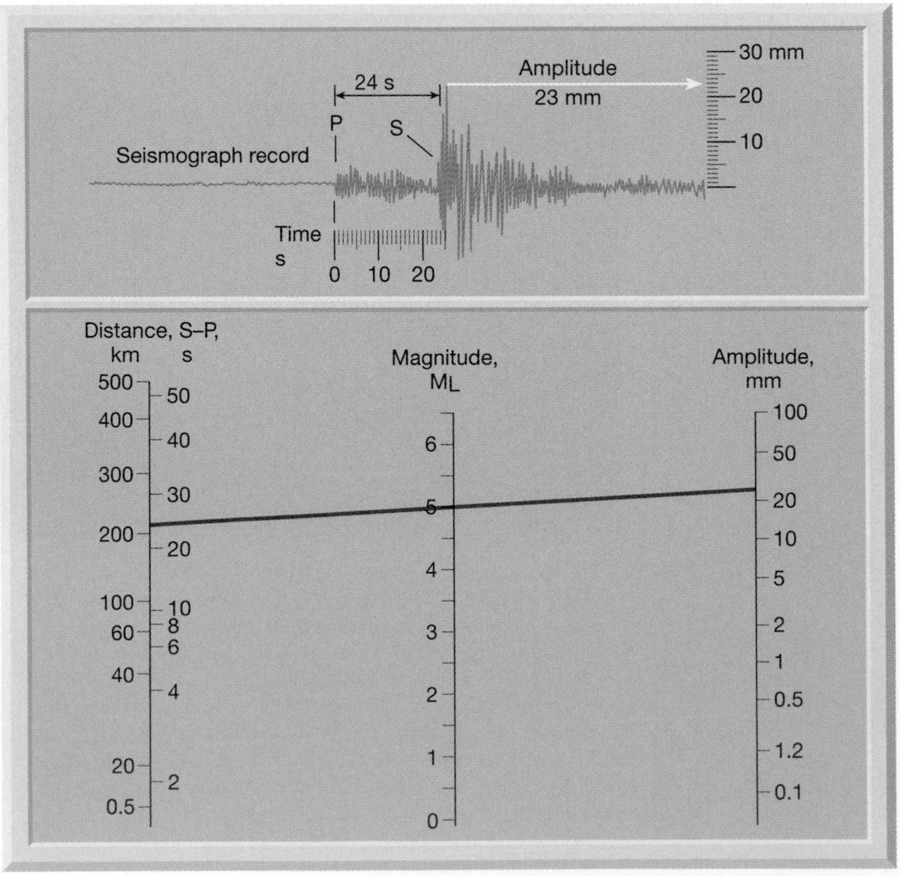

◆ **Figure 10.13** Illustration showing how the Richter magnitude of an earthquake can be determined graphically by using a seismograph record from a Wood-Anderson instrument. First, measure the height (amplitude) of the largest wave on the seismogram (23 millimetres) and then the distance to the focus by using the time interval between S and P waves (24 seconds). Next, draw a line between the distance scale (left) and the wave amplitude scale (right). By doing this, you obtain the Richter magnitude (M_L) of 5. (Data from California Institute of Technology)

TABLE 10.2 **Earthquake Magnitude and Energy Equivalence**

Earthquake Magnitude	Energy Released (millions of ergs)	Approximate Energy Equivalence
0	630,000	0.5 kilograms of explosives
1	20,000,000	
2	630,000,000	Energy of lightning bolt
3	20,000,000,000	
4	630,000,000,000	450 kilograms of explosives
5	20,000,000,000,000	
6	630,000,000,000,000	1946 Bikini atomic bomb test
		1994 Northridge earthquake
7	20,000,000,000,000,000	1989 Loma Prieta earthquake
8	630,000,000,000,000,000	1906 San Francisco earthquake
		1980 Eruption of Mount St. Helens
9	20,000,000,000,000,000,000	1964 Alaskan earthquake
		1960 Chilean earthquake
10	630,000,000,000,000,000,000	Annual U.S. energy consumption

Source: U.S. Geological Survey.
Note: For each unit increase in magnitude, the energy released increases 31.6 times.

quakes of southern California (shallow-focus earthquakes) into groups of large, medium, and small magnitude. Hence, Richter magnitude was designed to study nearby (or local) earthquakes and is denoted by the symbol (M_L)—where M is for *magnitude* and L is for *local*.

The convenience of describing the size of an earthquake by a single number that could be calculated quickly from seismograms makes the Richter scale a powerful tool. Further, unlike intensity scales that could only be applied to populated areas of the globe, Richter magnitudes could be assigned to earthquakes in more remote regions and even to events that occurred in the ocean basins. As a result, the method devised by Richter was adapted to a number of different seismographs located throughout the world. In time, seismologists modified Richter's work and developed new magnitude scales. These modified scales were initially calibrated to be equivalent to the Richter scale and have contributed to efforts to measure the size of earthquakes. However, despite their usefulness, none of these scales is adequate for describing very large earthquakes.

Moment Magnitude In recent years seismologists have been employing a more precise measure called **moment magnitude** (M_W), which is derived from the amount of displacement that occurs along a fault zone rather than by measuring the ground motion at some distant point. Moment magnitude is calculated by using a combination of factors that include the average amount of displacement along the fault, the area of the rupture surface, and the shear strength of the faulted rock—a measure of how much strain energy a rock can store before it suddenly slips and releases this energy in the form of an earthquake (and heat). For example, the energy involved in a 3-metre displacement of a rock body along a rupture a few hundred kilometres long would be much larger than that produced by a 1-metre displacement along a 10-kilometre-long rupture (assuming comparable rupture depths).

The moment magnitude can also be readily calculated from seismograms by examining very long period seismic waves. The values obtained have been calibrated so that small- and moderate-sized earthquakes have moment magnitudes that are roughly equivalent to Richter magnitudes. However, moment magnitudes are much better for describing very large earthquakes. For example, on the moment magnitude scale, the 1906 San Francisco earthquake, which had a surface-wave magnitude of 8.3, would be demoted to 7.9 on the moment magnitude scale, whereas the 1964 Alaskan earthquake with an 8.3 Richter magnitude would be increased to 9.2. The strongest earthquake on record is the 1960 Chilean earthquake with a moment magnitude of 9.5.

Moment magnitude has gained wide acceptance among seismologists and engineers because (1) it is the only magnitude scale that estimates adequately the size of very large earthquakes; (2) it is a measure established from the size of the rupture surface and the amount of displacement; thus, it better reflects the total energy released during an earthquake; and (3) it can be verified by two independent methods: field studies that are based on measurements of fault displacement and seismic methods by using long-period waves.

EARTHQUAKE DESTRUCTION

Many factors determine the degree of destruction that will accompany an earthquake. The most obvious is the magnitude of the earthquake and its proximity to a populated area. Fortunately, most earthquakes are small and occur in remote regions. However, about 20 major earthquakes are reported annually, one or two of which can be catastrophic.

Destruction from Seismic Vibrations

The 1964 Alaskan earthquake provided geologists with new insights into the role of ground shaking as a destructive force. As the energy released by an earthquake travels along Earth's surface, it causes the ground to vibrate in a complex manner by moving up and down as well as from side to side. The amount of structural damage attributable to the vibrations depends on several factors, including (1) the intensity of the vibrations, (2) the duration of the vibrations, (3) the nature of the material on which the structure rests, and (4) the design of the structure.

All of the multistorey structures in Anchorage were damaged by the vibrations. The more flexible wood-frame residential buildings fared best. However, many homes were destroyed when the ground failed. A striking example of how construction variations affect earthquake damage is shown in Figure 10.14. You can see that the steel-frame building on the left withstood the vibrations, whereas the poorly designed J. C. Penney building was badly damaged. Engineers have learned that unreinforced masonry buildings are the most serious safety threat in earthquakes.

Most large structures in Anchorage were damaged, even though they were built according to the earthquake building standards of the day. Perhaps some of that destruction can be attributed to the unusually long duration of this earthquake. Most quakes consist of tremors that last less than a minute. The Alaska quake was a notable exception: it reverberated for three to four minutes.

Amplification of Seismic Waves Although the region within 20 to 50 kilometres of the epicentre will experience about the same intensity of ground shaking, the destruction varies considerably within this area. This difference is mainly attributable to the nature of the ground on which the structures are built. Soft sediments, for example, generally amplify the vibrations more than solid bedrock. Thus, the buildings located in Anchorage, which were situated on unconsolidated sediments, experienced heavy structural damage. By contrast, most of the nearby town of Whittier, although much closer to the epicentre, rests on a firm foundation of granite and hence suffered much less damage. However, Whittier was damaged by a *tsunami* (described in the next section).

An earthquake that occurred in Mexico in 1985 gave seismologists and engineers a vivid reminder of what had been learned from the 1964 Alaskan earthquake. The Mexican coast, where the earthquake was centred, experienced unusually mild tremors despite the strength of the quake. As expected, the seismic waves became progressively weaker with increasing distance from the epicentre. However, in the central section of Mexico City, nearly 400 kilometres from

◆ **Figure 10.14** Damage caused to the five-storey J. C. Penney Co. building, Anchorage, Alaska. Very little structural damage was incurred by the adjacent building.
(Courtesy of NOAA/Seattle)

the source, the vibrations intensified to five times that experienced in outlying districts. Much of this amplified ground motion can be attributed to soft sediments, remnants of an ancient lake bed, that underlie portions of the city. The lake bed sediments were shaken by the earthquake, causing buildings to also shake and collapse (Figure 10.15).

Liquefaction In areas where unconsolidated materials are saturated with water, earthquake vibrations can generate a phenomenon known as **liquefaction** (*liqueo* = to be fluid, *facio* = to make). Under these conditions, what had been a stable soil turns into a mobile fluid that is not capable of supporting buildings or other structures (Figure 10.15). As a result, underground objects, such as storage tanks and sewer lines, can literally float to the surface of their newly liquefied environment. Buildings and other structures can settle and collapse. During the 1989 Loma Prieta earthquake in California, foundations failed and geysers of sand and water shot from the ground, indicating that liquefaction had occurred (Figure 10.16).

Tsunami

Most deaths associated with the 1964 Alaskan quake were caused by a **tsunami*** (*tsu* = harbour, *nami* = waves) or **seismic sea wave**. Before the catastrophic event that occurred on December 26, 2004 (Box 10.2), these destructive waves were commonly called *tidal waves* by the media. However, that name is incorrect; the waves are generated by earthquakes, not the tidal effect of the Moon or Sun.

Most tsunami result from vertical displacement along a fault located on the ocean floor (Figure 10.17), or some other severe undersea disturbance, such as a large volcanic eruption or submarine landslide. Once created, a tsunami resembles the ripples formed when a pebble is dropped into a pond. In contrast to ripples, tsunami advance across the ocean at amazing speeds: between 500 and 950 kilometres per hour. Despite this striking characteristic, a tsunami in the open ocean can pass undetected because its height is usually less than 1 metre and the distance between wave crests is great, ranging from 100 to 700 kilometres. However, on entering shallower coastal waters, these destructive waves are slowed down and the water begins to pile up to heights that occasionally exceed 30 metres (Figure 10.17). As the crest of a tsunami approaches the shore, it appears as a rapid rise in sea level, with

*Seismic sea waves were given the name *tsunami* by the Japanese, who have suffered a great deal from them. The term *tsunami* is now used worldwide.

◆ **Figure 10.15** Effects of liquefaction. This tilted building rests on unconsolidated sediment that behaved like quicksand during the 1985 Mexican earthquake.
(Photo by James L. Beck)

◆ **Figure 10.16** These "mud volcanoes" were produced by the Loma Prieta earthquake of 1989 in California. They formed when fountains of sand and water shot from the ground, an indication that liquefaction had occurred.
(Photo by Richard Hilton, courtesy of Dennis Fox)

BOX 10.2

Understanding Earth
2004 Boxing Day Tsunami

On December 26, 2004, the second-largest earthquake ever recorded by seismographs (9.3 M_W) occurred 150 kilometres off the northwest coast of Sumatra (Figure 10.C). The resulting tsunami damaged 11 countries around the Indian Ocean and Andaman Sea, claimed more than 200,000 human lives, and left more than 1 million people homeless (Figure 10.D). At the epicentre, located near the Sunda Trench, the ocean floor was thrust up to 5 metres and generated a wave up to 50 metres high. This wall of water smashed into the coasts of the Seychelles Islands and Somalia, some 2000 kilometres away, and was even recorded by tide gauges in California and New Jersey. The south and east coasts of Sri Lanka and India were hit hard as their shorelines suddenly pulled back

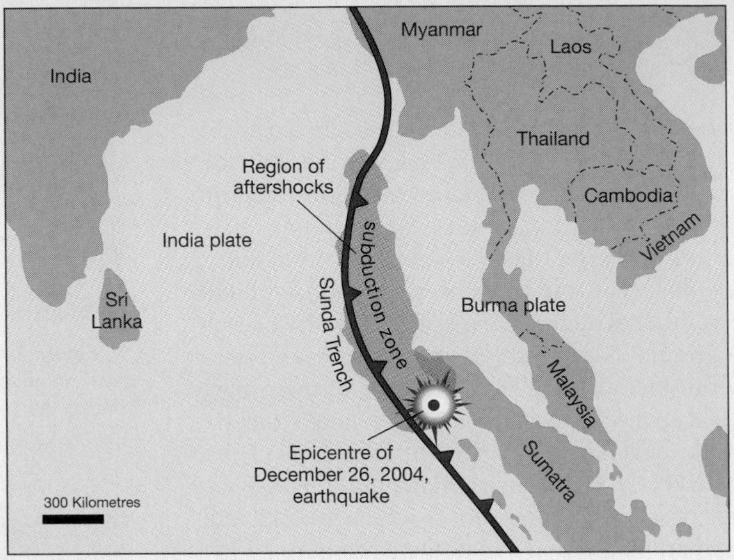

◆ **Figure 10.C** Map of eastern Indian Ocean showing the Sunda Trench, plate boundaries, and the epicentre of the 2004 earthquake.
(Courtesy of Tricouni Press Ltd.)

◆ **Figure 10.D** The village of Banda Aceh on the north shore of Sumatra before (**A**) and after (**B**) being hit by the 2004 tsunami.
(Photo by National Oceanic and Atmospheric Administration)

◆ **Figure 10.E** Aerial view of Kalutara (south coast of Sri Lanka) before (**A**) and during (**B**) shoreline withdrawal just before the tsunami surged inland.
(Photos courtesy of Digital Globe/Getty Images)

(Figure 10.E), exposing a large swath of sea bed as the tsunami crested then surged its way 2 kilometres inland, destroying property and people.

The earthquake focus was approximately 10 kilometres beneath the seafloor, generated by slippage deep beyond the Sunda Trench where the Australian-Indian plate subducts under the Burma subplate, part of the Eurasian plate. The epicentre is located near the intersection of two plates (Eurasian and Australian-Indian) that has generated several major earthquakes and tsunami, including the 1941 tsunami that killed 5000 people along the east coast of India. Interactions between these plates were also responsible for major volcanic eruptions including Krakatoa, Tambora, and Toba. In spite of this record, countries were taken by surprise when the Boxing Day tsunami hit. This region lacked the tide gauges, wave sensors, regional tsunami warning system, and communications network that the Pacific region has (see Box 10.3). By the time the Pacific network became aware of the disaster, it was too late to warn the Indian region, which underscores the need for a similar warning network there. The first step was taken in December 2006 by deploying a DART II tsunami buoy station in the Indian Ocean to collect wave data.

a turbulent and chaotic surface. Tsunami can be very destructive (see Boxes 10.2 and 10.3). Canadian examples include the 1929 tsunami that killed 28 people and damaged 40 villages along the Burin Peninsula of southern Newfoundland and Labrador (Figure 10.18A), and 1964 tsunami (generated by the great Alaskan earthquake) that caused extensive damage to Port Alberni on Vancouver Island (Figure 10.18B). The Burin tsunami was triggered by a magnitude 7.2 earthquake (epicentre 250 kilometres south of Newfoundland and Labrador) that caused a turbidity current of 200 cubic kilometres to

BOX 10.3

People and the Environment
Tsunami Warning System

Tsunami traverse large stretches of ocean before their energy is fully dissipated. The tsunami generated by a 1960 Chilean earthquake, in addition to destroying villages along an 800-kilometre stretch of coastal South America, travelled 17,000 kilometres across the Pacific to Japan. Here, about 22 hours after the quake, considerable damage occurred in south coastal villages. For several days afterward, tidal gauges in Hilo, Hawaii, detected these diminishing waves as they reverberated like echoes about the Pacific.

In 1946 a large tsunami struck the Hawaiian Islands without warning. A wave more than 15 metres high left several coastal villages in shambles. This destruction motivated the National Oceanic and Atmospheric Administration to establish a tsunami warning system for coastal areas of the Pacific. From seismic observatories throughout the region, large earthquakes are reported to the Pacific Tsunami Warning Center at Ewa Beach (near Honolulu), Hawaii. Scientists at the center use tidal gauges to determine whether a tsunami has been formed. Within an hour a warning is issued. Although tsunami travel very rapidly, there is sufficient time to evacuate all but the region nearest the epicentre (Figure 10.F). For example, a tsunami generated near the Aleutian Islands would take 5 hours to reach Hawaii, and one generated near the coast of Chile would travel 15 hours before reaching Hawaii.

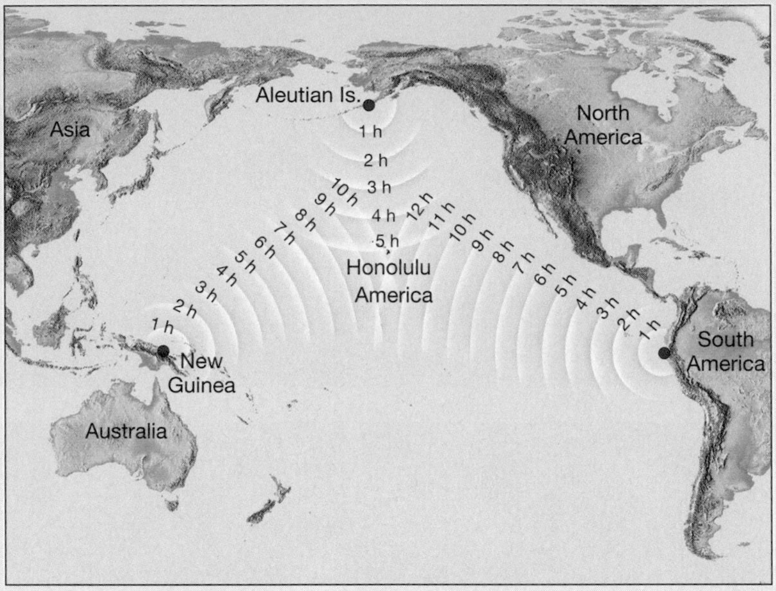

◆ **Figure 10.F** Tsunami travel times to Honolulu, Hawaii, from selected locations throughout the Pacific.
(Data from NOAA)

Fortunately, most earthquakes do not generate tsunami. On the average, only about 1.5 destructive tsunami are generated worldwide annually. Of these, only about 1 every 10 years is catastrophic.

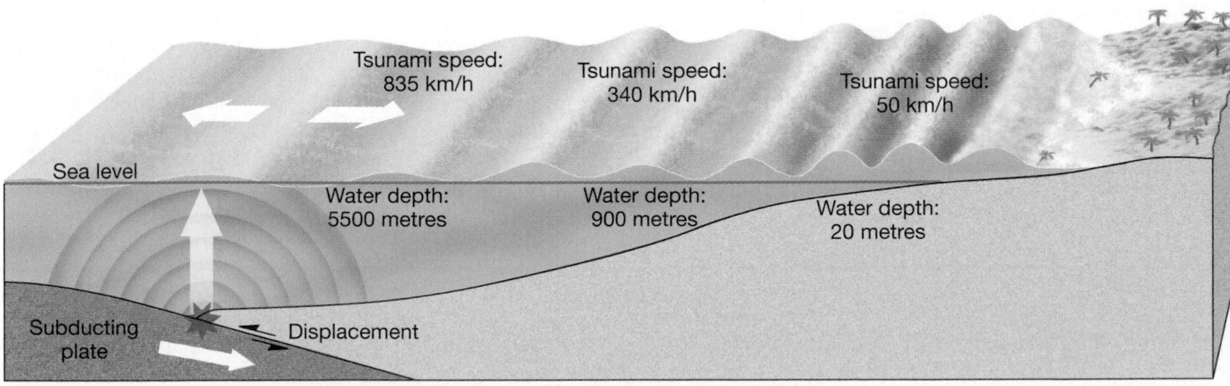

◆ **Figure 10.17** Schematic drawing of a tsunami generated by displacement of the ocean floor. The speed of a wave correlates with ocean depth. As shown, waves moving in deep water advance at speeds in excess of 800 kilometres per hour. Speed gradually slows to 50 kilometres per hour at depths of 20 metres. Decreasing depth slows the movement of the wave. As waves slow in shallow water, they grow in height until they topple and rush onto shore with tremendous force. The size and spacing of these swells are not to scale.

A

B

◆ **Figure 10.18** Examples of destruction by tsunami in Canada. **A.** Debris from houses, wharfs, boats, and fishing gear along the shore of the Burin Peninsula, Newfoundland and Labrador, following the tsunami generated by the Grand Banks earthquake of 1929. **B.** Damage to buildings associated with the tsunami that hit Port Alberni, British Columbia, in 1964. (Photo **A** courtesy of the Rooms Provincial Archives, A1–141/Parsons & Sons; photo **B** courtesy of UBC Library, Rare Books & Special Collections)

rush down the continental slope of the Grand Banks while rupturing 12 transatlantic cables and generating the tsunami. The wave rose to 27 metres and also reached the coasts of South Carolina and Portugal.

Usually, the first warning of an approaching tsunami is a relatively rapid withdrawal of water from beaches (see Box 10.2). Coastal residents have learned to heed this warning and move to higher ground because about 5 to 30 minutes later, the retreat of water is followed by a surge capable of extending hundreds of metres inland. In a successive fashion, each surge is followed by rapid oceanward retreat of the water.

Landslides and Ground Subsidence

In the 1964 Alaskan earthquake, the greatest damage to structures was from landslides and ground subsidence triggered by the vibrations. At Valdez and Seward, the violent shaking caused deltaic materials to experience liquefaction; the subsequent slumping carried both waterfronts away. Because of the threat of recurrence, the entire town of Valdez was relocated about 7 kilometres away on more stable ground. In Valdez, 31 people on a dock died when it slid into the sea.

Most of the damage in the city of Anchorage was also attributed to landslides. Many homes were destroyed in Turnagain Heights when a layer of clay lost its strength and more than 80 hectares of land slid toward the ocean (Figure 10.19). A portion of this spectacular landslide was left in its natural condition as a reminder of this destructive event. The site was appropriately named Earthquake Park. Downtown Anchorage was also disrupted as sections of the main business district dropped by as much as 3 metres.

Fire

The famous 1906 earthquake in San Francisco reminds us of the formidable threat of fire. The central city contained mostly large older wooden structures and brick buildings. Although many non-reinforced brick buildings were extensively damaged by vibrations, the greatest destruction was caused by fires when gas and electrical lines were severed. The

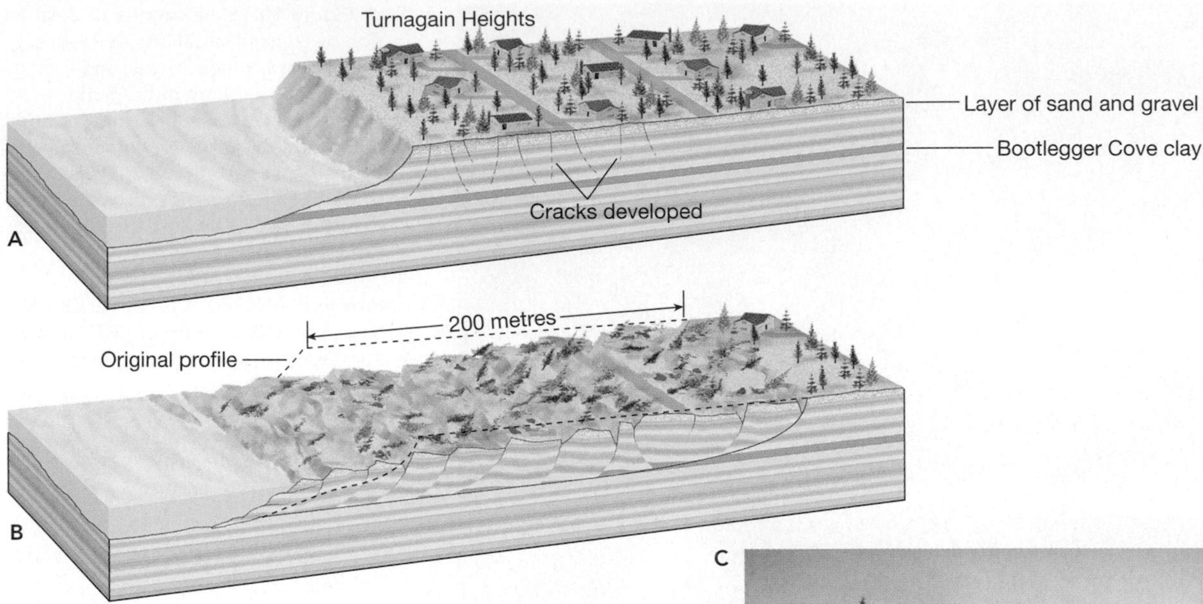

C

◆ **Figure 10.19** Turnagain Heights slide caused by the 1964 Alaskan earthquake. **A.** Vibrations from the earthquake caused cracks to appear near the edge of the bluff. **B.** Within seconds blocks of land began to slide toward the sea on a weak layer of clay. In less than five minutes, as much as 200 metres of the Turnagain Heights bluff area had been destroyed. **C.** Photo of a small portion of the Turnagain Heights slide.
(Photo **C** courtesy of U.S. Geological Survey)

fires raged out of control for three days and devastated more than 500 blocks of the city. The problem was compounded by the initial ground shaking, which broke the city's water lines into hundreds of unconnected pieces.

The fire was finally contained when buildings were dynamited along a wide boulevard to provide a firebreak, the same strategy used in fighting a forest fire. Although only a few deaths were attributed to the San Francisco fire, such is not always the case. A 1923 earthquake in Japan triggered an estimated 250 fires, which devastated the city of Yokohama and destroyed more than half the homes in Tokyo. More than 100,000 deaths were attributed to the fires, which were driven by unusually high winds.

CAN EARTHQUAKES BE PREDICTED?

The earthquake that shook Northridge, California, on January 17, 1994, was brief (about 40 seconds) and only of moderate rating (M_W 6.7), but it killed 57 people and caused about US$40 billion in damage. The amount of devastation caused by the earthquake was largely due to the fact that the area it affected was densely populated and highly developed. Seismologists warn that earthquakes of comparable or greater strength will occur along the San Andreas Fault system, which cuts a 1300-kilometre path through the state. The obvious question is, can earthquakes be predicted?

Short-Range Predictions

The goal of short-range earthquake prediction is to provide a warning of the location and magnitude of a large earthquake within a narrow time frame. We currently do not have an *absolutely* reliable method for making short-range earthquake predictions. However, substantial efforts to achieve this objective are being put forth in Japan, the United States, China, and Russia—countries where earthquake risks are high. This research has concentrated on monitoring possible *precursors*—phenomena that precede and thus provide a warning of a forthcoming earthquake. In California, for example, seismologists are measuring uplift, subsidence, and strain in the rocks near active faults. Some Japanese scientists are studying anomalous animal behaviour that may precede a quake. Other researchers are monitoring changes in groundwater levels, while still others are trying to predict earthquakes based on changes in the electrical conductivity of rocks.

Among the most ambitious earthquake experiments is one being conducted along a segment of the San Andreas Fault near the town of Parkfield in central California. Here, earthquakes of moderate intensity have occurred on a regular basis about once every 22 years since 1857. The most recent rupture was a magnitude 5.6 quake that occurred in 1966. With the next event already significantly overdue, the U.S. Geological Survey has established an elaborate monitoring network. Included are creepmeters, tiltmeters, and borehole strain meters that are used to measure the accumulation and release of strain. Seventy seismographs of various designs have been installed to record foreshocks and the main event. Finally, a network of distance-measuring devices that employ lasers measures movement across the fault (Figure 10.20). The object is to identify ground movements that may precede a sizeable rupture.

Long-Range Forecasts

In contrast to short-range predictions, which aim to predict earthquakes within hours or at most days, long-range forecasts give the probability of a certain magnitude earthquake occurring on a time scale of 30 to 100 years or more. Long-range forecasts are based on the premise that earthquakes are repetitive or cyclic, like the weather. In other words, as soon as one earthquake is over, the continuing motions of Earth's plates begin to build strain in the rocks again until they fail once more. This has led seismologists to study historical records of earthquakes, looking for any discernible patterns so that the probability of recurrence might be established.

With this concept in mind, a group of seismologists plotted the distribution of rupture zones associated with great earthquakes that have occurred in the seismically active regions of the Pacific Basin. The maps revealed that individual rupture zones tended to occur adjacent to one another without appreciable overlap, thereby tracing out a plate boundary. Recall that most earthquakes are generated along plate boundaries by the relative motion of large lithospheric blocks. Because plates are in continual motion, the researchers predicted that over one or two centuries, major earthquakes would occur along each segment of the Pacific plate boundary.

When the researchers studied historical records, they discovered that some zones had not produced a great earthquake in more than a century. These quiet zones, called **seismic gaps**, were identified as probable sites for major earthquakes in the next few decades (Figure 10.21). In the 25 years since the original studies were conducted, some of these gaps have ruptured. Included in this group is the

◆ **Figure 10.20** Lasers used to measure movement along the San Andreas Fault.
(Photo by John K. Nakata/U.S. Geological Survey)

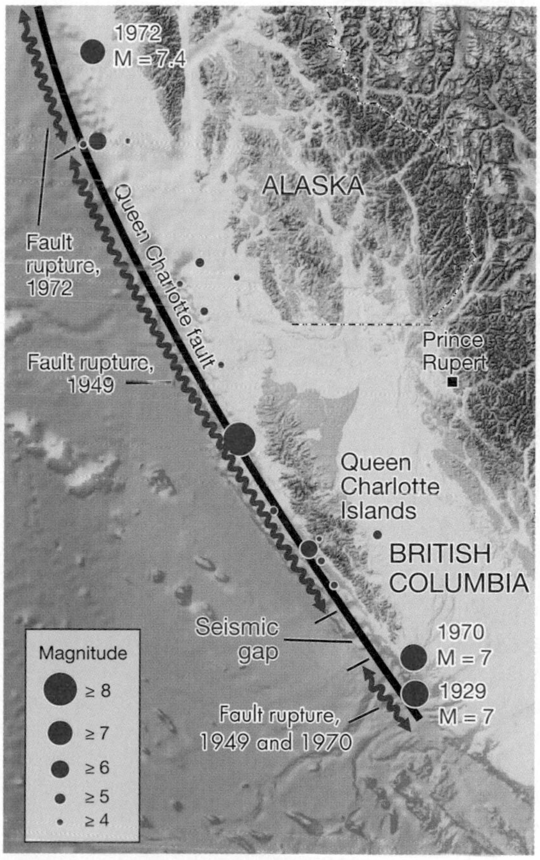

◆ **Figure 10.21** Map showing epicentres of large shallow earthquakes recorded from 1929 to 1972 along the northwest coast of British Columbia and the fault ruptures with which they were associated. The seismic gap located immediately west of the southern Queen Charlotte Islands denotes the most likely location for the next large earthquakes along the Queen Charlotte Fault.
(Courtesy of Tricouni Press Ltd.)

zone that produced the earthquake that devastated portions of Mexico City in September 1985.

Another method of long-term forecasting, known as *paleoseismology* (*palaios* = ancient, *seismos* = shake, *ology* = the study of), has been implemented. One technique involves studying layered deposits that were offset by prehistoric seismic disturbances. Researchers recently discovered strong evidence that very powerful earthquakes (magnitude of 8 or larger) have repeatedly struck the Pacific Northwest over the past several thousand years. The most recent event occurred about 300 years ago. As a result of these findings, public officials have taken steps to strengthen some of the region's existing dams, bridges, and water systems.

In summary, it appears that the best prospects for making useful earthquake predictions involve forecasting magnitudes and locations on time scales of years or perhaps even decades. These forecasts are important because they provide information used to develop earthquake building standards and to assist in land-use planning.

PROBING EARTH'S INTERIOR

GEODe EARTH Earth's Interior
↳ Earth's Layered Structure

Earth's interior lies just beneath us. However, direct access to it remains very limited. Wells drilled into the crust in search of oil, gas, and other natural resources have generally been confined to the upper 7 kilometres—only a small fraction of Earth's 6370-kilometre radius. Even the Kola Well, a super-deep research well located in a remote northern outpost of Russia, has penetrated to a depth of only 12.3 kilometres. Although volcanic activity is considered a window into Earth's interior because materials are brought up from below, it allows a glimpse of only the outer 200 kilometres of our planet.

Fortunately, geologists have learned a great deal about Earth's composition and structure through computer modelling, high-pressure laboratory experiments, and samples of the solar system (meteorites) that collide with Earth. In addition, many clues to the physical conditions inside our planet have been acquired through the study of seismic waves generated by earthquakes, nuclear explosions, and weaker, human-produced vibrations. As seismic waves pass through Earth, they carry information to the surface about the materials through which they were transmitted. Hence, when carefully analyzed, seismic records provide an image of materials below the surface. The Canadian LITHOPROBE project, for example, has yielded exciting insights on the deep lithosphere from the processing of seismic data (see Box 10.4).

Much of our knowledge of Earth's interior comes from the study of earthquake waves that penetrate Earth and emerge at some distant point.

BOX 10.4

Canadian Profile

LITHOPROBE: Probing the Depths of Canada

David Eaton*

Unlike the oceanic crust, continents preserve a record of Earth's early history, including how ancient mountains formed and how the continents grew and developed over time. Geoscientists are faced with a daunting challenge, however: to reconstruct this tectonic record from fragmentary evidence provided by rocks exposed at the surface. Canada's LITHOPROBE project, which commenced in 1984, is a bold 25-year multi-institutional endeavour to unravel the tectonic evolution of North America with a focus on the critical third dimension of geology: depth. With collaboration by more than 900 scientists working in academia, government agencies, and the petroleum and mining industries, LITHOPROBE has involved a significant segment of Canada's Earth science community in a coordinated research effort. The research program was divided into a series of transects that collectively span the evolution of the North American continent in time (about 4 billion years) and space.

To achieve adequate resolution of geologic features down to the base of the crust (approximately 40 kilometres) and the upper mantle, LITHOPROBE research has been spearheaded by multichannel seismic-reflection (MSR) profiling. Adapted from the petroleum industry, where it is used extensively for exploration of the top 10 kilometres of sedimentary basins, this technique makes use of P waves, usually generated mechanically by using vibroseis trucks, to record faint echoes produced at buried geologic contacts, faults, and shear zones. Much like medical imaging techniques, the seismic data are processed by computer to enhance the seismic reflections, which produces cross-sectional images that can be compared with geologic data to reveal the underlying anatomy of the lithosphere. Specialists in all areas of geology, geophysics, and geochemistry have collaborated on major geotectonic problems by using techniques that include basic mapping, precise geochronology, electromagnetic studies, seismic refraction, and paleomagnetism.

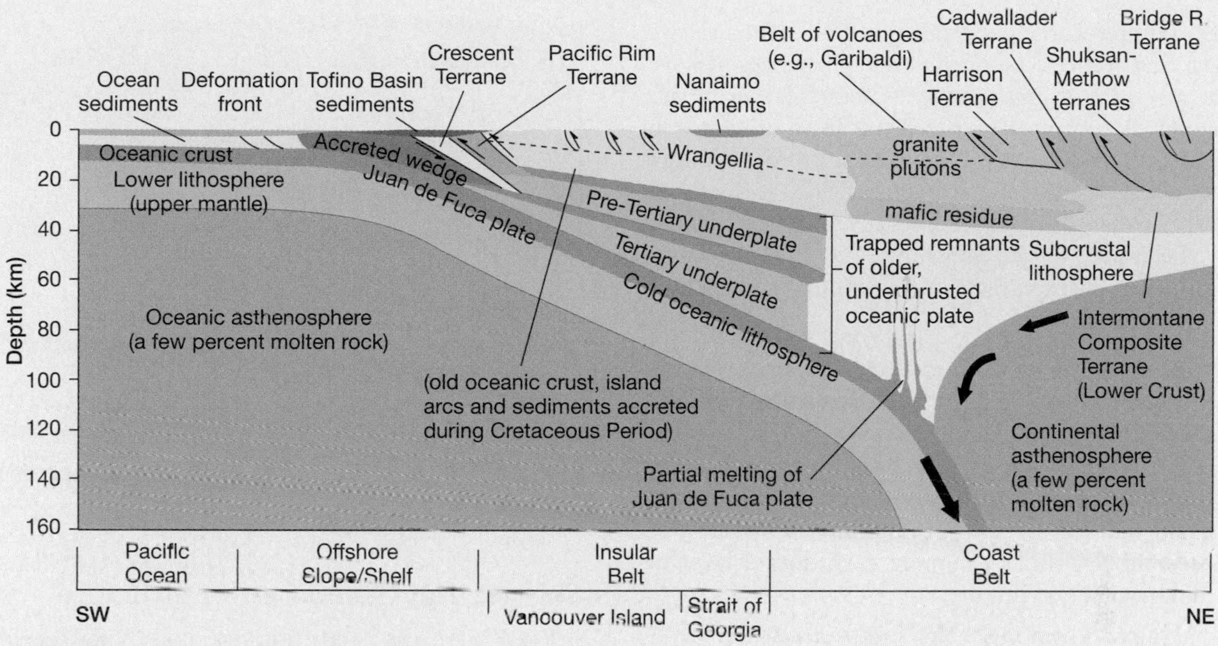

◆ **Figure 10.G** Part of the Canadian LITHOPROBE project involved the study of the lithospheric structure of western Canada. Among the exciting discoveries was the detection of lithospheric fragments (underplates) that remain lodged under the west coast region and have contributed to the growth of mountain roots. (Modified from image courtesy of R. M. Clowes)

LITHOPROBE's pilot study on Vancouver Island demonstrated that MSR profiling methods can be used to map layers near the top of the descending Juan de Fuca slab (Figure 10.G). It showed slabs of lithosphere welded to the continental lithosphere of western British Columbia as *underplates*. Results from this modern subduction system (Cascadia) have provided a template for understanding ancient subduction systems. Furthermore, subduction "scars" have been detected in the mantle beneath Archean rocks of the Superior craton in Québec and the Proterozoic Great Bear Arc in the Northwest Territories. These results establish that the subduction occurred in some areas in the late Archean and support the concept that subducted slabs can be accreted to the base of continental plates as part of the process of formation of deep lithospheric roots.

LITHOPROBE's main research focused on ancient shield and platform regions where North America is known to have grown via a series of mountain-building events. LITHOPROBE profiles have allowed geoscientists to trace structural contacts down to the base of the crust (Moho). This work has led to the discovery of previously unrecognized mountain belts that lie buried beneath undeformed sedimentary rocks.

For further information visit **www.lithoprobe.ca.**

---

*David Eaton is a professor in the Department of Earth Sciences at the University of Calgary.

The technique involves accurately measuring the time required for P and S waves to travel from an earthquake or nuclear explosion to a seismic station. Because the time required for P and S waves to travel through Earth depends on the properties of the materials encountered, seismologists search for variations in travel times that cannot be accounted for simply by differences in the distances travelled. These variations correspond to changes in the properties of the materials encountered.

One major problem is that to obtain accurate travel times, seismologists must establish the exact location and time of an earthquake. This is commonly a difficult task because most earthquakes occur in remote areas. By contrast, the time and location of a nuclear test explosion is always known precisely. Despite the limitations of studying seismic waves generated by earthquakes, seismologists in the first half of the twentieth century were able to use them to determine the major layers of Earth. It was not until the early 1960s, when nuclear testing was in its heyday and networks consisting of hundreds of sensitive seismographs were deployed, that the finer structures of Earth's interior were established with certainty.

The Nature of Seismic Waves

To examine Earth's composition and structure, we must first study some of the basic properties of wave transmission, or *propagation*. As stated earlier in this chapter, seismic energy travels out from its source in all directions as waves. For purposes of description, the common practice is to consider the paths taken by these waves as *rays*, or lines drawn perpendicular to the wave front, as shown in Figure 10.22. Significant characteristics of seismic waves include the following:

- The velocity of seismic waves depends on the density and elasticity of the intervening material. Seismic waves travel most rapidly in rigid materials that elastically spring back to their original shapes when the stress caused by a seismic wave is removed. For instance, crystalline rock transmits seismic waves more rapidly than does a layer of unconsolidated mud.
- Within a given layer the speed of seismic waves generally increases with depth because pressure increases and squeezes the rock into a more compact elastic material.
- Compressional waves (P waves), which vibrate back and forth in the same line as their direction of travel, are able to propagate through liquids as well as solids because when compressed, these materials behave elastically; that is, they resist a change in volume and, like a rubber band, return to their original shape as a wave passes.
- Shear waves (S waves), which vibrate at right angles to their direction of travel, cannot propagate through liquids because, unlike solids, liquids have no shear strength. That is, when liquids are subjected to forces that act to change their shapes, they simply flow.
- In all materials, P waves travel faster than S waves.
- When seismic waves pass from one material to another, the path of the wave is refracted (bent).* In addition, some of the energy is reflected from the **discontinuity** (the boundary between the two dissimilar materials). This is similar to what happens to light when it passes from air into water.

Thus, depending on the nature of the layers through which they pass, seismic waves speed up or slow down and can be refracted (bent) or reflected. These measurable changes in seismic wave motions enable seismologists to probe Earth's interior.

*Refraction occurs provided that the ray is not travelling perpendicular to the boundary.

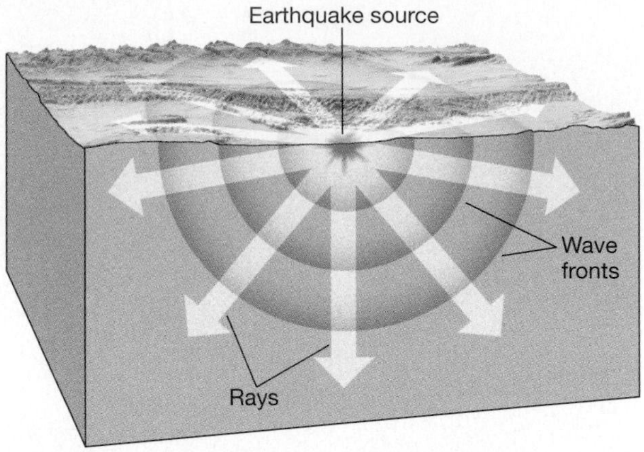

◆ **Figure 10.22** Seismic energy travels in all directions from an earthquake source (focus). The energy can be portrayed as expanding wave fronts or as rays drawn perpendicular to the wave fronts.

Seismic Waves and Earth's Structure

If Earth were a perfectly homogeneous body, seismic waves would spread through it in all directions. Such seismic waves would travel in a straight line at a constant speed. However, this is not the case for Earth. It so happens that the seismic waves reaching seismographs located farther from an earthquake travel at faster average speeds than those recorded at locations closer to the event. This general increase in speed with depth is a consequence of increased pressure, which enhances the elastic properties of deeply buried rock. As a result, the paths of seismic rays through Earth are refracted in the manner shown in Figure 10.23.

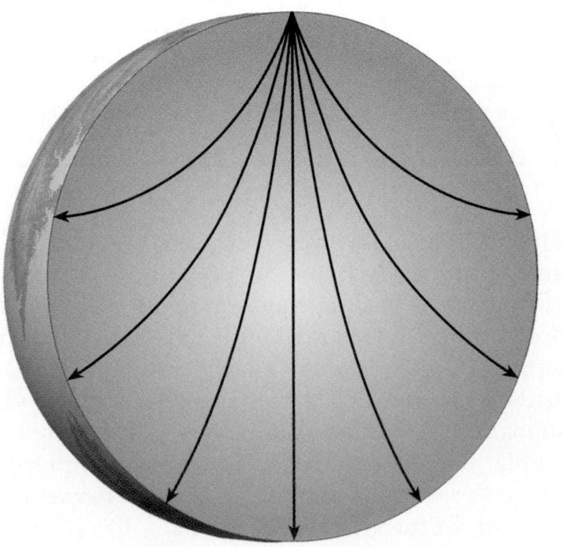

◆ **Figure 10.23** Wave paths through a planet where velocity increases with depth.

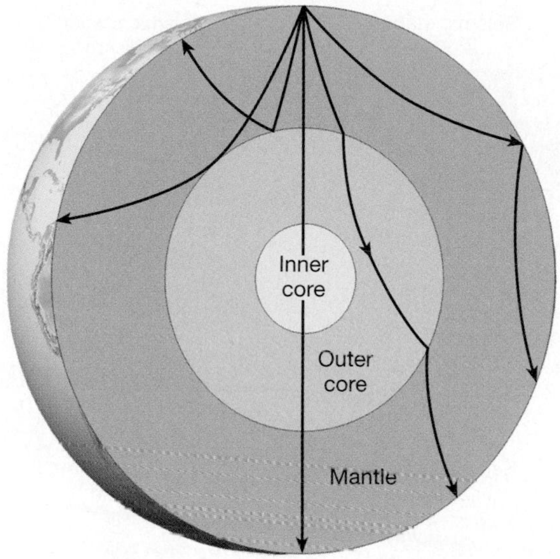

◆ **Figure 10.24** A few of the many possible paths that seismic rays take through Earth.

As more sensitive seismographs were developed, it became apparent that in addition to gradual changes in seismic wave velocities, rather abrupt velocity changes also occur at particular depths. Because these discontinuities were detected worldwide, seismologists concluded that Earth must be composed of distinct shells that have varying compositions or mechanical properties (Figure 10.24; see also Figure 1.19).

DISCOVERING EARTH'S MAJOR BOUNDARIES

Over the past century, seismic data gathered from many seismic stations have been compiled and analyzed. From this information, seismologists have developed a detailed image of Earth's interior (Figure 1.19). This model is continually being fine-tuned as more data become available and as new seismic techniques are employed. Furthermore, laboratory studies that experimentally determine the properties of various Earth materials under the extreme environments found deep in Earth add to this body of knowledge.

The Crust–Mantle Boundary (the Moho)

In 1909 a pioneering Yugoslavian seismologist, Andrija Mohorovičić, presented the first convincing evidence for layering within Earth. The boundary he discovered separates crustal materials from rocks of different composition in the underlying mantle, and it was named the **Mohorovičić discontinuity** in his honour. The name for this boundary was quickly shortened to **Moho**.

By carefully examining the seismograms of shallow earthquakes, Mohorovičić found that seismic stations located more than 200 kilometres from an earthquake obtained appreciably faster average travel velocities for P waves than did stations located nearer the quake (Figure 10.25). In particular, P waves that reached the closest stations first had velocities that averaged about 6 kilometres per second. By contrast, the seismic energy recorded at more distant stations travelled at speeds that approached 8 kilometres per second. This abrupt jump in velocity did not fit the general pattern that had been previously observed. From these data, Mohorovičić concluded that below 50 kilometres, a layer exists with properties markedly different from those of Earth's outer shell.

Figure 10.25 illustrates how Mohorovičić reached this important conclusion. Notice that the first wave to reach the seismograph located 100 kilometres from the epicentre travelled the shortest route directly through the crust. However, at the seismograph located 300 kilometres from the epicentre, the first P wave to arrive travelled through the mantle, a zone of higher velocity. Thus, although this wave travelled a greater distance, it reached the recording instrument sooner than did the rays taking the more direct route. This is because a large portion of its journey was through a region having a composition where seismic waves travel more rapidly. This principle is analogous to a driver taking a bypass route around a large city during rush hour. Although this alternative route is longer, it may be faster.

The Core–Mantle Boundary

A few years later, in 1914, the location of another major boundary was established by the German seismologist Beno Gutenberg.* This discovery was based primarily on the observation that P waves diminish and eventually die out completely about 105° from an earthquake (Figure 10.26). Then, about 140° away, the P waves reappear, but about two minutes later than would be expected based on the distance travelled. This belt, where direct seismic waves are absent, is about 35° wide and has been named the **P-wave shadow zone**** (Figure 10.26).

Gutenberg, and others before him, realized that the P-wave shadow zone could be explained if

*The core–mantle boundary had been predicted by R. D. Oldham in 1906, but his arguments for a central core did not receive wide acceptance.

**As more sensitive instruments were developed, weak and delayed P waves that enter this zone via reflection were detected.

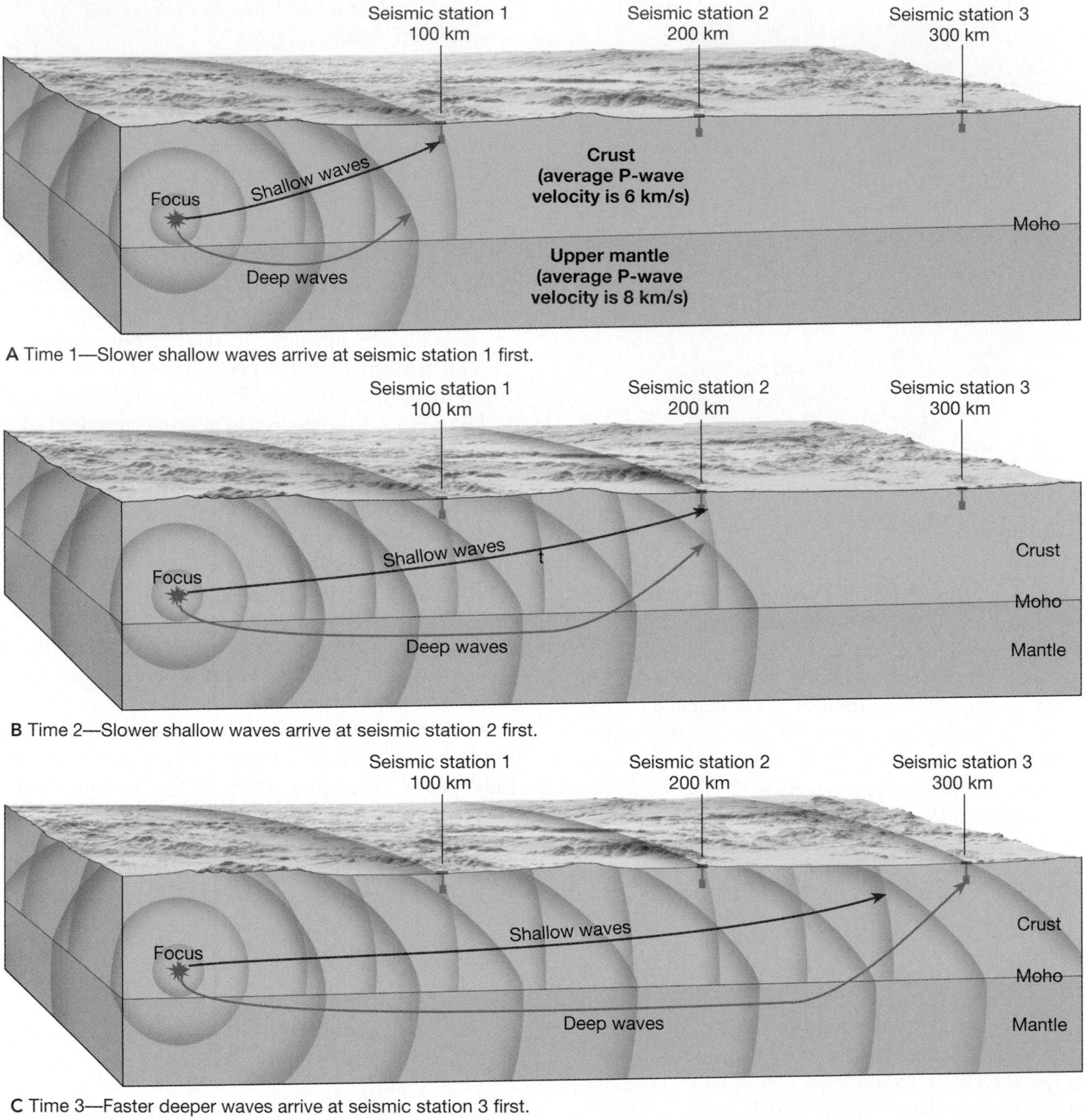

◆ **Figure 10.25** Idealized paths of seismic waves travelling from an earthquake focus to three seismic stations. In parts **A** and **B**, you can see that the two nearest recording stations receive the slower waves first because the waves travelled a shorter distance. However, as shown in part **C**, beyond 200 kilometres, the first waves received passed through the mantle, which is a zone of higher velocity.

Earth contained a core that was composed of material unlike the overlying mantle. The core, which Gutenberg calculated to be located at a depth of 2900 kilometres, must somehow hinder the transmission of P waves, similar to the way in which light rays are blocked by an object that casts a shadow. However, rather than actually stopping the P waves, the shadow zone is produced by bending (refracting) of the P waves, which enter the core, as shown in Figure 10.26.

It was further determined that S waves do not travel through the core. This fact led geologists to conclude that at least a portion of this region is liquid. This conclusion was further supported by the observation that P-wave velocities suddenly decrease by about 40 percent as they enter the core. Because

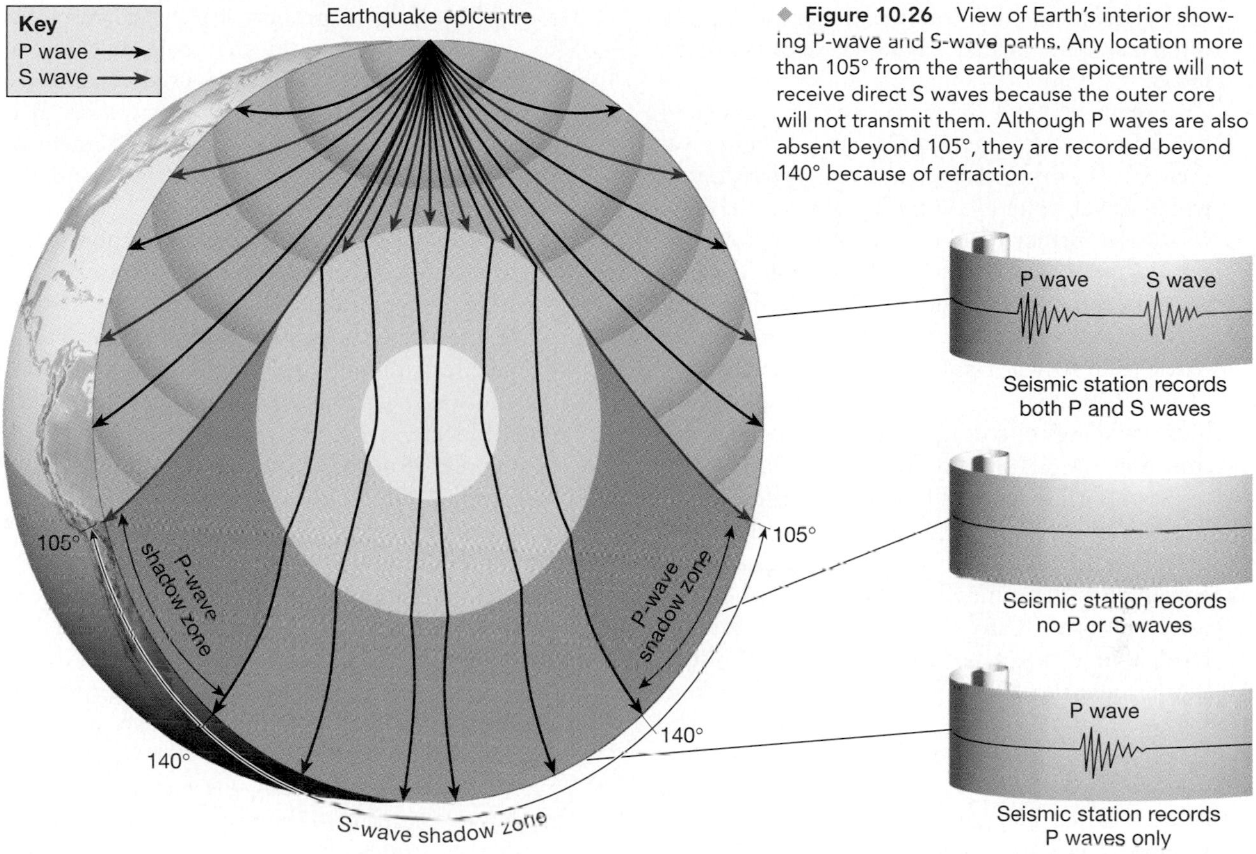

◆ **Figure 10.26** View of Earth's interior showing P-wave and S-wave paths. Any location more than 105° from the earthquake epicentre will not receive direct S waves because the outer core will not transmit them. Although P waves are also absent beyond 105°, they are recorded beyond 140° because of refraction.

melting reduces the elasticity of rock, this evidence pointed to the existence of a liquid layer below the rocky mantle.

Discovery of the Inner Core

In 1936 the last major subdivision of Earth's interior was predicted by Inge Lehmann, a Danish seismologist. Lehmann discovered a new region of seismic reflection and refraction within the core. Hence, a core within a core was discovered. The size of the **inner core** was not precisely established until the early 1960s, when underground nuclear tests were conducted in Nevada. Because the exact location and time of the explosions were known, echoes from seismic waves that bounced off the inner core provided a precise means of determining its size.

From these data, the inner core was found to have a radius of about 1216 kilometres. Furthermore, P waves passing through the inner core have appreciably faster average velocities than do those penetrating only the outer core. The apparent increase in the elasticity of the inner core is evidence that this innermost region is solid.

Chapter Summary

- *Earthquakes* are vibrations of Earth produced by the rapid release of energy from rocks that rupture because they have been subjected to stresses beyond their limit. This energy, which takes the form of waves, radiates in all directions from the earthquake's source, called the *focus*. The movements that produce most earthquakes occur along faults, which are usually associated with plate boundaries.
- Along a fault, rocks store energy as they are bent. As slippage occurs at the weakest point (the focus), displacement will exert stress farther along a fault, where additional slippage will occur until most of the built-up strain is released. An earthquake occurs as the rock elastically returns to its original shape. The "springing back" of the rock is termed *elastic rebound*. Small earthquakes, called *foreshocks*, often precede a major earthquake.

The adjustments that follow a major earthquake often generate smaller earthquakes called *aftershocks*.

- Two main types of seismic waves are generated during an earthquake: (1) *body waves*, which travel through Earth's interior, and (2) *surface waves*, which travel along the outer layer of Earth. Body waves are further divided into *primary waves*, or *P waves*, which push (compress) and pull (expand) rocks in the direction the wave is travelling, and *secondary waves*, or *S waves*, which "shake" the particles in rock at right angles to their direction of travel. P waves can travel through solids, liquids, and gases. Fluids (gases and liquids) will not transmit S waves. In any solid material, P waves travel about 1.7 times as fast as S waves do.
- The location on Earth's surface directly above the focus of an earthquake is the *epicentre*. An epicentre is determined by using the difference in velocities of P and S waves. By using the difference in arrival times between P and S waves, the distance separating a recording station from the earthquake can be determined. When the distances are known from three or more seismic stations, the epicentre can be located using a method called triangulation.
- A close correlation exists between earthquake epicentres and plate boundaries. The principal earthquake epicentre zones are along the outer margin of the Pacific Ocean, known as the circum-Pacific belt, and through the world's oceans along the oceanic ridge system.
- Seismologists use two fundamentally different measures to describe the size of an earthquake: intensity and magnitude. *Intensity* is a measure of the degree of ground shaking at a given locale based on the amount of damage. The *Modified Mercalli Intensity Scale* uses damage to buildings in California to estimate the intensity of ground shaking for a local earthquake. *Magnitude* is calculated from seismic records and estimates the amount of energy released at the source of an earthquake. Using the *Richter scale*, the magnitude of an earthquake is estimated by measuring the amplitude (maximum displacement) of the largest seismic wave recorded. A logarithmic scale is used to express magnitude, in which a tenfold increase in ground shaking corresponds to an increase of 1 on the magnitude scale. *Moment magnitude* is currently used to estimate the size of moderate and large earthquakes. It is calculated by using the average displacement of the fault, the area of the fault surface, and the sheer strength of the faulted rock.
- The most obvious factors determining the amount of destruction accompanying an earthquake are the magnitude of the earthquake and the proximity of the quake to a populated area. Structural damage attributable to earthquake vibrations depends on several factors, including (1) the wave amplitudes, (2) the duration of the vibrations, (3) the nature of the material on which the structure rests, and (4) the design of the structure. Secondary effects of earthquakes include *tsunami*, landslides, ground subsidence, and fire.
- Substantial research to predict earthquakes is underway in Japan, the United States, China, and Russia—countries where earthquake risk is high. No reliable method of short-range prediction has yet been devised. Long-range forecasts are based on the premise that earthquakes are repetitive or cyclic. Seismologists study the history of earthquakes for patterns so their occurrences might be predicted. Long-range forecasts are important because they provide information used to develop building standards and to assist in land-use planning.
- Much of our knowledge of Earth's interior comes from the study of earthquake waves that penetrate Earth and emerge at some distant point. In general, seismic waves travel faster in solid elastic materials and slower in weaker layers. Further, seismic energy is reflected and refracted (bent) at boundaries between compositionally or mechanically different materials. By carefully measuring the travel times of seismic waves, seismologists have been able to determine the major divisions of Earth's interior.
- The principal compositional layers of Earth include (1) the crust, Earth's comparatively thin outer skin; (2) the mantle, a solid rocky shell that extends to a depth of about 2900 kilometres; and (3) the core, a sphere that has a liquid outer part and a solid inner part.

Review Questions

1. What is an earthquake? Under what circumstances do earthquakes occur?
2. How are faults, foci, and epicentres related?
3. Who was first to explain the actual mechanism by which earthquakes are generated?
4. Explain what is meant by *elastic rebound*.

5. Faults that are experiencing no active movement can be considered "safe." Rebut or defend this statement.
6. Describe the principle of a seismograph.
7. List the major differences between P and S waves.
8. P waves move through solids, liquids, and gases, whereas S waves move only through solids. Explain.
9. Which type of seismic wave causes the greatest destruction to buildings?
10. Using Figure 10.9, determine the distance between an earthquake and a seismic station if the first S wave arrives three minutes after the first P wave.
11. For each increase of 1 on the Richter scale, wave amplitude increases __________ times.
12. An earthquake measuring 7 on the Richter scale releases about __________ times as much energy as an earthquake with a magnitude of 6.
13. List three reasons why the moment magnitude scale has gained popularity among seismologists.
14. List four factors that affect the amount of destruction caused by seismic vibrations.
15. What factor contributed most to the extensive damage that occurred in the central portion of Mexico City during the 1985 earthquake?
16. In addition to the destruction created directly by seismic vibrations, list three other types of destruction associated with earthquakes.
17. What is a tsunami? How is one generated?
18. Cite some reasons why an earthquake with a moderate magnitude might cause more extensive damage than a quake with a high magnitude.
19. Can earthquakes be predicted?
20. What is the value of long-range earthquake forecasts?
21. List six major characteristics of seismic waves.
22. What are the three compositional layers of Earth?
23. How does the boundary between the crust and mantle (Moho) differ from the boundary that occurs between the lithosphere and asthenosphere (Chapter 1)?
24. Briefly describe how the Moho was discovered.
25. What evidence did Beno Gutenberg use for the existence of Earth's central core?
26. Suppose the shadow zone for P waves were located between 120° and 160°, rather than between 105° and 140°. What would this indicate about the size of the core?
27. Describe the method first used to accurately measure the size of the inner core.
28. What evidence is provided by seismology to indicate that the outer core is liquid?

Key Terms

aftershock (p. 261)
body wave (p. 262)
discontinuity (p. 282)
earthquake (p. 259)
elastic rebound (p. 260)
epicentre (p. 265)
focus (p. 259)
foreshock (p. 261)
inertia (p. 261)
inner core (p. 285)
intensity (p. 268)
liquefaction (p. 273)
long (L) waves (p. 264)
magnitude (p. 268)
Modified Mercalli Intensity Scale (p. 268)
Mohorovičić discontinuity or Moho (p. 283)
moment magnitude (p. 271)
primary (P) waves (p. 262)
P-wave shadow zone (p. 283)
Richter scale (p. 270)
secondary (S) waves (p. 262)
seismic gaps (p. 279)
seismic sea wave (p. 273)
seismogram (p. 262)
seismograph (p. 261)
seismology (p. 261)
surface wave (p. 262)
tsunami (p. 273)

Web Resources

The *Earth* website uses the resources and flexibility of the internet to aid in your study of the topics in this chapter. Written and developed by geology instructors, this site will help improve your understanding of geology. Visit **www.pearsoned.ca/tarbuck** and click on the cover of the text to find

- online review quizzes
- Web-based critical thinking and writing exercises
- links to chapter-specific Web resources
- internet-wide key-term searches

www.pearsoned.ca/tarbuck

Chapter 11

The Ocean Floor

Mapping the Ocean Floor

Continental Margins
- Passive Continental Margins
- Submarine Canyons and Turbidity Currents
- Active Continental Margins

Features of the Deep-Ocean Basin
- Deep-Ocean Trenches
- Abyssal Plains
- Seamounts

Coral Reefs and Atolls

Seafloor Sediments
- Types of Seafloor Sediments

Mid-Ocean Ridges
- Seafloor Spreading
- Structure of the Oceanic Crust

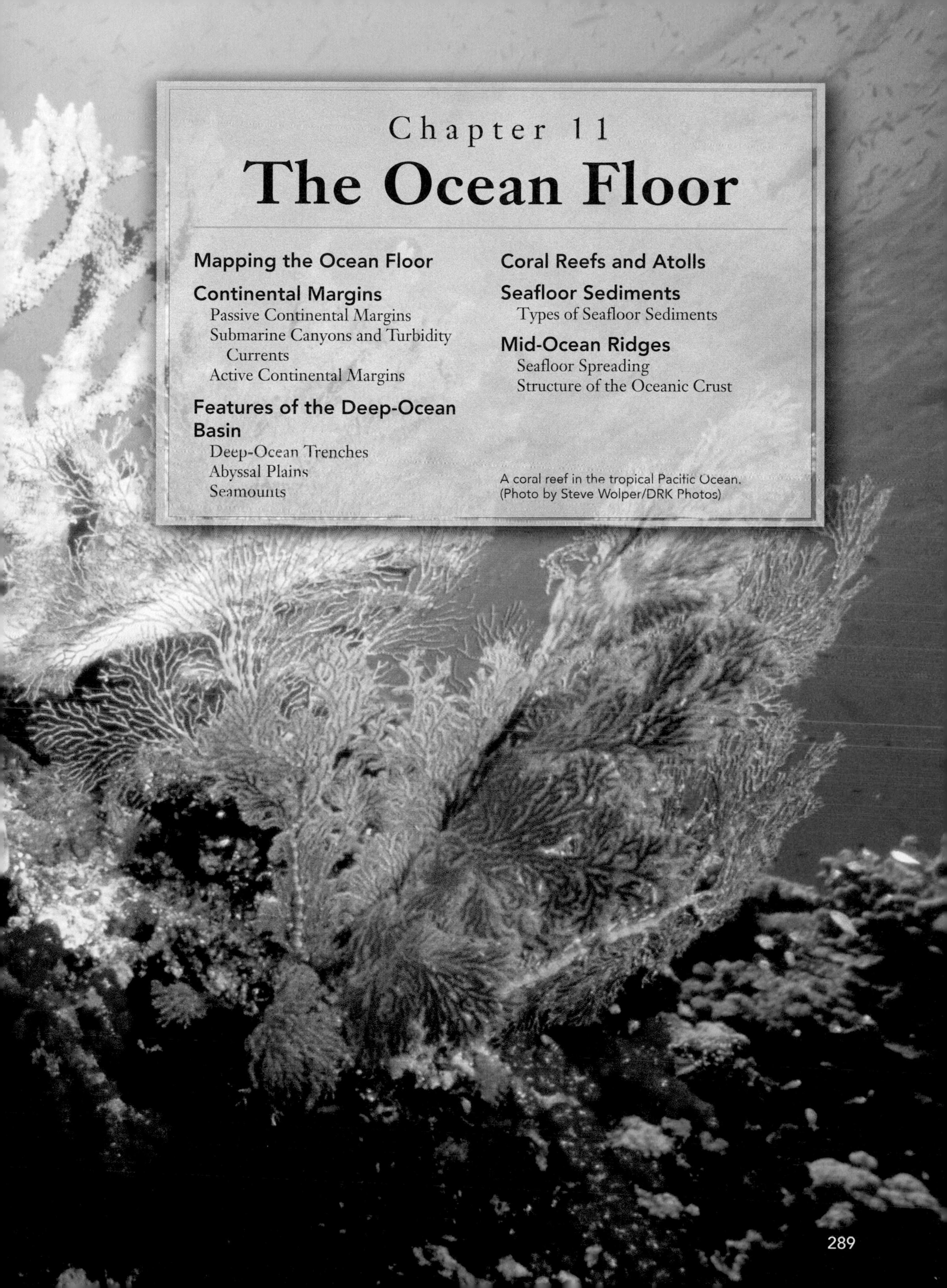

A coral reef in the tropical Pacific Ocean. (Photo by Steve Wolper/DRK Photos)

Because rock deformation and earthquakes often occur near lithospheric plate boundaries, and plate boundaries are commonly found offshore, we will now look at the topography and materials that compose the ocean floor. This information will prepare you to examine evidence for plate tectonics from the ocean floor in the next chapter, including magnetic, earthquake, and sedimentary data. As you will see in Chapter 12, that evidence convinced many scientists of the validity of the theory of plate tectonics.

If all water were drained from the ocean basins, we would see a great diversity of features, including linear chains of volcanoes, deep canyons, rift valleys, and large submarine plateaus. The scenery would be nearly as varied as that on the continents.

An understanding of the ocean floor's varied topography did not unfold until the historic three-year voyage of the H. M. S. *Challenger* (Figure 11.1). From December 1872 to May 1876, the *Challenger* expedition made the first, and still perhaps most comprehensive, study of the global ocean ever attempted by one agency. The 127,500-kilometre trip took the ship and its crew of scientists to every ocean except the Arctic. Throughout the voyage they sampled the depth of the water by laboriously lowering a weighted line overboard. Not many years later, the knowledge gained by the *Challenger* of the ocean's great depths and varied topography was further expanded with the laying of transatlantic cables. However, as long as ocean depth had to be measured with weighted line, our knowledge of the seafloor remained slight.

MAPPING THE OCEAN FLOOR

GEODe EARTH Divergent Boundaries
↳ Mapping the Ocean Floor

In the 1920s a technological breakthrough occurred with the invention of electronic depth-sounding equipment (**echo sounder**). (The echo sounder is also referred to as *sonar*, an acronym for *so*und *n*avigation *a*nd *r*anging.) The echo sounder works by transmitting sound waves toward the ocean bottom (Figure 11.2A). A sensitive receiver intercepts the echo reflected from the bottom, and a clock precisely measures the time interval to fractions of a second. By knowing the velocity of sound waves in water (about 1500 metres per second) and the time required for the energy pulse to reach the ocean floor and return, depth can be established. The depths determined from continuous monitoring of these echoes are plotted, creating a profile of the ocean floor. By laboriously combining profiles from several adjacent traverses, a chart of the seafloor is produced. Although much more complete and detailed than anything available before, these charts show only the largest topographic features of the ocean floor (see Figure 11.8).

◆ **Figure 11.1** The H. M. S. *Challenger*.
(From C. W. Thompson and Sir John Murray, *Report on the Scientific Results of the Voyage of the H. M. S.* Challenger, Vol. 1. Great Britain: Challenger Office, 1895, Plate 1, Library of Congress)

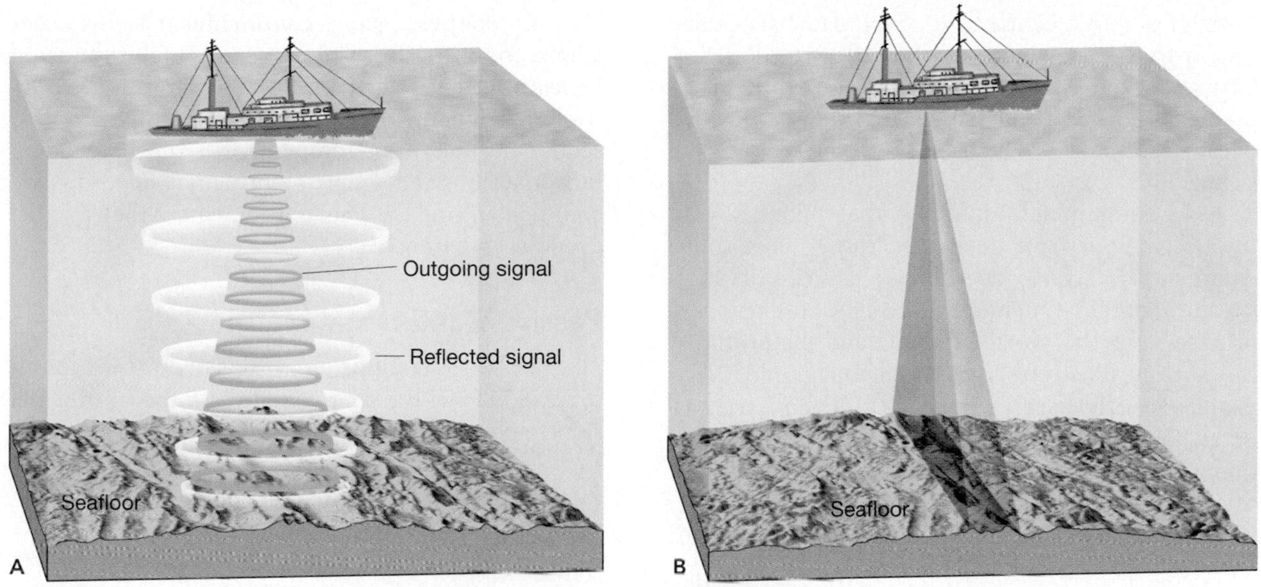

◆ **Figure 11.2** Echo sounders. **A.** An echo sounder determines the water depth by measuring the time interval required for an acoustic wave to travel from a ship to the seafloor and back. The speed of sound in water is 1500 metres per second. Therefore, depth = 1/2(1500 m/s × echo travel time). **B.** Modern multibeam sonar obtains a profile of a narrow swath of seafloor every few seconds.

In the last few decades, researchers have designed even more sophisticated echo sounders to map the ocean floor. In contrast to simple echo sounders, *multibeam sonar* employs an array of sound sources and listening devices. Thus, rather than obtaining the depth of a single point every few seconds, this technique obtains a profile of a narrow strip of seafloor (Figure 11.2B). These profiles are recorded every few seconds as the research vessel advances, building a continuous swath of relatively detailed coverage. (A ship will map a section of seafloor by travelling in a back-and-forth pattern like someone would use when mowing a lawn.)

Despite their greater efficiency and enhanced detail, research vessels equipped with multibeam sonar travel at a mere 10 to 20 kilometres per hour. It would take 100 vessels outfitted with this equipment hundreds of years to map the entire seafloor. Another technological breakthrough that has led to an enhanced understanding of the seafloor involves measuring the shape of the surface of the global ocean from space. After compensating for waves, tides, currents, and atmospheric effects, it was discovered that the water's surface is not perfectly flat; gravity attracts water toward regions where massive seafloor features occur. Therefore, mountains and ridges produce elevated areas on the ocean surface, and, conversely, canyons and trenches cause slight depressions. Satellites equipped with *radar altimeters* are able to measure these subtle differences by bouncing microwaves off the sea surface (Figure 11.3). These devices can measure variations

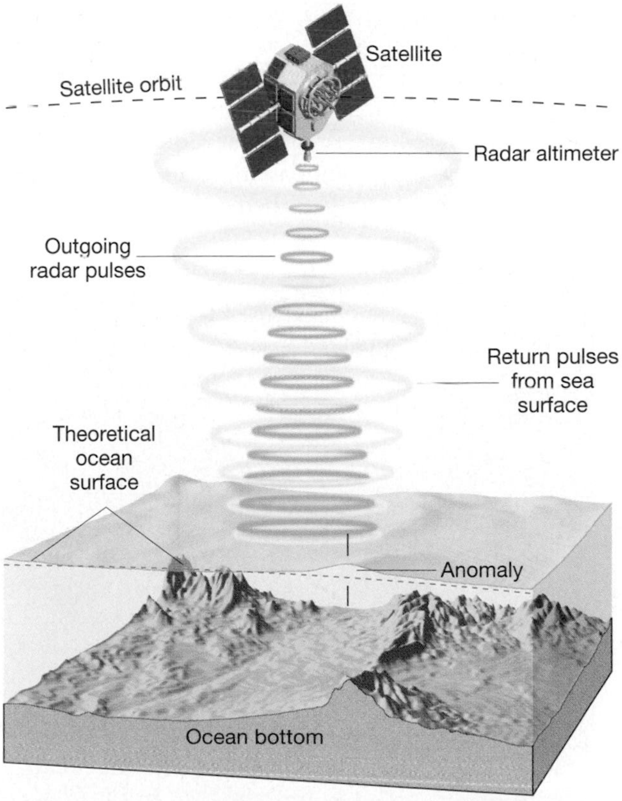

◆ **Figure 11.3** A satellite altimeter measures the variation in sea surface elevation, which is caused by gravitational attraction and mimics the shape of the seafloor. The sea surface anomaly is the difference between the measured and theoretical ocean surface.

as small as 3 to 6 centimetres. Such data have added greatly to the knowledge of ocean-floor topography. Cross-checked with traditional sonar depth measurements, the data are used to produce detailed ocean-floor maps, such as the one shown in Figure 11.8.

Oceanographers studying the topography of the ocean floor have delineated three major units: continental margins, deep-ocean basins, and mid-ocean ridges. The map in Figure 11.4 outlines these provinces for the North Atlantic, and the profile at the bottom illustrates the varied topography. Such profiles usually have their vertical dimension exaggerated many times—40 times in this case—to make topographic features more conspicuous. Because of this, the slopes shown in the seafloor profile appear to be *much* steeper than they actually are.

CONTINENTAL MARGINS

Two main types of **continental margins** have been identified: passive and active. Passive margins are found along most of the coastal areas that surround the Atlantic Ocean, including the east coasts of North and South America, as well as the coastal areas of western Europe and Africa. Passive margins are *not* associated with plate boundaries and therefore experience very little volcanism and few earthquakes. Here, weathered materials that eroded from the adjacent landmass accumulate to form a thick, broad wedge of relatively undisturbed sediments.

By contrast, active continental margins occur where oceanic lithosphere is being subducted beneath the edge of a continent. The result is a relatively narrow margin, consisting of highly deformed sediments that were scraped from the descending lithospheric slab. Active continental margins are common around the Pacific Rim, where they parallel deep oceanic trenches.

Passive Continental Margins

The features composing a **passive continental margin** include the continental shelf, the continental slope, and the continental rise (Figure 11.5).

Continental Shelf The **continental shelf** is a gently sloping submerged surface extending from the shoreline toward the deep-ocean basin. Because it is underlain by continental crust, it is clearly a flooded extension of the continents. The continental shelf varies greatly in width. Almost nonexistent along some continents, the shelf may extend seaward as far as 1500 kilometres along others. On average, the continental shelf is about 80 kilometres wide and 130 metres deep at the seaward edge. The average inclination of the continental shelf is only about 1/10 of 1 degree, a drop of about 2 metres per kilometre. The slope is so slight that it would appear to an observer to be a horizontal surface.

Although continental shelves represent only 7.5 percent of the total ocean area, they have eco-

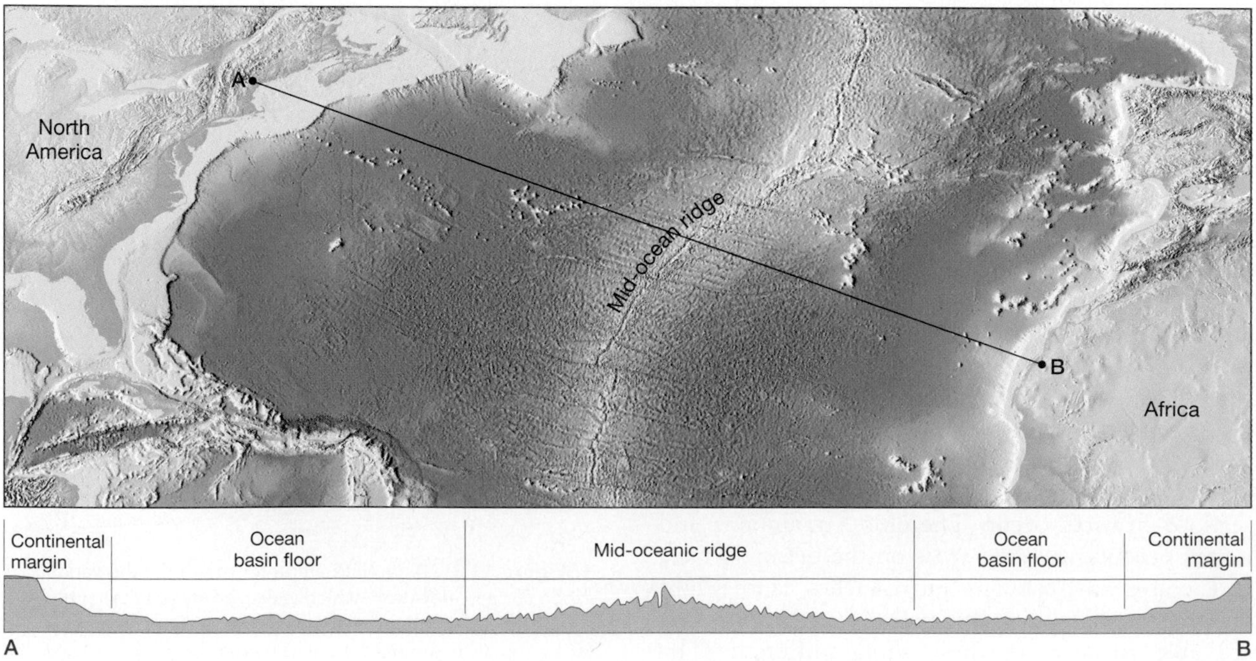

◆ **Figure 11.4** Major topographic divisions of the North Atlantic and a profile from the Maritimes to the coast of North Africa.

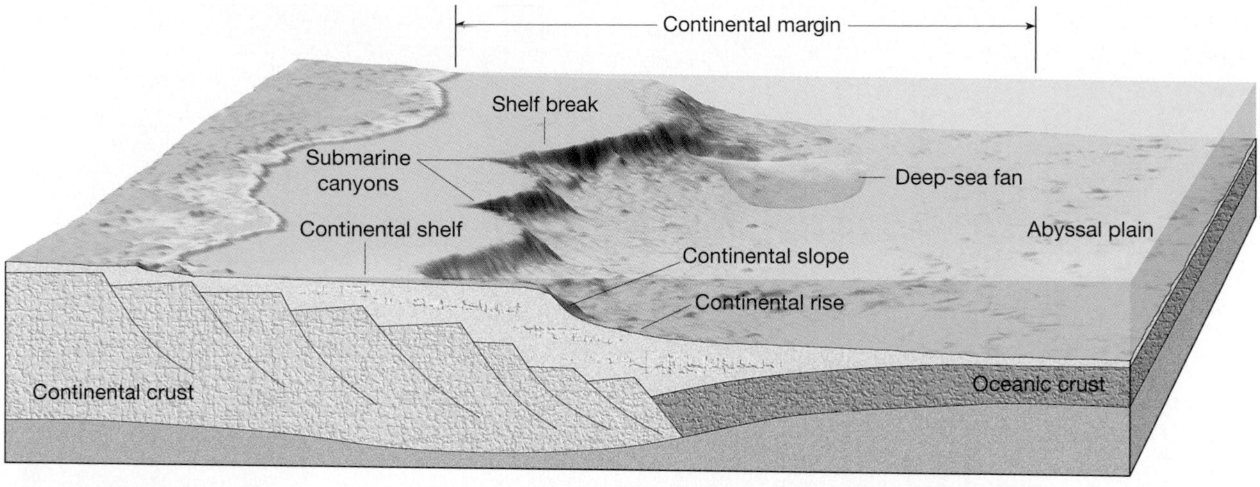

◆ **Figure 11.5** Schematic view showing the provinces of a passive continental margin. Note that the slopes shown for the continental shelf and continental slope are greatly exaggerated. The continental shelf has an average slope of 1/10 of 1 degree, while the continental slope has an average slope of about 5 degrees.

nomic, biologic, and political significance because they contain important mineral deposits, including large reservoirs of petroleum and natural gas, and huge sand and gravel deposits. The waters above the continental shelf contain many important fishing grounds that are significant sources of food.

Although the continental shelf is relatively featureless, some areas are mantled by extensive glacial deposits and are thus quite rugged. The most profound features are long valleys extending from the coastline into deeper waters. Many of these valleys are the seaward extensions of river valleys on the adjacent landmass. Such valleys appear to have been excavated during the Pleistocene Epoch (the last Ice Age).

During that time great quantities of water were contained in vast ice sheets on the continents, which caused sea level to drop by 100 metres or more, exposing large areas of the continental shelves (see Figure 17.5). Because of this drop in sea level, rivers extended their courses, and land-dwelling plants and animals inhabited the newly exposed portions of the continents. Dredging off the east coast of North America has produced the remains of numerous land dwellers, including mammoths, mastodons, and horses, adding to the evidence that portions of the continental shelves were once above sea level.

Most passive continental shelves, such as those along the east coast of Canada, consist of thick accumulations of shallow-water sediments. These sediments are frequently several kilometres thick and are interbedded with limestones that formed during earlier periods of coral reef building, a process that occurs only in shallow water. Such evidence led researchers to conclude that these thick accumulations of sediment are produced along a gradually subsiding continental margin.

Continental Slope Marking the seaward edge of the continental shelf is the **continental slope**, a relatively steep structure (compared with the shelf) that marks the boundary between continental crust and oceanic crust (Figure 11.5). As you will learn in Chapter 12, this boundary represents the original rift after a continent splits apart (the last major splitting was the breakup of the supercontinent Pangaea) and thus the true edge of a continent. Although the inclination of the continental slope varies greatly from place to place, it averages about 5 degrees and in places may increase to 25 degrees. Further, the continental slope is a relatively narrow feature, averaging only about 20 kilometres wide.

Continental Rise In regions where trenches do not exist, the continental slope merges into a more gradual incline known as the **continental rise**. Here the slope drops to about one third of a degree, or about 6 metres per kilometre. Whereas the width of the continental slope averages about 20 kilometres, the continental rise may extend for hundreds of kilometres into the deep-ocean basin.

The continental rise consists of a thick accumulation of sediment that moved downslope from the continental shelf to the deep-ocean floor. The sediments are delivered to the base of the continental slope by turbidity currents that follow submarine canyons (Figure 11.6). When these muddy currents emerge from the mouth of a canyon onto the relatively flat ocean floor, they deposit sediment that forms a **deep-sea fan**. As fans from adjacent submarine

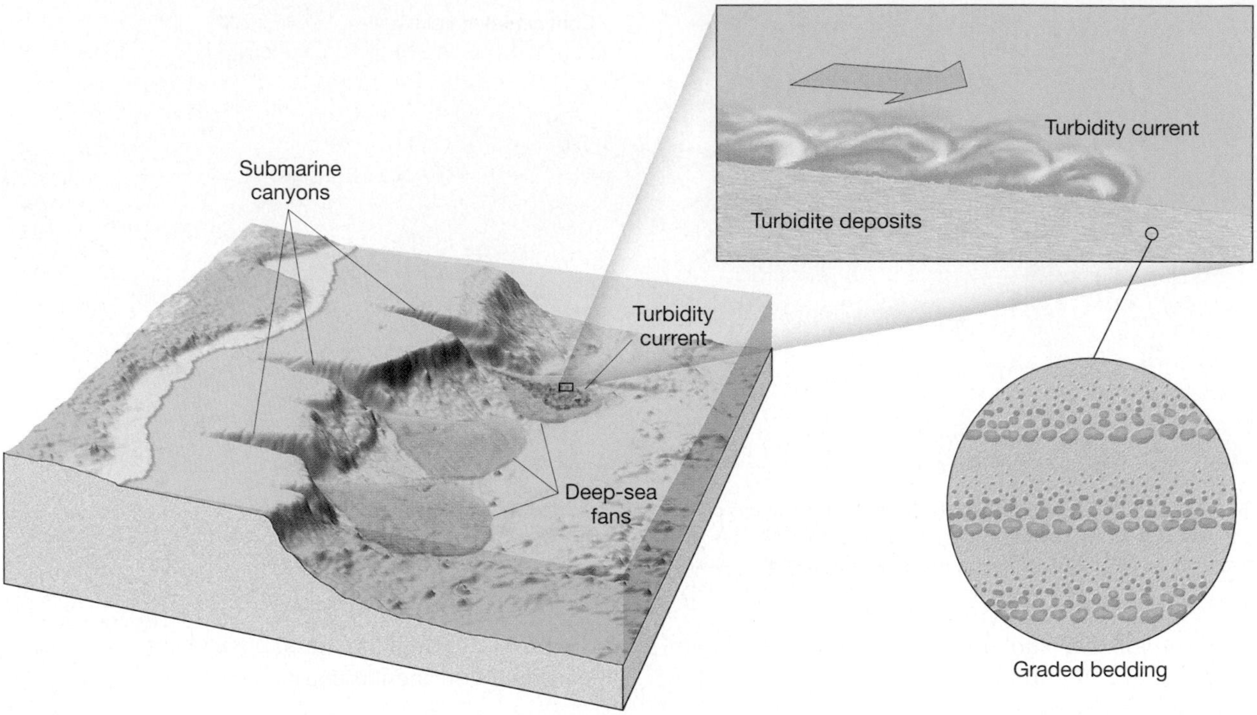

◆ **Figure 11.6** Turbidity currents move downslope, eroding the continental margin to enlarge submarine canyons. These sediment-laden high-density currents eventually lose momentum and deposit their loads of sediment as deep-sea fans. Beds deposited by these currents are called turbidites. Each event produces a single bed characterized by a decrease in sediment size from bottom to top, a feature known as a graded bed.

canyons grow, they coalesce to produce the continuous apron of sediment at the base of the continental slope that we call the continental rise.

Submarine Canyons and Turbidity Currents

Deep, steep-sided valleys known as **submarine canyons** are cut into the continental slope and may extend across the entire continental rise to the deep-ocean basin (Figure 11.6). Although some of the canyons appear to be the seaward extensions of river valleys, such as the Amazon River, others are not directly associated with existing river systems. Furthermore, because these canyons extend to depths far below the lowest level of the sea during the Ice Age, we cannot attribute their formation to stream erosion. These features must be created by some process that operates far below the ocean surface.

Most available information favours the view that submarine canyons have been eroded, at least in part, by turbidity currents (Figure 11.6). **Turbidity currents** are downslope movements of dense, sediment-laden water. They are created when sand and mud on the continental shelf and slope are dislodged, perhaps by an earthquake, and are thrown into suspension. Because such mud-choked water is denser than normal seawater, it flows downslope, eroding and accumulating more sediment. The erosional work repeatedly carried on by these muddy torrents is thought to be the major force in the growth of most submarine canyons.

Narrow continental margins (such as the one located along the California to British Columbia coast) are dissected by numerous submarine canyons. Here, headward erosion has extended many of these canyons landward into shallow water, where longshore currents are active. As a result, sediments carried to the coasts by rivers are transported along the shore until they reach a submarine canyon. This steady supply of sediment collects until it becomes unstable and moves as a massive underwater landslide (turbidity current) to the deep-ocean floor.

Turbidity currents eventually lose momentum and come to rest along the floor of the ocean basin (Figure 11.6). As these currents slow, the suspended sediments begin to settle out. First, the coarser, heavier sand is dropped, followed by successively finer deposits of silt and then clay. Consequently, these deposits, called **turbidites**, are characterized by a decrease in sediment grain size from bottom to top, producing **graded bedding** (Figure 11.6).

Although geologists still have more to learn about the complex workings of turbidity currents, it has been well established that they are an important mechanism of sediment transport in the ocean (Box 11.1). By the action of turbidity currents, submarine canyons are created and sediments are carried to the deep-ocean floor.

Active Continental Margins

Along some coasts the continental slope descends abruptly into a deep-ocean trench located between the continent and ocean basin. Thus, the landward wall of the trench and the continental slope are essentially the same feature. In such locations, the continental shelf is very narrow, if it exists at all.

Active continental margins are located primarily around the Pacific Ocean in areas where the leading edge of a continent is overrunning oceanic lithosphere (Figure 11.7). Here sediments from the ocean floor and pieces of oceanic crust are scraped from the descending oceanic plate and plastered against the edge of the overriding continent. This chaotic accumulation of deformed sediment and scraps of oceanic crust is called an **accretionary** (*ad* = toward, *crescere* = grow) **wedge**. Prolonged subduction, along with the accretion of sediments on the landward side of the trench, can produce a large accumulation of sediments along a continental margin. For example, a large accretionary wedge is found

BOX 11.1

Canadian Profile

Grand Banks Earthquake and Turbidity Current

On November 18, 1929, an earthquake measuring 7.2 on the Richter scale occurred at about 5:00 P.M. on the Laurentian Slope near the eastern edge of the Grand Banks. The quake was felt throughout the Atlantic provinces but produced only minor damage. At 7:30 P.M., however, a tsunami hit the Atlantic coast, causing great devastation, particularly in the Burin Peninsula of Newfoundland and Labrador, where 27 people drowned and boats and buildings were destroyed.

The earthquake occurred at a time when long-distance communication was limited to telegraph, a system that required extensive cable systems. Based on the timing of telegraph communication breaks, it was realized that a number of cables were severed at the precise time of the earthquake, near the epicentre. More difficult to explain was the sequence of cable breaks east of the epicentre (Figure 11.A); the last, and most easterly, cable, some 600 kilometres away, was cut 13 hours after the earthquake. It was not until the 1950s, when a lobe-shaped deposit (see Figure 11.A) of graded gravel and sand up to 1 metre thick was discovered on the deep-ocean floor, that the reason for the successive cable breaks was realized: the instantaneous cable breaks occurred because of slumping near the epicentre, and the later successive cable breaks resulted from the downslope movement of a turbidity current that deposited the sand.

The timing of the cable breaks in the deep sea provided the first indication of how fast turbidity currents can flow. It is estimated that the speed of the Grand Banks turbidity current reached 20 metres per second on the steepest part of the continental slope, slowing to 11 kilometres per second on the abyssal plain. The total area of deposition from this single event is estimated to be up to 250,000 square kilometres.

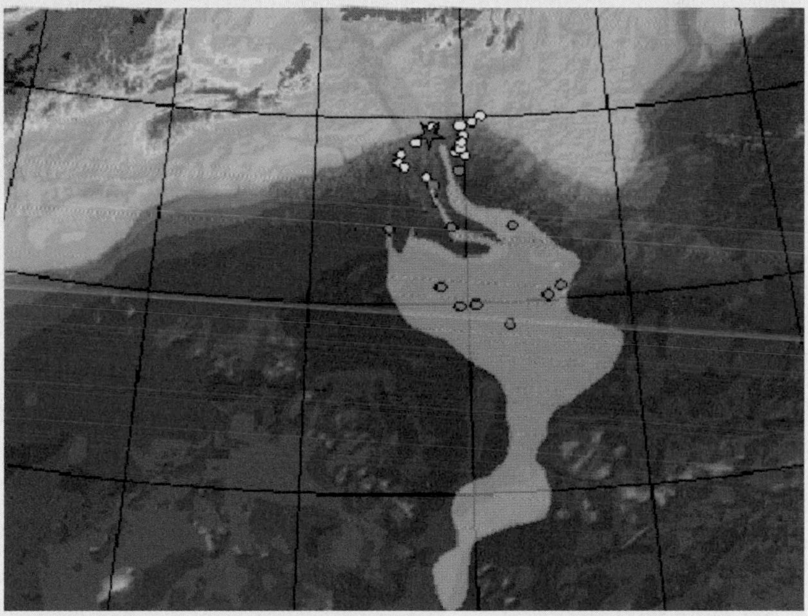

◆ **Figure 11.A** The distribution of the turbidite (light purple) deposited after the Grand Banks Earthquake of 1929. The orange star indicates the location of the earthquake epicentre. Yellow dots mark locations of telegraph cable breaks that occurred during the earthquake, whereas orange dots indicate locations of telegraph cable breaks recorded after the earthquake.
(Image from *The Last Billion Years*, Atlantic Geoscience Society)

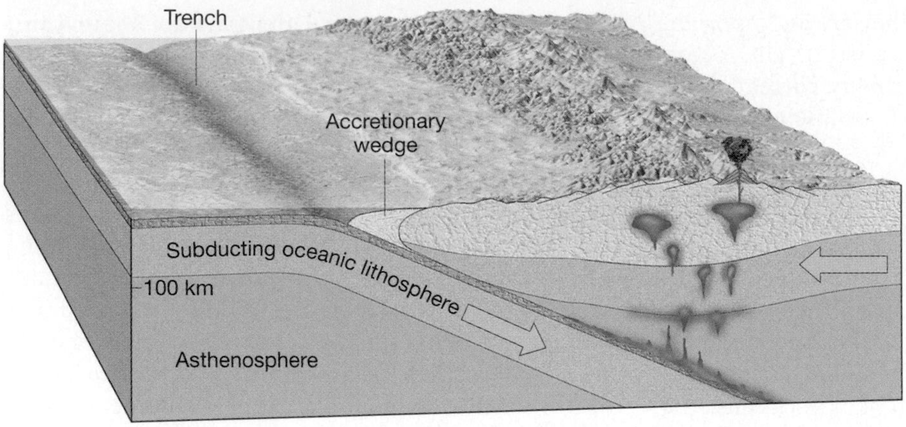

◆ **Figure 11.7** Active continental margin. Here sediments from the ocean floor are scraped from the descending plate and added to the continental crust as an accretionary wedge.

along the northern coast of Japan's Honshu island and pieces of an ancient wedge compose part of Newfoundland and Labrador.

Some subduction zones have little or no accumulation of sediments, indicating that ocean sediments are being carried into the mantle with the subducting plate. Here the continental margin is very narrow, as the trench may lie a mere 50 kilometres offshore.

FEATURES OF THE DEEP-OCEAN BASIN

Between the continental margin and the oceanic ridge system lies the **deep-ocean basin** (Box 11.2). The size of this region—almost 30 percent of Earth's surface—is roughly comparable to the percentage of the surface that projects above sea level as land. Here we find deep-ocean trenches, which are extremely deep linear depressions in the ocean floor; remarkably flat regions known as abyssal plains; and broad volcanic peaks called seamounts.

Deep-Ocean Trenches

Deep-ocean **trenches** are long, relatively narrow features that form the deepest parts of the ocean (Table 11.1). Most trenches are located in the Pacific Ocean, where some approach or exceed 10,000 metres in depth. At least a portion of one, the Challenger Deep, in the Mariana Trench, is more than 11,000 metres below sea level (Figure 11.8).

Although deep-ocean trenches represent only a very small portion of the area of the ocean floor, they are nevertheless significant geologic features. Trenches are the sites where moving lithospheric plates plunge back into the mantle. In addition to the earthquakes created as one plate descends beneath another, volcanic activity is also associated with these regions. Thus, trenches are commonly parallel to volcanic island arcs. Furthermore, volcanic mountains, such as those making up portions of the Andes, are located parallel to trenches that lie adjacent to continental margins. The release of volatiles (mainly water) from a descending plate triggers melting in the wedge of asthenosphere above it. This buoyant material slowly migrates upward and gives rise to volcanic activity at the surface.

Abyssal Plains

Abyssal (*a* = without, *byssus* = bottom) **plains** are incredibly flat features; in fact, these regions are likely the most level places on Earth. The abyssal plain found off the coast of Argentina, for example, has less than 3 metres of relief over a distance exceeding 1300 kilometres (Figure 11.8, dark area off southeast coast of South America). The monotonous topography of abyssal plains will occasionally be interrupted by the protruding summit of a partially buried volcanic peak.

Using seismic profilers, instruments whose signals penetrate far below the ocean floor, researchers have determined that abyssal plains owe their relatively featureless topography to thick accumulations of sediment that have buried an otherwise rugged ocean floor. The nature of the sediment indicates that these plains consist primarily of sediments transported far out to sea by turbidity currents.

Abyssal plains are found in all the oceans. However, because the Atlantic Ocean has fewer trenches to act as traps for the sediments carried down the continental slope, it has more extensive abyssal plains than does the Pacific.

Seamounts

Dotting the ocean floors are isolated volcanic peaks called **seamounts**. These features may rise hundreds of metres above the surrounding topography. Although these broad conical peaks have been dis-

BOX 11.2

Understanding Earth
Sampling the Ocean Floor

The *JOIDES Resolution* is the drilling ship of the Ocean Drilling Program. The *JOIDES* in the ship's name stands for Joint Oceanographic Institutions for Deep Earth Sampling and reflects the international commitment from the program's 19 member countries (including Canada). The *Resolution* part honours the H.M.S. *Resolution*, commanded more than 200 years ago by the well-known explorer Captain James Cook.

During cruises, holes are drilled deep into the seafloor. The cores of sediment and rock that are recovered represent millions of years of Earth history, and scientists use the cores to study many aspects of Earth science, including changes in global climate.

The ship is 143 metres long and 21 metres wide, with a derrick that towers 62 metres above the waterline. A computer-controlled positioning system maintains the ship over a specific location. The vessel can drill in water depths up to 8200 metres and can deploy as much as 9100 metres of drill pipe (Figure 11.B).

The *JOIDES Resolution* has living quarters for 50 scientists and technicians, plus a crew of 65. The 12 onboard laboratories are equipped with the largest and most varied array of seagoing research equipment in the world.

Since 1985, the ship has drilled in the Atlantic, Pacific, Indian, and Arctic oceans, as well as in several seas. The result has been the recovery of more than 210,000 metres of core samples.

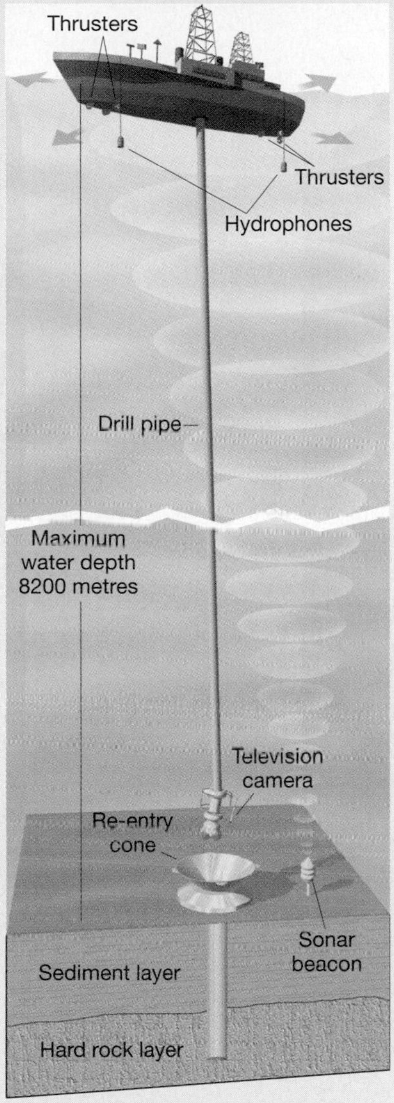

◆ **Figure 11.B** A *JOIDES Resolution* drill can re-enter holes in the seafloor years after initial drilling. The ship's dynamic positioning system consists of powerful thrusters (small propellers) that allow it to remain in place. Previous drill sites are located by bouncing sound waves between the ship's hydrophones and sonar beacons. A remote television camera aids in positioning the drill pipe into the re-entry cone.

covered in all the oceans (e.g., Flemish Cap in the north Atlantic: 560 kilometres east of St. John's and just off the upper right corner of Figure 11.A), the greatest number have been identified in the Pacific.

Many of these undersea volcanoes form near oceanic ridges, regions of seafloor spreading. If a volcano grows rapidly, it may emerge as an island. Examples of volcanic islands in the Atlantic include the Azores, Ascension, Tristan da Cunha, and St. Helena.

Although they exist as islands, some of these volcanoes are eroded to near sea

TABLE 11.1 **Dimensions of Some Deep-Ocean Trenches**

Trench	Depth (km)	Average Width (km)	Length (km)
Aleutian	7.7	50	3700
Central America	6.7	40	2800
Japan	8.4	100	800
Java	7.5	80	4500
Kurile–Kamchatka	10.5	120	2200
Mariana	11.0	70	2550
Peru–Chile	8.1	100	5900
Philippine	10.5	60	1400
Puerto Rico	8.4	120	1550
South Sandwich	8.4	90	1450
Tonga	10.8	55	1400

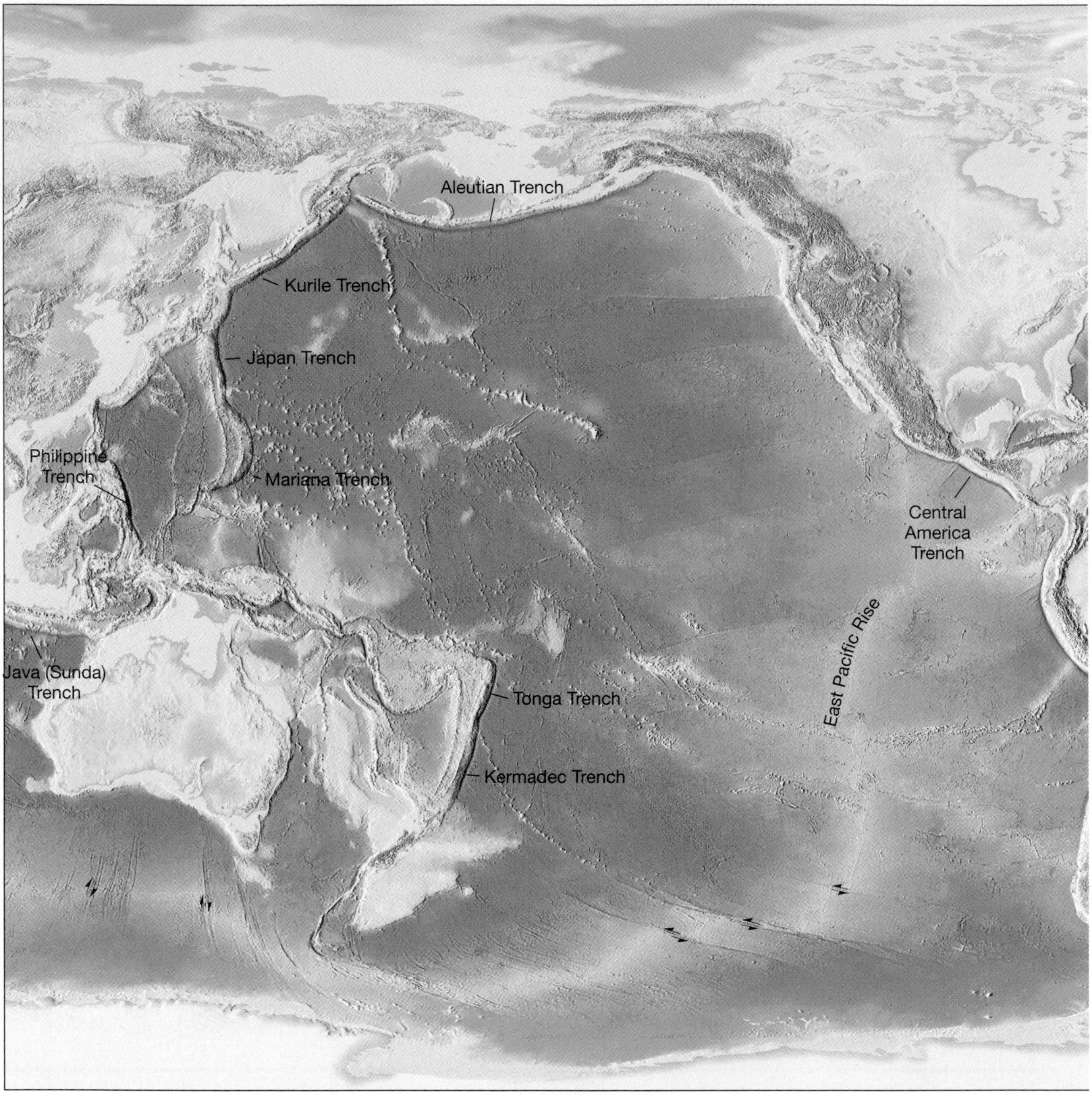

◆ **Figure 11.8** The topography of Earth's solid surface is shown on these two pages.

level by running water and wave action. Over millions of years the islands gradually sink as the moving plate slowly carries them from the oceanic ridge area. These submerged flat-topped seamounts are called **tablemounts** or **guyots.**[*] In other instances, guyots may be remnants of eroded volcanic islands that were formed away from the ridge crest, possibly by hot-spot activity. Here subsidence occurs after the volcanic activity ceases and the seafloor cools and contracts.

[*]The term *guyot* is named after Princeton University's first geology professor. It is pronounced "GEE-oh" with a hard *g* as in "give."

CORAL REEFS AND ATOLLS

Coral reefs are among the most picturesque features found in the ocean (see chapter-opening photo). They are constructed primarily from the calcareous (calcite-rich) skeletal remains and secretions of corals and certain algae. The term *coral reef* is somewhat misleading in that it makes no mention of the skeletons of many small animals and plants found inside

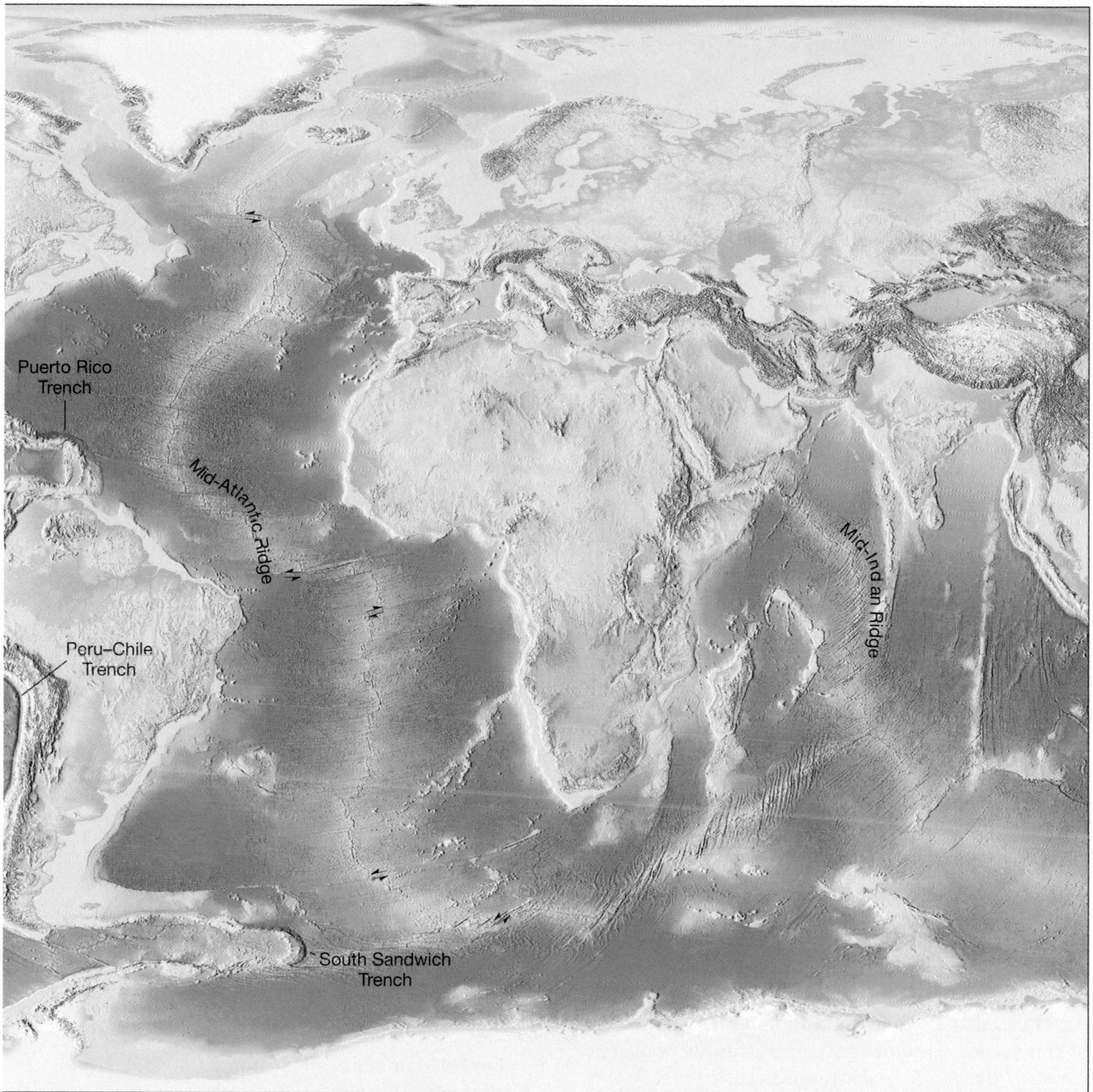

the branching framework built by the corals, and it does not reveal that secretions of algae help bind the entire structure together.

Coral reefs are confined largely to the warm, clear waters of the Pacific and Indian oceans, although a few occur elsewhere, such as in the Caribbean Sea. Reef-building corals grow best in waters with an average annual temperature of about 24°C. They can survive neither sudden temperature changes nor prolonged exposure to temperatures below 18°C. In addition, these reef-builders require clear sunlit water. Consequently, the limiting depth of active reef growth is only about 45 metres. Clear blue waters, such as those in the Florida Keys and Bahamas, support active reef building.

In 1831 the naturalist Charles Darwin set out aboard the British ship H. M. S. *Beagle* on its famous five-year expedition that circumnavigated the globe. One outcome of Darwin's studies was the development of a hypothesis on the formation of coral islands, called **atolls**. As Figure 11.9E illustrates, atolls consist of a nearly continuous ring of coral reef surrounding a central lagoon. Darwin's hypothesis explained what seemed to be a paradox; that is, how

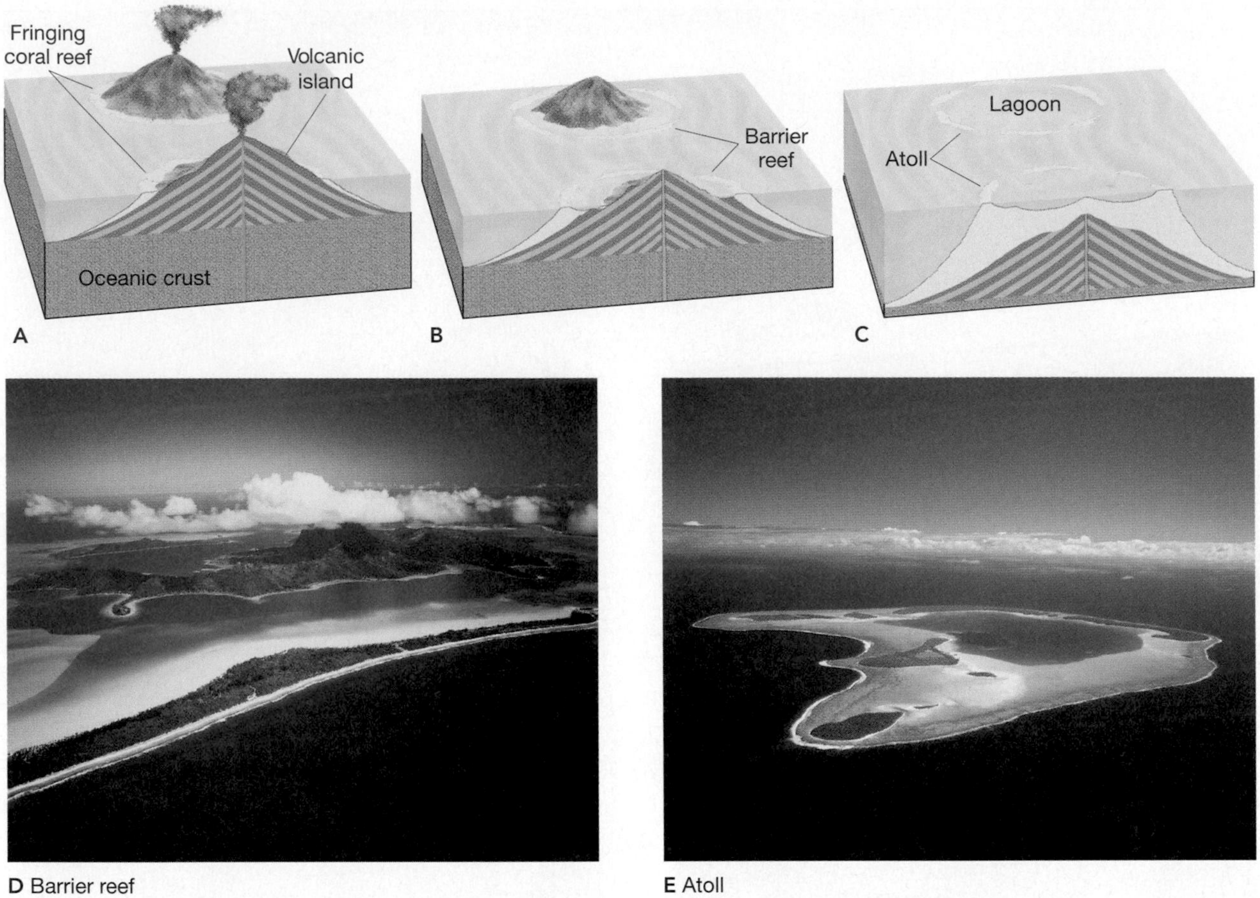

◆ **Figure 11.9** Formation of a coral atoll because of the gradual sinking of oceanic crust and upward growth of the coral reef. **A.** Fringing reef forms around volcanic island. **B.** As the volcanic island sinks, the fringing reef gradually becomes a barrier reef. **C.** Eventually, the volcano is completely submerged and an atoll remains. **D.** Aerial view of Bora Bora with surrounding barrier reef. **E.** Aerial view of Tetiaroa Atoll in the Pacific. The light blue waters of the relatively shallow lagoon contrast with the dark blue of the deep ocean surrounding the atoll. (Photo **D** by Tom Till/DRK Photo; photo **E** by Douglas Peebles Photography)

can corals, which require warm, shallow, sunlit water no deeper than a few dozen metres to live, create structures that reach thousands of metres to the floor of the ocean? Commenting on this in his book *The Voyage of the Beagle*, Darwin observed,

> from the fact of the reef-building corals not living at great depths, it is absolutely certain that throughout these vast areas, wherever there is now an atoll, a foundation must have originally existed within a depth of from 20 to 30 fathoms from the surface.*

The essence of Darwin's hypothesis was that coral reefs form on the flanks of sinking volcanic islands. As the island slowly sinks on moving oceanic crust (seafloor spreading), the corals continue to build the reef complex upward (Figure 11.9).

As Darwin further noted,

> For as mountain after mountain, and island after island slowly sank beneath the water, fresh bases would be successively afforded for the growth of the corals.

Thus, atolls, like guyots, are thought to owe their existence to the gradual sinking of oceanic crust. The succeeding years led to numerous challenges to Darwin's proposal. These arguments were not completely put to rest until after World War II, when the United States made extensive studies of two atolls (Eniwetok and Bikini), which became sites for testing atomic bombs. Drilling operations at these atolls revealed that volcanic rock did indeed underlie the thick coral reef structure. This finding was a striking confirmation of Darwin's explanation.

*One fathom (*fathme* = outstretched arms) equals 1.8 metres. This term is derived from how depth-sounding lines were brought back on board a vessel—by hauling in the line and counting the number of arm-lengths collected.

SEAFLOOR SEDIMENTS

Except for a few areas, such as near the crests of mid-ocean ridges, the ocean floor is mantled with sediment. Part of this material has been deposited by turbidity currents, and the rest has slowly settled to the bottom from above. The thickness of this carpet of debris varies greatly. In some trenches, which act as traps for sediments originating on the continental margin, accumulations can exceed 9 kilometres. In general, however, sediment accumulations are considerably less. In the Pacific Ocean, non-compacted sediment measures about 600 metres or less, while on the floor of the Atlantic, the thickness varies from 500 to 1000 metres.

Although deposits of sand-size particles are found on the deep-ocean floor, mud is the most common sediment covering this region. Mud also dominates on the continental shelf and slopes; however, the sediments in these areas are coarser overall because of greater quantities of sand.

Sampling has revealed that sand deposits are most prevalent as beach deposits along the shore. In some cases, though, coarse sediment, which we normally expect to be deposited near the shore, occurs in irregular patches at greater depths near the seaward limits of the continental shelves. Some sand may have been deposited by strong localized currents capable of moving coarse sediment far from shore; however, much of it appears to be the result of sand deposition on ancient beaches. Such beaches formed during the Ice Age, when sea level was much lower than today.

Types of Seafloor Sediments

Seafloor sediments can be classified according to their origin into three broad categories: (1) **terrigenous** (*terra* = the Earth, *generare* = to produce); (2) **biogenous** (*bio* = life, *generare* = to produce); and (3) **hydrogenous** (*hydro* = water, *generare* = to produce). Although each category is discussed separately, remember that all seafloor sediments are mixtures. No body of sediment comes from a single source.

Terrigenous Sediments Terrigenous sediment consists primarily of mineral grains that were weathered and eroded from continental rocks, and then transported to the ocean. The sand-size particles settle near shore. However, because the very smallest particles take years to settle to the ocean floor, they may be carried for thousands of kilometres by ocean currents. As a consequence, virtually every part of the ocean receives some terrigenous sediment. The rate at which this sediment accumulates on the deep-ocean floor, though, is very slow. From 5000 to 50,000 years are necessary for a 1-centimetre layer to form. Conversely, on the continental margins near the mouths of large rivers, terrigenous sediment accumulates rapidly. In the Gulf of Mexico, for example, the sediment carried by the Mississippi River has settled in a water depth of many kilometres.

Because fine particles remain suspended in the water for a very long time, ample opportunity exists for chemical reactions to occur. Because of this, the colours of the deep-sea sediments are often red or brown. This results when iron in the particles or in the water reacts with dissolved oxygen in the water and produces a coating of iron oxide (rust).

Biogenous Sediments Biogenous sediment consists of shells and skeletons of marine animals and plants (Figure 11.10). This debris is produced by microscopic organisms living near the ocean surface in sunlit waters. Once these organisms die, their remains rain down on the seafloor.

The most common biogenous sediments are known as *calcareous* ($CaCO_3$) *oozes*, and as their name implies, they have the consistency of thick mud. These sediments are produced by microscopic organisms, which inhabit warm surface waters. After death, their calcareous hard parts accumulate on the seafloor to form ooze. However, when calcareous

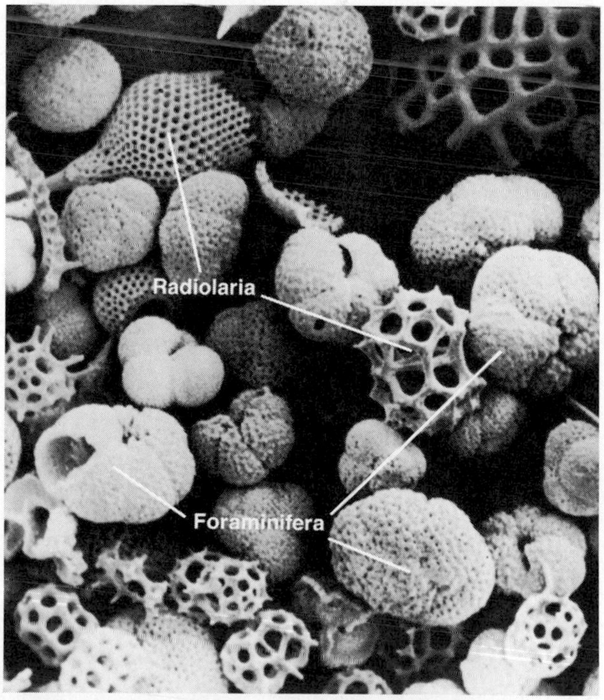

◆ **Figure 11.10** Microscopic hard parts of radiolarians (siliceous) and foraminifera (calcareous) are examples of biogenous sediments. This photomicrograph has been enlarged hundreds of times.
(Photo courtesy of Deep Sea Drilling Program, Scripps Institution of Oceanography, University of California, San Diego)

hard parts slowly sink through a cool layer of water, they begin to dissolve. This results because cold seawater is rich in carbon dioxide and is thus more acidic than warm water. In seawater deeper than about 4500 metres, calcareous shells will completely dissolve before they reach the bottom. Consequently, calcareous ooze does not accumulate in the deep-ocean basins.

Other biogenous sediments include *siliceous* (SiO_2) *oozes* and phosphate-rich materials. The former are composed primarily of opaline skeletons of diatoms (single-celled algae-like plants) and radiolarians (single-celled animals; Figure 11.10), whereas the latter are derived from the bones, teeth, and scales of fish and other marine organisms. Unlike calcareous shells, siliceous material is less soluble with water depth and does accumulate in deep-ocean basins.

Hydrogenous Sediments Hydrogenous sediment consists of minerals that crystallize directly from seawater through various chemical reactions. For example, some limestones are formed when calcium carbonate precipitates directly from the water; however, most limestone is composed of biogenous sediment.

Among the more interesting sediments on the ocean floor in terms of economic potential are **manganese nodules** (Figure 11.11). These rounded blackish lumps are composed of a complex mixture of minerals that form very slowly on the floors of the ocean basins. *Sulphide deposits* are another potential source of deep-ocean mineral resources. The richest submarine metallic sulphide deposits have been discovered in a series of deep basins along the axis of the Red Sea. The largest deposit ranks in size with the largest deposits on land. It may contain 100 million metric tonnes of potential ore with 29 percent iron, more than 3 percent zinc, 1 percent copper, and substantial gold and silver.

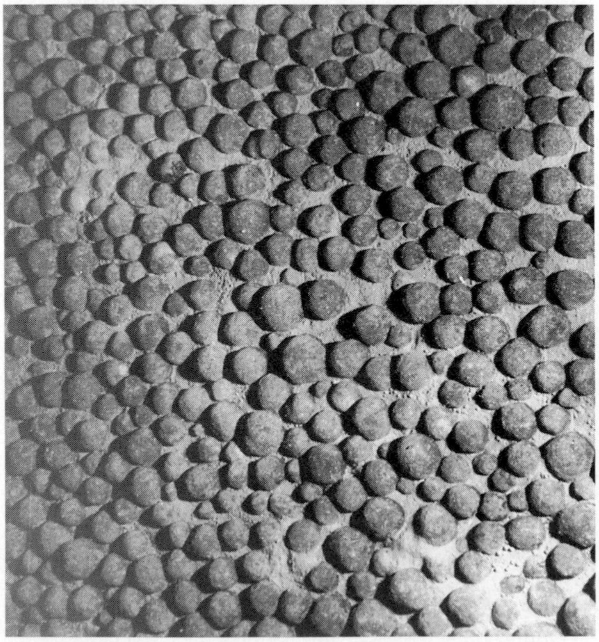

◆ **Figure 11.11** Manganese nodules photographed at a depth of 5323 metres beneath the *Robert Conrad* south of Tahiti.
(Photo courtesy of Lawrence Sullivan, Lamont-Doherty Earth Observatory/Columbia University)

MID-OCEAN RIDGES

GEODe EARTH Divergent Boundaries
↳ Oceanic Ridges and Seafloor Spreading

Our knowledge of **mid-ocean ridges** comes from soundings taken of the ocean floor, core samples obtained from deep-sea drilling, visual inspection by using deep-diving submersibles (Figure 11.12), and even first-hand inspection of slices of ocean floor that have been shoved up onto dry land (e.g., Newfoundland and Labrador). The ocean-ridge system is characterized by an elevated position, extensive faulting, and numerous volcanic structures that have developed on the newly formed crust (Figure 11.13).

The interconnected ocean-ridge system is the longest topographic feature on Earth's surface, exceeding 70,000 kilometres. Representing 20 percent of Earth's surface, the ocean-ridge system winds through all major oceans in a manner similar to the seam on a baseball (see Figure 11.8). The term *ridge* may be misleading, as these features are not narrow but have widths of from 1000 to 4000 kilometres and, in places, can occupy as much as half the total area of the ocean floor. An examination of Figure 11.8 shows that the ridge system is broken into segments that are offset by large transform faults. Further along the axis of some segments are deep down-faulted structures called **rift valleys**.

Although ocean ridges stand 2 to 3 kilometres above the floors of adjacent deep-ocean basins, they are much different from mountains found on the continents. Rather than consisting of thick sequences of folded and faulted sedimentary rocks, ocean ridges consist of layer on layer of basaltic rocks that have been faulted and uplifted.

The flanks of most ridges are topographically relatively featureless and rise very gradually (slope less than 1 degree) toward the ridge crest. Approaching the ridge crest, the topography begins to exhibit greater local relief as volcanic structures

◆ **Figure 11.12** The deep-diving submersible *Alvin* is 7.6 metres long, weighs 16 tonnes, has a cruising speed of 1 knot, and can reach depths as great as 4000 metres. A pilot and two scientific observers are along during a normal 6- to 10-hour dive.
(Photo courtesy of Rod Catanachy/ Woods Hole Oceanographic Institute)

and faulted valleys become more prominent. The most rugged topography is found on those ridges that exhibit large rift valleys.

Partly because of its accessibility to both American and European scientists, the Mid-Atlantic Ridge has been studied more thoroughly than other ridge systems (see Figure 11.8). The Mid-Atlantic Ridge is a broad submerged structure standing 2500 to 3000 metres above the adjacent ocean basin floor. In a few places, such as Iceland, the ridge has actually grown above sea level. Throughout most of its length, however, this divergent plate boundary lies 2500 metres below sea level. Another prominent feature of the Mid-Atlantic Ridge is its deep linear rift valley extending along the ridge axis. In places this rift valley is deeper than the Grand Canyon of the Colorado River and two or three times as wide. The name *rift valley* has been applied to this feature because it is so strikingly similar to continental rift valleys, such as the East African Rift Valley.

Seafloor Spreading

The concept of *seafloor spreading* (introduced in Chapter 1) was formulated in the early 1960s. Later geologists were able to verify that seafloor spreading occurs along relatively narrow zones, called **rift zones**, located at the crests of ocean ridges (see Box 11.3). As plates move apart, magma wells up into the newly created fractures and generates new slivers of oceanic lithosphere (Figure 11.13). This continually operating process generates new lithosphere that moves away from the ridge crest in a conveyor-belt fashion.

Active rift zones are characterized by frequent, but generally weak, earthquakes and a rate of heat flow that is greater than most other crustal segments. Here vertical displacement of large slabs of oceanic crust caused by faulting and the growth of volcanic piles contributes to the characteristically rugged topography of the oceanic ridge system. Further, the rocks along the ridge axis appear very fresh and are nearly devoid of sediment. Away from the ridge axis the topography becomes more subdued, and the thickness of the sediments and the depth of the water

◆ **Figure 11.13** A photograph taken from the *Alvin* during project FAMOUS shows lava extrusions in the rift valley of the Mid-Atlantic Ridge. Large toothpaste-like extrusions, such as this one, were common features. A mechanical arm is sampling an adjacent blister-like extrusion.
(Photo courtesy of Woods Hole Oceanographic Institution)

BOX 11.3

Canadian Profile
Deep-Sea Hydrothermal Vents in Canada's Backyard

Richard Léveillé*

Sitting in a computer-filled, darkened room, a group of geologists, biologists, and chemists peer intently at video monitors showing astonishing imagery of giant smoke-billowing, chimney-like rock formations and an abundance of bizarre animals. Is this a scene from Hollywood's latest sci-fi blockbuster? No, it's a typical scene from a research vessel located 250 kilometres southwest of Vancouver Island. The images are being relayed to the ship by the Canadian remotely controlled vehicle *ROPOS* (*Remotely Operated Platform for Ocean Science*), which is busy working more than 2 kilometres below the surface along the Juan de Fuca Ridge. This seafloor mountain chain is actively being created by the rifting and pulling apart of the Pacific and Juan de Fuca lithospheric plates and the production of new oceanic crust by upwelling magma.

◆ **Figure 11.C** A black smoker spewing hot, mineral-rich water along the East Pacific Rise. As heated solutions meet cold seawater, sulphides of copper, iron, and zinc precipitate immediately, forming mounds of minerals around these vents. (Photo by Dudley Foster, Woods Hole Oceanographic Institute)

Along ridges like the Juan de Fuca, cold seawater is entrained several hundreds of metres into the highly fractured basaltic crust, where it is then heated at depth by magmatic sources. Along the way, the heated water strips metals and elements, like sulphur, from the surrounding rocks. This heated fluid tends to rise upward because of convection, following conduits and fractures that are concentrated along the ridges. When it reaches the surface of the crust, the temperature of the fluid can be more than 400°C, but it does not boil because of the extremely high pressures caused by the water column above the vents. When this hydrothermal fluid comes into contact with the much colder seawater, minerals rapidly precipitate and form a shimmering smoke-like cloud, which gives *black smokers* their name (Figure 11.C). Some minerals immediately solidify and contribute to the formation of spectacular chimney-like structures, which can be as tall as a 15-storey building, and are appropriately given names like *Godzilla* and *Inferno*. In some cases, these chimneys and related deposits contain concentrated amounts of iron, copper, zinc, lead, silver, and even gold.

The Juan de Fuca vents are also remarkable for the biology that they support. In these environments completely devoid of sunlight, microorganisms take advantage of the mineral-rich hydrothermal fluid to perform what is known as chemosynthesis. The microbial communities, in turn, support larger, more complex animals, such as fish, crabs, worms, mussels, and clams. Some species at these vents are not found anywhere else on Earth. The most famous of these, and perhaps most unusual, is a particular type of tubeworm (Figure 11.D). With their white chitinous tubes and bright red plumes, these conspicuous creatures contain bacteria growing in their *trophosome*, an internal organ designed for harvesting bacteria. These *symbiotic* bacteria rely on the tubeworm to provide them with a suitable habitat and, in return, they provide carbon-based building blocks to the tubeworms.

◆ **Figure 11.D** Large tubeworms are among the organisms found in the extreme environment of mid-ocean ridges where sunlight is nonexistent. These organisms derive nourishment and energy from processes associated with hydrothermal vents. (Photo by Al Giddings/Al Giddings Images, Inc.)

---

*Richard Léveillé is a research scientist at the Canadian Space Agency and l'Université du Québec à Montréal.

increase. Gradually the ridge system grades into the flat, sediment-laden abyssal plains of the deep-ocean basin.

The primary reason for the elevated position of a ridge system is the fact that newly created oceanic crust is hot, and therefore it occupies more volume than cooler rocks of the deep-ocean basin. As the young lithosphere travels away from the spreading centre, it gradually cools and contracts. This thermal contraction accounts, in part, for the greater ocean depths that exist away from the ridge. It takes almost 80 million years before cooling and contraction cease completely. By this time, rock that was once part of an elevated ocean-ridge system is located in the deep-ocean basin, where it is mantled by thick accumulations of sediment.

During seafloor spreading, new material is equally added to the two diverging plates; hence, we would expect new ocean floor to grow symmetrically on each side of a centrally located ridge crest. Indeed, the ridge systems of the Atlantic and Indian oceans are located near the middle of these water bodies and as a consequence are named mid-ocean ridges. However, the East Pacific Rise is situated far from the centre of the Pacific Ocean. Despite uniform spreading along the East Pacific Rise, much of the Pacific Basin that once lay east of this spreading centre has been overridden by the westward migration of the North American plate.

Structure of the Oceanic Crust

Although most oceanic crust forms out of view, far below sea level, geologists have been able to examine the structure of the ocean floor first-hand. In such locations as Newfoundland and Labrador, Cyprus, and California, slivers of oceanic crust have been thrust high above sea level. From these outcrops, researchers conclude that the ocean floor consists of three distinct layers (Figure 11.14A). The upper layer is composed mainly of basaltic **pillow lavas**. The middle layer is made up of numerous interconnected dykes called **sheeted dykes**. Finally, the lower layer is made up of gabbro, the coarse-grained equivalent of basalt that crystallized at depth. This sequence of rocks is called an **ophiolite complex** (Figures 11.14 and 11.15). From studies of various ophiolite complexes and related data, geologists have

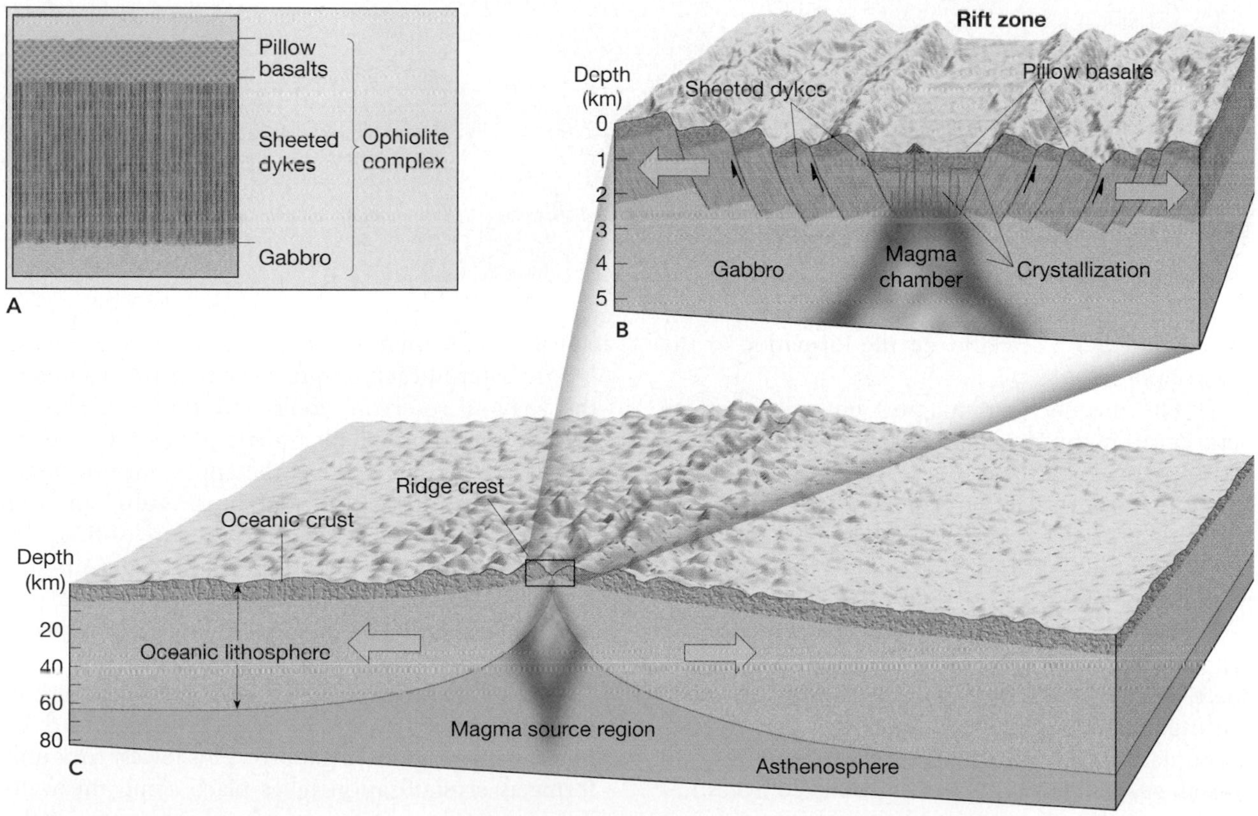

◆ **Figure 11.14** **A.** The structure of oceanic crust is thought to be equivalent to the ophiolite complexes that have been discovered elevated above sea level in such places as California and Newfoundland and Labrador. **B.** The formation of the three units of an ophiolite complex in the rift zone of an oceanic ridge. **C.** Diagram illustrating the site where new ocean crust is generated.

A

B

◆ **Figure 11.15** **A.** Ancient pillow lava at Trinity Bay, Newfoundland and Labrador. **B.** A rare glimpse of the Moho provided by the deepest levels of an ophiolite complex exposed in Table Mountain, Gros Morne National Park, Newfoundland and Labrador. The uppermost mantle and lower crust are represented by peridotite and gabbro, respectively. (Photo **A** courtesy of the Geological Survey of Canada, photo no. 152581; photo **B** by W. R. Church)

pieced together a scenario for the formation of the ocean floor.

The magma that migrates upward to create new ocean floor originates from partially melted peridotite in the asthenosphere. In the region of the rift zone, this magma source may lie no more than a few kilometres below the seafloor. Being molten and less dense than the surrounding solid rock, the magma gradually moves upward and enters large reservoirs located only a few kilometres below the ridge crest (Figure 11.14A). As the ocean floor moves apart, numerous fractures develop in the crust, permitting this magma to migrate to the surface. (Eventually magma in these vertical fractures will crystallize, generating the zone of sheeted dykes.)

During each eruptive phase, the initial lava flows are quite fluid and spread over the rift zone in broad, thin sheets. As new flows are added to the ocean floor, each is cut by fractures that allow additional lava to migrate upward and form overlying layers. Later in each eruptive cycle, as the magma in the shallow reservoir cools and thickens, shorter flows with a more characteristic pillow form occur. Recall that pillow lava has the appearance of large, elongate sandbags stacked one atop another (Figure 11.15A). Depending on the rate of flow, the thick pillow lavas may build into volcano-size mounds. These mounds will eventually be cut off from their supply of magma and be carried away from the ridge crest by seafloor spreading.

The magma that remains in the subterranean chamber will crystallize at depth to generate thick units of coarse-grained gabbro. This lowest rock unit forms as crystallization takes place along the walls and floor of the magma chamber. In this manner the processes at work along a ridge system generate the sequence of rocks found in an ophiolite complex (Figure 11.15B).

Chapter Summary

- Ocean depths are determined by using an *echo sounder*, a device carried by a ship that bounces sound off the ocean floor. The time it takes for the sound waves to make the round trip to the bottom and back to the ship is directly related to the depth. Continuous data from the echoes are plotted to produce a profile of the ocean floor. Although much of the ocean floor has been mapped by using echo sounders, only the large topographic features are shown.
- Oceanographers studying the topography of the ocean basins have delineated three major units: *continental margins*, *deep-ocean basins*, and *mid-ocean ridges*.
- The zones that collectively make up a *passive continental margin* include the *continental shelf* (a gently sloping, submerged surface extending from the shoreline toward the deep-ocean basin); *continental slope* (the true edge of the continent, which has a steeper slope that leads from the continental shelf into deep water); and *continental rise* (in regions where trenches do not exist, the steeper continental slope merges into a more gradual incline known as the *continental rise*). The continental rise consists of sediments that have moved downslope from the continental shelf to the deep-ocean floor.
- *Submarine canyons* are deep, steep-sided valleys that originate on the continental slope and can extend to depths of 3 kilometres. Some of these canyons appear to be the seaward extensions of river valleys. However, most information seems to favour the view that many submarine canyons are excavated by *turbidity currents*—downslope movements of dense, sediment-laden water. *Turbidites*, sediments deposited by turbidity currents, are characterized by a decrease in sediment grain size from bottom to top, a phenomenon known as *graded bedding*.
- *Active continental margins* are located primarily around the Pacific Ocean in areas where the leading edge of a continent is overrunning oceanic lithosphere. Here sediment scraped from the descending oceanic plate is plastered against the continent to form a collection of sediments called an *accretionary wedge*. An active continental margin generally has a narrow continental shelf, which grades into a deep-ocean trench.
- The deep-ocean basin lies between the continental margin and the mid-ocean ridge system. Its features include deep-ocean *trenches* (long, narrow depressions that are the deepest parts of the ocean and where moving lithospheric plates descend back into the mantle); *abyssal plains* (among the most level places on Earth, consisting of thick accumulations of sediments that were deposited atop the low, rough portions of the ocean floor by turbidity currents); and *seamounts* (isolated, steep-sided volcanic peaks on the ocean floor that originate near oceanic ridges or in association with volcanic hot spots).
- *Coral reefs*, which are confined largely to the warm, sunlit waters of the Pacific and Indian oceans, as well as such shallow seas as the Caribbean, are constructed over thousands of years primarily from the accumulation of skeletal remains and secretions of corals and certain algae. A coral island, called an *atoll*, consists of a continuous or broken ring of coral reef surrounding a central lagoon. Atolls form from corals that grow on the flanks of sinking volcanic islands, where the corals continue to build the reef complex upward as the island slowly sinks.
- There are three broad categories of seafloor sediments. *Terrigenous sediment* consists primarily of mineral grains that were weathered from continental rocks and transported to the ocean. *Biogenous sediment* consists of shells and skeletons of marine animals and plants. *Hydrogenous sediment* includes minerals that crystallize directly from seawater through various chemical reactions.
- Mid-ocean ridges, the sites of seafloor spreading, are found in all major oceans and represent more than 20 percent of Earth's surface. These broad features are certainly the most prominent features in the oceans, for they form an almost continuous mountain range. Ridges are characterized by an elevated position, extensive faulting, and volcanic structures that have developed on newly formed oceanic crust. Most of the geologic activity associated with ridges occurs along a narrow region on the ridge crest, called the *rift zone*, where magma from the asthenosphere moves upward to create new slivers of oceanic crust.
- New oceanic crust is formed in a continuous manner by the process of seafloor spreading. The upper crust is composed of *pillow lavas* of basaltic composition. Underlying this layer are numerous interconnected dykes (*sheeted dykes*) that are connected to a layer of gabbro. This entire sequence of rock is called an *ophiolite complex*.

Review Questions

1. Assuming that the average speed of sound waves in water is 1500 metres per second, determine the water depth if the signal sent out by an echo sounder requires 6 seconds to strike bottom and return to the recorder (see Figure 11.2).
2. List the three major features that compose the continental margin. Which of these features is considered a flooded extension of the continent? Which has the steepest slope?
3. Defend or rebut the following statement: "Most submarine canyons found on the continental slope and rise were formed during the Ice Age when rivers extended their valleys seaward."
4. What are turbidites? What evidence has been used to calculate the velocity of a turbidity current?
5. How does an active continental margin differ from a passive continental margin? Give examples of each type.
6. Why are abyssal plains more extensive on the floor of the Atlantic Ocean than on the floor of the Pacific Ocean?
7. What is an atoll? Describe Darwin's proposal on the origin of atolls. Was it ever confirmed?
8. Distinguish among the three basic types of seafloor sediment.
9. If you were to examine recently deposited biogenous sediment taken from a depth in excess of 4500 metres, would it more likely be rich in calcareous materials or siliceous materials? Explain.
10. How are mid-ocean ridges related to seafloor spreading?
11. What is the primary reason for the elevated position of the oceanic ridge system?

Key Terms

abyssal plain (p. 296)
accretionary wedge (p. 295)
active continental margin (p. 295)
atoll (p. 299)
biogenous sediment (p. 301)
continental margin (p. 292)
continental rise (p. 293)
continental shelf (p. 292)
continental slope (p. 293)
coral reef (p. 298)
deep-ocean basin (p. 296)
deep-sea fan (p. 293)
echo sounder (p. 290)
graded bedding (p. 294)
guyot (p. 298)
hydrogenous sediment (p. 301)
manganese nodule (p. 302)
mid-ocean ridge (p. 302)
ophiolite complex (p. 305)
passive continental margin (p. 292)
pillow lavas (p. 305)
rift valley (p. 302)
rift zone (p. 303)
seamount (p. 296)
sheeted dyke (p. 305)
submarine canyon (p. 294)
tablemount (p. 298)
terrigenous sediment (p. 301)
trench (p. 296)
turbidite (p. 294)
turbidity current (p. 294)

Web Resources

The *Earth* website uses the resources and flexibility of the internet to aid in your study of the topics in this chapter. Written and developed by geology instructors, this site will help improve your understanding of geology. Visit **www.pearsoned.ca/tarbuck** and click on the cover of the text to find

- online review quizzes
- Web-based critical thinking and writing exercises
- links to chapter-specific Web resources
- internet-wide key-term searches

www.pearsoned.ca/tarbuck

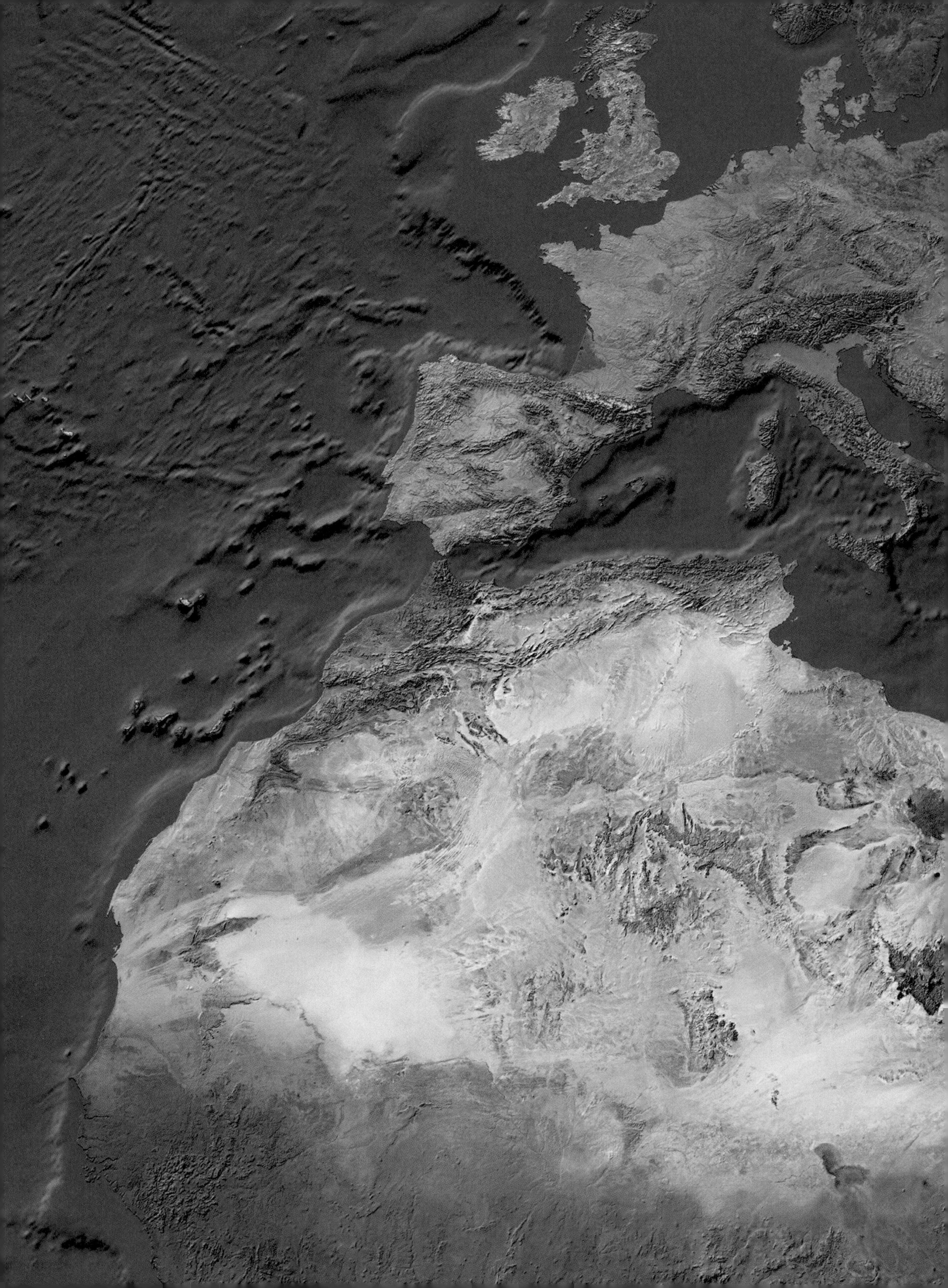

Chapter 12

Plate Tectonics: The Framework for Modern Geology

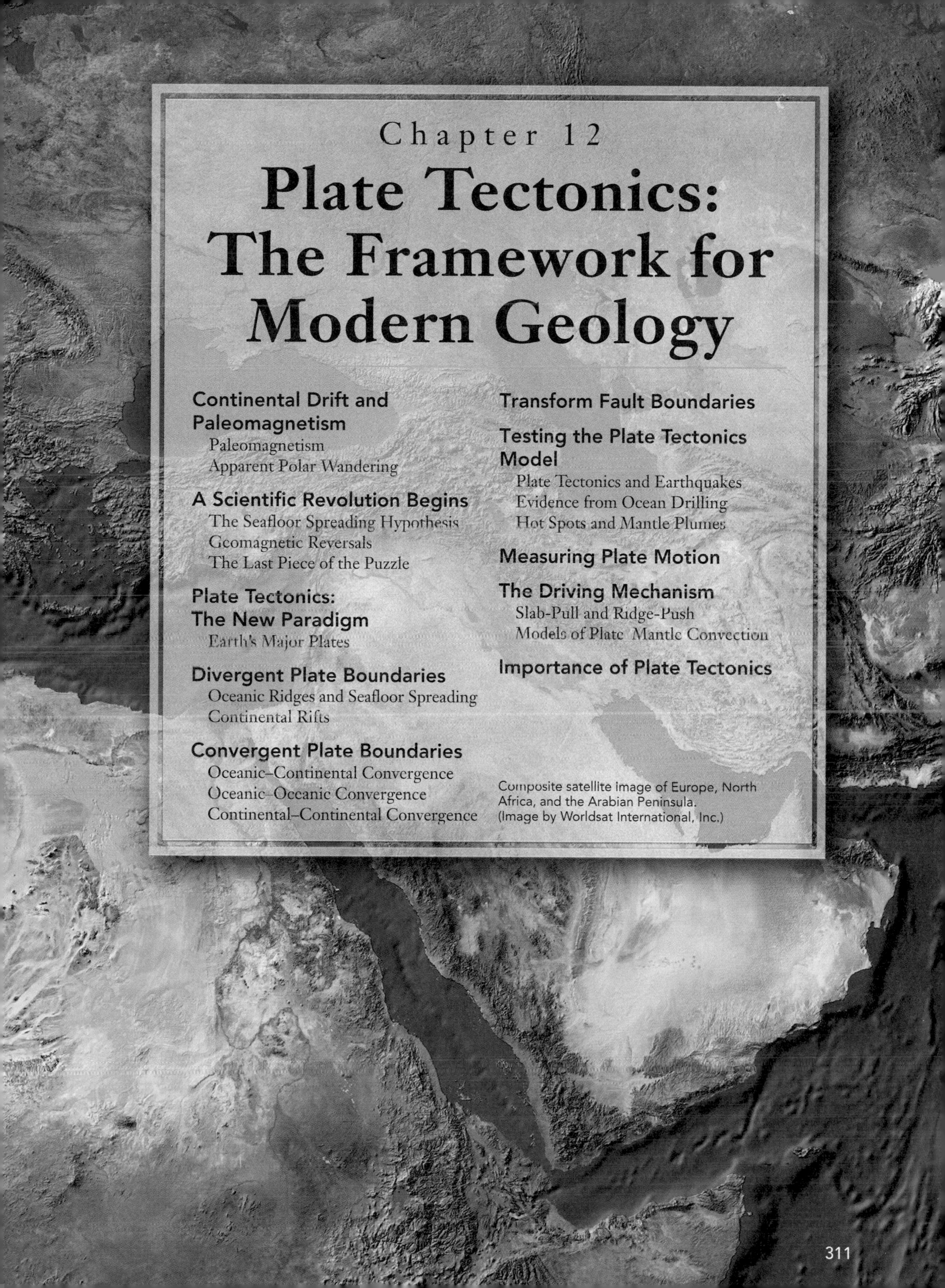

Composite satellite image of Europe, North Africa, and the Arabian Peninsula. (Image by Worldsat International, Inc.)

CONTINENTAL DRIFT AND PALEOMAGNETISM

In Chapter 1 we saw the early evidence that continents broke away from a former supercontinent called *Pangaea*. The evidence included the fit of continents, matching fossils and mountain chains now separated by ocean basins, and ancient glaciated rocks of the same age in many parts of the southern hemisphere. Recall that Alfred Wegener proposed a crude hypothesis of continental drift to account for the evidence that was effectively rejected in the first half of the twentieth century. Between the time of Wegener's death in 1930 and the early 1950s, very little new information became known about the continental drift hypothesis. For example, not much was known about the ocean floor (Chapter 11), which represents more than 70 percent of Earth's surface. This relatively unexplored area held the key to unravelling many secrets of our planet, especially rock magnetism.

Paleomagnetism

In many respects Earth's magnetic field is like that produced by a simple bar magnet. Invisible lines of force pass through Earth and extend from one pole to the other (Figure 12.1). A compass needle, itself a small magnet free to move about, aligns with these lines of force and thus points toward the magnetic poles.

The technique used to study ancient magnetic fields relies on the fact that certain rocks contain minerals that serve as "fossil compasses." These iron-rich minerals, such as magnetite, are abundant in lava flows of basaltic composition. As the lava cools, these minerals become magnetized in the direction parallel to the existing magnetic lines of force. Once the minerals solidify, the magnetism they possess will remain frozen in this direction. In this regard, they behave much like a compass needle: they point toward the existing magnetic poles at the time of their cooling. Then, if the rock is moved or if the magnetic pole changes position, the rock magnetism will in most instances retain its original alignment. Rocks that formed thousands or millions of years ago and recorded the location of the magnetic poles at that time are said to possess fossil magnetism, or **paleomagnetism**.

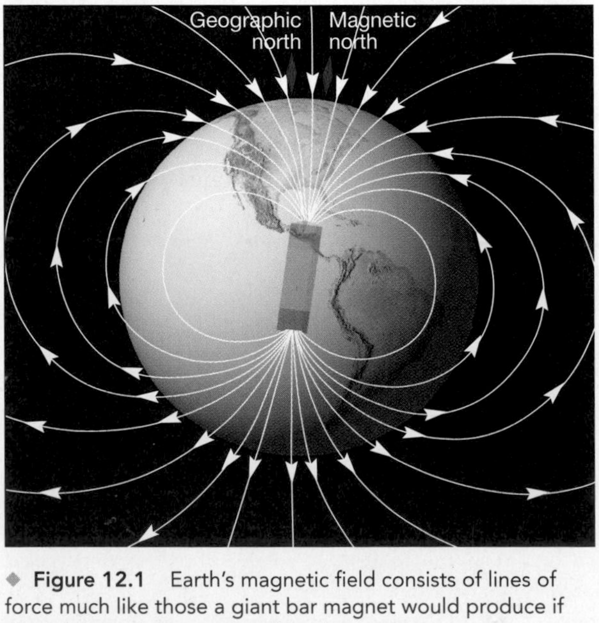

◆ **Figure 12.1** Earth's magnetic field consists of lines of force much like those a giant bar magnet would produce if placed through the centre of Earth.

Apparent Polar Wandering

During the 1950s S. K. Runcorn and his associates conducted a study by using rocks from European localities that led to an unexpected discovery: the magnetic alignment in the iron-rich minerals in lava flows of different ages varied widely. A plot of the apparent position of the magnetic north pole revealed that during the past 500 million years, the position of the pole has gradually wandered from a location in the Pacific Ocean northward to its present location in the Canadian Arctic (Figure 12.2). This was strong evidence that either the magnetic poles had migrated through time, an idea known as *polar wandering*, or that the lava flows moved—in other words, the continents had drifted.

Although the magnetic poles are known to move slightly in an erratic path around the geographic poles, studies of paleomagnetism from numerous locations show that the positions of the magnetic poles, averaged over thousands of years, correspond closely to the positions of the geographic poles. Therefore, the more acceptable explanation for the apparent polar wandering paths was provided by Wegener's hypothesis. If the magnetic poles remain stationary, their *apparent movement* is produced by continental drift.

Further evidence for continental drift came a few years later when another polar-wandering curve was constructed for North America (Figure 12.2A). To nearly everyone's surprise, the curves for North America and Europe had similar paths, except that they diverged to about 30 degrees longitude. When these rocks solidified, could there have been two magnetic north poles that migrated parallel to each other? This is very unlikely. The differences in these migration paths, however, can be reconciled if the two presently separated continents are placed next to each other, as we now believe they were before open-

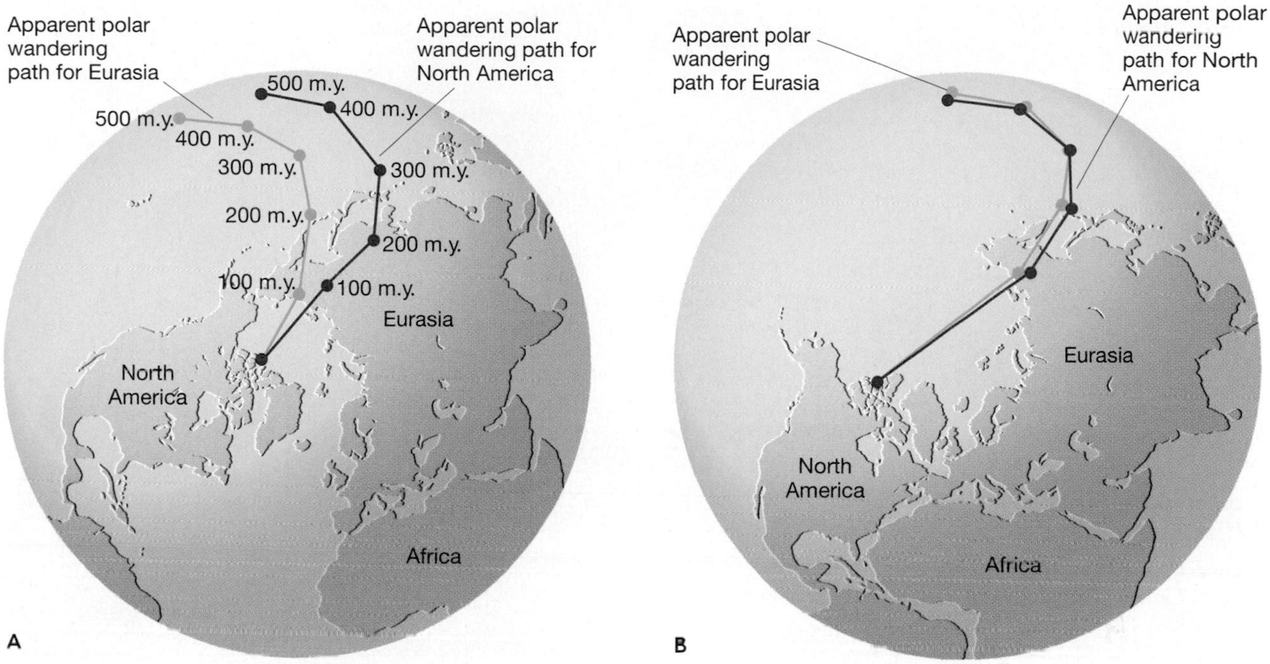

◆ **Figure 12.2** Simplified apparent polar-wandering paths as established from North American and Eurasian paleomagnetic data. **A.** The more westerly path determined from North American data was caused by the westward movement of North America by about 30 degrees from Eurasia. **B.** The positions of the wandering paths when the landmasses are reassembled. (Note that *m.y.* stands for "million years.")

ing of the Atlantic Ocean (Figure 12.2B). Then the two polar-wandering curves nearly overlap. This convinced some researchers that continental drift had indeed occurred. However, there was still the problem of identifying a mechanism, something that would allow continents to move closer together or farther apart while still connected by solid ocean floor. A new era had begun.

A SCIENTIFIC REVOLUTION BEGINS

During the 1950s and 1960s, great technological strides permitted extensive mapping of the ocean floor (Chapter 11). From this work came the discovery of the global oceanic ridge system. Furthermore, the Mid-Atlantic Ridge was found to parallel the continental margins on both sides of the Atlantic (see Figure 11.8). Also of importance was the discovery of a central rift valley extending the length of the Mid-Atlantic Ridge, an indication that great tensional forces were at work. In addition, high heat flow and volcanism were found to characterize the oceanic ridge system.

In other parts of the ocean additional discoveries were being made. Earthquake studies conducted near the deep-ocean trenches demonstrated that tectonic activity was occurring at great depths beneath the ocean. Flat-topped seamounts hundreds of metres below sea level showed signs of formerly being islands that somehow became submerged. Of equal importance, dredging of the oceanic crust did not bring up rock that was older than 180 million years. Could the ocean floor actually be a geologically young feature?

The Seafloor Spreading Hypothesis

In the early 1960s, Harry Hess of Princeton University put these newly discovered facts together into a hypothesis that was later named *seafloor spreading*. In Hess's now-classic paper, he proposed that the ocean ridges are located above zones of upwelling in the mantle (Figure 12.3). As rising material from the mantle spreads laterally, seafloor is carried in a conveyor-belt fashion away from the ridge crest. Here, tensional forces fracture the crust and provide pathways for magma to intrude and generate new slivers of oceanic crust. Thus, as the seafloor moves away from the ridge crest, newly formed crust replaces it. Hess further proposed that the deep-ocean trenches, such as the Peru–Chile Trench, are sites at which ocean crust is drawn back into the planet. Here the older portions of the seafloor are gradually consumed as they descend into the mantle. As one researcher summarized, "No wonder the ocean floor was young—it was constantly being renewed!"

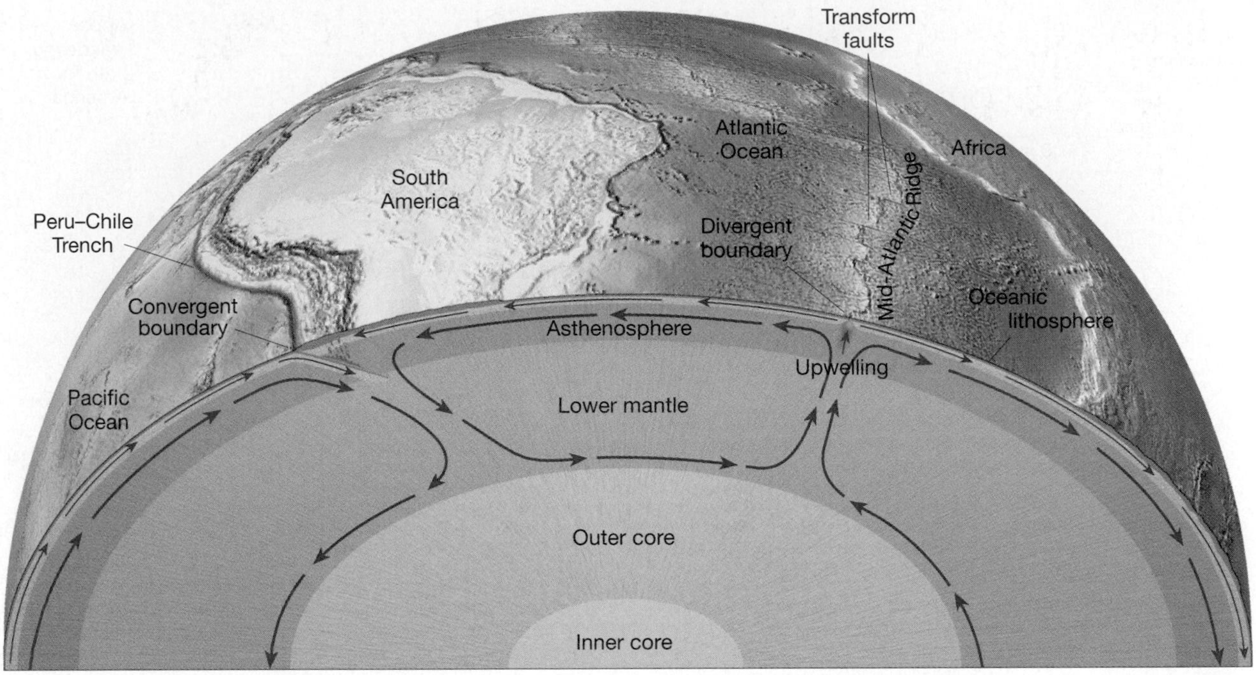

◆ **Figure 12.3** Seafloor spreading. Harry Hess proposed that upwelling of mantle material along the mid-ocean ridge system created new seafloor. The convective motion of mantle material carries the seafloor in a conveyor-belt fashion to the deep-ocean trenches, where the seafloor descends into the mantle.

With the seafloor-spreading hypothesis in place, Harry Hess had initiated another phase of this scientific revolution. The conclusive evidence to support his ideas came a few years later from studying magnetism of the seafloor.

Geomagnetic Reversals

About the time that Hess formulated seafloor spreading, geophysicists had begun to accept the fact the Earth's magnetic field periodically reverses polarity; that is, the north magnetic pole assumes a location near the south geographic pole, and vice versa (see Box 1.2). A rock solidifying during one of the periods of reverse polarity will be magnetized with the polarity opposite that of rocks being formed today. When rocks exhibit the same magnetism as the present magnetic field, they are said to possess **normal polarity**, whereas rocks exhibiting the opposite magnetism are said to have **reverse polarity**.

Evidence for magnetic reversals was obtained from lavas and sediments from around the world. Once the concept of magnetic reversals was confirmed, researchers set out to establish a time scale for polarity reversals. In many areas volcanic activity has occurred sporadically for periods of millions of years, so the task was to measure the polarity of paleomagnetism in numerous lava flows of various ages (Figure 12.4). These data, which were collected from around the globe, were used to determine the dates when the polarity of Earth's magnetic field changed. Figure 12.5 shows the time scale of polarity reversals established for the last few million years.

A significant relationship was uncovered between magnetic reversals and the seafloor-spreading hypothesis. Researchers discovered alternating stripes of high- and low-intensity magnetism that trend roughly parallel to the ridge crest. This was accomplished by using very sensitive instruments called **magnetometers**, which were towed by research vessels over segments of the ocean floor, as shown in Figure 12.6.

This relatively simple pattern of magnetic variation defied explanation until 1963, when Lawrence W. Morley of the Geological Survey of Canada, and British colleagues Fred Vine and D. H. Matthews, tied the discovery of the high- and low-intensity stripes to Hess's concept of seafloor spreading. They suggested that the stripes of high-intensity magnetism are regions where the paleomagnetism of the ocean crust exhibits normal polarity. Consequently, these rocks *enhance* (reinforce) the existing magnetic field (Figure 12.6A). Conversely, the low-intensity stripes are regions where the ocean crust is polarized in the reverse direction and therefore *weaken* the existing magnetic field. But how do parallel stripes of normally and reversely magnetized rock become distributed across the ocean floor?

Morley, Vine, and Matthews reasoned that as magma solidifies along narrow rifts at the crest of an

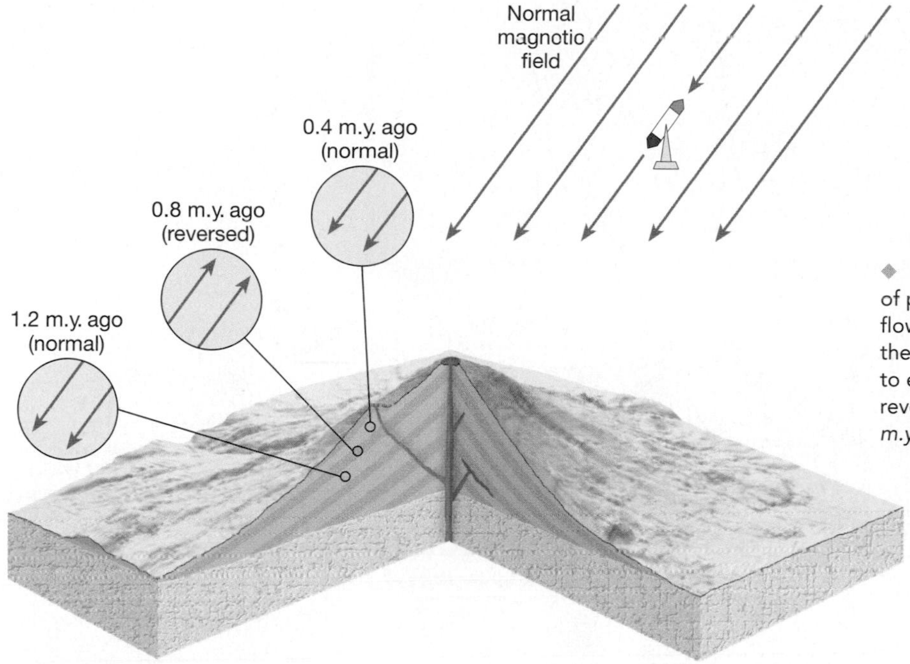

◆ **Figure 12.4** Schematic illustration of paleomagnetism preserved in lava flows of various ages. Such data as these from various locales were used to establish the time scale of polarity reversals shown in Figure 12.5. (Note: *m.y.* stands for "million years.")

oceanic ridge, it is magnetized with the polarity of the existing magnetic field (Figure 12.7). Because of seafloor spreading, this stripe of magnetized crust would gradually increase in width. When Earth's magnetic field reverses polarity, any newly formed seafloor (having the opposite polarity) would form in the middle of the old stripe. Gradually, the two parts of the old stripe are carried in opposite directions away from the ridge crest. Subsequent reversals would build a pattern of normal and reverse stripes, as shown in Figure 12.7. Because new rock is added in equal amounts to both trailing edges of the spreading ocean floor, we should expect the pattern of stripes (size and polarity) found on one side of an oceanic ridge to be a mirror image of the other side. A few years later a survey across the Mid-Atlantic Ridge just south of Iceland (Figure 12.6C) revealed a pattern of magnetic stripes exhibiting a remarkable degree of symmetry about the ridge axis (Figure 12.6B).

The Last Piece of the Puzzle

The 1960s have been characterized as a period of chaos in the tectonics debate. Some geologists believed in seafloor spreading and continental drift, whereas others held that an expanding Earth could better account for the displacement occurring at the crests of oceanic ridges. According to the latter view, landmasses once covered the entire surface of Earth, as shown in Figure 12.8. As Earth expanded, the continents split into their current configurations, while new seafloor "filled in" the space between them as they drifted apart (Figure 12.8). However, the expanding Earth theory is not valid because Earth's volume and diameter have remained constant for billions of years, and our planet has been gradually cooling.

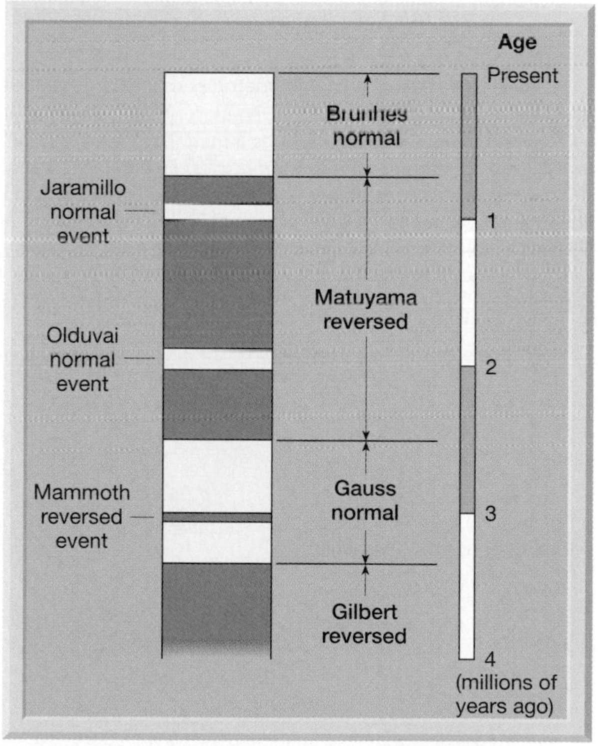

◆ **Figure 12.5** Time scale of Earth's magnetic field in the recent past. This time scale was developed by establishing the magnetic polarity for lava flows of known age. (Data from Allen Cox and G. B. Dalrymple)

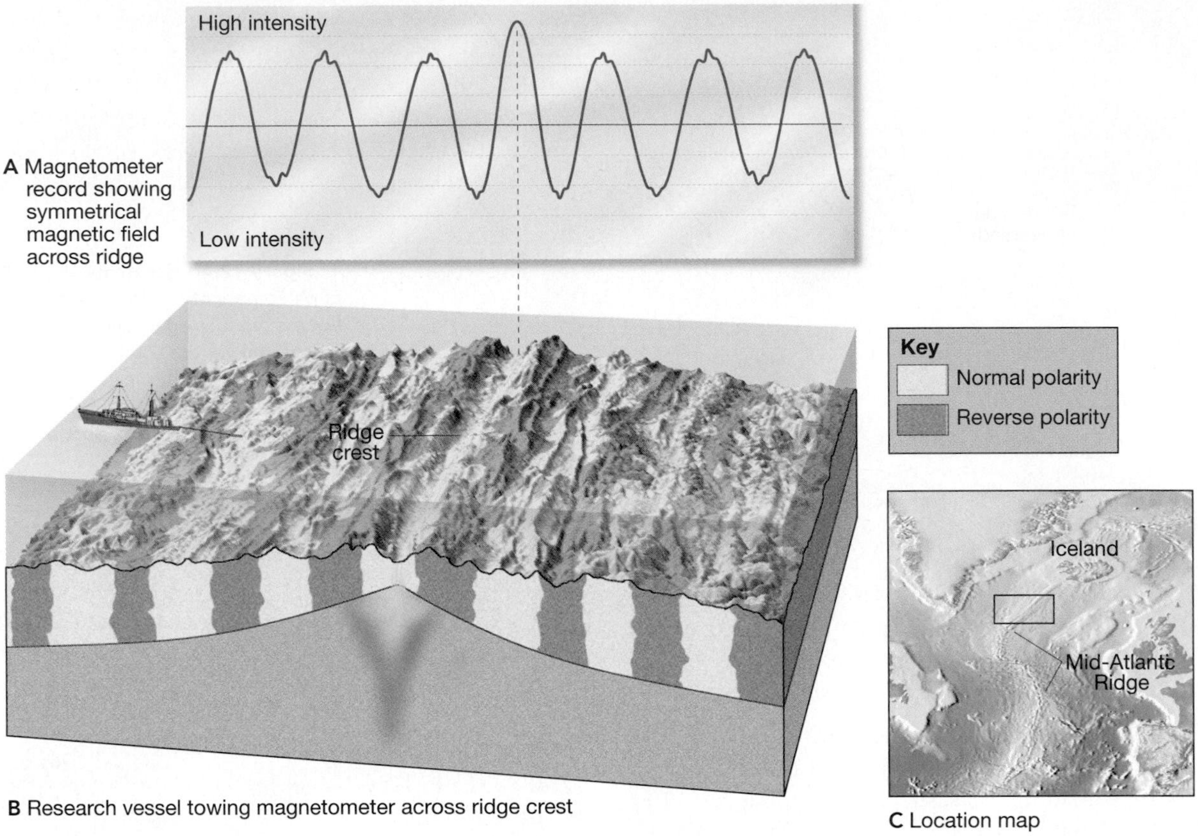

◆ **Figure 12.6** The ocean floor as a magnetic tape recorder. **A.** Schematic representation of magnetic intensities recorded as a magnetometer is towed across a segment of the Mid-Atlantic Ridge. **B.** Notice the symmetrical stripes of low- and high-intensity magnetism that parallel the ridge crest. Morley and colleagues suggested that the stripes of high-intensity magnetism occur where normally magnetized oceanic basalts enhance the existing magnetic field. Conversely, the low-intensity stripes are regions where the crust is polarized in the reverse direction, which weakens the existing magnetic field.

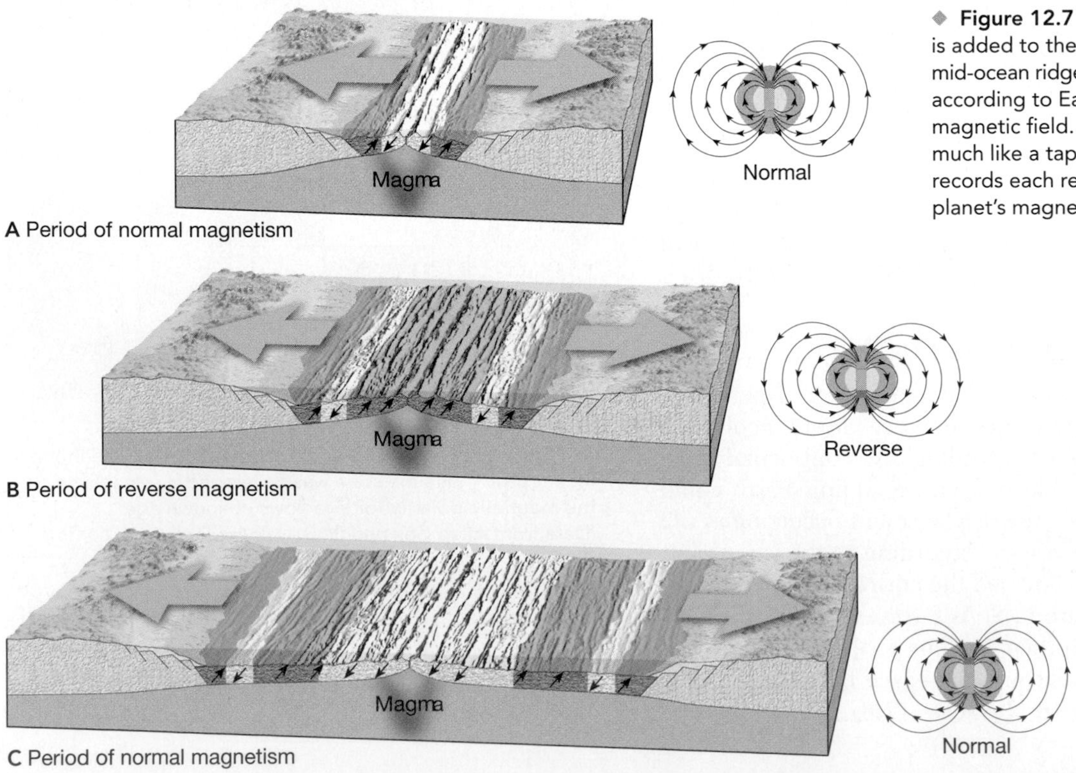

◆ **Figure 12.7** As new basalt is added to the ocean floor at mid-ocean ridges, it is magnetized according to Earth's existing magnetic field. Hence, it behaves much like a tape recorder as it records each reversal of the planet's magnetic field.

◆ **Figure 12.8** An alternative hypothesis to continental drift was an expanding Earth. According to this view the Earth was once only half its current diameter and covered by a layer of continents. As Earth expanded, the continents split into their current configurations, while new seafloor filled in the spaces as they drifted apart.

Against this background entered J. Tuzo Wilson, a Canadian geophysicist. In a paper published in 1965, Wilson provided the missing piece needed to formulate the theory of plate tectonics. Wilson suggested that large faults connected the global mobile belts into a continuous network that divides Earth's outer shell into several "rigid plates." In addition, Wilson described the three types of plate margins and how the solid blocks of Earth's outer shell moved relative to one another. At oceanic ridges, plates are moving apart, whereas along deep-ocean trenches, plates move together. Furthermore, along great faults—which he named *transform faults*—plates slide past one another. In a broad sense, Wilson had presented what would later be called the *theory of plate tectonics*.

Once the key concepts of plate tectonics were in place, the hypothesis-testing phase moved forward very quickly. Much of the supporting evidence for the plate tectonics model already existed. What this theory provided was a unified explanation for what seemed to be numerous unrelated observations from the fields of geology, paleontology, geophysics, and oceanography, among others.

By the end of the 1960s the tide of scientific opinion had indeed turned; however, some opposition to plate tectonics continued for at least a decade. Nevertheless, Wegener had been vindicated and the revolution in geology was nearing an end.

PLATE TECTONICS: THE NEW PARADIGM

GEODe EARTH Plate Tectonics
↳ Introduction

By 1968 the concepts of continental drift and seafloor spreading were united into a much more encompassing theory known as *plate tectonics*. Plate tectonics can be defined as the composite of a variety of ideas that explain the observed motion of Earth's lithosphere through the mechanisms of subduction and seafloor spreading, which, in turn, generate Earth's major features, including continents and ocean basins. The implications of plate tectonics are so far-reaching that this theory has become the basis for viewing most geologic processes.

Earth's Major Plates

As introduced in Chapter 1, according to the plate tectonics model, the uppermost mantle, along with the overlying crust, behaves as a strong, rigid layer, known as the **lithosphere**. This outermost shell overlies a weaker region in the mantle known as the **asthenosphere**. Further, the lithosphere is broken into numerous segments, called *plates*, that are in motion and are continually changing in shape and size. As shown in Figure 1.17, and discussed in Chapter 1, the seven major lithospheric plates are the North American, South American, Pacific, African, Eurasian, Australian-Indian, and Antarctic plates. The largest is the Pacific plate, which is located mostly within the Pacific Ocean. Several of the large plates include an entire continent and a large area of seafloor, such as the South American plate. This is a major departure from Wegener's continental drift hypothesis, which proposed that the continents moved through the ocean floor, not with it. Note also that none of the plates are defined entirely by the margins of a continent.

Intermediate-size plates include the Caribbean, Nazca, Philippine, Arabian, Cocos, and Scotia plates. More than a dozen smaller plates have been identified but are not shown in Figure 1.17. All major interactions among plates occur along or near their boundaries (divergent, convergent, and transform). These were discussed briefly in Chapter 1 and will now be covered in detail.

DIVERGENT PLATE BOUNDARIES

GEODe EARTH Plate Tectonics
↳ Divergent Boundaries

Most **divergent plate boundaries** (also called *spreading centres*) are located along the crests of oceanic ridges and can be thought of as *constructive plate margins* because this is where new oceanic lithosphere is generated (Figure 12.9). Here, as the plates move away from the ridge axis, the fractures created are filled with molten rock that wells up from the hot mantle below. Gradually, this magma cools to produce new slivers of seafloor. In a continuous manner,

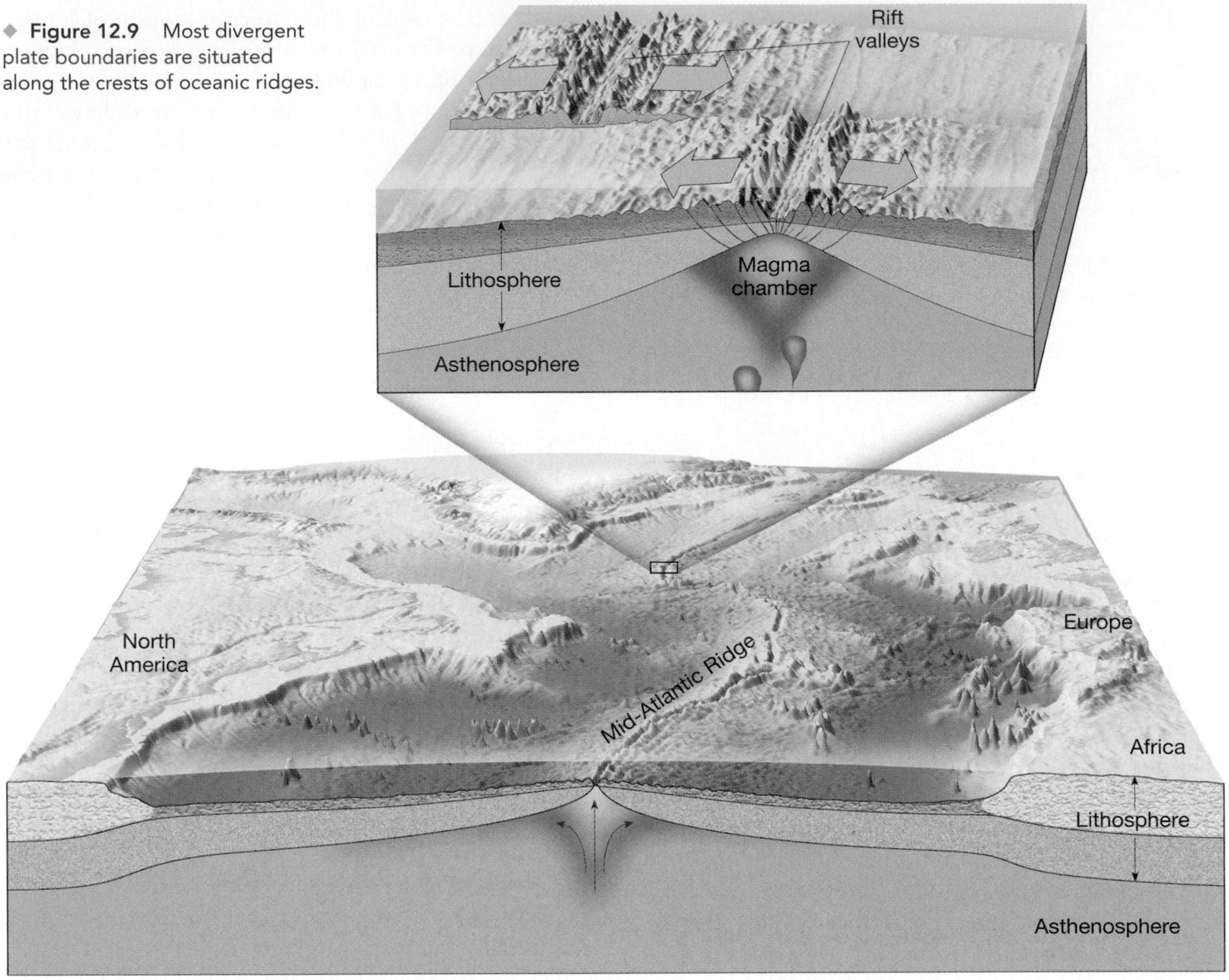

◆ **Figure 12.9** Most divergent plate boundaries are situated along the crests of oceanic ridges.

spreading and upwelling of magma adds oceanic lithosphere between the diverging plates. As you will see below, divergent boundaries can also form on the continents (see Box 12.1).

BOX 12.1

Understanding Earth
The Breakup of a Supercontinent

A great deal of evidence has been gathered to support the notion that Alfred Wegener's supercontinent of Pangaea began to break apart about 200 million years ago, as he had originally suggested (Figure 12.A, part A). An important consequence of this continental rifting was the creation of a "new" ocean basin, the Atlantic. As you can see in Figure 12.A, part B, the rifting that eventually resulted in the Atlantic basin occurred over an extended time. The first rift developed between North America and Africa and generated great volumes of Jurassic-age basalts. These basalts are present as weathered flows (e.g., North Mountain, Nova Scotia) and sills (e.g., Palisades Sill, New York) along the Eastern Seaboard of North America but primarily are buried beneath rocks that form the continental shelf. Radiometric dating of this material indicates that rifting began in various stages between 180 million and 165 million years ago. This span can be used as the birthdate for this section of the North Atlantic.

Rifting that formed the South Atlantic began about 130 million years ago near the tips of what are now Africa and South America. As this rift propagated northward, it gradually opened the South Atlantic (compare Figure 12.A, parts B and C). Continued rifting of the southern landmass of Gondwanaland sent India on a northward journey. By the early Cenozoic, about 50 million years ago, Australia began to separate from Antarctica, and the South Atlantic had emerged as a full-fledged ocean (Figure 12.A, part D).

A modern map (Figure 12.A, part E) shows that India eventually collided with Asia, an event that began about 45 million years ago and created the Himalayas and the Tibetan Plateau. About the same time, the separation of Greenland from Eurasia completed the breakup of the northern landmass (Laurasia). Also, notice the recent formation of the Baja Peninsula along with the Gulf of California. This event began less than 10 million years ago.

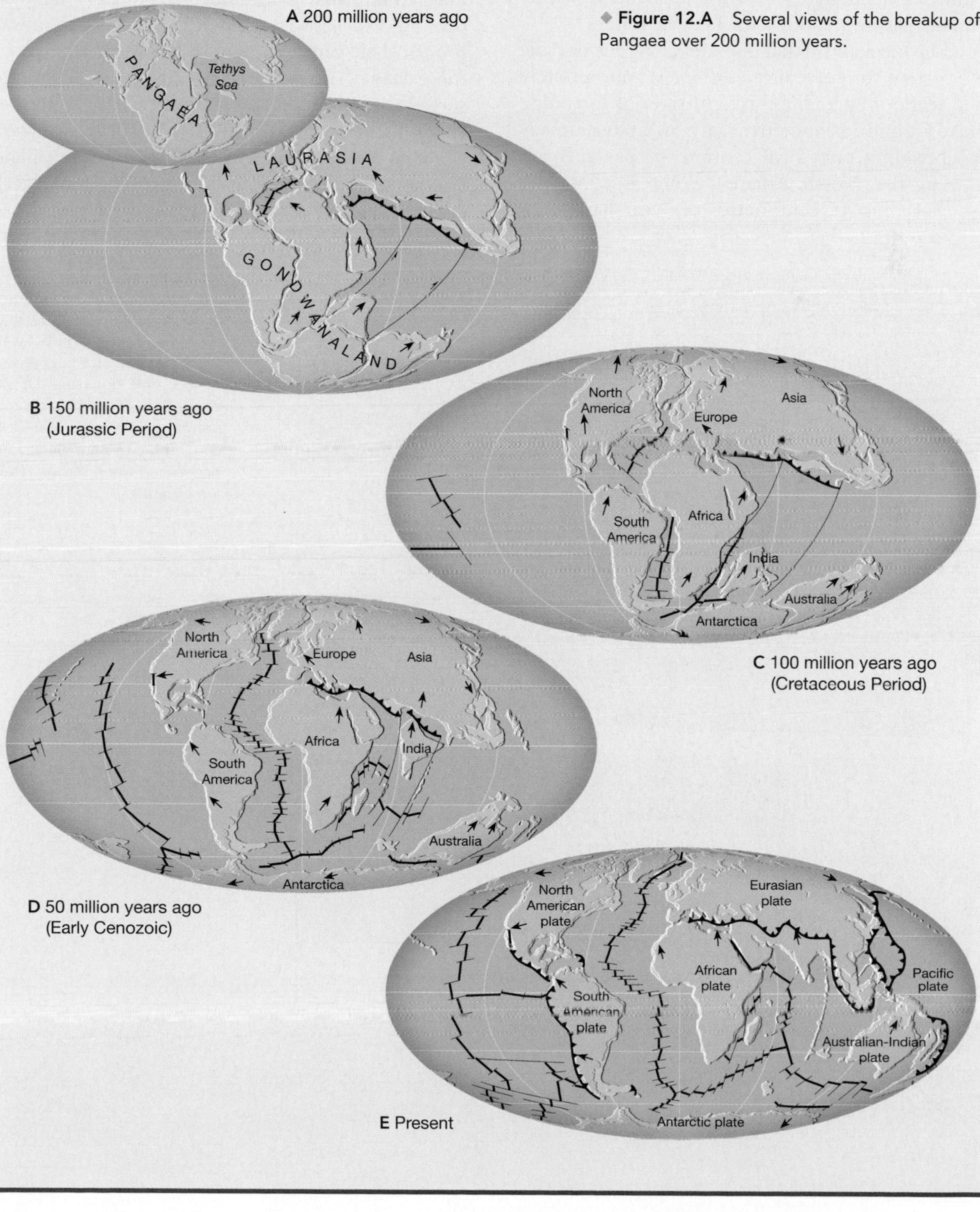

◆ **Figure 12.A** Several views of the breakup of Pangaea over 200 million years.

Oceanic Ridges and Seafloor Spreading

Along well-developed divergent plate boundaries, the seafloor is elevated, forming the **oceanic ridge**. As we learned in Chapter 11, the interconnected ocean ridge system is the longest topographic feature on Earth, stands higher than the floor of adjacent ocean basins, winds through all major ocean basins in a manner similar to the seam on a baseball, is broken up into segments by transform faults, and has some segments with wide, down-faulted rift valleys.

The mechanism that operates along the oceanic ridge system to create new seafloor is appropriately called seafloor spreading. Typical rates of spreading average around 5 centimetres per year. Comparatively slow spreading rates of 2 centimetres per year are found in the North Atlantic, whereas spreading rates exceeding 15 centimetres per year have been measured along sections of the East Pacific Rise. Although these rates of lithospheric production are slow on a human time scale, they are nevertheless rapid enough so that all of Earth's ocean basins could have been generated within the last 200 million years. As mentioned earlier, none of the ocean floor that has been dated exceeds 180 million years in age.

During seafloor spreading, the magma that is injected into newly developed fractures forms dykes that tend to cool from their outer borders inward toward their centres. Because the warm interiors of these newly formed dykes are weak, continued spreading produces new fractures that split these young rocks roughly in half. As a result, new material is added about equally to the two diverging plates. Consequently, new ocean floor grows symmetrically on each side of a centrally located ridge crest. As

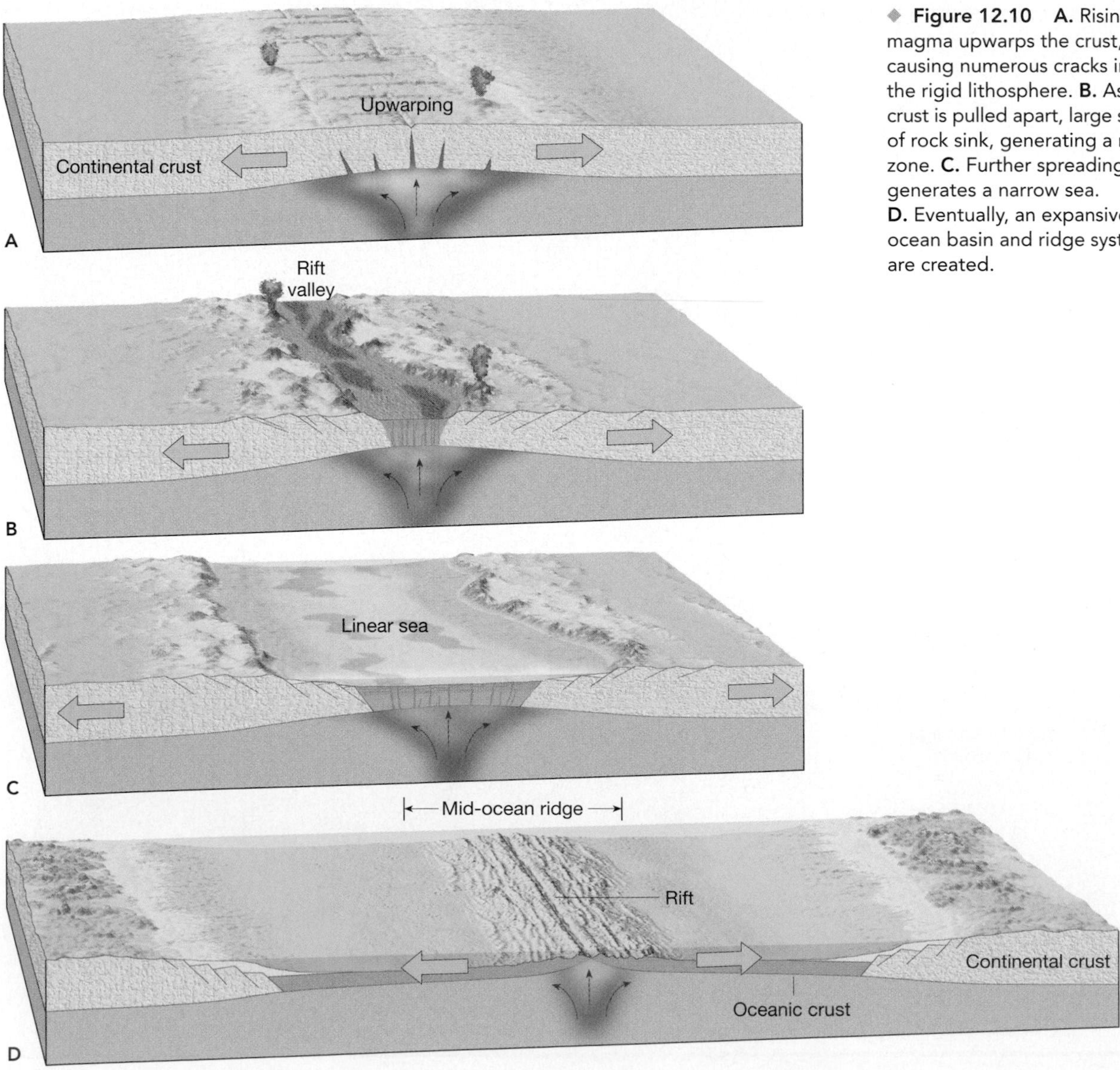

◆ **Figure 12.10** **A.** Rising magma upwarps the crust, causing numerous cracks in the rigid lithosphere. **B.** As the crust is pulled apart, large slabs of rock sink, generating a rift zone. **C.** Further spreading generates a narrow sea. **D.** Eventually, an expansive ocean basin and ridge system are created.

noted in Chapter 11, the ridge systems of the Atlantic and Indian oceans are located near the middle of these water bodies and as a consequence are called *mid-ocean ridges*. Conversely, the East Pacific Rise is situated far from the centre of the Pacific Ocean.

Continental Rifts

Spreading centres can also develop within a continent, in which case the landmass may split into two or more smaller segments, as Alfred Wegener had proposed for the breakup of Pangaea. Examples of active continental rifts include the East African rift valleys, the Baikal Rift in southcentral Siberia, the Rhine Valley (Northwest Europe), the Rio Grande Rift, and the Basin and Range province in western North America. Whether any of these rifts will continue to develop and eventually split a continent is a matter of much speculation.

The most widely accepted model for continental splitting suggests that extensional forces must be acting on the lithospheric plate. It appears that by themselves these extensional forces are not great enough to actually tear the lithosphere apart. Rather, the rupture of the lithosphere is initiated only in those settings where plumes of hot rock rise from the mantle. This activity weakens the lithosphere and domes the crust directly above the hot rising plume. Upwarping stretches and thins the crust, as shown in Figure 12.10A. Extension is accompanied by alternating episodes of faulting and volcanism that result in the development of a rift valley that resembles those found along the axes of some ridges (Figure 12.10B).

The East African rift valleys may represent the initial stage in the breakup of a continent as described above or they may be destined to become failed rift arms, like the Niger arm in Figure 12.11A. Large volcanic mountains, such as Mount Kilimanjaro and Mount Kenya, exemplify the extensive volcanic activity that accompanies continental rifting (Figure 12.11B).

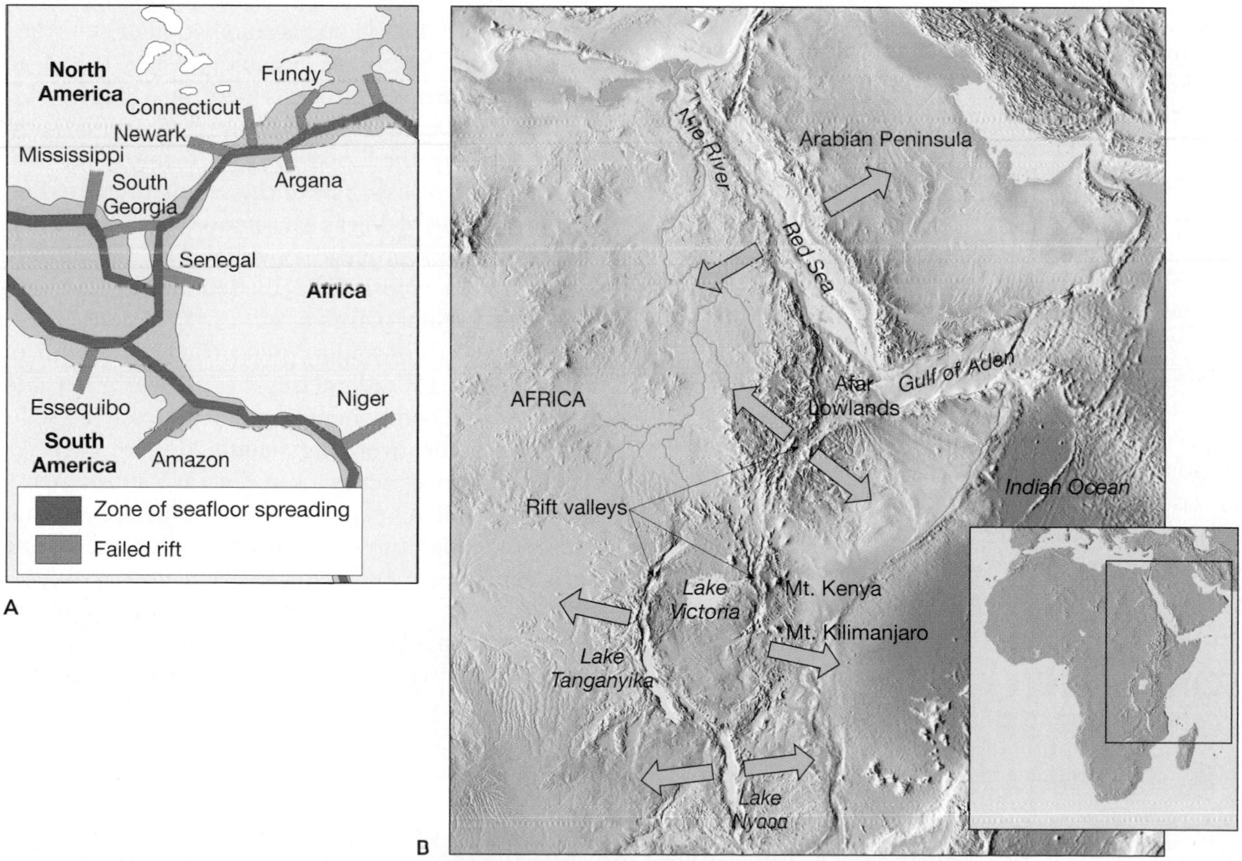

◆ **Figure 12.11** **A.** Cracks produced by mantle-plume-related doming of the lithosphere tend to produce rift zones that meet at triple junctions. Where two of the three rift arms in a particular triple-junction zone meet rift arms of other triple-junction systems, they form a composite rift zone, along which spreading can continue and ultimately form an ocean basin. The arms that do not connect with others eventually stop spreading and therefore become failed rifts that simply become filled with sediment. Some of the major river systems follow the trends of ancient failed rifts. This diagram shows the rift arms that developed just before the opening of the Atlantic Ocean. **B.** East African rift valleys and associated features.

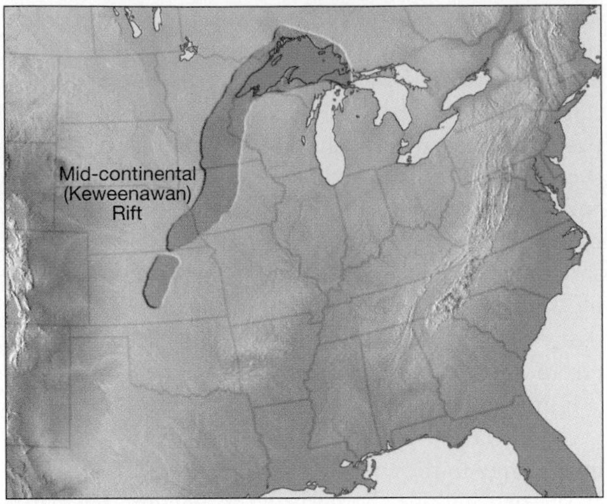

◆ **Figure 12.12** Map showing location of a failed rift extending from Lake Superior to Kansas.

Where the extensional forces are maintained, the rift valley will lengthen and deepen, eventually extending out to the margin of the plate, and split it in two (Figure 12.10C). At this point the rift becomes a narrow linear sea with an outlet to the ocean, similar to the Red Sea (Figure 12.11B). The Red Sea formed when the Arabian Peninsula rifted from Africa, an event that began about 20 million years ago. Consequently, the Red Sea provides oceanographers with a view of how the Atlantic Ocean may have looked in its infancy. The boundary between oceanic and continental crust (Figure 12.10D) represents the original rift or split of the former continent and becomes the true edge of the new continent. The surface expression of this crustal boundary is the *continental slope* discussed in Chapter 11.

Not all rift valleys develop into full-fledged spreading centres. Extending from Lake Superior to Kansas through central North America is a failed rift (Figure 12.12). This once active rift valley is filled with volcanic rocks that were extruded onto the crust more than a billion years ago.

CONVERGENT PLATE BOUNDARIES

GEODe EARTH Plate Tectonics
↳ Convergent Boundaries

Although new lithosphere is continually being added at the oceanic ridges, our planet is not growing larger—its total surface area remains constant. To accommodate the newly created lithosphere, older portions of oceanic plates return to the mantle along **convergent plate boundaries**. (Because lithosphere is "destroyed" at convergent boundaries, they are also called *destructive plate margins*.) As two plates slowly converge, the leading edge of one is bent downward, allowing it to slide beneath the other. The surface expression produced by the descending plate is an ocean *trench*, like the Peru–Chile Trench (Figure 12.13A). Trenches formed in this manner can be thousands of kilometres long, 8 to 12 kilometres deep, and between 50 and 100 kilometres wide (see Figure 11.8). Destructive plate margins where oceanic crust is being consumed in the mantle are called **subduction zones**.

Oceanic–Continental Convergence

Whenever the leading edge of a continental plate converges with an oceanic plate, the buoyant continental plate remains "floating," while the denser oceanic slab sinks into the asthenosphere (Figure 12.13A). As the oceanic slab descends, some of the sediments carried on the subducting plate, as well as pieces of oceanic crust, are scraped off and plastered against the edge of the overriding continental block. This chaotic accumulation of deformed sediment and scraps of oceanic crust is called an *accretionary wedge*, as described in Chapter 11. Studies conducted in the coastal regions of western Mexico, where the Cocos plate is being subducted, indicate that at least half of the sediment carried on the descending plate can be removed in this manner. Therefore, this process contributes to the already substantial accumulation of sediment deposited along continental margins.

When a descending plate reaches a depth of about 100 to 150 kilometres, heat drives water and other volatile components from the subducted sediments into the overlying mantle (Figure 12.13A). These substances act as a flux does at a steel-making foundry, inducing partial melting of mantle rocks at reduced temperatures. The partial melting of mantle rock generates magmas that have a mafic or occasionally intermediate composition. (Research has shown that in some settings the subducted oceanic lithosphere might also partially melt, generating some magma.) The newly formed magma, being less dense than the rocks of the mantle, will rise buoyantly. Often the magma, being denser than continental rocks, will pool beneath the overlying continental crust, where it may melt some of the silica-enriched rocks. Eventually some of this silica-rich magma may migrate to the surface, where it can give rise to volcanic eruptions, some of which are explosive.

Such mountains as the Andes, which were produced, in part, by volcanic activity associated with the subduction of oceanic lithosphere, are called

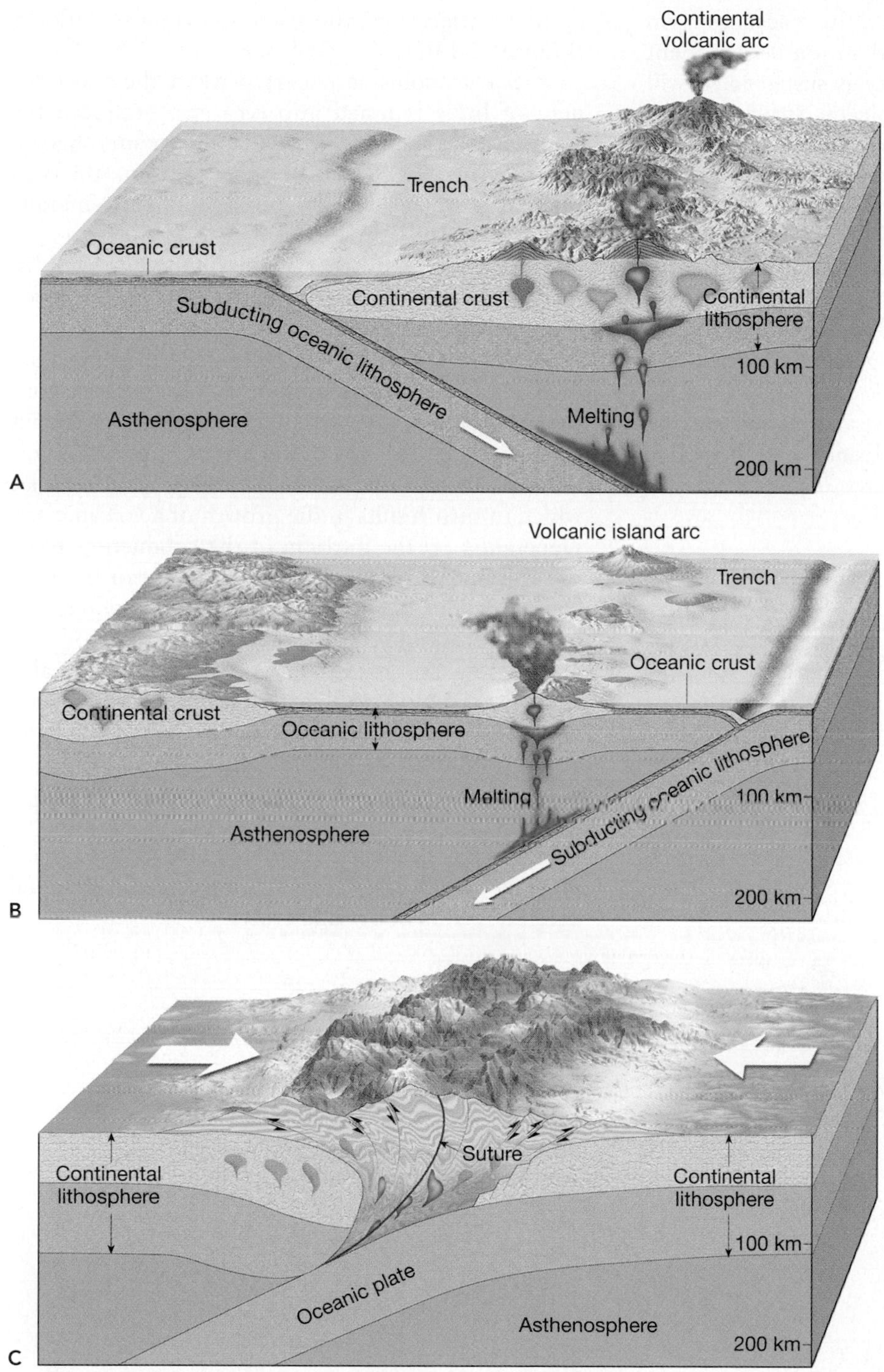

◆ **Figure 12.13** Zones of plate convergence. **A.** Oceanic–continental. **B.** Oceanic–oceanic. **C.** Continental–continental.

continental volcanic arcs. Another active continental volcanic arc is located in western North America. The Cascade Range of British Columbia, Washington, Oregon, and California consists of several well-known volcanic mountains, including Mount Baker, Mount St. Helens, Mount Rainier, and Mount Shasta (see Figure 4.18). The Cascade Range remains active as the continuing activity of Mount St. Helens testifies. The magma here arises from melting triggered by the subduction of a small remaining segment of the Farallon plate, of which the Juan de Fuca plate is the largest northern segment (see Figure 1.17).

Oceanic–Oceanic Convergence

When two oceanic slabs converge, one descends beneath the other, initiating volcanic activity in a manner similar to what occurs at an oceanic–continental boundary. In this case, however, the volcanoes form on the ocean floor rather than on a continent (Figure 12.13B). If this activity is sustained, it will eventually build a chain of volcanic structures that emerge as islands. The volcanic islands are spaced about 80 kilometres apart and are built on submerged ridges of volcanic material a few hundred kilometres wide. This newly formed land consisting of an arc-shaped chain of small volcanic islands is called a **volcanic island arc**. The Aleutian, Mariana, and Tonga islands are examples of volcanic island arcs. Island arcs, such as these, are generally located 200 to 300 kilometres from the trench axis. Located adjacent to the island arcs just mentioned are the Aleutian Trench, the Mariana Trench, and the Tonga Trench (see Figure 11.8). Most volcanic island arcs are located in the western Pacific.

Continental–Continental Convergence

As you saw earlier, when an oceanic plate is subducted beneath continental lithosphere, an Andean-type volcanic arc develops along the margin of the continent. However, if the subducting plate also contains continental lithosphere, continued subduction eventually brings the two continents together. Whereas oceanic lithosphere is relatively dense and sinks into the asthenosphere, continental lithosphere is buoyant, which prevents it from being subducted to any great depth. The result is a collision between the two continental blocks (Figure 12.13C).

Such a collision occurred when the subcontinent of India rammed into Asia and produced the Himalayas—the most spectacular mountain range on Earth (Figure 12.14). During this collision, the continental crust buckled, fractured, and was generally shortened and thickened. In addition to the Himalayas, several other major mountain systems, including the Alps, Appalachians, and Urals, formed during continental collisions.

Before a continental collision, the landmasses involved are separated by an ocean basin. As the continental blocks converge, the intervening seafloor is subducted beneath one of the plates. Subduction initiates partial melting in the overlying mantle rocks, which in turn results in the growth of a volcanic arc. Depending on the location of the subduction zone, the volcanic arc could develop on either of the converging landmasses, or if the subduction zone developed several hundred kilometres seaward from the coast, a volcanic island arc would form. Eventually, as the intervening seafloor is consumed, these continental masses collide. This folds and deforms the accumulation of sediments along the continental margin as if they had been placed in a gigantic vice. The result is the formation of a new mountain range composed of deformed and metamorphosed sedimentary rocks, fragments of the volcanic arc, and possibly slivers of oceanic crust.

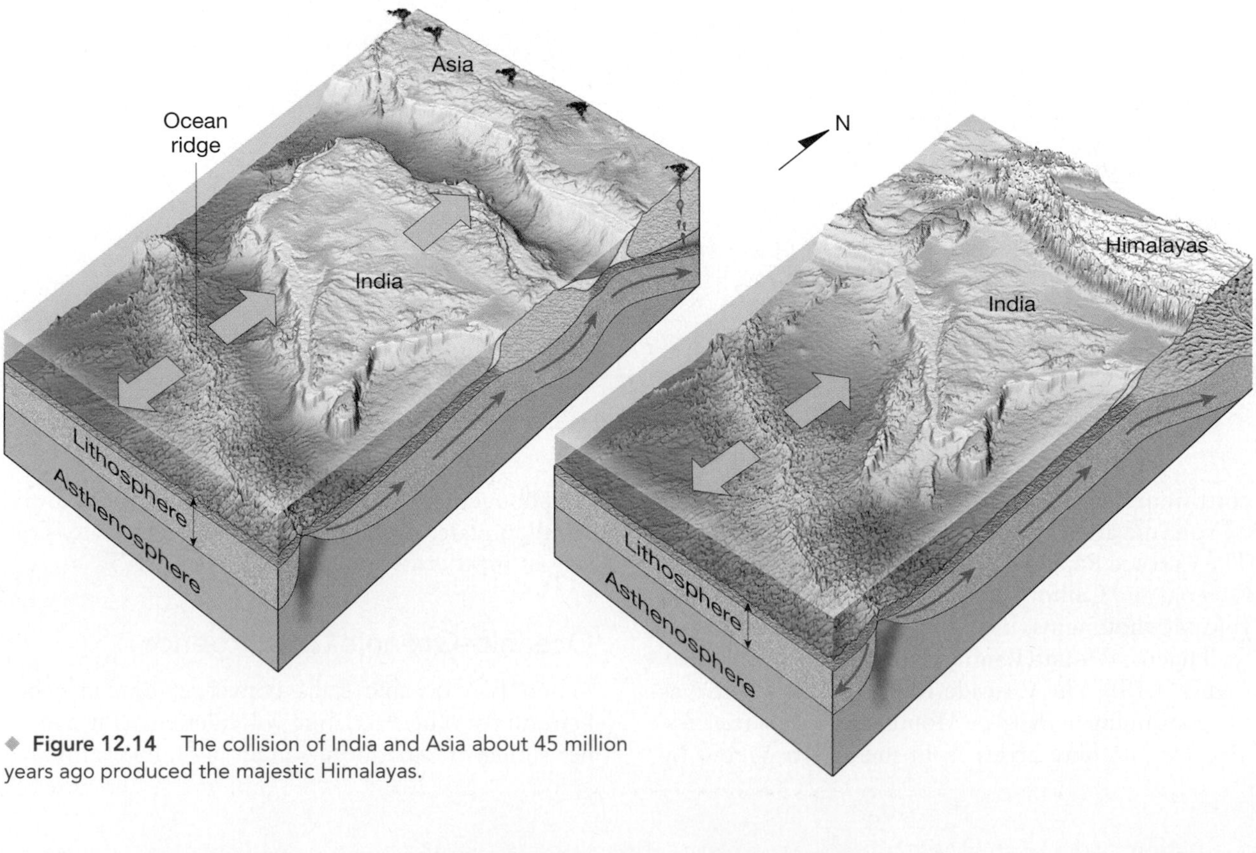

◆ **Figure 12.14** The collision of India and Asia about 45 million years ago produced the majestic Himalayas.

TRANSFORM FAULT BOUNDARIES

GEODe EARTH Plate Tectonics
↳ Transform Fault Boundaries

The third type of plate boundary is the **transform fault boundary**, which is characterized by strike-slip faulting, where plates move past one another without the production or destruction of lithosphere (*conservative plate margins*). Transform faults were first identified where they join offset segments of an ocean ridge (see Figure 11.8).

As noted earlier, they were discovered in 1965 by J. Tuzo Wilson of the University of Toronto (Box 12.2), when he suggested that these large faults connect the globally active belts into a network of several rigid plates. Thus, Wilson became the first to suggest that Earth was made of individual plates, while at the same time identifying the faults along which relative motion between the plates is made possible.

Most transform faults join two segments of a mid-ocean ridge (Figure 12.15). Here, they are part of prominent linear breaks in the oceanic crust known as **fracture zones**, which include both the transform faults and their inactive extensions into the plate interior. These fracture zones are present approximately every 100 kilometres along the trend of a ridge axis. As shown in Figure 12.15, active transform faults lie only *between* the two offset ridge segments. Here, seafloor produced at one ridge axis moves in the opposite direction from seafloor produced at an opposing ridge segment. Thus, between the ridge segments these adjacent slabs of oceanic crust are slipping past each other along a transform fault. Beyond the ridge crests are the inactive zones, where the fractures produced by strike-slip faulting

BOX 12.2

Canadian Profile

John Tuzo Wilson: Canada's Champion of Plate Tectonics

Vic Tyrer*

In the 1960s J. Tuzo Wilson (Figure 12.B) was one of a group of Earth scientists who developed the theory of plate tectonics. His many contributions to the theory include an explanation for the opening and closing of ocean basins, now known as the Wilson Cycle (see Chapter 13). In 1965 he proposed the existence of transform faults to explain the numerous narrow fracture zones and earthquakes found in oceanic crust. His idea of magma plumes rising through Earth's crust and creating local hot spots explained intraplate volcanoes, such as the Hawaiian Island chain.

Born in Ottawa, J. Tuzo Wilson was the first graduate of geophysics from the University of Toronto in 1930. He went on to become an assistant geologist with the Geological Survey of Canada from 1936 to 1939. Following service in the Canadian Army, he became a professor of geophysics at the University of Toronto from 1946 to 1974.

Wilson was the director general of the Ontario Science Centre from 1974 to 1985, where he combined his scientific vision with his commitment to public education. He was as comfortable in the Science Centre's classrooms as he was in the boardroom, frequently capturing the imagination of young students and adults alike with hands-on demonstrations of plate tectonics by using his familiar "lighter and paper" explanation of the Hawaiian Islands.

Wilson gave his last public lecture at the Ontario Science Centre in February 1992. His lecture, "With Zest to Go, in Quest to Know," recounted his lifetime travels of more than 3 million kilometres and seven continents in his quest to understand and teach the inner workings of Earth.

On May 3, 2001, the Ontario Science Centre unveiled a tribute to its former director general in the form of a geodetic monument. Central to the monument is the sculpture's large iron spike. Visitors are asked to imagine that the spike has been driven into the Earth's core. The iron spike remains fixed, seemingly gouging a trough in the surrounding concrete plaza as the North American plate "drifts" westward a few centimetres per year. The trough marks a total of 2.3 metres of tectonic movement during Tuzo Wilson's lifetime (1908–1993).

◆ **Figure 12.B** John Tuzo Wilson, Canadian pioneer of plate tectonics. (Photo courtesy of the Ontario Science Centre)

A notch on the spike marks a point calculated by using GPS technology. Geomatics, Canada's Geodetic Survey, located this site by monitoring the broadcast from numerous orbiting GPS satellites over 24 hours in July 1997.

---

*Vic Tyrer was the Earth science programmer at the Ontario Science Centre from 1978 to 1999.

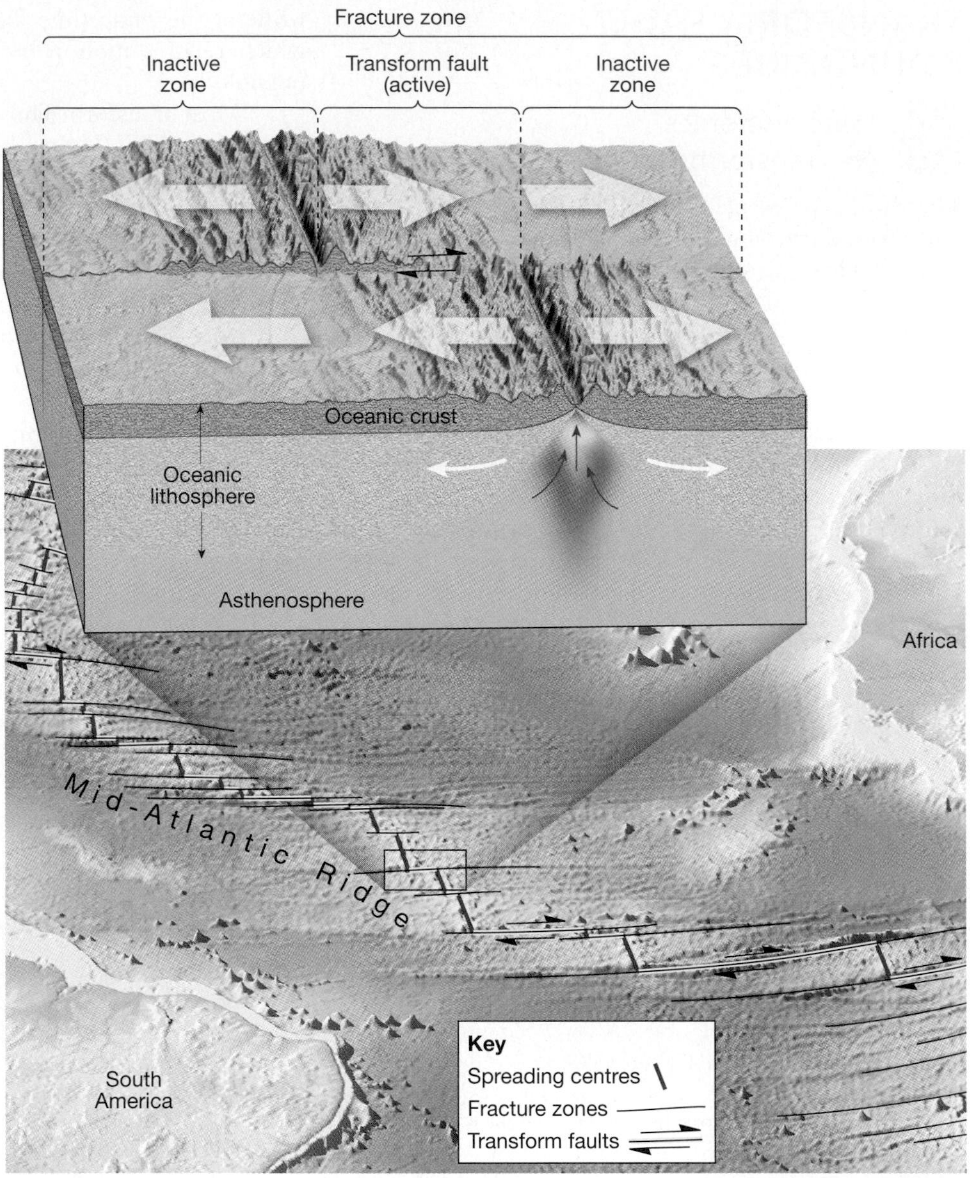

◆ **Figure 12.15** Diagram illustrating a transform fault boundary offsetting segments of the Mid-Atlantic Ridge.

are preserved as linear topographic scars. These fracture zones tend to curve such that small segments roughly parallel the direction of plate motion at the time of their formation.

Although most transform faults are located within the ocean basins, a few cut through continental crust. Two examples are the earthquake-prone San Andreas Fault of California and the Alpine Fault of New Zealand.

TESTING THE PLATE TECTONICS MODEL

With the development of plate tectonics, researchers from all Earth sciences began testing this model of how Earth works. We have already presented some of the evidence supporting continental drift and seafloor spreading; some of the evidence that was instrumental in solidifying the support for this new idea follows. Note that much of this evidence was not new; rather, the new interpretations of existing data turned the tide of opinion.

Plate Tectonics and Earthquakes

By 1968 the basic outline of global tectonics was firmly established. In that year, three seismologists published papers demonstrating how successfully the new plate tectonics model accounted for the global distribution of earthquakes (Figure 12.16). In particular, these scientists were able to account for the close association between deep-focus earthquakes and subduction zones. Furthermore, the absence of deep-focus earthquakes along the oceanic ridge system was shown to be consistent with the new theory.

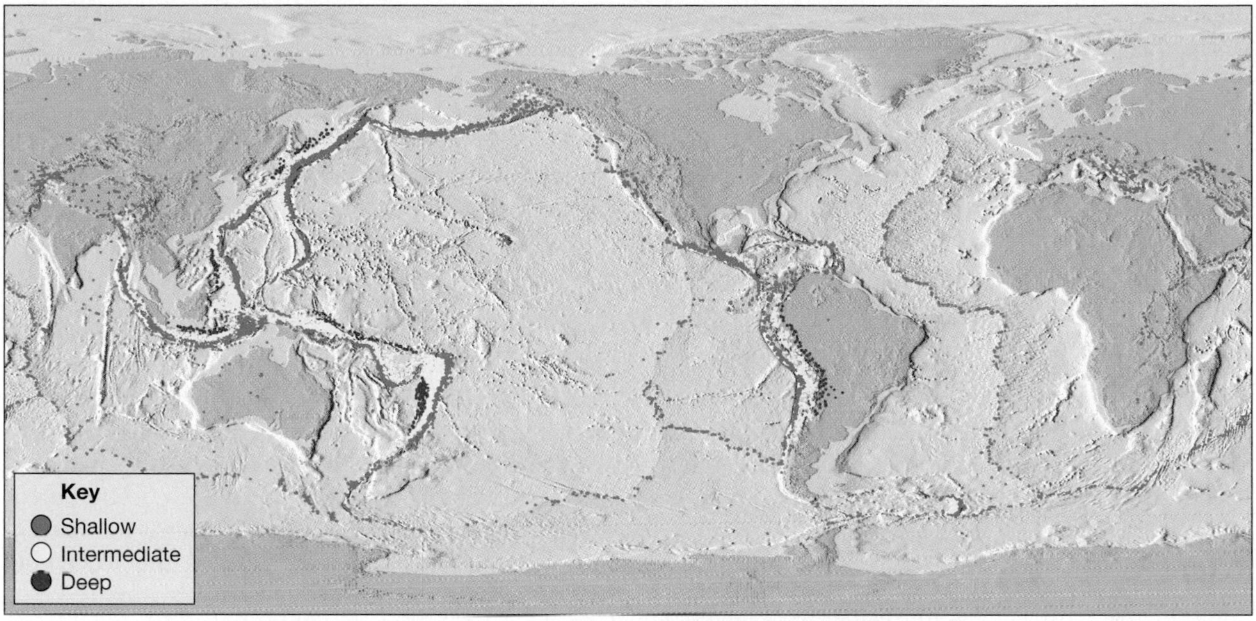

◆ **Figure 12.16** Distribution of shallow-, intermediate-, and deep-focus earthquakes. Note that deep-focus earthquakes occur only in association with convergent plate boundaries and subduction zones. (Data from NOAA)

Note the close association between plate boundaries and earthquakes by comparing the distribution of earthquakes shown in Figure 12.16 with the map of plate boundaries in Figure 1.17. In trench regions—where dense slabs of lithosphere descend into the mantle—this association is especially striking. When the depths of earthquake foci and their locations within the trench systems are plotted, an interesting pattern emerges. Figure 12.17 is an example of the distribution of earthquakes near the Japan Trench. Here, most shallow-focus earthquakes occur within or adjacent to the trench, whereas intermediate- and deep-focus earthquakes occur toward the mainland. A similar distribution pattern

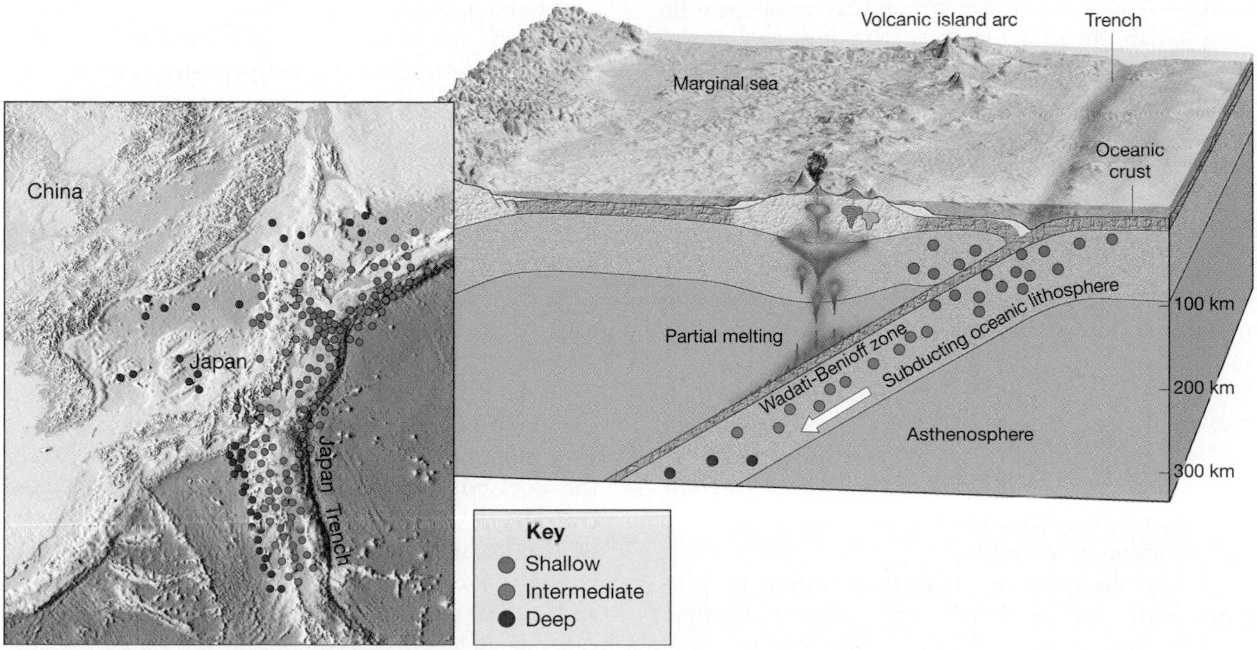

◆ **Figure 12.17** Distribution of earthquake foci near the Japan Trench. Note that intermediate- and deep-focus earthquakes occur only within the sinking slab of oceanic lithosphere. (Data from NOAA)

exists along the western margin of South America, where the Nazca plate is being subducted beneath the South American continent.

In the plate tectonics model, deep-ocean trenches form where dense slabs of oceanic lithosphere sink into the mantle (Figure 12.17). Shallow-focus earthquakes are produced as the descending plate interacts with the overriding lithosphere. As the slab descends farther into the asthenosphere, deeper-focus earthquakes are generated. Because the earthquakes occur within the rigid subducting plate (i.e., capable of faulting) rather than in the "plastic" mantle, they provide a method for tracking the plate's descent. Very few earthquakes have been recorded below 700 kilometres, possibly because the slab has been heated sufficiently to lose its rigidity.

Evidence from Ocean Drilling

Some of the most convincing evidence of seafloor spreading has come from drilling directly into ocean-floor sediment. From 1968 until 1983, the source of these important data was the Deep Sea Drilling Program, an international collaboration sponsored by several major oceanographic institutions.

At several sites, holes were drilled through the entire thickness of sediments to the mafic rock below. An important objective was to gather samples of sediment from just above the igneous crust as a means of dating the seafloor at each site.* Because sedimentation begins immediately after the oceanic crust forms, remains of microorganisms found in the oldest sediments—those resting directly on the basalt—can be used to date the ocean floor at that site.

When the oldest sediment from each drill site was plotted against its distance from the ridge crest, the plot demonstrated that the age of the sediment increased with growing distance from the ridge. This finding agreed with the seafloor-spreading hypothesis, which predicted that the youngest oceanic crust would be found at the ridge crest and that the oldest oceanic crust would be at the continental margins, where sediments have been accumulating on it longer.

The data from the Deep Sea Drilling Program also reinforced the idea that the ocean basins are geologically youthful because no sediment with an age in excess of 180 million years was found. By comparison, continental crust has been dated at more than 4 billion years old.

The thickness of ocean-floor sediments provided additional verification of seafloor spreading. Drill cores from the *Glomar Challenger* revealed that sediments are almost entirely absent on the ridge crest and that the sediment thickens with increasing distance from the ridge. Because the ridge crest is younger than the areas farther away from it, this pattern of sediment distribution should be expected if the seafloor-spreading hypothesis is correct.

The Ocean Drilling Program has succeeded the Deep Sea Drilling Program and, like its predecessor, it is a major international effort. The more technologically advanced drilling ship, the *JOIDES Resolution*, now continues the work of the *Glomar Challenger*.** The *JOIDES Resolution* can drill in water up to 8200 metres deep and contains onboard laboratories equipped with a large and varied array of seagoing scientific research equipment (Figure 12.18). The *JOIDES Resolution* is now part of a new international venture called the Integrated Ocean Drilling Program that also uses other research vessels, including the massive 210-metre-long *Chikyu* (meaning "planet Earth" in Japanese).

Hot Spots and Mantle Plumes

Mapping of seamounts in the Pacific Ocean revealed a chain of volcanic structures extending from the Hawaiian Islands to Midway Island and continuing northward toward the Aleutian Trench (Figure 12.19). Radiometric dating in this chain showed that the volcanoes increase in age with increasing distance from Hawaii. Hawaii has the youngest volcanoes in the chain and rose from the seafloor less than a million years ago, whereas Midway Island is 27 million years old and Suiko Seamount, near the Aleutian Trench, is 65 million years old (Figure 12.19).

Researchers are in agreement that a rising plume of mantle material is located beneath the island of Hawaii. Decompression melting of this hot rock as it enters the low-pressure environment near the surface generates a volcanic area known as a **hot spot**. As the Pacific plate moved over this hot spot, successive volcanic structures were built. The age of each volcano indicates the time when it was situated over the relatively stationary **mantle plume**.

This pattern is shown in Figure 12.19. Kauai is the oldest of the large islands in the Hawaiian chain. Five million years ago, when it was positioned over the hot spot, Kauai was the only Hawaiian Island (Figure 12.19). Evidence of Kauai's age can be seen by examining its well-developed red soils and extinct volcanoes, which have been eroded into jagged peaks and vast canyons. By contrast, the south slopes of the

*Radiometric dates of the ocean crust itself are unreliable because of the alteration of basalt by seawater.

***JOIDES* stands for Joint Oceanographic Institutions for Deep Earth Sampling (see Box 11.2).

◆ **Figure 12.18** The *JOIDES Resolution*, the drilling ship of the Ocean Drilling Program. This modern drilling ship has replaced the *Glomar Challenger* in the important work of sampling the floor of the world's oceans.
(Photo courtesy of Ocean Drilling Program)

comparatively young island of Hawaii consist of fresh lava flows, and two of Hawaii's volcanoes, Mauna Loa and Kilauea, remain active.

Two island groups parallel the Hawaiian Island–Emperor Seamount chain. One chain consists of the Tuamotu and Line islands, and the other includes the Austral, Gilbert, and Marshall islands. In each case, the most recent volcanic activity has occurred at the southeast end of the chain, and the islands get progressively older to the northwest. Thus, like the Hawaiian Island–Emperor Seamount chain, these volcanic structures apparently formed by the same motion of the Pacific plate over fixed mantle plumes. Not only does this evidence support the fact that the plates do indeed move relative to Earth's interior but the hot spot "tracks" also trace the direction of the plate motion. Notice in Figure 12.19, for example, that the Hawaiian Island–Emperor Seamount chain bends. This particular bend in the track occurred about 50 million years ago, when the motion of the Pacific plate changed from nearly due north to northwest. Similarly, hot spots found on the floor of the Atlantic have increased our understanding of the migration of landmasses following the breakup of Pangaea.

The existence of mantle plumes and their association with hot spots is well documented. Most mantle plumes are considered long-lived structures that appear to maintain relatively fixed positions within the mantle. Research suggests that at least some mantle plumes originate at great depth, perhaps at the mantle–core boundary. Others, however, may have a much shallower origin. Of the 40 or so hot spots that have been identified, more than a dozen are located near spreading centres. For example, the mantle plume located beneath Iceland is responsible for the large accumulation of volcanic rocks found along the northern section of the Mid-Atlantic Ridge.

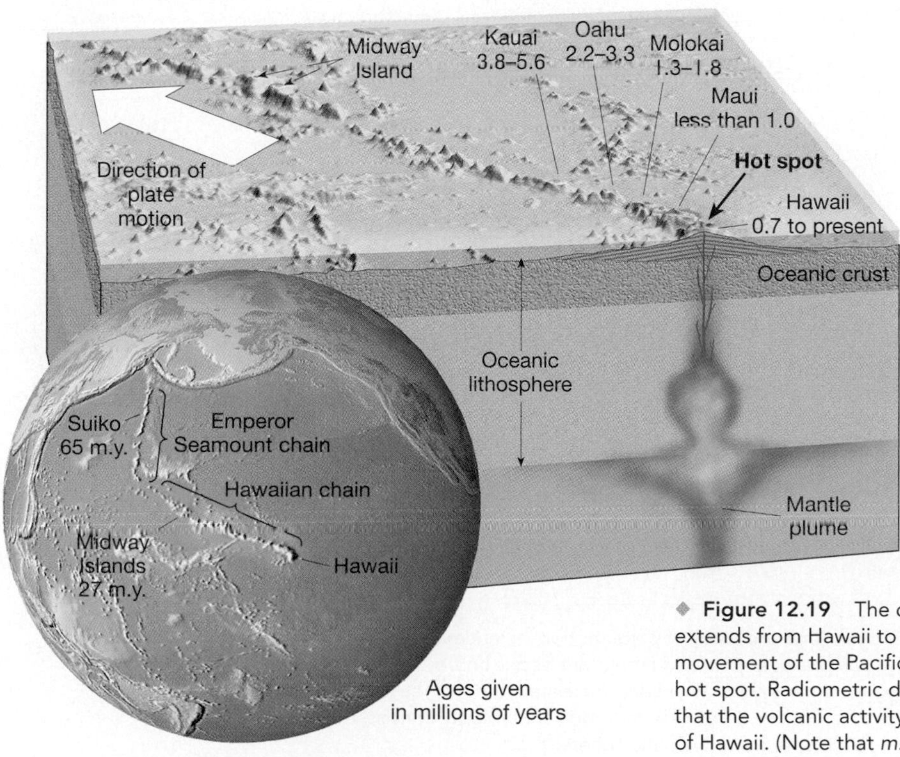

◆ **Figure 12.19** The chain of islands and seamounts that extends from Hawaii to the Aleutian Trench results from the movement of the Pacific plate over an apparently stationary hot spot. Radiometric dating of the Hawaiian Islands shows that the volcanic activity decreases in age toward the island of Hawaii. (Note that *m.y.* stands for "million years.")

MEASURING PLATE MOTION

A number of methods have been employed to establish the direction and rate of plate motion. As noted earlier, hot spot tracks, like those of the Hawaiian Island–Emperor Seamount chain, trace the movement of the Pacific plate relative to the mantle below. By measuring the length of this volcanic chain and the time interval between the formation of the oldest structure (Suiko Seamount) and youngest structure (Hawaii), we can calculate an average rate of plate motion. In this case the volcanic chain is roughly 3000 kilometres long and has formed over the past 65 million years—making the average rate of movement about 4.6 centimetres per year. The accuracy of this calculation hinges on the hot spot maintaining a fixed position in the mantle; recent evidence suggests that some hot spots may slowly migrate.

Recall that the magnetic stripes measured on the floor of the ocean (Figure 12.6B) also provide a method to measure rates of plate motion—at least as averaged over millions of years. By using paleomagnetism and other indirect techniques, researchers have been able to work out relative plate velocities, as shown on the map in Figure 12.20 (see Box 12.3).

It is currently possible, with the use of modern technology, to directly measure the relative motion between plates. This is accomplished by periodically establishing the exact locations of, and hence the distance between, two observing stations situated on opposite sides of a plate boundary. Two of the methods used for this calculation are *Very Long Baseline Interferometry* (VLBI) and a satellite positioning technique that employs the *global positioning system* (GPS). The VLBI system uses large radio telescopes to record signals from very distant quasars (quasi-stellar objects). Quasars lie billions of light-years from Earth, so they act as stationary reference points. The millisecond differences in the arrival times of the same signal at different earthbound observatories provide a means of establishing the precise distance between receivers. A typical survey may take a day to perform and involves two widely spaced radio telescopes observing perhaps a dozen quasars, five to ten times each. This scheme provides an estimate of the distance between these observatories, which is accurate to about 2 centimetres. By repeating this experiment at a later date, researchers can establish the relative motion of these sites. This method has been particularly useful in establishing large-scale plate motions, such as the separation that is occurring between North America and Europe.

You may be familiar with GPS, which uses numerous satellites to accurately locate any individual who is equipped with a handheld receiver. By using two spaced receivers, signals obtained by these instruments can be used to calculate the relative positions with considerable accuracy. Techniques that use GPS receivers have been useful in establishing small-scale

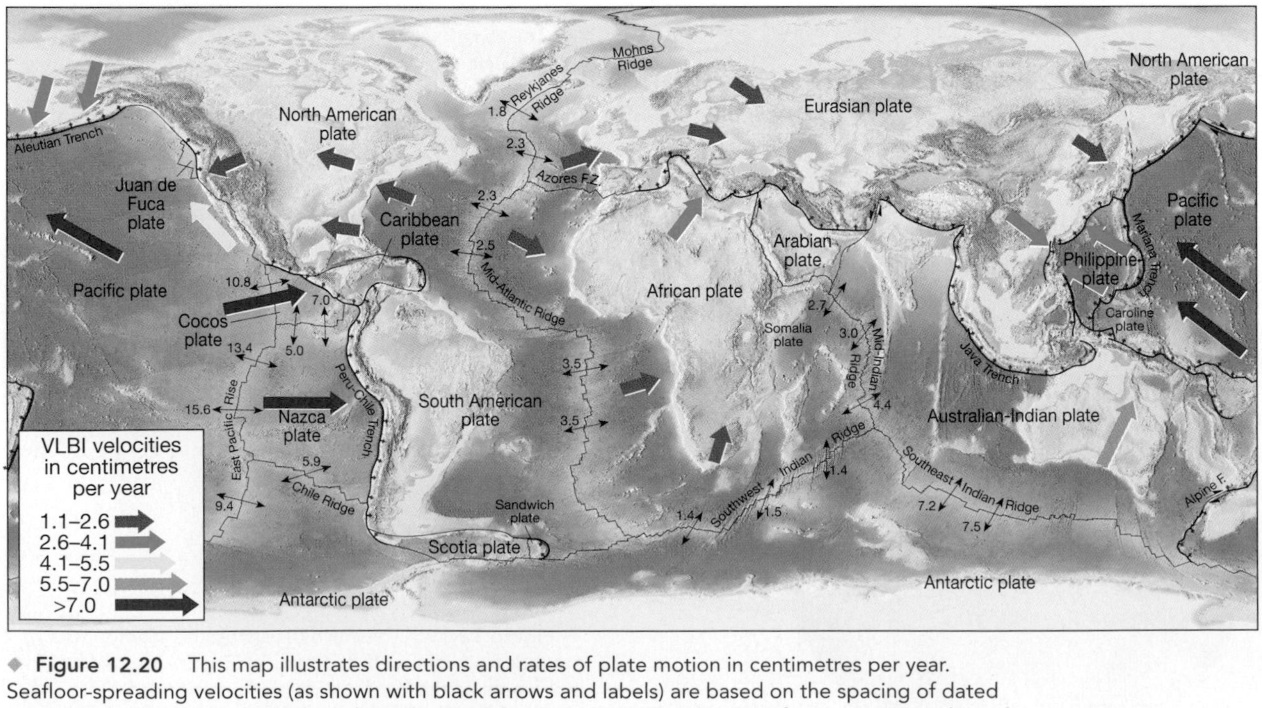

◆ **Figure 12.20** This map illustrates directions and rates of plate motion in centimetres per year. Seafloor-spreading velocities (as shown with black arrows and labels) are based on the spacing of dated magnetic stripes (anomalies). The coloured arrows show Very Long Baseline Interferometry (VLBI) data of plate motion at selected locations. The data obtained by these methods are typically consistent. (Seafloor data from DeMets and others, VLBI data from Ryan and others)

BOX 12.3

Understanding Earth
Plate Tectonics into the Future

Two geologists, Robert Dietz and John Holden, extrapolated present-day plate movements into the future. Figure 12.C illustrates where they envision Earth's landmasses will be 50 million years from now if present plate movements persist.

In North America we see that the Baja Peninsula and the portion of southern California that lies west of the San Andreas Fault will have slid past the North American plate. If this northward migration takes place, Los Angeles and San Francisco will pass each other in about 10 million years, and in about 60 million years Los Angeles will begin to descend into the Aleutian Trench.

Significant changes are seen in Africa, where a new sea emerges as East Africa parts company with the mainland. In addition, Africa will have moved slowly into Europe, perhaps initiating the next major mountain-building stage on our dynamic planet. Meanwhile, the Arabian Peninsula continues to diverge from Africa, allowing the Red Sea to widen and causing the Persian Gulf to close.

In other parts of the world, Australia is now astride the equator and, along with New Guinea, is on a collision course with Asia. Meanwhile, North and South America are beginning to separate, while the Atlantic and Indian oceans continue to grow at the expense of the Pacific Ocean.

These projections into the future, although interesting, must be viewed with caution because many assumptions must be correct for these events to unfold as just described. Nevertheless, changes in the shapes and positions of continents that are equally profound will undoubtedly occur for millions of years to come.

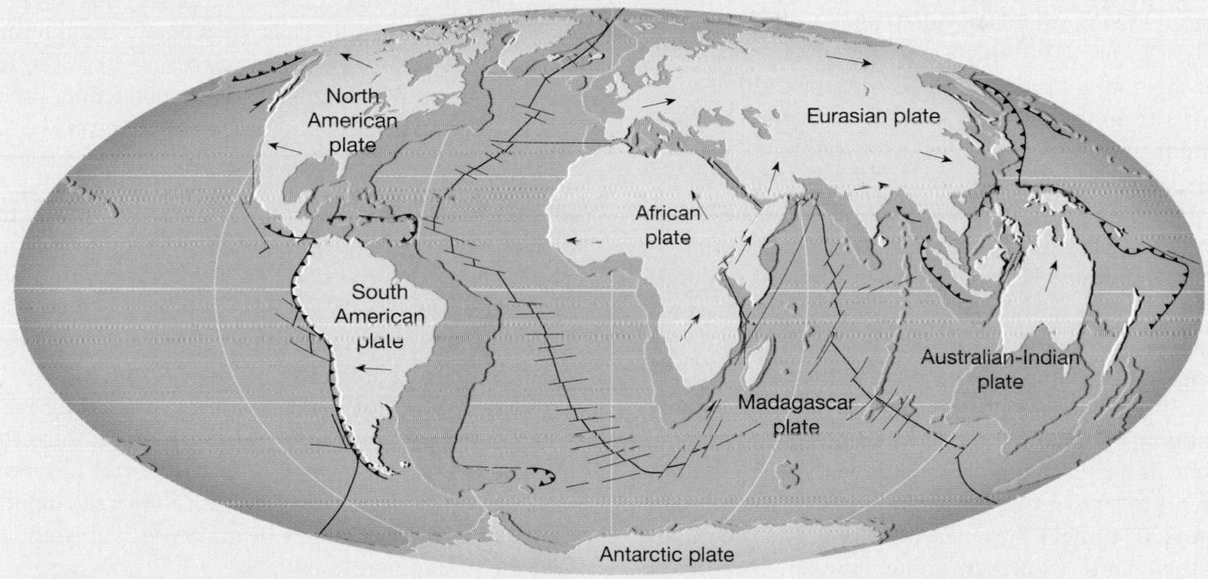

◆ **Figure 12.C** The world as it may look 50 million years from now.
(From "The Breakup of Pangaea," Robert S. Dietz and John C. Holden. Copyright 1970 by Scientific American, Inc., All rights reserved)

crustal movements, such as those that occur along local faults in regions known to be tectonically active.

THE DRIVING MECHANISM

The plate tectonics theory *describes* plate motion and the effects of this motion. Therefore, acceptance of this model does not rely on the mechanism that drives plate motion. This is fortunate, because none of the driving mechanisms yet proposed can account for all major facets of plate tectonics. Nevertheless, researchers generally agree on the following:

1. Convective flow in the rocky 2900-kilometre-thick mantle—in which warm, less dense rock rises and cooler, more dense material sinks—is the basic driving force for plate movement.
2. Mantle convection and plate tectonics are part of the same system. Subducting oceanic plates drive the cold downward-moving portion of convective flow, while shallow upwelling of hot rock along the oceanic ridge and buoyant mantle plumes are the upward-flowing arm of the convective mechanism.
3. The slow movements of the plates and mantle are driven by the unequal distribution of heat within

Earth's interior. This flow is the mechanism that transports heat away from Earth's core and up through the mantle.

What is not known with certainty is the precise nature of this convective flow.

Some researchers have argued that the mantle is like a giant layer cake, divided at a depth of 660 kilometres. Convection operates in both layers, but mixing between layers is minimal. At the other end of the spectrum is a model that loosely resembles a pot of just barely boiling water, churning ever so slowly from top to bottom over eons of geologic time. Neither model fits all of the available data.

Slab-Pull and Ridge-Push

Several mechanisms generate forces that contribute to plate motion. One relies on the fact that old oceanic crust, which is relatively cool and dense, sinks into the asthenosphere and "pulls" the trailing lithosphere along. This mechanism, called **slab-pull**, is thought to be the primary downward arm of the convective flow operating in the mantle. By contrast, **ridge-push** results from the elevated position of the oceanic ridge system and causes oceanic lithosphere to gravitationally slide down the flanks of the ridge. Ridge-push, although apparently active in some spreading centres, is probably less important than slab-pull.

Most models suggest that hot, buoyant plumes of rock are the upward-flowing arms in the convective mechanism at work in the mantle. These rising mantle plumes manifest themselves on Earth's surface as hot spots with their associated volcanic activity. Mapping of Earth's interior by using seismic tomography indicates that at least some of these hot plumes extend upward from the vicinity of the mantle-core boundary. Others, however, appear to originate higher in the mantle. Further, some upward flow in the mantle is not related to plumes and occurs just below the ridge crests as a result of seafloor spreading.

Models of Plate–Mantle Convection

Any model describing mantle convection must be consistent with the observed physical and chemical properties of the mantle. In particular, these models must explain why basalts that erupt along the oceanic ridge are fairly homogeneous in composition and depleted in certain trace elements. It is assumed that these ridge basalts are derived from rocks located in the upper mantle that experienced an earlier period of chemical differentiation in which trace elements were removed. By contrast, higher concentrations of these elements are evident in mafic eruptions associated with hot-spot volcanism. Because basalts that erupted in different settings have different concentrations of trace elements, they are thought to be derived from chemically distinct regions of the mantle. Basalts associated with mantle plumes are thought to come from a primitive (less differentiated) source, which more closely resembles the average chemical composition of the early mantle.

Layering at 660 Kilometres Earlier we mentioned the "layer cake" version of mantle convection. As shown in Figure 12.21A, one of these layered models has two zones of convection: a thin, convective layer above 660 kilometres, and a thick one located below. This model successfully explains why the basalts that erupt along the oceanic ridges have a somewhat different composition from those that erupt in Hawaii as a result of hot-spot activity. The oceanic ridge basalts come from the upper convective layer, which is well mixed, whereas the mantle plume that feeds the Hawaiian volcanoes taps a deeper, more primitive source that resides in the lower convective layer.

Despite evidence that supports this model, recent seismic imaging has shown that subducting slabs of cold oceanic lithosphere are able to penetrate the 660-kilometre boundary. The subducting lithosphere serves to mix the upper and lower layers together. As a result, the layered mantle structure is lost.

Whole–Mantle Convection Because of problems with the layered model, researchers began to favour whole-mantle convection. In a whole-mantle convection model, slabs of cold oceanic lithosphere descend into the lower mantle, providing the downward arm of convective flow (Figure 12.21B). Simultaneously, hot mantle plumes originating near the mantle-core boundary transport heat toward the surface. It was also suggested that at extremely slow rates of convection, primitive (not depleted) mantle rock would exist at depth in quantities sufficient to feed the rising mantle plumes.

Recent work, however, has shown that whole-mantle mixing would cause the lower mantle to become appreciably mixed in a matter of a few hundred million years. This mixing would tend to eliminate the source of primitive magma observed in hot-spot volcanism.

Deep-Layer Model A remaining possibility is layering deeper in the mantle. One deep-layer model has been described as analogous to a lava lamp on a low setting. As shown in Figure 12.21C, approximately the lower third of the mantle is like the coloured fluid in the bottom layer of a lava lamp. Like a lava lamp on low, heat from Earth's interior causes the two layers to slowly swell and shrink in complex patterns without substantial mixing. A small amount of material from the lower layer flows upward as mantle plumes to generate hot-spot volcanism at the surface.

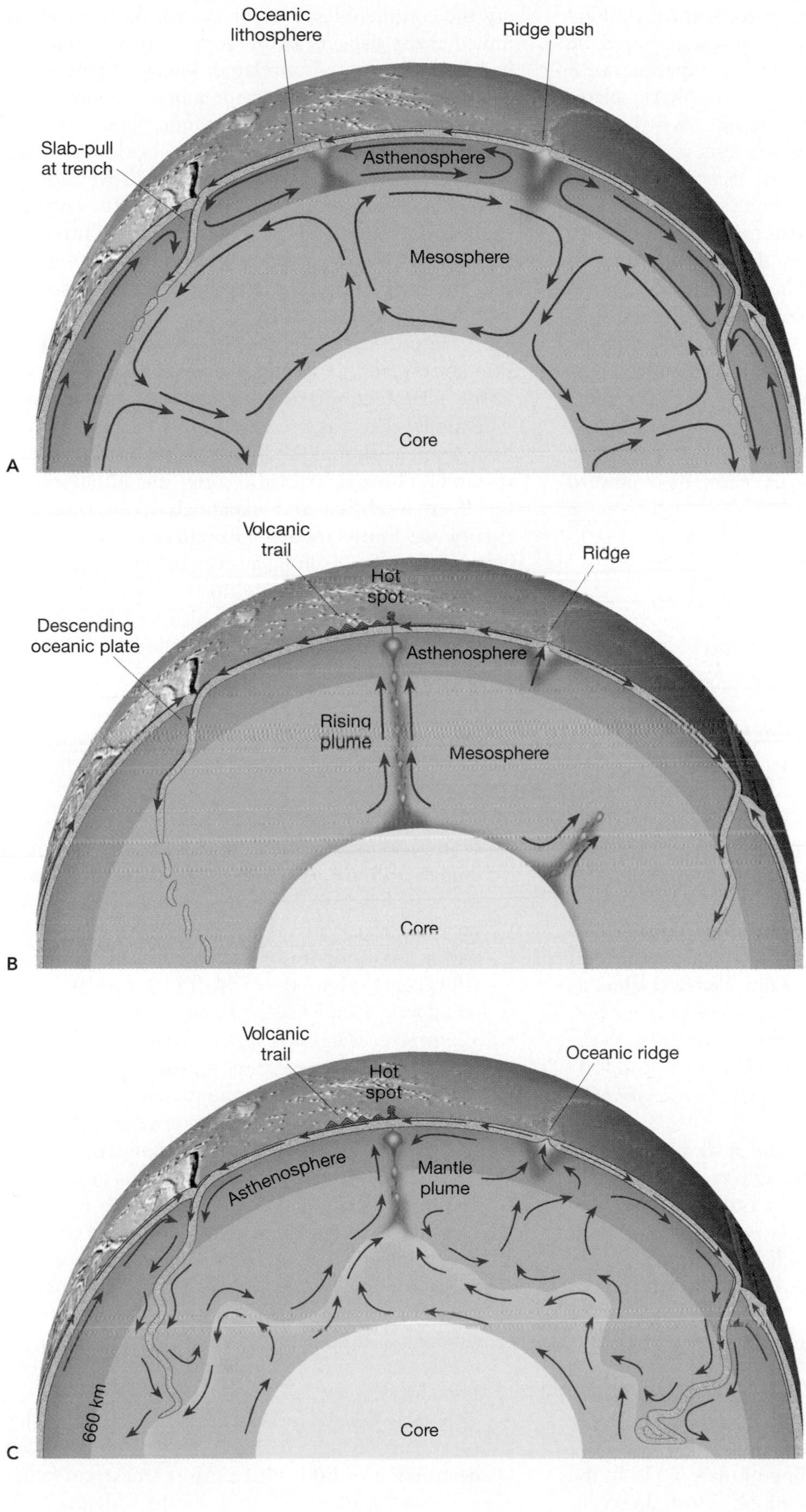

◆ **Figure 12.21** Proposed models for mantle convection. **A.** The model shown in this illustration consists of two convection layers: a thin, convective layer above 660 kilometres, and a thick one below. **B.** In this whole-mantle convection model, cold oceanic lithosphere descends into the lowermost mantle, while hot mantle plumes transport heat toward the surface. **C.** This deep-layer model suggests that the mantle operates similar to a lava lamp on a low setting. Earth's heat causes these layers of convection to slowly swell and shrink in complex patterns without substantial mixing. Some material from the lower layer flows upward as mantle plumes.

This model provides the two chemically different mantle sources for basalt that are required by observational data. Further, it is compatible with seismic images that show cold lithospheric plates sinking deep into the mantle. Despite its attractiveness, little seismic evidence suggests that a deep mantle layer of this nature exists, except for the very thin layer located at the core–mantle boundary.

Although Earth scientists still have much to learn about the mechanisms that cause plates to move, some facts are clear. The unequal distribution of heat in Earth generates some type of thermal convection that ultimately drives plate–mantle motion. The descending lithospheric plates are active components of downwelling, and they serve to transport cold material into the mantle (Figures 12.21B and 12.21C). Furthermore, mantle plumes generated near the core–mantle boundary carry heat upward from the core into the mantle.

IMPORTANCE OF PLATE TECTONICS

Plate tectonics is the first theory to provide a unified explanation of Earth's major surface features, including the continents and ocean basins. As such, it has linked many aspects of geology, which previously had been considered unrelated. Various branches of geology have joined to provide a better understanding of the workings of our dynamic planet. Within the framework of plate tectonics, geologists have found explanations for the geologic distribution of earthquakes, volcanoes, and mountain belts. Further, explanations for past distributions of plants and animals and the occurrence of economically significant mineral deposits have resulted from an understanding of plate tectonics.

Despite its usefulness in explaining many of the large-scale geologic processes operating on Earth, plate tectonics is not completely understood. The model that was presented in 1968 was simply a basic framework that left much of the detail to future research. Through critical testing, this initial model has been modified and expanded to become the theory we know today. The current theory will certainly be refined (and may even be replaced) as new technologies appear and additional data are obtained. The theory of plate tectonics, although a powerful tool, is nonetheless an evolving model of Earth's dynamic processes.

Chapter Summary

- From the study of *paleomagnetism*, researchers learned that the continents had wandered as Wegener proposed. In 1962, Harry Hess formulated the idea of seafloor spreading, which states that new seafloor is continually being generated at mid-oceanic ridges and old, dense seafloor is being consumed at the deep-ocean trenches. Support for seafloor spreading followed, with the discovery of alternating stripes of high- and low-intensity magnetism (*normal* and *reverse polarity*) that parallel the ridge crests.
- By 1968, continental drift and seafloor spreading were united into a far more encompassing theory known as plate tectonics. According to plate tectonics, Earth's rigid outer layer (*lithosphere*) overlies a weaker region called the *asthenosphere*. Further, the lithosphere is broken into seven large and numerous smaller segments called plates that are in motion and continually changing in shape and size. Plates move as relatively coherent units and are deformed mainly along their boundaries.
- *Divergent plate boundaries* occur where plates move apart, resulting in upwelling of material from the mantle to create new seafloor. Most divergent boundaries occur along the axis of the *oceanic ridge* system and are associated with seafloor spreading, which occurs at rates of 2 to 15 centimetres per year. New divergent boundaries may form within a continent (for example, the East African rift valleys), where they may fragment a landmass and develop a new ocean basin.
- *Convergent plate boundaries* occur where plates move together, resulting in the subduction of oceanic lithosphere into the mantle along a deep oceanic trench. Convergence between an oceanic and continental block results in subduction of the oceanic slab and the formation of a *continental volcanic arc* such as the Andes of South America. Oceanic–oceanic convergence results in an arc-shaped chain of volcanic islands called a *volcanic island arc*. When two plates carrying continental crust converge, both plates are too buoyant to be subducted. The result is a collision, resulting in the formation of a mountain belt, such as the Himalayas.
- *Transform fault boundaries* occur where plates slip past each other without the production or destruction of lithosphere. Most transform faults join two segments of a mid-oceanic ridge.

- The theory of plate tectonics is supported by (1) the global distribution of earthquakes and their close association with plate boundaries; (2) the ages and thickness of sediments from the floors of the deep-ocean basins; and (3) the existence of island chains that formed over *hot spots* and provide a frame of reference for tracing the direction of plate motion.
- Three basic models for mantle convection are currently being evaluated. Mechanisms that contribute to this convective flow are slab-pull, ridge-push, and mantle plumes. *Slab-pull* occurs where cold, dense oceanic lithosphere is subducted and pulls the trailing lithosphere along. *Ridge-push* results when gravity sets the elevated slabs astride ocean ridges in motion. Hot, buoyant *mantle plumes* are considered the upward flowing arms of mantle convection. One model suggests that mantle convection occurs in two layers separated at a depth of 660 kilometres. Another model proposes whole-mantle convection that stirs the entire 2900-kilometre-thick rocky mantle. Yet another model suggests that the bottom third of the mantle gradually bulges upward in some areas and sinks in others without appreciable mixing.

Review Questions

1. Briefly explain why the recent acceptance of plate tectonics has been described as a scientific "revolution."
2. What is meant by seafloor spreading? Who is credited with formulating the concept of seafloor spreading?
3. Describe how Lawrence Morley, Fred Vine, and D. H. Matthews related the seafloor-spreading hypothesis to magnetic reversals.
4. On what basis were plate boundaries first established?
5. Where is lithosphere being formed? Where is it being consumed? Why must the production and destruction of the lithosphere be going on at about the same rate?
6. Why is oceanic lithosphere subducted while continental lithosphere is not?
7. In what ways can the origin of the Japanese islands be considered similar to the formation of the Andes Mountains? How do they differ?
8. Differentiate between J. Tuzo Wilson's transform faults and the two other types of plate boundaries.
9. Applying the idea that hot spots remain fixed, in what direction was the Pacific plate moving while the Emperor Seamounts were being produced? (See Figure 12.19.) In what direction was it moving while the Hawaiian Islands were being produced?
10. With what type of plate boundary are the following places or features associated: Himalayas, Aleutian Islands, Red Sea, Andes Mountains, San Andreas Fault, Iceland, Japan, and Mount St. Helens? (Be as specific as possible.)
11. Briefly describe the three models proposed for plate–mantle convection. What is lacking in each model?

Key Terms

asthenosphere (p. 317)
continental volcanic arc (p. 323)
convergent plate boundaries (p. 322)
divergent plate boundaries (p. 317)
fracture zone (p. 325)
hot spot (p. 328)
lithosphere (p. 317)
magnetometer (p. 314)
mantle plume (p. 328)
normal polarity (p. 314)
oceanic ridge (p. 320)
paleomagnetism (p. 312)
reverse polarity (p. 314)
ridge-push (p. 332)
slab-pull (p. 332)
subduction zone (p. 322)
transform fault boundary (p. 325)
volcanic island arc (p. 324)

Web Resources

The *Earth* website uses the resources and flexibility of the internet to aid in your study of the topics in this chapter. Written and developed by geology instructors, this site will help improve your understanding of geology. Visit **www.pearsoned.ca/tarbuck** and click on the cover of the text to find

- online review quizzes
- Web-based critical thinking and writing exercises
- links to chapter-specific Web resources
- internet-wide key-term searches

www.pearsoned.ca/tarbuck

Chapter 13
Mountain Building and Continental Frameworks

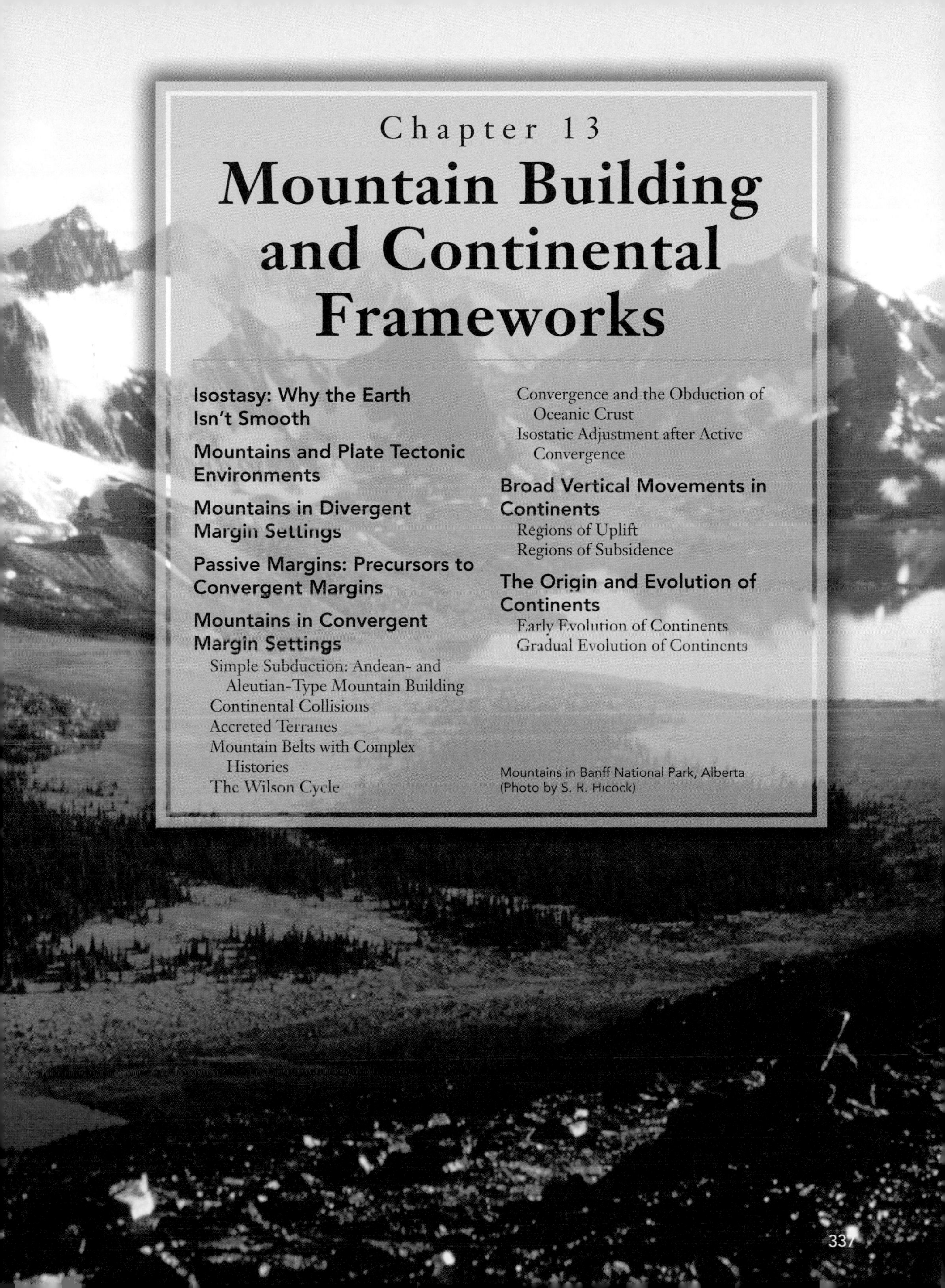

Mountains in Banff National Park, Alberta (Photo by S. R. Hicock)

Few geologic features of Earth have captured people's attention as much as mountains. Throughout the ages, mountains have inspired legends, appeared as prominent motifs in works of art, influenced the placement of political boundaries, and challenged the physical abilities of those bold enough to climb them.

To geologists, mountains are extremely important features for different reasons. First, mountains expose spectacular sedimentary rock sequences that are the basis for interpreting the sequence of events in Earth's history. Second, igneous and metamorphic rocks forced upward to the surface during mountain building provide information on processes that occur so deep in Earth's crust that they cannot be observed directly. Third, mountains supply geologists with information that is critical to understanding large-scale tectonic processes.

In the context of the Earth system, mountains influence drainage patterns of rivers, supply sediment that is the parent material for soil in lowland regions, and, in some areas of the world, greatly influence regional climatic conditions.

The fact that mountains differ in shape, size, and arrangement reflects differences in the processes that produce them as well as in the character and duration of the processes that act to wear them down (Figure 13.1). In this chapter, we discuss the manner in which mountains are believed to form, as well as their significance to the formation of continents.

ISOSTASY: WHY THE EARTH ISN'T SMOOTH

Continents stand higher than ocean basins because of **isostasy**, the state of gravitational equilibrium achieved by the flotation of buoyant lithosphere on top of the more dense material of the asthenosphere. Recall that the lower density and greater thickness of continental crust relative to oceanic crust allows the upper surface of a continent to stand at a significantly greater elevation than the ocean floor. On a slightly smaller scale, isostasy also explains why regions within a continental landmass can vary considerably in elevation.

Perhaps the easiest way to grasp the concept of how isostasy affects continental topography is to envision a series of wooden blocks of different heights floating in water, as shown in Figure 13.2. Note that the thin wooden blocks float only slightly above the water line, whereas the thick blocks stand very high. In a very general sense, the same principle applies to elevation differences in continents; regions underlain

A

B

◆ **Figure 13.1** Comparison of two of Canada's mountain systems. **A.** The relatively youthful mountains in the Western Cordillera have high, sharp peaks. **B.** The much older mountains in the Appalachians, as seen here along the Cabot Trail of Cape Breton Island, Nova Scotia, have been worn down to rolling hills.
(Photo **A** by Peter French/DRK Photo; photo **B** © J. A. Kraulis/Masterfile)

◆ **Figure 13.2** This drawing illustrates how wooden blocks of different thicknesses float in water. In a similar manner, thick sections of crustal material float higher than do thinner crustal slabs.

by thick continental lithosphere stand higher than those underlain by thin continental lithosphere.

This simple model of isostasy is a good starting point for explaining why certain features of Earth stand lower or higher than others on a regional scale. However, because it is a rather static depiction of the lithosphere, it does not give us insights as to *how*, *where*, or *when* such features are produced. Moreover, it does not account for the smaller scale deviations in elevation (e.g., high-standing volcanoes in rift zones) that complicate the overall appearance of certain physiographic regions. To address these aspects, it is necessary to examine mountains in the context of their tectonic history. The name for the processes that collectively produce mountains is **orogenesis** (*oros* = mountains, *genesis* = to come into being).

MOUNTAINS AND PLATE TECTONIC ENVIRONMENTS

GEODe EARTH Mountain Building and the Origin of Continents
↳ Introduction

A **mountain** can be loosely defined as a landform with an obvious peak that rises significantly above the land surrounding it, generally 300 metres or more. Such a definition, taken at face value, could imply that a mountain is no more than a big hill in the middle of nowhere. In the context of geology, however, nothing is further from the truth; when we consider mountains as part of the larger scale framework of continental features, it becomes obvious that the distribution of mountains is far from random (Figure 13.3).

Mountains tend to occur in linear patterns, ranging in scale from small **mountain ranges**, consisting simply of a linked series of mountains, to regionally extensive **mountain belts** that can be extremely complex both in relief and in internal structure. These linear features are generally oriented parallel to plate boundaries, where stresses generated by plate movement are the most intense. Because of isostasy, the modifications of crustal thickness that take place in extensional or compressional tectonic environments are accompanied by dramatic changes in land elevation.

In general, continental lithosphere subjected to extension is stretched and thinned, and it effectively collapses as fault-bounded blocks. In such cases,

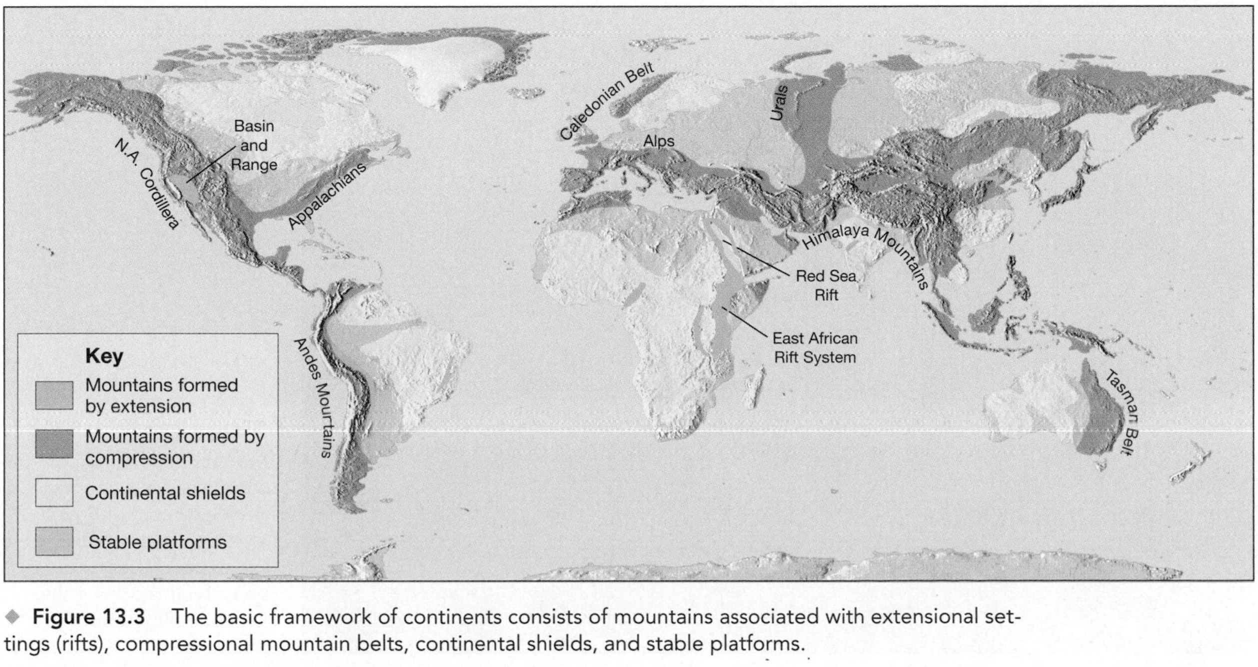

◆ **Figure 13.3** The basic framework of continents consists of mountains associated with extensional settings (rifts), compressional mountain belts, continental shields, and stable platforms.

mountainous relief is primarily due to the rotation of sinking lithospheric blocks, as observed in the formation of rift valleys. In contrast, continental lithosphere that has been compressed, deformed, and thickened, as observed along convergent margins, stands very high, producing towering highlands.

In addition to being important geologic entities in today's world, mountains have also left their mark on the formation and restructuring of continental masses through much of Earth's history. This is particularly true for mountains produced in convergent margins that, despite being worn down, have left evidence of their existence as deformed belts within the ancient shields of continental landmasses. These deformed belts, called *orogens*, indicate that large continents, such as North America, are the products of interactions with several crustal blocks. Before we explore this concept further, we will examine how various types of mountains fit into the plate tectonic scheme.

MOUNTAINS IN DIVERGENT MARGIN SETTINGS

GEODe EARTH Divergent Boundaries: Origin and Evolution of the Ocean Floor
↳ The Formation of Ocean Basins

Significant topographic relief is produced in some continental regions by the downward sliding and rotation of fault-bounded blocks associated with tensional forces within the crust. As already discussed in Chapter 12 (see Figure 12.10), continental crust can be put into a state of tension when an ascending mantle plume pushes upward on the base of the lithosphere, causing it to dome upward. In the process, the lithosphere thins and cracks to form rift valleys. Margins of rift valleys begin to collapse, causing blocks of lithosphere to slide downward relative to one another along normal faults. The resulting rift margins on both sides of the valley have a steplike appearance, with the blocks near the axis of the valley lying at lower elevations than those at the outer edges of the valley (Figure 13.4). The spectacular relief observed in the East African rift is largely the result of the downward sliding of such fault-bounded blocks (Figure 13.5).

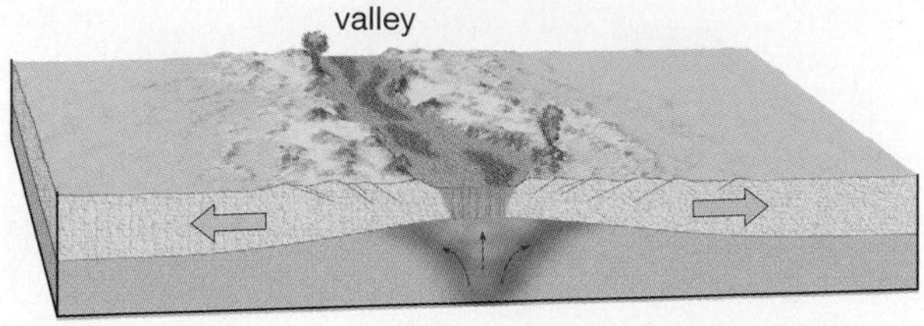

◆ **Figure 13.4** Linear mountains mark the tops of tilted fault blocks produced by crustal extension. Volcanoes are built by the extrusion of magma, adding to the rugged topography of rift regions.

Volcanism that accompanies the stretching and faulting of the crust contributes further to the high relief produced in continental rift margins. For example, Mount Kilimanjaro (5895 metres), located in Tanzania just adjacent to the Kenya border, was produced by mafic volcanism that accompanied the formation of the East African Rift.

◆ **Figure 13.5** Mountainous terrain of Jebel Zabara along the Red Sea coast of Egypt. The highlands represent the exposed edges of tilted fault blocks of the Red Sea rift system. (Photo by W. R. Church)

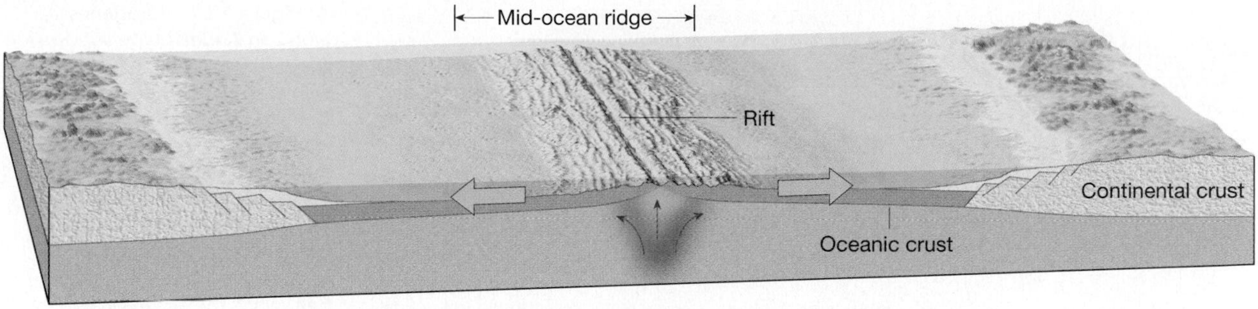

◆ **Figure 13.6** Rifting can ultimately lead to the development of an ocean basin, bordered by passive continental margins. The steplike topography inherited from the precursor rift valley is subdued by the accumulation of sediment on the resulting passive margins.

PASSIVE MARGINS: PRECURSORS TO CONVERGENT MARGINS

With continued divergence and continuation of mafic volcanism, a continental rift valley can evolve into an oceanic spreading centre. Under such circumstances, the originally narrow valley is transformed into a narrow sea and may develop further into a full-fledged ocean. The opposing walls of a rift valley therefore become the continental margins that border the spreading ocean (Figure 13.6). Such continental margins inherit a staircase-like profile from their rift valley precursors. We emphasize, however, that by the time the continental masses have separated, the extensional tectonic activity that produced the faulted margin has more or less ceased. During this episode the continental margin is a **passive margin**; that is, it is not a plate boundary but a part of the same plate as the adjoining oceanic crust.

Although passive margins are tectonically quiet, they do experience subtle crustal movements associated with loading. As marine sediment is deposited on the margin, it effectively weighs down the crust, causing it to sink. This sinking provides space for the deposition of more sediment, which causes further sinking, and so on. Thus, the general lack of tectonic activity with some large-scale subsidence in passive margins allows the gradual accumulation of thick sediment deposits, which drape over, and subdue, the rifted basement topography (Figure 13.6).

Not surprisingly, passive margins are particularly common around the edges of the currently spreading Atlantic Ocean. The eastern continental margins of North and South America and the western margins of Europe and Africa are all passive margins that were ultimately formed during the rifting and breakup of the supercontinent Pangaea. On each of these margins, deposition of sediment on the continental shelf produces a thick wedge of shallow-water sandstones, limestones, and shales (Figure 13.7A). Beyond the continental shelf, turbidity currents deposit sediments on the continental slope and rise (see Chapter 11).

MOUNTAINS IN CONVERGENT MARGIN SETTINGS

GEODe EARTH Convergent Boundaries
↳ Introduction

At the beginning of this chapter, we illustrated how the relative elevations of wooden blocks floating on water relate to their relative thicknesses: thick blocks stand higher than thin blocks by virtue of having thick "roots." Now visualize what would happen if another small block of wood were placed atop one of the blocks in Figure 13.2. The combined block would sink until a new isostatic balance was reached. However, the top of the combined block would be higher than before, and the bottom would be lower. This process of establishing a new level of gravitational equilibrium is called **isostatic adjustment**. In a similar manner, many mountain belts stand high above the surface because they have buoyant crustal roots that extend deeper into the supporting material below.

Simple Subduction: Andean- and Aleutian-Type Mountain Building

When a subduction zone is established at the edge of a continent, a passive margin is transformed into an active margin. The resulting convergence zone involving an oceanic plate and a plate whose leading edge contains continental crust leads to the formation of a volcanic arc and compressional tectonic features inland of the continental margin (Figure 13.7). This type of convergence zone is said to be of *Andean-type* because it is typified by the Andean region of South America, where the Nazca plate is currently being subducted beneath the South

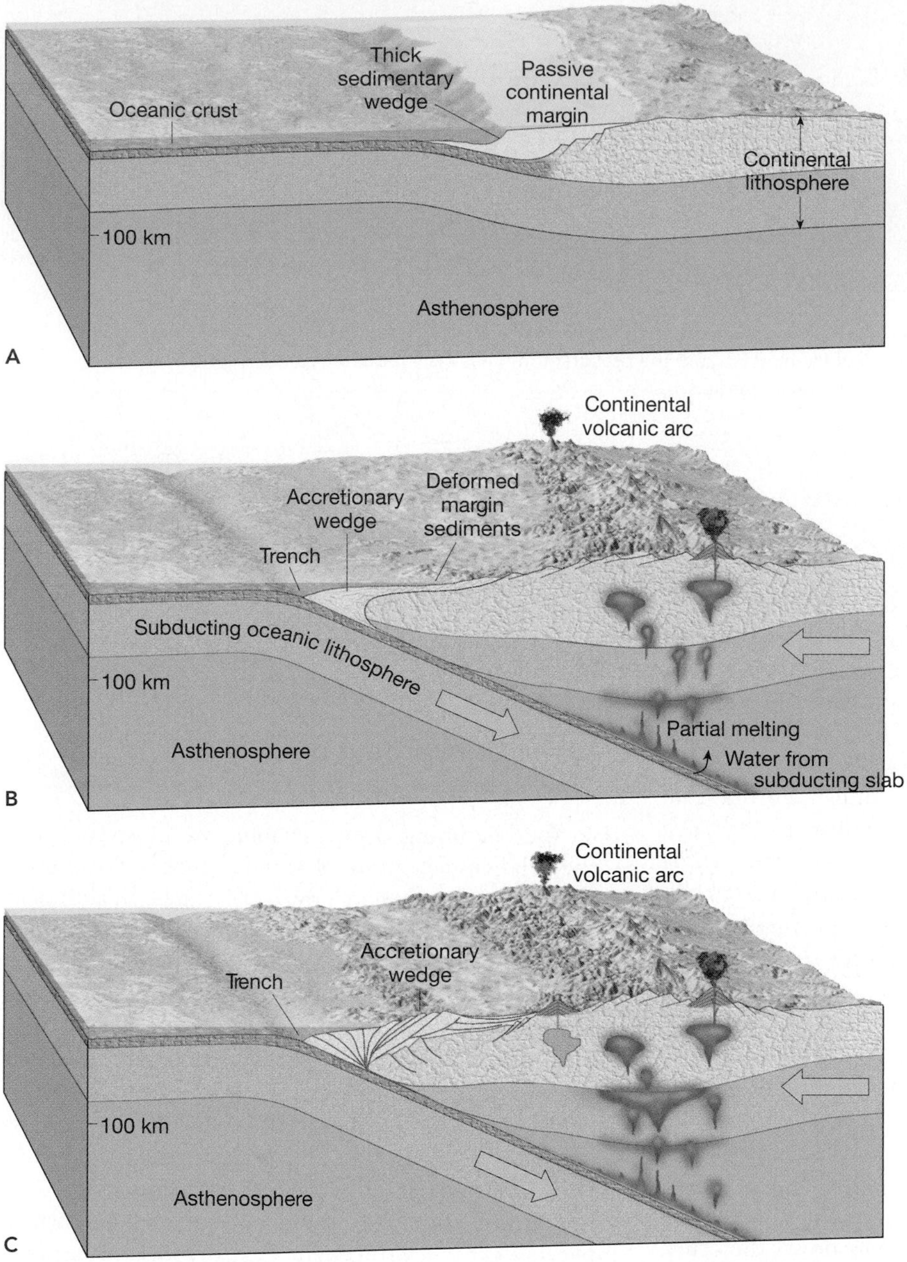

◆ **Figure 13.7** Orogenesis along an Andean-type subduction zone. **A.** Passive continental margin with extensive wedge of sediments. **B.** Plate convergence generates a subduction zone, and partial melting produces a developing volcanic arc. **C.** Continued convergence and igneous activity further deform and thicken the crust, elevating the mountain belt, while the accretionary wedge grows.

American plate along the Peru–Chile Trench (see Figure 11.8). This scenario differs from that of an *Aleutian-type* convergence zone, which involves the convergence of two oceanic plates and the formation of an island arc (Figure 13.8), as typified by the Aleutian Islands (Figure 13.9).

In an idealized Andean-type convergence zone, the subduction of an oceanic plate under a continental block leads to the deformation, metamorphism, and uplift of the continental margin. Once the oceanic plate descends to about 100 kilometres, partial melting of mantle rock above the subducting slab generates magma that migrates upward and further thickens the continental crust (Figure 13.7B). During the development of this continental volcanic arc, sediments derived from the land are scraped from the subducting plate and plastered against the landward side of the trench (Figure 13.7B). As described in Chapter 11, this chaotic accumulation of sedimentary and metamorphic rocks with occasional scraps of ocean crust is called an *accretionary wedge*. Prolonged subduction can build an accretionary wedge that is thick enough to stand above sea level (Figure 13.7C).

Andean-type mountain belts therefore contain two roughly parallel zones, each containing distinctive

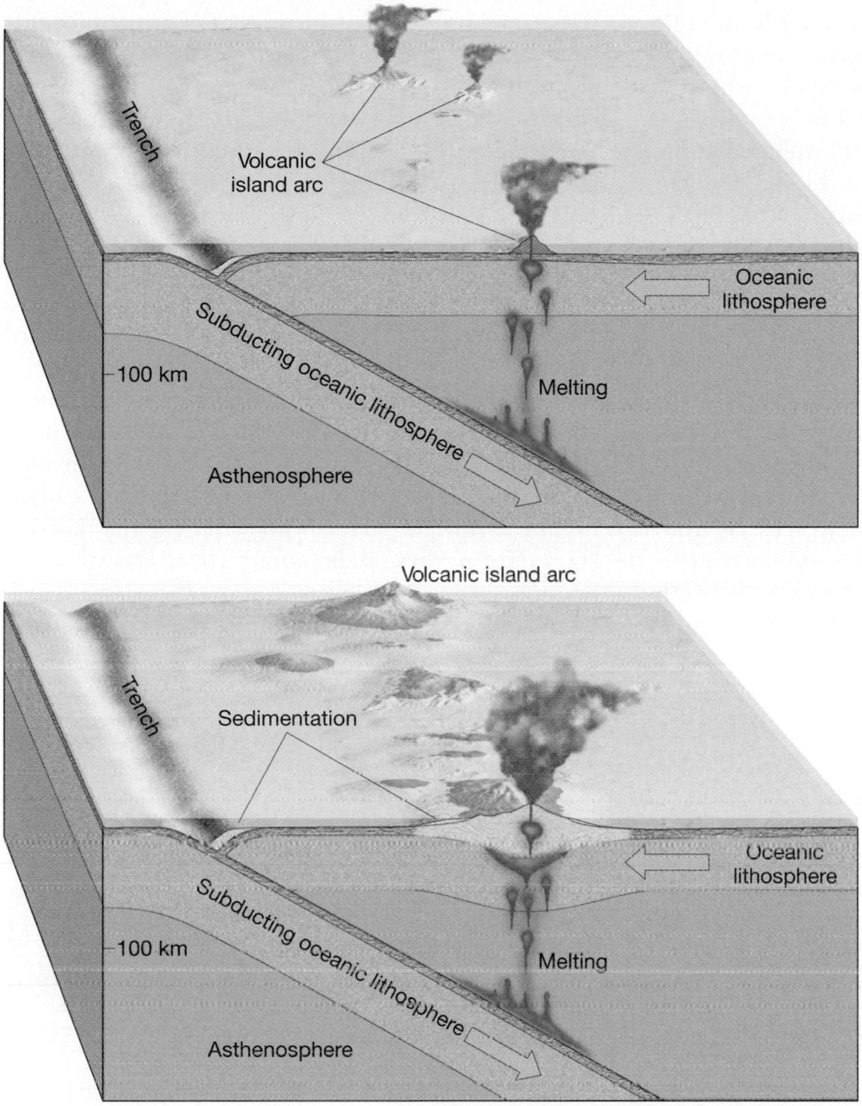

◆ **Figure 13.8** The development of a volcanic island arc by the convergence of two oceanic plates. Continuous subduction along these Aleutian-type convergent zones results in the development of thick units of continental-type crust.

◆ **Figure 13.9** Three of the many volcanic islands that compose the Aleutian arc. This narrow band of volcanism results from the subduction of the Pacific plate. In the distance is the Great Sitkin volcano (1772 metres), which the Aleuts call the "Great Emptier of Bowels," because of its frequent activity.
(Photo by Bruce D. Marsh)

suites of rock types. The continental block hosts volcanic rocks and large intrusive bodies intermixed with high-temperature metamorphic rocks, whereas the accretionary wedge that lies on the oceanic slab consists of folded, faulted, and metamorphosed sediments and volcanic debris (Figure 13.7C). North American examples of Andean-type mountain belts include the Coast Mountains of British Columbia and the Sierra Nevada of California.

Continental Collisions

Collisions of much greater magnitude are produced when two lithospheric plates carrying continental crust are brought into contact as the oceanic lithosphere on one plate is subducted under the other (Figure 13.10). Because continental crust is too buoyant to undergo any appreciable subduction, a spectacular collision between the continental masses results, and the two continental blocks fuse to become one. The mechanics of continental collision, crustal thickening, and the associated uplift are well displayed by the genesis of the Himalayas and the Tibetan Plateau. In fact, it was here that the concept of deep-rooted mountains was born (Box 13.1).

The Himalayas India, once part of Antarctica, split from that continent about 130 million years ago and over millions of years slowly drifted northward toward Eurasia (Figure 13.10A). The northward voyage of this continental block culminated in a head-on collision between India and Eurasia about 10 million years ago (Figure 13.10B). Although most of the oceanic crust that separated these landmasses before the collision was subducted, some was caught up in the squeeze, along with sediment that lay offshore. Today these sedimentary rocks and slivers of oceanic crust are elevated high above sea level. Geologists believe that following such a collision, the

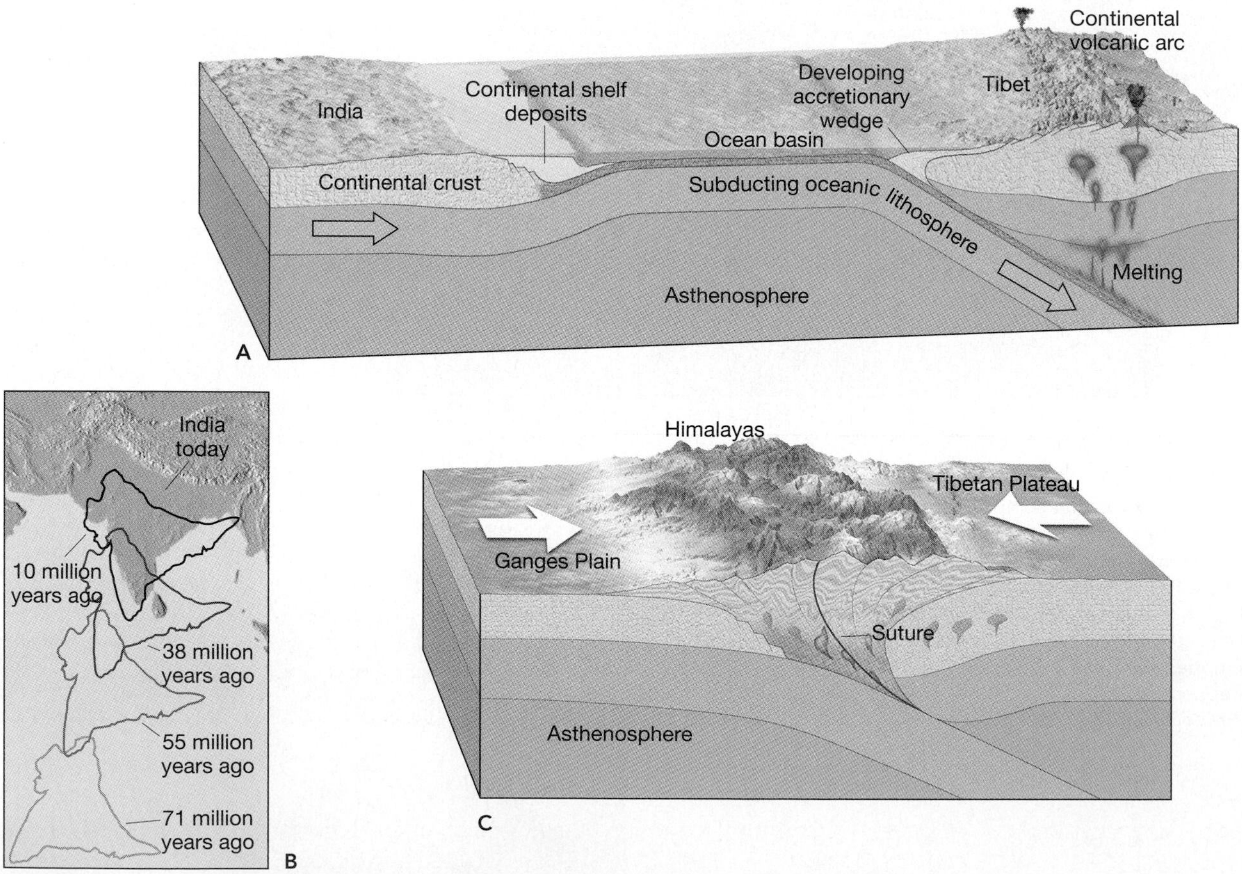

◆ **Figure 13.10** Simplified diagrams showing the northward migration and collision of India with the Eurasian plate. **A.** Converging plates generated a subduction zone, while partial melting of the subducting oceanic slab produced a continental volcanic arc. Sediments scraped from the subducting plate were added to the accretionary wedge. **B.** Position of India in relation to Eurasia at various times. **C.** Eventually, the two landmasses collided, deforming and elevating the accretionary wedge and continental shelf deposits. In addition, slices of the Indian crust were thrust up onto the Indian plate.
(Modified after Peter Molnar)

BOX 13.1

Understanding Earth
Do Mountains Have Roots?

One of the major advances in determining the structure of mountains occurred in the 1840s when Sir George Everest (after whom Mount Everest is named) conducted the first topographic survey in India. During this survey the distance between the towns of Kalianpur and Kaliana, located south of the Himalayan range, was measured by using two different methods. One method employed the conventional surveying technique of triangulation, and the other method determined the distance astronomically. Although the two techniques should have given similar results, the astronomical calculations placed these towns nearly 150 metres closer to each other than did the triangulation survey.

The discrepancy was attributed to the gravitational attraction exerted by the massive Himalayas on the plumb bob used for levelling the astronomical instrument. (A plumb bob is a metal weight suspended by a cord and used to determine a vertical orientation.) It was suggested that the deflection of the plumb bob would be greater at Kaliana than at Kalianpur because it is closer to the mountains (Figure 13.A).

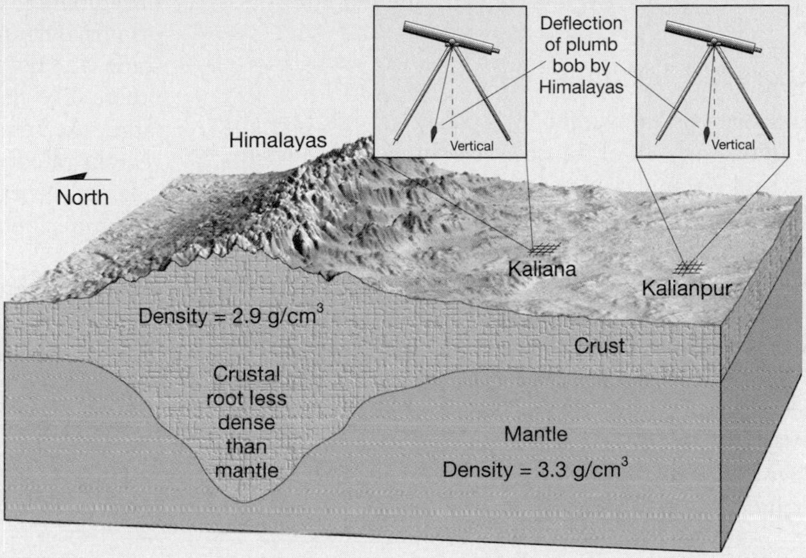

◆ **Figure 13.A** During the first survey of India, an error in measurement occurred because the plumb bob on an instrument was deflected by the massive Himalayas. Later work by George Airy predicted that the mountains have roots of light crustal rocks. Airy's model explained why the plumb bob was deflected much less than expected.

A few years later, J. H. Pratt estimated the mass of the Himalayas and calculated the error that should have been caused by the gravitational influence of the mountains. To his surprise, Pratt discovered that the mountains should have produced an error three times as large as was actually observed. Simply stated, the mountains were not "pulling their weight." It was as if they had a hollow central core.

A hypothesis to explain the apparent "missing" mass was developed by George Airy. Airy suggested that Earth's lighter crustal rocks float on the denser, more easily deformed mantle. He correctly argued that the crust must be thicker under mountains than beneath the adjacent lowlands. In other words, mountainous terrains are supported by light crustal material that extends as "roots" into the denser mantle (Figure 13.A). This phenomenon is exhibited by icebergs, which are buoyed up by the weight of the displaced water. If the Himalayas do have roots of light crustal rocks that extend far beneath them, then these mountains would exert less gravitational attraction, as Pratt had calculated. Hence, Airy's model explained why the plumb bob was deflected much less than expected.

Seismic and gravitational studies have confirmed the existence of crustal roots under some mountain ranges. The thickness of continental crust is normally about 35 kilometres, but crustal thicknesses exceeding 70 kilometres have been determined for some mountain belts.

subducted oceanic plate decouples from the rigid continental plate and continues its descent into the mantle.

The spreading centre that propelled India northward is still active; hence, India continues to be thrust into Asia at an estimated rate of a few centimetres each year. However, numerous earthquakes recorded off the southern coast of India indicate that a new subduction zone may be in the making. If formed, it would provide a subduction site for the floor of the Indian Ocean, which is continually being produced at a spreading centre located to the southwest. Should this occur, India's northward journey, relative to Asia, would come to an end and the growth of the Himalayas would cease.

A similar but much older collision is believed to have taken place when the European continent collided with the Asian continent to produce the

Ural Mountains, which extend in a north–south direction through Russia. Before the discovery of plate tectonics, geologists had difficulty explaining the existence of such mountain ranges as the Urals, which are located deep within continental interiors.

Accreted Terranes

Andean-type convergence is fairly straightforward in that nearly all of the material composing the subducting oceanic slab glides downward into the mantle and is consumed. Subduction is so efficient at such margins that the only traces of the subducted plate left at the surface are the small slivers of mafic oceanic crust and overlying sediments that have been shaved off and incorporated into the accretionary wedge. Convergence becomes more complicated when the leading edge of an oceanic plate carries features that are too thick and buoyant to be subducted. Such features vary widely in origin and include the following:

1. Micro-continents, small fragments of continental crust left over from continental rifting or sheared-off continental margins along transform faults, are rafted on oceanic plates. Recall that continental crust is thicker and more buoyant than oceanic crust and resists subduction.
2. Island arcs, produced by the convergence of two oceanic plates, are composed of crust that is largely andesitic in composition and therefore more buoyant than the adjacent mafic oceanic crust. As in the case of micro-continents, low crustal density and high crustal thickness prevent island arcs from being subducted.
3. Oceanic plateaus, as well as the hot-spot volcanoes and seamounts that compose such features as the Hawaiian Ridge, are prominent topographic features of the ocean floor produced by intraplate (mantle plume) volcanism. These features are mafic in composition and therefore of similar density to the crust of the surrounding ocean floor. However, because they are high-standing features, they are not readily forced under a continental plate by subduction.

The fate of a crustal component that resists subduction is to collide with, and become plastered against, the continental margin. Once the crustal fragment is firmly accreted to the continental margin and sheared off the subducting oceanic slab, it effectively becomes part of the continent itself. Packages of sedimentary deposits may also be added to the continent by virtue of being trapped between the crustal fragment and the continental margin.

Geologists refer to distinct units of material added to the edge of a continent as **terranes**. More formally, the term *terrane* designates any crustal fragment that has a geologic history distinct from that of the adjoining terranes. As a reflection of their diverse origins, terranes come in varied shapes and sizes; some are no larger than volcanic islands, whereas others, like the entire Indian subcontinent, are very large. Accreted terranes can compose substantial regions of continents, as observed along the western side of North America (Figure 13.11). British Columbia alone contains at least 39 distinct terranes

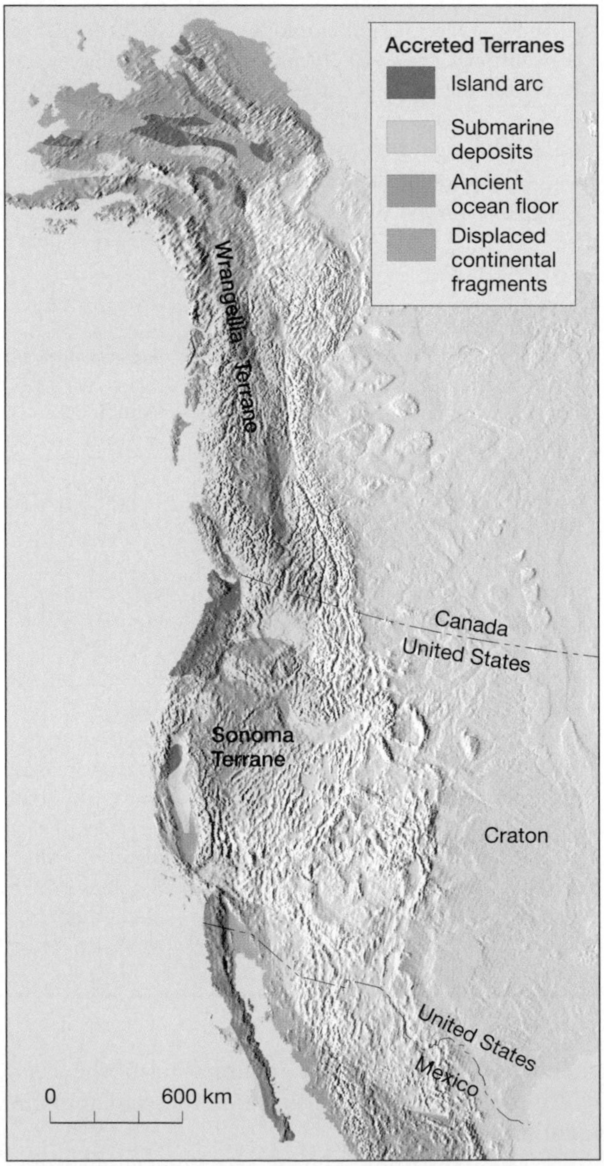

◆ **Figure 13.11** Map showing terranes that have been added to western North America during the past 200 million years. Data from paleomagnetic and fossil evidence indicate that some of these terranes originated thousands of kilometres south of their present location.
(After D. R. Hutchinson and others)

that together compose more than 80 percent of the province's land area and that have been added to North America within the past 200 million years. The Wrangellia Terrane is one of the largest of these accreted terranes.

Terrane accretion is accompanied by the generation of significant topographic relief inboard of the collision zone. As the buoyant crustal material is peeled from the subducting plate, it is thrust in relatively thin sheets onto the adjacent continental block. The material may later be overridden or displaced farther inland by the addition of other fragments. In turn, the shortening and thickening of the continental margin caused by collision promotes uplift and the formation of a mountain belt. The uplift of the North American Cordillera is a classic example of mountain building associated with terrane accretion. The compression generated by terrane accretion on the western margin of Canada can be appreciated by considering the deformation experienced in the Rocky Mountains of British Columbia and Alberta (Box 13.2).

BOX 13.2

Canadian Profile
Landscapes of the Canadian Rocky Mountains

The great compressional forces that accompanied the collision of terranes with the western margin of Canada resulted in a significant amount of crustal shortening that ultimately built the Canadian Rockies and their associated foothills (Figure 13.B). Huge sheets of rock bounded by westward dipping thrust faults were stacked atop one another and in some cases were deformed as they slid into their present positions. With progressive compression, older thrust sheets were carried in a piggyback fashion on younger thrust sheets that were generated successively eastward through time. In other words, thrust faults in the Rocky Mountain Foothills record

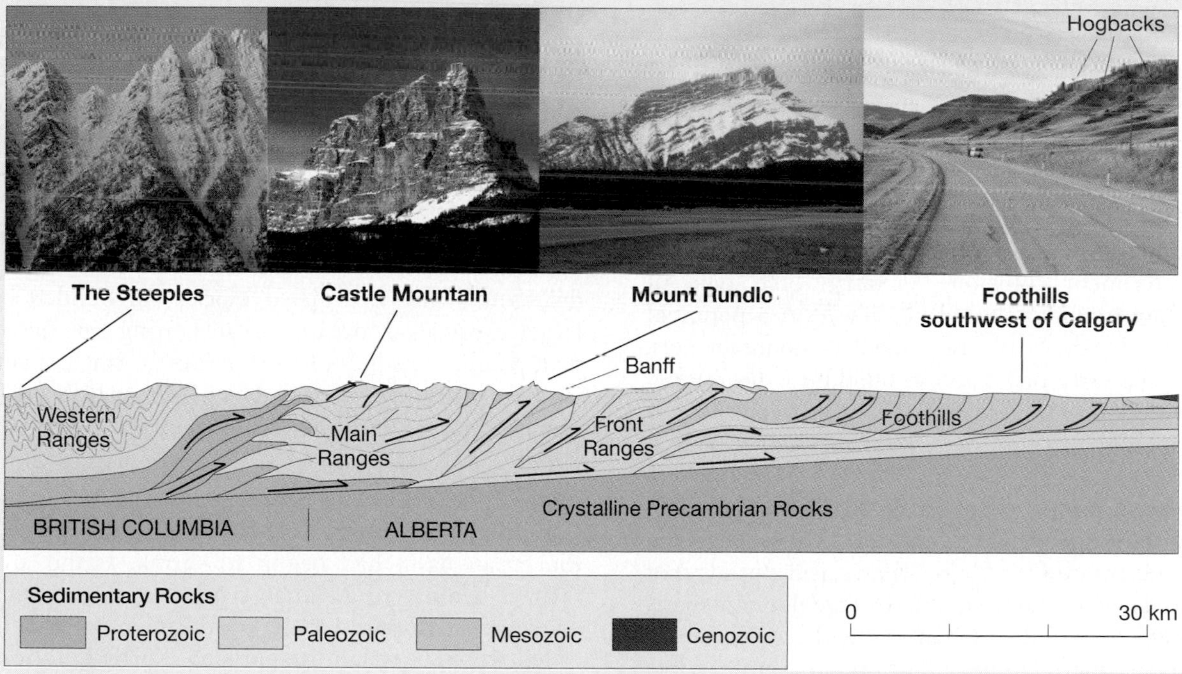

◆ **Figure 13.B** Shapes of mountains and foothills of the Canadian Rockies partly reflect the structure of their contained rocks. The jagged peaks of Western Range Mountains, such as the Steeples, reflect intense folding of shale-rich strata. The flatter peaks of the Main Range Mountains, such as Castle Mountain, manifest the flat-lying attitude of strata within thrust sheets. Front Range Mountains, such as Mount Rundle, have a more slanted appearance because of steeper slopes of underlying thrust faults. The foothills southwest of Calgary have a more subdued topography because their underlying Mesozoic rock is easier to erode than more resistant Paleozoic and Proterozoic rocks of the Rockies. The slightly greater resistance to erosion of sandstones and conglomerates (relative to adjacent shale) is indicated by protruding hogback ridges. Arrows indicate direction of movement along thrust faults.
(Photo of Steeples © Ron Straud/Masterfile; photo of Castle Mountain © Alec Pytlowany/Masterfile; photo of Mount Rundle by S. R. Hicock; photo of foothills by Christopher Collom)

the last stages of thrusting that occurred during the building of the mountain belt.

The landscapes of the Canadian Rockies and Rocky Mountain Foothills reflect the structural characteristics of their underlying rocks as well as differences in the erosion rates of various rock types. A transect through southeast British Columbia and southwest Alberta reveals four basic physiographic components: the Western Ranges, the Main Ranges, the Front Ranges, and the Foothills.

The Western Ranges, located in southeast British Columbia, are characterized by intensely folded, thinly bedded Paleozoic shales and carbonates. Enhanced erosion of shale-rich beds, relative to the more resistant beds of carbonate, imparts a jagged appearance to the mountains.

East of the Western Ranges, the Rockies are dominated by thick, massive units of Proterozoic and Paleozoic carbonates. Instead of folding like the strata of the Western Ranges, these rocks fractured and were thrust eastward in numerous fault-bounded sheets. The Main Ranges expose strata in a more or less horizontal orientation, reflecting the shallow dip of the thrust faults immediately underlying this area. Main Range peaks are characteristically castle-shaped, with steep cliffs on all sides. East of the Main Ranges are the Front Ranges, which occur as well-defined, linear ridges separated by linear valleys. In these ranges, the strata within each thrust sheet are significantly upturned and their bounding thrust faults are more steeply inclined. Manifesting the inclined attitude of the thrust sheets, the southwest slopes of Front Range mountains have a distinct, slanted appearance.

Finally, the Rocky Mountain Foothills mark the easternmost extent of significant deformation associated with the building of the Canadian Rocky Mountains. Like the Front Ranges, strata of the Foothills are significantly upturned because of having being forced upward in sheets over the steeply inclined segments of thrust faults. However, strata of the Foothills are predominantly late Mesozoic to early Cenozoic in age and therefore much younger than those of the true Rockies. As these rocks are more prone to erosion than the Paleozoic strata of the Rockies, they have been worn down to form more subtle linear hills. Even so, hogback ridges, composed of Cretaceous sandstones and conglomerates that are more resistant than the intervening shales, occur in some places. The Foothills thus mark a topographic transition zone between the Rockies to the west and the Plains to the east.

Mountain Belts with Complex Histories

Unsurprisingly, mountain belts can have extremely complex histories and can show evidence of more than one type of mountain-building process, including simple subduction, terrane accretion, and continent–continent collision. As such, each type of mountain building should be viewed as a potential stage in the evolution of a mature mountain belt. The complexity of mountain building is beautifully illustrated in the history of the Appalachian Mountain belt in eastern North America.

The Appalachians The Appalachian Mountain belt, stretching from Newfoundland and Labrador to the southeast coast of the United States, is the product of hundreds of millions of years of geologic activity. Through several decades of study, the evolution of the Appalachians has been interpreted to involve five basic phases of tectonic activity. In this section, the major events in the evolution of this complex mountain belt are briefly discussed, with an emphasis on Canadian features (Figure 13.12). The present-day distribution of major crustal components of the Appalachians is depicted in Figure 13.13.

Phase 1: Divergence During the late Precambrian, a supercontinent called Rodinia was split apart by continental rifting. Landmasses produced by this rifting included ancestral North America (part of Laurasia) and Africa (part of Gondwanaland), which drifted apart because of the spreading of the proto-Atlantic Ocean (Iapetus; Figures 13.12A and 13.12B). Smaller fragments of continental crust, also produced during the rifting process, were rafted on the diverging plates as isolated blocks, surrounded by larger expanses of oceanic crust. During this divergent phase, the edges of eastern North America and western Africa were occupied by passive margins that remained stable until the early Paleozoic.

Phase 2: Initial Convergence Sometime during the Cambrian, convergence was initiated in Iapetus and the ocean basin had begun to shrink. Island arcs formed because of Aleutian-type (oceanic–oceanic) convergence (Figure 13.12C), and a micro-continent called Avalonia began to approach North America's eastern margin.

Phase 3: Accretion of Terranes Continued closure of Iapetus brought eastern North America into contact with a number of crustal components that could not be consumed by subduction. The collision of these blocks with eastern North America is recorded in multiple mountain-building events. The first major event, called the Taconic Orogeny, involved the accretion of island arc complexes (Figure 13.12D)

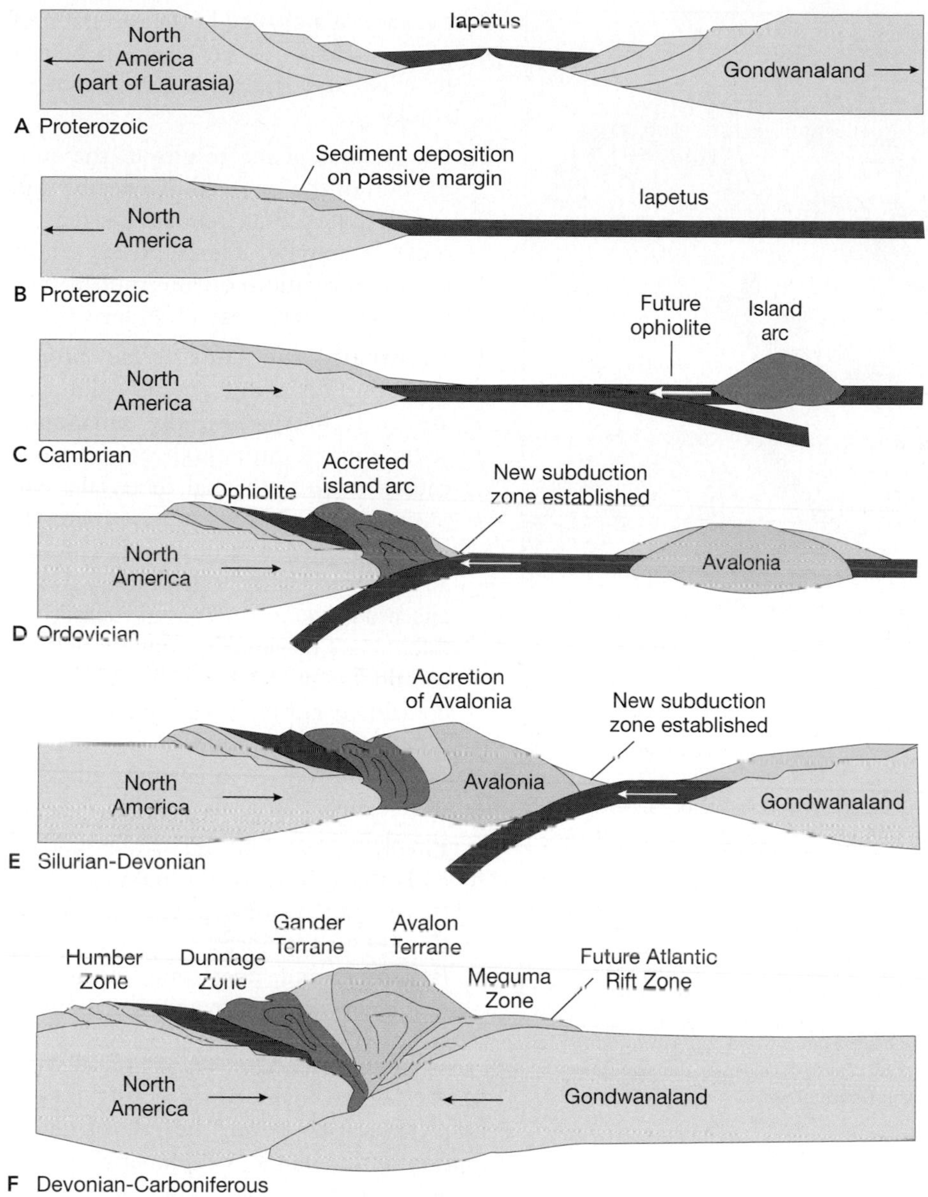

◆ **Figure 13.12** Principal tectonic events in the evolution of the northern Appalachian Mountains of eastern Canada. **A.** Rifting separates North America (then part of a continent called Laurasia) and Gondwanaland, forming the proto-Atlantic Ocean (Iapetus). **B.** With continued spreading of Iapetus, the eastern margin of North America exists as a passive margin on which land-derived sediments are deposited. **C.** Iapetus begins to close and Aleutian-type convergence is initiated in Iapetus, producing an island arc to the east of North America. **D.** With continued convergence, the volcanic arc is accreted to eastern North America, and a segment of its associated oceanic plate is plastered on as ophiolite. **E.** The micro continent Avalonia is accreted to the eastern margin of North America in the Middle Devonian. **F.** Gondwanaland collides with eastern North America.

in the Ordovician (represented by rocks of the Dunnage Zone in the Canada Appalachians). A later mountain-building episode called the Acadian Orogeny resulted from the docking of Avalonia (represented by rocks of the Avalon Terrane) along eastern North America, beginning in the Silurian and reaching its maximum in the Devonian (Figure 13.12E).

Phase 4: Continental Collision Iapetus eventually closed, bringing the western margin of Gondwanaland against eastern North America. The Meguma Zone in Nova Scotia is believed to represent a remnant of the Gondwanaland continental margin (possibly part of Africa or South America) that was welded to the North American continent during early stages of the closure of Iapetus (Figure 13.12F) and that was left stranded on North America when later rifting produced the Atlantic Ocean basin. The Meguma Zone apparently came into contact with North America as early as the Devonian (Figure 13.12F), but it was during the Carboniferous and Permian that the main episode of continental collision occurred. The final collision between the African part of Gondwanaland and eastern North America was centred in the southeast United States and resulted in the Allegheny Orogeny, the last mountain-building event in the Appalachians. This continental collision was only one of several that ultimately resulted in the formation of the supercontinent Pangaea by the late Permian.

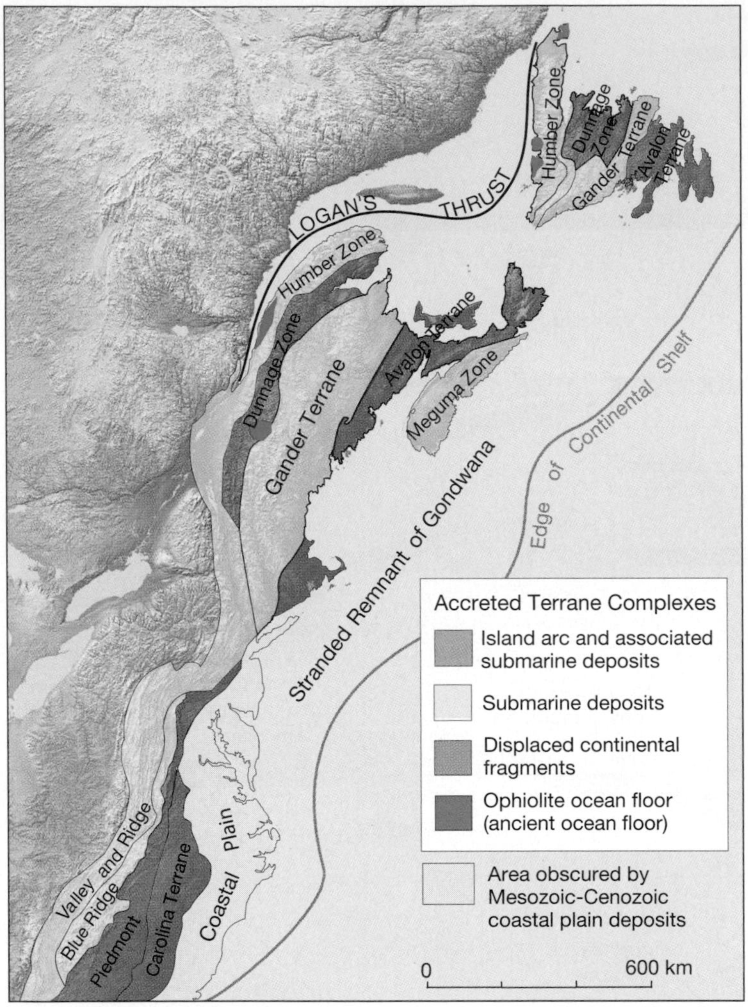

◆ **Figure 13.13** Accreted terrane complexes welded to eastern North America. Note that Paleozoic rocks of accreted terranes in the southeast United States are now obscured by thick sequences of Mesozoic and Cenozoic coastal plain deposits.

The Wilson Cycle

Studies of old, complex mountain chains, such as the Appalachians, have contributed greatly to the understanding of plate tectonics. From such studies, an idealized global tectonic cycle has been deduced, providing a valuable context for the understanding of the long-term consequences of the interactions of lithospheric plates. The Wilson Cycle, named after the famous Canadian geophysicist J. Tuzo Wilson (see Chapter 12), incorporates the major events that occur during the splitting apart and coming together of continental landmasses. The passage of a single Wilson cycle can be summarized as follows:

1. After the breakup of a continental landmass, a thick wedge of sediment is deposited along the passive continental margins, thereby increasing the size of the newly formed continent.
2. Because of a change in the direction of plate motion, the ocean basin begins to close and the continents begin to converge.
3. Plate convergence results in the subduction of the intervening oceanic slab and initiates an extended episode of igneous activity. This activity results in the formation of an Andean-type volcanic arc with associated intrusions.
4. Eventually the continental blocks collide. This event severely deforms and metamorphoses the entrapped sediments. Continental convergence causes these deformed materials, and occasionally slabs of crustal material, to be displaced up onto the plates along thrust faults. This activity shortens and thickens the crustal rocks, producing an elevated mountain belt. It should be noted here that the main collision event between the continental blocks may be preceded by smaller-scale collisions involving the docking of terranes.
5. Finally, a change in the plate boundary ends the growth of the mountains. At this point erosional processes become the dominant forces in altering the landscape, and, over time, the mountain chain is worn down to its roots.

This sequence of events is thought to have repeated many times during Earth's long history. However, the rate of deformation and geologic and climatic settings varied in each instance. Thus, the formation of each mountain chain must be regarded as a unique event.

Convergence and the Obduction of Oceanic Crust

As discussed in Chapter 11, much of our understanding of the composition and structure of oceanic plates comes from the study of ophiolite complexes. These slivers of oceanic material, now exposed in some of the world's greatest mountain ranges, have provided geologists rare glimpses of what goes on below the ocean floor.

Ophiolite complexes help us answer an important question: If continental crust stands high and oceanic crust stands low, how can oceanic crust end up exposed high above sea level? The answer appears to be that the subduction of oceanic crust is not always one hundred percent efficient. In rare cases, pieces of the oceanic plate can be broken off, thrust onto the continent, and lifted high and dry above sea level during mountain building. This process is called *obduction*.

Ophiolites, although originally produced as sections of oceanic crust settings, are emplaced in convergent tectonic settings. Some ophiolites occur as disrupted multiple shavings of oceanic crust scraped off a subducted plate and incorporated into an accretionary wedge, like that of the Franciscan Formation of California (Figure 13.7). Others, like the Bay of Islands Ophiolite in Newfoundland and Labrador, and the Thetford Mines Ophiolite of Quebec (Canada's source of crysotile asbestos), appear to have been emplaced as thicker, more intact blocks of material that were sliced off a subducting lithospheric slab, were thrust onto the edge of the continent during terrane accretion and were eventually uplifted when the continental block rose upward to achieve isostatic equilibrium (Figure 13.12). In such places as Gros Morne National Park, Newfoundland and Labrador, the ophiolite sequence is so complete that the base of the oceanic crust can be observed (see Figure 11.15B).

Thick slices of ophiolites also occur in mountain ranges that mark the collision of two continents, as seen in the Alps and the Himalayas. The scientific value of ophiolites preserved in the suture zones of such mountain ranges is obvious, for they provide tangible evidence of ocean basins that separated the continents before their collision.

Isostatic Adjustment after Active Convergence

At the beginning of this chapter, we used the example of wooden blocks of different heights floating in water to illustrate why some regions of Earth's surface stand higher than others. We noted that the thicker blocks have thicker roots and float higher than thinner blocks.

Applying the concept of isostasy, we should expect that when material is added to the top of a crustal block, such as the thrusted masses of rock piled up during mountain building, the root of the crustal block will subside to a deeper level. Accordingly, we should expect the original block to rebound and the thickness of its root to be reduced when weight is removed. (Visualize what happens to a ship as cargo is being loaded and unloaded.)

Much of our understanding of how the crust responds to the application and removal of loads has emerged from the study of the after-effects of the last Ice Age. When continental ice sheets occupied portions of North America during the Pleistocene Epoch, the added weight of 3-kilometre-thick masses of ice caused downwarping of Earth's crust by hundreds of metres. In the 8000 years since the last ice sheet melted, uplifting of as much as 330 metres has occurred in the Hudson Bay region, where the thickest ice had accumulated (see Figure 17.30).

Because of isostasy, deformed strata experience regional uplift both during mountain building and for an extended period afterward. Usually, little additional deformation is associated with the latter activity. As the crust rises, the processes of erosion accelerate, carving the deformed strata into a mountainous landscape.

One of the consequences of isostatic adjustment is that as erosion lowers the summits of mountains, the crust will rise in response to the reduced load (Figures 13.14A and 13.14B). The processes of uplifting and erosion will continue until the mountain block reaches "normal" crustal thickness. When this occurs, the mountains will be eroded to near sea level, and the once deeply buried interior of the mountain will be exposed at the surface. In addition, as mountains are worn down, the eroded sediment is deposited on adjacent landscapes, causing these areas to subside (Figure 13.14C). Isostatic adjustment is responsible for exposing the deep roots of the Appalachian Mountains in eastern North America and for contributing to the large amounts of sediment deposited along the Atlantic and Gulf Coastal Plain that now cover the older bedrock of accreted terranes (Figure 13.13).

BROAD VERTICAL MOVEMENTS IN CONTINENTS

Regions of Uplift

Although most young mountain belts, including the Alps, Andes, and Himalayas, have deep crustal roots and are supported by isostatic buoyancy, another important mechanism contributes to the elevated position of some landforms. With the development of the plate tectonics theory, it became clear that some form of up-and-down convective flow was occurring in the mantle. Although the exact nature of this movement is still not fully understood, it is known that zones of hot mantle upwelling underlie some landmasses. The buoyancy of this hot rising material accounts for broad upwarping in the overlying lithosphere, as is occurring under the Basin and Range province of the southwest United States.

Southern Africa is one area in which large-scale vertical motion is evident. Much of the region exists

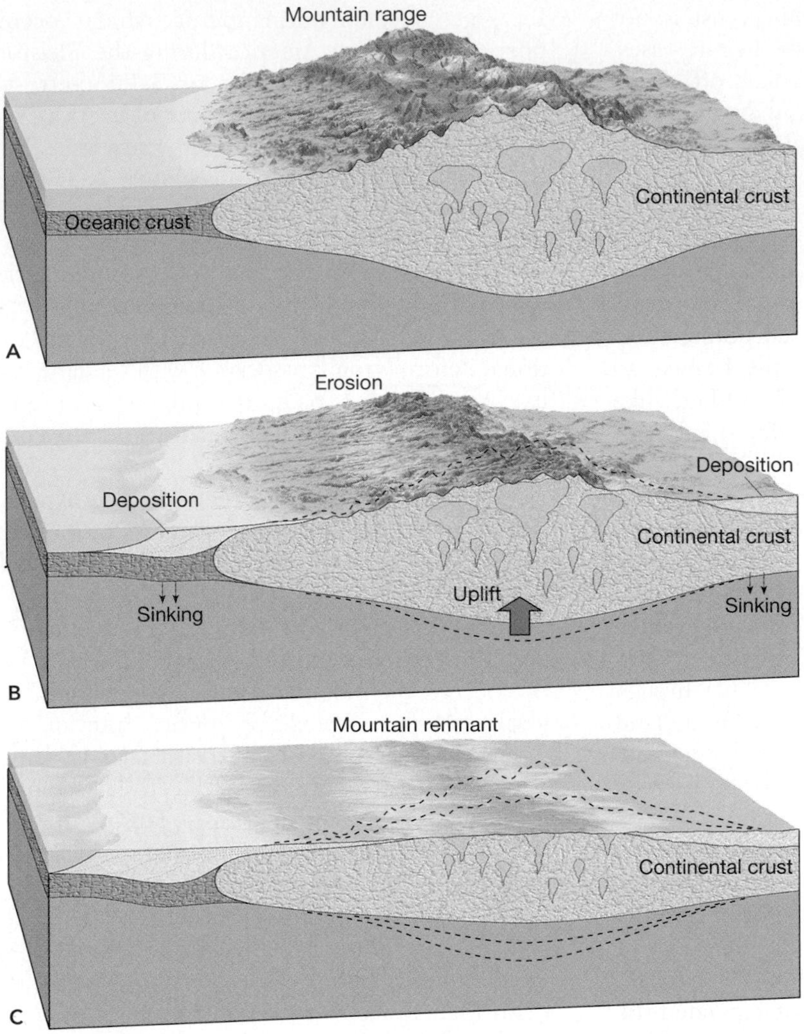

◆ **Figure 13.14** This sequence illustrates how the combined effect of erosion and isostatic adjustment results in a thinning of the crust in mountainous regions. **A.** When mountains are young, the continental crust is thickest. **B.** As erosion lowers the mountains, the crust rises in response to the reduced load. **C.** Erosion and uplift continue until the mountains reach "normal" crustal thickness.

as an expansive plateau that has an average elevation of nearly 1500 metres. Geologic evidence shows that southern Africa and the surrounding seafloor have been slowly rising for the past 100 million years, even though they have not experienced a plate collision for nearly 400 million years. Evidence from seismic tomography indicates that a large mushroom-shaped mass of hot mantle rock is centred below the southern tip of Africa. This *super-plume* extends upward about 2900 kilometres from the mantle–core boundary and spreads out over several thousand kilometres. Researchers have concluded that the upward flow of this huge mantle plume is sufficient to elevate southern Africa.

Regions of Subsidence

Although some continental regions show evidence of broad uplift, a host of others show evidence of gentle downwarping. We know that some downwarping is simply the result of an extra load being added to the crust, such as occurred during the last Ice Age. Other examples of crustal loading occur along the continental margins where sediments are being deposited. This phenomenon is particularly dramatic in regions like the Gulf of Mexico, where the Mississippi River has dumped enormous quantities of sediment. In the case of broad regional uplift, however, some downwarped areas may be linked to flow dynamics of the mantle.

Foreland and Intracratonic Basins Continental interiors, although having a more subdued topography than mountain belts along their margins, show a number of basins and intervening arches that manifest subtle deflections of the lithosphere. Of particular importance in North America are *foreland* and *intracratonic basins*, which have served as important catchment areas for sediments that now host significant volumes of oil and gas.

Foreland basins are elongate, asymmetrical, trough-like depressions (Figure 13.15) that are produced by the loading of a continental mass along one of its edges. Similar to the way the free end of a div-

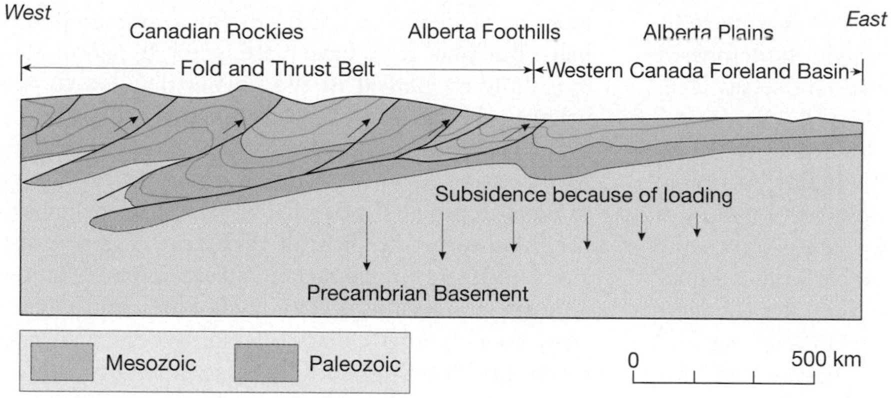

◆ **Figure 13.15** Simplified cross-section through Canadian Rocky Mountains, Alberta Foothills, and Alberta Plains. A foreland basin underlies the plains region because of loading by thrust sheets that accompanied the shortening of crust that formed the Rockies. Note that crustal shortening continued long after the main phase of foreland basin development. Thus, Mesozoic sedimentary rocks that originally accumulated in the western part of the foreland basin have been disturbed by thrust faulting.

ing board bends in response to the load of a diver, the lithosphere flexes downward under the increased mass of thickened crust. Among the best-known basins of this type in Canada is the Western Canada Foreland Basin.

This basin developed inland of the Rocky Mountains during the Mesozoic, in response to the crustal shortening and thickening that accompanied the accretion of terranes in British Columbia. Similarly, the Appalachian Foreland Basin in eastern Canada was produced by crustal thickening that accompanied the accretion of terranes and uplift of the early Appalachian Mountains during the Paleozoic.

Intracratonic basins are circular bowl-shaped depressions that develop well within continental interiors. Two classic examples of intracratonic basins are the Williston Basin, which underlies the southern part of the Canadian Prairies, and the Michigan Basin, the northern part of which underlies southwest Ontario (Figures 13.16 and 9.17). The origin of intracratonic basins is somewhat obscure and remains a subject of significant debate. A few geologists believe that the formation of such basins is linked to far-field compressive forces related to plate convergence, but most assert that the circular basin shape must indicate a mantle-related phenomenon acting independently of plate interactions. In the latter camp, it has been suggested that an intracratonic basin forms by lithospheric thinning and subsequent sagging associated with the ascent of mantle plumes. Others have suggested that intracratonic basins represent circular dimples produced by blobs of dense mantle material that attached to the base of the lithosphere and later sank because of their increased density on cooling.

Downwarping of Continental Margins and Interiors Evidence also suggests that much of the North American interior experienced a major episode of subsidence during the Cretaceous Period. Although sea level was no more than 120 metres higher than it is today, vast seas invaded much of the continent. The Cretaceous seas eventually retreated,

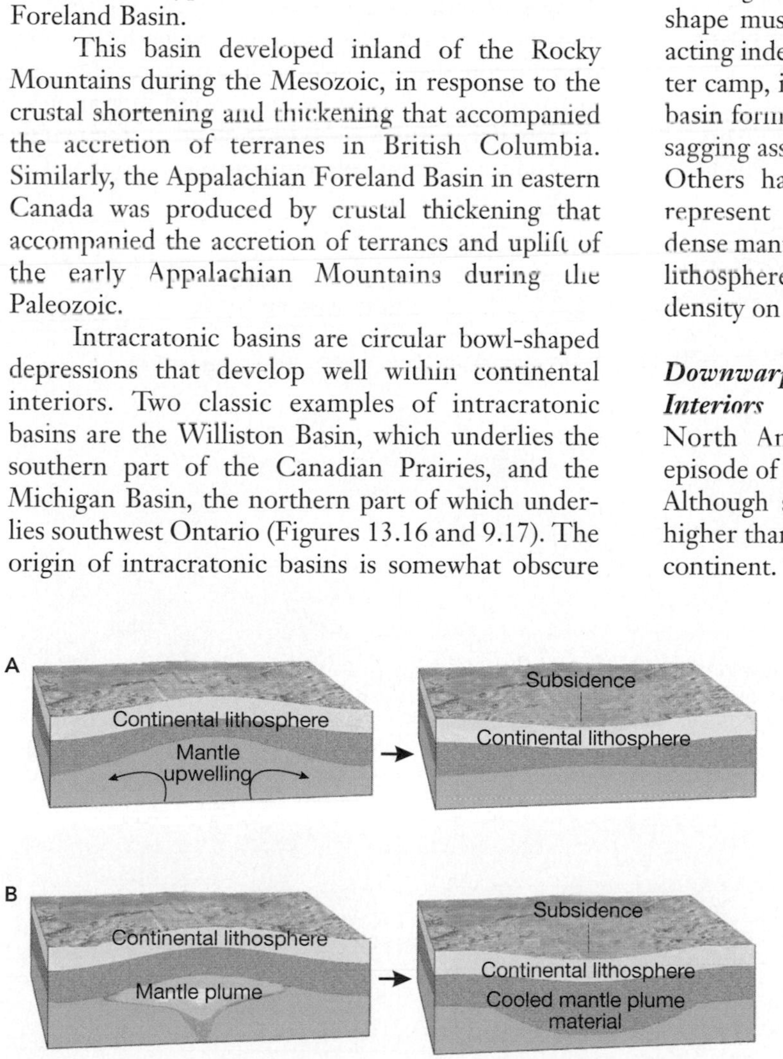

◆ **Figure 13.16** Two possible mechanisms responsible for forming a circular intracratonic basin. **A.** The lithosphere thins and sags because of localized mantle upwelling. **B.** The lithosphere is weighed down locally by a mass of mantle material that has attached to the base of the lithosphere and has sunk because of increased density on cooling.

leaving behind thick accumulations of marine sedimentary rocks. Today these largely undeformed strata are found hundreds of metres above sea level in the Canadian Prairies (Figure 13.17).

Similar episodes of large-scale downwarping are known on other continents, including Australia. The cause of these downward movements followed by rebound may be linked to subduction of oceanic lithosphere. One proposal suggests that when subduction ceases along a continental margin, the subducting slab detaches from the trailing lithosphere and continues its descent into the mantle. As this detached lithospheric slab sinks, it creates a downward flow in its wake that tugs on the base of the overriding continent. In some situations the crust is apparently pulled down enough to allow the ocean to extend inland. As the plate segment sinks deeper, the pull of the trailing wake weakens, and the continent "floats" back into isostatic balance. Although computer modelling supports this proposed mechanism, observational data to test this hypothesis has yet to be gathered.

THE ORIGIN AND EVOLUTION OF CONTINENTS

Earlier in this chapter, we learned that the theory of plate tectonics provides a model from which to examine the formation of Earth's major mountainous belts. But what roles have plate tectonics and mountain building played in the events that led to the origin and evolution of the continents?

The lack of agreement among geologists can be partly attributed to the complex nature and antiquity of most continental material, which makes deciphering its history very difficult. Whereas oceanic crust has a relatively simple layered structure and a rather uniform composition, the much older continental crust consists of a collage of highly deformed and metamorphosed igneous and sedimentary rocks. Moreover, in many places, such as the Canadian Prairies, the basement rocks are mantled by thick accumulations of much younger sedimentary rocks—a fact that inhibits detailed study. Nevertheless, during the last few decades, great strides have been made in unravelling the secrets held by the rocks that make up the stable continental interiors.

Early Evolution of Continents

At one extreme is a proposal that the continental crust formed early in Earth's history, perhaps in the first billion years. During this period, chemical differentiation resulted in the upward migration of the less-dense, silica-rich constituents of the mantle to produce a "scum" of continental-type rocks. The

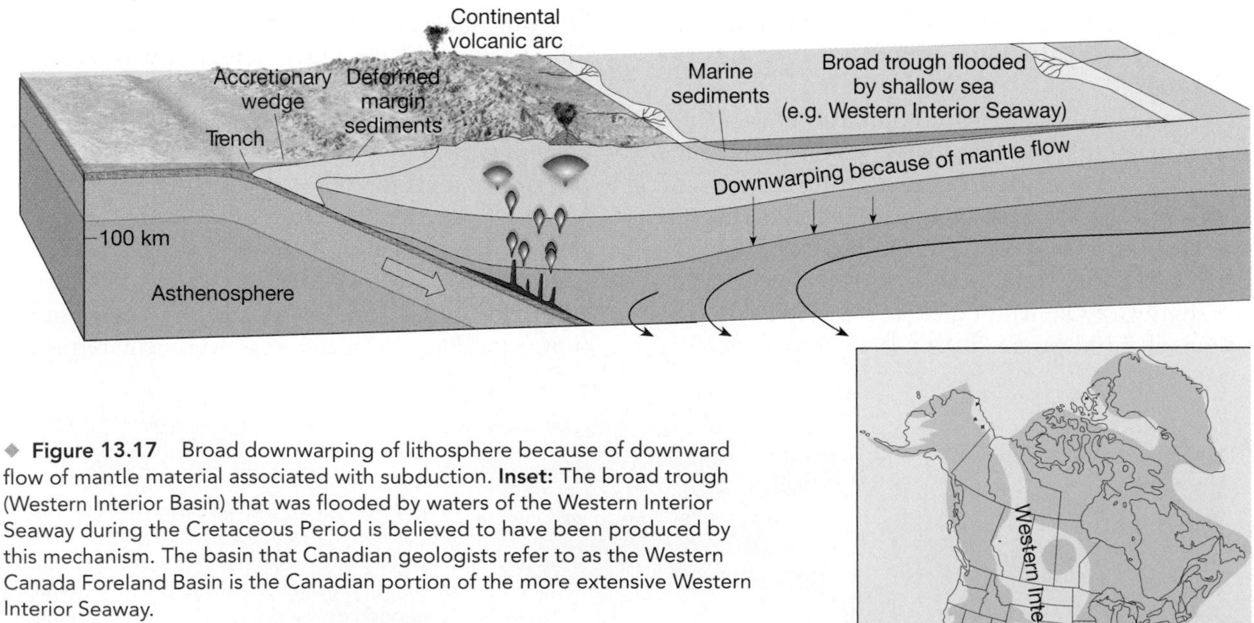

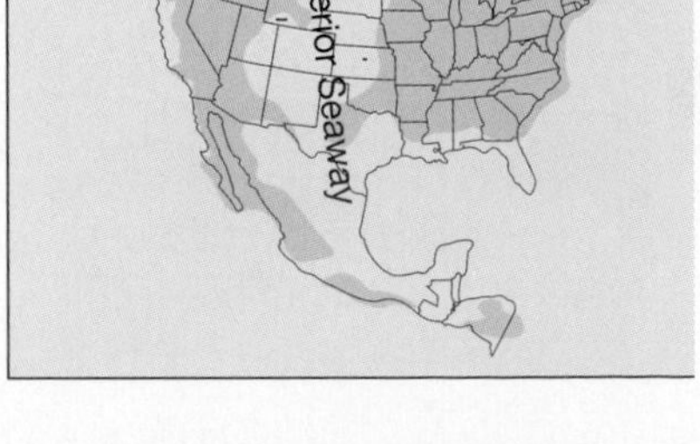

◆ **Figure 13.17** Broad downwarping of lithosphere because of downward flow of mantle material associated with subduction. **Inset:** The broad trough (Western Interior Basin) that was flooded by waters of the Western Interior Seaway during the Cretaceous Period is believed to have been produced by this mechanism. The basin that Canadian geologists refer to as the Western Canada Foreland Basin is the Canadian portion of the more extensive Western Interior Seaway.

more dense silicate minerals, those enriched in iron and magnesium, remained in the mantle.

Shortly after this period of chemical differentiation, a mechanism that may have resembled plate tectonics reworked and recycled the continental crust. Through such activity, the continental crust was deformed, metamorphosed, and even re-melted. However, because these silica-rich rocks were buoyant, they may not have been destroyed to any great extent or, if they were, they were replaced in roughly equal amounts by mantle-derived magmas. Thus, the essence of this hypothesis is that the total volume of continental crust has not changed appreciably since its origin—only the distribution and shape of the landmasses have been modified by tectonic activity.

Gradual Evolution of Continents

An opposing view contends that the continents have gradually grown larger through geologic time by the addition of material derived from the upper mantle. A main tenet of this hypothesis is that the primitive crust was of an oceanic type and the continents were small or possibly nonexistent. Then, through magmatic differentiation of mantle-derived magmas, the continents slowly grew over vast spans of geologic time.

According to this scenario, the earliest continental rocks came into existence at a few, isolated island arcs. Once formed, these island arcs coalesced to form larger continental masses, while deforming the volcanic and sedimentary rocks that were deposited in the intervening oceans. Eventually, this process generated blocks of continental crust that had the size and thickness of modern continents.

We can consider the growth of continents, as described above, to be a two-stage process. The first stage involves the formation of silica-rich rocks, which are the major constituents of the upper continental crust. As stated earlier, this process typically occurs at subduction zones, where mantle-derived magmas form crustal rocks in such settings as island arcs. The second stage involves the accretion of these terranes into larger crustal provinces, which in turn are sutured together to form continent-size crustal blocks. The latter event is associated with a major episode of mountain building.

North America provides an excellent example of the development of continental crust and its piecemeal assembly into a continent. Notice in Figure 13.18 that very little continental crust exists that is older than 3.5 billion years. In contrast, between 3 billion and 2.5 billion years ago there was a period of major crustal growth. During this span, the accretion of numerous island arcs and other

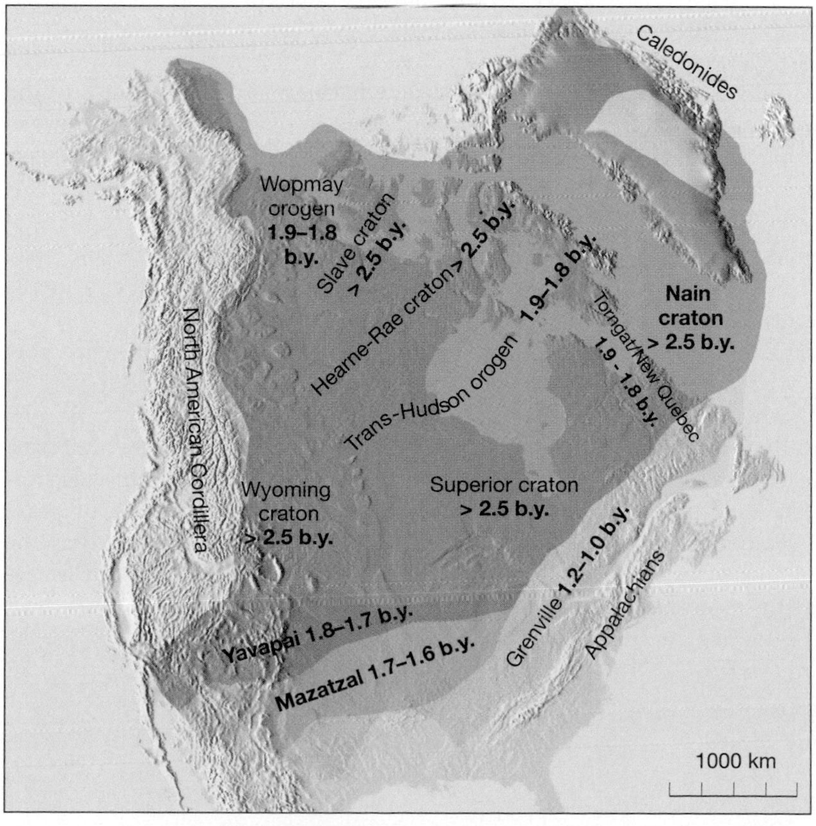

◆ **Figure 13.18** A map showing the major geologic provinces of North America and their ages in billions of years (b.y.). It appears that North America was joined by crustal blocks that were assembled by processes very similar to modern plate tectonics. These ancient collisions produced mountainous belts that include remnant volcanic island arcs trapped by the colliding continental fragments.

crustal fragments generated several large crustal provinces. North America contains some of these crustal provinces, including the Superior and Hearne/Rae cratons shown in Figure 13.18. The locations of these ancient continental blocks during their formation are not known. However, about 1.9 billion years ago these crustal provinces collided to produce the Trans-Hudson mountain belt (Figure 13.18). (This mountain-building episode was not restricted to North America, because ancient deformed strata of similar age are found on other continents.) This event built the core of North America, around which several large and numerous small crustal fragments were later added. Examples of these late arrivals include the Blue Ridge and Piedmont provinces of the Appalachians and several terranes that were added to the western margin of North America during the Mesozoic and Cenozoic eras.

We do not know with certainty how many major periods of mountain building have occurred since the formation of Earth. Each of these events probably marks the formation of a supercontinent. The last major period evidently coincided with the closing of the ancestral Atlantic during the formation of the supercontinent of Pangaea.

Chapter Summary

- Earth's less dense crust floats on top of the denser and deformable rocks of the mantle, much like wooden blocks floating in water. The concept of a floating crust in gravitational balance is called *isostasy*. Most mountainous topography is located where the crust has been shortened and thickened. Therefore, mountains have deep crustal roots that isostatically support them. As erosion lowers the peaks, *isostatic adjustment* gradually raises the mountains in response. The processes of uplifting and erosion will continue until the mountain block reaches "normal" crustal thickness.
- The name for processes that collectively produce a mountain system is *orogenesis*. Most *mountains* consist of roughly parallel ridges of folded and faulted sedimentary and volcanic rocks, portions of which have been strongly metamorphosed and intruded by younger igneous bodies.
- Major mountain systems form along convergent plate boundaries. Andean-type mountain building along continental margins involves the convergence of an oceanic plate and a plate whose leading edge contains continental crust. At some point in the formation of Andean-type mountains, a subduction zone forms, along with a continental volcanic arc. Sediment from the land, as well as material scraped from the subducting plate, becomes plastered against the landward side of the trench, forming an accretionary wedge. One of the best examples of an inactive Andean-type *mountain belt* is found in western Canada and includes the Coast Mountains in British Columbia.
- Continental collisions, in which both plates are carrying continental crust, have resulted in the formation of the Himalaya Mountains and the Tibetan Plateau. Continental collisions also formed many other mountain belts, including the Alps, Urals, and Appalachians.
- Recent investigations indicate that accretion, a third mechanism of orogenesis, takes place where small crustal fragments collide and accrete to continental margins along plate boundaries. The accreted crustal blocks are referred to as *terranes*. The mountainous topography of westernmost North America formed as the result of the accretion of terranes to North America.
- Convective flow in the mantle contributes to the up-and-down bobbing of the crust. The upward flow of a large super-plume located beneath southern Africa is thought to have elevated this region during the last 100 million years. Crustal subsidence has produced large basins and may have allowed the ocean to invade the continents several times in the geologic past.
- Geologists are trying to determine what role plate tectonics and mountain building play in the origin and evolution of continents. At one extreme is the view that most continental crust was formed early in Earth's history and has simply been reworked by the processes of plate tectonics. An opposing view contends that the continents have gradually grown larger by accretion of material derived from the mantle.

Review Questions

1. In the plate tectonics model, which type of plate boundary is most directly associated with mountain building?
2. Briefly describe the development of a volcanic island arc.
3. The formation of mountainous topography at a volcanic island arc, such as Japan, is considered just one phase in the development of a major mountain belt. Explain.
4. What is an accretionary wedge? Briefly describe its formation.
5. What is a passive margin? Give an example. Give an example of an active continental margin.
6. How does continental divergence produce mountains?
7. Suppose a sliver of oceanic crust was discovered in the interior of a continent. Would this support or refute the theory of plate tectonics? Explain.
8. Compare mountain building along an Andean-type convergent boundary and along a continent–continent convergent boundary.
9. How can the Appalachian Mountains be considered a collision-type mountain range when the nearest continent is 5000 kilometres away?
10. How does the plate tectonics theory help explain the existence of fossil marine life in rocks atop the Ural Mountains?
11. In your own words, briefly describe the stages in the formation of a major mountain system according to the plate tectonics model.
12. Define the term *terrane*. How is it different from the term *terrain*?
13. On the basis of current knowledge, describe the major difference between the evolution of the Appalachian Mountains and the North American Cordillera.
14. What evidence initially led geologists to conclude that mountains have deep crustal roots (see Box 13.1)?
15. Briefly describe the formation of the Canadian Rocky Mountains (see Box 13.2).
16. List some evidence that supports the concept of crustal uplift.
17. What happens to a floating object when weight is added? When it is subtracted? How does this principle apply to changes in the elevation of mountains? What term is applied to the adjustment that causes crustal uplift of this type?
18. How does the formation and melting of Pleistocene ice sheets support the idea that the lithosphere tries to remain in isostatic balance?
19. How do some researchers explain the elevated position of southern Africa?
20. What mechanism has been proposed to explain the subsidence in the interior of North America during the Cretaceous Period?
21. Briefly describe the difference between a foreland basin and an intracratonic basin.
22. Contrast the opposing views on the origin of the continental crust.

Key Terms

isostasy (p. 338)
isostatic adjustment (p. 341)
mountain (p. 339)
mountain belts (p. 339)
mountain ranges (p. 339)
orogenesis (p. 339)
passive margin (p. 341)
terrane (p. 346)

Web Resources

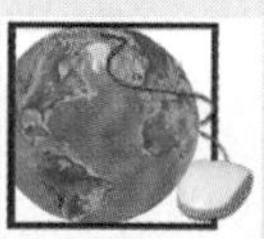

The *Earth* website uses the resources and flexibility of the internet to aid in your study of the topics in this chapter. Written and developed by geology instructors, this site will help improve your understanding of geology. Visit **www.pearsoned.ca/tarbuck** and click on the cover of the text to find

- online review quizzes
- Web-based critical thinking and writing exercises
- links to chapter-specific Web resources
- internet-wide key-term searches

www.pearsoned.ca/tarbuck

Chapter 14

Mass Wasting: The Work of Gravity

Mass Wasting and Landform Development
- The Role of Mass Wasting
- Slopes Change through Time

Controls and Triggers of Mass Wasting
- The Role of Water
- Oversteepened Slopes
- Removal of Vegetation
- Earthquakes as Triggers
- Liquefaction

Classification of Mass Wasting Processes
- Type of Material
- Type of Motion
- Rate of Movement

Slump

Rockslide

Debris Flow
- Lahars

Earthflow

Slow Movements
- Creep
- Solifluction
- Other Periglacial Features

Submarine Landslides

The Hope Slide (which occurred on January 9, 1965, in southwest British Columbia) is the largest historic landslide in western Canada. (Photo by Bill Cunningham/The Province)

Earth's surface is never perfectly flat; instead, it consists of slopes of different lengths and gradients. Slopes can be mantled with soil and vegetation or consist of barren rock and rubble. Taken together, slopes are important elements in our physical landscape. Although most slopes may appear to be stable and unchanging, the force of gravity ultimately causes material to move downslope. At one extreme, the movement can be gradual and practically imperceptible. At the other extreme, it can consist of a roaring debris flow or a thundering rockslide. When these hazardous natural processes lead to loss of life and property, they become natural disasters (Figure 14.1).

MASS WASTING AND LANDFORM DEVELOPMENT

Landslides (in the general sense) are examples of a basic geologic process called **mass wasting,** the downslope movement of rock, regolith, and soil under the direct influence of gravity. It is distinct from the erosional processes examined in subsequent chapters because mass wasting does not require a transporting medium, such as water, wind, or glacial ice.

The Role of Mass Wasting

Landforms developed as products of weathering are removed from the places where they originate. As mentioned in Chapter 5, once weathering weakens and breaks rock apart, mass wasting carries the debris downslope, where a stream, acting as a conveyor belt, usually carries it away. Although it may make many intermediate stops along the way, the sediment is eventually transported to the sea.

The combined effects of mass wasting and running water produce stream valleys, the most common and conspicuous of Earth's landforms. If streams alone were responsible for creating the valleys in which they flow, the valleys would be very narrow. The fact that most river valleys are much wider than they are deep indicates the significance of mass wasting processes in supplying material to streams. This fact is illustrated by the Grand Canyon (Figure 14.2). The walls of the canyon extend far from the Colorado River, owing to the transfer of weathered debris downslope to the river and its tributaries by mass wasting processes. In this manner, streams and mass wasting combine to sculpt the surface, along with groundwater, waves, and wind.

Slopes Change through Time

Clearly, if mass wasting is to occur, it needs slopes down which rock, soil, and regolith can move. It is Earth's mountain-building and volcanic processes that produce many of these slopes, sporadically changing the elevations of landmasses and the ocean floor. If dynamic internal processes did not continually produce regions of higher elevations, the transfer of debris to lower elevations would gradually slow and eventually cease.

A

B

◆ **Figure 14.1** The Hope Slide, the largest historic landslide in western Canada. **A.** Photo taken January 11, 1965, two days after the rockslide. **B.** Aerial view in 1988, when vegetation was re-established on the bottom part of the slide.
(Photo **A** Copyright © Province of British Columbia. All rights reserved. Reprinted with permission of the Province of British Columbia, www.ipp.gov.bc.ca; photo **B** used with permission of John Clague)

◆ **Figure 14.2** The walls of the Grand Canyon extend far from the channel of the Colorado River. This results primarily from the transfer of weathered debris downslope to the river and its tributaries by mass wasting processes.
(Photo by Tom and Susan Bean, Inc.)

Most extreme mass wasting events occur in areas of rugged, geologically young mountains. Newly formed mountains are rapidly eroded by rivers and glaciers, which produce steep and unstable slopes. It is in such settings that massive destructive landslides occur, such as the Hope disaster. As mountain building subsides, mass wasting and erosional processes lower the land. Over time, steep and rugged mountains are worn down to form gentler, more subdued terrain with smaller, less dramatic downslope movements.

CONTROLS AND TRIGGERS OF MASS WASTING

GEODe EARTH Mass Wasting
↳ Controls and Triggers of Mass Wasting

Gravity is the controlling force of mass wasting, but several factors play an important role in promoting downslope movements. Long before a landslide occurs, various processes work to weaken slope material, gradually making it more and more susceptible to failure. During this span, the slope becomes less stable. Eventually, the strength of the slope is weakened to the point that something **triggers**, or initiates, downslope movement. Remember that the trigger is not the sole cause of the mass wasting event but just the last of many causes. Among the common factors that trigger mass wasting processes are saturation of material with water, oversteepening of slopes, removal of anchoring vegetation, and ground vibrations from earthquakes.

The Role of Water

Mass wasting is sometimes triggered when heavy rains or periods of snowmelt saturate surface materials. This was the case in October 1998 when torrential downpours associated with Hurricane Mitch triggered devastating mudflows in Central America (Figure 14.3).

◆ **Figure 14.3** Heavy rains from Hurricane Mitch in the fall of 1998 triggered devastating mudflows in Central America. Water plays an important role in many mass wasting processes. (Photo by Noel Quidu/Liaison Agency, Inc.)

When the pores in sediment become filled with water, the cohesion among particles is destroyed, allowing them to slide past one another with relative ease. For example, when sand is slightly moist, it sticks together quite well. However, if enough water is added to fill the openings between the grains, the sand oozes out in all directions (Figure 14.4). Thus, saturation reduces the internal strength of materials, and they are then easily set in motion by the force of gravity. When clay is wetted, it becomes very slick and can act as a lubricating agent. Water also adds considerable weight to a mass of material. The added weight in itself may be enough to cause the material to slide or flow downslope.

Oversteepened Slopes

Oversteepening of slopes can also trigger mass movements. Oversteepening takes place in many natural settings. A stream or glacier undercutting a valley wall and waves pounding against the base of a cliff are two familiar examples. Furthermore, through their activities, people often create oversteepened and unstable slopes (Figure 14.5) that become prime sites for mass wasting (see Box 14.1).

Unconsolidated granular particles (sand-size or coarser) assume a stable slope called the **angle of repose** (*repose* = to be at rest). This is the steepest angle at which material remains stable. Depending on the size and shape of the particles, the angle varies from 25 to 40 degrees. The larger, more angular particles maintain the steepest slopes. If the angle is increased, the rock debris will adjust by moving downslope.

Oversteepening is not just important because it triggers movements of unconsolidated granular materials but also because it produces unstable slopes and mass movements in cohesive soils, regolith, and bedrock. The response will not be immediate, as with loose, granular material, but eventually one or more mass wasting processes will eliminate the oversteepening and restore stability to the slope.

Removal of Vegetation

Plants contribute to the stability of slopes because their root systems bind soil and regolith together. Their leaves can also protect the ground surface from the impact of raindrops. Where plants are lacking, mass wasting is enhanced, especially if slopes are

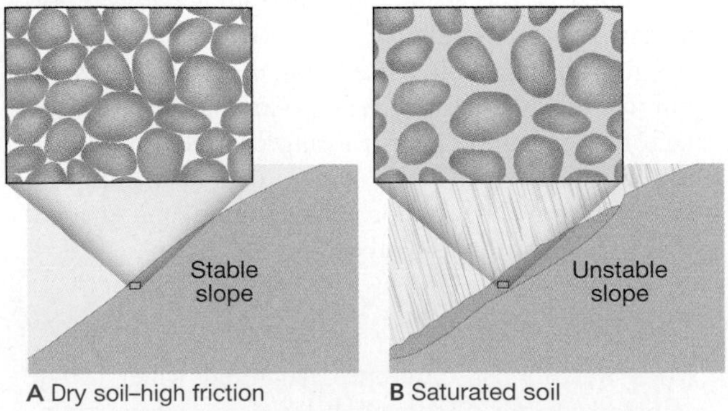

◆ **Figure 14.4** The effect of water on mass wasting can be great. **A.** When little or no water is present, friction among the closely packed soil particles on the slope holds them in place. **B.** When the soil is saturated, the grains are forced apart and friction is reduced, allowing the soil to move downslope.

◆ **Figure 14.5** Fractured rock was undercut and oversteepened to build this highway in British Columbia. Conspicuous joints dip parallel to the slope and are planes of weakness along which the rock can slide. (With permission of Tricouni Press Ltd.)

BOX 14.1

People and the Environment

Treacherous Slopes along the Sea-to-Sky Highway

During the 2010 Winter Olympics in Vancouver, Highway 99 from Vancouver to Whistler will be heavily used to shuttle people to outdoor events at Whistler. The problem is the stretch between West Vancouver and Squamish (Figure 14.A), which has a history of landslides that became more frequent after construction of the Sea-to-Sky Highway in the 1950s. The road was routed along the east side of Howe Sound, where joints in heavily fractured rocks dip parallel to the mountain slope. This structural setting, made worse by oversteepening to build the road (Figure 14.5) and heavy rains and snowmelts, results in rockfalls, rockslides, and debris flows that damage the highway, property, and people (see examples below). Increased highway congestion could result in more lives lost and longer traffic delays to remove debris from the road.

Rockfalls occur where talus slopes are seen beside the road. Attempts to inhibit rockfalls include bolting fractured rock with metal rods (Figure 14.B, left photo), covering slopes with heavy, coarse metal mesh (Figure 14.B, right photo), spraying slopes with cement, and drilling holes in the rock to increase drainage.

In 1915 a rockslide killed 56 people in a field camp above the mine site at Britannia Beach, British Columbia, when 100,000 cubic metres of rock and snow slid away from the steep mountainside and plowed into the camp. It may have been triggered by a spring thaw, infiltration of water, and blasting in tunnels under the mountain.

A classic debris flow (Figure 14.C) in British Columbia surged through Lions Bay in 1983, claiming two lives. It started as a slump into upper Alberta Creek, where water from an intense rainstorm and melting snow pooled behind a mass of logs and sediment that clogged the channel. When the dam broke, the slurry of debris grew to 10,000 cubic metres and travelled at 9 metres per second as it scoured more debris along its channel. Tongues of the debris flow overtopped the channel, smashed into homes and took out culverts and bridges.

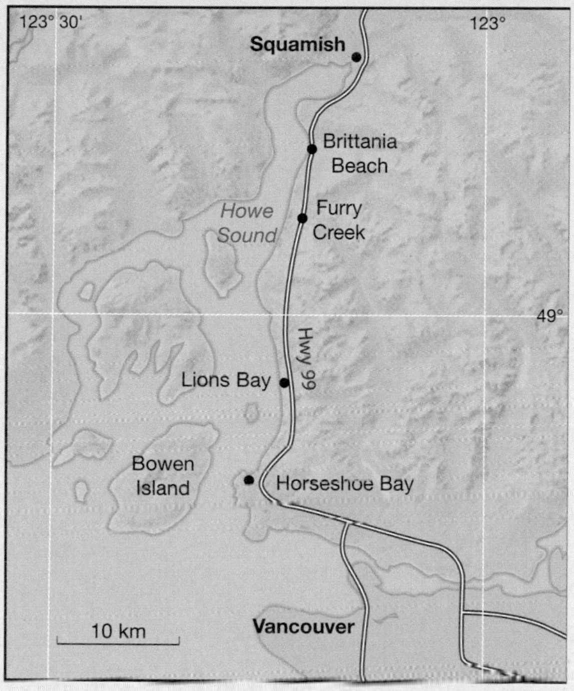

◆ **Figure 14.A** Map of the Howe Sound area between Vancouver and Squamish in British Columbia.

Along this highway, 2005 was another bad year for landslides. For example, earth fill in the backyard of a home at the top of a steep slope that failed during heavy rain swept downslope and into the houses below. The landslide picked up soil and trees as it travelled, adding to the destruction.

◆ **Figure 14.B** Rockfall mitigation attempts include inserting rock bolts into a grouted slope (left photo) and covering slopes with metal screen (right photo).
(With permission of Tricouni Press Ltd.)

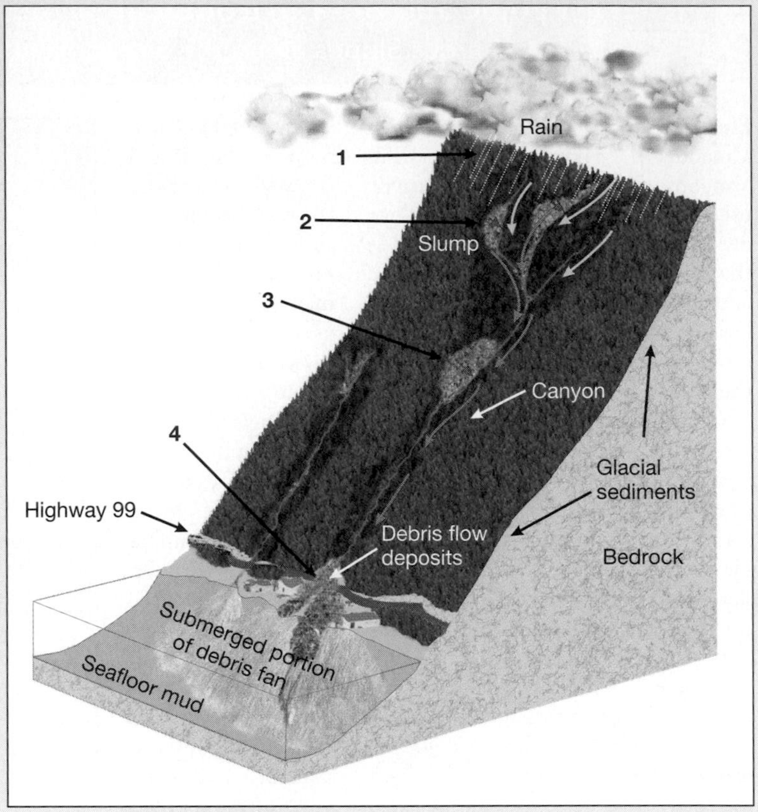

◆ **Figure 14.C** Anatomy of a Canadian debris flow. Sequence of events: (1) torrential rain swells streams near the mountain crest, (2) sediment slumps into a raging stream, triggering a debris flow that surges down the channel, (3) debris flow swells in volume as it picks up additional sediment and trees, and (4) debris flow emerges from the canyon onto a fan where it damages houses, roads, bridges, and railway.
(Reproduced with the permission of the Minister of Public Works and Government Services Canada, 2008, and courtesy of Natural Resources Canada)

steep and water is plentiful. When anchoring vegetation is removed by forest fires or by people (for timber, farming, or development), surface materials frequently move downslope.

An unusual example illustrating the anchoring effect of plants occurred several decades ago on steep slopes near Menton, France. Farmers replaced olive trees, which have deep roots, with a more profitable but shallow-rooted crop of carnations. When the slope became unstable and failed, the landslide took 11 lives.

During the summers of 1994 and 2000 severe wildfires swept hillsides of the western United States, denuding the slopes of vegetation (Figure 14.6). As a result, in September 1994 heavy rains in Colorado caused numerous debris flows, inundating a major highway with tonnes of rock, mud, and burned trees.

Earthquakes as Triggers

Conditions that favour mass wasting can exist in an area for a long time before movement occurs. An additional factor is sometimes necessary to trigger the movement. Among the more important and dramatic triggers are earthquakes. An earthquake and its aftershocks can dislodge enormous volumes of rock and unconsolidated material. Figure 14.7 illustrates one tragic example, and the Hope Slide in British Columbia (Figure 14.1) may also have been triggered this way.

Liquefaction

Intense ground shaking during earthquakes can cause water-saturated surface materials to lose their strength and behave as fluid-like masses that flow (see Chapter 10). This process, called *liquefaction*, is a major problem in the Ottawa-Saguenay region of eastern Ontario and western Quebec. In this area the Leda Clay (also known as *quick clay*) was deposited in the ancient Champlain Sea at the end of the last Ice Age. Slopes on this marine clay have failed many times, causing deaths, injuries, and property damage far beyond the site of failure. Even gentle slopes have failed because of liquefaction, in many cases induced by earthquakes, in others because of heavy rain, excavation, and overloading by heavy equipment and structures. The Fraser Delta in British Columbia is another example of potential failure because of liquefaction of its fine sediments. The communities of Delta, Richmond, and Steveston are at risk, especially in the event of an earthquake.

◆ **Figure 14.6** During the summer of 2000 wildfires raged in parts of the western United States. Hundreds of thousands of hectares were burned. The loss of anchoring vegetation sets the stage for accelerated mass wasting. This photo shows an area between Beavertail Hill and Bearmouth, Montana. (Photo by Derek Pruitt/The Montana Standard/AP/Wide World Photos)

Slope materials gradually weaken over time because of long-term weathering, infiltration of water, and other physical processes. Eventually, if the strength falls below what is necessary to maintain slope stability, a landslide will occur. The timing of such events is random, and thus accurate prediction is impossible.

◆ **Figure 14.7** Various forms of mass wasting can be triggered by earthquakes. This home was destroyed in Pacific Palisades, California, by a landslide triggered by the January 1994 Northridge earthquake. In some cases, damage from earthquake-induced mass wasting is greater than damage caused directly by an earthquake's ground vibrations. (Photo by Chromo Sohm/Corbis/The Stock Market)

CLASSIFICATION OF MASS WASTING PROCESSES

Geologists refer to a broad array of processes and classifications as mass wasting. Four main types are illustrated in Figure 14.8. Generally, the different types are classified based on the type of material involved, the kind of motion displayed, and the velocity of the movement.

Type of Material

The classification of mass wasting processes on the basis of the material involved in the movement depends on whether the descending mass began as unconsolidated material or as bedrock. If soil and regolith dominate, such terms as *debris* and *earth* are used in the description. In contrast, when a mass of mainly bedrock breaks loose and moves downslope, the term *rock* is commonly part of the description.

Type of Motion

In addition to characterizing the type of material involved in a mass wasting event, the way in which

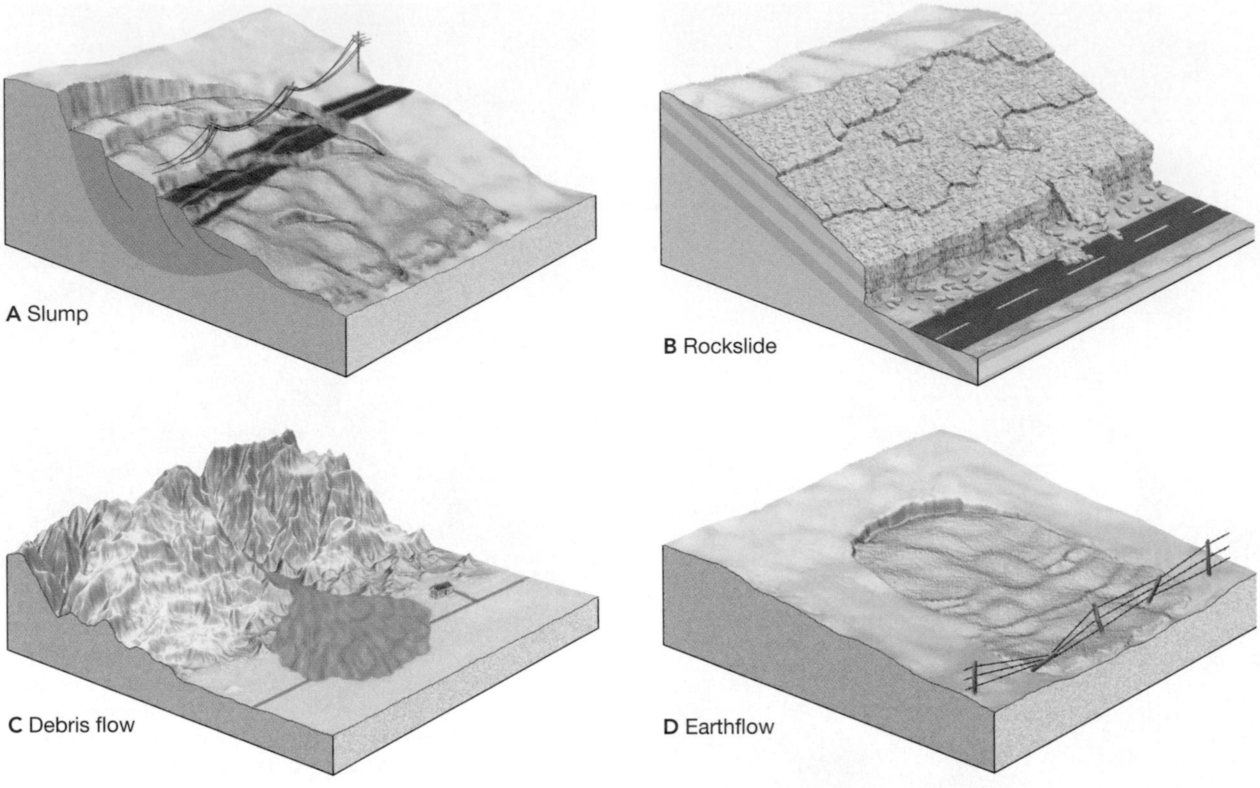

◆ **Figure 14.8** The four processes illustrated here are generally considered to be the main forms of mass wasting. Because material in **A.** slumps and **B.** rockslides move along well-defined surfaces, they are said to move by sliding. In contrast, when material moves downslope as a viscous fluid, the movement is described as a flow. **C.** Debris flow and **D.** earthflow advance downslope in this manner.

the material moves can also be important. Generally, the kind of motion is described as either a fall, a slide, or a flow.

Fall When the movement involves detached individual particles of any size dropping through the air, it is termed a **fall**. A fall is a common form of movement on slopes that are so steep that loose material cannot remain on the surface. The rock may fall directly to the base of the slope or move in a series of leaps and bounds over other rocks along the way. Many falls result when freeze and thaw cycles or the action of plant roots (see Figure 5.7) loosen rock to the point that gravity takes over (Figure 14.9). *Talus slopes* are built and maintained by such events (Figures 5.3 and 14.10).

Slide Many mass wasting processes are described as **slides**, which occur whenever material remains fairly coherent (negligible internal deformation) and moves along a well-defined surface. Sometimes the surface is a joint, a fault, or a bedding plane that parallels the slope. However, in the case of the movement called slump or *rotational slide*, the descending material moves en masse along a curved surface of rupture.

A note of clarification is appropriate at this point. Sometimes the word *slide* is used as a synonym for the word *landslide*, which has no specific definition in geology.

Flow The third type of movement common to mass wasting processes is termed **flow**, which occurs when material moves downslope as a viscous fluid. Most flows are saturated with water and typically move as lobes or tongues that experience internal deformation.

Rate of Movement

Rates of movement can be spectacularly sudden or exceptionally gradual. Although various types of mass wasting are commonly classified as either rapid or slow, such a distinction is highly subjective because a wide range of rates exists between the two extremes. Even the velocity of a single process at a particular site can vary considerably. This is why we present the main mass wasting processes according to the way they move, first those that move mainly by sliding, followed by those that move mainly by flow.

◆ **Figure 14.9** **A.** Rockfall blocking a highway near Bozeman, Montana. **B.** This road sign near Arthur's Pass, New Zealand, warns of falling rocks.
(Photo **A** by Phil Farnes/Photo Researchers, Inc.; photo **B** by Robert Essel/Corbis/Stock Market)

◆ **Figure 14.10** Talus is a slope built of angular rock fragments. Mechanical weathering, especially frost wedging, loosens the pieces of bedrock, which then fall to the base of the cliff. With time, a series of steep, cone-shaped accumulations build up at the base of the vertical slope. These talus cones are in Banff National Park, Alberta.
(Photo by Marli Miller)

SLUMP

GEODe EARTH Mass Wasting
↳ Types of Mass Wasting

Slump refers to the downward sliding of a mass of rock or unconsolidated material rotating as a unit along a curved surface (Figures 14.8A and 14.11). Usually, the slumped material travels neither spectacularly fast nor very far. This form of mass wasting is common along river valleys and eroding shorelines, especially in thick accumulations of cohesive materials, such as clay. The ruptured surface is characteristically spoon shaped and concave upward and outward. As the movement occurs, a crescent-shaped scarp is created at the head, and the block's upper surface is sometimes tilted backward because of rotation. Although slump can involve a single mass, it commonly consists of multiple blocks. Sometimes water collects between the base of the scarp and the top of the tilted block. As this water percolates downward along the surface of rupture, it may promote further instability and additional movement.

Slumping commonly occurs because a slope has been oversteepened. The material on the upper portion of a slope is held in place by the material at the bottom of the slope. As anchoring material at the base is removed, the material above is made unstable and reacts to the pull of gravity. One relatively common example is a valley wall that becomes oversteepened by a meandering river (Figure 14.12). Slumping can also occur when a slope is overloaded, causing internal stress on the material below. This type of

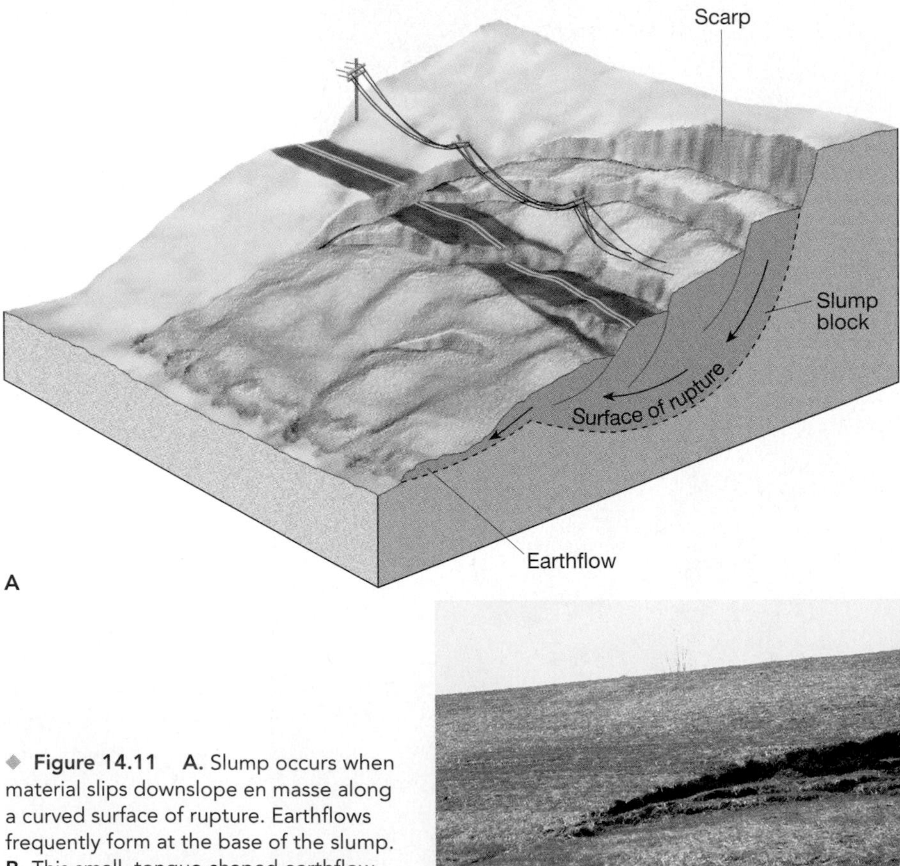

A

B

◆ **Figure 14.11** **A.** Slump occurs when material slips downslope en masse along a curved surface of rupture. Earthflows frequently form at the base of the slump. **B.** This small, tongue-shaped earthflow occurred on a newly formed slope along a recently constructed highway. It formed in clay-rich material following a period of heavy rain. Notice the small slump at the head of the earthflow.
(Photo by E. J. Tarbuck)

◆ **Figure 14.12** Slumps along the valley wall of the South Saskatchewan River near Medicine Hat, Alberta. (Photo by S. R. Hicock)

slump commonly occurs where weak, clay-rich material underlies layers of stronger, more resistant rock, such as sandstone. The seepage of water through the upper layers reduces the strength of the clay below, resulting in slope failure. It is common for the lower parts of slumps to break up and flow (Figure 14.11B).

ROCKSLIDE

GEODe EARTH Mass Wasting
↳ Types of Mass Wasting

Rockslides occur when blocks of mainly bedrock break loose and travel rapidly down a slope (see Figure 14.8B). Such events are among the fastest and most destructive mass movements. Usually, rockslides take place in a geologic setting where the rock strata are inclined, or where joints and fractures parallel the slope. When such a rock unit is undercut at the base of the slope, it loses support and the rock eventually gives way. Sometimes the rockslide is triggered when rain or melting snow destabilizes the underlying surface to the point where friction is no longer sufficient to hold the rock unit in place. As a result, rockslides tend to be more common during the spring, when heavy rains and melting snow are most prevalent. Commonly, rockslide blocks break up soon after failure, and then move by flowing rapidly downslope.

Earthquakes can trigger rockslides and other mass movements. The 1811 earthquake at New Madrid, Missouri, for example, caused slides in an area of more than 13,000 square kilometres along the Mississippi River Valley. A more recent example occurred on August 17, 1959, when a strong earthquake west of Yellowstone National Park triggered a massive slide in the canyon of the Madison River in southwest Montana. In a matter of moments an estimated 27 million cubic metres of rock, soil, and trees slid into the canyon. The debris dammed the river and buried a campground and highway. More than 20 campers perished.

Frank Slide, located in the Crowsnest Pass of the Alberta Rockies, is probably Canada's most famous rockslide disaster (Figure 14.13). Now a tourist attraction, Frank Slide was produced by the failure and rapid downslope movement of a huge body of rock from Turtle Mountain at 4:10 A.M., April 29, 1903.

◆ **Figure 14.13** The Frank Slide event occurred in the early morning of April 29, 1903, in the Crowsnest Pass, Alberta. At least 70 people in the town of Frank were killed in this famous Canadian disaster. (Photo by S. R. Hicock)

In less than 100 seconds, more than 80 million tonnes (30 million cubic metres) of rock tumbled from the top of Turtle Mountain, to spread out over 3 square kilometres of land at the base of the mountain. Within the path of the landslide was the coal-mining town of Frank. At least 70 people died in this disaster. Many more lives would probably have been spared if the event had taken place late in the day rather than in the early morning hours, when most people were still asleep. Although Frank Slide probably started as a true slide, it appears that on rock fragmentation, it evolved into a debris flow, travelling on a cushion of air, allowing the rock debris to travel partly up the opposite side of the valley.

Frank Slide is difficult to attribute to a single cause, and it is quite possible that it simply manifests the combined effect of a number of geologic and human factors. Beginning in the Cretaceous Period, extensive thrusting and deformation led to the sliding and bending of hard Paleozoic carbonate rocks over soft Mesozoic rocks, ultimately forming the lofty peaks of the Alberta Rockies. Associated with this disturbance was the development of stress cracks in the Paleozoic carbonates that allowed the infiltration of water and the widening of fissures and cavities by dissolution, which led to the structural weakening of Turtle Mountain limestones. Considerably later, glacial activity during the last Ice Age removed a significant amount of carbonate rock near the base of Turtle Mountain, exposing the much softer underlying Mesozoic sandstones and shales, and leaving the remaining carbonates near the peak prone to sliding like a dinner plate on a slanted table. It is suspected by some that deforestation and coal-mining activity (especially dynamite blasts) in the weak Mesozoic strata near the base of the slope contributed sufficient disturbance to trigger the mass wasting event. Then again, unseasonably warm weather preceding the event and unusually frigid conditions the night before the disaster suggest that frost wedging may have been the trigger.

This disaster, like many others, provides valuable information for the prevention of, or at least the reduction of, potential damage related to similar events in the future. Frank Slide also provides a reminder that Canadians are by no means immune to the types of natural disasters that we are so used to hearing about in other parts of the world. It is probably no coincidence, that long before the disaster that struck the town of Frank, the Blackfoot and Kutenai talked about Turtle Mountain as "the mountain that moves."

DEBRIS FLOW

GEODe EARTH Mass Wasting
↳ Types of Mass Wasting

Debris flow is a relatively rapid type of mass wasting that involves a flow of soil and regolith containing a large amount of water (Figure 14.8C). Debris flows are characteristic of mountainous regions, including some volcanoes. Because of their fluid properties, debris flows frequently follow canyons and stream channels. In populated areas, debris flows can pose a significant hazard to life and property.

When a cloudburst or rapidly melting mountain snows create a sudden flood, large quantities of soil and regolith can be washed into nearby stream channels. The end product is a flowing tongue of well-mixed mud, soil, rock, and water. Its consistency can range from that of wet concrete to that of soup. The rate of flow therefore depends not only on the slope but also on the water content. Dense debris flows are capable of carrying or pushing large boulders, trees, and even houses with relative ease.

Debris flows pose a serious hazard to development in mountainous areas, such as British Columbia (e.g., North and West Vancouver north to Pemberton; Box 14.1) and southern California. The construction of homes on canyon hillsides and the removal of native vegetation by brush fires and other means have increased the frequency of these destructive events (Figure 14.14). When a debris flow reaches the end of a steep, narrow canyon, it spreads out and covers the area beyond the mouth of the canyon with a mixture of wet debris. This material contributes to the buildup of fanlike deposits at canyon mouths. These structures, called alluvial fans, will be discussed in greater detail in Chapter 15.

The fans are relatively easy to build on, commonly have nice views, and are close to the mountains; in fact, like the nearby canyons, many have become preferred sites for development. Because debris flows occur only sporadically, the public is often unaware of the potential hazard of such sites.

Lahars

As described in Chapter 4, debris flows composed mostly of volcanic materials on the flanks of volcanoes are called *lahars*. The word originated in Indonesia, a volcanic region that has experienced many of these often-destructive events. Historically, lahars have been some of the deadliest volcanic hazards. They can occur either during an eruption or when a volcano is quiet. They take place when highly unstable layers of ash and debris become saturated with water and flow down steep volcanic slopes, generally following existing stream channels. Heavy rainfalls commonly trigger these flows. Others are initiated when large volumes of ice and snow are melted by heat flowing to the surface from within the volcano or by the hot gases and near-molten debris emitted during a violent eruption. The eruption of Mount St. Helens in May 1980 created several lahars (Figure 14.15).

◆ **Figure 14.14** On January 25, 1997, a mudflow buried this one-storey home in Mill Valley, California. Heavy rains from a powerful Pacific storm triggered the event.
(Justin Sullivan/AP/Wide World Photos)

◆ **Figure 14.15** A house damaged by a lahar along the Toutle River in Washington State, west-northwest of Mount St. Helens. The end section of the house was torn free and lodged against trees.
(Photo by D. R. Crandell, U.S. Geological Survey)

EARTHFLOW

GEODe EARTH Mass Wasting
↳ Types of Mass Wasting

We have seen that debris flows are fast and frequently confined to channels. In contrast, slower, viscous **earthflows** most commonly form on hillsides in humid areas during times of heavy precipitation or snowmelt (see Figure 14.8D). When water saturates the soil and regolith on a hillside, the material may break away, leaving a scar on the slope and forming a tongue- or teardrop-shaped mass that flows downslope (Figure 14.11B).

The materials most commonly involved are rich in clay and silt and contain only small proportions of sand and coarser particles. Earthflows range in size from bodies a few metres long, a few metres wide, and less than a metre deep to masses more than 1 kilometre long, several hundred metres wide, and more than 10 metres deep. They are characterized by a slow and persistent movement and can remain active for days or even years. Depending on the steepness of the slope and the material's consistency, measured velocities range from less than a millimetre a day up to several metres a day. Over the span that earthflows are active, movement is typically faster during wet periods than during drier times. In addition to occurring as isolated hillside phenomena, earthflows commonly take place in association with large slumps. In this situation, they may be seen as tongue-like flows at the base of the slump block (see Figure 14.11), which collapses following loss of support.

SLOW MOVEMENTS

GEODe EARTH Mass Wasting
↳ Types of Mass Wasting

Movements, such as rockslides and lahars, are certainly the most spectacular and catastrophic forms of mass wasting. Because these events can kill thousands, they deserve intensive study so that through more effective prediction, timely warnings, and better controls, more lives can be saved. However, because of their large size and spectacular nature, they give us a false impression of their importance as a mass wasting process. Indeed, sudden movements are responsible for moving less material than the slower and far subtler action of creep. Whereas rapid types of mass wasting are characteristic of mountains and steep hillsides, creep takes place on both steep and gentle slopes and is thus much more widespread.

Creep

Creep is a type of mass wasting that involves the gradual downhill movement of soil and regolith. One factor that contributes to creep is the alternate expansion and contraction of surface material caused by freezing and thawing or wetting and drying. As shown in Figure 14.16, freezing or wetting lifts particles at right angles to the slope, and thawing or drying allows the particles to fall back vertically to a slightly lower level. Each cycle therefore moves the material a tiny distance downslope. Creep is aided by anything that disturbs the soil, such as raindrop impact, plant roots, and burrowing animals. Creep is also promoted when the ground becomes saturated with water. Following a heavy rain or snowmelt, a waterlogged soil may lose its internal cohesion, allowing gravity to pull the material downslope. Because creep is imperceptibly slow, the process cannot be observed in action. What can be observed, however, are the effects of creep. Creep causes fences and utility poles to tilt and retaining walls to be displaced (Figure 14.17). Trees get tilted but continue to grow upward, resulting in curved trunks.

Solifluction

When soil is saturated with water, the soggy mass may flow downslope at a rate of a few millimetres or a few centimetres per day or per year. Such a process is called **solifluction** (literally, "soil flow"). It is a type of mass wasting that is common wherever water cannot escape from the saturated surface layer by infiltrating to deeper levels. A dense clay hardpan in soil or an impermeable bedrock layer can promote solifluction.

Solifluction is also common in regions underlain by **permafrost**, the permanently frozen ground that occurs in association with Earth's harsh polar

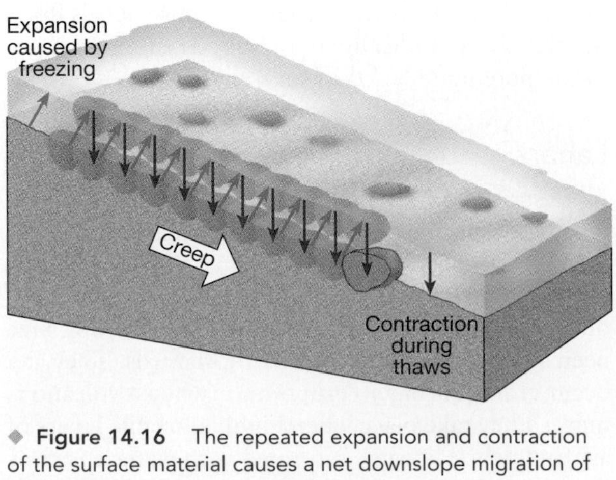

◆ **Figure 14.16** The repeated expansion and contraction of the surface material causes a net downslope migration of rock particles—a process called *creep*.

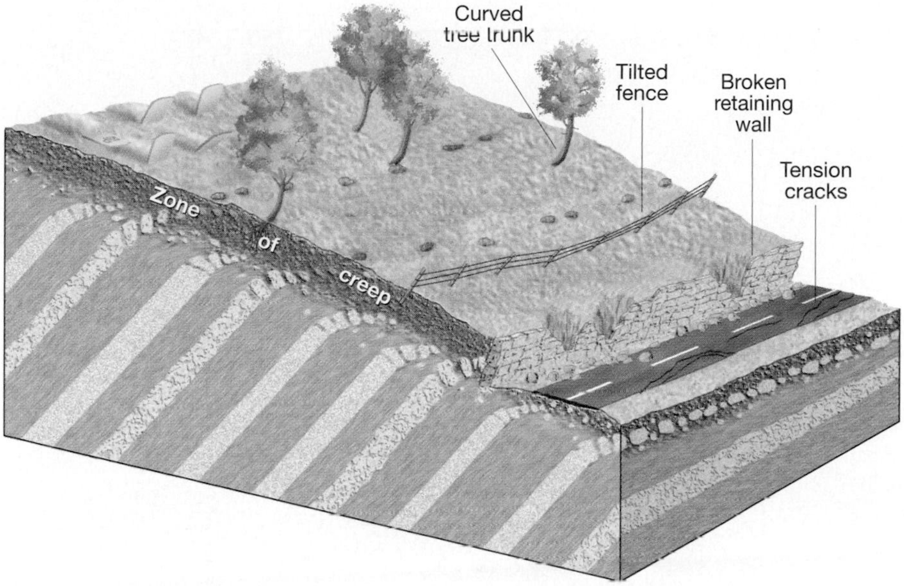

◆ **Figure 14.17** Although creep is an imperceptibly slow movement, its effects are commonly visible.

climates (see Box 14.2). Solifluction occurs in a zone above the permafrost called the **active layer**, which thaws to a depth of about a metre during the brief high-latitude summer and then refreezes in winter. During the summer season, water is unable to percolate into the impervious permafrost layer below. As a result, the active layer becomes saturated and slowly flows. The process can occur on slopes as gentle as 2 to 3 degrees. Where there is a well-developed mat of vegetation, a solifluction sheet may move in a series of well-defined lobes or as a series of partially overriding folds (Figure 14.18).

BOX 14.2

Understanding Earth

The Sensitive Permafrost Landscape

Many of the mass wasting events in this chapter have had sudden and disastrous impacts on people. When the activities of people cause ice contained in permanently frozen ground to melt, the impact is more gradual and less deadly. Nevertheless, because permafrost regions are sensitive and fragile landscapes, the scars resulting from poorly planned actions can remain for generations.

Permanently frozen ground, known as *permafrost*, occurs where summers are too cool to melt more than a shallow surface layer. Deeper ground remains frozen year-round. Strictly speaking, permafrost is defined only on the basis of temperature; that is, it is ground with temperatures that have remained below 0°C continuously for two years or more. The degree to which ice is present in the ground strongly affects the behaviour of the surface material. Knowing how much ice is present and where it is located is very important when it comes to constructing roads, buildings, and other projects in areas underlain by permafrost.

Permafrost underlies about 20 percent of Earth's land area. In addition to occurring in Antarctica and in some high mountain areas, permafrost is extensive in the lands surrounding the Arctic Ocean. It covers about 50 percent of Canada, a substantial portion of northern Siberia, and most of Alaska (Figure 14.D). Near the southern margins of the region, the permafrost consists of relatively thin, isolated masses. Farther north, the area and thickness gradually increase to the point where the permafrost is essentially continuous and its thickness may approach or even exceed 500 metres. In the discontinuous zone, land-use planning is frequently more difficult than in the continuous zone farther north because the occurrences of permafrost are patchy and difficult to predict.

When people disturb the surface, such as by removing the insulating vegetation mat or by building roads and buildings, the delicate thermal balance is disturbed, and the permafrost can thaw (Figure 14.E). Thawing produces unstable ground that may slide, slump, subside, and undergo severe frost heaving.

As Figure 14.F illustrates, when a heated structure is built directly on permafrost that contains a high proportion of ice, thawing creates soggy material into which a building can sink. One solution is to place buildings and other structures on piles, like stilts. Such piles allow subfreezing air to circulate between the floor of the building and the soil and thereby keep the ground frozen.

When oil was discovered on Alaska's North Slope, many people were concerned about the building of a pipeline linking the oil fields at Prudhoe Bay to the ice-free port of Valdez 1300 kilometres to the south. They voiced serious concern that such a massive project might damage the sensitive permafrost environment. Many also worried about possible oil spills.

Because oil must be heated to about 60°C to flow properly, special engineering procedures had to be developed to isolate this heat from the permafrost. Methods included insulating the pipe, elevating portions of the pipeline above ground level, and even placing cooling devices in the ground to keep it frozen. The Alaskan pipeline is clearly one of the most complex and costly projects ever built in the Arctic tundra. Detailed studies and careful engineering helped minimize adverse effects resulting from the disturbance of frozen ground.

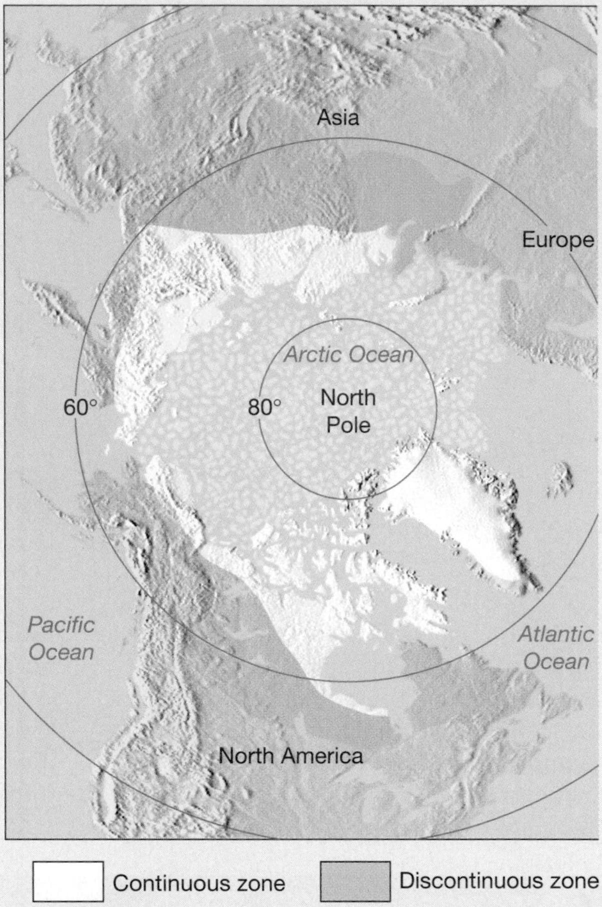

◆ **Figure 14.D** Distribution of permafrost in the Northern Hemisphere. About 50 percent of Canada and more than 80 percent of Alaska is underlain by permafrost. Two zones are recognized. In the *continuous zone*, the only ice-free areas are beneath deep lakes or rivers. The higher latitude portions of the *discontinuous zone* have only scattered islands of thawed ground. Moving southward, the percentage of unfrozen ground increases until all the ground is unfrozen.
(After the U.S. Geological Survey)

◆ **Figure 14.E** When a rail line was built across this permafrost landscape in Alaska, the ground subsided.
(Photo by Lynn A. Yehle, U.S. Geological Survey)

◆ **Figure 14.F** These buildings in Dawson, Yukon, are tilted because they rest directly on permafrost that is melting from the heat of the buildings.
(Photo by S. R. Hicock)

A B

◆ **Figure 14.18** **A.** Solifluction lobes northeast of Fairbanks, Alaska. Solifluction occurs in permafrost regions when the active layer thaws in summer. **B.** Solifluction lobes above Omega River near its mouth on north Baffin Island.
(Photo **A** by J. E. Patterson; photo **B** by S. R. Hicock)

Other Periglacial Features

Processes related to permafrost, and resulting features like solifluction lobes, are called **periglacial**. Because periglacial processes often initiate mass wasting events in cold environments, it is appropriate to mention them here. Box 14.2 explains *continuous* and *discontinuous zones* of permafrost and some associated environmental and industrial problems. Even in the continuous zone, unfrozen patches called *talik* can occur under the ground surface, usually under lakes. Some of these lakes gradually freeze to form ice-cored mounds covered with tundra vegetation, called **pingoes** (Figure 14.19A). Similar features are **palsas** (Figure 14.19B), but they are mounds of peat with ice lenses instead of a solid ice core. As you would expect, frost wedging (see Chapter 5) is common in periglacial environments where bedrock can be so shattered, the shards cover the ground as **felsenmeer** (Figure 14.19C), also known as a *block field*.

During winter the active layer freezes, inducing *frost heaving* of the ground surface (which can cause creep and solifluction on slopes) and *cryoturbation* (ice mixing) of soil horizons below. In periglacial areas the ground often cracks; where water enters the cracks in summer, it freezes to form *ice wedges*. These cracks and ice wedges (Figure 14.19D) are commonly connected in geometric patterns called **patterned ground** that are distinctive when viewed from above (Figure 14.19E). Frost heaving and cryoturbation gradually raise stones to the surface, where they tend to concentrate in ice wedges to form sorted stone polygons shaped like nets, circles, and stripes where gravity pulls polygons downslope.

Where permafrost melts (because of climate change, talik expansion, or human activities), irregular features form on the surface, resulting in **thermokarst** topography (as opposed to karst developed in limestone terrain) that commonly includes *thaw lakes* (Figure 14.19F). Thermokarst formation can damage roads, railways (Figure 14.E), pipelines, power lines, and buildings (Figure 14.F). Preventing human-induced melting of permafrost in this sensitive environment (Box 14.2) requires innovative engineering solutions.

SUBMARINE LANDSLIDES

As you might imagine, mass wasting processes are not confined to land. The development of high-quality instruments that perform ocean-floor imaging has allowed us to observe that submarine mass wasting is common and widespread. Large submarine landslides have been discovered on the flanks of the Hawaiian chain, as well as along the continental shelf and slope of North America (see Box 11.1). In fact, many submarine landslides, mostly in the form of slumps and debris flows, appear to be much larger than any similar mass wasting events that occur on land.

◆ **Figure 14.19** Selected periglacial features. **A.** Ice-cored pingo, Yukon. **B.** Small palsa on mainland Nunavut, south of Pelly Bay. **C.** Felsenmeer on north Baffin Island, south of Keele River. **D.** Ice wedge polygon near Kellet River, mainland Nunavut. **E.** Patterned ground near Pelly Bay, Nunavut. **F.** Thaw lakes west of Walker Lake, mainland Nunavut.
(Photo **A** © Staffan Widstrand/CORBIS; photos **B–F** by S. R. Hicock)

Among the most spectacular underwater landslides are those that occur on the flanks of *seamounts* and volcanic islands, such as Hawaii. One of the largest, known as the Nuuanu debris flow, is on the northeast side of Oahu. It extends for nearly 25 kilometres across the ocean floor, then rises up a 300-metre slope at its terminus, indicating that it must have had great power and momentum. This giant landslide transported giant blocks many kilometres across. It is probable that when such large and rapid events occur, they produce tsunami that race across the Pacific.*

The massive submarine slides discovered on the flanks of the Hawaiian Islands are almost certainly related to the movement of magma while a volcano is active. As huge quantities of lava are added to the seaward margin of a volcano, the buildup of material eventually triggers a great landslide. In the Hawaiian chain, it appears that this process of growth and collapse is repeated at intervals of 100,000 to 200,000 years while the volcano is active.

Along the continental margins of North America, large slumps and debris-flow scars mark the continental slope. These processes are triggered by the rapid buildup of unstable sediments or by such forces as storm waves and earthquakes (see Box 11.1). Submarine mass wasting is especially active near deltas, the massive deposits of sediment at the mouths of rivers. Here, as great loads of water-saturated clay and organic-rich sediments accumulate, they become unstable and readily flow down even gentle slopes. Some of these movements have been forceful enough to damage large offshore drilling platforms.

Mass wasting appears to be an integral part of the growth of passive continental margins, discussed in Chapter 11. Sediments supplied to the continental shelf by rivers move across the shelf to the upper continental slope. From here, slumps, slides, and debris flows (*turbidity currents*) move sediment down to the continental rise (coalesced *deep-sea fans*) and sometimes beyond.

*For more on these destructive waves, see the section on tsunamis in Chapter 10.

Chapter Summary

- *Mass wasting* refers to the downslope movement of rock, regolith, and soil under the direct influence of gravity. In the evolution of most landforms, mass wasting is the step that follows weathering. The combined effects of mass wasting and erosion by running water produce stream valleys.
- Gravity is the controlling force of mass wasting. Other factors that influence or *trigger* downslope movements are saturation of the material with water, oversteepening of slopes beyond a stable angle, removal of vegetation, and ground shaking by earthquakes.
- The various processes included under the name of mass wasting are divided and described on the basis of (1) the type of material involved (debris, earth, or rock); (2) the type of motion (*fall*, *slide*, or *flow*); and (3) the rate of movement (rapid or slow).
- The more rapid forms of mass wasting include *slump*, the downward sliding of a mass of rock or unconsolidated material moving as a unit along a curved surface; *rockslide*, blocks of bedrock break ing loose and sliding down slope; *debris flow*, a relatively rapid flow of soil and regolith containing a large amount of water; and *earthflow*, an unconfined flow of saturated clay-rich soil that most often occurs on a hillside in a humid area following heavy precipitation or snowmelt.
- The slowest forms of mass wasting include *creep*, the gradual downhill movement of soil and regolith; and *solifluction*, the gradual flow of a saturated surface layer that is underlain by an impermeable zone. Common sites for solifluction are regions underlain by *permafrost* (permanently frozen ground associated with tundra and ice-cap climates).
- Mass wasting is not confined to land; it also occurs underwater. Many submarine landslides, mostly slumps and debris avalanches, are much larger than those that occur on land.

Review Questions

1. Describe how mass wasting processes contribute to the development of stream valleys.
2. What is the controlling force of mass wasting?
3. How does water affect mass wasting processes?
4. Describe the significance of the angle of repose.
5. How might the removal of vegetation by fire or logging promote mass wasting?
6. How are earthquakes linked to landslides?
7. Distinguish among fall, slide, and flow.
8. Both slump and rockslide move by sliding. In what ways do these processes differ?
9. What factors led to the massive rockslide at Frank, Alberta?
10. Compare and contrast mudflow and earthflow.
11. Because creep is an imperceptibly slow process, what evidence might indicate that this phenomenon is affecting a slope?
12. What is permafrost? What portion of Earth's land surface is affected? (See Box 14.2.)
13. During what season does solifluction occur in permafrost regions?

Key Terms

active layer (p. 373)
angle of repose (p. 362)
creep (p. 372)
debris flow (p. 371)
earthflow (p. 372)
fall (p. 366)
felsenmeer (p. 375)
flow (p. 366)
mass wasting (p. 360)
palsa (p. 375)
patterned ground (p. 375)
periglacial (p. 375)
permafrost (p. 372)
pingo (p. 375)
rockslide (p. 369)
slide (p. 366)
slump (p. 368)
solifluction (p. 372)
thermokarst (p. 375)
trigger (p. 361)

Web Resources

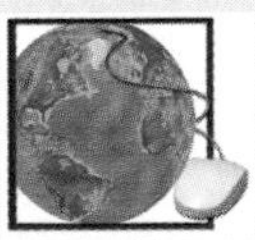

The *Earth* website uses the resources and flexibility of the internet to aid in your study of the topics in this chapter. Written and developed by geology instructors, this site will help improve your understanding of geology. Visit **www.pearsoned.ca/tarbuck** and click on the cover of the text to find

- online review quizzes
- Web-based critical thinking and writing exercises
- links to chapter-specific Web resources
- internet-wide key-term searches

www.pearsoned.ca/tarbuck

Chapter 15

Running Water

Earth as a System: The Hydrologic Cycle
- From Runoff to Stream Flow

Basic Components of a Stream

Characteristics and Controls of Stream Flow
- Gradient and Channel Characteristics
- Discharge

Changes from Upstream to Downstream

Stream Erosion

Transport of Sediment by Streams
- Dissolved Load
- Suspended Load
- Bed Load
- Capacity and Competence

Deposition of Sediment by Streams
- Channel Deposits
- Floodplain Deposits

The Graded Stream Concept and Base Level

Stream Valleys
- Narrow Valleys
- Wide Valleys

Types of Stream Systems
- Braided Streams
- Meandering Streams
- Anastomosed Streams

Alluvial Fans and Deltas
- Alluvial Fans
- Deltas

Drainage Networks
- Drainage Patterns
- Headward Erosion and Stream Piracy

Floods and Flood Control
- Causes and Types of Floods
- Methods of Flood Control

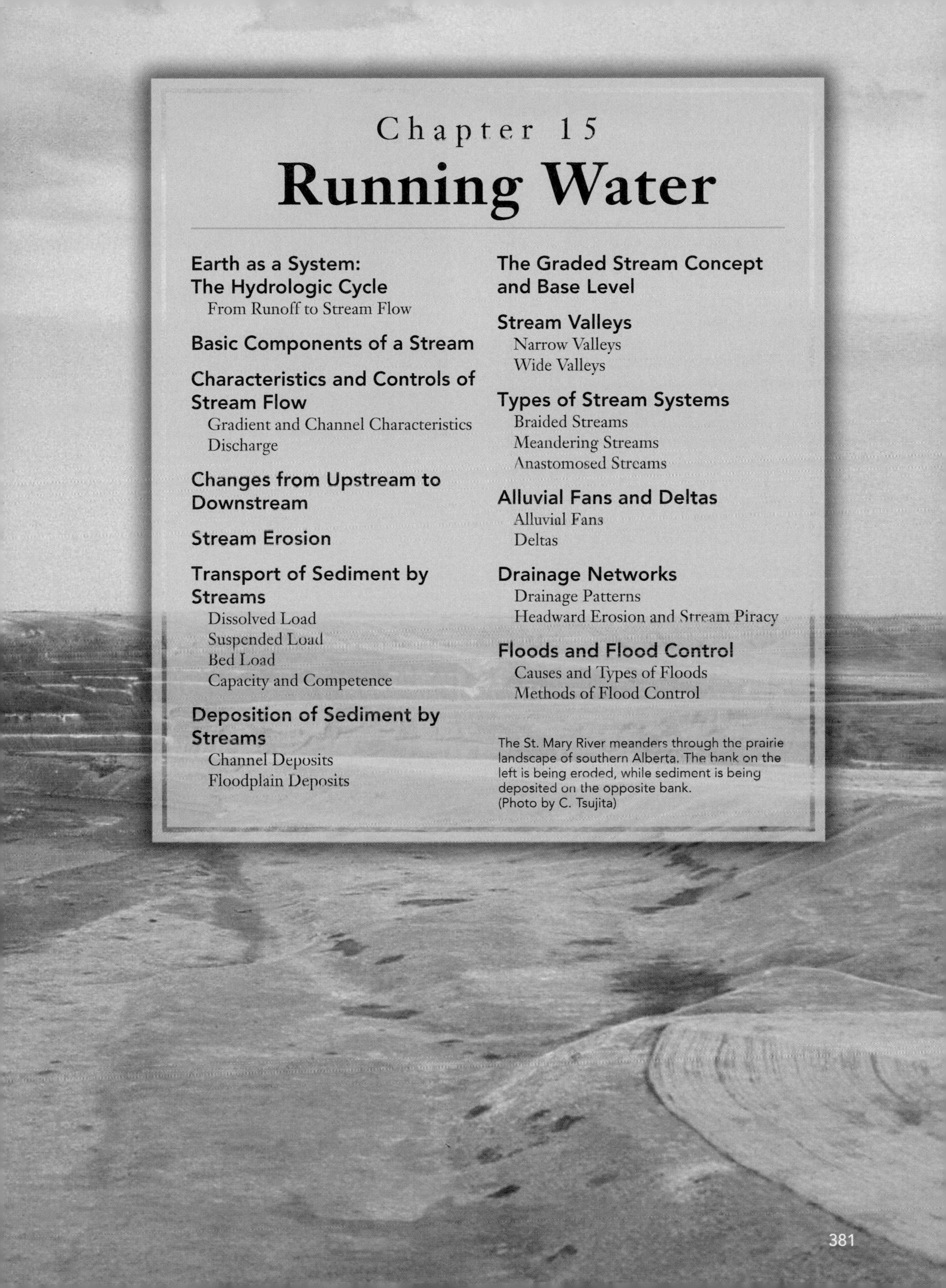

The St. Mary River meanders through the prairie landscape of southern Alberta. The bank on the left is being eroded, while sediment is being deposited on the opposite bank. (Photo by C. Tsujita)

Rivers are very important. We use them as routes for moving goods, as sources of water for irrigation, and as an energy source. Their fertile floodplains have been cultivated since the dawn of civilization. When viewed as part of the Earth system, rivers and streams represent a basic link in the constant cycling of the planet's water. Moreover, running water is the dominant agent of landscape alteration, eroding more terrain and transporting more sediment than any other process. Because so many people live near rivers, **floods** are among the most destructive of all geologic hazards. Despite huge investments in levees and dams, rivers cannot always be controlled (Figure 15.1). Finally, geologists interpret ancient river systems preserved in the rock record based on observations of modern rivers; such interpretations can be valuable in the exploration for petroleum and mineral deposits.

◆ **Figure 15.1** Most Canadians have witnessed stream flooding associated with the melting of snow during the spring. This photo shows a spring flood of the Thames River inundating a parking lot in London, Ontario. (Photo courtesy of S. R. Hicock)

EARTH AS A SYSTEM: THE HYDROLOGIC CYCLE

GEODe EARTH Running Water
↳ Stream Characteristics

Water is continually on the move, from the ocean to the land and back again in an endless cycle. Water is just about everywhere on Earth—in the oceans, glaciers, rivers, lakes, air, and soil, and in tissues of living things. All of these reservoirs constitute Earth's hydrosphere. In all, the water content of the hydrosphere is about 1.36 billion cubic kilometres.

The vast bulk of it, about 97.2 percent, is stored in the global oceans (Figure 15.2). Ice sheets and glaciers account for another 2.15 percent, leaving only 0.65 percent to be divided among lakes, streams, subsurface water, and the atmosphere (Figure 15.2). Although the percentages of Earth's water found in each of the latter sources (we could also add the biosphere) is just a small fraction of the total inventory, the absolute quantities are great.

The water found in each of the reservoirs depicted in Figure 15.2 does not remain in these places indefinitely. Water can readily change from one state of matter (solid, liquid, or gas) to another at the temperatures and pressures that occur at Earth's surface. Therefore, water is constantly moving among the hydrosphere, the atmosphere, the geosphere, and the biosphere. This unending circulation of Earth's water supply is called the **hydrologic cycle**. The cycle shows us the many critical interrelationships among different parts of the Earth system.

The hydrologic cycle is a gigantic worldwide system powered by energy from the Sun in which the atmosphere provides the vital link between the oceans and continents (Figure 15.3). Water evaporates into the atmosphere from the oceans and, to a much lesser extent, from the continents. Winds transport this moisture-laden air, often for great distances, until conditions cause the moisture to condense into clouds and precipitation to fall. The precipitation that falls into the ocean has completed its cycle and is ready to begin another. The water that falls on land, however, must make its way back to the ocean.

What happens to precipitation once it has fallen on the land? A portion of the water soaks into

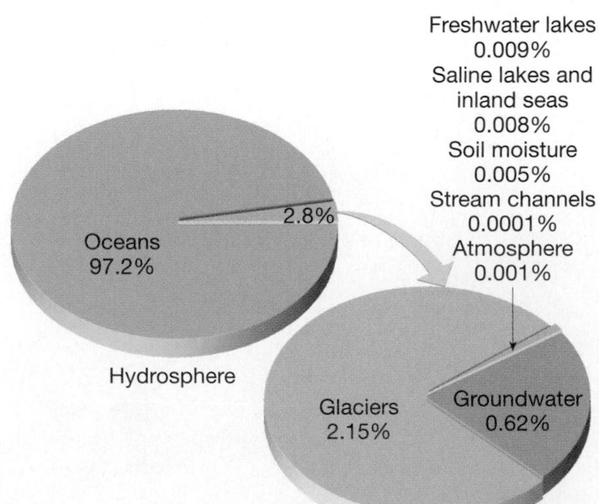

Figure 15.2 Distribution of Earth's water.

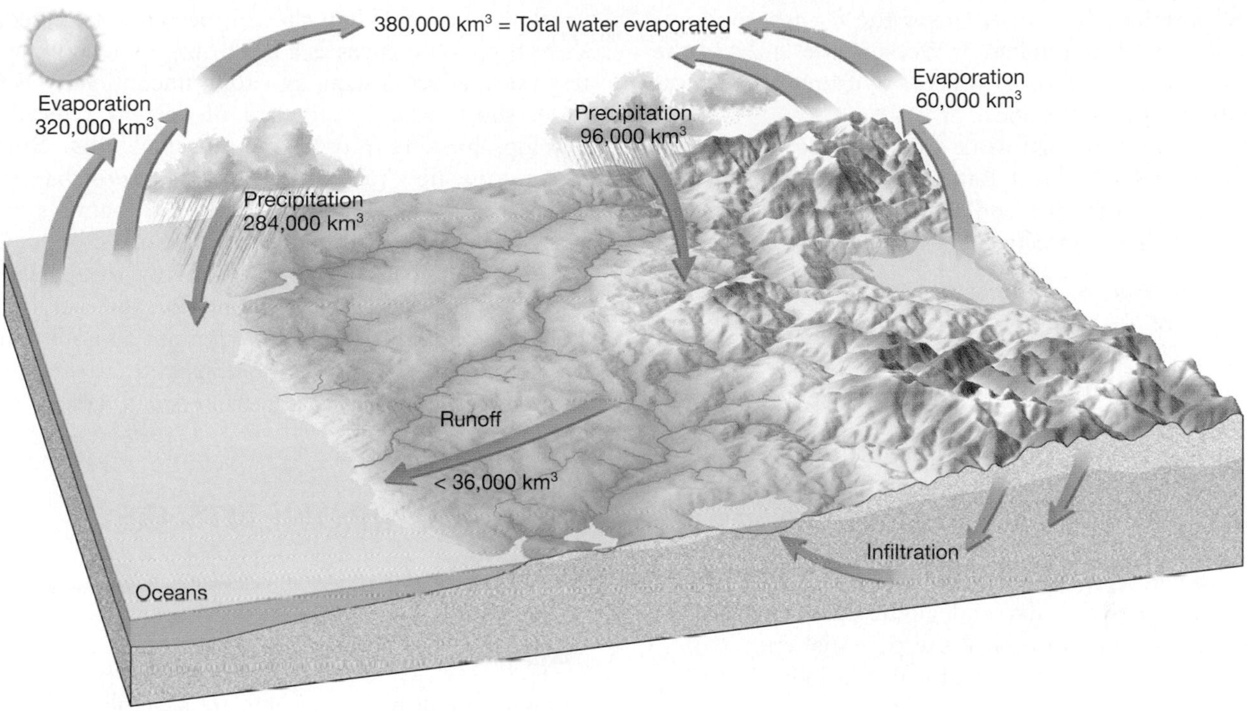

◆ **Figure 15.3** Earth's water balance. Each year, solar energy evaporates about 320,000 cubic kilometres of water from the oceans, while evaporation from the land (including lakes and streams) contributes 60,000 cubic kilometres of water. Of this total of 380,000 cubic kilometres of water, about 284,000 cubic kilometres falls back to the ocean, and the remaining 96,000 cubic kilometres falls on the land surface. Of that 96,000 cubic kilometres, approximately 60,000 cubic kilometres of water evaporates from the land. Assuming that not all of the water that infiltrated into the ground re-emerges as surface water, less than 36,000 cubic kilometres of water is left to erode the land during the journey back to the oceans.

the ground (called **infiltration**), moving downward, then laterally, and finally seeping into lakes and streams, or directly into the ocean. When the rate of rainfall is greater than the land's ability to absorb it, the additional water flows over the surface into lakes and streams, a process called **runoff**. Much of the water that infiltrates or runs off eventually finds its way back to the atmosphere because of evaporation from soil, lakes, and streams. Also, some of the water that infiltrates the ground is absorbed by plants, which later release it into the atmosphere. This process is called **transpiration** (*trans* = across, *spiro* = to breathe).

Each year a field of crops can transpire an amount of water equivalent to a layer 60 centimetres deep over the entire field. The same area of trees can pump twice this amount into the atmosphere. Because we cannot clearly distinguish between the amount of water that is evaporated and the amount that is transpired by plants, the term **evapotranspiration** is often used for the combined effect.

When precipitation falls in very cold areas—at high elevations or high latitudes—the water may not immediately soak in, run off, or evaporate. Instead, it may become part of a snowfield or, ultimately, a glacier. In this way, glaciers store large quantities of water on land. If present-day glaciers were to melt and release their stored water, sea level would rise by several tens of metres worldwide and submerge many heavily populated coastal areas. As you will see in Chapter 17, over the past 2 million years huge ice sheets have formed and melted on many occasions, each time changing the balance of the hydrologic cycle.

Figure 15.3 also shows Earth's overall *water balance*, or the volume of water that passes through each part of the cycle annually. The amount of water vapour in the air is just a tiny fraction of Earth's total water supply. But the absolute quantities that are cycled through the atmosphere in one year are immense—some 380,000 cubic kilometres. Estimates show that over North America, almost six times as much water is carried by moving currents of air as is transported by all the continent's rivers.

It is important to know that the hydrologic cycle is balanced. Because the total water vapour in the atmosphere remains about the same, average annual precipitation over Earth must be equal to the quantity of water evaporated. However, for all of the continents taken together, precipitation exceeds evaporation. Conversely, over the oceans, evaporation exceeds precipitation. Because the levels of the world oceans are not perpetually dropping, the system must be in balance.

The erosional work accomplished by the less-than 36,000 cubic kilometres of water that flows annually from the land to the ocean is enormous. Arthur Bloom effectively described it as follows:

> The average continental height is 823 metres above sea level . . . . If we assume that the 36,000 cubic kilometres of annual runoff flow downhill an average of 823 metres, the potential mechanical power of the system can be calculated. Potentially, the runoff from all lands would continuously generate almost 9×10^9 kW. If all this power were used to erode the land, it would be comparable to having . . . one horse-drawn scraper or scoop at work on each 3-acre piece of land, day and night, year round. Of course, a large part of the potential energy of runoff is wasted as frictional heat by turbulent flow and splashing of water.*

Although only a small percentage of the energy of running water is used to erode the surface, considered on a global scale, running water is *the single most important agent sculpting Earth's land surface*.

To summarize, the hydrologic cycle represents the continuous movement of water from the oceans to the atmosphere, from the atmosphere to the land, and from the land back to the sea. The wearing down of Earth's land surface is largely attributable to the last of these steps and is the primary focus of the remainder of this chapter.

From Runoff to Stream Flow

Although we have always depended to a great extent on running water, its source eluded us for centuries. Not until the sixteenth century did we realize that streams were supplied by surface runoff and underground water, which ultimately had their sources as rain and snow.

Runoff initially flows in broad, thin sheets across the ground, appropriately termed **sheet flow**. The amount of water that runs off in this manner rather than sinking into the ground depends on the **infiltration capacity** of the soil. Infiltration capacity is controlled by many factors, including (1) the intensity and duration of the rainfall, (2) the prior wetted condition of the soil, (3) the soil texture, (4) the slope of the land, and (5) the nature of the vegetative cover. When the soil becomes saturated, sheet flow commences as a layer only a few millimetres thick. After flowing as a thin, unconfined sheet for a short distance, threads of current typically develop, forming tiny channels called **rills**. Rills direct water flow to more prominent *gullies* that, in turn, feed larger and more stable channels of streams. To be considered a true **stream**, a body of water must be confined to one or more trough-like linear depressions, called **channels**, and to flow along a definite course. It is important to note that this term has no size connotations and embraces a wide spectrum of features, from small creeks to immense rivers.

---

*Arthur Bloom, *Geomorphology: A Systematic Analysis of Late Cenozoic Landforms* (Englewood Cliffs, NJ: Prentice Hall, 1978), p. 97.

BASIC COMPONENTS OF A STREAM

GEODe EARTH Running Water
↳ Stream Characteristics

Common to all major streams are a number of distinctive parts. Between its source area, called the **head** or **headwaters**, and its **mouth** (Figure 15.4), where it empties into another water body, a stream follows a well-defined path or **course**. Any given segment of a stream along its course is a **reach**. A major stream may be fed by several smaller streams or tributaries. Especially in low-lying areas, stream channels commonly develop snake-like bends or loops called **meanders** (named after the sinuous river Menderes in Turkey).

The bottom, or **bed**, of a stream channel is bounded on either side by **banks**, which confine the flowing water during times of normal flow. Under flood conditions, water overtops the stream's banks, inundating areas of land beyond the channel. These areas, which are only submerged during floods, are commonly flatter than the surrounding landscape, forming a broad **floodplain** (Figure 15.4) on which sediment is deposited. This is especially true in the middle to lower reaches of a stream, where slopes tend to be low.

On a larger scale, if we were to examine the **longitudinal profile** (or side view) of a major stream, we would notice that the slope or **gradient** of its channel is far from constant. Rather, we would see that it is a concave-upward curve, with steep slopes near the headwaters and a progressive decrease in gradient toward the mouth (Figure 15.4). The reason why streams tend to develop this shape will be discussed later in the chapter.

The remainder of this chapter will concentrate on that part of the hydrologic cycle in which the water moves in stream channels. The discussion will

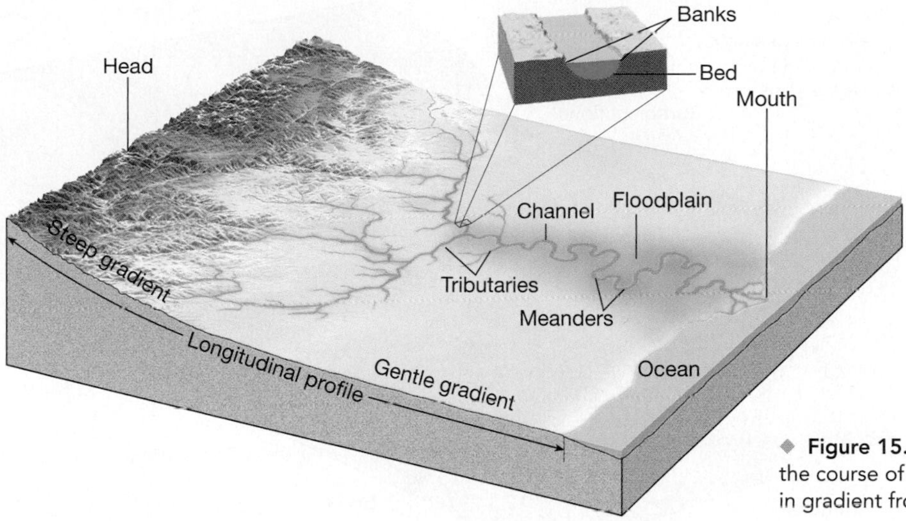

◆ **Figure 15.4** Basic features observed down the course of a major stream. Note the decrease in gradient from head to mouth.

deal primarily with streams in humid regions; the significance of streams in arid landscapes is examined in Chapter 18, Deserts and Winds.

CHARACTERISTICS AND CONTROLS OF STREAM FLOW

GEODe EARTH Running Water
↳ Stream Characteristics

Water can flow in one of two ways, either as **laminar flow** or as **turbulent flow** (Figure 15.5). When the movement is laminar, the water particles flow in straight paths that are parallel to the channel. By contrast, when the flow is turbulent, the water moves in a chaotic and erratic fashion that is commonly characterized by swirling, whirlpool-like eddies.

The stream's velocity is a primary factor that determines whether the flow is laminar or turbulent. Laminar flow is possible only when water is moving very slowly through a smooth channel. If the velocity increases or the channel becomes rough, laminar flow changes to turbulent flow. The movement of water in streams is usually fast enough that flow is turbulent. The multidirectional movement of turbulent flow is very effective both in eroding a stream's channel and in keeping sediment suspended within the water so that it can be transported downstream.

Flowing water makes its way to the sea under the influence of gravity. Some sluggish streams flow at less than 1 kilometre per hour, whereas a few rapid ones can exceed 30 kilometres per hour. Velocities are determined at gauging stations, where measurements are taken at several locations across the stream channel and then averaged. This is done because the rate of water movement is not uniform within a stream channel. When the channel is straight, the highest velocities occur in the centre, just below the surface (Figure 15.6). It is here that friction is least. Minimum velocities occur along the sides and bed of the channel, where friction is always greatest. When a stream channel is crooked or curved, the fastest flow is not in the centre; the zone of maximum velocity shifts toward the outside of each bend. As you will see later, this shift plays an important part in eroding the stream's channel on that side.

The ability of a stream to erode and transport material is directly related to its velocity. Even slight variations in velocity can lead to significant changes in the load of sediment that water can transport. Several factors determine the velocity of a stream and therefore control the amount of erosional work a stream can accomplish. These factors include (1) the gradient, (2) the shape, size, and roughness of the channel, and (3) the discharge.

Gradient and Channel Characteristics

Certainly one of the most obvious factors controlling stream velocity is the gradient of a stream channel because gravity works most effectively on slopes. Gradient is typically expressed as the vertical drop of a stream over a fixed distance. Gradients vary considerably from one stream to another, as well as along the course of a given stream.

Portions of the lower Mississippi River, for example, have very low gradients of 10 centimetres per kilometre and less. By way of contrast, some steep mountain stream channels decrease in elevation at a rate of more than 40 metres per kilometre, 400 times as abruptly as the lower Mississippi. The steeper the gradient, the more energy is available for stream flow. If two streams were identical in every respect

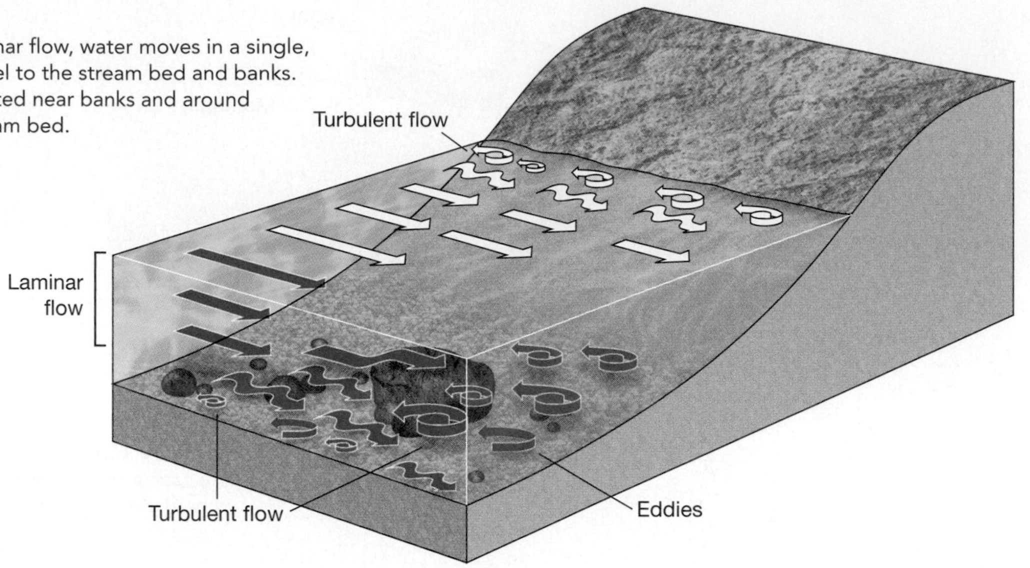

◆ **Figure 15.5** In laminar flow, water moves in a single, uniform direction, parallel to the stream bed and banks. Turbulent flow is generated near banks and around irregularities on the stream bed.

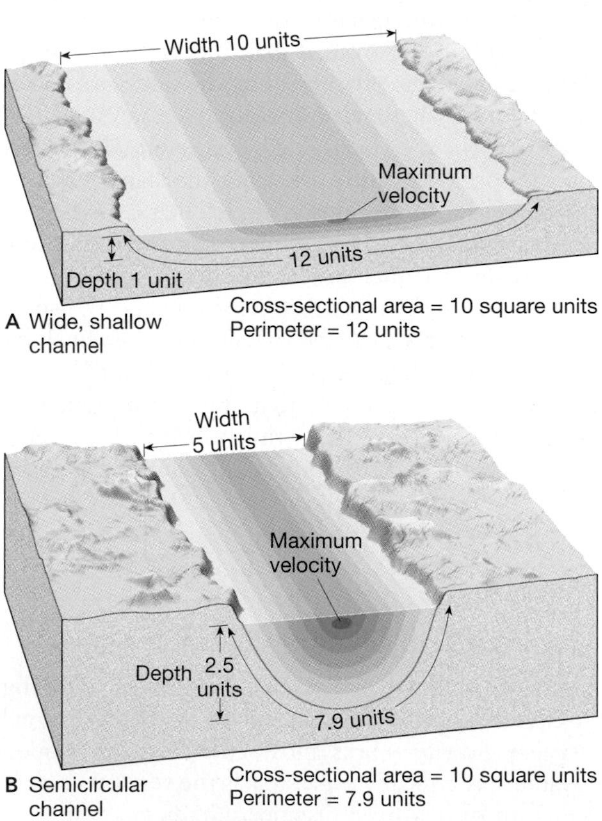

◆ **Figure 15.6** Influence of channel shape on velocity. **A.** The stream in this wide, shallow channel moves more slowly than does water in the semicircular channel because of greater frictional drag. **B.** The cross-sectional area of this semicircular channel is the same as the one in part A, but it has less water in contact with its channel and therefore less frictional drag. Thus, water will flow more rapidly in channel B, all other factors being equal. In both cases, maximum velocity is farthest from the banks.

except gradient, the stream with the higher gradient would obviously have the greater velocity.

The *cross-sectional shape* of a channel determines the amount of water in contact with the channel and hence affects the frictional drag. The most efficient channel is one with the least perimeter for its cross-sectional area. Figure 15.6 compares two channel shapes. Although the cross-sectional area of both is identical, the semicircular shape has less water in contact with the channel and therefore less frictional drag. As a result, if all other factors are equal, the water will flow more rapidly in the semicircular channel.

The size and roughness of the channel also affect the amount of friction. An increase in the size of a channel reduces the ratio of perimeter to cross-sectional area and therefore increases the efficiency of flow. The effect of roughness is obvious. A smooth channel promotes a more uniform flow, whereas an irregular channel creates enough turbulence to slow down the stream's forward motion. In extreme cases, where turbulent flow extends all the way up to the water surface because of the violent collision and diversion of flowing water around irregularities on the stream bed, **rapids** may form (Figure 15.7).

Discharge

The **discharge** of a stream is the amount of water flowing past a certain point in a given unit of time. This is usually measured in cubic metres per second (m^3/s). Discharge is determined by multiplying a stream's cross-sectional area by its velocity:

Discharge (m^3/s) =
Channel width (m) × Channel depth (m) × Velocity (m/s)

The largest river in North America, the Mississippi, discharges an average of 17,300 cubic metres per second. Although this is a huge quantity of water, it is nevertheless dwarfed by the mighty Amazon, the world's largest river. Draining an area that is nearly half the size of Canada and that averages about 200 centimetres of rainfall per year, the Amazon discharges 12 times as much water as the Mississippi. In fact, it has been estimated that the flow of the Amazon accounts for about 15 percent of all the fresh water discharged into the ocean by all of the world's rivers. Just one day's discharge would supply the water needs of Toronto for nearly 70 years!

The discharges of most rivers are far from constant because of such variables as rainfall and snowmelt. When discharge changes, the factors noted earlier must also change. When discharge increases, the width or depth of the channel must increase, the water must flow faster, or some combination of these factors must change. Indeed, measurements show that when the amount of water in a stream increases, the width, depth, and velocity all increase in an orderly fashion. To handle the additional water, the stream will increase the size of its channel by widening and deepening it. As we saw earlier, when the size of the channel increases, proportionally less of the water is in contact with the bed and banks of the channel. Friction, which acts to retard the flow, is reduced. The less friction there is, the more swiftly the water will flow.

Data collected from successive gauging stations along a river typically indicate a progressive increase in discharge downstream. This is mainly because the main channel of a stream system receives water from a progressively larger number of tributaries as it flows to its mouth. For example, by the time the Amazon River empties into the Atlantic Ocean, it has received water from as many as 1000 tributaries along its 6500-kilometre course. The cumulative input of water into a stream system, at least in non-arid environments, also increases downstream and probably contributes to the increase in discharge.

CHANGES FROM UPSTREAM TO DOWNSTREAM

GEODe EARTH Running Water
↳ Stream Characteristics

In the headwaters region where the gradient is steepest (Figure 15.4), the water must flow in a relatively small and often boulder-strewn channel. The small channel and rough bed create great drag and inhibit movement by sending water in all directions with almost as much backward motion as forward motion. However, progressing downstream, the material on the bed of the stream becomes much smaller, offering less resistance to flow, and the width and depth of the channel increase to accommodate the greater discharge. These factors permit water to flow more freely and hence more rapidly. A stream can therefore maintain a higher velocity near its mouth, where it has a lower gradient, than upstream because of the greater discharge, larger channel, and smoother bed.

STREAM EROSION

Streams erode their channels mainly by the plucking of loosened particles from their beds and by abrasion (Figure 15.8A). Some erosion can also result from the dissolution of soluble bedrock and channel debris; most dissolved material in a stream is contributed by inflows of groundwater.

◆ **Figure 15.7** Whitewater rafters enjoy turbulent conditions in the Ottawa River rapids.
(Photo by Henry George © JupiterImages/Comstock Corporation)

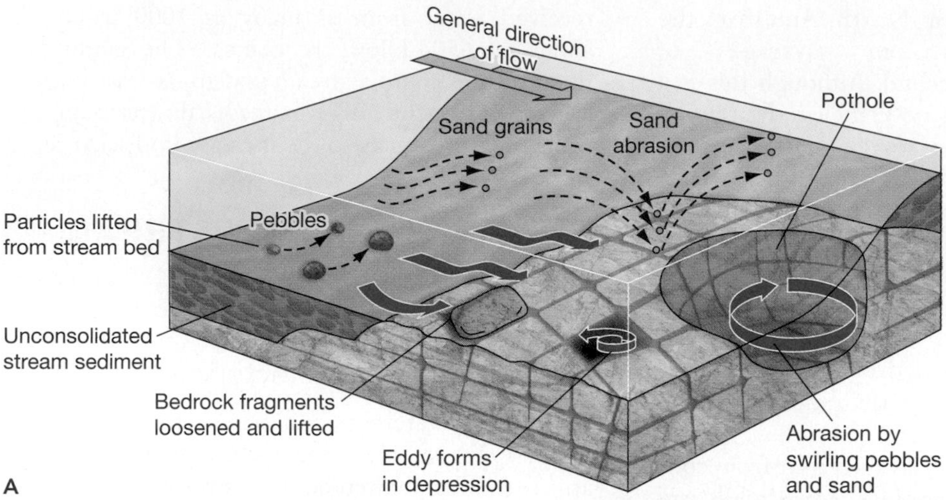

◆ **Figure 15.8** **A.** Erosional processes in a stream. Sedimentary particles can be loosened and plucked from unconsolidated sediment on the stream's bed and from bedrock by the lifting action of strong currents. Abrasion occurs because of the impact of sedimentary particles with bedrock surfaces and other particles residing on the bed. Particles swept into swirling eddies that develop in depressions on the bed (especially where bedrock is exposed) cause localized abrasion that can lead to the formation of potholes. **B.** These potholes in the bed of Kanaka Creek, British Columbia, were produced by the drilling action of swirling pebbles.
(Photo by S. R. Hicock)

As we learned earlier, when the flow of water is turbulent, the water swirls and eddies. When an eddy is sufficiently strong, it can dislodge particles from the channel and lift them into the moving water. In this manner, the force of running water swiftly erodes poorly consolidated materials on the bed and banks of the stream. The stronger the current, the more effectively the stream will lift particles. In some instances, water is forced into cracks and bedding planes with sufficient strength to actually pry up pieces of rock from the bed of the channel.

Observing a muddy stream demonstrates that currents of water can lift and carry debris. However, it is not as obvious that a stream is capable of eroding solid rock in a manner similar to sandpapering. Just as the particles of grit on sandpaper can wear down a piece of wood, so too can the sand and gravel carried by a stream abrade a bedrock channel. Many steep-sided gorges that are cut through solid rock by the ceaseless bombardment of particles against the bed and banks of a channel serve as testimony to this erosional strength (Figure 15.9). In addition, the individual sediment grains are also abraded by their many impacts with the channel and with one another. Thus, by scraping, rubbing, and bumping, abrasion erodes a bedrock channel and simultaneously smoothes and rounds the abrading particles.

Common features on some riverbeds are rounded depressions known as **potholes** (Figure 15.8B). They are created by the abrasive action of particles swirling in fast-moving eddies (Figure 15.8A). The rotational motion of the sand and pebbles acts like a drill to bore the holes. As the particles wear down to nothing, they are replaced by new ones that continue to drill the streambed. Eventually, smooth depressions several metres across and just as deep can result.

◆ **Figure 15.9** This steep-sided canyon in British Columbia has been cut through solid rock by stream erosion. Such canyons as this one are narrow because of a rapid rate of downcutting by the stream relative to the rate of mass wasting of the canyon walls.
(Photo by Mike Schering)

TRANSPORT OF SEDIMENT BY STREAMS

Streams are Earth's most important erosional agent. Not only do they have the ability to downcut their channels, but streams also have the capacity to transport the enormous quantities of sediment produced by weathering. Although erosion by running water in a stream's channel contributes significant amounts of material for transport, by far the greatest quantity of sediment carried by a stream is derived from the products of weathering. Weathering produces tremendous amounts of material that are delivered to the stream by sheet flow, mass wasting, and groundwater.

Streams transport their loads of sediment in three ways: (1) in solution (**dissolved load**), (2) in suspension (**suspended load**), and (3) along the bottom of the channel (**bed load**). (See Figure 15.10.) Let us now look at each of these.

Dissolved Load

The greatest portion of the dissolved load transported by most streams is supplied by groundwater. As water percolates through the ground, it first acquires soluble soil compounds. As the water seeps deeper through cracks and pores in the bedrock below, it may dissolve additional mineral matter. Eventually, much of this ion-rich water finds its way into streams.

The velocity of stream flow has essentially no effect on a stream's ability to carry its dissolved load. Once material is in solution, it goes wherever the stream goes, regardless of velocity. Precipitation occurs only when the chemistry of the water changes.

The quantity of material carried in solution is highly variable and depends on such factors as climate and the geologic setting. Usually, the dissolved load is expressed as parts of dissolved material per million parts of water (parts per million, or ppm). Although some rivers have a dissolved load of 1000 ppm or more, the average figure for the world's rivers is estimated at between 115 and 120 ppm. Almost 4 billion tonnes of dissolved mineral matter is supplied to the oceans each year by streams.

Suspended Load

Most streams (but not all) carry the largest part of their load in *suspension* (Figure 15.10A). Indeed, the visible cloud of sediment suspended in the water is the most obvious portion of a stream's load (Figure 15.10B). Usually only fine sand, silt, and clay particles can be carried this way, but during flood stage, larger particles are carried as well. Also during flood stage, the total quantity of material carried in suspension increases dramatically, as can be verified by people whose homes have become sites for the deposition of this material. During flood stage, the Hwang Ho (Yellow River) of China is reported to carry an amount of sediment equal in weight to the water that carries it. Rivers like this are appropriately

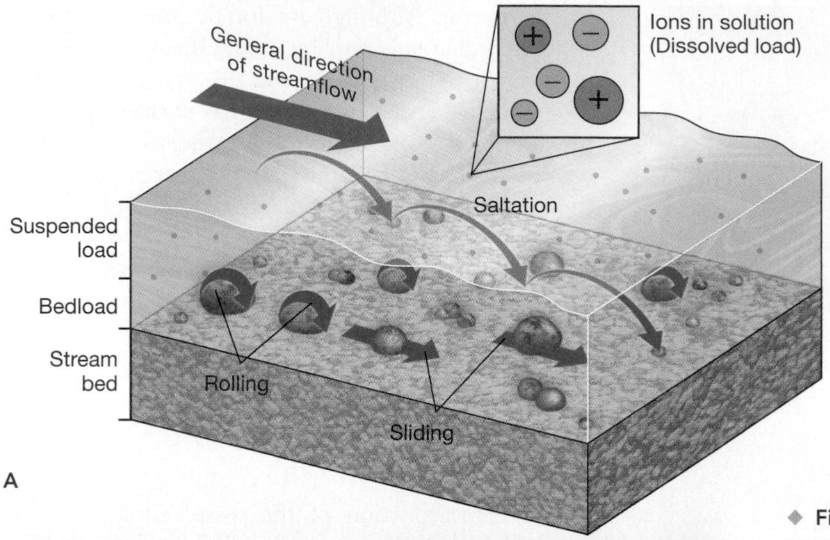

◆ **Figure 15.10** **A.** Sediment transport processes in a stream channel. A stream carries sediment as ions in solution (dissolved load), in suspension (suspended load), and as bed load. Components of the bed load can move by rolling, sliding, and saltation (alternating between bed and suspended loads). **B.** The muddy suspended load of British Columbia's Fraser River contrasts sharply with the clear water of its tributary, the Bridge River. (Photo by S. R. Hicock)

described as "too thick to drink but too thin to cultivate." The type and amount of material carried in suspension are controlled by two factors: the velocity of the water and the settling velocity of each sediment grain.

Settling velocity is defined as the speed at which a particle falls through a stationary fluid. The larger the particle, the more rapidly it settles toward the streambed. In addition to size, the shape and specific gravity of particles also influence settling velocity. Flat grains sink through water more slowly than do spherical grains, and dense particles fall toward the bed more rapidly than do less dense particles of the same size and shape. The slower the settling velocity and the stronger the turbulence, the longer a sediment particle will stay in suspension and the farther it will be carried downstream with the flowing water.

Bed Load

A portion of a stream's load of solid material consists of sediment that is too large to be carried in suspension. These coarser particles move along the bed of the stream and constitute the *bed load* (Figure 15.10A). In terms of the erosional work accomplished by a downcutting stream, the grinding action of the bed load is of great importance.

The particles that make up the bed load move along the bottom by rolling, sliding, and saltation. Sediment moving by **saltation** (*saltare* = to leap) appears to jump or skip along the streambed. This occurs as particles are propelled upward by collisions or lifted by the current and then carried downstream a short distance until gravity pulls them back to the bed of the stream. Particles that are too large or heavy to move by saltation either roll or slide along the bottom, depending on their shapes.

Unlike the suspended and dissolved loads, which are constantly in motion, the bed load is in motion only intermittently, when the force of the water is sufficient to move the larger particles. The bed load usually does not exceed 10 percent of a stream's total load, although it may constitute up to 50 percent of the total load of a few streams. For

◆ **Figure 15.11** Although the bed load of many rivers consists of sand, the bed load of this stream in British Columbia is made up of huge boulders. During floods, the seemingly immovable rocks in this channel are rolled along the bed of the stream and rounded by abrasion. The maximum size of particle a stream can move (its competence) is determined by the velocity of the water.
(Photo by Mike Schering)

example, consider the distribution of the 750 million tonnes of material carried to the Gulf of Mexico by the Mississippi River each year. Of this total, it is estimated that approximately 67 percent is carried in suspension, 26 percent in solution, and the remaining 7 percent as bed load. Estimates of a stream's bed load should be viewed cautiously, however, because this fraction of the load is very difficult to measure accurately. Not only is the bed load more inaccessible than the suspended and dissolved loads, but it also moves primarily during periods of flooding, when the bottom of a stream channel is most difficult to study.

Capacity and Competence

A stream's ability to carry solid particles is typically described by using two criteria. First, the maximum load of solid particles that a stream can transport is termed its **capacity**. The greater the amount of water flowing in a stream (discharge), the greater is the stream's capacity for hauling sediment. Second, the **competence** of a stream indicates the maximum particle size that a stream can transport. The stream's velocity determines its competence; the stronger the flow, the larger the particles it can carry in suspension and as bed load.

It is a general rule that the competence of a stream increases as the square of its velocity. Thus, if the velocity of a stream doubles, the impact force of the water increases four times; if the velocity triples, the force increases nine times, and so forth. Hence, the large boulders that are often visible during a low-water stage and that seem immovable can, in fact, be transported during flood stage because of the stream's increased competence (Figure 15.11).

By now it should be clear why the greatest erosion and transportation of sediment occur during floods (Figure 15.12). The increase in discharge results in greater capacity; the increased velocity produces greater competence. With rising velocity the water becomes more turbulent, and larger and larger particles are set in motion. In just a few days, or perhaps just a few hours, a stream in flood stage can erode and transport more sediment than it does during months of normal flow (see Box 15.1).

◆ **Figure 15.12** During floods, both capacity and competence increase. Therefore, the greatest erosion and sediment transport occur during these high-water periods. Here we see the sediment-filled floodwaters of Kenya's Mara River.
(Photo by Tim Davis/Stone)

BOX 15.1

People and the Environment
The 1997 Red River Floods

The Red River originates near the point where South Dakota, North Dakota, and Minnesota meet. It flows northward, finally emptying into Manitoba's Lake Winnipeg (Figure 15.A). Along most of its course in the United States, the river serves as the North Dakota–Minnesota boundary.

In April 1997, Grand Forks, North Dakota, and other communities along the Red River experienced disastrous flooding—the worst ever recorded in the region (Figure 15.B). The flood was preceded by an especially snowy winter. As April began, the winter snows were melting and flooding seemed imminent. Then on April 5 and 6 a final winter storm pounded the northern Great Plains. The blizzard rebuilt snowdrifts back to heights of 6 metres in some places. However, the drifts did not last long because rapidly rising temperatures melted the snow in a matter of days, causing rapid runoff into the Red River.

The discharge at Grand Forks jumped from about 70 cubic metres per second on April 1 to nearly 4200 cubic metres per second three weeks later. The floodwaters at Grand Forks crested at 17.7 metres, almost 8 metres above flood level! This exceeded the previous record flood stage set in 1897 by 1.2 metres. Roughly 2 million hectares of land were under water. A large portion of downtown Grand Forks was destroyed by water and fire, and more than 24,000 homes were either partially or totally destroyed by floodwaters. Only 27 homes in East Grand Forks, Minnesota, survived unscathed. The losses in Grand Forks and East Grand Forks were estimated to exceed $3.5 billion.

Farther downstream, the flood affected more than 200,000 hectares of land in southern Manitoba. In response to an earlier flood in 1950, a catastrophic event that forced some 100,000 people in the greater Winnipeg area out of their homes, an artificial floodway was built on the east side of Winnipeg to divert floodwaters from the city centre. The 1997 event displaced more than 25,000 people and produced at least $500 million in damages. However, it is certain that without the construction of the artificial floodway, losses would have been considerably higher, and most of Winnipeg would have been under water.

The 1997 Red River flood was truly a record-breaking event—a 500-year flood (that is, the statistical probability of such a flood is once in 500 years). Although such an extraordinary flood is rare, less severe flooding of broad areas along the Red River to the north is common. Why do floods here occur so frequently and over such large areas? Four factors seem to be especially important.

1. The Red River flows northward. When the spring thaw takes place, it proceeds in the same direction the river flows, from south to north. Therefore, runoff from the southern portion of the drainage basin progressively joins with newly created snowmelt from more northerly localities. If the south-to-north thaw is perfectly synchronized, extensive floods occur in the northern portion of the valley.
2. Ice derived from the southern valley meets with freshly broken ice in the central and northern valley. Such ice concentrations can slow or block the water flow, causing river levels to swell.
3. The Red River flows across a broad and extremely flat plain, the former floor of a now-abandoned lake. Therefore, when the river floods onto this plain, the area covered can be extensive.
4. The river's gradient is very low and decreases downstream. Near Fargo the gradient averages about 8 centimetres per kilometre. Farther north, near the Canadian border, the gradient drops to just 2.5 centimetres per kilometre. During floods in this border region, the river's lack of slope causes it to form what is essentially a massive shallow lake.

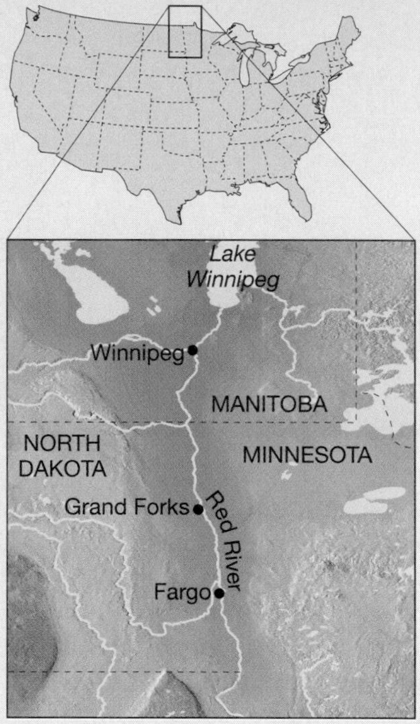

◆ **Figure 15.A** The Red River flows north into Manitoba's Lake Winnipeg.

◆ **Figure 15.B** A May 1997 photograph of St. Agathe, Manitoba, after the perimeter ring dyke broke during the Red River flood. (Photo by CP/Maclean's/Phill Snel)

DEPOSITION OF SEDIMENT BY STREAMS

Whenever a stream's velocity slows, its competence is reduced, and particles of sediment are deposited in definite order by size. As stream flow drops below the critical settling velocity of a certain particle size, sediment in that category begins to settle out. Thus, stream transport provides a mechanism by which solid particles of various sizes are separated. This process, called **sorting**, explains why particles of similar size are deposited together. The well-sorted material typically deposited by a stream, whether it is within its channel (channel deposits), on the valley floor adjacent to the channel (floodplain deposits), or at its mouth, is called **alluvium**.

Channel Deposits

Alluvium deposited within a stream's channel mostly comprises sand and gravel, the coarser components of a stream's load. Among the more obvious features constructed of such material that are directly associated with stream channels are **bars**. Depending on such factors as sediment load and stream flow behaviour, bars can assume a variety of forms. Under certain circumstances, sediment can locally accumulate on the channel bed as isolated mounds called **intrachannel bars**. In others, crescent-shaped buildups of sediment called **point bars** are constructed on the insides or *points* of meanders. In general, bars can be viewed as products of local reductions in the stream's competence. These features will be discussed later in this chapter in the context of meandering streams.

Floodplain Deposits

As its name implies, a *floodplain* is that part of a valley that is inundated when stream flow overtops riverbanks during a flood. Floodplains can range in width from a few metres to many kilometres. **Natural levees** (*lever* = to raise) are subtle, snake-like topographic features that flank the channels of some streams. Although levees are by no means limited to a certain type of stream, they are typically best developed in those that have a large suspended load of sand, silt, and clay, and occupy broad, flat floodplain floors. Natural levees are built by recurring floods over many years. When a stream overflows its banks onto the floodplain, the water flows over the surface as a broad sheet. Because such a flow pattern significantly reduces the water's velocity and turbulence, the coarser portion of the suspended load is deposited in strips bordering the channel. As the water spreads out over the floodplain, a lesser

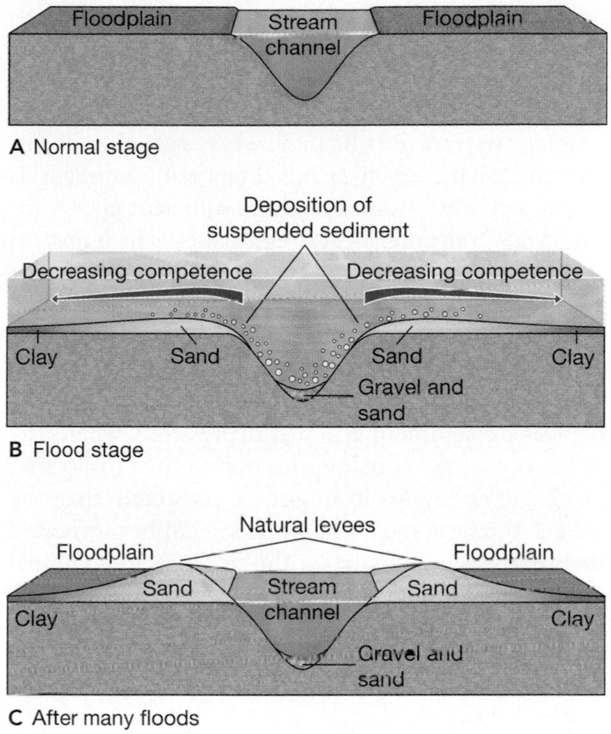

◆ **Figure 15.13** Schematic diagram, showing how natural levees form in relation to a stream channel (topography highly exaggerated). **A.** Under normal conditions, stream flow is confined to the stream channel. **B.** When a stream overtops its banks during a flood, its flow velocity decreases rapidly, thus reducing its capacity. Coarser grained material (usually sand) settles out closest to the channel, while finer grained material such as silt and clay settles farther away. The thickness of the resulting layer of sediment decreases with increasing distance from the channel banks. **C.** Over many years repeated flood deposition leads to the development of a ridge on both sides of the stream channel.

amount of finer sediment is laid down over the valley floor. This uneven distribution of material produces the gentle, almost imperceptible, slope of the natural levee (Figure 15.13).

THE GRADED STREAM CONCEPT AND BASE LEVEL

Like other complex systems, streams tend to naturally evolve toward a state of equilibrium, in which the parameters influencing their behaviour are in balance with one another and have reached their maximum efficiency. A stream that has attained such a balance is called a **graded stream**. In this condition, it is able to maintain just the amount of energy required to transport its load and experiences no net erosion or deposition.

As stated at the beginning of this chapter, the overall shape or longitudinal profile of a stream tends to be a smooth, concave-upward curve that progressively decreases in gradient from its headwaters to its mouth (Figure 15.4). The reason for this is that near its headwaters (where discharge is low and sediment is coarse), a stream must have a steep gradient to transport its load, whereas farther downstream (where discharge is high and sediment is finer), a gentle gradient provides sufficient energy for this task. Over time, local irregularities, which prevent the stream from flowing at its maximum efficiency, are smoothed out in a stream's longitudinal profile. This is accomplished by eroding local topographic highs where the stream's energy is above the optimum level for transporting sediment and, conversely, by depositing sediment in local depressions where the stream's energy is below the optimum transporting level. Accordingly, it might be expected that the longer the time over which the stream has increased its load-carrying efficiency, the closer its longitudinal profile would be to its ideal grade. This is not to say that time would restore the stream's original profile, but rather, that time would let the stream attain equilibrium with its new conditions. If no subsequent erosional changes were to occur, the profile would very slowly approach a flat gradient.

The graded stream concept is useful as a theoretical framework for predicting how perturbations in natural stream systems will affect their behaviour over time. Even though a natural stream may not ultimately attain true equilibrium, it will at least respond to disturbances in the same general manner as a graded stream. In other words, at the very least, a natural stream will adjust its characteristics to *approach* an ideal state of balance.

Stream profiles are strongly influenced by changes in **base level**—the lowest elevation to which a stream can erode its bed. Base level most commonly corresponds to the elevation at which a stream enters another water body where, on escaping the confinement of its channel, it rapidly loses velocity and, in turn, loses its ability to erode. Along its course, a stream can encounter one or more **local base levels** represented by the surface of a relatively small water body, such as a pond, a lake, or another stream. Because these features are not permanent,

◆ **Figure 15.14** The larger Canadian Horseshoe Falls at Niagara Falls. The river plunges over the falls and erodes the shale beneath the more resistant Lockport Dolostone. As a section of dolostone is undercut, it loses support and breaks off. (Photo by Alec Pytlowany © 2004 Masterfile Corporation)

they are also said to represent **temporary base levels**. A rock layer that is more resistant to erosion than are its overlying and underlying strata can also serve as a local base level by temporarily hindering the stream's ability to downcut. The Lockport Dolostone plays this role at Niagara Falls (Figure 15.14). Such a layer will commonly form a ledge that, because of undercutting and subsequent collapse, will maintain a steep slope over which water freely tumbles. The resulting feature is, of course, a **waterfall**.

Niagara Falls exemplifies the effects of variations in bedrock erodibility (Figure 15.14). Here, water falls over a resistant bed of dolostone that is underlain by less-resistant shale. As the water plunges over the lip of the falls, it erodes the weaker shale, undermining a section of dolostone, which eventually breaks off. In this manner the waterfall retains its vertical cliff while slowly but continually retreating upstream. Over the past 12,500 years, Niagara Falls has retreated more than 10 kilometres upstream. The course of the river itself has also changed substantially since pre-glacial times (Box 15.2).

Over time, a waterfall can migrate upstream a significant distance by headward erosion, but on reaching the point at which it is no longer an obstacle to flow, it ceases to be a local base level. In cases where a local change in gradient in the streambed disturbs stream flow, but not to the extent necessary to produce a waterfall, the irregularity may be marked by rapids. As mentioned previously, both of these features develop at locations where the

BOX 15.2

Canadian Profile
The History of Niagara Falls

Rick Cheel and Keith Tinkler*

Niagara Falls, on the Niagara River that is shared between Ontario and New York State, is certainly one of the best-known natural features in Canada. It was so well known to the native North Americans that Jacques Cartier was told about the great falls almost 80 years before the first European had the opportunity to witness its majesty. The name *Niagara* is derived from the Iroquois name *Onguiaahra*, meaning "the Strait."

Waters from lakes Superior, Michigan, Huron, and Erie all flow through the Niagara River where it passes over the falls. The current "natural" discharge of the river averages 5760 cubic metres per second (almost 500 million cubic metres per day). This discharge can vary because of a number of natural causes: ice dams at the mouth of the river can stop the discharge altogether, whereas winds that blow from west to east across Lake Erie can raise the water levels at the river's mouth and have produced a discharge as high as 9760 cubic metres per second. Today, the discharge over the falls is controlled so that some of the flow is re-routed through turbines to produce hydroelectricity on both the Canadian and U.S. sides of the river. To facilitate power production while maintaining a significant discharge over the falls for tourists, only 50 percent of the discharge of the river is routed through turbines during summer daytime hours, whereas 75 percent of the discharge is routed around the falls during summer evenings and over the winter months.

Niagara Falls exists because the Niagara River flows over the Niagara Escarpment. The action of the water flowing over the falls erodes the underlying bedrock so that its location recedes upstream over time, cutting the Niagara Gorge below the Falls. About 12,500 years ago the river fell over the brow of the escarpment (Figure 15.C) but it has eroded its gorge, and the position of the Falls, southward to its current position some 10 kilometres upstream. Before the onset of power generation (in 1907) Niagara Falls was eroding southward at a rate of 1.5 metres per year. However, because of the reduction of discharge and other measures to stop erosion of the bedrock, Niagara Falls is receding at a rate of only about 0.1 metres per year.

The evolution of the modern falls has been complex because of events associated with the last glaciation of North America. Before glaciation, the Niagara River followed a course that cut a gorge that extended to the northwest of the modern river, passing beyond the Niagara Escarpment, near the village of St. Davids (Figure 15.C). This old, now buried, gorge intersects the modern gorge at the Whirlpool (Figure 15.C); the location of the pre-glacial falls is shown in Figure 15.C. Because the area was covered by the thick sheet of sediment-laden continental ice, the old gorge became plugged with glacial sediment. When the glaciers receded from the area, the river bypassed the old gorge and flowed to the edge of the Niagara Escarpment, near Queenston, Ontario, where the modern gorge intersects the escarpment. Immediately following the retreat of the glaciers, discharge through the river was comparable to that of today; much of that discharge was derived from glacier ice melting as it retreated northward. The falls receded from the brow of the escarpment, cutting its gorge and moving the falls to a location approximately 2.2 kilometres to the south by 10,500 years ago. At that time the discharge through the river diminished dramatically because of events that took place to the north.

As the continental glaciers retreated to the region north of Sudbury, Ontario, the isostatically depressed land surface became the site of a major river known as the Nipissing Spillway (Figure 15.D). The Spillway captured all of the waters flowing from lakes Superior, Huron, and Michigan, and carried them to the Ottawa River. Being fed only by Lake Erie, flow through the Niagara River was greatly reduced and over the next 5000 years the falls receded by only 1.5 kilometres (Figure 15.C). By 5500 years ago, glacial isostatic rebound in the North Bay area was sufficient to stop the flow through the Nipissing Spillway, allowing water from all of the Great Lakes upstream of the falls to flow through the Niagara River. With the increase in discharge, the rate of erosion of the bedrock increased significantly and the falls progressed toward the Whirlpool. Once the falls had receded to the Whirlpool, it encountered the fill of glacial sediment that had plugged its earlier gorge.

The resistance to erosion of this sediment was much less than that of the bedrock that it had been eroding, so the rate of erosion, and the southward recession of the falls, was greatly speeded up. Within as little as two weeks, the falls had receded to its preglacial position, where erosion was once again of bedrock and progressed at a much slower rate, until it reached its present position (Figure 15.C).

*Rick Cheel and Keith Tinkler are professors in Department of Earth Sciences, Brock University.

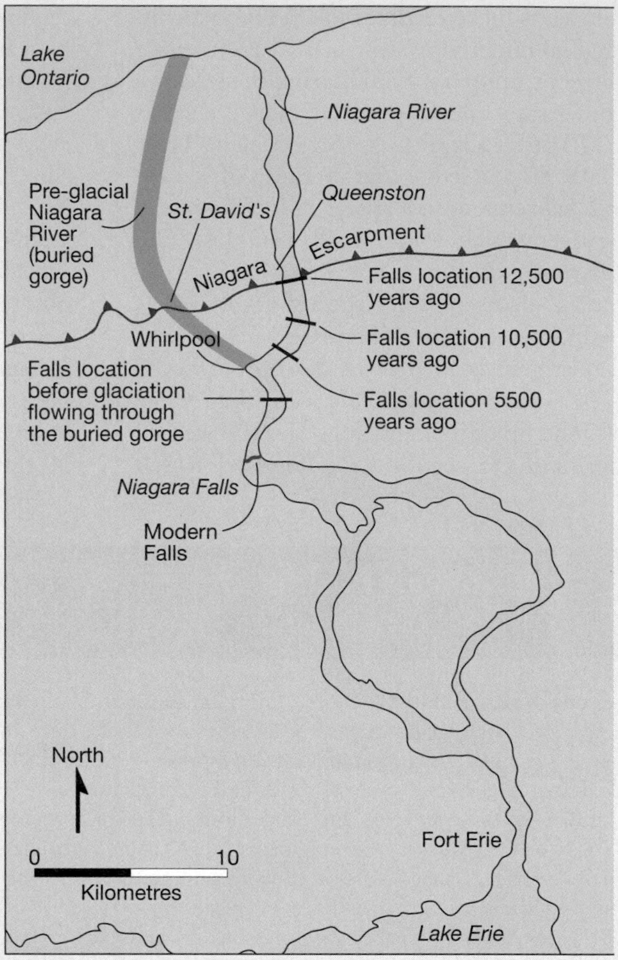

◆ **Figure 15.C** A map of the modern Niagara River and the buried Niagara Gorge showing past locations of the falls as it evolved since before the last glaciation.

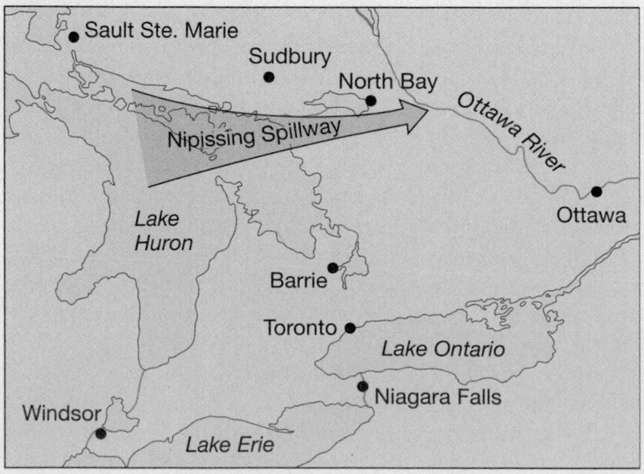

◆ **Figure 15.D** The route of the Nipissing Spillway, which captured flow from lakes Superior, Huron, and Michigan between 10,500 and 5500 years ago.

stream profile drops rapidly. Once erosion has eliminated the resistant rock, the stream profile smoothes out again.

Finally, the very lowest elevation to which any stream can erode, at least for practical purposes, is sea level. Accordingly, sea level is regarded as **ultimate base level**. In a stream close to grade, a rapid change in the base level, either local or ultimate, will cause a corresponding readjustment of the stream's activities in order to drive the system toward a new equilibrium. Sea level, and thus also ultimate base level, is of course a dynamic boundary that shifts relative to land, reflecting its own rise and fall (e.g., ice sheet expansion and melting) as well as tectonic movements of the land relative to it. Either way, fluctuations in relative sea level can profoundly change the dynamics of streams on a regional scale. If sea level falls relative to land, streams will tend to erode their bed until their longitudinal profile is adjusted to the lowered elevation of its mouth. If sea level rises relative to land, the stream will tend to raise its bed downstream by depositing more sediment, first at its mouth, then progressively upstream. Geologic evidence has indicated that such changes in stream activities occurred in the relatively recent past. Coastal streams carved deep valleys near their mouths as sea level dropped as much as 100 metres below its present position during the last Ice Age, when large amounts of water were locked up in ice sheets. By the end of the Ice Age, the release of water from ice sheets into the oceans led to a rise in sea level, resulting in backfilling of the deep valleys.

Changes in base level can also occur above sea level as smaller-scale features that interrupt a stream's flow are created and destroyed. For example, a stream will gradually adjust its profile as it cuts through a resistant rock layer that formerly impeded its flow, and then adjusts to the next lowest base level (Figure 15.15). In such a case, the lowering of base level will result in the merging of multiple, nested profiles into one. The construction of an artificial dam upstream of its mouth would, conversely, represent a rise in base level (Figure 15.16). Because the stream would lose velocity as it reached the reservoir behind the dam, its competence would be insufficient to transport its sediment load, and deposition would occur. (It is for this reason that dam reservoirs must be dredged to prevent them from filling with sediment.) Meanwhile, the water flowing downstream has more energy than it needs to transport its reduced sediment load and so expends this energy by cutting into its bed. The resulting profile is effectively split into two smaller segments, each adjusting to its own base level (Figure 15.16).

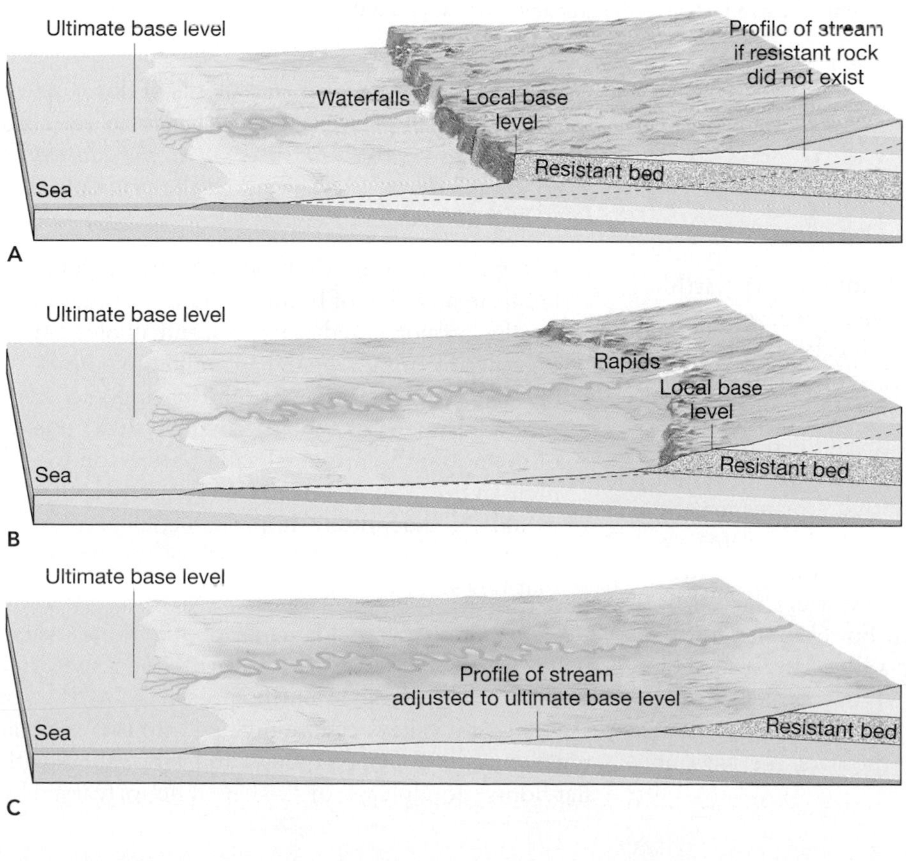

◆ **Figure 15.15** A resistant layer of rock can act as a local (temporary) base level. Because the durable layer is eroded more slowly, it limits the amount of downcutting upstream.

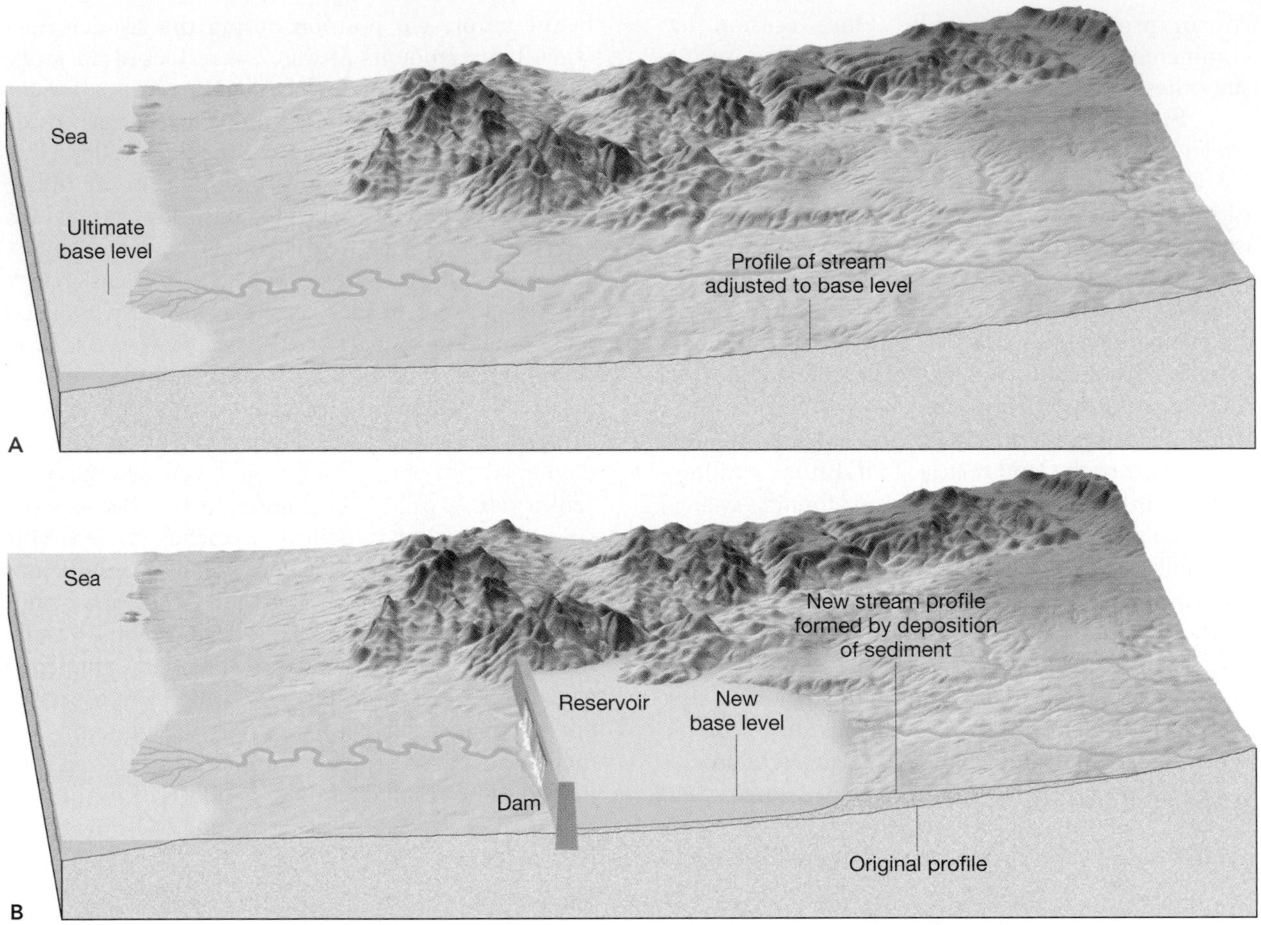

◆ **Figure 15.16** When a dam is built and a reservoir forms, the stream's base level is raised. This reduces the stream's velocity and leads to deposition and a reduction of the gradient upstream from the reservoir.

STREAM VALLEYS

GEODe EARTH Running Water
↳ Reviewing Valleys and Stream-Related Features

Valleys are the most common landforms on Earth's surface. In fact, they exist in such large numbers that they have never been counted except in limited areas used for study. Before the turn of the nineteenth century, it was generally believed that valleys were created by catastrophic events that pulled the crust apart and created troughs in which streams could flow. Today, however, we know that streams usually create their own valleys. However, some streams are very narrow compared with their valleys (called *misfit* streams) because their valleys were carved by glaciers or by glacial melt water. For example, few of Canada's major rivers fit their valleys because they occupy ancient *spillways* carved by former glacial meltwater streams that were much wider, and had much higher discharges, than those of the present rivers.

One of the first clear statements of this fact was made by English geologist John Playfair in 1802. In his well-known work *Illustrations of the Huttonian Theory of the Earth*, Playfair stated the principle that has come to be called **Playfair's law**:

> Every river appears to consist of a main trunk, fed from a variety of branches, each running in a valley proportioned to its size, and all of them together forming a system of valleys, communicating with one another, and having such a nice adjustment of their declivities, that none of them join the principal valley, either on too high or too low a level; a circumstance that would be indefinitely improbable, if each of these valleys were not the work of the stream that flows in it.

Not only were Playfair's observations essentially correct but they were also written in a style that is seldom achieved in scientific prose.

Stream valleys can be divided into two general types: narrow V-shaped valleys, and wide valleys with flat floors (floodplains) or U-shaped floors (carved by glaciers; see Chapter 17). These exist as the ideal forms, with many gradations in between.

◆ **Figure 15.17** V-shaped valley opening into Cambridge fjord, north Baffin Island. (Photo by S. R. Hicock)

Narrow Valleys

In some arid regions, where downcutting is rapid and weathering is slow, and in places where rock is particularly resistant, narrow valleys can have nearly vertical walls (see Figure 15.9). However, most valleys, even those that are narrow at the base, are much broader at the top than the width of the channel at the bottom. This would not be the case if the only agent responsible for eroding valleys were the streams flowing through them.

The sides of most valleys are shaped primarily by the combined processes of weathering, sheet flow, and mass wasting. Measurements and calculations have shown that stream channel erosion during periods of increased discharge can account for only a portion of the additional sediment transported by a stream. Therefore, much of the increased load must be delivered to the stream by sheet flow and mass wasting.

A narrow V-shaped valley (Figure 15.17) indicates that the primary work of the stream has been downcutting. If the erodibility of the material into which the stream channel is cutting varies significantly, especially where this material is solid bedrock, rapids and waterfalls can be common.

Wide Valleys

As a stream approaches base level and its gradient has decreased, less energy is expended in downcutting and more in lateral erosion. The result is the development of a meandering channel that widens the valley as it erodes first one bank and then the other (Figure 15.18). This side-to-side migration of the channel ultimately produces a broad *erosional floodplain*. If sediment is allowed to accumulate in an existing valley, as might be expected during a rise in base level, the valley floor aggrades and broadens, producing a *depositional floodplain*. The floodplain in California's Yosemite Valley is one such feature; it was produced when a glacier gouged the former stream valley about 300 metres deeper than it had been. After the glacial ice melted, the stream readjusted itself to its former base level by refilling the valley with alluvium. Further discussion of floodplain development in wide valleys is given in the next section on stream systems.

TYPES OF STREAM SYSTEMS

Depending on flow rate, gradient, sediment load, climate, and a host of other factors, streams can take on a number of forms. In this section, three basic types, braided, meandering, and anastomosed, are discussed. Keep in mind, however, that a wide spectrum of forms exist among these basic types and that a single stream can theoretically show characteristics of all these forms at various points along its course.

Braided Streams

Sometimes a stream deposits materials on the floor of its channel. If these accumulations become thick enough to act as significant obstacles, they can split the flow into multiple paths. What results is a broad channel containing a complex network of converging and diverging flow paths that thread their way among the bars (Figure 15.19A). Such a stream is said to be **braided**. Braided patterns most commonly form when the load supplied to a stream exceeds its competence or capacity. This can happen under a number of circumstances: (1) if a steeper, turbulent tributary enters a main stream, its rocky bed load

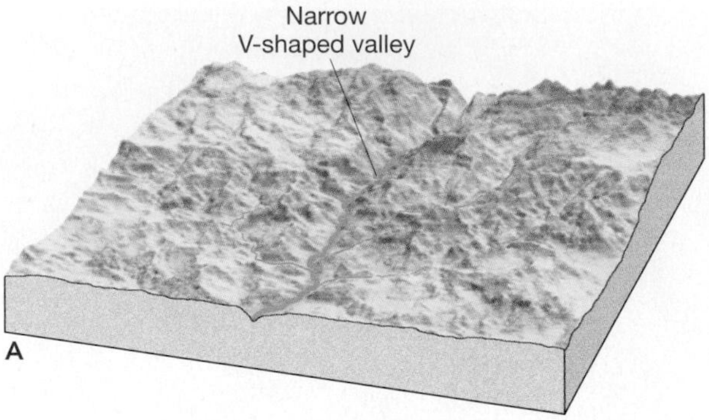

A

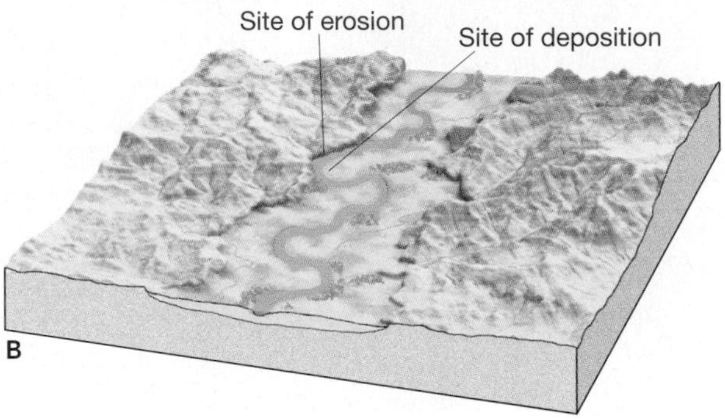

B

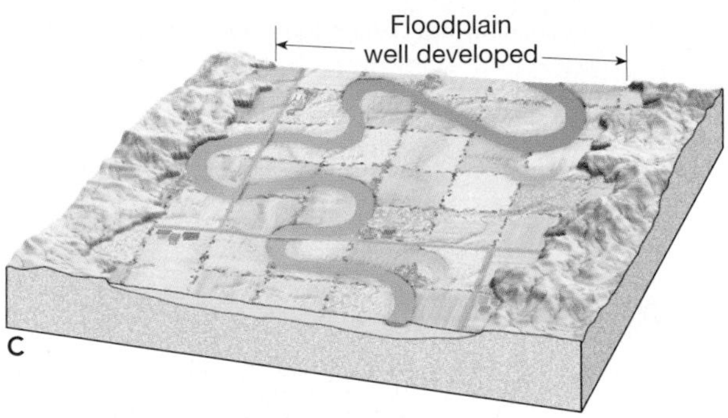

C

D

◆ **Figure 15.18** **A.** When a stream lies well above base level, stream erosion is directed predominantly downward, producing a V-shaped valley. **B.** As a stream bed approaches base level, the stream channel begins to meander, eroding both downward and laterally, widening its floodplain. **C.** When a stream bed has been lowered to an elevation close to base level, lateral erosion predominates, leading to the development of a very broad floodplain. **D.** Photograph of the St. Mary River, near Lethbridge, Alberta, eroding its floodplain. Note also the well-developed point bars and cutbanks in the meanders of the river. (Photo by C. Tsujita)

A

B

◆ **Figure 15.19** **A.** Modern braided stream choked with sediment near the edge of a melting glacier. **B.** Ancient (Triassic) sandy braided river deposits, Blomidon Formation, Tenneycape, Nova Scotia. The conglomerate lenses were deposited by migrating gravel bars in the stream bed.
(Photo **A** by Bradford Washburn; photo **B** by Guy Plint)

may be deposited at the junction because the velocity abruptly decreases; (2) excessive load can be provided when debris from barren slopes is flushed into a channel during a heavy downpour; or (3) excessive load can occur at the terminus of a glacier where ice-eroded sediment is dumped into a meltwater stream flowing away from the glacier. By splitting its flow into multiple paths, a braided stream also gains an increased ability to transport its load downstream.

Braided streams are common in areas adjacent to highlands, where steep gradients promote the supply of large volumes of coarse sediment through mass wasting. Braided streams also form when an abrupt decrease in gradient or a decrease in the stream's discharge occurs. The latter situation could result from a drop in rainfall in the area drained by the stream. It also commonly occurs when a stream leaves a humid area with many tributaries and enters a dry region with few tributaries. In this case, the loss of water to evaporation and seepage into the channel results in a diminished discharge, forcing the stream to deposit much of its load and to ultimately choke the stream with sediment.

Braided streams are dominated by coarse sediment (sand to gravel) bed load, the coarsest components commonly moulded into bars. Ancient deposits of braided rivers typically preserve cross bedded conglomerates that record the migration of such bars (Figure 15.19B).

Meandering Streams

As mentioned previously, streams frequently develop meanders along their courses. Those that occupy broad floodplains, whether erosional or depositional, commonly have a single channel with sweeping meanders. Meandering streams usually occur in areas of relatively low gradient, and their channels carry both fine-grained suspended sediment and coarser grained bed load.

What actually initiates the snake-like form of meandering rivers is uncertain, but the manner in which meanders are maintained is well known (Figure 15.20). Erosion occurs on the outside of the meander where velocity and turbulence are greatest. Most often, the outside bank is undermined, especially during periods of high water. As the bank becomes oversteepened, it fails by slumping into the channel. Because the outside of a meander is a zone of active erosion (Figure 15.21), it is often referred to as the **cut bank**. Much of the debris detached by the stream at the cut bank moves downstream and is soon deposited as point bars in zones of decreased velocity on the insides of meanders, while coarser debris may be left in the channel as lag gravel. In this manner the channel meanders migrate laterally, while keeping the same cross-sectional area, by eroding the outside of the bends and depositing on the inside. A point bar deposit can preserve **lateral accretion surfaces**, which mark the successive positions of the point bar surface as it built out laterally (Figure 15.22). These surfaces, which resemble cross bedding, but are significantly larger in scale, are hallmarks of meandering channels in ancient sedimentary deposits.

If we were to sample the floodplain alluvium associated with a meandering stream, we would find that some of it consists of coarse sands and gravels that were originally deposited as channel deposits

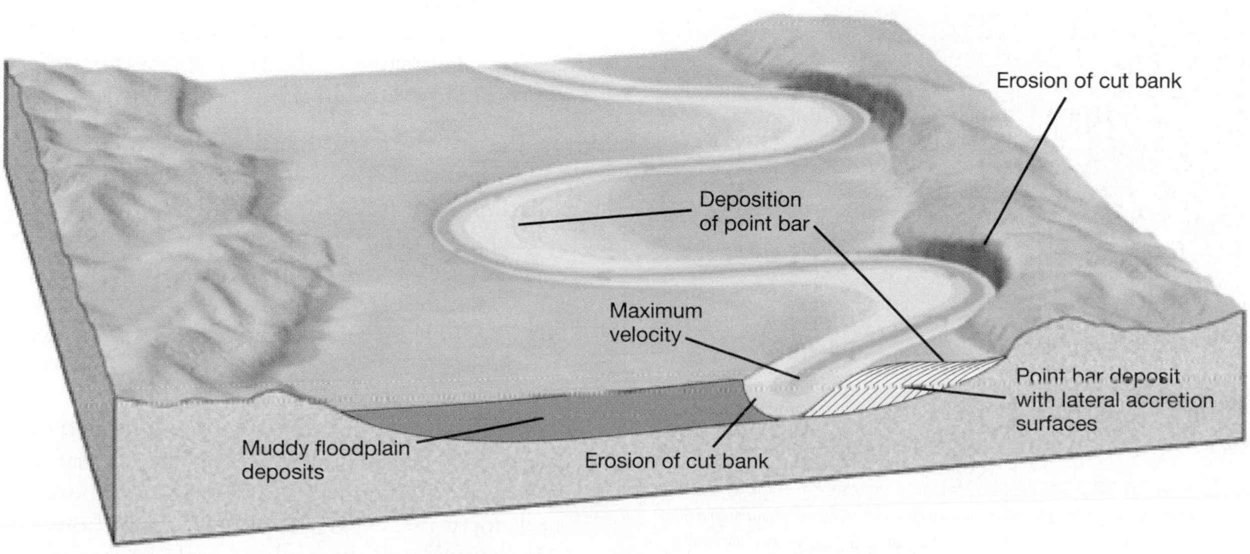

◆ **Figure 15.20** Schematic diagram showing the lateral migration of a meander by erosion of the cut bank and deposition on the point bar.

◆ **Figure 15.21** Erosion of a cut bank in action along the Newaukum River, Washington. **A.** January 1965. **B.** March 1965. Note the house about to be undermined by continued erosion of the cut bank. (Photos by P. A. Glancy, U.S. Geological Survey)

and point bars by meanders shifting laterally across the valley floor. Other sediments would be composed of fine sands, silts, and clays that were spread across the floodplain whenever water overtopped the channel banks during floods. Thus, a vertical sequence in which sediment gets finer as we move upward, changing from gravel to mud, can develop under a floodplain surface as stream meanders migrate back and forth over time.

Owing to the downslope gradient of the channel, erosion is more effective on the downstream side of a meander than on the upstream side.

◆ **Figure 15.22** Lateral accretion surfaces of ancient point bar deposits (upper part of photograph) record the migration of a meandering river channel. The lateral accretion surfaces dip toward the left side of the photograph, indicating that the channel was migrating in that direction. (Photo by Guy Plint)

Consequently, in addition to growing laterally, the bends also gradually migrate down the valley. Sometimes the downstream migration of a meander is slowed when it reaches a more resistant portion of the floodplain. This allows the next meander upstream to "catch up." Gradually the neck of land between the meanders is narrowed. When they get close enough, the river may erode through the narrow neck of land to the next loop (Figure 15.23A). The new, shorter channel segment is called a **cutoff**, and because of its shape, the abandoned bend is called an **oxbow lake** (Figures 15.23A and 15.23B). Over time, the oxbow lake fills with sediment to create a **meander scar** (Figure 15.23B).

The process of meander cutoff formation has the effect of shortening the river and was described humorously by Mark Twain in *Life on the Mississippi*:

> In the space of one hundred and seventy-six years the lower Mississippi has shortened itself two hundred and forty-two miles. This is an average of a trifle over one mile and a third per year. Therefore, any calm person, who is not blind or idiotic, can see that in the Old Oolitic Silurian Period, just a million years ago next November, the Lower Mississippi River was upwards of one million three hundred thousand miles long, and stuck out over the Gulf of Mexico like a fishing rod. And, by the same token, any person can see that seven hundred and forty-two years from now the Lower Mississippi will be only a mile and three quarters long, and Cairo and New Orleans will have joined their streets together, and be plod-

A

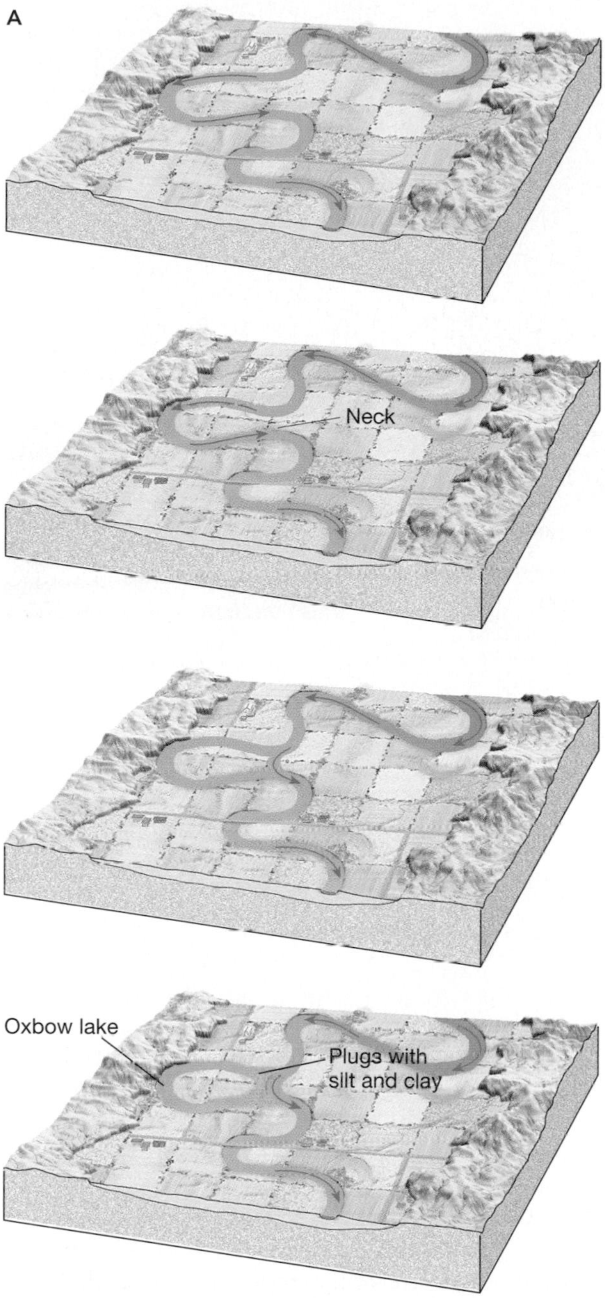

B

◆ **Figure 15.23** **A.** Formation of a cutoff and oxbow lake. **B.** Aerial view of Kenemich River at the foot of the Mealy Mountains, Newfoundland and Labrador, showing well-developed meanders, oxbow lakes, and meander scars. (Photo reproduced with the permission of the Minister of Public Works and Government Services Canada, 2008, and courtesy of Natural Resources Canada)

ding comfortably along under a single mayor and a mutual board of aldermen. One gets such wholesale returns of conjecture out of such a trifling investment of fact.

Although the data used by Mark Twain were reasonably accurate, he intentionally forgot to include the fact that the Mississippi also created many new meanders, thus lengthening its course by a similar amount. In fact, with the growth of its delta, the Mississippi is actually getting longer, not shorter.

Meandering streams commonly have well-developed natural levees that lie above the average level of their floodplains. For example, natural levees of the lower Mississippi River rise 6 metres above the lower portions of the valley floor. The area behind a natural levee is characteristically poorly drained for the obvious reason that water cannot flow up over the levee and back into the river (Figures 15.24A and 15.24B). When a tributary stream enters a valley that has substantial natural levees, it may not be able to make its way into the main channel. As a consequence, the tributary may flow through a **back swamp** parallel to the main river for many kilometres before crossing the natural levee and joining the main river. Such streams are called **yazoo tributaries** (Figure 15.24B), after the

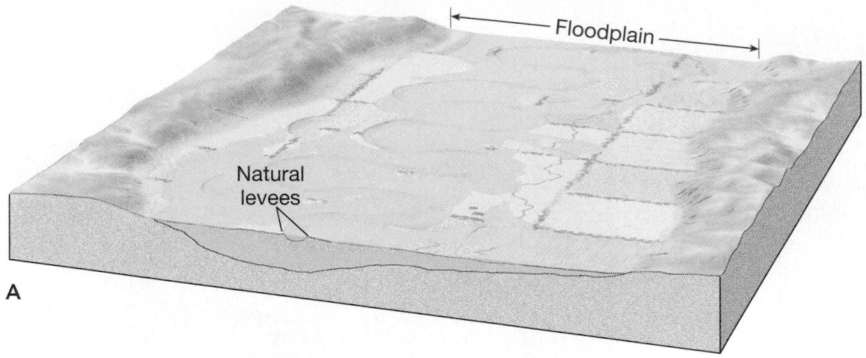

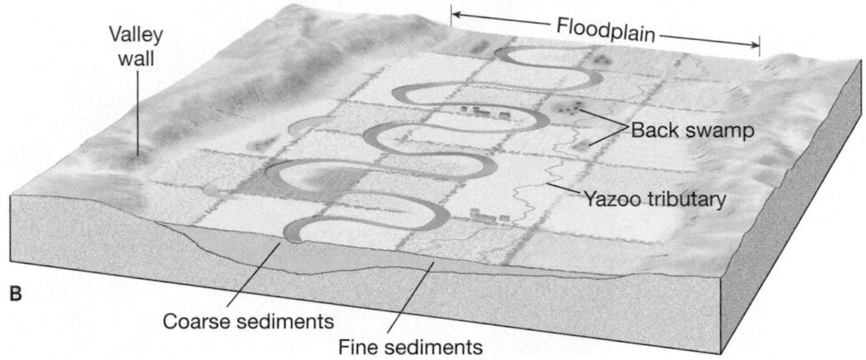

◆ **Figure 15.24** **A.** Natural levees are commonly built during floods in meandering river systems. **B.** After floodwaters recede, water may be prevented from draining into the main channel, resulting in the development of back swamps and yazoo tributaries that flow parallel to the main stream. **C.** A meandering stream near Swan Hills in central Alberta, showing slightly raised natural levees (bright green vegetated strips on both sides of the channel) and poorly drained back swamps.
(Photo reproduced with the permission of the Minister of Public Works and Government Services Canada, 2008, and courtesy of Natural Resources Canada)

◆ **Figure 15.25** Spectacular incised meanders of the Colorado River in Canyonlands National Park, Utah, that were formed in response to the uplift of the Colorado Plateau.
(Photo by Michael Collier)

Yazoo River, which parallels the lower Mississippi River for more than 300 kilometres. Back swamps also develop in the poorly drained conditions on the floodplain resulting from natural levee development (Figures 15.24B and 15.24C).

Certain meandering rivers flow in steep, narrow valleys. These meanders probably developed on the floodplain of a stream that was near base level. Then, a change in base level, either when it dropped or when the land on which the river was flowing was uplifted, caused the stream to begin downcutting.

During the last Ice Age, when large quantities of water were withdrawn from the ocean and locked up in glaciers on land (see Chapter 17), sea level (ultimate base level) dropped, causing rivers flowing into the ocean to begin to downcut. Of course, this activity ceased at the close of the last Ice Age when the glaciers melted and the ocean rose to its former level.

Regional uplift of the land, the second cause for incised meanders, is exemplified by the Colorado Plateau in the southwestern United States (Figure 15.25). As the plateau was gradually uplifted, numerous meandering rivers adjusted to being higher above base level by downcutting.

After a river has adjusted to a relative drop in base level by downcutting, it may once again produce a floodplain at a level below the old one. The remnants of a former floodplain are sometimes present in the form of flat surfaces called **terraces** (Figure 15.26).

Anastomosed Streams

Anastomosed streams look superficially like braided streams but differ greatly in their behaviour. Unlike a braided stream, the appearance of which basically reflects the diversion of flow around temporary bars of sediment in a single, shallow channel, an anastomosed stream has deep, interwoven, multiple channels separated by stable islands that are commonly heavily vegetated (Figure 15.27A). In other words, anastomosed streams are produced by the development of multiple true channels rather than by the local diversion of flow around buildups of sediment within a single channel. Also, anastomosed streams tend to be dominated by fine-grained suspended load as opposed to coarse-grained bed load.

Streams of anastomosed form tend to occur in areas of extremely low gradient and therefore possess little energy to carve their banks. Like meandering stream systems, anastomosed systems tend to have broad, muddy floodplains and levees along their channel banks.

The relatively small amounts of coarse-grained bed load in anastomosed systems are ultimately deposited in channels. However, unlike the channels of meandering streams that migrate laterally by eroding their outside bank and depositing sediment on point bars, those of anastomosed streams tend to become filled with sediment in a vertical direction with little or no lateral accretion and are ultimately abandoned. In the geologic record, channel deposits

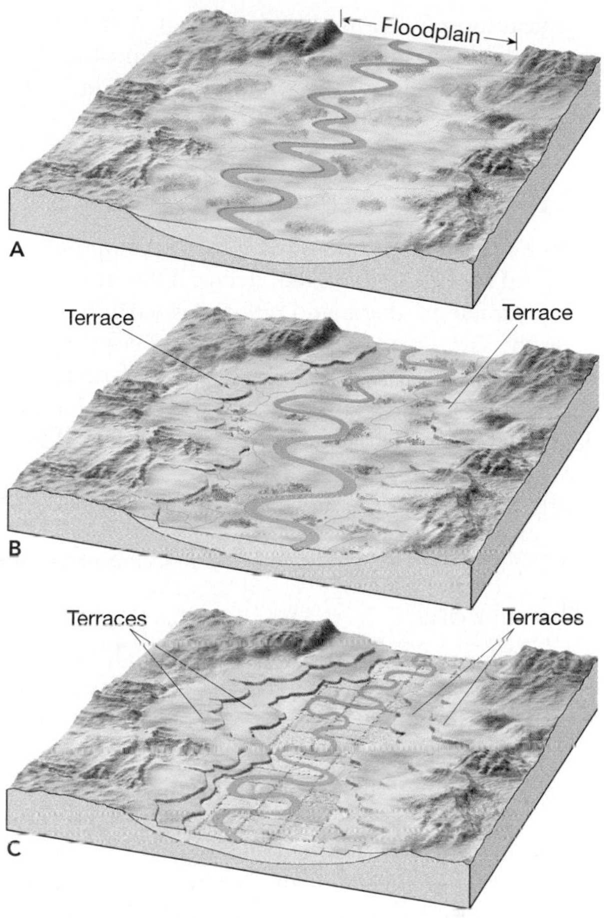

◆ **Figure 15.26** Terraces can form when a stream cuts down through previously deposited alluvium. This may occur in response to a lowering of elevation or as a result of regional uplift.

A B

◆ **Figure 15.27** **A.** The upper Columbia River in southeast British Columbia is a good example of an anastomosed stream. Note the multiple active channels and intervening islands with wetlands. **B.** A sand-filled channel (lightest coloured) of an ancient anastomosed river (Cretaceous Dunvegan Formation, Pine River area, British Columbia), encased in muddy floodplain deposits.
(Photo **A** by Norman D. Smith; photo **B** by Guy Plint)

of anastomosed streams can be recognized as lens-shaped bodies of horizontally bedded sandstones or conglomerates encased in muddy (floodplain) sediments (Figure 15.27B).

ALLUVIAL FANS AND DELTAS

Two of the most common landforms composed of alluvium are alluvial fans and deltas. They are sometimes similar in shape and are deposited for essentially the same reason: an abrupt loss of competence in a stream. The key distinction between them is that alluvial fans are deposited on land whereas deltas are deposited in a body of water. In addition, alluvial fans can be quite steep, but deltas are relatively flat, barely protruding above the level surface of the ocean or lake in which they formed.

Alluvial Fans

Alluvial fans typically develop where a high-gradient stream leaves a narrow valley in mountainous terrain and comes out suddenly onto a broad, flat plain or valley floor (Figure 15.28). Alluvial fans form in response to the abrupt drop in gradient combined with the change from a narrow channel of a mountain stream to less confined channels at the base of the mountains. The sudden drop in velocity causes the stream to dump its load of sediment quickly in a distinctive cone- or fan-shaped accumulation. As illustrated by Figure 15.28, the surface of the fan slopes outward in a broad arc from an apex at the mouth of the steep valley. Usually, coarse material is dropped near the apex of the fan, while finer material is carried toward the base of the deposit. As you learned in Chapter 14, steep canyons in dry regions are prime locations for debris flows. Therefore, many alluvial fans in arid areas have debris-flow deposits interbedded with the alluvium.

Deltas

In contrast to an alluvial fan, a **delta** forms when a stream enters an ocean or a lake. Figure 15.29A depicts the structure of a simple delta that might form in the relatively quiet waters of a lake. As the stream's forward motion is checked on entering the lake, the dying current deposits its load of sediments. These deposits occur in three types of beds. *Foreset beds* are composed of coarser particles that drop almost immediately on entering the lake to form layers that slope downcurrent on the *delta front*. The foreset beds are usually covered by thin, horizontal *topset beds*, which are deposited on the *delta plain* during floods. Topset beds tend to be dominated by mud and plant debris that accumulates in marshlands on the flat upper surface of the delta, but also contain the coarser grained material deposited within distributary channels. The finer silts and clays settle out some distance from the mouth in nearly horizontal layers called *bottomset beds* on an area called the *prodelta*.

As the delta grows outward, the stream's gradient continually lessens. This circumstance eventually causes the channel to become choked with sediment from the slowing water. As a consequence, the river seeks a shorter, higher-gradient route to base level, as

A

B

◆ **Figure 15.28** **A.** Alluvial fans develop where the gradient of a stream changes abruptly from steep to flat. Such a situation exists in Death Valley, California, where streams emerge from the mountains into a flat basin. As a result, Death Valley has many large alluvial fans. The highway will eventually be buried by fan buildup. **B.** Alluvial fans as viewed from the ground in Banff National Park, Alberta. (Photo **A** by Michael Collier; photo **B** by Bruce Wright)

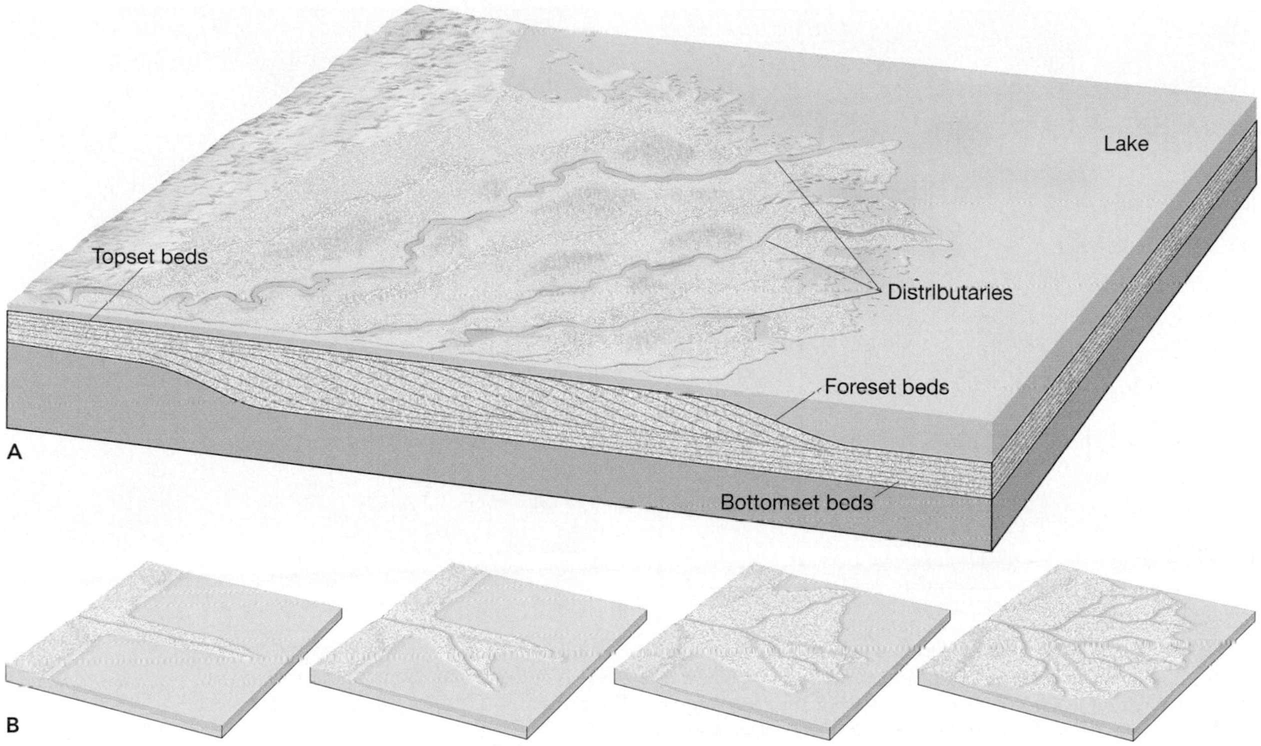

◆ **Figure 15.29** **A.** Structure of a simple delta that forms in the relatively quiet waters of a lake. **B.** Growth of a simple delta. As a stream extends its channel, the gradient is reduced. Frequently, during flood stage the river is diverted to a higher-gradient route, forming a new distributary. Old abandoned distributaries are gradually invaded by aquatic vegetation and fill with sediment.
(After Ward's Natural Science Establishment, Inc., Rochester, NY)

illustrated in Figure 15.29B. This illustration shows the main channel dividing into several smaller ones, called **distributaries.** Most deltas are characterized by these shifting channels, which act in the opposite way to tributaries. Rather than carrying water into the main channel, distributaries carry water *away* from the main channel in varying paths. After numerous shifts of the channel, the simple delta may grow into the triangular shape of the Greek letter delta (Δ), for which it was named. The Nile Delta (Figure 15.30) is affected by relatively strong wave activity that smears much of the sediment delivered to the river mouth against the shoreline; this has resulted in the development of the classic delta shape. Conversely, the Mississippi Delta is shaped more like a bird's foot, reflecting the high output of fine-grained, suspended sediment from its distributaries and relatively weak wave activity. Thus, depending on such factors as sediment load, shoreline shape, variations in the nature and strength of wave activity, a delta can assume different shapes (Figure 15.30).

Although deltas that form in the ocean generally exhibit the same basic form as the simple lake-deposited feature just described, most large marine deltas are far more complex and have foreset beds that are inclined at a much lower angle than those depicted in Figure 15.29A. Indeed, many of the world's great rivers have created massive deltas, each with its own peculiarities.

DRAINAGE NETWORKS

A stream is just a small component of a larger system. Each system consists of a **drainage basin**, the land area that contributes water to the stream. The drainage basin of one stream is separated from another by an elongated topographic high called a **divide** (Figures 15.31 and 15.32). Divides range in size from a ridge separating two small gullies to continental divides, which delineate enormous drainage basins. The Mississippi River has the largest drainage basin in North America. Extending between the Rocky Mountains in the West and the Appalachian Mountains in the East, the Mississippi River and its tributaries collect water from more than 3.2 million square kilometres of the continent.

Drainage Patterns

All drainage systems are made up of an interconnected network of streams that together form particular

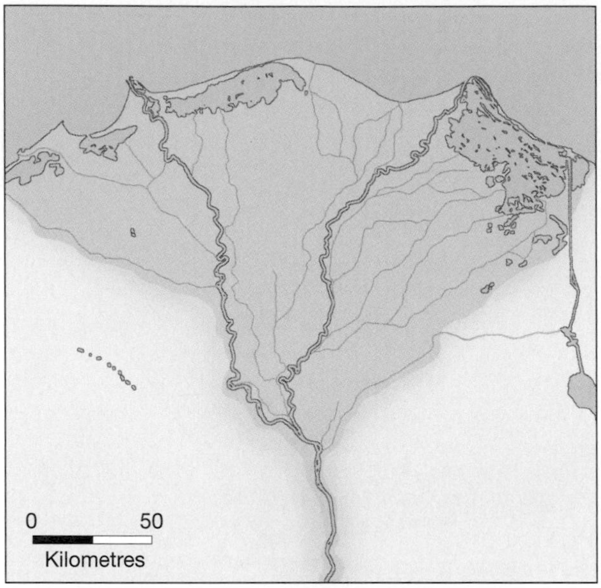

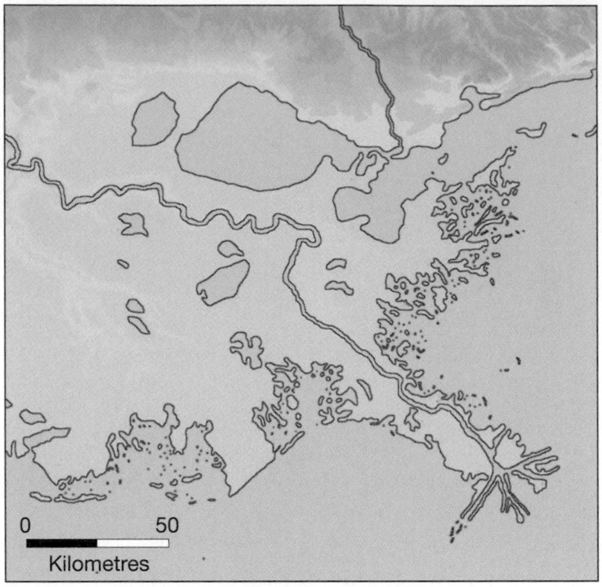

◆ **Figure 15.30** The shapes of deltas vary and depend on such factors as a river's sediment load and the strength and nature of shoreline processes. The triangular shape of the Nile Delta was the basis for naming this feature; here, waves tend to remove what the river deposits. The present Mississippi Delta is called a *bird-foot delta,* where river deposition dominates over wave erosion.

patterns. The nature of a drainage pattern can vary greatly from one type of terrain to another, primarily in response to the kinds of rock on which the streams developed or the structural pattern of faults and folds.

The most commonly encountered drainage pattern is the **dendritic pattern** (Figure 15.33A). This pattern is characterized by irregular branching of tributary streams that resembles the branching pattern of a deciduous tree. In fact, the word *dendritic* means "treelike." The dendritic pattern forms where underlying bedrock is relatively uniform, such as flat-lying sedimentary strata or massive igneous rocks. Because the underlying material is essentially

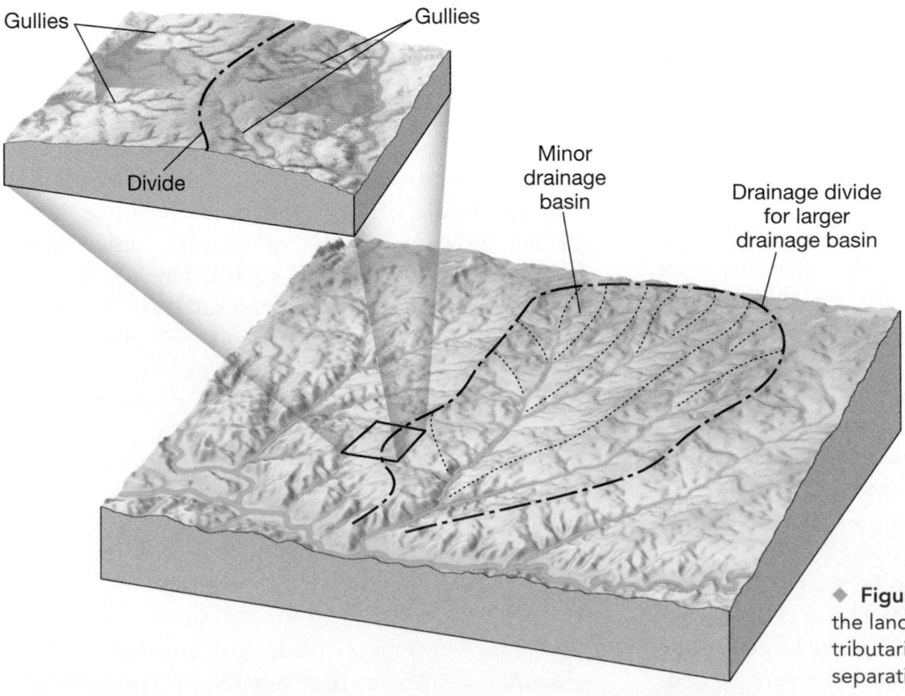

◆ **Figure 15.31** A *drainage basin* is the land area drained by a stream and its tributaries. *Divides* are the boundaries separating drainage basins.

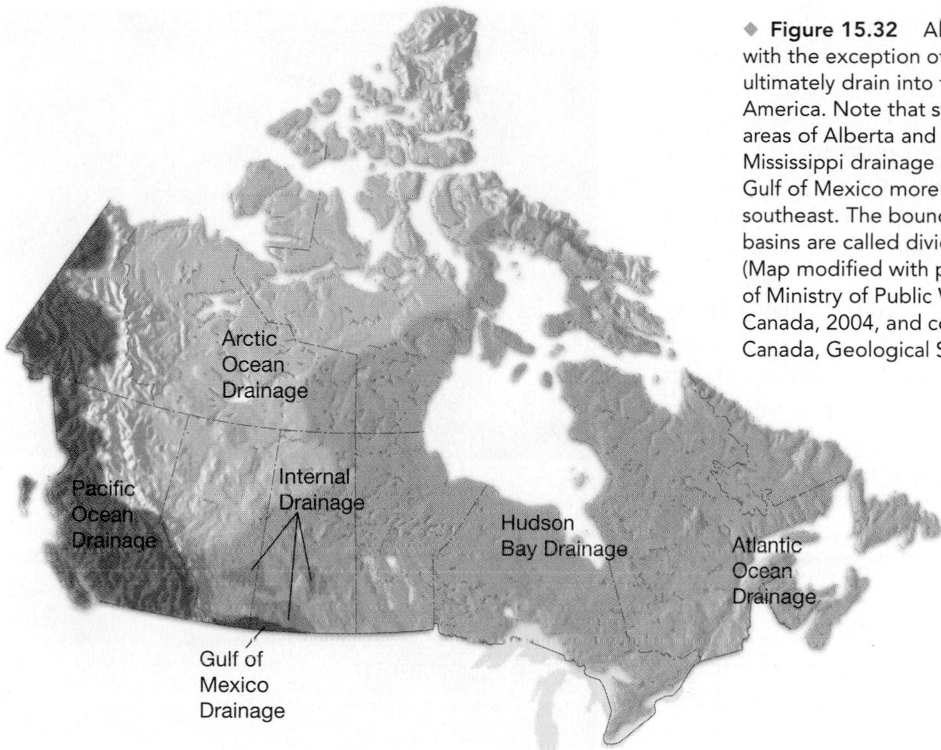

◆ **Figure 15.32** All major river systems in Canada, with the exception of a few in the Prairie provinces, ultimately drain into the oceans surrounding North America. Note that streams in the southernmost areas of Alberta and Saskatchewan feed into the Mississippi drainage system that empties into the Gulf of Mexico more than 6000 kilometres to the southeast. The boundaries between the drainage basins are called divides.
(Map modified with permission from image courtesy of Ministry of Public Works and Government Services Canada, 2004, and courtesy of Natural Resources Canada, Geological Survey of Canada)

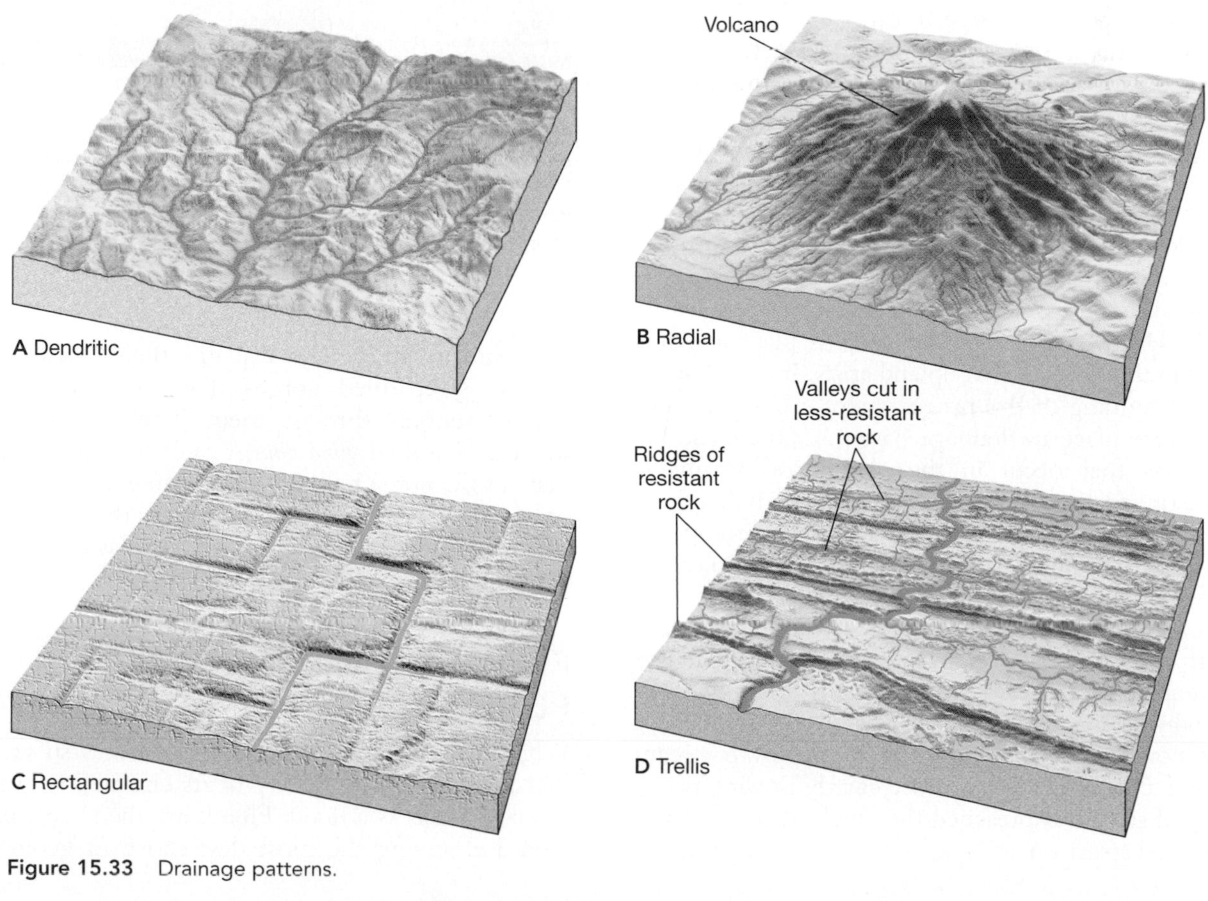

◆ **Figure 15.33** Drainage patterns.

uniform in its resistance to erosion, it does not control the pattern of stream flow. Rather, the pattern is determined chiefly by the direction of the slope of land.

When streams diverge from a central area, like spokes from the hub of a wheel, the pattern is said to be **radial** (Figure 15.33B). This pattern typically develops on isolated volcanic cones and domal uplifts.

Figure 15.33C illustrates a **rectangular pattern**, with many right-angle bends. This pattern develops when the bedrock is criss-crossed by a series of joints and faults. Because these structures are eroded more easily than unbroken rock, their geometric pattern guides the directions of streams as they carve their valleys.

Figure 15.33D illustrates a **trellis drainage pattern**, a rectangular pattern in which tributary streams are nearly parallel to one another and have the appearance of a garden trellis. This pattern forms in areas underlain by alternating bands of resistant and less resistant rock and is particularly well displayed in the Front Ranges of the Canadian Rockies, where both weak and strong strata crop out in nearly parallel belts.

Headward Erosion and Stream Piracy

We have seen that a stream can lengthen its course by building a delta at its mouth. A stream also lengthens its course by **headward erosion**, that is, by extending the head of its valley upslope. As sheet flow converges and becomes concentrated at the head of a stream channel, its velocity, and hence its power to erode, increases. The result can be vigorous erosion at the head of the valley. Thus, through headward erosion, the valley becomes extended into previously undissected terrain (Figure 15.34).

Headward erosion by streams plays a major role in the dissection of upland areas. In addition, an understanding of this process helps explain changes that take place in drainage patterns. One cause for changes that occur in the pattern of streams is **stream piracy**, the diversion of the drainage of one stream because of the headward erosion of another stream. Piracy can occur, for example, if a stream on one side of a divide has a steeper gradient than a stream on the other side. Because the stream with the steeper gradient has more energy, it can extend its valley headward, eventually breaking down the divide and capturing part or all of the drainage of the slower stream. In Figure 15.35 the flow of stream A was captured when a more swiftly flowing tributary of stream B breached the divide at its head and diverted stream A.

A

B

Figure 15.34 By headward erosion, valleys extend into previously undissected terrain. **A.** Aerial photo of the San Rafael River above its confluence with the Green River in Utah. **B.** Photo taken near Pelly Bay, Nunavut, showing the dissection of uplifted ancient seafloor mud.
(Photo **A** by Michael Collier; photo **B** by S. R. Hicock)

Stream piracy also explains the existence of narrow, steep-sided gorges that have no active streams running through them. These abandoned water gaps (called *wind gaps*) form when the stream that cut the notch has its course changed by a pirate stream. In Figure 15.35, one water gap that had been created by stream A became a wind gap as a result of stream piracy.

FLOODS AND FLOOD CONTROL

When the discharge of a stream becomes so great that it exceeds the capacity of its channel, it overflows its banks as a flood. Floods are the most common and among the most destructive of geologic

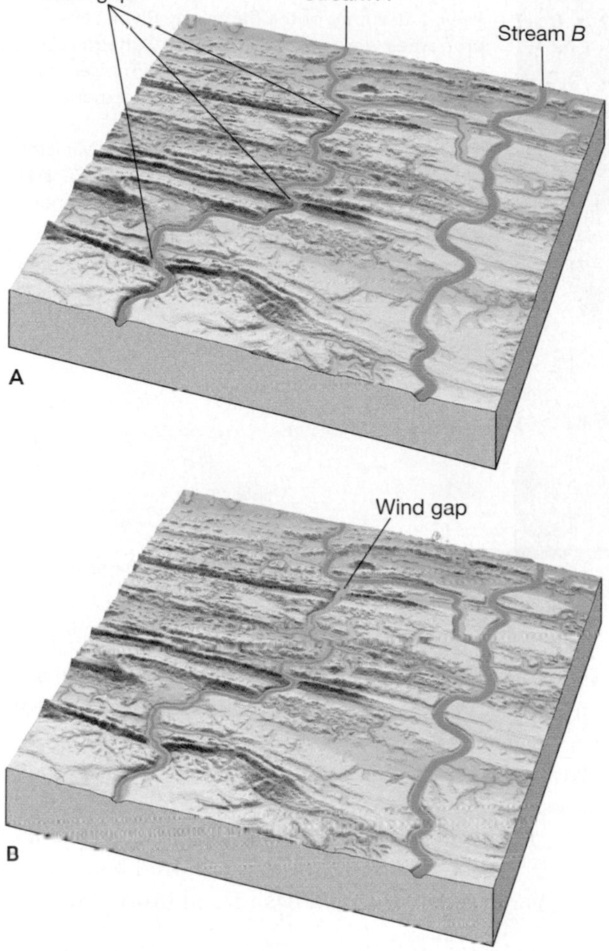

◆ **Figure 15.35** Stream piracy and the formation of wind gaps. A tributary of stream B erodes headward until it eventually captures and diverts stream A. A water gap through which stream A flowed is abandoned because of the piracy. As a result, this feature is now a wind gap. In this valley-and-ridge-type setting, the softer rocks in the valleys are eroded more easily than the resistant ridges. Consequently, as the valleys are lowered, the ridges and wind gaps become elevated relative to the valleys.

hazards. They are, nevertheless, simply part of the *natural* behaviour of streams.

Most floods have a meteorologic origin caused by atmospheric processes that can vary greatly in both time and space. Just an hour or less of intense thunderstorm rainfall can trigger floods in small valleys. By contrast, major floods in large river valleys are commonly the result of an extraordinary series of precipitation events over a broad region for an extended time.

Land-use planning in river basins requires an understanding of the frequency and magnitude of floods. Probably the greatest immediate practical use of the data collected at stream-gauging stations is estimating the probability of various flood magnitudes.

Floods are often described in terms of their **recurrence interval** or **return period**. This is the case when you hear about a 100-year flood (or a 30-year flood or the 500-year Red River flood described in Box 15.1). What does this mean? The flood discharge that has a 1 percent (1 in 100) probability of being exceeded in any one year is called a 100-year flood. This phrase is misleading because it leads people to believe that only one such flood will occur in a 100-year span or that such floods occur regularly every 100 years. Neither is accurate. The fact is that uncommonly big floods occur at irregular intervals and can happen in *any* year.

Many flood designations are re-evaluated and changed over time as more data are collected or when a river basin is altered in a way that affects the flow of water. Dams and urban development are examples of some human influences in a basin that can affect recurrence intervals.

Causes and Types of Floods

Floods can be the result of several naturally occurring and human-induced factors. Among the common types of floods are regional floods, flash floods, ice-jam floods, and dam-failure floods.

Regional Floods Some regional floods are seasonal. Rapid melting of snow in spring and heavy spring rains can overwhelm a river. The extensive 1948 flood of the Fraser River and the 1997 flood along the Red River (see Box 15.1) are notable examples of events triggered by rapid snowmelt. Early spring floods are sometimes made worse if the ground is frozen. This reduces infiltration into the soil, thereby increasing runoff. Extended wet periods any time of the year can create saturated soils, after which any additional rain runs off into streams until capacities are exceeded. Regional floods are commonly caused by slow-moving storm systems, including decaying hurricanes. For example, southern Quebec was subjected to torrential rain between July 19 and 21, 1996, when a storm system stalled over the region. The Saguenay area was particularly hard hit, receiving more than 200 millimetres of rain in 50 hours. Flooding of the Saguenay River and its tributaries caused more than $700 million in damage to the area, largely because of widespread erosion in some parts of the drainage basin and significant sediment deposition in others (Figure 15.36).

Flash Floods A flash flood can occur with little warning and can be deadly because it produces a rapid rise in water levels and can have a devastating flow velocity. Several factors influence flash flooding.

◆ **Figure 15.36** Downstream along Ha! Ha! River, a tributary of the Saguenay River, several properties were covered by up to 2 metres of sediment during the flood of 1996. The sediment was derived from upstream areas that experienced severe erosion during the flood.
(Reproduced with the permission of the Minister of Public Works and Government Services Canada, 2004, and courtesy of Natural Resources Canada, Geological Survey of Canada)

Among them are rainfall intensity and duration, surface conditions, and topography. Mountainous areas are susceptible because steep slopes can funnel runoff into narrow canyons, as occurs along the Sea-to-Sky Highway between Vancouver and Squamish, British Columbia.

Urban areas are susceptible to flash floods because a high percentage of the surface area is composed of impervious roofs, streets, and parking lots, where runoff is very rapid. To better understand the effect of urbanization on stream flow, examine Figure 15.37. The top part of the figure is a hypothetical hydrograph that shows the time relationship between a rainstorm and the occurrence of flooding. Notice that the water level in the stream does not rise at the onset of precipitation, because time is required for water to move from the place where it fell to the stream. This time difference is called the *lag time*. The hydrograph in the bottom part of Figure 15.37 depicts the same hypothetical area and rainfall event *after* urbanization. Notice that the peak discharge during a flood is greater and that the lag time between precipitation and flood peak is shorter than before urbanization. The explanation for this effect is straightforward. Streets, parking lots, and buildings cover the ground that once soaked up water. Thus, less water infiltrates, and the rate and amount of runoff increase. Further, because much less water soaks into the ground, the low-water (dry-season) flow in many urban streams, which is maintained by the movement of groundwater into the channel, is greatly reduced. As you might expect, the magnitude of these effects is a function of the percentage of land that is covered by impermeable surfaces.

Ice-Jam Floods Frozen rivers are susceptible to ice-jam floods. As the level of a stream rises, it will break up the ice and create ice floes that can pile up on channel obstructions. Such an ice jam creates a dam across the channel. Water upstream from the ice dam can rise rapidly and overflow the channel banks. When the ice dam fails, the water stored behind the dam is released, causing a flash flood downstream.

Dam-Failure Floods Human interference with a stream system can cause floods. A prime example is the failure of a dam or an artificial levee. Dams and artificial levees are built for flood protection. They are designed to contain floods of a certain magnitude. If a larger flood occurs, the dam or levee is overtopped. If the dam or levee fails or is washed out, the water behind it is released to become a flash flood.

Methods of Flood Control

Several strategies have been devised to eliminate or reduce the catastrophic effects of floods. Engineering efforts include the construction of artificial levees, the building of flood-control dams, and river channellization.

Artificial Levee Construction *Artificial levees* are earthen mounds built on the banks of a river to increase the volume of water the channel can hold. These most common of stream-containment structures have been used since ancient times and continue to be used today.

Artificial levees are usually easy to distinguish from natural levees because their slopes are much

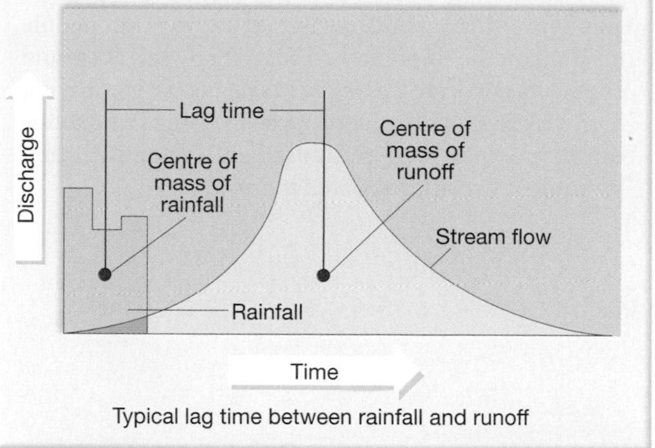

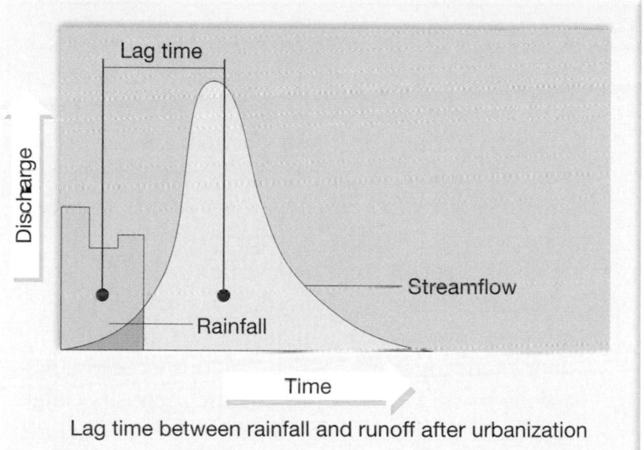

◆ **Figure 15.37** When an area changes from rural to urban, the lag time between rainfall and flood peak is shortened. The flood peak is also higher following urbanization. (After L. B. Leopold, U.S. Geological Survey)

◆ **Figure 15.38** Water rushes through a break in an artificial levee in Monroe County, Illinois. During the record breaking 1993 Midwest floods, many artificial levees could not withstand the force of the floodwaters. Sections of many weakened structures were overtopped or simply collapsed. (Photo by James A. Finley/AP/Wide World Photos)

steeper. When a river is confined by levees during periods of high water, it frequently deposits material in its channel as the discharge diminishes. This is sediment that otherwise would have been dropped on the floodplain. Thus, each time there is a high flow, deposits are left on the riverbed, and the bottom of the channel is built up. With the buildup of the bed, less water is required to overflow the original levee. As a result, the height of the levee may have to be raised periodically to protect the floodplain. Moreover, many artificial levees are not built to withstand periods of extreme flooding (Figure 15.B). For example, levee failures were numerous in the U.S. Midwest during the summer of 1993, when the upper Mississippi and many of its tributaries experienced record floods (Figure 15.38), and on the Mississippi Delta in 2006 when Hurricane Katrina hit New Orleans. In some urban areas (e.g., Winnipeg) concrete floodwalls are constructed that serve the same purpose as artificial levees.

Flood-Control Dams *Flood-control dams* are built to store floodwater and then let it out slowly. This lowers the flood crest by spreading it out over a longer time. Many dams have significant non-flood-related functions, such as providing water for irrigated agriculture and for hydroelectric power generation. Many reservoirs are also major regional recreational facilities.

Although dams can reduce flooding and provide other benefits, building these structures also has significant costs and consequences. For example, reservoirs created by dams may cover fertile farmland, useful forests, historic sites, and scenic valleys. Of course, dams trap sediment. Therefore, deltas and floodplains downstream erode because they are no longer replenished with silt during floods. Large dams can also cause significant ecological damage to river environments that took thousands of years to establish.

Building a dam is not a permanent solution to flooding. Sedimentation behind a dam means that the volume of its reservoir will gradually diminish, reducing the effectiveness of this flood-control measure.

Channellization *Channellization* involves altering a stream channel to speed the flow of water and prevent it from reaching flood height. This may simply involve clearing a channel of obstructions or dredging a channel to make it wider and deeper.

A more radical alteration involves straightening a channel by creating *artificial cutoffs*. The idea is that by shortening the stream, the gradient and the velocity are increased. By increasing velocity, the larger discharge associated with flooding can be dispersed more rapidly. However, because the river's tendency toward meandering still exists, preventing the river from returning to its previous course is difficult. Furthermore, artificial cutoffs increase a stream's velocity and the erosion of the bed and banks of the channel.

A Non-structural Approach The flood-control measures described involve structural solutions aimed at controlling a river. These solutions are expensive and often give a false sense of security to people residing on the floodplain. Today, many scientists and engineers advocate *floodplain management*: identifying high-risk areas so that appropriate zoning regulations can be implemented to minimize development and promote more appropriate land use.

Chapter Summary

- The *hydrologic cycle* describes the continuous interchange of water among the oceans, atmosphere, and continents. Powered by energy from the Sun, it is a global system in which the atmosphere provides the link between the oceans and continents. The processes involved in the hydrologic cycle include precipitation, evaporation, *infiltration* (the movement of water into rocks or soil through cracks and pore spaces), *runoff* (water that flows over the land), and *transpiration* (the release of water vapour to the atmosphere by plants). Running water is the single most important agent sculpting Earth's land surface.
- The amount of water running off the land—rather than sinking into the ground—depends on the *infiltration capacity* of the soil. Initially, runoff flows as broad, thin sheets across the ground, appropriately termed *sheet flow*. After a short distance, threads of current typically develop, and tiny channels called *rills* form, which then converge into *stream* channels.
- The factors that determine a stream's velocity are *gradient* (slope of the stream channel), cross-sectional shape, size, and roughness of the channel, and the stream's *discharge* (amount of water passing a given point per unit of time, frequently measured in cubic metres per second). Most often, the gradient and roughness of a stream decrease downstream, while width, depth, discharge, and velocity increase.
- Streams transport their load of sediment in solution (*dissolved load*), in suspension (*suspended load*), and along the bottom of the channel (*bed load*). Much of the dissolved load is contributed by groundwater. Most streams carry the greatest part of the load in suspension. The bed load moves only intermittently and usually represents the smallest portion of a stream's load.
- A stream's ability to transport solid particles is described using two criteria: *capacity* (the maximum load of solid particles a stream can carry) and *competence* (the maximum particle size a stream can transport). Competence increases as the square of stream velocity, so if velocity doubles, water's force increases fourfold.
- Streams deposit sediment when velocity slows and competence is reduced. This results in *sorting*—the process by which like-size particles are deposited together. Stream deposits are called *alluvium* and can occur as channel deposits called *bars*, and as floodplain deposits, which include *natural levees*.
- The two general types of *base level* (the lowest point to which a stream may erode its channel) are (1) *ultimate base level* (sea level) and (2) *temporary*, or *local*, *base level*. Any change in base level will cause a stream to adjust and establish a new balance. Lowering base level will cause a stream to erode, whereas raising base level results in deposition of material in the channel.
- Although many gradations exist, the two general types of stream valleys are (1) narrow V-shaped valleys and (2) wide valleys with flat floors. Because the dominant activity is down cutting, narrow valleys often contain *waterfalls* and *rapids*. When a stream has finished cutting downward, its energy is directed from side to side, and erosion produces a flat valley floor, or *floodplain*. Streams that flow on floodplains often move in sweeping bends called *meanders*. Widespread meandering may result in shorter channel segments, called *cutoffs*, and/or abandoned bends, called *oxbow lakes*. *Alluvial fans* or *deltas* form at the mouths of streams.
- The land area that contributes water to a stream is called a *drainage basin*. Drainage basins are

separated by an elongated topographic high called a *divide*. Common drainage patterns (the form of a network of streams) produced by a main channel and its tributaries include (1) *dendritic*, (2) *radial*, (3) *rectangular*, and (4) *trellis*.

- *Headward erosion* lengthens a stream course by extending the head of its valley upslope. This process can lead to *stream piracy* (the diversion of the drainage of one stream by another). Former water gaps, called wind gaps, can result from stream piracy.
- Floods are triggered by heavy rains or snowmelt. Sometimes human interference can worsen or even cause floods. Flood-control measures include the building of artificial levees and dams, as well as channellization, which could involve creating artificial cutoffs. Many scientists and engineers advocate a non-structural approach to flood control that involves more appropriate land use.

Review Questions

1. Describe the movement of water through the hydrologic cycle. Once precipitation has fallen on land, what paths are available to it?
2. Over the oceans, evaporation exceeds precipitation. Why does sea level not drop?
3. List several factors that influence infiltration capacity.
4. "Water in streams moves primarily in laminar flow." Briefly explain whether this statement is true or false.
5. A stream originates at 2000 metres above sea level and travels 250 kilometres to the ocean. What is its average gradient in metres per kilometre?
6. Suppose that the stream mentioned in question 5 developed extensive meanders so that its course was lengthened to 500 kilometres. Calculate this new gradient. How does meandering affect gradient?
7. When the discharge of a stream increases, what happens to the stream's velocity?
8. What typically happens to channel width, channel depth, velocity, and discharge from the point where a stream begins to the point where it ends? Briefly explain why these changes take place.
9. Why do most streams have low gradients near their mouths?
10. Describe three ways in which a stream can erode its channel. Which one of these is responsible for creating potholes?
11. If you were to collect a jar of water from a stream, what part of the load would settle to the bottom of the jar? What portion would remain in the water? What part of a stream's load would probably not be present in your sample?
12. What is settling velocity? What factors influence settling velocity?
13. Distinguish between capacity and competence.
14. What factors promote the frequent flooding of broad areas along the Red River? (See Box 15.1.)
15. Describe a situation that might cause a stream channel to become braided.
16. Briefly describe the formation of a natural levee. How is this feature related to back swamps and yazoo tributaries?
17. Define *base level*. Name the main river in your area. For what streams does it act a base level?
18. In what way is a delta similar to an alluvial fan? In what way are they different?
19. Why does a river flowing across a delta eventually change course?
20. Each of the following statements refers to a particular drainage pattern. Identify the pattern.
    (a) Streams diverging from a central high area, such as a dome
    (b) Branching, treelike pattern
    (c) A pattern that develops when bedrock is criss-crossed by joints and faults
21. Contrast regional floods and flash floods. Which type is deadliest?
22. List and briefly describe three basic flood-control strategies. What are some drawbacks of each?

Key Terms

alluvial fan (p. 406)
alluvium (p. 393)
anastomosed stream (p. 405)
back swamp (p. 403)
bank, stream (p. 384)
bar (p. 393)
base level (p. 394)
bed load (p. 389)
bed, stream (p. 384)
braided stream (p. 399)
capacity (p. 391)
competence (p. 391)
channel, stream (p. 384)
course, stream (p. 384)
cut bank (p. 401)
cutoff (p. 402)
delta (p. 406)
dendritic pattern (p. 408)
discharge (p. 386)
dissolved load (p. 389)
distributary (p. 407)
divide (p. 407)
drainage basin (p. 407)
evapotranspiration (p. 383)
flood (p. 382)
floodplain (p. 384)
graded stream (p. 393)
gradient (p. 384)
head (headwaters) (p. 384)
headward erosion (p. 410)
hydrologic cycle (p. 382)
infiltration (p. 383)
infiltration capacity (p. 384)
intrachannel bar (p. 393)
laminar flow (p. 385)
lateral accretion surface (p. 401)
local (temporary) base level (p. 394)
longitudinal profile (p. 384)
meander (p. 384)
meander scar (p. 402)
mouth (p. 384)
natural levee (p. 393)
oxbow lake (p. 402)
Playfair's law (p. 398)
point bar (p. 393)
pothole (p. 388)
radial pattern (p. 410)
rapids (p. 386)
reach, stream (p. 384)
rectangular pattern (p. 410)
recurrence interval (p. 411)
return period (p. 411)
rills (p. 384)
runoff (p. 383)
saltation (p. 390)
settling velocity (p. 390)
sheet flow (p. 384)
sorting (p.393)
stream (p. 384)
stream piracy (p. 410)
suspended load (p. 389)
temporary (local) base level (p. 395)
terrace (p. 405)
transpiration (p. 383)
trellis drainage pattern (p. 410)
turbulent flow (p. 385)
ultimate base level (p. 397)
waterfall (p. 395)
yazoo tributary (p. 403)

Web Resources

The *Earth* website uses the resources and flexibility of the internet to aid in your study of the topics in this chapter. Written and developed by geology instructors, this site will help improve your understanding of geology. Visit **www.pearsoned.ca/tarbuck** and click on the cover of the text to find

- online review quizzes
- Web-based critical thinking and writing exercises
- links to chapter-specific Web resources
- internet-wide key-term searches

www.pearsoned.ca/tarbuck

Chapter 16

Groundwater

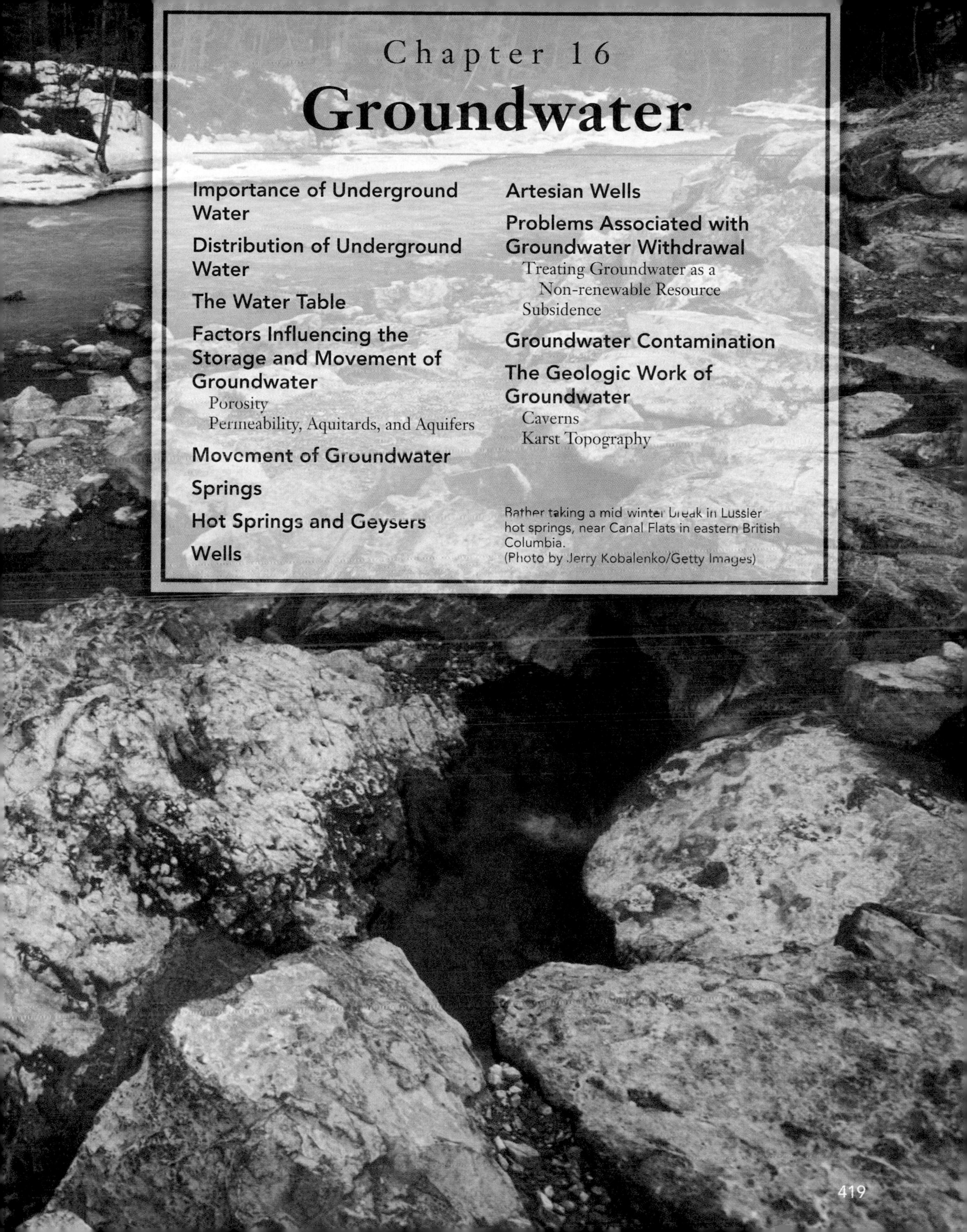

Bather taking a mid winter break in Lussier hot springs, near Canal Flats in eastern British Columbia.
(Photo by Jerry Kobalenko/Getty Images)

Worldwide, wells and springs provide water for cities, crops, livestock, and industry. Groundwater is the drinking water for more than 50 percent of the population, is 40 percent of the water used for irrigation, and provides more than 25 percent of industry's needs. In some areas, however, overuse of this basic resource has resulted in water shortage, stream flow depletion, land subsidence, increased pumping cost, and groundwater pollution.

IMPORTANCE OF UNDERGROUND WATER

GEODe EARTH Groundwater
↳ Importance and Distribution of Groundwater

Groundwater is one of our most important and widely available resources, yet people's perceptions of the subsurface environment from which it comes are commonly unclear and incorrect. The reason is that the groundwater environment is largely hidden from view except in caves and mines, and the impressions people gain from these subsurface openings are misleading. Observations made on the land surface give an impression that Earth is solid. This view remains when we enter a cave and see water flowing in a channel that appears to have been cut into solid rock.

Because of such observations, many people believe that groundwater occurs only in underground rivers. In reality, most of the subsurface environment is not solid at all. It includes countless tiny *pore spaces* between grains of soil and sediment, and narrow joints and fractures in bedrock. Together, these spaces add up to an immense volume. It is in these small openings that groundwater collects and moves.

Considering the entire hydrosphere, or all of Earth's water, only about 0.6 percent occurs underground. Nevertheless, this small percentage, stored in the rocks and sediments beneath Earth's surface, is a vast quantity. When the oceans are excluded and only sources of freshwater are considered, the significance of groundwater is more apparent.

Table 16.1 contains estimates of the distribution of fresh water in the hydrosphere. Clearly the largest volume occurs as glacial ice. Second in rank is groundwater, with slightly more than 14 percent of the total. However, when ice is excluded and just liquid water is considered, about 94 percent of all fresh water is groundwater. Without question, *groundwater represents the largest reservoir of fresh water that is readily available to humans*. Its value in terms of economics and human well-being is incalculable.

Geologically, groundwater is important as an erosional agent. The dissolving action of groundwater slowly removes soluble rock, such as limestone, allowing surface depressions known as sinkholes to form and creating subterranean caverns (Figure 16.1). Groundwater also moderates stream flow. Much of the water that flows in rivers is not direct runoff from rain and snowmelt. Rather, a large percentage of precipitation soaks in and then moves slowly underground to feed stream channels. Groundwater is thus a form of storage that sustains streams during periods when rain does not fall. The information in Table 16.1 reinforces this point. Here we see that the duration of exchange (residence time) for groundwater is 280 years. This figure represents the amount of time required to replace the water now stored underground. By contrast, the duration of water exchange for rivers is just slightly more than 11 days; if the groundwater supply to a river were cut off and no rain fell, the river would run dry in just more than 11 days. Thus, when we see water flowing in a river during a dry period, it represents rain that fell at some earlier time and was stored underground.

TABLE 16.1 **Fresh Water of the Hydrosphere**

Parts of the Hydrosphere	Volume of Fresh Water (km^3)	Share of Total Volume of Fresh Water (%)	Rate of Water Exchange
Ice sheets and glaciers	24,000,000	84.945	8000 years
Groundwater	4,000,000	14.158	280 years
Lakes and reservoirs	155,000	0.549	7 years
Soil moisture	83,000	0.294	1 year
Water vapour in the atmosphere	14,000	0.049	9.9 days
River water	1,200	0.004	11.3 days
Total	28,253,200	99.999	

Source: U.S. Geological Survey Water Supply Paper 2220, 1987.
Note: Total percentage does not equal exactly 100.000 because of rounding.

◆ **Figure 16.1** A view of the interior of Lehman Caves in Great Basin National Park, Nevada. The dissolving action of groundwater created the caverns. Later, groundwater deposited the limestone decorations.
(Photo by David Muench/David Muench Photography, Inc.)

DISTRIBUTION OF UNDERGROUND WATER

GEODe EARTH Groundwater
↳ Importance and Distribution of Groundwater

When rain falls, some of the water runs off, some evaporates, and the remainder infiltrates the ground. This last path is the primary source of practically all water underground. The amount of water that takes each of these paths, however, varies greatly in both time and space. Influential factors include steepness of slope, nature of surface material, intensity of rainfall, and type and amount of vegetation. Heavy rains falling on steep slopes underlain by impervious materials will obviously result in a high percentage of the water running off. Conversely, if rain falls steadily and gently on more gradual slopes composed of materials that are easily penetrated by the water, a much larger percentage of water soaks into the ground.

Some of the water that soaks in does not travel far because it is held by molecular attraction as a surface film on soil particles. This near-surface zone is called the **belt of soil moisture**. It is criss-crossed by roots, voids left by decayed roots, and animal and worm burrows that all enhance the infiltration of rainwater into the soil. Soil water is used in life functions and transpiration by plants. Some water also evaporates directly back into the atmosphere.

Water that is not held as soil moisture percolates downward until it reaches a zone where all of the open spaces in sediment and rock are completely filled with water (Figure 16.2). This is the **zone of saturation** or phreatic zone. Water within this zone is called **groundwater**.

The upper limit of this zone is known as the **water table**. Extending upward from the water table is the **capillary fringe** (*capillus* = hair). Here groundwater is held by surface tension in tiny passages between grains of soil or sediment. The area above the water table that includes the capillary fringe and the belt of soil moisture is called the **zone of aeration** or vadose zone. Although a considerable amount of water can be present in the zone of aeration, this water cannot be pumped by wells because it clings too tightly to rock and soil particles. By contrast, below the water table, the water pressure is great enough to allow water to enter wells, thus permitting groundwater to be withdrawn for use. We will examine wells more closely later in the chapter.

THE WATER TABLE

GEODe EARTH Groundwater
↳ Importance and Distribution of Groundwater

The water table, the upper limit of the zone of saturation, is a very significant feature of the groundwater system. The water table level is important in predicting the productivity of wells, explaining the changes in the flow of springs and streams, and accounting for fluctuations in the levels of lakes.

The depth of the water table is highly variable and can range from zero, at the surface, to hundreds of metres in some places. An important characteristic of the water table is that its configuration varies seasonally and yearly because the addition of water to the groundwater system is closely related to the quantity, distribution, and timing of precipitation.

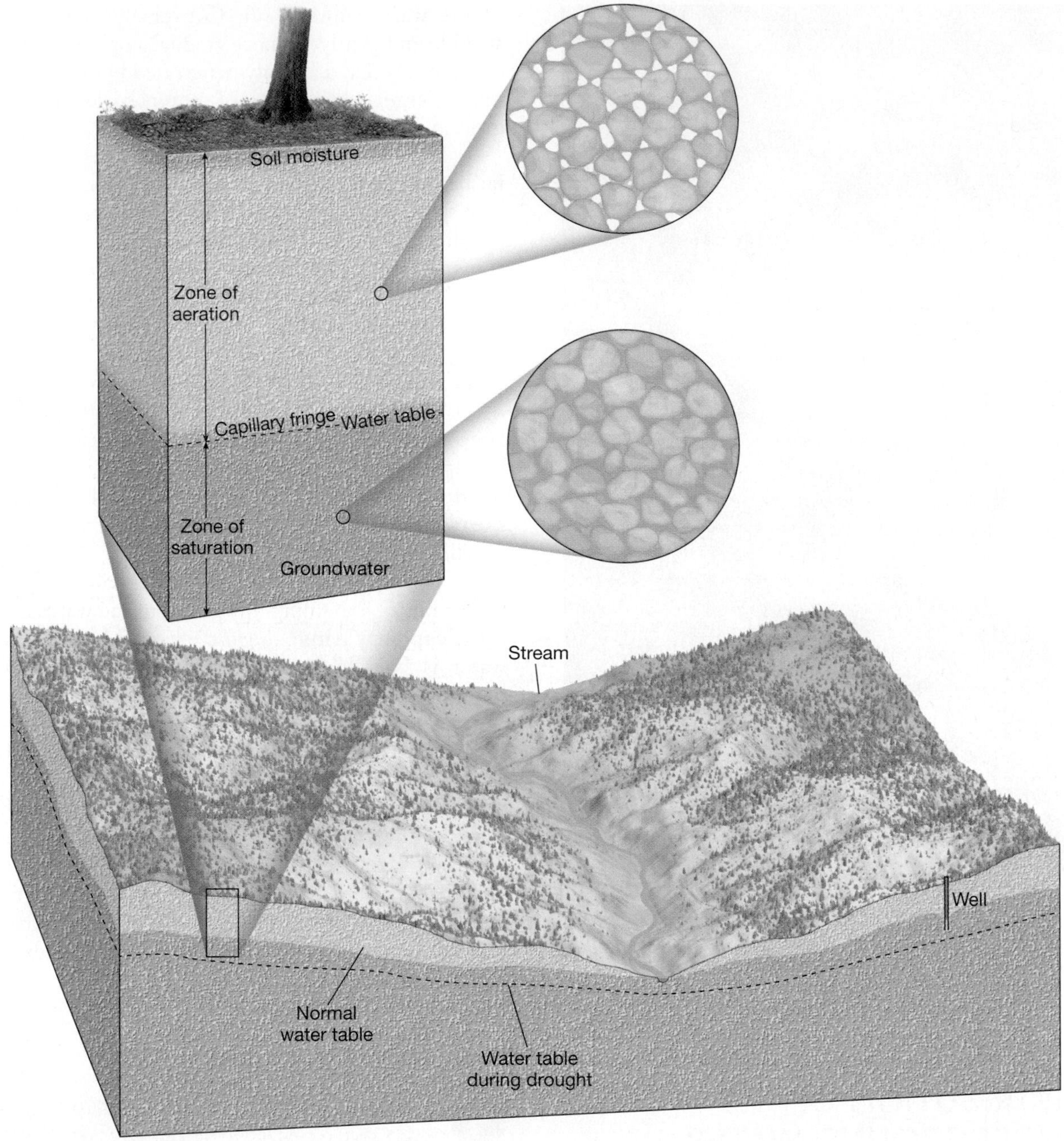

◆ **Figure 16.2** Distribution of underground water. The shape of the water table is usually a subdued replica of the surface topography. During periods of drought, the water table falls, reducing stream flow and drying up some wells.

Except where the water table is at the surface, we cannot observe it directly. Nevertheless, its elevation can be mapped and studied in detail where wells are numerous because the water level in wells coincides with the water table (Figure 16.3). Such maps reveal that the water table is rarely level, as we might expect a table to be. Instead, its shape is usually a subdued replica of the surface topography, reaching its highest elevations beneath hills and then descending toward valleys (Figure 16.2). Wetlands (swamps) occur where the water table is right at the surface. Lakes and streams generally occupy areas low enough that the water table is above the land surface.

Several factors contribute to the irregular surface of the water table. One important influence is the fact that groundwater moves very slowly and at varying rates under different conditions. Because of this, water tends to "pile up" beneath high areas between stream valleys. If rainfall were to cease completely, these water-table hills would slowly subside

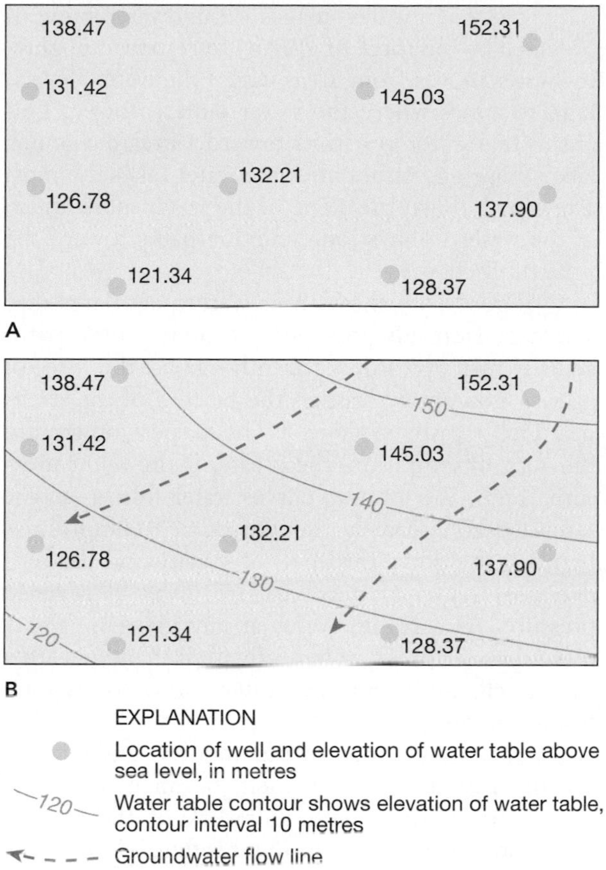

Figure 16.3 Preparing a map of the water table. The water level in wells coincides with the water table. **A.** First, the locations of wells and the elevation of the water table above sea level are plotted on a map. **B.** These data points are used to guide the drawing of water-table contour lines at regular intervals. On this sample map the interval is 10 metres. Groundwater flow lines can be added to show water movement in the upper portion of the zone of saturation. Groundwater tends to move approximately perpendicular to the contours and down the slope of the water table.

and gradually approach the level of the valleys. However, new supplies of rainwater are usually added frequently enough to prevent this. Nevertheless, in times of extended drought, the water table may drop enough to dry up shallow wells (Figure 16.2). Other causes for the uneven water table are variations in rainfall and permeability from place to place.

FACTORS INFLUENCING THE STORAGE AND MOVEMENT OF GROUNDWATER

The nature of subsurface materials strongly influences the rate of groundwater movement and the amount of groundwater that can be stored. Two factors are especially important: porosity and permeability.

Porosity

Water soaks into the ground because bedrock, sediment, and soil contain countless voids or openings. These openings are similar to those of a sponge and are commonly called pore spaces. The quantity of groundwater that can be stored depends on the **porosity** of the material, which is the percentage of the total volume of rock or sediment that consists of pore spaces. Voids most often are spaces between sedimentary particles, but also common are joints; faults; cavities formed by the dissolving of soluble rock, such as limestone; and vesicles (voids left by gases escaping from lava).

Variations in porosity can be great. Sediment is commonly quite porous, and open spaces may occupy 10 percent to 50 percent of the sediment's total volume. Pore space depends on the size and shape of the grains, how they are packed together, the degree of sorting, and, in sedimentary rocks, the amount of cementing material. For example, clay may have a porosity as high as 50 percent, whereas some gravels may have only 20 percent voids.

Where sediments of various sizes are mixed, the porosity is reduced because the finer particles tend to fill the openings among the larger grains. Most igneous and metamorphic rocks, as well as some sedimentary rocks, are composed of tightly interlocking crystals, so the voids between the grains may be negligible. In these rocks, fractures must provide the voids.

Permeability, Aquitards, and Aquifers

Porosity alone cannot measure a material's capacity to yield groundwater. Rock or sediment may be very porous yet still not allow water to move through it. The pores must be *connected* to allow water flow, and they must be *large enough* to allow flow. Thus, the **permeability** (*permeare* = to penetrate) of a material—its ability to *transmit* a fluid—is also very important.

Groundwater moves by twisting and turning through small, interconnected openings. The smaller the pore spaces, the slower the water moves. This idea is clearly illustrated by examining the information about the water-yielding potential of different materials in Table 16.2. Here groundwater is divided into two categories: (1) the portion that will drain under the influence of gravity (called *specific yield*) and (2) the part that is retained as a film on particle and rock surfaces and in tiny openings (called

TABLE 16.2 Selected Values of Porosity, Specific Yield, and Specific Retention*

Material	Porosity	Specific Yield	Specific Retention
Clay	50	2	48
Sand	25	22	3
Gravel	20	19	1
Limestone	20	18	2
Sandstone (semiconsolidated)	11	6	5
Granite	0.1	0.09	0.01
Basalt (fresh)	11	8	3

*Values in percentage by volume
Source: U.S. Geological Survey Water Supply Paper 2220, 1987.

specific retention). Specific yield indicates how much water is actually available for use, whereas specific retention indicates how much water remains bound in the material. For example, clay's ability to store water is great, owing to its high porosity, but its pore spaces are so small that water is unable to move through it. Thus, clay's porosity is high but because its permeability is poor, clay has a very low specific yield.

Impermeable layers that hinder or prevent water movement are termed **aquitards** (*aqua* = water, *tard* = slow). Clay is a good example. Conversely, larger particles, such as sand or gravel, have larger pore spaces. Therefore, the water moves with relative ease. Permeable rock strata or sediment that transmit groundwater freely are called **aquifers** (*aqua* = water, *fer* = carry). Sands and gravels are common examples.

In summary, you have seen that porosity is not always a reliable guide to the amount of groundwater that can be produced, and permeability is significant in determining the rate of groundwater movement and the quantity of water that can be pumped from a well.

MOVEMENT OF GROUNDWATER

We noted the common misconception that groundwater occurs in underground rivers that resemble surface streams. Although subsurface streams do exist, they are not common. Rather, as you learned in the preceding sections, groundwater exists in the pore spaces and fractures in rock and sediment. Thus, contrary to any impressions of rapid flow that an underground river might evoke, the movement of most groundwater from pore to pore is exceedingly slow—typically a few centimetres each day.

The energy that makes groundwater move is provided by the force of gravity. In response to gravity, water moves from areas where the water table is high to zones where the water table is lower. This means that water gravitates toward a stream channel, lake, or spring. Although some water takes the most direct path down the slope of the water table, much of the water follows long, curving paths toward the zone of discharge.

Figure 16.4 shows how water percolates into a stream from all possible directions. Some paths actually turn upward, apparently against the force of gravity, and enter through the bottom of the channel. This is easily explained: The deeper you go into the zone of saturation, the greater is the water pressure. Thus, the looping curves water follows in the saturated zone can be thought of as a compromise between the downward pull of gravity and the tendency of water to move toward areas of reduced pressure. As a result, water at any given height is under greater pressure beneath a hill than beneath a stream channel, and the water tends to migrate toward points of lower pressure.

The foundations of our modern understanding of groundwater movement began in the mid-nineteenth century with the work of the French engineer Henri Darcy. During this time, Darcy made measurements and conducted experiments in an attempt to determine whether the water needs of the city of Dijon in east-central France could be met by tapping local supplies of groundwater. Among the experiments carried out by Darcy was one that showed that the velocity of groundwater flow is proportional to the slope of the water table—the steeper the slope, the faster the water moves (because the steeper the slope, the greater the pressure difference between two points). The water-table slope, known as the **hydraulic gradient**, is determined by dividing

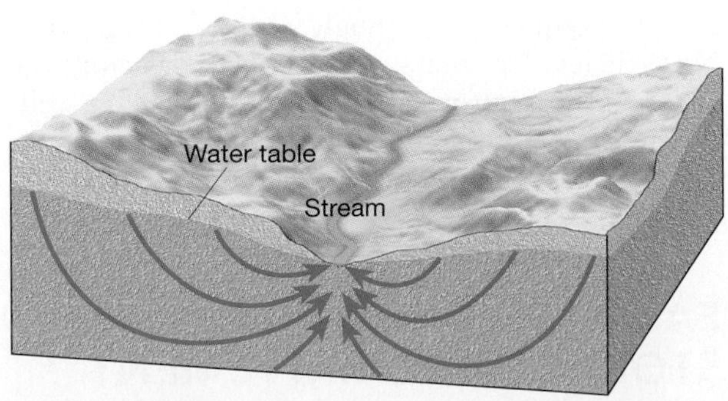

◆ **Figure 16.4** Arrows indicate groundwater movement through uniformly permeable material. The looping curves can be thought of as a compromise between the downward pull of gravity and the tendency of water to move toward areas of reduced pressure.

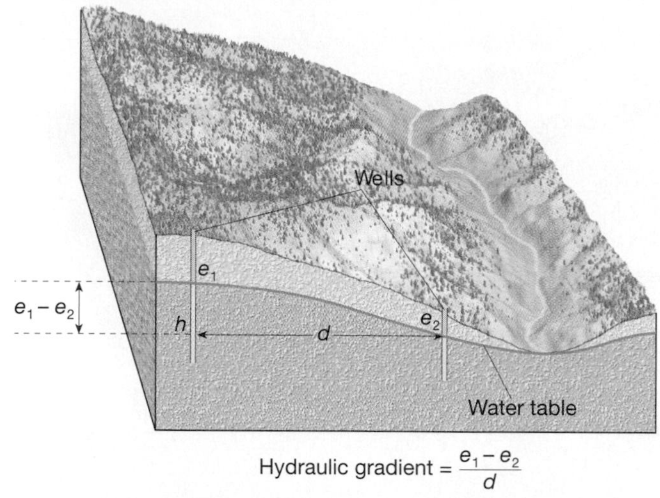

◆ **Figure 16.5** The hydraulic gradient is determined by measuring the difference in elevation between two points on the water table ($h_1 - h_2$) divided by the distance between them, *d*. Wells are used to determine the elevation of the water table.

the vertical difference between the recharge and discharge points (a quantity known as the **head**) by the length of flow between these points (Figure 16.5).

Darcy also experimented with different materials, such as coarse sand and fine sand, by measuring the rate of flow through sediment-filled tubes that were tilted at varying angles. He found that the flow velocity varied with the permeability of the sediment—groundwater flows more rapidly through sediments having greater permeability than through materials having lower permeability. This factor is known as **hydraulic conductivity** and is a coefficient that takes into account the permeability of the aquifer and the viscosity of the fluid. **Darcy's law**, named in honour of the pioneering French scientist-engineer, can be expressed by the following formula:

$$V = \frac{K}{n} \bullet \frac{h}{l}$$

where V represents groundwater velocity, n the porosity, h the head, l the length of flow, and K a coefficient that accounts for a material's permeability.

SPRINGS

GEODe EARTH Groundwater
↳ Springs and Wells

Springs have aroused people's curiosity and inspired wonder for thousands of years. The fact that springs were, and to some people still are, rather mysterious phenomena is not difficult to understand, for here is water flowing freely from the ground in all kinds of weather in seemingly inexhaustible supply, but with no obvious source.

Not until the middle of the seventeenth century did the French physicist Pierre Perrault invalidate the age-old assumption that precipitation could not adequately account for the amount of water emanating from springs and flowing in rivers. Over several years Perrault computed the quantity of water that fell on France's Seine River basin. He then calculated the mean annual runoff by measuring the river's discharge. After allowing for the loss of water by evaporation, he showed that sufficient water remained to feed the springs. Thanks to Perrault's pioneering efforts and the measurements by many others afterward, we now know that the source of springs is water from the zone of saturation and that the ultimate source of this water is precipitation.

Whenever the water table intersects Earth's surface, a natural outflow of groundwater results, which we call a **spring** (Figure 16.6). Springs, such as the one pictured in Figure 16.6, form when an aquitard

◆ **Figure 16.6** Spring in Arizona's Marble Canyon. (Photo by Michael Collier)

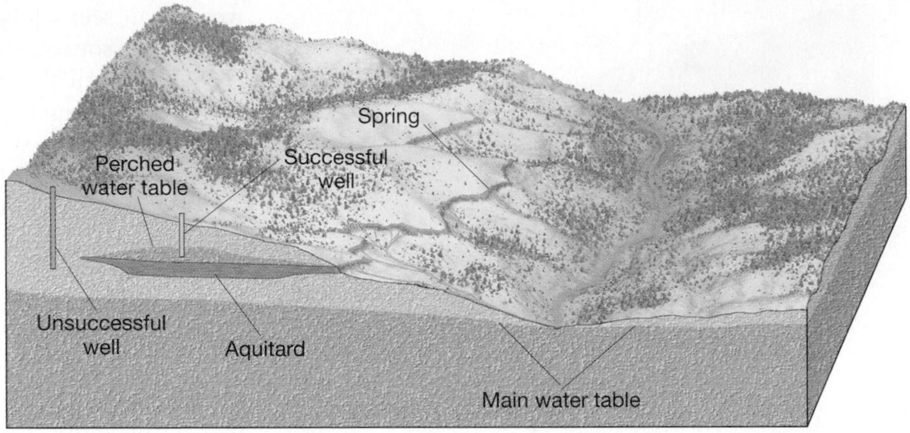

◆ **Figure 16.7** When an aquitard is situated above the main water table, a localized zone of saturation may result. Where the perched water table intersects the side of the valley, a spring flows. The perched water table also caused the well on the right to be successful, whereas the well on the left will be unsuccessful unless it is drilled to a greater depth.

blocks the downward movement of groundwater and forces it to move laterally. Where the permeable bed crops out, a spring results. Another situation leading to the formation of a spring is illustrated in Figure 16.7. Here, an aquitard is situated above the main water table. As water percolates downward, a portion of it is intercepted by the aquitard, thereby creating a localized zone of saturation and a **perched water table**.

Springs, however, are not confined to places where a perched water table creates a flow at the surface. Many geologic situations lead to the formation of springs because subsurface conditions vary greatly from place to place. Even in areas underlain by impermeable crystalline rocks, permeable zones may exist in the form of fractures or solution channels. If these openings fill with water and intersect the ground surface along a slope, a spring will result.

HOT SPRINGS AND GEYSERS

By definition, the water in **hot springs** is 6°C to 9°C warmer than the mean annual air temperature for the localities in which they occur. Temperatures in deep mines and oil wells usually rise with increasing depth, an average of about 2°C per 100 metres. Therefore, when groundwater circulates at great depths, it becomes heated. If it rises to the surface, the water may emerge as a hot spring. The water of some hot springs in the eastern United States is heated in this manner. However, the great majority (over 95 percent) of the hot springs (and geysers) in North America, including those in Banff (Figure 16.8), Alberta, and in Harrison, Lakelse, and Canal Flats, British Columbia (chapter-opening photo), are found in the west. The reason for such a distribution is that the source of heat for most hot

◆ **Figure 16.8** The hot springs in Banff, Alberta, attract tourists from all over the world. The water feeding these springs enters faults in the Alberta Rockies, where it is gently heated because of the high geothermal gradient in this region. The heated water emerges in springs located at the base of the mountains. (Photo by Kristin Singh)

springs is cooling igneous rock, and it is in the west that igneous activity has occurred more recently.

Geysers are intermittent hot springs or fountains in which columns of water are ejected with great force at various intervals, often rising 30 to 60 metres into the air. After the jet of water ceases, a column of steam rushes out, usually with a thunderous roar. Perhaps the most famous geyser in the world is Old Faithful in Yellowstone National Park, Wyoming, which erupts about once each hour (Figure 16.9). The great abundance, diversity, and spectacular nature of Yellowstone's geysers and other thermal features undoubtedly were the primary reason for it becoming the first national park in the United States. Geysers are also found in other parts of the world, notably New Zealand and Iceland. In fact, the Icelandic word *geysa*, "to gush," gives us the name *geyser*.

Geysers occur where extensive underground chambers exist within hot igneous rocks. How they operate is shown in Figure 16.10. As relatively cool groundwater enters the chambers, it is heated by the surrounding rock. At the bottom of the chambers, the water is under great pressure because of the weight of the overlying water. This great pressure

◆ **Figure 16.9** A wintertime eruption of Old Faithful, one of the world's most famous geysers. It emits as much as 45,000 litres of hot water and steam about once each hour. (Photo by Marc Muench, David Muench Photography, Inc.)

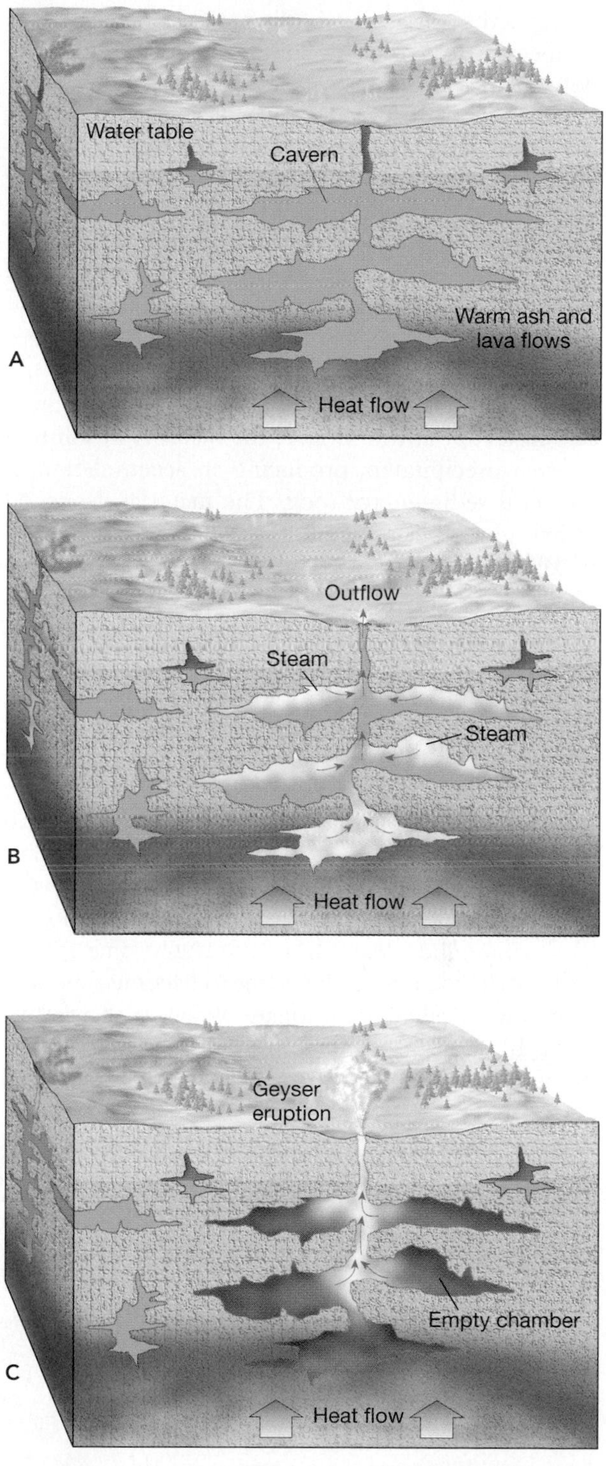

◆ **Figure 16.10** Idealized diagrams of a geyser. A geyser can form if the heat is not distributed by convection. **A.** In this figure, the water near the bottom is heated to near its boiling point. The boiling point is higher there than at the surface because the weight of the water above increases the pressure. **B.** The water higher in the geyser system is also heated; therefore, it expands and flows out at the top, reducing the pressure on the water at the bottom. **C.** At the reduced pressure on the bottom, boiling occurs. Some of the bottom water flashes into steam, and the expanding steam causes an eruption.

prevents the water from boiling at the normal surface temperature of 100°C. For example, water at the bottom of a 300-metre water-filled chamber must attain nearly 230°C before it will boil. The heating causes the water to expand, with the result that some is forced out at the surface. This loss of water reduces the pressure on the remaining water in the chamber, which lowers the boiling point. A portion of the water deep within the chamber quickly turns to steam, and the geyser erupts (Figure 16.10). Following eruption, cool groundwater again seeps into the chamber and the cycle begins anew.

When groundwater from hot springs and geysers flows out at the surface, the material in solution is often precipitated, producing an accumulation of chemical sedimentary rock. The material deposited at any given place commonly reflects the chemical makeup of the rock through which the water circulated. When the water contains dissolved silica, a material called *siliceous sinter* or *geyserite* is deposited around the spring. When the water contains dissolved calcium carbonate, a form of limestone called *travertine* or *calcareous tufa* is deposited. The latter term is used if the material is spongy and porous.

The deposits at Mammoth Hot Springs in Yellowstone National Park are more spectacular than most (Figure 16.11). As the hot water flows upward through a series of channels and then out at the surface, the reduced pressure allows carbon dioxide to separate and escape from the water. The loss of carbon dioxide causes the water to become supersaturated with calcium carbonate, which then precipitates. In addition to containing dissolved silica and calcium carbonate, some hot springs contain sulphur, which gives water a poor taste and unpleasant odour. Undoubtedly, Rotten Egg Spring, Nevada, is such a situation.

WELLS

GEODe EARTH Groundwater
↳ Springs and Wells

The most common method for removing groundwater is the **well**, a hole bored into the zone of saturation. Wells serve as small reservoirs into which groundwater migrates and from which it can be pumped to the surface. The use of wells dates back many centuries and continues to be an important method of obtaining water today. By far the single greatest use of this water in North America is irrigation for agriculture. More than 65 percent of the groundwater used each year serves this purpose. Industrial uses rank a distant second, followed by the amount used in city water systems and rural homes.

The water-table level may fluctuate considerably during the course of a year, dropping during the dry seasons and rising following periods of rain. Therefore, to ensure a continuous supply of water, a well must penetrate below the water table. Whenever water is withdrawn from a well, the water table around the well is lowered. This effect, termed **drawdown**, decreases with increasing distance from the well. The result is a depression in the water table, roughly conical in shape, known as a **cone of depression** (Figure 16.12). Because the cone of depression increases the hydraulic gradient near the well, groundwater will flow more rapidly toward the

◆ **Figure 16.11** Mammoth Hot Springs at Yellowstone National Park. Although most of the deposits associated with geysers and hot springs in Yellowstone Park are silica-rich geyserite, the deposits at Mammoth Hot Springs consist of a form of limestone called travertine. (Photo by Stephen Trimble)

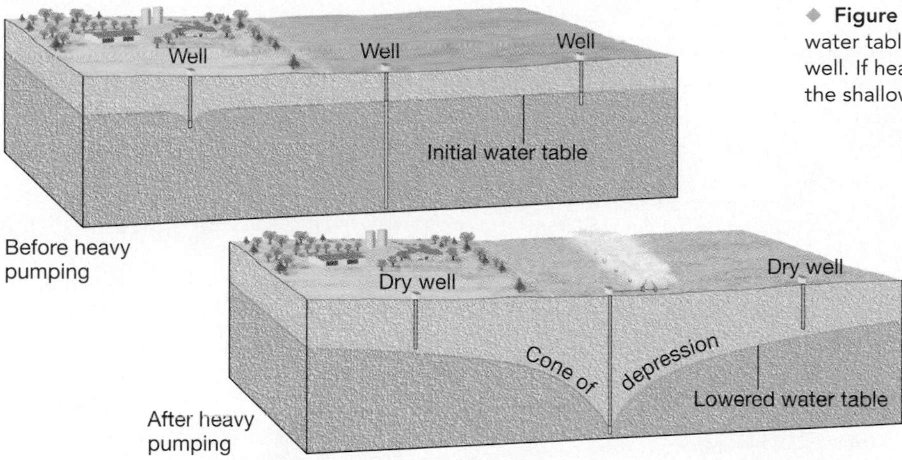

◆ **Figure 16.12** A cone of depression in the water table often forms around a pumping well. If heavy pumping lowers the water table, the shallow wells may be left dry.

opening. For smaller domestic wells, the cone of depression is negligible. However, when wells are heavily pumped for irrigation or for industrial purposes, the withdrawal of water can be great enough to create a very wide and steep cone of depression. This may substantially lower the water table in an area and cause nearby shallow wells to become dry. Figure 16.12 illustrates this situation.

Digging a successful well is a familiar problem for people in areas where groundwater is the primary source of supply. One well may be successful at a depth of 10 metres whereas a neighbour may have to go twice as deep to find an adequate supply. Still others may be forced to go deeper or try a different site altogether. When subsurface materials are heterogeneous, the amount of water a well is capable of providing may vary a great deal over short distances. For example, when two nearby wells are drilled to the same level and only one is successful, it may be caused by the presence of a perched water table beneath one of them. Such a case is shown in Figure 16.7. Massive igneous and metamorphic rocks provide a second example. These crystalline rocks are usually not very permeable except where they are cut by many intersecting joints and fractures. Therefore, when a well drilled into such rock does not intersect an adequate network of fractures, it is likely to be unproductive.

ARTESIAN WELLS

GEODe EARTH Groundwater
↳ Springs and Wells

In most wells, water cannot rise on its own. If water is first encountered at 30 metres depth, it remains at that level, fluctuating perhaps a metre or two with seasonal wet and dry periods. However, in some wells, water rises, sometimes overflowing at the surface. Such wells are abundant in the Artois region of northern France, and so we call these self-rising wells artesian.

To many people the term *artesian* is applied to any well drilled to great depths. This use of the term is incorrect. Others believe that an artesian well must flow freely at the surface (Figure 16.13). Although this is a more correct notion than the first, it represents too narrow a definition. The term **artesian** is applied to *any* situation in which groundwater under pressure rises above the level of the aquifer. As you will see, this does not always mean a free-flowing surface discharge.

For an artesian system to exist, two conditions must be met (Figure 16.14): (1) water must be confined to an aquifer that is inclined so that one end can receive water; and (2) aquitards, both above and below the aquifer (making it a *confined aquifer*), must be present to prevent the water from escaping. When such a layer is tapped, the pressure created by

◆ **Figure 16.13** Sometimes water flows freely at the surface when an artesian well is developed. However, for most artesian wells, the water must be pumped to the surface. (Photo by James E. Patterson)

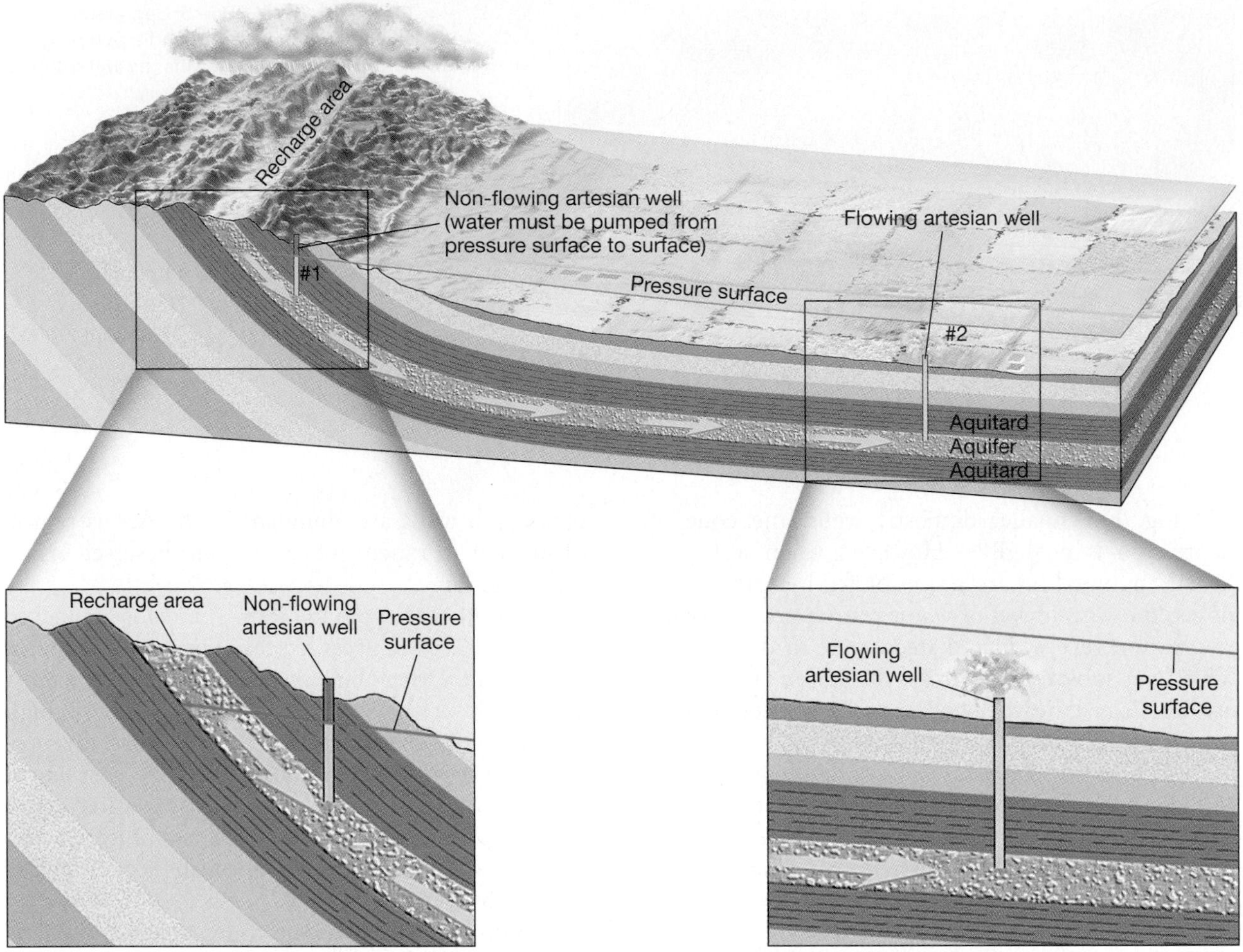

◆ **Figure 16.14** Artesian systems occur when an inclined aquifer is surrounded by impermeable beds.

the weight of the water above will force the water to rise. If there were no friction, the water in the well would rise to the level of the water at the top of the aquifer. However, friction reduces the height of the pressure surface. The greater the distance from the recharge area (where water enters the inclined aquifer), the greater the friction and the less the rise of water.

In Figure 16.14, well 1 is a **non-flowing artesian well**, because at this location the pressure surface is below ground level. When the pressure surface is above the ground and a well is drilled into the aquifer, a **flowing artesian well** is created (well 2, Figure 16.14, and Figure 16.15). Not all artesian systems are wells. *Artesian springs* also exist in which groundwater reaches the surface by rising through a natural fracture rather than through an artificially produced hole. In deserts, artesian springs can create an oasis.

Artesian systems act as conduits, often transmitting water great distances from remote areas of recharge to points of discharge. A well-known artesian system in South Dakota is a good example of this. In the western part of the state, the edges of a series of sedimentary layers have been bent up to the surface along the flanks of the Black Hills. One of these beds, the permeable Dakota Sandstone, is sandwiched between impermeable strata and gradually dips into the ground toward the east. When the aquifer was first tapped, water poured from the ground surface, creating fountains many metres high (Figure 16.15). In some places the force of the water was sufficient to power waterwheels. Such scenes as the one pictured in Figure 16.15, however, can no longer occur, because thousands of additional wells now tap the same aquifer. This depleted the reservoir, and the water table in the recharge area was lowered. As a consequence, the pressure dropped to the point where many wells stopped flowing altogether and had to be pumped.

On a different scale, city water systems can be considered examples of artificial artesian systems (Figure 16.16). The water tower, into which water is pumped, would represent the area of recharge, the

◆ **Figure 16.15** A gusher-like flowing artesian well in South Dakota in the early part of the twentieth century. Thousands of additional wells now tap the same confined aquifer; thus, the pressure has dropped to the point where many wells have stopped flowing altogether and have to be pumped. (Photo by N. H. Darton, U.S. Geological Survey)

pipes are the confined aquifer, and the faucets in homes are the flowing artesian wells.

PROBLEMS ASSOCIATED WITH GROUNDWATER WITHDRAWAL

As with many of our valuable natural resources, groundwater is being exploited at an increasing rate. In some areas, overuse threatens the groundwater supply. In other places, groundwater withdrawal has caused the ground and everything resting on it to sink. Still other localities are concerned with the possible contamination of the groundwater supply.

Treating Groundwater as a Non-renewable Resource

Many natural systems tend to establish a condition of equilibrium. The groundwater system is no exception. The water table's height reflects a balance between the rate of infiltration and the rate of discharge and withdrawal. Any imbalance will either raise or lower the water table. Long-term imbalances can lead to a significant drop in the water table if either a decrease in recharge because of prolonged drought or an increase in groundwater discharge or withdrawal occurs.

For many, groundwater appears to be an endlessly renewable resource because it is continually replenished by rainfall and melting snow. But in some regions, groundwater has been and is a *non-renewable* resource. Where this occurs, the water available to recharge the aquifer falls significantly short of the amount being withdrawn.

The High Plains of the United States provides one example, where an extensive agricultural economy is largely dependent on irrigation (Figure 16.17). In some parts of the region, where intense irrigation has been practised for an extended period, depletion of groundwater has been severe. Under these circumstances, it can be said that the groundwater is literally being mined. Even if pumping were to cease immediately, it could take hundreds or thousands of years for the groundwater to be fully replenished.

Subsidence

As you will see later in this chapter, surface subsidence can result from natural processes related to groundwater. However, the ground can also sink when water is pumped from wells faster than natural recharge processes can replace it. This effect is particularly pronounced in areas underlain by thick layers of unconsolidated sediments. As the water is withdrawn, the water pressure drops and the weight of the overburden is transferred to the sediment. The greater pressure packs the sediment grains tightly together, and the ground subsides.

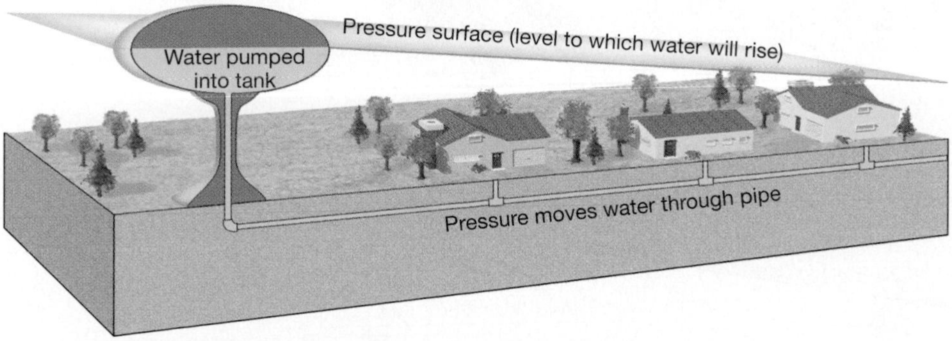

◆ **Figure 16.16** City water systems can be considered to be artificial artesian systems.

◆ **Figure 16.17** In some agricultural regions, water is pumped from the ground faster than it is replenished. In such instances, groundwater is being treated as a non-renewable resource. (Photo by Bill Kamin/Visuals Unlimited)

Many areas can be used to illustrate land subsidence caused by the excessive pumping of groundwater from relatively loose sediment, including the Italian coastal city of Venice. A classic example occurred in the San Joaquin Valley of California, where the ground surface subsided 8.5 metres between 1925 and 1977. Other cases of land subsidence because of groundwater pumping include Las Vegas, Nevada; New Orleans and Baton Rouge, Louisiana; and the Houston-Galveston area of Texas. In the low-lying coastal area between Houston and Galveston, land subsidence ranges from 1.5 to 3 metres. The result is that about 78 square kilometres are permanently flooded.

One of the most spectacular examples of subsidence occurred in Mexico City, which is built on a former lakebed. In the first half of the twentieth century, thousands of wells were sunk into the water-saturated sediments beneath the city. As water was withdrawn, portions of the city subsided by as much as 6 to 7 metres. In some places buildings have sunk so far that access to them from the street is located at what used to be the second-floor level!

GROUNDWATER CONTAMINATION

The pollution of groundwater is a serious matter, particularly in areas where aquifers provide a large part of the water supply. One common source of groundwater pollution is sewage. Its sources include an increasing number of septic tanks, inadequate or broken sewer systems, and farm wastes.

If sewage water that is contaminated with bacteria enters the groundwater system, it may become purified through natural processes. The harmful bacteria can be mechanically filtered by the sediment through which the water percolates, destroyed by chemical oxidation, or assimilated by other organisms.

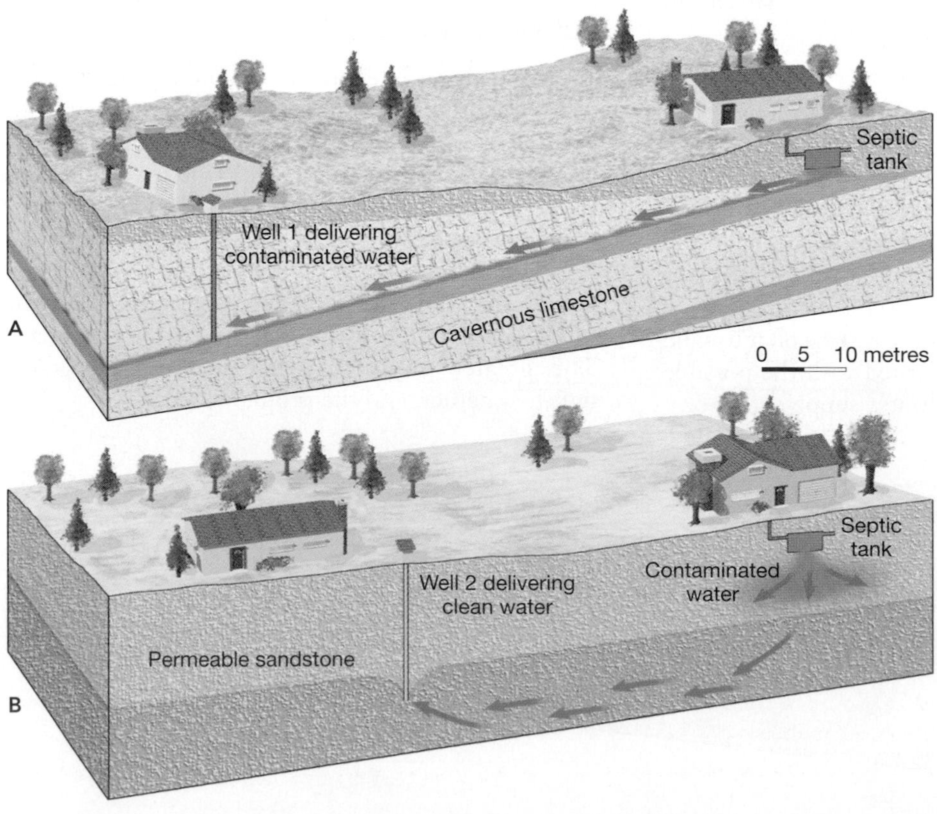

◆ **Figure 16.18** **A.** Although the contaminated water has travelled more than 100 metres before reaching well 1, the water moves too rapidly through the cavernous limestone to be purified. **B.** As the discharge from the septic tank percolates through the permeable sandstone, it is purified in a relatively short distance.

For purification to occur, however, the aquifer must be of the correct composition. For example, extremely permeable aquifers (such as highly fractured crystalline rock, coarse gravel, or cavernous limestone) have such large openings that contaminated groundwater can travel long distances without being cleansed. In this case, the water flows too rapidly and is not in contact with the surrounding material long enough for purification to occur. This is the problem at well 1 in Figure 16.18A. As learned by the people of Walkerton, Ontario, in 2000, such circumstances can lead to disaster (Box 16.1).

Conversely, when the aquifer is composed of sand or permeable sandstone, water can sometimes be

BOX 16.1

Canadian Profile

The Walkerton Tragedy: Geology Forms the Link

Robert A. Schincariol*

In May 2000 the people of Walkerton, Ontario, learned first hand how their groundwater-derived water supply was directly linked to surface activities. Seven people died and 2300 fell ill when their water system became contaminated with deadly bacteria, primarily *Escherichia coli* (E. coli O157:H7). This virulent form of E. coli is known to originate in the digestive system of cattle. The causes of this outbreak were investigated by the Walkerton Inquiry and resulted in a major overhaul of Ontario's drinking water regulations.

◆ **Figure 16.A** Aerial view of well 5 and adjacent farm near Walkerton, Ontario. Lot 20 contains the livestock barn and yard on which approximately 70 tonnes of manure was spread.
(Photo by Marc Bolduc, RCMP)

Although the cause of contamination was manure spread on a farm near one of the town's wells (well 5; Figure 16.A), ultimately the mistakes of many people and agencies allowed the problems to go undetected. If they had been more aware of the subsurface environment that provided the groundwater supply, the tragedy would not have happened. In fact, the inquiry report stated, "Both geology and hydrogeology are crucial factors in understanding why the contamination in May 2000 was able to enter well 5."

The problem revolved around well 5, which obtained water from a very shallow and vulnerable bedrock aquifer that was shown to be susceptible to contamination by bacteria because it was under the *direct influence* of surface water. In a secure groundwater source (no direct influence), surface water will infiltrate through overburden materials (topsoil, clay, silt, sand) and through bedrock. This infiltration process is slow (months, years, or even decades) and bacteria and viruses are usually filtered out or die off. However, where these overburden materials are thin or ineffective because of natural features (fractures, sand and gravel lenses) or human-induced features (fencepost holes, improperly abandoned or sealed wells) replenishment of the bedrock aquifer can be rapid. An interconnected network of fractures provides a ready pathway for groundwater flow. If the bedrock porosity of these fractured zones is very low, it can result in high groundwater velocities through fractures (see Darcy's law), allowing little time for filtration.

Well 5 was drilled in a weathered, fractured, and vertically jointed fine-grained dolostone. Overlying this shallow bedrock aquifer is as little as 2.4 metres of overburden deposits consisting of topsoil, till, sand, and gravel. Downhole testing at well 5 indicated that most pumped water was being derived from a zone between 5 and 7 metres below ground surface. The overburden and shallow bedrock aquifer are well interconnected, allowing rapid flow of groundwater and contaminants. In addition, a shallow water table existed at well 5 and heavy rainfall or ponded conditions resulted in the rapid downward migration of manure contaminants to the bedrock aquifer and into well 5.

Another avenue of surface water–groundwater connection was an unsealed test well, located only 6 metres from well 5, which provided a direct pathway for surface water or shallow groundwater to access the aquifer. This well likely provided a rapid route for groundwater flow, bypassing the natural aquifer materials that can filter out harmful microbes.

The incoming contamination overwhelmed the chlorine being added at the well and sufficient chlorine residuals were not maintained. This was aggravated by the fact that the operators of the Walkerton water system routinely used less chlorine than was required. Had continuous chlorine residual been maintained at well 5, the outbreak could have been prevented.

---

*Robert A. Schincariol is a professor in the Department of Earth Sciences at University of Western Ontario.

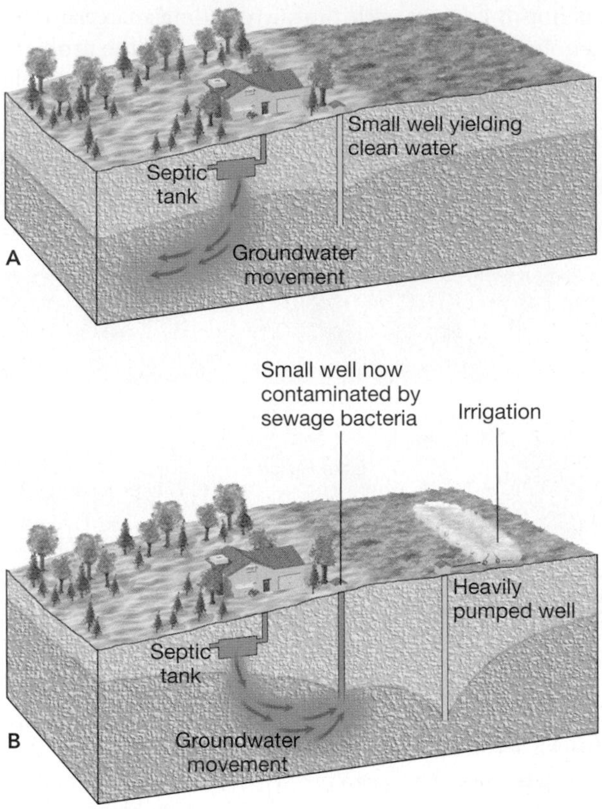

◆ **Figure 16.19** **A.** Originally the outflow from the septic tank moved away from the small well. **B.** The heavily pumped well changed the slope of the water table, causing contaminated groundwater to flow toward the small well.

purified after travelling only a few dozen metres through it. The openings between sand grains are large enough to permit water movement, yet the movement of the water is slow enough to allow ample time for its purification (well 2, Figure 16.18B).

Sometimes sinking a well can lead to groundwater pollution problems. If the well pumps a sufficient quantity of water, the cone of depression will locally increase the slope of the water table. In some instances the original slope can even be reversed. This could lead to the contamination of wells that yielded unpolluted water before heavy pumping began (Figure 16.19). Also recall that the rate of groundwater movement increases as the slope of the water table gets steeper. This could produce problems because a faster rate of movement allows less time for the water to be purified in the aquifer before it is pumped to the surface.

Other sources and types of contamination also threaten groundwater supplies (Figure 16.20). These include widely used substances, such as highway salt, fertilizers that are spread across the land surface, and pesticides. In addition, a wide array of chemicals and industrial materials may leak from pipelines, storage tanks, landfills, and holding ponds. Some of these pollutants are classified as *hazardous*, meaning that they are flammable, corrosive, explosive, or toxic. In landfill disposal, potential contaminants are heaped onto mounds or spread directly over the ground. As rainwater oozes through the refuse, it may dissolve a variety of organic and inorganic materials. If the

A

B

◆ **Figure 16.20** Sometimes agricultural chemicals (**A**) and materials leached from landfills (**B**) find their way into the groundwater. These are two of the potential sources of groundwater contamination. (Photo **A** by Roy Morsch/Corbis/The Stock Market; photo **B** by F. Rossotto/Corbis/The Stock Market) leached material reaches the water table, it will mix with the groundwater and contaminate the supply. Similar problems may result from leakage of shallow excavations, called holding ponds, into which a variety of liquid wastes are disposed.

Because groundwater movement is usually slow, polluted water can go undetected for a long time. In fact, contamination is commonly discovered only after drinking water has been affected and people become ill. By this time, the volume of polluted water may be very large, and even if the source of contamination is removed immediately, the problem is not solved. Although the sources of groundwater contamination are numerous, the solutions are relatively few.

Once the source of the problem has been identified and eliminated, the most common practice is simply to abandon the water supply and allow the pollutants to be flushed away gradually. This is the least costly and easiest solution, but the aquifer must remain unused for many years. To accelerate this process, polluted water is sometimes pumped out and treated. Following removal of the tainted water, the aquifer is allowed to recharge naturally, or in some cases the treated water or other fresh water is pumped back in. This process is costly and time-consuming, and it may be risky because we have no way to be certain that all of the contamination has been removed. Clearly, the most effective solution to groundwater contamination is prevention.

THE GEOLOGIC WORK OF GROUNDWATER

Groundwater dissolves rock. This fact is key to understanding how caverns and sinkholes form. Because soluble rocks, especially limestone, underlie millions of square kilometres of Earth's surface, it is here that the groundwater carries on its important role as an erosional agent. Limestone is nearly insoluble in pure water but is quite easily dissolved by water containing small quantities of carbonic acid, and most groundwater contains this acid. It forms because rainwater readily dissolves carbon dioxide from the air and from decaying plants. Therefore, when groundwater comes in contact with limestone, the carbonic acid reacts with the calcite (calcium carbonate) in the rocks to form calcium bicarbonate, a soluble material that is then carried away in solution.

Caverns

The most spectacular results of groundwater's erosional handiwork are limestone **caverns**. In Canada and the United States, more than 18,300 caves have been discovered and new ones are found every year. Although most are relatively small, some have spectacular dimensions. Mammoth Cave in Kentucky and Carlsbad Caverns in southeast New Mexico are famous examples. The Mammoth Cave system is the most extensive in the world, with more than 540 kilometres of interconnected passages. The dimensions at Carlsbad Caverns are impressive in a different way. Here we find the largest and perhaps most spectacular single chamber. The Big Room at Carlsbad Caverns has an area equivalent to 14 football fields and enough height to accommodate the Parliament buildings in Ottawa.

Most caverns are created at or just below the water table in the zone of saturation. Here acidic groundwater follows lines of weakness in the rock, such as joints and bedding planes. As time passes, the dissolving process slowly creates cavities and gradually enlarges them into caverns. Material that is dissolved by the groundwater is eventually discharged into streams and carried to the ocean.

In many caves, development has occurred at several levels, with the current cavern-forming activity occurring at the lowest elevation. This situation reflects the close relationship between the formation of major subterranean passages and the river valleys into which they drain. As streams cut their valleys deeper, the water table drops as the elevation of the river drops. Consequently, during periods when surface streams are rapidly downcutting, surrounding groundwater levels drop rapidly and cave passages are abandoned by water while the passages are still relatively small in cross-sectional area. Conversely, when the entrenchment of streams is slow or negligible, there is time for large cave passages to form.

Certainly the features that arouse the greatest curiosity for most cavern visitors are the stone formations that give some caverns a wonderland appearance. These are not erosional features, like the cavern itself, but depositional features created by the seemingly endless dripping of water over great spans of time. The calcium carbonate that is left behind produces the limestone we call travertine. These cave deposits, however, are also commonly called *dripstone*, an obvious reference to their mode of origin. Carbonate and salt minerals can also precipitate from water that forms pools on the cavern floor. Although the formation of caverns takes place in the zone of saturation, the deposition of calcium carbonate is not possible until the caverns are above the water table in the zone of aeration. As soon as the chamber is filled with air, the stage is set for the decoration phase of cavern building to begin.

The various cavern features produced by mineral precipitation are collectively called **speleothems** (*spelaion* = cave, *them* = put), no two of

◆ **Figure 16.21** Speleothems are of many types, including stalactites, stalagmites, and columns. Big Room, Carlsbad Caverns National Park. The large stalagmite is called the Totem Pole.
(Photo by David Muench/David Muench Photography)

which are exactly alike (Figure 16.21). Perhaps the most familiar speleothems are **stalactites** (*stalaktos* = trickling). These icicle-like pendants hang from the ceiling of the cavern and form where water seeps through cracks above. When the water reaches air in the cave, some of the dissolved carbon dioxide escapes from the drop, and calcite precipitates. Deposition occurs as a ring around the edge of the water drop. As drop after drop follows, each leaves a trace of calcite behind, and a hollow limestone tube is created. Water then moves through the tube, remains suspended momentarily at the end, contributes a tiny ring of calcite, and falls to the cavern floor. The stalactite just described is appropriately called a *soda straw* (Figure 16.22). Often the hollow tube of the soda straw becomes plugged or its supply of water increases. In either case, the water is forced to flow and hence deposit along the outside of the tube. As deposition continues, the stalactite takes on the more common conical shape.

Speleothems that form on the floor of a cavern and reach upward are called **stalagmites** (*stalagmos* = dropping). The water supplying the calcite for stalagmite growth falls from the ceiling and splatters over the surface. As a result, stalagmites do not have a central tube and are usually more massive in appearance and rounded on their upper ends than stalactites. Given enough time, a downward-growing stalactite and an upward-growing stalagmite can join to form a *column*.

Karst Topography

Many areas of the world have landscapes that, to a large extent, have been shaped by the dissolving power of groundwater. Such areas are said to exhibit **karst topography**, named for the Kras Plateau in Slovenia (formerly a part of Yugoslavia) located along the northeast shore of the Adriatic Sea, where such topography is strikingly developed. In North America karst landscapes occur in many areas that are underlain by limestone, including portions of the Atlantic provinces in Canada and Kentucky, Tennessee, Alabama, southern Indiana, and central and northern Florida in the United States. Generally, arid and semi-arid areas are too dry to develop karst topography. When solution features exist in such regions, they are likely to be remnants of a time when rainier conditions prevailed.

Karst areas typically have irregular terrain punctuated with many depressions, called **sinkholes** or **sinks**. The limestone areas of Florida, Kentucky, and southern Indiana have tens of thousands of these depressions, varying in depth from just a metre or two to more than 50 metres (Figure 16.23A).

Sinkholes commonly form in two ways. Some develop gradually over many years without any physical disturbance to the rock. In these situations the limestone immediately below the soil is dissolved by downward-seeping rainwater that is freshly charged with carbon dioxide. Over time the bedrock surface is lowered and the fractures into which the water seeps are enlarged. As the fractures grow, soil subsides into the widening voids, from which it is removed by groundwater flowing in the passages below. These depressions are usually shallow and have gentle slopes.

By contrast, sinkholes can form abruptly and without warning when the roof of a cavern collapses under its own weight. Typically, the depressions created in this manner are steep-sided and deep. In Canada, sinkholes are common in some parts of the Atlantic provinces that are underlain by easily dissolved evaporite and carbonate bedrock (Figure 16.23B).

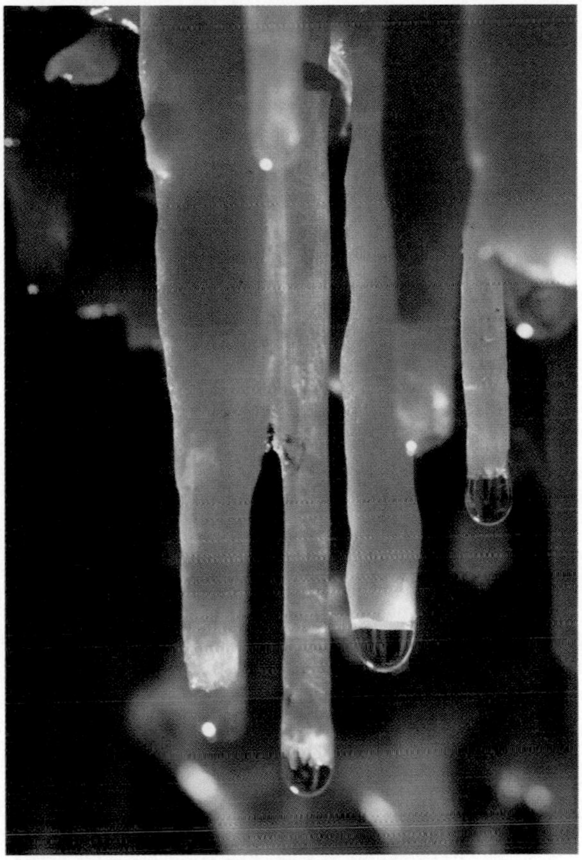

◆ **Figure 16.22** "Live" soda straw stalactites. Lehman Caves, Great Basin National Park, Nevada.
(Photo by Tom & Susan Bean, Inc.)

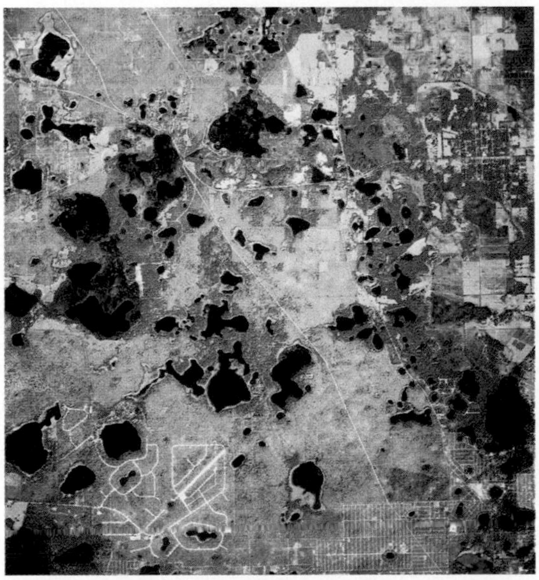

A

B

Figure 16.23 **A.** This high-altitude infrared image shows an area of karst topography in central Florida. The numerous lakes occupy sinkholes. **B.** Sinkhole in the Codroy Valley, western Newfoundland and Labrador. This sinkhole resulted from the collapse of a cave in gypsum bedrock.
(Photo **A** courtesy of USDA-ASCS; photo **B** by Trevor Bell)

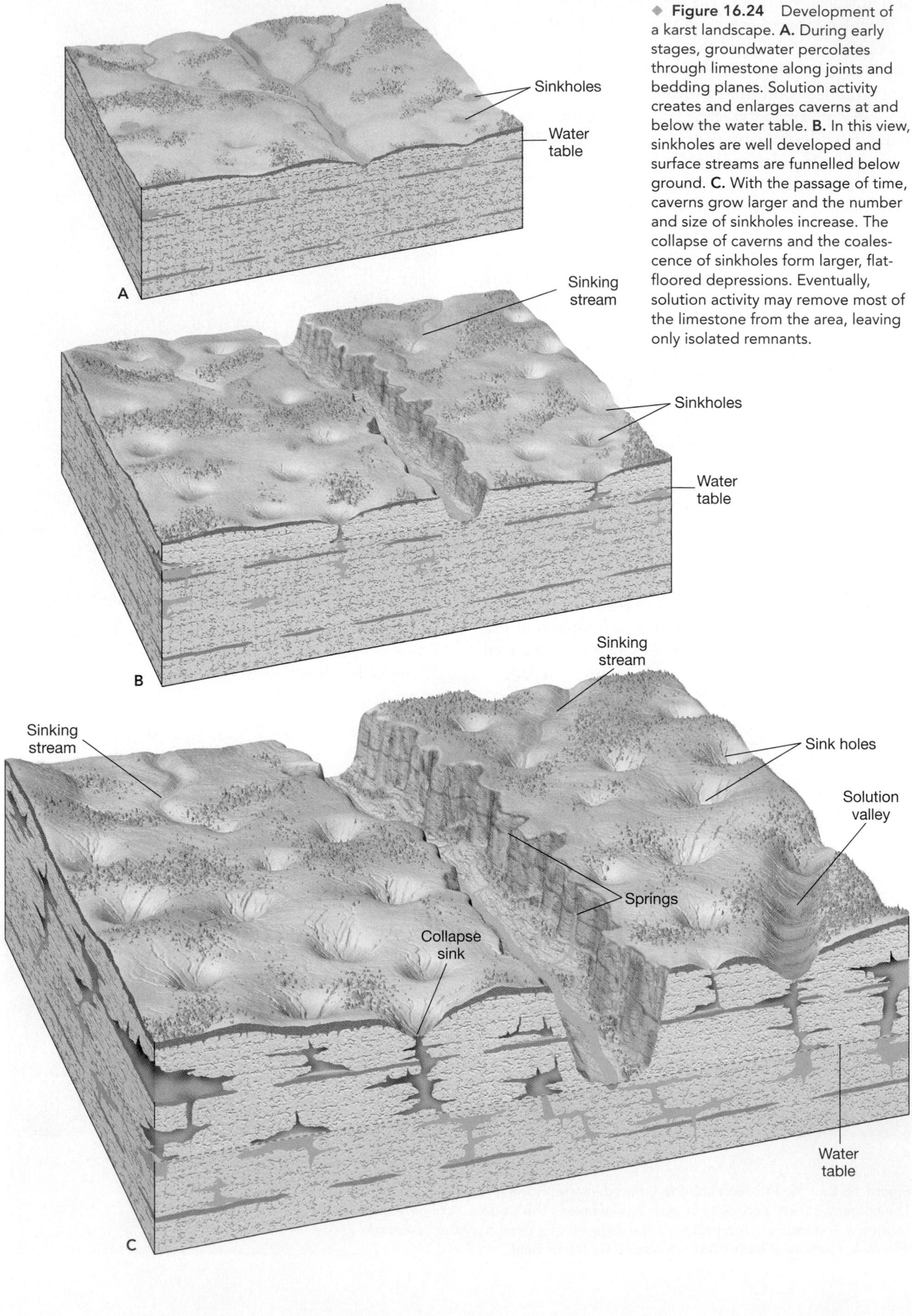

◆ **Figure 16.24** Development of a karst landscape. **A.** During early stages, groundwater percolates through limestone along joints and bedding planes. Solution activity creates and enlarges caverns at and below the water table. **B.** In this view, sinkholes are well developed and surface streams are funnelled below ground. **C.** With the passage of time, caverns grow larger and the number and size of sinkholes increase. The collapse of caverns and the coalescence of sinkholes form larger, flat-floored depressions. Eventually, solution activity may remove most of the limestone from the area, leaving only isolated remnants.

In addition to a surface pockmarked by sinkholes, karst regions characteristically show a striking lack of surface drainage (streams). Following a rainfall, the runoff is quickly funnelled below ground through sinks. It then flows through caverns until it finally reaches the water table. Where streams do exist at the surface, their paths are usually short. The names of such streams often give a clue to their fate. In the Mammoth Cave area of Kentucky, for example, there is Sinking Creek, Little Sinking Creek, and Sinking Branch. Some sinkholes become plugged with clay and debris, creating small lakes or ponds. The development of a karst landscape is depicted in Figure 16.24.

Some regions of karst development exhibit landscapes that look very different from the sinkhole-studded terrain depicted in Figure 16.24. One striking example is an extensive region in southern China that is described as exhibiting *tower karst*. As the image in Figure 16.25 shows, the term *tower* is appropriate because the landscape consists of a maze of isolated, steep-sided hills that rise abruptly from the ground. Each is riddled with interconnected caves and passageways. This type of karst topography forms in wet tropical and subtropical regions having thick beds of highly jointed limestone. Here groundwater has dissolved large volumes of limestone, leaving only these residual towers. Karst development is more rapid in tropical climates because of the abundant rainfall and the greater availability of carbon dioxide from the decay of lush tropical vegetation. The extra carbon dioxide in the soil means there is more carbonic acid for dissolving limestone. Other tropical areas of advanced karst development include portions of Puerto Rico, western Cuba, and northern Vietnam.

◆ **Figure 16.25** One of the best-known and most distinctive regions of tower karst development is the Guilin District of southeast China.
(Photo by Jose Fuste Raga/Corbis/The Stock Market)

Chapter Summary

- As a resource, *groundwater* represents the largest reservoir of fresh water that is readily available to humans. Geologically, the dissolving action of groundwater produces *caverns* and *sinkholes* or *sinks*. Groundwater is also an equalizer of stream flow.
- Groundwater is water that completely fills the pore spaces in sediment and rock in the subsurface *zone of saturation*. The upper limit of this zone is the *water table*. The *zone of aeration* is above the water table where the soil, sediment, and rock are not saturated.
- Materials with very small pore spaces (such as clay) hinder or prevent groundwater movement and are called *aquitards*. *Aquifers* consist of materials with larger, connected pore spaces (such as sand) that are permeable and transmit groundwater freely.
- Groundwater moves in looping curves that are a compromise between the downward pull of gravity and the tendency of water to move toward areas of reduced pressure.
- *Springs* occur whenever the water table intersects the land surface and a natural flow of groundwater

results. *Wells*, openings bored into the zone of saturation, withdraw groundwater and create roughly conical depressions in the water table known as *cones of depression*. *Artesian* wells occur when water rises above the level at which it was initially encountered.

- When groundwater circulates at great depths, it becomes heated. If it rises, the water may emerge as a *hot spring*. *Geysers* occur when groundwater is heated in underground chambers and expands, and some water quickly changes to steam, causing the geyser to erupt. The heat source for most hot springs and geysers is hot igneous rock.
- Some of the current environmental problems involving groundwater include (1) overuse by intense irrigation, (2) land subsidence caused by groundwater withdrawal, and (3) contamination by pollutants.
- Most caverns form in limestone at or below the water table when acidic groundwater dissolves rock along lines of weakness, such as joints and bedding planes. The various dripstone features found in caverns are collectively called *speleothems*. Landscapes that to a large extent have been shaped by the dissolving power of groundwater exhibit *karst topography*, an irregular terrain punctuated with many depressions, called sinkholes or sinks.

Review Questions

1. What percentage of fresh water is groundwater? If glacial ice is excluded and only liquid fresh water is considered, about what percentage is groundwater?
2. Geologically, groundwater is important as an erosional agent. Name another significant geologic role for groundwater.
3. Compare and contrast the zones of aeration and saturation. Which of these zones contains groundwater?
4. Although we usually think of tables as being flat, the water table generally is not. Explain.
5. Distinguish between porosity and permeability.
6. What is the difference between an aquitard and an aquifer?
7. Under what circumstances can a material have a high porosity but not be a good aquifer?
8. As illustrated in Figure 16.4, groundwater moves in looping curves. What factors cause the water to follow such paths?
9. Briefly describe the important contribution to our understanding of groundwater movement made by Henri Darcy.
10. When an aquitard is situated above the main water table, a localized saturated zone may be created. What term is applied to such a situation?
11. What is the heat source for most hot springs and geysers? How is this reflected in the distribution of these features?
12. Two neighbours each dig a well. Although both wells penetrate to the same depth, one neighbour is successful and the other is not. Describe a circumstance that might explain what happened.
13. What is meant by the term *artesian*?
14. For artesian wells to exist, two conditions must be present. List these conditions.
15. How was the Walkerton, Ontario, tragedy influenced by the geology of the area? (See Box 16.1.)
16. What problem is associated with the pumping of groundwater for irrigation?
17. Why does the rate of natural groundwater recharge decrease as urban areas develop?
18. Which aquifer would be most effective in purifying polluted groundwater: coarse gravel, sand, or cavernous limestone?
19. What is meant when a groundwater pollutant is classified as hazardous?
20. Name two common speleothems and distinguish between them.
21. Areas whose landscapes largely reflect the erosional work of groundwater are said to exhibit what kind of topography?
22. Describe two ways in which sinkholes are created.

Key Terms

aquifer (p. 424)
aquitard (p. 424)
artesian (p. 429)
belt of soil moisture (p. 421)
capillary fringe (p. 421)
cavern (p. 435)
cone of depression (p. 428)
Darcy's law (p. 425)
drawdown (p. 428)
flowing artesian well (p. 430)
geyser (p. 427)
groundwater (p. 421)
head (p. 425)
hot spring (p. 426)
hydraulic conductivity (p. 425)
hydraulic gradient (p. 424)
karst topography (p. 436)
non-flowing artesian well (p. 430)
perched water table (p. 426)
permeability (p.423)
porosity (p. 423)
sinkhole (sink) (p. 437)
speleothem (p. 435)
spring (p. 425)
stalactite (p. 436)
stalagmite (p. 436)
water table (p. 421)
well (p. 428)
zone of aeration (p. 421)
zone of saturation (p. 421)

Web Resources

The *Earth* website uses the resources and flexibility of the internet to aid in your study of the topics in this chapter. Written and developed by geology instructors, this site will help improve your understanding of geology. Visit **www.pearsoned.ca/tarbuck** and click on the cover of the text to find

- online review quizzes
- Web-based critical thinking and writing exercises
- links to chapter-specific Web resources
- internet-wide key-term searches

www.pearsoned.ca/tarbuck

Chapter 17

Glaciers and Glaciation

Shrinking Athabasca Glacier in Jasper National Park, Alberta.
(Photo by S. R. Hicock)

Climate has a strong influence on the nature and intensity of Earth's external processes. This fact is dramatically illustrated in this chapter because the existence and extent of glaciers is largely controlled by Earth's changing climate.

Today glaciers only cover about 10 percent of Earth's land surface. However, several nineteenth-century glacial geologists deduced that, in the recent geologic past (Pleistocene Epoch, see Figure 8.12), ice sheets were three times as extensive, covering vast areas with ice thousands of metres thick. Many regions still bear the mark of these ancient glaciers (Figure 17.1). The basic character of such diverse places as the Rocky Mountains, Canadian Shield, and Gros Morne National Park was fashioned by now-vanished masses of glacial ice. In fact, approximately 95 percent of Canada's landmass has been covered and shaped by ancient ice sheets, especially the Cordilleran and Laurentide ice sheets (see Figure 17.29). Moreover, the Great Lakes and the fjords of Norway and British Columbia all owe their existence to glaciers. Glaciers, of course, are not just a phenomenon of the geologic past. As you will see, they are still sculpting the landscape and depositing debris in many regions today.

GLACIERS: A PART OF TWO BASIC CYCLES

GEODe EARTH Glaciers and Glaciation
↳ Introduction

Glaciers are a part of two fundamental cycles in the Earth system: the hydrologic cycle and the rock cycle. In Chapter 15 you learned that the water of the hydrosphere is constantly cycled through the atmosphere, biosphere, and geosphere. Time and time again, the same water evaporates from the oceans into the atmosphere, precipitates on the land, and flows in rivers and underground back to the sea. However, when precipitation falls at high elevations or high latitudes, the water may not immediately make its way toward the sea. Instead, it may become part of a glacier. Although the ice will eventually melt, allowing the water to continue its path to the sea, water can be stored as glacial ice for many tens, hundreds, or even thousands of years. During the time that the water is locked up in a glacier, it can be a powerful erosional force. Erosional processes are an important part of the rock cycle. Like rivers and other erosional processes, moving

◆ **Figure 17.1** Moraine Lake and majestic peaks in Banff National Park, Alberta. (Photo by Christopher Collom)

ice modifies the landscape as it transports and deposits sediment.

A **glacier** is a thick ice mass that originates on land from the accumulation, compaction, and recrystallization of snow. Because glaciers are agents of erosion, they must *flow*, even though they appear to be stationary. Although glaciers are found in many parts of the world today, most are located at high altitudes and in high latitudes. Basic types of glaciers are presented next.

Ice Sheets

Ice sheets exist on a continental scale. The low total annual solar radiation reaching the poles makes these regions prone to great ice accumulations. Although many ice sheets have existed in the past, just two achieve this status at present (Figure 17.2). In the area near the North Pole, Greenland is covered by an imposing ice sheet that occupies 1.7 million square kilometres, or about 80 percent of this large island. Averaging nearly 1500 metres thick, the ice extends 3000 metres above the island's bedrock floor in some places.

In the South Polar realm, the huge Antarctic Ice Sheet attains a maximum thickness of nearly 4300 metres and covers an area of more than 13.9 million square kilometres. Because of the proportions of these huge features, they commonly are called *continental ice sheets*. Indeed, the combined areas of present-day continental ice sheets represent almost 10 percent of Earth's land area.

These enormous ice masses flow out in all directions from one or more snow-accumulation areas and completely obscure all but the highest areas of underlying terrain. Indeed, the ancient Laurentide Ice Sheet covered most of Canada. Even sharp variations in the topography beneath the glacier usually appear as relatively subdued undulations on the surface of the ice. Such topographic differences, however, do affect the behaviour of the ice sheets, especially near their margins, by guiding flow in certain directions and creating zones of faster and slower flow.

Along portions of the Antarctic coast, glacial ice flows into bays, creating features called **ice shelves**. These are large, relatively flat masses of floating ice that extend seaward from the coast but remain attached to the land along one or more sides. The shelves are thickest on their landward sides, and they become thinner seaward. They are sustained by ice from the adjacent ice sheet as well as being nourished by snowfall and the freezing of seawater to their bases. Antarctica's ice shelves extend over approximately 1.4 million square kilometres. The Ross and Filchner ice shelves are the largest, with the Ross Ice Shelf alone covering an area approximately the size of Manitoba (Figure 17.2).

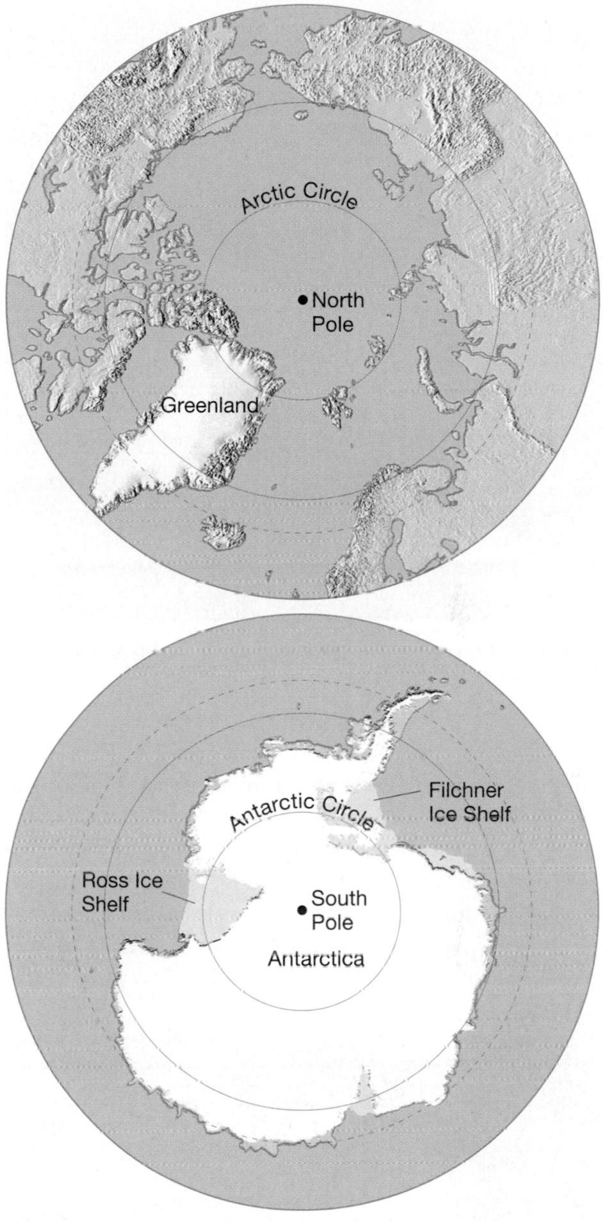

◆ **Figure 17.2** The only present-day ice sheets are those covering Greenland and Antarctica. Their combined areas represent almost 10 percent of Earth's land area. Greenland's ice sheet occupies 1.7 million square kilometres, or about 80 percent of the island. The area of the Antarctic Ice Sheet is almost 14 million square kilometres. Ice shelves occupy an additional 1.4 million square kilometres adjacent to the Antarctic Ice Sheet.

Valley (Alpine) Glaciers

Thousands of relatively small glaciers exist in lofty mountain areas, where they usually follow valleys

◆ **Figure 17.3** Merging valley glaciers on north Baffin Island, Nunavut.
(Photo by S. R. Hicock)

that were originally occupied by streams. Unlike the rivers that previously flowed in these valleys, the glaciers advance slowly, perhaps only a few centimetres per day. Because of their setting, these moving ice masses are termed **valley glaciers** or **alpine glaciers** (Figure 17.3). Each glacier is like a stream of ice, bounded by precipitous rock walls, that flows under its own weight down-valley from an accumulation area near its head. Like rivers, valley glaciers can be long or short, wide or narrow, single or with merging tributaries. Generally, the widths of alpine glaciers are small compared with their lengths. Some extend for just a fraction of a kilometre, whereas others go on for many tens of kilometres. The west branch of the Hubbard Glacier, for example, flows through 112 kilometres of mountainous terrain in Alaska and Yukon.

Other Types of Glaciers

In addition to valley glaciers and ice sheets, other types of glaciers are also identified. Covering some uplands and plateaus are masses of glacial ice called **ice caps**. Like ice sheets, ice caps completely bury the underlying landscape but are much smaller than the continental-scale features. Ice caps occur in many places, including Iceland (Figure 17.4A) and several of the large islands in Canada's Arctic Archipelago.

Often, ice caps and ice sheets feed **outlet glaciers**. These tongues of ice flow down valleys, extending outward from the margins of these larger ice masses. The tongues are essentially valley glaciers that are avenues for ice movement from an ice cap or ice sheet through mountainous terrain to the sea. Some outlet glaciers become fast-flowing **ice streams** that drain most of an ice sheet. Where they

A

B

◆ **Figure 17.4** **A.** The ice cap in this satellite image is the Vatnajökull in southeast Iceland (*jökull* means "ice cap" in Danish). **B.** Piedmont glaciers on north Baffin Island.
(Photo **A** *Landsat* image from NASA; photo **B** by S. R. Hicock)

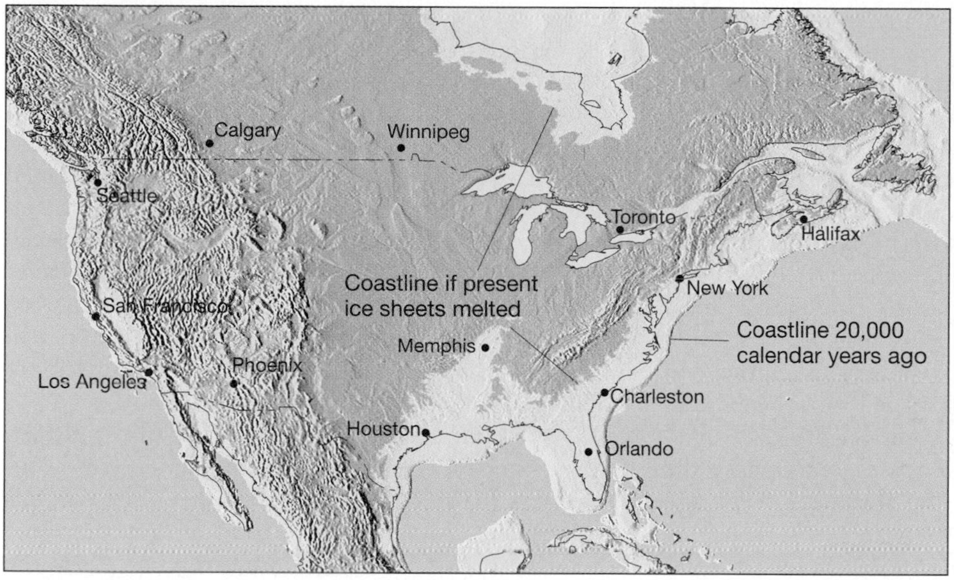

◆ **Figure 17.5** This map of a portion of North America shows the present-day coastline compared with the coastline that existed during the last Ice Age (about 20,000 years ago) and the coastline that would exist if present ice sheets on Greenland and Antarctica melted.
(After R. H. Dott, Jr., and R. L. Batten, *Evolution of the Earth*, New York: McGraw Hill, 1971. Reprinted by permission of the publisher.)

encounter the ocean, some outlet glaciers and ice streams spread out as floating ice shelves and produce large numbers of icebergs.

Piedmont glaciers occupy broad lowlands at the bases of steep mountains and form when one or more alpine glaciers emerge from the confining walls of mountain valleys (Figure 17.4B). Here, the advancing ice spreads out to form a broad sheet. The size of individual piedmont glaciers varies greatly. Among the largest in Canada is the broad piedmont lobe west of Lake Hazen on Ellesmere Island.

What If the Ice Melted?

How much water is stored as glacial ice? It is estimated by glaciologists that slightly more than 2 percent of the world's water is tied up in glaciers. But even 2 percent of a vast quantity is still large. The total volume of just valley glaciers is about 210,000 cubic kilometres, comparable to the combined volume of the world's largest saline and freshwater lakes.

As for ice sheets, the Antarctic Ice Sheet includes 80 percent of the world's ice and nearly two thirds of Earth's fresh water and covers an area similar to the total land area of Canada. If this ice melted, sea level would rise an estimated 60 to 70 metres and the ocean would inundate many densely populated coastal areas (Figure 17.5).

The hydrologic importance of Antarctic ice can be illustrated in another way. If the ice sheet were melted at a uniform rate, it could feed (1) the Mississippi River for more than 50,000 years, (2) all the rivers in the United States for about 17,000 years, (3) the Amazon River for approximately 5000 years, or (4) all the rivers of the world for about 750 years.

FORMATION OF GLACIAL ICE

GEODe EARTH Glaciers and Glaciation
↳ Budget of a Glacier

Snow is the raw material from which glacial ice originates; therefore, glaciers form in areas where more snow falls in winter than melts during the summer. Before a glacier is created, snow must be converted into glacial ice. This transformation is shown in Figure 17.6.

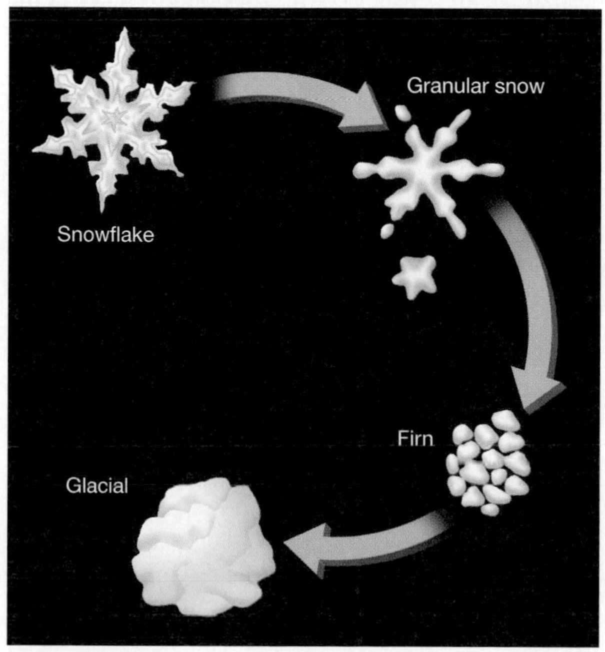

◆ **Figure 17.6** The conversion of freshly fallen snow into dense, crystalline glacial ice.

When temperatures remain below freezing following a snowfall, the fluffy accumulation of delicate hexagonal crystals soon changes. As air infiltrates the spaces between the crystals, the extremities of the crystals turn into water vapour, which condenses near the centres of the crystals. In this manner snowflakes become smaller, thicker, and more spherical, and the large pore spaces disappear. By this process, air is forced out and what was once light, fluffy snow is re-crystallized into a much denser mass of small grains having the consistency of coarse sand. This granular re-crystallized snow is called **firn** and is commonly found making up old snow banks near the end of winter. As more snow is added, the pressure on the lower layers increases, compacting the ice grains at depth. Once the thickness of ice and snow exceeds 50 metres, the weight is sufficient to fuse firn into a solid mass of interlocking ice crystals. Glacial ice has now been formed.

MOVEMENT OF A GLACIER

GEODe EARTH Glaciers and Glaciation
↳ Budget of a Glacier

The movement of glacial ice is generally referred to as *flow*. The fact that glacial movement is described in this way seems paradoxical—how can a solid flow? The way in which ice moves is complex and is of three basic types. The first of these, **internal deformation**, involves movement *within* the ice. Ice behaves as a brittle solid until the pressure on it is equivalent to the weight of about 50 metres of ice. Once that load is surpassed, ice behaves as a plastic material and flow begins. Such flow occurs because of the molecular structure of ice. Glacial ice consists of layers of molecules stacked one on the other. The bonds between layers are weaker than those within each layer. Therefore, when a stress exceeds the strength of the bonds between the layers, the layers remain intact and slide over one another.

A second and often equally important mechanism of glacial movement consists of the entire ice mass slipping along the ground. With the exception of some glaciers located in polar regions where the ice is mainly frozen to the solid bedrock floor, parts of many glaciers are thought to move by this sliding process, called **basal slip**. In this process, meltwater probably acts as a hydraulic jack allowing the ice to move over the rock. The source of the liquid water is related in part to the fact that the melting point of ice decreases as pressure increases. Therefore, deep within a glacier the ice can be at the melting point even though its temperature is below 0°C. In fact, parts of glacier bed can be wet and others dry, depending mainly on ice thickness.

The third mechanism is **soft bed deformation**, where sediment and fractured rock deform by friction of the overriding glacier. Water-saturated sediment and weak bedrock, such as shale, are easily deformed and offer little resistance to the power of the glacier. Figure 17.7 shows these three basic types of glacial movement. This vertical profile through a glacier also shows that not all the ice flows forward at the same rate. Frictional drag with the bedrock floor can cause the lower portions of the glacier to move more slowly.

In contrast to the lower portion of the glacier, the upper 50 metres or so is not under sufficient pressure to exhibit plastic flow. Rather, the ice in this uppermost zone is brittle and is appropriately referred to as the **zone of fracture**. The ice in the zone of fracture is carried along piggyback style by the ice below. When the glacier moves over irregular terrain, the zone of fracture is subjected to tension, resulting in cracks called **crevasses** (chapter-opening photo and Figure 17.8). These gaping cracks can make travel across glaciers dangerous and can extend to depths of 50 metres. Below this depth, plastic flow seals them off.

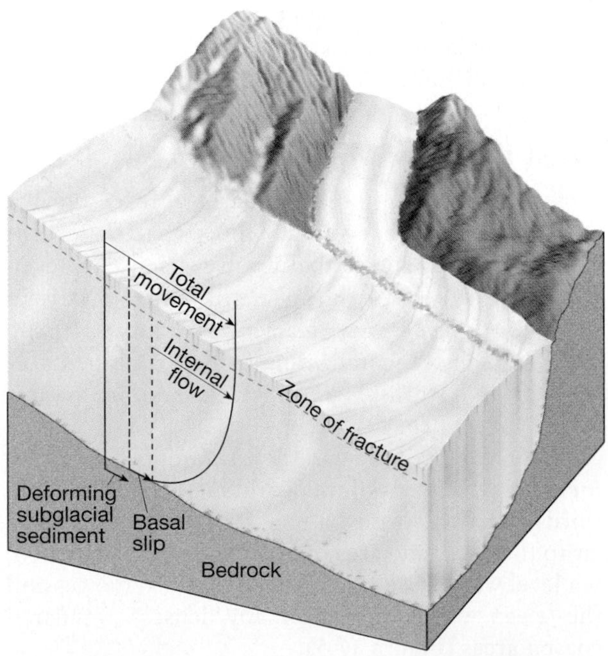

◆ **Figure 17.7** Cross-section through a glacier to illustrate ice movement, divided into three components. (1) Ice in the zone of fracture is carried passively on the main mass of ice. (2) Ice below approximately 50 metres behaves plastically and flows—it may even slip over the bed if wet. (3) Soft material under the ice may deform by frictional drag of the ice. Often the rate of movement is slowest at the base of the glacier, where frictional drag is greatest.

◆ **Figure 17.8** Crevasses form in the brittle ice of the zone of fracture. They can extend to depths of 50 metres and can make travel across glaciers dangerous.
(Photo by Galen Rowell/Mountain Light Photography, Inc.)

Rates of Glacial Movement

Unlike stream flow, glacial movement is not obvious. If we could watch an alpine glacier move, we would see that, like the water in a river, not all of the ice in the valley moves at an equal rate. Just as friction with the valley floor can slow the movement of the ice at the bottom of the glacier, the drag created by the valley walls causes the rate of flow to be greatest in the centre of the glacier. This was first demonstrated by experiments during the nineteenth century, in which markers were carefully placed in a straight line across the top of a valley glacier. Periodically, the positions of the stakes were recorded, revealing the type of movement just described.

How rapidly does glacial ice move? Average velocities vary considerably from one glacier to another. Some move so slowly that trees and other vegetation may become well established in the debris that has accumulated on the glacier's surface, whereas others may move at rates of up to several metres per day. For example, Byrd Glacier, an outlet glacier in Antarctica that was the subject of a 10-year study that used satellite images, moved at an average rate of 750 to 800 metres per year (about 2 metres per day). Other glaciers in the study advanced at one quarter that rate.

The advance of some glaciers is characterized by episodes of extremely rapid movements called **surges**. Glaciers that exhibit such movement flow along in an apparently normal manner, then speed up for a relatively short time, before returning to the normal rate again. The flow rates during surges are as much as 100 times the normal rate. Evidence indicates that many glaciers surge from time to time (Box 17.1).

Budget of a Glacier

Snow is the raw material from which glacial ice originates; therefore, as mentioned, glaciers form in areas where more snow falls in winter than melts during the summer. Glaciers are constantly gaining and losing ice. Snow accumulation and ice formation occur in the **zone of accumulation**. Its lower limit is defined by the **equilibrium line**. The elevation of the *snowline* (above which snow remains year-round) varies greatly. In polar regions it may be at sea level, whereas in tropical areas, the snowline exists only in high mountain areas, often at altitudes exceeding 4500 metres. Above the equilibrium line, in the zone of accumulation, the addition of snow thickens the glacier and promotes flow. The equilibrium line separates the zone of accumulation from the **zone of wastage** or **ablation**. Here, the glacier experiences a net loss, as all of the snow from the previous winter melts, as does some of the glacial ice (Figure 17.9).

In addition to melting, glaciers also waste as large pieces of ice break off the front of the glacier in a process called **calving**. Calving creates icebergs in places where the glacier has reached the sea or a lake (Figure 17.10). Because icebergs are just slightly less dense than seawater, they float very low in the water, with about 90 percent of their mass submerged. Along the margins of Antarctica's ice shelves, calving is the primary means by which these masses lose ice. The relatively flat icebergs produced here can be several kilometres across and 600 metres thick. By comparison, thousands of irregularly shaped icebergs are produced by outlet glaciers and ice streams flowing from the margins of the Greenland Ice Sheet. Many

BOX 17.1

Understanding Earth
Surging Glaciers

The copious snows that fall in the mountains of southeast Alaska, and adjacent Yukon, nurture an extensive system of valley glaciers. Because these glaciers are relatively accessible and exhibit a diversity of behaviours, they are of great interest to scientists. The ice lobes are used as natural laboratories for the study of glacial processes and climatic change.

Although many of these glaciers are retreating, others are advancing, and a few exhibit the comparatively rapid movements called surges. Hubbard Glacier is one example. From about 1900, when records of its movements were begun, until 1986, the ice within Hubbard Glacier moved forward at a relatively steady rate of 100 metres or so each year. Because loss of ice did not entirely offset this movement, the front of the ice gradually advanced. Then unexpectedly during the winter of 1986, Hubbard Glacier experienced a period of surging. At times the ice moved as fast as 14 metres a day. A tributary also surged forward at rates exceeding 30 metres a day.

Perhaps the most studied glacier exhibiting such surging movement is the 24-kilometre-long Variegated Glacier northwest of Juneau, Alaska (Figure 17.A). Unlike Hubbard Glacier, Variegated Glacier is known to surge at regular intervals. Since 1906, surges have occurred about once every 17 to 20 years. The most thoroughly investigated event took place in 1982–1983.* During this surge, the ice advanced as fast as 54 metres per day.

It is not yet clear whether the mechanism that triggers these rapid movements is the same for all surging-type glaciers. However, researchers studying Variegated Glacier have determined that the surges of this ice mass take the form of a rapid increase in basal sliding that is caused by increases in water pressure beneath the ice. The increased water pressure at the base of the glacier acts to reduce friction between the underlying bedrock and the moving ice. The pressure buildup, in turn, is related to changes in the system of passageways that conduct water along the glacier's bed and deliver it as outflow to the terminus.

*Barclay Kamb et al., "Glacier Surge Mechanism: 1982–1983 Surge of Variegated Glacier, Alaska," *Science* 227 (February 1985): 469.

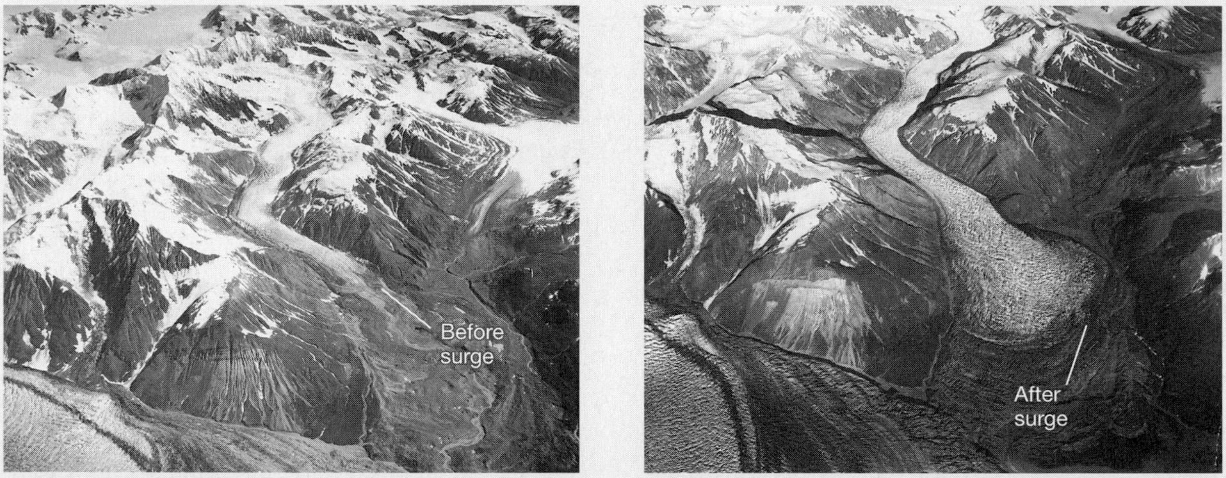

August 1964 August 1965

◆ **Figure 17.A** The surge of Variegated Glacier, a valley glacier near Yakutat, Alaska, northwest of Juneau, is captured in these two aerial photographs taken one year apart. During a surge, ice velocities in Variegated Glacier are 20 to 50 times as great as during normal flow.
(Photos by Austin Post, U.S. Geological Survey)

drift southward and find their way into the North Atlantic, where they can pose a hazard to navigation, as the captain of the *Titanic* discovered in 1912.

Whether the margin of a glacier is advancing, retreating, or remaining stationary depends on the budget of the glacier. The **glacial budget** or **mass balance** is the balance, or lack of balance, between accumulation at the upper end of the glacier and ablation (loss) at the lower end. If ice accumulation exceeds ablation, the glacial front advances until the two factors again come into balance. When this happens, the terminus (front edge) of the glacier becomes stationary.

If a warming trend increases ablation or if a drop in snowfall decreases accumulation, the ice front will retreat (chapter-opening photo). As the terminus

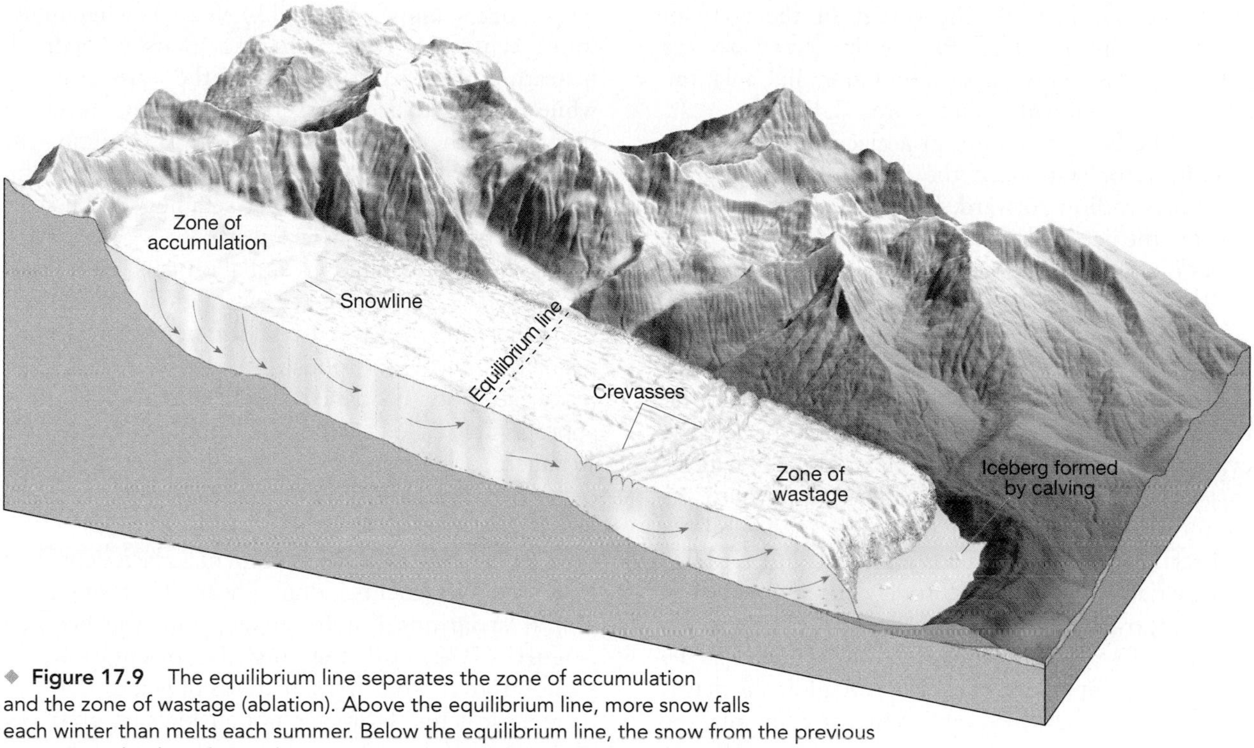

◆ **Figure 17.9** The equilibrium line separates the zone of accumulation and the zone of wastage (ablation). Above the equilibrium line, more snow falls each winter than melts each summer. Below the equilibrium line, the snow from the previous winter completely melts, as does some of the underlying ice. Whether the margin of a glacier advances, retreats, or remains stationary depends on the balance between accumulation and ablation. In any case internal flow (blue arrows) is toward the terminus. When a glacier moves across irregular terrain, crevasses form in the upper brittle portion.

Figure 17.10 Icebergs are created when large pieces calve from the front of a glacier after it reaches a water body. In this photo, ice pinnacles are about to calve from the terminus of a small outlet glacier in Greenland. Only about 10 percent of an iceberg protrudes above the water line.
(Photo by S. R. Hicock)

of the glacier retreats, the extent of the zone of wastage diminishes. Therefore, in time a new balance will be reached between accumulation and ablation, and the ice front will again become stationary.

Whether the margin of a glacier is advancing, retreating, or stationary, the ice within the glacier continues to flow forward. In the case of a receding glacier, the ice still flows forward but not rapidly enough to offset ablation.

GLACIAL EROSION

Glaciers are capable of great erosion. To anyone who has observed the terminus of an alpine glacier, the evidence of its erosive force is clear. You can witness first hand the release of rock material of various sizes from the ice as it melts; the ice has scraped, scoured, and torn rock from the floor and walls of the valley and carried it down-valley. Indeed, as a medium of sediment transport, ice has no equal.

Once rock debris is acquired by the glacier, the enormous competence of ice will not allow the debris to settle out like the load carried by a stream or by the wind. Consequently, glaciers can carry huge blocks that no other erosional agent could possibly budge (Figure 17.11). Although today's glaciers are of limited importance as erosional agents, much of the Canadian landscape was greatly modified by the Laurentide and Cordilleran ice sheets of the last Ice Age.

Glaciers erode the land primarily in two ways—plucking and abrasion. First, as a glacier flows over a fractured bedrock surface, it loosens and lifts blocks of rock and incorporates them into the ice. This process, known as **plucking**, occurs when meltwater penetrates the cracks and joints of bedrock beneath a glacier and freezes. As the water expands while turning to ice, it exerts tremendous leverage that pries the rock loose (see frost wedging in Chapter 5), and then freezes rock fragments to the base of the ice. In this manner sediment of all sizes becomes part of the glacier's load.

The second major erosional process is **abrasion** (Figure 17.12). As the ice with its load of rock fragments slides over bedrock, it functions like sandpaper to smooth and polish the surface below. The pulverized rock produced by the glacial gristmill is appropriately called **rock flour**. Abrasion can produce so much rock flour that meltwater streams flowing out of a glacier have the appearance of milk and offer visible evidence of the grinding power of ice.

When the ice at the bottom of a glacier contains large rock fragments, long, linear scratches called **glacial striations** can be gouged into the bedrock (Figure 17.12). By mapping the orientations of striations over large areas, patterns of glacial flow can be reconstructed. However, not all abrasion produces distinct striations. The rock surfaces over which the glacier moves may also become highly polished by the ice and its load of finer particles. The broad expanses of smoothly polished rock exposures in many parts of the Canadian Shield provide excellent examples.

As is the case with other agents of erosion, the rate of glacial erosion is highly variable. This differential erosion by ice is largely controlled by five factors: (1) rate of glacial movement; (2) thickness of the ice; (3) shape, abundance, and hardness of the

◆ **Figure 17.11** A large, glacially transported rock at Okotoks, Alberta. Such big rocks are called glacial erratics. (Photo by Christopher Collom)

◆ **Figure 17.12** Geologist Dr. Jack Armstrong examines glacial abrasion that created the striations and larger grooves in this volcanic bedrock at Victoria, British Columbia (arrows indicate direction of glacial flow).
(Photo by S. R. Hicock)

rock fragments contained in the ice at the base of the glacier; (4) the erodibility of the surface beneath the glacier; and (5) removal of rock flour to expose fresh bedrock for erosion. Variations in any or all of these factors from time to time or from place to place mean that the features, effects, and degree of landscape modification in glaciated regions can vary greatly.

LANDFORMS CREATED BY GLACIAL EROSION

GEODe EARTH Glaciers and Glaciation
↳ Reviewing Glacial Features

The erosional effects of valley glaciers and ice sheets are quite different. A visitor to a glaciated mountain region like the Canadian Rockies is likely to see a sharp and angular topography (see Figure 17.1). The reason is that as alpine glaciers move down-valley, they tend to accentuate the irregularities of the mountain landscape by creating steeper canyon walls and making bold peaks even more jagged. By contrast, ice sheets override the terrain and hence subdue rather than accentuate the irregularities they encounter (like the Canadian Shield). Although the erosional power of ice sheets is enormous, landforms carved by these huge ice masses usually do not inspire the same wonderment and awe that the erosional features created by valley glaciers do. Because much of the rugged mountain scenery so celebrated for its majestic beauty is the product of erosion by alpine glaciers, they are featured below. Figure 17.13 shows a hypothetical mountain area before, during, and after glaciation.

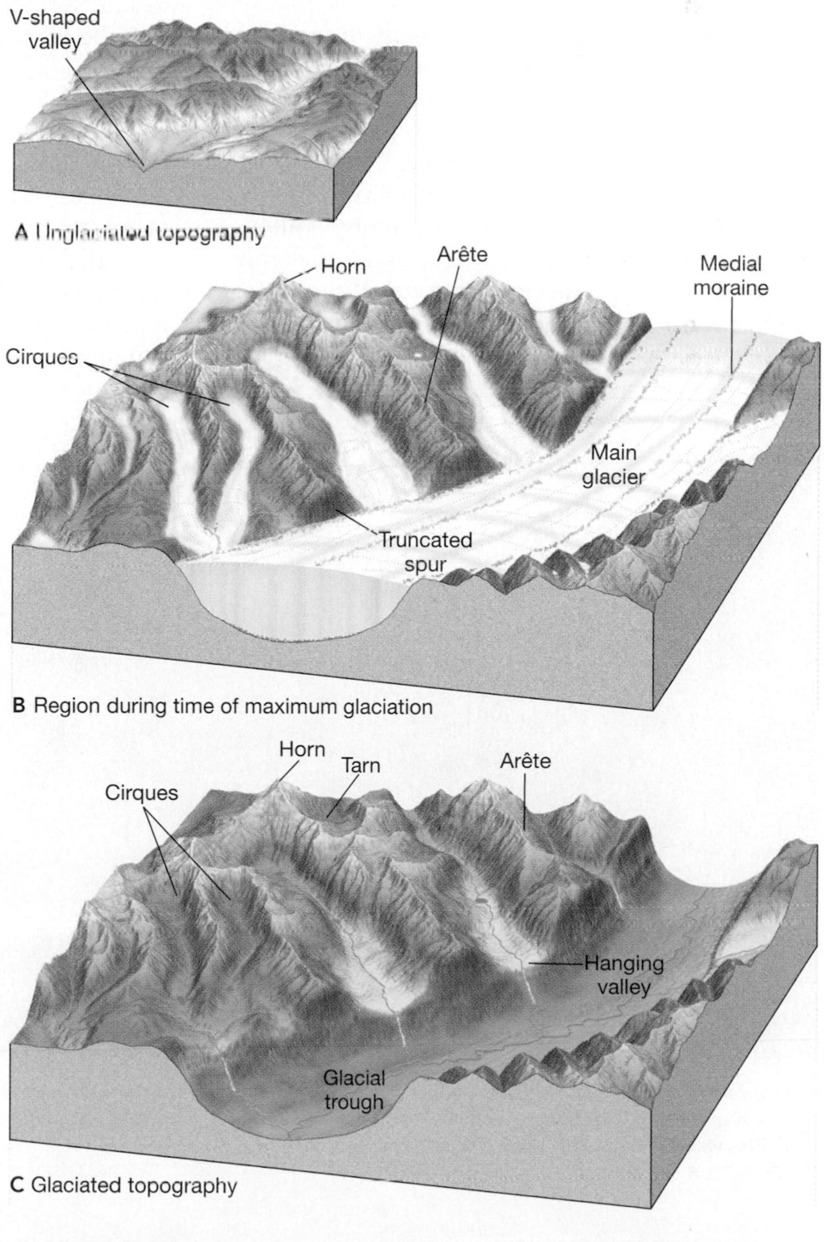

◆ **Figure 17.13** Erosional landforms created by alpine glaciers. The unglaciated landscape in part **A** is modified by valley glaciers in part **B.** After the ice recedes, in part **C**, the terrain looks very different than it did before glaciation.

Glaciated Valleys

A hike up a glaciated valley reveals a number of striking ice-created features. Unlike streams, which create their own valleys, glaciers take the path of least resistance by following the course of existing stream valleys. Before glaciation, mountain valleys are characteristically narrow and V-shaped because streams are downcutting. However, during glaciation these narrow valleys undergo a transformation as the glacier widens and deepens them, creating a U-shaped **glacial trough** (Figures 17.13C and 17.14). In addition to producing a broader and deeper valley, the glacier also straightens the valley. As ice flows around sharp curves, its great erosional force removes the spurs of land that extend into the valley. The results of this activity are triangular-shaped cliffs called **truncated spurs** (Figures 17.13B and 17.3, left of centre).

The intensity of glacial erosion depends in part on the thickness of the ice. Consequently, main glaciers, also called *trunk glaciers*, cut their valleys deeper than do their smaller tributary glaciers. Thus, when the glaciers eventually recede, the valleys of tributary glaciers are left standing above the main glacial trough and are termed **hanging valleys** (Figure 17.13C). Rivers flowing through hanging valleys can produce spectacular waterfalls, such as those in Butte Inlet, Toba Inlet, and Knight Inlet, British Columbia (Figure 17.15).

At the head of a glacial valley is a very characteristic and often imposing feature called a **cirque**. As Figure 17.16 illustrates, these bowl-shaped depressions have precipitous walls on three sides but are open on the down-valley side. The cirque is the focal point of the glacier's growth because it is the area of snow accumulation and ice formation. Cirques begin as irregularities in the mountainside that are subsequently enlarged by the frost wedging and plucking that occurs along the sides and bottom of the glacier. After the glacier has melted away, the cirque basin is commonly occupied by a small lake called a **tarn** (Figure 17.17).

Sometimes when two glaciers exist on opposite sides of a divide, each flowing away from the other, the dividing ridge between their cirques is largely eliminated as plucking and frost action enlarge each one. When this occurs, the two glacial troughs come to intersect, creating a gap or pass from one valley into the other. Such a feature is termed a **col**. Some important and well-known mountain passes that are cols include St. Gotthard Pass in the Swiss Alps, Chilkoot Pass ("the golden staircase") that gold miners had to scale during the Klondike gold rush in Yukon in 1898, and Tioga Pass in California's Sierra Nevada.

Before leaving the topic of glacial troughs and their associated features, we should discuss one more type of well-known feature: fjords. **Fjords** are deep, commonly spectacular, steep-sided inlets of the sea

◆ **Figure 17.14** Before glaciation, a mountain valley is typically narrow and V-shaped. During glaciation, an alpine glacier widens, deepens, and straightens the valley, creating the U-shaped glacial trough seen here. This valley is on north Baffin Island.
(Photo by S. R. Hicock)

◆ **Figure 17.15** Waterfall cascades down a hanging valley at Knight Inlet, British Columbia.
(Photo by John Marriott)

◆ **Figure 17.16** Glacier flowing from a cirque in Kluane National Park, Yukon. These bowl-shaped depressions are found at the heads of glacial valleys and represent a focal point of ice formation.
(Photo by Marli Miller)

that occur at high latitudes where mountains are adjacent to the ocean (Figures 17.18 and 17.4B background). They are drowned glacial troughs that became submerged as the ice left the valley and sea level rose following the Ice Age. The depths of fjords can exceed 1000 metres. However, the great depths of these flooded troughs are only partly explained by the post–Ice Age rise in sea level. Unlike the situation governing the downward erosional work of rivers, glaciers are capable of eroding their

◆ **Figure 17.17** A small lake occupying a cirque is called a tarn. Tombstone Mountains, Yukon. The sharp ridge separating the tarns is an arête.
(Photo by Stephen J. Krasemann)

◆ **Figure 17.18** Like other fjords, this one in the northeast coast of Baffin Island is a drowned glacial trough. (Photo by S. R. Hicock)

beds far below the surface of the sea. For example, a 300-metre-thick glacier can carve its valley floor more than 250 metres below sea level before downward erosion ceases and the ice begins to float. Norway, British Columbia, Greenland, New Zealand, Chile, and Alaska, for example, all have coastlines characterized by fjords.

Arêtes and Horns

A visit to the European Alps and the Canadian Rockies, or many other scenic mountain landscapes carved by valley glaciers, reveals more than the glacial troughs, cirques, and the other related features just discussed. You also are likely to see sinuous sharp-edged ridges called **arêtes** (French for "knife-edge") and sharp pyramid-like peaks called **horns** projecting above the surroundings. Both features can originate from the same basic process: the enlargement of cirques produced by plucking and frost wedging (Figures 17.13B and 17.13C). In the case of horns, groups of cirques around a single high mountain are responsible. As the cirques enlarge and converge, an isolated horn is produced. Noteworthy Canadian examples include Mt. Logan in Yukon's St. Elias Mountains and Mt. Assiniboine of the Alberta Rockies (Figure 17.19).

Arêtes can be formed in a similar manner, except that the cirques are not clustered around a point but rather exist on opposite sides of a divide. As the cirques grow, the divide separating them is reduced to a narrow knifelike partition (Figure 17.17). An arête, however, can also be created in another way: when two glaciers occupy parallel valleys, an arête can form when the divide separating the moving tongues of ice is progressively narrowed as the glaciers scour and widen their adjacent valleys (Figure 17.16; the glacier on the right is out of view).

◆ **Figure 17.19** Horns are sharp pyramid-like peaks shaped by cirque glaciers. This example is Mt. Assiniboine, Alberta. (Photo by J. C. Dueck)

Roches Moutonnées

In many glaciated landscapes, but most frequently where continental ice sheets have modified the terrain, the ice carves small streamlined hills from protruding bedrock knobs. Such an asymmetrical knob of bedrock is called a **roche moutonnée** (French for "sheep rock"). They are formed when glacial abrasion smoothes the gentle slope facing the oncoming ice sheet and plucking steepens the opposite side as the ice rides over the knob (Figure 17.20). Roches moutonnées indicate the direction of glacial flow because the gentler slope is generally on the side from which the ice advanced.

◆ **Figure 17.20** This roche moutonnée in Nunavut provides evidence of the direction of glacial ice movement. The gentle slope (under the backpack) was abraded and the steep side (under the geologist) was plucked, so the ice moved from right to left.
(Photo by S. R. Hicock)

GLACIAL DEPOSITS

GEODe EARTH Glaciers and Glaciation
↳ Reviewing Glacial Features

Glaciers pick up and transport a huge load of debris as they slowly advance across the land. Ultimately these materials are deposited when the ice melts. In regions where glacial sediment is deposited, it can play a truly significant role in forming the landscape. For example, in many areas once covered by the Laurentide and Cordilleran ice sheets of the last Ice Age, the bedrock is rarely exposed because glacial deposits that are tens or even hundreds of metres thick completely mantle the terrain. The general effect of these deposits is to reduce the local relief and thus level the topography. Indeed, rural country scenes that are familiar to many of us—rocky pastures in Ontario, wheat fields in Manitoba and Saskatchewan, rolling farmland in Alberta—result directly from glacial deposition by ancient ice sheets.

Long before the theory of an extensive Ice Age was ever proposed, much of the soil and rock debris covering portions of Europe was recognized as coming from somewhere else. At the time, these foreign materials were believed to have drifted into their present positions by floating ice during an ancient flood. As a consequence, the term *drift* was applied to this sediment. Although rooted in an incorrect concept, this term was so well established by the time the true glacial origin of the debris became widely recognized that it remained in the basic glacial vocabulary. Today **glacial drift** is an all-embracing term for sediments of glacial origin, no matter how, where, or in what shape they were deposited.

One of the features distinguishing drift from sediments deposited by other erosional agents is that glacial deposits consist primarily of mechanically weathered rock debris that underwent little or no chemical weathering before deposition. Thus, minerals that are notably prone to chemical decomposition, such as hornblende and the plagioclase feldspars, are commonly conspicuous components in glacial sediments.

Glacial drift is divided by geologists into two main types: (1) materials deposited directly by the glacier, known as **till**, and (2) sediments deposited by glacial meltwater, called **stratified drift**. We will now look at landforms made of each type.

LANDFORMS MADE OF TILL

Till is deposited as glacial ice melts and releases its load of rock fragments. Unlike moving water and wind, ice cannot sort the sediment it carries; therefore, deposits of till are characteristically poorly sorted mixtures of many particle sizes (Figure 17.21). A close examination of this sediment shows that many of the stones are scratched and polished as the result of being dragged by the glacier. Such stones help distinguish till from other deposits that are mixtures of different sediment sizes, such as debris flows or rockslides.

Earlier ice ages are indicated by deposits called **tillite**, a sedimentary rock formed when till becomes lithified (Figure 17.21B). Such deposits, found in strata of different ages, usually contain striated rock fragments, and some overlie grooved and polished bedrock surfaces or are associated with sandstones and conglomerates that show features of meltwater deposits. For example, two Precambrian glacial episodes have been identified in the geologic record, the first approximately 2 billion years ago (including evidence from the Canadian Shield) and the second about 600 million years ago (Box 17.2).

Boulders found in the till or lying free on the surface are called **glacial erratics** if they are different from the local bedrock (see Figure 17.11).

This means that they must have been derived from a source outside the area where they are found. Although the locality of origin for most erratics is unknown, the origin of some can be determined. In many cases, boulders were transported as far as 500 kilometres from their source area and, in a few

◆ **Figure 17.21** **A.** Till is a poorly sorted mixture of many different sediment sizes. A close examination reveals cobbles that have been scratched as they were dragged by the glacier. **B.** Rocks with virtually identical textural characteristics to till produced by modern glaciers occur in the geologic record and represent ice ages of Earth's deep past. This example of tillite from northern Ontario records a Precambrian glacial episode.
(Photo **A** by E. J. Tarbuck; photo **B** by Grant Young)

BOX 17.2

Canadian Profile

Snowball Earth: Canadian Cryospheric Controversy

Once Earth scientists had developed criteria for the recognition of recent glacial activity, they quickly realized that those same criteria could also be applied to ancient rocks. The Precambrian represents almost 90 percent of the 4.6 billion years of Earth history, but extensive glacial deposits have been recognized only at the beginning and end of the Proterozoic. The oldest extensive glacial deposits occur in Early Proterozoic rocks of North America, Finland, South Africa, and Western Australia, which are about 2.3 billion years old (Figure 17.B). Late Proterozoic glacial deposits occur on every continent.

The widespread nature of Late Proterozoic glacial deposits suggested to Canadian scientist Paul Hoffman (currently at Harvard University) that the entire surface of Earth could have been frozen (the snowball Earth hypothesis or SEH). Hoffman suggested that Earth, as its surface was progressively frozen, lost heat by reflection of solar radiation from ice-covered areas, causing rapid cooling and eventually leading to the planet being encapsulated in ice. Escape from the deep freeze is explained by release of greenhouse gases into the atmosphere from volcanoes, reversing the deep freeze into a "deep fry" interval. The appeal of this idea lies in its simplicity.

The SEH, however, has many problems. For example, the SEH calls for synchronous global-scale glaciation, but among the few glacial deposits that have been accurately dated are significant differences in age. Also, the thickness (many kilometres in some cases), and subaqueous origin, of many Precambrian glacial deposits are difficult to reconcile with a totally frozen planet because moving ice requires an active hydrologic cycle. Yet another problem concerns the limestone and dolostone cap carbonates that occur above many Late Proterozoic glacial deposits. According to the SEH, high levels of atmospheric CO_2 caused extreme global warming and increased weathering of silicate minerals, leading to saturation of the world's oceans with bicarbonate ions and widespread deposition of carbonate sediments. Mudstones deposited immediately after the glaciations ended should show signs of intense weathering. Field evidence, however, indicates the opposite—glacial muds that directly overlie the cap carbonates show less evidence of weathering than those that are stratigraphically higher.

Remnant magnetism in some rocks can be used to determine the latitude at which they formed. Several ancient glacial deposits appear to have formed at sea level in equatorial latitudes. Does this indicate that the entire planet was glaciated? The presence of varves (mudstones with annual layers) and fossil ice-wedge structures is puzzling because both require significant seasonal temperature variations that are not found in equatorial regions today. One possible explanation is the big tilt hypothesis (BTH), which invokes a highly tilted Earth (axis at greater than 54 degrees to the orbital plane) in the Precambrian. If Earth's axis were tilted at an extreme angle, equatorial regions would have experienced greater seasonality, possibly initiating glaciation on landmasses at low latitudes. Unfortunately, a mechanism that adequately explains *how* such a radical change in tilt could have been accomplished, and independent evidence substantiating this hypothesis, remains to be found.

Despite its shortcomings, the snowball Earth concept has stimulated lively discussions on other aspects of Precambrian history. For example, Canadian paleontologist Guy Narbonne and others suggest the evolution of complex life forms that eventually colonized Earth may be closely tied to these climatic and environmental changes.

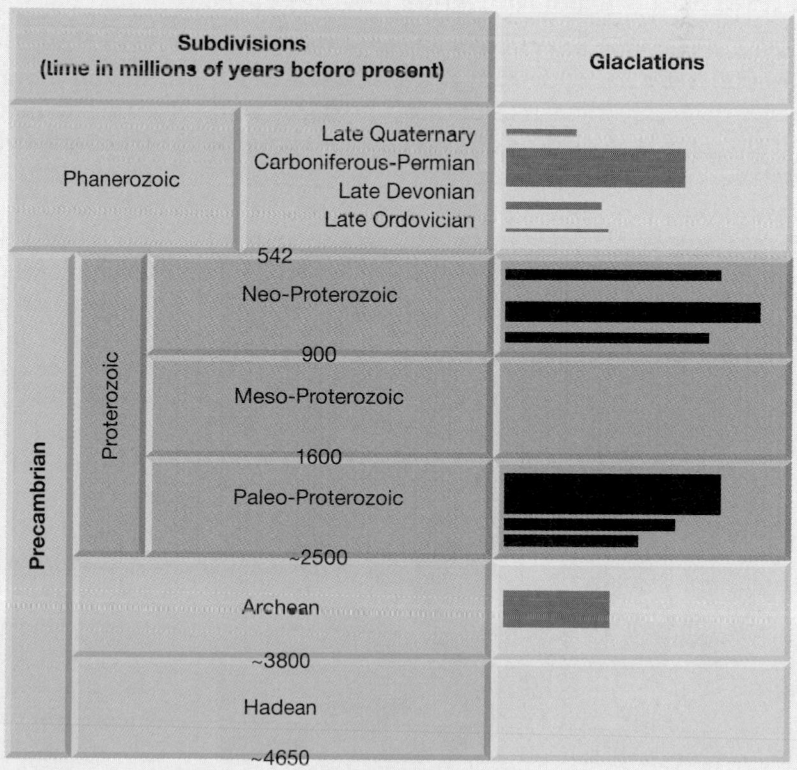

◆ **Figure 17.B** Major glacial episodes in Earth's history as indicated by horizontal bars.

instances, more than 1000 kilometres. The Foothills Erratics Train of southern Alberta is a classic example and the Big Rock near Okotoks (after the Blackfoot word for rock) is its most famous erratic (and reputedly the world's largest, weighing about 16,500 tonnes and standing 9 metres high; see Figure 17.11). The train is more than 600 kilometres long, made of a string of quartzite blocks derived from bedrock near Mt. Edith Cavell in Jasper National Park. A landslide dumped quartzite blocks onto a valley glacier that then carried the blocks eastward until the glacier merged with the edge of the last Laurentide Ice Sheet. Their combined southward flow and subsequent melting left the train of erratics that extends as far as Montana in the United States. Therefore, by studying glacial erratics as well as the mineral composition of the remaining till, geologists are sometimes able to trace the path of a lobe of ice.

In much of Canada, erratics dot pastures and farm fields once covered by ice sheets. In fact, in some places these large rocks were cleared from fields and piled to make fences, walls, and even houses (Figure 17.22). Keeping the fields clear, however, is an ongoing chore because each spring newly exposed erratics appear. Wintertime *frost heaving* has lifted them to the surface (see Chapter 14).

Lateral and Medial Moraines

The most common term for landforms made primarily of till is *moraine*. Originally this term was used by French peasants when referring to the ridges and embankments of rock debris found near the margins of glaciers in the French Alps.

◆ **Figure 17.22** Many older houses in southern Ontario are constructed of fieldstones (glacial erratics).
(Photo by C. Tsujita)

Alpine glaciers produce two types of moraines that occur exclusively in mountain valleys. The first of these is called a **lateral moraine** (Figure 17.23). As we learned earlier, when an alpine glacier moves down-valley, the ice erodes the sides of the valley with great efficiency. In addition, large quantities of debris are added to the glacier's surface as rubble falls or slides from higher on the valley walls and collects on the edges of the moving ice (see chapter-opening photo). When the ice eventually melts, this accumulation of debris is dropped next to the valley walls. These ridges of till parallel the sides of the valley and constitute the lateral moraines.

The second type of moraine that is unique to alpine glaciers is the **medial moraine** (Figures 17.24 and 17.3). Medial moraines are created when two alpine glaciers coalesce to form a wider valley glacier but the ice does not mix. The debris that was once carried along the sides of each glacier joins to form a single dark stripe of debris within the newly enlarged glacier. The creation of these dark stripes within the larger glacier is one obvious proof that glacial ice moves, because the moraine could not form if the ice did not flow down-valley. It is quite common to see several medial moraines within a single alpine glacier, because a streak of debris will form whenever a tributary glacier joins the main glacier.

End and Ground Moraines

An **end moraine** is a ridge of mainly till that forms at the terminus of an alpine glacier or ice sheet. These relatively common landforms are deposited when a state of equilibrium is attained between ice ablation and accumulation. That is, the end moraine forms when the ice is melting and evaporating near the end of the glacier at a rate equal to the forward advance of the glacier from its zone of accumulation. Although the terminus of the glacier is now stationary, the ice continues to flow forward, internally (see Figure 17.9), delivering a continuous supply of debris in the same manner as a conveyor belt delivers goods to the end of a production line. As the ice melts, the debris is dropped and the end moraine grows. The longer the ice front remains stationary, the larger the ridge of till will become. The glacier can also spread a sheet of till on the ground as it moves over it.

Eventually, ablation exceeds accumulation. At this point, the front of the glacier begins to recede in the direction from which it advanced. However, as the ice front retreats, the conveyor-belt action of the glacier continues to provide fresh supplies of debris to the terminus. In this manner a large quantity of till is deposited as the ice melts, creating a rock-strewn, undulating plain. This gently rolling layer of till

◆ **Figure 17.23** Well-developed lateral moraines deposited by the shrinking Athabasca Glacier in Jasper National Park.
(Photo by David Barnes/The Stock Market)

◆ **Figure 17.24** Medial moraines form when the lateral moraines of merging valley glaciers join. Kluane National Park, Yukon.
(Photo by Marli Miller)

deposited as the ice front advances then recedes is termed **ground moraine**. Ground moraine has a levelling effect, filling in low spots and clogging old stream channels, often leading to a derangement of the existing drainage system. The area between lateral moraines in Figure 17.23 is a mix of ground moraine and meltwater deposits. In areas where this layer of till is still relatively fresh, such as the northern Great Lakes region, poorly drained, swampy lands are common.

Periodically, a glacier will retreat to a point where ablation and accumulation once again balance. When this happens, the ice front stabilizes and a new end moraine forms.

The pattern of end moraine formation and ground moraine deposition may be repeated many times before the glacier completely vanishes. Such a pattern is illustrated by Figure 17.25, part of the legacy of the last Laurentide Ice Sheet. We should point out that the outermost end moraine marks the limit of the glacial advance. Because of its special status, this end moraine is also called the **terminal moraine**. Conversely, the end moraines that were created as the ice front occasionally stabilized during retreat are termed **recessional moraines**. Note that both terminal and recessional moraines are identical in origin; the only difference between them is their relative positions.

End moraines deposited during the last Ice Age are prominent features in many parts of Ontario. A well-known example north of Lake Ontario is the Oak Ridges Moraine that formed between two lobes of the Laurentide Ice Sheet. This hilly strip of glacial sediment extends westward from Trenton to Orangeville and is an important groundwater resource for the greater Toronto area (Figure 17.26). The moraine formed between the Simcoe and Ontario glacial lobes of the Laurentide Ice Sheet (Figure 17.25) and contains thick channel fills of sand and gravel that compose a large aquifer within and between till aquitards. It is a domestic source of water for Greater Toronto and also stores and discharges clean cool water that is vital to aquatic life in the area.

Figure 17.27 on pages 464 and 465 represents a hypothetical area during glaciation and following the retreat of Canadian ice sheets. It shows the moraines that were described in this section, as well as the depositional features that are discussed in the sections that follow. This figure depicts landscape features similar to what might be encountered if you were travelling in southern Canada during the last Ice Age or in Nunavut or Northwest Territories today. As you read the sections dealing with other glacial deposits, you will be referred to this figure several times.

Drumlins

Moraines are not the only landforms deposited by glaciers. In some areas that were once covered by

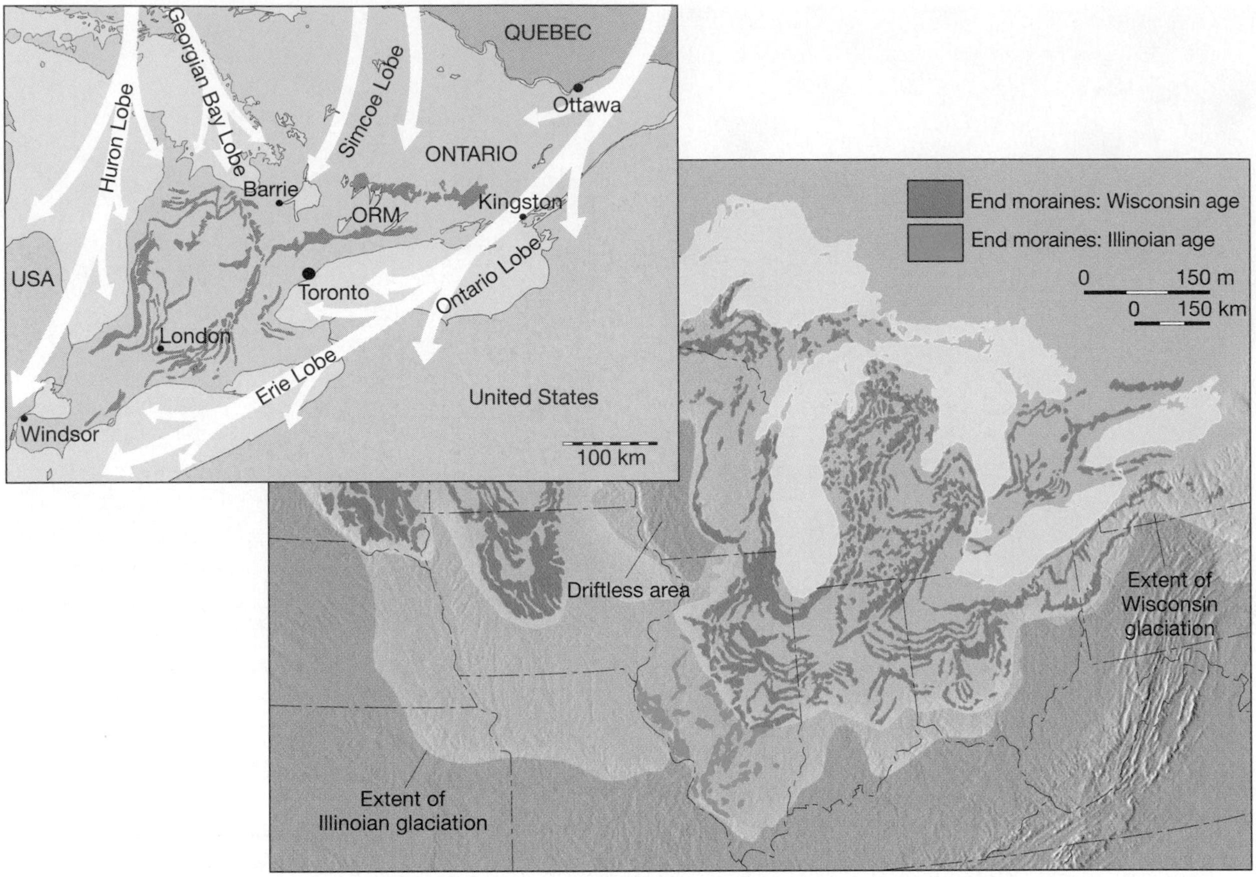

◆ **Figure 17.25** End moraines of central North America recording farthest advance of the Laurentide Ice Sheet during the last Ice Age. Moraines deposited during the most recent (Wisconsin) glaciation are most prominent. **Inset:** Close-up view of eastern Great Lakes region showing flow directions of major ice lobes; note that "ORM" marks the location of the Oak Ridges Moraine (shown in more detail in Figure 17.26, below).

◆ **Figure 17.26** Oak Ridges Moraine (pink) depicted in a digital elevation model image. The moraine is an important aquifer and aggregate reserve for the greater Toronto area.
(Reproduced with the permission of the Minister of Public Works and Government Services Canada, 2008, and courtesy of Natural Resources Canada)

continental ice sheets, a special variety of glacial landscape exists—one characterized by smooth, teardrop-shaped, parallel hills called **drumlins** (Figure 17.27). Good examples occur on islands off the Saanich Peninsula of southern Vancouver Island, British Columbia; on the Morley Flats near Calgary, Alberta (Figure 17.27B); in the Guelph and Peterborough areas of Ontario; and Gaetz Head near Halifax, Nova Scotia.

These streamlined asymmetrical hills are composed largely of till but can also contain sand and gravel. They range in height from about 15 to 50 metres and can be up to 1 kilometre long. The steep side of the hill faces the direction from which the ice advanced, whereas the gentler, longer slope points in the direction the ice moved. Drumlins are occasionally found as isolated landforms but usually occur in clusters called *drumlin fields* (Figure 17.28). Two such clusters occur near Peterborough and Guelph, Ontario. The Peterborough drumlin field alone is estimated to contain about 3000 drumlins. Although drumlin formation is not fully understood, their streamlined shape indicates that they were moulded under the zone of plastic flow of an active glacier. It is thought that many drumlins originate when glaciers advance over previously deposited drift and reshape the material.

LANDFORMS MADE OF STRATIFIED DRIFT

As the name implies, stratified drift is sorted according to the size and weight of the particles. Because ice is not capable of such sorting activity, these materials are not deposited directly by the glacier as till is but instead reflect the sorting action of glacial meltwater. Accumulations of stratified drift commonly comprise sand and gravel—that is, bed-load material—because the finer rock flour remains suspended and therefore is carried far from the glacier by the meltwater streams. The rock flour may settle in ponds and lakes, where it becomes laminated (called *varves* if they are annual layers). The laminations may be deformed by *dropstones* that melted out of icebergs and landed on the bottom of the lake. The sand and gravel provides aggregate for the construction industry to make concrete and asphalt (see Chapter 20). Buried deposits of sand and gravel make excellent aquifers, and clay from glacial lake deposits is used to make bricks and tile.

Outwash Plains and Valley Trains

At the same time as an end moraine is forming, water from the melting glacier cascades over the till, sweeping some of it out in front of the growing ridge of poorly sorted debris. Meltwater generally emerges from the ice in rapidly moving streams that are commonly choked with suspended material and carry a substantial bed load as well. As the water leaves the glacier, it moves onto the relatively flat surface beyond and rapidly loses velocity. As a consequence, much of its bed load is dropped and the meltwater begins weaving a complex pattern of braided channels (Figures 17.27 and 15.19A). In this way, a broad, ramplike surface composed of stratified drift is built adjacent to the downstream edge of most end moraines. When the feature is formed in association with an ice sheet, it is termed an **outwash plain**, and when largely confined to a mountain valley, it is usually referred to as a **valley train**.

Outwash plains and valley trains commonly are pockmarked with basins or depressions known as **kettles** (Figure 17.27). Kettles also occur in deposits of till. Kettles are formed when blocks of stagnant ice become wholly or partly buried in drift and eventually melt, leaving pits in the glacial sediment. Although most kettles do not exceed 2 kilometres in diameter, some with diameters exceeding 10 kilometres are known. In many cases water eventually fills the depression and forms a pond or lake. A good example is Sifton Bog in London, Ontario, the most southern large acidic bog in Canada.

Ice-Contact Deposits

When the melting terminus of a glacier shrinks to a critical point, flow virtually stops and the ice becomes stagnant. Meltwater that flows over, within, and at the base of the motionless ice deposits stratified drift. Then, as the supporting ice melts away, the stratified sediment is left behind in the form of hills, terraces, and ridges. Such accumulations are collectively termed **ice-contact deposits** and are classified according to their shapes.

When the ice-contact stratified drift is in the form of a mound or steep-sided hill, it is called a **kame** (Figure 17.27). Some kames represent bodies of sediment deposited by meltwater in openings within, or in depressions on top of, the ice. Others originate as deltas or fans built outward from the ice by meltwater streams. Later, when the stagnant ice melts away, these various accumulations of sediment collapse to form isolated, irregular mounds.

When glacial ice occupies a valley, **kame terraces** may be built along the sides of the valley. These features commonly are narrow masses of stratified drift deposited between the glacier and the side of the valley by streams that drop debris along the margins of the shrinking ice mass.

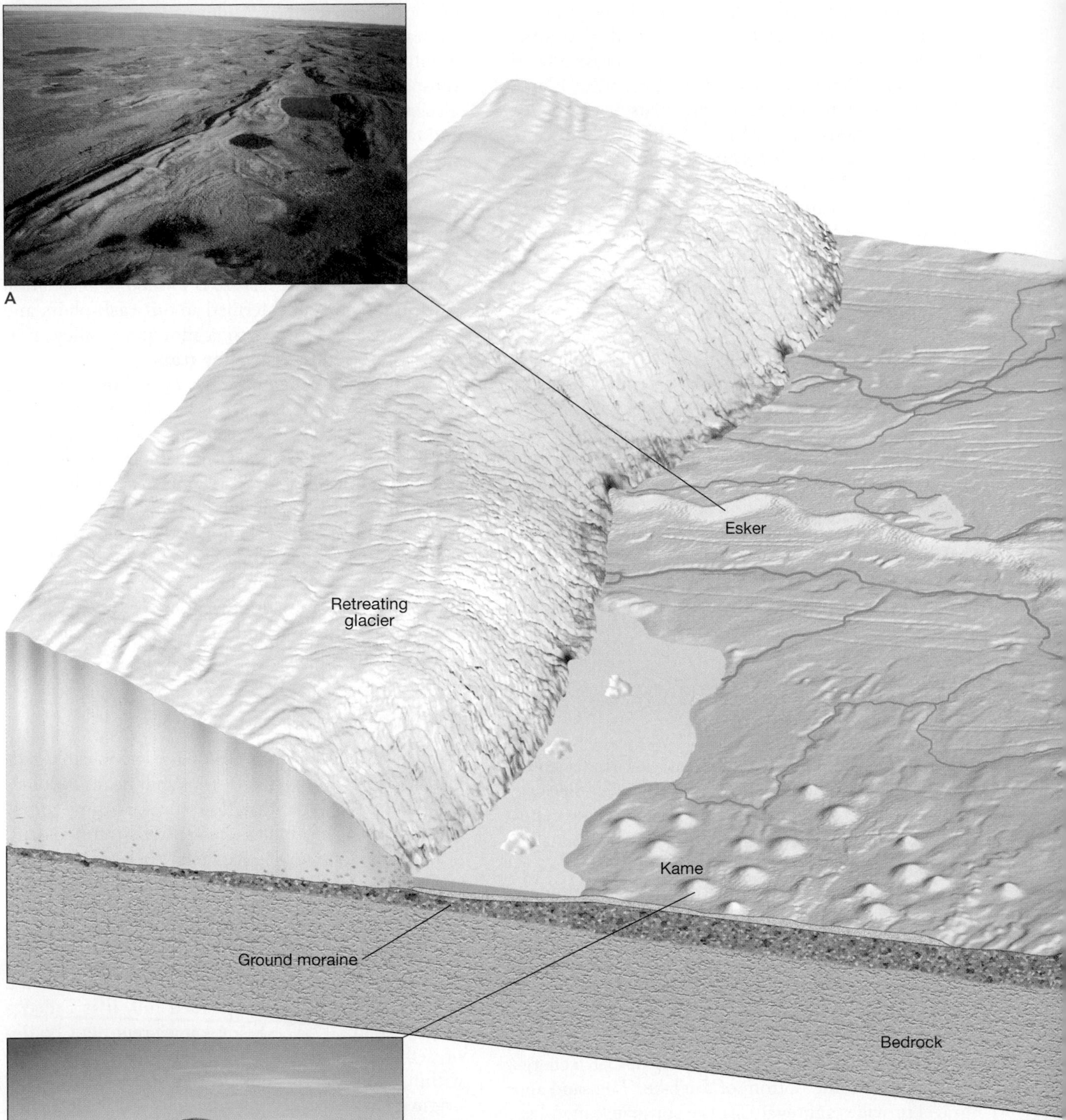

◆ **Figure 17.27** This hypothetical area in Canada illustrates many common landforms deposited by an ice sheet. **A.** Esker in Nunavut. **B.** Drumlin at Morley flats near Calgary. **C.** Kame in Nunavut. **D.** Kettle hole in Northwest Territories.
(Photos **A** and **C** by S. R. Hicock; photo **B** by Christopher Collom; photo **D** by Lynda Dredge. Reproduced with the permission of the Minister of Public Works and Government Services Canada, 2008, and courtesy of Natural Resources Canada, Geological Survey of Canada.)

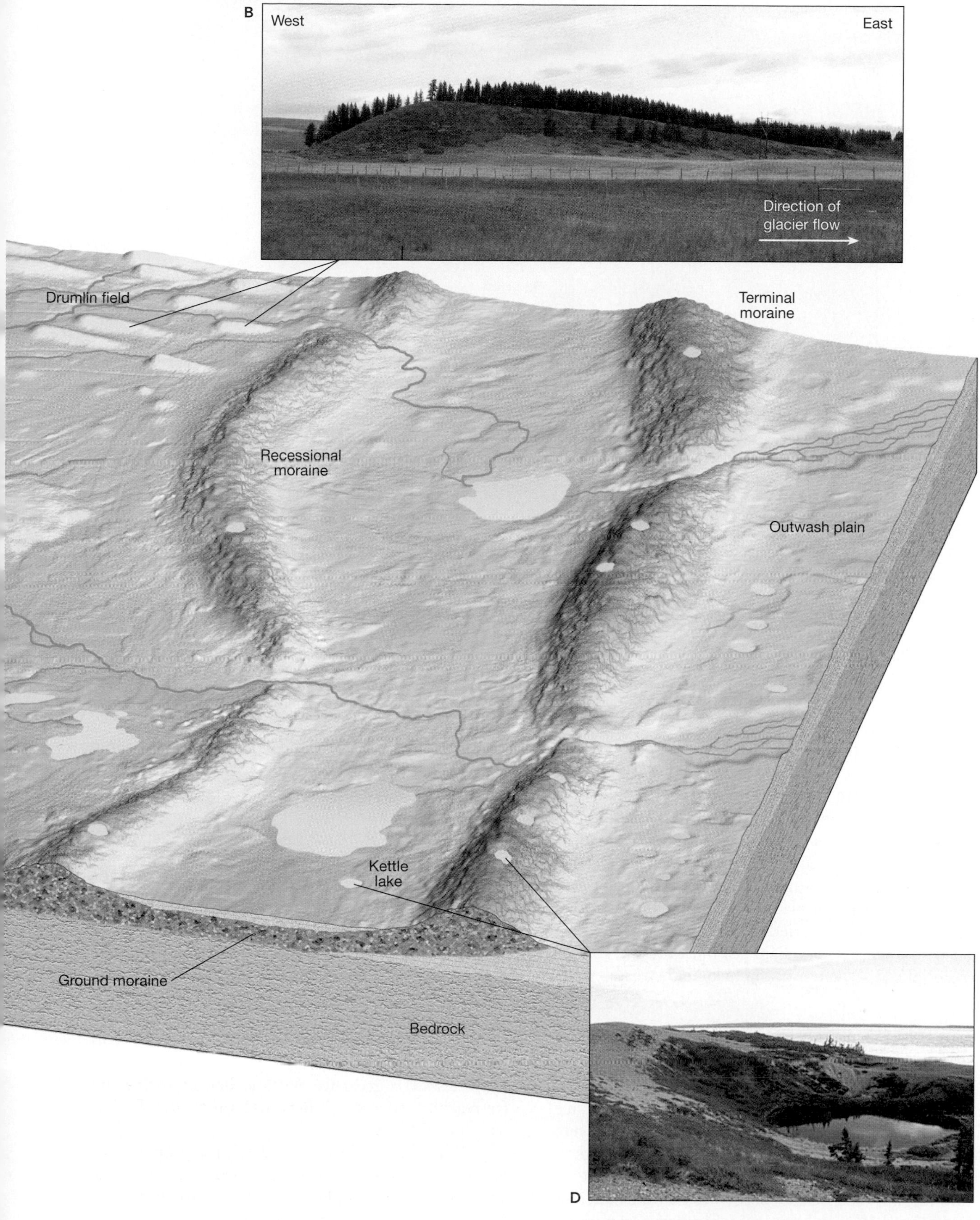
B
West
East
Direction of glacier flow
Drumlin field
Terminal moraine
Recessional moraine
Outwash plain
Kettle lake
Ground moraine
Bedrock
D

◆ **Figure 17.28** Map of Peterborough, Ontario, drumlin field.

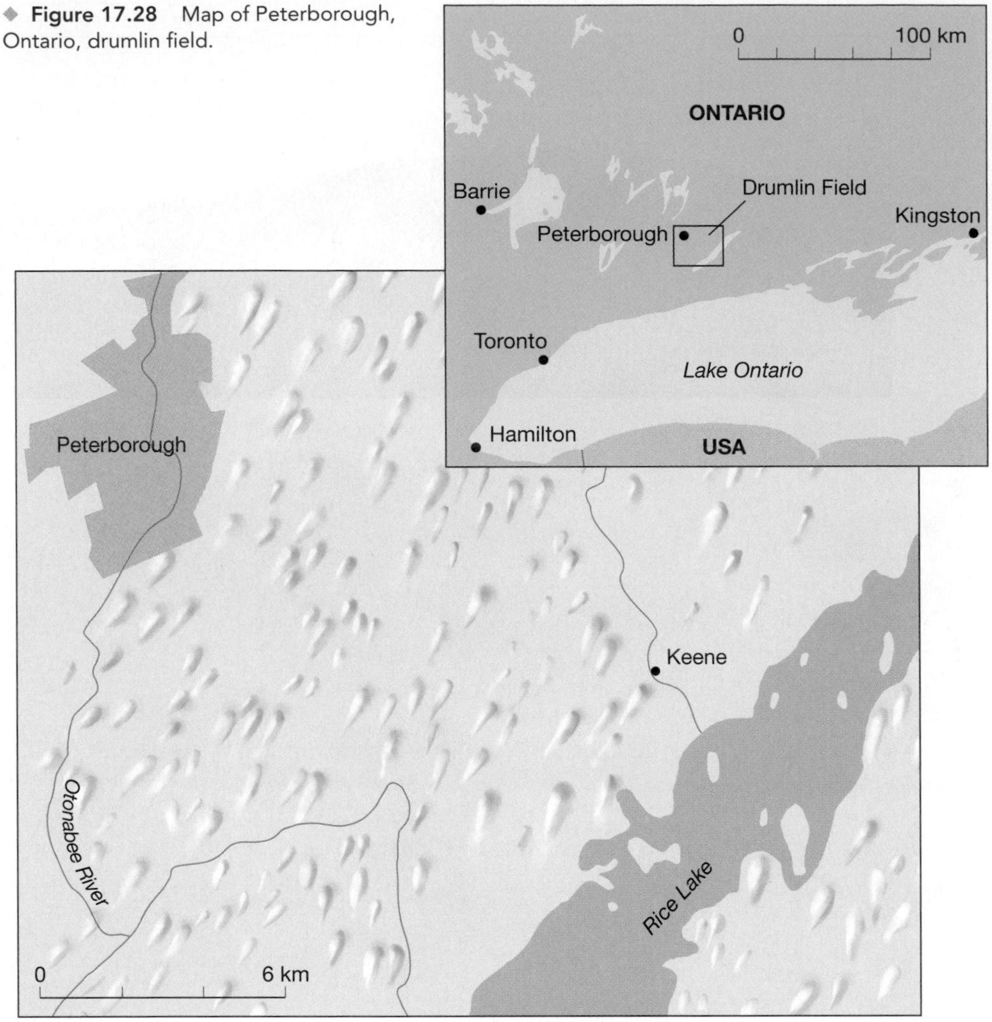

A third type of ice-contact deposit is a long, narrow, sinuous ridge composed largely of sand and gravel. Some are more than 100 metres high, with lengths in excess of 100 kilometres. The dimensions of many others are far less spectacular. Known as **eskers**, these ridges are deposited by meltwater rivers flowing within, on top of, and beneath a mass of motionless, stagnant glacial ice (Figure 17.27). Many sediment sizes are carried by the torrents of meltwater in the ice-banked channels, but only the coarser material can settle out of the turbulent stream.

THE GLACIAL THEORY AND THE ICE AGE

In the preceding pages we referred to the last Ice Age, a time when ice sheets and alpine glaciers were far more extensive than they are today. As noted, at one time the most popular explanation for what we now know to be glacial deposits was that the materials had been drifted in by means of icebergs or perhaps simply swept across the landscape by a catastrophic flood. What convinced geologists that an extensive Ice Age was responsible for these deposits and many other glacial features?

In 1821 a Swiss engineer, Ignaz Venetz, presented a paper suggesting that glacial landscape features occurred at considerable distances from the existing glaciers in the Alps. This implied that the glaciers had once been larger and occupied positions farther down-valley. Another Swiss scientist, Louis Agassiz, doubted the proposal of widespread glacial activity put forth by Venetz. He set out to prove that the idea was not valid. Ironically, his 1836 fieldwork in the Alps convinced him of the merits of his colleague's hypothesis. In fact, a year later Agassiz hypothesized a great ice age that had extensive and far-reaching effects—an idea that was to give Agassiz widespread fame.

The proof of the glacial theory proposed by Agassiz and others constitutes a classic example of applying the principle of uniformitarianism (see Chapter 1). Realizing that certain features are produced by no other known process but glacial action, they were able to begin reconstructing the extent of now-vanished ice sheets based on the presence of features and deposits found far beyond the margins of present-day glaciers. In this manner, the development and verification of the glacial theory continued during the nineteenth century, and through the efforts of many scientists, knowledge of the nature and extent of former ice sheets became clear.

By the beginning of the twentieth century, geologists had largely determined the aerial extent of the Ice Age glaciation. During their investigations, they had discovered that many glaciated regions had not one layer of drift but several. Moreover, close examination of these older deposits showed well-developed zones of chemical weathering and ancient soils, as well as the remains of plants that require warm temperatures. The evidence was clear: not just one glacial advance but many had occurred, each separated by extended intervals when climates were as warm or warmer than the present. The Ice Age had not simply been a time when the ice advanced over the land, lingered for a while, and then receded. Rather, it was a very complex event, characterized by a number of advances and withdrawals of glacial ice.

By the early twentieth century, a fourfold division of the Ice Age had been established for both North America and Europe. The divisions were based largely on studies of glacial deposits. In North America each of the four major stages was named for the midwest state of the United States where deposits of that stage were well exposed or were first studied. These were, in order from oldest to youngest: the Nebraskan, Kansan, Illinoian, and Wisconsin. These traditional divisions remained in place through most of the twentieth century, until it was learned that sediment cores from the ocean floor, and ice cores from ice sheets, contain a much more complete record of climate change during the last Ice Age. Unlike the glacial record on land, which is punctuated by many unconformities (since glaciers tend to destroy early deposits), seafloor sediments and ice cores provide an uninterrupted record of climatic cycles for the Ice Age because of minimal erosion. Studies of these cores showed that glacial/interglacial cycles had occurred about every 100,000 years. More than 20 such cycles of cooling and warming were identified for the span we call the Ice Age.

During the Ice Age, glaciers left their imprint on almost 30 percent of Earth's land area, including about 10 million square kilometres of North America, 5 million square kilometres of Europe, and 4 million square kilometres of Siberia (Figure 17.29). The amount of glacial ice in the Northern Hemisphere was roughly twice that of the Southern Hemisphere.

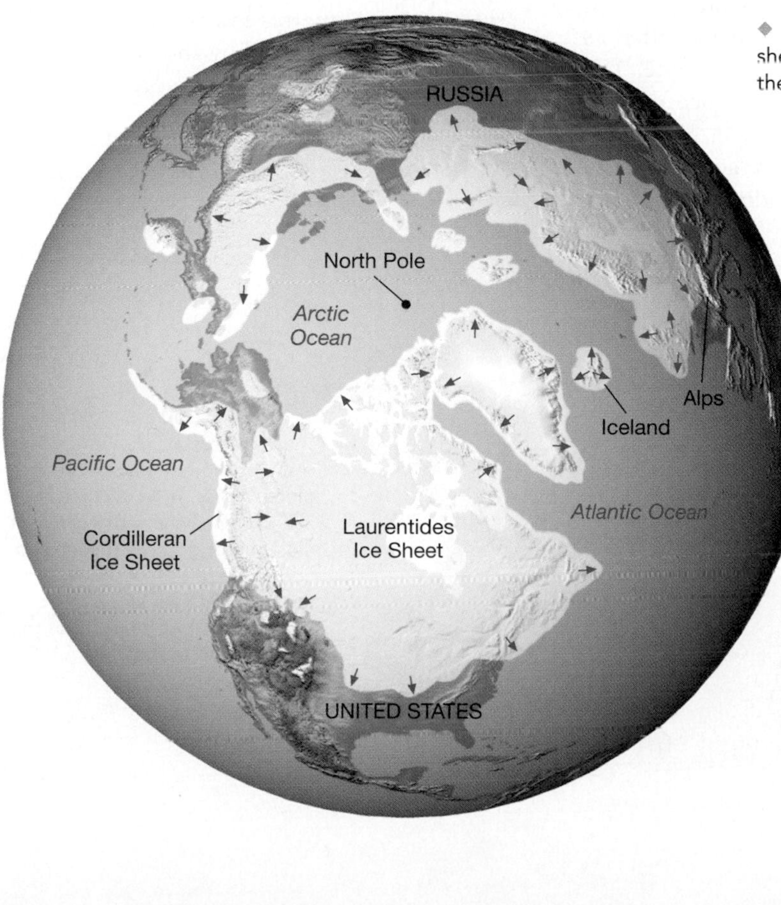

◆ **Figure 17.29** Maximum extent of ice sheets in the Northern Hemisphere during the last Ice Age, about 20,000 years ago.

The primary reason is that the southern polar ice could not spread far beyond the margins of Antarctica. By contrast, North America and Eurasia provided great expanses of land for the spread of ice sheets.

Today, we know that the Ice Age began between 3 million and 2 million years ago. This means that most of the major glacial stages occurred during a division of the geologic time scale called the Pleistocene Epoch (Chapter 8). Although the Pleistocene is commonly used as a synonym for the Ice Age, note that this epoch does not encompass all of the last glacial episode. The Antarctic Ice Sheet, for example, probably formed at least 20 million years ago.

SOME INDIRECT EFFECTS OF ICE-AGE GLACIERS

In addition to the massive erosional and depositional work carried on by Ice Age glaciers (Figure 17.29), the ice sheets had other, sometimes profound, effects on the landscape. For example, as the ice advanced and retreated, animals and plants were forced to migrate. This led to stresses that some organisms could not tolerate. Hence, a number of plants and animals became extinct.

Furthermore, many present-day stream courses bear little resemblance to their pre-glacial routes. Other rivers, called misfit streams (Chapter 15), that today carry only a trickle of water but nevertheless occupy broad channels called spillways (Chapter 15), are testimony to the fact that they once carried torrents of glacial meltwater.

In areas that were centres of ice accumulation, such as Scandinavia and the Canadian Shield, the land has been slowly rising over the past several thousand years. Uplifting of almost 300 metres has occurred in the Hudson Bay region. This, too, is the result of the ice sheets. But how can glacial ice cause such vertical crustal movement? We now understand that the land is rising because the added weight of a 3-kilometre-thick mass of ice like the Laurentide Ice Sheet caused downwarping of Earth's crust. Following the removal of this immense load, the crust has been adjusting by gradually rebounding ever since (Figure 17.30).*

Certainly, one of the most interesting and perhaps dramatic effects of the Ice Age was the fall and rise of sea level that accompanied the advance and retreat of the ice sheets. Earlier in the chapter we pointed out that sea level would rise by an estimated 60 or 70 metres if the water locked up in the Antarctic Ice Sheet were to melt completely. Such an occurrence would flood many densely populated coastal areas (see Figure 17.5).

Although the total volume of glacial ice today is great, exceeding 25 million cubic kilometres, during the Ice Age the volume of glacial ice amounted to about 70 million cubic kilometres (Figure 17.29), or 45 million cubic kilometres more than at present. Because we know that the snow from which glaciers are made ultimately comes from the evaporation of ocean water, the growth of ice sheets must have caused a worldwide drop in sea level (Figures 17.5 and 17.31). Indeed, estimates suggest that sea level was at least 100 metres lower than today. Thus, land that is presently flooded by the oceans was dry. The Atlantic Coast of Canada lay more than 100 kilome-

*For a more complete discussion of this concept, termed *isostatic adjustment*, see the section on isostasy in Chapter 13.

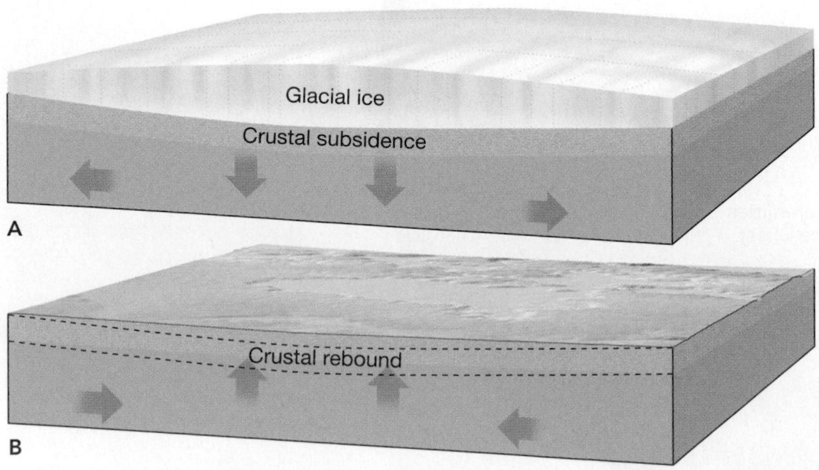

◆ **Figure 17.30** Simplified illustration showing crustal subsidence and rebound resulting from the addition and removal of ice sheets. **A.** In northern Canada and Scandinavia, where the greatest accumulation of glacial ice occurred, the added weight caused downwarping of the crust. **B.** Ever since the ice melted, gradual uplift or rebound of the crust has been occurring.

tres to the east of Nova Scotia; France and Britain were joined where the English Channel is today; Alaska and Siberia were connected across the Bering Strait; and Southeast Asia was tied by dry land to the islands of Indonesia.

Although formation and growth of ice sheets was an obvious response to significant changes in climate, the existence of the ice sheets triggered important climatic changes in the regions beyond their margins. In central Canada, glacial Lake Agassiz was the largest lake in North America (Figure 17.32) and may have discharged down the St. Lawrence River into the North Atlantic. It was dammed by the retreating margin of the Laurentide Ice Sheet and drained down the Mississippi into the Gulf of Mexico for most of its life. Lake Winnipeg is the largest remnant of Lake Agassiz. About the time of Lake Agassiz, strong winds blowing off the retreating Laurentide Ice Sheet picked up fine dust from freshly exposed ground moraine and stratified drift, and then deposited the dust in what is now the northern United States. These aeolian dust deposits are referred to as *loess* and today they make fertile farmland (more details in Chapter 18).

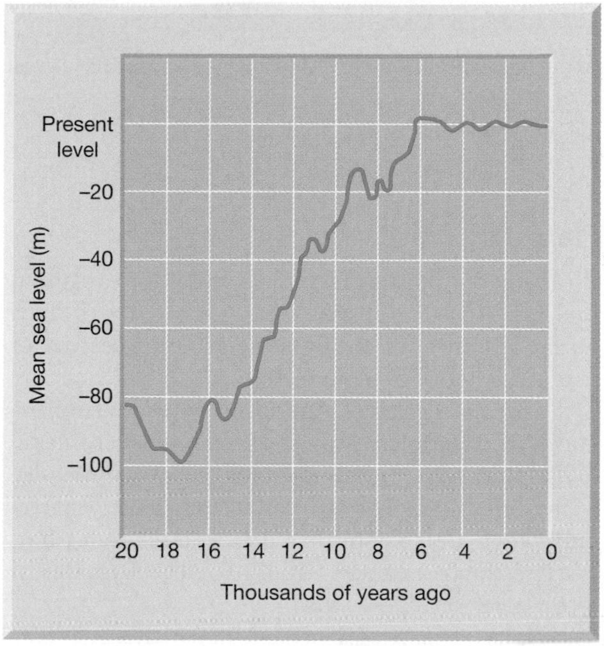

◆ **Figure 17.31** Changing sea level during the past 20,000 years (based on carbon-14 dating). The lowest level shown on the graph represents the time when the most recent Ice Age was at its maximum.

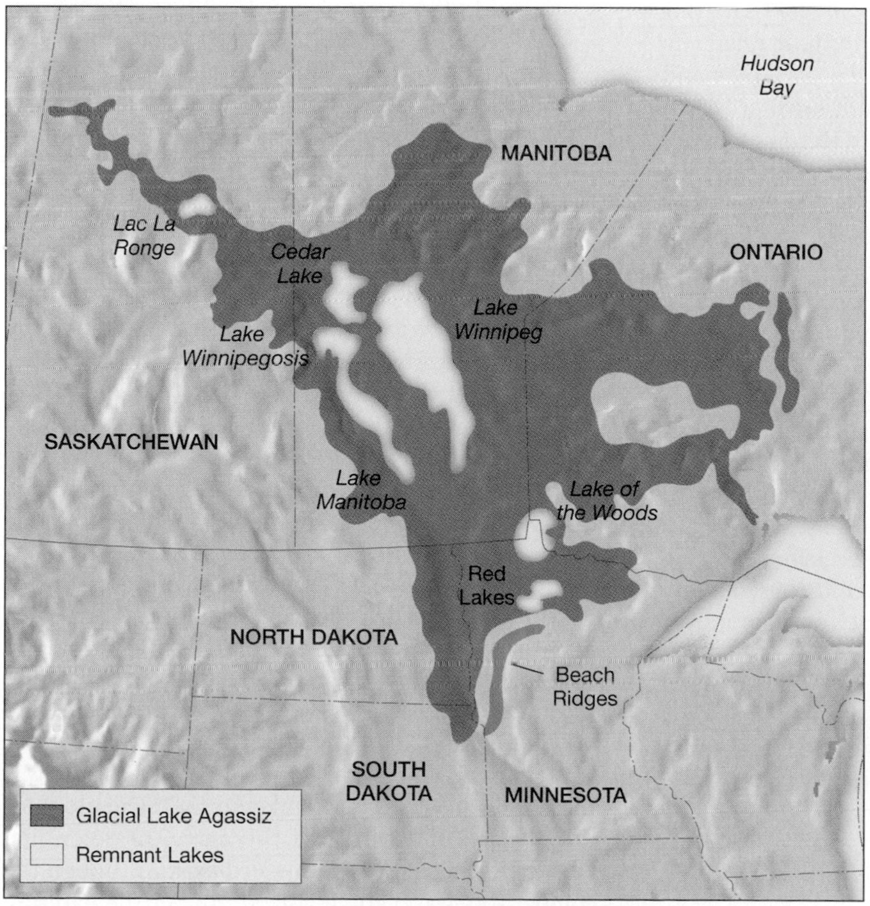

◆ **Figure 17.32** Glacial Lake Agassiz, in central Canada. (Image courtesy of the Minnesota Department of Natural Resources)

CAUSES OF ICE AGES

Although the literature of science contains a vast array of hypotheses relating to the possible *causes* of glacial episodes, we will discuss only a few major ideas to summarize current thought.

Plate Tectonics

Probably the most attractive proposal for explaining the fact that extensive ice ages of Earth have occurred only a few times in the geologic past comes from the theory of plate tectonics.*

Because glaciers can form only on land, we know that landmasses must exist somewhere in the higher latitudes before an ice age can commence. Many scientists suggest that ice ages have occurred only when Earth's shifting lithospheric plates have carried the continents from tropical latitudes to more pole-ward positions.

Glacial features in present-day Africa, Australia, South America, and India indicate that these regions, which are now tropical or subtropical, experienced an Ice Age near the end of the Paleozoic Era, about 250 million years ago (see Chapter 1). However, no evidence shows that ice sheets existed during this same episode in what are today the higher latitudes of North America and Eurasia. For many years this puzzled scientists. Was the climate in these relatively tropical latitudes once like it is today in Greenland and Antarctica? Why did glaciers not form in North America and Eurasia? Until the plate tectonics theory was formulated, we had no reasonable explanation.

Today scientists understand that the areas containing these ancient glacial features were joined together as a single supercontinent (Pangaea) located at latitudes far to the south of their present positions. Later this landmass broke apart and its pieces, each moving on a different plate, migrated toward their present locations (see Figure 1.16). Now we know that during the geologic past, plate movements accounted for many dramatic climatic changes as landmasses shifted in relation to one another and moved to different latitudinal positions. Changes in oceanic circulation also must have occurred, altering the transport of heat and moisture and consequently the climate as well. Because the rate of plate movement is very slow—a few centimetres annually—appreciable changes in the positions of the continents occur only over great spans of geologic time. Thus, climatic changes triggered by shifting plates are extremely gradual and happen on a scale of millions of years.

*A brief overview of the theory appears in Chapter 1, and a more extensive discussion is presented in Chapter 12.

Variations in Earth's Orbit

Because climatic changes brought about by moving plates are extremely gradual, the plate tectonics theory cannot be used to explain the alternation between glacial and interglacial climates that occurred during the Pleistocene Epoch. Therefore, we must look to some other triggering mechanism that might cause climatic change on a scale of thousands rather than millions of years. Many scientists today strongly suspect that the climatic oscillations that characterized the Pleistocene were linked to variations in Earth's orbit. This hypothesis was first developed by the Scottish scientist James Croll in the nineteenth century and later strongly advocated in the early twentieth century by the Serbian scientist Milutin Milankovitch. It is based on the premise that variations in incoming solar radiation are principal factors in controlling Earth's climate.

Milankovitch formulated a comprehensive mathematical model based on the following elements (Figure 17.33):

1. Variations in the shape (*eccentricity*) of Earth's orbit about the Sun
2. Changes in *obliquity*; that is, changes in the angle that the axis makes with the plane of Earth's orbit
3. The wobbling of Earth's axis, called *precession*

By using these factors, Milankovitch calculated variations in the receipt of solar energy and the corresponding surface temperature of Earth back into time in an attempt to correlate these changes with the climatic fluctuations of the Pleistocene. In explaining climatic changes that result from these three variables, note that they cause little or no variation in the total solar energy reaching the ground. Instead, their impact is felt because they change the degree of contrast between the seasons. Somewhat milder winters in the middle to high latitudes means greater snowfall totals, whereas cooler summers bring a reduction in snowmelt.

Later in the twentieth century, international teams of scientists added credibility to the astronomic theory of Milankovitch. Deep-sea sediments containing certain climatically sensitive microorganisms were analyzed to establish a chronology of temperature changes going back nearly half a million years. Ice cores containing remnant bubbles of Pleistocene greenhouse gases were also analyzed to corroborate the later part of that chronology.

This geologic time scale of climatic change was then compared with Milankovitch's calculations of eccentricity, obliquity, and precession to determine whether a correlation did indeed exist. Although the comparison was very involved and mathematically

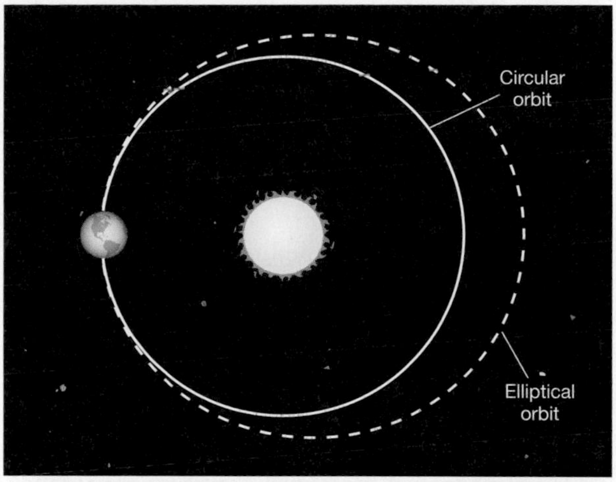

A

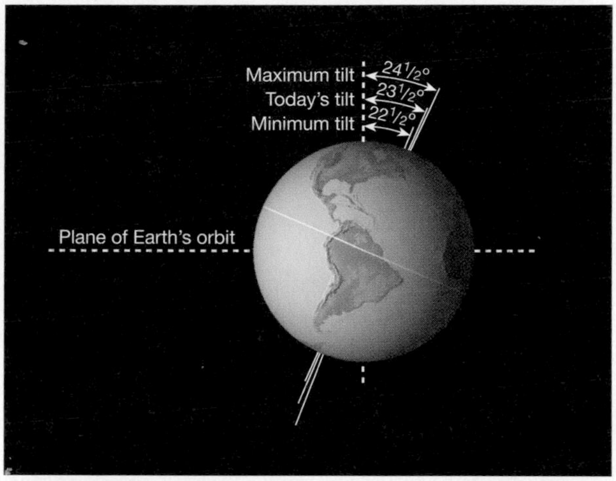

B

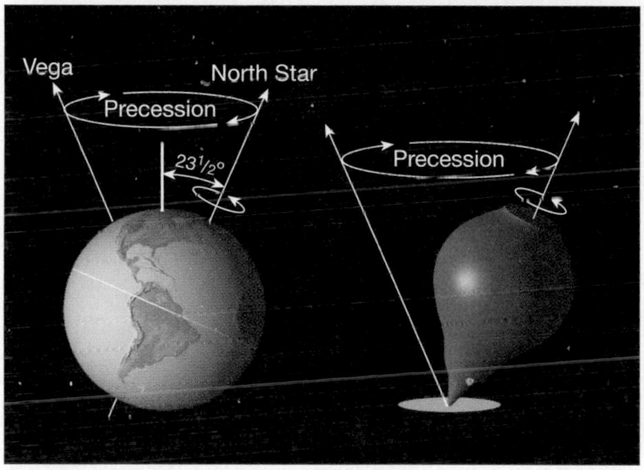

C

◆ **Figure 17.33** Orbital variations. **A.** Eccentricity. The shape of Earth's orbit changes during a cycle that spans about 100,000 years. It gradually changes from nearly circular to one that is more elliptical and back again. This diagram greatly exaggerates the amount of change. **B.** Obliquity. Today the axis of rotation is tilted about 23.5 degrees to the plane of Earth's orbit. During a cycle of 41,000 years, this angle varies from 21.5 degrees to 24.5 degrees. **C.** Precession. Earth's axis wobbles like that of a spinning top. Consequently, the axis points to different spots in the sky during a cycle of about 26,000 years.

complex, the conclusions were straightforward. The researchers found that major variations in climate over the past several hundred thousand years were closely associated with changes in the geometry of Earth's orbit; that is, cycles of climatic change were shown to correspond closely with the periods of obliquity, precession, and orbital eccentricity.

Let us briefly summarize the ideas that we just described. The theory of plate tectonics provides us with an explanation for the widely spaced and non-periodic onset of glacial conditions at various times in the geologic past, whereas the theory proposed by Milankovitch (and supported by later work) furnishes an explanation for the alternating glacial and interglacial episodes *within* the Pleistocene Epoch. Interdisciplinary research of the twenty-first century has been refining the details based on further analyses of terrestrial sediments, ice and deep-sea cores, and ancient and modern greenhouse gases (indicators of global warming). These data are used in constructing computer models of ice sheet behaviour, and oceanic and atmospheric circulation patterns in order to predict changes in global climate and sea level.

Chapter Summary

- A *glacier* is a thick mass of ice originating on land as a result of the compaction and re-crystallization of snow, and it shows evidence of past or present flow. *Ice sheets* exist on a continental scale, presently covering most of Greenland and Antarctica. Today *valley* or *alpine glaciers* are found in mountain areas, where they usually follow valleys that were originally occupied by streams.
- Near the surface of a glacier, in the *zone of fracture*, ice is brittle. However, below about 50 metres, pressure is great, causing ice to flow like plastic material. Other mechanisms of glacial movement involve the entire ice mass slipping over the bed or deforming the glacial bed.
- The average velocity of glacial movement is generally quite slow, but it varies considerably from one glacier to another. The advance of some glaciers is characterized by periods of extremely rapid movements called *surges*.
- Glaciers form in areas where more snow falls in winter than melts in summer. Snow accumulation and ice formation occur in the *zone of accumulation*, whose lower limit is defined by the *equilibrium line*. Beyond the equilibrium line is the *zone of wastage*, where there is a net loss to the glacier. The *glacial budget* is the balance, or lack of balance, between accumulation at the upper end of the glacier, and loss, called *ablation*, at the lower end.
- Glaciers erode land by *plucking* (lifting pieces of bedrock out of place) and *abrasion* (grinding and scraping of a rock surface). Erosional features produced by valley glaciers include *glacial troughs*, *hanging valleys*, *fjords*, *cirques*, *arêtes*, *horns*, and *roches moutonnées*.
- Any sediment of glacial origin is called drift. The two distinct types of *glacial drift* are (1) *till*, which is poorly sorted sediment deposited directly by the ice; and (2) *stratified drift*, which is relatively well sorted sediment deposited by glacial meltwater.
- The most widespread features created by glacial deposition are layers or ridges of till, called moraines. Associated with valley glaciers are *lateral moraines*, formed along the sides of the valley, and *medial moraines*, formed between two valley glaciers that have joined. *End moraines*, which mark the former position of the front of a glacier, and *ground moraines*, undulating layers of till deposited as the ice front advances then retreats, are common to both valley glaciers and ice sheets. An *outwash plain* is commonly associated with the end moraine of an ice sheet. A *valley train* may form when the glacier is confined to a valley. Other depositional features include *drumlins* (streamlined asymmetrical hills composed mainly of till), *eskers* (sinuous ridges composed largely of sand and gravel deposited by streams flowing in tunnels beneath the ice, near the terminus of a glacier), and *kames* (steep-sided hills consisting of sand and gravel).
- In addition to massive erosional and depositional work, other effects of Ice Age glaciers included the forced migration of organisms, changes in stream courses, adjustment of the crust by rebounding after the removal of the immense load of ice, and climate changes caused by the existence of the glaciers themselves. In the sea, the most far-reaching effect of the Ice Age was the worldwide change in sea level that accompanied each advance and retreat of the ice sheets.
- Ice ages appear to be caused primarily by the combined effects of plate tectonics moving large landmasses near the poles, and variations in Earth's orbital cycles around the Sun, including eccentricity (departure from circular) of the orbital plane, obliquity (tilt) of the rotational axis to the orbital plane, and precession (wobble) of the rotational axis.

Review Questions

1. Where are glaciers found today? What percentage of Earth's land area do they cover? How does this compare to the area covered by glaciers during the Ice Age?

2. Describe how glaciers fit into the hydrologic cycle. What role do they play in the rock cycle?

3. Each statement below refers to a particular type of glacier. Name the type of glacier.

(a) The term *continental* is often used to describe this type of glacier.

(b) This type of glacier is also called an *alpine glacier*.

(c) This is a body of ice flowing from the margin of an ice sheet through the mountains to the sea.

(d) This is a glacier formed when one or more valley glaciers spreads out at the base of a steep mountain front.

(e) Greenland is the only example in the Northern Hemisphere.

4. Describe the three components of glacial flow. At what rates do glaciers move? Vertically in a glacier, does all of the ice move at the same rate? Explain.
5. Why do crevasses form in the upper portion of a glacier but not below 50 metres?
6. Under what circumstances will the front of a glacier advance? Retreat? Remain stationary?
7. Describe the processes of glacial erosion.
8. How does a glaciated mountain valley differ in appearance from a mountain valley that was not glaciated?
9. List and describe the erosional features you might expect to see in an area where valley glaciers exist or have recently existed.
10. What is glacial drift? What is the difference between till and stratified drift? What general effect do glacial deposits have on the landscape?
11. List the four basic moraine types. What do all moraines have in common? What is the significance of terminal and recessional moraines?
12. Why are medial moraines proof that valley glaciers must move?
13. How do kettles form?
14. What direction was the ice sheet moving that affected the area shown in Figure 17.28? Explain how you were able to determine this.
15. What are ice-contact deposits? Distinguish between kames and eskers.
16. List three indirect effects of Ice Age glaciers.

Key Terms

ablation (p. 449)
abrasion (p. 452)
alpine glacier (p. 446)
arête (p. 456)
basal slip (p. 448)
calving (p. 449)
cirque (p. 454)
col (p. 454)
crevasse (p. 448)
drumlin (p. 463)
end moraine (p. 460)
equilibrium line (p. 449)
esker (p. 466)
firn (p. 448)
fjord (p. 454)
glacial budget (p. 450)
glacial drift (p. 457)
glacial erratic (p. 458)
glacial striations (p. 452)
glacial trough (p. 454)
glacier (p. 445)
ground moraine (p. 461)
hanging valley (p. 454)
horn (p. 456)
ice cap (p. 446)
ice-contact deposit (p. 463)
ice sheet (p. 445)
ice shelf (p. 445)
ice stream (p. 446)
internal deformation (p. 448)
kame (p. 463)
kame terrace (p. 463)
kettle (p. 463)
lateral moraine (p. 460)
mass balance (p. 450)
medial moraine (p. 460)
outlet glacier (p. 446)
outwash plain (p. 463)
piedmont glacier (p. 447)
plucking (p. 452)
recessional moraine (p. 461)
roche moutonnée (p. 456)
rock flour (p. 452)
soft bed deformation (p. 448)
stratified drift (p. 458)
surge (p. 449)
tarn (p. 454)
terminal moraine (p. 461)
till (p. 458)
tillite (p. 458)
truncated spur (p. 454)
valley glacier (p. 446)
valley train (p. 463)
zone of accumulation (p. 449)
zone of fracture (p. 448)
zone of wastage (p. 449)

Web Resources

The *Earth* website uses the resources and flexibility of the internet to aid in your study of the topics in this chapter. Written and developed by geology instructors, this site will help improve your understanding of geology. Visit **www.pearsoned.ca/tarbuck** and click on the cover of the text to find

- online review quizzes
- Web-based critical thinking and writing exercises
- links to chapter-specific Web resources
- internet-wide key-term searches

www.pearsoned.ca/tarbuck

Chapter 18
Deserts and Winds

Distribution and Causes of Dry Lands
- Low-Latitude Deserts
- Middle-Latitude Deserts
- Polar Deserts

Geologic Processes in Arid Climates
- Weathering
- The Role of Water

Transportation of Sediment by Wind
- Bed Load
- Suspended Load

Wind Erosion
- Deflation, Blowouts, and Desert Pavement
- Ventifacts and Yardangs

Wind Deposits
- Sand Deposits
- Types of Sand Dunes
- Loess (Silt) Deposits

The sand dunes in southeast Africa's Namib Desert are the largest in the world. (Photo by M. Harvey/DRK photo)

Climate has a strong influence on the nature and intensity of Earth's external processes, as was clearly demonstrated in the preceding chapter on glaciers. Another excellent example of the strong link between climate and geology is seen when we examine the development of arid landscapes. The word *desert* literally means "deserted" or "unoccupied." For many dry regions this is a very appropriate description, although where water is available in deserts, plants and animals thrive. Nevertheless, the world's dry regions are probably the least familiar land areas on Earth outside the polar realm.

Desert landscapes frequently appear stark. Their profiles are not softened by a carpet of soil and abundant plant life. Instead, barren rocky outcrops with steep, angular slopes are common. At some places the rocks are tinted orange and red. At others they are grey and brown and streaked with black. For many visitors, desert scenery exhibits a striking beauty; to others, the terrain seems bleak. No matter which feeling is elicited, it is clear that deserts are very different from the more humid places where most people live.

As you will see, arid regions are not dominated by a single geologic process. Rather, the effects of tectonic forces, running water, and wind are all apparent. Because these processes combine in different ways from place to place, the appearance of desert landscapes varies a great deal as well (Figure 18.1).

DISTRIBUTION AND CAUSES OF DRY LANDS

GEODe EARTH Deserts and Winds
↳ Distribution and Causes of Dry Lands

The dry regions of the world encompass about 42 million square kilometres, a surprising 30 percent of Earth's land surface. No other climatic group covers so large a land area. Within these water-deficient regions, two climatic types are commonly recognized: **desert**, or arid, and **steppe**, or semi-arid. The two share many features; their differences are primarily a matter of degree (see Box 18.1). The steppe is a marginal and more humid variant of the desert and is

◆ **Figure 18.1** A scene in the Sonoran Desert east of Phoenix, Arizona. The appearance of desert landscapes varies a great deal from place to place; contrast this landscape with that of the chapter-opening photo. (Photo by Tom Bean/DRK Photo)

BOX 18.1

Understanding Earth
What Is Meant by *Dry*?

Albuquerque, New Mexico, in the southwest United States, receives an average of 20.7 centimetres of rainfall annually. As you might expect, because Albuquerque's precipitation total is modest, this location is classified as a desert when standard climate classification is applied. The Russian city of Verkhoyansk is a remote location located near the Arctic Circle in Siberia. There, the yearly precipitation total averages 15.5 centimetres, about 5 centimetres less than Albuquerque's. Although Verkhoyansk receives less precipitation than Albuquerque, its classification is that of a humid climate. How can this occur?

We all recognize that deserts are dry places, but just what is meant by the term *dry*? That is, how much rain defines the boundary between humid and dry regions? Sometimes it is arbitrarily defined by a single rainfall figure, for example, 25 centimetres per year of precipitation. However, the concept of dryness is a relative one that refers to any situation in which a water deficiency exists. Hence, climatologists define *dry climate* as one in which yearly precipitation is not as great as the potential loss of water by evaporation. Dryness then not only is related to annual rainfall totals but also is a function of evaporation, which in turn is closely dependent on temperature.

As temperatures climb, potential evaporation also increases. Fifteen to 25 centimetres of precipitation may be sufficient to support coniferous forests in northern Scandinavia or Siberia, where evaporation into the cool, humid air is slight and a surplus of water remains in the soil. However, the same amount of rain falling on New Mexico or Iran supports only a sparse vegetative cover because evaporation into the hot, dry air is great. So, clearly, no specific amount of precipitation can serve as a universal boundary for dry climates.

To establish the boundary between dry and humid climates, the widely used Köppen classification system uses formulas that involve three variables: average annual precipitation, average annual temperature, and seasonal distribution of precipitation. The use of average annual temperature reflects its importance as an index of evaporation. The amount of rainfall defining the humid–dry boundary is larger where mean annual temperatures are high, and smaller where temperatures are low. The use of seasonal precipitation distribution as a variable is also related to this idea. If rain is concentrated in the warmest months, loss to evaporation is greater than if the precipitation is concentrated in the cooler months.

Table 18.A summarizes the precipitation amounts that divide dry and humid climates. Notice that a station with an annual mean of 20°C and a summer rainfall maximum of 68 centimetres is classified as dry. If the rain falls primarily in winter, however, the station need receive only 40 centimetres or more to be considered humid. If the precipitation is more evenly distributed, the figure defining the humid–dry boundary is in between the other two.

TABLE 18.A **Average Annual Precipitation Defining the Boundary between Dry and Humid Climates**

Average Annual Temperature (C°)	Winter Rainfall Maximum (centimetres)	Even Distribution (centimetres)	Summer Rainfall Maximum (centimetres)
5	10	24	38
10	20	34	48
15	30	44	58
20	40	54	68
25	50	64	78
30	60	74	88

a transition zone that surrounds the desert and separates it from bordering humid climates. The world map showing the distribution of desert and steppe regions reveals that dry lands are concentrated in the subtropics and in the middle latitudes (Figure 18.2).

Low-Latitude Deserts

The heart of the low-latitude dry climates lies in the vicinities of the tropics of Cancer and Capricorn. Figure 18.2 shows a virtually unbroken desert environment stretching for more than 9300 kilometres from the Atlantic coast of North Africa to the dry lands of northwest India. In addition to this single great expanse, the Northern Hemisphere contains another, much smaller, area of tropical desert and steppe in northern Mexico and the southwest United States.

In the Southern Hemisphere, dry climates dominate Australia. Almost 40 percent of the continent is desert, and much of the remainder is steppe. In addition, arid and semi-arid areas occur in southern Africa and make a limited appearance in coastal Chile and Peru.

What causes these bands of low-latitude desert? The answer is the global distribution of air pressure and winds. Figure 18.3 (an idealized diagram of Earth's general circulation) helps the visualization

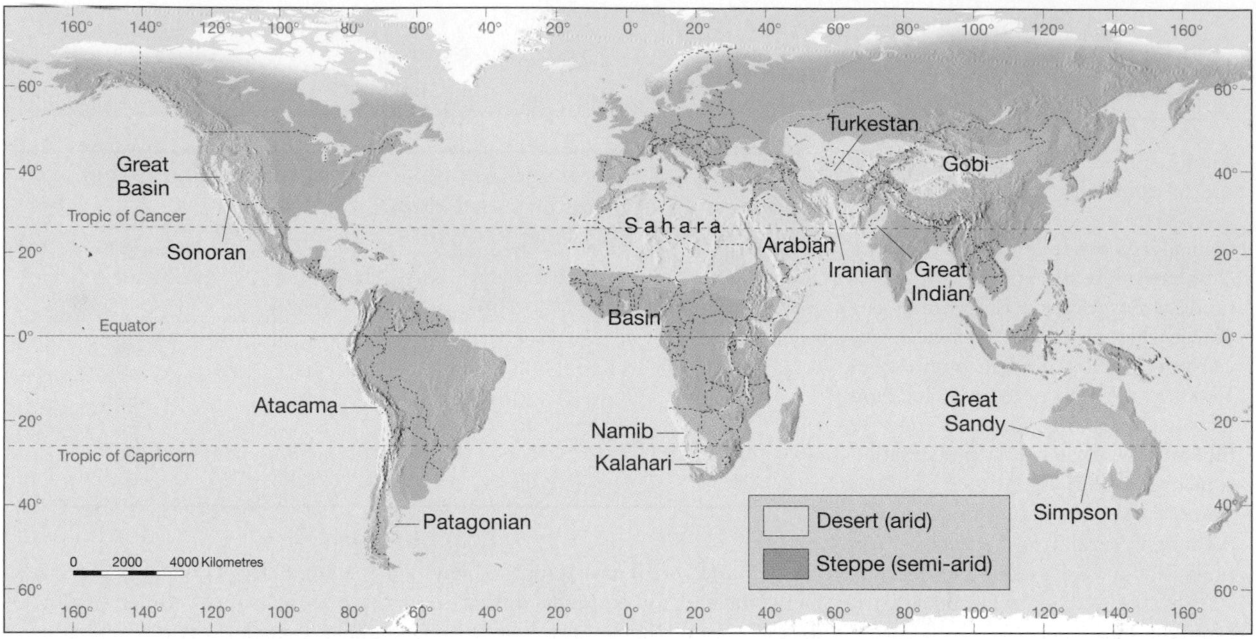

◆ **Figure 18.2** Arid and semi-arid climates cover about 30 percent of Earth's land surface. No other climate group covers so large an area.

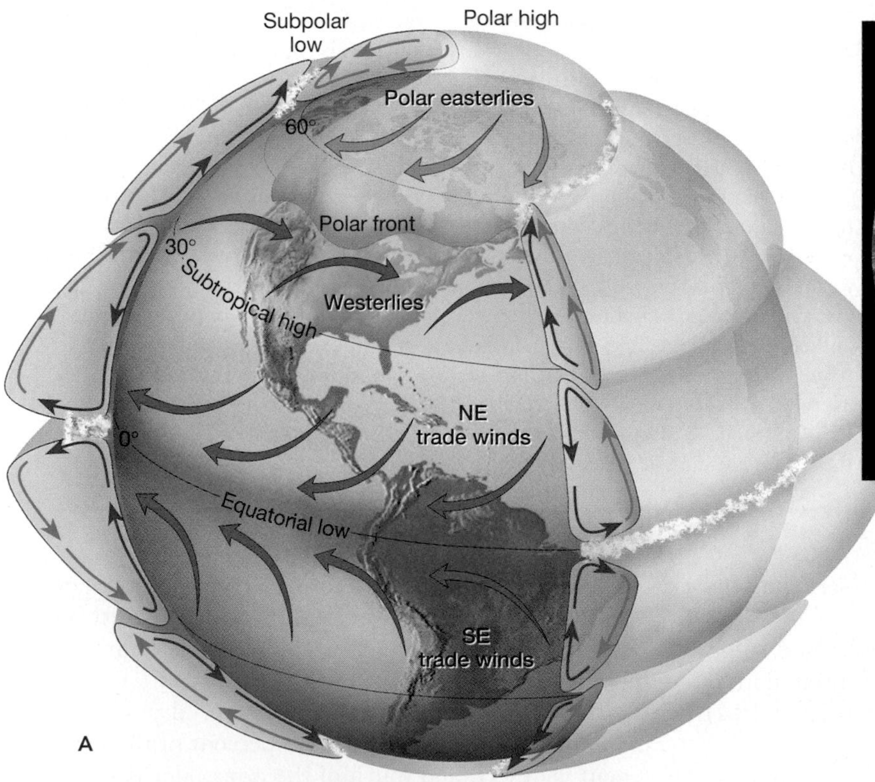

◆ **Figure 18.3** **A.** Idealized diagram of Earth's general circulation. The deserts and steppes that are centred in the latitude belt between 20° and 30° north and south coincide with the subtropical high-pressure belts. Here dry, subsiding air inhibits cloud formation and precipitation. By contrast, the pressure belt known as the equatorial low is associated with areas that are among the rainiest on Earth. **B.** In this view of Earth from space, North Africa's Sahara Desert, the adjacent Arabian Desert, and the Kalahari and Namib deserts in southern Africa are clearly visible as tan-coloured, cloud-free zones. The band of clouds that extends across central Africa and the adjacent oceans coincides with the equatorial low-pressure belt.
(Photo courtesy of NASA)

of the relationship. Heated air in the pressure belt known as the *equatorial low* rises to great heights (usually between 15 and 20 kilometres) and then spreads out. As the upper-level flow reaches 20° to 30° latitude, north or south, it sinks toward the surface. Air that rises through the atmosphere expands and cools, a process that leads to the development of clouds and precipitation. For this reason, the areas under the influence of the equatorial low are among the rainiest on Earth. Just the opposite is true for the regions near 30° north and south latitude, where high pressure predominates. Here, in the zones known as the *subtropical highs*, air is subsiding. When air sinks, it is compressed and warmed. Such conditions are just the opposite of what is needed to produce clouds and precipitation. Consequently, these regions are known for their clear skies, sunshine, and ongoing drought (Figure 18.3B).

Middle-Latitude Deserts

Unlike their low-latitude counterparts, middle-latitude deserts and steppes are not controlled by the subsiding air masses associated with high pressure. Instead, these dry lands exist principally because they are sheltered in the deep interiors of large landmasses. They are far removed from the ocean, which is the ultimate source of moisture for cloud formation and precipitation. One well-known example is the Gobi Desert of central Asia, north of India (Figure 18.2).

The presence of high mountains across the paths of prevailing winds further separates these areas from water-bearing, maritime air masses; the mountains also force the air to lose much of its water. The mechanism is simple: as prevailing winds meet mountain barriers, the air is forced to ascend. When air rises, it expands and cools, a process that can produce clouds and precipitation. The windward sides of mountains, therefore, commonly have high precipitation. By contrast, the leeward sides of mountains are usually much drier (Figure 18.4). This situation exists because air reaching the leeward side has lost much of its moisture, and if the air descends, it is compressed and warmed, making cloud formation even less likely. The dry region that results is often referred to as a **rain shadow desert**. Because many middle-latitude deserts occupy sites on the leeward sides of mountains, they can also be classified as rain shadow deserts.

In North America, the foremost mountain barriers to moisture from the Pacific are the Coast Ranges, Sierra Nevada, and Cascades (Figure 18.4). The Okanagan Valley of British Columbia lies in such a rain shadow area (Box 18.2). In Asia, the great Himalayan chain prevents the summertime monsoon flow of moist Indian Ocean air from reaching the interior (see Box 18.3).

Because the Southern Hemisphere lacks extensive land areas in the middle latitudes, only a small area of desert and steppe occurs in this latitude range, existing primarily near the southern tip of South America in the rain shadow of the towering Andes.

The middle-latitude deserts provide an example of how tectonic processes affect climate. Rain shadow deserts exist by virtue of the mountains produced when plates collide. Without such mountain-building episodes, wetter climates would prevail where many dry regions exist today.

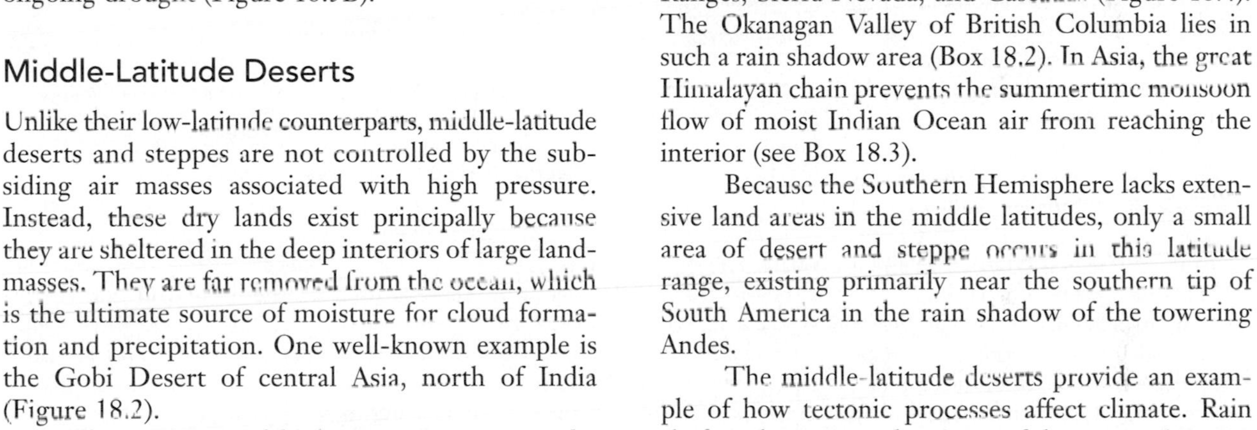

◆ **Figure 18.4** Many deserts in the middle latitudes are rain shadow deserts. As moving air meets a mountain barrier, it is forced to rise. Clouds and precipitation on the windward side often result. Air descending the leeward side is much drier. The mountains effectively cut the leeward side off from the sources of moisture, producing a rain shadow desert. The southern Okanagan desert of British Columbia occurs in the rain shadow of the Cascade Mountains.

BOX 18.2

Canadian Profile
The Okanagan Valley: A Canadian Desert

The Okanagan Valley in the interior of British Columbia is familiar to most Canadians as a fruit-growing and popular tourist region. However, many Canadians don't realize that the Okanagan Valley is also Canada's only non-polar desert. The valley, carved out by glaciers during the last Ice Age, is approximately 20 kilometres wide and about 250 kilometres long and extends from the British Columbia–Washington border to Vernon (see Figure 18.A).

Arid conditions prevail in the Okanagan Valley because of the rain shadow effect of the Cascade Mountains to the west, characterized by an average annual precipitation of about 25 centimetres. Because much of the moisture from westerly winds is depleted from the air by the time it reaches the Okanagan Valley, cloud cover tends to be minimal. Consequently, the region experiences about 2000 hours of sunshine per year.

An assortment of typical desert plants, such as sagebrush and prickly pear cactus, are found in the very dry, southern sector of the valley. The northern Okanagan is less arid and supports grasslands and scattered forests of Ponderosa pine.

Even though the region is a desert, it hosts a number of elongate lakes that include the Okanagan, Swan, Kalamalka, and Wood lakes. In fact, the very word *Okanagan* means "place of water" in Salish (the language of the First Nations people who settled in the valley). The successful agricultural and tourist industries of the region owe their existence to the water supplied from these lakes and associated rivers. The elongate shape of the lakes attests to the scouring action of glaciers during the last Ice Age.

◆ **Figure 18.A** Nk'Mip Canyon Desert Golf Course, southern Okanagan Valley. Note how irrigation has transformed part of the desert landscape into a lush, green fairway (foreground). Map: Location of the Okanagan Valley area. (Photo courtesy of Dave George, Nk'Mip Canyon Desert Golf Course)

The striking contrast between the lush green of a golf course and the nearly barren slopes of the surrounding hills in Figure 18.A illustrates the importance of irrigation in the Okanagan Valley. In addition to the availability of water, soil fertility contributes greatly to the success of agriculture in the region. Unlike many desert soils, those of the Okanagan are rich in nutrients, as their parent materials include the nutrient-rich deltaic sediments deposited after the last Ice Age.

Dairy and beef farming were established early in the settlement of the valley and remain important industries today. These activities are concentrated in the semi-arid, northern sector of the valley where little or no irrigation is required to support plant growth for grazing cattle. Fruit growing in the Okanagan was first established by missionaries in 1862 near Kelowna but only became significant in the 1890s when the Government of Canada provided incentives to develop the fruit-growing industry. At present, much Canadian fruit, such as apricots, cherries, peaches, pears, and plums, that is available in supermarkets across Canada comes from the Okanagan Valley. The Okanagan Valley has also become one of Canada's most successful wine regions and accounts for most of British Columbia's wine production.

Polar Deserts

The coldest of the world's deserts occur in the Earth's polar regions, where the constant descent of cold, dry air associated with stable high-pressure cells prevents the formation of rain clouds.

Much of Canada's Arctic region is polar desert (Figure 18.5). Polar desert conditions dominate most of the northern Arctic Archipelago, including most of Axel Heiberg and Ellesmere islands, a significant portion of Baffin Island, the majority of Somerset Island, and all of the remaining Queen Elizabeth Islands. The climate is very dry and cold, and mean summer temperatures in the northern reaches of the region are as low as –1.5°C (and as high as 2°C in the south, on the Lancaster Plateau in western Baffin

BOX 18.3

People and the Environment
The Shrinking Aral Sea

The Aral Sea (actually a lake basin) lies on the border between Uzbekistan and Kazakhstan in central Asia (Figure 18.B). The setting is the Turkestan desert, a middle-latitude desert in the rain shadow of Afghanistan's high mountains. In this region of interior drainage, two large rivers, the Amu Darya and the Syr Darya, carry water from the mountains of northern Afghanistan across the desert to the Aral Sea. Water leaves the sea by evaporation. Thus, the size of the water body depends on the balance between river inflow and evaporation.

In 1960 the Aral Sea was one of the world's largest inland water bodies, with an area of about 67,000 square kilometres. Only the Caspian Sea, Lake Superior, and Lake Victoria were larger. By the year 2000 the area of the Aral Sea had shrunk by 75 percent and split into two parts joined by a narrow passage. The water level had dropped 22 metres and the sea had lost 90 percent of its volume. The shrinking of this water body is depicted in Figure 18.C. By about 2010 all that will remain will be three small vestiges.

What caused the Aral Sea to dry up over the past 40 years? The answer is that the flow of water from the mountains that supplied the sea was significantly reduced and then all but eliminated. The waters of the Amu Darya and Syr Darya were diverted to supply a major expansion of irrigated agriculture in this dry region.

The intensive irrigation greatly increased agricultural productivity but not without a significant cost. Some of the effects are listed below.

- The once thriving fishing industry is dead, and the 24 species of fish that once lived in the Aral Sea are no longer there. The shoreline is now tens of kilometres from the towns that were once fishing centres (Figure 18.D).
- The shrinking sea has exposed thousands of hectares of former lake bed to sun and wind. The former lake bed is the source of an increasing number of dust storms that blow salts and toxic herbicides and pesticides into nearby towns, causing detrimental health effects.
- The deltas of the two major rivers have lost their wetlands, and wildlife has disappeared.
- The region has lost a moderating climatic influence. Without the large water body, there are greater extremes of temperature, a shorter growing season, and reduced local precipitation.

If enough fresh water were to once again flow into the Aral Sea, could the situation be reversed? Prospects appear grim. Experts estimate that restoring the Aral Sea to about twice its present size would require stopping all irrigation from the two major rivers for 50 years. This could not be done without ruining the economies of the countries that rely on that water.

The decline of the Aral Sea is a major environmental disaster that, sadly, is of human making.*

*For more on this, see R. Stone, "Coming to Grips with the Aral Sea's Grim Legacy," *Science* 284 (April 1999): 30–31; and C. Pala, "To Save a Vanishing Sea," *Science* 18 (February 2005): 1032–1034.

◆ **Figure 18.B** The Aral Sea lies east of the Caspian Sea in the Turkestan desert. Two rivers, the Amu Darya and Syr Darya, bring water from the mountains to the south.

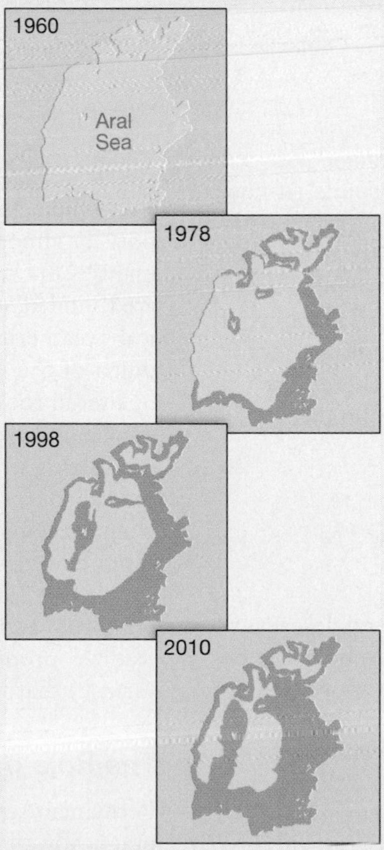

◆ **Figure 18.C** The shrinking Aral Sea. By the year 2010 all that will remain will be three small water bodies.

◆ **Figure 18.D** In the town of Jamboul, Kazakhstan, boats now lie in the sand because the Aral Sea has dried up. (Photo by Ergun Cagatay/Liaison Agency, Inc.)

Figure 18.5 Typical polar desert landscape on Cornwallis Island, Arctic Canada. (Photo by Alfred Lenz)

Island). Winter mean temperatures range between –32°C in the north and –23°C in the south. Annual precipitation is also very low, ranging mostly between 100 and 200 millimetres, with a few sites registering greater values (up to 400 millimetres) in the Baffin Island Uplands. The northern portions of the region, such as Ellesmere Island, generally receive less precipitation than anywhere else in Canada, sometimes as little as 50 millimetres in a single year.

GEOLOGIC PROCESSES IN ARID CLIMATES

The angular hills, sheer canyon walls, and desert surface of pebbles or sand contrast sharply with the rounded hills and curving slopes of more humid places. Indeed, to a visitor from a humid region, a desert landscape may seem to have been shaped by forces different from those operating in well-watered areas. However, although the contrasts may be striking, they do not reflect different processes. They merely disclose the differing effects of the same processes that operate under contrasting climatic conditions.

Weathering

In humid regions, relatively fine-textured soils support an almost continuous cover of vegetation that mantles the surface. Here the slopes and rock edges are rounded, reflecting the strong influence of chemical weathering in a humid climate. By contrast, much of the weathered debris in deserts consists of unaltered rock and mineral fragments—the result of mechanical weathering processes. In dry lands, rock weathering of any type is greatly reduced because of the lack of moisture and the scarcity of organic acids from decaying plants. However, chemical weathering is not completely lacking in deserts.

Over long spans of time, clays and thin soils do form, and many iron-bearing silicate minerals oxidize, producing the rust-coloured stain (desert varnish) that tints some desert landscapes.

The Role of Water

Permanent streams are normal in humid regions, but practically all desert stream beds are dry most of the time (Figure 18.6A). Deserts have **ephemeral** (*ephemero* = short-lived) **streams**, which means they carry water only in response to specific episodes of

A

B

◆ **Figure 18.6** **A.** Most of the time, desert stream channels are dry. **B.** An ephemeral stream shortly after a heavy shower. Although such floods are short lived, large amounts of erosion occur. (Photos by E. J. Tarbuck)

rainfall. A typical ephemeral stream might flow for only a few days or perhaps just a few hours during the year. In some years the channel might carry no water at all.

This fact is obvious even to the casual traveller who notices numerous bridges with no streams beneath them or numerous dips in the road where dry channels cross. However, when the rare heavy showers do come, so much rain falls in such a short time that all of it cannot soak in (Figure 18.7). Because desert vegetative cover is sparse, runoff is largely unhindered and consequently rapid, often

◆ **Figure 18.7** Desert thunderstorm over Tucson, Arizona. Often, many weeks, months, or occasionally even years separate periods of rain in the desert. When rains do occur, they are often heavy and of relatively short duration. Because the rainfall intensity is high, all of the water cannot soak in, and rapid runoff results.
(Photo by Warren Faidley/DRK Photo)

creating flash floods along valley floors (Figure 18.6B). Because much surface material in a desert is not anchored by vegetation, the amount of erosional work that occurs during a single short-lived rain event is impressive.

Humid regions are notable for their integrated drainage systems. But in arid regions, streams usually lack an extensive system of tributaries. In fact, a basic characteristic of desert streams is that they are small and die out before reaching the sea. Because the water table is usually far below the surface, few desert streams can draw on it as streams do in humid regions. Without a steady supply of water, the combination of evaporation and infiltration soon depletes the stream.

The few permanent streams that do cross arid regions, such as the Colorado and Nile rivers, originate *outside* the desert, commonly in well-watered mountains. Here the water supply must be great to compensate for the losses occurring as the stream crosses the desert. For example, after the Nile leaves its headwaters in the lakes and mountains of central Africa, it traverses almost 3000 kilometres of the Sahara without a single tributary. By contrast, in humid regions the discharge of a river grows as it flows downstream because tributaries and groundwater contribute additional water along the way.

It should be emphasized that *running water, although infrequent, nevertheless does most of the erosional work in deserts*. This is contrary to the common belief that wind is the most important erosional agent sculpting desert landscapes. Although wind erosion is indeed more significant in dry areas than elsewhere, most desert landforms are carved by running water. As you will see shortly, the main role of wind is in the transportation and deposition of sediment, which creates and shapes the ridges and mounds we call dunes.

TRANSPORTATION OF SEDIMENT BY WIND

Moving air, like moving water, is turbulent and able to pick up loose debris and transport it to other locations. Just as in a stream, the velocity of wind increases with height above the surface. Also like a stream, wind transports fine particles in suspension while heavier ones are carried as bed load (Figure 18.8). However, the transport of sediment by wind differs from that of running water in two significant ways. First, wind's lower density compared with water renders it less capable of picking up and transporting coarse materials. Second, because wind is not confined to channels, it can spread sediment over large areas, as well as high into the atmosphere.

Bed Load

The bed load carried by wind consists of sand grains. Observations in the field and experiments that use wind tunnels indicate that windblown sand moves by skipping and bouncing along the surface—a process termed saltation (Chapter 15).

The movement of sand grains begins when wind reaches a velocity sufficient to overcome the inertia of the resting particles. At first the sand rolls along the surface. When a moving sand grain strikes another grain, one or both of them may jump into the air. Once in the air, the grains are carried forward by the wind until gravity pulls them back toward the surface. When the sand hits the surface, it either bounces back into the air or dislodges other grains, which then jump upward. In this manner, a chain reaction is established, filling the air near the ground with saltating sand grains in a short interval of time (Figure 18.8).

Bouncing sand grains never travel far from the surface. Even when winds are very strong, the height of the saltating sand seldom exceeds a metre and usually is no greater than a half metre. Some sand grains are too large to be thrown into the air by impact from other particles. When this is the case, the energy provided by the impact of the smaller saltating grains drives the larger grains forward. This is called surface creep. Estimates indicate that between 20 percent and 25 percent of the sand transported in a sandstorm is moved in this way.

Suspended Load

Unlike sand, finer particles of dust can be swept high into the atmosphere by the wind. Because dust is commonly composed of rather flat particles that have large surface areas compared with their weight, it is relatively easy for turbulent air to counterbalance the pull of gravity and keep these fine particles airborne for hours or even days. Although both silt and clay can be carried in suspension, silt commonly makes up the bulk of the suspended load because the reduced level of chemical weathering in deserts provides only small amounts of clay.

Fine particles are easily carried by the wind, but they are not so easily picked up to begin with. The reason is that the wind velocity is practically zero within a very thin layer close to the ground. Thus, the wind cannot lift the sediment by itself. Instead, the dust must be ejected or spattered into the moving air by bouncing sand grains or other disturbances. This idea is illustrated nicely on a dry unpaved country road on a windy day. Left undisturbed, little dust is raised by the wind. However, as a car or truck moves over the road, the layer of silt is kicked up, creating a thick cloud of dust.

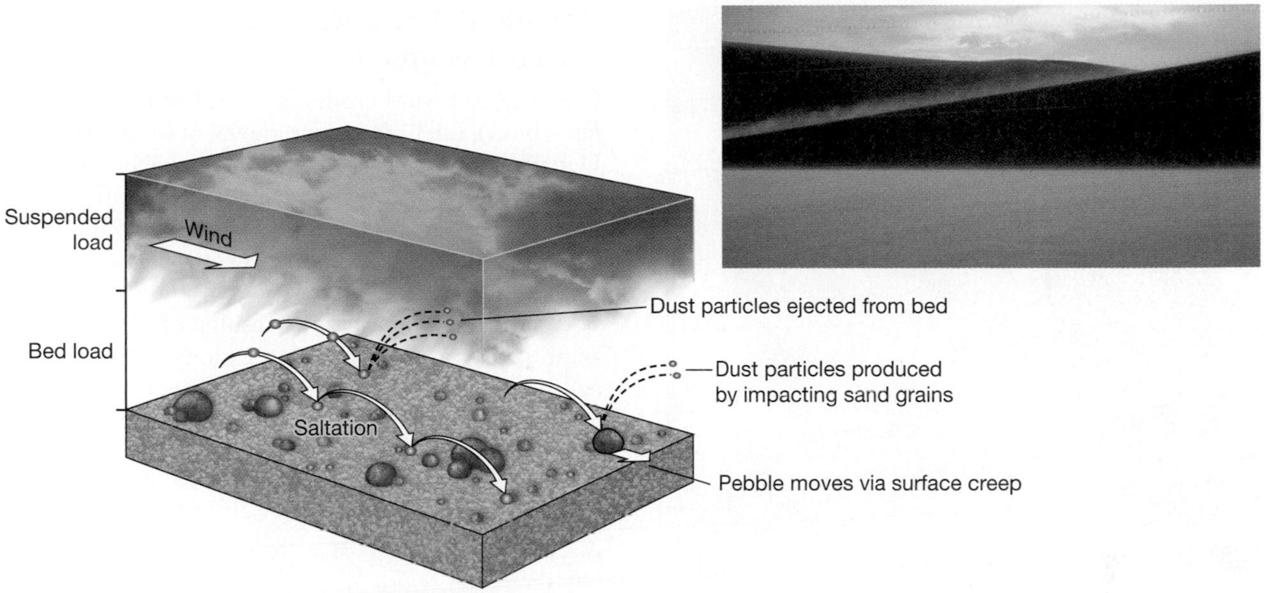

◆ **Figure 18.8** Schematic diagram illustrating suspended load, rolling bed load and saltation. Inset: A cloud of saltating sand grains moving up the gentle slope of a dune.
(Photo by Stephen Trimble)

Although the suspended load is usually deposited relatively near its source, high winds are capable of carrying large quantities of dust great distances (Figure 18.9). In the 1930s, silt that was picked up in Kansas was transported to New England and beyond into the North Atlantic. Similarly, dust blown from the Sahara has been traced as far as the West Indies (Figure 18.10).

◆ **Figure 18.9** Dust blackens the sky on May 21, 1937, near Elkhart, Kansas. It was because of storms like this that portions of the Great Plains were called the Dust Bowl in the 1930s.
(Photo reproduced from the collection of the Library of Congress)

◆ **Figure 18.10** This satellite image shows thick plumes of dust from the Sahara Desert blowing northwestward over the Canary Islands on March 12, 2003. Such dust storms are common in arid North Africa. In fact, this region is the largest dust source in the world. Satellites are excellent tools for studying the transport of dust on a global scale. They show that dust storms can cover huge areas and that dust can be transported great distances.
(Image courtesy of NASA)

WIND EROSION

GEODe EARTH Deserts and Winds
↳ Common Misconceptions about Deserts

Compared with running water and glaciers, wind is a relatively insignificant erosional agent. Recall that even in deserts, most erosion is performed by intermittent running water, not by the wind. Wind erosion is more effective in arid lands than in humid areas because in humid places moisture binds particles together and vegetation anchors the soil. For wind to be an effective erosional force, dryness and scanty vegetation are important prerequisites. When such circumstances exist, wind can pick up, transport, and deposit great quantities of fine sediment. During the 1930s, parts of the prairies experienced vast dust storms. The plowing under of the natural vegetative cover for farming, followed by severe drought, exposed the land to wind erosion and led to the area's being labelled the Dust Bowl.*

Deflation, Blowouts, and Desert Pavement

One way that wind erodes is by **deflation** (*de* = out, *flat* = blow), the lifting and removal of loose material. Deflation sometimes is difficult to notice because the entire surface is being lowered at the same time, but it can be significant. In portions of the 1930s Dust Bowl, vast areas of land were lowered by as much as a metre in only a few years.

The most noticeable results of deflation in some places are shallow depressions appropriately called **blowouts** (Figure 18.11). In the Great Plains region, from Alberta south to Texas, thousands of blowouts are visible on the landscape. They range

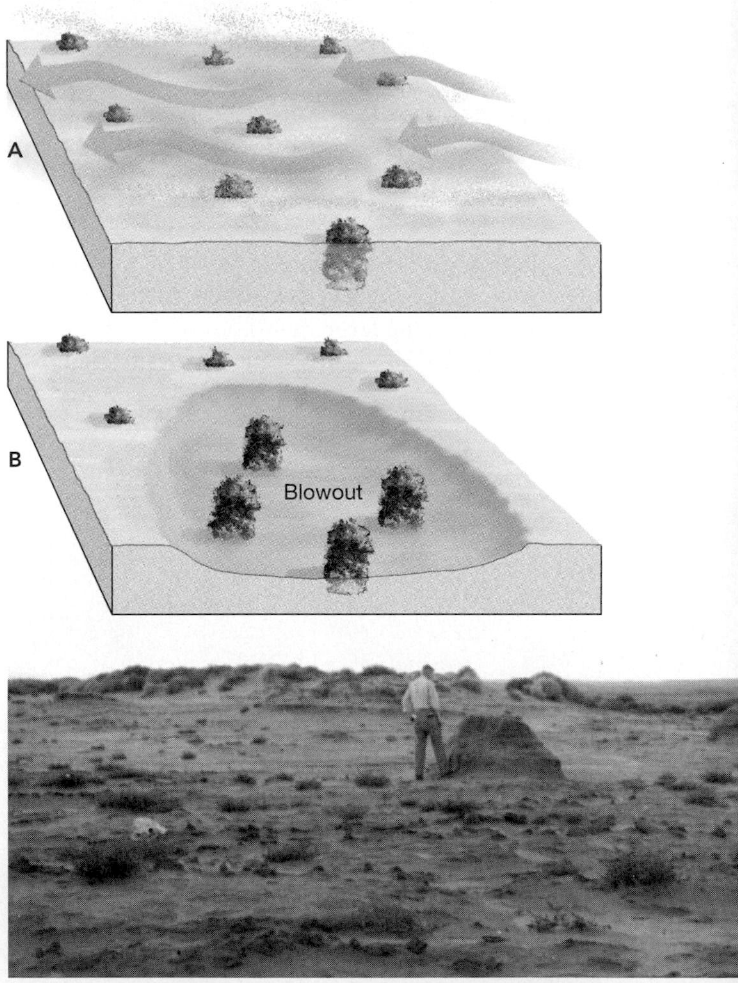

◆ **Figure 18.11** Formation of a blowout. **A.** Area before deflation. **B.** Area after deflation has created a shallow depression. **C.** This photo was taken in Saskatchewan in the 1930s during a prolonged drought. Strong winds removed the soil that was not anchored by vegetation. The mounds are more than 1 metre high and show the level of the land before deflation.
(Photo courtesy of the Saskatchewan Archives Board, photo R-A15082-3)

*For more information, see Box 5.2.

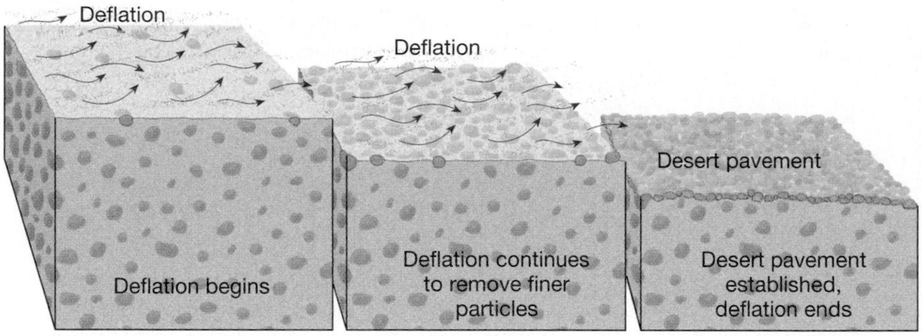

A

B

◆ **Figure 18.12** **A.** Formation of desert pavement. As these cross-sections illustrate, coarse particles gradually become concentrated into a tightly packed layer as deflation lowers the surface by removing sand and silt. **B.** If left undisturbed, desert pavement, such as this in Antarctica's Allan Hills, will protect the surface from further deflation (light-coloured boulder at the left edge of the photograph is about 30 centimetres across).
(Photo by S. R. Hicock)

from small dimples less than 1 metre deep and 3 metres wide to depressions that approach 50 metres deep and several kilometres across. The factor that controls the depths of these basins (that is, acts as base level) is the local water table. When blowouts are lowered to the water table, damp ground and vegetation prevent further deflation.

In portions of many deserts the surface is a closely packed layer of coarse pebbles and cobbles too large to be moved by the wind. This stony veneer is called a **desert pavement**. The common explanation for its formation is that deflation lowers the surface by removing sand and silt until eventually only a continuous cover of coarse particles remains (Figure 18.12). Once desert pavement becomes established, a process that can take hundreds of years, the surface is protected from further deflation if left undisturbed. However, because the layer is only one or two stones thick, disruption by vehicles or animals can dislodge the pavement and expose the fine-grained material below to deflation once again.

Ventifacts and Yardangs

Like glaciers and streams, wind also erodes by abrasion. In dry regions, as well as along some beaches, windblown sand cuts and polishes exposed rock surfaces. Abrasion sometimes creates interestingly shaped stones called **ventifacts** (Figure 18.13). The side of the stone exposed to the prevailing wind is abraded, leaving it polished, pitted, and with sharp edges. If the wind is not consistently from one direction, or if the pebble becomes reoriented, it may have several faceted surfaces.

Unfortunately, abrasion is often given credit for accomplishments beyond its capabilities. Such features as balanced rocks that stand high atop narrow pedestals and intricate detailing on tall pinnacles are not the results of abrasion. Sand seldom travels more than a metre above the surface, so the wind's sandblasting effect is obviously limited in vertical extent.

In addition to ventifacts, wind erosion is responsible for creating much larger features, called yardangs (from the Turkistani word *yar*, meaning "steep bank"). A **yardang** is a streamlined, wind-sculpted ridge that is oriented parallel to the prevailing wind. Yardangs commonly have the appearance of an inverted ship's hull. Individual yardangs are generally less than 10 metres high and 100 metres or so long, but can reach up to 10 times that size. They

◆ **Figure 18.13** Ventifacts are rocks that are polished and shaped by sandblasting, like these basalt boulders in the Allan Hills of Antarctica.
(Photo by S. R. Hicock)

often occur in groups and seem to be restricted to especially dry desert areas that have minimal plant cover and strong winds that blow predominantly from one direction.

WIND DEPOSITS

GEODe EARTH Deserts and Winds
↳ Reviewing Landforms and Landscapes

Although wind is relatively unimportant in producing *erosional* landforms, significant *depositional* landforms are created by the wind in some regions. Accumulations of windblown sediment are particularly conspicuous in the world's dry lands and along many sandy coasts. Wind deposits are of two distinctive types: (1) mounds and ridges of sand from the wind's bed load, which we call dunes, and (2) extensive blankets of silt, called loess, that once were carried in suspension.

Sand Deposits

As is the case with running water, wind drops its load of sediment when velocity falls and the energy available for transport diminishes. Thus, sand begins to accumulate wherever an obstruction across the path of the wind slows its movement. Unlike many deposits of silt, which form blanket-like layers over large areas, winds commonly deposit sand in mounds or ridges called **dunes** (Figure 18.14).

As moving air encounters an object, such as a clump of vegetation or a rock, the wind sweeps around and over it, leaving a shadow of slower-moving air behind the obstacle, as well as a smaller zone of quieter air just in front of the obstacle. Some of the saltating sand grains moving with the wind come to rest in these wind shadows. As the accumulation of sand continues, it becomes a more imposing barrier to the wind and thus a more efficient trap for even more sand. If the supply of sand is sufficient and the wind blows steadily long enough, the mound of sand grows into a dune.

Many dunes have an asymmetric profile, with the leeward (sheltered) slope being steep and the windward slope more gently inclined (Figure 18.15). Sand moves up the gentler slope on the windward side by saltation. Just beyond the crest of the dune, where the wind velocity is reduced, the sand accumulates. As more sand collects, the slope steepens and eventually some of it slides under the pull of gravity (Figure 18.14). In this way, the leeward slope of the dune, called the **slip face**, maintains an angle of about 34 degrees, the angle of repose for loose dry sand. (Recall from Chapter 14 that the angle of repose is the steepest angle at which loose material remains stable.) Continued sand accumulation, coupled with periodic slides down the slip face, results in the slow migration of the dune in the direction of air movement.

As sand is deposited on the slip face, layers form that are inclined in the direction the wind is blowing. These sloping layers are called **cross-beds** (Figure 18.15). When the dunes are eventually buried under other layers of sediment and become part of the sedimentary rock record, their asymmetric shape is destroyed, but the cross-beds remain as testimony to their origin. Nowhere is cross-bedding more prominent than in the sandstone walls of Zion Canyon in southern Utah (Figure 18.15D).

In some areas, moving sand is troublesome. For example, in Figure 18.16 dunes are advancing across irrigated fields in Egypt. In portions of the Middle East, valuable oil-rigs must be protected from encroaching dunes. In some cases, fences are built far enough upwind of the dunes to stop their migration. As sand continues to collect, however, the fences must be built higher. In

◆ **Figure 18.14** Sand sliding down the steep slip face of a dune in White Sands National Monument, New Mexico.
(Photo by Michael Collier)

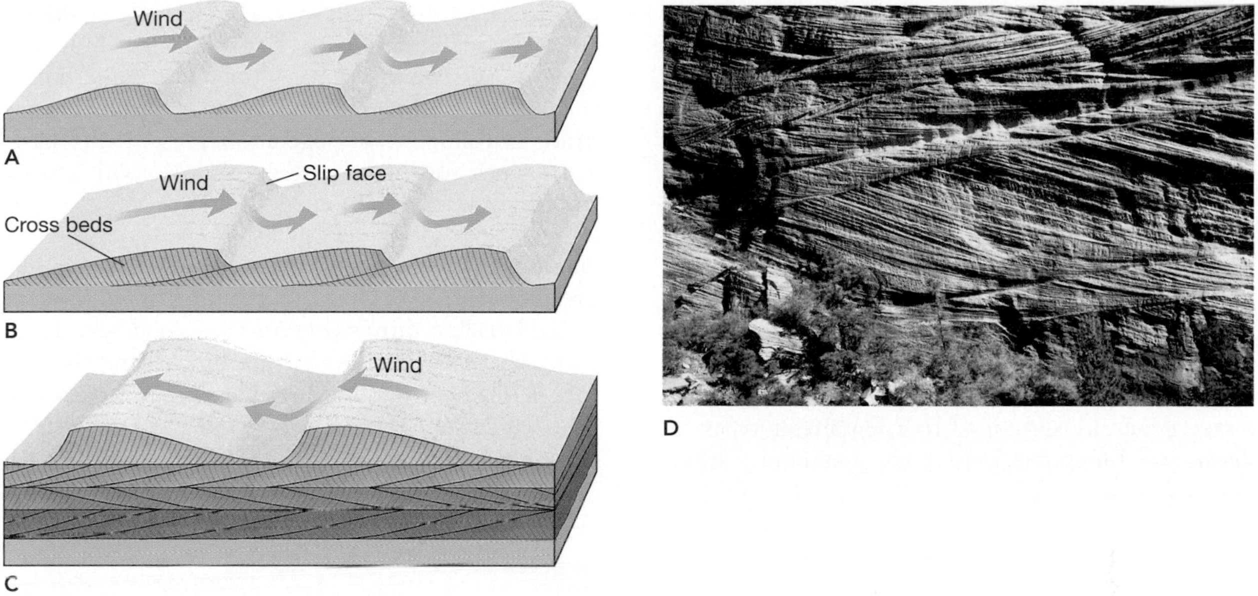

◆ **Figure 18.15** As parts **A** and **B** illustrate, dunes commonly have an asymmetrical shape. The steeper leeward side is called the slip face. Sand grains deposited on the slip face at the angle of repose create the cross-bedding of the dunes. **C.** A complex pattern develops in response to changes in wind direction. Also notice that when dunes are buried and become part of the sedimentary record, the cross-bedded structure is preserved. **D.** Cross-beds are an obvious characteristic of the Navajo Sandstone in Zion National Park, Utah.
(Photo by Marli Miller)

Kuwait, protective fences extend for almost 10 kilometres around one important oil field. Migrating dunes can also pose a problem for the construction and maintenance of highways and railroads that cross sandy desert regions. For example, to keep a portion of Highway 95 near Winnemucca, Nevada, open to

◆ **Figure 18.16** These desert dunes (called barchans) in Egypt are advancing from right to left across irrigated fields.
(Photo by Georg Gerster/Photo Researchers, Inc.)

traffic, sand must be taken away about three times a year. Each time, between 1500 and 4000 cubic metres of sand are removed. Attempts at stabilizing the dunes by planting different varieties of grasses have been unsuccessful because the meagre rainfall cannot support the plants.

Types of Sand Dunes

Dunes are not just random heaps of windblown sediment. Rather, they are accumulations that usually assume patterns that are surprisingly consistent (Figure 18.17). A broad assortment of dune forms exists, generally simplified to a few major types for discussion. Of course, gradations exist among different forms, as do irregularly shaped dunes that do not fit easily into any category. Several factors influence the form and size that dunes ultimately assume. These include wind direction and velocity, availability of sand, and amount of vegetation present. Six basic dune types are shown in Figure 18.17, with arrows indicating wind directions.

Barchan Dunes Solitary sand dunes shaped like crescents and with their tips pointing downwind are called **barchan dunes** (Figure 18.17A). These dunes form where supplies of sand are limited and the surface is relatively flat, hard, and lacking in vegetation. They migrate slowly with the wind at a rate of up to 15 metres per year. Their size is usually modest, with

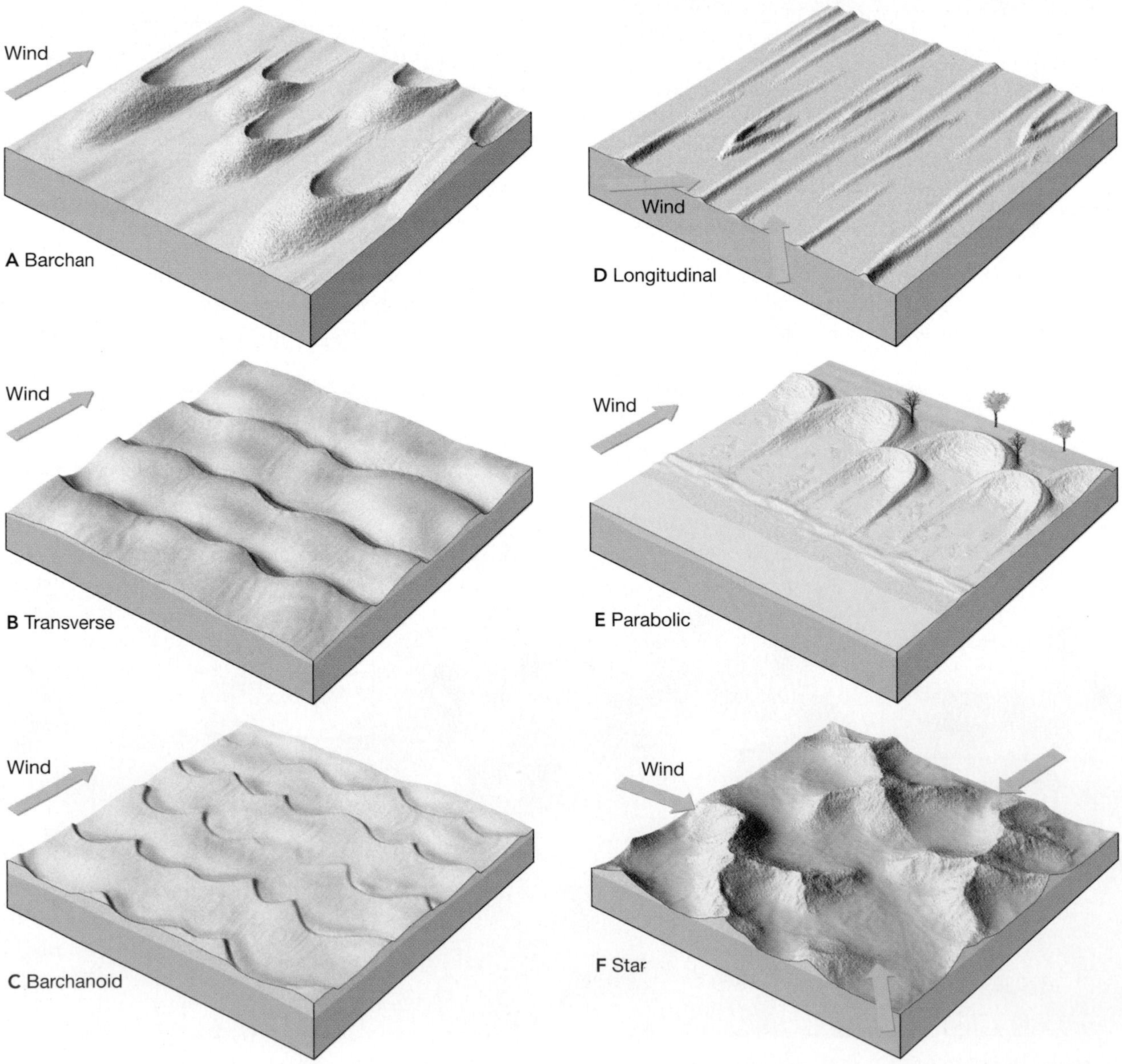

◆ **Figure 18.17** Sand dune types.

the largest barchans reaching heights of about 30 metres while the maximum spread between their horns approaches 300 metres. When the wind direction is nearly constant, the crescent form of these dunes is nearly symmetrical. However, when the wind direction is not perfectly fixed, one tip becomes larger than the other.

Transverse Dunes In regions where the prevailing winds are steady, sand is plentiful, and vegetation is sparse or absent, the dunes form a series of long ridges that are separated by troughs and oriented at right angles to the prevailing wind. Because of this orientation, they are termed **transverse dunes** (Figure 18.17B). Typically, many coastal dunes are of this type. In addition, transverse dunes are common in many arid regions where the extensive surface of wavy sand is sometimes called a *sand sea*. In some parts of the Sahara and Arabian deserts, transverse dunes reach heights of 200 metres, are 1 to 3 kilometres across, and can extend for distances of 100 kilometres or more.

A relatively common dune form is intermediate between isolated barchans and extensive waves of transverse dunes. Such dunes, called **barchanoid dunes**, form scalloped rows of sand oriented at right angles to the wind (Figures 18.17C and 18.18). The rows resemble a series of barchans that have been positioned side by side.

◆ **Figure 18.18** Barchanoid dunes represent a type that is intermediate between isolated barchans on the one hand and extensive transverse dunes on the other. The gypsum dunes at White Sands National Monument, New Mexico, are an example.
(Photo by Michael Collier)

Longitudinal Dunes **Longitudinal dunes** are long ridges of sand that form more or less parallel to the prevailing wind and where sand supplies are moderate (Figure 18.17D). Apparently, the prevailing wind direction must vary somewhat but still remain in the same quadrant of the compass. Although the smaller types are only 3 or 4 metres high and several dozens of metres long, in some large deserts longitudinal dunes can reach great size. For example, in portions of North Africa, Arabia, and central Australia, these dunes can approach a height of 100 metres and extend for distances of more than 100 kilometres.

Parabolic Dunes Unlike the other dunes that have been described thus far, **parabolic dunes** form where vegetation partially covers the sand. The shape of these dunes resembles the shape of barchans except that their tips point into the wind rather than downwind (Figure 18.17E). Parabolic dunes often form along coasts where there are strong onshore winds and abundant sand. If the sand's sparse vegetative cover is disturbed at some spot, deflation creates a blowout. Sand is then transported out of the depression and deposited as a curved rim, which grows higher as deflation enlarges the blowout.

Star Dunes Confined largely to parts of the Sahara and Arabian deserts, **star dunes** are isolated hills of sand that exhibit a complex form (Figures 18.17F and 18.19). Their name is derived from the fact that the bases of these dunes resemble multi-pointed stars. Usually three or four sharp-crested ridges diverge from a central high point that in some cases can approach a height of 90 metres. As their form suggests, star dunes develop where wind directions are variable.

Loess (Silt) Deposits

In some parts of the world the surface topography is mantled with deposits of windblown silt, called **loess**. Over periods of perhaps thousands of years, dust storms deposited this material. When loess is breached by streams or road cuts, it tends to maintain vertical cliffs and lacks any visible layers, as you can see in Figure 18.20.

The distribution of loess worldwide indicates that this sediment has two primary sources: deserts and glacial outwash deposits. The thickest and most

◆ **Figure 18.19** Star dune in the Namib Desert in southwest Africa. (Photo by Comstock)

In North America, deposits of loess are significant in many areas, including South Dakota, Nebraska, Iowa, Missouri, and Illinois, as well as portions of the Columbia Plateau in the Pacific Northwest. The correlation between the distribution of loess and important farming regions in the Midwest and eastern Washington State is not just a coincidence, because soils derived from this wind-deposited sediment are among the most fertile in the world.

Unlike the deposits in China, which originated in deserts, the loess in North America (and Europe) is an indirect product of glaciation. Its source includes deposits of stratified drift and till, much of it in ancestral Canada. During the retreat of the ice sheets, many river valleys were choked with sediment deposited by meltwater that was exposed to the air. Strong westerly winds sweeping across the barren floodplains and till plains picked up the finer sediment and dropped it as a blanket on the eastern sides of the valleys. Such an origin is confirmed by the fact that loess deposits are thickest and coarsest on the lee sides of such major glacial drainage outlets as the Mississippi and Illinois rivers and rapidly thin with increasing distance from the

extensive deposits of loess on Earth occur in western and northern China. They were blown there from the extensive desert basins of central Asia. Accumulations of 30 metres are common, and thicknesses of more than 100 metres have been measured. It is this fine buff-coloured sediment that gives the Yellow River (Hwang Ho) its name.

A

B

◆ **Figure 18.20** **A.** This vertical loess bluff near the Mississippi River in southern Illinois is about 3 metres high. **B.** Vegetated loess on south Vancouver Island (shovel is for scale). (Photo **A** by James E. Patterson; photo **B** by S. R. Hicock) valleys. Furthermore, the angular mechanically weathered particles composing the loess are essentially the same as the rock flour produced by the grinding action of glaciers.

Chapter Summary

- The concept of dryness is relative; it refers to any situation in which a water deficiency exists. Dry regions encompass about 30 percent of Earth's land surface. Two climatic types are commonly recognized: *desert*, which is arid, and *steppe* (a marginal and more humid variant of a desert), which is semi-arid. Low-latitude deserts coincide with the zones of subtropical highs in lower latitudes. Middle-latitude deserts exist principally because of their positions in the deep interiors of large landmasses far removed from the ocean.
- The same geologic processes that operate in humid regions also operate in deserts, but under contrasting climatic conditions. In dry lands rock weathering of any type is greatly reduced because of the lack of moisture and the scarcity of organic acids from decaying plants. Much of the weathered debris in deserts is the result of mechanical weathering. Practically all desert streams are dry most of the time and are said to be *ephemeral*. Stream courses in deserts are seldom well integrated and lack an extensive system of tributaries. Nevertheless, running water is responsible for most of the erosional work in a desert. Although wind erosion is more significant in dry areas than elsewhere, the main role of wind in a desert is in the transportation and deposition of sediment.
- The transport of sediment by wind differs from that by running water in two ways. First, wind has a low density compared with water; thus, it is not capable of picking up and transporting coarse materials. Second, because wind is not confined to channels, it can spread sediment over large areas. The bed load of wind consists of sand grains skipping and bouncing along the surface in a process termed saltation. Fine dust particles can be carried great distances by the wind as suspended load.
- Compared with running water and glaciers, wind is a relatively insignificant erosional agent. *Deflation*, the lifting and removal of loose material, often produces shallow depressions called *blowouts*. In portions of many deserts the surface, called *desert pavement*, is a layer of coarse pebbles and gravels too large to be moved by the wind. Wind also erodes by abrasion, often creating interestingly shaped stones called *ventifacts*. *Yardangs* are narrow, streamlined, wind-sculpted ridges that can be up to 90 metres high and 100 kilometres long.
- Wind deposits are of two distinct types: (1) mounds and ridges of sand, called *dunes*, which are formed from sediment that is carried as part of the wind's bed load; and (2) extensive blankets of silt, called *loess*, that once were carried by wind in suspension. The profile of a dune shows an asymmetrical shape with the leeward (sheltered) slope being steep and the windward slope more gently inclined. The types of sand dunes include (1) *barchan dunes*, (2) *transverse dunes*, (3) *barchanoid dunes*, (4) *longitudinal dunes*, (5) *parabolic dunes*, and (6) *star dunes*. The thickest and most extensive deposits of loess occur in western and northern China. Unlike the deposits in China, which originated in deserts, the loess in North America and Europe is an indirect product of glaciation.

Review Questions

1. How extensive are the desert and steppe regions of Earth?
2. What is the primary cause of subtropical deserts? Of middle-latitude deserts?
3. In which hemisphere (Northern or Southern) are middle-latitude deserts most common?
4. Why is the amount of precipitation that is used to determine whether a place has a dry climate or a humid climate a variable figure? (See Box 18.1.)
5. "Deserts are hot, lifeless, sand-covered landscapes shaped largely by the force of wind." The preceding statement summarizes the image of arid regions that many people hold, especially those living in more humid places. Is it an accurate view? Why or why not?
6. Why is rock weathering reduced in deserts?
7. As a permanent stream, such as the Nile River, crosses a desert, does discharge increase or decrease? How does this compare with a river in a humid region?
8. What is the most important erosional agent in deserts?
9. Why is sea level (ultimate base level) not a significant factor influencing erosion in desert regions?
10. Describe two places where true desert conditions occur in Canada.
11. Describe the way in which wind transports sand. During very strong winds, how high above the surface can sand be carried?
12. Why is wind erosion relatively more important in arid regions than in humid areas?
13. What factor limits the depths of blowouts?
14. How do sand dunes migrate?
15. List three factors that influence the form and size of a sand dune.
16. Six major dune types are recognized. Indicate which type of dune is associated with each of the following statements:
    - **(a)** Dunes whose tips point into the wind
    - **(b)** Long sand ridges oriented at right angles to the wind
    - **(c)** Dunes that often form along coasts where strong winds create a blowout
    - **(d)** Solitary dunes whose tips point downwind
    - **(e)** Long sand ridges that are oriented more or less parallel to the prevailing wind
    - **(f)** An isolated dune consisting of three or four sharp-crested ridges diverging from a central high point
    - **(g)** Scalloped rows of sand oriented at right angles to the wind
17. Although sand dunes are the best-known wind deposits, accumulations of loess are very significant in some parts of the world. What is loess? Where are such deposits found? What are the origins of this sediment?

Key Terms

barchan dune (p. 490)
barchanoid dune (p. 491)
blowout (p. 486)
cross-beds (p. 488)
deflation (p. 486)
desert (p. 476)
desert pavement (p. 487)
dune (p. 488)
ephemeral stream (p. 482)
loess (p. 491)
longitudinal dune (p. 491)
parabolic dune (p. 491)
rain shadow desert (p. 479)
slip face (p. 488)
star dune (p. 491)
steppe (p. 476)
transverse dune (p. 491)
ventifact (p. 487)
yardang (p. 487)

Web Resources

The *Earth* website uses the resources and flexibility of the internet to aid in your study of the topics in this chapter. Written and developed by geology instructors, this site will help improve your understanding of geology. Visit **www.pearsoned.ca/tarbuck** and click on the cover of the text to find

- online review quizzes
- Web-based critical thinking and writing exercises
- links to chapter-specific Web resources
- internet-wide key-term searches

www.pearsoned.ca/tarbuck

Chapter 19
Shorelines

The Shoreline: A Dynamic Interface

Waves
- Wave Characteristics
- Circular Orbital Motion
- Waves in the Surf Zone

Wave Erosion

Sand Movement on the Beach
- Wave Refraction
- Beach Drift and Longshore Currents

Tides
- Causes of Tides
- Spring and Neap Tides
- Tidal Currents

Shoreline Features
- Erosional Features
- Depositional Features
- The Evolving Shore

Ancient Detrital Coastal Deposits

Reefs

Stabilizing the Shore
- Hard Stabilization
- Alternatives to Hard Stabilization

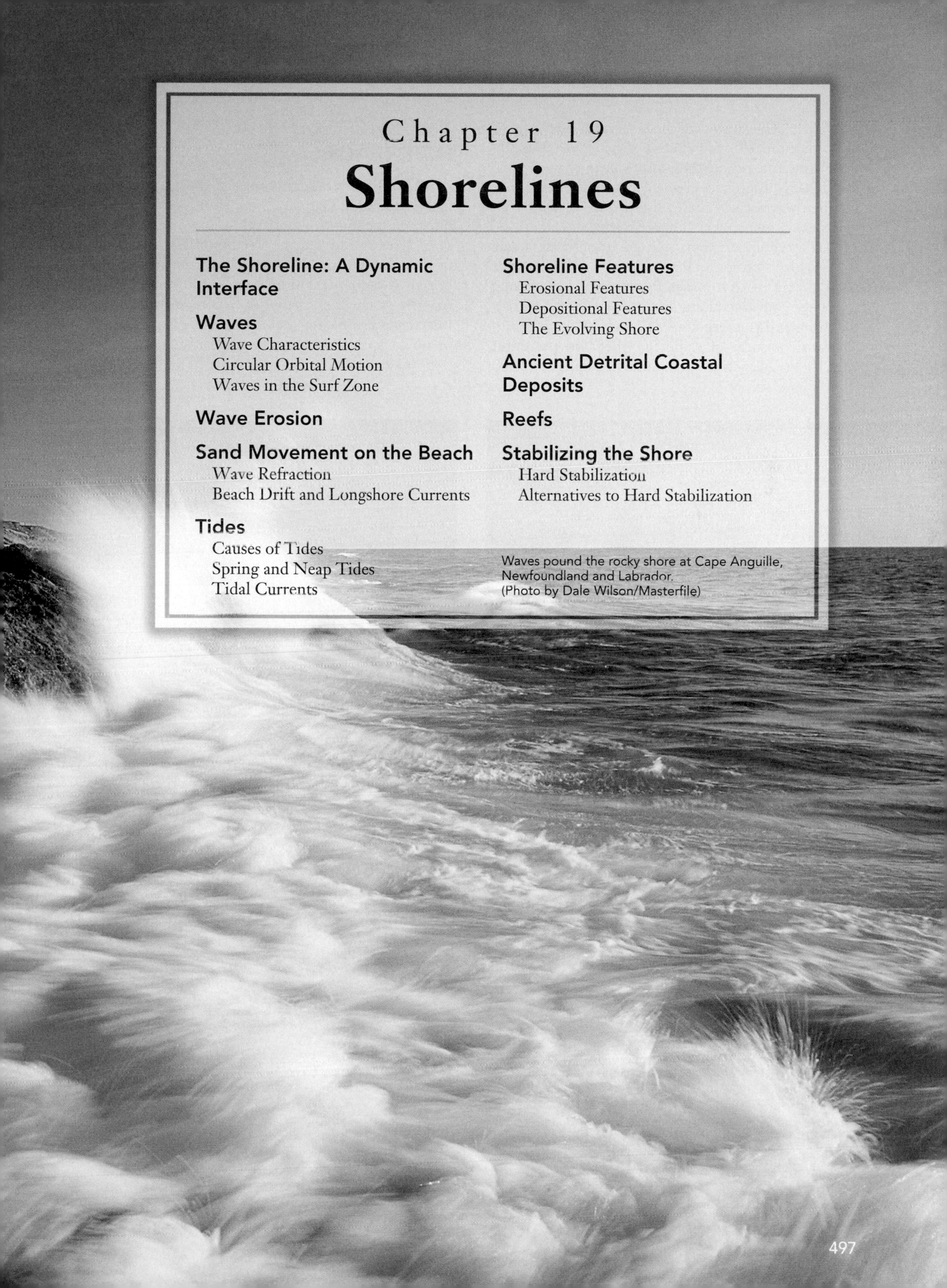

Waves pound the rocky shore at Cape Anguille, Newfoundland and Labrador. (Photo by Dale Wilson/Masterfile)

The restless waters of the ocean are constantly in motion. Winds generate surface currents, the gravity of the Moon and Sun produces tides, and density differences create deep-ocean circulation. Further, waves carry the energy from storms to distant shores, where their impact erodes the land.

Shorelines are dynamic environments. Their topography, geologic makeup, and climate vary greatly from place to place. Continental and oceanic processes converge along coasts to create landscapes that frequently undergo rapid change. When it comes to the deposition of sediment, they are transition zones between marine and continental environments.

THE SHORELINE: A DYNAMIC INTERFACE

Nowhere is the restless nature of the ocean's water more noticeable than along the shore—the dynamic interface (common boundary) among air, land, and sea. Here we can see the rhythmic rise and fall of tides and observe waves constantly rolling in and breaking. Sometimes the waves are low and gentle. At other times they pound the shore with awesome fury (chapter-opening photo). Although it may not be obvious, the shoreline is constantly being modified (Figure 19.1).

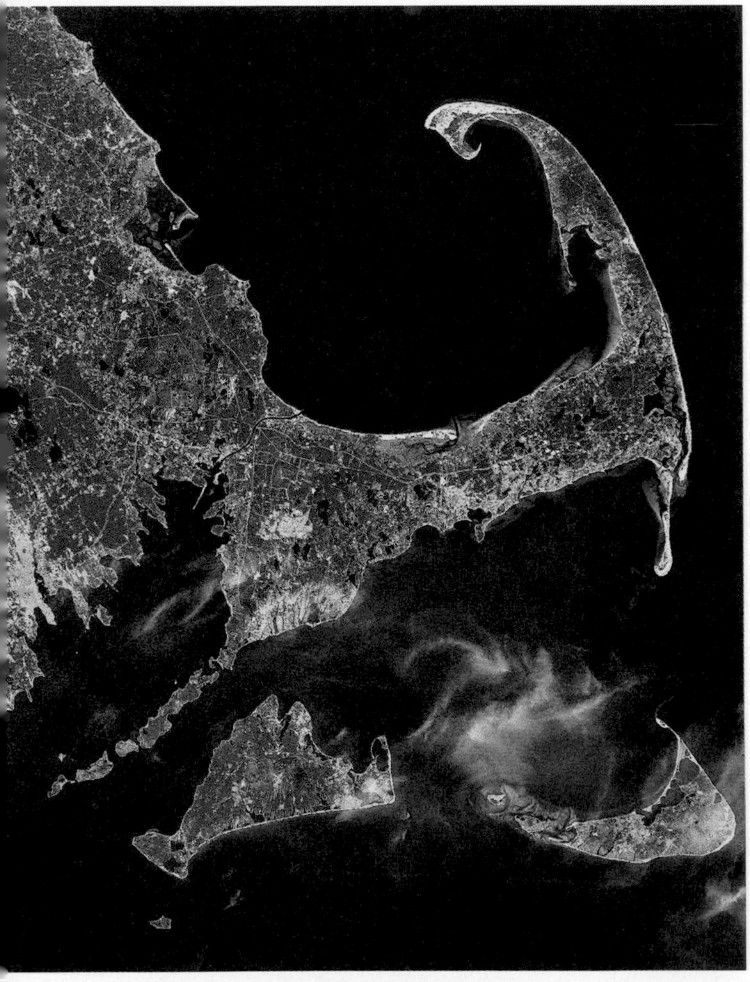

A

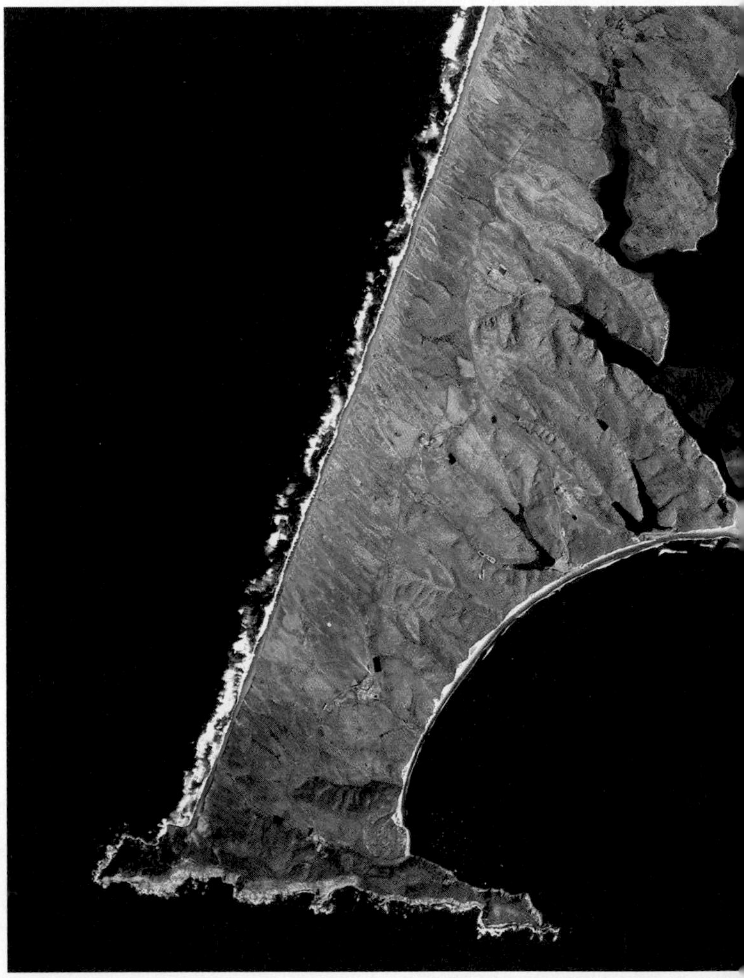

B

◆ **Figure 19.1** **A.** This satellite image includes the outline of Cape Cod, Massachusetts. Boston is to the upper left. The two large islands off the south shore of Cape Cod are Martha's Vineyard (left) and Nantucket (right). Although the work of waves constantly modifies this coastal landscape, shoreline processes are not responsible for creating it. Rather, the present size and shape of Cape Cod results from the positioning of moraines and other glacial materials deposited during the Pleistocene Epoch. **B.** High-altitude image of the Point Reyes area north of San Francisco, California. The 5.5-kilometre-long south-facing cliffs at Point Reyes (lower left corner) are exposed to the full force of the waves from the Pacific Ocean. Nevertheless, this promontory retreats slowly because the bedrock from which it formed is very resistant.
(Photo **A** satellite image courtesy of Earth Satellite Corporation/Science Photo Library/Photo Researchers, Inc.; photo **B** high-altitude image courtesy of USDA-ASCS)

The nature of present-day shorelines is not just the result of the relentless attack on the land by the sea. Indeed, the shore has a complex character that results from multiple geologic processes. For example, practically all coastal areas were affected by the worldwide rise in sea level that accompanied the melting of glaciers at the close of the last Ice Age. As the sea encroached landward, the shoreline retreated, becoming superimposed on existing landscapes resulting from such diverse processes as stream erosion, glaciation, volcanic activity, and the forces of mountain building.

Today the coastal zone is experiencing intensive human activity. Unfortunately, people often treat the shoreline as if it were a perpetually stable platform that is well suited for the construction of buildings. This attitude inevitably leads to conflicts between people and nature. As you will see, many coastal landforms, especially beaches and barrier islands, are relatively fragile, short-lived features that are inappropriate sites for development. This is because they experience the full impact of waves.

WAVES

GEODe EARTH Shorelines
↳ Waves and Beaches

Wind-generated waves provide most of the energy that shapes and modifies shorelines. Where the land and sea meet, waves that may have travelled unimpeded for hundreds or thousands of kilometres suddenly encounter a barrier that will not allow them to advance farther and that must absorb their energy. The conflict that results is continuous and sometimes dramatic.

Wave Characteristics

The undulations of the water surface (that we call waves) derive their energy and motion from the wind. If a breeze of less than 3 kilometres per hour starts to blow across still water, small wavelets appear almost instantly. When the breeze dies, the ripples disappear as suddenly as they formed. However, if the wind exceeds 3 kilometres per hour, more stable waves gradually form and advance with the wind.

All waves have the characteristics illustrated in Figure 19.2. The tops of the waves are *crests*, which are separated by *troughs*. The vertical distance between trough and crest is the **wave height**. The horizontal distance separating successive crests is the **wavelength**. The **wave period** is the time interval between the passage of two successive crests at a stationary point.

The height, length, and period that are eventually achieved by a wave depend on three factors: (1) the wind speed, (2) the length of time the wind has blown, and (3) the **fetch**, or distance that the wind has travelled across open water. As the quantity of energy transferred from the wind to the water increases, the height and steepness of the waves increases as well. Eventually a critical point is reached where waves grow so tall that they topple over, forming breakers called *whitecaps*.

A particular wind speed has a maximum fetch and duration of wind beyond which waves no longer

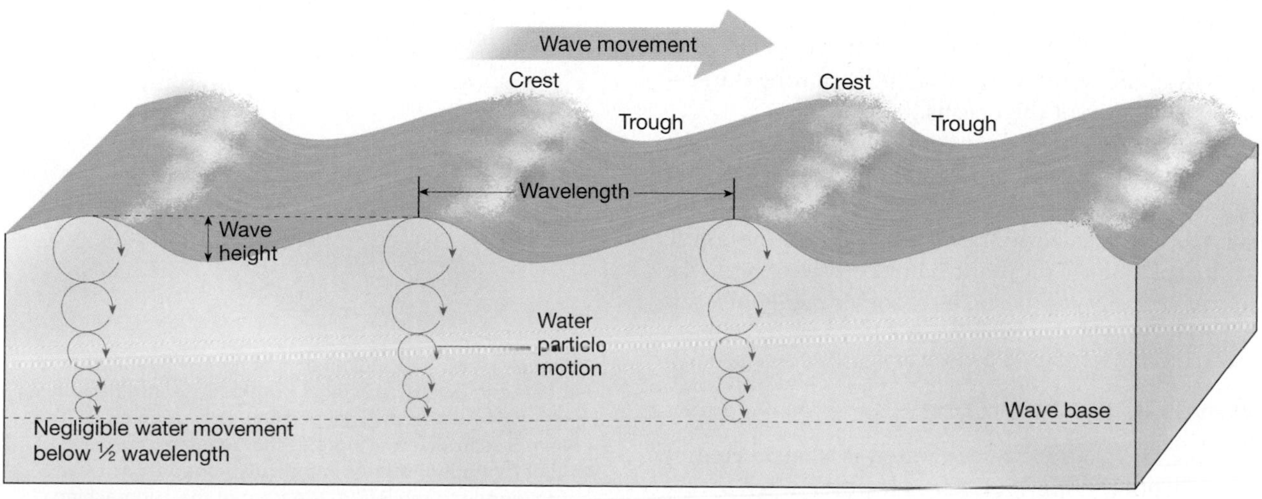

◆ **Figure 19.2** This diagram illustrates the basic parts of a wave as well as the movement of water particles with the passage of the wave. Negligible water movement occurs below a depth equal to one half the wavelength (the level of the dashed line).

increase in size. By this stage, waves lose as much energy through the breaking of whitecaps as they are receiving from the wind.

When wind stops or changes direction, or if waves leave the stormy area where they were created, they continue on without relation to local winds. The waves also undergo a gradual change to *swells*, which are lower and longer and can carry a storm's energy to distant shores. Because many independent wave systems exist at the same time, the sea surface acquires a complex, irregular pattern. Hence, the sea waves we watch from the shore are often a mixture of swells from faraway storms and waves created by local winds.

Circular Orbital Motion

When observing waves, always remember that you are watching *energy* travel through a medium (water). If you make waves by tossing a pebble into a pond, by splashing in a pool, or by blowing across the surface of a cup of coffee you are transferring *energy* to the water, and the waves you see are just the visible evidence of the energy passing through.

In open waters, it is the wave energy that moves forward, not the water itself. Each water particle moves in a circular path during the passage of a wave (Figure 19.2). As a wave passes, a water particle returns almost to its original position. The circular orbits followed by the water particles at the surface have a diameter equal to the wave height. When water is part of the wave crest, it moves in the same direction as the advancing waveform. In the trough, the water moves in the opposite direction. This is demonstrated by observing the behaviour of a floating object as a wave passes. The toy boat in Figure 19.3 merely seems to bob up and down and sway slightly back and forth without advancing appreciably from its original position. (The wind does drag the water forward slightly, causing the surface circulation of the oceans.)

The energy contributed by the wind to the water is transmitted not only along the surface of the sea but also downward. However, beneath the surface, the circular motion rapidly diminishes until, at a depth equal to about half the wavelength, the movement of water particles becomes negligible; this depth is called *wave base* (Figure 19.2).

Waves in the Surf Zone

As long as a wave is in deep water, it is unaffected by water depth (Figure 19.4, left). However, when a wave approaches the shore, the water becomes shallower and influences wave behaviour. The wave begins to

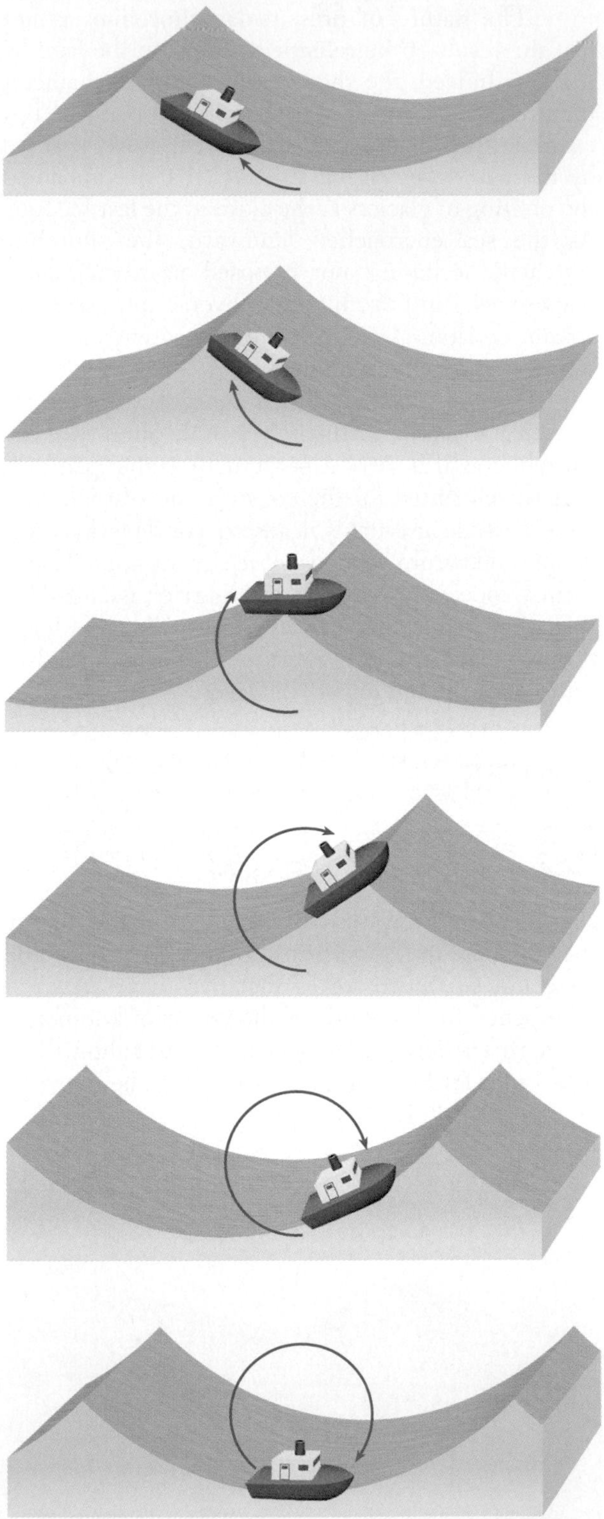

◆ **Figure 19.3** The movements of the toy boat illustrate that the wave energy advances but the water itself advances only slightly from its original position. In this sequence, the wave moves from left to right as the boat (and the water in which it is floating) rotates in a circular motion. The boat moves slightly to the left up the front of the approaching wave, and then, after reaching the crest, slides to the right down the back of the wave.

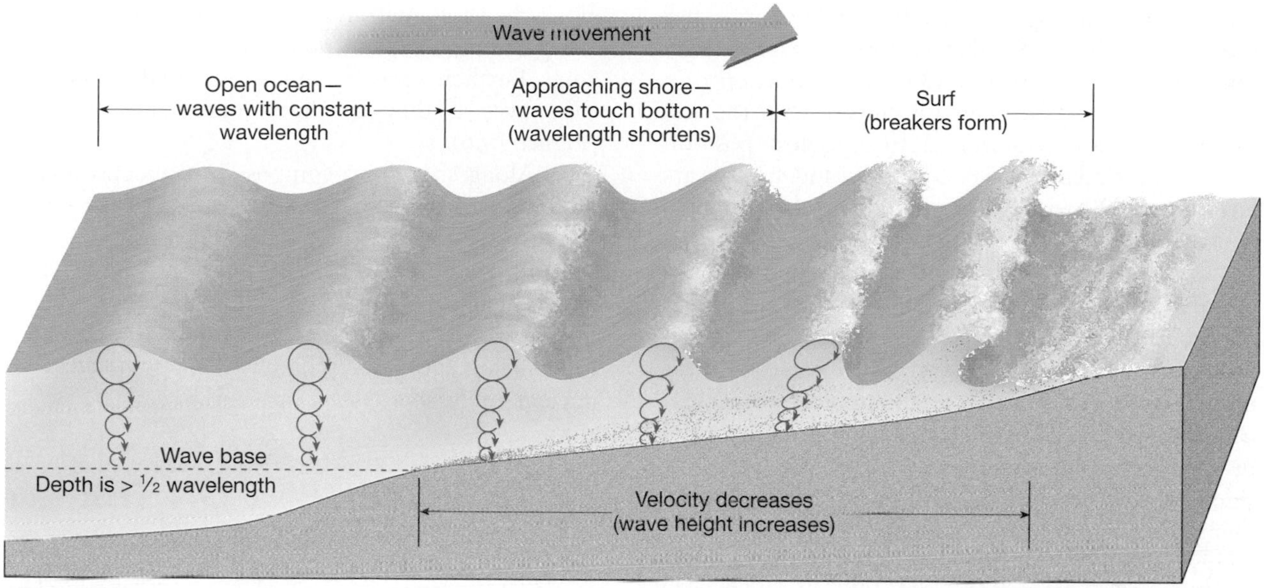

◆ **Figure 19.4** Changes that occur when a wave moves onto shore.

"feel bottom" at a water depth equal to about half its wavelength (wave base). Such depths interfere with water movement at the base of the wave and slow its advance (Figure 19.4, centre). As a wave advances toward the shore, the slightly faster waves farther out to sea catch up, decreasing the wavelength. As the speed and length of the wave diminish, the wave steadily grows higher. Finally, a critical point is reached when the steep wave front collapses, or *breaks* (Figure 19.4, right), and the water advances up the shore.

The turbulent water created by breaking waves is called **surf**. On the landward margin of the surf zone, the turbulent sheet of water from collapsing breakers, called *swash*, moves up the slope of the beach. When the energy of the swash has been expended, the water flows back down the beach toward the surf zone as *backwash*.

◆ **Figure 19.5** When waves break against the shore, the force of the water can be powerful and the erosional work that is accomplished can be great. Marin headlands, Golden Gate National Recreation Area, California. (Photo by Galen Rowell/Mountain Light Photography, Inc.)

WAVE EROSION

GEODe EARTH Shorelines
↳ Wave Erosion

During calm weather, wave action is minimal. However, just as streams do most of their work during floods, so too do waves accomplish most of their work during storms. The impact of high storm-induced waves against the shore can be awesome in its violence (Figure 19.5). Each breaking wave can hurl thousands of tonnes of water against the land, sometimes causing the ground to literally tremble. The pressures exerted by Atlantic waves in wintertime, for example, average nearly 10,000 kilograms per square metre. The force during storms is even greater. During one such storm a 1350-tonne portion of a steel-and-concrete barrier was ripped from the rest of the structure and moved to a useless position toward the shore at Wick Bay, Scotland. Five years later the 2600-tonne unit that replaced it met a similar fate.

Many such stories demonstrate the great force of breaking waves. It is no wonder that cracks and crevices are quickly opened in cliffs, seawalls, breakwaters, and anything else that is subjected to these enormous shocks. Water is forced into every opening, causing air in the cracks to become highly compressed by the thrust of crashing waves. When the wave subsides, the air expands rapidly, dislodging rock fragments and enlarging and extending fractures.

In addition to the erosion caused by wave impact and pressure, abrasion—the scouring and grinding action of the water armed with rock fragments—is also important. In fact, abrasion is probably more intense in the surf zone than in any other environment. Smooth, rounded stones and pebbles along the shore are obvious reminders of the relentless grinding action of rock against rock in the surf zone. Further, such fragments are used as tools by the waves as they cut horizontally into the land (Figure 19.6).

Along shorelines composed of unconsolidated material rather than hard rock, the rate of erosion by breaking waves can be extraordinary. In parts of Britain, where waves have the easy task of eroding glacial deposits of sand, gravel, and clay, the coast has been worn back 3 to 5 kilometres since Roman times (2000 years ago), sweeping away many villages and ancient landmarks.

SAND MOVEMENT ON THE BEACH

Beaches are sometimes called "rivers of sand." The reason is that the energy from breaking waves often causes large quantities of sand to move along the beach and in the surf zone, commonly by bending waves.

A B

◆ **Figure 19.6** **A.** Abrasion can be intense in the surf zone. Smooth rounded rocks along the shore are an obvious reminder of this fact. Garrapata State Park, California. **B.** Sandstone cliff undercut by wave erosion at Gabriola Island, British Columbia.
(Photo **A** by Carr Clifton; photo **B** by Fletcher and Baylis/Photo Researchers, Inc.)

Wave Refraction

The bending of waves, called **wave refraction**, plays an important part in shoreline processes (Figure 19.7). It affects the distribution of energy along the shore and thus strongly influences where and to what degree erosion, sediment transport, and deposition will take place.

Waves seldom approach the shore straight on and most move toward the shore at an angle. When they reach the shallow water of a smoothly sloping bottom, they are bent and tend to become parallel to the shore. Such bending occurs because the part of the wave nearest the shore reaches shallow water and slows first, whereas the end that is still in deep water continues forward at its full speed. The net result is a wave front that may approach nearly parallel to the shore regardless of the original direction of the wave.

Because of refraction, wave impact is concentrated against the sides and ends of headlands that project into the water, whereas wave attack is weakened in bays. This differential wave attack along irregular coastlines is illustrated in Figure 19.8. As the waves reach the shallow water in front of the headland sooner than they do in adjacent bays, they are bent more nearly parallel to the protruding land and strike it from all three sides. By contrast, refraction in the bays causes waves to diverge and expend less energy. In these zones of weakened wave activity, sediments can accumulate and form sandy beaches. Over a long period, erosion of the headlands and deposition in the bays will straighten an irregular shoreline.

◆ **Figure 19.7** Wave bending around the end of a beach at Stinson Beach, California.
(Photo by James E. Patterson)

Beach Drift and Longshore Currents

Although waves are refracted, most still reach the shore at some angle, however slight. Consequently, the uprush of water from each breaking wave (the swash) is oblique. However, the backwash is straight down the slope of the beach. The effect of this pattern of water movement is to transport sediment in a zigzag pattern along the beach (Figure 19.9). This movement is called **beach drift**, and it can transport sand and pebbles hundreds or even thousands of metres each day. However, typical rates are 5 to 10 metres per day.

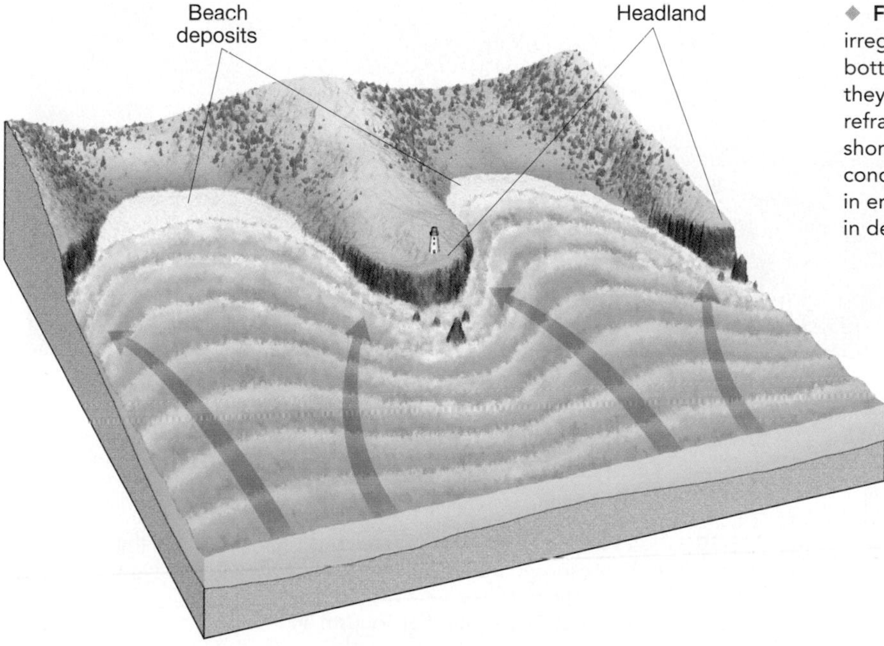

◆ **Figure 19.8** Wave refraction along an irregular coastline. As waves first touch bottom in the shallows off the headlands, they are slowed, causing the waves to refract and align nearly parallel to the shoreline. This causes wave energy to be concentrated on the headlands (resulting in erosion) and dispersed in bays (resulting in deposition).

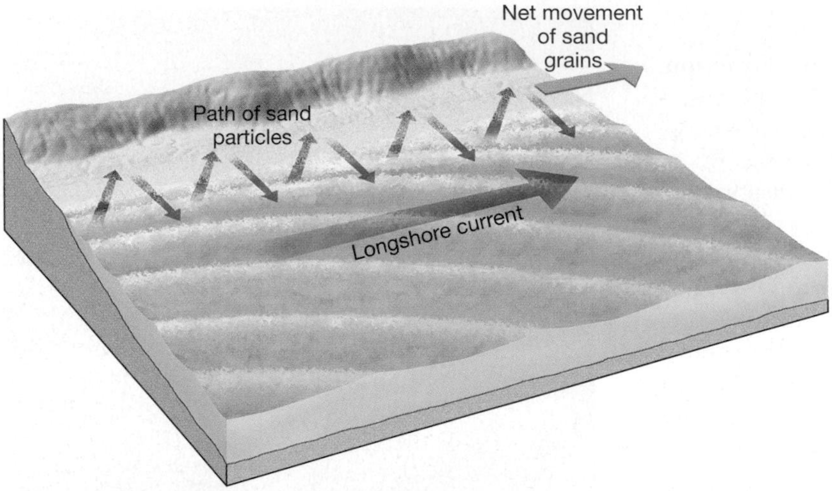

◆ **Figure 19.9** Beach drift and longshore currents are created by obliquely breaking waves. Beach drift occurs as incoming waves carry sand obliquely up the beach, while the water from spent waves carries it directly down the slope of the beach. Similar movements occur offshore in the surf zone to create the longshore current. These processes transport large quantities of material along the beach and in the surf zone.

Oblique waves also produce currents within the surf zone that flow parallel to the shore and move substantially more sediment than beach drift. Because the water here is turbulent, these **longshore currents** easily move the fine suspended sand and roll larger sand and gravel along the bottom. When the sediment transported by longshore currents is added to the quantity moved by beach drift, the total amount can be very large.

There should be little wonder why beaches are characterized as "rivers of sand." Any point along a beach is likely to have more sediment that was derived elsewhere than material eroded from the land immediately behind it. It is also worth noting that much of the sediment composing beaches is not wave-eroded debris. Rather, in many areas sediment-laden rivers that discharge into the ocean are the major sources of material. Hence, if it were not for beach drift and longshore currents, many beaches would be nearly sandless.

TIDES

Tides are familiar to most people as the daily changes in the elevation of the ocean surface (Figure 19.10). However, despite having been observed by countless individuals over the centuries, tides were not adequately explained until Sir Isaac Newton applied the law of gravitation to them. In essence, Newton discovered that tides are controlled by the gravitational attraction between Earth and the Moon, with a smaller influence from the Sun.

Figure 19.10 High tide and low tide on Nova Scotia's Minas Basin in the Bay of Fundy. The areas exposed during low tide and flooded during high tide are called tidal flats. The tidal flats here are extensive. (Courtesy of the Nova Scotia Department of Tourism and Culture)

Causes of Tides

Our perception of tides as the cyclic rising and falling of the ocean surface is a product of Earth's rotation relative to tidal bulges produced in the world's oceans by gravitational and inertial forces.

Tidal bulges are caused, as Newton discovered, by the pull of gravity and the equal and opposite force of inertia. Gravity is inversely proportional to the square of the distance between two objects, meaning simply that it quickly weakens with distance. In this case, the two objects are the Moon and Earth. Because the force of gravity decreases with distance, the Moon's gravitational pull on Earth is slightly greater on the near side of Earth than on the far side, exceeding the opposing force of inertia and producing a net tidal force directed toward the Moon. Although this differential pulling stretches (elongates) the solid only slightly, the world ocean, which is mobile, is deformed quite dramatically, producing a more prominent bulge toward the Moon (Figure 19.11).

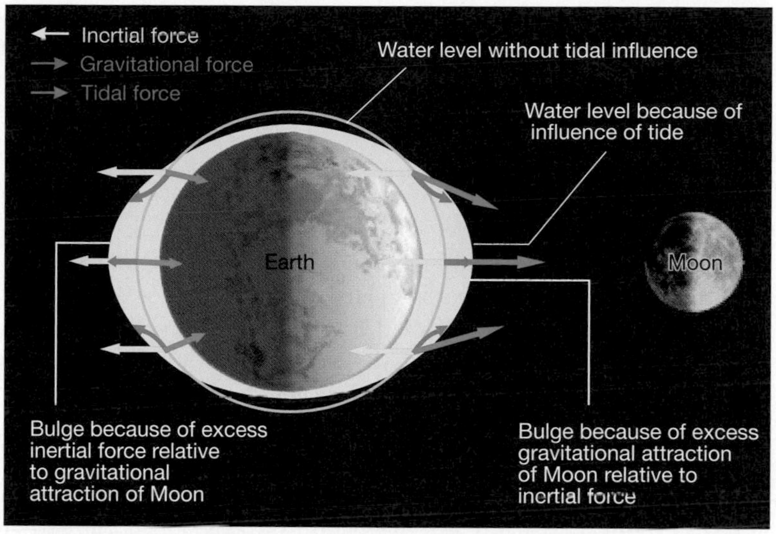

◆ **Figure 19.11** Schematic diagram showing the interaction of gravitational and inertial forces and the formation of tidal bulges in the ocean. Tidal forces are produced by the relative balance of gravitational attraction to the Moon and inertial forces of Earth. On the side of Earth facing the Moon, gravitational attraction is greater than the opposing inertial force and the reverse is true on the opposite side of Earth. Due to the ability of water to deform, the excess gravitational and inertial forces on opposing sides of Earth (in line with the Moon) produce two tidal bulges. These bulges are responsible for high tides.

It is easy to see how the Moon's gravitational force can cause the water to bulge on the side of Earth nearest the Moon, but why is an equally large tidal bulge produced on the side of Earth directly opposite the Moon? The reason is that although inertial force here is the same as on the Moon-facing side, the gravitational attraction to the Moon is much less. In this case, the inertial force exceeds the gravitational attraction to the Moon, producing a net tidal force directed away from the Moon and forming another tidal bulge. So the tidal bulge nearest the Moon is due to the dominance of gravitational attraction over the opposing force of inertia, but the tidal bulge farthest from the Moon is due to the dominance of inertia over gravitational attraction (Figure 19.11).

Because the position of the Moon changes only moderately in a single day, the tidal bulges remain in place while Earth rotates through them. For this reason, if you stand on the seashore for 24 hours, Earth will rotate you through alternating areas of deeper and shallower water. As you are carried into the regions of deeper water, the tide rises, and as you are carried away, the tide falls. Therefore, during one day you experience two high tides and two low tides.

Further, the tidal bulges migrate as the Moon revolves around Earth about every 29 days. As a result, the tides, like the time of moonrise, shift about 50 minutes later each day. After 29 days the cycle is complete and a new one begins. An inequality can exist between the high tides during a given day. Depending on the position of the Moon, the tidal bulges can be inclined to the equator, as in Figure 19.12. This figure illustrates that the first

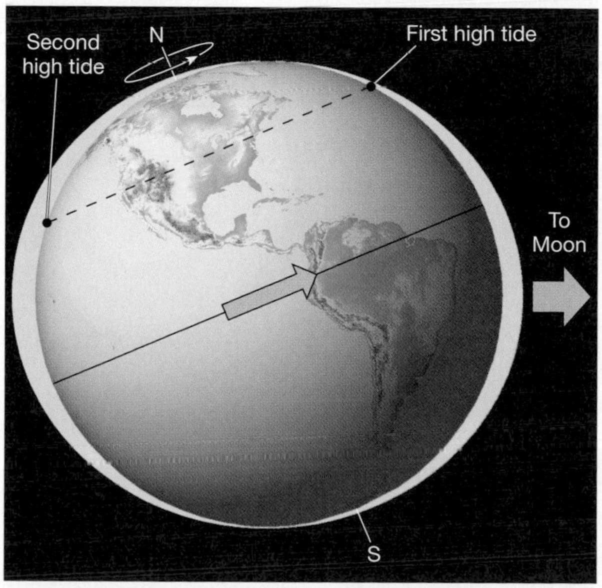

◆ **Figure 19.12** Tides on an Earth that is covered to a uniform depth with water. Depending on the Moon's position, tidal bulges can be inclined to the equator. In this situation, an observer will experience two unequal high tides.

high tide experienced by an observer in the Northern Hemisphere is considerably lower than the high tide half a day later. Conversely, a Southern Hemisphere observer would experience the opposite effect.

Spring and Neap Tides

The Sun also influences the tides. It is much larger than the Moon, but because it is so far away, its effect is considerably less than that of the Moon. In fact, the tide-generating potential of the Sun is slightly less than half that of the Moon.

Near the times of new and full moons, the Sun and Moon are aligned and their forces are added together (Figure 19.13A). Accordingly, the combined gravity of these two tide-producing bodies causes higher tidal bulges (high tides) and lower tidal troughs (low tides). These are called the **spring tides**. This term has no seasonal connotations but rather is derived from the old English word *springan*, meaning "jumping up." Spring tides create the largest daily tidal range—that is, the largest variation between high and low tides. Conversely, at about the time of the first and third quarters of the Moon, the gravitational forces of the Moon and Sun act on Earth at right angles, and each partially offsets the influence of the other (Figure 19.13B). As a result, the daily tidal range is less. These are called **neap tides**. The origin of the term neap tide is somewhat obscure, but may have been derived from the old Dutch word *nipen* meaning "to nip" perhaps referring to the tides being "nipped off" at this stage of the tidal cycle. Each month there are two spring tides and two neap tides, each about a week apart.

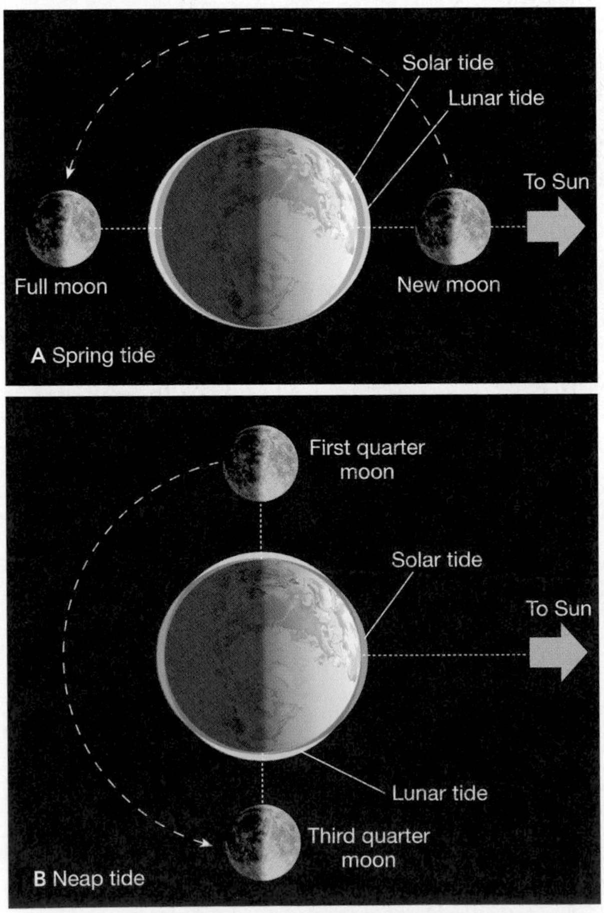

◆ **Figure 19.13** Relationship of the Moon to Earth during (**A**) spring tides and (**B**) neap tides.

In the Minas Basin of the Bay of Fundy, the average tidal range is 12 metres but can reach 17 metres during spring tides. The immense tides that have made the Bay of Fundy famous result primarily from two factors. First, the funnel-like shape of the Bay of Fundy progressively constricts the flow of water landward. Second, a resonance is produced by the rhythmic flood and ebb of the Fundy tides that can be likened to your body sliding back and forth in a bathtub. Just as the back and forth movement of water in a bathtub can amplify waves enough to flood your bathroom floor, so too can it amplify tidal range within a narrow body of water. The Minas Basin, being located at the head of the Bay of Fundy funnel, experiences the maximum effect of the combined factors.

Tidal Currents

Tidal current is the term used to describe the *horizontal* flow of water accompanying the rise and fall of the tide. These water movements, induced by tidal forces, are particularly impressive in such areas as the Bay of Fundy, where tidal flow rates of up to 25 million cubic metres per second are known. Tidal currents flow in one direction during a portion of the tidal cycle and reverse their flow during the remainder. Tidal currents that advance into the coastal zone as the tide rises are called **flood currents**. As the tide falls, seaward-moving water generates **ebb currents**. Periods of little or no current, called *slack water*, separate flood and ebb. The areas affected by these alternating tidal currents are **tidal flats** (see Figure 19.10). Depending on the nature of the coastal zone, tidal flats vary from narrow strips seaward of the beach to extensive zones that can extend for several kilometres.

Although tidal currents are not important in the open sea, they can be rapid in river **estuaries** (inlets of the sea formed at the mouths of streams), straits, and bays. Off the coast of Brittany in France, for example, tidal currents are known to attain a speed of 20 kilometres per hour. Although tidal currents are not generally major agents of erosion and sediment transport, notable exceptions occur where tides move through narrow inlets. Here, they constantly scour the small entrances to many good harbours that would otherwise be blocked.

SHORELINE FEATURES

A fascinating assortment of shoreline features can be observed along the world's coastal regions. These shoreline features vary depending on the type of rocks exposed along the shore, the intensity of wave activity, the nature of coastal currents, and whether the coast is stable, sinking, or rising. Features that owe their origin primarily to the work of erosion are called *erosional features*, whereas accumulations of sediment produce *depositional features*.

Erosional Features

Whether along the rugged and irregular Newfoundland and Labrador coast or along the steep shorelines of the Pacific Coast, the effects of wave erosion are often easy to see. **Wave-cut cliffs**, as the name implies, originate by the cutting action of the surf against the base of coastal land. As erosion progresses, rocks overhanging the notch at the base of the cliff crumble into the surf, and the cliff retreats (see Figure 19.6). A relatively flat, benchlike surface, called the **wave-cut platform**, is left behind by the receding cliff (Figure 19.14B). The platform broadens as the wave attack continues. Some of the debris produced by the breaking waves remains along the water's edge as part of the beach, while the remainder is transported farther seaward.

Headlands that extend into the sea are vigorously attacked by waves because of refraction. The surf erodes the rock selectively, wearing away the softer or more highly fractured rock at the fastest rate. At first, sea caves may form. When caves on opposite sides of a headland unite, a **sea arch** results (Figure 19.15). Eventually the arch falls in, leaving an isolated remnant, or **sea stack** (Figure 19.14), on the wave-cut platform. In time it too will be consumed by the action of the waves.

Depositional Features

Coastal regions dominated by deposition receive sediment primarily from river mouths (Chapter 15) and erosion-dominated regions of the coast. Because they are very dynamic, the depositional systems associated with coastal regions can be very complicated. However, most of them share a basic profile within which three main components, the offshore, shoreface, and beach (foreshore and backshore), can be distinguished (Figure 19.16).

A

B

◆ **Figure 19.14** **A.** Siwash Rock sea stack in Stanley Park, Vancouver, British Columbia. **B.** Elevated wave-cut platform and emergent sea stack near Trout River, Gros Morne area of Newfoundland and Labrador. (Photo **A** by S. R. Hicock; photo **B** by Bryan Monette and reproduced with the permission of the Minister of Public Works and Government Services Canada, 2008, and courtesy of Natural Resources Canada, Geological Survey of Canada)

◆ **Figure 19.15** Elephant Rock, a sea arch on the coast of Prince Edward Island. (Photo by Brian Sytnyk/Masterfile)

The base of a coastal profile is marked by the flat *offshore zone*, which is permanently submerged underwater and lies below the average depth at which waves touch the sea bottom during normal fair-weather conditions. This depth limit is commonly referred to as *fair-weather wave base*.

The *shoreface zone* lies landward of the offshore zone. It is characterized by constant day-to-day sediment transport in shallow water, between the fair-weather wave base and the low-tide mark. The shoreface normally has a concave-upward profile that is in equilibrium with the waves affecting it. The gradient of the shoreface ranges from nearly 0 degrees at its base to about 0.3 degrees at its upper boundary with the foreshore.

It is within the shoreface zone that most sediment is actively transported. Where waves approach the shore at an oblique angle, longshore currents transport sediment (usually sand) parallel to the shoreline landward of the breaker zone. In areas where wave approach is perpendicular to the shore, wave-generated currents form cells. In such cells, longshore currents converge and flow away from the shore as *rip currents*. Seaward of the surf zone, the rip currents diverge and dissipate, depositing sand in the lower shoreface.

A *beach* is an area of unconsolidated sediment that can be loosely considered to extend from the shoreface to the seaward limit of permanently vegetated land. In a more formal sense, the beach com-

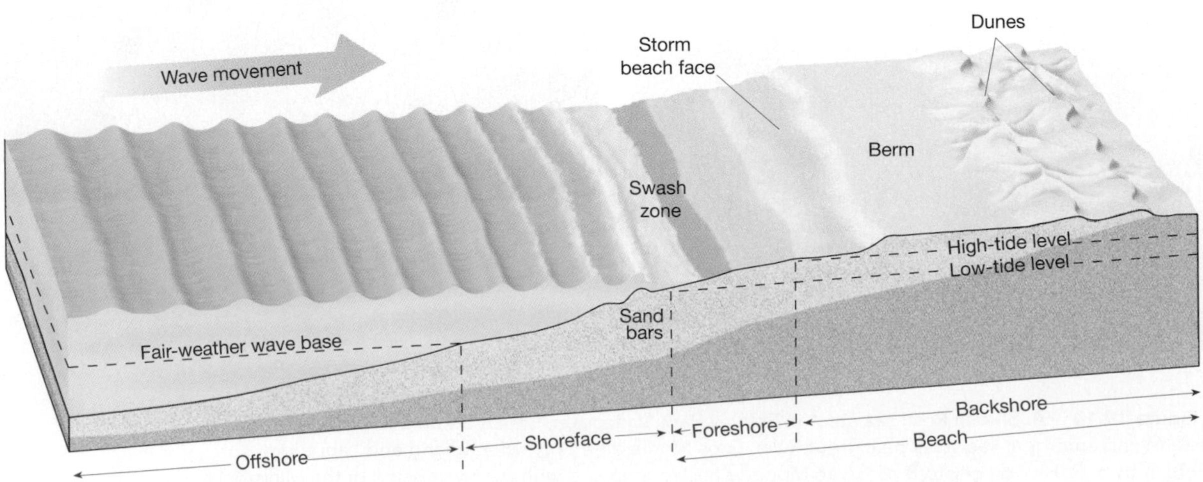

◆ **Figure 19.16** The coastal zone consists of several parts. The beach is an accumulation of sediment on the landward margin of the ocean or lake. It can be thought of as material in transit along the shore.

prises two zones, called the foreshore and the backshore. In its simplest form, the beach is attached to, and runs parallel to, the mainland. Such a beach is called a strand plain. It is worth restating that most of the sediment composing beaches is supplied by rivers that discharge into the ocean. Hence, if it were not for beach drift and longshore currents, many beaches would be nearly sandless.

The *foreshore zone* is the area of the beach directly affected by the repeated swash and retreating backwash of breaking waves, between the low-tide and high-tide watermarks of the coastal zone. Waves transport water onshore. When they break, they drive a thin sheet of water rapidly up the slope of the shore, depositing sediment in thin laminae. The rate of deposition by swash is slightly higher than erosion by backwash, resulting in a net gain of sediment.

The *backshore zone* lies landward of the foreshore, above the normal high-tide level. In some modern settings, a flat-lying to landward-sloping area adjacent to the foreshore, called a *berm*, is produced. The berm marks the uppermost limit of the water line that is reached only during the most severe storms and highest tides. Because it is normally exposed well above water level, sand in the backshore area is commonly moulded into dunes by wind. Vegetation may be temporarily established in moist, low-lying areas of the backshore that are transitional to inland areas stabilized by permanent vegetation. A good example is Ontario's Pinery Provincial Park along the west coast of Lake Huron.

Spits, Bars, and Tombolos Where beach drift and longshore currents are active, several features related to the movement of sediment along the shore may develop. A **spit** (*spit* = spine) is an elongated ridge of sand that projects from the land into the mouth of an adjacent bay. The end in the water commonly hooks landward in response to the dominant direction of the longshore current (Figures 19.17B and 19.17C). The term **baymouth bar** is applied to a sandbar that completely crosses a bay, sealing it off from the open ocean (Figure 19.17D). Such a feature tends to form across bays where currents are weak, allowing a spit

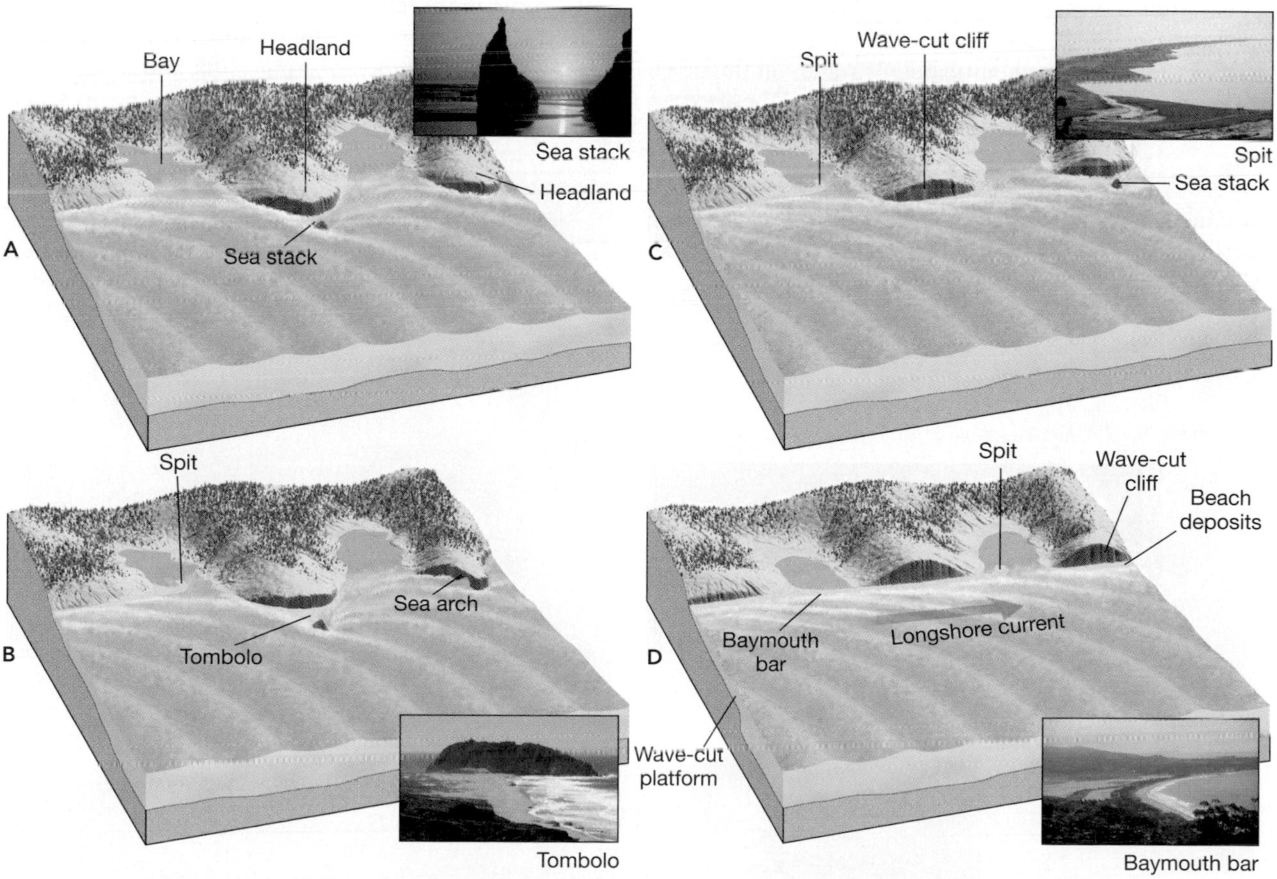

◆ **Figure 19.17** These diagrams illustrate the changes that can take place through time along an initially irregular coastline that remains relatively stable. The coastline shown in **A** gradually evolves to **B**, then **C**, and then **D**. The diagrams also serve to illustrate many of the features described in the section on shoreline features. (Photos by E. J. Tarbuck)

to extend to the other side. A **tombolo** (*tombolo* = mound), a ridge of sand that connects an island to the mainland or to another island (Figure 19.17B), forms in much the same manner as a spit.

Barrier Islands The Atlantic and Gulf Coastal Plains are relatively flat and slope gently seaward. The shore zone is characterized by **barrier islands**. These low ridges of land parallel the coast at distances from 3 to 30 kilometres offshore. From Cape Cod, Massachusetts, to Padre Island, Texas, nearly 300 barrier islands rim the coast (Figure 19.18).

Most barrier islands are from 1 to 5 kilometres wide and between 15 and 30 kilometres long. The tallest features are sand dunes, which usually reach heights of 5 to 10 metres; in a few areas, unvegetated dunes are more than 30 metres high. The lagoons separating these narrow islands from the shore represent zones of relatively quiet water that allow small craft travelling between New York and northern Florida to avoid the rough waters of the North Atlantic.

Barrier islands probably form in several ways. Some originate as spits that were subsequently severed from the mainland by wave erosion or by the general rise in sea level following the last Ice Age. Others are created when turbulent waters in the line of breakers heap up sand scoured from the bottom. Because these sand barriers rise above normal sea level, the piling of sand likely is the result of the work of storm waves at high tide. Finally, some barrier islands are former sand-dune ridges that originated along the shore during the last Ice Age, when sea level was lower. When the ice sheets melted, sea level rose and flooded the area behind the beach-dune complex. Associated with gaps along some barrier island (Figure 19.19A) and baymouth bar systems (Figure 19.19B) are **tidal deltas** that are created by tidal currents.

The Evolving Shore

A shoreline continually undergoes modification regardless of its initial configuration. At first most coastlines are irregular, although the degree of and reason for the irregularity may vary considerably from place to place. Along a coastline that is characterized by varied geology, the pounding surf may at first increase its irregularity because the waves will erode the weaker rocks more easily than the stronger ones. However, if a shoreline remains stable, marine erosion and deposition will eventually produce a straighter, more regular coast. Figure 19.17 illustrates the evolution of an initially irregular coast. As waves erode the headlands, creating cliffs and a wave-cut platform, sediment is carried along the shore. Some

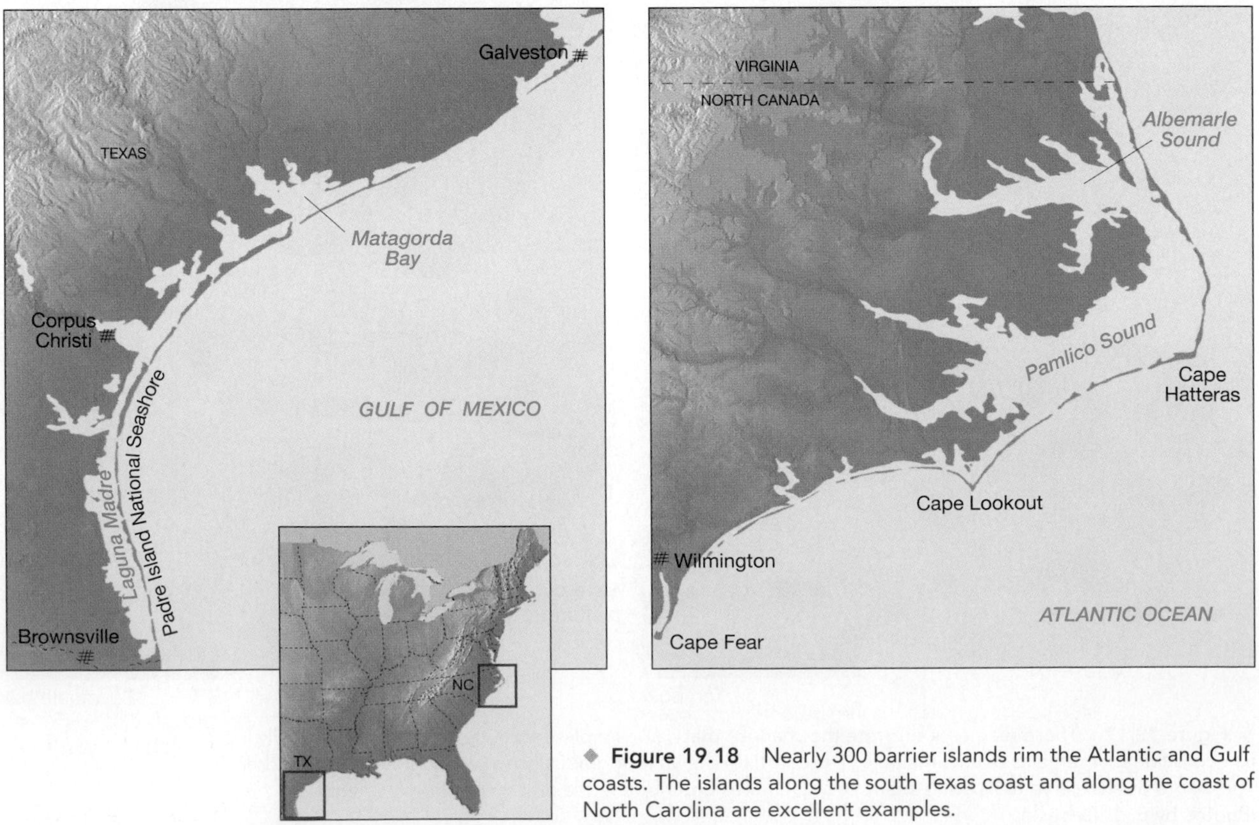

◆ **Figure 19.18** Nearly 300 barrier islands rim the Atlantic and Gulf coasts. The islands along the south Texas coast and along the coast of North Carolina are excellent examples.

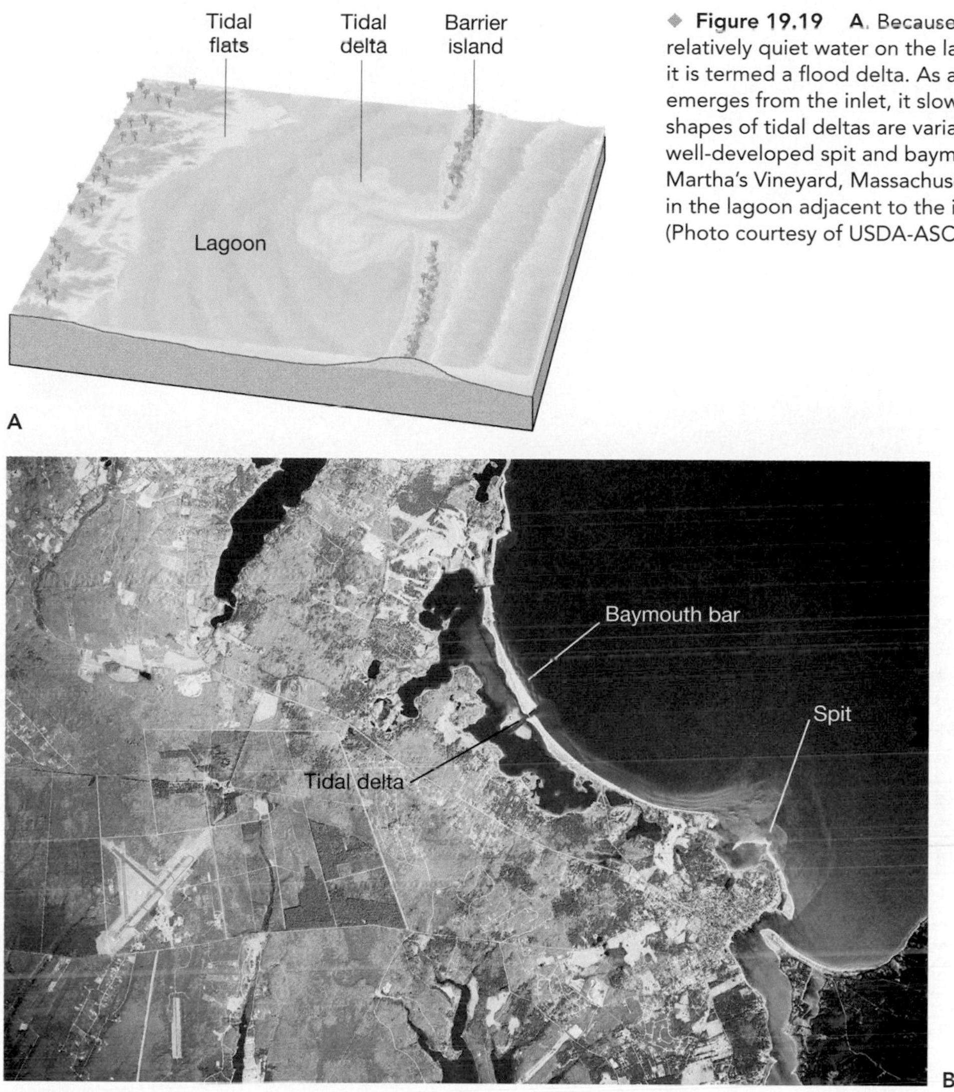

◆ **Figure 19.19** **A.** Because this tidal delta is forming in the relatively quiet water on the landward side of a barrier island, it is termed a flood delta. As a rapidly moving tidal current emerges from the inlet, it slows and deposits sediment. The shapes of tidal deltas are variable. **B.** High-altitude image of a well-developed spit and baymouth bar along the coast of Martha's Vineyard, Massachusetts. Also notice the tidal delta in the lagoon adjacent to the inlet through the baymouth bar. (Photo courtesy of USDA-ASCS)

material is deposited in the bays, while other debris is formed into spits and baymouth bars. At the same time, rivers fill the bays with sediment. Ultimately, a generally straight, smooth coast results.

ANCIENT DETRITAL COASTAL DEPOSITS

Unlike erosional coastlines, which are rarely preserved in the geologic record, ancient examples of depositional coasts are very common. Numerous studies of ancient coastal deposits have revealed that offshore, shoreface, foreshore, and backshore components can be recognized, based on their sedimentary characteristics and the relative stratigraphic positions of sedimentary units defined by these characteristics.

An interesting aspect of coastal sedimentation that has emerged from studies of ancient deposits is the importance of storms in the sediment dynamics of coastal systems, particularly in offshore and lower shoreface environments. Such studies have revealed that storms are responsible for depositing much of the sediment in the underwater portion of the coastal profile.

The basic sequence of units produced by the advance of a sandy shoreline (Figure 19.20) reflects the progressive overlap of offshore deposits by deposits of more landward environments. Accordingly, the vertical arrangement of strata produced by shoreline advance shows an upward shallowing trend, with offshore deposits at the bottom and backshore deposits at the top.

Offshore deposits are commonly characterized by the alternation of mudstone and sandstone beds (see Figure 19.20A), the latter preserving hummocky cross-stratification (see Chapter 6). Mudstone beds record episodes of fair-weather deposition, during which clay and silt particles settled from suspension

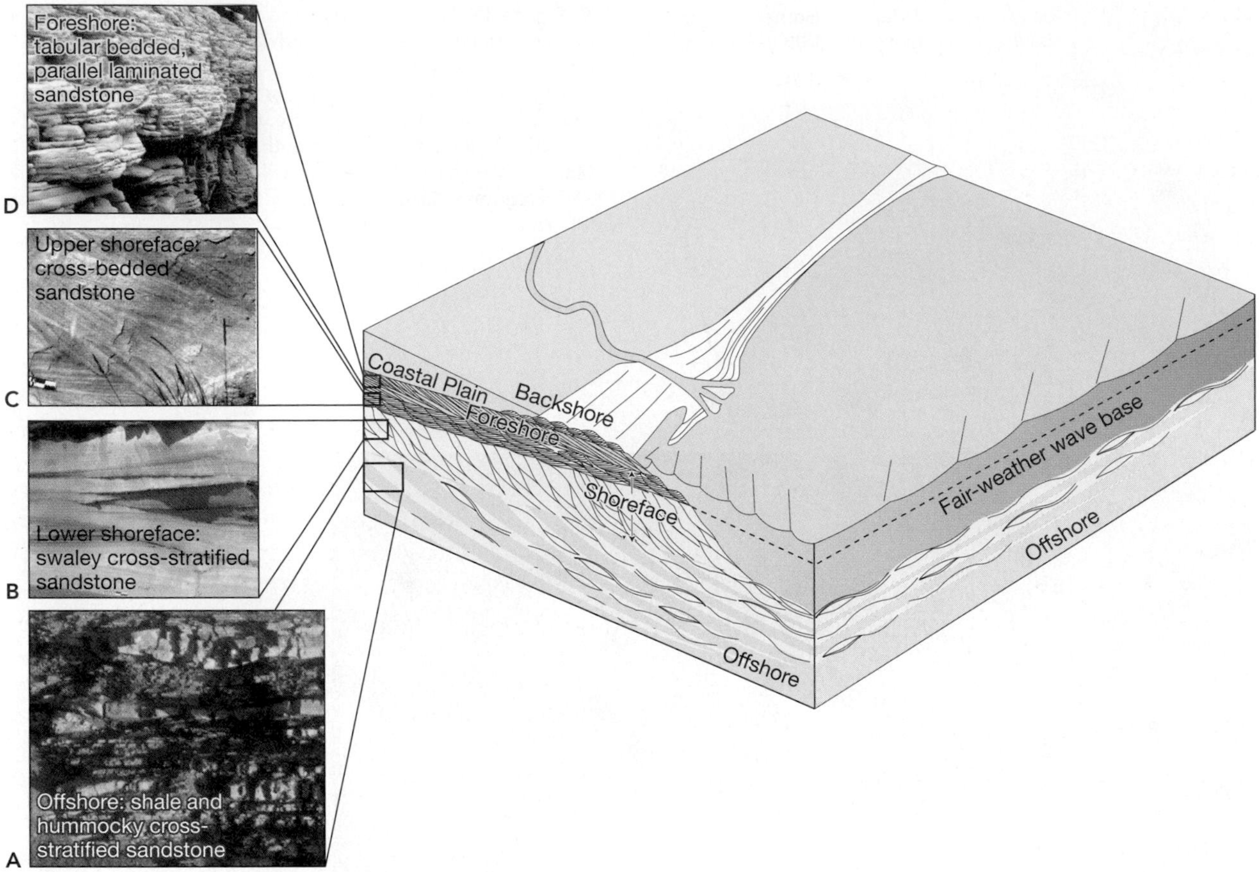

◆ **Figure 19.20** Schematic diagram showing deposits associated with an ancient coastal zone. The offshore zone is characterized by mud preserved as shale and hummocky stratified sands (**A**). The lower and upper portions of the shoreface are dominated by swaley (defined later) cross-stratified (**B**) and cross-bedded sands (**C**), respectively. Beach deposits are dominated by tabular bedded, parallel-laminated sands in the foreshore zone (**D**). Cross-bedded dune deposits can occur in the backshore zone but are rarely preserved.
(Photos by Guy Plint)

below fair-weather wave base. Sand deposition by storms is indicated by the presence of hummocky cross-stratification in the sandstone beds.

Shoreface deposits record depositional conditions above fair-weather wave base and are dominated by sand. Deposits of the lower shoreface do, however, tend to retain the signature of storms. Like offshore deposits, lower shoreface deposits contain sandstone beds with a draping internal structure similar to hummocky cross-stratification. Unlike offshore deposits, however, the sandstone beds lie directly on top of one another, with no intervening mudstone beds, and the tops of the upward-bulging hummocks are eroded off, producing a variation of hummocky cross-stratification called *swaley cross-stratification* (see Figure 19.20B). Fair-weather processes undoubtedly affect the lower shoreface, but it appears that the thin veneers of sediment deposited during fair-weather periods tend to be scoured away and replaced by thicker, storm-deposited beds that are more likely to be preserved in the long term. Swaley cross-stratified sandstone units have been noted to range from 2 to 15 metres thick.

Relative to the lower shoreface, the upper shoreface occupies a zone of much shallower water, where larger volumes of sand are transported on a day-to-day basis by fair-weather wave action. Consistent with this difference in depositional environment, upper shoreface deposits are usually dominated by cross-bedded sandstones that record the migration of ripples, dunes, and bars (Figure 19.20C). Such features are common in modern settings, particularly where wave-generated longshore and rip currents are active. Cross-bedded sandstone units, representing deposits of the upper shoreface, typically range in thickness from about 2 to 5 metres.

Foreshore (beach) deposits are typically preserved as thin sandstone units that cap the swaley cross-stratified or cross-bedded shoreface sandstones.

Internally, foreshore sandstones typically display tabular beds (see Figure 19.20D) of millimetre-scale parallel lamination defined by alternating layers of clean quartz sand and dark mineral concentrations. This lamination is the product of sand deposition by swash in the foreshore, and on modern beaches it is observed to gently dip toward the sea.

Backshore deposits vary greatly in their characteristics but are commonly represented by sandstone units containing large-scale cross-bedding. These units, in turn, represent migrating sand dunes produced by wind action well above high-tide level. Backshore deposits can also contain evidence of roots left by vegetation that became established in low-lying areas of the backshore, as well as local concentrations of organic matter deposited in areas of poor drainage of the coastal plain.

Coastal sedimentary successions of barrier islands contain all the above deposit types, as well as an additional component representing a lagoon. Lagoon deposits tend to be largely composed of organic-rich mudstone, representing the protected, low-energy conditions provided by the barrier. Minor beds of sandstone also occur, such as might be produced by the washover of sand from the barrier island into the lagoon during storms. In turn, the muddy lagoon deposits are commonly overlain by mudstones and sandstones with plant roots, indicating deposition along a coastal swamp at the edge of the mainland.

Clearly, the correlation of sedimentary processes with the observed characteristics of ancient shoreline deposits is extremely useful for the interpretation of sedimentary processes in the past that is important to oil and gas exploration. At the same time, however, it must be emphasized that the succession presented here is very simplified and that the details of any given ancient example can deviate significantly from this basic model.

REEFS

Reefs are prominent elements of some tropical coastal zones. Long coastline segments of continents can host reefs, provided that optimum conditions exist for the proliferation of reef-building organisms. Factors favouring reef growth include warm water temperatures averaging about 24°C; low nutrient levels that discourage leaf-like forms of algae from smothering reef-building organisms, such as corals; and normal salinity. Reef builders, such as corals, contain tiny forms of algae in their tissues that assist carbonate precipitation. Reefs also require lots of light to allow their symbiotic, skeleton-building helpers to photosynthesize.

The Great Barrier Reef, Earth's largest modern reef system, lies off the coast of Queensland, northeast Australia. This impressive coastal feature is 2500 kilometres long and has an area of 344,000 square kilometres. Its nearly 3000 individual carbonate buildups were constructed entirely by living organisms. Most reefs develop along continental coastlines either as fringing reefs that are attached to the coast or as barrier reefs that are separated from the mainland by a lagoon. Smaller versions of such reefs can also develop around volcanic islands in the open ocean, as discussed in Chapter 11.

As with coastal zones dominated by land-derived sediments, reefs contain sedimentary environments that reflect variations in water agitation. We emphasize, however, that the sediments produced in a reef setting are produced by living things and are therefore also influenced by factors controlling the life processes of the organisms involved.

The spectrum of sedimentary environments within reef settings is best illustrated in barrier reef systems (Figure 19.21). The hub of carbonate production lies in the reef crest, which is the highest

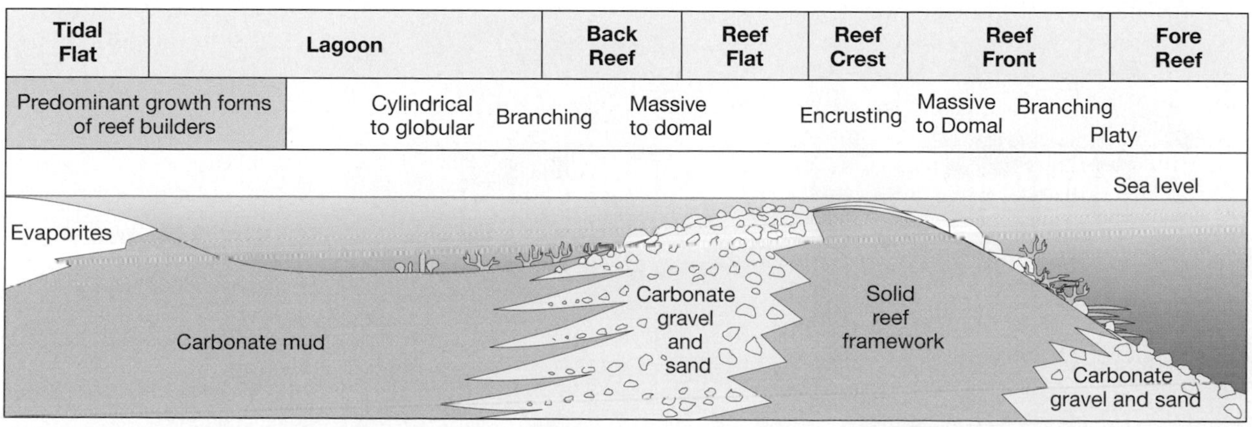

◆ **Figure 19.21** Principal zones of a barrier reef system.

part of the reef and stands nearest to the surface of the sea. The reef crest receives most of the wind and wave energy in the reef system and typically contains the most robust frame builders of the reef. Seaward of the reef crest is the reef front, typified by less robust reef builders and lots of carbonate debris shed from the reef crest. Still farther seaward is the fore reef, where low light levels discourage the establishment of reef-building organisms, and carbonate debris is abundant.

Landward of the reef crest is the reef flat, a plateau-like zone that is scoured by waves and where coarse-grained and well-sorted carbonate tends to accumulate. Still more landward is the lagoon, which is protected from wave action by the reef crest and reef flat, and is therefore an area where fine-grained carbonate sediment can settle out. Much of the carbonate mud within the lagoon is derived from types of algae that contain tiny grains of calcite and aragonite in their tissues. If the climate is arid, evaporite deposits can accumulate on tidal flats of the mainland adjacent to the lagoon.

STABILIZING THE SHORE

GEODe EARTH Shorelines
↳ Waves and Beaches

Today the coastal zone teems with human activity. Unfortunately, people often treat the shoreline as if it were permanently stable. One need only to consider the incredible devastation left in the wake of Hurricane Katrina in 2005 to appreciate the fact that a shoreline is not always a safe place to live.

Compared with natural hazards, such as earthquakes, volcanic eruptions, and landslides, shoreline erosion is commonly perceived to be a more continuous and predictable process that appears to cause relatively modest damage to limited areas. In reality, the shoreline is a dynamic place that can change rapidly in response to natural forces. Exceptional storms are capable of eroding beaches and cliffs at rates that are far in excess of the long-term average. Such bursts of accelerated erosion not only have a significant impact on the natural evolution of a coast but can also have a profound impact on people who reside in the coastal zone (Figure 19.22). Erosion along our coasts can cause significant property damage. Large sums are spent annually not only to repair damage but also to prevent or control erosion. Already a problem at many sites, shoreline erosion is certain to become an increasingly serious problem as extensive coastal development continues.

Although the same processes cause change along every coast, not all coasts respond in the same way. Interactions among different processes and the relative importance of each process depend on local factors. The factors include (1) the proximity of a coast to sediment-laden rivers, (2) the degree of tectonic activity, (3) the topography and composition of the land, (4) the prevailing winds and weather patterns, and (5) the configuration of the coastline and near-shore areas.

During the past 100 years, growing affluence and increasing demands for recreation have brought unprecedented development to many coastal areas. As both the number and the value of buildings have increased, so too have efforts to protect property from storm waves by stabilizing the shore. Also, con-

◆ **Figure 19.22** Wave erosion caused by strong storms forced abandonment of the highly developed shoreline area in Long Island, New York. Coastal areas are dynamic places that can change rapidly in response to natural forces.
(Photo by Mark Wexler/ Woodfin Camp & Associates)

trolling the natural migration of sand is an ongoing struggle in many coastal areas. Such interference can result in unwanted changes that are difficult and expensive to correct.

Hard Stabilization

Structures built to protect a coast from erosion or to prevent the movement of sand along a beach are known as **hard stabilization.** Hard stabilization can take many forms and often results in predictable yet unwanted outcomes. Hard stabilization includes jetties, groins, breakwaters, and seawalls.

Jetties From relatively early in North America's history, a principal goal in coastal areas was the development and maintenance of harbours. In many cases, this involved the construction of jetty systems. **Jetties** are usually built in pairs and extend into the ocean at the entrances to rivers and harbours. With the flow of water confined to a narrow zone, the ebb and flow caused by the rise and fall of the tides keep the sand in motion and prevent deposition in the channel. However, as illustrated in Figure 19.23, the jetty can act as a dam against which the longshore current and beach drift deposit sand. At the same time, wave activity removes sand on the other side. Because the other side is not receiving any new sand, soon it has no beach at all.

Groins To maintain or widen beaches that are losing sand, groins are sometimes constructed. A **groin** (*groin* = ground) is a barrier built at a right angle to the beach to trap sand that is moving parallel to the shore. Groins are usually constructed of large rocks but can also be composed of wood. These structures often do their job so effectively that the longshore current beyond the groin becomes sand-starved. As a result, the current erodes sand from the beach on the downstream side of the groin.

To offset this effect, property owners downstream from the structure may erect a groin on their property. In this manner, the number of groins multiplies, resulting in a *groin field* (Figure 19.24). An example of such proliferation is the shoreline of New Jersey, where hundreds of these structures have been built. Because it has been shown that groins often do not provide a satisfactory solution, they are no longer the preferred method of keeping beach erosion in check.

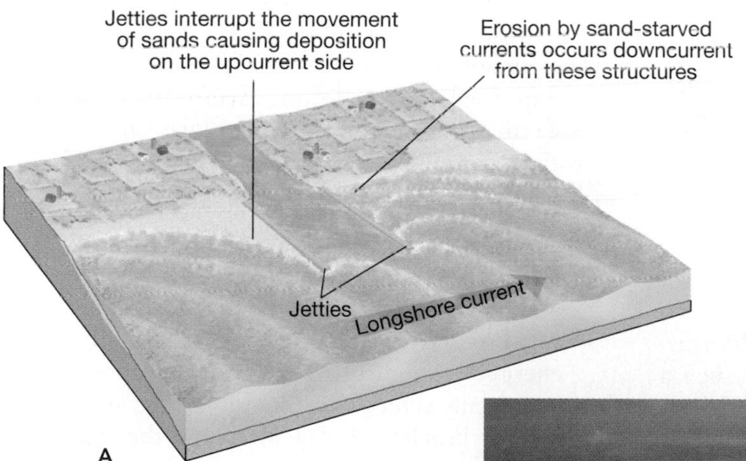

A

B

◆ **Figure 19.23** **A.** Jetties are built at the entrances to rivers and harbours and are intended to prevent deposition in the navigation channel. Jetties interrupt the movement of sand by beach drift and longshore currents. Beach erosion often results down current from the site of the structure. **B.** Stevenson Jetty at the mouth of the Fraser River, near Richmond, British Columbia. (Photo by S. R. Hicock)

◆ **Figure 19.24** Groins along the New Jersey shore at Cape May.
(Photo by John S. Shelton)

◆ **Figure 19.25** Aerial view of a breakwater at Santa Monica, California. The breakwater appears as a faint line in the water behind which many boats are anchored. The construction of the breakwater disrupted longshore transport and caused the seaward growth of the beach.
(Photo by John S. Shelton)

Breakwaters and Seawalls Hard stabilization can also be built parallel to the shoreline. One such structure is a **breakwater**, the purpose of which is to protect boats from the force of large breaking waves by creating a quiet water zone near the shoreline. However, when this is done, the reduced wave activity along the shore behind the structure can allow sand to accumulate. If this happens, the marina will eventually fill with sand while the downstream beach erodes and retreats. At Santa Monica, California, where the building of a breakwater created such a problem, the city uses a dredge to remove sand from the protected quiet-water zone and deposit it downstream, where longshore currents and beach drift continue to move the sand down the coast (Figure 19.25).

Another type of hard stabilization built parallel to the shoreline is a **seawall**, which is designed to armour the coast and defend property from the force of breaking waves (Figure 19.26A). Waves expend much of their energy as they move across an open beach. Seawalls cut this process short by reflecting the force of unspent waves seaward. As a consequence, the beach to the seaward side of the seawall experiences significant erosion and can in some instances be eliminated entirely. Once the width of the beach is reduced, the seawall is subjected to even greater pounding by the waves (Figure 19.26B). Eventually this battering will cause the wall to fail, and a larger, more expensive wall must be built to take its place.

The wisdom of building temporary protective structures along shorelines is increasingly questioned. The opinions of many coastal scientists and engineers are expressed in the following excerpt from a position paper that grew out of a conference on America's eroding shoreline:

> It is now clear that halting the receding shoreline with protective structures benefits only a few and seriously degrades or destroys the natural beach and the value it holds for the majority. Protective structures divert the ocean's energy temporarily from private properties, but usually refocus that energy on the adjacent natural beaches. Many interrupt the natural sand flow in coastal currents, robbing many beaches of vital sand replacement.*

Alternatives to Hard Stabilization

Armouring the coast with hard stabilization has several potential drawbacks, including the cost of the structure and the loss of sand on the beach.

*J. D. Howard, W. Kaufman, and O. H. Pilkey, "Strategy for Beach Preservation Proposed," *Geotimes* 30, no. 12 (December 1985): 15.

A B

◆ **Figure 19.26** **A.** Seawall around Stanley Park, Vancouver, British Columbia. **B.** Seabright in northern New Jersey once had a broad, sandy beach. A seawall 5 to 6 metres high, and 8 kilometres long, was built to protect the town and the railroad that brought tourists to the beach. As you can see, after the wall was built, the beach narrowed dramatically.
(Photo A by S. R. Hicock, photo B by Raphael Macia/Photo Researchers, Inc.)

Alternatives to hard stabilization include beach nourishment and relocation.

Beach Nourishment **Beach nourishment** represents an approach to stabilizing shoreline sands without hard stabilization. As the term implies, this practice simply involves the addition of large quantities of sand to the beach system (Figure 19.27). By building the beaches seaward, beach quality and storm protection are improved. Beach nourishment, however, is not a permanent solution to the problem of shrinking beaches. The same processes that removed the sand in the first place will eventually remove the replacement sand as well. In addition, beach nourishment is very expensive because huge volumes of sand must be transported to the beach from offshore areas, nearby rivers, or other source areas.

In some instances, beach nourishment can lead to unwanted environmental effects. For example, beach replenishment at Waikiki Beach, Hawaii,

A B

◆ **Figure 19.27** Miami Beach, Florida. **A.** Before beach nourishment. **B.** After beach nourishment.
(Photos courtesy of the U.S. Army Corps of Engineers, Vicksburg District)

BOX 19.1

People and the Environment
Coastal Vulnerability to Sea-Level Rise

Human activities, especially the combustion of fossil fuels, have been adding vast amounts of carbon dioxide and other trace gases to the atmosphere for 200 years or more. Emissions of these gases is likely to increase during the twenty-first century. One consequence of this change in the composition of the atmosphere is an enhancement of Earth's greenhouse effect with a resulting increase in global temperatures. During the twentieth century, average global temperatures increased by about 0.6°C. During the twenty-first century, the increase is projected to be considerably greater.*

One probable impact of a human-induced global warming is a rise in sea level (Figure 19.A). How is a warmer atmosphere related to a global rise in sea level? The most obvious connection—the melting of glaciers—is important but not the most significant factor. More significant is that a warmer atmosphere causes an increase in ocean volume because of thermal expansion. Higher air temperatures warm the adjacent upper layers of the ocean, which in turn causes the water to expand and sea level to rise.

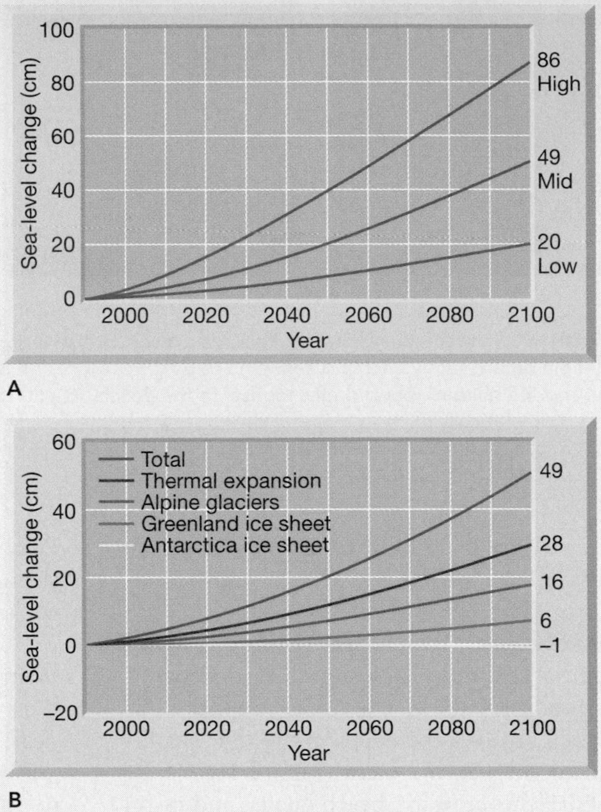

◆ **Figure 19.A** **A.** High, middle, and low projections of global sea-level rise, 1990–2100. **B.** Projected individual contributions to global sea-level change, 1990–2100, for the middle projection in part **A.** Thermal expansion is responsible for 28 centimetres of the sea-level rise. Melting alpine glaciers and ice caps contribute another 16 centimetres. The impact shown for Antarctica indicates that this massive ice sheet is projected to grow larger during this period.

*For more on this, see the section "Environmental Effects of Fossil Fuel Use" in Chapter 20.

involved replacing coarse calcareous sand with softer, muddier calcareous sediment. Destruction of the soft beach sand by breaking waves increased the water's turbidity and killed offshore coral reefs. At Miami Beach increased turbidity also damaged local coral communities.

Beach nourishment appears to be an economically viable long-range solution to the beach preservation problem only in areas where dense development, large supplies of sand, relatively low-wave energy, and reconcilable environmental issues exist. Unfortunately, few areas possess all these attributes.

Relocation Instead of building structures, such as groins and seawalls, to hold the beach in place, or adding sand to replenish eroding beaches, another option is available. Many coastal scientists and planners are calling for a policy shift from defending and rebuilding beaches and coastal property in high hazard areas to *relocating* storm-damaged buildings in those places and letting nature reclaim the beach. This approach is similar to that adopted by the United States for river floodplains following the devastating 1993 Mississippi River floods in which vulnerable structures are abandoned and relocated on higher, safer ground.

Such proposals, of course, are controversial. People with significant near-shore investments shudder at the thought of not rebuilding and defending coastal developments from the erosional wrath of the sea. Others, however, argue that with sea level rising, the impact of coastal storms will only get worse in

Research indicates that sea level has risen between 10 and 25 centimetres over the past century and that the trend will continue at an accelerated rate. Some models indicate that the rise may approach or even exceed 50 centimetres by the year 2100 (Figure 19.A). Such a change may seem modest, but scientists realize that any rise in sea level along a *gently* sloping shoreline, such as the Atlantic and Arctic coasts of Canada, will lead to significant erosion and severe permanent inland flooding (Figure 19.B). If this happens, many beaches and wetlands will be eliminated, and coastal civilization would be severely disrupted.

Because rising sea level is a gradual phenomenon, it may be overlooked as an important contributor to shoreline erosion problems. Rather, the blame may be assigned to other forces, especially storm activity. Although a given storm may be the immediate cause, the magnitude of its destruction may result from the relatively small sea-level rise that allowed the storm's power to cross a much greater land area. Although most of the severe hurricanes born in the tropical Atlantic and Gulf of Mexico dissipate before they can reach Canadian shores, storms such as Hurricane Juan in 2003 are important reminders that Canada is by no means immune to the damaging effects of storms. Some scientists predict that as a result of continued global warming, hurricanes will strike Atlantic Canada more frequently and with greater destructive power than has been so over the past few decades.

One of the most challenging problems for coastal scientists today is determining the physical response of the coastline to sea-level rise. Predicting shoreline retreat and land-loss rates is critical to formulating coastal management strategies. To date, long-term planning for our shorelines has been piecemeal, if at all. Consequently, development continues without adequate consideration of the potential costs of erosion, flooding, and storm damage.

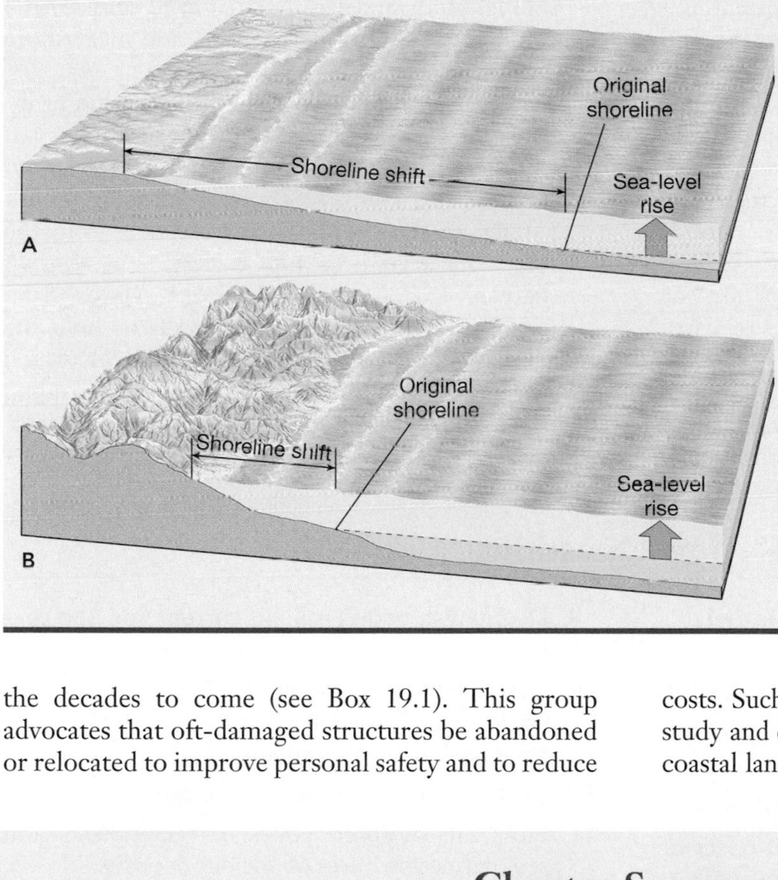

◆ **Figure 19.B** The slope of a shoreline is critical to determining the degree to which sea-level changes will affect it. **A.** When the slope is gentle, small changes in sea level cause a substantial shift. **B.** The same sea-level rise along a steep coast results in only a small shoreline shift.

the decades to come (see Box 19.1). This group advocates that oft-damaged structures be abandoned or relocated to improve personal safety and to reduce costs. Such ideas will no doubt be the focus of much study and debate as communities evaluate and revise coastal land-use policies.

Chapter Summary

- The three factors that influence the height, *wavelength*, and period of a wave are (1) wind speed, (2) length of time the wind has blown, and (3) *fetch*, the distance that the wind has travelled across the open water.
- Wind-generated wave forms advance as the water particles move in circular orbits; the turbulent advance of water near the shore causes waves to collapse, or break, and form *surf*.
- Wave erosion is caused by wave impact pressure and abrasion (the scouring and grinding action of water armed with rock fragments). The bending of waves is called *wave refraction*. Owing to refraction, wave impact is concentrated against the sides and ends of headlands.

- Most waves reach the shore at an angle. The uprush (swash) and backwash of water from each breaking wave moves the sediment in a zigzag pattern along the beach. This movement, called *beach drift*, can transport sand hundreds or even thousands of metres each day. Oblique waves also produce *longshore currents* within the surf zone that flow parallel to the shore.
- Features produced by shoreline erosion include *wave-cut cliffs* (which originate from the cutting action of the surf against the base of coastal land), *wave-cut platforms* (relatively flat, benchlike surfaces left behind by receding cliffs), *sea arches* (formed when a headland is eroded and two caves from opposite sides unite), and *sea stacks* (formed when the roof of a sea arch collapses).
- *Tides*, the daily rise and fall in the elevation of the ocean surface, are caused by the gravitational attraction of the Moon and, to a lesser extent, the Sun. Near the times of new and full moons, the Sun and Moon are aligned, and their gravitational forces are added together to produce especially high and low tides. These are called the *spring tides*. Conversely, at about the times of the first and third quarters of the Moon, when the gravitational forces of the Moon and Sun are at right angles, the daily tidal range is less. These are called *neap tides*.
- *Tidal currents* are horizontal movements of water that accompany the rise and fall of tides. *Tidal flats* are the areas that are affected by the advancing and retreating tidal currents. When tidal currents slow after emerging from narrow inlets, they deposit sediment that may eventually create *tidal deltas*.
- Some of the depositional features that form when sediment is moved by beach drift and longshore currents are *spits* (elongated ridges of sand that project from the land into the mouth of an adjacent bay), *baymouth bars* (sandbars that completely cross a bay), and *tombolos* (ridges of sand that connect an island to the mainland or to another island). Along the Atlantic and Gulf Coastal Plains of the United States, the shore zone is characterized by *barrier islands*, low ridges of sand that parallel the coast at distances of 3 to 30 kilometres offshore.
- Local factors that influence shoreline erosion are (1) the proximity of a coast to sediment-laden rivers, (2) the degree of tectonic activity, (3) the topography and composition of the land, (4) prevailing winds and weather patterns, and (5) the configuration of the coastline and near-shore areas.
- Three basic responses to shoreline erosion problems are (1) building structures, such as *groins* (short walls built at a right angle to the shore to trap moving sand), *breakwaters* (structures built parallel to the shoreline to protect it from the force of large breaking waves), and *seawalls* (barriers constructed to prevent waves from reaching the area behind the wall) to hold the shoreline in place; (2) *beach nourishment*, which involves the addition of sand to replenish eroding beaches; and (3) relocating buildings away from the beach.

Review Questions

1. List three factors that determine the height, length, and period of a wave.
2. Describe the motion of a water particle as a wave passes.
3. Explain what happens when a wave breaks.
4. Describe two ways in which waves cause erosion.
5. What is wave refraction? What is the effect of this process along irregular coastlines?
6. Discuss the origin of ocean tides.
7. How does the Sun influence tides?
8. Distinguish between flood current and ebb current.
9. Describe the formation of the following features: wave-cut cliff, wave-cut platform, sea stack, spit, baymouth bar, and tombolo.
10. Explain how barrier islands are formed.
11. How can shoreline zones be recognized from sedimentary features of ancient deposits?
12. How might a seawall lead to increased beach erosion?
13. What are the drawbacks of beach nourishment?

Key Terms

barrier island (p. 510)
baymouth bar (p. 509)
beach drift (p. 503)
beach nourishment (p. 517)
breakwater (p. 516)
ebb current (p. 506)
estuaries (p. 506)
fetch (p. 499)
flood current (p. 506)
groin (p. 515)
hard stabilizers (p. 515)
jetty (p. 515)
longshore current (p. 504)
neap tide (p. 506)
sea arch (p. 507)
sea stack (p. 507)
seawall (p. 516)
spit (p. 509)
spring tide (p. 506)
surf (p. 501)
tidal current (p. 506)
tidal delta (p. 510)
tidal flats (p. 506)
tide (p. 504)
tombolo (p. 510)
wave-cut cliff (p. 507)
wave-cut platform (p. 507)
wave height (p. 499)
wavelength (p. 499)
wave period (p. 499)
wave refraction (p. 503)

Web Resources

The *Earth* website uses the resources and flexibility of the internet to aid in your study of the topics in this chapter. Written and developed by geology instructors, this site will help improve your understanding of geology. Visit **www.pearsoned.ca/tarbuck** and click on the cover of the text to find

- online review quizzes
- Web-based critical thinking and writing exercises
- links to chapter-specific Web resources
- internet-wide key-term searches

www.pearsoned.ca/tarbuck

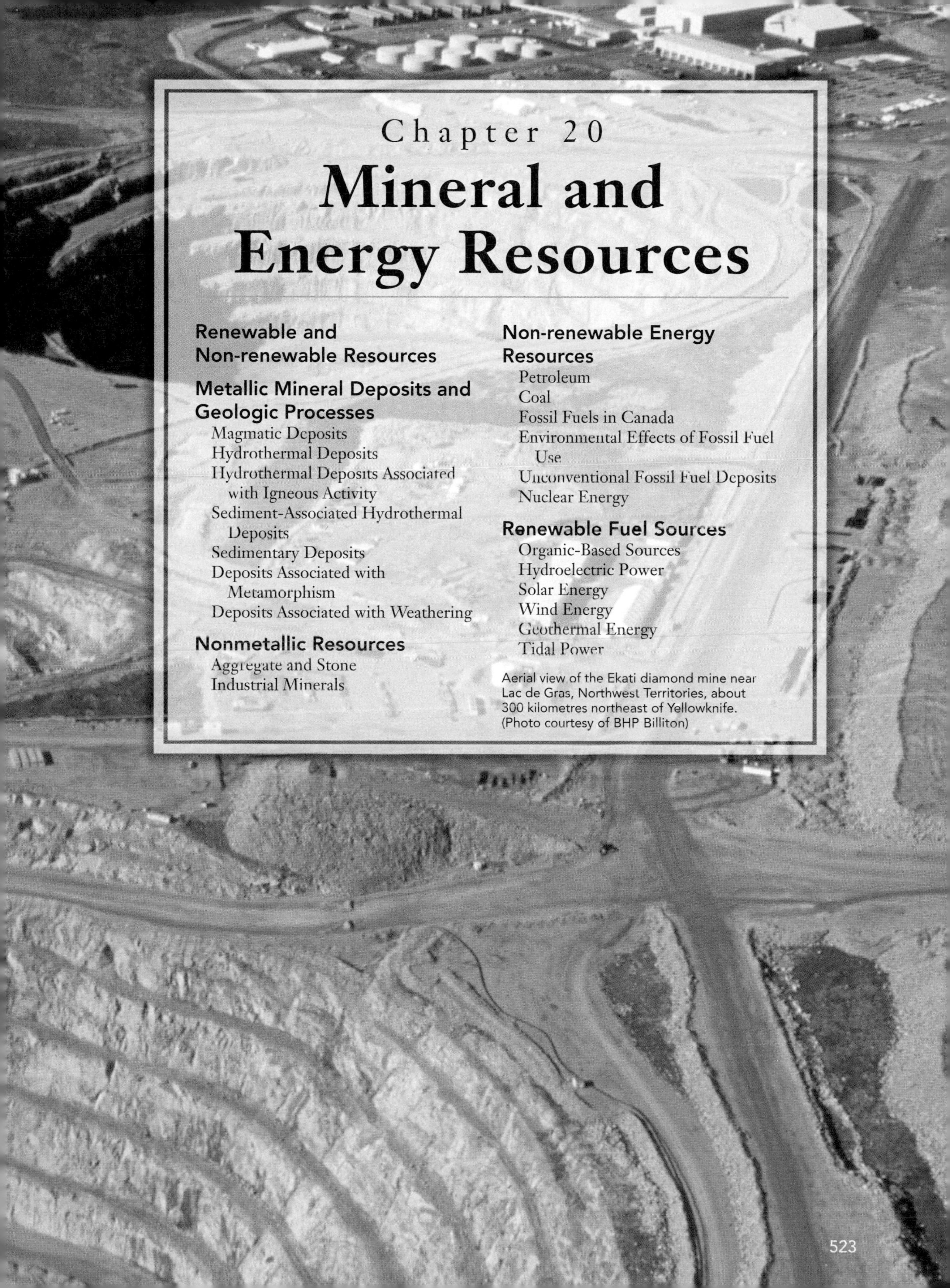

Chapter 20

Mineral and Energy Resources

Renewable and Non-renewable Resources

Metallic Mineral Deposits and Geologic Processes
- Magmatic Deposits
- Hydrothermal Deposits
- Hydrothermal Deposits Associated with Igneous Activity
- Sediment-Associated Hydrothermal Deposits
- Sedimentary Deposits
- Deposits Associated with Metamorphism
- Deposits Associated with Weathering

Nonmetallic Resources
- Aggregate and Stone
- Industrial Minerals

Non-renewable Energy Resources
- Petroleum
- Coal
- Fossil Fuels in Canada
- Environmental Effects of Fossil Fuel Use
- Unconventional Fossil Fuel Deposits
- Nuclear Energy

Renewable Fuel Sources
- Organic-Based Sources
- Hydroelectric Power
- Solar Energy
- Wind Energy
- Geothermal Energy
- Tidal Power

Aerial view of the Ekati diamond mine near Lac de Gras, Northwest Territories, about 300 kilometres northeast of Yellowknife. (Photo courtesy of BHP Billiton)

A popular saying among geologists is "if it can't be grown, it's gotta be mined." Materials extracted from Earth are the basis for modern civilization (Figure 20.1). Everything we use in our lives that is not derived from living things comes from the geosphere. We depend on Earth's resources so much that we generally take this fact for granted. Chances are that most of the metals, plastics, and energy sources that you are using today are derived from Earth resources that were ultimately discovered and developed with the help of geoscientists. For example, when you turn on your television or computer, you are using materials derived from Earth. From the silicon chips to the copper in the wires, and from the glass screen to the energy that powers the computer, nearly all aspects of these high-tech devices are linked to mineral and energy resources. The economic uses of several minerals, both metallic and nonmetallic, are indicated in Table 2.3.

The mining industry is a vital contributor to the Canadian economy. The mining and mineral-processing industries contribute more than $35 billion to the Canadian economy, amounting to more than $1060 per person. Canada is also one of the world's largest exporters of minerals and mineral products. At least 80 percent of Canada's mineral and metal production is exported. Canada ranks first in the world for the production of potash and uranium, is the second-largest producer of nickel and asbestos, and ranks in the top five for the production of zinc, cadmium, titanium concentrate, aluminum, platinum group metals, salt, gold, molybdenum, copper, gypsum, cobalt, and lead. The five most important minerals in Canada with respect to production value are gold, nickel, potash, copper, and zinc.

◆ **Figure 20.1** Toronto at night. As this scene reminds us, mineral and energy resources are the basis of modern civilization. (Photo © Lloyd Sutton/Masterfile)

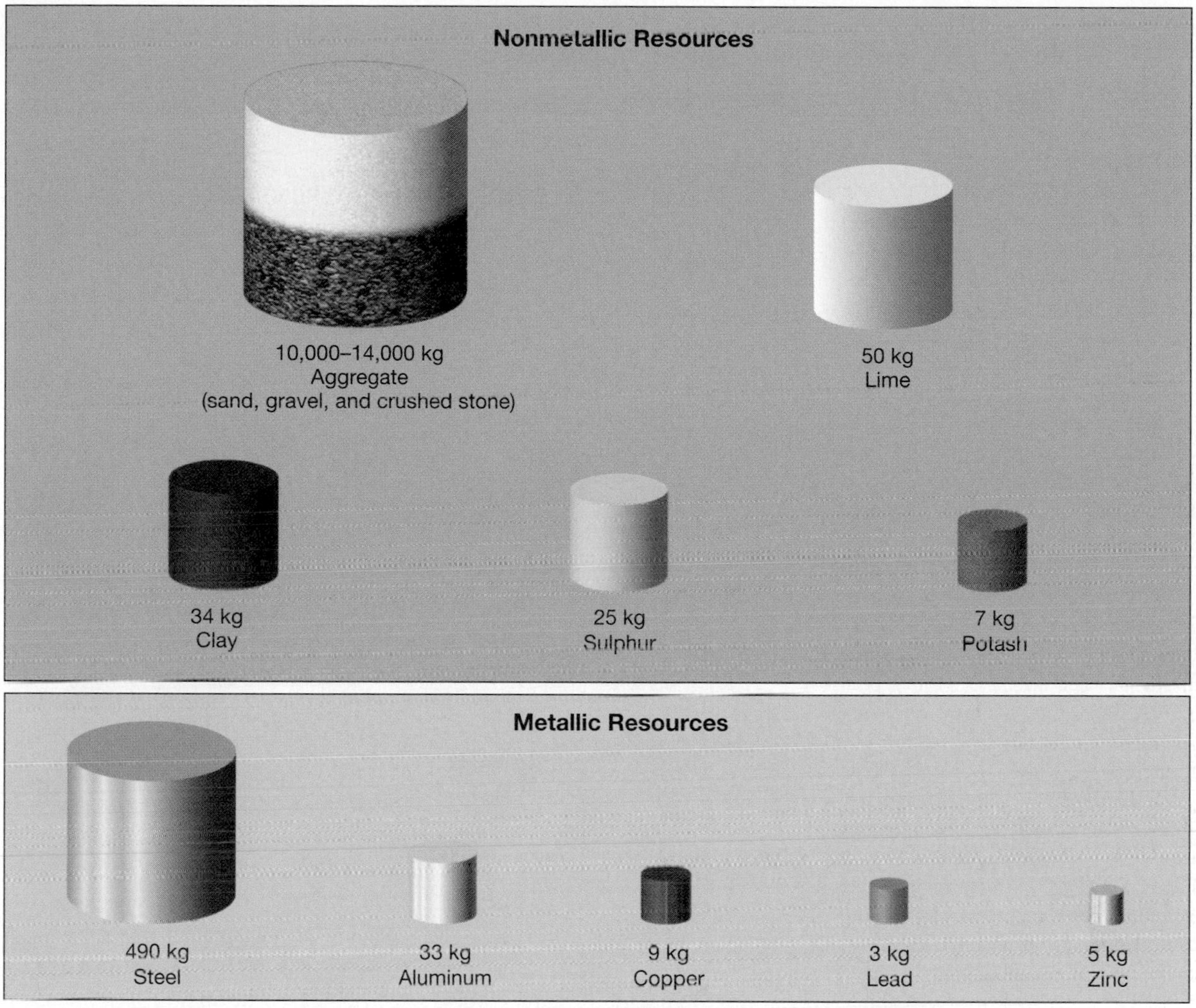

◆ **Figure 20.2** The annual per capita consumption of selected mineral resources for Canada. (Based on data from Statistics Canada, Aggregate Producers of British Columbia, and Canadian Steel Producers Association)

The number of different **mineral resources** required by modern industries is immense (Figure 20.2), and although some countries, like Canada and the United States, have rich supplies of many important minerals, no nation is completely self-sufficient. Consequently, the resources of Earth have long been the basis of world trade, have driven great waves of immigration, and have even generated wars.

Geoscientists are indispensable in many aspects of mineral and energy resource discovery, measurement, and management. These include predicting where an economically important resource might occur, determining the most effective way of extracting it, and determining the conditions of mineral deposit formation to aid in the discovery of similar deposits. At the same time, geoscientists are mindful of the great responsibilities nations face in their exploitation and utilization of natural resources (Box 20.1), and they play crucial roles in assessing the possible environmental impacts of mineral extraction and developing techniques for environmental remediation.

RENEWABLE AND NON-RENEWABLE RESOURCES

Resources are the endowment of materials held in reserve that are useful to people and are ultimately available commercially. Resources are commonly divided into two broad categories: renewable and non-renewable.

Renewable resources can be replenished over relatively short time spans, such as months, years, or decades. Common examples are plants and animals for food, natural fibres for clothing, and trees for lumber and paper. Energy from flowing water, wind, and the Sun are also considered renewable. By

BOX 20.1

People and the Environment

Resource Consumption and Sustainability: A Global Perspective

Mike Powell*

In a global context, resources include not only minerals and fuel but also anything else held in reserve that can be used in the future. For many of us, resources are those things that we use in excess to maintain our quality of life, or high standard of living (consumables, energy, etc.); this is a view embraced mainly by people living in developed countries. However, for most of the world's population, locally available resources are those things that simply maintain life on a daily basis (food, shelter, etc.). Many small countries possess a single resource (e.g., sandy white beaches or a pleasant climate), which translates into tourism dollars. From a global perspective, resources include the vast reservoirs of less tangible commodities, such as air, water, and soil quality, as well as plant and animal species. Global resource consumption is not equitable or evenly distributed on a per capita basis. The vast majority of worldwide resources are channelled into economies that have the financial capacity to buy commodities.

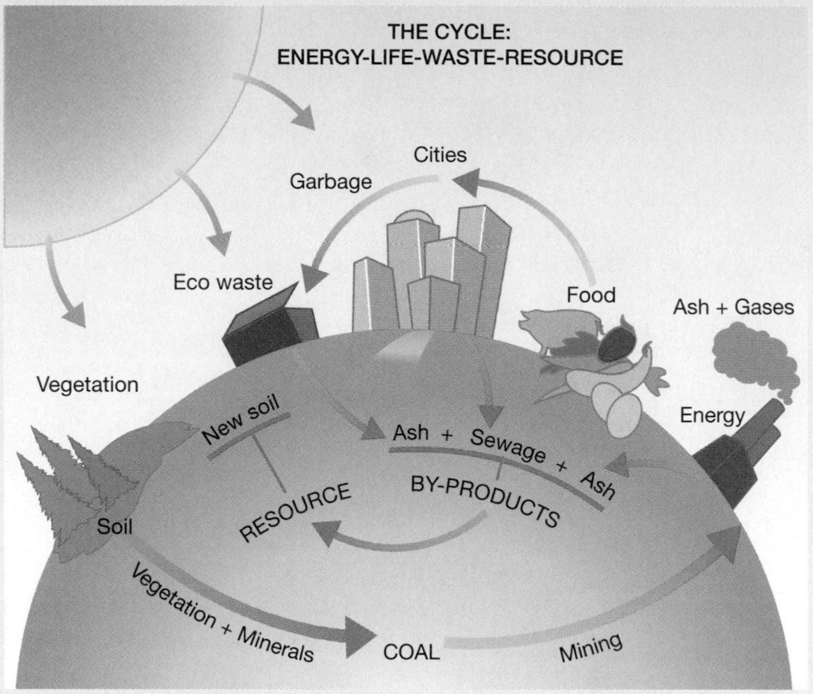

◆ **Figure 20.A** Uses of waste resources from by-products. (Courtesy of Mike Powell)

Earth can be thought of as a single mixed reservoir of all resources that are consumed mostly by a single component (people). The rate of resource consumption is a product of population size and rate of consumption. The rate of population growth has accelerated exponentially throughout history. It took more than 100,000 years for Earth to reach the 1 billion population mark. About 130 years later, population doubled to 2 billion. By 1975 it doubled again to 4 billion, and by 2015 it may exceed 7 billion. Increases in economic activity worldwide show that the richest 20 percent of people consume 85 percent of the resources, while the poorest 25 percent use less than 1.5 percent. To put this into perspective, consider a scenario where China consumed resources at the same rate as North America. Estimating conservatively, China would use the entire worldwide production of nearly all resources each year! Another interesting perspective is to consider how long the total static resources would last if all the people in the world used resources at the same rate as North Americans—not very long, not even a generation.

Energy is the single most important resource. Per capita consumption is a measure of quality of life (and life expectancy) and industrial status worldwide. Approximately 25 percent of the global population use 75 percent of the total energy produced annually. North America (5 percent of the total population) uses twice as much energy as all developing countries combined, and Western Europe (9 percent of the total population) uses about the same amount. On a per capita basis, people in developed countries use between 10 and 30 times as much energy as people in developing countries. Canada (sixth-largest consumer worldwide) uses 3.7 percent of the world's total generated electricity for a population of only 33 million. India (seventh-largest consumer worldwide), with a population of more than 1 billion, uses less.

How long global resources will last depends on future population growth and consumption trends. Even at a conservative across-the-board increase of 1 percent, most of our proven mineral and energy reserves will last for fewer than 200 years. If the rate of consumption increases by 2 percent, static levels of resources will last for fewer than 100 years. So, whether or not we use resources in a sustainable way will be a complicated issue in the future, and one of the greatest problems facing future generations. The question remains: can we keep adding 100 million people to the surface of Earth each year and still pretend that resource consumption can be tailored to sustainability? Figure 20.A shows the relationship between some types of waste and the need for new resources.

*Mike Powell is a consulting geoscientist.

contrast, **non-renewable resources** continue to be formed in Earth, but the processes that create them are so slow that significant deposits may take millions of years to accumulate. For our purposes, Earth contains fixed quantities of these substances.

When the present supplies have been mined or pumped from the ground, there will be no more. Examples are fuels (e.g., coal, oil, natural gas) and many important metals (e.g., iron, copper, uranium, gold). Some of these non-renewable resources, such as aluminum, can be used over and over again; others, such as coal, cannot be recycled. Some resources can be placed in either category, depending on how they are used. Groundwater is one such example. Where it is pumped from the ground at a rate that can be replenished, groundwater can be classified as a renewable resource. However, in places where groundwater is withdrawn faster than it is replenished, the water table drops steadily. In this case, the groundwater is being "mined" just like other non-renewable resources (see Chapter 16).

Resources include **reserves**, the already identified deposits from which minerals and fuel materials can be extracted profitably and known deposits that are not yet economically or technologically recoverable. Resources can also include deposits that have not yet been discovered but are inferred to exist by some evidence.

METALLIC MINERAL DEPOSITS AND GEOLOGIC PROCESSES

An important point to be made about Earth's resources concerns the natural abundance of elements sought after; even the common metals, such as aluminum and iron, compose less than 10 percent of average continental crust. When we examine the distribution of mines and the primary mineral resources they extract, it becomes obvious that the various metals and other resources we rely on are not uniformly distributed across the globe—they are naturally concentrated only in particular areas. This uneven distribution is inherent in the Earth system. Not only does the composition of crust vary in different regions but the effects of tectonic processes, weathering, sedimentation rates, the movement of fluids, and various other factors are also expected to be subdued in some areas and enhanced in others. These circumstances, combined with the economics of extracting the resources, limit the localities on Earth where the mining of particular materials is practical.

Most of us have heard the term **ore**, which is generally used to denote those useful metallic minerals (and a few nonmetallic minerals, such as fluorite and sulphur) of sufficient concentrations to be mined at a profit. A rock body can be considered an ore one day and not the next because of economic factors. These can include fluctuations in the price of the material sought after, the price of fuel required for the running of machinery, and the efficiency of mining equipment. Note that the term *ore* is not applied to all materials of economic interest. Most nonmetallic minerals used for such purposes as building stone, aggregate, abrasives, ceramics, and fertilizers are not usually called ores but are generally classified as **industrial minerals**.

In this section, a few of the most important types of metallic mineral deposits are discussed. The primary types of deposits discussed in this section and their contained metals are summarized in Table 20.1 and depicted in the context of plate tectonic environments in Figure 20.3. Canadian metallic mineral deposits of present and historical significance are shown in Figure 20.4.

Magmatic Deposits

Many of the world's most valuable metallic mineral resources are directly associated with magma that ultimately forms igneous rocks. Certain metals are naturally enriched in certain magmas, but most only reach economically viable concentrations on further enrichment during the cooling process. In both cases, it is the characteristics of the magma itself that are responsible for the formation of mineral deposits.

Gravitational Settling The igneous processes that generate some metal deposits are fairly straightforward. For example, some economically important minerals are concentrated by simple gravitational settling within a magma chamber. In essence, crystals of heavy minerals that form during early stages of crystallization settle at the bottom of a magmatic body, such as a batholith or sill, concentrating layers of minerals (Figure 20.5). Such deposits, commonly called *cumulate* deposits, are important sources for chrome (in the mineral chromite), iron (in the mineral magnetite), and platinum. They typically form from mafic igneous magmas enriched in these elements. Examples of mafic intrusions that host such deposits are the Bird River Sill of Manitoba, the Muskox Intrusion of Northwest Territories, the Stillwater Complex of Montana, and the Bushveld Complex of South Africa.

Immiscibility Some metal deposits, such as the nickel deposits of Sudbury, Ontario, and Voisey's Bay, Newfoundland and Labrador, are probably produced by the separation of liquid components of magma in a manner similar to the separation of oil

TABLE 20.1 Occurrence of Metallic Minerals

Metal	Principal Ores	Geologic Occurrences
Aluminum	Bauxite	Residual product of weathering
Chromium	Chromite	Magmatic segregation
Copper	Chalcopyrite Bornite Chalcocite	Hydrothermal deposits; contact metamorphism; enrichment by weathering processes
Gold	Native gold	Hydrothermal deposits; placers
Iron	Hematite Magnetite Limonite	Banded sedimentary formations; magmatic segregation; residual product of weathering
Lead	Galena	Hydrothermal deposits
Magnesium	Magnesite Dolomite	Hydrothermal deposits
Manganese	Pyrolusite	Residual product of weathering
Mercury	Cinnabar	Hydrothermal deposits
Molybdenum	Molybdenite	Hydrothermal deposits
Nickel	Pentlandite	Magmatic segregation
Platinum	Native platinum	Magmatic segregation; placers
Silver	Native silver Argentite	Hydrothermal deposits; enrichment by weathering processes
Tin	Cassiterite	Hydrothermal deposits; placers
Titanium	Ilmenite Rutile	Magmatic segregation; placers
Tungsten	Wolframite Scheelite	Pegmatites; contact metamorphic deposits; placers
Uranium	Uraninite (pitchblende)	Pegmatites; sedimentary deposits
Zinc	Sphalerite	Hydrothermal deposits

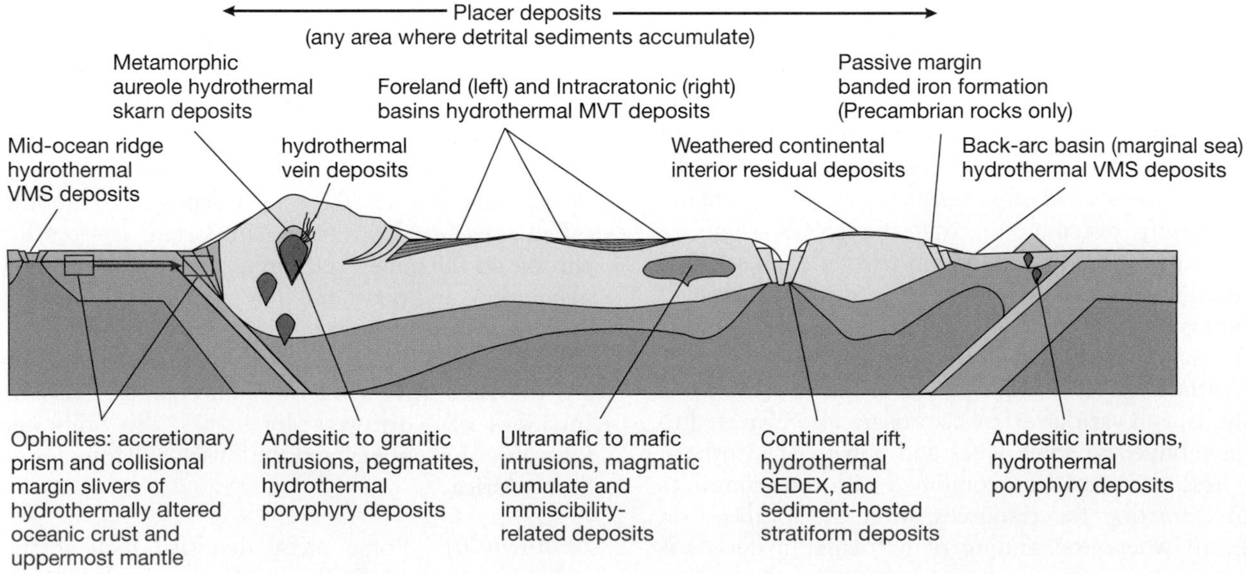

◆ **Figure 20.3** Distribution of common mineral deposit types and their contained metals with respect to plate tectonic environments (explained later). Abbreviations used for types of hydrothermal deposits: VMS = volcanogenic massive sulphide, SEDEX = sedimentary exhalative, MVT = Mississippi Valley type.

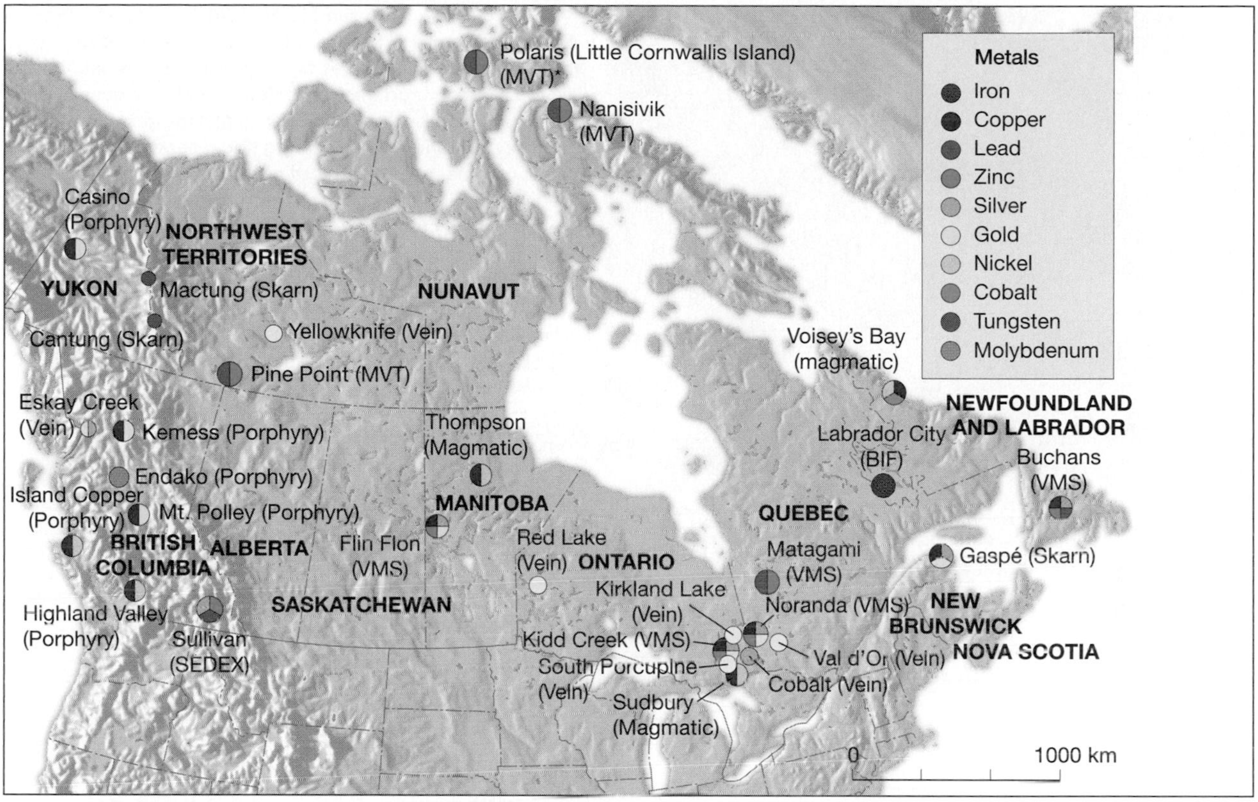

◆ **Figure 20.4** Locations of important metallic resources and important mining centres in Canada.
*Recently closed.

and water in salad dressing left to stand on a kitchen counter. Such non-mixing of liquid phases is called *immiscibility*.

Mantle-sourced magmas of mafic to ultramafic composition are naturally enriched in elements, such as nickel and copper, relative to felsic magmas. Because these elements are readily incorporated into silicate minerals, such as olivine and pyroxene, substituting for atoms of iron and magnesium, they are usually too dispersed within mafic intrusive rocks to be mined at a profit. In some cases, however, these elements can be scavenged from the melt by small droplets of immiscible iron sulphide liquid that eventually sink to the base of the intrusion and accumulate to form an orebody. The resulting deposit (Figure 20.6A) is dominated by the iron sulphide mineral *pyrrhotite*, with intergrowths of the nickel-bearing sulphide mineral *pentlandite* [$(Ni,Fe)_9S_8$], as well as chalcopyrite [$(Cu,Fe)S_2$] and some precious metals, such as platinum.

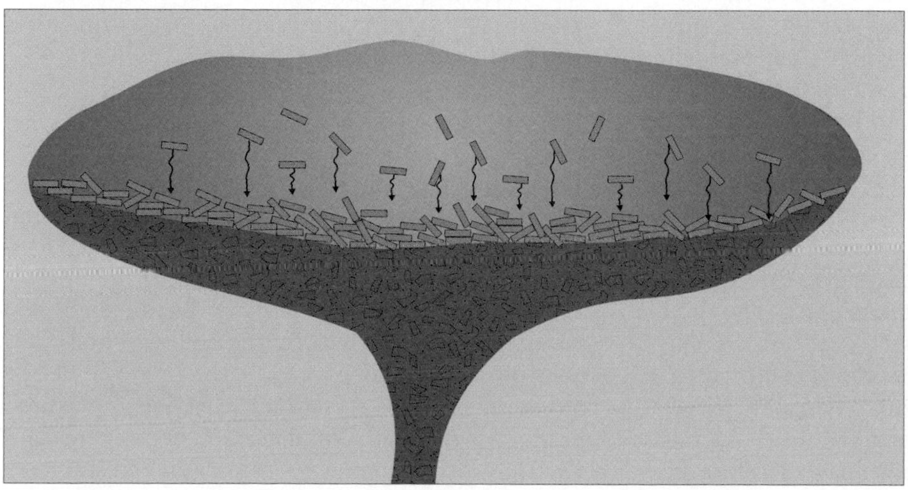

◆ **Figure 20.5** High-density minerals, such as chromite and magnetite, crystallize during the early stages of magma crystallization. The crystals can sink to the bottom of the magma chamber, forming concentrated layers of these minerals.

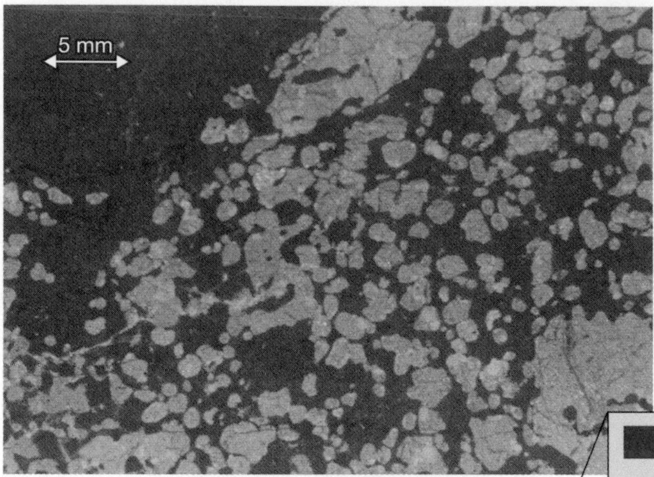

A

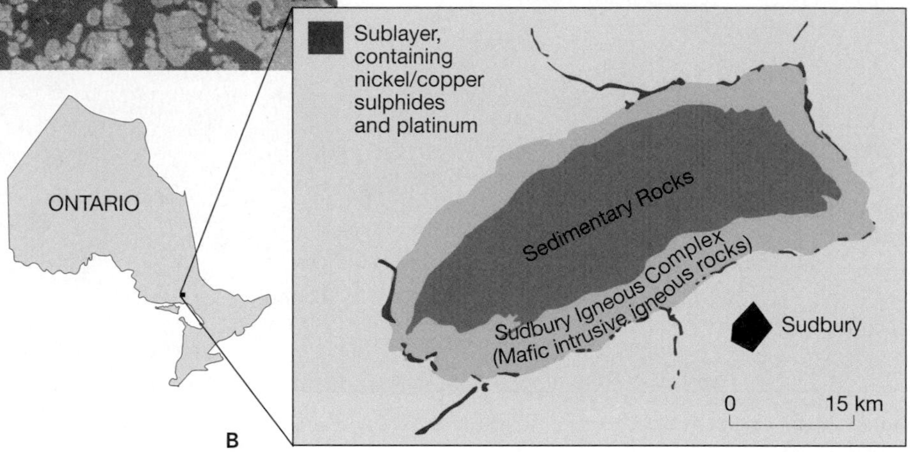

B

◆ **Figure 20.6** **A.** A sample of nickel-bearing rock from Sudbury. The nickel occurs in the rounded bodies of bronze-coloured sulphides that crystallized from immiscible fluid. Dark-coloured mafic silicate minerals surround the metal sulphide bodies. Scale bar: 5 millimetres. **B.** In Sudbury, Ontario, nickel-bearing liquid separated from mafic magma, eventually settling to form a sublayer beneath a silicate-dominated, mafic intrusive body and becoming injected into fractures that emanated from the impact structure. The magmatic materials are believed to have escaped from the mantle because of a meteorite impact during the Proterozoic. The Sudbury Basin impact structure has since been deformed into an oval shape. (Photo courtesy of R. W. Hodder)

Although the nickel deposits of Sudbury and Voisey's Bay share similar origins from mantle-derived magma, the mechanisms believed to have triggered igneous activity in each case differ markedly. In Sudbury, the generation and emplacement of mafic magma is linked to the impact of a large meteorite that occurred about 1.9 billion years ago. The impact is believed to have produced fractures that penetrated into the mantle and acted as passageways for magma that contained the required sulphide droplets. The Sudbury orebody occurs at the base of a mafic igneous intrusion and is exposed at the surface as an oval ring-shaped structure (Figure 20.6B). In contrast, the Voisey's Bay orebody (1.3 billion years old) occurs at the base of a mafic igneous intrusion that appears to have been fed by mantle-penetrating fractures generated by an ascending mantle plume.

Pegmatites As an igneous body cools, the most abundant components of the magma that are able to crystallize are removed from the magma. The melt remaining during the very last stages of cooling becomes enriched in volatile components (e.g., water) and rare elements that are not readily incorporated into common igneous minerals. Minerals that crystallize from such a melt may therefore be very unusual in their chemical composition, containing some of the least abundant elements found in Earth's crust. Because the melt is very fluid, it is readily injected into cracks surrounding the cooling igneous body and allows the growth of unusually large crystals (see Box 3.3).

The resulting rocks, called **pegmatites**, typically occur in dykes and small veins within and around plutons (Figures 20.7 and 20.9) and are generally felsic in composition. Elements of economic value that are mined from pegmatites include uranium, thorium, beryllium, lithium, tantalum, and niobium. Industrial minerals mined from pegmatites include feldspar and muscovite.

Hydrothermal Deposits

Among the best-known and most important ore deposits are those generated from **hydrothermal (hot-water) solutions**, which may be produced during the late-stage cooling of magma, by the heating of groundwater or seawater, or by metamorphic processes. A critical factor in the ability of hot water to dissolve metals appears to be the presence of dissolved salts, such as sodium chloride, potassium chloride, and calcium sulphate. Whereas metals are effectively insoluble in pure water, salt-rich *brines* are

◆ **Figure 20.7** Pegmatite dyke cuts through gneiss on mainland Nunavut, south of Pelly Bay. Note large orthoclase crystals at centre bottom. Knife is 20 centimetres long. Pegmatites, formed during the late stages of crystallization in felsic magmas, can be rich sources of rare earth elements, such as beryllium and lithium.
(Photo by S. R. Hicock)

capable of dissolving at least small amounts of metallic elements (e.g., gold, silver, copper, lead, zinc, and mercury). High temperatures further increase the ability of brines to hold metals in solution. Because of their mobility, brines can migrate great distances before they eventually cool, lose their ability to keep metals in solution, and deposit the metals (usually in the form of sulphide minerals).

Companies mining hydrothermal ores must take great care in managing the waste materials (tailings) as the sulphide minerals contained in the ores readily react with water and produce substances that can be harmful to living things, if released into the environment (Box 20.2).

Hydrothermal Deposits Associated with Igneous Activity

Studies of modern hydrothermal systems have shown that igneous activity serves as a powerful heat engine that drives the production and circulation of mineral-rich fluids. As is evident in the hot springs of Yellowstone National Park, Wyoming, the ordinary groundwater can invade a zone of recent igneous activity and be heated to increase its capacity to dissolve minerals. In such an environment, migrating hot waters can remove metallic ions from intrusive igneous rocks and carry them upward, where they may be deposited as an orebody.

The role of igneous activity in producing ore deposits is also evident in the depths of the oceans. Since the mid-1970s, active hot springs and metal-rich sulphide deposits have been detected at several sites, including study areas along the East Pacific Rise and Juan de Fuca Ridge. The deposits are forming where heated seawater, rich in dissolved metals and sulphur, gushes from the seafloor as particle-filled clouds called *black smokers*. As shown in Figure 20.8, seawater infiltrates the hot oceanic crust along the flanks of the ridge. As the water moves through the newly formed material, it is heated and chemically interacts with the basalt, extracting and transporting sulphur, iron, copper, and other metals. Near the ridge axis, the hot, metal-rich fluid rises along faults. On reaching the seafloor, the spewing liquid mixes with the cold seawater and the sulphides precipitate to form massive sulphide deposits.

Vein Deposits Hydrothermal fluids generated by cooling magmas can rise to the surface through fractures, faults, and other features that result from the brittle deformation of the overlying rocks. Fluids passing through the fractures eventually cool, allowing minerals to precipitate (Figure 20.9). The precipitated minerals, generally dominated by quartz or calcite, but sometimes including metallic minerals, fill the fractures to produce veins (Figure 20.10) that can range in width from a few centimetres to a few metres. The fluids can also react with the rocks immediately adjacent to the fractures to produce new minerals. Mineral deposits that occur in veins, or at least are intimately associated with vein systems, are called **vein** (or *lode*) **deposits**. These are important sources of valuable ore minerals, such as native gold and silver, as well as copper and zinc sulphides. The hydrothermal environment in which some vein deposits were formed probably resembled that of Yellowstone. However, networks of metal-rich veins are also associated with fracture systems of other hydrothermal environments.

Mineral deposits of particular importance in Canada are vein gold deposits, which occur throughout the Archean greenstone belts of the Superior and Slave provinces of the Canadian Shield. More than 4000 tonnes of gold have been extracted from the many individual deposits in these areas. Among the most famous producers are the mines of the Porcupine, Red Lake, Kirkland Lake, Malartic-Val d'Or, and Yellowknife districts. Vein silver deposits are also important in some parts of Canada, particularly British Columbia. Historically significant to Canada are the lode silver deposits of Cobalt, Ontario, which spawned a remarkable mining boom in the early 1900s.

BOX 20.2

People and the Environment
Acid Mine Drainage (AMD) in Canada

Gordon Southam*

Base and precious metal mining in Canada (and globally) is focused on the recovery of metals (e.g., nickel, copper, or gold) from geologic deposits. In an existing mine, rock is blasted and brought to the surface or removed from an open pit, crushed in rod and ball mills, and then undergoes a series of flotation steps leading toward metal purification. After the minerals of economic interest—for example, millerite (NiS) or chalcopyrite $(Cu,Fe)S_2$—are recovered, the gangue materials (waste rock) are disposed of in massive holding (waste) ponds. These wastes include silicates, base metals containing sulphide minerals that were not recovered during flotation, and, typically, pyrite. Mining can also result in the generation of waste rock possessing pyrite. On removal, this waste rock is usually stored above ground in large free-draining piles.

The disposal of sulphide-bearing mine wastes (rock and tailings) as open deposits results in the formation of unique acid-generating ecosystems (Figure 20.B). Acid formation is biocatalyzed by acidophilic ("acid-loving") bacteria, (e.g., *Acidithiobacillus ferrooxidans*), which oxidize sulphide minerals, generating dilute solutions of sulphuric acid that contain soluble, toxic heavy metals. This acid mine drainage (AMD) seeps into and damages surrounding aquatic and terrestrial environments.

Although abiotic chemical oxidation of pyrite can occur (see Reaction 1), it is slow and on its own will not lead to the formation of AMD. Under normal, natural water conditions (pH near 7), the iron that's released from Reaction 1 will oxidize (Reaction 2) to Fe^{3+}, which will then break down water molecules, producing three protons (acid; Reaction 3). The net acid generating capacity of Reactions 1–3 (4 protons) additionally cannot produce AMD.

$$FeS_2 + 3\tfrac{1}{2}O_2 + H_2O \rightarrow Fe^{2+} + 2SO_4^{2-} + 2H^+ \quad (1)$$

$$Fe^{2+} + \tfrac{1}{4}O_2 + H^+ \rightarrow Fe^{3+} + \tfrac{1}{2}H_2O \quad (2)$$

$$Fe^{3+} + 3H_2O \rightarrow Fe(OH)_3 \text{ (iron hydroxide; the rust colour)} + 3H^+ \quad (3)$$

Under acidic conditions (i.e., pH < 4) Fe^{2+} is generally stable and soluble (Reaction 2 slows down). Therefore, the net acid generation should slow as well, but it doesn't. This is where the acidophilic lithotrophic (*lithos* = rock, *trophic* = food or eating) bacteria become important. The key to the formation of acid mine drainage is the bacteria's ability to oxidize iron under acidic conditions. (They can also catalyze Reaction 2.) In the presence of water and acid conditions, Fe^{3+} will attack pyrite (Reaction 4), producing lots of Fe^{2+} (more food for the bacteria) and lots of acid.

$$FeS_2 + 14Fe^{3+} + 8H_2O \rightarrow 15Fe^{2+} + 2SO_4^{2-} + 16H^+ \quad (4)$$

The chemical oxidation of pyrite (Reaction 4) occurs extremely quickly under acid conditions—typically faster than the bacteria can oxidize the Fe^{2+}. Therefore, the rate-limiting step in the formation of AMD is the oxidation of Fe^{2+} by the bacteria (biocatalyzed Reaction 2). It should be noted that Fe^{3+} can also chemically attack other base metals (e.g., Cu_2S) that will, in turn, release soluble toxic heavy metals (e.g., Cu^{2+}).

The Canadian mineral industry generates 1 million tonnes of waste rock and 950,000 tonnes of tailings per day, exceeding 710 million tonnes of total waste per year. Canada has an estimated 351 million tonnes of waste rock, 510 million tonnes of sulphide tailings, and more than 55 million tonnes of other mining sources that have the potential to cause AMD.[1]

Once in a tailings pile, bacteria get their O_2 and CO_2 from the air (they're autotrophic, similar to plants) and their energy from the sulphide minerals (e.g., pyrite), ultimately forming AMD. Acid mine drainage is the mining industry's greatest environmental problem and its greatest liability.[2] The water pollution resulting from the bio-oxidation of mine wastes may need to be managed for centuries after mine closure; the cleanup at existing acid-generating mines in Canada will cost billions of dollars.

◆ **Figure 20.B** Metal mine tailings at the Lamoine mine near Chibougamau, Quebec, which appeared benign at first glance, were revealed to be highly oxidized immediately below the surface (inset). This zone of oxidation extended approximately 40 centimetres down into the tailings.
(Photos by Gordon Southam)

1. Government of Canada, *The State of Canada's Environment* (Ottawa: Ministry of Supply and Services, 1991), pp. 11–19.
2. P. C. Singer and W. Stumm, "Acidic Mine Drainage: The Rate-Determining Step," *Science* 167 (1970): 1121–1123.

*Gordon Southam is a professor and Canada research chair in the Department of Earth Sciences at the University of Western Ontario.

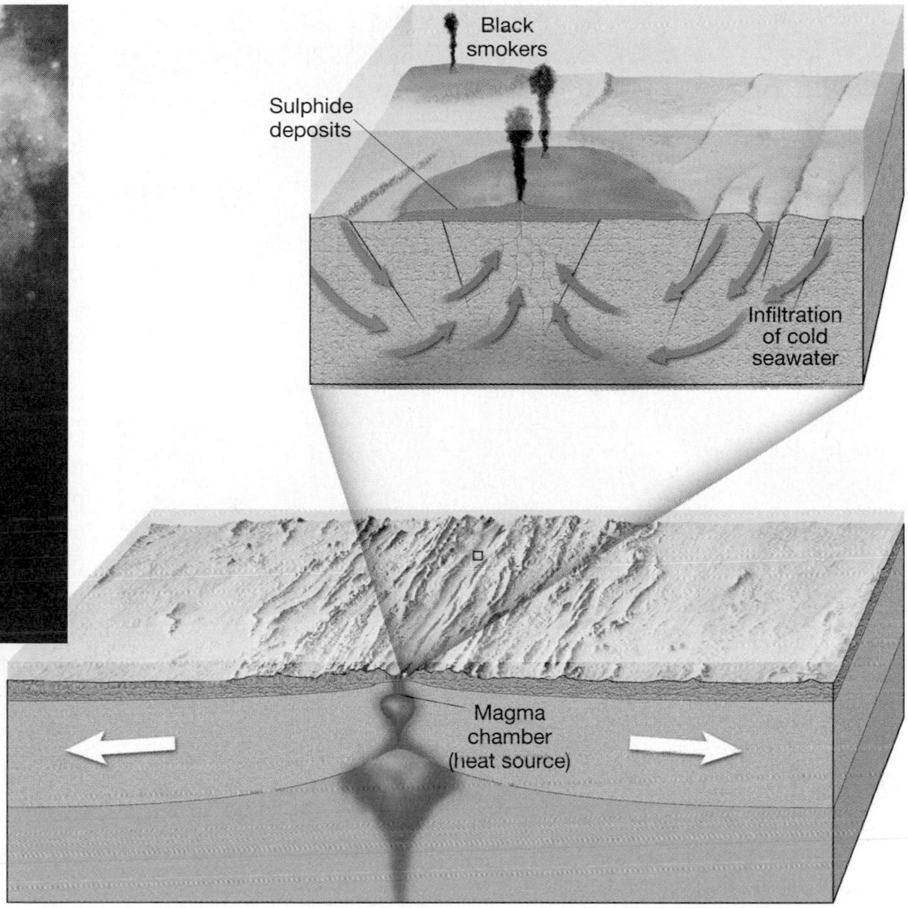

◆ **Figure 20.8** Massive sulphide deposits can result from the circulation of seawater through the oceanic crust along active spreading centres. As seawater infiltrates the hot mafic crust, it leaches out sulphur, iron, copper, and other metals. The hot, enriched fluid returns to the seafloor near the ridge axis along faults and fractures. Some metal sulphides may be precipitated in these channels as the rising fluid begins to cool. When the hot liquid emerges from the seafloor and mixes with cold seawater, the sulphides precipitate to form massive deposits. Photo shows a close-up view of a black smoker spewing hot, mineral-rich seawater along the East Pacific Rise. (Photo © Robert Ballard, Woods Hole Oceanographic Institution)

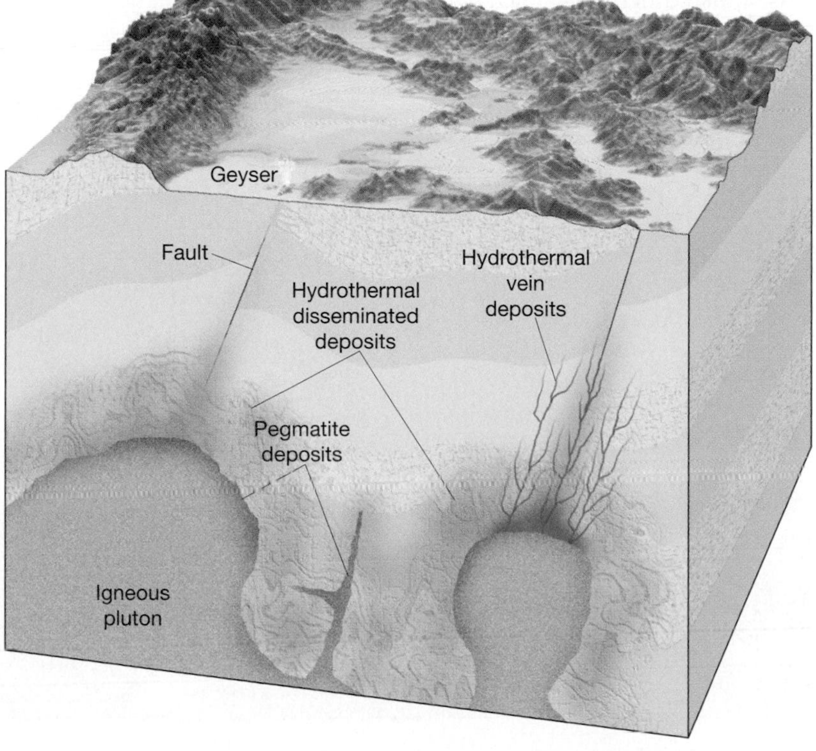

◆ **Figure 20.9** Illustration of the relationship between a parent igneous body and the associated pegmatite and hydrothermal deposits.

◆ **Figure 20.10** Gneiss laced with quartz veins at Diablo Lake Overlook, North Cascades National Park, Washington. (Photo by James E. Patterson)

Disseminated Deposits Another important type of accumulation generated by magma-sourced hydrothermal fluids is called a **disseminated deposit**. Rather than being concentrated in well-defined veins, these ores are distributed in small masses throughout a large rock body. Most of the world's copper and molybdenum, and smaller quantities of other metals, such as gold and silver, are mined from disseminated deposits called *porphyry deposits*. These are so named because of their close association with porphyritic igneous rocks.

When silicate minerals, such as feldspars, crystallize around the edges of an intrusion during the early cooling of a pluton, the water content of the remaining melt increases to the extent that steam pressure shatters the already crystallized rock and, in some cases, the surrounding host rock.

The fractures thus produced are then filled with the hydrothermal fluid condensed from the steam and, in turn, are filled with metal sulphides precipitated from the fluid. This cycle can be repeated several times until the plutonic rock and some of the host rock is riddled with minute sulphide-filled fractures rarely exceeding a few millimetres in thickness. The result is a swarm or *stockwork* of thin (at times microscopic) metal sulphide veinlets scattered throughout porphyritic rocks of the cooled pluton, as well as in the surrounding host rocks (Figures 20.9 and 20.11). Porphyry deposits are generally associated with magma chambers that feed stratovolcanoes (composite cones) and are found accordingly in convergent margin settings.

Porphyry deposits have a very low ore grade. For example, porphyry copper deposits contain only 0.4 percent to 0.8 percent copper. However, the ore occurs in such large volumes and so close to

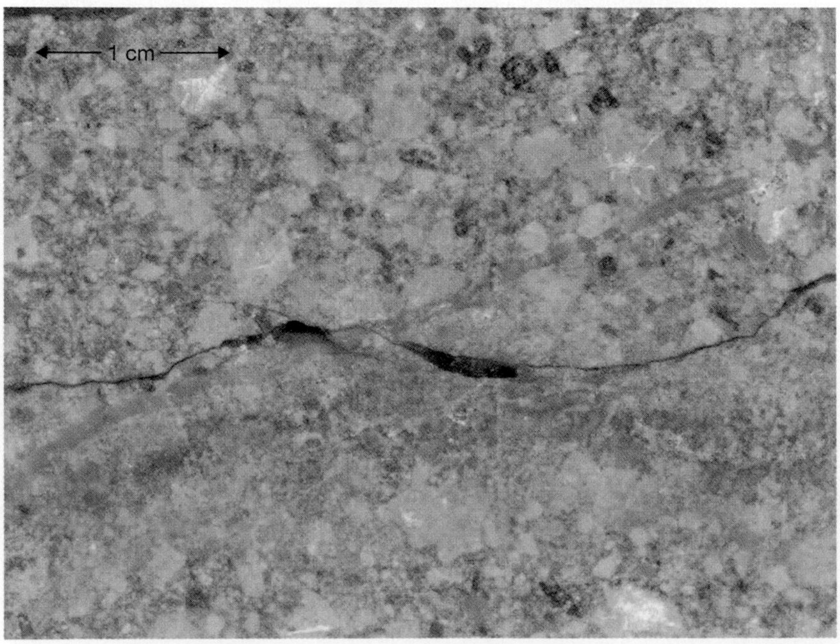

◆ **Figure 20.11** Sample of a porphyry molybdenum deposit from British Columbia. Mineralization has occurred in the dark groundmass of this andesitic igneous rock. (Photo by C. Tsujita)

the surface that they are well worth mining. Large deposits of porphyry copper and molybdenum figure prominently in the mining industry of British Columbia.

Volcanogenic Massive Sulphide Deposits Some hydrothermal deposits form pod-shaped bodies of *massive sulphides* that are almost entirely composed of interlocking sulphide minerals and are intimately associated with volcanic (usually mafic) rock. These are called *volcanogenic massive sulphide* (VMS) *deposits*.

The hydrothermal systems associated with the black smokers we see in today's mid-ocean ridge settings are considered to be similar to those that produced VMS deposits in ancient rocks. As discussed earlier, the convective fluid flow that develops in centres of seafloor spreading leaches metals from oceanic crust, transports them through fractures, and deposits them as sulphide minerals in mounds that surround volcanic vents (Figure 20.8). VMS deposits appear to represent these large sulphide bodies (Figure 20.12).

VMS deposits are extremely important worldwide as they commonly contain economically valuable concentrations of copper, zinc, lead, silver, and gold. VMS deposits occur in all provinces and territories of Canada, except Alberta and Prince Edward Island, and most of them are hosted in Precambrian greenstone belts. Among the better-known VMS deposits in Canada are those of Kidd Creek, Ontario; Matagami and Noranda, Quebec; Flin Flon, Manitoba; and Buchans, Newfoundland and Labrador.

Sediment-Associated Hydrothermal Deposits

Some mineral deposits are intimately associated with sedimentary rocks and appear to have involved mineral precipitation from hydrothermal fluids at relatively low temperatures. For most of these deposits, the source of the metals is believed to be brine that was flushed from sediments buried deep within the sedimentary pile of a sedimentary basin, although deep-seated igneous activity (e.g., in rift basins) may be responsible for contributing heat to the hydrothermal system.

Sedimentary Exhalative (SEDEX) Deposits Some mineral deposits feature thin layers of massive sulphide that are interbedded with detrital or chemical sedimentary rocks (Figure 20.13A). These deposits are called *sedimentary exhalative* (SEDEX) *deposits*, as they are not only intimately related to sedimentary strata (most commonly mudrocks, chert, and fine-grained carbonates) but are also thought to be associated with the mineral precipitation from fluids that were "exhaled" from hydrothermal vents onto the seafloor. SEDEX deposits typically form sheet to lens-like bodies that are vertically stacked within the sediment fill of failed continental rifts (Figure 20.13B) and fault-bounded basins of rifted continental margins. Hot brines, derived from deep areas within rift basins, are believed to have leached metallic ions from sediments and to have carried them in solution along faults, ultimately emerging at

◆ **Figure 20.12** Massive sulphide deposit at Noranda, Quebec. This deposit contains mainly pyrite (light-coloured material), but thin, dark-coloured bands of galena are also visible. The rusty-coloured patches are iron oxides produced by the weathering of the pyrite.
(Photo courtesy of R. W. Hodder)

A

◆ **Figure 20.13** **A.** A sample of a SEDEX mineral deposit from the Sullivan mine near Kimberley, British Columbia, showing distinct, highly reflective beds of lead/zinc sulphides and dark-coloured beds of mudstone. **B.** Sedimentary-exhalative (SEDEX) deposits are interpreted to result from the precipitation of sulphide minerals from hydrothermal vents in fault-bounded depressions on the seafloor. SEDEX deposits typically occur in the sediment fill of rift basins.
(Photo by C. Tsujita)

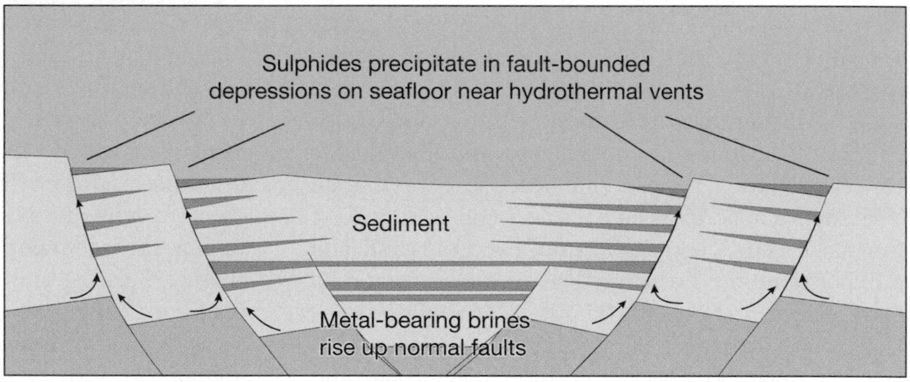

B

the seafloor from hydrothermal vents. It is further speculated that the brines formed dense pools in fault-bounded depressions on the seafloor, ultimately precipitating metals in the form of sulphide minerals. The role of normal faults in the migration of hydrothermal fluids is indicated by the preservation of subvertical vein networks, apparently representing feeder vents, associated with some SEDEX deposits. In addition, concentrations of lead, zinc, and silver decrease with distance away from these vein networks. The floor of the present-day Red Sea bears pools of hydrothermal brines that are believed to be similar to those that formed ancient SEDEX deposits.

Canada's most famous SEDEX deposit of this type is an impressive lead-zinc deposit that was the foundation of the Sullivan mine in southwest British Columbia (Figure 20.13A). This mine closed in 2001 after 92 years of production.

Sediment-Hosted Stratiform Deposits Highly enigmatic in terms of their origin are strata-like bodies of metallic minerals called *sediment-hosted stratiform deposits*, which occur within sedimentary units of some ancient rift basins. A key characteristic of these deposits, most of which are rich in copper sulphides, is that the ore minerals occur as pore-filling material of the host rock, rather than as pure bands (Figure 20.14A). Also significant is the tendency of such deposits to occur in the basal portions of marine shales that abruptly overlie nearshore and non-marine sandstones.

Some geologists believe that sediment-hosted stratiform deposits are produced because of mineral precipitation from submarine brine pools, as envisaged for SEDEX deposits. However, more recent interpretations favour a mechanism by which oxygenated, copper-bearing brines travelling through a coarse-grained sedimentary unit are forced upward into an overlying unit of oxygen-poor, sulphide-rich mud, thereby promoting the precipitation of copper sulphide minerals among the tiny particles of clay and other detrital grains (Figure 20.14B). The most commonly cited deposit of this type is the

A

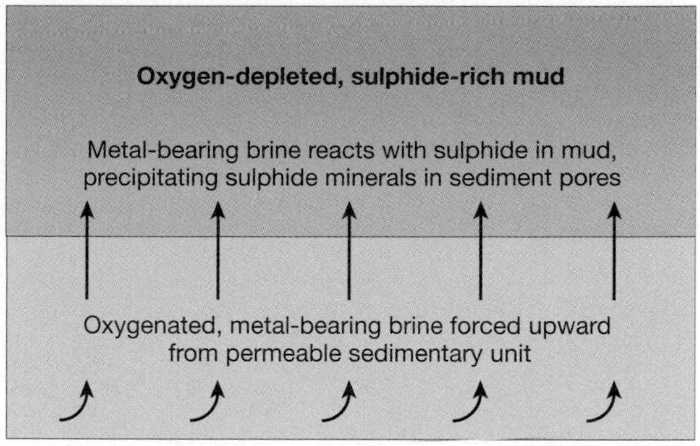

B

◆ **Figure 20.14** **A.** Sample of the Kupferschiefer shale from Germany. Note the greenish tinge in this sample imparted by copper oxide that was produced by the weathering of the contained copper sulphide minerals. **B.** Sediment-hosted stratiform copper deposits are formed by the interaction of oxygenated brine with overlying sulphide-rich sediment.
(Photo by C. Tsujita)

Kupferschiefer of Germany (Figure 20.14A), but similar deposits are known in the Coppermine District in the Northwest Territories.

Mississippi Valley-Type Deposits *Mississippi Valley-type* (MVT) *deposits* are unusual hydrothermal deposits that, as their name implies, are well developed in southeast North America. Similar deposits have, however, also been found on nearly all other continents. It has been suggested that the compaction of shales deep within a sedimentary basin can release metal-bearing brines that migrate toward the edges of the basin, where they react with limestones (Figure 20.15A). More recently, it has been proposed that the mineralizing fluids are sourced from fractured Precambrian basement rocks. MVT deposits show evidence of significant calcite dissolution and replacement by other minerals, particularly sphalerite and galena (Figure 20.15B). Cavities developed in limestones hosting MVT deposits can be sufficiently large to permit the growth of huge crystals of sulphide minerals. In Canada, MVT deposits are actively mined for lead and zinc in Nunavut and the Northwest Territories.

Sedimentary Deposits

Banded Iron Formations As already briefly mentioned in Chapter 6, a peculiar chemical sedimentary rock called **banded iron formation** was formed during the Archean and Proterozoic. The common *Superior-type banded iron formation* is Proterozoic in age and typically consists of alternating bands of iron oxides (magnetite or hematite) and chert (Figure 20.16). Because of the generally reducing conditions that prevailed through much of the Precambrian, a great deal of iron occurred in the soluble ferrous state and was dissolved in large quantities from weathered rocks and delivered to the sea. Large quantities of iron were probably also produced from hydrothermal vents.

It is believed that the oxygen liberated from photosynthesizing bacteria eventually accumulated in sufficient quantities in the oceans to oxidize some of the iron, resulting in the deposition of insoluble iron oxide minerals. It appears that such oxygenation occurred in pulses, such that the iron oxides were deposited in more or less distinct bands. During intervening periods when iron oxide precipitation was low, silica was deposited as a gel that eventually lithified to form chert.

Despite the presence of oxygen in the oceans when banded iron formations were formed, oxygen had not yet reached sufficient quantities to occur in a gaseous state in the atmosphere. Iron formations are not formed today because of our oxygen-rich atmosphere. In today's world, iron is immediately oxidized into the insoluble ferric state and therefore does not accumulate in a dissolved form to the degree it did during the Precambrian. In addition, much of the dissolved silica in today's oceans is taken up by organisms (e.g., radiolarians, diatoms, and sponges) to make their skeletons and therefore does not precipitate in large quantities to form chert.

In Canada and the northern United States, banded iron formations occur abundantly in the Lake Superior area of the Canadian Shield. They also reach ore grade in Newfoundland and Labrador. Banded iron formations presently compose the main sources of iron in North America.

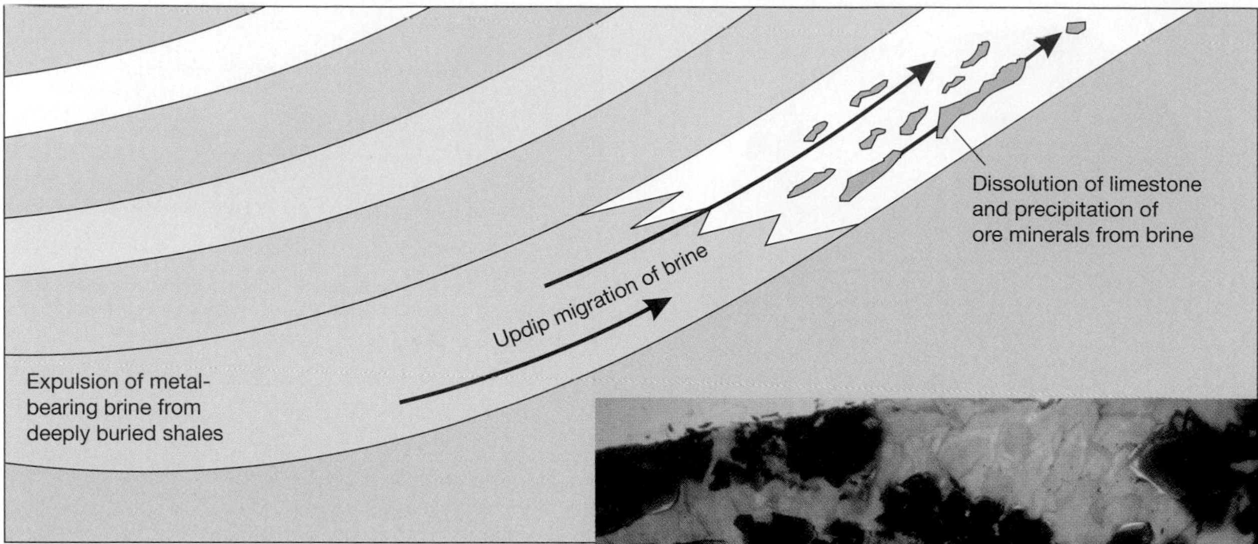

A

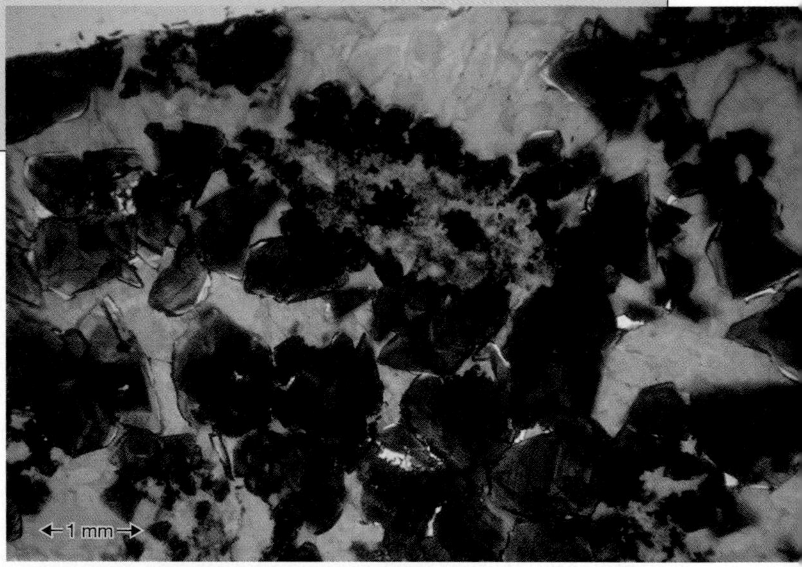

B

◆ **Figure 20.15** **A.** Mississippi Valley-type deposits have traditionally been interpreted to form by sulphide mineral precipitation from metal-bearing brines that migrate from deeply buried sediments of a sedimentary basin. **B.** Zinc ore from the Mississippi Valley-type Pine Point deposit in the Northwest Territories, as seen under a microscope. In this sample, cavities within a carbonate sedimentary rock have been filled with crystals of sphalerite (yellowish brown) and dolomite (white).
(Photo courtesy of R. W. Hodder)

◆ **Figure 20.16** Banded iron formation has historically been an important source of iron in the Lake Superior area of Ontario and the northern United States. This example is from a Proterozoic sequence in Northern Ontario. The dark bands are composed of magnetite and hematite and the red bands are iron-stained chert (called *jasper*).
(Photo by Grant Young)

Placer Deposits The formation of **placer** deposits relates to the sorting action of running water. As you will recall from Chapter 6, large, heavy sediment grains tend to be deposited in more agitated water than do smaller, lighter ones. In the same sense, mineral particles of high density can be concentrated because of the sorting out and washing away of mineral particles of lower density. The concentrations of heavy minerals that form in this manner are called placers and are associated with areas of high water agitation, such as streams and beaches.

Placer deposits of gold were the foundation of the famous gold rushes in California and Yukon, and they continue to perpetuate images of old, haggard-looking prospectors panning river sediment, with their mules standing close by. It is in placer deposits that the familiar *nuggets* of gold are found, their commonly rounded appearance attesting to the rigours of sediment transport. It has traditionally been assumed that nuggets are sourced from hydrothermal veins as large sedimentary particles and become increasingly smaller as they are transported away from their host rocks by water action. More recently, however, some geologists have pondered the possibility that gold nuggets might actually grow due to bacterially mediated gold precipitation from surface waters.

Panning is a simple, small-scale method of concentrating gold that takes advantage of essentially the same process responsible for concentrating heavy minerals in natural deposits. Water and a bit of sediment are scooped into a pan and swirled to suspend the light rock particles. When the pan is tipped, the suspended sediment is dumped out with the water, and the heavy minerals are left behind in the pan as a residue. Most other methods of extracting heavy minerals, including sluicing and hydraulic monitoring, are based on the same principle (Figure 20.17).

Additional minerals extracted from placer deposits include magnetite, rutile, and ilmenite (titanium oxides), platinum, and diamonds. Ancient placer deposits, such as conglomerate in the Witwatersrand of South Africa, are also mined for precious minerals.

Deposits Associated with Metamorphism

The role of metamorphism in producing mineral deposits is frequently tied to igneous processes. For example, many of the most important metamorphic ore deposits are produced by contact metamorphism. The host rock is re-crystallized and chemically altered by heat, pressure, and hydrothermal solutions emanating from an intruding igneous body. The extent to which the host rock is altered depends on the nature of the intruding igneous mass as well as the nature of the host rock.

Some resistant materials, such as quartz sandstone, may show little alteration, whereas others,

A B

◆ **Figure 20.17** **A.** It was placer deposits that led to the 1898 Klondike gold rush in Yukon. Here, a group of placer miners (in 1901 on Last Chance Creek) operate a sluice box that separates sand and gravel from flecks of gold by using running water. **B.** Gold mining in 2002 of a placer deposit along the same creek shown in **A.** Still using water, the hydraulic monitor thaws frozen gravel in the creek bank.
(Photo **A** courtesy of Yukon Archives, Adams and Larkin fonds, #9163; photo **B** by Peter Rotheisler)

including limestone (readily metamorphosed to marble), may exhibit the effects of metamorphism for several kilometres from the igneous pluton. As hot, iron-rich fluids move through limestone, chemical reactions take place. These reactions release carbon dioxide, which greatly facilitates the mobilization of metallic ions. These extensive aureoles of metal-rich deposits are called *skarns* and commonly surround igneous plutons that have invaded limestone strata (Figure 20.18).

The most common metallic minerals associated with contact metamorphism are sphalerite (zinc), galena (lead), chalcopyrite (copper), magnetite (iron), and bornite (copper). The hydrothermal ore deposits may be disseminated throughout the altered zone or as concentrated masses either next to the intrusive body or along the margins of the metamorphic zone.

As you might expect by their similar geologic setting, skarns can be closely associated with porphyry deposits. Two of Canada's best-known skarn deposits are the Copper Mountain deposit of British Columbia and Mines Gaspé copper deposits of Quebec. A number of tungsten and gold skarns occur in British Columbia and Yukon.

Deposits Associated with Weathering

Weathering creates many important mineral deposits by concentrating minor amounts of metals that are scattered through unweathered rock into economically valuable reserves. Such a transformation is often termed **secondary enrichment** and takes place in one of two ways. In one situation, chemical weathering coupled with downward-percolating water removes undesirable materials from decomposing rock, leaving the desirable elements enriched in the upper zones of the soil. The second situation is basically the reverse of the first. That is, the desirable elements that are found in low concentrations near the surface are removed and carried to lower zones, where they are redeposited and become more concentrated.

Bauxite The metal most often cited in discussions on the relationships between weathering and ore deposit formation is aluminum. Although aluminum is one of the most common metallic elements on Earth and a primary component of many silicates, it is generally so tightly bonded with other elements that the energy required to extract the aluminum outstrips the value of the metal. Fortunately, aluminum also occurs in oxide form. Aluminum oxides are generally produced by the weathering of aluminum-bearing silicates in warm, humid tropical regions of the world. In such areas, soils tend to have very deep profiles and are severely leached in their upper horizons. Infiltration of groundwater removes soluble ions, such as calcium, sodium, and potassium, from the upper soil profile, leaving a residue of less soluble iron and aluminum oxides and hydroxides. The resulting *residual deposit*, called *bauxite* (Figures 20.19 and 5.C), is an aluminum-rich laterite (see also Chapter 5). Similarly, the olivine of nickel-bearing ultramafic rocks may weather to form silicate minerals containing up to 5 percent nickel.

Great concern surrounds the mining of bauxite and other residual deposits because they tend to occur in the humid, environmentally sensitive areas of the tropics. Not only does the clearcutting of forest, which necessarily precedes mining, destroy rainforest ecosystems, but the thin, moisture-retaining layer of organic matter that naturally covers the soil is also disturbed. When allowed to dry in the hot sun, the exposed soil becomes hard as brick, loses its moisture-retaining abilities, and can no longer support vegetation for farming or forest growth. The long-term consequences of bauxite mining are

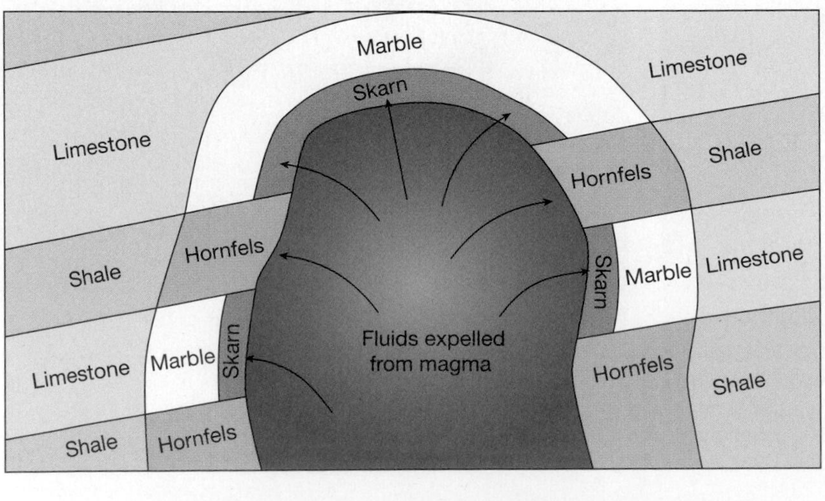

◆ **Figure 20.18** Skarns are associated with contact metamorphism. In this example, the intrusion of magma into sedimentary rock layers has metamorphosed limestone to marble and shale to hornfels. Infiltration of magmatic fluids into the zones of marble promotes the reaction of the fluids with minerals of the various intruded rocks, the dissolution of calcium carbonate, and the precipitation of metallic minerals in permeable zones. Hornfels lacks significant porosity and permeability and therefore does not host skarn deposits.

◆ **Figure 20.19** Bauxite is the ore of aluminum and forms as a result of weathering processes under tropical conditions. Its colour varies from red or brown to nearly white. (Photo by E. J. Tarbuck)

obvious and continue to be points of concern for the many developing countries of the tropics.

Other Deposits Many copper and silver deposits result when weathering processes concentrate metals that are deposited through a low-grade primary ore. Usually, such enrichment occurs in deposits containing pyrite (FeS_2), the most common and widespread sulphide mineral. Pyrite is important because when it chemically weathers, sulphuric acid forms, which enables percolating waters to dissolve the ore minerals. Once dissolved, the metals gradually migrate downward through the primary orebody until they are precipitated. Deposition takes place because of changes that occur in the chemistry of the solution when it reaches the saturated zone (the zone beneath the surface where all pore spaces are filled with water; see Chapter 16). In this manner, the small percentage of dispersed metal can be removed from a large volume of rock and redeposited as a higher-grade ore in a smaller volume of rock. This enrichment process is responsible for the economic success of some metallic mineral deposits, particularly those containing copper.

NONMETALLIC RESOURCES

Earth materials that are not used as fuels, or processed for metals, are referred to as **nonmetallic mineral resources**. Realize the use of the word *mineral* is very broad in the economic context and is quite different from the geologist's strict definition of mineral found in Chapter 2. Nonmetallic mineral resources are extracted and processed either for the nonmetallic elements they contain or for their desirable physical or chemical properties.

People often do not realize the importance of nonmetallic minerals because they see only the products that result from their use, not the minerals themselves. That is, many nonmetallics are used up in the process of creating other products. Examples include the fluorite and limestone that are part of the steelmaking process, the abrasives required to make a piece of machinery, and fertilizers needed to grow a food crop. Accordingly, the quantities of nonmetallics used in construction and other applications are huge.

Nonmetallic mineral resources are divided into two broad groups here: aggregate and stone, and industrial minerals. Because some substances have many uses, they can technically belong to either category. Limestone, for example, is used as crushed rock and building stone in its raw form, but its main mineral constituent, calcite, is important in its own right as the key ingredient for the manufacture of cement and as a component in a score of other products, including cosmetics and pharmaceuticals.

Aggregate and Stone

Because most building materials are widely distributed and present in almost unlimited quantities, they have little intrinsic value. Their economic worth comes only after the materials are removed from the ground and processed. Because their per-tonne value compared with metals and industrial minerals is low, mining and quarrying operations are usually undertaken to satisfy local needs. Except for special types of cut stone used for building and monuments, transportation costs greatly limit the distance most building materials can be moved. The aggregate and stone industry is very important in the lives of Canadians, as reflected in the thousands of sand and gravel pits and stone quarries that exist in our country.

Natural aggregate consists of crushed stone, sand, and gravel. From the standpoint of quantity and value, aggregate is a very important building material. It is produced in all provinces and territories in Canada and is used in nearly all road and building construction (Figure 20.20A). Thanks to the large volume of sand and gravel in Canada deposited as glacial outwash during and at the end of the last Ice Age, every province and territory has an ample supply of aggregates for construction. Aggregate is used as-is in various construction applications and is also important in the manufacture of concrete and road asphalt. To appreciate the importance of aggregate in our daily lives, we only need to consider that just one kilometre of a four-lane highway, such

◆ **Figure 20.20** Examples of nonmetallic resources. **A.** Aggregate pits are located in all provinces and territories of Canada. This pit is near Aldergrove, British Columbia. **B.** Cut stone set into the floor of a building in Iqaluit, capital city of Nunavut.
(Photos by S. R. Hicock)

as Highway 401 in Ontario, requires more than 40 tonnes of aggregate.

Attesting to the diversity of Canada's geologic makeup, many varieties of solid stone are quarried throughout the country, including rocks of igneous (e.g., granite), metamorphic (e.g., marble, gneiss, and slate), and sedimentary (e.g., sandstone, limestone, and dolostone) origin. Cut stone is largely used for aesthetic applications in construction, such as decorative facings, walkways (Figure 20.20B), and countertops.

Industrial Minerals

Many nonmetallic resources are classified as industrial minerals. In some instances these materials are important because they contain specific chemical elements or compounds used in fertilizers or industrial chemicals. Some minerals possess useful physical properties. For example, garnet is both relatively hard and fairly common, making it a handy substance for the manufacture of abrasive products, such as sandpaper. Other industrial minerals are used in the manufacture of products used in construction as fillers, coaters, and extenders in plastics, paints, and paper products and as heat-resistant materials, in addition to a host of other applications. Common industrial minerals and their uses are listed in Table 20.2. Some industrial minerals of particular importance in Canada, and their geologic occurrences, are indicated in Figure 20.21 and discussed next.

Diamonds Diamonds are familiar as gemstones, but diamond is also extremely valuable as an abrasive by virtue of being the hardest natural substance known. Only about one quarter of all diamonds mined are used as gemstones.

The vast majority of diamonds are found in a unique ultramafic igneous rock called **kimberlite**. Magmas that produce kimberlite are believed to be generated by a small amount of partial melting in the asthenosphere at depths greater than 150 kilometres below Earth's surface. The diamonds themselves do not crystallize from kimberlitic magma. Rather, they are produced in the deep roots of the solid, lithospheric mantle beneath areas of old, stable continental crust at depths of more than 120 kilometres (Figure 20.22). It is only here that high temperatures (between 900°C and 1200°C) and pressures (more than 40 kilobar) remain stable for geologically long enough periods of time to allow the formation of diamonds.

Kimberlitic magma rapidly rises to the surface, acting as a sort of geologic elevator that picks up chunks of lithospheric mantle material and crustal rock during its ascent. If kimberlitic magma passes through the deep areas of lithospheric mantle where diamonds reside, diamonds can be naturally sampled

TABLE 20.2 **Occurrences and Uses of Nonmetallic Minerals**

Mineral	Uses	Geologic Occurrences
Apatite	Phosphorus fertilizers	Sedimentary deposits
Asbestos (chrysotile)	Incombustible fibres	Metamorphic alteration
Barite	Drilling mud; cement; paint; paper	Hydrothermal deposits
Calcite	Aggregate; steelmaking; soil conditioning; chemicals; cement; building stone	Sedimentary deposits
Clay minerals (kaolinite)	Ceramics; china	Residual product of weathering
Corundum	Gemstones; abrasives	Metamorphic deposits
Diamond	Gemstones; abrasives	Kimberlite pipes; placers
Fluorite	Steelmaking; aluminum refining; glass; chemicals	Hydrothermal deposits
Garnet	Abrasives; gemstones	Metamorphic deposits
Graphite	Pencil lead; lubricant; refractories	Metamorphic deposits
Gypsum	Plaster of Paris; drywall	Evaporite deposits
Halite	Table salt; chemicals; ice control	Evaporite deposits; salt domes
Muscovite	Insulator in electrical applications	Pegmatites
Quartz	Primary ingredient in glass	Igneous intrusions; sedimentary deposits
Sulphur	Chemicals; fertilizer manufacture	Sedimentary deposits; hydrothermal deposits
Sylvite	Potassium fertilizers	Evaporite deposits
Talc	Powder used in paints, cosmetics, etc.	Metamorphic deposits

◆ **Figure 20.21** Significant industrial mineral deposits in Canada.
(Reproduced with the permission of the Minister of Public Works and Government Services Canada, 2008, and courtesy of Natural Resources Canada)

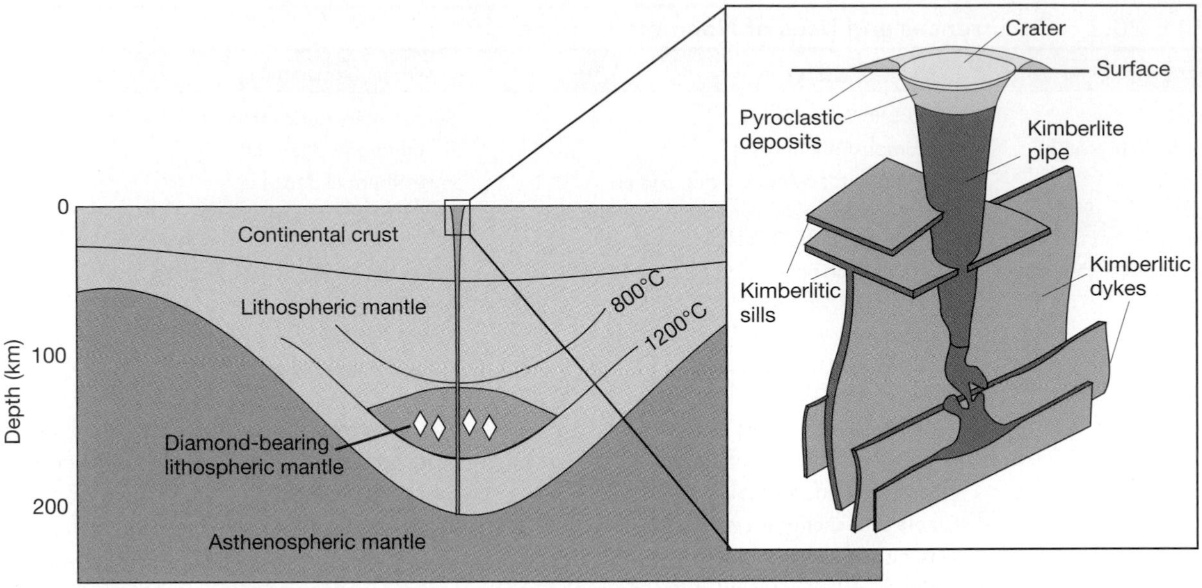

◆ **Figure 20.22** Kimberlite pipes are carrot-shaped igneous bodies that are formed when mantle-sourced magma is violently extruded to Earth's surface. At the Ekati mine in the Northwest Territories (see chapter-opening photo), diamonds are mined from this rare type of igneous body.

from this material as xenocrysts (foreign crystals) and as crystal components of xenoliths (foreign rock fragments) and can be carried upward by the magma.

During the last stage of magma ascent, the rapid escape of carbon dioxide from the magma and the interaction of the hot kimberlitic magma with groundwater, an explosive volcanic eruption and a pipe-shaped vent are produced (Figure 20.22). The fractures and cavities within the vent are ultimately filled with kimberlite and shattered fragments of the surrounding rock. Associated with the main, carrot-shaped kimberlite pipe are ultramafic dykes and sills at depth and pyroclastic volcanic deposits at the surface.

Major producers of diamonds include South Africa (the hub of the early diamond industry), Australia, Namibia, and Russia. Canada has recently entered the diamond market through discoveries in the Northwest Territories. The Ekati mine, the first Canadian diamond mine, began production in 1998; the nearby Diavik mine under Lac de Gras reached full production in 2004. More recent mining projects include Snap Lake, Jericho, and Victor (Figure 20.21). It is projected that Canada may well supply 15 percent to 20 percent of the world's diamonds within the next decade.

Clays Clays, the fine-grained, platy minerals formed by the weathering and hydration of aluminosilicate minerals, are important industrial minerals. Certain clay minerals can form economically important deposits at the place of origin in masses of weathered material. However, much larger quantities of clay minerals occur in sedimentary deposits of seas and lakes, having been transported long distances by wind or water from their site of formation. Major Canadian producers of clay include Saskatchewan, Ontario, and British Columbia.

The diverse physical and chemical properties of clays make them extremely useful in many applications. For example, sediment dominated by the clay mineral kaolinite (but also generally containing minor amounts of other minerals) is extensively mined for the production of bricks, sewer pipes, and pottery. As an industrial mineral, kaolinite is also used in the production of wall and floor tiles, porcelain, insulation products, and ion-exchange products; as a filler (and natural whitener) for paint, adhesives, sealants, pharmaceuticals, and cosmetics; and as a coater in paper. It might surprise you that the glossy finish on the pages of magazines is actually a thin layer of kaolinite.

Clay minerals, such as *montmorillonite* (a weathering product of volcanic ash), readily absorb moisture and are therefore useful as absorbents in products, such as clumping cat litter. Montmorillonite is also an important ingredient contributing to the lubricating properties of drilling mud in the petroleum industry. In addition, because of their high capacity for ion exchange, clays are used in oil refining and in waste treatment.

Carbonate Minerals As discussed in Chapter 6, calcium carbonate in the form of calcite (and to a lesser extent, aragonite) is an important component of many sedimentary rocks. Vast quantities of limestone, most representing accumulations of calcareous skeletal material secreted by organisms, are quarried worldwide. Although some limestone is quarried raw in the form of building stone, a great deal of it is extracted for its calcium carbonate content.

Large volumes of limestone are quarried and processed for the manufacture of cement. The principal raw materials used in the making of common cements are calcite (from limestone), with smaller amounts of silica (from sand), clay (from shale), and iron oxide. These provide the necessary ingredients—calcium, silica, alumina, and iron—that chemically interact to produce the desired qualities of cement. The raw materials are crushed into a powder and fed into the top of a tower containing a series of heating chambers. As the powdered substance drops through the series of chambers, it is heated to nearly 900°C, and then is fed through a kiln that heats the mixture further, to about 1500°C–1600°C, and converts the raw material into a substance called clinker. The key substance formed during this heating process is calcium silicate. The clinker is cooled, mixed with a small amount of gypsum (a regulator of cement setting time), and milled into a fine powder that is then ready for use as cement. When water is added to the cement powder, crystals of calcium silicate hydrate form an interlocking network that gives concrete its strength for construction purposes.

Calcium carbonate is also used in a great many other applications. It is used as a filler in asphalt, fertilizers, insecticides, paints, rubber, and plastics; as a fluxing agent; as a mild abrasive in some toothpastes; as an acid neutralizer in a wide variety of cosmetic, medicinal, and paper products; and as a dietary supplement. In all likelihood, the very page you are reading in this text has a thin coat of calcium carbonate that has been added to the paper to provide a smooth, uniform surface for printing. People also use dolomite as a gentle abrasive and a dietary supplement.

Evaporite Salts Evaporite deposits are important sources of many industrial minerals, particularly chloride and sulphate salts, and some carbonate minerals. During many times in Earth's past, widespread evaporite deposits were formed in shallow basins that were periodically flooded by seawater but dried up because of intense evaporation under arid conditions.

Normal seawater contains about 3.5 percent (by weight) dissolved matter that can be precipitated in mineral form when the water is evaporated. As observed in a glass of salty water left on the counter for several days, evaporation reduces the total volume of liquid, increasing the concentration of the dissolved matter to the point that salt can be precipitated. Partly because of differences in the relative concentrations of dissolved ions in seawater, minerals of different composition are precipitated sequentially as evaporation removes more and more water from the brine. In order of appearance, the principal minerals that form during progressive evaporation are calcite, gypsum, halite, and finally sylvite. Few evaporite deposits contain sylvite, probably because of the dilution of brines by episodic influxes of normal seawater from the adjacent ocean. Note that thick evaporite deposits represent several cycles of seawater influx, evaporation, and mineral precipitation rather than a single drying-up event in a basin.

Gypsum is primarily used for the manufacture of plaster products used in construction and other applications. Gypsum ($CaSO_4 \bullet 2H_2O$) is heated to about 180°C to drive off about three quarters of its water (producing $CaSO_4 \bullet {}^1/_2H_2O$), milled to a fine powder, and sold as plaster. When water is added to the powder, it rehydrates the material to produce tiny, interlocking crystals of gypsum that give plaster products their strength for interior construction applications. A plaster product familiar to most people is drywall (also called wallboard or gyprock), which consists of a sheet of plaster sandwiched between two sheets of paper. Physicians also commonly use plaster to make casts for patients who require their limbs to be stabilized as their fractured bones heal. Gypsum is also widely used as a filler or additive in many products, including cosmetics, pharmaceuticals, fertilizers, paints, and plastics. Significant deposits of gypsum occur in British Columbia, Manitoba, Ontario, Nova Scotia, and Newfoundland and Labrador.

Halite, or salt, as it is more commonly known, is another important resource mined from evaporite deposits. The consumption of salt in Canada is very high, averaging about 360 kilograms of salt per person per year. This high figure reflects not only our liberal use of salt in the de-icing of roads but also the extensive use of halite in the manufacture of important substances used in the chemical industry, such as chlorine, caustic soda, baking soda, and washing soda. Halite, of course, is also used to season and preserve foods. Salt is a common evaporite and thick deposits are exploited by using conventional underground mining and brining, which involves dissolving salt underground and re-precipitating it at the surface. In Canada, extensive Paleozoic salt deposits occur in the sedimentary basins of the Prairie provinces, southwest Ontario, Quebec, and the Maritime provinces. Globally, salt is extracted directly from seawater in arid, coastal areas by using the natural evaporating abilities of the Sun's heat.

The mining of potash, an evaporite rock containing the potassium-bearing minerals sylvite (KCl) and carnallite ($KClMgCl_2 \cdot 6H_2O$), is a huge industry in Canada. Most of Canada's potash is mined from immense deposits in Saskatchewan, where it occurs in horizontal layers up to 3 metres thick (Figure 2.30). Potash deposits also occur in the Maritime provinces and are actively mined in New Brunswick. About 95 percent of all potash mined in Canada is exported to other countries, where it is primarily used in the production of fertilizers. It is also used in de-icing products, in the manufacture of soaps and detergents, and as an additive in glass and ceramic products.

Phosphate Phosphate, contained in the mineral apatite, is mined primarily for the production of phosphoric acid for fertilizers, additives for livestock feed, industrial chemicals, and some home products. Although generally scarce in nature, phosphate can reach high concentrations in sedimentary rocks. The manner in which these deposits form is somewhat enigmatic, but appears to require a combination of high primary productivity, low oxygen, and low input rates of detrital sediment in a marine environment. Such conditions appear to be fairly common in oceanic environments influenced by upwelling cold, nutrient-rich seawater. North America's major phosphate mines are in the states of Florida, North Carolina, Idaho, and Utah, although sedimentary phosphate deposits are known to exist in British Columbia. Canada's only active phosphate mine is located in Kapuskasing, Ontario, where the weathering of an igneous intrusion has left a rich residue of apatite crystals.

Sulphur Because of its many uses, sulphur is an important nonmetallic resource. Sulphur is a major component of sulphuric acid and fertilizers; it is also used in matches and gunpowder. Sources of sulphur include deposits of native sulphur associated with salt domes and volcanic areas and sulphide minerals, such as pyrite. Canada's main source of sulphur is natural gas; huge amounts are scrubbed from natural gas as a measure to reduce the content of corrosive sulphur-bearing compounds and to ensure a cleaner-burning product.

Other Industrial Mineral Deposits In addition to igneous and sedimentary deposits of industrial minerals, deposits of metamorphic origin also occur. Recall that, at convergent plate boundaries, the oceanic crust and sediments that have accumulated at the continental margins are carried to great depths. In these high-temperature, high-pressure environments, the mineralogy and texture of the subducted material are altered, producing deposits of nonmetallic minerals, such as talc (used widely in cosmetic products) and graphite (used in the manufacture of steel products, lubricants, and pencils). Chrysotile asbestos is another product of metamorphism, resulting from the flushing of fluids through ultramafic rock. Zeolite minerals are used to extract ions in water softeners. Concentrations of industrial minerals can also be produced in association with skarns during contact metamorphism. These minerals include garnet and corundum, used in abrasive products.

NON-RENEWABLE ENERGY RESOURCES

Petroleum

Petroleum is the group of hydrocarbons that includes oil and gas, and is presently a vital resource for our daily activities. It is mainly used as fuel, but it also composes the main ingredients in plastics that find their way into synthetic fabrics, product packaging, casings, and a wide range of other products.

How Petroleum Is Formed The origin of petroleum ultimately lies in organic matter contained in the tissues of living things. The vast majority of petroleum is derived from the remains of simple, aquatic organisms (mostly planktonic algae) that constitute most of the plankton in the seas and other large bodies of water, although some land-derived organic matter may also contribute to petroleum generation. Organic matter has a rather low preservation potential in most aquatic environments, because scavenging organisms and aerobic microbes naturally recycle it. However, it often accumulates in the quiet-water environments of shallow seas and lakes, where low-oxygen conditions prevail. Accordingly, organic-rich sediments are typically fine-grained and are represented in ancient deposits by shales and fine-grained carbonate rocks. Because they are the principal sources of organic matter from which petroleum is generated, these organic-rich rocks are called *source rocks*.

Although organic matter stands a better chance of survival under low-oxygen conditions, it is by no means immune to microbial attack. Organic-rich sediment can initially yield significant quantities of *biogenic gas* (principally methane) because of the breakdown of organic matter by anaerobic microbes (Figure 20.23). This microbial attack also removes

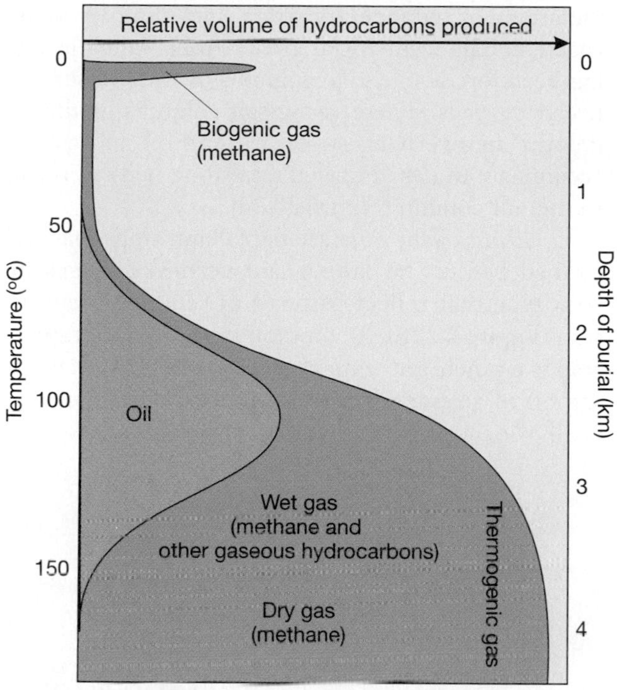

◆ **Figure 20.23** The temperatures and corresponding depths of burial at which oil and gas are generated. Note that biogenic gas is only produced at low temperatures, whereas thermogenic gas produced by the thermal cracking of organic molecules dominates at higher temperatures. Oil generation is restricted to a temperature window between approximately 50°C and 150°C. Note also the large amounts of natural gas produced at the expense of oil as hydrocarbons are cracked to progressively simpler molecular forms.

much of the oxygen, nitrogen, phosphorus, and sulphur from the organic matter, leaving a residue that is enriched in hydrocarbons. With progressive burial, the production of biogenic gas ceases, the organic-rich sediment undergoes lithification, and heat becomes the main agent in the breakdown of the organic matter.

As the hydrocarbon-rich organic matter of a source rock is subjected to higher and higher temperatures, it is transformed into a solid waxy substance called *kerogen*. At temperatures above about 50°C, carbon–carbon bonds within the kerogen break, producing the lighter, less complex hydrocarbon molecules. This process is called cracking. As the temperature rises, more carbon–carbon bonds are broken, both in the kerogen and in the hydrocarbon molecules that formed previously, generating oil (Figure 20.23). Oil generation peaks at a temperature of about 100°C, beyond which the kerogen is depleted of its hydrocarbon supply, and significant amounts of thermogenic natural gas are produced (Figure 20.23). The natural gas produced at temperatures just above that of peak oil generation is commonly called *wet gas* because, in addition to its primary constituent, methane, it contains gaseous components, such as ethane, propane, and butane, that can be separated by condensation. At temperatures above about 150°C, only *dry gas*, consisting almost entirely of methane, is generated.

It should be noted that the specific proportions of oil and gas generated in any given source rock depend not only on burial depth and duration of cooking but also on the composition of the organic matter from which the hydrocarbons are derived. Whereas organic matter from marine sources is *oil prone*, land-derived organic matter tends to be more *gas prone*. Because land-derived organic matter can be transported into aquatic environments, some source rocks can be expected to be more gas prone than others.

Petroleum Migration Unlike the organic matter from which they form, oil and gas are mobile. These fluids are gradually squeezed from the compacting fine-grained source rocks where they originate into adjacent permeable beds, such as sandstone, where openings between sediment grains are larger. Because this occurs underwater, the rock layers containing the oil and gas are saturated with water. Because oil and gas are less dense than water, they migrate upward through the water-filled pore spaces of the enclosing rocks. Unless something halts this upward migration, the fluids will eventually reach the surface, at which point the volatile components will evaporate.

Petroleum Traps Sometimes the upward migration of oil and gas is halted. A geologic environment that enables economically significant amounts of oil and gas to accumulate underground is called a **petroleum trap**. Several geologic structures can act as petroleum traps, but all have two basic conditions in common: a porous, permeable **reservoir rock** that will yield oil and natural gas in sufficient quantities to make drilling worthwhile; and a **cap rock**, such as shale, that is virtually impermeable to oil and gas. The cap rock halts the upwardly mobile oil and gas and keeps them from escaping to the surface. Petroleum traps can be produced in a number of ways, but they can be separated into two groups: structural traps and stratigraphic traps.

Structural traps are petroleum traps that form because of the structural deformation of the rock layer that contains the hydrocarbons. One of the simplest structural traps is an anticline, an up-arched succession of sedimentary strata (Figure 20.24A). As the strata are bent, the rising oil and gas collect at the apex (top) of the fold. Because of its lower density, the natural gas collects above the oil. In turn, the oil rests on the denser water that saturates the reservoir rock. One of the world's largest oil fields, El Nala in Saudi Arabia, is the result of anticlinal traps, as is the famous Teapot Dome in Wyoming.

Fault traps form when strata are displaced in such a manner as to bring a dipping reservoir rock into position opposite an impermeable bed, as shown in Figure 20.24B. In this case the upward migration of the oil and gas is halted where it encounters the fault.

In the Gulf coastal plain region of the United States, important accumulations of oil occur in association with *salt domes*. Such areas have thick accumulations of sedimentary strata, including layers of rock salt. Salt occurring at great depths is ductile and has been forced to rise in columns by the pressure of overlying beds. These rising salt columns gradually deform the overlying strata, causing oil and gas to accumulate in the upturned sandstone beds adjacent to the salt column (Figure 20.24C).

Stratigraphic traps are petroleum traps that are formed because of lateral and vertical changes in rock type that reflect patterns of sediment deposition (Figure 20.25). A common type of stratigraphic trap is a pinch-out trap, characterized by the tapering off of a reservoir unit into a body of imperme-

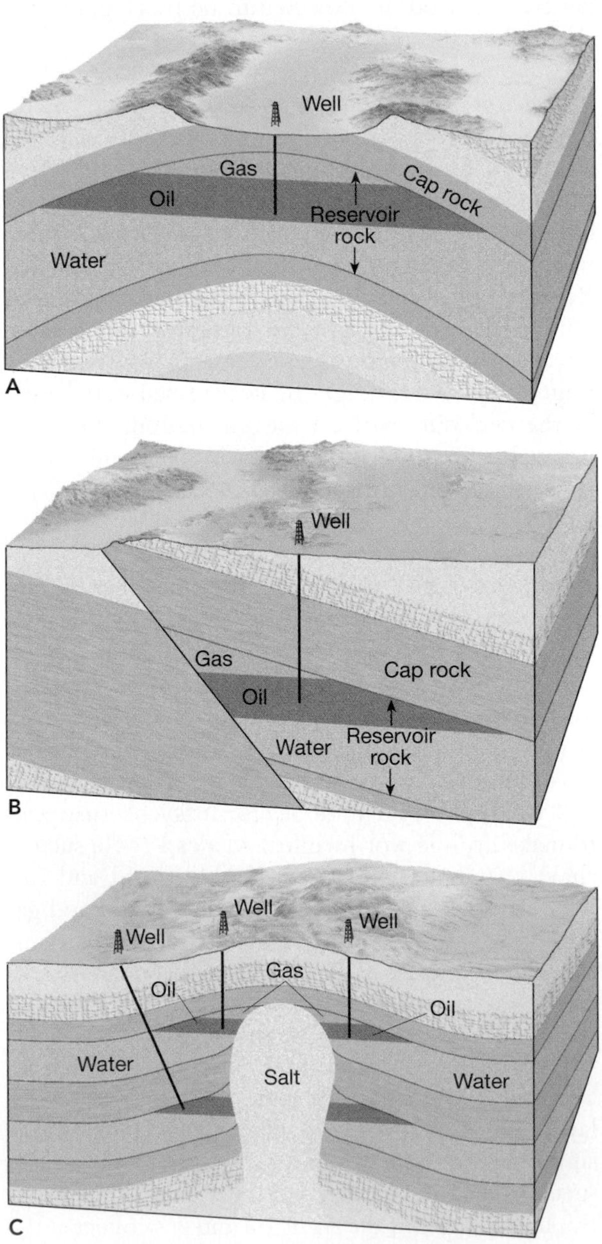

◆ **Figure 20.24** Common structural petroleum traps. **A.** Anticline. **B.** Fault trap. **C.** Salt dome.

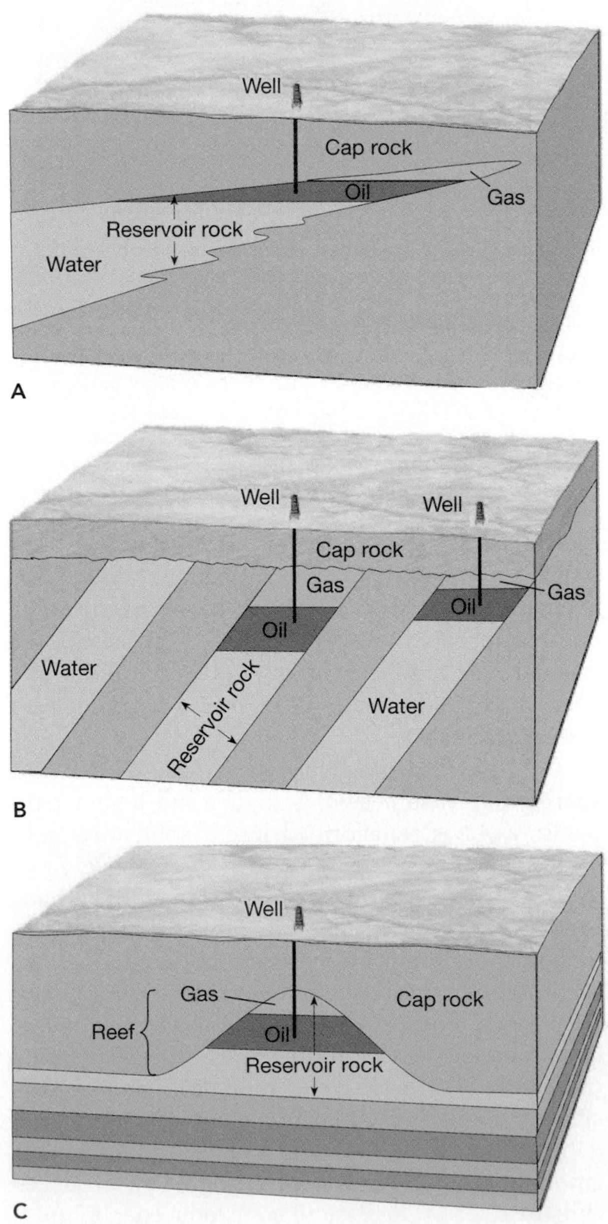

◆ **Figure 20.25** Common stratigraphic petroleum traps. **A.** Pinch-out trap. **B.** Unconformity trap. **C.** Limestone reef.

able rock. An unconformity trap results from the truncation of a reservoir unit by erosion, followed by the deposition of impermeable cap rock sediments. Reefs also form important stratigraphic traps, by virtue of representing lens-shaped bodies of porous, permeable limestone that are commonly encased by impermeable shales.

Coal

Whereas petroleum is generally sourced from organic matter provided by aquatic plankton, coal is largely derived from the fibrous and woody remains of land plants. Similar to petroleum, the organic remains that form coal can only accumulate in appreciable quantities in oxygen-poor environments. Accordingly, accumulations of coal-forming organic matter tend to be restricted to such areas as swamps. In a swamp, the decomposition of organic matter consumes so much oxygen from the water that much of the organic matter escapes decomposition. The organic matter that survives decomposition is buried to progressively greater depths, where it is gradually cooked and compressed to form coal. This was discussed in greater detail in Chapter 6.

Coal has been an important fuel for centuries. In the nineteenth and early twentieth centuries, cheap and plentiful coal powered the Industrial Revolution. Until the 1950s, coal was an important domestic fuel as well as a power source for industry. However, its direct use in the home has largely been replaced by oil, natural gas, and electricity. These fuels are preferred because they are more readily available (delivered via pipes, tanks, or wiring) and cleaner to use. Nevertheless, coal remains the major fuel used by many nations.

Although coal is plentiful, its recovery and use present a number of problems. Surface mining can turn the countryside into a scarred wasteland if careful (and costly) reclamation is not carried out to restore the land. Although underground mining does not scar the landscape to the same degree, it has been costly in terms of human life and health.

Underground mining long ago ceased to be a pick-and-shovel operation and is today a highly mechanized and computerized process (Figure 20.26). However, the hazards of collapsing roofs, gas explosions, and working with heavy equipment remain.

Air pollution is a major problem associated with the burning of coal. Much coal contains significant quantities of sulphur. Despite efforts to remove sulphur before it is burned, the sulphur is converted into noxious sulphur oxide gases. Through a series of complex chemical reactions in the atmosphere, the

◆ **Figure 20.26** Modern underground coal mining is highly mechanized. Strip mining (**inset**) of coal at Black Mesa, Arizona. Surface mining is common when coal seams are near the surface.
(**Main** photo by Melvin Grubb/ Grubb Photo Services, Inc.; **inset** photo by Richard W. Brooks/ Photo Researchers, Inc.)

sulphur oxides are converted to sulphuric acid, which then falls to Earth's surface as rain or snow. This acid precipitation can have adverse ecological effects over widespread areas (see Box 5.1).

As none of the problems just mentioned is likely to prevent the increased use of this important and abundant fuel, stronger efforts must be made to correct the problems associated with the mining and use of coal. Disposal of fly ash produced by coal burning also poses problems. However, as indicated in Figure 20.A, this material may well prove to be a future resource in itself. For example, at Wabamun, Alberta, fly ash produced from coal burning for power generation is used in making high-quality cement.

Fossil Fuels in Canada

Canada is fortunate to host large quantities of coal and petroleum—so much that most of it is exported. The overwhelming majority of Canada's petroleum is produced in the southern areas of the Prairie provinces and British Columbia that overlie strata of the Western Canada Sedimentary Basin (Figure 20.27). Through much of Paleozoic and Mesozoic time, warm, shallow seas, within which

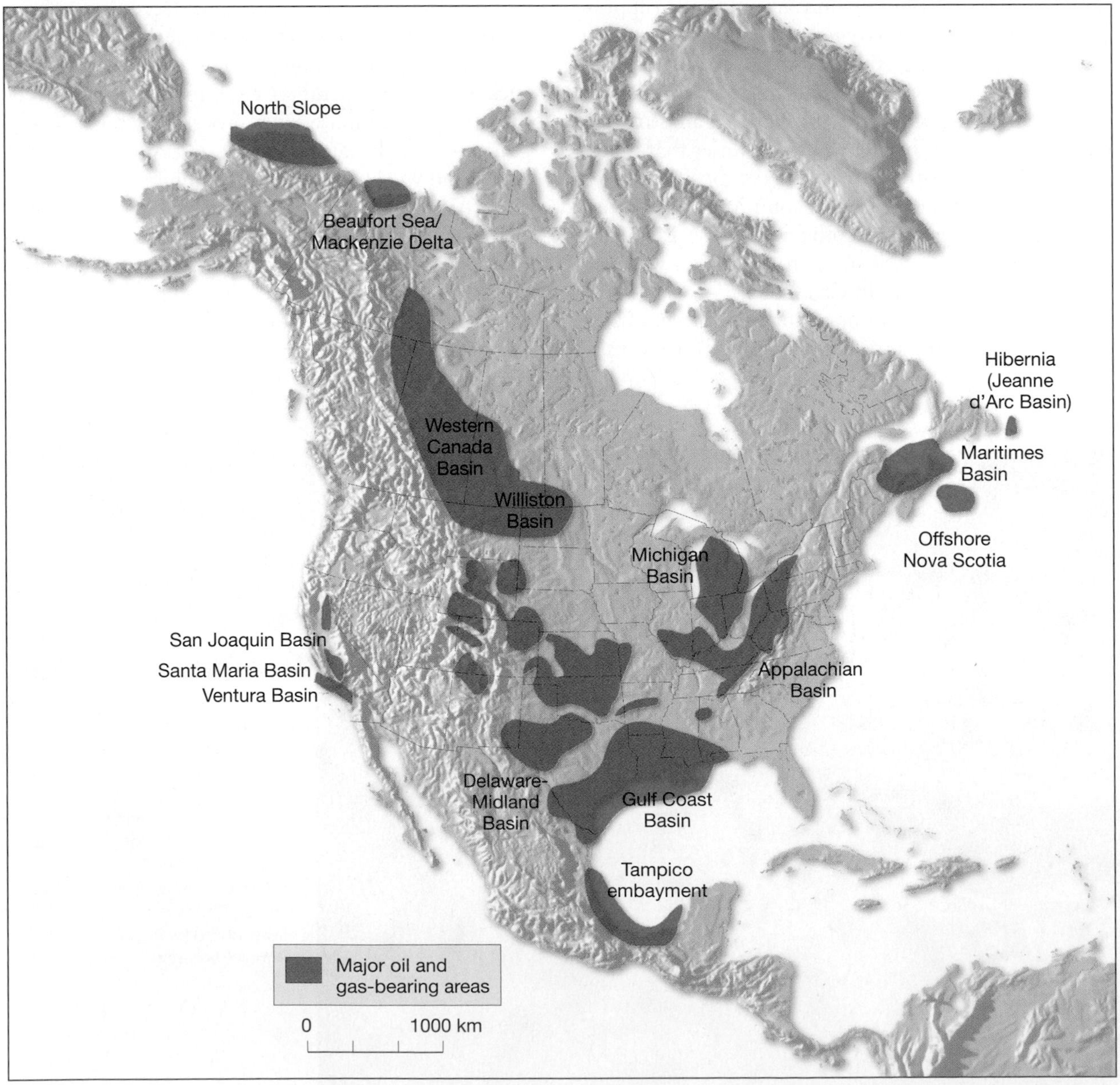

◆ **Figure 20.27** Distribution of important oil- and gas-bearing areas of North America. (Reproduced with the permission of the Minister of Public Works and Government Services Canada, 2008, and courtesy of Natural Resources Canada)

organic-rich sediments were deposited, occupied this area of Canada. Hydrocarbons were squeezed out of the organic-rich sediments and migrated to the permeable, low-pressure areas of the rock column, such as Paleozoic reefs and units of Mesozoic sandstone. Similar circumstances allowed oil to be produced and trapped in basins and the continental shelf areas of Newfoundland and Labrador (Hibernia project), Yukon, Northwest Territories, Nunavut, and, to a lesser degree, British Columbia and Nova Scotia. Modest quantities of oil and gas are also extracted from Paleozoic sedimentary rocks of the Michigan Basin in Ontario (Figure 20.27), where North America's oil industry started. As discussed in Box 20.3, Canadians have played major roles in the development of the North American oil industry.

BOX 20.3

Canadian Profile

The Hard Oilers of Enniskillen Township and Canada's Petroleum Industry

Claudia Cochrane*

In the early 1850s, the Industrial Revolution was well under way in both Europe and the New World. As in ancient times, asphalt was needed for ship construction and for paving streets and sidewalks, and fuel was required for illumination. Although the Victorians had been using whale oil for their lamps, the great whales had been hunted almost to extinction. The world was desperate for a cheap source of petroleum. It was in the swampy hinterland of Lambton County's Enniskillen Township, Ontario, that the North American oil industry was born.

In response to the demand for oil, the enterprising Tripp Brothers, Henry and Charles, following their noses as well as reports from the Geological Survey of Canada, found their way to the site of the Lambton County oil seeps. In 1852 they started digging and manufacturing asphalt, which they sold for ships and roads. "The International Mining & Manufacturing Company," chartered in 1854, was the first oil company in North America.

Initially, the Tripps were immensely successful. Only a year after incorporation, their asphalt was displayed at the Paris Universal Exhibition and received honourable mention from Emperor Napoleon III. More important, they received an order for asphalt to pave the streets of Paris. That winter the Enniskillen gum was transported overland by sled to Port Sarnia, and then by ship across the Atlantic Ocean to France. In 1854, another enterprising Canadian and government geologist, Abraham Gesner, was experimenting with oil seeps in the colony of Nova Scotia. He had just invented and patented a method of extracting kerosene lamp fuel from the liquid oil component of natural seeps. When he set up a factory in New York the world suddenly lit up, and the search for crude oil was on.

Others, driven by dreams of profitable lighting, quickly followed the Tripps to Enniskillen Township and in 1858 James Miller Williams produced oil from sandy lenses at the base of the Tripp's gum bed. Initially pumped by hand and later by steam, his well yielded about 50 whiskey barrels a day. It was the first producing oil well in North America. By early winter, using a simple iron kettle distiller, he was refining kerosene. Although the resulting product was not very clean (it was called "skunk juice"), his was also the first oil refinery in North America. On the other side of Lake Erie, near Titusville in Pennsylvania, the Americans were exploiting gum beds as well, and a year later "Colonel" Edwin Drake, drilling all the way through into bedrock, encountered oil.

By 1860 word got out in both countries and the twin oil rush was on. In Enniskillen Township workers flocked to the new village of Oil Springs, and within a year there were 400 wells in the field; some of them also drilled into bedrock, each producing 50 to 500 barrels a day. In 1862 one of these wells brought in a gusher, reputed to produce 2000 barrels a day, and the rush compounded. Oil Springs boomed and soon 1000 wells covered 2.5 square kilometres around Black Creek (Figure 20.C). A forest of shifting ash-pole service-derricks replaced the native woodland. The oil flowed freely and there was often no need to pump. Indeed sometimes it flowed too freely, running into Black Creek and into Lake St. Clair, where it produced an oil slick several centimetres thick. Oil Springs and Titusville have often produced conflicting claims for the position of "first in North America," but neither has cared to take credit for the continent's first petroleum-related environmental debacle!

One of the more successful drillers, John Henry Fairbank, devised an ingenious method of pumping numerous wells efficiently and economically. The well pumps were linked each to another, and thereby all were connected up to a central power source by a series of parallel wooden rods. Known as the "jerker rod system," it could pump more than 200 wells from 1 large central steam engine. Fairbank eventually expanded his operation over a large part of the Oil Springs field that is still operated by his descendants today. The Oil Springs boom was short-lived—less than eight years. The gushers "watered out" (depleted) and oil was discovered in Petrolia and further afield in Texas. Production went up, the oil prices went down as the market became saturated, and Oil Springs became a ghost town.

But for Enniskillen Township, the story was not finished. The producers and the party simply moved several kilometres north to Petrolia, which produced its first gusher in 1866. This time, with a better infrastructure already in place, the boom was sustained for decades and Petrolia thrived as the oil capital of Canada. The only intrusion on this refined lifestyle was the indelicate smell of sour crude that wafted over the town when the wind was blowing in the wrong direction—the townspeople referred to it as "the smell of money."

It was in Petrolia that the energetic drillers came to call themselves "hard oilers." Although the exact origin of the label is obscure, it has been said that a team of resolute Petrolia oil workers were threatened by their opponents at a ball game with a "hard oil finish" and that the term was born on their victory. Many of the Petrolia Hard Oilers went on to open new oil fields abroad—in North Africa, Asia, and South America. Dubbed "the foreign drillers," they returned to Petrolia, full of exotic stories and souvenirs from strange lands. In all, they eventually went to 87 countries and were present in the 1920s and 1930s when giant oil fields were found in Iraq and other parts of the Middle East.

Price fluctuations were one of the greatest banes of the oil producers' lives. In an attempt to control supply, Jacob Englehart bought up several refineries in Petrolia and the nearby city of London, where he and several other Ontario financiers established the Imperial Oil Company in 1880. Three years later, after a major fire in London, all of the operations were moved to Petrolia.

By 1893, Imperial Oil, still operating out of Petrolia, was a great refining success, with 23 branches all over Canada. But as demand outstripped supply, Imperial needed capital for expansion. As Canada was in a recession, the directors initially approached British investors, but were unsuccessful in securing funds. The only option left was to sell to the Americans. Standard Oil had already bought many small refineries in the United States, including Abraham Gesner's New York kerosene factory, and had been casting a covetous eye on Canada's flagship firm for several years. The conditions of the takeover, effected in 1898, were unequivocal: the Imperial name was kept; Canadian headquarters and refineries were moved from Petrolia to Sarnia; and Imperial Oil went on to participate in developing the industry in other parts of Canada over the next century.

◆ **Figure 20.C** A photo taken in the late nineteenth century of drilling rigs in the Petrolia oilfield of southern Ontario, the birthplace of the Canadian oil industry. (Photo courtesy of Charles Fairbank)

One of the new frontiers of petroleum exploration was western Canada. The first exploration well in Alberta was drilled in 1902 at the site of an oil seep near Cameron Brook, which is now part of the Waterton Lakes National Park. It produced a brief boomtown of Oil Springs that suffered the same fate as its namesake in Ontario. But the nearby Turner Valley field, discovered in 1914 and drilled with the assistance of Petrolia Hard Oilers, established that Alberta was indeed a fertile ground for petroleum production.

After 20 years and 133 dry holes, Imperial Oil encountered Canada's first giant oil field at Leduc, Alberta, in 1947. Pipelines to Sarnia, Vancouver, and the United States were quickly built and Canada became a world-class oil-producing nation. But oil is not the only economically important hydrocarbon. In fact, natural gas is cleaner and requires no refining. Commercial natural gas production was pioneered in Alberta and Ontario. In 1883, CPR workers, drilling for water for their steam engines at Langevin in southern Alberta, hit an unexpected flow of natural gas that ignited and destroyed their derrick. George Dawson of the Geological Survey of Canada, observing that the strata that contained the gas were continuous over much of western Canada, predicted large volumes of gas from the territory. Indeed, George Dawson's prediction was well fulfilled in that the reserves of the Western Interior Basin are 80 percent gas prone.

Looking further afield for oil, Imperial pioneered exploration in the north with Canada's first Arctic discovery at Norman Wells in the Northwest Territories in 1920. The first well was drilled in the vicinity of yet another oil seep that had been originally noted by the intrepid explorer Alexander Mackenzie. The field was produced only intermittently over the years until it was connected to the Canadian pipeline system in 1985.

The east coast of Canada was also considered to be prime exploration territory and, at about the same time as the Leduc discovery, drillers were exploring underwater in the Atlantic Ocean near Prince Edward Island. This first effort at offshore drilling in Canada was not economically encouraging, but the technology was off to a good start. Half a century later, in 1979, the Hibernia Field was discovered 315 kilometres off the coast of Newfoundland and Labrador.

Today, Canada and its neighbours are encountering new petroleum challenges. Conventional sources of crude oil and natural gas are being depleted, and other more technologically sophisticated methods of extraction will be required. The Canadian oil sands, North Atlantic offshore drilling, and Arctic reserves are all potential sources of hydrocarbon energy. However, their exploitation will require not only more advanced and expensive technology but also recognition of environmental hazards and social concerns. In the Kyoto Accord, which was ratified by Ottawa in 2002, Canada pledged to reduce the emissions of greenhouse gases over the next 10 years. As well, Canada's First Nations are asserting their right to a share of the wealth, and long-ignored land claims must ultimately be negotiated. Therefore the future of the petroleum industry in Canada and elsewhere will depend not only on technological growth, as in the past, but on the development of sober and responsible social and ecological policies as well.

At the start of the twenty-first century, the fourth generation of Fairbank Oil celebrated its 140th anniversary in tiny Oil Springs, Ontario (population 800). North America's first oil discovery field remains a commercially viable operation as the 14th-largest oil producer in Ontario. Victorian technology is still largely utilized and, remarkably, the original jerker rod system, designed by J. H. Fairbank early in the 1860s, remains in place. This is the oldest continuously operated oil company in the world.

*Claudia Cochrane is a consulting geologist with Cairnlins Resources Limited and an adjunct professor in the Department of Earth Sciences at the University of Western Ontario.

In the Prairie provinces, the shallow seas that supplied marine organic matter to form oil were rimmed with coastal lowlands where land plants thrived and supplied their fibrous remains to form coal. About 98 percent of Canada's coal is produced in British Columbia, Alberta, and Saskatchewan and is of Mesozoic age (Figure 20.28). The famous coal beds of Nova Scotia are somewhat older, dating to

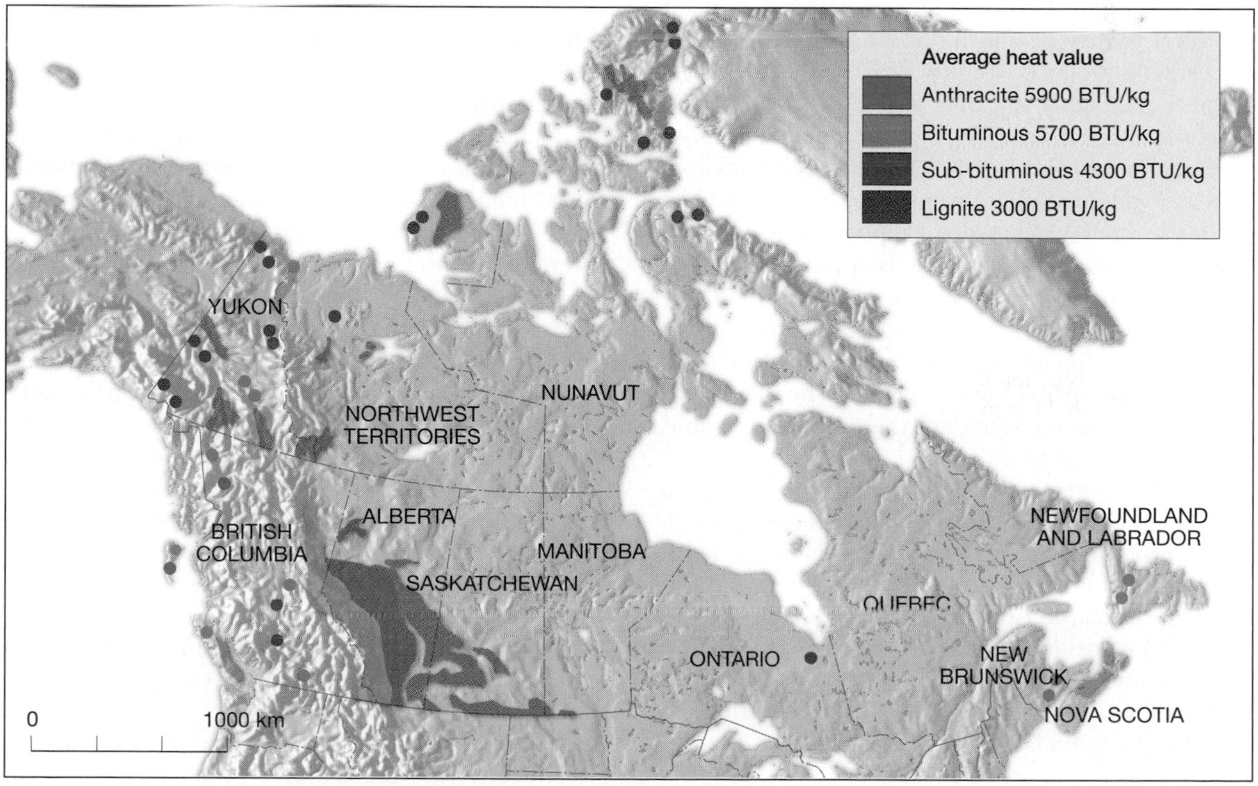

◆ **Figure 20.28** Distribution of coal deposits in Canada.
(Modified from an image courtesy of the Coal Association of Canada)

the Late Paleozoic, and contributed greatly to the Canadian coal output for more than 100 years. By 2001, Canada's coal production was becoming a multibillion-dollar industry. Canada supplies more than 20 countries (but mainly Japan and Korea) with coal and ranks as one of the world's leading coal exporters. A large proportion of coal remains in Canada to supply energy required for steel production.

Environmental Effects of Fossil Fuel Use

We face a broad array of human-caused environmental problems. Among the most serious are the impacts on the atmosphere that occur because of **fossil fuel** combustion (see Box 20.4). As world population continues its explosive growth (Figure 20.29), environmental problems associated with fossil fuel emissions will continue to grow unless drastic measures are taken to decrease them. Rural and urban air pollution, acid rain, and global greenhouse warming are all closely linked to the use of these basic energy resources.

Air Pollution *Air pollutants* are airborne particles and gases that occur in concentrations that endanger the health of organisms or disrupt the orderly function of the environment.

The human population constitutes a giant chemical factory producing a remarkable variety of undesirable products. Figure 20.30 shows the major primary pollutants and their sources. *Primary pollutants* are emitted directly from identifiable sources. They pollute the air immediately on their emission. Much of the air pollution in Canada is particulate matter, most of which comes simply from dust blown from open sources, such as roads and fields. For the remainder of pollution sources, the significance of the industrial and transportation categories is obvious. Industry (including fuel-generating plants) and the hundreds of millions of vehicles on the roads, and airplanes in the skies, are the greatest contributors in this category.

When chemical reactions take place among primary pollutants, *secondary pollutants* are formed. The noxious mixture of gases and particles that make up urban smog is an important example that is created when volatile organic compounds and sulphur and nitrogen oxides react in the presence of sunlight. The burning of fossil fuels by industry and various modes of transportation are the greatest contributors of these compounds.

Carbon Dioxide and Global Warming Warming of the lower atmosphere is global in scale. Unlike acid rain and urban air pollution, this issue is not associated with any of the primary pollutants in Figure 20.30. Rather, the connection between global warming and burning of fossil fuels relates to a basic product of combustion: carbon dioxide.

Carbon dioxide (CO_2) is a gas that occurs naturally in the atmosphere and is augmented by fuel combustion. Although CO_2 represents only about 0.038 percent of clean, dry air, it is nevertheless meteorologically significant. The importance of carbon dioxide lies in the fact that it is transparent to incoming short-wave solar radiation but is not transparent to some of the longer wavelength outgoing radiation emitted by Earth. A portion of the energy leaving the ground is absorbed by carbon dioxide and subsequently re-emitted, part of it toward the surface, thereby keeping the air near the ground warmer than it would be without carbon dioxide. Thus, carbon dioxide is one of the gases responsible for warming the atmosphere. This process is called the *greenhouse effect* (Figure 20.31). Because carbon dioxide is an important heat absorber, any change in the air's carbon dioxide content could alter temperatures in the lower atmosphere.

Although the proportion of carbon dioxide in the air is relatively uniform at any given time, its percentage has been rising steadily for more than a century (Figure 20.32). Much of this rise is the result of burning increasing quantities of fossil fuels. From the mid-nineteenth century until 2000, the carbon dioxide content of the air increased by more than 25 percent.

Have global temperatures already increased as a result of the rising carbon dioxide level? This appears to be the case, according to the Intergovernmental Panel on Climate Change (IPCC). During the twentieth century the increase was about 0.6°C. Moreover, recent years have been among the warmest on record. Globally, the 1990s were the warmest decade and 1998 and 2005 the warmest years since 1861, when reliable instrument records began (Figure 20.33). Other studies indicate that the increase in temperature in the twentieth century is likely to have been the largest of any century during the past millennium. Are these temperatures caused by human activities or would they have occurred anyway? In January the IPCC declared that most of the observed warming over the past 50 years is likely due to the increase in carbon dioxide and other greenhouse gases that humans contribute to the atmosphere.

If fossil fuel use continues to increase at projected rates, the present carbon dioxide content of 360 parts per million (ppm) will climb to between 540 ppm and 970 ppm by 2100. With such an

BOX 20.4

People and the Environment
Aerosols from the "Human Volcano"

Increasing the levels of carbon dioxide and other greenhouse gases in the atmosphere is the most direct human influence on global climate. But it is not the only impact. Global climate is also affected by human activities that contribute to the atmosphere's aerosol content. *Aerosols* are the tiny, often microscopic, liquid and solid particles that are suspended in the air. Atmospheric aerosols are composed of many different materials, including soil, smoke, sea salt, and sulphuric acid. Natural sources are numerous and include such phenomena as dust storms and volcanoes. In Chapter 4 you learned that some explosive volcanoes (such as Mount Pinatubo) emit large quantities of sulphur dioxide gas high into the atmosphere. This gas combines with water vapour to produce clouds of tiny sulphuric acid aerosols that can lower air temperatures near the surface by reflecting solar energy back to space. So it is with sulphuric acid aerosols produced by human activities.

◆ **Figure 20.D** One source of human-generated aerosols is power plants. (Photo by Bruce Forstery/Tony Stone Images)

Presently the human contribution of aerosols to the atmosphere *equals* the quantity emitted by natural sources. Most human-generated aerosols come from the sulphur dioxide emitted during the combustion of fossil fuels (Figure 20.D) and as a consequence of burning vegetation to clear agricultural land (Figure 20.A). Chemical reactions in the atmosphere convert the sulphur dioxide into aerosols, the same material that produces acid precipitation (see Box 5.1).

The aerosols produced by human activity act directly by reflecting sunlight back to space and indirectly by making clouds brighter reflectors. The second effect relates to the fact that sulphuric acid aerosols attract water and thus are especially effective as cloud condensation nuclei (tiny particles on which water vapour condenses). The large quantity of aerosols produced by human activities (especially industrial emissions and airplanes) trigger an increase in the number of cloud droplets that form within a cloud. A greater number of small droplets increases the cloud's brightness—that is, more sunlight is reflected back to space.

By reducing the amount of solar energy available to the climate system, aerosols have a net cooling effect. Studies indicate that the cooling effect of human-generated aerosols could offset a portion of the global warming caused by the growing quantities of greenhouse gases in the atmosphere. Unfortunately, the magnitude and extent of the cooling effect of aerosols is highly uncertain. This uncertainty is a significant hurdle in advancing our understanding of how humans alter Earth's climate.

It is important to point out some significant differences between global warming by greenhouse gases and aerosol cooling. After being emitted, greenhouse gases, such as carbon dioxide, remain in the atmosphere for many decades. By contrast, aerosols released into the lower atmosphere remain there for only a few days or, at most, a few weeks before they are washed out by precipitation. Because of their short lifetime in the atmosphere, human-generated aerosols are distributed unevenly over the globe. As expected, they are concentrated near the areas that produce them, namely industrialized regions that burn fossil fuels and land areas where vegetation is burned.

Because the lifetime of human-generated aerosols in the atmosphere is short, the effect of the "human volcano" on today's climate is determined by the quantity of material emitted during the preceding couple of weeks. By contrast, the carbon dioxide released into the atmosphere remains for much longer spans and thus influences climate for many decades.

increase, the greenhouse effect would be much more dramatic and measurable than in the past. The predicted result would be an average global surface temperature increase of 1.4°C to 5.8°C. The warming of the lower atmosphere will not be the same everywhere. Rather, the temperature response in the polar

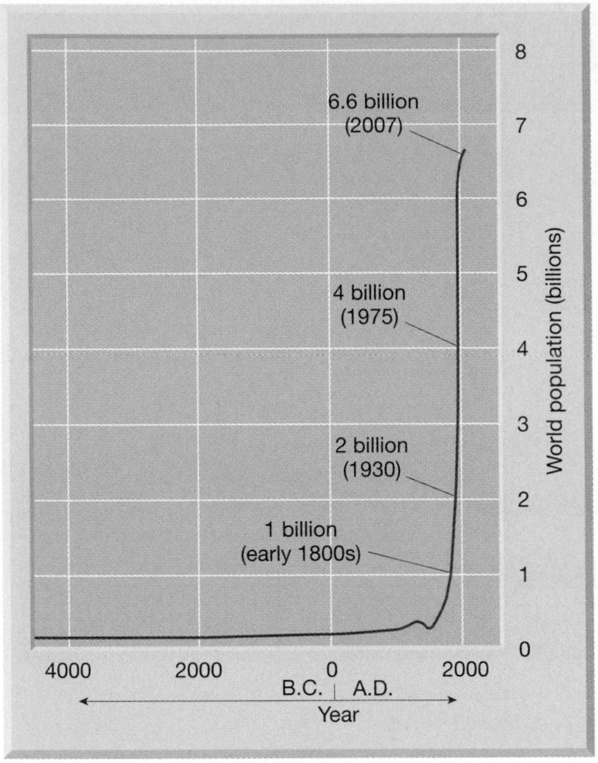

◆ **Figure 20.29** Growth of world population. It took until 1800 for the number to reach 1 billion. By the year 2015, more than 7 billion people may inhabit the planet. The demand for basic resources is growing faster than the rate of population increase.
(Data from the Population Reference Bureau)

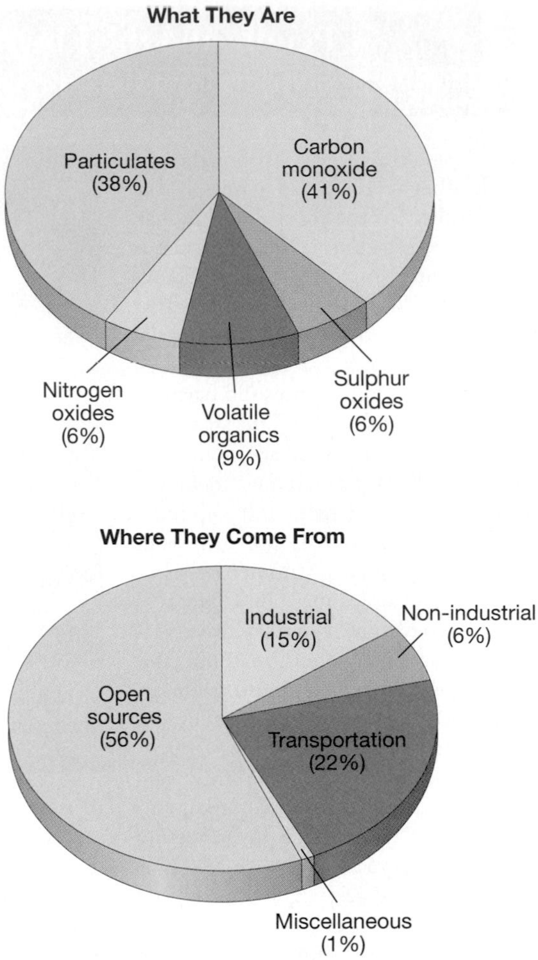

◆ **Figure 20.30** Principal types and sources of air pollution in Canada per unit mass. Although particulates from non-industrial sources, such as fields and roads, compose a large proportion of pollutants, the remaining pollutants can be linked largely to industrial and transportation-related emissions.
(Pie charts based on data from *Criteria Air Contaminants Emission Summaries*, Environment Canada, www.ec.gc.ca/pdb/ape/cape_home-e.cfm)

regions could be much greater than the global average, while some low-latitude regions would experience much smaller fluctuations. According to the IPCC, the projected rate of warming during the next century will be much larger than the observed changes in the last century and is very likely without precedent during the last 10,000 years. However, the possible effects of aerosol emissions from fossil fuel combustion complicate this outlook considerably.

In December 1997, Canada and more than 160 other countries met in Kyoto, Japan, and agreed on targets to reduce greenhouse gas emissions. The Kyoto Protocol includes the ratification of these targets and the proposed methods of achieving them. Canada's target is to reduce its greenhouse gas emissions to 6 percent below 1990 levels by 2012. In December 2002, the federal Government of Canada officially ratified Canada's commitment to the Kyoto Protocol.

Unconventional Fossil Fuel Deposits

As supplies of petroleum and coal that can be extracted by conventional methods dwindle, we can expect that an increasing volume of fossil fuel will be produced from lower-grade deposits that require innovative, unconventional methods of extraction (Figure 20.34). Two main types of deposits that are being developed for hydrocarbon extraction are heavy oil sands and oil shales.

Heavy Oil Sands *Heavy oil sands*, also commonly called tar sands, are mixtures of sediment, water, and abundant, black, tar-like bitumen. It is thought that such deposits result from a very high level of interaction between regular crude oil and groundwater linked to long-distance and near-surface oil migration. A popular explanation for the origin of the tarry oil is that cool, oxygen-rich groundwater provided optimal conditions for certain bacteria to preferen-

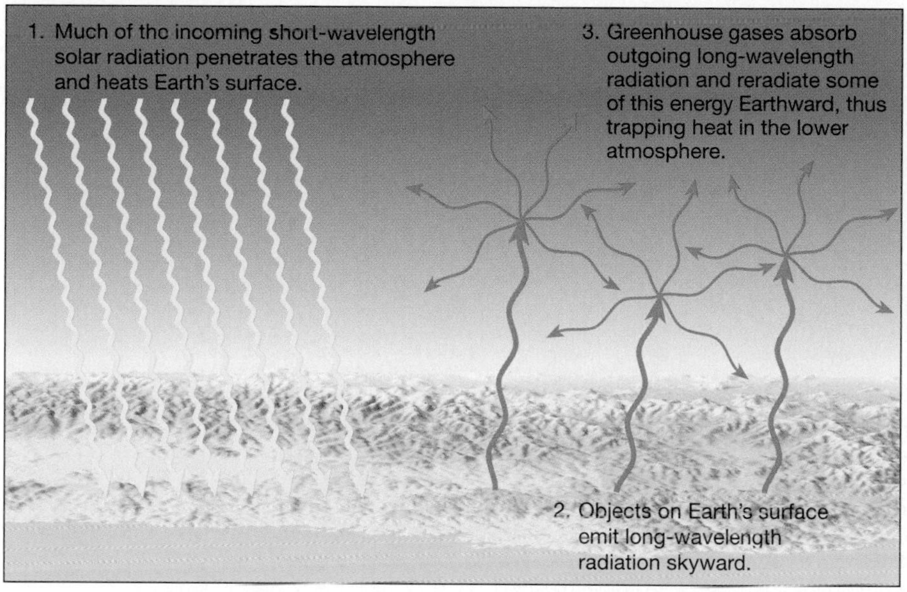

◆ **Figure 20.31** The heating of the atmosphere. Most of the short-wavelength radiation from the Sun that is not reflected back to space passes through the atmosphere and is absorbed by Earth's land-sea surface. This energy is then emitted from the surface as longer-wavelength radiation, much of which is absorbed by certain gases in the atmosphere. Some of the energy absorbed by the atmosphere will be radiated Earthward. This so-called greenhouse effect is responsible for keeping Earth's surface much warmer than it would be otherwise.

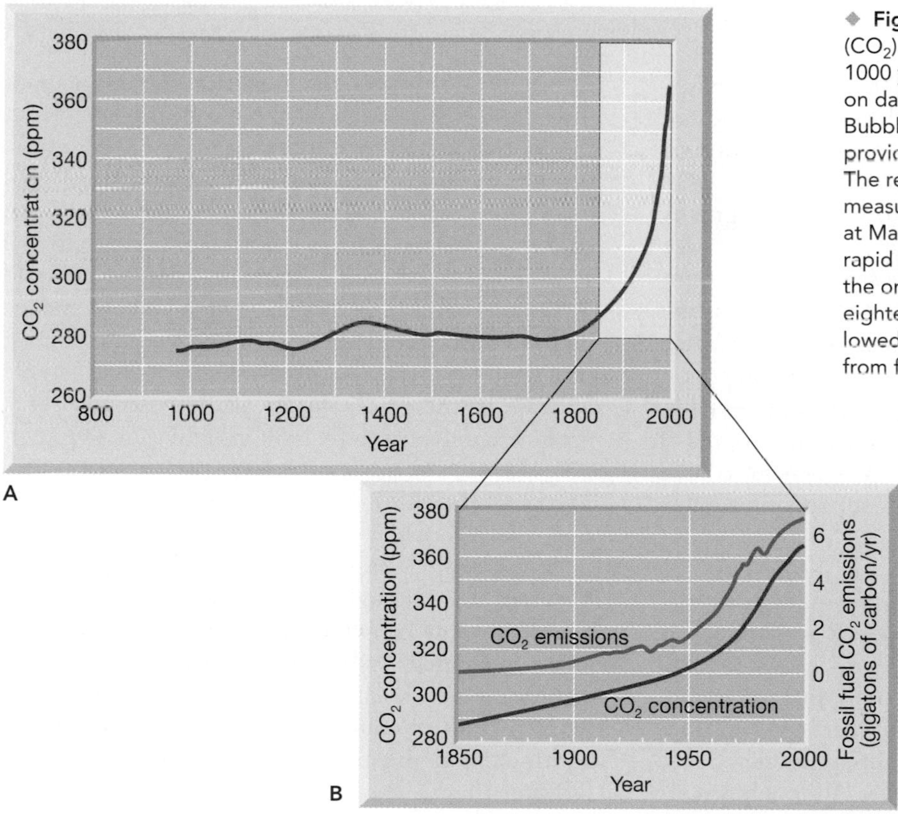

◆ **Figure 20.32** **A.** Carbon dioxide (CO_2) concentrations over the past 1000 years. Most of the record is based on data obtained from Antarctic ice cores. Bubbles of air trapped in the glacial ice provide samples of past atmospheres. The record since 1958 comes from direct measurements of atmospheric CO_2 taken at Mauna Loa Observatory, Hawaii. **B.** The rapid increase in CO_2 concentration since the onset of industrialization in the late eighteenth century is clear and has followed closely the rise in CO_2 emissions from fossil fuels.

tially consume light components of the oil, thus leaving behind a heavy residue. Exposure of petroleum to air at the surface of Earth also allows its light components to evaporate and could also contribute to enrichment of the heavier components of the petroleum. In any case, the hydrocarbons of the tar sands appear to represent degraded oil. Heavy oil sands occur in abundance in Alberta (Figure 20.34), the most famous of which are the Athabasca Tar Sands located northeast of Edmonton. Alberta's vast deposits are the source of about 15 percent of Canada's oil production.

Because of their high viscosity, hydrocarbons that occur in heavy oil sands cannot be pumped from

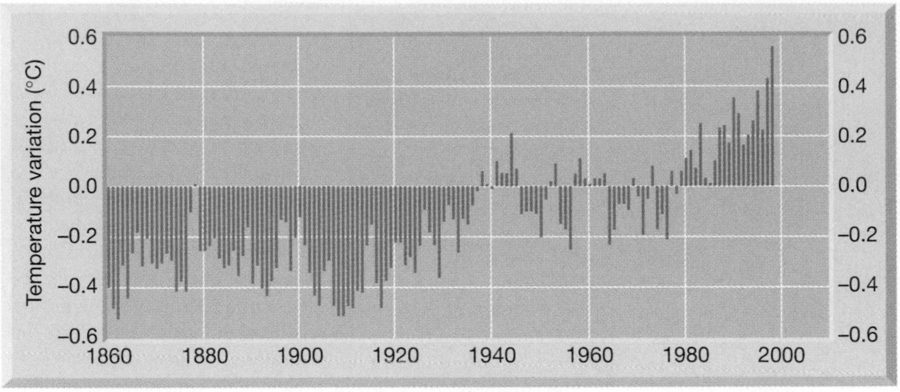

◆ **Figure 20.33** Annual average global temperature variations for the period 1860–1998. The basis for comparison is the average for the period 1961–1990 (the 0.0 line on the graph). Each narrow bar on the graph represents the departure of the global mean temperature from the 1961–1990 average for one year. For example, the global mean temperature for 1862 was more than 0.5°C *below* the 1961–1990 average, whereas the global mean for 1998 was more than 0.5°C above. (Specifically, 1998 was 0.56°C warmer.) The bar graph clearly indicates that there can be *significant variations from year to year*. But the graph also shows a trend. Estimated global mean temperatures have been above the 1961–1990 average every year since 1978. Also, the three warmest years in the 138-year record shown here were 1995, 1997, and 1998. (After G. Bell et al. "Climate Assessment for 1998," *Bulletin of the American Meteorological Society*, Vol. 80, No. 5, May 1999, p. 54.)

a well like conventional oil. The tar sand is effectively mined at the surface and heated to mobilize the hydrocarbons, which are upgraded to a synthetic crude with the addition of hydrogen and removal of impurities. Such projects as steam-assisted gravity drainage, whereby steam is injected directly into the tar sand deposit to mobilize the hydrocarbons, now bypass the mining process and oil is then recovered from pipes much like conventional crude oil. Much energy must be expended in the recovery process—about half as much as the end product yields. Nonetheless, Alberta's tar sands are a major source of petroleum and will undoubtedly play a major role in fossil-fuel production as global supplies inevitably decrease.

Oil Shale In some cases, fine-grained, organic-rich sedimentary rocks are not subjected to sufficiently high temperatures and pressures to liberate liquid and gas hydrocarbons, and they instead retain organic matter in the form of kerogen. A fine-grained sedimentary rock containing an abundance of kerogen is called an *oil shale*. Although widely used, this term is somewhat misleading because most oil shales are not shales at all, but fine-grained limestones (Figure 20.35). In any case, oil shales contain enormous amounts of hydrocarbons and can be artificially heated to crack their kerogen into liquid petroleum. Huge deposits of Cenozoic-age oil shale composing the Green River Formation occur in Colorado, Utah, and Wyoming, and represent fine-grained lake sediments deposited during the Eocene Epoch. Paleozoic oil shales occur in a number of places in Canada, including New Brunswick, Nova Scotia, and southern Ontario, and a few Mesozoic deposits have also been identified (Figure 20.34). Oil extraction from Canadian oil shales has been attempted but is not yet profitable. Similar to the case of heavy oil sands, the extraction of a liquid product from oil shale involves a high input of energy, both because it must be mined and because it must be heated to liberate oil. Accordingly, a considerable increase in the price of oil will be necessary for a profitable industry to be built around this resource.

Methane Hydrate *Methane hydrate* is a solid substance formed when water molecules form cages that surround single molecules of methane. Methane hydrates, once thought to be oddities in the natural world, are now known to be common in permafrost areas associated with methane seeps. Even more significant are vast methane hydrate deposits found in deep areas of continental shelves of nearly every continent on Earth, including North America (Figure 20.36). In those places, the methane-ice complexes are kept stable because of high pressures and cold temperatures at the seafloor. At least some of these deposits are associated with communities of microbes that produce methane as part of their normal metabolic activities. Methane hydrates are sufficiently high in methane content to produce a flame when ignited with a match.

Although the thought of exploiting this large reservoir of methane is appealing, many concerns

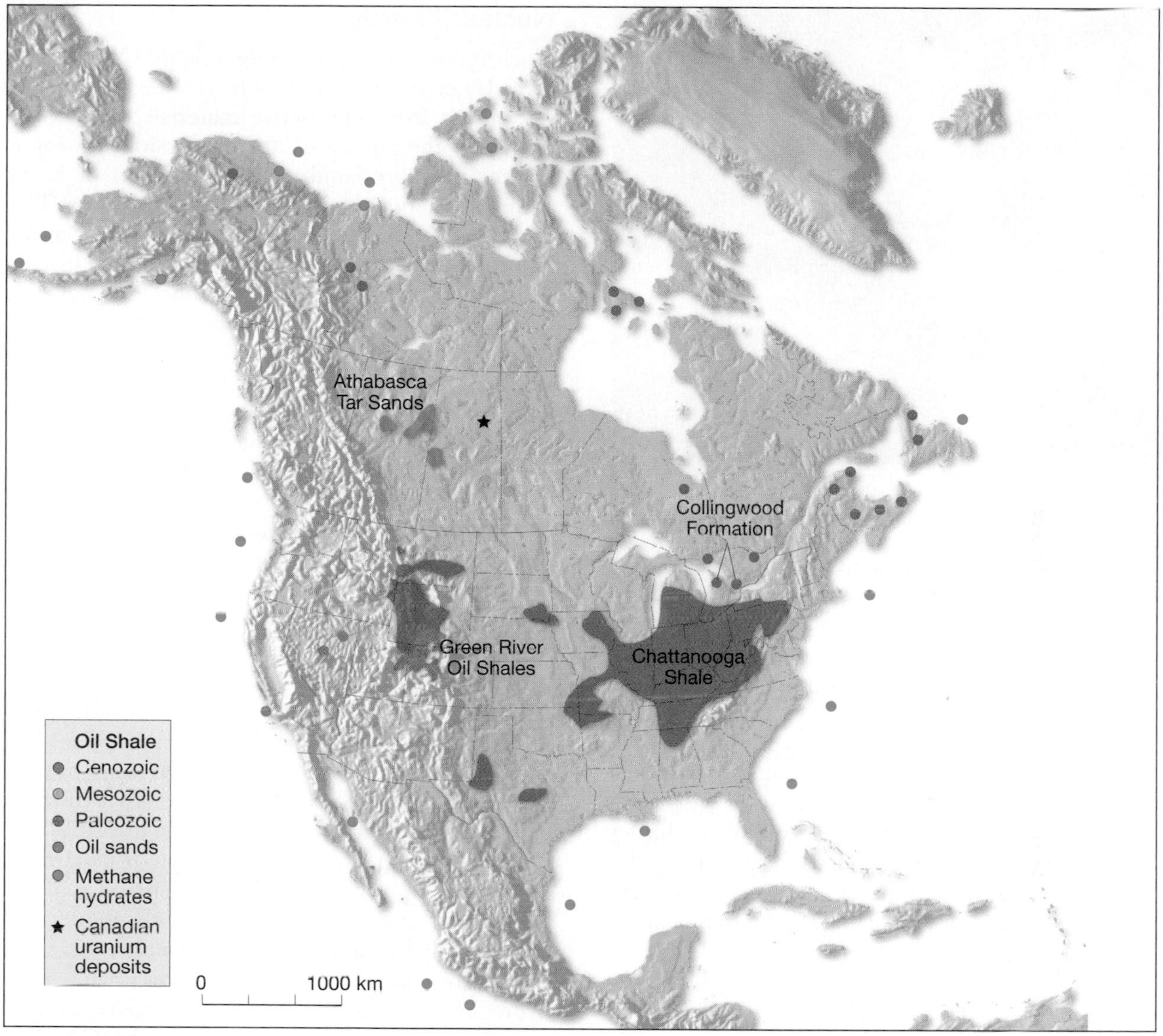

◆ **Figure 20.34** Unconventional fossil fuel resources (oil sands, oil shales, and methane hydrates) in North America and uranium deposits of northern Saskatchewan.

◆ **Figure 20.35** Outcrop of thinly bedded, kerogen-rich, Ordovician limestones ("oil shales") of the Collingwood Formation on the southern shore of Georgian Bay, Ontario.
(Photo by C. Tsujita)

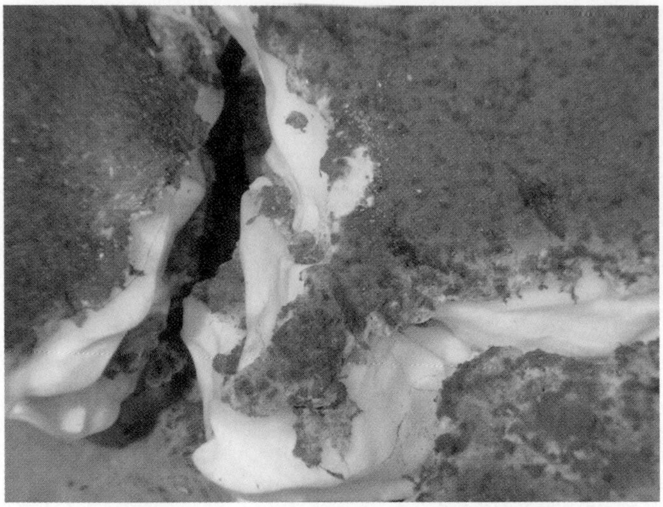

◆ **Figure 20.36** A body of methane hydrate (yellowish-white) photographed on the seafloor some 850 metres below sea level, off the west coast of Vancouver Island, British Columbia. (Photo courtesy of Ross Chapman)

surround the use of this potential energy source. As with all unconventional hydrocarbon resources, the feasibility and cost of extraction is questionable at the present time. More serious, however, are the environmental impacts of extraction, both in terms of disturbing the seafloor and in terms of the potential leakage of methane into the atmosphere during extraction. The warming effect of methane in the atmosphere is at least 20 times as high as that of carbon dioxide, and thus methane leakage from seafloor hydrates is a legitimate concern.

Coal-Bed Methane The slow heating of fibrous organic matter derived from land plants not only produces solid coal but also liberates methane. This *coal-bed methane* is trapped in the pore spaces of coal seams and associated detrital sediments. Because it is confined in the pores of sedimentary rocks, it is difficult to extract by conventional means. However, many projects and wells are extracting the gas in Canada. It has been found that coal-bed methane can be released by pumping large quantities of water from a coal seam through several wells. The merits of this practice have, however, been questioned because of concerns about surface-water and groundwater contamination, groundwater depletion, and the possible escape of the methane into the atmosphere. Still, coal-bed methane is attractive as a clean-burning alternative to conventional fossil fuels, such as oil and coal. As more efficient extraction technologies are developed, coal-bed methane is likely to become more important as a fuel source in the future.

Nuclear Energy

Nuclear power plants generate roughly 12 percent of Canada's electricity supply. The fuel for these facilities comes from radioactive materials that release energy by the process of **nuclear fission**. Fission is accomplished by bombarding the nuclei of heavy atoms, commonly uranium-235, with neutrons. This causes the uranium nuclei to split into smaller nuclei and to emit neutrons and heat energy. The ejected neutrons, in turn, bombard the nuclei of adjacent uranium atoms, producing a chain reaction. If the supply of fissionable material is sufficient and if the reaction is allowed to proceed in an uncontrolled manner, an enormous amount of energy is released in the form of an atomic explosion. In most nuclear reactors, the chain reaction is regulated through the use of materials called *moderators*, which slow neutrons down to allow them to react with the uranium atoms in a controlled manner. Most reactors also use neutron-absorbing materials in control rods to prevent the participation of too many neutrons in the reaction at any one time.

CANDU Reactors The production of nuclear power in Canada is centred on the CANDU (Canadian Deuterium-Uranium) design, which uses natural uranium-235 as fuel and deuterium oxide as a moderator and heat transport medium (Figure 20.37).

Deuterium is a stable isotope of hydrogen containing a proton and a neutron. Because of the higher mass of deuterium, relative to the more common light hydrogen that contains a single proton and no neutrons, deuterium oxide is heavier than regular hydrogen oxide (water). Deuterium oxide is therefore commonly called *heavy water*. The CANDU design allows on-power refuelling, does not require fuel reprocessing, and can potentially use spent fuel from other reactors. The versatility of CANDU reactors is a major factor that has contributed to their use in a number of countries outside North America, including Argentina, India, Korea, Pakistan, and Romania.

Uranium Occurrences Although technically a metal, uranium is discussed in this section by virtue of being a fuel source. Uranium-235 is the only naturally occurring isotope that is readily fissionable and is therefore the primary fuel used in nuclear power plants. Although large quantities of uranium ore have been discovered, most contain less than 0.05 percent uranium. Of this small amount, 99.3 percent is the non-fissionable isotope uranium-238 and just 0.7 percent consists of the fissionable isotope uranium-235. Because most nuclear reactors operate with fuels that

◆ **Figure 20.37** A significant amount of electricity in Canada is produced by nuclear fission. Canadian nuclear reactors, such as those at the Pickering Nuclear Power Plant in Ontario, are of CANDU (Canadian Deuterium-Uranium) design.
(Photo by CP/Kevin Frayer)

are at least 3 percent uranium-235, the two isotopes must be separated to concentrate the fissionable isotope. The process of separating the uranium isotopes is difficult, secretive, and substantially increases the cost of nuclear power.

In addition to being scarce, the size of the uranium atom generally prevents it from being incorporated into the crystal lattice of most rock-forming minerals. In addition, uranium is highly soluble in oxidizing environments and therefore requires unusual conditions to be precipitated in minerals at Earth's surface. Uranium ores are extremely diverse in their geologic settings, but it appears that a critical factor controlling the precipitation of uranium-bearing minerals is the absence of oxygen.

Uranium can be enriched in residual fluids of felsic magmas, reaching concentrations over a hundred parts per million and incorporated as a trace element in minerals such as zircon and apatite. In sufficient concentrations, however, uranium forms an oxide mineral (UO_2) called uraninite (pitchblende if very fine grained), which can occur in veins associated with felsic igneous intrusions. Ores of uranium-bearing minerals also occur as placers in Precambrian rocks, reflecting the oxygen-free atmosphere of those times. The uranium ores of Elliot Lake, Ontario, that formerly supplied a significant proportion of Canada's uranium represent such uranium placers.

The fact that uranium is soluble in oxidizing environments and insoluble in reducing environments can also contribute to the formation of uranium ores. For example, the rich uranium deposits of northern Saskatchewan's Athabasca Basin (Figure 20.34), which currently account for Canada's entire uranium production, appear to have been formed by the interaction of deep-sourced, oxygen-free fluid with shallow-sourced oxygenated fluid that carried dissolved uranium. In this case, this fluid interaction was focused in small areas where fault breccias intersect a nonconformity separating highly deformed metamorphic rocks from overlying sedimentary rocks. Uranium can also be dissolved near Earth's surface by oxygenated groundwater and carried through permeable, coarse-grained sedimentary rocks (e.g., sandstone). The uranium-charged fluid precipitates uranium in the mineral carnotite when it mixes with oxygen-poor water. Most of the uranium mined in Arizona, New Mexico, and Utah is contained in this type of ore. The close association of uranium and organic matter is also apparent in the slightly elevated concentration of uranium in organic-rich shales and phosphate deposits, relative to other sedimentary rock types.

Obstacles to Development At one time, nuclear power was heralded as the clean, cheap source of energy to replace fossil fuels. However, several obstacles have emerged to hinder the development of nuclear power as a major energy source, not the least of which is the enormous cost of building the facilities that contain numerous safety features. More important, perhaps, is the concern over the possibility of a serious accident at one of the nearly 200 nuclear plants that exist worldwide. The Three Mile Island (Harrisburg, Pennsylvania) accident in 1979 brought this point home. Here, a malfunction led the plant operators to believe there was too much water in the primary system rather than too little and allowed the reactor core to lie uncovered for several hours. Although the reactor sustained considerable damage, the public was fortunately spared great harm.

Unfortunately, the 1986 accident at Chernobyl in the former Soviet Union was far more serious. In this incident, the reactor ran out of control and two pressure-related explosions lifted the roof of the structure, allowing radioactive material to be strewn over the immediate area. During the 10 days that it took to quench the fire that ensued, high levels of radioactive material were carried by the atmosphere and detected as far away as Norway. In addition to the 18 people who died within six weeks of the accident, many thousands more face an increased risk of death from radioactive-fallout-related illnesses.

We emphasize that the concentrations of fissionable uranium-235 and the design of reactors are such that nuclear power plants cannot explode like an atomic bomb. The dangers arise from the possible escape of radioactive debris during a meltdown of the core or other malfunction. In addition, hazards, such as the disposal of nuclear waste and the relationship that exists between nuclear energy programs and the proliferation of nuclear weapons, must be considered as we evaluate the pros and cons of employing nuclear power.

RENEWABLE FUEL SOURCES

Organic-Based Sources

Landfill Methane Methane produced by the microbial decomposition of organic matter in landfills is a significant contributor of greenhouse gases to the atmosphere, although it usually escapes attention from the media. Thus, with the continued rise in global population, methane production from landfills can only increase in total volume and production rate. One way to deal with both the volume of methane released to the atmosphere and the demand for energy is to use this methane as fuel. About one quarter of all landfill methane is presently being collected in Canada, about 70 percent of which is used for energy production. Although the use of landfill methane does significantly decrease total greenhouse emissions, it does not eliminate them, because carbon dioxide, although less potent than methane as a greenhouse gas, is produced from its combustion.

Biomass Energy Biomass energy is derived from the tissues of organisms, specifically plants, and provided the first organic fuel used by humans. Plants, through photosynthesis, produce their structural tissues and sugars by using solar energy, and this stored energy can later be released through combustion. You release this kind of biomass energy every time you burn wood in a campfire.

Biomass fuel is a primary source of energy in developing countries in the form of wood and dung, but has been largely replaced in developed countries by fossil fuels. Recently, however, the use of biomass fuel has been seriously considered as a clean, renewable energy source.

One very important biomass fuel is ethanol, which is a product of anaerobic (oxygen-free) fermentation. In Canada, such industries as forestry generate lots of waste material that could support large ethanol-producing operations. Although not used as fuel in its pure form, ethanol can be used as an additive to gasoline and has been found to reduce carbon monoxide and carbon dioxide emissions. A form of biodiesel has been developed from vegetable oils and could also be used as an additive to conventional fuel. Although biomass fuels are far from replacing conventional fossil fuels, they are, at the very least, renewable and can reduce the total volume of greenhouse gas emissions.

Hydroelectric Power

Falling water has been an energy source for centuries. Through most of history, the mechanical energy produced by waterwheels was used to power mills and other machinery. Today, the power generated by falling water drives turbines that produce electricity, hence the term **hydroelectric power**. Canada is a world leader in the production of hydroelectricity, as it contributes to the production of 58 percent of Canada's total electricity generation (Figure 20.38). Most of this energy is produced at large dams, which allow controlled flow of water (Figure 20.39). The water impounded in a reservoir is a form of stored (potential) energy that can be released at any time to produce electricity.

Although water power is considered a renewable resource, the dams built to provide hydroelectricity have finite lifetimes and there are always negative environmental effects. All rivers carry sus-

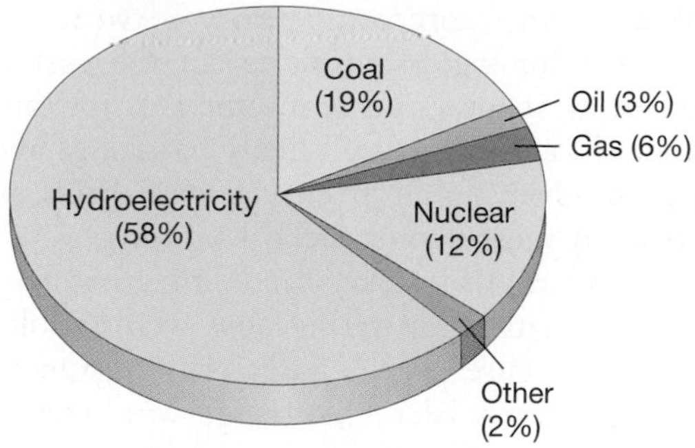

◆ **Figure 20.38** Electricity generation sources in Canada, 2003. Note the extremely high contribution of electricity from hydroelectric sources compared with fossil fuels and nuclear power generation.
(Data for the pie chart from Canadian Electricity Association, 2006, Power Generation in Canada: A Guide, p. 5, www.canelect.ca/en/Pdfs/HandBook.pdf)

◆ **Figure 20.39** Daniel Johnson Manicouagan (Manic) 5 Hydroelectric Dam in Quebec.
(Photo by Walter Muma)

pended sediment that is deposited behind the dam as soon as it is built. Eventually the sediment will completely fill the reservoir. This takes 50 to 300 years, depending on the quantity of suspended material transported by the river. An example is Egypt's huge Aswan High Dam, which was completed in the 1960s. It is estimated that half of the reservoir will be filled with sediment from the Nile River by the year 2025.

The availability of appropriate sites is an important limiting factor in the development of large hydroelectric power plants. A good site provides a significant height for the water to fall and a high rate of flow. Most of the best U.S. sites have already been developed, limiting the future expansion of hydroelectric power. Canada still has many rivers that have not been dammed for hydroelectric power, but many of these are in remote areas that are particularly sensitive to environmental disturbance.

Recently a different type of hydroelectric power production has come into use. Called a *pumped water-storage system*, it is actually a type of energy management. During times when demand for electricity is low, unneeded power produced by nonhydroelectric sources is used to pump water from a lower reservoir to a storage area at a higher elevation. Then, when demand for electricity is great, the water stored in the higher reservoir is available to drive turbines and produce electricity to supplement the power supply.

Solar Energy

The direct use of *solar energy* has gained much appeal as an alternative resource on a small scale. Many people use south-facing windows in their homes as *passive solar collectors* that allow objects in a room to absorb the energy of the Sun's rays and to re-emit the energy as heat. Together with more efficient insulation, south-facing windows are featured in many modern homes as a measure of heat conservation. More elaborate systems used in homes feature an active solar collector that utilizes large glass-covered boxes to collect energy. This energy heats air or water that is, in turn, circulated through the house in pipes to supply heat where it is needed.

The use of solar energy on a large scale is becoming more practical as technology advances, but is still relatively insignificant compared with the energy used from conventional fuel resources. So if solar energy is free, why isn't it used more? The reason lies in economics; although solar energy is free, the equipment required for its exploitation is expensive. As supplies of non-renewable fuels decrease, and as solar-collecting technology becomes more advanced, solar energy will surely increase in popularity and might even become cost-effective in the near future. Another major impetus for the conversion to solar energy will be the continued quest for non-polluting energy sources.

Research is currently under way to improve sunlight-collecting technologies, and experimental installations are becoming increasingly common throughout North America. One method currently under investigation in Barstow, California, involves the use of some 2000 sun-tracking mirrors that continually focus reflected light on a central receiving tower. The light energy collected by the receiver heats water in pressurized panels. This water is then transferred to turbines that generate electrical power. Another type of collector uses photovoltaic cells that collect sunlight and convert it directly into electricity. Examples of large experimental photovoltaic installations in Canada are the roof arrays of the Hugh MacMillan Rehabilitation Centre in Toronto, Ontario; the CANMET Energy Technology Centre in Varennes, Quebec; and the EPCOR office building in Edmonton, Alberta (Figure 20.40). Small rooftop photovoltaic systems have begun to be used in developing countries, such as the Dominican Republic, Sri Lanka, and Zimbabwe. The units are about as small as an open briefcase and use a battery to store electricity that is generated from sunlight during the day. These small photovoltaic systems can run a television or radio, plus a few light bulbs, for up to four hours. Although much cheaper than the construction of conventional electric generators, the units are still too expensive for poor families. Consequently, an estimated 2 billion people in developing countries still lack electricity.

Wind Energy

Approximately 0.25 percent of the solar energy that reaches the lower atmosphere is transformed into wind. Despite this deceptively minuscule figure, the total amount of energy that can be collected from the wind is enormous.

Wind has, of course, been used for centuries as an almost free and non-polluting source of energy. Sailboats and windmills are two common forms of wind-powered devices used long ago. In addition, settlers of rural North America relied heavily on wind power for the pumping of water and other applications.

As technology has improved, efficiency has increased and the costs of wind-generated electricity have become more competitive. Between 1983 and 2005, technological advances cut the cost of wind power by about 85 percent. One area for the expansion of wind energy will likely be islands and other regions that are far from electrical grids and that presently must import fuel for power generation.

Wind turbines are becoming commonplace in Canada, with wind farms now well established in Alberta (Figure 20.41), Saskatchewan, Quebec, and Prince Edward Island. Although wind generation is still modest in Canada, the energy produced in 2006 was equivalent to that used by more than 400,000 Canadian homes in a year.

Although the future for wind power is promising, it is not without difficulties. In addition to technical advances that must continue to be made, noise pollution and costs of large tracts of land in populated areas present significant obstacles to development, including the fact that it is intermittent. If wind were to constitute a high proportion of the total energy supply, any shortfall could cause severe economic disruptions. Better means of storage would allow wind to contribute a significantly higher percentage of our energy needs. One proposal would use wind energy to produce hydrogen by electrolysis of water. This combustible gas would then be distributed and stored in a manner similar to natural gas.

◆ **Figure 20.40** Photograph of the EPCOR Solar Panel Array, located on EPCOR's corporate head office in downtown Edmonton, Alberta. The array has a generating capacity of 13.4 kilowatts. This building's integrated photovoltaic system, which converts sunlight directly into electricity, is connected to the Alberta grid. When installed in 1996, it was the largest of its kind in Canada, as well as the world's highest. (Photo used with permission of EPCOR Utilities Inc.)

Geothermal Energy

People have taken advantage of water that has been heated by Earth for centuries. In the modern age, such **geothermal energy** is now becoming popular for home and commercial heating, and it is also being used in innovative applications, such as the heating of greenhouses that can grow fruit and vegetable crops year-round. Another novel use of geothermal heat can be found in Springhill, Nova Scotia, where water that has been slightly warmed by the natural geothermal gradient in abandoned shafts of coalmines is pumped to provide space heating for an industrial development.

The use of geothermal energy for the generation of electricity is a relatively new development and is focused on areas where groundwater is heated by near-surface volcanic activity. Geothermal power plants are presently well established in Iceland (Figure 20.42), Italy, New Zealand, and the United States. In these facilities, the steam and superheated water generated by hot springs is tapped and piped to turbines that generate electric power.

However, we must recognize that geothermal power is not inexhaustible. When hot fluids are pumped from volcanically heated reservoirs, water cannot be replaced and then heated sufficiently to

◆ **Figure 20.41** Blue Ridge Wind Turbine, Waterton Wind Turbines Facility near Hillspring, Alberta.
(Photo courtesy of Vision Quest Windelectric Inc.)

recharge the reservoir. Experience shows that steam and hot water from individual wells usually lasts no more than 10 to 15 years, so more wells must be drilled to maintain power production. Eventually the field is depleted. As with other alternative methods of power production, geothermal sources are not expected to provide a high percentage of the world's growing energy needs. Nevertheless, in regions where its potential can be developed, its use will no doubt continue to grow.

Tidal Power

The ocean contains a huge amount of physical energy in the form of tides. Although harnessing this energy presently involves sophisticated technology, the principle of electricity generation from tidal energy is fairly simple. The most common method involves trapping ocean water in reservoirs at high tide and later releasing it through hydroelectric turbines as the tide goes down (Figure 20.43). The largest tidal

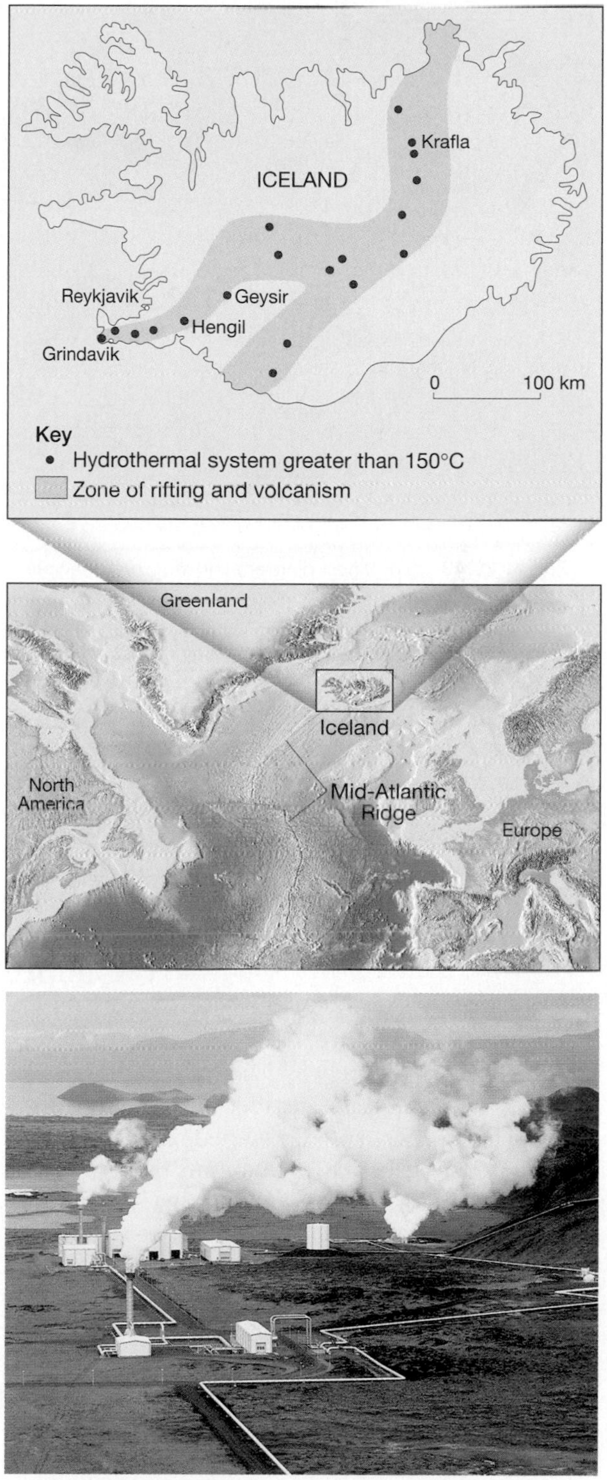

◆ **Figure 20.42** Iceland straddles the Mid-Atlantic Ridge. This divergent plate boundary is the site of numerous active volcanoes and geothermal systems. Because the entire country consists of geologically young volcanic rocks, warm water can be encountered in holes drilled almost anywhere. More than 45 percent of Iceland's energy comes from geothermal sources. The photo shows a power station in southwest Iceland. The steam is used to generate electricity. Hot (83°C) water from the plant is sent via an insulated pipeline to Reykjavik for space heating.
(Photo by Simon Fraser/Science Photo Library)

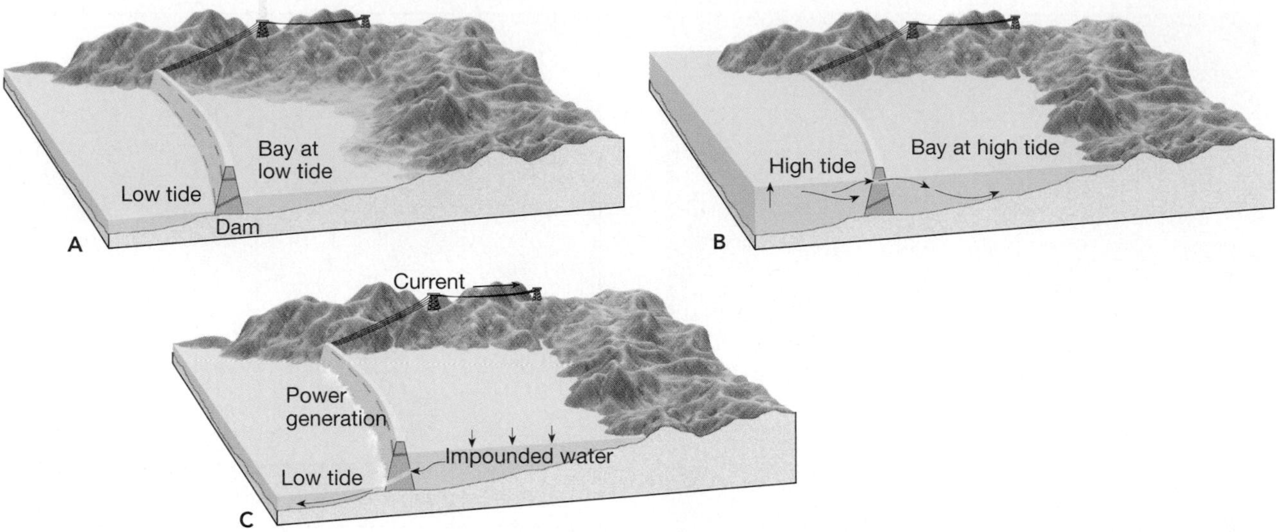

◆ **Figure 20.43** Simplified diagram showing the principle of the tidal dam.

energy plant is located on the La Rance River in France, which generates 240 megawatts of power. The Annapolis Tidal Power Generation Station in the Bay of Fundy, Nova Scotia, is the only tidal plant in North America and generates about 20 megawatts. Although tidal power is a good non-polluting form of energy, its use is limited to areas where the tidal range is high and water turbidity is low. Thus, the focus of its further development will probably be on supplementing other forms of energy rather than replacing them.

Chapter Summary

- *Mineral resources* are the endowment of useful minerals ultimately available commercially. *Resources* include already identified deposits from which minerals can be extracted profitably, called *reserves*, as well as known deposits that are not yet economically or technologically recoverable. Deposits inferred to exist but not yet discovered are also considered mineral resources. The term *ore* is used to denote those useful metallic minerals that can be mined for a profit, as well as some nonmetallic minerals, such as fluorite and sulphur, that contain useful substances.
- Some of the most important accumulations of metals, such as gold, silver, lead, and copper, are associated with igneous processes. The best-known and most important ore deposits are generated from *hydrothermal (hot-water) solutions*. Hydrothermal deposits can originate from hot, metal-rich fluids that are remnants of late-stage magmatic processes. These ion-rich solutions move along fractures or bedding planes, cool, and precipitate the metallic ions to produce *vein deposits*. In a *disseminated deposit* (e.g., much of the world's copper deposits) the ores from hydrothermal solutions are distributed as minute masses throughout the entire rock mass. Hydrothermal deposits can also be produced by mineral precipitation from fluids that picked up metals from volcanic or sedimentary rocks.
- Sedimentary deposits include *banded iron formation* of alternating bands of iron oxide and red chert deposited with help from bacteria under reducing conditions of the Precambrian Eon. *Placer* deposits were sorted by running water, and discoveries of gold-bearing placers led to the Cariboo (British Columbia) and Klondike (Yukon) rushes in previous centuries.
- Many of the most important metamorphic ore deposits are produced by contact metamorphism. Extensive aureoles of metal-rich deposits commonly surround igneous bodies where ions have invaded limestone strata. The most common metallic minerals associated with contact metamorphism are sphalerite (zinc), galena (lead), chalcopyrite (copper), magnetite (iron), and bornite (copper). Of equal economic importance

are the metamorphic rocks themselves. In many regions, slate, marble, and quartzite are quarried for a variety of construction purposes.

- Weathering creates ore deposits by concentrating minor amounts of metals into economically valuable deposits. The process, often called *secondary enrichment*, is accomplished by either (1) removing undesirable materials and leaving the desired elements enriched in the upper zones of the soil, or (2) removing and carrying the desirable elements to lower zones where they are redeposited and become more concentrated. Bauxite, the principal ore of aluminum, is one important ore created as a result of enrichment by weathering processes. In addition, many copper deposits result when weathering processes concentrate metals that were formerly dispersed through low-grade primary ore.
- Earth materials that are not used as fuels or processed for the metals they contain are referred to as *nonmetallic resources*. Many are sediments or sedimentary rocks. The two broad groups of nonmetallic resources are aggregate and stone and industrial minerals. Limestone, perhaps the most versatile and widely used rock of all, is found in both groups.
- *Renewable resources* can be replenished over relatively short spans. Examples include natural fibres for clothing and trees for lumber. *Non-renewable resources* form so slowly that, from our standpoint, Earth contains fixed supplies. Examples include fuels, such as oil and coal, and metals, such as copper and gold. A rapidly growing world population and the desire for an improved living standard cause non-renewable resources to become depleted at an increasing rate.
- Oil and natural gas, which commonly occur together in the pore spaces of some sedimentary rocks, consist of various hydrocarbon compounds (compounds made of hydrogen and carbon) mixed together. Petroleum formation is associated with the accumulation of sediment in ocean areas that are rich in plant and animal remains that become buried and isolated in an oxygen-deficient environment. As the mobile petroleum and natural gas form, they migrate and accumulate in adjacent permeable beds, such as sandstone. If their upward migration is halted by an impermeable rock layer, referred to as a *cap rock*, a *petroleum trap* develops that allows economically significant amounts of oil and gas to accumulate underground. The two basic conditions common to all petroleum traps are (1) a porous, permeable *reservoir rock* that will yield petroleum or natural gas in sufficient quantities, and (2) a cap rock.
- Coal, petroleum, and natural gas, the *fossil fuels* of our modern economy, are all associated with sedimentary rocks. Coal originates from large quantities of plant remains that accumulate in an oxygen-deficient environment, such as a swamp. Much of the present-day coal usage is for the generation of electricity. Air pollution produced by the sulphur oxide gases that form from burning most types of coal is a significant environmental problem.
- Environmental problems associated with burning fossil fuels include urban air pollution and global warming. The primary pollutants emitted by sources, such as motor vehicles, can react in the atmosphere to produce the secondary pollutants that make up urban smog. Combustion of fossil fuels is one of the ways that humans are increasing the atmosphere's carbon dioxide content. Greater quantities of this heat-absorbing gas contribute to global warming.
- When conventional petroleum resources are no longer adequate, fuels derived from tar sands and oil shale may become substitutes. Presently, tar sands in Alberta are the source of about 15 percent of Canada's oil production. Oil from oil shale is presently uneconomical to produce. Oil production from both tar sands and oil shale has significant environmental drawbacks.
- Much of our energy is derived from non-fossil fuels. *Hydroelectric power* provides 58 percent of Canada's electricity. Another important alternative energy source is *nuclear fission*. Other alternative energy sources are locally important but collectively provide little of the demand. These include solar power, *geothermal energy*, wind energy, and tidal power.

Review Questions

1. Contrast renewable and non-renewable resources. Give one or more examples of each.

2. What is the estimated world population for the year 2015? How does this compare with the figures for 1930 and 1975? Is demand for resources growing as rapidly as world population?

3. Most coal in Canada is used for what purpose?

4. Describe two impacts on the atmospheric environment of burning fossil fuels.
5. What is a petroleum trap? List two conditions common to all petroleum traps.
6. List two drawbacks associated with the processing of tar sands recovered by surface mining.
7. North America has huge oil shale deposits but does not produce oil shale commercially. Explain.
8. What is the main fuel for nuclear fission reactors?
9. List two obstacles that have hindered the development of nuclear power as a major energy source.
10. Briefly describe two methods by which solar energy might be used to produce electricity.
11. Explain why dams built to provide hydroelectricity do not last indefinitely.
12. Is geothermal power considered an inexhaustible energy source? Explain.
13. What advantages does tidal power production offer? Is it likely that tides will ever provide a significant proportion of the world's electrical energy requirements?
14. Contrast *resource* and *reserve*.
15. What might cause a mineral deposit that had not been considered an ore to be reclassified as an ore?
16. List two general types of hydrothermal deposits.
17. Metamorphic ore deposits are often related to igneous processes. Provide an example.
18. Name the primary ore of aluminum and describe its formation.
19. Briefly describe the way in which minerals accumulate in placers. List four minerals that are mined from such deposits.
20. Describe the effects of metal mining in Canada on the natural environment.
21. Nonmetallic resources are commonly divided into two broad groups. List the two groups and some examples of materials that belong to each. Which group is most widely distributed?

Key Terms

banded iron formation (p. 537)
cap rock (p. 547)
disseminated deposit (p. 534)
fossil fuel (p. 554)
geothermal energy (p. 564)
hydroelectric power (p. 562)
hydrothermal (hot-water) solution (p. 530)
industrial minerals (p. 527)
kimberlite (p. 542)
mineral resource (p. 525)
nonmetallic mineral resource (p. 541)
non-renewable resource (p. 527)
nuclear fission (p. 560)
ore (p. 527)
pegmatite (p. 530)
petroleum trap (p. 547)
placer (p. 539)
renewable resource (p. 525)
reserves (p. 527)
reservoir rock (p. 547)
resources (p. 525)
secondary enrichment (p. 540)
vein deposit (p. 531)

Web Resources

The *Earth* website uses the resources and flexibility of the internet to aid in your study of the topics in this chapter. Written and developed by geology instructors, this site will help improve your understanding of geology. Visit **www.pearsoned.ca/tarbuck** and click on the cover of the text to find

- online review quizzes
- Web-based critical thinking and writing exercises
- links to chapter-specific Web resources
- internet-wide key-term searches

www.pearsoned.ca/tarbuck

Glossary

Aa flow A type of lava flow that has a jagged, blocky surface.
Ablation A general term for the loss of ice and snow from a glacier.
Abrasion The grinding and scraping of a rock surface by the friction and impact of rock particles carried by water, wind, and ice.
Abyssal plain A very level area of the deep-ocean floor, usually lying at the foot of the continental rise.
Accretionary wedge A large wedge-shaped mass of sediment that accumulates in subduction zones. Sediment is scraped from the subducting oceanic plate and accreted to the overriding crustal block.

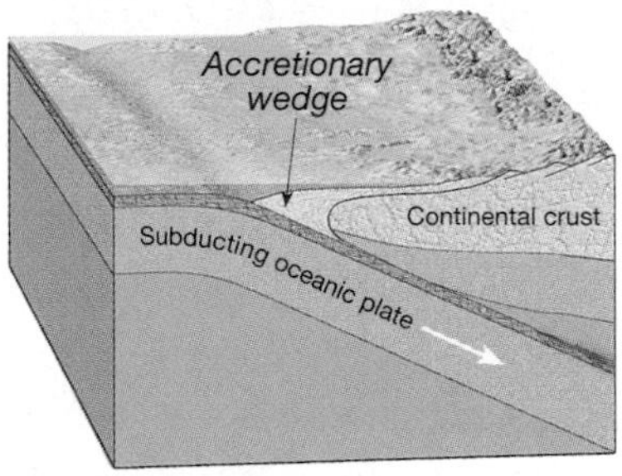

Active continental margin Usually narrow and consisting of highly deformed sediments. Such margins occur where oceanic lithosphere is being subducted beneath the margin of a continent.
Active layer The zone above the permafrost that thaws in summer and refreezes in winter.
Aftershock A smaller earthquake that follows the main earthquake.
Alluvial fan A fan-shaped deposit of sediment formed where a stream's slope abruptly reduces.

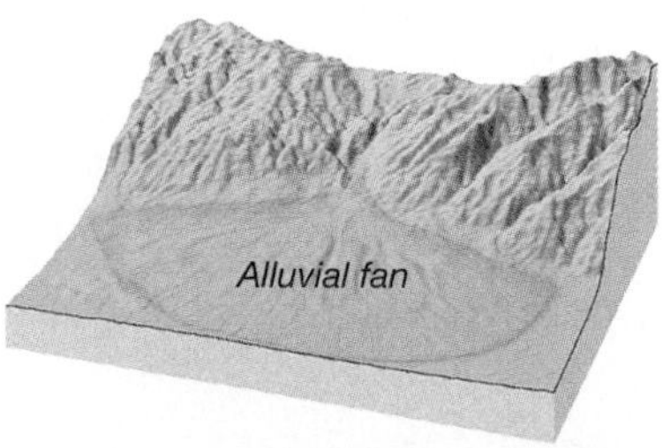

Alluvium The unconsolidated sediment deposited by a stream.
Alpine glacier A glacier confined to a mountain valley, which in most instances was previously a stream valley.
Anastomosed stream A stream with deep, interwoven, multiple channels separated by stable islands that are commonly heavily vegetated.
Andesitic composition See *Intermediate composition.*
Angle of repose The steepest angle at which loose material remains stationary without sliding downslope.
Angular unconformity An unconformity in which the older strata dip at an angle different from that of the younger beds.

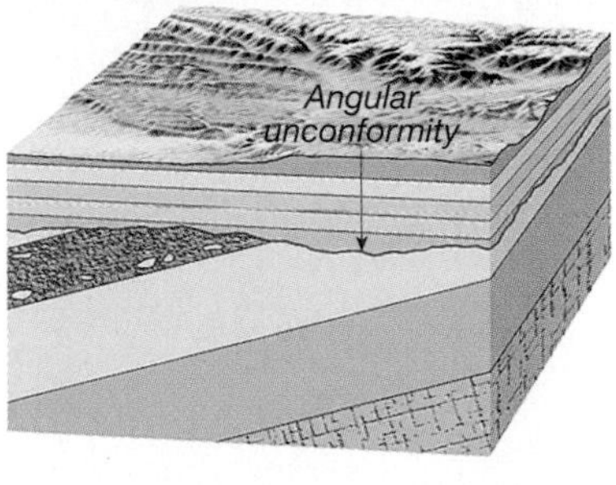

Anticline A fold in sedimentary strata that resembles an arch.

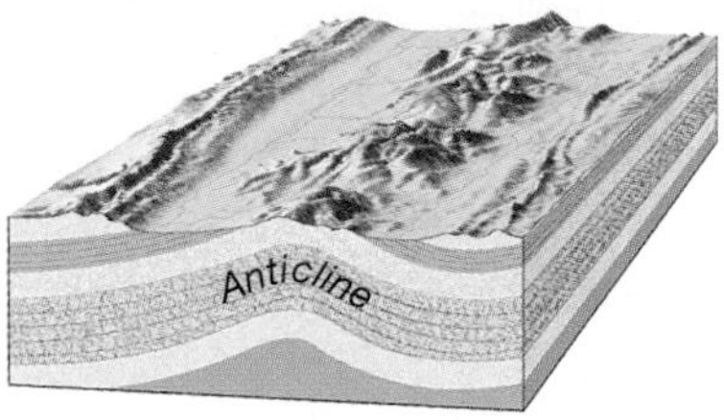

Aphanitic texture A texture of igneous rocks in which the crystals are too small for individual minerals to be distinguished without the aid of a microscope.
Aquifer The rock or sediment through which groundwater moves easily.
Aquitard An impermeable bed that hinders or prevents groundwater movement.
Archean Eon The second eon of Precambrian time. The eon following the Hadean and preceding the Proterozoic. It extends between approximately 3.8 billion and 2.5 billion years ago.
Arête A narrow, knifelike ridge separating two adjacent glaciated valleys.
Artesian well A well in which the water rises above the level where it was initially encountered.
Assimilation In igneous activity, the process of incorporating country rock into a magma body.
Asthenosphere A subdivision of the mantle situated below the lithosphere.
Atmosphere The gaseous portion of a planet; the planet's envelope of air. One of the traditional subdivisions of Earth's physical environment.
Atoll A coral island consisting of a nearly continuous ring of coral reef surrounding a central lagoon.

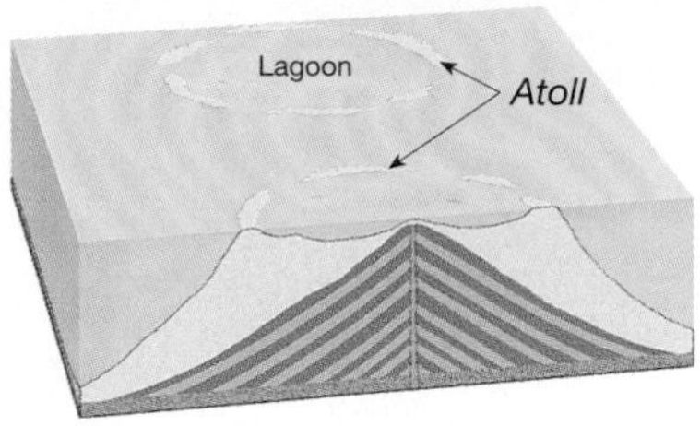

Atom The smallest particle that exists as an element.
Atomic number The number of protons in the nucleus of an atom.
Atomic weight The average of the atomic masses of the isotopes for a given element.
Aureole A zone or halo of contact metamorphism found in the country rock surrounding an igneous intrusion.

Back swamp A poorly drained area on a floodplain that results when natural levees are present.
Banded iron formation A chemical sedimentary rock consisting of alternating bands of iron oxide minerals and chert. Restricted to the Precambrian and most widespread in Proterozoic rock sequences.
Bank, stream The sides of a stream channel.
Bar A common term for sand and gravel deposits in a stream channel.
Barchan dune A solitary sand dune shaped like a crescent with its tips pointing downwind.

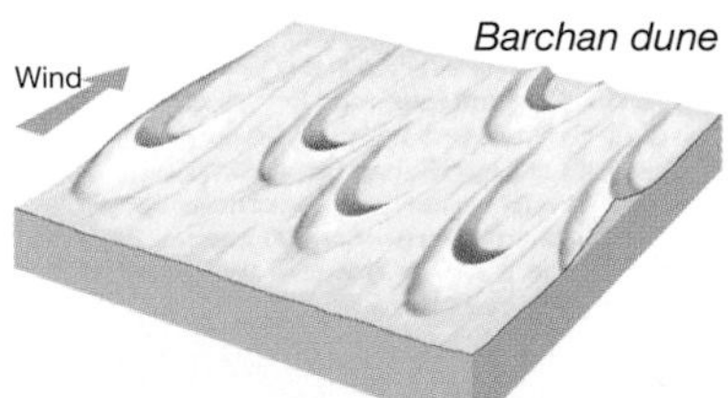

Barchanoid dune Dunes that form scalloped rows of sand oriented at right angles to the wind. This form is intermediate between isolated barchans and extensive waves of transverse dunes.
Barrier island A low, elongate ridge of sand that parallels the coast.

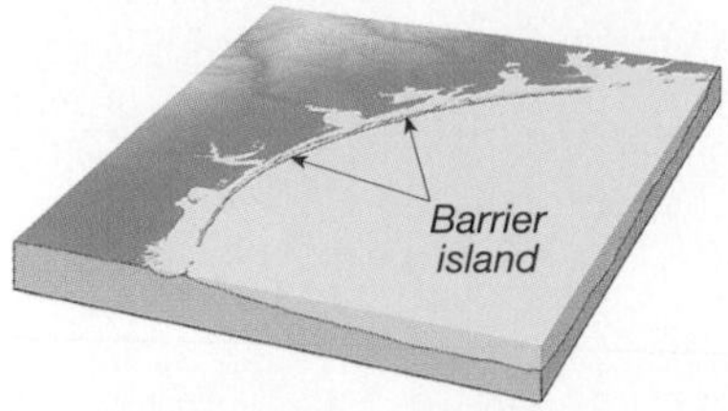

Basal slip A mechanism of glacial movement in which the ice mass slides over the wet surface below.
Basaltic composition See *Mafic composition*.
Base level The level below which a stream cannot erode.
Basin A circular downfolded structure.

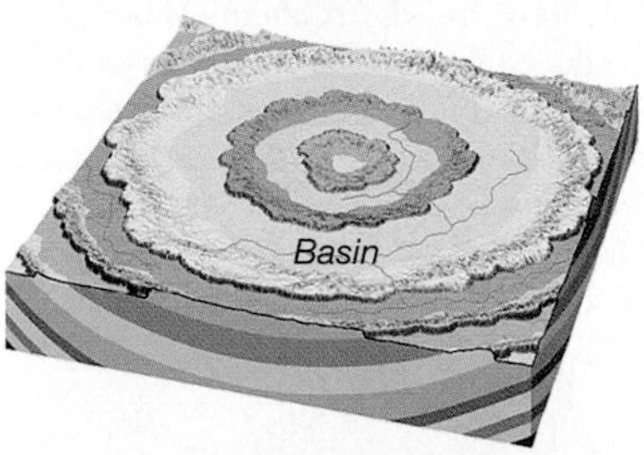

Batholith A large mass of igneous rock that formed when magma was emplaced at depth, crystallized, and subsequently exposed by erosion.
Baymouth bar A sandbar that completely crosses a bay, sealing it off from the main body of water.

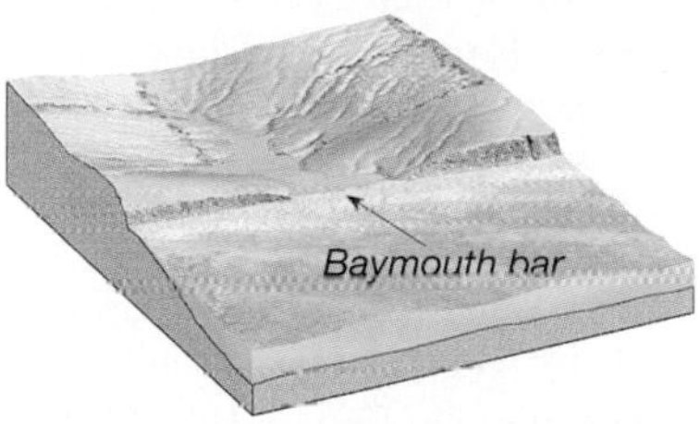

Beach drift The transport of sediment in a zigzag pattern along a beach, caused by the uprush of water from obliquely breaking waves.
Beach nourishment The process in which large quantities of sand are added to the beach system to offset losses caused by wave erosion. Building beaches seaward improves beach quality and storm protection.
Beds See *Strata*.
Bed load Sediment moved along the bottom of a stream by moving water, or particles moved along the ground surface by wind.
Bed, stream The bottom of a stream channel.
Bedding plane A nearly flat surface separating two beds of sedimentary rock. Each bedding plane marks the end of one deposit and the beginning of another having different characteristics.
Belt of soil moisture A zone in which water is held as a film on the surface of soil particles and can be used by plants or withdrawn by evaporation. The uppermost subdivision of the zone of aeration.
Biochemical A type of chemical sediment that forms when material dissolved in water is precipitated by water-dwelling organisms. Shells are common examples.
Bioclastic Term used when clastic particles are of biological origin.
Biogenous sediment Seafloor sediments consisting of material of marine-organic origin.
Biosphere The totality of life forms on Earth.
Blowout A depression excavated by wind in easily eroded materials.

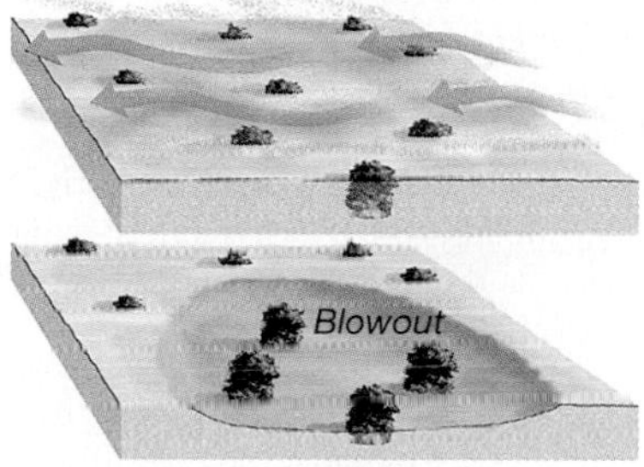

Body wave A seismic wave that travels through Earth's interior.
Bowen's reaction series A concept proposed by N. L. Bowen that illustrates the relationships between magma and the minerals crystallizing from it during the formation of igneous rocks.
Braided stream A stream consisting of numerous intertwining channels.
Breakwater A structure protecting a nearshore area from breaking waves.
Brittle deformation (failure) Deformation that involves the fracturing of rock. Associated with rocks near the surface.
Burial metamorphism Low-grade metamorphism that occurs in the lowest layers of very thick accumulations of sedimentary strata.

Caldera A large depression typically caused by collapse or ejection of the summit area of a volcano.

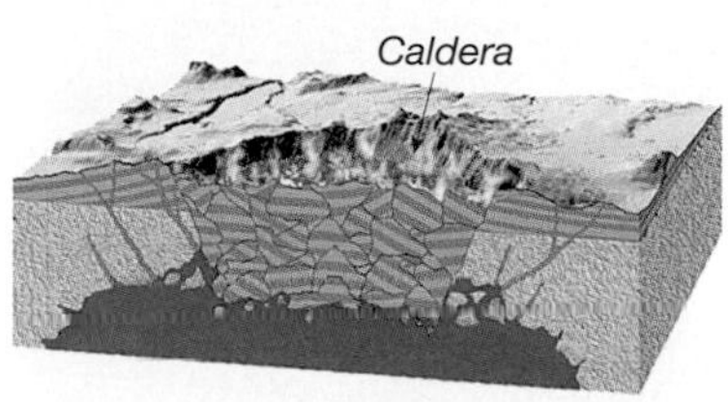

Caliche A hard layer, rich in calcium carbonate, that forms beneath the *B* horizon in soils of arid regions.
Calving Wastage of a glacier that occurs when large pieces of ice break into the water.
Capacity The total amount of sediment a stream is able to transport.
Capillary fringe A relatively narrow zone at the base of the zone of aeration. Water rises from the water table in tiny threadlike openings between grains of soil or sediment.
Cap rock A necessary part of an oil trap. The cap rock is impermeable and hence keeps upwardly mobile oil and gas from escaping at the surface.
Catastrophism The concept that Earth was shaped by catastrophic events of a short-term nature.
Cavern A naturally formed underground chamber or series of chambers most commonly produced by solution activity in limestone.
Cementation One way in which sedimentary rocks are lithified. As material precipitates from water that percolates through the sediment, open spaces are filled and particles are joined into a solid mass.
Cenozoic Era A span on the geologic time scale beginning about 65.5 million years ago, following the Mesozoic Era.
Channel, stream A natural passageway or depression of flowing water.
Chemically active fluid A fluid composed mainly of water but also containing chemical components that can react with the rock body through which the fluid penetrates.
Chemical sedimentary rock Sedimentary rock consisting of material that was precipitated from water by either inorganic or organic means.
Chemical weathering The processes by which the internal structure of a mineral is altered by the removal or addition of elements.
Cinder cone A rather small volcano built primarily of ejected lava fragments that consist mostly of pea- to walnut-size lapilli.

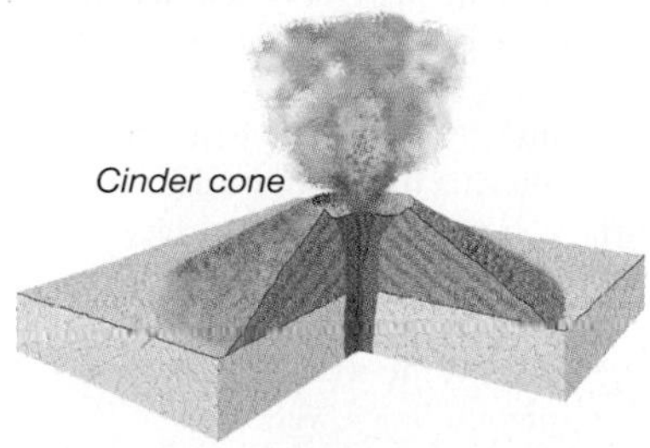

Cirque An amphitheatre-shaped basin at the head of a glaciated valley produced by frost wedging and plucking.
Clastic A sedimentary rock texture consisting of broken fragments of preexisting rock.

Cleavage The tendency of a mineral to break along planes of weak bonding.

Col A pass between mountain valleys where the headwalls of two cirques intersect.

Colour A phenomenon of light by which otherwise identical objects can be differentiated.

Columnar joints A pattern of cracks that form during cooling of molten rock to generate columns.

Compaction A type of lithification in which the weight of overlying material compresses more deeply buried sediment. It is most important in fine-grained sedimentary rocks, such as shale.

Competence A measure of the largest particle a stream can transport; a factor dependent on velocity.

Composite cone A volcano composed of both lava flows and pyroclastic material.

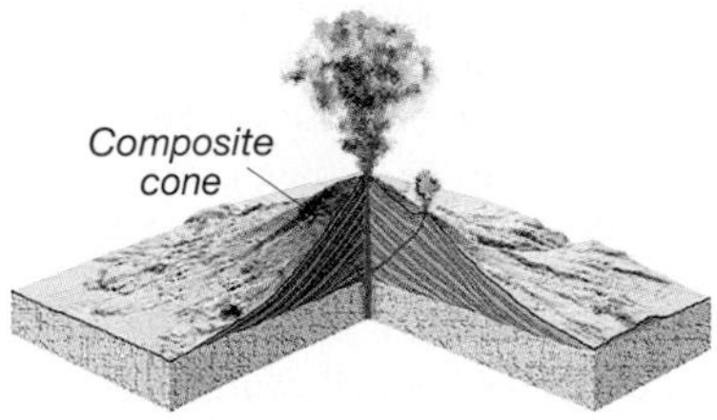

Compound A substance formed by the chemical combination of two or more elements in definite proportions and usually having properties different from those of its constituent elements.

Compressional stress The differential stress that shortens a rock body.

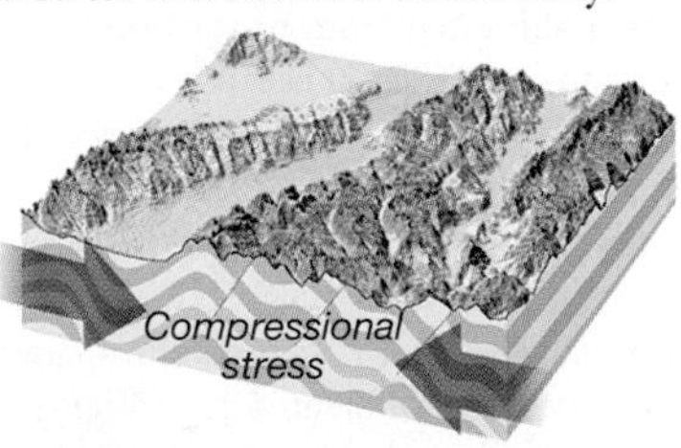

Concordant A term used to describe intrusive igneous masses that form parallel to the bedding of the surrounding rock.

Conduit A pipelike opening through which magma moves toward Earth's surface. It terminates at a surface opening called a vent.

Cone of depression A cone-shaped depression in the water table immediately surrounding a well.

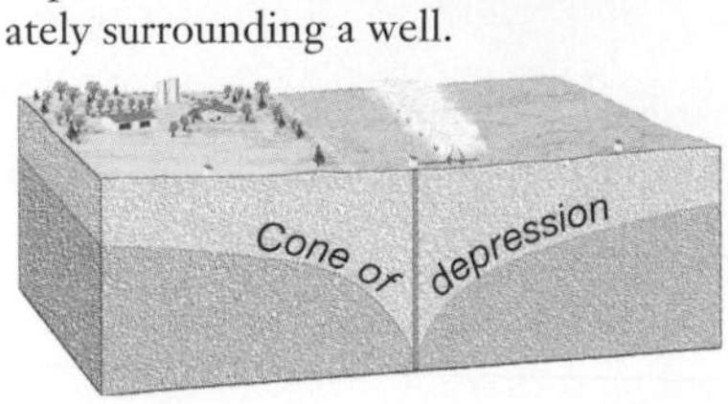

Confining pressure See *Uniform stress.*

Conformable layers Rock layers that were deposited without interruption.

Contact metamorphism The changes in rock caused by the heat from a nearby magma body.

Continental drift A hypothesis, credited largely to Alfred Wegener, that suggested all present continents once existed as a single supercontinent. Further, beginning about 200 million years ago, the supercontinent began breaking into smaller continents, which then drifted to their present positions.

Continental margin That portion of the seafloor adjacent to the continents. It may include the continental shelf, continental slope, and continental rise.

Continental rise The gently sloping surface at the base of the continental slope.

Continental shelf The gently sloping submerged portion of the continental margin, extending from the shoreline to the continental slope.

Continental slope The steep gradient that leads to the deep-ocean floor and marks the seaward edge of the continental shelf.

Continental volcanic arc Mountains formed in part by igneous activity associated with the subduction of oceanic lithosphere beneath a continent. Examples include the Andes and the Cascades.

Convection The transfer of heat by the mass movement or circulation of a substance.

Convergent plate boundary A boundary in which two plates move together, resulting in oceanic lithosphere being thrust beneath an overriding plate, eventually to be reabsorbed into the mantle. It can also involve the collision of two continental plates to create a mountain system.

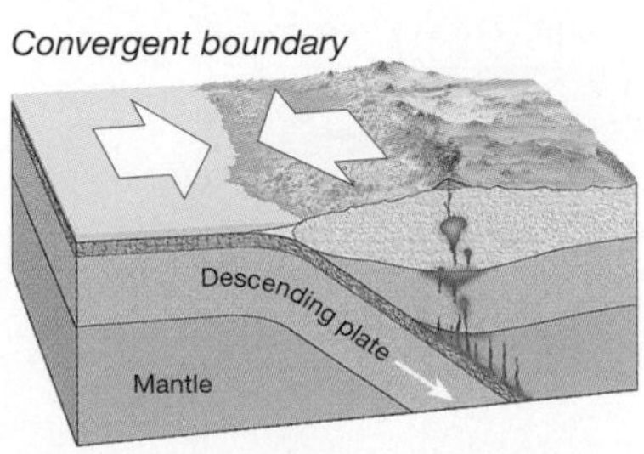

Coral reef A structure formed in a warm, shallow, sunlit ocean environment that consists primarily of the calcite-rich remains of corals as well as the limy secretions of algae and the hard parts of many other small organisms.

Core The innermost layer of Earth based on composition. It is thought to be largely an iron-nickel alloy with minor amounts of oxygen, silicon, and sulphur.

Correlation The equivalence of rocks of similar age in different areas.

Course, stream The path or route of a stream.

Covalent bond A chemical bond produced by the sharing of electrons.

Crater The depression at the summit of a volcano or one produced by a meteorite impact.

Creep The slow downhill movement of soil and regolith.

Crevasse A deep crack in the brittle surface of a glacier.

Cross-beds or cross-bedding A structure in which relatively thin layers are inclined at an angle to the main bedding. Formed by currents of wind or water.

Cross-cutting relations A principle of relative dating. A rock or fault is younger than any rock (or fault) through which it cuts.

Crust The very thin outermost layer of Earth.

Crystal form The external appearance of a mineral as determined by its internal arrangement of atoms.

Crystallization The formation and growth of a crystalline solid from a liquid or gas.

Crystal settling During the crystallization of magma, the earlier-formed minerals are denser than the liquid portion and settle to the bottom of the magma chamber.

Cut bank The area of active erosion on the outside of a meander.

Cutoff A short channel segment created when a river erodes through the narrow neck of land between meanders.

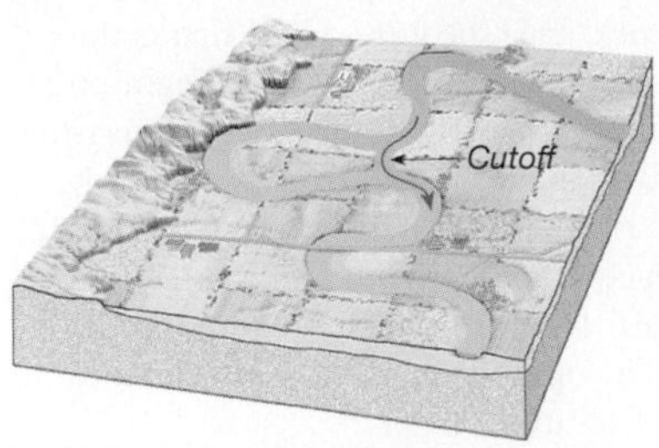

Darcy's law When permeability is uniform, the velocity of groundwater increases as the slope of the water table increases. It is expressed by the formula: $V = \frac{K}{n} \bullet \frac{h}{l}$, where V is velocity, n the porosity, h the head, l the length of flow, and K the coefficient of permeability.
Dark silicate Silicate minerals that contain ions of iron or magnesium (or both) in their structure. They are dark in colour and have a higher specific gravity than nonferromagnesian silicates.
Debris flow A flow of soil and regolith containing a large amount of water. Most common in mountainous regions and on the slopes of some volcanoes.
Decompression melting The melting that occurs because of a drop in confining pressure as rock ascends.
Deep-ocean basin The portion of seafloor that lies between the continental margin and the oceanic ridge system. This region composes almost 30 percent of Earth's surface.
Deep-sea fan A cone-shaped deposit at the base of the continental slope. The sediment is transported to the fan by turbidity currents that follow submarine canyons.
Deflation The lifting and removal of loose material by wind.
Deformation A general term for the processes of folding, faulting, shearing, compression, or extension of rocks as the result of various natural forces.
Delta An accumulation of sediment formed where a stream enters a lake or an ocean.

Dendritic pattern A stream system that resembles the pattern of a branching tree.

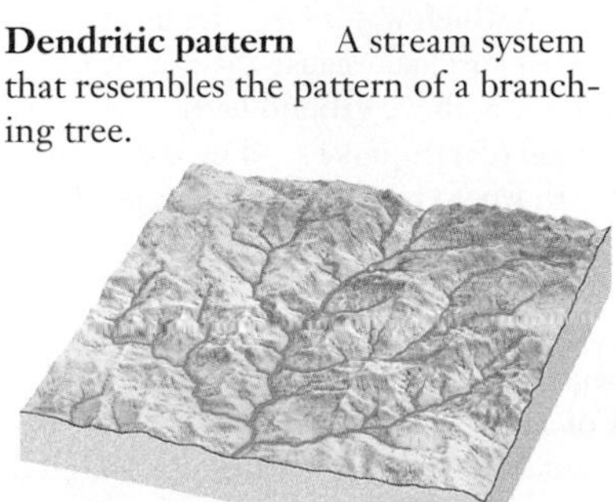

Dendritic pattern

Desert One of the two types of dry climate; the driest of the dry climates.
Desert pavement A layer of coarse pebbles and gravel created when wind removes the finer material.
Detrital sedimentary rocks Rocks that form from the accumulation of materials that originate and are transported as solid particles derived from both mechanical and chemical weathering.
Diagenesis A collective term for all the chemical, physical, and biologic changes that take place after sediments are deposited and during and after lithification.
Differential stress See *Directed pressure*.
Differential weathering The variation in the rate and degree of weathering caused by such factors as mineral makeup, degree of jointing, and climate.
Dip The angle at which a rock layer or fault is inclined from the horizontal. The direction of dip is at a right angle to the strike.
Dip-slip fault A fault in which the movement is parallel to the dip of the fault.
Directed pressure Forces that are unequal in different directions.
Discharge The quantity of water in a stream that passes a given point in an interval of time.
Disconformity A type of unconformity in which the beds above and below are parallel.
Discontinuity A sudden change with depth in one or more of the physical properties of the material making up Earth's interior. The boundary between two dissimilar materials in Earth's interior as determined by the behaviour of seismic waves.
Discordant A term used to describe plutons that cut across existing rock structures, such as bedding planes.
Disseminated deposit Any economic mineral deposit in which the desired mineral occurs as scattered particles in the rock but in sufficient quantity to make the deposit an ore.
Dissolution A common form of chemical weathering, it is the process of dissolving into a homogeneous solution, as when an acidic solution dissolves limestone.
Dissolved load That portion of a stream's load carried in solution.
Distributary A section of a stream that leaves the main flow.
Divergent plate boundary A boundary in which two plates move apart, resulting in upwelling of material from the mantle to create new seafloor.

Divergent boundary

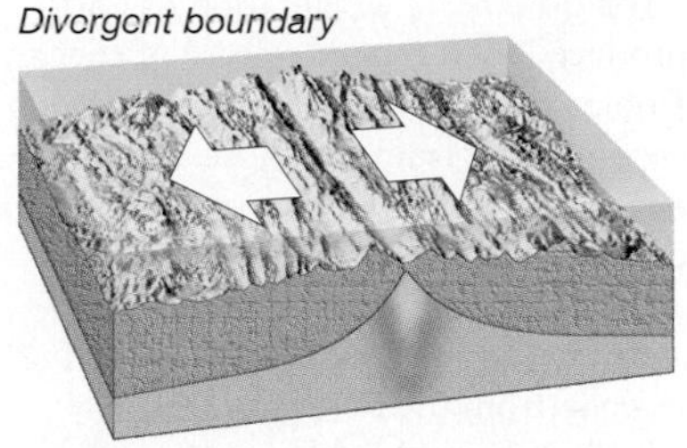

Divide An imaginary line that separates the drainage of two streams, often found along a ridge.

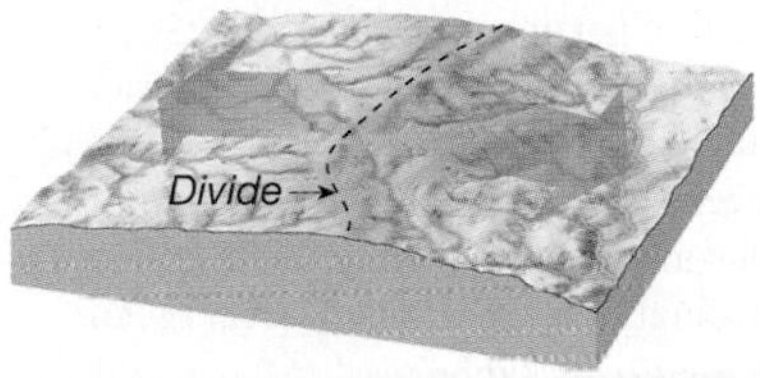

Dome A roughly circular upfolded structure.

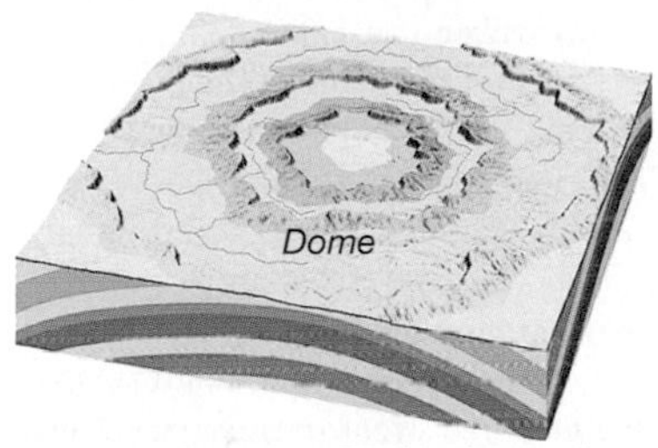

Drainage basin The land area that contributes water to a stream.
Drawdown The difference in height between the bottom of a cone of depression and the original height of the water table.
Drumlin A streamlined, symmetrical hill composed of till. The steep side of the hill faces the direction from which the ice advanced.
Ductile deformation A type of solid-state flow that produces a change in the size and shape of a rock body without fracturing. It occurs at depths where temperatures and confining pressures are high.
Dune A hill or ridge of wind-deposited sand.
Dyke A tabular-shaped intrusive igneous feature that cuts through the surrounding rock.

Earthflow The downslope movement of water-saturated, clay-rich sediment. It is most characteristic of humid regions.

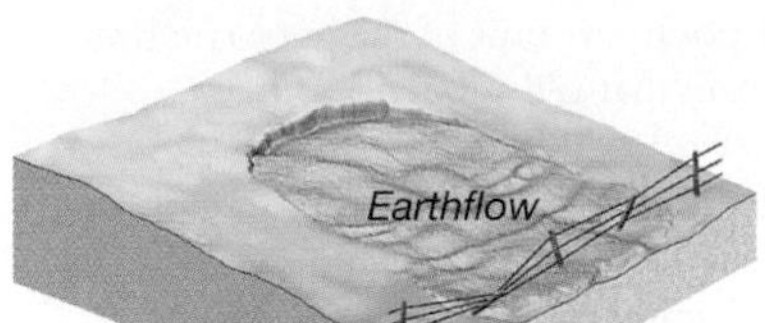

Earthquake The vibration of Earth produced by the rapid release of energy.
Ebb current The movement of tidal current away from the shore.
Echo sounder An instrument used to determine the depth of water by measuring the time interval between emission of a sound signal and the return of its echo from the bottom.
Elastic rebound The sudden release of stored strain in rocks that results in movement along a fault.
Electron A negatively charged subatomic particle that has a negligible mass and is found outside an atom's nucleus.
Element A substance that cannot be decomposed into simpler substances by ordinary chemical or physical means.
Eluviation The washing out of fine soil components from the *E* horizon by downward-percolating water.
End moraine A ridge of till marking a former position of the front of a glacier.
Energy levels The spherically shaped, negatively charged zones that surround the nucleus of an atom.
Environment of deposition A geographic setting where sediment accumulates. Each site is characterized by a particular combination of geologic processes and environmental conditions.
Eon The largest time unit on the geologic time scale, next in order of magnitude above an era.
Ephemeral stream A stream that is usually dry because it carries water only in response to specific episodes of rainfall. Most desert streams are of this type.
Epicentre The location on Earth's surface that lies directly above the focus of an earthquake.

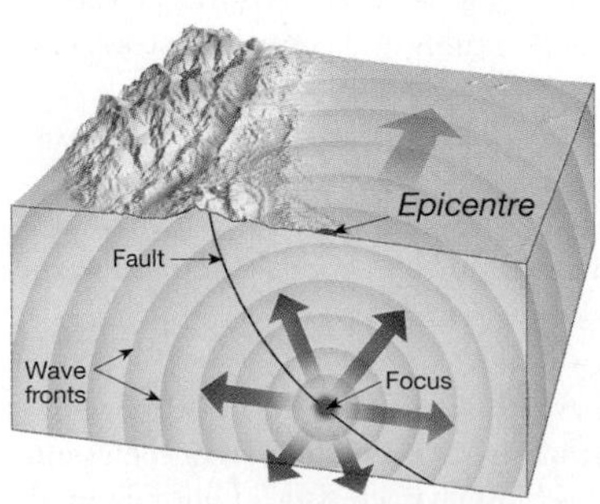

Epoch A unit of the geologic time scale that is a subdivision of a period.
Equilibrium line The boundary between net snow accumulation and wastage on a glacier.
Era A major division on the geologic time scale; eras are divided into shorter units called periods.
Erosion The incorporation and transportation of material by a mobile agent, such as water, wind, or ice.
Eruption column Buoyant plumes of hot, ash-laden gases that can extend thousands of metres into the atmosphere.
Esker A sinuous ridge composed largely of sand and gravel deposited by a stream flowing in a tunnel beneath a glacier near its terminus.
Estuary A funnel-shaped, tidally influenced inlet of the sea that formed when a rise in sea level or subsidence of land caused the mouth of a river to be flooded.

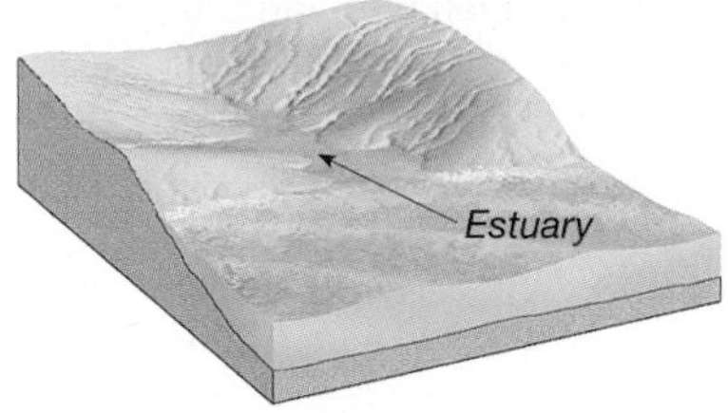

Evaporite A sedimentary rock formed of material deposited from solution by evaporation of the water.
Evapotranspiration The combined effect of evaporation and transpiration.
Exfoliation dome A large, dome-shaped structure, usually composed of granite, formed by sheeting.
External process A process, such as weathering, mass wasting, or erosion, that is powered by the Sun and contributes to the transformation of solid rock into sediment.
Extrusive The igneous activity that occurs at Earth's surface.

Fall A type of movement common to mass-wasting processes that refers to detached individual pieces of any size dropping through the air.
Fault A break in a rock mass along which movement has occurred.
Fault scarp A cliff created by movement along a fault. It represents the exposed surface of the fault before modification by weathering and erosion.
Felsenmeer A thin accumulation of angular blocks on bedrock where no steep slopes (sources) occur nearby.
Felsic composition A compositional group of igneous rocks indicating the rock is composed almost entirely of light-coloured silicates.
Ferromagnesian silicate See *Dark silicate*.
Fetch The distance that the wind has travelled across the open water.
Firn Granular re-crystallized snow. A transitional stage between snow and glacial ice.
Fissility The property of splitting easily into thin layers along closely spaced, parallel surfaces, such as bedding planes in shale.
Fissure A crack in rock along which there is a distinct separation.
Fissure eruption An eruption in which lava is extruded from narrow fractures or cracks in the crust.
Fjord A steep-sided inlet of the sea formed when a glacial trough was partially submerged.
Flood The overflow of a stream channel that occurs when discharge exceeds the channel's capacity. The most common and destructive geologic hazard.
Flood basalts The flows of basaltic lava that issue from numerous cracks or fissures and commonly cover extensive areas to thicknesses of hundreds of metres.
Flood current The tidal current associated with the increase in the height of the tide.
Floodplain The flat, low-lying portion of a stream valley subject to periodic inundation.

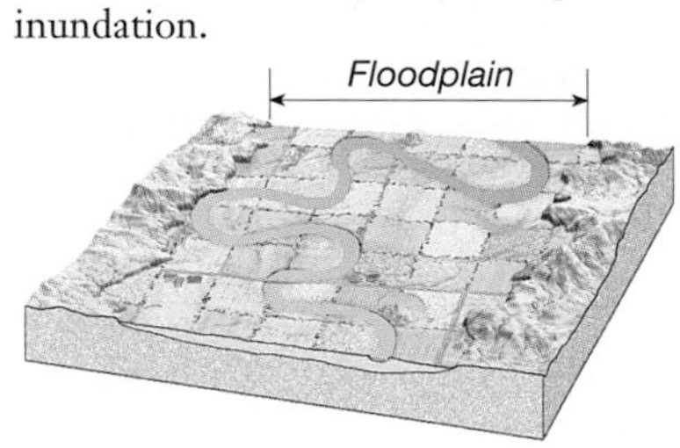

Flow A type of movement common to mass-wasting processes in which water-saturated material moves downslope as a viscous fluid. Also, internal movement of a glacier.
Flowing artesian well An artesian well in which water flows freely at Earth's surface because the pressure surface is above ground level.
Focus (earthquake) The zone within Earth where rock displacement produces an earthquake.
Fold A bent layer or a series of layers that were originally horizontal and subsequently deformed.
Foliation A term for a linear arrangement of textural features often exhibited by metamorphic rocks.
Force Any influence that tends to put stationary objects in motion or change the motion of moving bodies.

Foreshocks Small earthquakes that often precede a major earthquake.
Fossil The remains or traces of organisms preserved from the geologic past.
Fossil fuel A general term for any hydrocarbon that can be used as a fuel, including coal, oil, natural gas, bitumen from tar sands, and shale oil.
Fossil succession, principle of Fossil organisms succeed one another in a definite and determinable order, and any time period can be recognized by its fossil content.
Fracture Any break or rupture in rock along which no appreciable movement has taken place.
Fracture zone A linear zone of irregular topography on the deep-ocean floor that follows transform faults and their inactive extensions.
Fragmental texture See *Pyroclastic texture*.
Frost wedging The mechanical breakup of rock caused by the expansion of freezing water in cracks and crevices.

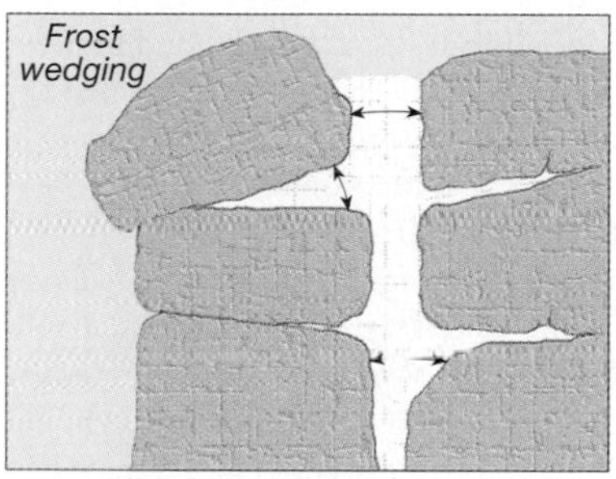

Fumarole A vent in a volcanic area from which fumes or gases escape.

Geologic time scale The division of Earth history into blocks of time: eons, eras, periods, and epochs. The time scale was created by using relative dating principles.
Geologist A person who is trained in and works in the geologic sciences.
Geology The science that examines Earth, its form and composition, and the changes that it has undergone and is undergoing.
Geothermal energy Natural steam used for power generation.
Geothermal gradient The gradual increase in temperature with depth in the crust. The average is 30°C per kilometre in the upper crust.
Geyser A fountain of hot water ejected periodically from the ground.
Glacial budget The balance, or lack of balance, between ice formation at the upper end of a glacier and ice loss in the zone of wastage.
Glacial drift An all-embracing term for sediments of glacial origin, no matter how, where, or in what shape they were deposited.
Glacial erratic An ice-transported boulder that was not derived from the bedrock near its present site.
Glacial striations The scratches and grooves on bedrock caused by glacial abrasion.
Glacial trough A mountain valley that has been widened, deepened, and straightened by a glacier.
Glacier A thick mass of ice originating on land from the compaction and re-crystallization of snow that shows evidence of past or present flow.
Glass (volcanic) The natural glass produced when molten lava cools too rapidly to permit re-crystallization. Volcanic glass is a solid composed of unordered atoms.
Glassy A term used to describe the texture of certain igneous rocks, such as obsidian, that contain no crystals.
Gneissic texture A texture of metamorphic rocks in which dark and light silicate minerals are separated, giving the rock a banded appearance.
Graben A valley formed by the downward displacement of a fault-bounded block.

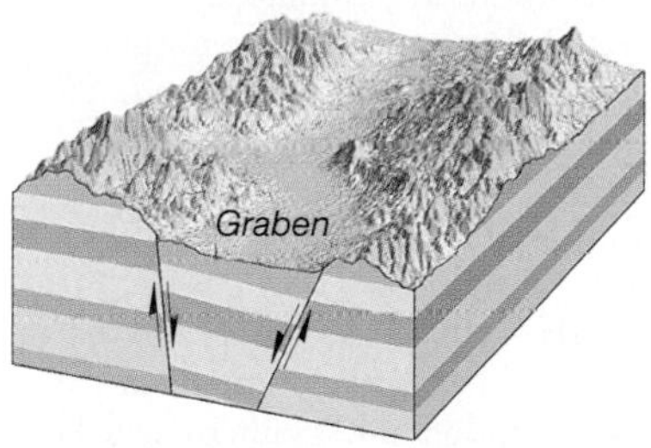

Graded bed or graded bedding A sediment layer characterized by a decrease in sediment size from bottom to top.
Graded stream A stream that has the correct channel characteristics to maintain exactly the velocity required to transport the material supplied to it.
Gradient The slope of a stream, generally expressed as the vertical drop over a fixed distance.
Granitic composition See *Felsic composition*.
Groin A short wall built at a right angle to the seashore to trap moving sand.

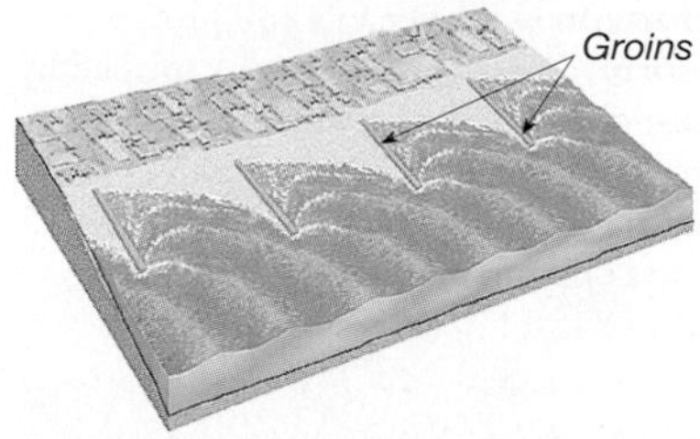

Groundmass The matrix of smaller crystals within an igneous rock that has porphyritic texture.
Ground moraine An undulating layer of till deposited as the ice front retreats.
Groundwater The water in the zone of saturation.
Guyot A submerged flat-topped seamount.

Hadean Eon The first eon on the geologic time scale. The eon ending approximately 3.8 billion years ago that preceded the Archean Eon.
Half-life The time required for one half of the atoms of a radioactive substance to decay.
Hanging valley A tributary valley that enters a glacial trough at a considerable height above the floor of the trough.

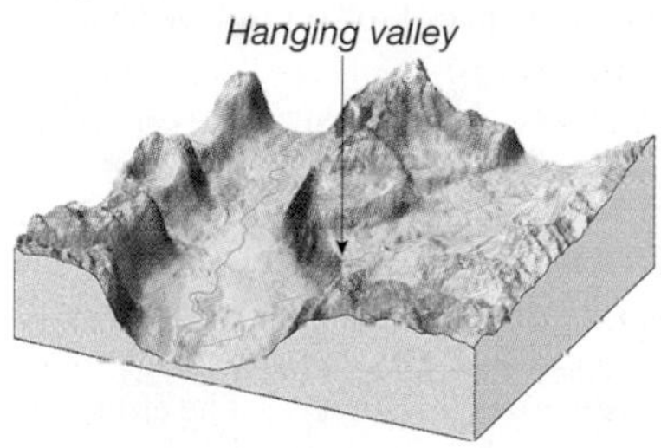

Hardness A mineral's resistance to scratching and abrasion.
Hardpan A general term for a relatively hard, impervious layer of sediment or soil just below the ground surface.
Hard stabilizers The structures built to protect a coast from erosion or to prevent the movement of sand along a beach.
Head (headwaters) The beginning or source area for a stream.
Headward erosion The extension upslope of the head of a valley because of erosion.
Historical geology A major division of geology that deals with the origin of Earth and its development through time. It usually involves the study of fossils and their sequence in rock beds.
Hogback A narrow, sharp-crested ridge formed by the upturned edge of a steeply dipping bed of resistant rock.

Horizon A layer in a soil profile.
Horn A pyramid-like peak formed by glacial action in three or more cirques surrounding a mountain summit.
Horst An elongate, uplifted block of crust bounded by faults.

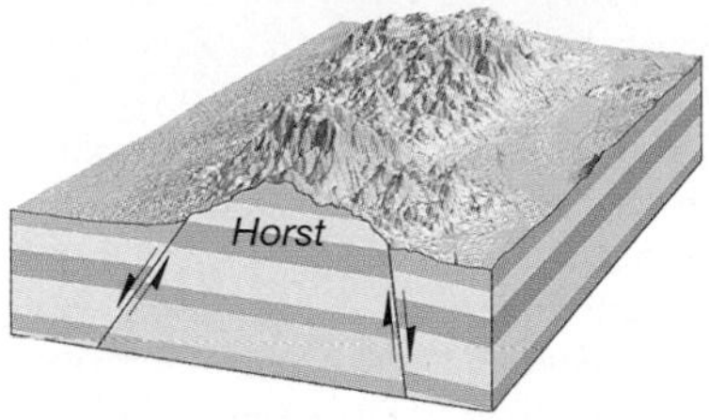

Hot spot A concentration of heat in the mantle capable of producing magma that, in turn, extrudes onto Earth's surface. The intraplate volcanism that produced the Hawaiian Islands is one example.
Hot spring A spring in which the water is 6°C to 9°C warmer than the mean annual air temperature of its locality.
Hummocky cross-stratification A sedimentary structure characterized by draped laminations that dip away from a central high (hummock). Hummocks are typically about 1 metre in diameter and are believed to be produced by storm waves.
Humus The organic matter in soil produced by the decomposition of plants and animals.
Hydraulic gradient The slope of the water table. Expressed as h/l, where h is the head and l the length of flow.
Hydroelectric power The electricity generated by falling water that is used to drive turbines.
Hydrogenous sediment Seafloor sediment consisting of minerals that crystallize from seawater. An important example is manganese nodules.
Hydrologic cycle The unending circulation of Earth's water supply. The cycle is powered by energy from the Sun and is characterized by continuous exchanges of water among the oceans, the atmosphere, and the continents.
Hydrolysis A chemical weathering process in which minerals are altered by chemically reacting with water and acids.
Hydrosphere The water portion of our planet; one of the traditional subdivisions of Earth's physical environment.
Hydrothermal (hot-water) solution The hot, watery solution that escapes from a mass of magma during the later stages of crystallization. Such solutions can alter the surrounding country rock and are commonly the source of ore deposits.

Ice cap A mass of glacial ice covering a high upland or plateau and spreading out radially.
Ice sheet A very large, thick mass of glacial ice flowing outward in all directions from one or more accumulation centres.
Ice-contact deposit An accumulation of stratified drift deposited in contact with a supporting mass of ice.
Ice shelf Forming where glacial ice flows into bays, it is a large, relatively flat mass of floating ice that extends seaward from the coast but remains attached to the land along one or more sides.
Ice stream A zone of ice within an ice sheet or ice cap that flows more rapidly than the surrounding ice; it is usually not constrained by exposed bedrock.
Igneous rock Rock formed from the crystallization of magma.
Inclusion A piece of one rock unit contained within another. Inclusions are used in relative dating. The rock mass adjacent to the one containing the inclusion must have been there first in order to provide the fragment.
Index fossil A fossil that is associated with a particular span of geologic time.
Index mineral A mineral that is a good indicator of the metamorphic environment in which it formed. It is used to distinguish different zones of regional metamorphism.
Industrial minerals Useful nonmetallic resources.
Inertia Objects at rest tend to remain at rest, and objects in motion tend to stay in motion unless either is acted on by an outside force.
Infiltration The movement of surface water into rock or soil through cracks and pore spaces.
Infiltration capacity The maximum rate at which soil can absorb water.
Inner core The solid innermost layer of Earth, about 1216 kilometres in radius.

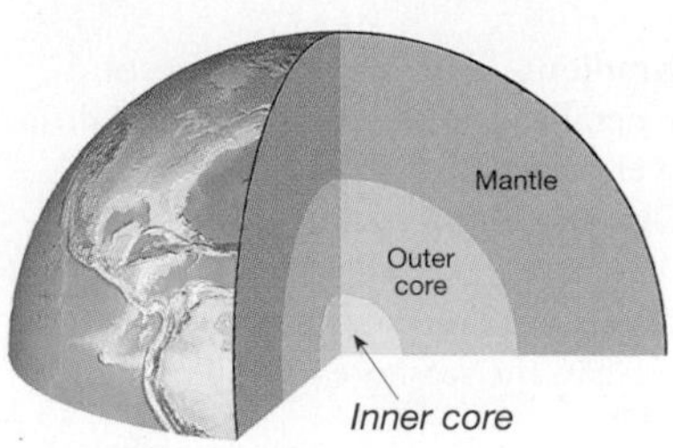

Intensity (earthquake) A measure of the degree of earthquake shaking at a given locale based on the amount of damage.
Intermediate composition A compositional group of igneous rocks, indicating that the rock contains at least 25 percent dark silicate minerals. The other dominant mineral is plagioclase feldspar.
Internal deformation The recrystallization and ductile flow of ice within a glacier.
Internal process A process, such as mountain building or volcanism, that derives its energy from Earth's interior and elevates Earth's surface.
Intrachannel bar A sand and gravel bar between channels of a stream.
Intraplate volcanism The igneous activity that occurs within a tectonic plate away from plate boundaries.
Intrusive rock The igneous rock that formed below Earth's surface.
Ion An atom or a molecule that possesses an electrical charge.
Ionic bond A chemical bond between two oppositely charged ions formed by the transfer of valence electrons from one atom to the other.
Isostasy The concept that Earth's crust is floating in gravitational balance on the material of the mantle.
Isotatic adjustment The compensation of the lithosphere when weight is added or removed. When weight is added, the lithosphere will respond by subsiding, and when weight is removed, there will be uplift.
Isotopes The varieties of the same element that have different mass numbers; their nuclei contain the same number of protons but different numbers of neutrons.

Jetties A pair of structures extending into the ocean at the entrance to a harbour or river that are built for the purpose of protecting against storm waves and sediment deposition.

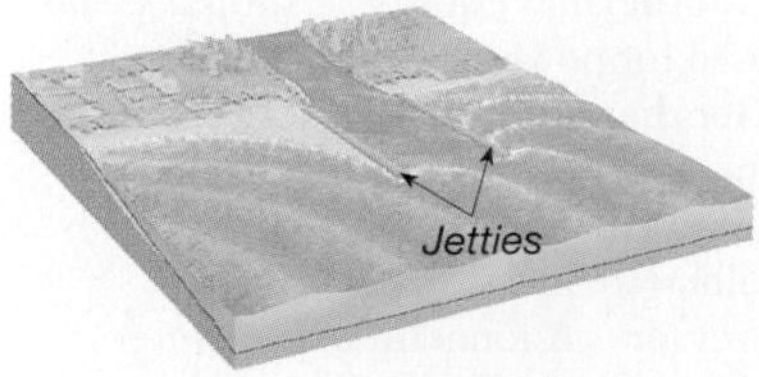

Joint A fracture in rock along which there has been no movement.

Kame A steep-sided hill composed of sand and gravel, originating when sediment collected in openings in stagnant glacial ice.
Kame terrace A narrow, terrace-like mass of stratified drift deposited between a glacier and an adjacent valley wall.
Karst topography A type of topography formed on soluble rock (especially limestone) primarily by dissolution. It is characterized by sinkholes, caves, and underground drainage.
Kettles The depressions created when blocks of ice become lodged in glacial deposits and subsequently melt.
Kimberlite A rare ultramafic rock that commonly contains diamonds.
Klippe A remnant or an outlier of a thrust sheet that was isolated by erosion.

Laccolith A massive igneous body intruded between preexisting strata.

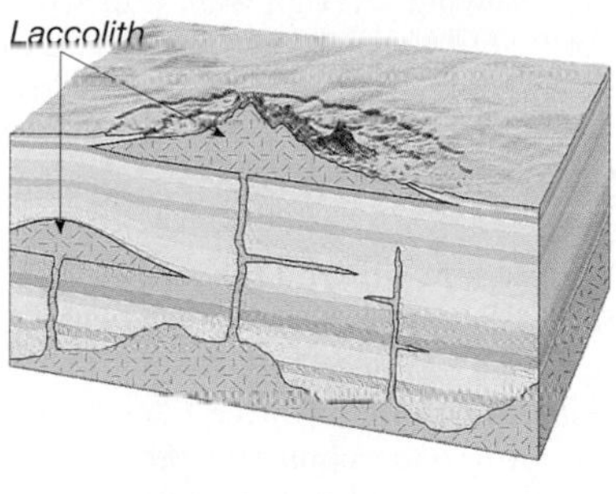

Lahar The debris flows on the slopes of volcanoes that result when unstable layers of ash and debris become saturated and flow downslope, usually following stream channels.
Laminar flow The movement of water particles in straight paths that are parallel to the channel. The water particles move downstream without mixing.
Lateral accretion surfaces Gently dipping sedimentary structures preserved within point bar deposits of meandering streams. These surfaces mark former positions of an accreting point bar.
Lateral moraine A ridge of till along the sides of a valley glacier composed primarily of debris that fell to the glacier from the valley walls.
Laterite A red, highly leached soil type found in the tropics that is rich in oxides of iron and aluminum.
Lava The magma that reaches Earth's surface.
Lava dome A bulbous mass associated with an old-age volcano, produced when thick lava is slowly squeezed from the vent. Lava domes can act as plugs to deflect subsequent gaseous eruptions.

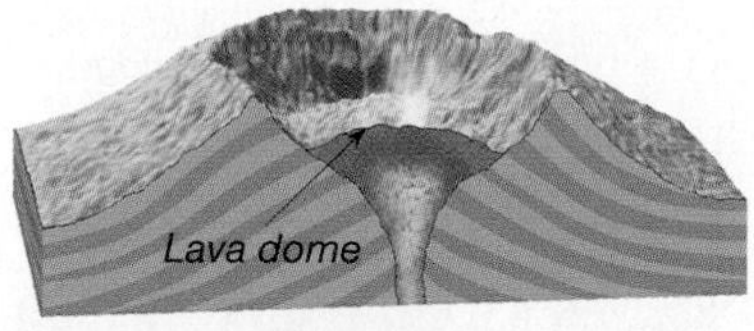

Lava tube A tunnel in hardened lava that acts as a horizontal conduit for lava flowing from a volcanic vent. Lava tubes allow fluid lavas to advance great distances.
Leaching The depletion of soluble materials from the upper soil by downward-percolating water.
Light silicates Silicate minerals that lack iron or magnesium. They are generally lighter in colour and have lower specific gravities than dark silicates.
Liquefaction The transformation of a stable soil into a fluid that is often unable to support buildings or other structures.
Lithification The process, generally cementation or compaction, of converting sediments to solid rock.
Lithosphere The rigid outer layer of Earth, including the crust and upper mantle.

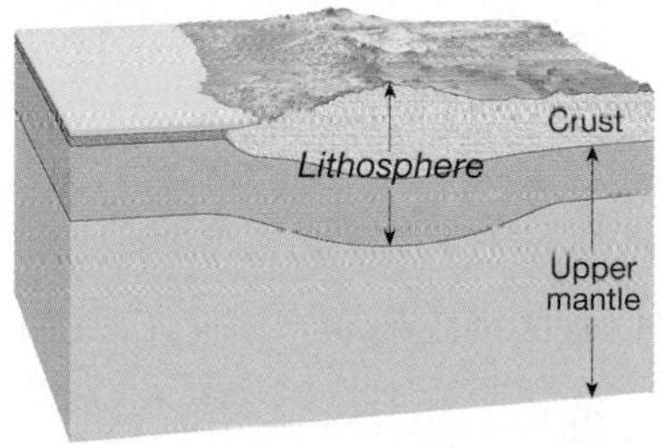

Local base level See *Temporary base level.*
Loess The deposits of windblown silt that lack visible layers, are generally buff-coloured, and are capable of maintaining a nearly vertical cliff.
Longitudinal dunes Long ridges of sand oriented parallel to the prevailing wind; these dunes form where sand supplies are limited.

Longitudinal profile A cross-section of a stream channel along its descending course from the head to the mouth.
Long (L) waves These earthquake-generated waves travel along the outer layer of Earth and are responsible for most of the surface damage. L waves have longer periods than other seismic waves.
Longshore current A nearshore current that flows parallel to the shore.
Lower mantle See *Mesosphere.*
Lustre The appearance or quality of light reflected from the surface of a mineral.

Mafic composition A compositional group of igneous rocks indicating that the rock contains substantial dark silicate minerals and calcium-rich plagioclase feldspar.
Magma A body of molten rock found at depth, including any dissolved gases and crystals.
Magma mixing The process of altering the composition of a magma through the mixing of material from another magma body.
Magmatic differentiation The process of generating more than one rock type from a single magma.
Magnetometer A sensitive instrument used to measure the intensity of Earth's magnetic field at various points.
Magnitude (earthquake) An estimate of the total amount of energy released during an earthquake, based on seismic records.
Manganese nodules A type of hydrogenous sediment scattered on the ocean floor, consisting mainly of manganese and iron and usually containing small amounts of copper, nickel, and cobalt.
Mantle One of Earth's compositional layers. The solid rocky shell that extends from the base of the crust to a depth of 2900 kilometres.
Mantle plume A mass of hotter than normal mantle material that ascends toward the surface, where it may lead to igneous activity. These plumes of solid yet mobile material may originate as deep as the core-mantle boundary.
Mass balance The difference between gain (accumulation) and loss (ablation) of ice in a glacier, determined as a change of mass over some time interval.
Massive An igneous pluton that is not tabular in shape.
Mass number The sum of the number of neutrons and protons in the nucleus of an atom.
Mass wasting The downslope movement of rock, regolith, and soil under the direct influence of gravity.

Meander A looplike bend in the course of a stream.

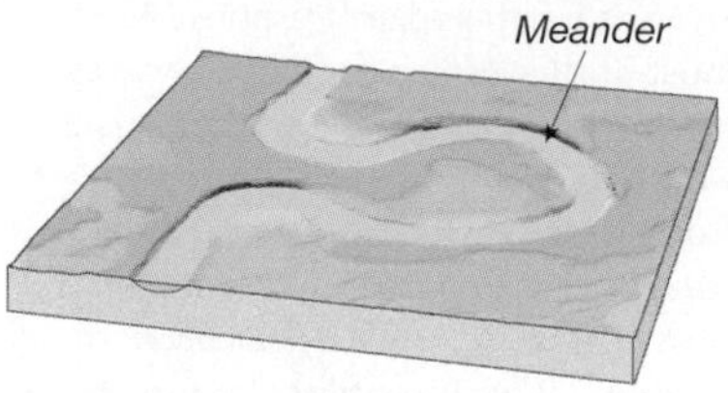

Meander scar A floodplain feature created when an oxbow lake becomes filled with sediment.

Mechanical weathering The physical disintegration of rock, resulting in smaller fragments.

Medial moraine A ridge of till formed when lateral moraines join from two coalescing alpine glaciers.

Melt The liquid portion of magma excluding the solid crystals.

Mesosphere The part of the mantle that extends from the core–mantle boundary to a depth of 2900 kilometres. It is also known as the lower mantle.

Mesozoic Era A time span on the geologic time scale between the Paleozoic and Cenozoic Eras—from about 251 million to 65.5 million years ago.

Metallic bond A chemical bond present in all metals that can be characterized as an extreme type of electron sharing in which the electrons move freely from atom to atom.

Metamorphic facies A distinctive assemblage of minerals that can be used to designate a particular set of metamorphic environmental conditions recorded in a metamorphic rock.

Metamorphic grade The intensity of metamorphism as measured by the degree of difference between the original rock and the metamorphic rock.

Metamorphic rock Rock formed by the alteration of preexisting rock deep within Earth (but still in the solid state) by heat, pressure, or chemically active fluids.

Metamorphism The changes in mineral composition and texture of a rock subjected to high temperatures and pressures within Earth.

Mid-ocean ridge A continuous mountainous ridge on the floor of all the major ocean basins and varying in width from 500 to 5000 kilometres. The rifts at the crests of these ridges represent divergent plate boundaries.

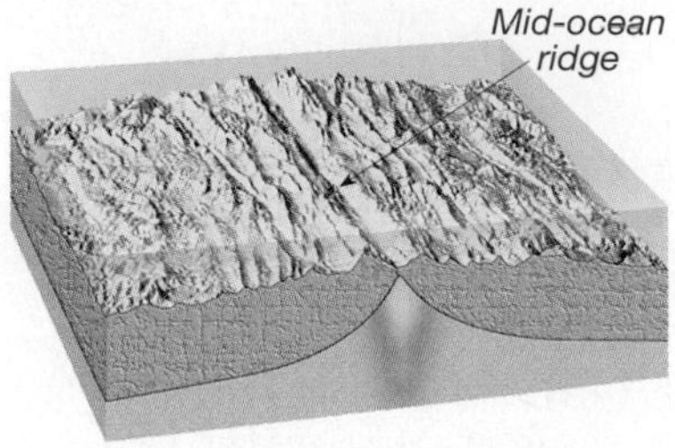

Migmatite A rock exhibiting both igneous and metamorphic rock characteristics. Such rocks can form when light-coloured silicate minerals melt and then crystallize while the dark silicate minerals remain solid.

Mineral A naturally occurring, inorganic crystalline material with a unique chemical structure.

Mineralogy The study of minerals.

Mineral resource All discovered and undiscovered deposits of a useful mineral that can be extracted now or in the future.

Modified Mercalli Intensity Scale A 12-point scale developed to evaluate earthquake intensity based on the amount of damage to various structures.

Mohorovičić discontinuity (Moho) The boundary separating the crust and the mantle, discernible by an increase in seismic velocity.

Mohs scale A series of 10 minerals used as a standard in determining hardness.

Moment magnitude A more precise measure of earthquake magnitude than the Richter scale that is derived from the amount of displacement that occurs along a fault zone.

Monocline A one-limbed flexure in strata. The strata are usually flat-lying or very gently dipping on both sides of the monocline.

Mountain A landform with an obvious peak that rises significantly above the land surrounding it, generally about 300 metres or more.

Mountain belt A regionally extensive group of mountains composed of multiple mountain ranges.

Mountain range A linked series of mountains.

Mouth The point downstream where a river empties into another stream or water body.

Mud crack A feature in some sedimentary rocks that forms when wet mud dries out, shrinks, and cracks.

Natural levee An elevated landform composed of alluvium that parallels some streams and acts to confine their waters, except during floodstage.

Neap tide The lowest tidal range, occurring near the times of the first and third quarters of the Moon.

Nebular hypothesis A model for the origin of the solar system that supposes a rotating nebula of dust and gases that contracted to form the Sun and planets.

Neutron A subatomic particle found in the nucleus of an atom. The neutron is electrically neutral, with a mass approximately equal to that of a proton.

Nonclastic A term for the texture of sedimentary rocks in which the minerals form a pattern of interlocking crystals.

Nonconformity An unconformity in which older metamorphic or intrusive igneous rocks are overlain by younger sedimentary strata.

Nonferromagnesian silicates See *Light silicates*.

Non-flowing artesian well An artesian well in which water does not rise to the surface, because the pressure surface is below ground level.

Nonfoliated Metamorphic rocks that do not exhibit foliation.

Nonmetallic mineral resource A mineral resource that is not a fuel or processed for the metals it contains.

Non-renewable resource A resource that forms or accumulates over such long time spans that it must be considered as fixed in total quantity.

Normal fault A fault in which the rock above the fault plane has moved down relative to the rock below.

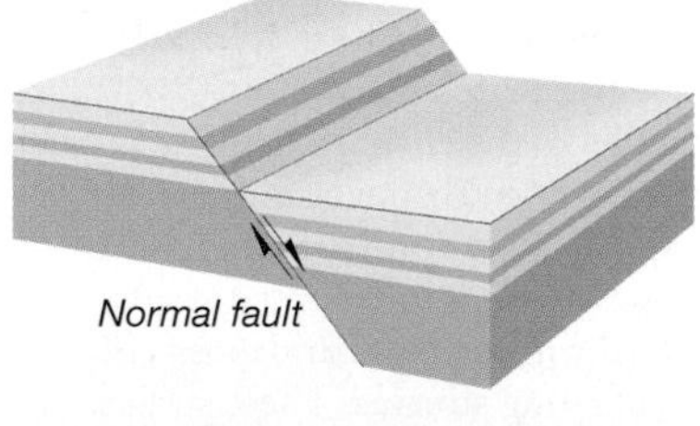

Normal polarity A magnetic field the same as the one that presently exists.

Nuclear fission The splitting of atomic nuclei into smaller nuclei, causing neutrons to be emitted and heat energy to be released.

Nucleus The small, heavy core of an atom that contains all of its positive charge and most of its mass.

Nuée ardente Incandescent volcanic debris buoyed up by hot gases that moves downslope in an avalanche fashion.

Numeric date The number of years that have passed since an event occurred.

Oceanic ridge See *Mid-ocean ridge*.

Octet rule The order in which atoms combine so that each can have the electron arrangement of a noble gas; that is, the outer energy level contains eight neutrons.

Ophiolite complex The sequence of rocks that make up the oceanic crust. The three-layer sequence includes an upper layer of pillow basalts, a middle zone of sheeted dykes, and a lower layer of gabbro.

Ore A useful metallic mineral that can be mined at a profit. The term is also applied to certain nonmetallic minerals, such as fluorite and sulphur.

Original horizontality, principle of The layers of sediment that are generally deposited in a horizontal or nearly horizontal position.

Orogenesis The processes that collectively result in the formation of mountains.

Outcrops The bedrock exposed at the ground surface.

Outer core A layer beneath the mantle about 2270 kilometres thick, which has the properties of a liquid.

Outlet glacier A tongue of ice normally flowing rapidly outward from an ice cap or ice sheet, usually through mountainous terrain to the sea.

Outwash plain A relatively flat, gently sloping plain consisting of materials deposited by meltwater streams in front of the margin of an ice sheet.

Oxbow lake A curved lake produced when a stream cuts off a meander.

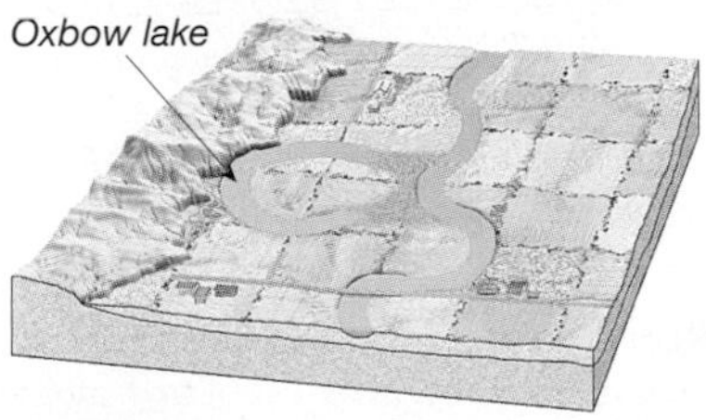

Oxidation The removal of one or more electrons from an atom or ion. So named because elements commonly combine with oxygen.

Pahoehoe flow A lava flow with a smooth to ropy surface.

Paleomagnetism The natural remnant magnetism in rock bodies. The permanent magnetization acquired by rock that can be used to determine the location of the magnetic poles at the time the rock became magnetized.

Paleozoic Era A time span on the geologic time scale between the Precambrian and Mesozoic Eras, from about 542 million to 251 million years ago.

Palsa A domelike frost mound of peat with ice lenses, commonly found in the Arctic.

Pangaea The proposed supercontinent that 200 million years ago began to break apart and form the present landmasses.

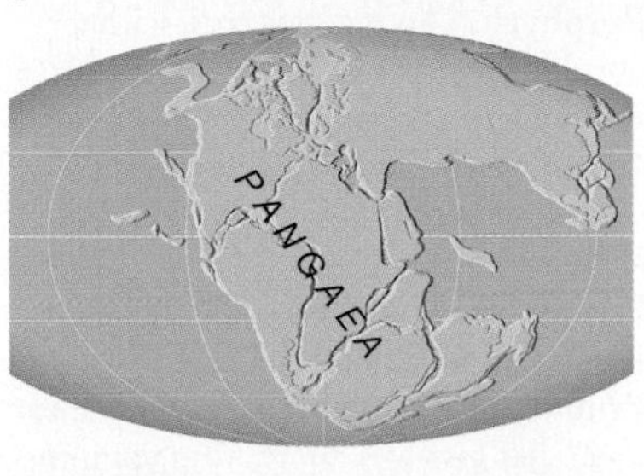

Parabolic dune A sand dune similar in shape to a barchan dune except that its tips point into the wind. These dunes often form along coasts that have strong onshore winds, abundant sand, and vegetation that partly covers the sand.

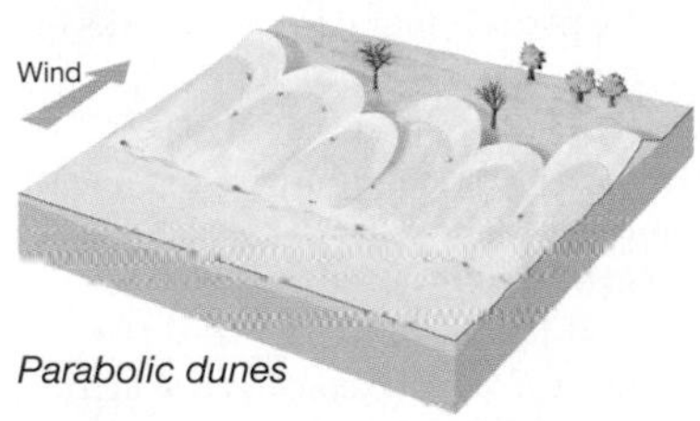

Parabolic dunes

Paradigm A theory that is held with a very high degree of confidence and is comprehensive in scope.

Parasitic cone A volcanic cone that forms on the flank of a larger volcano.

Parent material The material on which a soil develops.

Parent rock The rock from which a metamorphic rock formed.

Partial melting The process by which most igneous rocks melt. Because individual minerals have different melting points, most igneous rocks melt over a temperature range of a few hundred degrees. If the liquid is squeezed out after some melting has occurred, a melt with a higher silica content results.

Passive continental margin or passive margin A margin that consists of a continental shelf, continental slope, and continental rise. It is not associated with plate boundaries and therefore experiences little volcanism and few earthquakes.

Patterned ground The general term for circles, polygons, nets, and stripes in surface material subjected to intense frost action (e.g., frost wedging and heaving). It is common in polar regions.

Pedalfer The soil of humid regions characterized by the accumulation of iron oxides and aluminum-rich clays in the *B* horizon.

Pedocal The soil associated with drier regions and characterized by an accumulation of calcium carbonate in the upper horizons.

Pegmatite A very coarse-grained igneous rock (typically granite) commonly found as a dyke associated with a large mass of plutonic rock that has smaller crystals. Crystallization in a water-rich environment is believed to be responsible for the very large crystals.

Pegmatitic texture A texture of igneous rocks in which the interlocking crystals are all larger than 1 centimetre in diameter.

Perched water table A localized zone of saturation above the main water table, created by an impermeable layer.

Periglacial An environment in which frost action is the main process shaping the landscape.

Period A basic unit of the geologic time scale that is a subdivision of an era. Periods can be divided into smaller units called epochs.

Permafrost Any permanently frozen subsoil. It is usually found in the sub-Arctic and Arctic regions.

Permeability A measure of a material's ability to transmit water.

Petroleum trap A geologic structure that allows for significant amounts of oil and gas to accumulate.

Phaneritic texture An igneous rock texture in which the crystals are roughly equal in size and large enough so the individual minerals can be identified without the aid of a microscope.

Phanerozoic Eon That part of geologic time represented by rocks that contain abundant fossil evidence. The eon extending from the end of the Proterozoic Eon (542 million years ago) to the present.

Phenocryst A conspicuously large crystal embedded in a matrix of finer-grained crystals.

Physical geology A major division of geology that examines the materials of Earth and seeks to understand the processes and forces acting beneath and on Earth's surface.

Piedmont glacier A glacier that forms when one or more alpine glaciers emerge from the confining walls of mountain valleys and spread out to create a broad sheet in the lowlands at the base of the mountains.

Pillow lava Basaltic lava that solidifies in an underwater environment and develops a structure that resembles a pile of pillows.
Pingo A large conical mound of soil-covered ice raised mainly by water pressure within or below permafrost in Arctic regions.
Pipe A vertical conduit through which magmatic materials have passed.
Placer A deposit formed when heavy minerals are mechanically concentrated by currents, most commonly streams and waves. Placers are sources of gold, tin, platinum, diamonds, and other valuable minerals.
Plate One of numerous rigid sections of the lithosphere that moves as a unit over the material of the asthenosphere.
Plate tectonics The theory that proposes that Earth's outer shell consists of individual plates that interact in various ways and thereby produce earthquakes, volcanoes, mountains, and the crust itself.
Playfair's law A well-known and oft-quoted statement by John Playfair that states that a valley is the result of the work of the stream that flows in it.
Plucking The process by which pieces of bedrock are lifted out of place by a glacier.
Pluton A structure that results from the emplacement and crystallization of magma beneath the surface of Earth.
Plutonic rock The igneous rock that forms at depth. Named after Pluto, the god of the lower world in classical mythology.
Point bar A crescent-shaped accumulation of sand and gravel deposited on the inside of a meander.

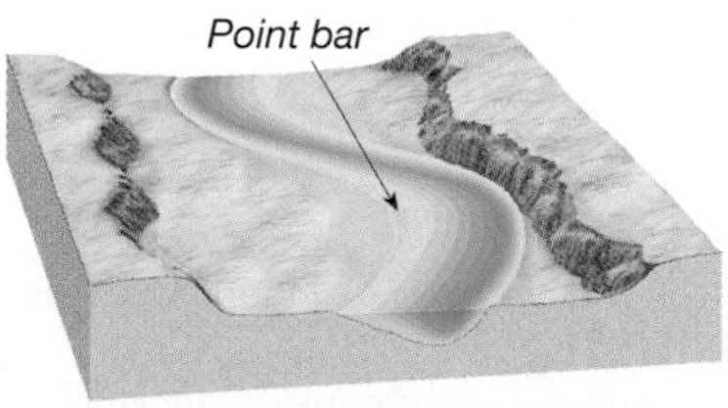

Polymorphs Two or more minerals that have the same chemical composition but different crystalline structures. They are exemplified by the diamond and graphite forms of carbon.
Pore space The open spaces in a rock, in sediment, or in soil.
Porosity The volume of open spaces in rock or soil.
Porphyritic texture An igneous rock texture characterized by two distinctively different crystal sizes. The larger crystals are called phenocrysts, whereas the matrix of smaller crystals is termed the groundmass.
Porphyroblastic texture A texture of metamorphic rocks in which particularly large grains (porphyroblasts) are surrounded by a fine-grained matrix of other minerals.
Porphyry An igneous rock with a porphyritic texture.
Pothole A depression formed in a stream channel by the abrasive corkscrew action of the water's sediment load.
Precambrian All geologic time before the Paleozoic Era.
Primary (P) wave A type of seismic wave that involves alternating compression and expansion of the material through which it passes.
Proterozoic Eon The eon following the Archean and preceding the Phanerozoic. It extends between 2500 million and 542 million years ago.
Proton A positively charged subatomic particle found in the nucleus of an atom.
Pumice A light-coloured glassy vesicular rock commonly having a felsic composition.
P-wave shadow zone The zone between 105 and 140 degrees distance from an earthquake epicentre, which direct waves do not penetrate because of refraction by Earth's core.
Pyroclastic flow A highly heated mixture, largely of ash and pumice fragments, travelling down the flanks of a volcano or along the surface of the ground.
Pyroclastic material The volcanic rock ejected during an eruption. Pyroclastics include ash, bombs, and blocks.
Pyroclastic texture An igneous rock texture that results from the consolidation of individual rock fragments that are ejected during a violent volcanic eruption.

Radial pattern A system of streams running in all directions away from a central elevated structure, such as a volcano.

Radial pattern

Radioactive decay The spontaneous decay of certain unstable atomic nuclei.
Radioactivity The spontaneous decay of certain unstable atomic nuclei.
Radiocarbon dating Using the radioactive isotope of carbon to date organic fossils of the recent geologic past.
Radiometric dating The procedure of calculating the absolute ages of rocks and minerals that contain certain radioactive isotopes.
Rain shadow desert A dry area on the lee side of a mountain range. Many middle-latitude deserts are of this type.

Rain shadow desert

Rapids A part of a stream channel in which the water suddenly begins flowing more swiftly and turbulently because of an abrupt steepening of the gradient.
Reach, stream A relatively straight segment of a stream.
Recessional moraine An end moraine formed as the ice front stagnated during glacial retreat.
Rectangular pattern A drainage pattern that is characterized by numerous right-angle bends and that develops on jointed or fractured bedrock.

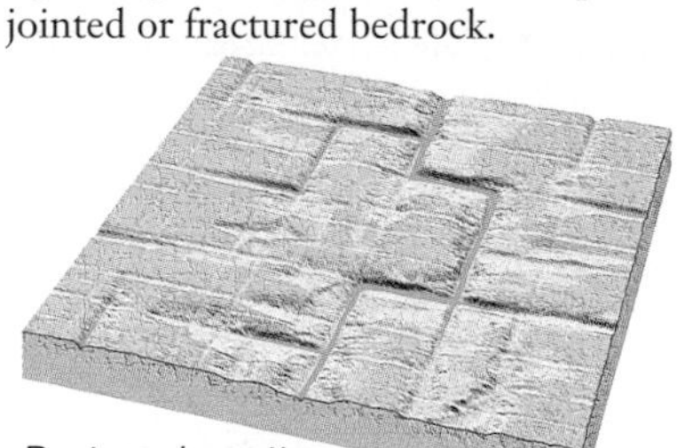
Rectangular pattern

Recurrence interval The average time between occurrences of hydrologic events, such as floods of a given or greater magnitude.
Regional metamorphism The metamorphism associated with large-scale mountain building.
Regolith The layer of rock and mineral fragments that nearly everywhere covers Earth's land surface.
Relative dating The placing of rocks and structures in their proper sequence or order. Only the chronologic order of events is determined.
Renewable resource A resource that is virtually inexhaustible or that can be replenished over relatively short time spans.

Reserve The already identified deposits from which minerals can be extracted profitably.

Reservoir rock The porous, permeable portion of an oil trap that yields oil and gas.

Resources The endowment of materials held in reserve that are useful to people and are ultimately available commercially.

Return period See *Recurrence interval.*

Reverse fault A fault in which the material above the fault plane moves up in relation to the material below.

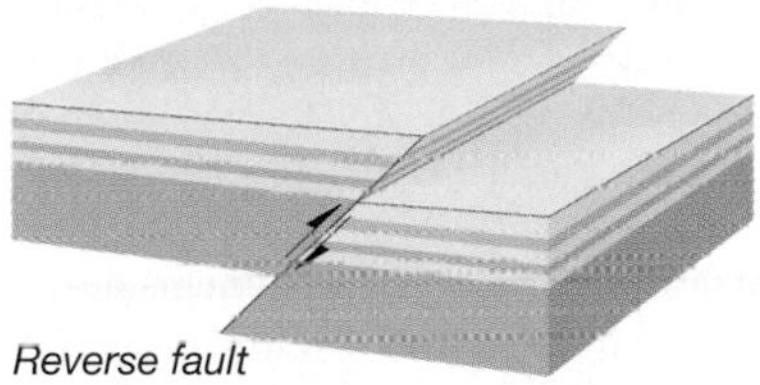

Reverse polarity A magnetic field opposite to the one that presently exists.

Richter scale A scale of earthquake magnitude based on the amplitude of the largest seismic wave.

Ridge-push A mechanism that can contribute to plate motion. It involves the oceanic lithosphere sliding down the oceanic ridge under the pull of gravity.

Rift valley A long, narrow trough bounded by normal faults. It represents a region where divergence is taking place.

Rift zone A zone of tension and normal faulting where two lithospheric plates move away from each other.

Rills The tiny channels that develop as unconfined flow begins producing threads of current.

Ripple marks The small waves of sand that develop on the surface of a sediment layer by the action of moving water or air.

Roche moutonnée An asymmetrical knob of bedrock formed when glacial abrasion smoothes the gentle slope facing the advancing ice sheet and plucking steepens the opposite side as the ice overrides the knob.

Rock A consolidated mixture of minerals.

Rock cleavage The tendency of rocks to split along parallel, closely spaced surfaces. These surfaces are often highly inclined to the bedding planes in the rock.

Rock cycle A model that illustrates the origin of the three basic rock types and the interrelatedness of Earth materials and processes.

Rock flour The ground-up rock produced by the grinding effect of a glacier.

Rockslide The rapid slide of a mass of rock downslope along planes of weakness.

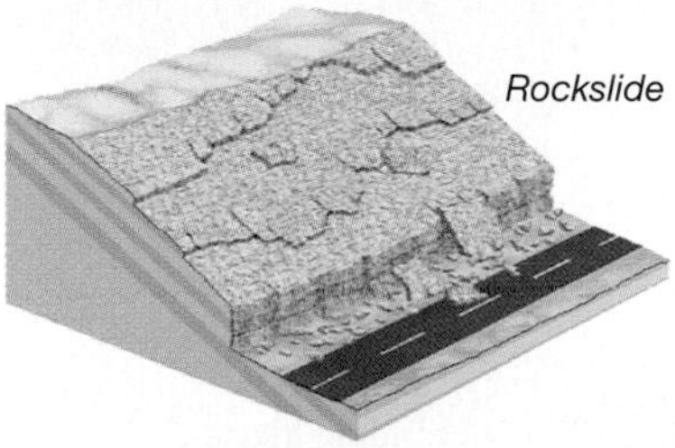

Rock structure All features created by the processes of deformation, from minor fractures in bedrock to a major mountain chain.

Runoff The water that flows over the land rather than infiltrating into the ground.

Saltation The transportation of sediment through a series of leaps or bounces.

Salt flat A white crust on the ground produced when water evaporates and leaves its dissolved materials behind.

Schistosity A type of foliation characteristic of coarser-grained metamorphic rocks. Such rocks have a parallel arrangement of platy minerals, such as the micas.

Scoria The vesicular ejecta that is the product of basaltic magma.

Scoria cone See *Cinder cone.*

Sea arch An arch formed by wave erosion when caves on opposite sides of a headland unite.

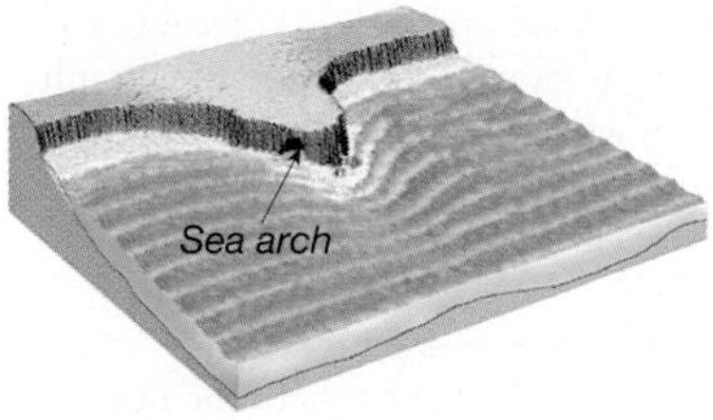

Seafloor spreading The hypothesis first proposed in the 1960s by Harry Hess that suggested that new oceanic crust is produced at the crests of mid-ocean ridges, which are the sites of divergence.

Seamount An isolated volcanic peak that rises at least 1000 metres above the deep-ocean floor.

Sea stack An isolated mass of rock standing just offshore, produced by wave erosion of a headland.

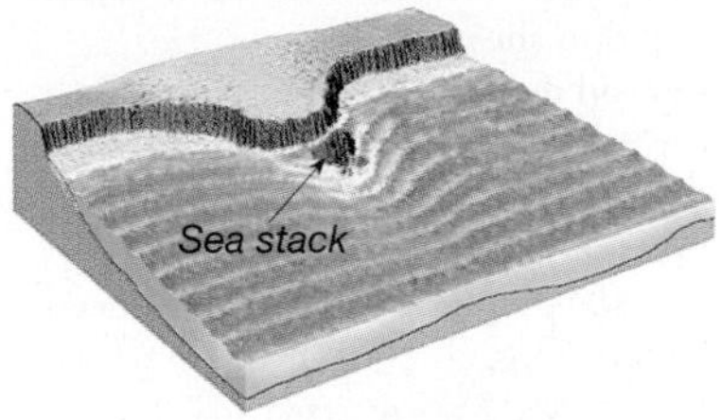

Seawall A barrier constructed to prevent waves from reaching the area behind the wall. Its purpose is to defend property from the force of breaking waves.

Secondary enrichment The concentration of minor amounts of metals that are scattered through unweathered rock into economically valuable concentrations by weathering processes.

Secondary (S) wave A seismic wave that involves oscillation perpendicular to the direction of propagation.

Sediment Unconsolidated particles created by the weathering and erosion of rock, by chemical precipitation from solution in water, or from the secretions of organisms, and then transported by water, wind, or glaciers.

Sedimentary environment See *Environment of deposition.*

Sedimentary facies The characteristics of a rock unit that reflect its environment of deposition and differentiate the rock unit from time-equivalent units adjacent to it.

Sedimentary rock The rock formed from the weathered products of preexisting rocks that have been transported, deposited, and lithified.

Seismic gap A segment of an active fault zone that has not experienced a major earthquake over a span when most other segments have. Such segments are probable sites for future major earthquakes.

Seismic sea wave A rapidly moving ocean wave generated by earthquake activity, which is capable of inflicting heavy damage in coastal regions.

Seismogram The record made by a seismograph.

Seismograph An instrument that records earthquake waves.

Seismology The study of earthquakes and seismic waves.

Settling velocity The speed at which a particle falls through a still fluid. The size, shape, and specific gravity of particles influence settling velocity.

Shear The stress that causes two adjacent parts of a body to slide past each other.
Sheet flow Runoff moving in unconfined thin sheets.
Sheeted dykes A large group of nearly parallel dykes.
Sheeting A mechanical weathering process characterized by the splitting off of slablike sheets of rock produced by unloading.
Shells See *Energy levels*.
Shield A large, relatively flat expanse of ancient metamorphic rock within the stable continental interior.
Shield volcano A broad, gently sloping volcano built from fluid basaltic lavas.

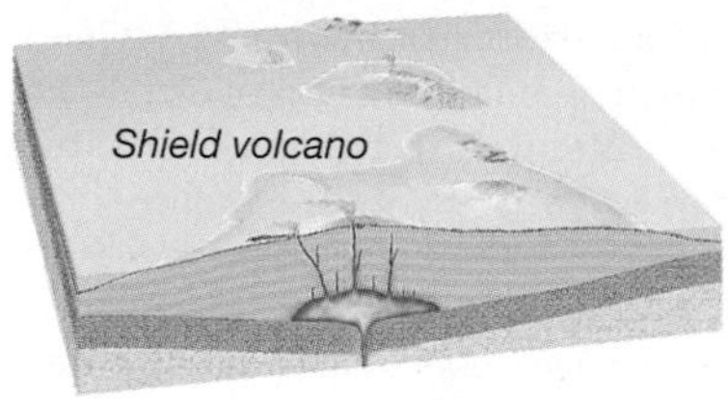

Silicate Any one of numerous minerals that have the silicon–oxygen tetrahedron as their basic structure.
Silicon–oxygen tetrahedron A structure composed of four oxygen atoms surrounding a silicon atom that constitutes the basic building block of silicate minerals.
Sill A tabular igneous body that was intruded parallel to the layering of preexisting rock.
Sinkhole (sink) A depression produced in a region where soluble rock has been removed by groundwater.

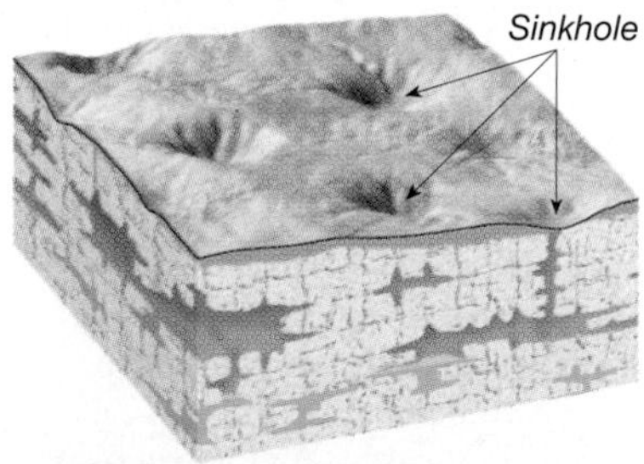

Slab-pull A mechanism that contributes to plate motion in which cool, dense oceanic crust sinks into the mantle and pulls the trailing lithosphere along.
Slide A movement common to mass-wasting processes in which the material moving downslope remains fairly coherent and moves along a well-defined surface.
Slip face The steep, leeward surface of a sand dune that maintains a slope of about 34 degrees.
Slump The downward slipping of a mass of rock or unconsolidated material moving as a unit along a curved surface.

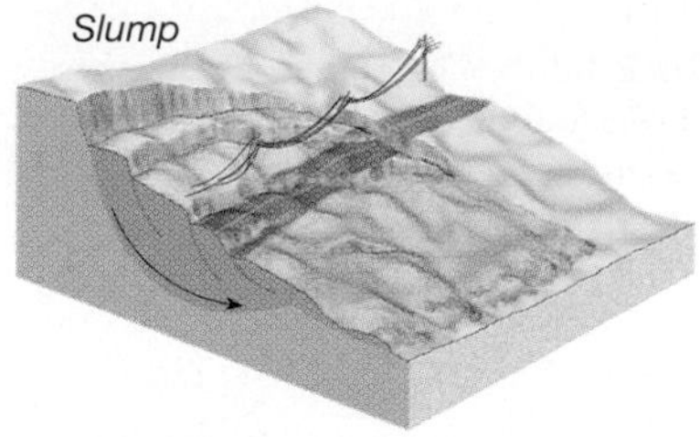

Soft bed deformation The deformation of water-saturated subglacial fine sediment or weak bedrock by frictional drag of the overriding glacier.
Soil A combination of mineral and organic matter, water, and air; the portion of the regolith that supports plant growth.
Soil profile A vertical section through a soil that shows its succession of horizons and the underlying parent material.
Solifluction The slow downslope flow of water-saturated materials common to permafrost areas.
Solum The *O*, *A*, and *B* horizons in a soil profile. Living roots and other plant and animal life are largely confined to this zone.
Sorting The degree of similarity in particle size in sediment or sedimentary rock.
Specific gravity The ratio of a substance's weight to the weight of an equal volume of water.
Speleothem A collective term for the dripstone features found in caverns.
Spheroidal weathering Any weathering process that tends to produce a spherical shape from an initially blocky shape.
Spit An elongate ridge of sand that projects from the land into the mouth of an adjacent bay.
Spring A flow of groundwater that emerges naturally at the ground surface.
Spring tide The highest tidal range. It occurs near the times of the new and full moons.
Stalactite The icicle-like structure that hangs from the ceiling of a cavern.
Stalagmite The columnlike form that grows upward from the floor of a cavern.
Star dune An isolated hill of sand that exhibits a complex form and develops where wind directions are variable.

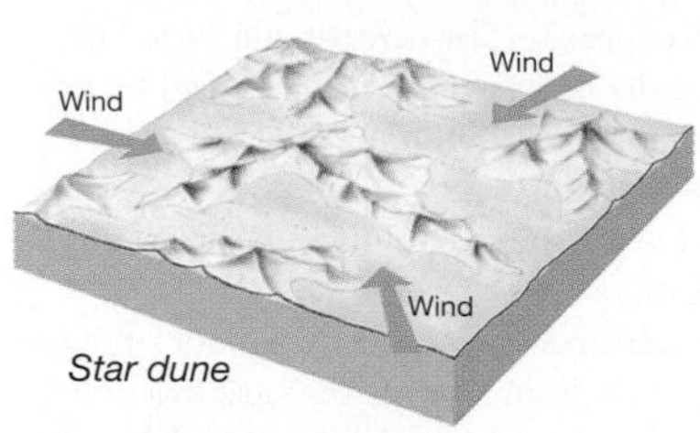

Steppe One of the two types of dry climate. A marginal and more humid variant of the desert that separates it from bordering humid climates.
Stock A pluton similar to but smaller than a batholith.
Strain An irreversible change in the shape and size of a rock body caused by stress.
Strata Parallel layers of sedimentary rock.
Stratified drift The sediments deposited by glacial meltwater.
Stratovolcano See *Composite cone*.
Streak The colour of a mineral in powdered form.
Stream A general term to denote the flow of water within any natural channel. Thus, a small creek and a large river are both streams.
Stream piracy The diversion of the drainage of one stream, resulting from the headward erosion of another stream.
Stress The force per unit area acting on any surface within a solid.
Strike The compass direction of the line of intersection created by a dipping bed or fault and a horizontal surface. Strike is always perpendicular to the direction of dip.
Strike-slip fault A fault along which the movement is horizontal.
Subduction The process by which oceanic lithosphere plunges into the mantle along a convergent zone.

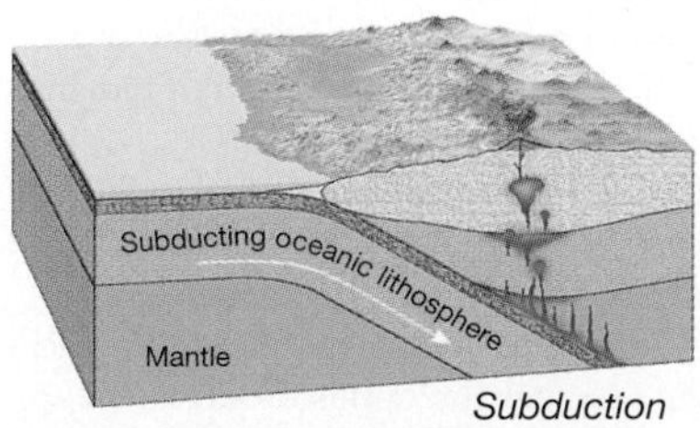

Subduction zone A long, narrow zone in which one lithospheric plate descends beneath another.
Subduction zone metamorphism Metamorphism in the region of a subducted slab under very high pressures but relatively low temperatures.
Submarine canyon A seaward extension of a valley that was cut on the con-

tinental shelf during a time when sea level was lower, or a canyon carved into the outer continental shelf, slope, and rise by turbidity currents.
Superposition, law of In any undeformed sequence of sedimentary rocks, each bed is older than the one above and younger than the one below.
Surf A collective term for breakers; also the wave activity in the area between the shoreline and the outer limit of breakers.
Surface waves The seismic waves that travel along the outer layer of Earth.
Surge A period of rapid glacial advance. Surges are typically sporadic and short-lived.
Suspended load The fine sediment carried within the body of flowing water or air.
Syncline A linear downfold in sedimentary strata; the opposite of anticline.

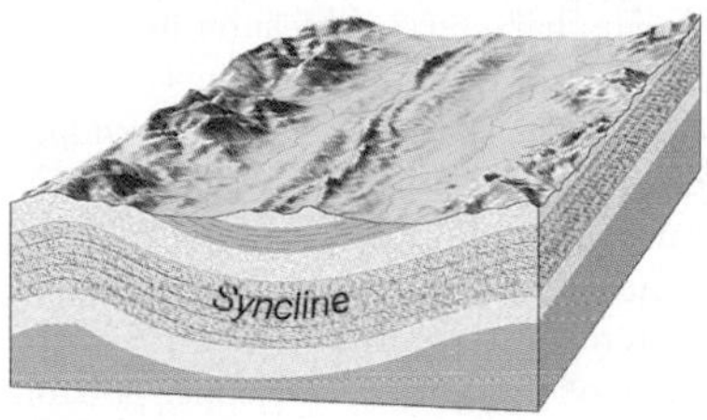

System A group of interacting or interdependent parts that form a complex whole.

Tablemount See *Guyot*.
Tabular The description of a feature, such as an igneous pluton, that has two dimensions that are much longer than the third.
Talus An accumulation of rock debris at the base of a cliff.

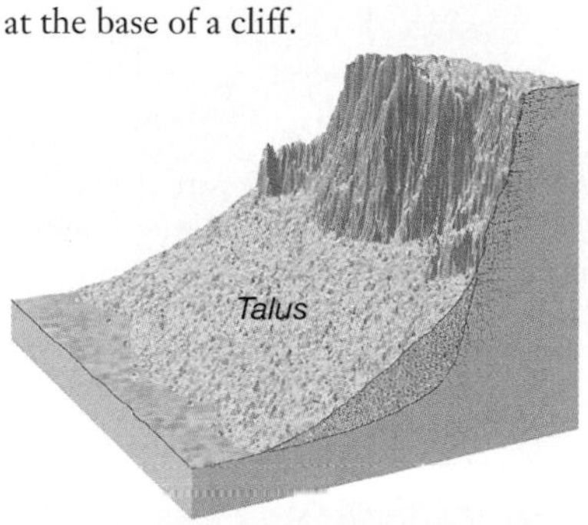

Tarn A small lake in a cirque.
Temporary base level The level of a lake, resistant rock layer, or any other base level that stands above sea level.
Tensional stress The type of stress that tends to pull a body apart.
Terminal moraine The end moraine marking the farthest advance of a glacier.
Terrace A flat, benchlike structure produced by a stream, which was left elevated as the stream cut downward.
Terrane A crustal block bounded by faults, whose geologic history is distinct from the histories of adjoining crustal blocks.
Terrigenous sediment The seafloor sediments derived from terrestrial weathering and erosion.
Texture The size, shape, and distribution of the particles that collectively constitute a rock.
Thermokarst The karstlike ponds produced in a permafrost region by the local melting of ground ice and resultant settling of the ground.
Thrust fault A low-angle reverse fault.

Tidal current The alternating horizontal movement of water associated with the rise and fall of the tide.
Tidal delta A deltalike feature created when a rapidly moving tidal current emerges from a narrow inlet and slows, depositing its load of sediment.
Tidal flat A marshy or muddy area that is alternately covered and uncovered by the rise and fall of the tide.
Tide The periodic change in the elevation of the ocean surface.
Till The poorly sorted sediment deposited directly by a glacier.
Tillite A rock formed when till is lithified.
Tombolo A ridge of sand that connects an island to the mainland or to another island.

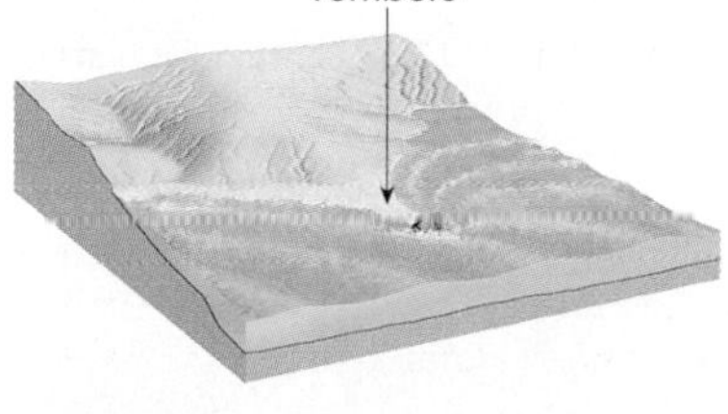

Transform fault A major strike-slip fault that cuts through the lithosphere and accommodates motion between two plates.
Transform fault boundary A boundary in which two plates slide past each other without creating or destroying lithosphere.

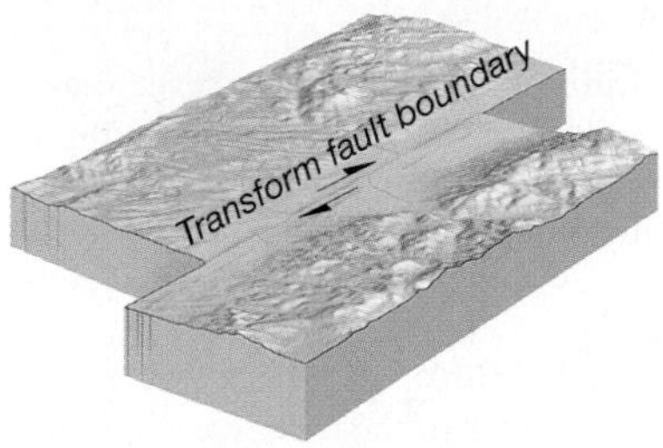

Transpiration The release of water vapour to the atmosphere by plants.
Transverse dunes A series of long ridges oriented at right angles to the prevailing wind; these dunes form where vegetation is sparse and sand is very plentiful.
Trellis drainage pattern A system of streams in which nearly parallel tributaries occupy valleys cut in folded strata.

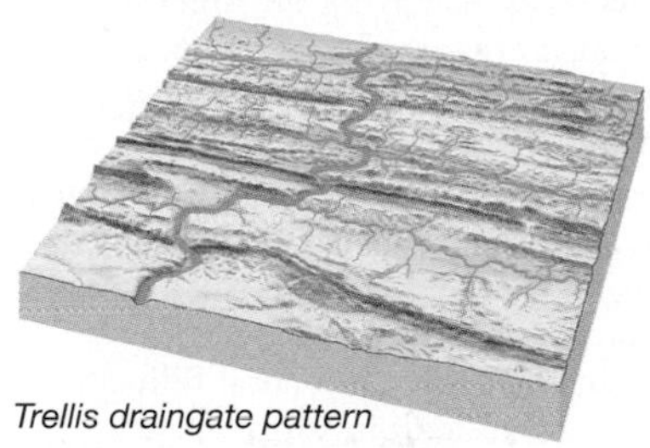

Trench An elongate depression in the seafloor produced by bending of oceanic crust during subduction.
Trigger A factor that initiates an event, such as an episode of mass wasting.
Truncated spurs Triangular-shaped cliffs produced when spurs of land that extend into a valley are removed by the great erosional force of a valley glacier.
Tsunami The Japanese word for a seismic sea wave.
Turbidite Turbidity current deposit characterized by graded bedding.
Turbidity current A downslope movement of dense, sediment-laden water created when sand and mud on the continental shelf and slope are dislodged and thrown into suspension.

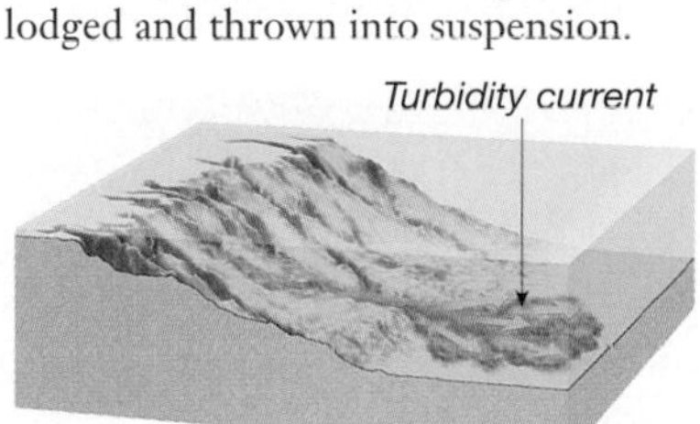

Turbulent flow The movement of water in an erratic fashion often characterized by swirling, whirlpool-like eddies. Most streamflow is of this type.

Ultimate base level Sea level; the lowest level to which stream erosion could lower the land.
Ultramafic composition A compositional group of igneous rocks that contain mostly olivine and pyroxene.
Unconformity A surface that represents a break in the rock record, caused by erosion and nondeposition.
Uniformitarianism The concept that the processes that have shaped Earth in the geologic past are essentially the same as those operating today.
Uniform stress Forces that are equal in all directions.

Valence electron The electrons involved in the bonding process; the electrons occupying the highest principal energy level of an atom.
Valley glacier See *Alpine glacier*.
Valley train A relatively narrow body of stratified drift deposited on a valley floor by meltwater streams that issue from the terminus of an alpine glacier.
Vein deposit A mineral filling a fracture or fault in a host rock. Such deposits have a sheetlike, or tabular, form.
Vent The surface opening of a conduit or pipe.
Ventifact A cobble or pebble polished and shaped by the sandblasting effect of wind.
Vesicular texture A term applied to aphanitic igneous rocks that contain many small cavities called vesicles.
Viscosity A measure of a fluid's resistance to flow.
Volatiles The gaseous components of magma dissolved in the melt. Volatiles readily vaporize (form a gas) at surface pressures.
Volcanic Pertaining to the activities, structures, or rock types of a volcano.
Volcanic island arc A chain of volcanic islands generally located a few hundred kilometres from a trench, where there is active subduction of one oceanic plate beneath another.
Volcanic neck An isolated, steep-sided, erosional remnant consisting of lava that once occupied the vent of a volcano.

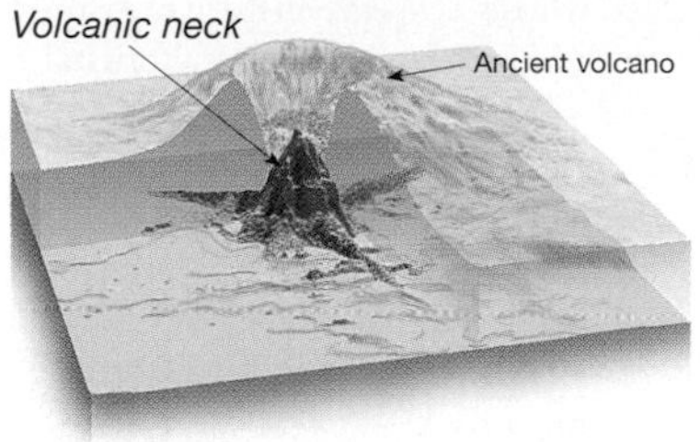

Volcano A mountain formed from lava or pyroclastics.

Waterfall A precipitous drop in a stream channel that causes water to fall to a lower level.
Water table The upper level of the saturated zone of groundwater.

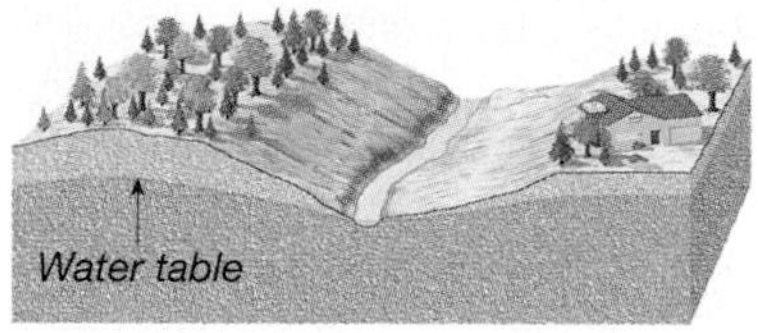

Wave-cut cliff A seaward-facing cliff along a steep shoreline, formed by wave erosion at its base and mass wasting.
Wave-cut platform A bench or shelf along a shore at sea level, cut by wave erosion.
Wave height The vertical distance between the trough and crest of a wave.
Wavelength The horizontal distance separating successive crests or troughs.
Wave period The time interval between the passage of successive crests at a stationary point.
Wave refraction A change in direction of waves as they enter shallow water. The portion of the wave in shallow water is slowed, which causes the waves to bend and align with the underwater contours.
Weathering The disintegration and decomposition of rock at or near the surface of Earth.
Well An opening bored into the zone of saturation.

Xenolith An inclusion of unmelted country rock in an igneous pluton.

Yardang A streamlined, wind-sculpted ridge that has the appearance of an inverted ship's hull oriented parallel to the prevailing wind.
Yazoo tributary A tributary that flows parallel to the main stream because a natural levee is present.

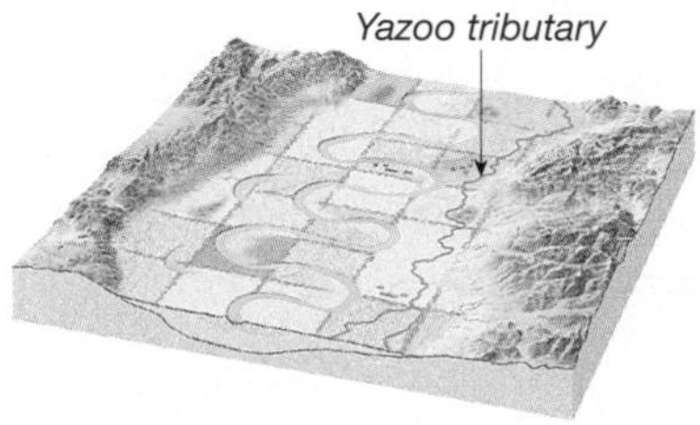

Zone of accumulation The part of a glacier characterized by snow accumulation and ice formation. The lower limit of this zone is the equilibrium line.
Zone of aeration The area above the water table where openings in soil, sediment, and rock are not saturated but filled mainly with air.
Zone of fracture The upper portion of a glacier that consists of brittle ice.
Zone of saturation The zone where all open spaces in sediment and rock are completely filled with water.

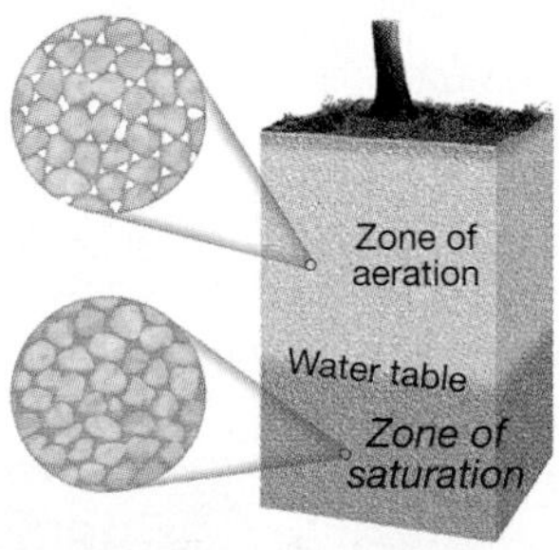

Zone of wastage The part of a glacier below the equilibrium line where annually there is a net loss of ice.

Index

Note: *f* denotes a figure, *t* denotes a table, and *n* denotes a footnote.

H

I

N

O

"AS IS" LICENSE AGREEMENT AND LIMITED WARRANTY

READ THIS LICENSE CAREFULLY BEFORE OPENING THIS PACKAGE. BY OPENING THIS PACKAGE, YOU ARE AGREEING TO THE TERMS AND CONDITIONS OF THIS LICENSE. IF YOU DO NOT AGREE, DO NOT OPEN THE PACKAGE. PROMPTLY RETURN THE UNOPENED PACKAGE AND ALL ACCOMPANYING ITEMS TO THE PLACE YOU OBTAINED THEM. ***THESE TERMS APPLY TO ALL LICENSED SOFTWARE ON THE DISK EXCEPT THAT THE TERMS FOR USE OF ANY SHAREWARE OR FREEWARE ON THE DISKETTES ARE AS SET FORTH IN THE ELECTRONIC LICENSE LOCATED ON THE DISK:***

1. GRANT OF LICENSE and OWNERSHIP: The enclosed computer programs <<and any data>> ("Software") are licensed, not sold, to you by Pearson Canada Inc. ("We" or the "Company") in consideration of your adoption of the accompanying Company textbooks and/or other materials, and your agreement to these terms. You own only the disk(s) but we and/or our licensors own the Software itself. This license allows instructors and students enrolled in the course using the Company textbook that accompanies this Software (the "Course") to use and display the enclosed copy of the Software for academic use only, so long as you comply with the terms of this Agreement. You may make one copy for back up only. We reserve any rights not granted to you.

2. USE RESTRICTIONS: You may not sell or license copies of the Software or the Documentation to others. You may not transfer, distribute or make available the Software or the Documentation, except to instructors and students in your school who are users of the adopted Company textbook that accompanies this Software in connection with the course for which the textbook was adopted. You may not reverse engineer, disassemble, decompile, modify, adapt, translate or create derivative works based on the Software or the Documentation. You may be held legally responsible for any copying or copyright infringement which is caused by your failure to abide by the terms of these restrictions.

3. TERMINATION: This license is effective until terminated. This license will terminate automatically without notice from the Company if you fail to comply with any provisions or limitations of this license. Upon termination, you shall destroy the Documentation and all copies of the Software. All provisions of this Agreement as to limitation and disclaimer of warranties, limitation of liability, remedies or damages, and our ownership rights shall survive termination.

4. DISCLAIMER OF WARRANTY: THE COMPANY AND ITS LICENSORS MAKE NO WARRANTIES ABOUT THE SOFTWARE, WHICH IS PROVIDED "AS-IS." IF THE DISK IS DEFECTIVE IN MATERIALS OR WORKMANSHIP, YOUR ONLY REMEDY IS TO RETURN IT TO THE COMPANY WITHIN 30 DAYS FOR REPLACEMENT UNLESS THE COMPANY DETERMINES IN GOOD FAITH THAT THE DISK HAS BEEN MISUSED OR IMPROPERLY INSTALLED, REPAIRED, ALTERED OR DAMAGED. THE COMPANY DISCLAIMS ALL WARRANTIES, EXPRESS OR IMPLIED, INCLUDING WITHOUT LIMITATION, THE IMPLIED WARRANTIES OF MERCHANTABILITY AND FITNESS FOR A PARTICULAR PURPOSE. THE COMPANY DOES NOT WARRANT, GUARANTEE OR MAKE ANY REPRESENTATION REGARDING THE ACCURACY, RELIABILITY, CURRENTNESS, USE, OR RESULTS OF USE, OF THE SOFTWARE.

5. LIMITATION OF REMEDIES AND DAMAGES: IN NO EVENT, SHALL THE COMPANY OR ITS EMPLOYEES, AGENTS, LICENSORS OR CONTRACTORS BE LIABLE FOR ANY INCIDENTAL, INDIRECT, SPECIAL OR CONSEQUENTIAL DAMAGES ARISING OUT OF OR IN CONNECTION WITH THIS LICENSE OR THE SOFTWARE, INCLUDING, WITHOUT LIMITATION, LOSS OF USE, LOSS OF DATA, LOSS OF INCOME OR PROFIT, OR OTHER LOSSES SUSTAINED AS A RESULT OF INJURY TO ANY PERSON, OR LOSS OF OR DAMAGE TO PROPERTY, OR CLAIMS OF THIRD PARTIES, EVEN IF THE COMPANY OR AN AUTHORIZED REPRESENTATIVE OF THE COMPANY HAS BEEN ADVISED OF THE POSSIBILITY OF SUCH DAMAGES. SOME JURISDICTIONS DO NOT ALLOW THE LIMITATION OF DAMAGES IN CERTAIN CIRCUMSTANCES, SO THE ABOVE LIMITATIONS MAY NOT ALWAYS APPLY.

6. GENERAL: THIS AGREEMENT SHALL BE CONSTRUED AND INTERPRETED ACCORDING TO THE LAWS OF THE PROVINCE OF ONTARIO. This Agreement is the complete and exclusive statement of the agreement between you and the Company and supersedes all proposals, prior agreements, oral or written, and any other communications between you and the company or any of its representatives relating to the subject matter.

Should you have any questions concerning this agreement or if you wish to contact the Company for any reason, please contact in writing: Permissions, Pearson Canada Inc., 26 Prince Andrew Place, Toronto, Ontario, M3C 2T8.